THE INTERNATIONAL COVENANT ON ECONOMIC, SOCIAL AND CULTURAL RIGHTS

Advance Praise

The International Covenant on Economic, Social and Cultural Rights is the most misunderstood instrument in the international human rights system. It has sparked considerable controversy, being both lauded for its understanding of the economic aspects of exploitation and dismissed as a set of Utopian rights guarantees. With the entry into force of an Optional Protocol allowing individual complaints and other enforcement procedures, the Covenant is poised to become a significant frontier in human rights law.

This book will quickly become an essential companion to anyone interested in this field. It offers a comprehensive and nuanced account of the rights set out in the Covenant, explaining their historical and jurisprudential context and how they have been and might be deployed. It unpacks the concept of 'progressive realization' of economic, social, and cultural rights, rejecting an interpretation that views it as an alibi for inaction. The book transcends the rather static debates between supporters and critics of the Covenant by focusing on how its rights have been protected in practice and the authors emphasize the limits of a narrow legal approach in this area. This is a book packed with important information and sophisticated analyses and it will change the way that the Covenant is understood.

PROFESSOR HILARY CHARLESWORTH

Australian Research Council Laureate Fellow;
Director, Centre for International Governance and Justice,
Regulatory Institutions Network College of Asia and the Pacific,
Australian National University

THE INTERNATIONAL COVENANT ON ECONOMIC, SOCIAL AND CULTURAL RIGHTS

Commentary, Cases, and Materials

BEN SAUL

DAVID KINLEY

and

JACQUELINE MOWBRAY

OXFORD
UNIVERSITY PRESS

OXFORD
UNIVERSITY PRESS

Great Clarendon Street, Oxford, OX2 6DP,
United Kingdom

Oxford University Press is a department of the University of Oxford.
It furthers the University's objective of excellence in research, scholarship,
and education by publishing worldwide. Oxford is a registered trade mark of
Oxford University Press in the UK and in certain other countries

First published 2014
First published in paperback 2016

Published in the United States of America by Oxford University Press
198 Madison Avenue, New York, NY 10016, United States of America

British Library Cataloguing in Publication Data
Data available

Library of Congress Cataloging in Publication Data
Data available

ISBN 978–0–19–964030–0 (Hbk.)
ISBN 978–0–19–879046–4 (Pbk.)

Printed and bound by
CPI Group (UK) Ltd, Croydon, CR0 4YY

Foreword

The publication of this volume marks something of a coming of age for the International Covenant on Economic, Social and Cultural Rights. The United Nations doctrine affirming the indivisibility of the two sets of human rights has long been belied by the priority given by governments, international organizations, and by scholars to civil and political rights at the expense of their 'poor cousins', economic, social, and cultural rights. In enthusiastically welcoming the publication of the present volume it is instructive to situate it within the scholarly history of English language publications analysing the two International Covenants. For the most part, that history consists of a series of landmark publications dealing with the ICCPR, none of which had, at the time of their publication or since, a fully fledged counterpart dealing with the ICESCR. The most prominent of these works are Louis Henkin's groundbreaking edited 1981 volume of essays undertaking a systematic legal analysis of the ICCPR's principal rights,[1] Marc Bossuyt's compilation of that Covenant's travaux préparatoires in 1987,[2] and Manfred Nowak's excellent 1993 Commentary.[3] While some important works were published on the ICESCR during this period,[4] the absence of a counterpart to each of these three volumes made it even easier for casebooks on human rights and other teaching materials either to minimize or entirely omit the treatment of economic, social, and cultural rights. In 2000 Sarah Joseph, Jenny Schultz and Melissa Castan published their collection of cases, materials, and commentary on the ICCPR,[5] thereby making the key sources and interpretive materials relating to that Covenant more readily available to both scholars and practitioners. Fourteen years later, a degree of equality has now been achieved through the publication of this splendid volume and Ben Saul,

[1] Louis Henkin, *The International Bill of Rights: The Covenant on Civil and Political Rights* (Columbia University Press, New York, 1981).

[2] Marc J. Bossuyt, *Guide to the "Travaux Préparatoires" of the International Covenant on Civil and Political Rights* (Martinus Nijhoff, Dordrecht, 1987).

[3] Manfred Nowak, *U.N. Covenant on Civil and Political Rights: CCPR Commentary* (N.P. Engel, Kehl, 1993).

[4] See especially Matthew C. R. Craven, *The International Covenant on Economic, Social and Cultural Rights: A Perspective on its Development* (Clarendon Press, Oxford, 1995).

[5] Sarah Joseph, Jenny Schultz, and Melissa Castan, *The International Covenant on Civil and Political Rights: Cases, Materials and Commentary*, (Oxford University Press, Oxford, 2000).

David Kinley, and Jacqueline Mowbray are to be very warmly congratulated for having brought it to fruition.

The reader might wonder why this Foreword places such emphasis on scholarship in a field in which it might be thought to be the actions of governments, courts, and perhaps international monitoring bodies that really matter. But in fact there are some areas of international law in which the role of scholars has been of unique importance, and goes significantly beyond the usual role of communicating and analysing practice, and trying to fit it into an overall narrative of the field. This seems to me to be clearly the case in relation to much of international criminal law because of the novelty of the issues being raised in an international context and because of the limited utility of any one national criminal law regime or jurisdiction in shedding light on a determinedly hybrid civil/common law approach. Judges of international courts and tribunals who are called upon to interpret open-ended provisions inevitably rely significantly on available scholarship to assist and sometimes even guide them. The same is true in relation to economic, social, and cultural rights, an area in which national precedents are of limited direct transposability to the international domain and in which relatively few important precedents have emerged from the more coherent regional judicial institutions (notably the European Court of Human Rights and the Inter-American Court of Human Rights) which played such an important role in building the international jurisprudence of civil and political rights.

In the absence of international judicial institutions one might have expected an important role to be played by alternative international institutional arrangements in generating a deeper understanding of the normative implications of economic, social, and cultural rights. But for much of the latter part of the twentieth century governments seemed intent on ensuring that such institutions were not created. For example, rather than setting up a committee of independent experts to monitor and encourage compliance, as they did with the ICCPR, they formed an inter-governmental committee which achieved very little of value until it was replaced by the Committee on Economic, Social and Cultural Rights in 1987. And while the Commission on Human Rights began in 1981 to appoint special rapporteurs and other experts to promote respect for a range of civil and political rights, it conspicuously refused to do so for any of the economic, social, and cultural rights until 1998. Similarly, while the Human Rights Committee began generating important jurisprudence through the examination of complaints alleging violations of civil and political rights obligations in the late 1970s, its counterpart committee dealing with the other set of rights is only now—some thirty-five years later—gearing up to begin the same process. At the same time as they were avoiding the establishment of expert mechanisms at the international level, governments operating within the political organs of the United Nations contented themselves with engagement in sterile ideological debates which purported to reflect on the deeper nature and philosophical foundations of economic, social, and cultural rights. Such debates were only rarely heard in relation to civil and political rights, but were pursued enthusiastically to overshadow much of the inter-governmental reflection on economic, social, and cultural rights and divert it into a cul-de-sac.

There is, of course, a measure of circularity in the phenomena I have described above. In the absence of international expert bodies capable of generating jurisprudential insights, there were fewer materials for scholars to work with and fewer incentives for them to invest their time and intellectual resources into this field.

Nevertheless, some scholars have made important contributions to the development of the international community's understanding of the nature and scope of the obligations reflected in the ICESCR. This has occurred especially through the writings of international lawyers and philosophers, an important example of the latter being the groundbreaking work of Henry Shue. In the early 1980s, he drew attention to the obligations side of the rights and duties balance sheet with his identification of separate obligations to respect, protect, and fulfill in relation to 'subsistence rights.' This typology, abundantly reflected in its adjusted form in much of the analysis in the present volume, underscored the fact that the obligation to expend resources which had previously pre-occupied most commentators in relation to economic, social and cultural rights was only one part of the set of obligations incumbent upon governments that were parties to the Covenant. Other important scholarly contributions also came in the form of collaborative efforts such as the highly influential Limburg Principles on the Implementation of the ICESCR, the thrust of which is again evident in much of the analysis in this volume. Those Principles foreshadowed the approach adopted by the UN Committee on ESCR in its landmark General Comment No. 3 which, in turn, laid the foundations for the initial foray by the South African Constitutional Court into developing a coherent jurisprudence surrounding these rights.

In brief, scholarly contributions are crucial for the development of a coherent, systematic, and persuasive jurisprudence relating to economic, social, and cultural rights. This volume performs a formidable service by providing such an insightful synthesis of the most important elements of this emerging jurisprudence. It also helps to expose the relative paucity in the literature of engaged but critical analyses of this jurisprudence, and thus highlights the need for the next generation of scholars to engage in a more robust and challenging way with the materials brought together in this volume.

PHILIP ALSTON
John Norton Pomeroy Professor of Law,
New York University School of Law;
Chair, UN Committee on Economic, Social and Cultural Rights 1991–98

Acknowledgements

This book was some years in the making. We are foremost grateful to our long-suffering research assistants who amassed and analysed a vast array of primary materials, particularly extensive drafting records, treaty body practice, and the decisions of regional and national tribunals. They also drafted briefs for us on particular issues and intensively prepared the manuscript. They never complained and were always willing to do more. All of them are or were law students at the University of Sydney and are talented and hard-working. They are Naomi Hart, Giselle Kenny, Vanessa Austen, Katherine Bones, Kathleen Heath, Ella Alexander, Harrison Grace, Alexander Horne, and Alice Gardoll.

For assistance in obtaining ICESCR drafting records from the 1950s and 1960s, we thank the University of Sydney Library; State Library of New South Wales (Sydney); National Library of Australia (Canberra); and Dag Hammarskjöld Library of the United Nations in New York.

Various colleagues at Sydney Law School provided helpful insights, including Ron McCallum, Irene Baghoomians, Terry Carney, and Judith Cashmore, and our colleagues in the Sydney Centre for International Law (including Tim Stephens, Fleur Johns, Chester Brown, Emily Crawford, Mary Crock, Luke Nottage, John Pace, Alison Pert, Ivan Shearer and Laura Smith-Khan). Countless law students in our undergraduate and postgraduate human rights classes have also contributed to our ideas. We make special mention of our Nepalese and Australian students in our Himalayan Field School course, 'Law, Development and Human Rights', held annually in Nepal with Kathmandu School of Law. Jacqui also notes the contributions of the students of the European Regional MA in Human Rights and Democracy in South East Europe.

Elsewhere we are grateful for discussions with experts, colleagues, or friends including Philip Alston, Daniel Augenstein, Danny Bradlow, Takele Bulto, Aldo Caliari, Allison Corkery, Mac Darrow, Costas Douzinas, Mary Dowell-Jones, Conor Gearty, Christof Heynes, Malcolm Langford, Bonita Meyersfeld, Sri Palupi, Geeta Pathak Sangroula, Yubaraj Sangroula, Magdalena Sepúlveda Carmona, Ahmed Shahid, Shiyan Sun, and Frans Viljoen. We also thank the many online contributors to ESCR-NET and the members of the Human Rights Council of Australia. Personally, Ben Saul thanks Jane McAdam and Jacqui

Mowbray thanks Tim Sherman. Any errors or omissions in this book are, of course, our own.

We acknowledge assistance from the Australian Research Council, including a Future Fellowship (Saul) and a Discovery Project (Kinley, DPI096521: 'Financing Human Rights: Global Problems and Possibilities'); and from the Legal Scholarship Support Fund at Sydney Law School. The academic environment at the University of Sydney made this project possible. In a world where many universities and academics are struggling, we are grateful that Australian universities, and ours in particular, enable and support large, complex, multi-year research projects. This book is collectively authored, although each of us took the lead on certain chapters (Ben on Articles 1/25, 4/5/24, 6, 7, 8, 9, and 10 (with Kathleen Heath); David on Articles 2(1), 11, and 12, and Jacqui on Articles 2(2), 2(3), 3, 13, 14, and 15).

We thank Oxford University Press for their patience during the long gestation of this book. John Louth embraced the idea and Merel Alstein and Anthony Hinton helped us execute it.

Sydney, September 2013

Contents

Each of these appendices can be found in full online here at<http://ukcatalogue.oup.com/product/9780199640300.do>

Table of Cases

INTERNATIONAL DECISIONS

African Commission on Human and Peoples' Rights

DOMESTIC DECISIONS

Argentina

Australia

Canada

Colombia

Iceland

India

Table of Instruments

INTERNATIONAL TREATIES

REGIONAL TREATIES

NATIONAL LAWS

Algeria

List of Abbreviations

ACHR	American Convention on Human Rights
ACHPR	African Commission on Human and Peoples' Rights
ADB	Asian Development Bank
ANZSIL	Australian and New Zealand Society of International Law
APSED	Asia-Pacific Strategy on Emerging Diseases
ARV	anti-retrovirals
ASEAN	Association of Southeast Asian Nations
ASIO	Australian Security Intelligence Organisation
AU	African Union
BPL	below poverty line
CAT	Convention against Torture
CCPR	[International] Covenant on Civil and Political Rights
CCT	conditional cash transfer
CEACR	ILO Committee of Experts on the Application of Conventions and Recommendations
CEDAW	Convention on the Elimination of All Forms of Discrimination against Women
CEDAW Committee	[UN] Committee on the Elimination of Discrimination against Women
CERD	[UN] Committee on the Elimination of Racial Discrimination
CESCR	[UN] Committee on Economic, Social and Cultural Rights
CESR	Center for Economic and Social Rights
CHC	community health centre
CHR	[UN] Commission on Human Rights
CIS	Commonwealth of Independent States
CMW	[UN] Committee on Migrant Workers
CRC	[UN] Committee on the Rights of the Child
CROC	Convention on the Rights of the Child
CRPD	Convention on the Rights of Persons with Disabilities
CRPD Committee	[UN] Committee on the Rights of Persons with Disabilities

DPSP	Directive Principle of State Policy
DRC	Democratic Republic of Congo
EC	European Community
EC Treaty	Treaty Establishing the European Community
ECHR	European Convention on Human Rights
ECJ	European Court of Justice
ECOSOC	[UN] Economic and Social Council
ECSR	European Committee on Social Rights
ECT	electro-convulsive therapy
ECtHR	European Court of Human Rights
EFA	Education for All
EPZ	export processing zone
ESC	European Social Charter 1961
EU	European Union
EXCOM	Executive Committee of the Programme of the UNHCR
FAO	Food and Agriculture Organization
FCGH	Framework Convention on Global Health
FCNM	European Framework Convention for the Protection of National Minorities
FCTC	Framework Convention on Tobacco Control
FEANTSA	Federation of National Organisations Working with the Homeless
FGM	female genital mutilation
FYROM	Former Yugoslavian Republic of Macedonia
GATT	General Agreement on Tariffs and Trade 1947
GDP	gross domestic product
GNP	gross national product
GUF	Global Union Federation
HKSAR	Hong Kong Special Administrative Region
HMDC	home for mentally disabled children
HRBA	human rights-based approach
HRC	[UN] Human Rights Committee
IAASTD	International Assessment of Agricultural Science and Technology for Development
IACHR	Inter-American Court of Human Rights
ICAO	International Civil Aviation Organization
ICC	International Criminal Court
ICERD	Convention on the Elimination of All Forms of Racial Discrimination
ICDS	Integrated Child Development Scheme
ICCPR	International Covenant on Civil and Political Rights
ICERD	International Convention on the Elimination of All Forms of Racial Discrimination

ICESCR	International Covenant on Economic, Social and Cultural Rights
ICFTU	International Confederation of Free Trade Unions
ICJ	International Court of Justice
ICMW	International Convention on the Protection of the Rights of All Migrant Workers and Members of Their Families
ICTR	International Criminal Tribunal for Rwanda
ICTY	International Criminal Tribunal for the former Yugoslavia
IDP	internally displaced person
IE	Independent Expert
IFAD	International Fund for Agricultural Development
IFC	International Finance Corporation
IFM	international framework agreement
IHL	international humanitarian law
IHR	International Health Regulations
ILC	International Law Commission
ILO	International Labour Organization
ILO CEACR	ILO Committee of Experts on the Application of Conventions and Recommendations
IMF	International Monetary Fund
IOE	International Organisation of Employers
IPR	intellectual property right
IPRA	Indigenous Peoples Rights Act 1997 (Philippines)
ISO	International Organization for Standardization
ISSA	International Social Security Association
ITUC	International Trade Union Confederation
KFOR	Kosovo Force (NATO)
KRL	Christianity, religion and philosophy
LTTE	Liberation Tigers of Tamil Eelam
MDG	Millennium Development Goal
MDMS	Mid Day Meal Scheme (India)
MINPROFF	Ministère de la Promotion de la Femme et de la Famille (Cameroon)
MINURCAT	UN Mission in the Central African Republic and Chad
MOH	Ministry of Health
MRT	Moldovan Republic of Transdniestria
MTEF	Medium-Term Expenditure Framework
NAFTA	North American Free Trade Agreement
NATO	North Atlantic Treaty Organization
NCD	non-communicable disease
NFBS	National Family Benefit Scheme
NGO	non-governmental organisation
NHRC	National Human Rights Commission
NHSP	National Health Strategy Plan

NMBS	National Maternity Benefit Scheme
NRHM	National Rural Health Mission framework
OAS	Organization of American States
OAU	Organization of African Unity
OCHA	UN Office for the Coordination of Humanitarian Affairs
OECD	Organisation for Economic Cooperation and Development
OHCHR	UN Office of the High Commissioner for Human Rights
OIC	Organisation of Islamic Cooperation
OP	Optional Protocol
OPEC	Organization of the Petroleum Exporting Countries
OSCE	Organization for Security and Cooperation in Europe
PHC	primary health care
POW	prisoner of war
PRHW	People's Rural Health Watch
RTD	right to development
SERAC	Social and Economic Rights Action Center
SPF	Social Protection Floor
SPFS	FAO Special Programme for Food Security
SRSG	Special Representative of the UN Secretary-General
STI	sexually transmitted infection
SWAp	Sector-wide Approach
TBKP	Türkiye Birlesik Komünist Partisi (United Communist Party of Turkey)
THE	total health expenditure
TPDS	Targeted Public Distribution System
TRIPS	Trade-Related Aspects of Intellectual Property Rights
TUAC	Trade Union Advisory Committee to the OECD
TVE	technical and vocational education
UAR	United Arab Republic
UDHR	Universal Declaration of Human Rights
UK	United Kingdom of Great Britain and Northern Ireland
UN	United Nations
UNAIDS	Joint UN Programme on HIV/AIDS
UNCHR	UN Commission on Human Rights
UNDG	UN Development Group
UNDP	UN Development Programme
UNEP	UN Environment Programme
UNESCO	UN Educational, Scientific and Cultural Organization
UNFPA	UN Population Fund (formerly UN Fund for Population Activities)
UNGA	UN General Assembly
UNGAOR	UN General Assembly Official Records
UNHCR	UN High Commissioner for Refugees

UNICEF	UN Children's Fund
UNMIK	UN Interim Administration Mission in Kosovo
UNSGAB	UN Secretary-General's Advisory Board on Water and Sanitation
UPDF	Uganda People's Defence Force
US	United States of America
USAID	US Agency for International Development
USSR	Union of Soviet Socialist Republics
VEA	Veterans' Entitlement Act 1986 (Australia)
WCL	World Confederation of Labour
WFP	Water for People
WGIP	Working Group of Experts on Indigenous Populations
WHO	World Health Organization
WTO	World Trade Organization
ZUS	Zones Urbaines Sensibles (Sensitive Urban Areas)

1
Introduction

Despite the much-emphasized indivisibility of human rights, economic, social and cultural rights have long been seen as the poor cousins of civil and political rights. The different trajectory of each category of rights was set by the splintering of human rights into the two separate covenants of 1966, in the protracted and complicated process of juridifying the Universal Declaration of Human Rights (UDHR) of 1948. The story is well known. Civil and political rights were largely seen as immediately applicable and typically justiciable, whereas economic, social and cultural rights were viewed as subject only to progressive realization through measures of state policy. Civil and political rights were often viewed as negative freedoms from state interference, whereas economic, social and cultural rights were thought to involve positive obligations on the state, which in turn implied politically sensitive claims on public resources. Civil and political rights were also more familiar to many national constitutional and legal traditions (as the 'first generation' of individual rights), whereas economic, social and cultural rights were more novel and less familiar (sequentially 'second' generation, and partly 'collective' in orientation). These fault lines were ultimately reflected in differences in state obligations of implementation between the International Covenant on Economic, Social and Cultural Rights (ICESCR or 'the Covenant') and the International Covenant on Civil and Political Rights (ICCPR).

The burgeoning scholarship in recent decades has exhaustively demonstrated how these supposed fault lines are both too simplistic and overly deterministic.[1] Civil and political rights also involve positive demands on the state as much as negative freedoms from interference; they too can be expensive (for instance, to run a prison service which ensures humane conditions of detention, or to fund an accessible law enforcement and judicial system capable of protecting rights from interference). On the other hand, many aspects of economic, social and cultural rights are immediately applicable and capable of judicial application or supervision (for example, protecting the freedom of association of trade unions and their members, prohibiting forced labour or unjustified dismissal, or guaranteeing non-discrimination in access to education or health services).

[1] See, eg, Matthew Craven, *The International Covenant on Economic, Social and Cultural Rights: A Perspective on its Development* (Clarendon Press, Oxford, 1995), 7–9; Jeff Kenner, 'Economic and Social Rights in the EU Legal Order: The Mirage of Indivisibility' in Tamara Hervey and Jeff Kenner (eds), *Economic and Social Rights under the EU Charter of Fundamental Rights* (Hart, Oxford, 2003), 1–4; Conor Gearty and Virginia Mantouvalou, *Debating Social Rights* (Hart, Oxford, 2011), 97–107; Daphne Barak-Erez and Aeyal M Gross, 'Introduction: Do We Need Social Rights? Questions in the Era of Globalisation, Privatisation, and the Diminished Welfare State' in Daphne Barak-Erez and Aeyal M Gross (eds), *Exploring Social Rights: Between Theory and Practice* (Hart, Oxford, 2011), 5.

Further, it has become clear that the principle of progressive realization is not an unbounded or elastic prerogative of states to choose, at their discretion, when they wish to confer or withhold rights. The United Nations Committee on Economic, Social and Cultural Rights (CESCR) has demonstrated that 'progressive realization' requires a rational devotion of state effort to achieve rights within the maximum of available resources, in the shortest possible time, while preserving a minimum irreducible core of rights and safeguarding the most vulnerable. These components of progressive realization are themselves amenable to judicial oversight of various kinds.

If socio-economic rights were historically unfamiliar to many legal systems, that too has changed: there are now numerous judicial or quasi-judicial applications of such rights, and an evolving jurisprudence at the national, regional and international levels. Even the assumption of the novelty of such rights is problematic. Our own country, the developed welfare state of Australia, which still has no bill of rights, is a case in point. There, certain socio-economic rights were well protected by statute long before many civil and political rights, including those in relation to work and trade unions, social security, education, health and an adequate standard of living (encompassing rights to food, water, clothing and housing). Yet, there is still no enforceable freedom from arbitrary or indefinite detention in Australia, or from cruel, inhuman or degrading treatment;[2] and even torture was only prohibited a few short years ago.

At the same time, socio-economic rights discourse and practice have also demonstrated that judicial enforceability is not the litmus test of what is truly 'law' in this field of rights. Many socio-economic rights are well advanced through national policies and action plans, and often more ably so than through the narrow aperture of courts. In addition, the international community's preoccupation with economic development in recent decades has focused increased attention on the achievement of economic and social rights in 'development'. As a result, such rights can no longer be considered 'novel' or marginal within international law, but are rather central to the mainstream of international development activity, including in its economic and financial dimensions.

An increasing interest in a 'human rights-based approach' to development has also led donors and international actors to develop more 'scientific' technical indicators or benchmarks to measure the implementation of socio-economic rights, potentially giving more traction to their implementation and enforcement. Conspicuous inattention to socio-economic rights has also provoked much controversy in this context. For instance, the absence of express reference to human rights in the Millennium Development Goals (MDGs) and in the suggested means and methods of their attainment has spawned much debate, including whether—and if so, to what extent—this omission matters in terms of rights outcomes. Similarly, the now thirty-plus year debate over the international community's formal recognition of a 'right to development' has been dogged by

[2] See *F.K.A.G. et al v Australia*, HRC Communication No. 2094/2011 (26 July 2013); *M.M.M. et al v Australia*, HRC Communication No. 2136/2012 (25 July 2013).

the rude intrusion of unavoidable political and economic realities upon the high principles of economic equity and fairness between states, peoples and individuals. Like the idea of happiness, few would deny its desirability for all; but equally few can agree upon whom the responsibility lies to achieve it, and how they ought to go about getting there.

Overall, though, economic, social and cultural rights have moved from the subject of theoretical debates (are they 'real' and 'enforceable' rights?) to being increasingly accepted as important international norms with significant practical application. The adoption of the Optional Protocol to the International Covenant on Economic, Social and Cultural Rights in 2008 (and its coming into force in May 2013) is indicative of this change in perception, with individuals now able to complain to the CESCR of violations of their Covenant rights.

One purpose of this book is to respond to this shift: to look beyond the more abstract and ideological discussions of the nature of socio-economic rights in order to engage empirically with how such rights have manifested in international practice. In doing so, the book takes its cue from the sophisticated and influential resources which have long existed in respect of the ICCPR: Manfred Nowak's encyclopedic *CCPR Commentary*,[3] and Sarah Joseph and Melissa Castan's utilitarian *ICCPR Cases, Materials and Commentary*.[4] The former engages in depth with the drafting records as well as the supervisory practice of the UN Human Rights Committee; the latter focuses principally on the Human Rights Committee's practice and particularly its 'Views' in individual communications under the ICCPR Optional Protocol complaints procedure. Further, while Nowak digests and analyses the key decisions and materials, Joseph and Castan extract key passages from the primary materials with the aim of letting them speak for themselves, while also providing a certain amount of critical commentary.

This book hybridizes these two approaches in examining the ICESCR. It examines the drafting records (acknowledging the more detailed treatment of much, though not all, of the drafting by Matthew Craven's *The International Covenant on Economic, Social and Cultural Rights: A Perspective on its Development*);[5] considers the supervisory practice of the CESCR; extracts key primary materials; provides a critical commentary; and generally builds on Craven's excellent, but more restricted and somewhat dated, 1995 work. While this book is something of a companion tome to Joseph and Castan's work on the ICCPR, it is entitled *Commentary, Cases and Materials* (not *Cases, Materials and Commentary*) to reflect that the book is comparatively less weighted towards extracting primary materials and contains a proportionately higher analytical content. The book also strikes out in certain new directions, not least necessitated by the availability and limitations of relevant primary source materials.

[3] Manfred Nowak, *UN Covenant on Civil and Political Rights: CCPR Commentary* (2nd edn, Clarendon Press, Oxford, 2005).

[4] Sarah Joseph and Melissa Castan, *The International Covenant on Civil and Political Rights: Cases, Materials and Commentary* (3rd edn, Oxford University Press, Oxford, 2013).

[5] Craven, *The ICESCR*.

Methodologically, in interpreting the ICESCR, an obvious starting point is the drafting records. Following the drafting of the UDHR between 1947 and 1948, the UN Commission on Human Rights (UNCHR) commenced drafting an international covenant on human rights in 1950, with an almost exclusive focus on civil and political rights. By February 1952, it was apparent that it would be necessary to draft two separate instruments because of division over the appropriate means of implementing civil and political compared with economic, social and cultural rights. The drafting of a covenant on the latter commenced in 1953 in the UNCHR. The drafting discussions were then spread across the UNHCR and the General Assembly's Third Committee between 1954 and 1966, with some overall direction provided by the General Assembly. This book makes reference to the drafting debates where relevant, including occasional consideration of the drafting of comparable ICCPR provisions (such as the extent and immediacy of legal obligations, self-determination, non-discrimination and equality, the prohibition on forced labour and freedom of association/trade union rights).

Looking beyond the drafting, this book next looks to the products of the ICESCR's monitoring system, and particularly the work of the CESCR. The ICESCR entered into force on 3 January 1976. Part IV of the ICESCR provides for the Economic and Social Council (ECOSOC) to monitor states' implementation of their obligations. It requires states to submit regular reports on the measures they have taken and the progress they have made in implementing the ICESCR. Upon entry into force of the Covenant, monitoring of state reports was conducted by ECOSOC, first by its Sessional Working Group on the Implementation of the ICESCR, and from 1982 by the Sessional Working Group of Governmental Experts on the Implementation of the International Covenant.

The supervision system was modernized in 1985, when an ECOSOC resolution established the CESCR as a subsidiary body of ECOSOC, to assume the monitoring functions.[6] The CESCR's legal pedigree is thus somewhat more precarious than that of the Human Rights Committee, which is embedded in the ICCPR itself. But the composition and functions of the two committees are comparable. The CESCR consists of eighteen members, 'experts with recognized competence in the field of human rights, serving in their personal capacity', elected with 'due consideration . . . to equitable geographical distribution and to the representation of different forms of social and legal systems'.[7]

The CESCR is the body ultimately responsible for the international interpretation and supervision of the ICESCR, and so this book relies extensively on its documents as evidence of the meaning and application of the Covenant. First, the CESCR's guidelines for state reporting, issued in 1991 and revised in 2008 (after

[6] ECOSOC Res. 1985/17, Review of the Composition, Organisation and Administrative Arrangements of the Sessional Working Group of Governmental Experts on the Implementation of the International Covenant on Economic, Social and Cultural Rights, E/RES/1985/17 (28 May 1985).

[7] Review of the Composition, Organisation and Administrative Arrangements of the Sessional Working Group of Governmental Experts on the Implementation of the ICESCR, [b].

reforms to simplify UN treaty body reporting as a whole),[8] give a brief indication of the scope of each right in setting the parameters of reporting.

Secondly, with respect to a number of rights and issues, the CESCR has issued authoritative statements of its opinions and practice in the form of twenty-one 'General Comments' between 1989 and 2009. These General Comments, which draw on the CESCR's experience in monitoring state reports, are not formally binding, but are highly influential in setting out the scope of rights and standards under the ICESCR, and provide an excellent starting point for examining its normative content. This is particularly the case with respect to more recent General Comments, which are more detailed and comprehensive than some of the earlier ones. There are, however, still significant gaps in their coverage. In particular, there are no General Comments on the rights to just and favourable conditions of work (Article 7), to form and join trade unions and to strike (Article 8), and to the protection of families, mothers and children (Article 10).

Thirdly, the CESCR has issued over 300 Concluding Observations or like-comments in its monitoring of states' periodic reports, and these constitute the majority of the core primary materials that this book relies upon to build up an interpretive picture of the ICESCR. States are required to produce their initial report within two years of becoming parties to the ICESCR, and to report every five years thereafter. We collected and analyzed the CESCR's observations on all reporting states between the years 1989 and 2012 inclusive. We also analyzed a good number of observations produced between 1980 and 1989.

Concluding Observations in their present form have been issued since at least 1992, when states' objections to issuing state-specific comments—previously seen as interference in domestic affairs—eroded after the end of the Cold War.[9] Before then, the CESCR's dialogue with states was recorded in collective comments addressed to states in general and sometimes by publication of the entire dialogue between the CESCR and a state party.[10] The increasing sophistication of the current form of Concluding Observations, which has been broadly uniform since 2002, provides a more elaborate understanding of what the ICESCR requires. Examining the Concluding Observations in their totality, across all states and over time, enables the repeated core concerns of the CESCR to be identified. It also highlights what is considered more peripheral or has not thus far received attention at all. In this book we have given a little more prominence to more recent Concluding Observations, in part because the CESCR's approach has tended to become more comprehensive and sophisticated as it has refined its consideration of issues. But we also identify earlier practice in order to chart shifts in the CESCR's approach over time.

[8] CESCR, Guidelines on Treaty-Specific Documents to be Submitted by States Parties under Articles 16 and 17 of the International Covenant on Economic, Social and Cultural Rights, E/C.12/2008/2 (24 March 2009).

[9] See Michael O'Flaherty, 'The Concluding Observations of the United Nations Human Rights Treaty Bodies' (2006) 6(1) *Human Rights Law Review* 27, 29–30.

[10] O'Flaherty, 'Concluding Observations', 27 and 29.

Thus far, the book largely follows the methodology of Nowak, Joseph and Castan, and Craven in focusing on the drafting of one of the twin covenants and the work of its committee as guides to interpretation. Where we depart substantially from their script is in the scope and breadth of primary materials considered. This is for two reasons. The first is that, unlike the ICCPR, the ICESCR has not yet given rise to a body of 'jurisprudence' stemming from Views issued by the CESCR in deciding communications under an individual complaints procedure. Between 1979 and mid 2013, the Human Rights Committee issued almost 800 Views under the Optional Protocol to the ICCPR. These provide the core content for Joseph and Castan's work and (beyond the drafting) Nowak's. In contrast, the Optional Protocol to the ICESCR, allowing individual communications, only entered into force in May 2013, and so there is as yet no such jurisprudence, although complaints are already rolling in.

At the same time, the CESCR's General Comments and Concluding Observations are typically limited to consideration of systemic issues at a certain level of abstraction, and rarely grapple with socio-economic rights at the level of individual disputes, controversies or cases. As a result, we have had to look elsewhere for the kind of granular, fact-specific jurisprudence capable of more fully fleshing out the meaning of the ICESCR. Consequently, this book makes extensive use of a comparative, analogical and legally plural methodology (with all the risks of imprecision that this entails).

In the first place, this book draws extensively on primary materials from other UN human rights treaty bodies (particularly the Human Rights Committee, Committee on the Elimination of All Forms of Discrimination against Women, and Committee on the Elimination of All Forms of Racial Discrimination, but also those concerning children, migrant workers and persons with disabilities). While each of the UN human rights treaties establishes its own formally autonomous legal regime, we have chosen to read them consistently or harmoniously as far as their legal texts permit, on the basis that the UN treaties are also an inter-related normative system as much as islands unto themselves.

Those other bodies have often produced more specialized guidelines on the application of socio-economic rights to the groups in question, which are of benefit in unpacking the ICESCR. At the level of individual jurisprudence, we have drawn on relevant Human Rights Committee communications under the ICCPR where the ICESCR shares the norms in question (for instance, in relation to self-determination, non-discrimination and equality, the prohibition on forced labour, trade union rights and cultural rights). The book also considers the relevant UN special procedures or mechanisms in the area of socio-economic rights, such as special rapporteurs and independent experts whose thematic mandates have engaged directly with ICESCR rights (including mandates which scrutinize adequate housing, cultural rights, education, extreme poverty, health, and water and sanitation).

Secondly, the book also draws upon the decisions of regional and domestic courts, tribunals or bodies which have considered socio-economic rights, particularly where the language of the relevant legal standards approximates those of the ICESCR. European social rights jurisprudence features particularly prominently (under the European Social Charter and Revised European Social Charter), since those instruments are the closest mirror of the ICESCR at the regional level. But jurisprudence is also drawn from regional systems with a predominant focus on civil and political rights, as under the European Convention on Human Rights, American Convention on Human Rights, African Convention on Human and People's Rights, and very occasionally the Arab Charter on Human Rights, the Commonwealth of Independent States' Human Rights Convention, and the Association of Southeast Asian Nations (ASEAN) Declaration on Human Rights. This strategy allows the book to provide a richer, deeper account of the range of possibilities available when interpreting economic, social and cultural rights, particularly where there are gaps in the CESCR's practice to date, and to illustrate where the CESCR's practice is more progressive—or has gone wrong.

Thus, as will be seen, the global picture is one of convergence and divergence: whereas private prison labour is permitted under European human rights law, the ICESCR forbids it; and whereas Europe has permited restrictions on one's freedom not to join a trade union (in order to advance collective trade union interests), the ICESCR takes a stricter approach and privileges individual over collective rights.

Thirdly, the ICESCR is a more open-textured legal instrument than certain other human rights treaties; it is far from being a self-contained normative regime. As a result, certain ICESCR rights can only be understood against the background of special norms in the particular area. For instance, the right of self-determination is necessarily shackled to general international law and UN principles on self-determination. The various work-related rights (Articles 6 to 9), the right to social security (Article 9), and certain rights of families, mothers and children (Article 10) are closely connected to the numerous International Labour Organization (ILO) conventions and soft law standards developed over the more than ninety years since the establishment of the ILO in 1919. The ICESCR provisions simply make no sense without reference to the ILO standards.

This is true also in other areas, such as with respect to UNESCO's standard setting in the areas of education and culture, the work of the World Health Organization in the field of health, the efforts of the Food and Agriculture Association in relation to the right to food, UNICEF on disabilities and socio-economic rights, UNHCR on refugees and socio-economic rights, and so on. Further, the connection between socio-economic rights and development means that these rights must be understood in the context of international work to promote development and alleviate poverty, such as the UN Guiding Principles on Extreme Poverty and Human Rights[11] or the work of the UN Development Programme. This book therefore draws heavily on the pertinent norms and practices of relevant specialized regimes and organizations.

Finally, perhaps due to the historical controversy as to the status and meaning of economic, social and cultural rights, or to the historical scarcity of 'jurisprudence' on these rights, the work of independent human rights experts has been particularly influential in providing normative guidance on interpreting and implementing the ICESCR and identifying the current state of the law. Particularly significant 'soft law' materials developed by experts include the Limburg Principles on the Implementation of the ICESCR[12] and the Maastricht Guidelines on Violations of Economic, Social and Cultural Rights,[13] which have been embraced by international bodies and influenced national legal systems. Other sources include the Maastricht Principles on Extraterritorial Obligations of States in the area of Economic, Social and Cultural Rights 2011[14] and the Montréal Principles on Women's Economic, Social and Cultural Rights.[15] All of these reflect efforts to progressively develop or clarify some of the ambiguities or controversies under the ICESCR.

Throughout this book, we also invoke the views of jurists from time to time, although our main purpose is not to reproduce scholarly critiques, but to agglomerate the primary legal materials in an effort to divine their cumulative essence, coherence and contradiction. Where the state of the law is in flux or problematic, we also permit our own critical voices to intrude occasionally, in an attempt to explain and resolve competing interpretive or policy differences, and perhaps even to nudge the development of the law in the 'right' direction.

In that context, it is perhaps worth saying something of how we see the field of economic, social and cultural rights evolving. Clearly, the most significant impact on the ICESCR over the coming years will be the effect of the entry into force of the Optional Protocol in May 2013. The process of drafting the Optional Protocol reopened many familiar debates about the justiciability of economic, social and cultural rights, with some states remaining skeptical about the appropriateness of

[11] Human Rights Council, Final Draft of the Guiding Principles on Extreme Poverty and Human Rights, submitted by the Special Rapporteur on extreme poverty and human rights, A/HRC/21/39 (18 July 2012).

[12] Limburg Principles on the Implementation of the ICESCR, reproduced in UN Commission on Human Rights, Note Verbale dated 5 December 1986 from the Permanent Mission of the Netherlands to the UN Office at Geneva addressed to the Centre for Human Rights, E/CN.4/1987/17 (8 January 1987).

[13] CESCR, Substantive Issues Arising in the Implementation of the ICESCR: Maastricht Guidelines on Violations of Economic, Social and Cultural Rights, E/C.12/2000/13 (2 October 2000).

[14] Maastricht Principles on Extraterritorial Obligations of States in the Area of Economic, Social and Cultural Rights (28 September 2011), reproduced in Olivier de Schutter, Asbjorn Eide, Ashfaq Khalfan, Marcos Orellana, Margot Salomon and Ian Seiderman, 'Commentary to the Maastricht Principles on the Extraterritorial Obligations of States in the Area of Economic, Social and Cultural Rights' (2012) 34(4) *Human Rights Quarterly* 1085, 1085–98.

[15] International Federation for Human Rights, Montréal Principles on Women's Economic, Social and Cultural Rights (December 2002), reproduced in (2004) 26 *Human Rights Quarterly* 760.

a communications procedure.[16] Despite this, an Optional Protocol encompassing all ICESCR rights was adopted, thus providing a strong affirmation of the quasi-'justiciability' of economic, social and cultural rights (even if the final Views are not strictly binding, like under the ICCPR Optional Protocol), and creating an important future means of standard setting under the ICESCR.

The Optional Protocol establishes three new procedures for the protection and enforcement of rights under the ICESCR: an individual complaints procedure; an inter-state complaints procedure; and an inquiry procedure that is engaged when the CESCR receives 'reliable information indicating grave or systematic violations'. The individual complaints mechanism largely mirrors that under the ICCPR, with some minor differences: there is express provision for communications to be submitted on behalf of groups,[17] and communications may be declared inadmissible where they are 'manifestly ill-founded, not sufficiently substantiated or exclusively based on reports disseminated by mass media',[18] or submitted more than one year after the exhaustion of domestic remedies.[19] There is also a discretion not to consider a communication that does not reveal a 'clear disadvantage' to the author, unless the CESCR considers 'that the communication raises a serious issue of general importance'.[20]

The inter-state communication mechanism allows a state party to refer a matter to the CESCR if it considers that another state is not fulfilling its obligations under the Covenant.[21] The mechanism can only be invoked where both states have made declarations that they recognize the competence of the CESCR to hear such communications. The provisions under the Optional Protocol are modelled on, and very similar to, the equivalent (but seldom used) procedure in Article 41 of the ICCPR.

In contrast, the further inquiry procedure established under Article 11 of the Optional Protocol has no equivalent in the ICCPR system, although there is an almost identical mechanism under the Optional Protocol to the Convention on

[16] While a comprehensive approach to the enforcement of all ICESCR rights was ultimately settled on, many states pushed strongly for what was deemed an *à la carte* approach, where states could either opt-in to, or opt-out of, the enforcement of specific rights, depending on the model chosen: see Commission on Human Rights, Elements for an Optional Protocol to the International Covenant on Economic, Social and Cultural Rights: Analytical paper by the Chairperson-Rapporteur, Catarina de Albuquerque, E/CN.4/2006/WG.23/2 (30 November 2005), 4. Some states also displayed a strong reluctance to permit any interference by the CESCR in national decisions on resource allocation (see Commission on Human Rights, Status of the International Covenants on Human Rights: Report of the independent expert (Mr Hatem Kotrane), E/CN.4/2002/57 (12 February 2012), [18]), and insisted that the 'reasonableness' of the steps taken by the state party should be considered before a violation was found (see Explanatory Memorandum in Human Rights Council, Draft Optional Protocol to the International Covenant on Economic, Social and Cultural Rights, A/HRC/7/WG.4/2 (23 April 2007), [29]).

[17] Optional Protocol to the International Covenant on Economic, Social and Cultural Rights (adopted 10 December 2008, entered into force 5 May 2013), Article 5(2)(b).

[18] Optional Protocol to the ICESCR, Article 3(2)(e).

[19] Optional Protocol to the ICESCR, Article 3(2)(a) (unless the author can demonstrate that it was not possible to meet that time limit).

[20] Optional Protocol to the ICESCR, Article 4.

[21] Optional Protocol to the ICESCR, Article 10.

the Elimination of All Forms of Discrimination against Women.[22] Under this procedure, the CESCR may designate one or more of its members to conduct an inquiry into reports of grave or systemic violations of rights under the Covenant and report urgently to the CESCR. However, a country must opt-in to the inquiry procedure,[23] and an inquiry can only include a visit to a state's territory with its consent.[24]

These procedures, and particularly the individual communications mechanism, will provide important opportunities for the CESCR to clarify the meaning and scope of the ICESCR. As more states ratify the Optional Protocol, and individual communications are submitted and decided, the CESCR's Views in communications will become an increasingly important guide to interpretation. In future editions of this book, we will integrate and analyse these Views, and address the communications procedure (including admissibility) in more detail.

In addition to the influence of the Optional Protocol, the future development of economic, social and cultural rights seems likely to be shaped by the CESCR's approach to a number of emerging issues. Foremost among these will be the role of non-state actors, especially corporations, and their impact (both positive and negative) on the rights guaranteed by the ICESCR. In recent years, the CESCR (as well as a number of special rapporteurs holding related mandates) has increasingly focused on the effects of corporate actions (and inactions) on peoples' enjoyment of economic, social and cultural rights, and especially the implications for states' obligations under the Covenant.

From the evolving jurisprudence of the Human Rights Committee, as well as that of the regional human rights systems in Europe and the Americas, it now seems clear that states can be held responsible, under certain circumstances, not only for rights-infringing actions of private actors within their territory, but also extra-territorially. The nature and dimensions of these circumstances and attendant conditions will certainly be matters of interest and debate for the CESCR for years to come, particularly given the economic and social effects of globalization. The precise extent and weight of states' responsibilities to render 'international assistance and cooperation' as demanded by Articles 2(1) and 11 (and by implication, 12 and 13) of the Covenant is also likely to tax the jurisprudential boundary-setting capabilities of the CESCR.

The accumulation and systematization of primary legal materials in this book establishes beyond doubt that there is now a fairly comprehensive, integrated and sophisticated international law of social, economic and cultural rights. Such rights are no longer the poor cousins of civil and political rights, even if there is much room for further consolidation and refinement of the jurisprudence; and more room still for the strengthening of mechanisms, institutions and procedures for their implementation, enforcement and protection.

[22] Optional Protocol to the ICESCR, Article 8.
[23] Optional Protocol to the ICESCR, Article 11(1).
[24] Optional Protocol to the ICESCR, Article 11(3).

Interest in the theory and practice of the ICESCR is set to accelerate with its coming of age through the cases arising under the Optional Protocol. This process of concretising or grounding rights will be assisted by the coalescence of the many vanguard international human rights issues already mentioned: the implications of globalization and economic development; public sector responsibilities for private sector rights violations; states' extra-territorial obligations; and the inter-relationship between the ICESCR and relevant specialized norms and legal regimes.

While this book is far from the last word on the Covenant, its modest aim is to provide a detailed guide to how, where and when the Covenant's journey began, where it has gone thus far, and where it may travel in future.

Sydney, September 2013

2

Article 1: The Right of Peoples of Self-Determination

Article 25: The Right to Freely Utilize Natural Resources

Article 1

1. All peoples have the right of self-determination. By virtue of that right they freely determine their political status and freely pursue their economic, social and cultural development.

2. All peoples may, for their own ends, freely dispose of their natural wealth and resources without prejudice to any obligations arising out of international economic co-operation, based upon the principle of mutual benefit, and international law. In no case may a people be deprived of its own means of subsistence.

3. The States Parties to the present Covenant, including those having responsibility for the administration of Non-Self-Governing and Trust Territories, shall promote the realization of the right of self-determination, and shall respect that right, in conformity with the provisions of the Charter of the United Nations.

Article 25

Nothing in the present Covenant shall be interpreted as impairing the inherent right of all peoples to enjoy and utilize fully and freely their natural wealth and resources.

Introduction and Origins

The right of self-determination is expressed in identical terms in common Article 1 of the ICESCR and ICCPR, and springs immediately from the references to self-determination in the United Nations Charter 1945 (though it does not appear in the Universal Declaration of Human Rights 1948). Its earlier international law origins lie in the First World War peace settlement at Versailles, embodied in US President Woodrow Wilson's 'Fourteen Points', and the inter-war law and practice of the League of Nations, particularly through the colonial mandate system and in the protection of European minorities.[1]

[1] On the history of international law on self-determination, see generally Antonio Cassese, *Self-Determination of Peoples: A Legal Reappraisal* (Oxford University Press, Oxford, 1996).

According to the Human Rights Committee (HRC), the articulation of self-determination as a human right is of foundational importance and underpins all other human rights:

> The right of self-determination is of particular importance because its realization is an essential condition for the effective guarantee and observance of individual human rights and for the promotion and strengthening of those rights.[2]

Article 1 is considered of such importance that the HRC noted in General Comment No. 24 that a reservation to the ICCPR [or ICESCR] denying the right of self-determination would be incompatible with the object and purpose of the Covenant.[3] As discussed below, self-determination is also a peremptory norm of general international law (*jus cogens*), admitting no derogation and taking priority in the event of a conflict with norms of a lesser status.

While Article 1 of the ICESCR is identical to Article 1 of the ICCPR, given its place in an instrument on socio-economic rights, the former may be understood to emphasize the economic dimensions of self-determination, whereas the latter focuses on its political aspects. Both dimensions are, however, inextricably intertwined: full economic self-determination depends on political self-determination, although as will be seen it is still possible to realize aspects of economic self-determination even in the absence of political autonomy.

The scope and meaning of Article 1 of the ICESCR can only be properly understood in the light of the background of norms on self-determination in the ICCPR and the law of the United Nations. Certain shared concepts, including the meaning of a 'people' entitled to exercise the right, the political forms it may take, and the obligations of other states, will necessarily be considered in this chapter, although the focus is on its economic dimensions.

The late and rather confused inclusion of Article 25 of the ICESCR is also vital to the scope of Article 1. It is a clause 'saving' 'the inherent right of all peoples to enjoy and utilize fully and freely their natural wealth and resources' from being impaired by anything in the ICESCR. It is of particular relevance in potentially 'trumping' or mitigating the subjection, in Article 1(2), of a people's right to freely dispose of their natural wealth and resources to 'any obligations arising out of international economic co-operation'.

To situate it in its legal context, Article 1 of the ICESCR derives from, builds on and juridifies the brief references to self-determination in Articles 1 and 55 of the UN Charter.[4] Article 1(2) of the Charter provides that it is a 'purpose' of the United Nations '[t]o develop friendly relations among nations based on

[2] HRC, General Comment No. 12, The right to self-determination of peoples (Art. 1), HRI/GEN/1/Rev.1 (13 March 1984), [1] ('General Comment No. 12').

[3] HRC, General Comment No. 24, Issues relating to reservations made upon ratification or accession to the Covenant or the Optional Protocols thereto, or in relation to declarations under Article 41 of the Covenant, CCPR/C/21/Rev.1/Add.6 (4 November 1994), [9]. As discussed below, the Indian and Bangladeshi reservations to Article 1 of the ICESCR are particularly problematic.

[4] UNGA Third Committee, A/3077 (8 December 1955), 12.

respect for the principle of equal rights and self-determination of peoples…'. Article 55 of the Charter further links self-determination to economic and security policy:

With a view to the creation of conditions of stability and well-being which are necessary for peaceful and friendly relations among nations based on respect for the principle of equal rights and self-determination of peoples, the United Nations shall promote:

a. higher standards of living, full employment, and conditions of economic and social progress and development;

b. solutions of international economic, social, health, and related problems; and international cultural and educational cooperation; and

c. universal respect for, and observance of, human rights and fundamental freedoms for all without distinction as to race, sex, language, or religion.

Chapter XI of the Charter concerning non-self-governing territories does not expressly mention self-determination, but applies the principle in that context.[5] Article 73 provides:

Members of the United Nations which have or assume responsibilities for the administration of territories whose peoples have not yet attained a full measure of self-government recognize the principle that the interests of the inhabitants of these territories are paramount, and accept as a sacred trust the obligation to promote to the utmost, within the system of international peace and security established by the present Charter, the well-being of the inhabitants of these territories, and, to this end:

a. to ensure, with due respect for the culture of the peoples concerned, their political, economic, social, and educational advancement, their just treatment, and their protection against abuses;

b. to develop self-government, to take due account of the political aspirations of the peoples, and to assist them in the progressive development of their free political institutions, according to the particular circumstances of each territory and its peoples and their varying stages of advancement;

c. to further international peace and security;

d. to promote constructive measures of development, to encourage research, and to co-operate with one another and, when and where appropriate, with specialized international bodies with a view to the practical achievement of the social, economic, and scientific purposes set forth in this Article; and

e. to transmit regularly to the Secretary-General for information purposes, subject to such limitation as security and constitutional considerations may require, statistical and other information of a technical nature relating to economic, social, and educational conditions in the territories for which they are respectively responsible other than those territories to which Chapters XII and XIII apply.

[5] Daniel Thürer and Thomas Burri, 'Self-Determination', *Max Planck Encyclopaedia of Public International Law Online*, [6] (accessed 24 January 2013).

Chapter XII of the Charter, concerning the international trusteeship system, likewise implicitly engages the principle of self-determination. Article 76(b) of the Charter provides that the 'basic objectives' of the trusteeship system shall be:

b. to promote the political, economic, social, and educational advancement of the inhabitants of the trust territories, and their progressive development towards self-government or independence as may be appropriate to the particular circumstances of each territory and its peoples and the freely expressed wishes of the peoples concerned, and as may be provided by the terms of each trusteeship agreement...

The content and scope of the principle were elaborated further in the UN General Assembly Declaration on the Granting of Independence to Colonial Countries and Peoples (Resolution 1514 (XV), 14 December 1960), which declared that:

1. The subjection of peoples to alien subjugation, domination and exploitation constitutes a denial of fundamental human rights, is contrary to the Charter of the United Nations and is an impediment to the promotion of world peace and co-operation.

2. All peoples have the right to self-determination; by virtue of that right they freely determine their political status and freely pursue their economic, social and cultural development.

3. Inadequacy of political, economic, social or educational preparedness should never serve as a pretext for delaying independence.

4. All armed action or repressive measures of all kinds directed against dependent peoples shall cease in order to enable them to exercise peacefully and freely their right to complete independence, and the integrity of their national territory shall be respected.

5. Immediate steps shall be taken, in Trust and Non-Self-Governing Territories or all other territories which have not yet attained independence, to transfer all powers to the peoples of those territories, without any conditions or reservations, in accordance with their freely expressed will and desire, without any distinction as to race, creed or colour, in order to enable them to enjoy complete independence and freedom.

6. Any attempt aimed at the partial or total disruption of the national unity and the territorial integrity of a country is incompatible with the purposes and principles of the Charter of the United Nations.

7. All States shall observe faithfully and strictly the provisions of the Charter of the United Nations, the Universal Declaration of Human Rights and the present Declaration on the basis of equality, non-interference in the internal affairs of all States, and respect for the sovereign rights of all peoples and their territorial integrity.[6]

The language of paragraph 2 of the Declaration (of 1960) is reflected in Article 1 of the ICESCR and ICCPR as adopted in 1966. However, that language was settled during the drafting of the twin covenants in 1955, such that the Declaration did not decisively influence the formulation of the ICESCR's language.

[6] UNGA Res. 1514 [XV], Declaration on the Granting of Independence to Colonial Countries and Peoples (14 December 1960) [preamble omitted].

Resolution 1541 of 15 December 1960 also laid down 'Principles' to guide states in respect of their reporting obligations concerning non-self-governing territories under Article 73 of the Charter.[7] Principles VI to IX relevantly outline the forms of political self-determination:

Principle VI

A Non-Self-Governing Territory can be said to have reached a full measure of self-government by:

(a) Emergence as a sovereign independent State;

(b) Free association with an independent State; or

(c) Integration with an independent State.

Principle VII

(a) Free association should be the result of a free and voluntary choice by the peoples of the territory concerned expressed through informed and democratic processes. It should be one which respects the individuality and the cultural characteristics of the territory and its peoples, and retains for the peoples of the territory which is associated with an independent State the freedom to modify the status of that territory through the expression of their will by democratic means and through constitutional processes.

(b) The associated territory should have the right to determine its internal constitution without outside interference, in accordance with due constitutional processes and the freely expressed wishes of the people. This does not preclude consultations as appropriate or necessary under the terms of the free association agreed upon.

Principle VIII

Integration with an independent State should be on the basis of complete equality between the peoples of the erstwhile Non-Self-Governing Territory and those of the independent country with which it is integrated. The peoples of both territories should have equal status and rights of citizenship and equal guarantees of fundamental rights and freedoms without any distinction or discrimination; both should have equal rights and opportunities for representation and effective participation at all levels in the executive, legislative and judicial organs of government.

Principle IX

Integration should have come about in the following circumstances:

(a) The integrating territory should have attained an advanced stage of self-government with free political institutions, so that its peoples would have the capacity to make a responsible choice through informed and democratic processes;

(b) The integration should be the result of the freely expressed wishes of the territory's peoples acting with full knowledge of the change in their status, their wishes having been expressed through informed and democratic processes, impartially

[7] UNGA Res. 1541, Principles which should guide Members in determining whether or not an obligation exists to transmit the information called for under Article 73e of the Charter (15 December 1960).

conducted and based on universal adult suffrage. The United Nations could, when it deems it necessary, supervise these processes.

Early in the drafting of the twin covenants, there was no provision for self-determination. The Universal Declaration of Human Rights of 1948 had not mentioned it, although it refers to rights of political participation and various economic and cultural rights. In 1950, the General Assembly requested ECOSOC and the Commission on Human Rights to study ways and means of protecting the right of self-determination.[8] The study was not completed by the time the Assembly decided in 1952 to include in the draft covenant(s) 'the right of all peoples and nations to self-determination, in reaffirmation of the principle enunciated in the Charter'.[9] The Assembly also stipulated some of the wording to be included:

This article shall be drafted in the following terms: 'All peoples shall have the right of self-determination', and shall stipulate that all States, including those have responsibility for the administration of Non-Self-Governing Territories, should promote the realization of that right, in conformity with the Purposes and Principles of the United Nations, and that States having responsibility for the administration of Non-Self-Governing Territories should promote the realization of that right in relation to the peoples of such Territories.[10]

The drafting proceeded on the basis of that formulation, with the final text as adopted in 1966 being essentially settled by 1955.

Subsequent Normative Developments

The HRC has opined that 'other international instruments' concerning self-determination are relevant to the interpretation of Article 1:

In connection with article 1 of the Covenant, the Committee refers to other international instruments concerning the right of all peoples to self-determination, in particular the Declaration on Principles of International Law concerning Friendly Relations and Co-operation among States in accordance with the Charter of the United Nations, adopted by the General Assembly on 24 October 1970 (General Assembly resolution 2625 (XXV)).[11]

The 1970 Declaration on Friendly Relations[12] first mentions self-determination when elaborating on the principle of the non-use of force by states in international relations:

Every State has the duty to refrain from any forcible action which deprives peoples referred to in the elaboration of the principle of equal rights and self-determination of their right to self-determination and freedom and independence…

[8] UNGA Res. 421 (V)(D), Draft International Covenant on Human Rights and measures of implementation: future work of the Commission on Human Rights (4 December 1950), [6].

[9] UNGA Res. 545 (VI), Inclusion in the International Covenant or Covenants on Human Rights of an article relating to the rights of peoples to self-determination (5 February 1952), [1].

[10] UNGA Res. 545 (VI), [1].

[11] HRC, General Comment No. 12 (Vol. I), 184, [7].

[12] UNGA Res. 2625 (XXV), Declaration on Principles of International Law concerning Friendly Relations and Co-operation among States in accordance with the Charter of the United Nations (24 October 1970).

The Declaration then sets out the 'principle of equal rights and self-determination of peoples':

By virtue of the principle of equal rights and self-determination of peoples enshrined in the Charter of the United Nations, all peoples have the right freely to determine, without external interference, their political status and to pursue their economic, social and cultural development, and every State has the duty to respect this right in accordance with the provisions of the Charter.

Every State has the duty to promote, through joint and separate action, realization of the principle of equal rights and self-determination of peoples, in accordance with the provisions of the Charter, and to render assistance to the United Nations in carrying out the responsibilities entrusted to it by the Charter regarding the implementation of the principle, in order:

(a) To promote friendly relations and co-operation among States; and

(b) To bring a speedy end to colonialism, having due regard to the freely expressed will of the peoples concerned;

and bearing in mind that subjection of peoples to alien subjugation, domination and exploitation constitutes a violation of the principle, as well as a denial of fundamental human rights, and is contrary to the Charter.

Every State has the duty to promote through joint and separate action universal respect for and observance of human rights and fundamental freedoms in accordance with the Charter.

The establishment of a sovereign and independent State, the free association or integration with an independent State or the emergence into any other political status freely determined by a people constitute modes of implementing the right of self-determination by that people.

Every State has the duty to refrain from any forcible action which deprives peoples referred to above in the elaboration of the present principle of their right to self-determination and freedom and independence. In their actions against, and resistance to, such forcible action in pursuit of the exercise of their right to self-determination, such peoples are entitled to seek and to receive support in accordance with the purposes and principles of the Charter.

The territory of a colony or other Non-Self-Governing Territory has, under the Charter, a status separate and distinct from the territory of the State administering it; and such separate and distinct status under the Charter shall exist until the people of the colony or Non-Self-Governing Territory have exercised their right of self-determination in accordance with the Charter, and particularly its purposes and principles.

Nothing in the foregoing paragraphs shall be construed as authorizing or encouraging any action which would dismember or impair, totally or in part, the territorial integrity or political unity of sovereign and independent States conducting themselves in compliance with the principle of equal rights and self-determination of peoples as described above and thus possessed of a government representing the whole people belonging to the territory without distinction as to race, creed or colour.

Every State shall refrain from any action aimed at the partial or total disruption of the national unity and territorial integrity of any other State or country.

The 1970 Declaration is significant for a number of reasons. It prohibits forcible external intervention to deny self-determination, thus outlawing a foreign state from assisting another state to internally repress self-determination movements. It goes a step further by entitling self-determination movements 'to seek and receive' support when opposing states which forcibly deny self-determination, although customary law remained unsettled whether such support could lawfully include military assistance.

The Declaration also illustrates some of the forms which self-determination may take (such as independent, free association or integration, or some other status). Finally, it precludes the territorial dismemberment of states which internally respect self-determination through representative, non-discriminatory government. Minority secession is thus excluded (absent extreme circumstances of systematic repression) and the *uti possidetis* principle upholding the sanctity of existing territorial boundaries is preserved.

As will be seen, other instruments are relevant to the interpretation of particular aspects of Article 1. As regards economic self-determination, pertinent instruments discussed below include the General Assembly's 1962 Declaration on Permanent Sovereignty over Natural Resources;[13] 1974 Declaration on the Establishment of a New International Economic Order;[14] 1974 Charter of Economic Rights and Duties of States;[15] and 1986 Declaration on the Right to Development.[16] The International Labour Organization's (ILO) Convention No. 169 on Indigenous and Tribal Peoples in Independent Countries of 1989 and the General Assembly's 2007 Declaration on the Rights of Indigenous Peoples are also significant.[17]

Regional Standards

Instruments of regional organizations may also shed light on wider state practice regarding the right of self-determination. Only a few regional human rights systems have expressly embraced self-determination. There is no reference to it in the European Convention on Human Rights, European Social Charter, American Convention on Human Rights, or ASEAN Human Rights Declaration. The Arab Charter on Human Rights 2004 refers briefly to it in Article 2(1):

> All peoples have the right of self-determination and control over their natural wealth and resources and, accordingly, have the right to freely determine the form of their political structure and to freely pursue their economic, social and cultural development.[18]

[13] UNGA Res. 1803 (XVII), Permanent Sovereignty over Natural Resources (14 December 1962).

[14] UNGA Res. 3201 (S-VI), Declaration on the Establishment of a New International Economic Order (1 May 1974).

[15] UNGA Res. 3281 (XXIX), Charter of Economic Rights and Duties of States (12 December 1974).

[16] UNGA Res. 41/128, Declaration on the Right to Development (4 December 1986).

[17] ILO Convention No. 169 on Indigenous and Tribal Peoples in Independent Countries (adopted 27 June 1989, entered into force 5 September 1991); UNGA Res. 61/295, UN Declaration on the Rights of Indigenous Peoples (13 September 2007).

[18] Arab Charter on Human Rights (adopted 22 May 2004, entered into force 15 March 2008), Article 2(1) (the original Arab Charter was adopted on 15 September 1994, but never entered into force; an identical provision on self-determination was found in Article 1(a)).

The most elaborate regional articulation of the right of self-determination is in the inter-related Articles 20 to 22 of the African Charter on Human and Peoples' Rights 1981.[19] The provisions draw inspiration from Article 1 of the twin covenants, but go further by specifying the consequences of its denial, including obligations of restitution and compensation for the spoliation of people's property. Article 20 recognizes the right of self-determination of all peoples; Article 21 entitles people to freely dispose of their natural resources; and Article 22 is a right of peoples to development:

Article 20

1. All peoples shall have the right to existence. They shall have the unquestionable and inalienable right to self-determination. They shall freely determine their political status and shall pursue their economic and social development according to the policy they have freely chosen.

2. Colonized or oppressed peoples shall have the right to free themselves from the bonds of domination by resorting to any means recognized by the international community.

3. All peoples shall have the right to the assistance of the States parties to the present Charter in their liberation struggle against foreign domination, be it political, economic or cultural.

Article 21

1. All peoples shall freely dispose of their wealth and natural resources. This right shall be exercised in the exclusive interest of the people. In no case shall a people be deprived of it.

2. In case of spoliation the dispossessed people shall have the right to the lawful recovery of its property as well as to an adequate compensation.

3. The free disposal of wealth and natural resources shall be exercised without prejudice to the obligation of promoting international economic cooperation based on mutual respect, equitable exchange and the principles of international law.

4. States parties to the present Charter shall individually and collectively exercise the right to free disposal of their wealth and natural resources with a view to strengthening African unity and solidarity.

5. States parties to the present Charter shall undertake to eliminate all forms of foreign economic exploitation particularly that practiced by international monopolies so as to enable their peoples to fully benefit from the advantages derived from their national resources.

Article 22

1. All peoples shall have the right to their economic, social and cultural development with due regard to their freedom and identity and in the equal enjoyment of the common heritage of mankind.

[19] African Charter on Human and Peoples' Rights (adopted 27 June 1981, 1520 UNTS 217, entered into force 21 October 1986).

2. States shall have the duty, individually or collectively, to ensure the exercise of the right to development.

While the African Commission has paid little attention to the economic aspects of the right to self-determination in Article 20,[20] the provision should be interpreted in conjunction with the right of a people to development under Article 22,[21] and the right of a people to freely dispose of their wealth and resources under Article 21 (which in turn is connected to the further right to property under Article 14 of the African Charter).[22]

There is no express right of self-determination in the American Convention on Human Rights. However, as discussed below, the Inter-American human rights system has implied self-determination into the interpretation of other American Convention rights, such as rights to life and property, including in the case of indigenous or tribal peoples.

National judicial decisions concerning self-determination are especially rare, with a few exceptions,[23] principally because national legal systems seldom constitutionalize or otherwise legislate for its existence in domestic law. National courts are also (understandably) reluctant to destroy their own jurisdiction by ruling on the lawfulness of the acquisition of their own state's territory or statehood and thus calling into question the authority of its institutions.[24]

Approach to Interpretation by United Nations Treaty Bodies

The UN treaty bodies have only partially illuminated the scope of the right of self-determination under common Article 1. The CESCR has not issued any General Comment on it and has not yet decided any individual communications under the Optional Protocol procedure, which entered into force on 5 May 2013.[25] Its observations in the periodic state reporting process have, however, shed considerable interpretive light on the economic aspects of the right, as discussed throughout this chapter. Far less attention has been paid to the social or cultural aspects of the right, with the exception of situations involving indigenous peoples.

[20] Apart from brief attention in the reporting guidelines on Article 20: see, eg, African Commission, Guidelines for National Periodic Reports, Second Activity Report (June 1989), Annex II, [III.2]: 'All communities are allowed full participation in political activities and are allowed equal opportunities in the economic activities of the country both of which should be according to the choices they have made independently'.

[21] Clive Baldwin and Cynthia Morel, 'Group Rights' in Malcolm Evans and Rachel Murray (eds), *The African Charter on Human and Peoples' Rights: The System in Practice, 1986–2006* (Cambridge University Press, Cambridge, 2010), 244, 261. The right to development is not discussed in this chapter; on Article 22 of the African Charter, see infra, 270–79.

[22] Baldwin and Morel, 'Group Rights', 266.

[23] *Reference re Secession of Quebec* [1998] 2 SCR 217, [112].

[24] In *Mabo v Queensland (No 2)* (1992) 175 CLR 1, [31–2] (Brennan J), the High Court of Australia found that the acquisition of territory by a sovereign state for the first time is an act of state which cannot be challenged, controlled or interfered with by that state's courts (though the case did not concern self-determination per se).

[25] As at mid 2013.

For its part, in its General Comment on Article 1 of the ICCPR, the HRC briefly addresses the economic aspects of the right in common Article 1(2) and (3). It has, however, often considered self-determination in its concluding observations on states' periodic reports under the ICCPR, albeit with a focus on the right's political dimensions. The Committee on the Elimination of Racial Discrimination (CERD) has also given attention to the scope of rights-holders, which may inform ICESCR interpretation.

The HRC has generally refused, however, to consider self-determination claims in adjudicating communications under the First Optional Protocol to the ICCPR, on the basis that the procedure only allows individuals to claim violations of individual rights. In *Ominayak v Canada*, the HRC found:

32.1 …The Optional Protocol provides a procedure under which individuals can claim that their individual rights have been violated. These rights are set out in part III of the Covenant, articles 6 to 27, inclusive. There is, however, no objection to a group of individuals, who can claim to be similarly affected, collectively to submit a communication about alleged breaches of their rights.[26]

The HRC thus ruled inadmissible this claim by a leader of Cree Indians in Alberta, Canada, who claimed that the taking of Indian land for commercial and industrial development (such as timber and oil concessions), and consequent adverse economic and environmental effects, would violate their self-determination rights by destroying their means of subsistence and their ability to freely dispose of their natural resources. Only a violation of Article 27 (minority rights) was found.

The HRC's requirement to be a 'victim' personally affected by a violation has been found to preclude public interest standing in later cases, as the HRC stated in *EP v Colombia*:

8.2 …The Committee further notes no individual, or group of individuals, can in the abstract, by way of *actio popularis*, challenge a law or practice deemed to be contrary to the Covenant. An individual, or a group of individuals, can only claim to be a victim in the sense of article 1 of the Optional Protocol if he or she, or they, are actually affected.[27]

The HRC conceded, however, in *Diergaardt et al v Namibia*, that 'the provisions of article 1 may be relevant in the interpretation of other rights protected by the Covenant, in particular articles 25, 26 and 27'.[28] In that case, the HRC found that the diminished influence of the minority Baster community on public life in Namibia after independence did not adversely affect individual community members' political rights under Article 25 of the ICCPR. One member of the HRC,

[26] *Chief Bernard Ominayak and Lubicon Lake Band v Canada*, HRC Communication No. 167/1984 (26 March 1990), [32.1].

[27] *E.P. v Colombia*, HRC Communication No. 318/1988 (10 June 1988), [8.2].

[28] *Diergaardt et al v Namibia*, HRC Communication No. 760/1997 (25 July 2000) [2.3–2.5, 10.3, 10.8] and Individual Opinion of Martin Scheinin (concurring). See also *Gillot v France*, HRC Communication No. 932/2000 (15 July 2002), [13.4]; *Mahuika et al v New Zealand*, HRC Communication No. 547/1993 (27 October 2000), [9.2].

Martin Scheinin, while agreeing with the decision, believed that greater weight ought to have been accorded to Article 1 in the interpretation of Article 25:

I share the Committee's conclusions in relation to all aspects of the case. On one particular point, however, I find that the Committee's reasoning is not fully consistent with the general line of its argumentation. In paragraph 10.8, the Committee, in my opinion unnecessarily, emphasizes the individual nature of rights of participation under article 25. In my view there are situations where article 25 calls for special arrangements for rights of participation to be enjoyed by members of minorities and, in particular, indigenous peoples. When such a situation arises, it is not sufficient under article 25 to afford individual members of such communities the individual right to vote in general elections. Some forms of local, regional or cultural autonomy may be called for in order to comply with the requirement of effective rights of participation. As is emphasized at the end of paragraph 10.3 of the Views, the right of self-determination under article 1 affects the interpretation of article 25. This obiter statement represents, in my opinion, proper recognition of the interdependence between the various rights protected by the Covenant, including article 1 which according to the Committee's jurisprudence cannot, on its own, serve as the basis for individual communications under the Optional Protocol.[29]

Invoking Article 1 in the interpretation of other ICCPR rights is an important and creative means of securing partial protection for some aspects of the right of self-determination, as long as the HRC insists that Article 1 proper is non-justiciable. It is a route which the CESCR may be tempted to follow under its own Protocol for individual communications.

The broader question remains, however, whether the HRC is correct to dismiss Article 1 claims per se—and whether the CESCR should take a different path. Article 1 of the First Optional Protocol to the ICCPR provides that complaints may be made in respect of a violation of 'any' ICCPR right.[30] Article 1 complaints are thus not expressly excluded. The HRC's restrictive approach rests on a fallacious conceptualization of self-determination rights as exclusively 'collective' and thus as inappropriate for individual vindication, and on an overly restrictive approach to standing.

In an appropriate case, where the author(s) of a communication is recognized as the legitimate representative of a 'people', it is hard to see why a blanket inadmissibility rule should be upheld. Collective rights can only be enjoyed by individuals who comprise the group, and the general international law on self-determination contains certain principles to identify a people's legitimate representatives (such as through recognition by a relevant regional organization or UN procedures).

In an early case, the HRC dismissed a complaint brought by a Canadian indigenous leader (a Grand Captain of the Mikmaq tribe), but appeared to contemplate that, on the right facts, a claim may be admissible if a person 'is authorized to act as representative on behalf of' a group.[31] It would remain necessary for the

[29] *Diergaardt et al v Namibia*, Individual Opinion of Martin Scheinin (concurring), [15–26].

[30] Optional Protocol to the International Covenant on Civil and Political Rights (adopted 16 December 1966, 999 UNTS 171, entered into force 23 March 1976).

[31] *A.D. (The Mikmaq Tribal Society) v Canada*, HRC Communication No. 78/1980 (29 July 1984), [8.2].

person to prove that s/he was individually affected by the violation of the group's rights, but that too is conceivable in the right case. Under the Optional Protocol to the ICESCR (unlike under the Optional Protocol to the ICCPR), there is express provision for communications to be submitted on behalf of groups,[32] lending further support to the view that collective claims of self-determination ought to be recognized.

Article 1(1)

'ALL PEOPLES'

There has been long-running debate about the meaning of 'peoples'. As the following extracts from the drafting records suggest, the intended meaning of the phrase is somewhat unclear, given the significant differences of opinion expressed by states. Attempts were variously made to understand the term by reference to the legal status of territories, the inherent characteristics of groups, or the aspirations of political movements:

37. It was said further that the right of self-determination might also be understood to refer to peoples at present struggling for their independence. The view was expressed that the Commission should define self-determination and should attempt to decide how far mere separatist movements or vague aspirations to self-government should be included in the concept.

38. Some members expressed the view that the right of peoples to self-determination was also applicable to peoples which had already formed independent national States whose independence was threatened.

40. The opinion was expressed that it was unnecessary to attempt to define self-determination, which should be proclaimed for all peoples with special emphasis on the peoples of Non-Self-Governing Territories.

41. With regard to the word 'peoples', it was said that no distinction should be made on the grounds that peoples were under the sovereignty of another country, that they lived in a particular continent, that they were independent territories or were within the territory of a sovereign State.

42. It was also suggested that 'peoples' should be interpreted to mean all peoples that could exercise the right of self-determination, that such a people should inhabit a compact territory and that its members should be related ethnically or in some other way.

43. Other views were that 'peoples' should apply to large compact national groups; that the right of self-determination should be granted only to those who made a conscious demand for it; and that peoples who were politically undeveloped should be placed under the protection of the International Trusteeship System, which would prepare them for the exercise of the right of self-determination.[33]

[32] Human Rights Council, Optional Protocol to the International Covenant on Economic, Social and Cultural Rights (adopted on 10 December 2008, entered into force 5 May 2013), Article 5(2)(b).
[33] Commission on Human Rights, E/2256 (14 April–14 June 1952), 5–6 [37, 38, 40–43].

The core of self-determination was certainly seen to involve colonial situations, but that did not necessarily exhaust the concept of peoples:

39. Much of the discussion on article 1 had related the question of self-determination to the colonial issue, but that was only because the peoples of Trust and Non-Self-Governing Territories had not yet attained independence. The right would be proclaimed in the covenants as a universal right for all time. The dangers of including the article had been exaggerated. It was true that the right could and had been misused, but that did not invalidate it. It was said that the article was not concerned with minorities or the right of secession, and the terms 'peoples' and 'nations' were not intended to cover such questions.[34]

Some delegations wished self-determination to apply to 'nations' in addition to 'peoples':

44. It was thought, by those who wished to include a reference to 'nations' in the article to be inserted in the covenants, that this addition would result in a more precise and comprehensive statement of the principle. It was pointed out that General Assembly resolution 421 D (V) had referred to 'peoples and nations' and that resolution 545 (VI), now before the Commission, also referred to 'peoples and nations' in the first and second paragraphs of the preamble to the resolution and in paragraph 1 of the operative part.[35]

Likewise:

10. The text of the clause, as it appeared in General Assembly resolution 545 (VI), read: 'All peoples shall have the right of self-determination.' The words 'all nations' were added in order to emphasize the universal character of the right. There were nations which had formerly been sovereign but were no longer masters of their own destinies; and nations, now independent, which might lose their right of self-determination.[36]

Reference to 'nations' was subsequently omitted. The wider term 'peoples' arguably already encompasses many 'nations', although not necessarily 'nations' constituted by sub-state minorities.[37] Difficulty in identifying 'peoples' resulted in a compromise in 1955 to leave it undefined, albeit subject to a general understanding that minorities were not covered by it:[38]

9. The word 'peoples' was understood to mean peoples in all countries and territories, whether independent, trust or non-self-governing. Suggestions were made to the effect that 'peoples' should apply to 'large compact national groups', to 'ethnic, religious or linguistic minorities', to 'racial units inhabiting well-defined territories', etc. It was thought, however, that the term 'peoples' should be understood in its most general sense and that no definition was necessary. Furthermore, the right of minorities was a separate problem of great complexity.[39]

On becoming parties to the ICESCR, a number of states lodged reservations or declarations on the scope of Article 1. Most prominently, India declared that the right applies 'only to the peoples under foreign domination and that these words do not apply to sovereign independent States or to a section of a people

[34] UNGA Third Committee, A/3077 (8 December 1955), 14.
[35] Commission on Human Rights, E/2256 (14 April–14 June 1952), 5–6 [44].
[36] UNGAOR, A/2929 (1 July 1955), 42. [37] See further below.
[38] See further below. [39] UNGAOR, A/2929 (1 July 1955), 42.

or nation—which is the essence of national integrity'. That statement attracted objections from France, Germany, the Netherlands, Pakistan and Sweden, principally on the basis that it attached impermissible conditions or limitations on a right which applies to all peoples and not only those under foreign domination. Bangladesh also understood Article 1 as applying in 'the historical context of colonial rule, administration, foreign domination, occupation and similar situations', attracting objections on similar grounds from France and the Netherlands, the latter on the basis that the Bangladeshi position was inconsistent with the Declaration on Friendly Relations 1970.

On ratification, Indonesia declared that Article 1 does 'not apply to a section of people within a sovereign independent state and cannot be construed as authorizing or encouraging any action which would dismember or impair, totally or in part, the territorial integrity or political unity of sovereign and independent states'. In support of this view, it invoked the Declaration on Friendly Relations 1970, the Declaration on the Granting of Independence to Colonial Countries and Peoples, and the Vienna Declaration and Program of Action 1993. Thailand similarly declared that Article 1(1) 'shall be interpreted as being compatible with that expressed in the Vienna Declaration'. Neither declaration attracted objections, in contrast to the Indian and Bangladeshi statements. The latter provoked greater reactions because it sought to exclude the right of self-determination of the peoples of independent states, whereas the latter less controversially excluded internal minority self-determination.

The absence of a definition of 'peoples' was admittedly thought to make it 'difficult for the proposed human rights committee or any machinery established to act in any particular case'.[40] The treaty bodies have nonetheless given shape and form to the term 'peoples' over time. The CERD's General Recommendation No. 21 of 1996 is the most explicit general statement on the scope of self-determination by any of the treaty bodies:

> 4. In respect of the self-determination of peoples two aspects have to be distinguished. The right to self-determination of peoples has an internal aspect, that is to say, the rights of all peoples to pursue freely their economic, social and cultural development without outside interference. In that respect there exists a link with the right of every citizen to take part in the conduct of public affairs at any level, as referred to in article 5(c) of the International Convention on the Elimination of All Forms of Racial Discrimination. In consequence, Governments are to represent the whole population without distinction as to race, colour, descent or national or ethnic origin. The external aspect of self-determination implies that all peoples have the right to determine freely their political status and their place in the international community based upon the principle of equal rights and exemplified by the liberation of peoples from colonialism and by the prohibition to subject peoples to alien subjugation, domination and exploitation.[41]

[40] UNGA Third Committee, A/3077 (8 December 1955), 12.

[41] Committee on the Elimination of Racial Discrimination (CERD), General Recommendation No. 21: Right to self-determination, A/51/18 (23 August 1996).

The international law of internal self-determination may not yet require, however, full democratic political governance of the state for the benefit of its people, with the emphasis instead on freedom from foreign interference, the sovereign equality of states,[42] and various rights of political participation which do not also presuppose a particular political system. Practically, however, democracy is the form of governance most compatible with such rights.

As regards external self-determination, in its *Kosovo Advisory Opinion* in 2010, the International Court of Justice (ICJ) affirmed that it includes 'a right to independence for the peoples of non-self-governing territories and peoples subject to alien subjugation, domination and exploitation'.[43] It found it unnecessary, however, to consider whether any other groups (such as minorities) were entitled to self-determination. Other ICJ cases involving self-determination were likewise limited to similar situations of colonialism or occupation (such as Namibia, East Timor and Palestine).

In the *Quebec Secession* case in 1998, the Canadian Supreme Court shared the CERD's classification of self-determination into internal and external varieties:

> 126. …The recognized sources of international law establish that the right to self-determination of a people is normally fulfilled through internal self-determination—a people's pursuit of its political, economic, social and cultural development within the framework of an existing state. A right to external self-determination (which in this case potentially takes the form of the assertion of a right to unilateral secession) arises in only the most extreme of cases and, even then, under carefully defined circumstances.[44]

Internal self-determination is ordinarily exercised through the population enjoying political representation and rights of equality and non-discrimination:

> 130. While the *International Covenant on Economic, Social and Cultural Rights* and the *International Covenant on Civil and Political Rights* do not specifically refer to the protection of territorial integrity, they both define the ambit of the right to self-determination in terms that are normally attainable within the framework of an existing state. There is no necessary incompatibility between the maintenance of the territorial integrity of existing states, including Canada, and the right of a 'people' to achieve a full measure of self-determination. A state whose government represents the whole of the people or peoples resident within its territory, on a basis of equality and without discrimination, and respects the principles of self-determination in its own internal arrangements, is entitled to the protection under international law of its territorial integrity.[45]

According to the Supreme Court, external self-determination is limited to three situations:

> 138. In summary, the international law right to self-determination only generates, at best, a right to external self-determination in situations of former colonies; where a people is oppressed, as for example under foreign military occupation; or where a definable group

[42] Thürer and Burri, 'Self-Determination', [17].
[43] *Accordance with International Law of the Unilateral Declaration of Independence in Respect of Kosovo (Advisory Opinion)* ('*Kosovo Advisory Opinion*'), 22 July 2010, (2010) ICJ Reports 403, [79].
[44] *Reference re Secession of Quebec* [1998] 2 SCR 217, [126].
[45] *Reference re Secession of Quebec* [1998] 2 SCR 217, [130].

is denied meaningful access to government to pursue their political, economic, social and cultural development. In all three situations, the people in question are entitled to a right to external self-determination because they have been denied the ability to exert internally their right to self-determination.[46]

The Court left open the possibility—avoided and declared controversial by the ICJ in the *Kosovo Advisory Opinion*—of remedial self-determination for groups whose rights are systematically violated. On the facts, the people of Québec were not such a group. Under the right conditions, however, persecuted minorities may be entitled to exercise self-determination through secession, beyond ordinary rights of political participation and minority cultural rights. As discussed later, the African Commission has expressly admitted the possibility, but in no case to date has it upheld such right on the facts.

As Nowak presciently observes, if internal self-determination requires the observance of various political rights, 'it contains the seeds of a right of revolution against dictatorships that systematically and grossly violate human rights'.[47] A conceptual link may be drawn here to a clause of the preamble to the Universal Declaration of Human Rights, which states:

Whereas it is essential, if man is not to be compelled to have recourse, as a last resort, to rebellion against tyranny and oppression, that human rights should be protected by the rule of law…

MINORITIES

Historically, state practice has been equivocal on whether minorities are entitled to self-determination. (The definition of minorities is considered in the chapter on Article 15 of the ICESCR.) Since the time of the League of Nations, questions of minority protection and self-determination were often co-mingled in situations where a state is in transition, as the *Aaland Islands* case of 1921 suggests:

THE PRINCIPLE OF SELF-DETERMINATION AND THE RIGHTS OF PEOPLES

…Positive International Law does not recognise the right of national groups, as such, to separate themselves from the State of which they form part by the simple expression of a wish, any more than it recognises the right of other States to claim such a separation.

Generally speaking, the grant or refusal of the right to a portion of its population of determining its own political fate by plebiscite or by some other method, is, exclusively, an attribute of the sovereignty of every State which is definitively constituted…

DE FACTO AND DE JURE CONSIDERATIONS. THEIR INTERNATIONAL CHARACTER.

3. It must, however, be observed that all that has been said concerning the attributes of the sovereignty of a State, generally speaking, only applies to a nation which is definitively

[46] *Reference re Secession of Quebec* [1998] 2 SCR 217, [138].

[47] Manfred Nowak, *UN Covenant on Civil and Political Rights: CCPR Commentary* (2nd edn, NP Engel, Kehl, 2005) ('*CCPR Commentary*'), 23.

constituted as a sovereign State and an independent member of the international community, and so long as it continues to possess these characteristics.

From the point of view of both domestic and international law, the formation, transformation and dismemberment of States as a result of revolutions and wars create situations of fact which, to a large extent, cannot be met by the application of the normal rules of positive law. This amounts to a statement that if the essential basis of these rules, that is to say, territorial sovereignty, is lacking, either because the State is not yet fully formed or because it is undergoing transformation or dissolution, the situation is obscure and uncertain from a legal point of view, and will not become clear until the period of development is completed and a definite new situation, which is normal in respect to territorial sovereignty, has been established.

This transition from a de facto situation to a normal situation de jure cannot be considered as one confined entirely within the domestic jurisdiction of a State…

SELF-DETERMINATION AS APPLIED TO DE FACTO SITUATIONS. ITS FORMS.

Under such circumstances, the principle of self-determination of peoples may be called into play. New aspirations of certain sections of a nation, which are sometimes based on old traditions or on a common language and civilisation, may come to the surface and produce effects which must be taken into account in the interests of the internal and external peace of nations.

The principle recognising the rights of peoples to determine their political fate may be applied in various ways; the most important of these are, on the one hand the formation of an independent State, and on the other hand the right of choice between two existing States. This principle, however, must be brought into line with that of the protection of minorities; both have a common object—to assure to some national Group the maintenance and free development of its social, ethnical or religious characteristics.

The protection of minorities is already provided for, to a very varying extent, in a fairly large number of constitutions. This principle appears to be one of the essential characteristics of liberty at the present time. Under certain circumstances, however, it has been thought necessary to go further, and to guarantee, by international treaties, some particular situation to certain racial or religious minorities. Thus, in some recent treaties a special legal régime, under the control and guarantee of the League of Nations, has been established for certain sections of the population of a State.

The fact must, however, not be lost sight of that the principle that nations must have the right of self-determination is not the only one to be taken into account. Even though it be regarded as the most important of the principles governing the formation of States, geographical, economic and other similar considerations may put obstacles in the way of its complete recognition. Under such circumstances, a solution in the nature of a compromise, based on an extensive grant of liberty to minorities, may appear necessary according to international legal conception and may even be dictated by the interests of peace.[48]

[48] *Report of the International Committee of Jurists entrusted by the Council of the League of Nations with the task of giving an advisory opinion upon the legal aspects of the Aaland Islands question*, League of Nations Council Document B7 21/68/106 (1921), [2–3].

During the drafting of the twin covenants, Russia proposed a provision on the protection of minorities within the article on self-determination:

...the State shall ensure to national minorities the right to use the native tongue and to have the national schools, libraries, museums and other cultural and educational institutions.[49]

Opinion amongst delegates was mixed:

56. ...It was said that that right could not be fully ensured without guaranteeing the right of national minorities to use their native tongue and to have their own cultural and educational institutions. Others thought that the question of minorities was a separate issue and should be dealt with elsewhere. It was pointed out that if the principle that all national aspirations should be fulfilled were interpreted broadly, then any minority which could claim to be a 'people' could claim the right to self-determination. It was also said that to attempt to introduce the question of the rights of minorities into the article on self-determination would tend to discourage States from ratifying the covenant. It was also argued, however, that, under the Charter, all peoples had the right of self-determination, that it mentioned no exception, and that hence a people could not be debarred from exercising that right on the pretext that it formed a national minority.[50]

Ultimately, by 1955 the proposal had been rejected for a combination of reasons:

22. ...One view was that such a proposal would retard the process of assimilation of immigrants to a new country and prevent the formation of a homogeneous society. Another view was that it might encourage separatist or irredentist movements and might bring about a multiplication of barriers and frontiers. (It may be noted that the rights of minorities are dealt with in article 25 of the draft covenant on civil and political rights.)[51]

A number of treaty bodies have initially sought to draw sharp distinctions between minorities and peoples. Thus, the HRC has distinguished (individual) minority rights under Article 27 of the ICCPR from (collective) self-determination in Article 1:

The Covenant draws a distinction between the right to self-determination and the rights protected under Article 27. The former is expressed to be a right belonging to peoples and is dealt with under a separate part (Part I) of the Covenant.[52]

Likewise, in its General Recommendation No. 21 on self-determination of 1996, the CERD emphasized that minorities are foremost entitled to general human rights and minority rights:

1. The Committee notes that ethnic or religious groups or minorities frequently refer to the right to self-determination as a basis for an alleged right to secession.

...

[49] UNGAOR (10th Session), A/2929 (1 July 1955), Annexes, 15 [22]; see also Commission on Human Rights, E/CN.4/L.21 (15 April 1952); Commission on Human Rights, E/2256 (14 April–14 June 1952), 6–7.

[50] Commission on Human Rights, E/2256, 7.

[51] UNGAOR (10th Session), A/2929 (1 July 1955), Annexes, 15.

[52] HRC, General Comment No. 23, The rights of minorities (Article 27), CCPR/C/21/Rev.1/Add.5 (8 April 1994).

5. In order to respect fully the rights of all peoples within a State, Governments are again called upon to adhere to and implement fully the international human rights instruments and in particular the International Convention on the Elimination of All Forms of Racial Discrimination. Concern for the protection of individual rights without discrimination on racial, ethnic, tribal, religious or other grounds must guide the policies of Governments. In accordance with article 2 of the International Convention on the Elimination of All Forms of Racial Discrimination and other relevant international documents, Governments should be sensitive towards the rights of persons belonging to ethnic groups, particularly their right to lead lives of dignity, to preserve their culture, to share equitably in the fruits of national growth and to play their part in the Government of the country of which they are citizens. Also, Governments should consider, within their respective constitutional frameworks, vesting persons belonging to ethnic or linguistic groups comprised of their citizens, where appropriate, with the right to engage in activities which are particularly relevant to the preservation of the identity of such persons or groups.

6. The Committee emphasizes that, in accordance with the Declaration on Friendly Relations, none of the Committee's actions shall be construed as authorizing or encouraging any action which would dismember or impair, totally or in part, the territorial integrity or political unity of sovereign and independent States conducting themselves in compliance with the principle of equal rights and self-determination of peoples and possessing a Government representing the whole people belonging to the territory, without distinction as to race, creed or colour. In the view of the Committee, international law has not recognized a general right of peoples unilaterally to declare secession from a State. In this respect, the Committee follows the views expressed in An Agenda for Peace (paras. 17 and following), namely, that a fragmentation of States may be detrimental to the protection of human rights, as well as to the preservation of peace and security. This does not, however, exclude the possibility of arrangements reached by free agreements of all parties concerned.[53]

For the CERD, minorities are primarily entitled to enjoy freedom from discrimination, cultural rights, and political participation rights (as citizens). A closer reading suggests, however, that the CERD does not specifically exclude minorities from self-determination altogether, but rather observes that they enjoy no right of secession. It thus leaves open a middle ground position in which minorities may be entitled to a limited form of self-determination not involving secession. At the very least the CESCR has recognized that minorities are also part of the state's wider population and their interests must be protected in the state's social and cultural life; they too are part of the state's 'people' as a whole, in addition to enjoying minority rights:

32. In the Committee's view, article 15, paragraph 1(a) of the Covenant also includes the right of minorities and of persons belonging to minorities to take part in the cultural life of society, and also to conserve, promote and develop their own culture.[54] This right entails

[53] CERD, General Recommendation No. 21: Right to self-determination, A/51/18 (23 August 1996), [1, 5–6].

[54] ICCPR, Article 27; UNGA Res. 47/135, Declaration on the Rights of Persons Belonging to National or Ethnic, Religious and Linguistic Minorities (18 December 1992), [1(1)].

the obligation of States parties to recognize, respect and protect minority cultures as an essential component of the identity of the States themselves…

33. Minorities, as well as persons belonging to minorities, have the right not only to their own identity but also to development in all areas of cultural life. Any programme intended to promote the constructive integration of minorities and persons belonging to minorities into the society of a State party should thus be based on inclusion, participation and non-discrimination, with a view to preserving the distinctive character of minority cultures.[55]

Since the early 1990s, there has been a liberalization of attitudes towards minorities and self-determination rights. The European Commission's Badinter Arbitration Committee characterized the break-up of Yugoslavia in the 1990s as the legal dissolution of a federal state.[56] But it also linked minority rights and self-determination in *Opinion No. 2*:[57]

1. The Committee considers that, whatever the circumstances, the right to self-determination must not involve changes to existing frontiers at the time of independence *(uti possidetis juris)* except where the states concerned agree otherwise.

2. Where there are one or more groups within a state constituting one or more ethnic, religious or language communities, they have the right to recognition of their identity under international law.

As the Committee emphasized in its Opinion No. 1 of 29 November 1991, published on 7 December, the—now peremptory—norms of international law require states to ensure respect for the rights of minorities. This requirement applies to all the Republics *vis-a-vis* the minorities on their territory.

The Serbian population in Bosnia-Herzegovina and Croatia must therefore be afforded every right accorded to minorities under international convention as well as national and international guarantees consistent with the principles of international law and the provisions of Chapter II of the draft Convention of 4 November 1991, which has been accepted by these Republics.

3. Article 1 of the two 1986 International Covenants on human rights establishes that the principle of the right to self-determination serves to safeguard human rights. By virtue of that right every individual may choose to belong to whatever ethnic, religious or language community he or she wishes.

In the Committee's view one possible consequence of this principle might be for the members of the Serbian population in Bosnia-Herzegovina and Croatia to be recognized under agreements between the Republics as having the nationality of their choice, with all the rights and obligations which that entails with respect to the states concerned.

[55] CESCR, General Comment No. 21, Right of everyone to take part in cultural life (Article 15, para. 1(a) of the ICESCR), E/C.12/GC/21 (21 December 2009), ('General Comment No. 21), [32–3].

[56] Conference on Yugoslavia Arbitration Committee ('Badinter Committee'), *Opinions on Questions Arising from the Dissolution of Yugoslavia, Opinion No. 1* (1992) 31 *International Legal Materials* 1494.

[57] Alain Pellet, 'The Opinions of the Badinter Arbitration Committee: A Second Breath for the Self-Determination of Peoples' (1992) 3 *European Journal of International Law* 178, 179.

4. The Arbitration Committee is therefore of the opinion:

(i) that the Serbian population in Bosnia-Herzegovina and Croatia is entitled to all the rights concerned to minorities and ethnic groups under international law and under the provisions of the draft Convention of the Conference on Yugoslavia of 4 November 1991, to which the Republics of Bosnia-Herzegovina and Croatia have undertaken to give effect; and

(ii) that the Republics must afford the members of those minorities and ethnic groups all the human rights and fundamental freedoms recognized in international law, including, where appropriate, the right to choose their nationality.[58]

The Badinter Committee's view is significant for a number of reasons. Minorities emerge as beneficiaries of limited self-determination rights (in contrast to their exclusion from such rights in the *Aaland Islands* case above).[59] First, the collective right of self-determination involves individual rights to choose one's cultural identity. Article 1 of the ICESCR and ICCPR (including the notion of cultural self-determination) are thus linked with Article 15(1)(e) and Article 27 respectively of the twin covenants. The untenable distinction sometimes drawn between self-determination as a collective right and minority rights as individual rights is eroded, as both sets of rights are recognized to involve both group and individual dimensions.

Secondly, while minorities may not be entitled to secede from the state—which may infringe the self-determination rights of the majority population—in the context of dissolving a federal state their cultural self-determination may justify special treatment such as the right to choose their nationality. Self-determination is thus decoupled from the primacy of state territory; minority groups resident in one state may pursue their self-determination through the attachment of citizenship to another state.

In 2000, the CESCR urged Yugoslavia 'to facilitate the exercise of the right of self-determination by all peoples in the Federal Republic of Yugoslavia'.[60] The CESCR accordingly implied that an independent federal state may be constituted not by a single 'people' (the population as a whole, subsuming minorities within it), but by a plurality of sub-national 'peoples'. The most pressing contemporaneous example was Kosovo, which was legally part of Yugoslavia but subject to UN administration (UNMIK) and a NATO peacekeeping force (KFOR), following acute inter-ethnic violence in 1999. As early as 1992, the CESCR had faulted Yugoslavia in relation to self-determination:

With reference to article 1 of the Covenant, the fact that there was no procedure under domestic law for implementation of the right to secede recognized in the federal Constitution, which would have enabled the crisis to be settled peacefully is regretted, as

[58] Badinter Committee, *Opinions on Questions Arising from the Dissolution of Yugoslavia, Opinion No. 2* (1992) 31 *International Legal Materials* 1497.

[59] *Report of the International Committee of Jurists entrusted by the Council of the League of Nations with the Task of Giving an Advisory Opinion upon the Legal Aspects of the Aaland Islands Question*, League of Nations Council Document B7 21/68/106 (1921).

[60] CESCR, Preliminary Recommendations: Yugoslavia, E/2001/22 (2001), [503].

is the fact that, under the state of emergency proclaimed in the province of Kosovo, excessive steps have been taken to limit the rights and freedoms guaranteed by the Covenant.[61]

In its *Kosovo Advisory Opinion* of 2010, the ICJ did not decide whether the Kosovar minority in Yugoslavia was a 'people' entitled to self-determination, or whether any such self-determination right supported a claim of secession. Kosovo eventually declared independence unilaterally in 2008, prior to the conclusion of final status negotiations envisaged by Security Council Resolution 1244 (1999). The ICJ declared simply that international law does not prohibit declarations of independence,[62] a view advanced in 1998 by the Canadian Supreme Court in the *Quebec Secession* case.[63] The ICJ made only incidental observations on self-determination:

79. …During the second half of the twentieth century, the international law of self-determination developed in such a way as to create a right to independence for the peoples of non-self-governing territories and peoples subject to alien subjugation, domination and exploitation (cf. *Legal Consequences for States of the Continued Presence of South Africa in Namibia (South West Africa) notwithstanding Security Council Resolution 276 (1970), Advisory Opinion, I.C.J. Reports 1971*, pp. 31–32, paras. 52–53; *East Timor (Portugal* v. *Australia), Judgment, I.C.J. Reports 1995*, p. 102, para. 29; *Legal Consequences of the Construction of a Wall in the Occupied Palestinian Territory, Advisory Opinion, I.C.J. Reports 2004 (I)*, pp. 171–172, para. 88). A great many new States have come into existence as a result of the exercise of this right. There were, however, also instances of declarations of independence outside this context…

…

82. A number of participants in the present proceedings have claimed, although in almost every instance only as a secondary argument, that the population of Kosovo has the right to create an independent State either as a manifestation of a right to self-determination or pursuant to what they described as a right of 'remedial secession' in the face of the situation in Kosovo.

The Court has already noted (see paragraph 79 above) that one of the major developments of international law during the second half of the twentieth century has been the evolution of the right of self-determination. Whether, outside the context of non-self-governing territories and peoples subject to alien subjugation, domination and exploitation, the international law of self-determination confers upon part of the population of an existing State a right to separate from that State is, however, a subject on which radically different views were expressed by those taking part in the proceedings and expressing a position on the question. Similar differences existed regarding whether international law provides for a right of 'remedial secession' and, if so, in what circumstances. There was also a sharp difference of views as to whether the circumstances which some participants maintained would give rise to a right of 'remedial secession' were actually present in Kosovo.

83. The Court considers that it is not necessary to resolve these questions in the present case. The General Assembly has requested the Court's opinion only on whether or not the

[61] HRC, Report: Yugoslavia, A/47/40 (1994), 103, [465].
[62] *Kosovo Advisory Opinion*, [79].
[63] *Reference re Secession of Quebec* [1998] 2 SCR 217, [112].

declaration of independence is in accordance with international law. Debates regarding the extent of the right of self-determination and the existence of any right of 'remedial secession', however, concern the right to separate from a State. As the Court has already noted (see paragraphs 49 to 56 above), and as almost all participants agreed, that issue is beyond the scope of the question posed by the General Assembly. To answer that question, the Court need only determine whether the declaration of independence violated either general international law or the *lex specialis* created by Security Council resolution 1244 (1999).

The ICJ therefore left unanswered the 'radically' contested question of '[w]hether, outside the context of non-self-governing territories and peoples subject to alien subjugation, domination and exploitation, the international law of self-determination confers upon part of the population of an existing State a right to separate from that State'.[64] Nor was the Court called upon to otherwise specify the content of the right of self-determination where secession was not at issue. It may be noted, however, that the Independent International Commission on Kosovo recognized 'the right of self-determination for the people of Kosovo'.[65]

A superior national court, the Canadian Supreme Court, touched on some of these questions in its decision in the *Quebec Secession* case over a decade earlier in 1998.[66] Acknowledging the uncertainty surrounding the interpretation of 'peoples' under international law, the Supreme Court nonetheless accepted that a people 'may include only a portion of the population of an existing state'.[67] It found it unnecessary to answer, however, whether the people of Québec, or the aboriginal population of Québec, were a people entitled to self-determination, finding instead that self-determination in any case does not ground a right to unilateral secession:

(i) Defining 'Peoples'

123. International law grants the right to self-determination to 'peoples'. Accordingly, access to the right requires the threshold step of characterizing as a people the group seeking self-determination. However, as the right to self-determination has developed by virtue of a combination of international agreements and conventions, coupled with state practice, with little formal elaboration of the definition of 'peoples', the result has been that the precise meaning of the term 'people' remains somewhat uncertain.

124. It is clear that 'a people' may include only a portion of the population of an existing state. The right to self-determination has developed largely as a human right, and is generally used in documents that simultaneously contain references to 'nation' and 'state'. The juxtaposition of these terms is indicative that the reference to 'people' does not necessarily mean the entirety of a state's population. To restrict the definition of the term to the population of existing states would render the granting of a right to self-determination largely

[64] *Kosovo Advisory Opinion*, [82].

[65] Independent International Commission on Kosovo, *The Kosovo Report: Conflict, International Response, Lessons Learned* (Oxford University Press, Oxford, 2000), 186.

[66] *Reference re Secession of Quebec* [1998] 2 SCR 217.

[67] *Reference re Secession of Quebec*, [124].

duplicative, given the parallel emphasis within the majority of the source documents on the need to protect the territorial integrity of existing states, and would frustrate its remedial purpose.

125. While much of the Quebec population certainly shares many of the characteristics (such as a common language and culture) that would be considered in determining whether a specific group is a 'people', as do other groups within Quebec and/or Canada, it is not necessary to explore this legal characterization to resolve Question 2 appropriately. Similarly, it is not necessary for the Court to determine whether, should a Quebec people exist within the definition of public international law, such a people encompasses the entirety of the provincial population or just a portion thereof. Nor is it necessary to examine the position of the aboriginal population within Quebec. As the following discussion of the scope of the right to self-determination will make clear, whatever be the correct application of the definition of people(s) in this context, their right of self-determination cannot in the present circumstances be said to ground a right to unilateral secession.

The HRC too has gradually widened the scope of 'peoples' with regard to minorities. The HRC 'regretted' the narrow view of self-determination taken by Azerbaijan and recalled that 'under Article 1 of the Covenant, that principle applies to all peoples, and not merely colonized peoples'.[68] The HRC was responding to Azerbaijan's claim that self-determination should be limited to former colonies, so as to avoid 'micronationalism' and its attendant violation of sovereignty. Azerbaijan had thus stated:

4. At the same time the Azerbaijani Republic, foreseeing a danger of micronationalism when many small groupings want to set up independent States, and of ultranationalism when a number of States do not accept the applicable principles of operation of the United Nations or interpret them in their own interests chiefly in pursuance of their own policy, maintains that self-determination should be applied exclusively to former colonies. This principle cannot be used for regional groupings within a State. Otherwise, other basic principles—sovereignty and the inviolability of frontiers—are violated.

An example of the pernicious consequences attendant upon violation of these principles is the aggression which has been continuing for more than five years against the Azerbaijani Republic and the occupation of its territory by the neighbouring Republic of Armenia, which is using the right of self-determination of peoples, in particular that of the Armenian minority in the Nagorny Karabakh region of the Azerbaijani Republic, as a factor in concealing its far-reaching plans to seize the territories of others.[69]

Aside from the special circumstances of Yugoslavia mentioned earlier, the CESCR has infrequently linked minorities to self-determination. In 2010 it was concerned with the adverse impacts of infrastructure, development and mining projects on Afro-Colombian communities—descendants of African slaves—in Colombia,[70]

[68] HRC, Concluding Observations: Azerbaijan, CCPR/C/79/Add.38 (3 August 1994), [6].

[69] HRC, Addendum to the Initial Reports of States Parties Due in 1993: Azerbaijan, CCPR/C/81/Add.2 (8 March 1994).

[70] CESCR, Concluding Observations: Colombia, E/C.12/COL/CO/5 (12 May 2010), [9].

and also by the impact of free trade agreements on the same communities.[71] The CESCR has also highlighted land-based 'inter-ethnic' conflict in the Ituri province of the Democratic Republic of Congo as engaging Article 1.[72]

The CESCR's practice remains, however, inconsistent, or at least opaque. It has not, for instance, invoked Article 1 in the context of the bitter ethnic conflict between Sinhalese and Tamil Sri Lankans either during or after the civil war that ended in 2009, despite that conflict being a candidate for 'remedial self-determination' in the context of suppressed minority rights. It would be generally helpful for the CESCR to more precisely articulate when it believes Article 1 is or is not engaged by particular group-oriented rights problems.

Regional human rights bodies have developed the concept of 'peoples' further in the direction of encompassing certain minorities within independent states. In *Katangese Peoples' Congress v Zaire*, the African Commission noted that there may be 'controversy as to the definition of peoples', but implied that it might include an ethnic minority within a state.[73] On the facts, the Commission found it unnecessary to determine the question because the case was disposed of on the basis that the relevant group did not meet other conditions for exercising self-determination.[74]

In a later case involving a self-determination claim by the people of southern Cameroon against the Republic of Cameroon, *Mgwanga Gunme v Cameroon*, the African Commission elaborated at length on the problem of the definition of 'peoples' for the purposes of Articles 20 to 22 of the African Charter (dealing with various aspects of self-determination):

169. The Commission shall clarify its understanding of 'peoples' rights' under the African Charter. The Commission is aware the controversial nature of the issue, due to the political connotation that it carries. That controversy is as old as the Charter. The drafters of the Charter refrained deliberately from defining it. To date, the concept has not been defined under international law. However, there is recognition that certain objective features attributable to a collective of individuals, may warrant them to be considered as 'people'.

170. A group of international law experts commissioned by UNESCO to reflect on the concept of 'people' concluded that where a group of people manifest some of the following characteristics; a common historical tradition, a racial or ethnic identity, cultural homogeneity, linguistic unity, religious and ideological affinities, territorial connection, and a common economic life, it may be considered to be a 'people'. Such a group may

[71] CESCR, Concluding Observations: Colombia, E/C.12/COL/CO/5 (12 May 2010), [10].

[72] CESCR, Concluding Observations: Democratic Republic of Congo, E/C.12/COD/CO/4 (16 December 2009), [15].

[73] *Katangese Peoples' Congress v Zaire*, African Commission on Human and Peoples' Rights Communication No. 75/92 (1995), (2000) AHRLR 72, [4]: 'The issue in the case is not self-determination for all Zaireoise as a people but specifically for the Katangese. Whether the Katangese consist of one or more ethnic groups is, for this purpose, immaterial and no evidence has been adduced to that effect.'

[74] *Katangese Peoples' Congress v Zaire*, [6].

also identify itself as a people, by virtue of their consciousness that they are a people. This characterisation does not bind the Commission but can only be used as a guide.

171. In the context of the African Charter, the notion of 'people' is closely related to collective rights. Collective rights enumerated under Articles 19 to 24 of the Charter can be exercised by a people, bound together by their historical, traditional, racial, ethnic, cultural, linguistic, religious, ideological, geographical, economic identities and affinities, or other bonds.

172. The drafters of the Charter provided for the protection of 'peoples rights' under the Charter. In his book, entitled; [sic] *The Law of the African (Banjul) Charter on Human and Peoples' Rights*, Justice Hassan B. Jallow, an eminent African Jurist, who participated in the drafting [of] the African Charter, sheds light on this issue. He says that:

'[t]he concept of peoples' rights, to which a whole chapter had been devoted in the draft did not mean there was any grading of rights. There were economic, social and cultural rights which have particular importance to developing countries and which together with civil rights and political rights in one complementary whole should henceforth be given an important place.'

…

174. The African Commission has itself dealt with the issues of peoples' rights without defining the term 'people' or 'peoples' rights'. In its acclaimed Report of the Working Group of Experts on Indigenous Populations/Communities, the African Commission described its dilemma of defining the concepts in the following terms:

'[d]espite its mandate to interpret all provisions of the African Charter as per Article 45.3, the African Commission initially shied away from interpreting the concept of "peoples". The African Charter itself does not define the concept. Initially the African Commission did not feel at ease in developing rights where there was little concrete international jurisprudence. The ICCPR and the ICESR do not define "peoples". It is evident that the drafters of the African Charter intended to distinguish between the traditional individual rights where the sections preceding Article 17 make reference to "every individual".

Article 18 serves as a break by referring to the family. Articles 19–24 make specific reference to "all peoples."'

175. It continues:

'Given such specificity, it is surprising that the African Charter fails to define "peoples" unless it was trusted that its meaning could be discerned from the prevailing international instruments and norms. Two conclusions can be drawn from this. One, that the African Charter seeks to make provision for group or collective rights, that is, that set of rights that can conceivably be enjoyed only in a collective manner like the right to self determination or independence or sovereignty…'.

176. The Commission deduces from the foregoing discourse that peoples' rights are equally important as are individual rights. They deserve, and must be given protection. The minimum that can be said of peoples' rights is that, each member of the group carries with him/her the individual rights into the group, on top of what the group enjoys in its

collectivity, i.e. common rights which benefit the community such as the right to development, peace, security, a healthy environment, self-determination and the right to equitable share of their resources.[75]

On the facts, the Commission accepted that 'the people of Southern Cameroon can legitimately claim to be a "people"'.[76] Significantly, the basis of its decision was that they shared a distinct identity (akin to a minority), not also—as claimed by the complainants—that they were victims of a botched decolonization process. The Commission ruled that the latter question was beyond its jurisdiction,[77] such that the people of Southern Cameroon could not be viewed as a still colonized people subject to foreign domination and still entitled to obtain independence:

178. …Besides the individual rights due to Southern Cameroon[ians], they have a distinct identity which attracts certain collective rights. The UNESCO Group of Experts report referred to hereinabove, states that for a collective of individuals to constitute a 'people' they need to manifest some, or all the identified attributes. The Commission agrees with the Respondent State that a 'people' may manifest ethno-anthropological attributes. Ethno-anthropological attributes may be added to the characteristics of a 'people'. Such attributes are necessary only when determining indigenology of a 'people' [quote], but cannot be used as the only determinant factor to accord or deny the enjoyment or protection of peoples' rights. Was *[sic]* it the intention of the State Parties to rely on ethno-anthropological roots only to determine [quote] 'peoples' rights,' they would have said so in the African Charter? As it is, the African Charter guarantees equal protection to people on the continent, including other racial groups whose ethno-anthropological roots are not African.

179. Based on that reasoning, the Commission finds that 'the people of Southern Cameroon' qualify to be referred to as a 'people' because they manifest numerous characteristics and affinities, which include a common history, linguistic tradition, territorial connection and political outlook. More importantly they identify themselves as a people with a separate and distinct identity. Identity is an innate characteristic within a people. It is up to other external people to recognise such existence, but not to deny it.

180. The Respondent State might not recognise such innate characteristics. That shall not resolve the question of self-identification of Southern Cameroonians. It might actually postpone the solution to the problems in Southern Cameroon, including those already highlighted hereinabove. The Respondent State acknowledges that there have been problems created regularly by the secessionist SCNC and SCAPO, in that part of its territory, which calls itself the 'Southern Cameroon'.

181. The Commission is aware that post-colonial Africa has witnessed numerous cases of domination of one group of people over others, either on the basis of race, religion, or ethnicity, without such domination constituting colonialism in the classical sense. Civil wars and internal conflicts on the continent are testimony to that fact. It is incumbent on State Parties, therefore, whenever faced with allegations of the nature contained in the

[75] *Mgwanga Gunme v Cameroon*, African Commission on Human and Peoples' Rights Communication No. 266/03 (13–27 May 2009), (2009) AHRLR 9.

[76] *Mgwanga Gunme v Cameroon*, [178]. [77] *Mgwanga Gunme v Cameroon*, [155].

present communication, to address them rather than ignore them under the guise of sovereignty and territorial integrity. Mechanisms such as the African Commission were established to resolve disputes in an amicable and peaceful manner. If such mechanisms are utilised in good faith, they can spare the continent valuable human and material resources, otherwise lost due to conflicts fighting against ethnic, religious domination or economic marginalisation.

It did not follow, however, that the people of Southern Cameroon were entitled to secession, as opposed to more limited forms of self-determination, an issue considered further below.

INDIGENOUS AND TRIBAL GROUPS

Article 1 of the ICESCR does not specifically mention 'indigenous' peoples nor are they expressly mentioned elsewhere in the ICESCR. Indigenous peoples were scarcely visible in drafting of the twin covenants in the 1950s, although they evidently present a narrower category than the whole field of 'minorities'. Until recently the CESCR did not generally refer to indigenous peoples in the context of Article 1. However, since the early to mid 2000s, the CESCR has expressly recognized indigenous peoples under Article 1 in its observations on Brazil, Cambodia, Colombia, Democratic Republic of Congo, Russia and Sweden.[78]

While the CESCR has not offered a definition of indigenous peoples, it has repeatedly invoked the International Labour Organization's Convention (No. 169) concerning Indigenous and Tribal Peoples in Independent Countries as a key normative framework linked to the interpretation of Article 1 of the ICESCR. Convention No. 169 stipulates its scope of application in Article 1:

1. This Convention applies to:

   (a) Tribal peoples in independent countries whose social, cultural and economic conditions distinguish them from other sections of the national community, and whose status is regulated wholly or partially by their own customs or traditions or by special laws or regulations;

   (b) Peoples in independent countries who are regarded as indigenous on account of their descent from the populations which inhabited the country, or a geographical region to which the country belongs, at the time of conquest or colonisation or the establishment of present State boundaries and who, irrespective of their legal status, retain some or all of their own social, economic, cultural and political institutions.

2. Self-identification as indigenous or tribal shall be regarded as a fundamental criterion for determining the groups to which the provisions of this Convention apply.

[78] CESCR, Concluding Observations: Cambodia, E/C.12/KHM/CO/1 (12 June 2009), [15]–[16]; Colombia, E/C.12/COL/CO/5 (7 June 2010), [9–10]; Democratic Republic of Congo, E/C.12/COD/CO/4 (16 December 2009), [13]–[14]; Ecuador, E/C.12/1/Add.100 (4 June 2004), [12], [35]; Philippines, E/C.12/PHL/CO/4 (1 December 2008), [6], [16]; Russian Federation, E/C.12/1/Add.94 (12 December 2003), [11], [39]; Sweden, E/C.12/SWE/CO/5 (1 December 2008), [15]; Brazil, E/C.12/BRA/CO/2 (12 June 2009), [9].

3. The use of the term 'peoples' in this Convention shall not be construed as having any implications as regards the rights which may attach to the term under international law.

With the General Assembly's adoption of the 2007 Declaration on the Rights of Indigenous Peoples, it may be expected that the CESCR will draw in future upon that new UN 'soft law' standard in reinforcing its understanding that indigenous groups are 'peoples' entitled to self-determination under Article 1 of the ICESCR. The language of the Declaration (in Article 3) deliberately mirrors part of the text of the ICESCR and ICCPR:

Indigenous peoples have the right of self-determination. By virtue of that right they freely determine their political status and freely pursue their economic, social and cultural development.

The 2007 Declaration does not define 'indigenous peoples', which was thought unnecessary. However, the UN system generally accepts[79] the functional working definition suggested in 1986 by a UN Special Rapporteur, Jose R. Martinez Cobo, in his study on discrimination against indigenous populations:

34. ... Indigenous populations are composed of the existing descendants of the peoples who inhabited the present territory of a country wholly or partially at the time when persons of a different culture or ethnic origin arrived there from other parts of the world, overcame them and, by conquest, settlement or other means, reduced them to a non-dominant or colonial condition; who today live more in conformity with their particular social, economic and cultural customs and traditions than with the institutions of the country of which they now form part, under a State structure which incorporates mainly the national, social and cultural characteristics of other segments of the population which are predominant.[80]

The Cobo study also articulated various factors or characteristics which may assist in identifying indigenous peoples:

379. Indigenous communities, peoples and nations are those which, having a historical continuity with pre-invasion and pre-colonial societies that developed on their territories, consider themselves distinct from other sectors of the societies now prevailing on those territories, or parts of them. They form at present non-dominant sectors of society and are determined to preserve, develop and transmit to future generations their ancestral territories, and their ethnic identity, as the basis of their continued existence as peoples, in accordance with their own cultural patterns, social institutions and legal system.

[79] UN Department of Economic and Social Affairs, Division for Social Policy and Development, Secretariat of the Permanent Forum on Indigenous Issues, Workshop on Data Collection and Disaggregation for Indigenous Peoples, 'The Concept of Indigenous Peoples: Background Paper Prepared by the Secretariat of the Permanent Forum on Indigenous Issues', PFII/2004/WS.1/3 (19–21 January 2004), [8].

[80] Jose R. Martinez Cobo, Special Rapporteur of the Sub-Commission on Prevention of Discrimination and Protection of Minorities, 'Study on the Problem of Discrimination against Indigenous Populations', E/CN.4/SUB.2/1986/7/ADD.4 (1986), [34].

380. This historical continuity may consist of the continuation, for an extended period reaching into the present of one or more of the following factors:

(a) Occupation of ancestral lands, or at least of part of them;

(b) Common ancestry with the original occupants of these lands;

(c) Culture in general, or in specific manifestations (such as religion, living under a tribal system, membership of an indigenous community, dress, means of livelihood, lifestyle, etc.);

(d) Language (whether used as the only language, as mother-tongue, as the habitual means of communication at home or in the family, or as the main, preferred, habitual, general or normal language);

(e) Residence on certain parts of the country, or in certain regions of the world;

(f) Other relevant factors.

381. On an individual basis, an indigenous person is one who belongs to these indigenous populations through self-identification as indigenous (group consciousness) and is recognized and accepted by these populations as one of its members (acceptance by the group).

382. This preserves for these communities the sovereign right and power to decide who belongs to them, without external interference.[81]

In some societies, it is relatively straightforward to identify indigenous groups in relation to majority immigrant populations which dispossessed them, as in 'white settler' societies in North America, Australia or New Zealand. In other situations, the application of the definition is more complicated, particularly in independent African and Asian states where there are no white majorities but many different 'indigenous' groups (including 'tribal' groups) which have historical associations with land, and distinct cultural practices, yet some are politically dominant and others are disadvantaged. In practice, definitions of indigeneity in national law may be under-inclusive from an international law perspective, for instance as a result of deliberate state policies of exclusion.

Conceptually there may be no bright lines between 'indigenous' and 'minority' groups in some situations,[82] given that both groups may have long and deep attachments to land, possess distinctive culture, and suffer from past injustice and current disadvantage. The political construction of both concepts has also led to shifting self-identification in practice, with groups previously designated as 'minorities' re-identifying as 'indigenous', or as hybrid 'indigenous nationalities' (as in Nepal) to claim or assert the stronger level of rights protection associated with the law on indigenous peoples.

[81] Cobo, 'Study on the Problem of Discrimination against Indigenous Populations', [379–82].

[82] Kristin Henrard, 'Minorities, International Protection', *Max Planck Encyclopedia of Public International Law Online*, [17] (accessed 24 January 2013).

There is also ongoing inconsistency among UN treaty bodies in the framing of indigenous rights. The CERD, for instance, still routinely deals with indigenous peoples through the prism of minority rights rather than by invoking self-determination. The CERD remains guided by its General Recommendation XXIII of 1997 on indigenous peoples, which does not mention self-determination, even though it implicitly incorporates aspects of it:

1. … the Committee has consistently affirmed that discrimination against indigenous peoples falls under the scope of the Convention and that all appropriate means must be taken to combat and eliminate such discrimination.

…

3. The Committee is conscious of the fact that in many regions of the world indigenous peoples have been, and are still being, discriminated against and deprived of their human rights and fundamental freedoms and in particular that they have lost their land and resources to colonists, commercial companies and State enterprises. Consequently, the preservation of their culture and their historical identity has been and still is jeopardized.

4. The Committee calls in particular upon States parties to:

(a) Recognize and respect indigenous distinct culture, history, language and way of life as an enrichment of the State's cultural identity and to promote its preservation;

(b) Ensure that members of indigenous peoples are free and equal in dignity and rights and free from any discrimination, in particular that based on indigenous origin or identity;

(c) Provide indigenous peoples with conditions allowing for a sustainable economic and social development compatible with their cultural characteristics;

(d) Ensure that members of indigenous peoples have equal rights in respect of effective participation in public life and that no decisions directly relating to their rights and interests are taken without their informed consent;

(e) Ensure that indigenous communities can exercise their rights to practise and revitalize their cultural traditions and customs and to preserve and to practise their languages.

5. The Committee especially calls upon States parties to recognize and protect the rights of indigenous peoples to own, develop, control and use their communal lands, territories and resources and, where they have been deprived of their lands and territories traditionally owned or otherwise inhabited or used without their free and informed consent, to take steps to return those lands and territories. Only when this is for factual reasons not possible, the right to restitution should be substituted by the right to just, fair and prompt compensation. Such compensation should as far as possible take the form of lands and territories.[83]

As will be seen below, there is also inconsistency of treatment by the CESCR and HRC, both of which sometimes invoke self-determination, other times minority or cultural rights, and in yet other circumstances both approaches.

[83] CERD, General Recommendation No. 23: Rights of Indigenous Peoples, A/52/18, annex V (1997).

Certain international institutions have also developed their own guidelines for recognizing indigenous peoples. A case in point is World Bank Operational Manual OP 4.10:

3. *Identification.* Because of the varied and changing contexts in which Indigenous Peoples live and because there is no universally accepted definition of 'Indigenous Peoples,' this policy does not define the term. Indigenous Peoples may be referred to in different countries by such terms as 'indigenous ethnic minorities,' 'aboriginals,' 'hill tribes,' 'minority nationalities,' 'scheduled tribes,' or 'tribal groups.'

4. For purposes of this policy, the term 'Indigenous Peoples' is used in a generic sense to refer to a distinct, vulnerable, social and cultural group possessing the following characteristics in varying degrees:

(a) self-identification as members of a distinct indigenous cultural group and recognition of this identity by others;

(b) collective attachment to geographically distinct habitats or ancestral territories in the project area and to the natural resources in these habitats and territories;[7]

(c) customary cultural, economic, social, or political institutions that are separate from those of the dominant society and culture; and

(d) an indigenous language, often different from the official language of the country or region.

A group that has lost 'collective attachment to geographically distinct habitats or ancestral territories in the project area'; (paragraph 4(b)) because of forced severance remains eligible for coverage under this policy…[84]

Developments in regional human rights law have been influenced by international norms recognizing indigenous self-determination. In an advisory opinion on the 2007 Declaration, the African Commission endorsed a right of self-determination for indigenous peoples and sought to clarify their characteristics, but without defining the concept:

10. …the ACHPR is of the view that, a definition is not necessary or useful as there is no universally agreed definition of the term and no single definition can capture the characteristics of indigenous populations. Rather, it is much more relevant and constructive to try to bring out the main characteristics allowing the identification of the indigenous populations and communities in Africa.

11. Thus, the major characteristics, which allow the identification of Africa's Indigenous Communities is the favored approach adopted, and it is the same approach at the international level…

12. The concept in effect embodies the following constitutive elements or characteristics, among others…:

(a) Self-identification;

[84] World Bank, Operational Manual: Indigenous Peoples, OP 4.10 (July 2005).

(b) A special attachment to and use of their traditional land whereby their ancestral land and territory have a fundamental importance for their collective physical and cultural survival as peoples;

(c) A state of subjugation, marginalisation, dispossession, exclusion, or discrimination because these peoples have different cultures, ways of life or mode of production than the national hegemonic and dominant model.

13. Moreover, in Africa, the term indigenous populations does not mean 'first inhabitants' in reference to aboriginality as opposed to non-African communities or those having come from elsewhere. This peculiarity distinguishes Africa from the other Continents where native communities have been almost annihilated by non-native populations. Therefore, the ACHPR considers that any African can legitimately consider him/herself as indigene to the Continent.[85]

In the case of *Endorois Welfare Council v Kenya*, for instance, the African Commission accepted that the Endorois people of Kenya were 'indigenous', in a case involving the indigenous right to freely dispose of natural resources under Article 21 of the African Charter, discussed further below.[86] The Commission discussed at length the notion of 'peoples' and indigenous peoples in African and international human rights law, arguing for an expansive and flexible approach in African jurisprudence:

147. …the African Commission notes that the concepts of 'peoples' and 'indigenous peoples/communities' are contested terms. As far as 'indigenous peoples' are concerned, there is no universal and unambiguous definition of the concept, since no single accepted definition captures the diversity of indigenous cultures, histories and current circumstances. The relationships between indigenous peoples and dominant or mainstream groups in society vary from country to country. The same is true of the concept of 'peoples.' The African Commission is thus aware of the political connotation that these concepts carry. Those controversies led the drafters of the African Charter to deliberately refrain from proposing any definitions for the notion of 'people(s).' …

148. The African Commission, nevertheless, notes that while the terms 'peoples' and 'indigenous community' arouse emotive debates, some marginalised and vulnerable groups in Africa are suffering from particular problems. It is aware that many of these groups have not been accommodated by dominating development paradigms and in many cases they are being victimised by mainstream development policies and thinking and their basic human rights violated. The African Commission is also aware that indigenous peoples have, due to past and ongoing processes, become marginalised in their own country and they need recognition and protection of their basic human rights and fundamental freedoms.

149. The African Commission also notes that normatively, the African Charter is an innovative and unique human rights document compared to other regional human rights

[85] African Commission on Human and Peoples' Rights (41st Session), *Advisory Opinion on the United Nations Declaration on the Rights of Indigenous Peoples*, 16–30 May 2007, 63.

[86] *Centre for Minority Rights Development (Kenya) and Minority Rights Group International on behalf of Endorois Welfare Council v Kenya*, African Commission on Human and Peoples' Rights Communication No. 276/2003, 2009 AHRLR 75, 4 February 2010.

instruments, in placing special emphasis on the rights of 'peoples.' It substantially departs from the narrow formulations of other regional and universal human rights instruments by weaving a tapestry which includes the three 'generations' of rights: civil and political rights; economic, social, and cultural rights; and group and peoples' rights. In that regard, the African Commission notes its own observation that the term 'indigenous' is also not intended to create a special class of citizens, but rather to address historical and present-day injustices and inequalities. This is the sense in which the term has been applied in the African context by the Working Group on Indigenous Populations/Communities of the African Commission. In the context of the African Charter, the Working Group notes that the notion of 'peoples' is closely related to collective rights.

150. The African Commission also notes that the African Charter, in Articles 20 through 24, provides for peoples to retain rights as peoples, that is, as collectives. The African Commission through its Working Group of Experts on Indigenous Populations/ Communities has set out four criteria for identifying indigenous peoples. These are: the occupation and use of a specific territory; the voluntary perpetuation of cultural distinctiveness; self-identification as a distinct collectivity, as well as recognition by other groups; an experience of subjugation, marginalisation, dispossession, exclusion or discrimination. The Working Group also demarcated some of the shared characteristics of African indigenous groups:

...first and foremost (but not exclusively) different groups of hunter-gatherers or former hunter-gatherers and certain groups of pastoralists...

...A key characteristic for most of them is that the survival of their particular way of life depends on access and rights to their traditional land and the natural resources thereon.

151. The African Commission is thus aware that there is an emerging consensus on some objective features that a collective of individuals should manifest to be considered as 'peoples', viz: a common historical tradition, racial or ethnic identity, cultural homogeneity, linguistic unity, religious and ideological affinities, territorial connection, and a common economic life or other bonds, identities and affinities they collectively enjoy—especially rights enumerated under Articles 19 to 24 of the African Charter—or suffer collectively from the deprivation of such rights. What is clear is that all attempts to define the concept of indigenous peoples recognize the linkages between peoples, their land, and culture and that such a group expresses its desire to be identified as a people or have the consciousness that they are a people.

152. As far as the present matter is concerned, the African Commission is also enjoined under Article 61 of the African Charter to be inspired by other subsidiary sources of international law or general principles in determining rights under the African Charter. It takes note of the working definition proposed by the UN Working Group on Indigenous Populations:

...that indigenous peoples are...those which, having a historical continuity with pre-invasion and pre-colonial societies that developed on their territories, consider themselves distinct from other sectors of the societies now prevailing in those territories, or parts of them. They form at present non-dominant sectors of society and are determined to preserve, develop and transmit to future generations their ancestral territories, and their

ethnic identity, as the basis of their continued existence as peoples, in accordance with their own cultural patterns, social institutions and legal systems.

153. But this working definition should be read in conjunction with the 2003 Report of the African Commission's Working Group of Experts on Indigenous Populations/Communities, which is the basis of its 'definition' of indigenous populations. Similarly it notes that the International Labour Organisation has proffered a definition of indigenous peoples in Convention No. 169 concerning Indigenous and Tribal Peoples in Independent Countries…

154. The African Commission is also aware that though some indigenous populations might be first inhabitants, validation of rights is not automatically afforded to such pre-invasion and pre-colonial claims. In terms of ILO Convention 169, even though many African countries have not signed and ratified the said Convention, and like the UN Working Groups' conceptualisation of the term, the African Commission notes that there is a common thread that runs through all the various criteria that attempts to describe indigenous peoples—that indigenous peoples have an unambiguous relationship to a distinct territory and that all attempts to define the concept recognise the linkages between people, their land, and culture.

On the facts, the African Commission found that the Endorois are an indigenous people:

154. …the African Commission notes the observation of the UN Special Rapporteur, where he states that in Kenya indigenous populations/communities include pastoralist communities such as the *Endorois*, Borana, Gabra, Maasai, Pokot, Samburu, Turkana, and Somali, and hunter-gatherer communities whose livelihoods remain connected to the forest, such as the Awer (Boni), Ogiek, Sengwer, or Yaaku. The UN Special Rapporteur further observed that the Endorois community have lived for centuries in their traditional territory around Lake Bogoria, which was declared a wildlife sanctuary in 1973…

156. …the African Commission is of the view that Endorois culture, religion, and traditional way of life are intimately intertwined with their ancestral lands—Lake Bogoria and the surrounding area. It agrees that Lake Bogoria and the Monchongoi Forest are central to the Endorois' way of life and without access to their ancestral land, the Endorois are unable to fully exercise their cultural and religious rights, and feel disconnected from their land and ancestors.

157. In addition to a sacred relationship to their land, self-identification is another important criterion for determining indigenous peoples. The UN Special Rapporteur on the Rights and Fundamental Freedoms of Indigenous People also supports self-identification as a key criterion for determining who is indeed indigenous. The African Commission is aware that today many indigenous peoples are still excluded from society and often even deprived of their rights as equal citizens of a state. Nevertheless, many of these communities are determined to preserve, develop and transmit to future generations their ancestral territories and their ethnic identity. It accepts the arguments that the continued existence of indigenous communities as 'peoples' is closely connected to the possibility of them influencing their own fate and to living in accordance with their own cultural patterns, social institutions and religious systems. The African Commission further notes

that the Report of the African Commission's Working Group of Experts on Indigenous Populations/Communities (WGIP) emphasises that peoples' self-identification is an important ingredient to the concept of peoples' rights as laid out in the Charter. It agrees that the alleged violations of the African Charter by the Respondent State are those that go to the heart of indigenous rights—the right to preserve one's identity through identification with ancestral lands, cultural patterns, social institutions and religious systems. The African Commission, therefore, accepts that self-identification for Endorois as indigenous individuals and acceptance as such by the group is an essential component of their sense of identity.

158. Furthermore, in drawing inspiration from international law on human and peoples' rights, the African Commission notes that the IACtHR has dealt with cases of self-identification where Afro-descendent communities were living in a collective manner, and had, for over 2–3 centuries, developed an ancestral link to their land. Moreover, the way of life of these communities depended heavily on the traditional use of their land, as did their cultural and spiritual survival due to the existence of ancestral graves on these lands.

159. The African Commission notes that while it has already accepted the existence of indigenous peoples in Africa through its WGIP reports, and through the adoption of its Advisory Opinion on the UN Declaration on the Rights of Indigenous Peoples, it notes the fact that the Inter-American Court has not hesitated in granting the collective rights protection to groups beyond the 'narrow/aboriginal/pre-Colombian' understanding of indigenous peoples traditionally adopted in the Americas. In that regard, the African Commission notes two relevant decisions from the IACtHR: *Moiwana v Suriname* and *Saramaka v Suriname*. The Saramaka case is of particular relevance to the Endorois case, given the views expressed by the Respondent State during the oral hearings on the Merits.

...

161. Like the State of Suriname, the Respondent State (Kenya) in the instant Communication is arguing that the inclusion of the Endorois in 'modern society' has affected their cultural distinctiveness, such that it would be difficult to define them as a distinct group that is very different from the Tugen sub-tribe or indeed the larger Kalenjin tribe. That is, the Respondent State is questioning whether the Endorois can be defined in a way that takes into account the different degrees to which various members of the Endorois community adhere to traditional laws, customs, and economy, particularly those living within the Lake Bogoria area. In the Saramaka case, the IACtHR disagreed with the State of Suriname that the Saramaka could not be considered a distinct group of people just because a few members do not identify with the larger group. In the instant case, the African Commission, from all the evidence submitted to it, is satisfied that the Endorois can be defined as a distinct tribal group whose members enjoy and exercise certain rights, such as the right to property, in a distinctly collective manner from the Tugen sub-tribe or indeed the larger Kalenjin tribe.

162. The IACtHR also noted that the fact that some individual members of the Saramaka community may live outside of the traditional Saramaka territory and in a way that may differ from other Saramakas who live within the traditional territory and in accordance with Saramaka customs does not affect the distinctiveness of this

tribal group, nor its communal use and enjoyment of their property. In the case of the Endorois, the African Commission is of the view that the question of whether certain members of the community may assert certain communal rights on behalf of the group is a question that must be resolved by the Endorois themselves in accordance with their own traditional customs and norms and not by the State. The Endorois cannot be denied a right to juridical personality just because there is a lack of individual identification with the traditions and laws of the Endorois by some members of the community.

From all the evidence (both oral and written and video testimony) submitted to the African Commission, the African Commission agrees that the Endorois are an indigenous community and that they fulfil the criterion of 'distinctiveness.' The African Commission agrees that the Endorois consider themselves to be a distinct people, sharing a common history, culture and religion. The African Commission is satisfied that the Endorois are a 'people', a status that entitles them to benefit from provisions of the African Charter that protect collective rights. The African Commission is of the view that the alleged violations of the African Charter are those that go to the heart of indigenous rights—the right to preserve one's identity through identification with ancestral lands.[87]

In the Inter-American case referred to by the African Commission, *Saramaka People v Suriname*, the Inter-American Court recognized a tribal group—descendants of African slaves in Suriname known as Maroons—as legally analogous to indigenous peoples for the purpose of the right to property under Article 21 of the American Convention. As discussed later, the interpretation of that right has been influenced by international standards on self-determination. The Inter-American Court held:

79. First of all, the Court observes that the Saramaka people are not indigenous to the region they inhabit; they were instead brought to what is now known as Suriname during the colonization period…

81. Their social structure is different from other sectors of society inasmuch as the Saramaka people are organized in matrilineal clans (*lös*), and they regulate themselves, at least partially, by their own customs and traditions…

82. Their culture is also similar to that of tribal peoples insofar as the members of the Saramaka people maintain a strong spiritual relationship with the ancestral territory they have traditionally used and occupied. Land is more than merely a source of subsistence for them; it is also a necessary source for the continuation of the life and cultural identity of the Saramaka people. The lands and resources of the Saramaka people are part of their social, ancestral, and spiritual essence. In this territory, the Saramaka people hunt, fish, and farm, and they gather water, plants for medicinal purposes, oils, minerals, and wood. Their sacred sites are scattered throughout the territory, while at the same time the territory itself has a sacred value to them. In particular, the identity of the members of the Saramaka people with the land is inextricably linked to their historical fight for freedom from slavery, called the sacred 'first time'. During the public

[87] *Endorois Welfare Council v Kenya.*

hearing in this case, Head Captain Wazen Eduards described their special relationship with the land as follows:

The forest is like our market place; it is where we get our medicines, our medicinal plants. It is where we hunt to have meat to eat. The forest is truly our entire life. When our ancestors fled into the forest they did not carry anything with them. They learned how to live, what plants to eat, how to deal with subsistence needs once they got to the forest. It is our whole life.

83. Furthermore, their economy can also be characterized as tribal. According to the expert testimony of Dr. Richard Price, for example, 'the very great bulk of food that Saramaka eat comes from [...] farms [and] gardens' traditionally cultivated by Saramaka women. The men, according to Dr. Price, fish and 'hunt wild pig, deer, tapir, all sorts of monkeys, different kinds of birds, everything that Saramakas eat'. Furthermore, the women gather various fruits, plants and minerals, which they use in a variety of ways, including making baskets, cooking oil, and roofs for their dwellings.

84. Thus, in accordance with all of the above, the Court considers that the members of the Saramaka people make up a tribal community whose social, cultural and economic characteristics are different from other sections of the national community, particularly because of their special relationship with their ancestral territories, and because they regulate themselves, at least partially, by their own norms, customs, and/or traditions...

86. ...this Tribunal declares that the members of the Saramaka people are to be considered a tribal community, and that the Court's jurisprudence regarding indigenous peoples' right to property is also applicable to tribal peoples because both share distinct social, cultural, and economic characteristics, including a special relationship with their ancestral territories, that require special measures under international human rights law in order to guarantee their physical and cultural survival.[88]

It is notable that some regions have explicitly sought to identify indigenous peoples by treaty. For example, the draft Nordic Saami Convention 2005, drafted by three Nordic states and their Saami parliaments, and with a view to finalization by 2016, recognizes that '[t]he Saami people is the indigenous people of Finland, Norway and Sweden' (Article 2). Article 3 provides for Saami self-determination:

As a people, the Saami has the right of self-determination in accordance with the rules and provisions of international law and of this Convention. In so far as it follows from these rules and provisions, the Saami people has the right to determine its own economic, social and cultural development and to dispose, to their own benefit, over its own natural resources.

Significantly, Article 4 attempts to define who is Saami:

The Convention applies to persons residing in Finland, Norway or Sweden that identify themselves as Saami and who

1. have Saami as their domestic language or have at least one parent or grandparent who has or has had Saami as his or her domestic language, or

[88] *Case of the Saramaka People v Suriname*, Preliminary Objections, Merits, Reparations and Costs, 28 November 2007, IACHR (Ser. C) No. 172.

2. have a right to pursue Saami reindeer husbandry in Norway or Sweden, or

3. fulfil the requirements to be eligible to vote in elections to the Saami parliament in Finland, Norway or Sweden, or

4. are children of a person referred to in 1, 2 or 3.

As discussed later in this chapter, recognition of a right of self-determination for indigenous peoples does not mean that such groups are entitled to assert the full spectrum of entitlements classically enjoyed by colonized peoples during the decolonization process (such as the nomadic peoples in the *Western Sahara Advisory Opinion*[89]). Specifically, the right appears more limited or qualified for indigenous peoples within an existing independent state in that it does not carry with it a right of secession or independence from an existing state.

Despite many indigenous peoples experiencing colonialism, they are not treated as colonized 'peoples' entitled to full external self-determination from independent states (which did secure independence from a foreign colonial power). Where colonial ventures succeeded in 'populating others'' territories with a new majority of their own 'settlers', such majority came to constitute the relevant 'people' entitled to exercise self-determination against colonial rule. The construction of self-determination still has not gone one level deeper.

Apart from minority and indigenous groups, the CESCR's consideration of state reports has incrementally fleshed out which other groups enjoy self-determination in Article 1.

THE GENERAL PUBLIC

The CESCR has endorsed the 'internal' aspect of self-determination by insisting that states are procedurally accountable to the 'general public', as the relevant 'people', in their dealings with the state's natural resources. Thus, the CESCR found that the privatization of Azerbaijan's oil resources required the provision of public information, participation and transparency to the 'general public' to comply with Article 1.[90] It was also concerned that land acquisition by foreign investors in Madagascar prejudiced the right to food of 'the Malagasy population' and engaged Article 1.[91]

VULNERABLE SECTIONS OF THE PUBLIC

The CESCR has taken its endorsement of internal self-determination a step further by suggesting that sub-sections of the public in a state, such as particularly vulnerable or disadvantaged groups, may engage the right of self-determination. Thus, the CESCR was concerned that the granting of economic land concessions in Cambodia adversely affected the livelihoods of rural communities who depend

[89] *Western Sahara Advisory Opinion,* 16 October 1975, (1975) ICJ Reports 12.
[90] CESCR, Concluding Observations: Azerbaijan, E/C.12/1/Add.20 (22 December 1997).
[91] CESCR, Concluding Observations: Madagascar, E/C.12/MDG/CO/2 (16 December 2009), [12].

on land and forest resources for their survival.[92] Likewise, the CESCR was concerned about the adverse impacts of free trade agreements on the livelihoods of the rural poor in Colombia.[93] Article 1 also arose in relation to land acquisitions by foreign investors in Madagascar which adversely impacted 'on the access of peasants and people living in rural areas' to land and natural resources.[94]

In addition to economic disadvantage as an identifying criterion, the CESCR has relied upon political geography as a delimiting factor. Thus, it criticized the illegal or exploitative mining of natural resources to the detriment of 'the people' of Katanga province in the Democratic Republic of Congo.[95] The CESCR implied that economic self-determination can operate at a sub-national level by calling on the state to ensure that mining revenues in Katanga 'are allocated for the development of the province' and its poor inhabitants. It is thus not only the population of Congo as a whole that constitutes the relevant 'people'. The CESCR raised separate concerns under Article 1 about the plight of peasant farmers expelled from their land by mining in Katanga.[96]

INHABITANTS OF NON-SELF-GOVERNING TERRITORIES

On a number of occasions, the CESCR has expressed concern that self-determination has not been exercised in Western Sahara, in accordance with UN Security Council proposals,[97] and in respect of 'the people of Western Sahara'.[98] The CESCR criticized Morocco's 'population transfer' which prejudiced the rights of 'the relevant population'.[99] The implication is that the Saharawi people (presumably including Saharawi refugees expelled or who fled from the territory) constitute the relevant 'people', not also the many Moroccan settlers who moved there after the Moroccan invasion and occupation in 1975. Identification of voters for the purposes of the proposed UN plebiscite in Western Sahara is precisely the sticking point in resolving the future of that territory, with Morocco naturally wishing to count its settlers.

The CESCR has also raised self-determination in its observations on the United Kingdom in the context of both efforts to promote self-rule in various dependent territories, as well as 'the situation of Gibraltar'.[100] The CESCR vaguely avoided specifying who constitutes the relevant 'people' for the purpose

[92] CESCR, Concluding Observations: Cambodia, E/C.12/KHM/CO/1 (12 June 2009), [15].
[93] CESCR, Concluding Observations: Colombia, E/C.12/COL/CO/5 (7 June 2010), [10].
[94] CESCR, Concluding Observations: Madagascar, E/C.12/MDG/CO/2 (16 December 2009), [12].
[95] CESCR, Concluding Observations: Democratic Republic of Congo, E/C.12/COD/CO/4 (16 December 2009), [13].
[96] CESCR, Concluding Observations: Democratic Republic of Congo, E/C.12/COD/CO/4 (16 December 2009), [15].
[97] CESCR, Concluding Observations: Morocco, E/C.12/1994/5 (30 May 1994), [10]. See also Morocco, E/C.12/1/Add.55 (1 December 2000).
[98] CESCR, Concluding Observations: Morocco, E/C.12/MAR/CO/3 (4 September 2006), [35].
[99] CESCR, Concluding Observations: Morocco, E/C.12/MAR/CO/3 (4 September 2006), [35].
[100] CESCR, Concluding Observations: UK and its Dependent Territories (except Hong Kong), E/C.12/1994/19 (21 December 1994), [5] and [9] respectively.

of self-determination in Gibraltar, noting only 'the concern expressed to it' about self-determination there and calling on 'all parties to the existing situation to ensure full respect for all of the rights' in the ICESCR.[101] Since Britain has succeeded in populating Gibraltar with largely British people, it is unsurprising that Britain regards their choice to remain with Britain (in a 1967 referendum) as an expression of their self-determination. Spain, on the other hand, regards Gibraltar as part of sovereign Spanish territory, in which Gibraltans are part of the Spanish people as a whole.[102] Mention may similarly be made of the Falkland Islands / Malvinas in this context, where the settler population is pro-British, but British sovereignty over the islands is contested by Argentina.

In total, sixteen territories (including both Gibraltar and the Falkland Islands) remain listed by the United Nations as non-self-governing territories (as of mid 2013).[103] Of these, Britain is listed as the administering power for ten territories, the United States for three, France and New Zealand one each, and the remaining territory, Western Sahara, is under the de facto control of Morocco.

Article 1 also specifically mentions the inhabitants of trust territories, but this is now of only historical interest. Palau's attainment of independence from the United States in 1994 brought to an end the last UN trust territory arrangement.[104] The Trusteeshp Council no longer meets annually and recommendations were made in 2005 in the context of UN reform to wind up the Council altogether.

INHABITANTS OF OCCUPIED TERRITORIES

The CESCR condemned the impact of frequent 'general closures' in the West Bank and Gaza Strip since 1993 for cutting off Palestinian residents from their land and resources, depriving them of subsistence and resulting in 'widespread violations' of Article 1(2).[105] In the *Israel Wall Advisory Opinion*, the ICJ stated that the right of the Palestinian people to self-determination is 'no longer in issue'.[106] The precise basis for the Palestinian right of self-determination was not specified. The ICJ referred to the United Nations' condemnation of the acquisition of territory by force,[107] implying that Palestinian self-determination partly arises by way of occupation. International recognition of the right was also highlighted, including in UN practice.

[101] CESCR, Concluding Observations: UK and its Dependent Territories (except Hong Kong), E/C.12/1994/19 (21 December 1994), [9].

[102] Antonio Cassese, *Self-Determination of Peoples: A Legal Reappraisal* (Oxford University Press, Oxford, 1996), 206–14.

[103] These are: Western Sahara; Anguilla; Bermuda; British Virgin Islands; Cayman Islands; Falkland Islands (Malvinas); Montserrat; St Helena; Turks and Caicos Islands; US Virgin Islands; Gibraltar; American Samoa; Guam; New Caledonia; Pitcairn; and Tokelau: <http://www.un.org/en/decolonization/nonselfgovterritories.shtml>.

[104] UN, Non-Self-Governing Territories, <http://www.un.org/en/decolonization/its.shtml>.

[105] CESCR, Concluding Observations: Israel, E/C.12/1/Add.27 (4 December 1998), [17], [39].

[106] *Legal Consequences of the Construction of a Wall in the Occupied Palestinian Territory* Advisory Opinion, 9 July 2004, (2004) ICJ Reports 136, ('*Israel Wall Advisory Opinion*'), [118].

[107] *Israel Wall Advisory Opinion*, [117].

CERTAIN PALESTINIANS IN THE DIASPORA

Israel's discriminatory *Law of Return* was criticized by the CESCR for making it prohibitively difficult for 'Palestinians in the diaspora' to resume their domicile in Israel, thus infringing Article 1(2).[108] The implication is that Palestinians born in but exiled from Israel are properly part of the Israeli 'people' and entitled to a share in its self-determination on that account (including the freedom to return to one's own country). It is questionable whether invoking Article 1 adds anything meaningful when Article 12(4) of the ICCPR already precludes a person from being arbitrarily deprived of the right to enter their own country, but it is pertinent where persons have been unlawfully denationalized.

It is not clear whether the CESCR would also recognize restrictions on the 'right of return' of Palestinian refugees generally to the Palestinian occupied territories (as opposed to Israel), or restrictions on the right of any refugees to return to their home countries, as also engaging Article 1. The wider implications for stateless persons generally are also left unresolved.

'FREELY DETERMINE THEIR POLITICAL STATUS AND FREELY PURSUE THEIR ECONOMIC, SOCIAL AND CULTURAL DEVELOPMENT'

Common Article 1 refers to both the political aspects and the economic, social and cultural dimensions of self-determination. The drafters viewed these different facets as indivisible:

14. A suggestion was made that the right of a people or nation to determine its 'political status' should be written into the article to be included in the Covenant on Civil and Political Rights, and that the right to determine its 'economic, social and cultural status' in the article to be included in the Covenant on Economic, Social and Cultural Rights. However, this suggestion was thought to be based upon an artificial distinction between political status and economic, social and cultural status. Every people or nation was or should be an integrated entity. A people or nation that could not freely determine its political status could hardly determine its economic, social and cultural status and *vice versa*.[109]

An early draft had referred more simply to a right of peoples to 'freely to determine their political, economic, social and cultural *status*' [emphasis added]. That language was changed because it was agreed that while a people can choose their political 'status', that concept did not make sense in relation to the economic, social or cultural life of a people:

43. …The definition of the right of self-determination contained in paragraph 1 was also criticized. It was said that a nation could determine its political status, but the expression 'economic, social and cultural status' had little meaning.[110]

108 CESCR, Concluding Observations: Israel, E/C.12/1/Add.27 (4 December 1998), [13], [36].
109 UNGAOR (10th Session), A/2929 (1 July 1955), Annexes, [14].
110 UNGA Third Committee, A/3077 (8 December 1955), 15, [43].

The draft was thus amended to differentiate a people's right to 'freely determine their political status' from their right to 'freely pursue their economic, social and cultural development'.[111] The change in language recognizes that whereas a people can consciously choose their political status, social and cultural development are somewhat more organic and less structured processes.

It must be acknowledged, however, that many liberation movements and modern democratic states alike attempt to consciously engineer particular political visions of culture and society. Particularly where peoples are denied self-determination, culture often emerges as a site of political expression in shaping the identity of the group in opposition to the oppressor. In some senses, social and cultural life are deliberately constructed in a process of 'imagining' community,[112] just as political institutions are consciously selected. A people can also choose their economic 'status', even if economic life also 'develops' organically in various ways.

The essential point of Article 1 is that the freedom to shape political, economic, social and cultural life is vested with the 'people' rather than foreign actors (even if freedom from external influence is never absolute and always relative). The essence of Article 1's 'very comprehensive' conception of self-determination was described in the drafting thus:

> Every people or nation should be free to establish its own political institutions, to develop its own economic resources, and to direct its own social and cultural evolution, without the interference of other peoples or nations.[113]

ECONOMIC SELF-DETERMINATION

Despite the seemingly equal weighting of the political, economic, social and cultural aspects of self-determination in Article 1, in subsequent international practice and doctrine the political aspects of self-determination have received the most attention. This includes in debates over: the definition of 'peoples' (from colonized populations to internal minorities and indigenous peoples); its juridical character as a 'right' or 'principle'; the possible forms of political status (from independent statehood to internal autonomy); its internal and external aspects; and the procedures for realizing it (from referendum to armed struggle).[114]

In contrast, the economic, social and cultural dimensions of self-determination have often been overshadowed by the emphasis on resolving political status. The subordination of the economic to the political is in part inevitable, because the attainment of political self-determination empowers economic decision-making (or social and cultural freedoms), while persisting foreign political domination

[111] UNGA Third Committee, A/3077 (8 December 1955), 20.

[112] Benedict Anderson, *Imagined Communities: Reflections on the Origin and Spread of Nationalism* (Verso, London, 2006).

[113] UNGAOR (10th Session), A/2929 (1 July 1955), Annexes, 14, [12].

[114] See generally Cassese, *Self-Determination of Peoples*; James Crawford, 'The Right of Self-Determination in International Law: Its Development and Future' in Philip Alston (ed), *Peoples' Rights* (Oxford University Press, Oxford, 2001).

makes economic autonomy (or socio-cultural expression) more difficult. Indeed, the purpose of political domination is often precisely to control others' resources.

As noted earlier, during the drafting the attempt to enshrine 'permanent sovereignty over natural resources' was diluted by reference instead to free disposition of resources. Economic self-determination was given renewed impetus, however, in normative efforts to reshape the international economic order in the 1970s. The 1974 Declaration on the Establishment of a New International Economic Order and the 1974 Charter of Economic Rights and Duties of States both invoke the right of self-determination in articulating new economic principles, albeit by recasting economic freedoms as a prerogative of states not 'peoples'. The 1974 Declaration on the Establishment of a New International Economic Order provides for:

> [4] d. The right of every country to adopt the economic and social system that it deems the most appropriate for its own development and not to be subjected to discrimination of any kind as a result...[115]

Likewise, the 1974 Charter of Economic Rights and Duties of States provides that:

> Every State has the sovereign and inalienable right to choose its economic system as well as it political, social and cultural systems in accordance with the will of its people, without outside interference, coercion or threat in any form whatsoever.[116]

The emphasis of the new international economic order sought to create fairer economic conditions for developing states, in which they could genuinely exercise their economic autonomy without being subject to the hegemonic interests of developed states. Nowak writes that the 'failure thus far to achieve a New International Economic Order, the continually spiraling difference between over- and under-development and the current debt crisis in countries of the Third World show that most peoples of the South are still far removed from true self-determination'.[117] Paradoxically, however, the thrust of the new economic order was to create a more collaborative or cooperative vision of global economic relations, to promote the interests of developing states and circumscribe the rampant economic freedoms of the developed states. In this sense, such a paradigm undercuts Article 1's emphasis on economic self-determination, which rests on a more atomized conception of people freely (including unilaterally) choosing their own economic path.

With the fading of efforts to establish a new international economic order by the late 1980s, new paradigms also emerged which overshadowed self-determination as the orienting principle of economic activity. The emergence of environmental ideas about 'sustainable development' at the United Nations' Stockholm Conference on the Human Environment in 1972 succeeded in generating new normative limits on the freedom to exploit natural resources over time. Thus, the

[115] Declaration on the Establishment of a New International Economic Order, [4(d)].
[116] Charter of Economic Rights and Duties of States, Article 1.
[117] Nowak, *CCPR Commentary*, 8.

United Nations' Rio Declaration on Environment and Development 1992 recognizes a state's right to exploit its own resources (Principle 1), but subjects it to environmental limits (Principles 3 and 4):

Principle 2

States have, in accordance with the Charter of the United Nations and the principles of international law, the sovereign right to exploit their own resources pursuant to their own environmental and developmental policies, and the responsibility to ensure that activities within their jurisdiction or control do not cause damage to the environment of other States or of areas beyond the limits of national jurisdiction.

Principle 3

The right to development must be fulfilled so as to equitably meet developmental and environmental needs of present and future generations.

Principle 4

In order to achieve sustainable development, environmental protection shall constitute an integral part of the development process and cannot be considered in isolation from it.[118]

Further, the push since the mid 1980s to recognize a 'right to development' further diffused the primacy of self-determination as the prevailing rights-based principle governing economic life. Articulated in the General Assembly's 1986 Declaration on the Right to Development, the emerging right to development drew explicit linkages with self-determination:

Recalling the right of peoples to self-determination, by virtue of which they have the right freely to determine their political status and to pursue their economic, social and cultural development,

Recalling also the right of peoples to exercise, subject to the relevant provisions of both International Covenants on Human Rights, full and complete sovereignty over all their natural wealth and resources…

Article 1

…

2. The human right to development also implies the full realization of the right of peoples to self-determination, which includes, subject to the relevant provisions of both International Covenants on Human Rights, the exercise of their inalienable right to full sovereignty over all their natural wealth and resources.

Development thus encompasses self-determination, but is distinct from it and perhaps wider. Significantly, whereas self-determination is characterized as a group right, the right to development has both collective and individual aspects, with individuals at the core of the right. Older statist notions of development, pursued by newly independent states after decolonization from the 1950s onwards, are

[118] UNGA, Rio Declaration on Environment and Development, A/CONF.151/26 (Vol. I) (12 August 1992).

replaced by a human-centred vision of development, including as regards use of natural resources. The state is relegated to being a vehicle for the development of the population and individuals, rather than being a rights-holder. Article 2 of the 1986 Declaration thus provides:

1. The human person is the central subject of development and should be the active participant and beneficiary of the right to development.

2. All human beings have a responsibility for development, individually and collectively, taking into account the need for full respect for their human rights and fundamental freedoms as well as their duties to the community, which alone can ensure the free and complete fulfilment of the human being, and they should therefore promote and protect an appropriate political, social and economic order for development.

3. States have the right and the duty to formulate appropriate national development policies that aim at the constant improvement of the well-being of the entire population and of all individuals, on the basis of their active, free and meaningful participation in development and in the fair distribution of the benefits resulting therefrom.

As discussed further below, the intensification of international economic law in many areas—particularly trade, investment and finance—has also eaten away at ideas about economic self-determination, subjecting economic life instead to different ideas about global cooperation and interdependency rather than autonomy and independence. In some ways, then, economic self-determination is a shell of its former self, hollowed out, its potency diluted or circumvented by changing paradigms and its promise unfulfilled.

Economic self-determination can nonetheless possess content independent of political self-determination, state's rights, other conceptual frameworks such as sustainable development or the right to development, and notwithstanding the constraints of international economic law. Forms of economic self-determination can precede the resolution of political status, as examples considered below demonstrate. For instance, colonial powers or foreign occupants have sometimes devolved control over certain economic activities while retaining overall political control. More recently, the economic, social and cultural self-determination rights of indigenous peoples have been recognized despite final political status remaining unresolved or subordinate to the sovereignty of an existing state.

Like all human rights, the political and economic aspects of self-determination are indivisible. Ultimately, it is not possible to fully exercise political self-determination without the capacity to make political decisions about economic resources (or social and cultural affairs). It is equally impossible for a people to fully mobilize its economic resources, or to develop its culture and social life, without the ability to make political decisions about their utilization or development. Any disjuncture between these two sides of the self-determination coin impedes the enjoyment of the right, even if a temporary separation is sometimes thought expedient.

Within independent states, a people's right to freely pursue its economic development in principle entails the freedom to choose its own economic system, whether market-based, socialist, collectivist, mixed, subsistence, agrarian and so on. In reality, however, such autonomy and the associated freedom from foreign interference is necessarily relative and highly circumscribed by prevailing global liberal market conditions—a freedom without choice. As shown below, Article 1(2) limits the freedom by reference to a range of obligations under international law, particularly international economic law. The freedoms protected by the right of self-determination are necessarily relative, not absolute.

Aside from formal legal obligations, the degree of factual global interdependence of national economies is such that peoples would find it extremely hard to realistically choose an economic system other than the prevailing global liberal economic order. Global financial institutions, the United Nations' development agenda, private companies and so on are oriented towards that particular economic model. While such model enables (or tolerates) a level of diversity within the system, there are outer limits of its logic which may make opting out of that system unbearably costly. (The economic aspects of self-determination are naturally examined in considering Article 1(2) below, concerning the free disposition of natural wealth and resources.)

SOCIAL AND CULTURAL DEVELOPMENT

If the political aspects of self-determination have overshadowed its economic aspects, in turn its economic aspects have overshadowed its social and cultural dimensions. There was little attention during the drafting to the latter, and consideration of social and cultural self-determination is fairly scarce in the practice of the UN treaty bodies. Where such aspects are considered, the 'social' is typically subsumed by attention to culture.

Again, in a globalized world of interdependent societies, cultures and technology, the idea that a people is an island entitled to shape its own unique destiny is somewhat antiquated or unreal, and seeks to statically (and parochially or patriotically) fix 'authentic' local cultures in relation to unwanted foreign ones. During the drafting of Article 1, concern was expressed, for instance, that (cultural) self-determination should not be seen to 'sanction the burning of foreign books'.[119] The CESCR, in the different context of cultural rights under Article 15 of the ICESCR, accepts a dynamic and syncretic vision of culture.

> 11. In the Committee's view, culture is a broad, inclusive concept encompassing all manifestations of human existence. The expression 'cultural life' is an explicit reference to culture as a living process, historical, dynamic and evolving, with a past, a present and a future.
>
> 12. The concept of culture must be seen not as a series of isolated manifestations or hermetic compartments, but as an interactive process whereby individuals and communities, while preserving their specificities and purposes, give expression to the culture of humanity. This concept takes account of the individuality and otherness of culture as the creation and product of society.[120]

[119] UNGAOR (10th Session), A/2929 (1 July 1955), Annexes, 14, [13].
[120] CESCR, General Comment No. 21, E/C.12/GC/21 (21 December 2009), [11–12].

At the same time, there is no singular model of global culture, despite the seepage of particularly powerful national cultures into many others. Many peoples are genuinely and legitimately concerned to express their own distinctive cultural identities, even if what they consider distinctive may be found surprisingly often in other cultural traditions. Article 1 provides for such relative autonomy from external interference, as well as internal safeguards for a people vis-à-vis culturally repressive practices of their own governments.

A key reason for the paucity of practice concerning social and cultural self-determination appears to be that cultural and minority rights are more concretely and specifically addressed by other provisions of the twin covenants, namely Article 27 of the ICCPR and Article 15(1)(a) of the ICESCR. Those provisions break down cultural rights into their component parts and give the protection of culture more bite than is perhaps possible (or obvious) under common Article 1.

In this way, cultural self-determination has often been assigned a subsidiary interpretive role in relation to other Covenant rights. As noted earlier, this has occurred in relation to individual communications under the First Optional Protocol to the ICCPR, where the HRC has refused to consider direct violations of Article 1 in individual complaints, but has accepted that Article 1 may be relevant in interpreting individual rights, including to culture.

In General Comment No. 21 on the right to take part in cultural life under Article 15(1)(a) of the ICESCR, the CESCR stated more generally that:

> The right to take part in cultural life is also interdependent on other rights enshrined in the Covenant, including the right of all peoples to self-determination (art. 1) and the right to an adequate standard of living (art. 11).[121]

Cultural rights are considered in the chapter in this book on Article 15, including the definition of 'culture'[122] and the scope of interests protected. Whether the right of cultural self-determination retains any autonomous meaning—that is, independent of the specific cultural rights in the twin covenants—is an open question in the jurisprudence.

Certainly, cultural and minority rights have often been characterized as individual rights, in contrast to the collective nature of self-determination. Such binary classification is, however, wholly inaccurate, given that cultural, minority and self-determination rights all involve individual and collective dimensions. Confusion has sometimes arisen because jurisdictional limitations have been conflated with substantive considerations. Further, there is no reason why the same facts establishing a breach of particular cultural or minority rights might not also ground a breach of cultural self-determination rights in a given case, at least where the scale or nature of the harm is sufficient to engage the cultural freedoms of the whole 'people'. Related areas of international law should also be mentioned here in the context of severe attacks on culture, such as the protection of cultural

[121] CESCR, General Comment No. 21, [2].
[122] CESCR, General Comment No. 21, [10–13].

objects in armed conflict under international humanitarian law, and the cultural dimensions of the international crime of genocide.

One area in which human rights bodies have been particularly attentive to culture in the context of self-determination is in relation to indigenous peoples, considered further below.

Article 1(2)

'FREELY DISPOSE OF THEIR NATURAL WEALTH AND RESOURCES'

The core economic component of the right of self-determination in Article 1 is a people's entitlement to 'freely dispose of their natural wealth and resources' in paragraph 2. According to the HRC in General Comment No. 12:

> 5. Paragraph 2 affirms a particular aspect of the economic content of the right of self-determination, namely the right of peoples, for their own ends, freely to 'dispose of their natural wealth and resources without prejudice to any obligations arising out of international economic cooperation, based upon the principle of mutual benefit, and international law. In no case may a people be deprived of its own means of subsistence'. This right entails corresponding duties for all States and the international community. States should indicate any factors or difficulties which prevent the free disposal of their natural wealth and resources contrary to the provisions of this paragraph and to what extent that affects the enjoyment of other rights set forth in the Covenant.[123]

As the HRC observes, the freedom to deal with natural resources involves a correlative duty of other states not to interfere in such freedom. During the drafting, control over natural resources was seen as elementary to sustaining a people's political life.

> 45. Some members expressed the view that the right of peoples to self-determination should not be regarded solely from the political point of view but should also be considered from the economic aspect, since political independence was based on economic independence, and that the right of peoples freely to dispose of their own natural resources should be recognized. It was said that that would not mean that States would arbitrarily denounce agreements, but would settle the matter of relations between nations and foreign private undertakings, which made large profits by exploiting a country's natural resources without, in most cases, being affected by its legislation. The realization of the right of peoples to self-determination, in accordance with United Nations principles, should enable any State to acquire complete control of its own natural resources and should place that State in a position to apply its national legislation to any private industry, even if the legislation sanctioned the expropriation or nationalization of certain undertakings on fair conditions.[124]

[123] HRC, General Comment No. 12 (Vol. I), 184, [5].

[124] Commission on Human Rights, E/2256 (14 April–14 June 1952), 6.

The text of Article 1(2) drew upon General Assembly Resolution 626 (VII) on the 'Right to Exploit Freely Natural Wealth and Resources'.

The General Assembly,

Bearing in mind the need for encouraging the under-developed countries in their proper use and exploitation of their natural wealth and resources;

Considering that the economic development of the under-developed countries is one of the fundamental requisites for the strengthening of universal peace;

Remembering that the right of peoples freely to use and exploit their natural wealth and resources is inherent in their sovereignty and is in accordance with the Purposes and Principles of the Charter of the United Nations,

1. *Recommends* all Member States, in the exercise of their right freely to use and exploit their natural wealth and resources wherever deemed desirable by them for their own progress and economic development, to have due regard, consistently with their sovereignty, to the need for maintaining the flow of capital in conditions of security, mutual confidence and economic cooperation among nations;

2. *Further recommends* all Member States to refrain from acts, direct or indirect, designed to impede the exercise of the sovereignty of any State over its natural resources.[125]

That Resolution had influenced some state practice, for instance when Japanese and Italian courts upheld the lawfulness of Iranian nationalization laws in 1953 to 1955.[126] General Assembly Resolution 1515 (XV) of 1960 reiterated 'the sovereign right of every State to dispose of its wealth and its natural resources should be respected in conformity with the rights and duties of States under international law'.[127]

During the drafting, there was considerable controversy over the extent of a people's economic freedoms. In particular, there was a Chilean proposal in 1952 to cast Article 1 in stronger terms, to refer to a people's 'permanent sovereignty over their natural wealth and resources'.[128] Mention of 'permanent sovereignty' was controversial due to stark differences of opinion between developed, developing and socialist states about the international economic order:

20. Against this text it was suggested that 'permanent sovereignty' was not a tenable concept as any State could voluntarily limit its own sovereignty at any time. Furthermore, the proposition was considered dangerous in that it would sanction unwarranted expropriation or confiscation of foreign property and would subject international agreements and arrangements to unilateral renunciation.

[125] UNGA Res. 626 (VII), Right to Exploit Freely Natural Wealth and Resources (21 December 1952), Article 1(2).

[126] Oji Umozurike, *Self-Determination in International Law* (Archon Books, Connecticut, 1972), 205.

[127] UNGA Res. 1515 (XV), 'Concerted Action for Economic Development of Economically Less Developed Countries' (15 December 1960), [5].

[128] UNGAOR (10th Session), A/2929 (1 July 1955), Annexes, 15, [19]. For a discussion of the drafting, see Nico Schrijver, *Sovereignty over Natural Resources: Balancing Rights and Duties* (Cambridge University Press, Cambridge, 2008), 49–53.

21. On the other hand, it was stated that the right of self-determination certainly included the simple and elementary principle that a nation or people should be master of its own natural wealth or resources. The proposal, it was emphasized, was not intended to frighten off foreign investment by a threat of expropriation or confiscation; it was intended rather to warn against such foreign exploitation as might result in depriving the local population of its own means of subsistence.[129]

Further:

44. Both sentences in paragraph 3 were criticized as being imprecise and dangerous in their present wording. Some opposed the inclusion of any provision relating to a peoples' right to sovereignty over their natural wealth and resources in an article on self-determination. Some said that the paragraph as drafted was either superfluous, or it was dangerous because it might introduce obstacles to international cooperation. The first sentence was criticised on the grounds that 'permanent sovereignty' had little meaning. Objection was raised to the second sentence on the grounds that, as drafted, its consequences might be too far-reaching and infringe upon existing international treaties and agreements between States. It could be interpreted to mean expropriation with just compensation. It could discourage foreign investors and, in particular, could harm the policy of assistance to under-developed countries. Those who supported this paragraph recognised that some amendment might be called for to meet some of these objections.[130]

The draft text concerning permanent sovereignty was ultimately amended in 1955 to delete reference to 'permanent sovereignty' and to refer only to a people's right to 'freely dispose of their natural wealth and resources', but remained controversial and only narrowly passed.[131] As discussed below, however, the linkage to permanent sovereignty was later revived by the addition of Article 25 of the ICESCR late in the drafting in 1966.

The amendment (temporarily) decoupled Article 1(2) from the development of the notion of permanent sovereignty in the General Assembly, which adopted a Declaration on Permanent Sovereignty over Natural Resources in 1962[132]—prior to the adoption of the twin covenants in 1966, but after the text of Article 1 was settled in 1955. The preamble to the 1962 Declaration nonetheless linked permanent sovereignty to self-determination:

Bearing in mind its resolution 1314(XIII) of 12 December 1958, by which it established the Commission on Permanent Sovereignty over Natural Resources and instructed it to conduct a full survey of the status of permanent sovereignty over natural wealth and resources as a basic constituent of the right to self-determination…

…

Considering that any measure in this respect must be based on the recognition of the inalienable right of all States freely to dispose of their natural wealth and resources in

[129] UNGAOR (10th Session), A/2929 (1 July 1955), Annexes, 15.

[130] UNGA Third Committee, A/3077 (8 December 1955), 15.

[131] By twenty-five votes in favour, eighteen against and fifteen abstentions: see Nowak, *CCPR Commentary*, 12.

[132] UNGA Res. 1803 (XVII), Permanent Sovereignty over Natural Resources. See also UNGA Res. 2158 (XXI), Permanent Sovereignty over Natural Resources (25 November 1966).

accordance with their national interests, and on respect for the economic independence of States,

. . .

Considering that it is desirable to promote international co-operation for the economic development of developing countries, and that economic and financial agreements between the developed and the developing countries must be based on the principles of equality and of the right of peoples and nations to self-determination . . .

Paragraph 1 of the 1962 Declaration recognized the principle of permanent sovereignty:

1. The right of peoples and nations to permanent sovereignty over their natural wealth and resources must be exercised in the interest of their national development and of the well-being of the people of the State concerned.

The conceptual attempt to link self-determination with permanent sovereignty after the adoption of the twin covenants continued in the General Assembly's standard-setting efforts in the 1970s. Both the 1974 Declaration on the Establishment of a New International Economic Order and the 1974 Charter of Economic Rights and Duties of States referred to self-determination as a founding or governing principle of the international economic order.[133] Both instruments also elaborated on the content of permanent sovereignty over natural resources. The 1974 Declaration on the Establishment of a New International Economic Order provided:

[4] e. Full permanent sovereignty of every State over its natural resources and all economic activities. In order to safeguard these resources, each State is entitled to exercise effective control over them and their exploitation with means suitable to its own situation, including the right to nationalization or transfer of ownership to its nationals, this right being an expression of the full permanent sovereignty of the State. No State may be subjected to economic, political or any other type of coercion to prevent the free and full exercise of this inalienable right . . .[134]

Similarly, Article 2 of the 1974 Charter of Economic Rights and Duties of States declared:

1. Every State has and shall freely exercise full permanent sovereignty, including possession, use and disposal, over all its wealth, natural resources and economic activities.

2. Each State has the right:

   a. To regulate and exercise authority over foreign investment within its national jurisdiction in accordance with its laws and regulations and in conformity with its national objectives and priorities. No State shall be compelled to grant preferential treatment to foreign investment;

   b. To regulate and supervise the activities of transnational corporations within its national jurisdiction and take measures to ensure that such activities comply with

[133] Declaration on the Establishment of a New International Economic Order, [4(a)]; Charter of Economic Rights and Duties of States, Chapter 1(g).

[134] Declaration on the Establishment of a New International Economic Order, [4(e)].

its laws, rules and regulations and conform with its economic and social policies. Transnational corporations shall not intervene in the internal affairs of a host State. Every State should, with full regard for its sovereign rights, cooperate with other States in the exercise of the right set forth in this subparagraph;

c. To nationalize, expropriate or transfer ownership of foreign property, in which case appropriate compensation should be paid by the State adopting such measures, taking into account its relevant laws and regulations and all circumstances that the State considers pertinent. In any case where the question of compensation gives rise to a controversy, it shall be settled under the domestic law of the nationalizing State and by its tribunals, unless it is freely and mutually agreed by all States concerned that other peaceful means be sought on the basis of the sovereign equality of States and in accordance with the principle of free choice of means.[135]

The most contentious aspect of efforts to recognize permanent sovereignty and construct a 'new international economic order' concerned state liability for the expropriation or nationalization of foreign property. That issue was the fulcrum of ideological division and legal uncertainties for about three decades (the 1960s to the 1980s) over the scope of economic self-determination, for it defined the circumstances and terms in which peoples—particularly in newly independent decolonized states—could reassert fuller control over national resources otherwise denied to them by foreign proprietary, concessionary and contractual interests. That issue is considered further below.

While the drafters were primarily concerned about external interference in a people's economic self-determination, Article 1(2) has an important internal aspect, as Antonio Cassese explains:

Given that the people of every sovereign State have a permanent right to choose by whom they are governed, it is only logical that they should have the right to demand that the chosen central authorities exploit the territory's natural resources so as to benefit the people. Herein enters Article 1(2), which provides that the right to control and benefit from a territory's natural resources lies with the inhabitants of that territory. This right, and the corresponding duty of the central government to use the resources in a manner which coincides with the interests of the people, is the natural consequence of the right to political self-determination.

The problem lies not in understanding the nature of the right but in ensuring State compliance. Decisions concerning the exploitation of natural resources require a wide measure of discretionary power and generally turn on a host of technical and economic factors. Therefore it is often hard for peoples to police their governments. Nevertheless, Article 1(2) can have an impact in extreme situations, where it is relatively easy to demonstrate that a government is exploiting the natural resources in the exclusive interest of a small segment of the population and is thereby disregarding the needs of the vast majority of its nationals. Similarly, it may be invoked with some success where it is apparent that a government has surrendered control over its natural resources to another State or to foreign private corporations without ensuring that the people will be the primary beneficiaries of such an

[135] Charter of Economic Rights and Duties of States, Article 2.

arrangement. Either of these situations would constitute a clear violation of Article 1(2) of the Covenants.[136]

In the practice of the CESCR and other relevant human rights bodies, attention to both the internal and external aspects of economic self-determination is evident. Such practice, particularly as regards the internal aspects of the right, also indicates that self-determination is now understood as an ongoing process rather than a one-off event. Self-determination is not realized simply upon the attainment of independence or the selection of an economic system; its political, economic, social and cultural freedoms are continuing obligations in independent states, in which state institutions are accountable to the 'people'.

INTERNAL ASPECT

A people's protection from its own government

The internal aspect of the right of economic self-determination involves both the protection of a population (or certain groups within it) against economic exploitation by the state, as well as their protection by the state from exploitative private actors. The CESCR has dealt with a number of different situations engaging economic self-determination in these contexts.

In one of its earlier decisions on the issue, the CESCR found in 1997 that the privatization of Azerbaijan's oil resources required the provision of public information, participation and transparency to comply with Article 1:

16. With respect to specific provisions of the Covenant, the Committee calls attention to article 1 on the right of self-determination. The Committee regrets that, due to lack of information, it is unable to assess to what extent the general public is able to participate in the privatization process. It stresses the importance of managing this process in a way that is sufficiently transparent to ensure fairness and accountability.

…

29. The Committee notes that the ability of people to defend their own economic, social and cultural rights depends significantly on the availability of public information. Efforts to ensure accountability and to combat corruption also require such information in order to be effective. In this regard it is important that the privatization process should be conducted in an open and transparent manner and that the conditions under which oil concessions are granted should always be made public.[137]

Economic self-determination is not, therefore, automatically protected by the mere existence of independent national political institutions, but rather involves continuing procedural obligations on state authorities to ensure transparency in disposing of public resources. Human rights standards in this respect have been heavily influenced by procedural principles arising in other areas of international law. The principle of public participation (and related principles of public

[136] Cassese, *Self-Determination of Peoples*, 55–6.

[137] CESCR, Concluding Observations: Azerbaijan, E/C.12/1/Add.20 (22 December 1997).

information and access to justice) in decision-making about public resources and development emerged in international environmental law from the 1970s,[138] crystallizing in Principle 10 of the UN Rio Declaration on Environment and Development 1992:

> Environmental issues are best handled with the participation of all concerned citizens, at the relevant level. At the national level, each individual shall have appropriate access to information concerning the environment that is held by public authorities, including information on hazardous materials and activities in their communities, and the opportunity to participate in decision-making processes. States shall facilitate and encourage public awareness and participation by making information widely available.[139]

Such principles have been elaborated more fully in a binding instrument in Europe (the 'Aarhus Convention'[140]); the interpretation of human rights standards in regional human rights systems in the Americas and Africa;[141] the development of binding norms (such as ILO Convention No. 169) and 'soft law' standards (such as the 2007 Declaration on Indigenous Peoples) concerning indigenous peoples;[142] and has influenced national laws and the practices and guidelines of international institutions from the World Bank to the UN Development Programme.[143]

Principles of public participation have also been incorporated into the right to development, with Article 8(2) of the 1986 Declaration on the Right to Development urging states to 'encourage popular participation in all spheres as an important factor in development and in the full realization of all human rights'. The CESCR too has explicitly endorsed public participation in decision-making as part of human rights law, including for those living in poverty:

> 12. …the international human rights normative framework includes the right of those affected by key decisions to participate in the relevant decision-making processes. The right

[138] Starting with the 1972 UN Conference on the Human Environment, Stockholm, 5–16 June 1972.

[139] UNGA Rio Declaration on Environment and Development, A/CONF.151/26 (Vol. I) (12 August 1992), Principle 10.

[140] UN Convention on Access to Information, Public Participation in Decision-Making and Access to Justice in Environmental Matters (adopted 25 June 1998, 2161 UNTS 447, entered into force 20 October 2001).

[141] *Social and Economic Rights Action Center and the Center for Economic and Social Rights v Nigeria*, African Commission on Human and Peoples' Rights Communication No. 155/96 (27 October 2001), (2001) AHRLR 60. The Commission construed the right to a 'general satisfactory environment favourable to their development', under Article 24 of the African Charter on Human and Peoples' Rights, as including a duty on the state to provide relevant information as well as meaningful opportunities for individuals to be heard and to participate in the development decisions that affect their communities. The Inter-American Commission on Human Rights in *Maya Indigenous Community of the Toledo District v Belize* (Case 12.053), Report on the Merits No. 40/04, 12 October 2004, held that by failing to provide for effective consultation and the informed consent of the Maya people, with resulting environmental damage when granting logging and oil concessions, Belize had violated the right to property of the Maya people (Ninth International Conference of American States, American Declaration on the Rights and Duties of Man, Bogota, Colombia, 2 May 1948, Article 23).

[142] UN Declaration on the Rights of Indigenous Peoples.

[143] See, eg, World Bank, 'Operational Manual: Indigenous Peoples', OP 4.10 (July 2005); UNDP, 'UNDP and Indigenous Peoples: A Policy of Engagement' (1 June 2001); UN Development Group, 'United Nations Development Group Guidelines on Indigenous Peoples' Issues' (February 2008).

to participate is reflected in numerous international instruments, including the International Covenant on Economic, Social and Cultural Rights and the Declaration on the Right to Development. In the Committee's experience, a policy or programme that is formulated without the active and informed participation of those affected is most unlikely to be effective. Although free and fair elections are a crucial component of the right to participate, they are not enough to ensure that those living in poverty enjoy the right to participate in key decisions affecting their lives.[144]

In subsequent country reports, the CESCR has raised the procedural aspects of Article 1, particularly in the context of indigenous peoples (considered below). Thus, the CESCR emphasized the procedural safeguards necessary to ensure economic self-determination in commenting on the illegal exploitation of mineral resources in the Democratic Republic of Congo, and also identified a substantive infringement of Article 1(2). In this case, the infringement involved the grant of mining concessions to foreign companies which were detrimental to the Congolese people and in ways which lacked the necessary transparency:

13. The Committee is concerned that, in spite of the adoption of a mining code in 2002 and a mining plan in 2004, as well as the current review of all mining contracts, the illegal exploitation and mismanagement of the natural resources of the State party continue with the involvement of foreign companies. The Committee also notes with great concern that in the resource-rich province of Katanga which is under effective Government control, its extensive mining industry continues to be exploited to the detriment of the rights of people of this province who remain extremely poor and deprived of basic social services and infrastructure. The Committee is further concerned about the lack of transparency surrounding the current revision of mining contracts and the granting of new contracts to foreign companies, such as the exclusive concession granted in the field of uranium extraction. (article 1.2)

The Committee urges the State party to take all appropriate measures to ensure that its natural resources are not subjected to illegal exploitation and mismanagement; to review without delay the mining contracts in a transparent and participatory way; repeal all contracts which are detrimental to the Congolese people; and ensure that future contracts are concluded in a transparent and public way. The Committee also encourages the State party to implement the Extractive Industries Transparency Initiative (EITI) for which it has been a candidate country since 2008, in particular as regards the regular disclosure of revenues received from oil, gas and mining to a wide audience in a publicly accessible, comprehensive and comprehensible manner. The State party should also adopt appropriate measures to control the export of minerals and to impose drastic sanctions on those involved in the illicit trade in natural resources. The Committee further calls upon the State party to ensure that revenues derived from the mining sector are allocated for the development of the province of Katanga and that its inhabitants are provided with basic social services and infrastructure so that their living conditions may be improved.[145]

[144] CESCR, Poverty and the ICESCR, E/C.12/2001/10 (10 May 2001), [12].

[145] CESCR, Concluding Observations: Democratic Republic of Congo, E/C.12/COD/CO/4 (16 December 2009).

The CESCR was also concerned by the expulsion or displacement of peasant farmers and inter-ethnic land disputes, in part due to mining, in the Congo:

15. The Committee is concerned that land-related disputes which were at the heart of the Ituri conflict and continue to be the source of conflicts in many provinces, remain unresolved and therefore may lead to new inter-ethnic confrontation. The Committee is especially concerned that the consultation process to revise the Land Law, although announced in the State party report, has not yet formally begun and that no other initiative is foreseen to prevent future land dispute. The Committee expresses further concern at the numerous cases of peasants expelled from their land due to mining operations in Kijiba, Kaposhi, Ngaleshi, Kifunga and Chimanga (Katanga). (article 1.2)

The Committee calls upon the State party to urgently launch a consultation process with a view to revising the current Land Law and securing land tenure. Until such a law is adopted and implemented, the State party should take all the necessary measures in consultation with local and regional authorities to solve the existing land conflicts and prevent further disputes. As part of its efforts, the State party should envisage financially supporting the sensitization and mediation activities of the Land Commission established in February 2008 in the province of Ituri and creating community-based land commissions in the other provinces. The State party should also inquire into the expulsion of farmers in Katanga and provide them with compensation and alternative locations for agriculture.[146]

In another context, the granting of land and agricultural concessions to foreign investors in Madagascar was criticized by the CESCR for adversely impacting on the rights of peasants and rural people, and the right to food of the 'Malagasy population'.

12. The Committee is concerned that Law No. 2007-036 of 14 January 2008, relating to investment law which allows land acquisition by foreign investors, including for agricultural purposes, has an adverse impact on the access of peasants and people living in rural areas to cultivable lands, as well as to their natural resources. The Committee is also concerned that such land acquisition leads to a negative impact on the realization by the Malagasy population of the right to food. (art. 1)

The Committee recommends that the State party revise Law No. 2007-037 and facilitate the acquisition of land by peasants and persons living in rural areas, as well as their access to natural resources. It also recommends that the State party carry out a national debate on investment in agriculture and seek, prior to any contracts with foreign companies, the free and informed consent of the persons concerned.[147]

Regional human rights systems have similarly recognized that economic self-determination requires the protection of a people from exploitative private interests. In *Social and Economic Rights Action Centre (SERAC) v Nigeria*, the African Commission on Human and Peoples' Rights found that the Nigerian

[146] CESCR, Concluding Observations: Democratic Republic of Congo, E/C.12/COD/CO/4 (16 December 2009).

[147] CESCR, Concluding Observations: Madagascar, E/C.12/MDG/CO/2 (16 December 2009).

Government violated Article 21 of the African Charter by failing to prevent the destruction of the Ogoni people's lands by foreign oil companies:

55. The Complainants also allege a violation of Article 21 of the African Charter by the government of Nigeria. The Complainants allege that the Military government of Nigeria was involved in oil production and thus did not monitor or regulate the operations of the oil companies and in so doing paved a way for the Oil Consortiums to exploit oil reserves in Ogoniland. Furthermore, in all their dealings with the Oil Consortiums, the government did not involve the Ogoni Communities in the decisions that affected the development of Ogoniland. The destructive and selfish role-played by oil development in Ogoniland, closely tied with repressive tactics of the Nigerian Government, and the lack of material benefits accruing to the local population, may well be said to constitute a violation of Article 21.

[Text of Article 21 omitted.]…

56. The origin of this provision may be traced to colonialism, during which the human and material resources of Africa were largely exploited for the benefit of outside powers, creating tragedy for Africans themselves, depriving them of their birthright and alienating them from the land. The aftermath of colonial exploitation has left Africa's precious resources and people still vulnerable to foreign misappropriation. The drafters of the Charter obviously wanted to remind African governments of the continent's painful legacy and restore co-operative economic development to its traditional place at the heart of African Society.

57. Governments have a duty to protect their citizens, not only through appropriate legislation and effective enforcement but also by protecting them from damaging acts that may be perpetrated by private parties. This duty calls for positive action on part of governments in fulfilling their obligation under human rights instruments…

58. The Commission notes that in the present case, despite its obligation to protect persons against interferences in the enjoyment of their rights, the Government of Nigeria facilitated the destruction of the Ogoniland. Contrary to its Charter obligations and despite such internationally established principles, the Nigerian Government has given the green light to private actors, and the oil Companies in particular, to devastatingly affect the well-being of the Ogonis. By any measure of standards, its practice falls short of the minimum conduct expected of governments, and therefore, is in violation of Article 21 of the African Charter.[148]

The African Commission failed, however, to elaborate on the concept of 'peoples' in the African Charter,[149] an omission not remedied until its later decision in *Endorois Welfare Council v Kenya*, discussed earlier.[150]

In another African Commission case, *Mgwanga Gunme v Cameroon*, a portion of Cameroon's population, the people of Southern Cameroon, were recognized

[148] *Social and Economic Rights Action Center and the Center for Economic and Social Rights v Nigeria*, African Commission on Human and Peoples' Rights Communication No. 155/96, (2001) AHRLR 60, 27 October 2001), [55–8].

[149] Frans Viljoen, *International Human Rights Law in Africa* (Oxford University Press, Oxford, 2007), 246.

[150] *Endorois Welfare Council v Kenya.*

as a distinct 'people' under Articles 20 to 22 of the African Charter.[151] The complainants argued that they were economically marginalized, politically oppressed, unequally represented and discriminated against in the constitutional and political structures of Cameroon. The Commission found, however, that they were entitled to neither secede from Cameroon nor exercise any right of self-determination less than secession, other than forms of political participation already provided for by the state:

190. The Commission notes that the Republic of Cameroon is a party to the Constitutive Act (and was a State party to the OAU Charter). It is a party to the African Charter on Human and Peoples' Rights as well. The Commission is obliged to uphold the territorial integrity of the Respondent State. As a consequence, the Commission cannot envisage, condone or encourage secession, as a form of self-determination for the Southern Cameroons. That will jeopardise the territorial integrity of the Republic of Cameroon.

191. The Commission states that secession is not the sole avenue open to Southern Cameroonians to exercise the right to self-determination. The African Charter cannot be invoked by a Complainant to threaten the sovereignty and territorial integrity of a State party. The Commission has however accepted that autonomy within a sovereign state, in the context of self-government, confederacy, or federation, while preserving territorial integrity of a State party, can be exercised under the Charter. In their submission, the Respondent State implicitly accepted that self-determination may be exercisable by the Complainants on condition that they establish cases of massive violations of human rights, or denial of participation in public affairs.

192. The Complainants have submitted that the people of the Southern Cameroon are marginalised, oppressed, and discriminated against to such an extent that they demand to exert their right to self-determination.

193. The Respondent States submitted that the 1996 Constitution was adopted by the National Assembly, which included representatives of the people of Southern Cameroon. The Respondent State argues that, within the framework of the 1996 Constitution, three laws on decentralisation, which 'will enable Cameroon to resume the development of local potentials,' were adopted by the Parliament. The Respondent State submits further that since 2004 measures are being taken to give more autonomy to regions. Whether the laws shall be applied to address the concerns of South Cameroonians, will depend on the goodwill of both sides.

194. The Commission has so far found that the Respondent has violated Articles 2, 4, 5, 6, 7, 11 and 19 of the Charter. It is the view of the Commission, however that, in order for such violations to constitute the basis for the exercise of the right to self determination under the African Charter, they must meet the test set out in the Katanga case, that is, there must be:

'concrete evidence of violations of human rights to the point that the territorial integrity of the State Party should be called to question, coupled with the denial of the people,

[151] *Mgwanga Gunme v Cameroon*, African Commission on Human and Peoples' Rights Communication No. 266/03, (2009) AHRLR 9, 13–27 May 2009, [178–81].

their right to participate in the government as guaranteed by Article 13.1.' (emphasis added)

195. The Commission has already made a finding that Article 13 was not violated. The Commission saw ample evidence that the people of Southern Cameroon are represented in the National Assembly, at least through an opposition party, the SDF. Information on the record suggests that there has been some form of representation of the people of Southern Cameroon in the national institutions prior to, and after 18 December 1989. The Complainants may not recognise the representatives elected to the national institutions under the current constitutional arrangement. The Respondent State on the other hand may not share the same views or even recognise the SCNC and SCAPO as representing a section of the people of Southern Cameroon.

196. The Complainants' main complaint is that the people of Southern Cameroon are denied equal status in the determination of national issues. They allege that their constitutional demands have been ignored by the Respondent State. In other words they assert their right to exist and hence the right to determine their own political, social and economic affairs under Article 20.1.

197. The Commission is not convinced that the Respondent State violated Article 20 of the Charter. The Commission holds the view that when a Complainant seeks to invoke Article 20 of the African Charter, it must satisfy the Commission that the two conditions under Article 20.2 namely oppression and domination have been met.

198. The Complainants have not demonstrated if these conditions have been met to warrant invoking the right to self-determination. The basic demands of the SCNC and SCAPO as well as the two Anglophone Conferences, is the holding of constitutional negotiations to address economic marginalisation, unequal representation and access to economic benefits. Secession was the last option after the demands of Buea and Bamenda Conferences were ignored by the Respondent State.

199. Going by the Katanga decision, the right to self-determination cannot be exercised, in the absence of proof of massive violation of human rights under the Charter. The Respondent State holds the same view. The Commission states that the various forms of governance or self-determination such as federalism, local government, unitarism, confederacy, and self-government can be exercised only subject to conformity with state sovereignty and territorial integrity of a State party. It must take into account the popular will of the entire population, exercised through democratic means, such as by way of a referendum, or other means of creating national consensus. Such forms of governance cannot be imposed on a State Party or a people by the African Commission.

200. The African Commission finds that the people of Southern Cameroon cannot engage in secession, except within the terms expressed hereinabove, since secession is not recognised as a variant of the right to self-determination within the context of the African Charter.

201. The Commission, however, finds also that the Respondent State violated various rights protected by the African Charter in respect of Southern Cameroonians. It urges the Respondent State to address the grievances expressed by the Southern Cameroonians through its democratic institutions. The 1993 Buea and 1994 Bamenda Anglophone conferences raised constitutional and human rights issues which have been a matter of concern

to a sizable section of the Southern Cameroonian population for quite a long time. The demand for these rights has lead to civil unrest, demonstrations, arrests, detention, and the deaths of various people, which culminated in the demand for secession.

202. The Respondent State implicitly acknowledges the existence of this unwelcome state of affairs. It is evident that the 1995 Constitution did not address the Southern Cameroonians' demands, particularly since it did not accommodate the concerns expressed through the 1993 Buea Declaration and 1994 Bamenda Proclamation.

203. The Commission believes that the Southern Cameroonians' grievances cannot be resolved through secession but through a comprehensive national dialogue.[152]

The complainants were also unsuccessful in arguing that Cameroon had infringed their Article 21 right to freely dispose of their wealth and natural resources, on the basis that they had failed to bring any evidence to support that allegation.[153] They also failed in their claim that their Article 22 right to (economic, social and cultural) development had been violated because of economic marginalization and lack of economic infrastructure.[154] Here the Commission invoked the principle of progressive realization in approaching the state's responsibility:

206. The Commission is cognisant of the fact that the realisation of the right to development is a big challenge to the Respondent State, as it is for State Parties to the Charter, which are developing countries with scarce resources. The Respondent State gave explanations and statistical data showing its allocation of development resources in various socio-economic sectors. The Respondent State is under obligation to invest its resources in the best way possible to attain the progressive realisation of the right to development, and other economic, social and cultural rights. This may not reach all parts of its territory to the satisfaction of all individuals and peoples, hence generating grievances. This alone cannot be a basis for the finding of a violation. The Commission does not a find a violation of Article 22.

The Commission was satisfied with the state's explanation and justification of its allocation of resources in that case. This was despite the Commission's own finding that Article 19 of the African Charter had been violated because 'the relocation of business enterprises and location of economic projects to Francophone Cameroon . . . generated negative effects on the economic life of Southern Cameroon'.[155] Article 19 relevantly protects the equal rights of peoples and prohibits 'the domination of a people by another'. In light of the information presented by the complainants on the intensity of economic inequality and marginalization in Southern Cameroon, it may be questioned whether the Commission paid sufficiently intense scrutiny to Cameroon's economic policies, even accounting for the principle of progressive realization.[156]

[152] *Mgwanga Gunme v Cameroon*, African Commission on Human and Peoples' Rights Communication No. 266/03, (2009) AHRLR 9, 13–27 May 2009.

[153] *Mgwanga Gunme v Cameroon*, [204]. [154] *Mgwanga Gunme v Cameroon*, [205–6].

[155] *Mgwanga Gunme v Cameroon*, [162].

[156] Progressive realization under the ICESCR is considered in the next chapter on Article 2(1).

The Commission in *Mgwanga Gunme v Cameroon* invoked the *Katanga* case to define the circumstances in which self-determination accrues. In *Katanga*, it was held that:

4. The Commission believes that self-determination may be exercised in any of the following ways independence, self-government, local government, federalism, confederalism, unitarism or any other form of relations that accords with the wishes of the people but fully cognisant of other recognised principles such as sovereignty and territorial integrity.

5. The Commission is obligated to uphold the sovereignty and territorial integrity of Zaire, member of the OAU and a party to the African Charter on Human and Peoples' Rights.

6. In the absence of concrete evidence of violations of human rights to the point that the territorial integrity of Zaire should be called to question and in the absence of evidence that the people of Katanga are denied the right to participate in Government as guaranteed by Article 13(1) of the African Charter, the Commission holds the view that Katanga is obliged to exercise a variant of self-determination that is compatible with the sovereignty and territorial integrity of Zaire.[157]

The *Katanga* case establishes that the African Charter may contemplate the secession of parts of the population of an independent state, but only where very serious human rights abuses are involved. In cases where political representation is denied contrary to Article 13, a people may be entitled to the benefits of other forms of self-determination not involving secession. In all other cases, a people (here, 'the people of Katanga') enjoys only the rights of self-determination enjoyed in concert with other members of the state's population, including the political and economic choices made by that whole population (or larger unit of 'people').

Mere interference in an individual's private property rights will not amount to interference in a people's economic self-determination under Article 21 of the African Charter. In a case before the African Commission, *Bissangou v Republic of Congo*, the complainant's property was damaged by soldiers, armed bands and renegade police during socio-political upheavals in the Republic of Congo in 1993, and the state had failed to uphold a judgment of a national court finding in his favour. The Commission found that the 'movable and immovable property of the Complainant that had been destroyed during the socio-political events which shook the country in 1993 does not constitute the wealth and natural resources of a people but rather individual assets'; and that the complaintant was acting on his own behalf and not for an affected group.[158] The Commission acknowledged, however, that claims brought by groups might be treated differently, for instance where the scale of their assets collectively constitute the natural resources of the people (or some significant part of it).

[157] *Katangese Peoples' Congress v Zaire*, African Commission on Human and Peoples' Rights Communication No. 75/92, (2000) AHRLR 72, 1995), [4–6].

[158] *Bissangou v Democratic Republic of Congo*, African Commission on Human and Peoples' Rights Communication No. 253/2002, (2006) AHRLR 80, 15–29 November 2006.

Protection of indigenous peoples' rights

The acceptance of indigenous peoples as entitled to limited internal self-determination was described earlier. On numerous occasions the CESCR has invoked Article 1 in relation to the adverse impacts on indigenous peoples of the state's exploitation of natural resources, or the state's failure to protect such groups from private exploitation of resources.

The CESCR thus criticized rapid deforestation and the granting of economic land concessions in Cambodia for interfering in the self-determination of indigenous peoples and rural communities, particularly absent public participation and informed decision-making:

15. …The Committee is also concerned about the reports that the rapid increase in economic land concessions in the last several years, even within the protected zones, is the major factor in the degradation of natural resources, adversely affecting the ecology and biodiversity, resulting in the displacement of indigenous peoples from their lands without just compensation and resettlement, and in the loss of livelihood for rural communities who depend on land and forest resources for their survival. (art. 1)

The Committee urges the State party to review its policy regarding the conversion of protected zones into economic concessions, by conducting environmental and social impact assessments including consultations with relevant stakeholders and communities with due regard to their right to participate in informed decisions that affect their lives. The Committee strongly recommends that the granting of economic concessions take into account the need for sustainable development and for all Cambodians to share in the benefits of progress rather than for private gain alone…[159]

Cambodia's failure to implement a domestic law protecting communal land title for indigenous peoples, and the adverse impacts of mining and oil operations on indigenous lands, were also viewed by the CESCR as raising Article 1 concerns:

16. The Committee notes with concern that the 2001 Land Law, which provides for the titling of indigenous communities' communal lands, has not been implemented effectively and that so far, no indigenous community has received any land title. The Committee also notes with concern, the adverse effects of the exploitation of natural resources, in particular mining operations and oil exploration that are being carried out in indigenous territories, contravening the right of indigenous peoples to their ancestral domains, lands and natural resources. (art. 1)

The Committee urges the State party to implement the 2001 Land Law without further delay and to ensure that its policies on registration of communal lands do not contravene the spirit of this law. The Committee emphasizes the need for carrying out environmental and social impact assessments and consultations with affected communities with regard to economic activities including mining and oil explorations, with a view to ensuring that these activities do not deprive the indigenous peoples of the full enjoyment of their rights to their ancestral lands and natural resources. The Committee encourages the State

[159] CESCR, Concluding Observations: Cambodia, E/C.12/KHM/CO/1 (12 June 2009).

party to consider ratifying ILO Convention No. 169 on Indigenous and Tribal Peoples in Independent Countries.[160]

Similarly, the CESCR was concerned at Brazil's slow progress in land reform and demarcation, affecting indigenous self-determination under Article 1(1):

9. The Committee is concerned at the slow progress in the land reform process notwithstanding the constitutional rights to property and self-determination, as well as the enactment of legislation to facilitate the demarcation of land belonging to the indigenous peoples, the State party's adoption of the United Nations Declaration on the Rights of Indigenous Peoples (adopted in 2007) and its ratification of ILO Convention No. 169. (art. 1, para. 1)

The Committee recalls the recommendation made in its concluding observations on the State party's initial report in this regard and recommends that the State party expeditiously complete the process of demarcation and allocation of indigenous land in accordance with the Constitution and existing laws.[161]

Concerning Colombia, the CESCR criticized the adverse impacts of infrastructure, development and mega-mining projects on indigenous peoples and Afro-Colombians, which prejudiced their self-determination rights:

9. The Committee is concerned that infrastructure, development and mining mega-projects are being carried out in the State party without the free, prior and informed consent of the affected indigenous and Afro-Colombian communities. The Committee is also concerned that, according to the Constitutional Court, the legitimate representatives of the Afro-Colombian communities did not participate in the process of consultation and the authorities did not provide accurate information on the scope and the impact of the mining mega-project of Chocò and Antioquia. The Committee is further concerned that the Presidential Directive No. 001 aimed at establishing a general framework for prior consultation may not be sufficient and that indigenous and Afro-Colombian peoples were not consulted regarding the draft bill elaborated by the Working Party on Prior Consultation of the Ministry of the Interior that, therefore, does not create the adequate framework for the process of genuine consultation (art. 1).

The Committee recommends that the State party take practical measures to review the processes concerning infrastructure, development and mining projects and fully implement decisions of the Constitutional Court in this regard. The Committee also recommends that the State party review the Presidential Directive No. 001 and the draft bill elaborated by the Working Party on Prior Consultation of the Ministry of the Interior. The Committee further recommends that the State party adopt legislation in consultation with and the participation of indigenous and Afro-Colombian people, that clearly establishes the right to free, prior and informed consent in conformity with International Labour Organization Convention No. 169 concerning Indigenous and Tribal Peoples in Independent Countries, as well as the relevant decisions of the Constitutional Court.[162]

160 CESCR, Concluding Observations: Cambodia, E/C.12/KHM/CO/1 (12 June 2009).
161 CESCR, Concluding Observations: Brazil, E/C.12/BRA/CO/2 (12 June 2009).
162 CESCR, Concluding Observations: Colombia, E/C.12/COL/CO/5 (7 June 2010).

The CESCR also raised Article 1 in criticizing the failure of the Philippines to implement existing domestic laws providing for the protection of indigenous peoples and their land from the adverse effects of the economic exploitation of natural resources, especially mining:

16. The Committee notes with concern the adverse effects that economic activities connected with the exploitation of natural resources, especially mining operations, carried out in indigenous territories continue to have on the right of indigenous peoples to their ancestral domains, lands and natural resources, as recognized in the 1997 Indigenous Peoples Rights Act (IPRA). The Committee is concerned about the conflict of laws between the 1995 Mining Act and IPRA, and notes in particular that section 56 of the IPRA, which provides for the protection of property rights already existing within the ancestral domains, de facto risks to undermine the protection of the rights recognized to indigenous peoples under the Act. (arts. 1, 11, 12 and 15) The Committee urges the State party to fully implement the 1997 Indigenous Peoples Rights Act (IPRA), in particular by ensuring the effective enjoyment by indigenous peoples of their rights to ancestral domains, lands and natural resources, and avoiding that economic activities, especially mining, carried out on indigenous territories adversely affect the protection of the rights recognized to indigenous peoples under the Act.[163]

The CESCR found that illegal logging in the Congo engaged Article 1(2) because it adversely affected the forest environment, resources and lands on which indigenous peoples depend:

14. The Committee is concerned that despite the adoption of the Forestry Code and a moratorium on concessions, illicit trade of wood and abusive exploitation of the country's forests continue to adversely affect the ecology and biodiversity and undermine the rights of indigenous populations, especially pygmies, to live in their ancestral lands and manage their forests according to their traditional practices. The Committee also expresses concern that representatives of indigenous communities were not invited to take part in the second session of the inter-ministerial commission in charge of reviewing illicit logging contracts, although the session was devoted to the signature of contracts between local authorities and logging companies. (article 1.2)

The Committee urges the State party to enforce the moratorium on concessions until the mapping and zoning exercise is completed and to ensure that future forest concessions do not deprive the indigenous peoples of the full enjoyment of their rights to their ancestral lands and natural resources, and that the benefits thereof contribute to their poverty alleviation. The State party should ensure that forestry projects are centred on advancing the rights of forest-dependent peoples and conducted only after comprehensive studies are carried out, with the participation of the peoples concerned, to assess the social, spiritual, cultural and environmental impact on them of planned activities. The Committee encourages the State party to consider ratifying ILO Convention No. 169 (1989) on Indigenous and Tribal Peoples in Independent Countries.[164]

[163] CESCR, Concluding Observations: Philippines, E/C.12/PHL/CO/4 (1 December 2008).

[164] CESCR, Concluding Observations: Democratic Republic of Congo, E/C.12/COD/CO/4 (16 December 2009).

The 'precarious situation' of indigenous peoples in the Russian Federation was found by the CESCR to raise Article 1 concerns, including because existing laws to demarcate indigenous territory and protect indigenous lands had not been implemented:

11. The Committee is concerned about the precarious situation of indigenous communities in the State party, affecting their right to self-determination under article 1 of the Covenant. The Committee notes that the Law of 2001 On Territories of Traditional Nature Use of Indigenous Numerically Small Peoples of the North, Siberia and the Far East of the Russian Federation, which provides for the demarcation of indigenous territories and protection of indigenous land rights, has still not been implemented.

…

39. The Committee, recalling the right to self-determination enshrined in article 1 of the Covenant, urges the State party to intensify its efforts to improve the situation of the indigenous peoples and to ensure that they are not deprived of their means of subsistence. The Committee also encourages the State party to ensure the effective implementation of the Law on Territories and Traditional Nature Use.[165]

In earlier observations on Russia, while not mentioning self-determination, the CESCR had specifically outlined that poverty, inadequate food (including from traditional resources such as fishing and reindeer stocks), environmental pollution, and illegal or exploitative oil and gas concessions adversely affected indigenous peoples.[166]

The CESCR criticized Sweden's failure to resolve Saami land rights as affecting Saami culture and way of life, particularly reindeer herding, thus raising self-determination issues under Article 1:

15. The Committee, while welcoming the initiative of a Nordic Sami Convention, reiterates its concern that the Sami land rights have not yet been resolved and that this fact negatively affects their right to maintain and develop their traditional culture and way of life, particularly reindeer herding. The Committee also reiterates its regret that the State party has not yet ratified ILO Convention No. 169 concerning Indigenous and Tribal People. (arts. 1, 2.2, and 15) The Committee urges the State party to ensure the adoption of the Nordic Sami Convention and consider ratifying ILO Convention No. 169. It also recommends the expeditious resolution of the Sami land and resource rights issues by introducing appropriate legislation, in cooperation with the Sami communities.[167]

The CESCR has also been prepared to criticize the effects of a state's economic choices in its international relations where such choices have adverse impacts for the self-determination of marginalized and disadvantaged groups. In doing so, the CESCR implies that the economic freedom of the state to enter into treaties is limited by the internal self-determination rights of those constituent groups

[165] CESCR, Concluding Observations: Russian Federation, E/C.12/1/Add.94 (12 December 2003).
[166] CESCR, Concluding Observations: Russian Federation, E/C.12/1/Add.13 (20 May 1997), [14] and [30].
[167] CESCR, Concluding Observations: Sweden, E/C.12/SWE/CO/5 (1 December 2008).

comprising part of the state's population. It thus criticized the negative impacts of free trade agreements on indigenous, Afro-Colombian and rural people in Colombia:

10. The Committee is concerned that bilateral and multilateral trade agreements signed by the State party may affect the enjoyment of economic, social and cultural rights, in particular of disadvantaged and marginalized groups, such as indigenous and Afro-Colombian peoples and persons living in rural areas...(arts. 1, 12).

The Committee recommends that the State party take effective measures to ensure that economic, social and cultural rights are taken into account in all free trade and bilateral and multilateral trade agreements, and develop effective policies to protect the rights of the population, in particular the marginalized and disadvantaged groups, against the negative impact of such agreements...[168]

Human Rights Committee practice under Article 1 of the ICCPR

The HRC too has occasionally referred to the economic and cultural self-determination rights of indigenous peoples. It found that Canada's 'practice of extinguishing inherent aboriginal rights is incompatible with article 1 and should be abandoned'.[169] The HRC was concerned that Australia had not taken sufficient action to protect indigenous self-determination and asked it to 'take the necessary steps in order to secure for the indigenous inhabitants a stronger role in decision-making over their traditional lands and natural resources (art. 1, para. 2)'.[170] It was also concerned for Mexico to enable indigenous peoples to enjoy the usufruct of their lands and natural resources:

All necessary measures should be taken to safeguard for the indigenous communities respect for the rights and freedoms to which they are entitled individually and as a group; to eradicate the abuses to which they are subjected; and to respect their customs and culture and their traditional patterns of living, enabling them to enjoy the usufruct of their lands and natural resources. Appropriate measures should also be taken to increase their participation in the country's institutions and the exercise of the right to self-determination.[171]

Similarly, Sweden was criticized for unduly limiting the role of the Saami in making decisions about their traditional lands and economic activities, and the impact of various development projects on their environment and means of subsistence:

The Committee is concerned at the limited extent to which the Sami Parliament can have a significant role in the decision-making process on issues affecting the traditional lands and economic activities of the indigenous Sami people, such as projects in the fields of hydroelectricity, mining and forestry, as well as the privatization of land (articles 1, 25 and 27 of the Covenant).

[168] CESCR, Concluding Observations: Colombia, E/C.12/COL/CO/5 (7 June 2010).
[169] HRC, Report: Canada (ICCPR), A/54/40 vol. I (1999), [230].
[170] HRC, Report: Australia (ICCPR), A/55/40 vol. I (2000), [506–[507].
[171] HRC, Report: Mexico (ICCPR), A/54/40 vol. I (1999), [331].

The State party should take steps to involve the Sami by giving them greater influence in decision-making affecting their natural environment and their means of subsistence.[172]

Finland too came under Article 1 (and 27) scrutiny for failing to settle Saami land rights and the impact of other land users on their traditional means of subsistence, namely reindeer breeding:

The Committee regrets that it has not received a clear answer concerning the rights of the Sami as an indigenous people (Constitution, sect. 17, subsect. 3), in the light of article 1 of the Covenant. It reiterates its concern over the failure to settle the question of Sami rights to land ownership and the various public and private uses of land that affect the Sami's traditional means of subsistence—in particular reindeer breeding—thus endangering their traditional culture and way of life, and hence their identity.

The State party should, in conjunction with the Sami people, swiftly take decisive action to arrive at an appropriate solution to the land dispute with due regard for the need to preserve the Sami identity in accordance with article 27 of the Covenant. Meanwhile it is requested to refrain from any action that might adversely prejudice settlement of the issue of Sami land rights.[173]

In certain other cases, minority groups also recognized as indigenous for the purpose of Article 27 of the ICCPR has not resulted in the HRC expressing concern about self-determination, even where the people's subsistence is threatened and their group economic or land rights are engaged.[174] It is not always clear, however, why the HRC refers to some groups as 'minorities' and others as 'indigenous', whether in respect of Article 1 or 27 of the ICCPR, since it seldom elaborates on the characteristics of either group in applying the concepts to the facts of a given case. In many cases, only minorities have been recognized (for example, 'Highlanders' in Thailand),[175] as discussed in the chapter in this book on Article 15 concerning cultural rights and minorities, even where such groups have indigenous-like attachments to land.

Other relevant normative standards on indigenous self-determination

As is apparent from the above extracts, the CESCR has often invoked ILO Convention No. 169 on Indigenous and Tribal Peoples in Independent Countries as a 'best practice' normative standard relevant to the exercise of indigenous self-determination under Article 1, even though that Convention does not specifically mention self-determination. While Convention No. 169 has only been ratified by twenty-two states (with Latin-American states particularly represented), it 'has gained recognition well beyond the number of actual ratifications…[and]

[172] HRC, Report: Sweden (ICCPR), A/57/40 vol. I (2002), [79(15)].

[173] HRC, Report: Finland (ICCPR), A/60/40 vol. I (2004), [81(17)].

[174] HRC, Report: Suriname (ICCPR), A/59/40 vol. I (2004), [69(21)] (concerning 'indigenous and tribal' Maroon and Amerindian communities, whose land and resources were affected by logging and mining concessions imposed without notice or consultation, and involving the release of mercury which affected their life, health and environment).

[175] HRC, Report: Thailand (ICCPR), A/60/40 vol. I (2005), 95(24).

influenced numerous policy documents, debates and legal decisions at the regional and international levels, as well as national legislation and policies'.[176]

In addition to providing guidance on identifying indigenous peoples as noted earlier,[177] the Convention extensively recognizes indigenous land and economic rights in Articles 13 to 19, including rights in natural resources (Article 15) and against forced relocation (Article 16):

Article 13

1. In applying the provisions of this Part of the Convention governments shall respect the special importance for the cultures and spiritual values of the peoples concerned of their relationship with the lands or territories, or both as applicable, which they occupy or otherwise use, and in particular the collective aspects of this relationship.

2. The use of the term 'lands' in Articles 15 and 16 shall include the concept of territories, which covers the total environment of the areas which the peoples concerned occupy or otherwise use.

Article 14

1. The rights of ownership and possession of the peoples concerned over the lands which they traditionally occupy shall be recognised. In addition, measures shall be taken in appropriate cases to safeguard the right of the peoples concerned to use lands not exclusively occupied by them, but to which they have traditionally had access for their subsistence and traditional activities. Particular attention shall be paid to the situation of nomadic peoples and shifting cultivators in this respect.

2. Governments shall take steps as necessary to identify the lands which the peoples concerned traditionally occupy, and to guarantee effective protection of their rights of ownership and possession.

3. Adequate procedures shall be established within the national legal system to resolve land claims by the peoples concerned.

Article 15

1. The rights of the peoples concerned to the natural resources pertaining to their lands shall be specially safeguarded. These rights include the right of these peoples to participate in the use, management and conservation of these resources.

2. In cases in which the State retains the ownership of mineral or sub-surface resources or rights to other resources pertaining to lands, governments shall establish or maintain procedures through which they shall consult these peoples, with a view to ascertaining whether and to what degree their interests would be prejudiced, before undertaking or permitting any programmes for the exploration or exploitation of such resources pertaining to their lands. The peoples concerned shall wherever possible participate in the benefits of such activities, and shall receive fair compensation for any damages which they may sustain as a result of such activities.

[176] ILO, 'Convention No. 169', <http://www.ilo.org/indigenous/Conventions/no169/lang--en/index.htm>.
[177] ILO Convention No. 169, Article 1.

Article 16

1. Subject to the following paragraphs of this Article, the peoples concerned shall not be removed from the lands which they occupy.

2. Where the relocation of these peoples is considered necessary as an exceptional measure, such relocation shall take place only with their free and informed consent. Where their consent cannot be obtained, such relocation shall take place only following appropriate procedures established by national laws and regulations, including public inquiries where appropriate, which provide the opportunity for effective representation of the peoples concerned.

3. Whenever possible, these peoples shall have the right to return to their traditional lands, as soon as the grounds for relocation cease to exist.

4. When such return is not possible, as determined by agreement or, in the absence of such agreement, through appropriate procedures, these peoples shall be provided in all possible cases with lands of quality and legal status at least equal to that of the lands previously occupied by them, suitable to provide for their present needs and future development. Where the peoples concerned express a preference for compensation in money or in kind, they shall be so compensated under appropriate guarantees.

5. Persons thus relocated shall be fully compensated for any resulting loss or injury.

Article 17

1. Procedures established by the peoples concerned for the transmission of land rights among members of these peoples shall be respected.

2. The peoples concerned shall be consulted whenever consideration is being given to their capacity to alienate their lands or otherwise transmit their rights outside their own community.

3. Persons not belonging to these peoples shall be prevented from taking advantage of their customs or of lack of understanding of the laws on the part of their members to secure the ownership, possession or use of land belonging to them.

Article 18

Adequate penalties shall be established by law for unauthorised intrusion upon, or use of, the lands of the peoples concerned, and governments shall take measures to prevent such offences.

Article 19

National agrarian programmes shall secure to the peoples concerned treatment equivalent to that accorded to other sectors of the population with regard to:

(a) The provision of more land for these peoples when they have not the area necessary for providing the essentials of a normal existence, or for any possible increase in their numbers;

(b) The provision of the means required to promote the development of the lands which these peoples already possess.

The CESCR has regarded as particularly significant the procedural obligations on states to consult with indigenous peoples, involve them in decision-making, and seek their consent, including in development, under Articles 6 and 7 of the ILO Convention:

Article 6

1. In applying the provisions of this Convention, Governments shall:

(a) Consult the peoples concerned, through appropriate procedures and in particular through their representative institutions, whenever consideration is being given to legislative or administrative measures which may affect them directly;

(b) Establish means by which these peoples can freely participate, to at least the same extent as other sectors of the population, at all levels of decision-making in elective institutions and administrative and other bodies responsible for policies and programmes which concern them;

(c) Establish means for the full development of these peoples' own institutions and initiatives, and in appropriate cases provide the resources necessary for this purpose.

2. The consultations carried out in application of this Convention shall be undertaken, in good faith and in a form appropriate to the circumstances, with the objective of achieving agreement or consent to the proposed measures.

Article 7

1. The peoples concerned shall have the right to decide their own priorities for the process of development as it affects their lives, beliefs, institutions and spiritual well-being and the lands they occupy or otherwise use, and to exercise control, to the extent possible, over their own economic, social and cultural development. In addition, they shall participate in the formulation, implementation and evaluation of plans and programmes for national and regional development which may affect them directly.

2. The improvement of the conditions of life and work and levels of health and education of the peoples concerned, with their participation and co-operation, shall be a matter of priority in plans for the overall economic development of areas they inhabit. Special projects for development of the areas in question shall also be so designed as to promote such improvement.

3. Governments shall ensure that, whenever appropriate, studies are carried out, in co-operation with the peoples concerned, to assess the social, spiritual, cultural and environmental impact on them of planned development activities. The results of these studies shall be considered as fundamental criteria for the implementation of these activities.

4. Governments shall take measures, in co-operation with the peoples concerned, to protect and preserve the environment of the territories they inhabit.

With the adoption of the General Assembly's 2007 Declaration on the Rights of Indigenous Peoples, it may be expected that in future the CESCR will increasingly refer to that instrument to guide its approach to the economic self-determination of indigenous peoples.[178] Already the CESCR invoked the Declaration in commenting on Brazil in 2009.[179]

While the 2007 Declaration is not a binding treaty, it has been endorsed by the overwhelming majority of states. When adopted as a UN resolution in 2007, 144 states voted in favour, four against (Australia, Canada, New Zealand and the United States) and eleven abstained.[180] Some of the states voting against, such as Australia, have since supported the Declaration. In 2009, 182 states at the Durban Review Conference expressed consensus support for the adoption of the UN Declaration and urged states to implement the rights of indigenous peoples.[181] The Declaration is also intended as a restatement of existing international law affecting indigenous peoples, rather than creating new law. In this sense, the Declaration likely has even wider normative or juridical effects than ILO Convention No. 169 (with only twenty ratifications).

The Declaration expressly mentions self-determination twice in the preamble:

Acknowledging that the Charter of the United Nations, the International Covenant on Economic, Social and Cultural Rights and the International Covenant on Civil and Political Rights as well as the Vienna Declaration and Programme of Action, affirm the fundamental importance of the right of self-determination of all peoples, by virtue of which they freely determine their political status and freely pursue their economic, social and cultural development,

Bearing in mind that nothing in this Declaration may be used to deny any peoples their right of self-determination, exercised in conformity with international law…

It then operatively refers to self-determination in Articles 3 and 4:

Article 3

Indigenous peoples have the right of self-determination. By virtue of that right they freely determine their political status and freely pursue their economic, social and cultural development.

Article 4

Indigenous peoples, in exercising their right to self-determination, have the right to autonomy or self-government in matters relating to their internal and local affairs, as well as ways and means for financing their autonomous functions.

Article 5 of the Declaration relevantly focuses on the identity rights of indigenous peoples:

Indigenous peoples have the right to maintain and strengthen their distinct political, legal, economic, social and cultural institutions, while retaining their rights to participate fully, if they so choose, in the political, economic, social and cultural life of the State.

178 On discussion of self-determination in the drafting of the Declaration, see Caroline Foster, 'Articulating Self-Determination in the Draft Declaration on the Rights of Indigenous Peoples' (2001) 12 *European Journal of International Law* 141.

179 CESCR, Concluding Observations: Brazil, E/C.12/BRA/CO/2 (12 June 2009).

180 UN Declaration on the Rights of Indigenous Peoples: Azerbaijan, Bangladesh, Bhutan, Burundi, Colombia, Georgia, Kenya, Nigeria, Russian Federation, Samoa and Ukraine.

181 UN Office of the High Commissioner for Human Rights, *Outcome Document of the Durban Review Conference*, 24 April 2009, [73].

Building on the procedural rights in Article 6 of the ILO Convention No. 169, the Declaration provides for indigenous rights of participation and consultation in all decisions affecting them, under Articles 18 and 19:

Article 18

Indigenous peoples have the right to participate in decision-making in matters which would affect their rights, through representatives chosen by themselves in accordance with their own procedures, as well as to maintain and develop their own indigenous decision-making institutions.

Article 19

States shall consult and cooperate in good faith with the indigenous peoples concerned through their own representative institutions in order to obtain their free, prior and informed consent before adopting and implementing legislative or administrative measures that may affect them.

Various provisions in the Declaration are relevant to particular aspects of self-determination. As regards cultural self-determination, mention may be made of the provisions on group membership (Article 9), culture (Article 11), cultural heritage (Article 31), religion (Article 12), language (Article 13) and education (Article 14). On economic self-determination, Articles 20 and 21 of the Declaration set out the overarching framework for indigenous economic rights:

Article 20

1. Indigenous peoples have the right to maintain and develop their political, economic and social systems or institutions, to be secure in the enjoyment of their own means of subsistence and development, and to engage freely in all their traditional and other economic activities.

2. Indigenous peoples deprived of their means of subsistence and development are entitled to just and fair redress.

Article 21

1. Indigenous peoples have the right, without discrimination, to the improvement of their economic and social conditions, including, inter alia, in the areas of education, employment, vocational training and retraining, housing, sanitation, health and social security.

2. States shall take effective measures and, where appropriate, special measures to ensure continuing improvement of their economic and social conditions. Particular attention shall be paid to the rights and special needs of indigenous elders, women, youth, children and persons with disabilities.

Article 23 of the Declaration echoes but strengthens Article 7 of ILO Convention No. 169 on indigenous control over development, by referring to it as a 'right', not merely a 'process':

Indigenous peoples have the right to determine and develop priorities and strategies for exercising their right to development. In particular, indigenous peoples have the right to be actively involved in developing and determining health, housing and other economic and social programmes affecting them and, as far as possible, to administer such programmes through their own institutions.

A large number of provisions in the Declaration (Articles 10, 25 to 30 and 32) focus on land as a particularly significant source of economic (as well as cultural, religious and environmental) rights. Article 10 prohibits forced removals from indigenous lands. Article 25 recognizes indigenous rights to maintain distinctive relationships with land, while Article 26 acknowledges indigenous land rights. Article 27 provides for fair procedures to recognize and adjudicate land rights and Article 28 requires compensation for the taking of land. Environmental protection of indigenous lands and resources is recognized by Article 29, as is freedom from military activities on their land in Article 30. Article 32 particularizes the right of indigenous control over development (Article 23) by applying a similar principle to development of lands and resources:

Article 10

Indigenous peoples shall not be forcibly removed from their lands or territories. No relocation shall take place without the free, prior and informed consent of the indigenous peoples concerned and after agreement on just and fair compensation and, where possible, with the option of return.

. . .

Article 25

Indigenous peoples have the right to maintain and strengthen their distinctive spiritual relationship with their traditionally owned or otherwise occupied and used lands, territories, waters and coastal seas and other resources and to uphold their responsibilities to future generations in this regard.

Article 26

1. Indigenous peoples have the right to the lands, territories and resources which they have traditionally owned, occupied or otherwise used or acquired.

2. Indigenous peoples have the right to own, use, develop and control the lands, territories and resources that they possess by reason of traditional ownership or other traditional occupation or use, as well as those which they have otherwise acquired.

3. States shall give legal recognition and protection to these lands, territories and resources. Such recognition shall be conducted with due respect to the customs, traditions and land tenure systems of the indigenous peoples concerned.

Article 27

States shall establish and implement, in conjunction with indigenous peoples concerned, a fair, independent, impartial, open and transparent process, giving due recognition to indigenous peoples' laws, traditions, customs and land tenure systems, to recognize and adjudicate the rights of indigenous peoples pertaining to their lands, territories and resources, including those which were traditionally owned or otherwise occupied or used. Indigenous peoples shall have the right to participate in this process.

Article 28

1. Indigenous peoples have the right to redress, by means that can include restitution or, when this is not possible, of a just, fair and equitable compensation, for the lands, territories and resources which they have traditionally owned or otherwise occupied or used, and which have been confiscated, taken, occupied, used or damaged without their free, prior and informed consent.

2. Unless otherwise freely agreed upon by the peoples concerned, compensation shall take the form of lands, territories and resources equal in quality, size and legal status or of monetary compensation or other appropriate redress.

Article 29

1. Indigenous peoples have the right to the conservation and protection of the environment and the productive capacity of their lands or territories and resources. States shall establish and implement assistance programmes for indigenous peoples for such conservation and protection, without discrimination.

2. States shall take effective measures to ensure that no storage or disposal of hazardous materials shall take place in the lands or territories of indigenous peoples without their free, prior and informed consent.

3. States shall also take effective measures to ensure, as needed, that programmes for monitoring, maintaining and restoring the health of indigenous peoples, as developed and implemented by the peoples affected by such materials, are duly implemented.

Article 30

1. Military activities shall not take place in the lands or territories of indigenous peoples, unless justified by a relevant public interest or otherwise freely agreed with or requested by the indigenous peoples concerned.

2. States shall undertake effective consultations with the indigenous peoples concerned, through appropriate procedures and in particular through their representative institutions, prior to using their lands or territories for military activities.

…

Article 32

1. Indigenous peoples have the right to determine and develop priorities and strategies for the development or use of their lands or territories and other resources.

2. States shall consult and cooperate in good faith with the indigenous peoples concerned through their own representative institutions in order to obtain their free and informed consent prior to the approval of any project affecting their lands or territories and other resources, particularly in connection with the development, utilization or exploitation of mineral, water or other resources.

3. States shall provide effective mechanisms for just and fair redress for any such activities, and appropriate measures shall be taken to mitigate adverse environmental, economic, social, cultural or spiritual impact.

Article 32 importantly imposes obligations on states to consult and cooperate in good faith with indigenous peoples to obtain their free and informed consent. There has been some controversy over whether development decisions affecting indigenous peoples' lands or resources *require* their consent in order to proceed (as opposed to merely *seeking* their consent). ILO Convention No. 169 requires consultation and indigenous participation in decisions, but only 'with the objective of achieving agreement or consent to the proposed measures' (Article 6(2)).

In contrast, Article 32(2) of the 2007 Declaration appears to raise the threshold by requiring consultation 'in order to obtain their free and informed consent prior to the approval of any project'. This would appear to give a veto to indigenous peoples over development projects approved by national governments, in effect privileging indigenous self-determination rights over the economic self-determination priorities of the national authorities. The test for a justified interference in indigenous rights is thus higher than is the case for an ordinary interference in individual property rights, as a UN Special Rapporteur observes:

> Limitations, if any, on the right to indigenous peoples to their natural resources must flow only from the most urgent and compelling interest of the state. Few, if any, limitations on indigenous resource rights are appropriate, because the indigenous ownership of the resources is associated with the most important and fundamental human rights, including the right to life, food, the right to self-determination, to shelter, and the right to exist as a people.[182]

While in many cases a negotiated outcome is possible, there may be cases where the economic interests of the nation collide with those of an indigenous people implacably opposed to a particular development. Article 36 of the draft Saami Nordic Convention attempts to steer a middle path between ILO Convention No. 169 and the 2007 Declaration by providing an indigenous veto, but only in more limited circumstances:

> Permit for prospecting or extraction of natural resources shall not be granted if the activity would make it impossible or substantially more difficult for the Saami to continue to utilize the areas concerned, and this utilization is essential to the Saami culture, unless so consented by the Saami parliament and the affected Saami…

The Declaration recognizes some key limitations on the indigenous right of self-determination. Drawing directly upon the language of the 1970 Declaration on Friendly Relations, Article 46(1) precludes the invocation of self-determination to disrupt the territorial integrity or political unity of sovereign, independent states:

> 1. Nothing in this Declaration may be interpreted as implying for any State, people, group or person any right to engage in any activity or to perform any act contrary to the Charter of the United Nations or construed as authorizing or encouraging any action which would dismember or impair totally or in part, the territorial integrity or political unity of sovereign and independent States.

[182] Special Rapporteur of the UN Sub-Commission for the Promotion and Protection of Human Rights, quoted in *Endorois Welfare Council v Kenya*, [212].

As noted earlier, the African Commission has applied a similar principle in the context of minority secession claims to self-determination under the African Charter. The preamble of the Declaration also notes that 'nothing in this Declaration may be used to deny any peoples their right of self-determination, exercised in conformity with international law', intimating that the self-determination rights of the population as a whole in an independent state may prevail over narrower claims of indigenous groups.

Article 46(2) of the Declaration also envisages that the need to ensure respect for other human rights and freedoms may justifiably limit the exercise of rights in the Declaration, necessarily including self-determination where it collides with other fundamental rights:

> 2. In the exercise of the rights enunciated in the present Declaration, human rights and fundamental freedoms of all shall be respected. The exercise of the rights set forth in this Declaration shall be subject only to such limitations as are determined by law, and in accordance with international human rights obligations. Any such limitations shall be non-discriminatory and strictly necessary solely for the purpose of securing due recognition and respect for the rights and freedoms of others and for meeting the just and most compelling requirements of a democratic society.

As noted earlier, in dealing with indigenous issues the CERD has tended to invoke its own General Recommendation XXIII of 1997 on indigenous peoples,[183] which does not mention self-determination, and it has not generally referenced either ILO Convention No. 169 or the 2007 Declaration. General Recommendation XXIII is extracted above and recognizes indigenous cultural and identity rights (paragraph 4(a)), economic and social development (paragraph 4(c)), political participation rights (paragraph 4(d)), cultural rights (paragraph 4(e)), and land and resource rights (paragraph 5), including prior free and informed consent and compensation.[184]

As is self-evident, however, General Recommendation XXIII is less detailed in its proscriptions for indigenous peoples than ILO Convention No. 169 and the 2007 Declaration, and unlike the latter, falls short of explicitly linking indigenous rights to self-determination. It remains to be seen whether it will draw upon these other standards to expand its approach to indigenous rights in the future. For its part, the CESCR has generally avoided drawing upon General Recommendation XXIII as a relevant standard for indigenous peoples, instead preferring ILO Convention No. 169 and more recently the 2007 Declaration.

Certain indigenous economic activities may also be an expression of the right to culture under Article 15(1)(a) of the ICESCR. In General Comment No. 21, the CESCR emphasized that indigenous peoples may exercise their cultural

[183] For example, see CERD, Reports: Ecuador, A/58/18 (2003), [59], [62]; Bolivia, [335], [339]; Finland, [405]; Norway, [481]; Brazil, [60]; Nepal, [128]; Nigeria, A/60/18 (2005), [294]; Venezuela (Bolivarian Republic of), A/60/18 (2005), [382].

[184] CERD, General Recommendation No. 23: Indigenous Peoples, A/52/18 (18 August 1997), annex V.

rights collectively and in ways which are inextricably connected with their lands and economic activities:

36. States parties should take measures to guarantee that the exercise of the right to take part in cultural life takes due account of the values of cultural life, which may be strongly communal or which can only be expressed and enjoyed as a community by indigenous peoples. The strong communal dimension of indigenous peoples' cultural life is indispensable to their existence, well-being and full development, and includes the right to the lands, territories and resources which they have traditionally owned, occupied or otherwise used or acquired. Indigenous peoples' cultural values and rights associated with their ancestral lands and their relationship with nature should be regarded with respect and protected, in order to prevent the degradation of their particular way of life, including their means of subsistence, the loss of their natural resources and, ultimately, their cultural identity. States parties must therefore take measures to recognize and protect the rights of indigenous peoples to own, develop, control and use their communal lands, territories and resources, and, where they have been otherwise inhabited or used without their free and informed consent, take steps to return these lands and territories.

37. Indigenous peoples have the right to act collectively to ensure respect for their right to maintain, control, protect and develop their cultural heritage, traditional knowledge and traditional cultural expressions, as well as the manifestations of their sciences, technologies and cultures, including human and genetic resources, seeds, medicines, knowledge of the properties of fauna and flora, oral traditions, literature, designs, sports and traditional games, and visual and performing arts. States parties should respect the principle of free, prior and informed consent of indigenous peoples in all matters covered by their specific rights.[185]

In this context, it may be noted that the HRC addressed similar questions in its General Comment on Article 27 of the ICCPR,[186] as well as in an individual communication involving indigenous cultural rights under Article 27. In *Mahuika et al v New Zealand*, the HRC stated that 'economic activities may come within the ambit of article 27, if they are an essential element of the culture of a community'.[187] It recognized the economic significance of Maori fishing rights as an exercise of cultural rights, including not only as a traditional means of livelihood, but also as a means adapted to a modern way of life and technology.[188] Such rights may not be interfered with unless the indigenous people has had the 'opportunity to participate in the decision-making process' and as long as 'they will continue to benefit from their traditional economy'.[189]

To extrapolate to the self-determination context, it may be that Article 1 is infringed where interference in the economic aspects of cultural rights deprives a people of subsistence, or involves a failure to adequately consult or enable the participation and consent of indigenous peoples in decisions about natural resources.

185 CESCR, General Comment No. 21, E/C.12/GC/21 (21 December 2009), [36].

186 HRC, General Comment No. 23, The Rights of Minorities (Article 27), CCPR/C/21/Rev.1/Add.5 (8 April 1994).

187 *Mahuika et al v New Zealand*, HRC Communication No. 547/1993 (27 October 2000), [9.3].

188 *Mahuika et al v New Zealand*, [9.4]. 189 *Mahuika et al v New Zealand*, [9.5].

Certain regional arrangements have developed more extensive protections for indigenous economic self-determination. To mention one example, the draft Nordic Saami Convention (between Finland, Norway and Sweden) recognizes the Saami customary economic resource of *transboundary* reindeer husbandry in Article 43. Protection of this transboundary economic and cultural practice progressively acknowledges that indigenous livelihoods do not necessarily coincide with national boundaries and that indigenous self-determination is capable of—and may necessitate—being jointly protected across sovereign borders.

Indigenous self-determination by implication

The CESCR has frequently expressed concern for indigenous peoples, but without specifically invoking the right of self-determination. It is sometimes plausible to infer or deduce that the CESCR is implicitly concerned about self-determination because of the nature of the issues it raises in its observations and the manner in which it expresses its concerns.

Thus, the CESCR was concerned about: the rights of the Saami people in Norway to participate in the management and control of natural resources;[190] the failure of Ecuador to consult and obtain the full consent of indigenous peoples before granting natural resource concessions to foreign companies which affected their land, culture, health and the ecosystem;[191] the expulsion of indigenous groups from their lands in Paraguay by cattle ranchers or industrial enterprises, and the government's failure to enable indigenous access to land through agrarian land reform, resulting in hunger and also affecting landless mestizo peasants;[192] and the adverse affects of mining on the health, living environment and way of life of indigenous populations in Venezuela.[193] It was also concerned by the privatization of customary communal land in the Solomon Islands, which 'may undermine the foundations of Solomon Islands society and could lead to the dispossession of the majority of people, thereby depriving them of their basic source of income';[194] and Canada's failure to restore and respect an aboriginal land and resource base adequate to achieve a sustainable aboriginal economy and culture.[195] In some cases, the impacts of interference in indigenous lands may deprive indigenous peoples of their means of subsistence, contrary to Article 1(2) of the ICESCR.

Other regional practice in indigenous / tribal self-determination

There is no express right of self-determination in the instruments of the Inter-American human rights system. However, the right to property in Article 21 of the American

[190] CESCR, Concluding Observations: Norway, E/C.12/1/Add.109 (23 June 2005), [26].
[191] CESCR, Concluding Observations: Ecuador, E/C.12/1/Add.100 (4 June 2004), [12, 35].
[192] CESCR, Concluding Observations: Paraguay, E/C.12/1/Add.1 (28 May 1996), [9].
[193] CESCR, Concluding Observations: Venezuela, E/C.12/1/Add.56 (21 May 2001), [12, 22].
[194] CESCR, Concluding Observations: Solomon Islands, E/C.12/1/Add.33 (14 May 1999), [20].
[195] CESCR, Consideration of States Reports: Canada, E/1999/22 (1998), [418].

Convention,[196] which is articulated in individual terms, has been progressively interpreted by the Inter-American human rights bodies to protect the communal property interests of tribal or indigenous groups. Thus, the Inter-American Court has accepted that indigenous attachment to land creates communal property rights under Article 21 of the Convention, including interests in the natural resources of such lands.[197] Similar proprietary rights were also recognized as vesting in tribal peoples (such as Maroons in Suriname),[198] in addition to indigenous peoples.

In *Saramaka People v Suriname*, the Inter-American Court went further by invoking the international right of self-determination to interpret and expand the scope of the right to property under Article 21 of the American Convention. The case was brought by a tribal people whose use of traditional lands was adversely affected by the state's granting of logging and mining concessions.[199] The Saramaka people are a Maroon tribe whose ancestors were slaves brought by Dutch colonists in the seventeenth century and who escaped to form distinct communities. As noted earlier, while they are not strictly 'indigenous', the Inter-American Court drew an analogy between the legal situation of tribal and indigenous peoples under the American Convention to recognize communal tribal property rights. The Court then drew upon the right of self-determination in common Article 1 of the ICESCR and ICCPR to help delimit the right to property in the American Convention:

93. … Suriname's domestic legislation does not recognize a right to communal property of members of its tribal communities, and it has not ratified ILO Convention 169. Nevertheless, Suriname has ratified both the International Covenant on Civil and Political

[196] American Convention on Human Rights (adopted 22 November 1969, 1144 UNTS 143, entered into force 18 July 1978), Article 21:

'Right to Property:

1. Everyone has the right to the use and enjoyment of his property. The law may subordinate such use and enjoyment to the interest of society.
2. No one shall be deprived of his property except upon payment of just compensation, for reasons of public utility or social interest, and in the cases and according to the forms established by law.
3. Usury and any other form of exploitation of man by man shall be prohibited by law.'

[197] See, eg, *Case of The Mayagna (Sumo) Awas Tingni Community v Nicaragua*, Merits, Reparations and Costs, 31 August 2001, IACHR (Ser. C) No. 79, [148–9], [151] (where the state violated the indigenous people's right to the use enjoy their property, by granting concessions to third parties to utilize their property and resources); *Case of the Indigenous Community Sawhoyamaxa v Paraguay*, Merits, Reparations and Costs, 29 March 2006, IACHR (Ser. C) No. 146, [118]–[121], [131]; *Case of the Indigenous Community Yakye Axa v Paraguay*, Merits, Reparations and Costs, 17 June 2005, IACHR (Ser. C) No. 125, [124], [131], [135]–[137] (where the state had prevented indigenous people from accessing their traditional means of livelihood); *Matter of Pueblo Indígena de Sarayaku Regarding Ecuador*, Provisional Measures, 17 June 2005, IACHR (Ser. E) No. 21, [2]. See also *Maya Indigenous Community of the Toledo District v Belize* (Case 12.053), Report on the Merits No. 40/04, 12 October 2004 (Inter-American Commission on Human Rights).

[198] *Case of the Moiwana Community v Suriname*, Preliminary Objections, Merits, Reparations and Costs, 15 June 2005, IACHR (Ser. C) No. 124, [132]–[133].

[199] *Case of the Saramaka People v Suriname*, Preliminary Objections, Merits, Reparations and Costs, 28 November 2007, IACHR (Ser. C) No. 172, [92]–[196]; see also Lisl Brunner, 'The Rise of Peoples' Rights in the Americas: The Saramaka People Decision of the Inter-American Court of Human Rights' (2008) 7 *Chinese Journal of International Law* 699.

Rights as well as the International Covenant on Economic, Social, and Cultural Rights. The Committee on Economic, Social, and Cultural Rights, which is the body of independent experts that supervises State parties' implementation of the ICESCR, has interpreted common Article 1 of said instruments as being applicable to indigenous peoples. Accordingly, by virtue of the right of indigenous peoples to self-determination recognized under said Article 1, they may 'freely pursue their economic, social and cultural development', and may 'freely dispose of their natural wealth and resources' so as not to be 'deprived of [their] own means of subsistence'. Pursuant to Article 29(b) of the American Convention, this Court may not interpret the provisions of Article 21 of the American Convention in a manner that restricts its enjoyment and exercise to a lesser degree than what is recognized in said covenants. This Court considers that the same rationale applies to tribal peoples due to the similar social, cultural, and economic characteristics they share with indigenous peoples (*supra* paras. 80–86).

94. Similarly, the Human Rights Committee has analyzed the obligations of State Parties to the ICCPR under Article 27 of such instrument, including Suriname, and observed that 'minorities shall not be denied the right, in community with the other members of their group, to enjoy their own culture [which] may consist in a way of life which is closely associated with territory and use of its resources. This may particularly be true of members of indigenous communities constituting a minority'.

95. The above analysis supports an interpretation of Article 21 of the American Convention to the effect of calling for the right of members of indigenous and tribal communities to freely determine and enjoy their own social, cultural and economic development, which includes the right to enjoy their particular spiritual relationship with the territory they have traditionally used and occupied. Thus, in the present case, the right to property protected under Article 21 of the American Convention, interpreted in light of the rights recognized under common Article 1 and Article 27 of the ICCPR, which may not be restricted when interpreting the American Convention, grants to the members of the Saramaka community the right to enjoy property in accordance with their communal tradition.

96. Applying the aforementioned criteria to the present case, the Court thus concludes that the members of the Saramaka people make up a tribal community protected by international human rights law that secures the right to the communal territory they have traditionally used and occupied, derived from their longstanding use and occupation of the land and resources necessary for their physical and cultural survival, and that the State has an obligation to adopt special measures to recognize, respect, protect and guarantee the communal property right of the members of the Saramaka community to said territory.[200]

Suriname acknowledged that the Saramakas enjoyed rights to use and occupy traditional lands, but disputed that such rights encompassed ownership of minerals in the subsoil (which were owned by the state)[201] or extended to resources not traditionally used by the tribe for subsistence (traditional uses being agriculture, hunting, fishing and so on). The Inter-American Court found, however, that tribal

[200] *Case of the Saramaka People v Suriname*, Preliminary Objections, Merits, Reparations and Costs, 28 November 2007, IACHR (Ser. C) No. 172, [93]–[96].

[201] *Case of the Saramaka People v Suriname*, [119], [125].

and indigenous peoples have a right to the natural resources in land for the same reason that they enjoy a right to the land itself: to ensure their physical and cultural survival as a community and to preserve their way of life:

121. In accordance with this Court's jurisprudence as stated in the *Yakye Axa* and *Sawhoyamaxa* cases, members of tribal and indigenous communities have the right to own the natural resources they have traditionally used within their territory for the same reasons that they have a right to own the land they have traditionally used and occupied for centuries. Without them, the very physical and cultural survival of such peoples is at stake. Hence the need to protect the lands and resources they have traditionally used to prevent their extinction as a people. That is, the aim and purpose of the special measures required on behalf of the members of indigenous and tribal communities is to guarantee that they may continue living their traditional way of life, and that their distinct cultural identity, social structure, economic system, customs, beliefs and traditions are respected, guaranteed and protected by States.

122. ...due to the inextricable connection members of indigenous and tribal peoples have with their territory, the protection of their right to property over such territory, in accordance with Article 21 of the Convention, is necessary to guarantee their very survival. Accordingly, the right to use and enjoy their territory would be meaningless in the context of indigenous and tribal communities if said right were not connected to the natural resources that lie on and within the land. That is, the demand for collective land ownership by members of indigenous and tribal peoples derives from the need to ensure the security and permanence of their control and use of the natural resources, which in turn maintains their very way of life. This connectedness between the territory and the natural resources necessary for their physical and cultural survival is precisely what needs to be protected under Article 21 of the Convention in order to guarantee the members of indigenous and tribal communities' right to the use and enjoyment of their property. From this analysis, it follows that the natural resources found on and within indigenous and tribal people's territories that are protected under Article 21 are those natural resources traditionally used and necessary for the very survival, development and continuation of such people's way of life...[202]

The Court acknowledged, however, that tribal and indigenous rights over land and natural resources are not absolute, but are subject to certain limitations:

127. ...the protection of the right to property under Article 21 of the Convention is not absolute...Although the Court recognizes the interconnectedness between the right of members of indigenous and tribal peoples to the use and enjoyment of their lands and their right to those resources necessary for their survival, said property rights, like many other rights recognized in the Convention, are subject to certain limitations and restrictions. In this sense, Article 21 of the Convention states that the 'law may subordinate [the] use and enjoyment [of property] to the interest of society'. Thus, the Court has previously held that, in accordance with Article 21 of the Convention, a State may restrict the use and enjoyment of the right to property where the restrictions are: (a) previously established by law; (b) necessary; (c) proportional; and (d) with the aim of achieving a legitimate objective in a democratic society. In accordance with this Article, and the Court's jurisprudence, the State will be able to restrict, under certain circumstances, the Saramakas' property rights, including their rights to natural resources found on and within the territory.

[202] *Case of the Saramaka People v Suriname*, [121]–[122].

128. Furthermore, in analyzing whether restrictions on the property right of members of indigenous and tribal peoples are permissible, especially regarding the use and enjoyment of their traditionally owned lands and natural resources, another crucial factor to be considered is whether the restriction amounts to a denial of their traditions and customs in a way that endangers the very survival of the group and of its members. That is, under Article 21 of the Convention, the State may restrict the Saramakas' right to use and enjoy their traditionally owned lands and natural resources only when such restriction complies with the aforementioned requirements and, additionally, when it does not deny their survival as a tribal people (*supra* paras. 120–122).[203]

The Inter-American Court also demanded that the state comply with certain procedural safeguards in issuing concessions over natural resources, namely: (a) the participation of the affected community in decisions; (b) a reasonable benefit from exploitation must accrue to the community; and (c) prior social and environmental impact assessments must be completed:

129. In this particular case, the restrictions in question pertain to the issuance of logging and mining concessions for the exploration and extraction of certain natural resources found within Saramaka territory. Thus, in accordance with Article 1(1) of the Convention, in order to guarantee that restrictions to the property rights of the members of the Saramaka people by the issuance of concessions within their territory does not amount to a denial of their survival as a tribal people, the State must abide by the following three safeguards: First, the State must ensure the effective participation of the members of the Saramaka people, in conformity with their customs and traditions, regarding any development, investment, exploration or extraction plan (hereinafter 'development or investment plan') within Saramaka territory. Second, the State must guarantee that the Saramakas will receive a reasonable benefit from any such plan within their territory. Thirdly, the State must ensure that no concession will be issued within Saramaka territory unless and until independent and technically capable entities, with the State's supervision, perform a prior environmental and social impact assessment. These safeguards are intended to preserve, protect and guarantee the special relationship that the members of the Saramaka community have with their territory, which in turn ensures their survival as a tribal people.[204]

The right of participation in development decisions includes duties on the state to consult in good faith and in a culturally appropriate manner, on the basis of sufficient information. Large projects with serious impacts further require the free, prior and informed consent of the community:

133. …in ensuring the effective participation of members of the Saramaka people in development or investment plans within their territory, the State has a duty to actively consult with said community according to their customs and traditions (*supra* para. 129). This duty requires the State to both accept and disseminate information, and entails constant communication between the parties. These consultations must be in good faith, through culturally appropriate procedures and with the objective of reaching an agreement. Furthermore, the Saramakas must be consulted, in accordance with their own traditions, at the early stages of a development or investment plan, not only when the need arises to obtain approval from the community, if such is the case. Early notice provides time for internal discussion within

[203] *Case of the Saramaka People v Suriname*, [127]–[128].

[204] *Case of the Saramaka People v Suriname*, [129].

communities and for proper feedback to the State. The State must also ensure that members of the Saramaka people are aware of possible risks, including environmental and health risks, in order that the proposed development or investment plan is accepted knowingly and voluntarily. Finally, consultation should take account of the Saramaka people's traditional methods of decision-making. Additionally, the Court considers that, regarding large-scale development or investment projects that would have a major impact within Saramaka territory, the State has a duty, not only to consult with the Saramakas, but also to obtain their free, prior, and informed consent, according to their customs and traditions…[205]

Finally, the right to share in the benefits of any projects flowed from the right to be compensated for the deprivation of property under Article 21(2) of the Convention:

138. The second safeguard the State must ensure when considering development or investment plans within Saramaka territory is that of reasonably sharing the benefits of the project with the Saramaka people. The concept of benefit-sharing, which can be found in various international instruments regarding indigenous and tribal peoples' rights, can be said to be inherent to the right of compensation recognized under Article 21(2) of the Convention, which states that [n]o one shall be deprived of his property except upon payment of just compensation, for reasons of public utility or social interest, and in the cases and according to the forms established by law.

139. The Court considers that the right to obtain compensation under Article 21(2) of the Convention extends not only to the total deprivation of property title by way of expropriation by the State, for example, but also to the deprivation of the regular use and enjoyment of such property. In the present context, the right to obtain 'just compensation' pursuant to Article 21(2) of the Convention translates into a right of the members of the Saramaka people to reasonably share in the benefits made as a result of a restriction or deprivation of their right to the use and enjoyment of their traditional lands and of those natural resources necessary for their survival.[206]

On the facts, the Inter-American Court found that the concessions granted by Suriname did not comply with the various safeguards.

Other decisions of the Inter-American Court have addressed the economic aspects of indigenous land rights in relation to other Convention rights, such as the right to life, including where an indigenous people was deprived of subsistence, resulting in deaths.[207]

The African Commission has also recognized and protected indigenous self-determination rights against predatory governments and private interests. The case of *Endorois Welfare Council v Kenya*[208] was brought by the indigenous Endorois people, who were evicted from their traditional lands by the government's granting of mining concessions. Their eviction denied them vital economic resources (namely, medicinal salt licks, fertile soil and unpolluted water in the Lake Bogoria region) which kept their cattle healthy and sustained their

[205] *Case of the Saramaka People v Suriname*, [133].

[206] *Case of the Saramaka People v Suriname*, [139].

[207] *Case of the Indigenous Community Yakye Axa v Paraguay*, Merits, Reparations and Costs, 17 June 2005, IACHR (Ser. C) No. 125.

[208] *Endorois Welfare Council v Kenya*.

livelihoods. In 2010, the African Commission found that Kenya had unlawfully interfered with the Endorois' right, under Article 21 of the African Charter, to freely dispose of their wealth and natural resources in consultation with the state. Their right to freely dispose of resources extended to those which were not traditionally utilized by them, such as rubies.

In reaching its decision, the African Commission drew heavily on the Inter-American Court's decision in *Saramaka People v Suriname*. Specifically, the African Commission endorsed and transposed the Inter-American Court's strict legal test governing when the right to property of tribal peoples (under Article 21 of the American Convention) can be lawfully limited as the relevant test for limiting indigenous/tribal rights to self-determination in land (under Article 21 of the African Charter).[209] The African Commission analogously reasoned:

266. The Saramaka case is analogous to the instant case with respect to ruby mining. The IACtHR analysed whether gold-mining concessions within traditional Saramaka territory have affected natural resources that have been traditionally used and are necessary for the survival of the members of the Saramaka community. According to the evidence submitted before the Court, the Saramaka community, traditionally, did not use gold as part of their cultural identity or economic system. Despite possible individual exceptions, the Saramaka community do not identify themselves with gold nor have demonstrated a particular relationship with this natural resource, other than claiming a general right to 'own everything, from the very top of the trees to the very deepest place that you could go under the ground.' Nevertheless, the Court stated that, because any gold mining activity within Saramaka territory will necessarily affect other natural resources necessary for the survival of the Saramakas, such as waterways, the State has a duty to consult with them, in conformity with their traditions and customs, regarding any proposed mining concession within Saramaka territory, as well as allow the members of the community to reasonably participate in the benefits derived from any such possible concession, and perform or supervise an assessment on the environmental and social impact prior to the commencement of the project. The same analysis would apply regarding concessions in the instant case of the Endorois.

267. In the instant case of the Endorois, the Respondent State has a duty to evaluate whether a restriction of these private property rights is necessary to preserve the survival of the Endorois community. The African Commission is aware that the Endoroids do not have an attachment to ruby. Nevertheless, it is instructive to note that the African Commission decided in *The Ogoni case* that the right to natural resources contained within their traditional lands vested in the indigenous people. This decision made clear that a people inhabiting a specific region within a state can claim the protection of Article 21. Article 14 of the African Charter indicates that the two-pronged test of 'in the interest of public need or in the general interest of the community' and 'in accordance with appropriate laws' should be satisfied.

268. As far as the African Commission is aware, that has not been done by the Respondent State. The African Commission is of the view the Endorois have the right to freely dispose of their wealth and natural resources in consultation with the Respondent State. Article 21(2)

[209] *Endorois Welfare Council v Kenya*, [256] and [262].

also concerns the obligations of a State Party to the African Charter in cases of a violation by spoliation, through provision for restitution and compensation. *The Endorois have never received adequate compensation or restitution of their land. Accordingly, the Respondent State is found to have violated Article 21 of the Charter.*[210]

The *Ogoni* case was mentioned earlier.[211] While the African Commission invoked the right of self-determination in that case, it did not define the Ogoni people as 'indigenous', but appeared to treat them as a distinct group within Nigeria's larger population.

EXTERNAL ASPECT

Economic rights in occupation, armed conflict or dependencies

It may be recalled that the origins of self-determination lay in a concern that foreign domination, including colonial exploitation of economic resources, was a key cause of war and insecurity. The international use of force, armed conflict or occupation may severely affect the economic rights of peoples under Article 1(2).

The CESCR has considered a number of problematic situations. In relation to Israel's occupation of Palestinian territories, mentioned earlier, the CESCR has identified Israel's policy of 'general closures' as interfering in the economic self-determination of Palestinian residents:

17. The Committee regrets that the Government of Israel has maintained 'general closures' continuously since 1993, thereby restricting and controlling the movement of people and goods between Israel and the West Bank and the Gaza Strip, between Jerusalem and the West Bank and between the West Bank and the Gaza Strip. The Committee notes with concern that these restrictions apply only to Palestinians and not to Jewish Israeli citizens. The Committee is of the view that closures have cut off Palestinians from their own land and resources, resulting in widespread violations of their economic, social and cultural rights, including in particular those contained in article 1(2) of the Covenant.

18. The Committee notes with grave concern the severe consequences of closure on the Palestinian population. Closures have prevented access to health care, first and foremost during medical emergencies, which at times have tragically ended in death at checkpoints and elsewhere. Workers from the occupied territories are prevented from reaching their workplaces, depriving them of income and livelihood and the enjoyment of their rights under the Covenant. Poverty and lack of food aggravated by closures particularly affect children, pregnant women and the elderly who are most vulnerable to malnutrition.

…

39. The Committee urges the State party to respect the right to self-determination as recognized in article 1 (2) of the Covenant, which provides that 'in no way may a people

[210] *Endorois Welfare Council v Kenya*, [256] and [262].

[211] *Social and Economic Rights Action Center and the Center for Economic and Social Rights v Nigeria*, African Commission on Human and Peoples' Rights Communication No. 155/96, (2001) AHRLR 60, 27 October 2001.

be deprived of its own means of subsistence'. Closure restricts the movement of people and goods, cutting off access to external markets and to income derived from employment and livelihood. The Committee also calls upon the Government to give full effect to its obligations under the Covenant and, as a matter of the highest priority, to undertake to ensure safe passage at checkpoints for Palestinian medical staff and people seeking treatment, the unhampered flow of essential foodstuffs and supplies, the safe conduct of students and teachers to and from schools, and the reunification of families separated by closures.[212]

The CESCR also criticized (in 2003) Israel's security fence or wall as interfering in Palestinians' economic resources, but without specifically mentioning Article 1(2):

24. The Committee is particularly concerned about information received concerning the construction of a 'security fence' around the occupied territories, which allegedly would infringe upon the surface area of the occupied territories and which would limit or even impede access by Palestinian individuals and communities to land and water resources. The Committee regrets the fact that the delegation did not respond to questions by the Committee concerning the security fence or wall during the dialogue.[213]

In its *Israel Wall Advisory Opinion* of 2004, the ICJ found that the security wall unjustifiably interfered in Palestinian self-determination, although it was more focused on issues of political rather than economic self-determination:

121. Whilst the Court notes the assurance given by Israel that the construction of the wall does not amount to annexation and that the wall is of a temporary nature (see paragraph 116 above), it nevertheless cannot remain indifferent to certain fears expressed to it that the route of the wall will prejudge the future frontier between Israel and Palestine, and the fear that Israel may integrate the settlements and their means of access. The Court considers that the construction of the wall and its associated régime create a 'fait accompli' on the ground that could well become permanent, in which case, and notwithstanding the formal characterization of the wall by Israel, it would be tantamount to *de facto* annexation.

122. The Court recalls moreover that, according to the report of the Secretary-General, the planned route would incorporate in the area between the Green Line and the wall more than 16 per cent of the territory of the West Bank. Around 80 per cent of the settlers living in the Occupied Palestinian Territory, that is 320,000 individuals, would reside in that area, as well as 237,000 Palestinians. Moreover, as a result of the construction of the wall, around 160,000 other Palestinians would reside in almost completely encircled communities (see paragraphs 84, 85 and 119 above). In other terms, the route chosen for the wall gives expression in *loco* to the illegal measures taken by Israel with regard to Jerusalem and the settlements, as deplored by the Security Council (see paragraphs 75 and 120 above). There is also a risk of further alterations to the demographic composition of the Occupied Palestinian Territory resulting from the construction of the wall

[212] CESCR, Concluding Observations: Israel, E/C.12/1/Add.27 (4 December 1998).
[213] CESCR, Concluding Observations: Israel, E/C.12/1/Add.90 (26 June 2003).

inasmuch as it is contributing, as will be further explained in paragraph 133 below, to the departure of Palestinian populations from certain areas. That construction, along with measures taken previously, thus severely impedes the exercise by the Palestinian people of its right to self-determination, and is therefore a breach of Israel's obligation to respect that right.[214]

The ICJ nevertheless found that the wall involved violations of a bundle of socio-economic rights,[215] without linking them specifically to the infringement of self-determination.

In other cases where the CESCR has commented on self-determination of peoples subject to foreign occupation, it has not expressly invoked any economic aspects of Article 1, although the subject matter in question necessarily has economic implications for the persons concerned. One example is Israel's discriminatory exclusion of the Palestinian diaspora from a right to return to and live in Israel as their place of birth:

13. The Committee notes with concern that the Law of Return, which allows any Jew from anywhere in the world to immigrate and thereby virtually automatically enjoy residence and obtain citizenship in Israel, discriminates against Palestinians in the diaspora upon whom the Government of Israel has imposed restrictive requirements which make it almost impossible to return to their land of birth.

…

36. In order to ensure respect of article 1(2) of the Covenant and to ensure equality of treatment and nondiscrimination, the Committee strongly recommends a review of reentry policies for Palestinians who wish to reestablish their domicile in their homeland, with a view to bringing such policies level with the Law of Return as applied to Jews.[216]

Another example is Western Sahara, where the CESCR has supported the realization of self-determination and drawn attention to rights violations (including economic ones) there, including as a result of Morocco's policy of population transfer. In 1994, the CESCR stated:

10. As regards Western Sahara the Committee is concerned that the right to self-determination has not been exercised and expresses its hope that it will be exercised in full compliance with the provisions of article 1 of the Covenant, in accordance with plans approved by the United Nations Security Council. The Committee expresses its preoccupation about the negative consequences of the Western Sahara policy of Morocco for the enjoyment of the economic, social and cultural rights of the relevant population, particularly through population transfer.[217]

214 *Israel Wall Advisory Opinion*, [121–2].

215 *Israel Wall Advisory Opinion*, [134], including: the right to work, to health, to education and to an adequate standard of living under the ICESCR and CRC.

216 CESCR, Concluding Observations: Israel, E/C.12/1/Add.27 (4 December 1998).

217 CESCR, Concluding Observations: Morocco, E/C.12/1994/5 (30 May 1994). The African Commission has also addressed the right of self-determination in Western Sahara under Article 20 of the African Charter: see, eg, African Commission, Resolution on Western Sahara (2000).

In 2000 and 2006, the CESCR further regretted the failure to resolve the self-determination issue and urged a resolution,[218] while also lamenting the situation of displaced persons.[219]

In *Congo v Uganda*, while the ICJ did not deal specifically with economic self-determination, it rejected an argument that looting, pillage and exploitation of natural resources in occupied territory violated the victim state's permanent sovereignty over natural resources:

244. The Court finds that it cannot uphold the contention of the DRC that Uganda violated the principle of the DRC's sovereignty over its natural resources (see paragraph 226 above). The Court recalls that the principle of permanent sovereignty over natural resources is expressed in General Assembly resolution 1803 (XVII) of 14 December 1962 and further elaborated in the Declaration on the Establishment of a New International Economic Order (General Assembly resolution 3201 (S.VI) of 1 May 1974) and the Charter of Economic Rights and Duties of States (General Assembly resolution 3281 (XXIX) of 12 December 1974). While recognizing the importance of this principle, which is a principle of customary international law, the Court notes that there is nothing in these General Assembly resolutions which suggests that they are applicable to the specific situation of looting, pillage and exploitation of certain natural resources by members of the army of a State militarily intervening in another State, which is the subject-matter of the DRC's third submission. The Court does not believe that this principle is applicable to this type of situation.

245. As the Court has already stated (see paragraph 180 above), the acts and omissions of members of Uganda's military forces in the DRC engage Uganda's international responsibility in all circumstances, whether it was an occupying Power in particular regions or not. Thus, whenever members of the UPDF were involved in the looting, plundering and exploitation of natural resources in the territory of the DRC, they acted in violation of the *jus in bello*, which prohibits the commission of such acts by a foreign army in the territory where it is present. The Court notes in this regard that both Article 47 of the Hague Regulations of 1907 and Article 33 of the Fourth Geneva Convention of 1949 prohibit pillage. The Court further observes that both the DRC and Uganda are parties to the African Charter on Human and Peoples' Rights of 27 June 1981, which in paragraph 2 of Article 21, states that '[i]n case of spoliation the dispossessed people shall have the right to the lawful recovery of its property as well as to an adequate compensation'.[220]

The ICJ's reasoning is rather unclear. On one hand, it could be implicitly invoking a *lex specialis* rule, whereby international humanitarian law and regional human rights law are the special law governing the illegal taking of resources in situations of armed conflict, to the exclusion of the principle of permanent sovereignty. The provisions of humanitarian law serve a comparable purpose to the principle of permanent sovereignty, by requiring occupying powers to act in trust for the

[218] CESCR, Concluding Observations: Morocco, E/C.12/1/Add.55 (1 December 2000), [13] and [35].
[219] CESCR, Concluding Observations: Morocco, E/C.12/MAR/CO/3 (4 September 2006), [13] and [35].
[220] *Armed Activities on the Territory of the Congo (Democratic Republic of the Congo v Uganda)*, Judgment, 19 December 2005, (2005) ICJ Reports 168 (*'Armed Activities Case'*).

benefit of the local people in any dealings with their resources—as Article 55 of the Hague Regulations 1907 provides:

The occupying State shall be regarded only as administrator and usufructuary of public buildings, real estate, forests and agricultural estates belonging to the hostile State, and situated in the occupied territory. It must safeguard the capital of these properties, and administer them in accordance with the rules of usufruct.[221]

Alternatively, the ICJ may be suggesting that the looting, plundering and exploitation of natural resources by their nature do not affect *permanent* sovereignty, for instance because the scale of exploitation was insufficient or the harm was temporary since it could be remedied through restitution. Or it may be simply that the exploitation by individual Ugandan soldiers was not shown to be part of a governmental policy. Judge Koroma certainly thought that permanent sovereignty still applied in principle 'during armed conflict and occupation',[222] whereas Judge ad hoc Kateka thought the principle was confined to decolonization and was thus inapplicable to relations between independent African states.[223]

In any case, it does not follow that the right of self-determination in Article 1 would be treated similarly by the ICJ. As noted earlier, reference to permanent sovereignty was omitted from Article 1, which instead protects a people's right to freely dispose of their natural resources. Article 1 may thus be activated at a different threshold from the principle of permanent sovereignty: looting, plunder and exploitation of natural resources in armed conflict plainly disrupt the freedom of a people to freely dispose of their resources (even if it does not affect permanent sovereignty). Nor has the ICJ displaced self-determination pursuant to any *lex specialis* rule where violations of other international laws are involved. As the *Israel Wall Advisory Opinion* establishes, violations of humanitarian law and human rights law can occur alongside a violation of self-determination. Indeed, international humanitarian law and international human rights law apply concurrently in armed conflict.[224] Moreover, self-determination is *jus cogens* and is thus arguably not displaced by the *lex specialis* principle.

The African Commission has precisely found violations of economic self-determination (under the African Charter) in war time in *Congo v Burundi, Rwanda and Uganda*.[225] After first finding that the use of armed force by the respondent states violated the right of self-determination of the Congolese people under Article 20(1) of the African Charter, the Commission found that the illegal exploitation of natural resources by foreign states violated the right of economic

[221] For example, Hague Convention (IV) respecting the Laws and Customs of War on Land and its annex: Regulations concerning the Laws and Customs of War on Land (adopted 19 October 1907, entered into force 26 January 1910), Article 55 (designating the occupying state as administrator and usufructuary of public immovable property in occupied territory).

[222] *Armed Activities Case*, [11] (Declaration of Judge Koroma).

[223] *Armed Activities Case*, [56] (Dissenting Opinion of Judge ad hoc Kateka).

[224] *Israel Wall Advisory Opinion; Legality of the Threat or Use of Nuclear Weapons (Advisory Opinion)*, 8 July 1996, (1996) ICJ Reports 266.

[225] *Democratic Republic of Congo v Burundi, Rwanda and Uganda*, African Commission on Human and Peoples' Rights Communication No. 227/99, (2004) AHRLR 19, 29 May 2003.

self-determination in Article 21 of the African Charter and the right to development in Article 22:

The Complainant State alleges that between October and December 1998, the gold produced by the OKIMO firm and by local diggers yielded $100,000,000 (one hundred million US dollars) to Rwanda. By its calculation, the coffee produced in the region and in North Kivu yielded about $70,000,000 (seventy million US dollars) to Uganda in the same period. Furthermore, Rwanda and Uganda took over control of the fiscal and customs revenue collected respectively by the Directorate General of Taxes. The plunder of the riches of the eastern provinces of Congo is also affecting endangered animal species such as okapis, mountain gorillas, rhinoceros [sic], and elephants.

Indeed, the respondent States, especially, Uganda, has refuted these allegations, pretending for example that its troops never stepped in some of the regions they are accused of human rights violations and looting of the natural resources of the complainant States. However, the African Commission has evidence that some of these facts did take place and are imputable to the armies and agents of the respondent states. In fact, the United Nations have acknowledged that during the period when the armies of the Respondent States were in effective control over parts of the territory of the Complainant State, there were lootings of the natural resources of the Complainant State. The United Nations set up a Panel of Experts to investigate this matter.

The report of the Panel of Experts, submitted to the Security Council of the United Nations in April 2001 (under reference S/2001/357) identified all the Respondent States among others actors, as involved in the conflict in the Democratic Republic of Congo. The report profusely provides evidence of the involvement of the Respondent states in the illegal exploitation of the natural resources of the Complainant State. It is stated in paragraph 5 of the Summary of the report: '*During this first phase* (called Mass-scale looting phase by the experts), *stockpiles of minerals, coffee, wood, livestock and money that were available in territories conquered by the armies of Burundi, Rwanda and Uganda were taken, and either transferred to those countries or exported to international markets by their forces and nationals.*'

Paragraph 25 of the reports further states: '*The illegal exploitation of resources (of the Democratic Republic of Congo) by Burundi, Rwanda and Uganda took different forms, including confiscation, extraction, forced monopoly and price-fixing. Of these, the first two reached proportions that made the war in the Democratic Republic of the Congo a very lucrative business.*'

The Commission therefore finds the illegal exploitation/looting of the natural resources of the complainant state in contravention of Article 21 of the African Charter…

The deprivation of the right of the people of the Democratic Republic of Congo, in this case, to freely dispose of their wealth and natural resources, has also occasioned another violation—their right to their economic, social and cultural development and of the general duty of States to individually or collectively ensure the exercise of the right to development, guaranteed under Article 22 of the African Charter.[226]

The nexus between the right of (economic) self-determination and the right to development was noted earlier.

There may be other cases where economic self-determination is infringed under Article 1(2) concurrently with breaches of other international obligations,

[226] *Democratic Republic of Congo v Burundi, Rwanda and Uganda.*

such as the principle of trusteeship over public resources of occupied territory under the law of occupation. Mention may be made of allegations, for instance, that American companies were preferentially awarded oil contracts during the United States' occupation of Iraq in 2003 to 2004, in ways which did not benefit Iraqis. An occupying power is only permitted to exploit the resources of occupied territory for the benefit of its population, or otherwise in accordance with international humanitarian law.

Dependent territories

As noted earlier, the CESCR has raised self-determination when commenting on states which administer or control non-self-governing territories, namely Britain (concerning Gibraltar and other territories) and Morocco (concerning Western Sahara). Aside from general calls to implement self-determination under Article 1, the CESCR has tended not to specifically address the economic or cultural dimensions of self-determination.

Freedom from foreign interference

Apart from the exceptional situations of colonialism, dependency, occupation or armed conflict, the CESCR has seldom identified situations where the economic self-determination of the people of one state has been jeopardized by external interference by another state. This aspect of economic self-determination—the right to be free from external interference—crosses over with other long-established principles of international law.

The prohibition on the use of force by states in their international affairs, under Article 2(4) of the UN Charter and customary international law,[227] forbids the use of military force to acquire the economic resources or territory of another state. The mere provision of financial support to private military actors (who, for instance, appropriate such resources by force) may not, however, constitute a prohibited use of force by the supporting state, where the latter does not control the former.[228] It is also well accepted that mere economic coercion does not amount to a use of force.[229]

The related principle of non-intervention in the internal affairs of another state may, however, capture such conduct.[230] The 1970 Declaration on Friendly Relations sets out the prohibition:

No State or group of States has the right to intervene, directly or indirectly, for any reason whatever, in the internal or external affairs of any other State. Consequently, armed

[227] *Military and Paramilitary Activities in and against Nicaragua*, Jurisdiction and Admissibility, Judgment, 26 November 1984, (1984) ICJ Reports 392, ('*Nicaragua v United States of America*').

[228] *Nicaragua v United States of America*.

[229] James Crawford, *Brownlie's Principles of Public International Law* (8th edn, Oxford University Press, Oxford, 2012), 747; but some suggest that this is still in dispute between developing and developed states: Christine Gray, *International Law and the Use of Force* (3rd edn, Oxford University Press, Oxford, 2008), 30.

[230] See, eg, *Nicaragua v United States of America*, Jurisdiction and Admissibility, Judgment, 26 November 1984, (1984) ICJ Reports 392.

intervention and all other forms of interference or attempted threats against the personality of the State or against its political, economic and cultural elements, are in violation of international law.

No State may use or encourage the use of economic political or any other type of measures to coerce another State in order to obtain from it the subordination of the exercise of its sovereign rights and to secure from it advantages of any kind. Also, no State shall organize, assist, foment, finance, incite or tolerate subversive, terrorist or armed activities directed towards the violent overthrow of the regime of another State, or interfere in civil strife in another State.

The use of force to deprive peoples of their national identity constitutes a violation of their inalienable rights and of the principle of non-intervention.

Every State has an inalienable right to choose its political, economic, social and cultural systems, without interference in any form by another State…[231]

There is a conceptual question of whether a prohibited intervention is coterminous with a denial of self-determination, or whether they involve thresholds. But the real difficulty lies in practically identifying what constitutes prohibited forms of economic interference, whether under the non-intervention principle or the freedom from external interference that is part of the right of self-determination. All states utilize their economic leverage to pursue foreign policy objectives and merely bringing competitive economic pressure to bear on another state can hardly be seen as a prohibited intervention or a denial of its people's economic self-determination.

Even economic sanctions are generally not treated as prohibited interventions under international law, despite attempts by developing states to change the law in that direction.[232] In the *Nicaragua (Merits)* case, Nicaragua alleged that the United States' economic sanctions (including a comprehensive trade embargo) violated non-intervention, but the ICJ was 'unable to regard such action on the economic plane as a breach of the customary-law principle of non-intervention'.[233] While various UN resolutions have attempted to prohibit economic coercion by unilateral sanctions,[234] with many developing states supporting such efforts,[235] there is strong opposition from certain developed countries which utilize such sanctions

[231] See also UNGA Res. 2131 (XX), Declaration on the Inadmissibility of Intervention in the Domestic Affairs of States and the Protection of their Independence and Sovereignty (21 December 1965).

[232] Alain Pellet and Alina Miron, 'Sanctions', *Max Planck Encyclopedia of Public International Law Online*, [30] (accessed 24 January 2013).

[233] *Nicaragua v United States of America*, Merits, Judgment, 27 June 1986, (1986) ICJ Reports 14, [126].

[234] UNGA Res. 48/168, Economic Measures as a means of Political and Economic Coercion against Developing Countries (21 December 1993). See also UNGA Res. 44/215, Economic Measures as a means of Political and Economic Coercion against Developing Countries (22 December 1989); UNGA Res. 46/210, Economic Measures as a means of Political and Economic Coercion against Developing Countries (20 December 1991).

[235] See, eg, UNGA, Report of the Secretary-General, Unilateral Economic Measures as a means of Political and Economic Coercion against Developing Countries, A/66/138 (14 July 2011).

and thus insufficient consensus on a prohibition.[236] Sanctions may, however, breach Article 1(2) where their imposition separately violates obligations under international economic law, such as the WTO free trade regime.[237]

There may, of course, be clearer cases where a line is crossed. Unilateral economic sanctions (as opposed to multilateral UN measures under Chapter VII of the Charter) imposed by one state on another, to compel that state to change a particular political or economic policy, could amount to a prohibited intervention and a denial of self-determination. So too could certain discriminatory economic policies, such as trade preferences, which arbitrarily limit the economic freedoms and opportunities of those states which are excluded from certain markets.

Further, a state which engages in cyber-crime or espionage against the economic institutions or corporate or industrial sectors of another state, causing economic harm due to the exposure of economically sensitive information, might amount to a prohibited intervention and, if on a sufficient scale, also to an infringement of economic self-determination. A more brazen cyber-attack on financial institutions or stock markets, causing major economic loss to a foreign state, could equally engage the protections.

Mention has already been made of the role of foreign private corporations in extractive industries and the adverse impacts on indigenous rights. The right of economic self-determination implies a freedom not only from unwanted external state interference, but also from external private actors such as transnational corporations or private security companies. Self-determination entails the relative freedom of a state to determine the terms on which foreign companies are entitled to do business, subject to respect for other relevant international obligations (including as provided for in Article 1 itself) and domestic law (as well as prudential considerations such as the willingness of foreign companies to accept the terms imposed by particular states).

OTHER POSSIBLE SITUATIONS—INTERNAL AND EXTERNAL

The Committee's comments on state reports often do not mention any specific article of the ICESCR which is engaged by a particular issue. This can make it difficult to identify concerns about self-determination, other than by implication. In many of these cases it is simply not clear whether the CESCR is interested for reasons of self-determination or other rights grounds (such as minority rights, non-discrimination or political representation).

For instance, as regards possible instances of internal self-determination, the CESCR commended the holding of free and fair elections in Mongolia as 'reflecting the will of the population';[238] urged Nepal to design its new constitution to include

[236] UNGA, Note by the Secretary-General, Economic Measures as a means of Political and Economic Coercion against Developing Countries, A/48/535 (25 October 1993), [Agenda Item 91(a), [1]]; Pellet and Miron, 'Sanctions', [30].

[237] Discussed further below.

[238] CESCR, Concluding Observations: Mongolia, E/C.12/1/Add.47 (1 September 2000), [3].

'all sectors of society, including disadvantaged and marginalized groups, in particular the Dalit [lower castes], the Madhesi [a rural-based ethnic movement] and indigenous communities…in decision-making bodies at all levels';[239] and noted the significant autonomy granted to indigenous people in Sweden through an elected Saami parliament and in education, cultural and economic activities.[240] It also acknowledged Ukraine's progress in the representation of Crimean Tartars in the Crimean Parliament and in reintegrating Tartars into the region;[241] called for Sri Lanka to implement its peace plan to devolve authority to regional governments through constitutional reform, to settle ethnic conflict;[242] and welcomed a peace settlement in Sudan.[243]

In relation to external self-determination, the CESCR endorsed Portugal's political decolonization of Macau and East Timor.[244] In its notification that the ICESCR applied to Macau, Portugal had earlier declared that Article 1 'shall in no way effect the status of Macau as defined in the Constitution of the Portuguese Republic and in the Organic Statute of Macau'.[245] A state may not subjectively self-characterize whether self-determination has been achieved in one of its colonial territories; the people of Macau are entitled to choose the form of their self-determination, and Portugal's purported limitation of it was arguably contrary to the object and purpose of the ICESCR, given the central importance of Article 1.

LIMITS ON THE FREE DISPOSITION OF RESOURCES

The right to freely dispose of natural wealth and resources in Article 1(2) was qualified to ensure that it would not do 'prejudice to any obligations arising out of international economic co-operation, based upon the principle of mutual benefit, and international law'.[246] This was a concession to developed states concerned during the drafting to preserve their favoured international economic order, namely a climate conducive to free and competitive international trade (as opposed to cartelization or economic isolationism or self-sufficiency) and protective of foreign investment and the free flow of capital. The drafting record notes:

> 46. Other members argued that, in order to correct past abuses of rights granted under contractual arrangements, it would be more appropriate to incorporate limitations in such agreements rather than to include statements in a treaty which might invalidate contracts and make international co-operation impossible. It was also argued that to include such a provision in the covenant would mean that international agreements might be arbitrarily

239 CESCR, Concluding Observations: Nepal, E/C.12/NPL/CO/2 (16 January 2008), [30].
240 CESCR, Concluding Observations: Sweden, E/C.12/1995/5 (7 June 1995), [5].
241 CESCR, Concluding Observations: Ukraine, E/C.12/1995/15 (28 December 1995), [4].
242 CESCR, Concluding Observations: Sri Lanka, E/C.12/LKA/CO/2-4 (9 December 2010), [6].
243 CESCR, Concluding Observations: Sudan, E/C.12/1/Add.48 (1 September 2000), [9].
244 CESCR, Concluding Observations: Portugal, E/C.12/1995/4 (7 June 1995), [7] (Macau) and Portugal, E/C.12/1/Add.53 (1 December 2000), [6] (East Timor).
245 See Appendix II of this book.
246 UNGA Third Committee, A/3077 (8 December 1955), 23.

revoked, and that it might discourage foreign investments in the under-developed areas as well as any kind of technical assistance programmes. Another view was that to attempt to define the relations between States owning resources and States or their nationals seeking to develop such resources was not appropriate for inclusion in a covenant on human rights because they concerned rights of States rather than rights of individuals.[247]

The meaning of the qualification is considered below.

'WITHOUT PREJUDICE TO ANY OBLIGATIONS ARISING OUT OF INTERNATIONAL ECONOMIC CO-OPERATION'

Expropriation and nationalization and Article 25 of the ICESCR

At the time of drafting, the key limitation envisaged by this qualifying phrase on the right to freely dispose of natural resources was the international customary law on the expropriation or nationalization of foreign property. Western states long took the view that an international minimum standard applied to protect foreign property in cases of expropriation, namely that the 'Hull' standard of 'prompt, adequate and effective' compensation (meaning fair market value) applied to the taking of property. Such states were keen to ensure that Article 1 did not diminish that extant level of protection. Neither the ICESCR nor ICCPR explicitly provided for the protection of property rights.

In contrast, influenced by the Latin-American 'Calvo doctrine', developing states and the Soviet Union argued in the General Assembly for national law alone to govern expropriation, thus allowing rectification of historical injustices and national necessity to prevail over foreign investors' interests. There was also a concern to remedy colonial injustices by voiding 'unequal treaties' which had granted concessionary resource contracts to Western interests on highly disadvantageous terms for developing states. The creation of many newly independent states as a result of decolonization gradually tilted the balance of majority opinion in the United Nations towards the developing states.

Faced with such division, the 1962 Declaration on Permanent Sovereignty over Natural Resources settled upon compromise language which did not resolve the competing viewpoints:

> 4. Nationalization, expropriation or requisitioning shall be based on grounds or reasons of public utility, security or the national interest which are recognized as overriding purely individual or private interests, both domestic and foreign. In such cases the owner shall be paid appropriate compensation, in accordance with the rules in force in the State taking such measures in the exercise of its sovereignty and in accordance with international law…[248]

The Declaration iterates the 'public purpose' test for expropriation which subsequently found acceptance in international law. But its iteration of a standard

[247] Commission on Human Rights, E/2256 (14 April–14 June 1952), 6.
[248] UNGA Res. 1803 (XVII), Permanent Sovereignty over Natural Resources.

of 'appropriate' compensation confirmed neither the Hull approach favoured by developed states nor the Calvo doctrine preferred by the developing states.[249] The uncertainty was clarified a little by the Declaration's acceptance that foreign investment agreements *freely* entered into by states should be observed in good faith:

8. Foreign investment agreements freely entered into by or between sovereign States shall be observed in good faith; States and international organizations shall strictly and conscientiously respect the sovereignty of peoples and nations over their natural wealth and resources in accordance with the Charter and the principles set forth in the present resolution.

As noted earlier, the text of Article 1 of the twin covenants was settled by 1955. By contrast, Article 25 of the ICESCR (and its equivalent, Article 47 of the ICCPR, which was modelled on it[250]) was adopted in October 1966, near the end of the drafting of the covenants. In the meantime, new developing states had joined as UN members and were participating in the later drafting phases.[251] Article 25 as adopted provides that: 'Nothing in the present Covenant shall be interpreted as impairing the inherent right of all peoples to enjoy and utilize fully and freely their natural wealth and resources'.

The proposal for Article 25, submitted by a large number of developing states,[252] caused strong disagreement during the drafting. Those in favour argued that permanent sovereignty over natural resources is 'a sacred right'[253] or right 'of a special character',[254] which is 'absolute' and not subject to the restrictions in Article 1 of the ICESCR (namely, those concerning international cooperation).[255] It was said that 'a country could not be master of its fate unless it was completely free to utilize and enjoy its natural resources'.[256] While developing states were not opposed to international cooperation, it was felt that 'certain obligations were no longer valid',[257] namely the 'odious rights of capitalism'[258] (including treaties made under duress[259]) which had allowed the 'neo-colonialists'[260] and

[249] Rudolf Dolzer and Christoph Schreuer, *Principles of International Investment Law* (Oxford University Press, Oxford, 2008), 14. On the controversy, see Schrijver, *Sovereignty over Natural Resources*, 352–9.

[250] Nowak, *CCPR Commentary*, 800.

[251] UNGA Third Committee, A/C.3/AR.1405 (27 October 1966), 157 (Ceylon), 159 (Algeria).

[252] UNGA Third Committee, A/6546 (13 December 1966), 17–18 (Chile, Ghana, Guinea, India, Iran, Iraq, Nepal, Nigeria, Pakistan, Sudan, UAR, Tanzania, Venezuela, Yugoslavia, and joined by Afghanistan, Algeria, Congo, Jordan, Libya, Mauritania, Mongolia, Panama, Ethiopia, Kuwait, Liberia, Mali, Rwanda, Saudi Arabia, Syria, Zambia).

[253] UNGA Third Committee, A/C.3/AR.1405 (27 October 1966), 159 (Iran).

[254] UNGA Third Committee, A/C.3/AR.1404 (26 October 1966), 155 (India).

[255] UNGA Third Committee, A/C.3/AR.1404 (26 October 1966), 155 (Iraq); UNGA Third Committee, A/C.3/AR.1405 (27 October 1966), 157 (Ceylon); UNGA Third Committee, A/6546 (13 December 1966), 18.

[256] UNGA Third Committee, A/C.3/AR.1405 (27 October 1966), 159 (Tunisia).

[257] UNGA Third Committee, A/C.3/AR.1405 (27 October 1966), 159 (Tunisia).

[258] UNGA Third Committee, A/C.3/AR.1405 (27 October 1966), 157 (Cuba).

[259] UNGA Third Committee, A/6546 (13 December 1966), 18.

[260] UNGA Third Committee, A/C.3/AR.1405 (27 October 1966), 159 (Iran).

'imperialist' powers[261] to exploit the resources of developing states. Syria warned of the danger that the duty of international cooperation under Article 1(2) could otherwise be interpreted so that 'the ultimate victory would lie with the strongest, with the result that the rich countries would become increasingly richer at the expense of the developing countries' and could 'perpetuate their dominion'.[262]

Those against argued that self-determination should not be absolute or prevail over all other rights;[263] and that such approach is not in the interests of developing states themselves, who benefit from international cooperation (including through development assistance and solidarity).[264] It was further argued that Article 25 would give rise to difficulties of interpretation or confusion in relation to Article 1(2). Some considered it to be out of place in a part of the ICESCR on measures of implementation,[265] which was thought to be an inappropriate means of altering or derogating from an earlier substantive right.[266] Some states also thought that the ICESCR should not prejudge the contemporaneous consideration of permanent sovereignty over natural resources by other UN bodies examining the issue.[267]

Article 25 was nonetheless adopted by an overwhelming majority, with only the United States, the United Kingdom, Norway and New Zealand voting against it.[268] Many states felt that the substantive importance of Article 25 outweighed any procedural irregularities,[269] and it was too late to reopen the text of Article 1, settled over a decade previously. Article 25 operates as a 'specific interpretational rule' amending Article 1.[270]

To the extent that permanent sovereignty over natural resources (in Article 25) is coextensive with economic self-determination in Article 1,[271] the former 'trumps' obligations of international cooperation under the latter to the extent of any inconsistency. Technically, Article 25 leads to a conflict of obligations between the ICESCR and treaties imposing economic obligations inconsistent with it. Article 25 may then be invoked (as between parties to the same treaties)

261 UNGA Third Committee, A/C.3/AR.1405 (27 October 1966), 157 (Ethiopia).

262 UNGA Third Committee, A/C.3/AR.1405 (27 October 1966), 157 (Syria); see also UNGA Third Committee, A/6546 (13 December 1966), 18.

263 UNGA Third Committee, A/6546 (13 December 1966), 18; UNGA Third Committee, A/C.3/AR.1404 (26 October 1966), 155 (France).

264 UNGA Third Committee, A/C.3/AR.1405 (27 October 1966), 160 (France).

265 UNGA Third Committee, A/C.3/AR.1405 (27 October 1966), 158 (UK), 159 (Netherlands), 160 (Finland); A/C.3/AR.1406 (27 October 1966), 163 (Madagascar, Japan, Norway, New Zealand), 165 (US).

266 UNGA Third Committee, A/C.3/AR.1405 (27 October 1966), 158 (UK).

267 UNGA Third Committee, A/C.3/AR.1405 (27 October 1966), 158 (UK).

268 By seventy-four votes to four, with twenty abstentions: UNGA Third Committee, A/6546 (13 December 1966), 18.

269 UNGA Third Committee, A/C.3/AR.1406 (27 October 1966), 166 (Cyprus).

270 Nowak, *CCPR Commentary*, 801 (concerning the identical Article 47 of the ICCPR).

271 This was the dominant assumption during the drafting, although the Philippines suggested that self-determination was subordinate to the more fundamental right of resource sovereignty: '[t]he right in question was an essential element of State sovereignty and should be established as a basic and primary right from which article 1, paragraph 2, of the Covenant derived its existence and validity' (UNGA Third Committee, A/C.3/AR.1405 (27 October 1966), 157 (Philippines)).

as: a 'later in time' provision (for treaty obligations assumed prior to those under the ICESCR); as the more 'special' law (*lex specialis*, taking precedence over general obligations of economic cooperation under other treaties, including those later in time); or as a superior norm in all cases (*jus cogens*, since sovereignty over resources, as an expression of unqualified self-determination, is a peremptory norm).

The legal consequence of Article 25 may be relatively less uncontroversial where the international obligation in question stemmed from an 'unequal treaty' coercively imposed in a pre-independence colonial context and which is sought to be invoked post-independence. Such obligations may in any event be abrogated under the law of state succession, such that there may be no residual necessity to apply Article 25.

More difficult is where a now independent developing state freely enters into international economic obligations and later seeks to rely on Article 25 to evade them. The strict text of Article 25 may appear to permit this result. However, freely entering into a treaty is itself an exercise of sovereignty over natural resources (namely, the freedom to deal with such resources as the state wishes), such that there is no inconsistency between Articles 25 and 1(2) in such cases. Also, the drafting record suggests that Article 25 was principally directed at the unequal treaty scenario, rather than contemporary, lesser inequalities of treaty bargaining power between independent developing and developed states.

A different problem arises where a non-representative government enters into a treaty obligation which compromizes the sovereignty of its 'people' over their natural resources, for instance by enriching the state's political leadership, but failing to secure a fair price for the resources or a fair distribution of their bounty. As noted earlier, self-determination and resource sovereignty are the rights of a 'people', not the legal person of the state; Article 25 may have a role in negativing international obligations which conflict with the rights of the 'people' under Article 25 (and 1).

In practice, the adoption of Article 25 of the ICESCR in 1966 did not resolve the underlying disagreement between states. Debate over expropriation intensified in the 1970s as developing states pushed for a 'new international economic order'. Thus, the 1974 Charter adopts some of the same language on expropriation as the 1962 Declaration, but leaves disputes potentially subject only to national law. The 1974 Declaration on the Establishment of a New International Economic Order does not mention compensation at all for expropriation, but mentions only compensation for victims of foreign exploitation:

> 4(f). The right of all States, territories and peoples under foreign occupation, alien and colonial domination or apartheid to restitution and full compensation for the exploitation arid depletion of, and damages to, the natural resources and all other resources of those States, territories and peoples…[272]

[272] Declaration on the Establishment of a New International Economic Order, [4(f)].

The heated debates about the standard of compensation under customary international law between 1960 and 1990 have largely dissipated in practice because of the rise of a treaty-based consensus that fair market value (akin to the Hull 'adequate' approach) is the standard.[273] The change resulted from a combination of factors, including the collapse of the Soviet Union by 1990, a financial crisis in Latin America in the 1990s, and increasing global consensus on the importance of foreign investment.[274] The Latin-American states abandoned the Calvo doctrine and came to accept bilateral investment treaties which protected foreign property; developing countries increasingly pursued foreign investment treaties; and the General Assembly discontinued its call for permanent sovereignty over natural resources.[275]

The contemporary patchwork of bilateral and multilateral investment treaties significantly resolves uncertainties about the scope of Articles 1(2) and 25. Plainly, a state cannot invoke Article 25 to avoid an investor protection obligation freely entered into by treaty; in practice, Article 25 has not been so invoked by states. Such obligations are now extensive and go well beyond protection in case of expropriation to include matters such as fair and equitable treatment, full protection and security, non-discriminatory and non-arbitrary treatment, national treatment, and most-favoured-nation treatment.[276]

In addition, there may be gaps in the patchwork coverage of investment treaties in some cases. Recourse to international customary law may then remain necessary to resolve whether a state has acted lawfully in expropriating foreign property and in permissibly exercising economic self-determination under Article 1(2). It may be that a proliferation of widespread and consistent investment treaty law has resolved the debate about customary law by generating a modern customary iteration of the Hull rule. But that brings the matter full circle to the problematic savings clause, which may then be invoked to override whatever is the (non-peremptory) customary law obligation.

Regulatory measures

Connected with expropriation is the complicated issue of when an interference with foreign property amounts to permissible regulatory measures in the public interest (such as for taxation, economic policy, environmental protection and so on) as opposed to an indirect, compensable expropriation of property.[277] If the latter, state action may be within the right to freely dispose of natural resources under Article 1, subject to international economic obligations (treaty or customary) governing compensation. If the former, since there is no taking of property there is no question of the disposition of resources under Article 1(2), but equally no international obligation to compensate. Rather, the matter subject to regulation

[273] Dolzer and Schreuer, *Principles of International Investment Law*, 91.

[274] Dolzer and Schreuer, *Principles of International Investment Law*, 15.

[275] Dolzer and Schreuer, *Principles of International Investment Law*, 15–16.

[276] Christoph Schreuer, 'Investments: International Protection', *Max Planck Encyclopedia of Public International Law Online*, [48] (accessed 24 January 2013).

[277] Dolzer and Schreuer, *Principles of International Investment Law*, 109–12.

falls within the reserved domain of domestic jurisdiction of a sovereign state and the general right of a people under Article 1(1) to freely pursue their political status and economic development.

The characterization of a measure as a permissible regulatory one is nonetheless governed by international standards. Reasonable measures in the public interest, adopted in a a fair and non-discriminatory manner and not as disguised expropriation, will not be regarded as compensable takings of property. As stated by an arbitral tribunal in *Methanex v USA*:

> …as a matter of general international law, a non-discriminatory regulation for a public purpose, which is enacted in accordance with due process and, which affects, inter alios, a foreign investor or investment is not deemed expropriatory and compensable unless specific commitments had been given by the regulating government to the then putative foreign investor contemplating investment that the government would refrain from such regulation.[278]

States are limited by other relevant international economic obligations under Article 1(2).

Cartels

Aside from controversies over expropriation, the 1974 Charter of Economic Rights and Duties of States—coming after the OPEC oil crisis of 1973—was also controversial for its promotion in Article 5 of commodity cartels, a move strongly opposed by Western states:

> All States have the right to associate in organizations of primary commodity producers in order to develop their national economies, to achieve stable financing for their development and, in pursuance of their aims, to assist in the promotion of sustained growth of the world economy. In particular accelerating the development of developing countries. Correspondingly, all States have the duty to respect that right by refraining from applying economic and political measures that would limit it.

There is no general prohibition of cartels under international law, particularly given that the development of any 'international competition law' is still in its infancy. However, it may be noted that many commodities (including mining, energy and agriculture) have now been brought within the multilateral trading system and are therefore now subject to WTO rules.[279] The economic freedom of states to organize production through cartels is thus increasingly curtailed and subject to the limit under Article 1(2) to respect international economic obligations.

International trade law

Modern international trade law, constituted by the multilateral agreements of the World Trade Organization, and other bilateral, regional or multilateral free trade

[278] *Methanex Corp v United States*, Final Award of the Tribunal on Jurisdiction and Merits, 3 August 2005, 44 ILM (2005) 1345, [Part IV, Chapter D, 4, [7]].

[279] Melaku Geboye Desta, 'Commodities, International Regulation of Production and Trade', *Max Planck Encyclopedia of Public International Law Online*, [34] (accessed 24 January 2013).

agreements, is a relevant source of international economic obligation limiting economic freedom under Article 1(2). Such agreements require states that wish to trade in their natural resources to do so in accordance with agreed rules and procedures, thus limiting the freedom to trade however the state sees fit under Article 1(2) (for instance, by applying protectionist measures such as subsidies or tariffs (which favour one's own nationals) or discriminatory preferential treatment in market access (which favour some states over others)).

While such agreements thus limit economic freedom in one sense, three observations are pertinent. First, entry into such treaty arrangements is itself an exercise of economic sovereignty and self-determination, signified by voluntary acceptance of treaty commitments.

Secondly, the very purpose of free trade agreements is to expand states' economic freedoms, by enlarging access to foreign markets for their exports, including natural resources. This was indeed a view shared by developing states advocating a new international economic order, such that economic self-determination and free trade aligned rather than collided. The UN Conference on Trade and Development thus declared in 1964 that 'every country has the sovereign right freely to trade with other countries, and freely to dispose of its natural resources in the interest of the economic development and well-being of its own people'.[280] A caveat is that current international trade law may still prevent free trade in certain sectors or commodities, as in the area of agriculture, where protectionism persists.

Thirdly, trade law itself has built into it certain concessions to national autonomy, thus protecting political and economic freedoms of states in a range of areas, including security, public health, environmental protection, culture[281] and so on. In addition, less developed countries are entitled to special privileges according to their needs,[282] to help create a more level playing field in a world of economically unequal states. There is thus typically little need to invoke Article 1 to trump trade law where it is designed (at a meta-level) to enable states' economic freedoms.

Particular areas of trade law raise difficulties for the right of self-determination. For instance, international treaties on intellectual property (the Trade-Related Aspects of Intellectual Property Rights ('TRIPs') Agreements) may come into conflict with the intellectual property rights of indigenous peoples in their own traditional resources. Thus, both the state's population as a whole and indigenous groups within the state may be restricted under international agreements in how they may deal with international property resources.

280 UN Conference on Trade and Development, Final Act and Report, E/CONF.46/141, Vol. I (15 June 1964), General Principle Three, [54].

281 UNESCO Convention on the Protection and Promotion of the Diversity of Cultural Expressions (adopted 20 October 2005, 2440 UNTS 311, entered into force 18 March 2007).

282 See WTO (Committee on Trade and Development), 'Special and Differential Treatment for Least-Developed Countries', Note by the Secretariat, WT/COMTD/W/135 (5 October 2004).

International financial obligations

All states enter into financial obligations of various kinds with foreign lenders (state, international and private), and some transactions are governed by international law rather than purely private or commercial law. Developing countries in particular may enter into arrangements for monetary cooperation or economic development with international financial institutions such as the World Bank group, International Monetary Fund and regional development banks. Many states also incur debts by borrowing from other states, while foreign aid and development assistance also involve a myriad of binding financial commitments. Finance for development may cover a spectrum of activities, such as loans, concessional credits, grants, guarantees, derivatives, equity participations, technical assistance and advisory services, and in areas from infrastructure to social development, governance, security and legal reform.[283]

In one sense, international financial obligations are incurred voluntarily by a state, whether by choosing to borrow from a particular source or through consensual membership of international financial institutions. There is therefore no formal derogation of economic autonomy under Article 1, but rather a free exercise of it. That does not, however, account for the unequal bargaining power of poor developing states vis-à-vis richer states or global financial institutions such as the Bretton Woods institutions, which are largely able to dictate the terms of transactions. Criticisms of the conditionality and structural adjustment requirements imposed on certain developing countries in the past are well known, and weak states may be faced with little real choice in shaping their economic destiny in some circumstances. At the same time, economic self-determination cannot confer on states a licence to borrow in bad faith, or to otherwise pursue economic programmes which rely on the benefits of external capital but reject its burdens. Economic self-determination is not a right to freely spend other people's money.

'IN NO CASE MAY A PEOPLE BE DEPRIVED OF ITS OWN MEANS OF SUBSISTENCE'

A particularly extreme denial of economic self-determination might arise if a people were deprived of its own means of subsistence and Article 1(2) safeguards against this risk. The protection applies equally to populations denied subsistence by foreign actors (state or private) as well as domestic actors (such as a people's own state—as in the Soviet forced famine in the Ukraine in the 1930s—or private actors tolerated by it).

An example given in the drafting was Britain's exploitation and depletion of Nauru's phosphate resources.[284] A comparable example is the destruction of Ocean Island (now part of Kiribati) by British phosphate mining, destroying

[283] Maurizio Ragazzi, 'Financial Institutions, International', *Max Planck Encyclopedia of Public International Law Online*, [7] (accessed 24 January 2013).

[284] Nowak, *CCPR Commentary*, 25.

the land and its habitability and compelling the relocation of the entire Banaban people to Rabi Island in Fiji in 1945.[285] Another example of mass relocation of a people was Britain's removal of the Chagos Islanders from their Indian Ocean territory.[286] The dispossession of indigenous peoples from their lands and livelihoods would also now qualify. The threshold is, however, a high one and would not preclude the ordinary issue of proprietary rights to private actors to develop resources.

This aspect of Article 1(2) is closely related to certain other human rights, such as survival rights to life, food, water, employment and social assistance, and the prohibition on inhuman or degrading treatment. The CESCR linked this aspect of Article 1(2) to the right to water in General Comment No. 15 on Articles 11 and 12 of the ICESCR:

7. The Committee notes the importance of ensuring sustainable access to water resources for agriculture to realize the right to adequate food (see general comment no.12 (1999) on the right to adequate food (article 11 of the Covenant), in particular paragraphs 12 and 13). Attention should be given to ensuring that disadvantaged and marginalized farmers, including women farmers, have equitable access to water and water management systems, including sustainable rain harvesting and irrigation technology. Taking note of the duty in article 1, paragraph 2, of the Covenant, which provides that a people may not 'be deprived of its own means of subsistence', States parties should ensure that there is adequate access to water for subsistence farming and for securing the livelihoods of indigenous peoples.[287]

Other branches of international law may also be engaged, such as prohibitions in international humanitarian law on using starvation as a method of war or the destruction of objects indispensible to civilian survival.[288] International criminal law obligations are also connected, such as prohibitions on genocide (by inflicting such conditions on a group as to destroy it) or crimes against humanity (such as extermination).

The imposition of economic sanctions on a state may raise special risks of depriving a people of its means of subsistence. In its General Comment No. 8, the CESCR highlighted the potentially negative impacts of economic sanctions on respect for economic, social and cultural rights:

3. While the impact of sanctions varies from one case to another, the Committee is aware that they almost always have a dramatic impact on the rights recognized in the Covenant. Thus, for example, they often cause significant disruption in the distribution of food, pharmaceuticals and sanitation supplies, jeopardize the quality of food and the availability of

285 Gil Tabucanon, 'The Banaban Resettlement: Implications for Pacific Environmental Migration' (2012) 35 *Pacific Studies* 1; see also earlier litigation in Britain in *Tito v Waddell* [1977] 2 WLR 496 (Chancery Division).

286 Currently subject to litigation: *Chagos Islanders v United Kingdom* (App. 35622/04), 11 December 2012, [2012] ECHR 2094.

287 CESCR, General Comment No. 15, The right to water (Articles 11 and 12 of the Covenant), E/C.12/2002/11 (20 January 2003), [7].

288 Geneva Convention Relative to the Protection of Civilian Persons in Time of War (adopted 12 August 1949, 75 UNTS 287, entered into force 21 October 1950).

clean drinking water, severely interfere with the functioning of basic health and education systems, and undermine the right to work. In addition, their unintended consequences can include reinforcement of the power of oppressive élites, the emergence, almost invariably, of a black market and the generation of huge windfall profits for the privileged élites which manage it, enhancement of the control of the governing élites over the population at large, and restriction of opportunities to seek asylum or to manifest political opposition. While the phenomena mentioned in the preceding sentence are essentially political in nature, they also have a major additional impact on the enjoyment of economic, social and cultural rights.[289]

The CESCR did not suggest that the impact of sanctions might also constitute a violation of self-determination. Nonetheless, it is plain that in a given case, universally imposed sanctions regimes, which are insufficiently tailored or targeted and which lack adequate humanitarian exemptions, could have the cumulative effect of depriving a population, or substantial sections of it, of their means of subsistence. The CESCR notes that a Security Council decision to impose sanctions in the interests of international security does not render ICESCR rights inoperative:

7. The Committee considers that the provisions of the Covenant, virtually all of which are also reflected in a range of other human rights treaties as well as the Universal Declaration of Human Rights, cannot be considered to be inoperative, or in any way inapplicable, solely because a decision has been taken that considerations of international peace and security warrant the imposition of sanctions. Just as the international community insists that any targeted State must respect the civil and political rights of its citizens, so too must that State and the international community itself do everything possible to protect at least the core content of the economic, social and cultural rights of the affected peoples of that State (see also General Comment 3 (1990), paragraph 10).[290]

The CESCR also emphasizes that both sanctioned and sanctioning states retain responsibility for implementing their ICESCR obligations, the former in fully utilizing their remaining available resources, negotiating internationally and protecting the vulnerable, and the latter in designing and monitoring sanctions, and alleviating disproportionate suffering.[291]

Certainly the Security Council could not override core ICESCR rights by mere implication. The express abrogation of such rights would raise the question whether Article 103 of the UN Charter would require states to implement the sanctions and override their inconsistent ICESCR obligations. The CESCR has not gone so far as to qualify minimum core rights as *jus cogens*; even if they were, the Charter obligation to maintain peace and security is a norm of equivalent status and is thus still capable of prevailing in this specific context. In practice it is extremely difficult to envisage the Council ordering states to violate minimum core ICESCR rights. If it did, it would almost certainly be faced with significant

[289] CESCR, General Comment No. 8, The Relationship between Economic Sanctions and Respect for Economic, Social and Cultural Rights, E/C.12/1997/8 (12 December 1997), [3].
[290] CESCR, General Comment No. 8, [7].
[291] CESCR, General Comment No. 8, [10–14].

non-compliance by many states. Acute legal questions would also arise whether the Council was acting outside its own legal authority by not respecting fundamental human rights.

It was noted earlier that certain measures taken by an occupying power in occupied territory, namely Israel's 'general closures' policy in the West Bank, was faulted by the CESCR for depriving a people of their means of subsistence, contrary to Article 1(2).[292] The use of the distinct strategy of 'blockade' in armed conflict also carries heightened risks of depriving a people of subsistence. The Report to the Human Rights Council of the international fact-finding mission into Israel's interception of a flotilla near Gaza in 2010 described the impact of Israel's blockade of the Gaza Strip:

> 40. According to information provided to the Mission by the United Nations Office for the Coordination of Humanitarian Affairs (OCHA) in the occupied Palestinian territory, the blockade exacerbated the already existing difficulties of the population in Gaza in terms of livelihoods and brought to new peaks the severe human dignity crisis resulting from the deteriorated public services, widespread poverty, food insecurity, over 40 per cent unemployment and 80 per cent aid dependence (i.e. some 80 per cent of the population receives humanitarian assistance, mainly food). People's lives were reduced to a daily struggle in an attempt to secure the most basic needs.
>
> 41. 'Abject poverty' among refugees has tripled since the imposition of the blockade from 100,000 to 300,000 and 61 per cent of households are food insecure. There has been a shift in diet (from protein rich to low cost and high carbohydrate foods), triggering concerns over mineral and vitamin deficiencies. Moreover, Gaza has been affected by a protracted energy crisis, with the power plant operating at 30 per cent of its capacity, scheduled cuts of 8–12 hours per day, leaving households with partial food refrigeration. Services and utilities are forced to rely on generators and UPS units vulnerable due to inconsistent supply of spare parts.
>
> 42. Water and sanitation services have deteriorated and resulted in over 40 per cent of water loss due to leakages. On a daily basis, eighty million litres of untreated and partially treated sewage is discharged into the environment. Polluted sea water has led to increased health risks and as a result of sewage infiltrating into the aquifer only between five and ten per cent of the extracted water is safe. Challenges to the health system include the impossibility of ensuring that medical equipment is available and properly maintained, while referral abroad is subject to long and arduous permit processing and medical staff are prevented from upgrading knowledge and skills.[293]

The Human Rights Council Report found that the blockade inflicted disproportionate damage on Gazan civilians and was illegal under international humanitarian law, also for imposing collective punishment.[294] In contrast, the subsequent 2011 Report of the Secretary-General's Panel of Inquiry on the 31 May 2010 Flotilla

[292] CESCR, Concluding Observations: Israel, E/C.12/1/Add.27 (4 December 1998), [39].

[293] Human Rights Council, Report of the international fact-finding mission to investigate violations of International law, including international humanitarian and human rights law, resulting from the Israeli attacks on the flotilla of ships carrying humanitarian assistance, A/HRC/15/21 (27 September 2010), [40]–[42].

[294] Human Rights Council, Report of the international fact-finding mission, [53–4].

Incident ('Palmer Inquiry') found the blockade to be lawful,[295] on the basis that it pursued a legitimate military purpose and it did not disproportionately harm civilians. The Palmer Inquiry found that Israel's land border closures, rather than its naval blockade, impacted most heavily on civilians, whereas the Human Rights Council Report treated the land and sea restrictions as part of a single disproportionate closure regime.[296] The Palmer Inquiry nonetheless found that the land restrictions had acutely negative humanitarian effects in Gaza:

> 151. The Panel underlines the reaffirmation by the Quartet on 21 June 2010, shortly after the flotilla incident, that the situation in Gaza, including the humanitarian and human rights situation of the civilian population, was unsustainable, unacceptable and not in the interests of any of those concerned. That appears also to be a widespread view in the international community. It is clear that the restrictions Israel has placed on goods and persons entering and leaving Gaza via the land crossings continue to be a significant cause of that situation.
>
> …
>
> 153. Gaza occupies an area of 360 square kilometres and contains a population of 1.43 million, of whom one million are refugees—that is to say 70 percent of the population. It has a high population density, 3,881 persons per square kilometre. A high percentage of the population is young—54 percent are under the age of 18. The unemployment rate is very high, 39 percent. This is one of the highest unemployment rates in the world. Similarly, the poverty rate is high and the area is heavily dependent upon foreign aid. Furthermore, socio-economic conditions in Gaza have deteriorated badly in the aftermath of the Hamas take-over and the Israeli-imposed restrictions on goods entering Gaza via the land crossings. Since these restrictions began in 2007, most private businesses have closed. The functioning of hospitals has been severely affected. The provision of electricity has been reduced and is intermittent. There has been a deterioration of water supply and sanitation services. The demand for housing and social services is climbing. Israel's report admits Israel's land crossings policies have an adverse impact on the daily life of the civilian population, and that they were designed to weaken the economy in order to undermine Hamas's ability to attack Israel.[297]

While neither report mentions self-determination, it may be recalled that the CESCR criticized the general closures policy in respect of Article 1(2) of the ICESCR. The wider principle is that an indiscriminate blockade—by land, sea or air—is potentially capable of depriving a people—of a state, or occupied territory—of their means of subsistence, thus infringing Article 1(2).

Where such measures do not rise to the level of such deprivation, they may nonetheless still infringe Article 1 by reason of interfering unlawfully in the economic freedoms of the people in question. In such circumstances, international humanitarian law governing blockades (and/or occupation) will supply the *lex specialis* to determine whether such measures constitute a lawful limitation on

[295] Report of the Secretary-General's Panel of Inquiry on the 31 May 2010 Flotilla Incident, September 2011, [81].

[296] HRC, Report of the International Fact-finding Mission, [59].

[297] Palmer Inquiry, [151], [153].

self-determination in the special situation of armed conflict. Such law already carefully protects the humanitarian needs of civilians so that any deviation it justifies from the right of self-determination at large (by restricting national or peoples' economic freedoms in war) will not, in any event, deprive them of their means of subsistence.

While Article 1(2) recognizes that economic self-determination may be subject to international economic obligations, it should be noted that such obligations could not justify depriving a people of their means of subsistence, where those two aspects of Article 1(2) are in conflict. The latter element of Article 1(2) is framed in the strongest, unqualified, non-derogable terms—'in no case may a people be deprived of its own means of subsistence'—and follows the earlier qualification on international economic obligations.

As such, where international economic obligations require a state to repay a high and unserviceable foreign debt, or surrender natural resources at a very low price, or displace indigenous people to provide land to foreign businesses, and its people (or parts of it) were consequently deprived of subsistence, a breach of Article 1(2) may still arise. Mention may be made of structural adjustment programmes introduced in certain developing countries by their governments in conjunction with international financial institutions in the past, which aggravated famine and the impoverishment of large sections of some populations.

LIMITS NECESSITATED BY RESPECT FOR OTHER HUMAN RIGHTS

The CESCR has implicitly recognized that the need to ensure respect for other fundamental rights and freedoms may justify limitations on the state's economic choices. In other words, although not mentioning self-determination in the following contexts, the CESCR's comments indicate a willingness to intrude upon the economic autonomy of states, where its policies would infringe other ICESCR rights (including internal self-determination). In doing so, the CESCR has not overtly invoked the 'limitations clause' in Article 5 of the ICESCR (which is considered in a later chapter).

To give some examples in the economic field, the CESCR has criticized national structural adjustment programmes for impeding the implementation of various rights under the ICESCR. It has recommended that states allocate more revenue to fulfil Covenant obligations. The CESCR has also intervened in the conduct of a state's international economic relations, for instance by requesting states to ensure that ICESCR obligations are taken into account in negotiations with international financial institutions; or to ensure that free trade agreements do not infringe the self-determination rights of disadvantaged and marginalized groups, such as indigenous, Afro-Colombian or rural communities in Colombia.[298]

The above cases can be explained in either of two ways. First, where the state's economic choices are ordinarily viewed as an expression of its people's economic

[298] CESCR, Concluding Observations: Colombia, E/C.12/COL/CO/5 (7 June 2010).

self-determination, such expression must be limited by respect for other basic socio-economic rights of individuals. The group's rights in such cases are subordinated to an individual's subsistence or survival rights, pursuant to a limitations analysis,[299] and notwithstanding the notion that self-determination is *jus cogens*. Secondly, and alternatively, in some cases the CESCR treats the state not as the sole repository of the people's self-determination at all, but rather duty-bound to deal with the state's resources in ways which respect the self-determination of groups within the state, such as indigenous peoples.

The right of self-determination also gives rise to potential conflicts with individual rights under the ICCPR. For instance, a state's economic decision to fundamentally restructure its economy through large-scale expropriations of its citizens' property may be seen as an exercise of economic self-determination, which is not limited by international economic obligations protecting *foreign* property. There is no individual right to property in the ICCPR and ICESCR, although it may sometimes be incidentally protected where other rights (such as non-discrimination, or arbitrary interference in the home) are engaged.

In such cases, a question arises whether self-determination 'trumps' individual rights (either by overriding them, or providing a legitimate public purpose in 'limiting' them), or whether more specific individual rights prevail over the more general and rather vague notion of the group's self-determination. The approach to resolving such real or apparent conflicts of obligation also affect the state's duty to compensate and the individual's remedy in benefiting from it. Limitations on rights are considered in the chapter on Article 4 below.

LIMITS NECESSITATED BY RESPECT FOR OTHER INTERNATIONAL OBLIGATIONS

While Article 1(2) expressly limits self-determination by reference to international economic obligations, it does not mention limitations flowing from other specified areas of law. It does, however, state that the freedom to dispose of resources is to be 'based upon the principle of mutual benefit, and international law'. In this way Article 1(2) opens the door to a range of other international obligations being taken into account when peoples exploit their resources.

Of particular relevance is international environmental law, which restricts the manner in which states are free to develop their resources—and fundamentally alters assumptions about what 'permanent sovereignty' over resources can now legitimately entail. During the drafting, a few states were concerned that the freedom to dispose of resources should not involve an absolute freedom to exploit the seas (for instance, by depleting common fish stocks) or to exploit international watercourses to deprive downstream riparian states.[300]

International environmental law was still in its infancy at the time of the drafting of the ICESCR in the 1950s and 1960s. Now such law relevantly includes

[299] See the chapter below on Articles 4 and 5 of the ICESCR.
[300] Schrijver, *Sovereignty over Natural Resources*, 63–4.

norms governing: transboundary environmental harm; sustainable development; the precautionary principle; inter-generational equity; waste and pollution; carbon emissions; biodiversity; conservation; protected areas; World Heritage status; the human 'right' to a healthy environment; and so forth. Developments in the international law of the sea too have enabled states to exploit their maritime resources (for instance, by strengthening sovereignty or rights in adjacent maritime areas) while imposing environmental limits.

It is unsurprising that the UN human rights treaty bodies that are not explicitly mandated to apply international environmental law have not drawn heavily on those norms in disposing of human rights problems, including questions of self-determination. Even so, the treaty bodies have recognized the interdependence of human rights and the environment in certain cases. As discussed earlier, the economic and cultural dependence of indigenous peoples on environmental resources (from land to forests) has featured in the CESCR's consideration of Article 1, and also informed related concerns about the right to health. It is thus open to the CESCR in future to draw in more detail on international environmental standards in defining situations in which peoples—whether whole populations or parts of it—have been denied self-determination as a result of the despoliation of their natural resources or environment.

Article 1(3)

'STATES PARTIES...SHALL PROMOTE THE REALIZATION OF THE RIGHT OF SELF-DETERMINATION'

In General Comment No. 12 on Article 1 of the ICCPR, the HRC notes that the freedoms in Article 1 generally impose correlative duties on states:

2. ...The article imposes on all States parties corresponding obligations. This right and the corresponding obligations concerning its implementation are interrelated with other provisions of the Covenant and rules of international law.

...

4. With regard to paragraph 1 of article 1, States parties should describe the constitutional and political processes which in practice allow the exercise of this right.[301]

The specific obligation in Article 1(3) to promote the realization of self-determination is not limited to colonial states that administer trust or non-self-governing territories (as originally envisaged in the drafting[302]), nor to states solely in relation to their own peoples. As the HRC further observes:

6. Paragraph 3, in the Committee's opinion, is particularly important in that it imposes specific obligations on States parties, not only in relation to their own peoples but vis-à-vis all peoples which have not been able to exercise or have been deprived of the possibility

[301] HRC, General Comment No. 12 (Vol. I), [2, 4].

[302] Nowak, *CCPR Commentary*, 12.

of exercising their right to self-determination. The general nature of this paragraph is confirmed by its drafting history…The obligations exist irrespective of whether a people entitled to self-determination depends on a State party to the Covenant or not. It follows that all States parties to the Covenant should take positive action to facilitate realization of and respect for the right of peoples to self-determination. Such positive action must be consistent with the States' obligations under the Charter of the United Nations and under international law: in particular, States must refrain from interfering in the internal affairs of other States and thereby adversely affecting the exercise of the right to self-determination. The reports should contain information on the performance of these obligations and the measures taken to that end.[303]

The duty is also restated in the 1970 Declaration on Friendly Relations:

Every State has the duty to promote, through joint and separate action, realization of the principle of equal rights and self-determination of peoples, in accordance with the provisions of the Charter, and to render assistance to the United Nations in carrying out the responsibilities entrusted to it by the Charter regarding the implementation of the principle…[304]

So too in Article 5 of the 1986 Declaration on the Right to Development:

States shall take resolute steps to eliminate the massive and flagrant violations of the human rights of peoples and human beings affected by situations such as those resulting from…refusal to recognize the fundamental right of peoples to self-determination.[305]

Article 1(3) implies both a negative duty not to interfere in the exercise of self-determination and a positive obligation to promote its realization. As regards non-self-governing territories, the duties of an administering state are straightforward: not to forcibly repress self-determination, and to facilitate the exercise of free choice, such as through a plebiscite or referendum.

Concerning independent states, the state's obligations towards its own people (that is, after independence) have already been considered, namely to enable its people (and relevant segments of it, such as indigenous peoples, certain minorities and vulnerable groups) to continuously exercise control of their political, economic and cultural destiny, through such means as political representation, public participation in resource governance, and so on. The legally uncertain question of internal 'remedial self-determination' for oppressed groups, or a broader right of rebellion of the population at large, is also relevant here.

SELF-DETERMINATION ELSEWHERE—NEGATIVE DUTIES

As regards the obligations of a states vis-à-vis foreign 'peoples' in the territory or jurisdiction of another state, the scope of the negative duty can be reasonably well

[303] HRC, General Comment No. 12 (Vol. I), [6].

[304] Declaration on Principles of International Law concerning Friendly Relations and Co-operation among States in accordance with the Charter of the United Nations. See HRC, General Comment No. 12 (Vol. I), [7].

[305] Declaration on the Right to Development.

defined by reference to certain other international obligations, such as the prohibition on the use of force and the duty of non-intervention, discussed earlier. As the 1970 Declaration on Friendly Relations provides:

Every State has the duty to refrain from any forcible action which deprives peoples referred to in the elaboration of the principle of equal rights and self-determination of their right to self-determination and freedom and independence…

Outside the context of the use of force, the ICJ has assisted a little in clarifying the scope of a state's duty not to interfere in the exercise of self-determination elsewhere. In the *East Timor* case, the ICJ recognized that self-determination has an *erga omnes* character.[306] The implications of such characterization were spelled out in the *Israel Wall Advisory Opinion*:

155. The Court would observe that the obligations violated by Israel include certain obligations *erga omnes*. As the Court indicated in the *Barcelona Traction* case, such obligations are by their very nature 'the concern of all States' and, 'In view of the importance of the rights involved, all States can be held to have a legal interest in their protection' (*Barcelona Traction, Light and Power Company, Limited, Second Phase, Judgment, I.C.J. Reports 1970*, p. 32, para. 33). The obligations *erga ommes* violated by Israel are the obligation to respect the right of the Palestinian people to self-determination, and certain of its obligations under international humanitarian law.

156. As regards the first of these, the Court has already observed (paragraph 88 above) that in the *East Timor* case, it described as 'irreproachable' the assertion that 'the right of peoples to self-determination, as it evolved from the Charter and from United Nations practice, has an *erga omnes* character' (*I.C.J. Reports 1995*, p. 102, para. 29). The Court would also recall that under the terms of General Assembly resolution 2625 (XXV), already mentioned above (see paragraph 88),

'Every State has the duty to promote, through joint and separate action, realization of the principle of equal rights and self-determination of peoples, in accordance with the provisions of the Charter, and to render assistance to the United Nations in carrying out the responsibilities entrusted to it by the Charter regarding the implementation of the principle…'

…

159. Given the character and the importance of the rights and obligations involved, the Court is of the view that all States are under an obligation not to recognize the illegal situation resulting from the construction of the wall in the Occupied Palestinian Territory, including in and around East Jerusalem. They are also under an obligation not to render aid or assistance in maintaining the situation created by such construction. It is also for all States, while respecting the United Nations Charter and international law, to see to it that any impediment, resulting from the construction of the wall, to the exercise by the Palestinian people of its right to self-determination is brought to an end…

160. Finally, the Court is of the view that the United Nations, and especially the General Assembly and the Security Council, should consider what further action is required to

[306] *East Timor (Portugal v Australia)*, Judgment, (1995) ICJ Reports 90, [29].

bring to an end the illegal situation resulting from the construction of the wall and the associated régime, taking due account of the present Advisory Opinion.[307]

The *erga omnes* character of self-determination requires all states not to recognize an illegal situation resulting from its denial, nor aid or assist in maintaining that illegal situation. On the facts of that case, the implications were that no state should recognize the route of Israel's security wall as predetermining the boundaries of a Palestinian state, or accept the lawfulness of the Israeli settlements which seek to change demographic facts on the ground. States also must not assist Israel in the construction, maintenance or operation of the wall and its infrastructure.

DEALINGS WITH ILLEGALLY EXPLOITED RESOURCES

In practice, the negative duty of states not to interfere in self-determination abroad may be of most significance in relation to illegally extracted natural resources. It was noted earlier that the CESCR has faulted states for exploiting their own resources in ways which are either procedurally deficient under Article 1 or not for the benefit of the population or parts of it. A question arises whether a state is also required not to be complicit in the illegal exploitation of a foreign people's natural resources by a foreign state. The situation arises most prominently in relation to non-self-governing or occupied territories, but it also potentially arises where an independent state deprives its own people of its resources and other states are implicated.

The means by which a state may be implicated in illegal resource exploitation by a foreign state are manifold, for instance by: financing the illegal extraction of foreign resources; purchasing the resulting exports or products; supplying technical assistance, services, labour or goods to facilitate exploitation; transporting the exploited resources; or permitting its nationals or companies to take part in the foreign exploitation. In situations of armed conflict, such acts may separately involve violations of humanitarian law and other provisions of human rights law.

The self-determination issue has not, however, been directly addressed by any international tribunal. In the *East Timor* case, for jurisdictional reasons the ICJ did not rule on the merits of whether Australia had infringed the Timorese people's right of self-determination, since to do so would impermissibly determine the legal position of a third (non-party) state, Indonesia. Assuming that Indonesia's invasion of Portuguese Timor involved a denial of self-determination (as is certain), Australia's agreement with Indonesia to exploit Timor's oil and gas resources breached its own obligation not to interfere in Timor's economic self-determination. (So too did Australia's recognition of Indonesian sovereignty over Timor, including through maritime boundary

[307] *Israel Wall Advisory Opinion*, [155]–[160].

agreements, constitute a denial of political and economic self-determination more generally.)

Other examples may be given, such as where one state imports resources illegally extracted in foreign territory in denial of self-determination, as in the export of Israeli settler products acquired from the Palestinian Occupied Territories. The international law of self-determination may require all states to boycott imports of goods from companies of any nationality operating in the Palestinian territories where such business is not conducted for the benefit of the Palestinian people and with the consent of that people.

In relation to Western Sahara, the UN Legal Counsel, Hans Correll, provided a legal opinion in 2002 to the Security Council on the legality of Morocco concluding mining contracts with foreign companies in Western Sahara. The opinion answered the question by analogy to the international law on permanent sovereignty over natural resources in non-self-governing territories, but the close connection of such law to the right of self-determination suggests that the opinion may be relevant to the latter legal issue as well. Correll reviewed state practice (including on East Timor's maritime resources, Nauru's phosphates, Western Sahara's phosphates and Namibia's uranium) and concluded:

21. The question addressed to me by the Security Council namely, 'the legality…of actions allegedly taken by the Moroccan authorities consisting in the offering and signing of contracts with foreign companies for the exploration of mineral resources in Western Sahara', has been analysed by analogy as part of the more general question of whether mineral resource activities in a Non-Self-Governing Territory by an administering Power is illegal, as such, or only if conducted in disregard of the needs and interests of the people of that territory. An analysis of the relevant provisions of the United Nations Charter, General Assembly resolutions, the case law of the International Court of Justice and the practice of States, supports the latter conclusion.

22. The principle that the interests of the peoples of Non-Self-Governing Territories are paramount, and their well-being and development is the 'sacred trust' of their respective administering Powers, was established in the Charter of the United Nations and further developed in General Assembly by resolutions on the question of decolonization and economic activities in Non-Self-Governing Territories. In recognizing the inalienable rights of the peoples of Non-Self-Governing Territories to the natural resources in their territories, the General Assembly has consistently condemned the exploitation and plundering of natural resources and any economic activities which are detrimental to the interests of the peoples of these territories and deprive them of their legitimate rights over their natural resource. It recognized, however, the value of economic activities which are undertaken in accordance with the wishes of the peoples of those territories, and their contribution to the development of such territories.

23. In the Cases of East Timor and Nauru, the International Court of Justice did not pronounce itself on the question of the legality of economic activities in Non-Self-Governing Territories. It should be noted, however, that in neither case was it alleged that mineral resource exploitation in such territories was illegal per se. In the Case of East Timor, the conclusion of an oil exploitation agreement was allegedly illegal because it was not concluded with the administering Power (Portugal); in the Nauru Case, the illegality allegedly arose because the mineral resource exploitation depleted unnecessarily or inequitably the overlaying lands.

24. The recent State practice, though limited, is illustrative of an opinio juris on the part of both administering Powers and third States: where resource exploitation activities are concluded in Non-Self-Governing Territories for the benefit of the peoples of these territories, on their behalf, or in consultation with their representatives, they are considered compatible with the Charter obligations of the administering Power, and in conformity with the General Assembly resolutions and the principle of 'permanent sovereignty over natural resources' enshrined therein.

25. The foregoing legal principles established in the practice of States and the United Nations pertain to economic activities in Non-Self-Governing Territories, in general, and mineral resource exploitation, in particular. It must be recognized, however, that in the present case, the contracts for oil reconnaissance and evaluation do not entail exploitation or the physical removal of the mineral resources, and no benefits have as of yet accrued. The conclusion is, therefore, that, while the specific contracts which are the subject of the Security Council's request are not in themselves illegal, if further exploration and exploitation activities were to proceed in disregard of the interests and wishes of the people of Western Sahara, they would be in violation of the international law principles applicable to mineral resource activities in Non-Self-Governing Territories.[308]

The opinion did not rest upon other areas of international law, such as the law of occupation (given Morocco's unlawful invasion and conquest of Spanish Sahara in 1975, resulting in an armed conflict and ceasefire stalemate) or human rights law. It was noted earlier that the ICJ refused to find a breach of permanent sovereignty over natural resources in dealing with illegally plundered resources, in breach of humanitarian law, in *Congo v Uganda*. The existence of an armed conflict (via occupation) in Western Sahara might therefore affect whether the ICJ would agree with the Correll opinion, though unlike Sahara, Congo is not a non-self-governing territory and so those different considerations may well still apply.

To extrapolate to economic self-determination, assume that one state has exploited the natural resources of a people (whether its own, or the inhabitants of a non-self-governing territory or occupied territory), and such exploitation is not for the benefit of such people (according to the law of self-determination under Article 1(2), which may overlap with concurrent violations of the law of non-self-governing territories, the law of permanent sovereignty over resources and the law of occupation). Assume further that in doing so, it has contracted to export the extracted commodities to a second state (or the second state has otherwise assisted by investing in or providing material support for the venture).

In such a scenario, there is little doubt that the second state has breached its obligation under Article 1(3) to respect the right of self-determination and to promote its realization, namely by infringing its negative duty not to interfere in the exercise of self-determination by others. The *erga omnes* character of self-determination demands that a state must not recognize an illegal situation

[308] UN Security Council, Letter dated 29 January 2002 from the Under-Secretary-General for Legal Affairs, the Legal Counsel, addressed to the President of the Security Council, S/2002/161 (12 February 2002), [21]–[25].

brought about by another state's denial of it, including where the other state arrogates to itself a purported proprietary or sovereign right to deal with the natural resources of a repressed people.

If a state is thus forbidden from dealing with resources extracted contrary to Article 1(2) by another, the duty must extend to an obligation to prevent similar activity by private parties within the first state's territory or jurisdiction (such as mining companies which operate abroad). A pertinent example is the continuing importation of Saharan phosphate by Australian companies; or foreign companies or individuals that invest in Israeli settlement activities; or private security companies which provide services to companies or governments to sustain exploitation. Further support may be found in Article 16(2) of the Charter of Economic Rights and Duties of States 1974, which provides that '[n]o State has the right to promote or encourage investments that may constitute an obstacle to the liberation of a territory occupied by force'.

Outside the context of natural resources, the negative aspect of Article 1(3) may extend to other situations. Logically the obligation entails a duty not to suppress the lawful political activities of members of a foreign 'people' present in a state's territory and working towards their self-determination elsewhere—activities also protected by various ICCPR political rights (for instance, freedom of expression, association, assembly, movement and so on). That includes criticism, for instance, of the economic or environmental activities of a foreign state.

Mention was also made earlier of the CESCR's criticism of a state's adoption of a free trade agreement which adversely impacts on vulnerable sections of its population. By implication, the other state party(s) to the agreement might share responsibility for the harmful impacts of the agreement on the economic self-determination of the foreign population.

SELF-DETERMINATION ELSEWHERE—POSITIVE DUTIES

The scope of the positive duty on states to promote self-determination abroad is less clear, given that there is a broad spectrum of acts of lesser to higher intensity that are capable of promoting the right. These might include privately or publicly expressing support for a cause; voting favourably in UN fora; diplomatically pressuring other states to support a particular cause; taking positions favourable to developing economies in WTO or climate change negotiations; submitting matters to the ICJ or other legal procedures; unilaterally imposing economic or other sanctions, or otherwise preventing nationals or companies from dealing with a repressive state; directly or concretely assisting self-determination movements (such as by providing financing, training or information); and participating in UN-authorized interventions.

None of these methods is specifically stipulated as obligatory by Article 1(3), even if they are possible; and practice suggests that a state which fails to take all steps within its power to promote self-determination in any or every case abroad is generally not regarded as in breach of Article 1(3). The choice of means in promoting self-determination elsewhere is rather left to a state's discretion, perhaps taking into account what is reasonable or achievable given the relative capabilities of the state in question. Certainly states which have particular links to a foreign territory where self-determination is at issue—for instance, through trade, bonds of nationality, diplomatic influence or historical ties—might be expected to do more. This aspect of Article 1(3) may well be more of a legal principle than a rule, given the difficulty in identifying consensus on any binding 'checklist' of positive acts a state must take to discharge its duty.

Other provisions of the ICESCR may help to give content to the positive duty in Article 1(3). For example, Article 2(1) of the ICESCR requires states to 'take steps, individually and through international assistance and co-operation' to progressively realize ICESCR obligations. In supervising states, the CESCR has frequently called on developed states to increase their foreign aid allocations to meet the UN target of 0.7 per cent of GNP, thus incidentally promoting economic self-determination. It has also called on developing states to place more emphasis in donors' official development assistance on support for particular social adjustment programmes, such as financing low-interest credit for poor farmers, slum-upgrading and housing for the poor.[309] It has also urged states to seek technical assistance to achieve their anti-poverty goals or to otherwise realize ICESCR obligations. These are just a few of the material ways in which states can promote the economic freedoms of other peoples, in the context of the international economic and social order envisaged by Article 55 of the UN Charter and Article 28 of the Universal Declaration of Human Rights.

MILITARY INTERVENTION OR ASSISTANCE

One vexed issue in relation to states' positive duty to promote self-determination concerns the use of military force to assist a people to realize self-determination.[310] Many developing states long argued for a right of military assistance to national liberation movements which were being forcibly repressed by a colonial power, although such claim was contested by developed states.

Outside that now rare situation (setting aside Palestine and Western Sahara), as noted earlier, the HRC has stated that any positive action to assist self-determination must be consistent with international law and 'States must refrain from interfering in the internal affairs of other States and thereby adversely affecting the exercise of the right to self-determination'.[311] The 1970 Declaration generally rules out external intervention in independent states:

> Nothing in the foregoing paragraphs shall be construed as authorizing or encouraging any action which would dismember or impair, totally or in part, the territorial integrity or political unity of sovereign and independent States conducting themselves in compliance with the principle of equal rights and self-determination of peoples as described above and thus

[309] CESCR, Concluding Observations: Philippines, E/C.12/PHL/CO/4 (1 December 2008).
[310] See, eg, James Crawford, 'The Right of Self-Determination in International Law: Its Development and Future' in Alston (ed), *Peoples' Rights*, 7, [40]–[47].
[311] HRC, General Comment No. 12 (Vol. I), [6].

possessed of a government representing the whole people belonging to the territory without distinction as to race, creed or colour.

Every State shall refrain from any action aimed at the partial or total disruption of the national unity and territorial integrity of any other State or country.

Ordinarily, external military intervention or assistance would be a prohibited use of force under Article 2(4) of the Charter and violate the principle of non-intervention. Collective self-defence in aid of an existing independent state against an aggressor state is a lawful exception under Article 51 of the UN Charter, which necessarily serves to protect the right of self-determination of the victim people. In the case of non-independent peoples, the only possible caveat in the 1970 Declaration concerns the rare case of remedial self-determination, that is, where a state is no longer conducting itself 'in compliance with the principle of equal rights and self-determination of peoples' and no longer represents its people in a non-discriminatory fashion.

As noted earlier, any right of remedial self-determination is unsettled. But the HRC's assumption that external military interference in a foreign state's internal affairs would adversely affect self-determination would be misconceived in such situations, for the HRC conflates 'state' with 'people'. Interference in a state's internal affairs—on the side of the *people*, against the *state*—may be precisely necessary to realize a right of self-determination otherwise in abeyance.

State practice is mixed but still supports the restrictive view of the prohibition on the use of force. Much of the legal discussion of intervention has concerned claims of humanitarian intervention rather than self-determination, as in Kosovo, where questions of political settlement followed rather than precipitated intervention. (Humanitarian intervention is, in any case, disputed, but likely contrary to Article 2(4) of the Charter.) Much of the legal discussion of self-determination and intervention has also concerned *minorities and secession*,[312] rather than *majorities overthrowing governments*.

During the 'Arab Spring', various states offered support for rebel or resistance movements opposed to their governments, typically following severe repression of protests by governments. In Libya, such support took the form of direct military intervention by Arab states and NATO, but the legal basis was a (disputed) UN Security Council resolution, not unilateral intervention. By contrast, in Syria, where the Security Council could not agree on intervention, a number of states unilaterally provided military assistance to rebel forces, sometimes announcing that the Assad regime in Syria had lost its 'legitimacy'.

Where rebels represent a clear majority of the population, and a government's repression is egregious, such an example might be a genuine case of remedial self-determination by aggrieved citizens. In such cases, external military intervention might be viewed as supporting self-determination rather than infringing it, assuming it is possible for external powers to: accurately gauge the balance

[312] See, eg, Marc Weller, *Escaping the Self-Determination Trap* (Martinus Nijhoff, Leiden, 2008), Chapter V.

of domestic opinion in the foreign state; only intervene at the right threshold of severity of rights violations; exhaust peaceful means; and act relatively disinterestedly.

On the other hand, a strict view of non-intervention rests on the notion that civil war itself is an expression of self-determination, such that external intervention is prohibited precisely so as not to interfere in the free resolution of the people's destiny (by siding with the government or rebels). That view cannot be right in principle because it does not account for the disparity in the machinery of violence as between governments and rebels, at least at the outset of a conflict; abstinence implicitly favours the status quo, that is, the supremacy of the government. It is also not accepted in practice, given that states often provide military assistance to other governments (on request) to repress insurgencies, and such assistance is sometimes considered lawful or acquiesced in.

There is still, however, insufficient state practice to sustain a view that unilateral military intervention in support of remedial self-determination is lawful, so as to dislodge the prohibition on the use of force under Article 2(4) of the UN Charter. In many cases of internal repression by governments, there has been no offer of external military support to rebels, from Russia's war in Chechnya to Sri Lanka's conflict with the LTTE. The prohibition on the use of force is a norm of *jus cogens* and while self-determination too is *jus cogens*, no further right of intervention to aid self-determination is yet recognized as part of the principle. At most, an intervention in aid of self-determination might be judged less harshly by the international community in its aftermath, affecting the treatment of the delinquent state and the resolution or settlement of the situation.

As regards the sub-set of economic self-determination, there is virtually no state practice evidencing support for a right of a state to militarily intervene to assist a foreign population to restore control over natural resources depleted or misused by their government (for example, where Nigeria permits destructive oil exploitation in the Niger delta; or where a state impoverishes its people to enrich its leaders). The situation might be different where economic violations are accompanied by widespread political violence of the kind ordinarily thought to engage the notion of remedial self-determination.

3

Article 2(1): Progressive Realization of ICESCR Rights

Article 2

1. Each State Party to the present Covenant undertakes to take steps, individually and through international assistance and co-operation, especially economic and technical, to the maximum of its available resources, with a view to achieving progressively the full realization of the rights recognized in the present Covenant by all appropriate means, including particularly the adoption of legislative measures.

2. The States Parties to the present Covenant undertake to guarantee that the rights enunciated in the present Covenant will be exercised without discrimination of any kind as to race, colour, sex, language, religion, political or other opinion, national or social origin, property, birth or other status.

3. Developing countries, with due regard to human rights and their national economy, may determine to what extent they would guarantee the economic rights recognized in the present Covenant to non-nationals.

Article 2 comprises key umbrella provisions of the Covenant that stipulate the nature and extent of the obligations imposed on states parties in respect of their implementation of the substantive rights contained in the rest of the Covenant (namely Articles 3 to 15). Paragraphs 1 and 2 are universal in their coverage—concerning how states must implement in terms of extent and speed (paragraph 1), and that they must do so without discrimination (paragraph 2). Paragraph 3, however, is somewhat different, relating to an exception that applies only to 'developing countries', and only in respect of 'economic rights' (and not, apparently, to social or cultural rights, although that remains somewhat in dispute, as we discuss below).

The Realities of Realization

The provisions in Article 2(1) are as remarkable for what they do not say, as for what they do say. The tone and nature of the demands made of states are quite different here from the equivalent Article 2(1) in the ICCPR,[1] being more exhortatory than mandatory; more progressive, than immediate. The significance of this difference—or at least how significant the difference is perceived to be—has been the source for much of the opinion that the ICESCR rights are less demanding of states—less legal (or even non-justiciable) and more policy-oriented (setting aspirational goals, rather than immutable minimum standards).

This was quite deliberate of course, even if the profound consequences were not entirely understood by the Convention's framers. During a series of meetings of the General Assembly's Third Committee in late 1962,[2] the texts of the two Articles were considered side by side. There was a broad consensus among delegates, across developing as well as developed states, that there was a need to treat the two sets of rights differently in terms of the strictures of their attainment and enforcement. In this respect, the reported intervention by the United Kingdom's delegate Sir Douglas Glover was broadly representative:

> ... civil and political rights ... were capable of precise formulation and immediate application and when any state became a party to the Covenant it should undertake to ensure to its nationals the enjoyment of the rights enumerated in that Covenant [the ICCPR] ... A clause to permit progressive legislative action would be contrary to the structure and spirit of the draft Covenant on Civil and Political Rights, where it was entirely appropriate in the draft Covenant on Economic, Social and Cultural Rights which set forth rights of a different nature.[3]

And while during these meetings there were some discussions over how the term 'achieving progressively' in ICESCR Article 2(1) might be tightened up—ranging from suggestions as to how to ensure against stagnation or delayed progress, through to calls for inserting adverbs like 'rapid' or 'accelerated', and even consideration of defining periods within which progressive achievements might reasonably be expected to occur (from 'immediate' for wealthier states to 'realistic'

[1] Article 2(1) of the International Covenant on Civil and Political Rights (ICCPR) (adopted 16 December 1966, 999 UNTS 171, entered into force 23 March 1976) reads: 'Each State Party to the present Covenant undertakes to respect and to ensure to all individuals within its territory and subject to its jurisdiction the rights recognized in the present Covenant, without distinction of any kind, such as race, colour, sex, language, religion, political or other opinion, national or social origin, property, birth or other status.'

[2] UNGA Third Committee, A/C.3/SR.1181 (13 November 1962) to UNGA Third Committee, A/C.3/SR.1206 (10 December 1962).

[3] UNGA Third Committee, A/C.3/SR.1181 (13 November 1962), 235. The reference to a state's 'nationals' was soon to be superseded, with the relevant clause in ICCPR Article 2(1) eventually to read: 'all individuals within its territory and subject to its jurisdiction'.

for poorer ones)—there was little suggestion that progressivity was to be removed and/or replaced by the language of immediacy or imperativity.[4]

In fact, the core elements of the paragraph's programmatic language were established relatively early in the drafting process. The text before the UN General Assembly's Third Committee in December 1955 differed from that which was to become the final form in just two respects: (i) the earlier draft referred only to 'international co-operation', without any additional mention of international 'assistance', and nor was mention made of the especial need for 'economic and technical' assistance/cooperation; and (ii) the 'means' by which states were expected to implement the rights in the Covenant were expressed in slightly looser terms: 'by legislative as well as other means', rather than as was finally agreed to in 1966: 'by all appropriate means, including particularly the adoption of legislative measures'.

The stipulation of international assistance, both in economic[5] and technical terms, was an important—indeed vital—addition, and heralded the deep and continuing debates over both the incapacity of many states to provide adequate coverage for the Covenant's rights, and the existence and extent of obligations on the part of states parties to assist each other in their respective realization of those rights.

> 49. All speakers recognised that in view of the inadequacy of resources in many countries and the time needed to develop them, it was important to impose on States Parties to the Covenant only the obligation of achieving 'progressively' the realization of economic, social and cultural rights. The considerable difficulties which would be experienced by the developing countries desirous of applying the Covenant were mentioned.
>
> 50. It was agreed that the development of resources in each country depended on the continuation and intensification of assistance and international co-operation. The amendment submitted by Bolivia, Chile, Colombia, Mali and Uruguay... stressed that idea and particularly the importance of economic and technical co-operation.
>
> 51. Some representatives felt that the proposal concerning certain aspects of international co-operation was out of place in the draft Covenant and tended to underestimate the importance of such co-operation in other fields. Other speakers expressed fear that by making international assistance an essential condition for the application of the Covenant, the five-Power amendment might have the effect of subordinating economic, social and cultural progress, in the last analysis, to the good will of countries providing such assistance.[6]

The question of the means by which Article 2(1)'s obligations ought to be implemented centred upon a series of propositions sponsored by the United Kingdom.

[4] Although see discussion below of a proposal to impose a time limit made by the representative of Congo, Léopoldville, text at n. 45 below.

[5] It should be noted that the five sponsoring states (mentioned at [50] of the above extract) had originally sponsored an amendment that referred to 'financial' assistance, rather than 'economic', but, in apparent recognition of the latter's desirably broader remit, they revised the wording accordingly: UNGA Third Committee, A/5365 (17 December 1962), [39].

[6] UNGA Third Committee, A/5365 (17 December 1962), [49]–[51].

During Third Committee discussions in the General Assembly's Tenth Session in 1955:

> ...the United Kingdom submitted an amendment to replace the words 'as well as' by the word 'or'. This amendment was intended to leave the States free to employ either 'legislative' or 'other means'—instead of the obliging them to employ both 'legislative' and 'other means'—in order to achieve the realisation of the rights recognized in the covenants.[7]

This rather strange amendment (in the sense that from today's perspective we would expect legislation to be the primary means of implementation) was something of an echo of the United Kingdom's common law tradition, whereby judge-made law more commonly protected rights than parliamentary legislation (although it must be said that that circumstance was by then fast reversing under the deluge of legislation that marked the United Kingdom's post-war recovery). Perhaps in part recognition of such change, and certainly on account of the arguments advanced by the overwhelming majority of delegates who contributed to the debate that in making the legislative action 'optional', the United Kingdom's amendment 'would weaken the article and the practical defence of human rights',[8] the United Kingdom modified its stance during the General Assembly's Seventeenth Session in 1962. It first abandoned its mutual exclusivity stance and instead promoted the phrase 'by all appropriate means, including legislative measures',[9] and then was prepared to accept Ghana's additional amendment to insert the word 'particularly' before 'legislative'.[10] It was in this form that the provision was finally approved by the Third Committee and subsequently by the General Assembly in late December 1962.

Identifying Obligations

The obligations imposed on states parties arising from Article 2(1) can be broken down into four key sections: (i) the undertaking to take steps; (ii) to utilize maximum available resources; (iii) to achieving progressively the full realization of rights; and (iv) doing so by employing all appropriate means. We now address each of these in turn.

[7] UNGA Third Committee, A/3077 (5 December 1955), [86]. Note that at this time the Committee was considering wording that might apply to both Covenants (ICCPR and ICESCR) jointly—hence the plural last word in the quote above.

[8] UNGA Third Committee, A/C.3/SR.1183 (14 November 1962), [1].

[9] Emphasis added. These were the reported words in respect of the Ukrainian Soviet Socialist Republic: UNGA Third Committee, A/5365 (17 December 1962), [41]. In subsequent interventions that day and in the remaining Third Committee meetings across this Seventeenth Session, delegates from Austria, Argentina, Brazil, Chile, Cuba, Czechoslovakia, Ecuador, Ghana, Guatemala, Indonesia, Italy, Iraq, Nigeria, Saudi Arabia, Uruguay and the USSR all made comments similar to or supportive of the Ukrainian line. See UNGA Third Committee, A/C.3/SR.1181 (13 November 1962) to UNGA Third Committee, A/C.3/SR.1206 (10 December 1962).

[10] UNGA Third Committee, A/5365 (17 December 1962), [41].

(I) UNDERTAKING TO TAKE STEPS

This is the Covenant's foundational obligation—the 'undertaking' that states have made—which is at once admonitory and concrete, while at the same time, by the words 'to take steps' that immediately follow, qualified and fluid. The matters towards which the steps will be taken that comprise the remainder of Article 2(1) bear out this bipolarity. The Committee's General Comment No. 3[11] underscores the point by referring to Article 2 as having a 'dynamic relationship' with all the other rights provisions in the Covenant. In the same paragraph of this General Comment, the Committee goes on to distinguish between obligations of conduct and obligations of result', which amounts, in effect, to an attempt to reconcile the apparently mixed messages of the text. For, whereas the obligations of result are evidently qualified and largely indeterminate—there are no precisely identified outcomes, but rather stipulated states of transition—the obligations of conduct are more tangible. The General Comment notes that there are, in particular, two such obligations which are of 'immediate effect'. One is the undertaking contained in Article 2(2), that all of the Convention's rights 'will be exercised without discrimination' (on which see the next chapters on Articles 2(2) and (3)), and the second is as follows:

2. The other is the undertaking in article 2 (1) 'to take steps', which in itself, is not qualified or limited by other considerations. The full meaning of the phrase can also be gauged by noting some of the different language versions. In English the undertaking is 'to take steps', in French it is 'to act' ('s'engage à agir') and in Spanish it is 'to adopt measures' ('a adoptar medidas'). Thus while the full realization of the relevant rights may be achieved progressively, steps towards that goal must be taken within a reasonably short time after the Covenant's entry into force for the States concerned. Such steps should be deliberate, concrete and targeted as clearly as possible towards meeting the obligations recognized in the Covenant.

3. The means which should be used in order to satisfy the obligation to take steps are stated in article 2 (1) to be 'all appropriate means, including particularly the adoption of legislative measures'. The Committee recognizes that in many instances legislation is highly desirable and in some cases may even be indispensable. For example, it may be difficult to combat discrimination effectively in the absence of a sound legislative foundation for the necessary measures. In fields such as health, the protection of children and mothers, and education, as well as in respect of the matters dealt with in articles 6 to 9, legislation may also be an indispensable element for many purposes.[12]

In trying to explain what is meant by this seminal 'undertaking' obligation, it is clear from both of the above paragraphs how the Committee sees its unavoidable intersection with the Article's other provisions. The undertaking has further layers that bear significantly on its extent and nature. One of these relates to the

[11] CESCR, General Comment No. 3, The Nature of State Parties' Obligations (Art. 2, Para.1, of the Covenant) ('General Comment No. 3'), E/1991/23 (14 December 1990), [1].

[12] CESCR, General Comment No. 3, [2] and [3].

jurisdiction of 'each state party', and another, to the economic nature of the states' obligations. In terms of jurisdiction, it is critical that it be recognized not merely that states undertake to fulfil the demands of Article 2 in respect of their own national jurisdictions, but that they are also subject to some degree of duty to render 'international assistance and co-operation, especially economic and technical'. In practical terms, this is taken to mean that richer states assist poorer ones. This was evident in the tenor and substance of the Third Committee discussions of the original text. In leading a group of five nations jointly proposing an amendment (A/C.3/L.1046) that would emphasize the need for international assistance, the Chilean representative, Mr Diaz Casanueva, argued forcefully for the need to treat the obligation to respect economic, social and cultural rights differently in this respect from civil and political rights:

12. It must be understood that the guarantee of economic, social and cultural rights raised problems of a material nature, which the guarantee of civil and political rights did not. The former group of rights could not be ensured simply by enacting legislation and providing for enforcement, but depended on the level and rate of economic development. It was well known, however, that the economic development of the less developed countries was bound up with factors that the highly industrialized countries had more control that the developing countries themselves. The need for active cooperation and assistance from the industrial nations was becoming increasingly apparent and, fortunately, was gaining wider recognition, as could be seen from programs such as the Alliance for Progress [a then newly established initiative aimed at promoting economic relations between the US and Latin American states]. It was also being recognized that to narrow the gap between the developed and the underdeveloped countries would be in the interests of all concerned, for it would mean the universal enjoyment of the rights and privileges exercised today only by the industrial nations, and hence a world safer from conflict and upheaval. That was the new philosophy of international cooperation.[13]

The proposed amendment was not in the end carried, although it was recognized in debate that in any case the level of assistance implied in the form or words that were finally agreed to was thoroughly capable of connoting direct, positive and (where needs be) substantial economic and technical assistance from developed states to developing ones. It is fair to say, however, that since those early days, the connotations attributed to this part of Article 2(1) have been somewhat more muted than this. Not least this was due to the dynamics of international economic and political relations over the nearly three decades that were to follow, which hardened rather than softened the differences between rich and poor states as ironically exemplified by the swift demise of the Alliance for Progress in the Americas referred to above.

Indeed, in General Comment No. 3, the Committee avoids any direct attribution of responsibility or duty on the part of the richer states in particular, or the international community more generally, to provide assistance and cooperation to less well-off states. Rather, the Committee ducks the issue by tying the question

[13] UNGA Third Committee, A/C.3/SR.1203 (5 December 1962), 342.

of international assistance back to the base domestic responsibility of individual states when it notes that:

…the phrase 'to the maximum of its available resources' was intended by the drafters of the Covenant to refer to both the resources existing within a state and those available from the international community through international cooperation and assistance.[14]

It is, in other words, largely up to the individual state to avail itself of those opportunities for assistance that are available, rather than there being any specific obligation on other countries or international organizations to make such assistance available, still less any duty on them to render assistance. In fact, the Committee focuses on the rather more open-ended notion of international cooperation. Immediately following the above quotation from paragraph 13, the Committee underscores 'the essential role of such cooperation in facilitating the full realization' of the Covenant's rights, and points to the provisions in various Articles that allude to states parties' collective responsibilities to cooperate regarding equitable food distribution (Article 11), the conservation, development and diffusion of scientific and cultural benefits (Article 15), and, alongside UN bodies and specialized agencies, the rendering of technical assistance that promotes implementation of the Covenant (Articles 22 and 23).

The final paragraph of General Comment No. 3 provides the clearest indication of who or what the Committee sees as the mechanism that will do the heavy-lifting of assigning responsibility for international assistance:

14. The Committee wishes to emphasize that in accordance with Articles 55 and 56 of the Charter of the United Nations, with well-established principles of international law, and with the provisions of the Covenant itself, international cooperation for development and thus for the realization of economic, social and cultural rights is an obligation of all States. It is particularly incumbent upon those States which are in a position to assist others in this regard. The Committee notes in particular the importance of the Declaration on the Right to Development adopted by the General Assembly in its resolution 41/128 of 4 December 1986 and the need for States parties to take full account of all of the principles recognized therein. It emphasizes that, in the absence of an active programme of international assistance and cooperation on the part of all those States that are in a position to undertake one, the full realization of economic, social and cultural rights will remain an unfulfilled aspiration in many countries. In this respect, the Committee also recalls the terms of its General Comment 2 (1990).[15]

This statement is both revealing and sobering. It shows how the Committee views the Covenant as merely one of a suite of four obligation-imposing vehicles by which cooperation in development is promoted and thereby ('and thus', in the above passage) economic, social and cultural rights are realized. Of the

[14] CESCR, General Comment No. 3, [13].

[15] CESCR, General Comment No. 3, [14]. CESCR, General Comment No. 2, International technical assistance measures (Art. 22), E/1990/23 (2 February 1990) amplifies how and what sorts of measures UN organs and specialized agencies might take in order to provide technical assistance to signatory states in their implementation of the Covenant.

other three, the provisions of Articles 55 and 56 of the Charter—though broadly couched—are indisputable, but the assertion that there are 'well-established principles of international law' that oblige states to so cooperate is simply incorrect. That states ought so to cooperate is a principle often and rightly advanced in legal and non-legal circles. That, beyond this, there may be grounds to argue that there already exists (or nearly so) a duty to cooperate in international law is also a contention not infrequently advanced in international legal debates. But to maintain still further, not only that the principle exists (the 'ought' being now accepted as an 'is'), but that it is a matter 'well-established', is hyperbole.

The cause of the problem likely lies in the Committee's over-enthusiastic embrace of the fourth and final vehicle nominated in the above passage—namely, the then relatively recently concluded Declaration on the Right to Development (RTD) in December 1986.[16] One of the intended consequences, if not indeed a central objective of the Declaration, was certainly to enhance the means, methods and magnitude of international development assistance and cooperation in the realization of economic, social and cultural rights. And the Committee was right to state the important (albeit obvious) point that to fail to do so would mean that such realization 'will remain an unfulfilled aspiration in many countries'. But, as the subsequently troubled history of the RTD generally, and the ignominious fate of the Declaration in particular, have since shown, such noble sentiments may neither be easily transposed into the legal (or even semi-legal) language of a UN Declaration (and certainly not into a well-established principle of international law), nor readily attract the political support needed for them to be honoured in practice. The Committee was perhaps investing more hope and expectation in the Declaration than it was capable of bearing (on the RTD, see further below in this chapter).

The final layer of the states' undertaking in this Article is more subliminal than explicit and yet it is perhaps the most significant of all. The economic nature of the signatory states' obligations is assumed within all aspects of Article 2(1) and yet in the legal analytical fervour that tends to dominate the discussion and definition of what we can expect and indeed demand of states under the Covenant, serious engagement with the relevant economic circumstances is skirted over or left off the agenda altogether. This much has been noted in dialogue between the Committee and commentators over the years.[17] In the following extract reporting remarks made by Professor Mathew Craven, it is noted that while he saw the establishment of the Committee having yielded legal benefits (enforceability and a promotion of the fact that ESC rights are not that different from CP rights in format and application), the same could not be said of its economic competences and capacity:

30. Turning to the question of whether the Committee could develop its role beyond the narrowly quasi-judicial, he hoped that the Committee would take in good part any

[16] UNGA Res. 41/128, Declaration on the Right to Development, A/RES/41/128 (4 December 1986).

[17] See, in particular, Mary Dowell-Jones, *Contextualising the International Covenant on Economic, Social and Cultural Rights: Assessing the Economic Deficit* (Martinus Nijhoff, Leiden, 2004), chapters 3 and 4.

criticisms he might make. It was clearly not able to solve the broad issues of poverty or deprivation; it could not prevent outbreaks of violence or the accession of dictatorial regimes; it would not save the world. Nor had it been able to assist States in developing social programmes or restructuring their economic relations; it lacked the technical, administrative or financial means to do so. States did not generally expect assistance, but scrutiny by some sort of judicial body. He did not think, either, that the Committee would significantly alter the way in which aid was given by the international financial community. The Committee was, therefore, left with an essentially marginal role, dealing with States that had overstepped the mark in some way through arbitrary or indiscriminate action. A possible approach, as the Committee had outlined in its first general comment, was to ensure that there were appropriate decision-making policies at national level; such an aim could continue to be achieved through the reporting procedure. That did not exclude the possibility of the Committee's undertaking a more expansive role, but it would need more expert knowledge, either developed within itself or brought in from outside. So far it had been incapable of either, particularly in relation to such technical issues as International Labour Organization standards, which figured in articles 6–9. Individual members might have some knowledge, but the general level of expertise was low. He understood the constraints within which the Committee worked, but more expert knowledge would need to be imported if the Committee was to expand its work.[18]

The situation, however, is improving, with the Committee's Concluding Observations in respect of states parties' periodic reports now increasingly wrestling with the economic and political realities of states, alongside the adamancy of the legal obligation to safeguard economic, social and cultural rights. Thus, while it can be said that in its earlier engagements with states the Committee stressed the disadvantages that individuals and groups were facing in terms especially of whether or how they were able to seek or obtain redress, in more recent times (post 2000, approximately), such concerns are now accompanied by much more sophisticated and demanding economic awareness. This extract from Concluding Observations regarding South Korea in 2009 is representative of this newer approach:

26. The Committee notes with concern that, in spite of a high GDP growth rate, the extent and depth of poverty continue to increase (art. 11). The Committee recommends that the State party allocate sufficient funds for the full implementation of its poverty eradication strategy. While noting the existence of a formal poverty line to determine the minimum cost of living, the Committee recommends that the State party monitor effectively the impact of its poverty eradication strategy on disadvantaged and marginalized individuals and groups. The Committee urges the State party to ensure the full integration of economic, social and cultural rights in the strategy, as recommended by the Committee in its statement on poverty and the International Covenant on Economic, Social and Cultural Rights (E/C.12/2001/10). The Committee requests the State party to include in its next periodic report detailed information on the results of the measures taken under the strategy, including updated statistical data, on an annual basis, on the percentage of the population living in

[18] CESCR, Summary Record of the 22nd Meeting, E/C.12/1995/SR.22 (18 May 1995), [30] (per Mr Craven).

poverty, disaggregated by gender, age, number of children per household, number of single parent households, rural/urban population and ethnic group.[19]

The Committee has also engaged with the question of the impact of the private sector on the enjoyment of economic, social and cultural rights, and especially the reach of states parties' jurisdiction to encompass private sector economic actors over which they have regulatory authority. In a review of all the Committee's Concluding Observations since 2004, we identified more than 100 references to the role of corporations and/or the private sector, with an increasing instance in more recent years. References are being made not only to the activities of, and responsibilities for, local (domestic) corporations, but foreign or transnational ones as well; to corporations undertaking public functions (ie on behalf of, or under contract to, the state) or purely 'private' enterprise; and to the rights benefits as well as problems that corporations can bring.[20] These concerns culminated in a Statement made by the Committee in 2011 that focused specifically on the corporate sector and the attendant obligations of states:

1. As a result of globalization and the growing role played by non-state actors, the Committee increasingly addresses the obligations of States Parties regarding the impact of the corporate sector on the implementation of the rights under the Covenant. The corporate sector in many instances contributes to the realization of economic, social and cultural rights enshrined in the Covenant through inter alia input to economic development, employment generation, and productive investment. However, the Committee has also frequently observed that corporate activities can adversely affect the enjoyment of Covenant rights. Multiple examples of the related problems range from child labour and unsafe working conditions through restrictions on trade union rights and discrimination against female workers, to harmful impact on the right to health, standard of living, of including indigenous peoples, the natural environment, as well as to the destructive role of corruption. The Committee reiterates the obligation of States Parties to ensure that all economic, social and cultural rights laid down in the Covenant are fully respected and rights holders adequately protected in the context of corporate activities.

[19] CESCR, Concluding Observations: Republic of Korea, E/C.12/KOR/CO/3 (17 December 2009), [26].

[20] The Committee's observations in these respects have covered a range of states. For example: CESCR, Concluding Observations: Cambodia, E/C.12/KHM/CO/1 (12 June 2009), [30], regarding 'the granting of concessions over vast tracts of land to private companies' with little or no redress available to prior owners or occupiers; the Democratic Republic of Congo, E/C.12/COD/CO/4 (16 December 2009), [13] and [14], regarding the endangering of environmental rights and rights of indigenous peoples by mining and logging multinational corporations; Ecuador, E/C.12/1/Add.100 (7 June 2004), [12] and [35], regarding the ecological impact of resource-extracting companies on the land, livelihood and cultural rights of local people; India, E/C.12/IND/CO/5 (8 August 2008), [29], regarding local private sector land acquisitions and the use of genetically modified seed by multinational agribusinesses; and Ukraine, E/C.12/UKR/CO/5 (4 January 2008), [36], regarding discrimination against women in private sector employment. The Committee has not, however, gone so far as the Committee on the Elimination of Racial Discrimination, which has developed a line of argument in recent Concluding Observations that states have extra-territorial responsibilities regarding the human-rights-infringing actions of companies over which they have jurisdiction (principally those domiciled or incorporated within their territorial boundaries)—see CERD, Concluding Observations: Canada, CERD/C/CAN/CO/18 (25 May 2007), [17]; United States of America, CERD/C/USA/CO/6 (8 May 2008), [30]; Australia, CERD/C/AUS/CO/15-17 (27 August 2010), [13]; and the United Kingdom, CERD/C/GBR/CO/18-20 (14 September 2011), [29].

...

3. States Parties have the primary obligation to respect, protect and fulfil the Covenant rights of all persons under their jurisdiction in the context of corporate activities, undertaken by state-owned or private enterprises. This results from Article 2(1) of the Covenant that defines the nature of the obligations of States Parties, referring to legislative and other appropriate implementation steps, which include administrative, financial, educational, social measures, domestic and global needs assessments, and the provision of judicial or other effective remedies.[21]

(II) UTILIZING THE MAXIMUM AVAILABLE RESOURCES

There is an unavoidable subjectivity in the command that a state utilize 'the maximum of its available resources'. There has also been a tendency to view the resources available in purely or mainly financial terms. The questions of whom or what is to determine which resources are available, and what is their maximum, must inevitably rest heavily, or at least initially, on the shoulders of the state under consideration. Certainly, as we discussed above, resources may be available beyond a state's boundaries and the international community has certain responsibilities to supply or make available, and not to deny,[22] resources where necessary. And equally, the resources of the private sector can and should be employed, or at least directed, towards the Covenant's goals, either through the expansion of opportunities for private gain, or by way of more equitable public distribution of private wealth. In this latter respect, a government's fiscal policy—that is, how it raises and spends revenue—is critical. The question of available resources is one that necessarily engages both sides of the fiscal equation. And whereas there has been considerable attention paid to the expenditure side—addressing

[21] CESCR, Statement on the Obligations of States Parties Regarding the Corporate Sector and Economic, Social and Cultural Rights, E/C.12/2011/1 (20 May 2011). This Statement was in part prompted by, and in part reflects, the work of the former Special Representative of the UN Secretary-General on the Issue of Human Rights and Transnational Corporations and Other Business Enterprises (2005-11), and subsequently by the UN Working Group of the same name. See <http://www.ohchr.org/EN/Issues/Business/Pages/SRSGTransCorpIndex.aspx>.

[22] This prescription not to deny international assistance has a number of important facets, including to ensure that where trade sanctions are imposed on a state, the imposing state(s) must guard against unduly hindering the target state from meeting its international human rights obligations by anticipating and tracking sanctions impacts and taking actions to ensure that 'vulnerable groups within the targeted state' do not experience any 'disproportionate suffering' (see CESCR, General Comment No. 8, The relationship between economic sanctions and respect for economic, social and cultural rights (E/C.12/1997/8 (12 December 1997), [11]–[14]). Asbjørn Eide, a former Special Rapporteur on the right to food, has also noted that the right to self-determination under Article 1 in regard to the control and disposition of sovereign resources and wealth must be respected by other states (and, by implication, by corporations) who might otherwise exploit a state's resources to the latter's disadvantage: see Commission on Human Rights, The New International Economic Order and the Promotion of Human Rights: Report on the right to adequate food as a human right submitted by Asbjørn Eide, Special Rapporteur, E/CN.4/Sub.2/1987/23 (7 July 1987), [196]–[203], especially [199], which states that such level of respect 'includes refraining from using or encouraging the use of economic, political or any other type of measure to coerce another state in order to obtain from it the subordination of the exercise of its sovereign rights...'.

the questions of how much, and spent on what—there has, in more recent times, been increased focus on questions relating to the raising of revenue as well.[23] Aside from debt and obtaining funds through international assistance and cooperation, taxation constitutes a vital source of revenue. This being so, the design and structure of a state's taxation framework, as well as its capacity to implement and enforce the regulatory system flowing from it, are matters of fundamental importance. Thus, as a policy brief on Taxes and Human Rights from the Tax Justice Network argues, tax-related obstacles and problems for states in raising the maximum available resources include: the extent of regressive taxation; the form and nature of tax incentives; the weakness of tax authorities; the extent of tax evasion and avoidance; and the size of the informal (ie untaxed) sector.[24]

Whatever the answers to these questions and however these problems are addressed, ultimately the quantum, quality and utility of resources to be made available for the realization of economic, social and cultural rights will in practice be very largely determined by the state itself, precisely because it must (except in the most dysfunctional of states) necessarily be through the state that such resources are to be applied or their application overseen.

The fact that the term 'resources' needs to be understood to encompass more than financial means (critical though they are) further complicates the matter of their identification, calculation and utilization. A state's capacity to deliver on human rights guarantees also includes the extent, fairness and efficacy of its systems of governance, its institutions of administration and its means of dispute-resolution, as well as the existence and strength of its basic infrastructure of public amenities (in transport, health, education, sanitation, power and communication).[25]

The pairing in Article 2(1) of 'economic and technical' as resources upon which states should draw to realize the rights in the Convention clearly points to matters beyond financial means, even if linked closely to them. This much was recognized in the earlier days of the Human Rights Commission's consideration of this provision in the Convention, with, for example, Mr Azkoul, the French representative, arguing that 'the resources of a State should be interpreted broadly to include budgetary appropriations and also technical assistance, international co-operation and other elements'.[26] Indeed, as Maria Socorro Dikono

[23] In this respect initiatives such as the *Social and Economic Rights Fulfilment Index* and the *OPERA Framework* seek to measure and evaluate the relative revenue capacities of states and thereby to assess the degree to which they are fulfilling their obligations to utilize their maximum available resources. See respectively: <http://www.serfindex.org/data/> and <http://www.cesr.org/section.php?id=179>.

[24] Wolfgang Obenland, 'Taxes and Human Rights', Info Steuergerechtigkeit #08e, Policy Brief, Global Policy Forum and Tax Justice Network Germany, February 2013, 2–3.

[25] This broad, contextual approach is reflected in recent studies on the matter—eg, the Queen's University Belfast, *Budget Analysis and the Advancement of Economic and Social Rights in Northern Ireland*, at <http://www.qub.ac.uk/schools/SchoolofLaw/Research/HumanRightsCentre/ResearchProjects/BudgetAnalysis/> and Radhika Balakrishnan, Diane Elson, James Heintz and Nicholas Lusiani (Centre for Women's Global Leadership), 'Maximum Available Resources and Human Rights' (2011), 2–5.

[26] UNGA, Draft International Covenants on Human Rights, E/CN.4/SR.271 (14 May 1952), 5.

makes clear in the following extract, the process of budgetary appropriation and expenditure that state governments typically and regularly go through amply illustrates how integrated are the financial, administrative and technical aspects of any programme that bears on economic and social rights outcomes.

ESC rights advocates can no longer ignore the national budget. The budget is important because it reflects what the state is doing or intends to do. The budget is a translation in financial terms of the action program of the state, coordinating planned expenditures with expected revenue collections and proposed borrowing operations—hence a national plan that cuts across departmental boundaries and ties together all plans and projects. It is the instrument through which a state attempts to carry out the full range of its activities. It converts state development plans and priorities into a program of action.[27]

The African Commission on Human and Peoples' Rights, adopts a similar stance in its Principles and Guidelines on Economic, Social and Cultural Rights in the African Charter on Human and Peoples' Rights, while emphasizing both the revenue raising and expenditure sides of the budgetary equation:

States need sufficient resources to progressively realise economic, social and cultural rights. There are a variety of means through which states may raise these resources, including taxation. The duty of the individual to pay taxes imposed by the African Charter [in Article 29(6)] implies that there is an obligation on the State to institute an effective and fair taxation system and a budgeting process that ensures that economic, social and cultural rights are prioritised in the distribution of resources.[28]

It can be fairly said that the two most compelling features of Article 2(1) comprise questions of the extent of resources, and their nature, and, further, that it has been with these two questions that much of the labour of the Committee on Economic, Social and Cultural Rights has ultimately been concerned. For while it has to be accepted that the logistical and computational exigencies of resource management demand that the target states themselves principally determine whether and how rights are protected, the Committee does not and must not remain impassive. The Committee, naturally, heeds national indicators, measurement and evaluation processes, and resultant data regarding resource capacities and availability, but it also continually strives to impose objective standards and expectations upon the national positions in order to provide some means of comparison and accountability. In particular, the Committee has adopted a baseline perspective to try to establish 'minimum' or 'core' standards of rights protection, beneath which no state can be permitted to fall. Thus, even when economic times are most straitened—indeed, especially then—no state can rightfully claim that the poorest and most vulnerable must suffer (further) diminution of their enjoyment of economic, social and cultural rights. It is precisely in such dire circumstances that, as Bruno Simma, a former member of the Committee, has

[27] Maria Socorro Dikono, 'A Rights-Based Approach towards Budget Analysis; paper commissioned by International Human Rights Internship Program' (1999), 6.

[28] Principles and Guidelines on Economic, Social and Cultural Rights in the African Charter on Human and Peoples' Rights (adopted on 24 October 2011), para. 15.

argued, the ICESCR 'should assume its most important function—that of a last ditch defence for the most vulnerable'.[29] This sentiment is, importantly, reflected in General Comment No. 3:

10. On the basis of the extensive experience gained by the Committee, as well as by the body that preceded it, over a period of more than a decade of examining States parties' reports the Committee is of the view that a minimum core obligation to ensure the satisfaction of, at the very least, minimum essential levels of each of the rights is incumbent upon every State party. Thus, for example, a State party in which any significant number of individuals is deprived of essential foodstuffs, of essential primary health care, of basic shelter and housing, or of the most basic forms of education is, prima facie, failing to discharge its obligations under the Covenant. If the Covenant were to be read in such a way as not to establish such a minimum core obligation, it would be largely deprived of its raison d'être. By the same token, it must be noted that any assessment as to whether a State has discharged its minimum core obligation must also take account of resource constraints applying within the country concerned. Article 2(1) obligates each State party to take the necessary steps 'to the maximum of its available resources'. In order for a State party to be able to attribute its failure to meet at least its minimum core obligations to a lack of available resources it must demonstrate that every effort has been made to use all resources that are at its disposition in an effort to satisfy, as a matter of priority, those minimum obligations.

11. The Committee wishes to emphasize, however, that even where the available resources are demonstrably inadequate, the obligation remains for a State party to strive to ensure the widest possible enjoyment of the relevant rights under the prevailing circumstances. Moreover, the obligations to monitor the extent of the realization, or more especially of the non-realization, of economic, social and cultural rights, and to devise strategies and programmes for their promotion, are not in any way eliminated as a result of resource constraints. The Committee has already dealt with these issues in its General Comment 1 (1989). [These requirements of monitoring and taking appropriate action are elaborated on below, in section (iv) Employing all appropriate means].

12. Similarly, the Committee underlines the fact that even in times of severe resources constraints whether caused by a process of adjustment, of economic recession, or by other factors the vulnerable members of society can and indeed must be protected by the adoption of relatively low-cost targeted programmes. In support of this approach the Committee takes note of the analysis prepared by UNICEF entitled 'Adjustment with a human face: protecting the vulnerable and promoting growth', the analysis by UNDP in its Human Development Report 1990 and the analysis by the World Bank in the World Development Report 1990.[30]

[29] CESCR, Consideration of Report Submitted by State Party: Jamaica, E/C.12/1990/SR.15 (30 January 1990), [7].

[30] CESCR, General Comment No. 3. The reference to these various reports points towards some of the early work—since very substantially enlarged—on the incorporation of human-rights-based approaches to development programming. The *UN Common Statement of Understanding on Human Rights Based-Approach to Development Co-operation and Programming* (2003), available (along with other relevant documents) through the United Nation's HRBA Portal, <http://hrbaportal.org/the-un-and-hrba>, is perhaps the most authoritative of these subsequent initiatives.

Although the concept of 'minimum core obligations' may provide an intellectual framework with which one might be able to establish objective standards against which the states' efforts to protect economic, social and cultural rights can be measured, it still lacks precision, or even easy application in practice. Since its endorsement by the Committee in this General Comment, the notion of there being minimum core obligations has become a central feature in the Covenant's landscape, being cited and further explained in terms of its application in principle, policy and practice to all the Covenant's rights. The idea will therefore be found discussed regularly and often in specific contexts throughout the chapters of this book.[31] Fundamentally, it concerns not only what states must do, but also when, and, increasingly, how—albeit, in all these respects, with qualifications and conditions attached. Thus, it demands that certain minimum standards have to be met immediately by states (the timing question), and that in so doing states must, where necessary, make the required priorities and policy changes (the how question). It is not enough for a state to claim that such are its circumstances that even these minimum standards are beyond its capacity, for when such a claim is made, the burden of proof lies with the state itself to demonstrate why it is unable to shift whatever resources it does have (for example, from spending on the military to primary education, or from subsidising privileged elites to funding basic medical and sanitation services for all).[32] This is what the Committee means by its proclamation in paragraph 11 of the above extract, that a state's obligations to monitor, plan for and realize the Convention's rights are 'not in any way eliminated as a result of resource constraints'.

The 1987 Limburg Principles also reflect these essential obligations of states:

'to the maximum of its available resources'

25. States Parties are obligated, regardless of the level of economic development, to ensure respect for minimum subsistence rights for all.

26. 'Its available resources' refers to both the resources within a State and those available from the international community through international co-operation and assistance.

27. In determining whether adequate measures have been taken for the realization of the rights recognized in the Covenant attention shall be paid to equitable and effective use of and access to the available resources.

[31] In respect, in particular, to labour rights (chapters 8, 9 and 10), the rights to social security (chapter 11), to an adequate standard of living (housing, clothing, food and water) (chapter 13), health (chapter 14), education (chapters 15 and 16), as well as rights to enjoying cultural expression and scientific progress (chapter 17).

[32] The 2003 African Union, Protocol to the African Charter on Human and Peoples' Rights on the Rights of Women (adopted 11 July 2003, 1 AHRLJ 40, entered into force 25 November 2005) makes specific provision for such prioritization, by proclaiming, in Article 10(3), that 'States Parties shall take the necessary measures to reduce military expenditure significantly in favour of spending on social development in general, and the promotion of women in particular', and, in Article 26(2), that 'States Parties undertake to adopt all necessary measures and in particular shall provide budgetary and other resources for the full and effective implementation of the rights herein recognised'.

28. In the use of the available resources due priority shall be given to the realization of rights recognized in the Covenant, mindful of the need to assure to everyone the satisfaction of subsistence requirements as well as the provision of essential services.[33]

Proclamations alone, however, do not prevent continuing abuse or neglect of economic, social and cultural rights, even at the minimum level. The allocation of scarce resources is invariably subject to an array of political, economic, cultural and philosophical demands, of which human rights standards are but one claim. And no matter how fervently we might wish it otherwise, that is the *Realpolitik*.

This much was, in fact, recognized by the Maastricht Guidelines on Violations of Economic, Social and Cultural Rights[34] which, building on the Limburg Principles, were formulated in 1997, on the tenth anniversary of the latter. For while the Guidelines expressly reiterate (in paragraph 10) the four principles extracted above, they also concede the difficulties in meeting them in practice:

1. Since the Limburg Principles were adopted in 1986, the economic and social conditions have declined at alarming rates for over 1.6 billion people, while they have advanced also at a dramatic pace for more than a quarter of the world's population. The gap between rich and poor has doubled in the last three decades, with the poorest fifth of the world's population receiving 1.4% of the global income and the richest fifth 85%. The impact of these disparities on the lives of people—especially the poor—is dramatic and renders the enjoyment of economic, social and cultural rights illusory for a significant portion of humanity.

2. Since the end of the Cold War, there has been a trend in all regions of the world to reduce the role of the state and to rely on the market to resolve problems of human welfare, often in response to conditions generated by international and national financial markets and institutions and in an effort to attract investments from the multinational enterprises whose wealth and power exceed that of many states. It is no longer taken for granted that the realization of economic, social and cultural rights depends significantly on action by the state, although, as a matter of international law, the state remains ultimately responsible for guaranteeing the realization of these rights. While the challenge of addressing

[33] Limburg Principles on the Implementation of the International Covenant on Economic, Social and Cultural Rights, as contained in Commission on Human Rights, Note Verbale dated 5 December 1986 from the Permanent Mission of the Netherlands to the United Nations Office at Geneva addressed to the Centre for Human Rights ('Limburg Principles'), E/CN.4/1987/17 (8 January 1987). The Introduction to the Limburg Principles explains their provenance as follows: 'A group of distinguished experts in international law, convened by the International Commission of Jurists, the Faculty of Law of the University of Limburg (Maastricht, the Netherlands) and the Urban Morgan Institute for Human Rights, University of Cincinnati (Ohio, United States of America), met in Maastricht on 2–6 June 1986 to consider the nature and scope of the obligations of States Parties to the International Covenant on Economic, Social and Cultural Rights, the consideration of States Parties reports by the newly constituted ECOSOC Committee on Economic, Social and Cultural Rights, and international co-operation under Part IV of the Covenant'.

[34] Like the Limburg Principles, the Maastricht Guidelines were the collective effort of thirty experts in the field. In the Introduction to the Guidelines, they are described as being 'designed to be of use to all who are concerned with understanding and determining violations of economic, social and cultural rights and in providing remedies thereto, in particular monitoring and adjudicating bodies at the national, regional and international levels': Maastricht Guidelines on Violations of Economic, Social and Cultural Rights ('Maastricht Guidelines'), E/C.12/2000/13 (26 January 1997), as contained in CESCR, Substantive Issues arising in the implementation of the International Covenant on Economic, Social and Cultural Rights, E/C.12/2000/13 (2 October 2000), 16.

violations of economic, social and cultural rights is rendered more complicated by these trends, it is more urgent than ever to take these rights seriously and, therefore, to deal with the accountability of governments for failure to meet their obligations in this area.[35]

The matter of resources—their composition, availability, utilization and impact—continues to be a vexed and highly complicated question of political opinion, policy choice and practical implementation. And there have been clear signs that with the potential for such a question to be the subject of individual complaints under the Optional Protocol, the Committee is especially mindful of the need to state more precisely what level and extent of obligation, the 'maximum available resources', provision imposes upon states.

1. The Committee on Economic, Social and Cultural Rights welcomes the decision by the Human Rights Council to draft an optional protocol to the Covenant. Such a protocol granting it authority to consider individual and collective communications will assist the Committee in monitoring the implementation of the Covenant by complementing the periodic review of reports, thus strengthening the Committee's interpretation of the Covenant.

2. The Committee is aware of States parties' interest in obtaining further clarification on how it would apply the obligation under article 2(1) 'to take steps ... to the maximum of its available resources' to achieve progressively the full realization of the rights recognized in the Covenant. Of particular relevance is how the Committee would examine communications concerning this obligation, while fully respecting the authority vested in relevant State organs to adopt what it considers to be its most appropriate policies and to allocate resources accordingly. On the basis of its practice under the periodic reporting process, the Committee in this present statement seeks to clarify how it might consider States Parties' obligations under article 2(1) in the context of an individual communications procedure.

...

8. In considering a communication concerning an alleged failure of a State party to take steps to the maximum of available resources, the Committee will examine the measures that the State party has effectively taken, legislative or otherwise. In assessing whether they are 'adequate' or 'reasonable', the Committee may take into account, inter alia, the following considerations:

(a) the extent to which the measures taken were deliberate, concrete and targeted towards the fulfilment of economic, social and cultural rights;

(b) whether the State party exercised its discretion in a non-discriminatory and non arbitrary manner;

(c) whether the State party's decision (not) to allocate available resources is in accordance with international human rights standards;

(d) where several policy options are available, whether the State party adopts the option that least restricts Covenant rights;

(e) the time frame in which the steps were taken;

[35] Maastricht Guidelines, paras. 1 and 2.

(f) whether the steps had taken into account the precarious situation of disadvantaged and marginalized individuals or groups and, whether they were non-discriminatory, and whether they prioritized grave situations or situations of risk.

9. The Committee notes that in case of failure to take any steps or of the adoption of retrogressive steps, the burden of proof rests with the State party to show that such a course of action was based on the most careful consideration and can be justified by reference to the totality of the rights provided for in the Covenant and by the fact that full use was made of available resources.

10. Should a State party use 'resource constraints' as an explanation for any retrogressive steps taken, the Committee would consider such information on a country-by- country basis in the light of objective criteria such as:

(a) the country's level of development;

(b) the severity of the alleged breach, in particular whether the situation concerned the enjoyment of the minimum core content of the Covenant;

(c) the country's current economic situation, in particular whether the country was undergoing a period of economic recession;

(d) the existence of other serious claims on the State party's limited resources; for example, resulting from a recent natural disaster or from recent internal or international armed conflict.

(e) whether the State party had sought to identify low-cost options; and

(f) whether the State party had sought cooperation and assistance or rejected offers of resources from the international community for the purposes of implementing the provisions of the Covenant without sufficient reason.

11. In its assessment of whether a State party has taken reasonable steps to the maximum of its available resources to achieve progressively the realization of the provisions of the Covenant, the Committee places great importance on transparent and participative decision-making processes at the national level. At all times the Committee bears in mind its own role as an international treaty body and the role of the State in formulating or adopting, funding and implementing laws and policies concerning economic, social and cultural rights. To this end, and in accordance with the practice of judicial and other quasi-judicial human rights treaty bodies, the Committee always respects the margin of appreciation of States to take steps and adopt measures most suited to their specific circumstances.

12. Where the Committee considers that a State party has not taken reasonable or adequate steps, it will make relevant recommendations to the State party. In line with the practice of other treaty bodies, the Committee will respect the margin of appreciation of the State party to determine the optimum use of its resources and to adopt national policies and prioritize certain resource demands over others.

13. In the context of an optional protocol, the Committee could make recommendations, inter alia, along four principal lines:

(a) recommending remedial action, such as compensation, to the victim, as appropriate;

(b) calling upon the State party to remedy the circumstances leading to a violation. In doing so, the Committee might suggest goals and parameters to assist the State party in identifying appropriate measures. These parameters could include suggesting overall priorities to ensure that resource allocation conformed with the State party's obligations under the Covenant; provision for the disadvantaged and marginalized individuals and groups; protection against grave threats to the enjoyment of economic, social and cultural rights; and respect for non-discrimination in the adoption and implementation of measures;

(c) suggesting, on a case-by-case basis, a range of measures to assist the State party in implementing the recommendations, with particular emphasis on low-cost measures. The State party would nonetheless still have the option of adopting its own alternative measures;

(d) recommending a follow-up mechanism to ensure ongoing accountability of the State party; for example, by including a requirement that in its next periodic report the State party explain the steps taken to redress the violation.[36]

What is perhaps most evident in this Statement is the Committee's anticipation of having to address resources questions in the context of litigation or quasi-litigation and not just as a matter of policy analysis. However, rather than that yielding clearly defined lines of what is compliant with the provision and what is not, this heightened recognition of the legal boundaries heralds a focus on the reasonableness of a state's actions or excuses for the levels of protection it affords economic, social and cultural rights. In the language of rights obligations, this is a demarcation between obligations of outcome (the actual levels of rights protection) and obligations of conduct (the nature of the efforts to achieve protection).

It is perhaps not surprising to see this shift in emphasis in advance of the OP coming into force—and especially as it borrows directly from the path-breaking jurisprudence of the South African Constitutional Court on this very point[37]—but now that it is in force, we can expect to see from the Committee more of this type of insistence on the states attaining certain levels of care, attention and reasonableness in their actions and justifications regarding their meeting the maximum available resources obligation under the Convention.

(III) ACHIEVING PROGRESSIVELY THE FULL REALIZATION OF RIGHTS

The key to this provision of Article 2(1) is that the full realization of the Convention rights is to be achieved 'progressively'. That is, while it is accepted on the one hand that that full realization may often not be possible immediately, nonetheless, the Committee maintains that the steps to be taken by states ought to be ones that progress towards that goal, not ones that regress.

9. The principal obligation of result reflected in article 2(1) is to take steps 'with a view to achieving progressively the full realization of the rights recognized' in the Covenant. The term 'progressive realization' is often used to describe the intent of this phrase. The

[36] CESCR, Statement: An evaluation of the obligation to take steps to the 'maximum available resources' under an Optional Protocol to the Covenant, E/C.12/2007/1 (10 May 2007).

[37] See further below, text at n. 90.

concept of progressive realization constitutes a recognition of the fact that full realization of all economic, social and cultural rights will generally not be able to be achieved in a short period of time. In this sense the obligation differs significantly from that contained in article 2 of the International Covenant on Civil and Political Rights which embodies an immediate obligation to respect and ensure all of the relevant rights. Nevertheless, the fact that realization over time, or in other words progressively, is foreseen under the Covenant should not be misinterpreted as depriving the obligation of all meaningful content. It is on the one hand a necessary flexibility device, reflecting the realities of the real world and the difficulties involved for any country in ensuring full realization of economic, social and cultural rights. On the other hand, the phrase must be read in the light of the overall objective, indeed the raison d'être, of the Covenant which is to establish clear obligations for States parties in respect of the full realization of the rights in question. It thus imposes an obligation to move as expeditiously and effectively as possible towards that goal. Moreover, any deliberately retrogressive measures in that regard would require the most careful consideration and would need to be fully justified by reference to the totality of the rights provided for in the Covenant and in the context of the full use of the maximum available resources.[38]

In paragraph 2 of the same General Comment,[39] the Committee elaborates on the progressive nature of the steps that are to be taken—that is, that they 'should be deliberate, concrete and targeted as clearly as possible towards meeting the obligations recognized in the Covenant'. Where, however, 'deliberately retrogressive measures' are taken by states, the Committee makes clear in the last sentence of paragraph 9 that they must be carefully considered and 'fully justified'. Plainly, the Committee is reluctant to concede any ground at all on this point, but, once again, it feels obliged to bow to the reality of how states sometimes behave and what circumstances they sometimes find themselves in. The Committee has since underscored these provisos in its 2007 Statement regarding the Optional Protocol to the Covenant,[40] adding, in appropriate litigious terms, that the 'burden of proof rests with the state party' to show that it has abided by these conditions of justification for any retrogressive steps it might take (at paragraph 9).

As we have noted earlier during our discussion of minimum core standards,[41] these standards oblige states to provide protection that has immediate effect. That is—at least on the face of it—that no excuses are acceptable in the view of the Committee for not so providing. Thus, for example, the Committee has made clear that security concerns, including (indeed, especially) in situations of conflict, are not justifiable reasons for the neglect of basic Convention rights.

31. The Committee recognizes that the State party has serious security concerns, which must be balanced with its efforts to comply with its obligations under international human rights law. However, the Committee reaffirms its view that the State party's obligations under the Covenant apply to all territories and populations under its effective control. The Committee repeats its position that even in a situation of armed conflict, fundamental

[38] CESCR, General Comment No. 3, [9].
[39] Extracted above at n. 12.
[40] Extracted above at n. 36.
[41] Above text accompanying n. 31.

human rights must be respected and that basic economic, social and cultural rights, as part of the minimum standards of human rights, are guaranteed under customary international law and are also prescribed by international humanitarian law. Moreover, the applicability of rules of humanitarian law does not by itself impede the application of the Covenant or the accountability of the State under article 2(1) for the actions of its authorities. The Committee therefore requests that the State party provide more extensive information on the enjoyment of economic, social and cultural rights enshrined in the Covenant by those living in the occupied territories in its next periodic report.[42]

And yet, it remains the case that inadequate implementation, even of these 'floor level' standards, is not uncommon, including in respect of countries which are now considered 'emerging economies' and therefore apparently able to afford adequate protection. Thus, for example, there is more than a hint of exasperation on this point in the following extract from the Committee's Concluding Observations in respect of India and what it perceives to be the state's inability to deliver, despite having the resources to do so.

45. The Committee is of the view that the State party has within its power the ability to immediately implement the rights in Part II of the Covenant as required, and to meet, at the least, its core obligations for the progressive realization of the rights in Part III of the Covenant. The Committee therefore urges the State party to review its position regarding its legal obligations arising under the Covenant in light of the Committee's statement on the evaluation of the obligation to take steps to the 'maximum of its available resources' under an optional protocol to the Covenant (E/C.12/2007/1), and its general comments No. 13 (1999) and No. 14 (2000) in relation to core obligations. The Committee also encourages the State party to ensure that the provisions of the Covenant are taken into consideration in legislative and administrative policy and decision-making processes.[43]

The Committee has made much the same argument in respect of the Philippines, with the addition of explicit mention of the connection between the obligations to use maximum available resources and to realize rights fulfilment progressively:

17. The Committee notes with concern that, in spite of a high GDP growth rate, the national spending on social services such as housing, health and education remains low, and has in fact decreased over the years. The Committee draws the attention of the State party to its statement on 'An evaluation of the obligation to take steps to the "maximum of its available resources" under an Optional Protocol to the Covenant' (E/C.12/2007/1), and recommends that the State party increase its national spending on social services such as housing, health and education so as to achieve, in accordance with article 2, paragraph 1, the progressive realization of the economic, social and cultural rights provided for in the Covenant.[44]

Inclusion of the notion of the 'progressive' realization of rights in Article 2(1) was not uncritically accepted by all of those involved in drafting the provision. For while it is evident from the Official Records of the travaux préparatoires that it was generally understood and accepted that the notion of progressiveness would grant to poorer states some latitude in meeting their obligations, there was also

[42] CESCR, Concluding Observations: Israel, E/C.12/1/Add.90 (26 June 2003), [31].
[43] CESCR, Concluding Observations: India, E/C.12/IND/CO/5 (8 August 2008), [45].
[44] CESCR, Concluding Observations: the Philippines, E/C.12/PHL/CO/4 (1 December 2008), [17].

some concern that the notion might be used by richer states and the international community at large to justify the provision of stilted or restricted (or no) assistance to developing states, thereby hampering the fulfilment of rights protection in those countries.

29. Mr SITA (Congo, Léopoldville [now the Democratic Republic of the Congo]) emphasized that economic, cultural and social rights were of great importance for the developing countries, for true political independence and human dignity were unthinkable without a genuine independence in economic, social and cultural matters. He therefore thought it was essential to include the idea of a reasonable time limit in article 2 of the draft Covenant on Economic, Social and Cultural Rights. In his view, the principle of progressive implementation was so elastic that it left room for deliberate misinterpretation and as a result the developing countries might be unable to set up development programmes which would ensure to them true economic independence.

30. As an illustration, he cited the example of developing countries which, like his own, produced mainly raw materials for countries with processing industries. If, under article 2, paragraph 1 of the draft Covenant the States Parties undertook to grant assistance to the under-developed countries, there was a danger that, instead of helping those countries, their assistance would in fact, under the cover of progressive implementation, be aimed solely at a long-range consolidation of their own economies. Moreover, it was to be feared that such foreign aid would only benefit those privileged groups, generally white, which were sometimes to be found in developing countries side by side with poverty-stricken indigenous masses. He recalled in that connexion, that, on the basis of statistics relating to the period preceding his country's independence [in 1960, from Belgium], it had been possible to claim that the country had a prosperous economy. In actual fact, there had been little islands of civilization, with a very high of living, in the midst of a far less privileged rural population. In such cases, if a reasonable time-limit were provided, the developing countries would be enabled to draw up plans for their economy, taking into account not only the view of privileged groups but of the entire population, the text should therefore be strengthened in order to avert what might be called the economic, social and cultural colonization of certain countries.[45]

Whether or not Mr Sita's concerns over this international assistance 'Trojan Horse' have been borne out over the decades since is a matter of debate. But there can be no doubt that many of the scourges he identified stubbornly remain in most developing countries (including the DRC) more than fifty years later: elite capture; poverty; stark inequalities; poor governance; and, often, a lack of 'genuine independence' in economic matters.

That said, it is highly unlikely that, if a time limit had been inserted in the provision, matters would have been any better. As intimated already, the reality of the political and practical exigencies faced by many countries are such that even today they are unable fully to meet the minimum demands of the Covenant. So while the notion of progressive realization may not have averted this circumstance, it has a least allowed flexibility on all sides in seeking to achieve the goal,

[45] UNGA Third Committee, A/C.3/SR.1181 (13 November 1962), [29] and [30].

without the certainty of 'failure' that would have accompanied any imposition of a 'reasonable time limit'.

It is notable in this regard that explicit time limits for the realization of economic, social or cultural rights have not been imposed in any other UN human rights treaty, nor indeed in any of the regional human rights treaties. Thus, for example, whereas neither the American Convention on Human Rights,[46] nor the African Charter on Human and People's Rights,[47] impose specific time scales on when states must effect their rights guarantees, it is evident that the supervisory organs of both interpret states' undertaking to be of immediate effect, even if the implementation is accepted to be incremental to various degrees. This compromise is well illustrated in the Inter-American Court of Human Rights case of *Acevedo Buendia et al v Peru*,[48] in which retirees argued that the state's arbitrary cessation and devaluation of their pension funds violated Peru's obligations under the American Convention on Human Rights. On the one hand, in extending a degree of flexibility to the state, the Court denied that Peru had infringed its duty under Article 26 to 'achieve progressively…the rights implicit in the economic, social, educational, scientific, and cultural standards set forth in the Charter of the Organization of American States'. In doing so, the Court expressly relied upon the view of the ESCR Committee that the notion of 'progressive' implementation 'is a necessary flexibility device, reflecting the realities of the real world […] and the difficulties involved for any country in ensuring full realization of economic, social and cultural right'.[49] However, on the other hand, the Court insisted that Peru had infringed the right to property under Article 21 of the Convention (and specifically Article 21(2) that mandates 'just compensation' when property is compulsorily acquired for public interest reasons), as well as the right to be provided with adequate judicial protection, including remedies for rights breaches, as required under Article 25 of the Convention, when it failed to comply with a domestic court order to compensate the complainants for deprivation of their pension assets.[50]

An apparently less malleable approach has been adopted in the ICERD[51] and the CEDAW,[52] both of which stipulate that policies to eliminate discrimination in their respective spheres are to be pursued by states 'without delay'. The corresponding provision in the CRC (1989), what is more, yields much the same result by declaring that states 'shall respect and ensure the rights set forth in the present Convention' (Article 2(1)). It can be argued that these textual formulae, though hardly precise, are nonetheless more akin to the terms under

[46] American Convention on Human Rights (adopted 22 November 1969, 1144 UNTS 123, entered into force 18 July 1978).

[47] African Charter on Human and Peoples' Rights (adopted 27 June 1981, 1520 UNTS 217, entered into force 21 October 1986).

[48] *Acevedo Buendia et al [Discharged and Retired Employees of the Comptroller] v Peru*, 1 July 2009, Series C No. 198.

[49] *Acevedo Buendia et al v Peru*, [102].

[50] *Acevedo Buendia et al v Peru*, [81] and [91].

[51] International Convention on the Elimination of All Forms of Racial Discrimination (ICERD) (adopted 21 December 1965, 660 UNTS 195, entered into force 4 January 1969), Article 2(1).

[52] Convention on the Elimination of All Forms of Discrimination Against Women (CEDAW) (adopted 20 December 1979, entered into force 3 September 1981), Article 2.

which civil and political rights are expected to be honoured. Given that each of the above instruments blends economic, social and cultural rights with civil and political ones, these nuanced compromises on temporal implementation are unsurprising.

It is therefore of especial interest that the 'progressive realization' formula, having been eschewed in these other instruments, made a reappearance in the Convention on the Rights of Persons with Disabilities (CRPD),[53] which also embraces both categories of rights. What is notable about the CRPD is that for persons with disabilities, it singles out their economic, social and cultural rights alone as being subject to terms of implementation that are almost identical to those used in ICESCR's Article 2(1).[54] In this respect, the United Nations' handbook on *Monitoring the Convention on the Rights of Persons with Disabilities* notes that:

> …with regard to economic, social and cultural rights, the Convention on the Rights of Persons with Disabilities reaffirms the obligation of States to progressively implement them, as already recognized in article 2 of the International Covenant on Economic, Social and Cultural Rights and article 4 of the Convention on the Rights of the Child. The recognition that the full realization of economic, social and cultural rights may be constrained by limited resources is balanced by the requirement that measures should be taken to the maximum of a State's available resources and, where needed, within the framework of international cooperation [as enunciated in the] Convention on the Rights of Persons with Disabilities, arts. 4(2) and 32.[55]

It states further that:

> Several aspects of the progressive realization of economic, social and cultural rights are important for implementation and monitoring purposes:
>
> – Discrimination on any grounds, including disability, is always forbidden, regardless of the level of realization of economic, social and cultural rights;
>
> – States have an immediate obligation to ensure a minimum essential level of enjoyment of each economic, social and cultural right;
>
> – States have an obligation to take steps towards the progressive realization of these rights. A State, for example, can develop a plan of action which should include: (a) a time frame for implementing economic, social and cultural rights; (b) time-bound benchmarks of achievement; and (c) indicators of success;
>
> – States are forbidden from taking regressive steps or measures that diminish the enjoyment of economic, social and cultural rights.[56]

[53] Convention on the Rights of Persons with Disabilities (CRPD) (adopted 13 December 2006, 2515 UNTS 3, entered into force 3 May 2008).

[54] CRPD, Article 4(2) reads: 'With regard to economic, social and cultural rights, each State Party undertakes to take measures to the maximum of its available resources and, where needed, within the framework of international cooperation, with a view to achieving progressively the full realization of these rights, without prejudice to those obligations contained in the present Convention that are immediately applicable according to international law.'

[55] UN Office of the High Commissioner for Human Rights, *Monitoring the Convention on the Rights of Persons with Disabilities*, Guidance for Human Rights Monitors (Professional Training Series No. 17), 28.

[56] UN Office of the High Commissioner for Human Rights, *Monitoring the Convention on the Rights of Persons with Disabilities*, 28.

In light of these other formulations, what is clear about how the term as it appears in Article 2(1) of the ICESCR is to be read by states is that progressive realization entails the taking of steps of the sort elsewhere specified in the provision. This is the tenor of the following extract from a Statement by the Committee, which also provides an appropriate segue into the fourth and final of our elements of the Article 2(1) obligations:

3. Having already examined the terms of article 2(1) in its General Comment No. 3, the Committee reiterates that in order to achieve progressively the full realization of the Covenant, States parties must take deliberate, concrete and targeted steps within a reasonably short time after the Covenant's entry into force for the States concerned. The steps should include 'all appropriate means, including particularly the adoption of legislative measures'. In addition to legislation, the Committee understands the term 'appropriate means' to include the provision of judicial or other remedies, where appropriate, as well as 'administrative, financial, educational and social measures' (General Comment No. 3, para. 7, General Comment No. 9, paras. 3–5, 7).[57]

(IV) EMPLOYING ALL APPROPRIATE MEANS

This criterion in many ways both encapsulates and is the culmination of the other three discussed above. The appropriateness of the means employed will directly determine whether: (i) adequate steps have been taken; (ii) realization has been progressive; and (iii) all available resources have been used. Accordingly, the Committee and other relevant adjudicatory and supervisory bodies have scrutinized this issue more carefully and rigorously. And it is for this reason that we dwell on this criterion for longer than the others.

As noted earlier in this chapter, the question of whether legislation is a necessary means for implementation of the Covenant's rights engendered animated debate during the Convention's drafting, resulting, ultimately, in the stipulation that it must, at least, be one of the means considered to be appropriate. Hardly a ringing endorsement of the need—or indeed the instance, in fact—for legislative action, but the phrase nonetheless serves the valuable purpose of marking one end of the spectrum of measures—both legal and non-legal—that might be adopted. Government policies and goals, administrative guidelines and best practices, economic incentives and rewards, and perceptions of community standards, as well as statutes, secondary rules and judicial and other arbitral body determinations are all part of the panoply of 'appropriate means' that are typically invoked by states in their efforts to promote and protect economic, social and cultural rights:

4. The Committee notes that States parties have generally been conscientious in detailing at least some of the legislative measures that they have taken in this regard. It wishes to emphasize, however, that the adoption of legislative measures, as specifically foreseen by the Covenant, is by no means exhaustive of the obligations of States parties. Rather,

[57] CESCR, Statement: An evaluation of the obligation to take steps to the 'maximum available resources' under an Optional Protocol to the Covenant, E/C.12/2007/1 (10 May 2007).

the phrase 'by all appropriate means' must be given its full and natural meaning. While each State party must decide for itself which means are the most appropriate under the circumstances with respect to each of the rights, the 'appropriateness' of the means chosen will not always be self-evident. It is therefore desirable that States parties' reports should indicate not only the measures that have been taken but also the basis on which they are considered to be the most 'appropriate' under the circumstances. However, the ultimate determination as to whether all appropriate measures have been taken remains one for the Committee to make.

5. Among the measures which might be considered appropriate, in addition to legislation, is the provision of judicial remedies with respect to rights which may, in accordance with the national legal system, be considered justiciable. The Committee notes, for example, that the enjoyment of the rights recognized, without discrimination, will often be appropriately promoted, in part, through the provision of judicial or other effective remedies. Indeed, those States parties which are also parties to the International Covenant on Civil and Political Rights are already obligated (by virtue of arts. 2 (paras. 1 and 3), 3 and 26) of that Covenant to ensure that any person whose rights or freedoms (including the right to equality and non-discrimination) recognized in that Covenant are violated, 'shall have an effective remedy' (art. 2(3)(a)). In addition, there are a number of other provisions in the International Covenant on Economic, Social and Cultural Rights, including articles 3, 7(a)(i), 8, 10(3), 13(2)(a), (3) and (4) and 15(3) which would seem to be capable of immediate application by judicial and other organs in many national legal systems. Any suggestion that the provisions indicated are inherently non-self-executing would seem to be difficult to sustain.

6. Where specific policies aimed directly at the realization of the rights recognized in the Covenant have been adopted in legislative form, the Committee would wish to be informed, *inter alia*, as to whether such laws create any right of action on behalf of individuals or groups who feel that their rights are not being fully realized. In cases where constitutional recognition has been accorded to specific economic, social and cultural rights, or where the provisions of the Covenant have been incorporated directly into national law, the Committee would wish to receive information as to the extent to which these rights are considered to be justiciable (i.e. able to be invoked before the courts). The Committee would also wish to receive specific information as to any instances in which existing constitutional provisions relating to economic, social and cultural rights have been weakened or significantly changed.

7. Other measures which may also be considered 'appropriate' for the purposes of article 2(1) include, but are not limited to, administrative, financial, educational and social measures.[58]

Clearly, therefore, the Committee sees the requirement that states give effect to the Convention's rights 'by all appropriate means', as providing them with 'a broad and flexible approach which enables the particularities of the legal and administrative systems of each State, as well as other relevant considerations, to be taken into account'.[59] The breadth and depth of the provision was, in fact, the result of some deliberation in the Third Committee drafting negotiations. Thus, over a series of

[58] CESCR, General Comment No. 3, [4]–[7].

[59] CESCR, General Comment No. 9, Substantive Issues Arising in the Implementation of the ICESCR ('General Comment No. 9'), E/C.12/1998/24 (3 December 1998), [1].

debates in late 1962,[60] the terms of the provision moved from an original formulation that required both legislative and other measures (what the UK delegate referred to as an impractical 'double obligation'),[61] through a suggestion that states be given a choice of which types of measure they preferred[62] (which many delegates saw as an undesirable weakening of provision), to the finally agreed terms whereby, in the words of the Uruguayan delegate, Mrs Cattarossi, it is 'imperative to stipulate that Member States should undertake to adopt inter alia, legislative measures with a view to achieving the realization of the rights recognized in the Covenant'.[63] The United Kingdom's revised amendment (A/C.3/L.1026/Rev.1)[64] duly reflected that inclusive approach, which, by way of a second revision (A/C.3/L.1026/Rev.2), was supplemented, importantly, with the inclusion of the word 'particularly' to stress the significance of adopting legislative measures.

This significance has been borne out in the practice of the Committee's work. For while it is true, as Mr Herndl, the Austrian Delegate, remarked in regard to the finalized wording, that 'what mattered in the last analysis was not the use of a particular procedure but the effective application of the Covenant, whether by legislative, administrative or other measures',[65] the Committee has nonetheless subsequently made very clear the importance it attaches to states enacting legislation (and enforcing it) as effective means to realize the Covenant's rights. In particular, as General Comment No. 9 makes clear, the provision of remedies and redress for breaches is essential, and that, by implication, is best ensured through statutory means.

> 2. But this flexibility coexists with the obligation upon each State party to use all the means at its disposal to give effect to the rights recognized in the Covenant. In this respect, the fundamental requirements of international human rights law must be borne in mind. Thus the Covenant norms must be recognized in appropriate ways within the domestic legal order, appropriate means of redress, or remedies, must be available to any aggrieved individual or group, and appropriate means of ensuring governmental accountability must be put in place.[66]

The Committee regularly commends states for taking such positive actions, and condemns those that do not, or do so inadequately or ineffectually. So, while it acknowledges other measures, including policy initiatives, administrative rules and practical assistance and guidance, the Committee is especially keen to 'urge' and 'recommend' that states do more in terms of 'hard law' implementation—that is by way of statutes and courts. The following five

[60] UNGA Third Committee, Meetings 1181 to 1185 (UNGA Third Committee, A/C.3/SR.1181 (13 November 1962) to UNGA Third Committee, A/C.3/SR.1185 (16 December 1982)), and 1202 to 1206 (UNGA Third Committee, A/C.3/SR.1202 (5 December 1962) to UNGA Third Committee, A/C.3/SR.1206 (10 December 1962)).

[61] UNGA Third Committee, A/C.3/SR.1182 (14 November 1962), [19].

[62] As proposed by the UK Delegation, UNGA Third Committee, A/C.3/SR.1182 (14 November 1962), per amendment A/C.3/L.1026.

[63] UNGA Third Committee, A/C.3/SR.1185 (16 November 1962), [21].

[64] UNGA Third Committee, A/C.3/SR.1185 (16 November 1962), [39] (per Sir Douglas Glover (UK)).

[65] UNGA Third Committee, A/C.3/SR.1205 (7 December 1962), [3].

[66] CESCR, General Comment No. 9, [2].

extracts from Concluding Observations of the Committee clearly illustrate the concerns and objects of its thinking in this regard. Here we can see the Committee exhorting states to incorporate or entrench in law, or otherwise make justiciable,[67] the provisions of the Convention, to address the inadequate implementation of the Convention in courts, across all levels of government and through human rights commissions and civil society organizations, and to monitor the progress in doing so.

For example, in relation to the United Kingdom:

10. The Committee also finds disturbing the position of the State party that provisions of the Covenant, with certain minor exceptions, constitute principles and programmatic objectives rather than legal obligations, and that consequently the provisions of the Covenant cannot be given legislative effect.[68]

…21. The Committee suggests that the State party take appropriate steps to introduce into legislation the International Covenant on Economic, Social and Cultural Rights, so that the rights covered by the Covenant may be fully implemented…[69]

New Zealand:

11. The Committee notes with regret the view expressed by the State party's delegation that economic, social and cultural rights are not necessarily justiciable…

21. Affirming the principle of the interdependence and indivisibility of all human rights, the Committee encourages the State party to reconsider its position regarding the justiciability of economic, social and cultural rights. Moreover, the Committee points out that the State party remains under an obligation to give full effect to the Covenant in its domestic legal order, providing for judicial and other remedies for violations of economic, social and cultural rights. In this respect, the Committee draws the attention of the State party to its general comment No. 9 on the domestic application of the Covenant.[70]

Australia:

C. Factors and difficulties impeding the implementation of the Covenant

13. In spite of existing guarantees pertaining to economic, social and cultural rights in the State party's domestic legislation, the Covenant continues to have no legal status at the federal and state level, thereby impeding the full recognition and applicability of its provisions.

D. Principal subjects of concern

14. The Committee regrets that, because the Covenant has not been entrenched as law in the domestic legal order, its provisions cannot be invoked before a court of law…

[67] See discussion in following section regarding the 'justiciability' of economic, social and cultural rights.

[68] The Committee used the same condemnatory tone in its 'disagreement' with a very similar stance adopted by Switzerland: CESCR, Concluding Observations: Switzerland, E/C.12/1/Add.30 (7 December 1998), [10].

[69] CESCR, Concluding Observations: The United Kingdom of Great Britain and Northern Ireland, E/C.12/1/Add.19 (12 December 1997), [10] and [21].

[70] CESCR, Concluding Observations: New Zealand, E/C.12/1/Add.88 (26 June 2003), [11] and [21].

24. The Committee strongly recommends that the State party incorporate the Covenant in its legislation, in order to ensure the applicability of the provisions of the Covenant in the domestic courts. The Committee urges the State party to ensure that no conflicts occur between Commonwealth and state law in this respect. The Committee encourages the State party to follow the High Court's position concerning 'legitimate expectations' arising from the ratification of the Covenant.[71]

Canada (1998):

52. …The Committee consequently urges the Federal Government to take concrete steps to ensure that the provinces and territories are made aware of their legal obligations under the Covenant and that the Covenant rights are enforceable within the provinces and territories through legislation or policy measures and the establishment of independent and appropriate monitoring and adjudication mechanisms.[72]

Canada (2006):

11. The Committee regrets that most of its 1993 and 1998 recommendations in relation to the second and third periodic reports have not been implemented, and that the State party has not addressed in an effective manner the following principal subjects of concern, which are still relevant: (a) The State party's restrictive interpretation of its obligations under the Covenant, in particular its position that it may implement the legal obligations set forth in the Covenant by adopting specific measures and policies rather than by enacting legislation specifically recognizing economic, social and cultural rights, and the consequent lack of awareness, in the provinces and territories, of the State party's legal obligations under the Covenant; (b) The lack of legal redress available to individuals when governments fail to implement the Covenant, resulting from the insufficient coverage in domestic legislation of economic, social and cultural rights, as spelled out in the Covenant; the lack of effective enforcement mechanisms for these rights; the practice of governments of urging upon their courts an interpretation of the Canadian Charter of Rights and Freedoms denying protection of Covenant rights, and the inadequate availability of civil legal aid, particularly for economic, social and cultural rights…

35. The Committee reiterates its recommendation that the federal Government take concrete steps to ensure that provinces and territories are made aware of the State party's legal obligations under the Covenant, that the Covenant rights should be enforceable within provinces and territories through legislation or policy measures, and that independent and appropriate monitoring and adjudication mechanisms be established in this regard. In particular, the State party should establish transparent and effective mechanisms, involving all levels of government as well as civil society, including indigenous peoples, with the specific mandate to follow up on the Committee's concluding observations.[73]

And India:

9. The Committee is concerned that, despite the significant role played by the Supreme Court of India in interpreting the Constitution with a view to achieving justiciability of economic, social and cultural rights, the Covenant is not given its full effect in the legal system

[71] CESCR, Concluding Observations: Australia, E/C.12/1/Add.50 (11 September 2000), [13], [14] and [24].

[72] CESCR, Concluding Observations: Canada, E/C.12/1/Add.31 (10 December 1998), [52].

[73] CESCR, Concluding Observations: Canada, E/C.12/CAN/CO/4 (22 May 2006), [11] and [35].

of the State party due to the absence of relevant domestic legislation. The Committee is also concerned by the non-implementation of court decisions by state authorities.

10. The Committee is concerned about the absence of effective mechanisms to coordinate and ensure, at both the federal and state levels, administrative and policy measures relating to economic, social and cultural rights, which constitutes a major impediment to the equal and effective implementation of the Covenant in the State party.

11. The Committee notes with concern that the National Human Rights Commission (NHRC) and the State Human Rights Commissions are not supported by adequate financial and other resources. The Committee is also concerned that the establishment of Human Rights Courts at the district level as envisaged by the 1993 Human Rights Act has not been implemented in most parts of the country, and that the mandate of the Human Rights Courts does not cover violations of economic, social and cultural rights.[74]

The incorporation of economic, social and cultural rights at the level of constitutional law would seem to be the most secure (and elevated) manner of legal implementation. As the Committee notes in General Comment No. 9, incorporation of the Convention into domestic law 'has often been done by means of constitutional provisions according priority to the provisions of international human rights treaties over any inconsistent domestic laws'.[75] And many countries, more especially those in the Civil Law tradition (it is no mere coincidence that all five of the above extracts relate to common law jurisdictions), have indeed pursued this path. It is clear, however, that there are often significant gaps between promise and practice.

In respect of some states, such as Greece, the constitutional guarantee of Convention rights is clear, but what is missing is sufficient 'awareness of the individual entitlements under the Covenant and of the justiciable elements of all rights contained therein as defined in the Committee's general comments, among members of the legal professions, in particular judges and attorneys, as well as among the general public'.[76] The Committee has also raised almost identical concerns with the Philippines,[77] with Japan—albeit there focusing on the need for greater recognition of constitutional guarantees in the state's law-making, administrative and judicial processes[78]—and with Lithuania, where it recommended that the state 'take measures to raise awareness of the Covenant and of the possibility of invoking its provisions before the courts among the public at large and the judiciary'.[79]

For other states, however, the problems of constitutional incorporation are more complex. Thus, for example, the Committee has voiced its concern over the fact that despite the constitutionally protected status in both Austria[80] and

[74] CESCR, Concluding Observations: India, E/C.12/IND/CO/5 (8 August 2008), [9]–[11].
[75] CESCR, General Comment No. 9, [9].
[76] CESCR, Concluding Observations: Greece, E/C.12/1/Add.97 (7 June 2004), [30].
[77] CESCR, Concluding Observations: the Philippines, E/C.12/PHL/CO/4 (1 December 2008), [12].
[78] CESCR, Concluding Observations: Japan, E/C.12/1/Add.67 (24 September 2001), [10].
[79] CESCR, Concluding Observations: Lithuania, E/C.12/1/Add.96 (7 June 2004), [30].
[80] CESCR, Concluding Observations: Austria, E/C.12/1994/16 (14 December 1994), [10]. The Committee adds, ruefully, that this is 'unlike the European Convention for the Protection of Human Rights and Fundamental Freedoms, which has been incorporated into domestic legislation and has the force of constitutional law', [10].

Madagascar,[81] the Convention cannot be directly invoked in either of their respective domestic courts. And with South Korea, the Committee notes with some dismay that while the Constitution grants protection to Covenant rights, it does so only as the same level as ordinary domestic legislation (and can, therefore, be overridden), and that, additionally, there is a 'lack of clarity as to whether all Covenant rights can be invoked in domestic courts'.[82]

There is, further, a sort of 'half-way house' between full constitutional incorporation of the Covenant and proclaiming that the rights it contains are merely desirable policy goals. Some constitutions contain so-called 'Directive Principles of State Policy' (DPSP), which though non-justiciable,[83] nonetheless have the added force of being enshrined in a state's constitution and not simply a policy initiative of government, a minister or a departmental bureaucracy. The Constitutions of India and Ireland, contain such provisions which, by their exhortation for the state to 'strive to promote the welfare of the whole people by securing and protecting as effectively as it may a social order in which justice and charity shall inform all the institutions of the national life' (as Article 45(1) of the Irish Constitution puts it), directly promote many economic, social and cultural rights. Such broad-based Directive Principles are also found in the Constitutions of Nigeria, Lesotho and Sierra Leone, while in the other African states of Ethiopia, Ghana and Uganda, specific economic, social and cultural rights are expressed in both justiciable and non-justiciable formulations in their respective constitutions.[84] Aside from the obvious intention that all such principles provide a template for directing the policies and practices of governments (being 'fundamental in the governance of the country', as the Indian Constitution puts it),[85] they have also proved on occasion to obtain the force of law, as our discussion of the so-called *Bombay Pavement Dwellers* case in chapter 13 below on the right to an adequate standard of living strikingly illustrates in respect of that right.[86]

Meeting Obligations in Practice

We conclude this chapter by considering four key features of the actual practice of states meeting the obligations imposed upon them by Article 2(1). These are: the supposedly vexed issue of the justiciability of economic, social and cultural

[81] CESCR, Concluding Observations: Madagascar, E/C.12/MDG/CO/2 (16 December 2009), [8].

[82] CESCR, Concluding Observations: Republic of Korea, E/C.12/1/Add.59 (21 May 2001), [15].

[83] Usually explicitly so—the Constitution of India, for example, states in section 37 that the DPSP 'shall not be enforceable by any court', but it then adds that 'the principles therein laid down are nevertheless fundamental in the governance of the country and it shall be the duty of the State to apply these principles in making laws fundamental in the governance of the country and it shall be the duty of the State to apply these principles in making laws'.

[84] For discussion of these provisions in the named African states, see Frans Viljoen, *International Human Rights in Africa* (Oxford University Press, Oxford, 2007), 576–81.

[85] Section 37 of the Indian Constitution.

[86] That is, *Tellis v Bombay Municipal Corporation*, 10 July 1985, (1987) LRC (Const) 351 (Supreme Court of India).

rights; the necessity of adequate planning for and implementation of appropriate laws and policies; the question of who (or what) determines which of these means (or others) are indeed appropriate; and finally, addressing the unavoidable pressures placed by domestic and international politics on states regarding implementation of the rights guaranteed under the Covenant.

JUSTICIABILITY

The question of the justiciability of economic, social and cultural rights has reserved for itself a special place in the jurisprudence and practice of human rights generally. In respect of the Covenant in particular—and reflecting the nature of the Covenant drafting debates over the purported differences in the curial enforceability of civil and political rights as compared to those in the ICESCR—the Committee devoted some effort to explaining what it considered to be the correct interpretation of the situation in its General Comment No. 9:

Justiciability

10. In relation to civil and political rights, it is generally taken for granted that judicial remedies for violations are essential. Regrettably, the contrary assumption is too often made in relation to economic, social and cultural rights. This discrepancy is not warranted either by the nature of the rights or by the relevant Covenant provisions. The Committee has already made clear that it considers many of the provisions in the Covenant to be capable of immediate implementation. Thus, in General Comment No. 3 it cited, by way of example, articles 3, 7(a)(i), 8, 10.3, 13.2(a), 13.3, 13.4 and 15.3. It is important in this regard to distinguish between justiciability (which refers to those matters which are appropriately resolved by the courts) and norms which are self-executing (capable of being applied by courts without further elaboration). While the general approach of each legal system needs to be taken into account, there is no Covenant right which could not, in the great majority of systems, be considered to possess at least some significant justiciable dimensions. *It is sometimes suggested that matters involving the allocation of resources should be left to the political authorities rather than the courts. While the respective competences of the various branches of government must be respected, it is appropriate to acknowledge that courts are generally already involved in a considerable range of matters which have important resource implications.* The adoption of a rigid classification of economic, social and cultural rights which puts them, by definition, beyond the reach of the courts would thus be arbitrary and incompatible with the principle that the two sets of human rights are indivisible and interdependent. It would also drastically curtail the capacity of the courts to protect the rights of the most vulnerable and disadvantaged groups in society.[87]

The essentially contested feature of the justiciability of economic, social and cultural rights is captured by the sentences that we have highlighted in the above extract. In fact, what the Committee does not here add is that the most important and indeed pervasive way in which 'courts are already generally involved' in the

[87] CESCR, General Comment No. 9, [10] (emphasis added).

field of resource allocation is through administrative law. The time-honoured and straight-forwardness of this means of holding governments to account for their many actions or inactions, including in respect of economic, social and cultural rights, may seem to be as obvious as it is profound. But it is a curious fact that until the implications of the iconoclastic decision of the Constitutional Court of South Africa in *Soobramoney v Minister of Health (Kwazulu-Natal)*[88] became widely appreciated (and it is interesting to note that the case was decided fully one year before the Committee General Comment was published), the notion that the basic principles of administrative law provide an excellent vehicle to advance such rights before the courts had barely been considered. But they did, and they do. In the *Soobramoney* case (and in a steady stream of South African cases that pursue the same line of reasoning),[89] the court has made clear that constitutionally enshrined rights such as the right to emergency health care in section 27(3) of the South African Constitution are not absolute, but that any limitations that are imposed need to be reasonable in aim and format, and be 'applied fairly and rationally'.[90]

It follows therefore, that where states fail to act, act unreasonably or otherwise in disregard of their rights' obligations, then adjudicatory bodies will likely find them to have violated those obligations. Thus, for example, the African Commission on Human and Peoples' Rights in *SERAC v Nigeria*[91] held that the Government of Nigeria had violated numerous economic and social rights under the African Charter on Human and Peoples' Rights (including to the rights to life, physical safety, health, property and environment) by failing to 'move its machinery towards the actual realisation of the rights' by way of, for example, 'direct provision of basic needs such as food or resources that can be used for food (direct food aid and social security)'. The Commission underscored this obligation with an express reference to the relevance of 'all appropriate means' formulation in Article 2(1) of the ICESCR, adding that 'depending on the type of rights under consideration... [s]ometimes the need meaningfully to enjoy some of the rights demands a concerted action from the state in terms of more than one of the said duties [ie to employ legislative, policy or court-enforced means]'.[92]

In a similar vein, in another judicial review case, the High Court of Malawi, in *Masangano v Attorney-General*,[93] found that the chronic overcrowding in the country's prisons, and the severe maltreatment of inmates who were routinely denied sufficient food, clothing, shelter, physical safety and access to health care, amounted to cruel, inhuman and degrading treatment contrary to section 44 of the Malawi Constitution. After dismissing the pleas of the state that it lacked sufficient resources and that, in any case, matters of socio-economic rights as were

[88] ('*Soobramoney*'), 27 November 1997, CCT32/97, [1997] ZACC 17.

[89] Danie Brand, 'Introduction to Socio-Economic Rights in the South African Constitution' in Danie Brand and Christof Heyns (eds), *Socio-Economic Rights in South Africa* (Pretoria University Law Press, Pretoria, 2005), 1–56.

[90] *Soobramoney*, [25].

[91] *SERAC v Nigeria*, 13–27 October 2001, (2001) AHRLR 60.

[92] *SERAC v Nigeria*, [47] and [48].

[93] 9 November 2009, (2009) AHRLR 353.

at issue in this case were non-justiciable under the Malawian Constitution,[94] the court directed that the state was:

> ...to comply with this judgment within a period of 18 months by taking concrete steps in reducing prison overcrowding by half, thereafter periodically reducing the remainder to eliminate overcrowding and by improving the ventilation in our prisons and, further, by improving prison conditions generally. Parliament through the Prisons Act and Prison Regulations set minimum standards on the treatment of prisoners in Malawi, which standards are in tandem with international minimum standards in the area. Parliament should therefore make available to the respondents adequate financial resources to enable them meet their obligations under the law to comply with this judgment and the minimum standards set in the Prisons Act and Prison Regulations.[95]

The fact of the justiciability of socio-economic rights points very clearly to the way in which the Committee will interpret and apply the rights under the Covenant in the individual communications that now come before it. This is one effective step towards making economic, social and cultural rights more tangible in law and practice.

PLANNING AND IMPLEMENTATION

Another step in this direction is the Committee's insistence that at the very least, states earnestly engage with their obligations by devising strategies and policy programmes that will fulfil them. Thus, it states in General Comment No. 3 that 'the obligations to monitor the extent of the realization, or more especially of the non-realization, of economic, social and cultural rights, and to devise strategies and programmes for their promotion, are not in any way eliminated as a result of resource constraints'.[96] This focus on planning as an appropriate means of implementation is in fact a reflection of how all four of the elements of Article 2(1) that we have discussed in this chapter intersect and co-depend. Planning is one of the first concrete steps states can take towards progressive realization, which requires not only consideration of which measures to employ, but also what resources are needed to achieve the declared goals. The Committee captured the essence and importance of planning in its General Comment No. 5, which although focusing on fulfilment of the rights of disabled people nevertheless applies generally to implementation of the Covenant's obligations:

> 13. The methods to be used by States parties in seeking to implement their obligations under the Covenant towards persons with disabilities are essentially the same as

[94] The non-justiciability contention was based, in part, on the argument that the human dignity standards (to health, welfare and safety of the people generally) claimed by the applicants were merely directive principles under section 13 of the Constitution, and thus were non-binding. But the Court dismissed that argument by noting that under section 14 of the Constitution, these principles 'could be used by courts in interpreting and applying any provisions of this Constitution or any law or in determining the validity of decisions of the executive and in the interpretation of the provisions of this Constitution': *Masangano v Attorney-General*, [19] and [28].

[95] *Masangano v Attorney-General*, [52].

[96] CESCR, General Comment No. 3, [11] (as extracted above at n. 30).

> those available in relation to other obligations (see General Comment No. 1 (Third session, 1989)). They include the need to ascertain, through regular monitoring, the nature and scope of the problems existing within the State; the need to adopt appropriately tailored policies and programmes to respond to the requirements thus identified; the need to legislate where necessary and to eliminate any existing discriminatory legislation; and the need to make appropriate budgetary provisions or, where necessary, seek international cooperation and assistance. In the latter respect, international cooperation in accordance with articles 22 and 23 of the Covenant is likely to be a particularly important element in enabling some developing countries to fulfil their obligations under the Covenant.[97]

Articles 22 and 23 of the ICESCR, as referred to above, read as follows:

Article 22

The Economic and Social Council may bring to the attention of other organs of the United Nations, their subsidiary organs and specialized agencies concerned with furnishing technical assistance any matters arising out of the reports referred to in this part of the present Covenant which may assist such bodies in deciding, each within its field of competence, on the advisability of international measures likely to contribute to the effective progressive implementation of the present Covenant.

Article 23

The States Parties to the present Covenant agree that international action for the achievement of the rights recognized in the present Covenant includes such methods as the conclusion of conventions, the adoption of recommendations, the furnishing of technical assistance and the holding of regional meetings and technical meetings for the purpose of consultation and study organized in conjunction with the Governments concerned.

The Committee is, therefore, looking for evidence of Member States making plans for how they will implement obligations, as much as their fulfilment, and where such planning is absent or deficient, then states are failing to meet their commitments. An indication of what this can mean in practice is provided by the South African Constitutional Court in *Minister of Health et al v Treatment Action Campaign et al.*[98] In this case a group of civil society organizations lead by Treatment Action Campaign successfully argued that the shortcomings of the South African Government's treatment programme for combatting HIV/AIDS in the community were contrary to the state's obligations under section 27 of the South African Constitution to provide access to health care services and to take appropriate steps towards realizing that right of access.[99] The Court found that the government's programme had *not* reasonably addressed the need to reduce the risk of HIV-positive mothers transmitting the disease to their babies at birth. More specifically, the Court held that the government had acted unreasonably

[97] CESCR, General Comment No. 5, Persons with Disabilities ('General Comment No. 5'), E/1994/22 (9 December 1994), [13].

[98] 5 July 2002, (2002) Case No. CCT 8/02, (2002) AHRLR 189.

[99] Which section reads: '(1) Everyone has the right to have access to (a) health care services, including reproductive health care ... [and] (2) The state must take reasonable legislative and other measures, within its available resources, to achieve the progressive realisation of each of these rights.'

in: (a) refusing to make the antiretroviral drug Nevirapine available in the public health sector where the attending doctor considered it medically indicated; and (b) not setting a time frame for the institution of a national programme to prevent mother-to-child transmission of HIV. Further, the Court's order contained the following directions to the government as to the manner and form of its policy formulation:

It is declared that:

(a) Sections 27(1) and (2) of the Constitution require the government to devise and implement within its available resources a comprehensive and co-ordinated programme to realise progressively the rights of pregnant women and their newborn children to have access to health services to combat mother-to-child transmission of HIV.

(b) The programme to be realised progressively within available resources must include reasonable measures for counselling and testing pregnant women for HIV, counselling HIV-positive pregnant women on the options open to them to reduce the risk of mother-to-child transmission of HIV, and making appropriate treatment available to them for such purposes.

(c) The policy for reducing the risk of mother-to-child transmission of HIV as formulated and implemented by government fell short of compliance with the requirements in sub-paragraphs (a) and (b) in that:

(i) Doctors at public hospitals and clinics other than the research and training sites were not enabled to prescribe nevirapine to reduce the risk of mother-to-child transmission of HIV even where it was medically indicated and adequate facilities existed for the testing and counselling of the pregnant women concerned.

(ii) The policy failed to make provision for counsellors at hospitals and clinics other than at research and training sites to be trained in counselling for the use of nevirapine as a means of reducing the risk of mother-to-child transmission of HIV.[100]

The Committee on Economic, Social and Cultural Rights has endorsed the so-called human rights-based approach (HRBA) to the realization of development goals that directly impact thereby fulfilment of the Covenant's rights. Such an approach—according to the United Nations—adopts the view that international human rights instruments ought to 'guide all development cooperation and programming in all sectors and in all phases of the programming process', thereby 'contribut[ing] to the development of the capacities of "duty-bearers" to meet their obligations and/or of "rights-holders" to claim their rights'.[101] Thus, for example, in a number of Concluding Observations, the Committee has urged that states

[100] *Minister of Health et al v Treatment Action Campaign et al (No. 2)* (CCT8/02) [2002] ZACC 15; 2002 (5) SA 721; 2002 (10) BCLR 1033 (5 July 2002), [135].

[101] The UN Human Rights Based Approach to Development Cooperation: Towards a Common Understanding Among UN Agencies ('The Common Understanding'), which was adopted by the UNDG in 2003. The Introduction to the Statement proclaims that 'the purpose behind developing a common understanding was to ensure that UN agencies, funds and programmes apply a consistent Human Rights-Based Approach to common programming processes at global and regional levels, and especially at the country level…'. See The UN's Human Rights Practitioners' Portal onto

incorporate a HRBA into existing strategies or programmes, such as Afghanistan's National Development Strategy,[102] Bosnia-Herzegovina's terms of reference for its State Ombudsman[103] and Ireland's National Anti-Poverty Strategy.[104] In respect of the critical issue of data collection, the Committee has emphasized (to South Korea) 'that a human rights approach to government actions must begin with a proper understanding of the actual situation in respect of each right, accurate identification of the most vulnerable groups, and the formulation of appropriate laws, programmes and policies. It urges the national statistical agencies and relevant ministries to review the ways in which data relating to all rights are collected through the lens of the Covenant.'[105]

WHO DETERMINES WHAT IS 'APPROPRIATE'?

A final comment on the 'all appropriate means' provision is borne of the latitude we have seen that the provision allows to states in their choice of means of implementation, together with the very *fact* of the various means they employ in practice. For this circumstance appears to have compelled the Committee to adopt a strong supervisory stance over what means it considers to be 'appropriate' and whether they have been taken or not. Thus, in General Comment No. 3, in the final sentence of paragraph 4 (extracted above), the Committee arrogates to itself the position of final arbiter of these questions.[106] It may be well and good for the Committee to claim as much, but the fact remains that in practice its determinations are delivered as particularized recommendations (in Concluding Observations, as we see above, and now in views on individual communications, regarding specific states), or more broadly, through General Comments, rather than dispositive determinations. In respect of General Comments, for example, these recommendations range from the obvious and generic ('means used should be appropriate in the sense of producing results which are consistent with the full discharge of [a state's] obligations'),[107] to the more practical and precise (consider the detailed policy and practice suggestions in General Comment No. 5).[108]

Human Rights Based Approaches to Programming at <http://hrbaportal.org/the-human-rights-based-approach-to-development-cooperation-towards-a-common-understanding-among-un-agencies>.

102 CESCR, Concluding Observations: Afghanistan, E/C.12/AFG/CO/2-4 (7 June 2010), [14].

103 CESCR, Concluding Observations: Bosnia-Herzegovina, E/C.12/BIH/CO/1 (24 January 2006), [30].

104 CESCR, Concluding Observations: Republic of Ireland, E/C.12/1/Add.77 (5 June 2002), [25].

105 CESCR, Concluding Observations: Republic of Korea, E/C.12/1/Add.59 (21 May 2001), [34].

106 It is noticeable that the language used in General Comment No. 9 is significantly less strident in this regard, simply noting that 'the means chosen are also subject to review as part of the Committee's examination of the State Party's compliance with its obligations under the Covenant': CESCR, General Comment No. 9, [5].

107 CESCR, General Comment No. 9, [5].

108 CESCR, General Comment No. 5, [19]–[35]. These paragraphs stipulate specific examples of how the rights of persons with disabilities under the Covenant can be more effectively protected, including, for example, that states should ensure that public places and workplaces are designed so as to accommodate wheelchairs – [22]; and that teachers are trained to educate children with disabilities within regular schools and that the necessary equipment and support be provided, such as—for deaf children—recognizing sign language as a separate language to which all children should have access – [35].

In the end, however, such is the diversity of means of implementation—simple and complex; direct and indirect; orthodox and heterodox; effective and less effective—they will elude rigid standardization and, for reasons of practice and politics, their appropriateness will continue to be assessed by the Committee on a case-by-case basis.

THE POLITICS OF IMPLEMENTATION

Indeed, the acid test for the Committee—as well as for all others wishing to assess compliance with the terms of Article 2(1) of the Covenant—is much more than merely what states have committed themselves to observe (necessary though that be), but whether and how they honour their obligations. As the preceding analyses of the fourfold aspects of states parties' obligations bear out, the manner and form by which states 'take steps' using 'all available resources' and by 'all appropriate means' to 'progressively realise' the Covenant's rights, and how well they are adjudged to do so, is complex and intertwined, rather than simple and linear. States approach their obligations regarding economic, social and cultural rights synthetically, whereby, typically, they combine broad-brush approaches (for example, overarching social welfare, health, housing or education goals and policies) with very particular programmes of action (for example, water sanitation; access to health care and/or educational services for persons with disabilities; occupational health and safety standards, and laws protecting cultural heritage) to try to fulfil their duties. As such, the wider circumstantial contexts of each state will invariably impact on the state's capacity, opportunity and willingness to deliver what is demanded of it. The political and economic contexts are necessarily and fundamentally determinative, precisely because of the promissory (ie political) and productive (ie economic) commitments that Article 2(1) requires of signatory states.

The question of how far these economic and political factors can be allowed to determine economic, social and cultural rights outcomes before one can say that they themselves must be changed is, as we have seen, a moot point in respect of this Article. To what extent, in other words, is it acceptable for states to point to such factors as the (or the primary) reasons for their poor record of rights protection? When are they indeed victims of circumstance—and so some latitude may be extended to them? And when are they the architect of their plight—and so ill-deserving of leniency? Much of the 'line-drawing' undertaken by the Committee in its General Comments and Concluding Observations is predicated on addressing these very questions, with the notion of 'minimum core obligations' as discussed above being a foremost example of such a stance.

The Committee has, however, adopted a somewhat ambiguous stance as regards what type or types of political and economic system are acceptable vehicles for guaranteeing rights, as illustrated in the following extract from General Comment No. 3. For while, on the one hand, the Committee proclaims that steps and measures to be taken by states under the terms of Article 2(1) do not 'require or preclude' any particular version of political economy, it then insists in the same sentence precisely to do so, by imposing the condition that it must be democratic. The remainder of the relevant paragraph in the General Comment as extracted below does little to disentangle either where that leaves states that are, or are professed to be, non-democratic, or what precisely are the boundaries of 'democratic':

8. The Committee notes that the undertaking 'to take steps ... by all appropriate means including particularly the adoption of legislative measures' neither requires nor precludes any particular form of government or economic system being used as the vehicle for the steps in question, provided only that it is democratic and that all human rights are thereby respected. Thus, in terms of political and economic systems the Covenant is neutral and its principles cannot accurately be described as being predicated exclusively upon the need for, or the desirability of a socialist or a capitalist system, or a mixed, centrally planned, or *laissez-faire* economy, or upon any other particular approach. In this regard, the Committee reaffirms that the rights recognized in the Covenant are susceptible of realization within the context of a wide variety of economic and political systems, provided only that the interdependence and indivisibility of the two sets of human rights, as affirmed *inter alia* in the preamble to the Covenant, is recognized and reflected in the system in question. The Committee also notes the relevance in this regard of other human rights and in particular the right to development.[109]

In terms specifically of the role of law and legal means in meeting the Covenant's obligations, the political and economic contexts are also vitally important. The law is, in fact, both a player and stage in this respect. It reflects the mores and practicalities of the particular political economy in which it operates, but it is also a tool by which that political economy is fashioned. And while both necessary and useful, too much cannot, and should not, be expected of the law to deliver the complete package of human rights protections—more especially, when those rights are economic, social and cultural in form. Conor Gearty, a human rights law professor, warns that '[l]aw is simply not good at securing the kinds of changes we need to make if we are serious (as we ought to be) about embedding social rights in our culture. It is politically insensitive and sociologically illiterate, and no end of excellence on the part of its well-meaning practitioners can change these brute facts.'[110] The limits of the law in respect of obtaining the desirable goals of human rights is also underscored—albeit less surprisingly—by certain economists. Amartya Sen (an economics and philosophy professor), for example, argues that the legal routes to understanding and implementing human rights—while nearly always essential—are not alone sufficient, as the concept of 'human rights' (and we might add here, especially economic, social and cultural rights)

[109] CESCR, General Comment No. 3, [8].

[110] Conor Gearty, 'Against Judicial Enforcement' in Conor Gearty and Virginia Mantouvalou, *Debating Social Rights* (Hart, Oxford, 2011), 2.

encompasses political, social and economic dimensions, as well as that of the law.[111]

So, as the reader embarks on the rest of this book's journey through the Covenant's substantive rights, it is as well to heed these caveats, as indeed the Committee itself will be doing as it grapples with the first wave of individual complaints under Optional Protocol.

[111] Amartya Sen, 'Human Rights and the Limits of the Law' (2006) 27(6) *Cardozo Law Review* 2913, 2913–27.

4

Article 2(2): Non-Discrimination

Article 2(2)

The States Parties to the present Covenant undertake to guarantee that the rights enunciated in the present Covenant will be exercised without discrimination of any kind as to race, colour, sex, language, religion, political or other opinion, national or social origin, property, birth or other status.

Article 2(2) prohibits discrimination in relation to the substantive rights contained in the Covenant. In contrast to the obligations imposed on states under Article 2(1), which are for the most part subject to progressive realization, the prohibition on discrimination contained in Article 2(2) is effective immediately. As a result, Article 2(2) imposes concrete and immediate obligations on states to eliminate discrimination with respect to the rights contained in the Covenant.

Background and Context

Non-discrimination (or its corollary, equality) has been described as 'the dominant single theme of the Covenant'.[1] According to the Preamble, the Covenant is based on 'recognition of the inherent dignity and of the equal and inalienable rights of all members of the human family'. And the substantive rights contained in the Covenant are guaranteed to 'everyone'. Further, certain provisions of the Covenant specifically require equality in the implementation of rights. Article 3 requires states to 'ensure the equal right of men and women to the enjoyment of all economic, social and cultural rights'. Article 7 provides for 'equal remuneration for work of equal value without distinction of any kind' and 'equal opportunity for everyone to be promoted' in employment. And Article 13 provides that rights in relation to primary, secondary and higher education shall be available 'to all'. The theme of non-discrimination therefore runs through the Covenant as a whole. However, it finds particular expression in Article 2(2), which specifically applies a non-discrimination requirement to all rights recognized in the Covenant.

Article 2(2) is substantially identical to Article 2(1) of the International Covenant on Civil and Political Rights (ICCPR).[2] Together, these provisions highlight the central role of non-discrimination within human rights and international law as a whole. As the Committee has indicated in its General Comment No. 20 on non-discrimination in economic, social and cultural rights,

[1] Matthew Craven, *The International Covenant on Economic, Social and Cultural Rights: A Perspective on Its Development* (Clarendon Press, Oxford, 1998), 153–4, quoting Bertrand Ramcharan, 'Equality and Non-discrimination' in Louis Henkin (ed), *The International Bill of Rights: The Covenant on Civil and Political Rights* (Columbia University Press, New York, 1981), 246.

[2] International Covenant on Civil and Political Rights (adopted 16 December 1966, 999 UNTS 171, entered into force 23 March 1976) ('ICCPR').

principles of equal rights and non-discrimination are recognized in the UN Charter,[3] and have been reflected in all international human rights instruments, starting with the Universal Declaration of Human Rights (UDHR).[4] The relevant provisions of international law include both free-standing prohibitions on discrimination—which prohibit discrimination per se—and 'subordinate' provisions—which prohibit discrimination only with respect to the rights contained in the relevant instrument. As discussed further below, Article 2(2) falls into this latter category, together with Article 2(1) of the ICCPR, Article 2 of the UDHR, and several provisions in regional instruments.[5] Free-standing prohibitions on discrimination are found in Article 7 of the UDHR, Article 26 of the ICCPR, and regional instruments.[6] Article 26 of the ICCPR, for example, provides as follows:

> All persons are equal before the law and are entitled without any discrimination to the equal protection of the law. In this respect, the law shall prohibit any discrimination and guarantee to all persons equal and effective protection against discrimination on any ground such as race, colour, sex, language, religion, political or other opinion, national or social origin, property, birth or other status.

In addition to these general non-discrimination provisions, a range of international instruments prohibit discrimination against particular persons or groups of persons. These instruments include the International Convention on the Elimination of All Forms of Racial Discrimination;[7] the Convention on the Elimination of All Forms of Discrimination Against Women;[8] the Convention Relating to the Status of Refugees;[9] the Convention Relating to the Status of Stateless Persons;[10] the Convention on the Rights of the Child;[11] the International Convention on the

[3] Charter of the United Nations (adopted 26 June 1945, 1 UNTS XVI, entered into force 24 October 1945), Preamble, Articles 1(3) and 55; CECSR, General Comment No. 20, Non-discrimination in economic, social and cultural rights (art. 2, para. 2, of the International Covenant on Economic, Social and Cultural Rights) ('General Comment No. 20'), E/C.12/GC/20 (2 July 2009), [5].

[4] UNGA Res. 217 A (III), Universal Declaration of Human Rights, A/810 (10 December 1948) ('UDHR'), Articles 2 and 7.

[5] European Convention for the Protection of Human Rights and Fundamental Freedoms ('ECHR') (adopted 4 November 1950, 213 UNTS 2, entered into force 3 September 1953), Article 14; American Convention on Human Rights (adopted 22 November 1969, 1144 UNTS 123, entered into force 18 July 1978), Article 1(1); and African Charter on Human and Peoples' Rights ('African Charter') (adopted 27 June 1981, 1520 UNTS 217, entered into force 21 October 1986), Article 2.

[6] Protocol 12 to the ECHR on the Prohibition of Discrimination (adopted 4 November 2000 ETS 177, entered into force 1 April 2005); American Convention on Human Rights, Article 4; African Charter, Article 3.

[7] International Convention on the Elimination of All Forms of Racial Discrimination (CERD) (adopted 21 December 1965, 660 UNTS 195, entered into force 4 January 1969).

[8] Convention on the Elimination of All Forms of Discrimination Against Women (adopted 18 December 1979, 1249 UNTS 13, entered into force 3 September 1981).

[9] Convention Relating to the Status of Refugees (adopted 28 July 1951, 189 UNTS 137, entered into force 22 April 1954).

[10] Convention Relating to the Status of Stateless Persons (adopted 28 September 1954, 360 UNTS 117, entered into force 6 June 1960).

[11] Convention on the Rights of the Child (adopted 20 November 1989, 1577 UNTS 3, entered into force 2 September 1990).

Protection of the Rights of all Migrant Workers and Members of their Families;[12] and the Convention on the Rights of Persons with Disabilities.[13] Other international instruments prohibit discrimination in specific areas, such as in relation to education[14] and employment.[15] The principle of non-discrimination is in fact so widely recognized in international law that certain forms of discrimination, at least, are seen to be contrary to customary international law and the obligations of states *erga omnes*. Thus, in the *Barcelona Traction case*,[16] the International Court of Justice listed racial discrimination among the obligations of states *erga omnes*.[17]

There is thus a wealth of international law, and corresponding practice on the part of relevant international bodies, addressing the issue of non-discrimination. This chapter will not attempt to cover all this material, but will limit its focus to non-discrimination in the enjoyment of economic, social and cultural rights, as considered by the CESCR when interpreting and applying Article 2(2). Nonetheless, it is important to be aware of other international legal provisions and bodies addressing the issue of non-discrimination for two reasons. The first is that the approaches taken by other international bodies may inform the approach taken by the Committee. In relation to sex discrimination, for example, it is not surprising that the Committee is influenced by the standards developed within the framework of the Convention on the Elimination of All Forms of Discrimination Against Women, as discussed further in relation to Article 3, below.

Secondly, the equal enjoyment of economic, social and cultural rights may be protected not only by Article 2(2), but also under other international instruments. In particular, the free-standing non-discrimination provision in Article 26 of the ICCPR has been used to enforce non-discrimination in relation to economic, social and cultural rights. So, for example, in the case of *Broeks v Netherlands*,[18] the Human Rights Committee considered a claim of discrimination in relation to the payment of unemployment benefits.[19] And in *Waldman v Canada*,[20] the Committee considered the issue of state funding to schools of certain religious faiths but not others. Following the entry into force of the Optional Protocol to the ICESCR, such complaints may now be framed in terms of violations of Article 2(2) of the ICESCR, in conjunction with the rights protected under that

[12] International Convention on the Protection of the Rights of All Migrants and Members of Their Families (adopted 18 December 1990, 2220 UNTS 39481, entered into force 1 July 2003).

[13] Convention on the Rights of Persons with Disabilities (adopted 13 December 2006, 2515 UNTS 3, entered into force 3 May 2008).

[14] UNESCO Convention Against Discrimination in Education (adopted 14 December 1960, 429 UNTS 93, entered into force 22 May 1962).

[15] See, eg, ILO Convention 111 concerning Discrimination in Respect of Employment and Occupation (adopted 25 June 1958, entered into force 15 June 1960).

[16] *Barcelona Traction, Light and Power Company, Limited (Belgium v Spain); Second Phase* ('*Barcelona Traction case*'), 5 February 1970, (1970) ICJ Rep 3.

[17] *Barcelona Traction* case, 33–4.

[18] HRC Communication No. 172/84 (9 April 1987).

[19] See also, eg, *Sprenger v Netherlands*, HRC Communication No. 395/90 (31 March 1992); and *Van Oord v Netherlands*, HRC Communication No. 658/95 (23 July 1997).

[20] HRC Communication No. 694/96 (3 November 1999).

Covenant, rather than as violations of the free-standing non-discrimination provision in Article 26 of the ICCPR. However, the reasoning in the Article 26 ICCPR cases seems likely to influence the reasoning of the Committee when hearing such complaints in future.

In focusing on the Committee's general approach to Article 2(2), this chapter will also not consider the specifics of how Article 2(2) is interpreted and applied in the context of the particular substantive rights protected under the Covenant. This will be considered in more detail in relation to each of the substantive rights in the relevant chapters below. The discussion in this chapter will focus instead on the Committee's general approach to Article 2(2), and the theoretical issues which this raises.

Definition

The notion of equality is notoriously difficult to define and can require a range of different outcomes, yet the concept of discrimination is not defined in the Covenant, and there is very little indication of what form of equality was envisaged by the drafters when including the non-discrimination provision in Article 2(2).

The initial draft of Article 2(2) submitted by the Commission on Human Rights used the term 'distinction' instead of the term 'discrimination'. Although the word 'distinction' was used in the Charter of the United Nations and the UDHR, and was retained in Article 2(1) of the ICCPR:[21]

> 57. A number of…representatives felt that the word 'distinction' was too broad in its meaning and would have the effect of prohibiting the adoption of legitimate measures designed precisely to safeguard and promote the rights of certain categories of persons.
>
> 58. It was generally recognized, for instance, that the protective measures taken by various States for the benefit of certain socially and educationally backward groups of the population were aimed at re-establishing equality and could not, therefore, be violations of Article 2. It was decided that that interpretation of paragraph 2, which was accepted unanimously by the Committee, should be specially mentioned in the report.
>
> …
>
> 60. The majority of the Committee took the view that the word 'discrimination', proposed by Argentina, Italy and Mexico…would prevent arbitrary action more effectively than the word' distinction', while at the same time it allowed for the adoption of legitimate measures of the kind referred to above. Moreover, the word 'discrimination' was being increasingly used in texts adopted by the United Nations and the specialized agencies.[22]

[21] Despite the difference in wording between Article 2(1) of the ICCPR and Article 2(2) of the ICESCR, it is generally accepted that there is no difference in substance between the provisions. See, eg, Yvonne Klerk, 'Working Paper on Article 2(2) and Article 3 of the International Covenant on Economic, Social and Cultural Rights' (1987) 9 *Human Rights Quarterly* 250, 252.

[22] UNGA, Draft International Covenants on Human Rights: Report of the Third Committee (Rapporteur Mrs Marie Sivomey (Togo)), A/5365 (17 December 1962), 18–19.

The purpose of the introduction of the word 'discrimination' was therefore to allow certain measures to promote or improve the position of disadvantaged groups, and to indicate that not all distinctions, only those which were unjustified or for which there was no proper purpose, would be contrary to the Covenant.

The *travaux préparatoires* otherwise offer little guidance as to the meaning which the drafters intended to give to the term 'discrimination'. However, the Committee has now provided a definition of discrimination in its General Comment No. 20:

> [D]iscrimination constitutes any distinction, exclusion, restriction or preference or other differential treatment that is directly or indirectly based on the prohibited grounds of discrimination and which has the intention or effect of nullifying or impairing the recognition, enjoyment or exercise, on an equal footing, of Covenant rights. Discrimination also includes incitement to discriminate and harassment.[23]

This definition closely follows those contained in other international instruments, such as the International Convention on the Elimination of all Forms of Racial Discrimination and the Convention on the Elimination of all Forms of Discrimination Against Women,[24] and consists of four elements:

- differential treatment;
- based upon certain prohibited grounds;
- which has a specific intention or effect;
- in relation to Covenant rights.

DIFFERENTIAL TREATMENT

Not all differential treatment will constitute discrimination contrary to Article 2(2). According to General Comment No. 20:

> Differential treatment based on prohibited grounds will be viewed as discriminatory unless the justification for differentiation is reasonable and objective. This will include an assessment as to whether the aim and effects of the measures or omissions are legitimate, compatible with the nature of the Covenant rights and solely for the purpose of promoting the general welfare in a democratic society. In addition, there must be a clear and reasonable relationship of proportionality between the aim sought to be realized and the measures or omissions and their effects.[25]

The Committee thus follows the formulation first established in the *Belgian Linguistics case* before the European Court of Human Rights, which held that differential treatment will not constitute discrimination contrary to Article 14 of the ECHR, provided there is an 'objective and reasonable justification' for the difference, and a 'reasonable relationship of proportionality between the means employed and the aims sought to be realized'.

[23] CECSR, General Comment No. 20, [7]. [24] See CERD, Article 1(1); and CEDAW, Article 1.
[25] CECSR, General Comment No. 20, [13].

This raises issues of what constitutes an 'objective and reasonable justification' for differential treatment. The Concluding Observations of the Committee do not consider such questions in detail. However, it is clear from the General Comment that the Committee will consider whether the aim and effects of the differentiation are legitimate, compatible with Covenant rights and 'solely for the purpose of promoting the general welfare in a democratic society'.

Further, since the Committee is adopting the same test applied by other international bodies, including the European Court of Human Rights and the Human Rights Committee, decisions of these bodies are likely to inform the approach which the Committee takes to this issue. Although this chapter will not undertake a detailed analysis of this significant body of jurisprudence,[26] consideration of two cases decided by the Human Rights Committee under Article 26 of the ICCPR with respect to economic, social and cultural rights may serve to highlight the general approach the Committee is likely to follow.

In the case of *Love et al v Australia*,[27] the Human Rights Committee considered a complaint by a number of individuals that they had been discriminated against on the basis of age, as a result of their compulsory dismissal by an airline at the age of 60. The state party argued that there were objective and reasonable justifications for the compulsory dismissal at age 60, including concerns for passenger safety. The Committee accepted these arguments, reasoning as follows:

> 8.2 The issue to be decided by the Committee on the merits is whether the author(s) have been subject to discrimination, contrary to article 26 of the Covenant. The Committee recalls its constant jurisprudence that not every distinction constitutes discrimination, in violation of article 26, but that distinctions must be justified on reasonable and objective grounds, in pursuit of an aim that is legitimate under the Covenant. While age as such is not mentioned as one of the enumerated grounds of prohibited discrimination in the second sentence of article 26, the Committee takes the view that a distinction related to age which is not based on reasonable and objective criteria may amount to discrimination on the ground of 'other status' under the clause in question, or to a denial of the equal protection of the law within the meaning of the first sentence of article 26…
>
> 8.3 In the present case, as the State party notes, the aim of maximising safety to passengers, crew and persons otherwise affected by flight travel was a legitimate aim under the Covenant. As to the reasonable and objective nature of the distinction made on the basis of age, the Committee takes into account the widespread national and international practice, at the time of the author's dismissals, of imposing a mandatory retirement age of 60. In order to justify the practice of dismissals maintained at the relevant time, the State party has referred to the ICAO [International Civil Aviation Organization] regime which was aimed at, and understood as, maximising flight safety. In the circumstances, the Committee cannot conclude that the distinction made was not, at the time of Mr Love's dismissal, based on objective and reasonable considerations. Consequently, the Committee is of the view that it cannot establish a violation of article 26.

[26] See Sarah Joseph, Jenny Schultz and Melissa Castan, *The International Covenant on Civil and Political Rights: Cases and Commentary* (Oxford University Press, Oxford, 2004), 700–28.

[27] HRC Communication No. 983/01 (25 March 2003).

In contrast, in the case of *Gueye et al v France*,[28] the Committee found a violation of Article 26 of the ICCPR in relation to pension rights. The authors of the communication were Senegalese soldiers who served in the French Army prior to the independence of Senegal in 1960. Their pension rights were the same as those of French soldiers until a new law froze the rate of their pensions at the rate paid on 1 January 1975, while allowing for the pensions of French veterans to be increased from time to time. After finding that there was a difference in treatment based on 'other status', the Committee went on to consider whether it was 'based on reasonable and objective criteria':[29]

> 9.5 In determining whether the treatment of the authors is based on reasonable and objective criteria, the Committee notes that it was not the question of nationality which determined the granting of pensions to the authors but the services rendered by them in the past. They had served in the French Armed Forces under the same conditions as French citizens; for 14 years subsequent to the independence of Senegal they were treated in the same way as their French counterparts for the purpose of pension rights, although their nationality was not French but Senegalese. A subsequent change in nationality cannot by itself be considered as a sufficient justification for different treatment, since the basis for the grant of the pension was the same service which both they and the soldiers who remained French had provided. Nor can differences in the economic, financial and social conditions as between France and Senegal be invoked as a legitimate justification. If one compared the case of retired soldiers of Senegalese nationality living in Senegal with that of retired soldiers of French nationality in Senegal, it would appear that they enjoy the same economic and social conditions. Yet, their treatment for the purpose of pension entitlements would differ. Finally, the fact that the State party claims that it can no longer carry out checks of identity and family situation, so as to prevent abuses in the administration of pension schemes cannot justify a difference in treatment. In the Committee's opinion, mere administrative inconvenience or the possibility of some abuse of pension rights cannot be invoked to justify unequal treatment. The Committee concludes that the difference in treatment of the authors is not based on reasonable and objective criteria and constitutes discrimination prohibited by the Covenant.

PROHIBITED GROUNDS

The Covenant prohibits 'discrimination of any kind *as to* race, colour, sex, language, religion, political or other opinion, national or social origin, property, birth or other status' (emphasis added). Interestingly, this wording differs from that in Article 2(1) of the ICCPR, which prohibits 'distinction of any kind, *such as* race, colour, sex, language, religion, political or other opinion, national or social origin, property, birth or other status' (emphasis added). As noted above, the difference in terminology between the Covenants as regards use of the word 'discrimination' or 'distinction' does not appear to affect their substantive meaning. But what of the reference to discrimination 'as to' certain specified grounds in the ICESCR? Does this indicate that the list of specified grounds is exhaustive,

[28] HRC Communication No. 196/85 (3 April 1989).
[29] *Gueye v France*, [9.4].

rather than illustrative? Although some commentators formed this view, based on the wording of Article 2(2),[30] the Committee has now clarified, in General Comment No. 20, that the prohibited grounds of discrimination specified in Article 2(2) are illustrative, rather than exhaustive. According to the Committee, 'the inclusion of "other status" indicates that this list is not exhaustive and other grounds may be incorporated in this category'.[31]

Each of the prohibited grounds of discrimination is discussed in more detail below.

INTENTION OR EFFECT

In order for differential treatment to constitute discrimination contrary to Article 2(2), it is not necessary for the state to *intend* to discriminate against the group in question. The fact that a particular act or omission has the *effect* of treating certain groups differently will be sufficient. The concept of discrimination employed by the Committee is therefore a broad one, and the Committee has indicated, in General Comment No. 20, that Article 2(2) covers both formal and substantive discrimination, direct and indirect discrimination, and systemic discrimination.

Formal/substantive discrimination

According to the Committee, the purpose of Article 2(2) is not only to ensure formal equality, that is, equality according to law, but also to secure substantive equality between different groups in terms of how they enjoy the rights under the Covenant in practice. Significantly, the Committee has indicated that achieving substantive equality may require states to address the historic or pre-existing disadvantage suffered by particular groups by adopting 'temporary special measures', designed to address the underlying conditions which perpetuate discrimination against these groups.[32]

According to the General Comment:

8. In order for States parties to 'guarantee' that the Covenant rights will be exercised without discrimination of any kind, discrimination must be eliminated both formally and substantively:

(a) *Formal discrimination*: Eliminating formal discrimination requires ensuring that a State's constitution, laws and policy documents do not discriminate on prohibited grounds; for example, laws should not deny equal social security benefits to women on the basis of their marital status;

(b) *Substantive discrimination*: Merely addressing formal discrimination will not ensure substantive equality as envisaged and defined by article 2, paragraph 2. The effective enjoyment of Covenant rights is often influenced by whether a person is

[30] See, eg, Anne Bayefsky, 'The Principle of Equality or Non-Discrimination in International Law' (1990) 11 *Human Rights Law Journal* 1, 1–2.

[31] CECSR, General Comment No. 20, [15].

[32] This issue of 'temporary special measures' is discussed further below.

a member of a group characterized by the prohibited grounds of discrimination. Eliminating discrimination in practice requires paying sufficient attention to groups of individuals which suffer historical or persistent prejudice instead of merely comparing the formal treatment of individuals in similar situations. States parties must therefore immediately adopt the necessary measures to prevent, diminish and eliminate the conditions and attitudes which cause or perpetuate substantive or de facto discrimination. For example, ensuring that all individuals have equal access to adequate housing, water and sanitation will help to overcome discrimination against women and girl children and persons living in informal settlements and rural areas.

9. In order to eliminate substantive discrimination, States parties may be, and in some cases are, under an obligation to adopt special measures to attenuate or suppress conditions that perpetuate discrimination. Such measures are legitimate to the extent that they represent reasonable, objective and proportional means to redress de facto discrimination and are discontinued when substantive equality has been sustainably achieved. Such positive measures may exceptionally, however, need to be of a permanent nature, such as interpretation services for linguistic minorities and reasonable accommodation of persons with sensory impairments in accessing health-care facilities.

The Committee is thus concerned with both de jure and de facto discrimination, that is, with inequality both in law and in fact. The Committee's Concluding Observations on Poland provide a good example of the way in which the Committee addresses both forms of discrimination:

The Committee continues to be concerned at the de facto discrimination experienced by some disadvantaged and marginalized individuals and groups, such as ethnic minorities, persons with disabilities, and lesbian, gay, bisexual and transgender persons in the enjoyment of their economic, social and cultural rights, despite the appointment of the Plenipotentiary for Equal Treatment in April 2008. The Committee is further concerned that the draft act on implementation of some European Union directives in the field of equal treatment does not provide comprehensive protection against all forms of discrimination in all areas related to Covenant rights (art. 2.2). The Committee strongly urges the State party to amend the provisions of the draft act on implementation of some European Union directives in the field of equal treatment, to bring it into conformity with the Committee's General Comment No. 20 on non-discrimination in economic, social and cultural rights. The Committee also recommends that the State party ensure effective enforcement of existing anti-discrimination legislation, and strengthen measures to combat de facto discrimination, including through campaigns aimed at combatting stereotypes, especially concerning disadvantaged and marginalized individuals and groups.[33]

Since the Committee is concerned with both de jure and de facto discrimination, the *intention* of the state concerned is irrelevant: states can be found in violation of Article 2(2) even where they have adopted legal measures to address discrimination. Thus, for example, in relation to Azerbaijan:

While noting that the constitutional guarantee of the enjoyment of all rights and freedoms is extended to all foreign citizens and stateless persons, the Committee is concerned about

[33] CESCR, Concluding Observations: Poland, E/C.12/POL/CO/5 (2 December 2009), [12].

the persistent de facto discrimination against foreign citizens, ethnic minorities and stateless persons in the fields of housing, employment and education.[34]

Similarly, in relation to Belgium:

The Committee notes that despite the measures adopted by the State party to enhance its legal and institutional mechanisms aimed at combatting racial discrimination, de facto discrimination against foreigners and persons belonging to ethnic and national minorities, in particular migrant workers and members of their families, members of the Muslim community and Roma, is still widespread among some sectors of the population, especially in the fields of employment, housing and access to public places such as restaurants and bars.[35]

On the other hand, the existence of de jure discrimination allows the Committee to find discriminatory intent, without having to consider the further question of whether there is a discriminatory effect. So, for example, in relation to Bolivia, the Committee 'deplores the *de jure* discrimination of salaried domestic workers established in Chapter II of the General Labour Code, with regard to daily and weekly rest and annual paid vacation, dismissal, social benefits and salary'.[36]

Direct/indirect discrimination

The concepts of direct and indirect discrimination are well established in international law. While direct discrimination involves *intention* to discriminate, indirect discrimination arises where measures are formally neutral but have the *effect* of discriminating against certain groups. Under the Committee's definition of discrimination, therefore, both forms of discrimination are contrary to Article 2(2). General Comment No. 20 provides as follows:

10. Both direct and indirect forms of differential treatment can amount to discrimination under article 2, paragraph 2, of the Covenant:

(a) *Direct discrimination* occurs when an individual is treated less favourably than another person in a similar situation for a reason related to a prohibited ground; e.g. where employment in educational or cultural institutions or membership of a trade union is based on the political opinions of applicants or employees. Direct discrimination also includes detrimental acts or omissions on the basis of prohibited grounds where there is no comparable similar situation (e.g. the case of a woman who is pregnant);

(b) *Indirect discrimination* refers to laws, policies or practices which appear neutral at face value, but have a disproportionate impact on the exercise of Covenant rights as distinguished by prohibited grounds of discrimination. For instance, requiring a birth registration certificate for school enrolment may discriminate against ethnic minorities or non-nationals who do not possess, or have been denied, such certificates.

[34] CESCR, Concluding Observations: Azerbaijan, E/C.12/1/Add.104 (14 December 2004), [15].
[35] CESCR, Concluding Observations: Belgium, E/C.12/BEL/CO/3 (4 January 2008), [14].
[36] CESCR, Concluding Observations: Bolivia, E/C.12/1/Add.60 (21 May 2001), [16]. See also, eg, CESCR, Concluding Observations: Benin, E/C.12/BEN/CO/2 (9 June 2008), [13].

Direct discrimination will usually be fairly obvious. Thus, for example, in relation to Benin, the Committee is 'concerned that children born out of wedlock have the same rights and obligations as "legitimate children" only if they are recognized by their father and under certain conditions relating to inheritance rights'.[37] However, the Committee is also sensitive to circumstances of indirect discrimination. For example, in relation to Bosnia and Herzegovina, the Committee has expressed concern about laws for the compensation and protection of civilian war victims, which do not give the status of civilian war victims to victims of sexual violence. The Committee has indicated its concern that these laws 'are gender-insensitive and provide inadequate social protection for victims of sexual violence'.[38]

Similarly, the Committee has expressed concern about laws and policies requiring residence papers or other documents to access social services, for although these requirements apply to all, they often have a disproportionate impact on refugees and non-nationals, who have difficulty obtaining such documents. For example, in relation to Serbia and Montenegro:

> The Committee expresses its deep concern about the uncertain residence status of and the limited access by refugees, returnees from third countries and internally displaced persons, including internally displaced Roma, to personal identification documents, which are a requirement for numerous entitlements such as eligibility to work, to apply for unemployment and other social security benefits, or to register for schools.[39]

Systemic discrimination

According to General Comment No. 20:

> The Committee has regularly found that discrimination against some groups is pervasive and persistent and deeply entrenched in social behaviour and organization, often involving unchallenged or indirect discrimination. Such systemic discrimination can be understood as legal rules, policies, practices or predominant cultural attitudes in either the public or private sector which create relative disadvantages for some groups, and privileges for other groups.[40]

Systemic discrimination will not be addressed by legal prohibitions which focus on discriminatory intent or simply require formally equal treatment. Such approaches ignore the pre-existing and entrenched disadvantage suffered by certain groups across the board, and the fact that treating all groups equally may leave in place existing structures of disadvantage, or even entrench or exacerbate them.[41] As a result, the Committee notes that:

> States parties must adopt an active approach to eliminating systemic discrimination and segregation in practice. Tackling such discrimination will usually require a comprehensive

[37] CESCR, Concluding Observations: Benin, E/C.12/BEN/CO/2 (9 June 2008), [11].

[38] CESCR, Concluding Observations: Bosnia and Herzegovina, E/C.12/BIH/CO/1 (24 January 2006), [19]. See also [41].

[39] CESCR, Concluding Observations: Serbia and Montenegro, E/C.12/1/Add.108 (23 June 2005), [14].

[40] CECSR, General Comment No. 20, [12].

[41] See CESCR, General Comment No. 16, The equal right of men and women to the enjoyment of all economic, social and cultural rights (art. 3 of the International Covenant on Economic, Social and Cultural Rights) ('General Comment No. 16'), E/C.12/2005/4 (11 August 2005), [13].

approach with a range of laws, policies and programmes, including temporary special measures. States parties should consider using incentives to encourage public and private actors to change their attitudes and behaviour in relation to individuals and groups of individuals facing systemic discrimination, or penalize them in case of non-compliance. Public leadership and programmes to raise awareness about systemic discrimination and the adoption of strict measures against incitement to discrimination are often necessary. Eliminating systemic discrimination will frequently require devoting greater resources to traditionally neglected groups. Given the persistent hostility towards some groups, particular attention will need to be given to ensuring that laws and policies are implemented by officials and others in practice.[42]

Although the Committee's Concluding Observations do not specifically discuss the issue of systemic discrimination as such, a number of the Concluding Observations demonstrate awareness of this issue and the need for states to take particular steps to address it, including through the adoption of temporary special measures. A good example is provided by the Committee's Concluding Observations on Hungary in 2008, in which the Committee shows awareness of the widespread and entrenched disadvantage suffered by the Roma.[43] In these Concluding Observations, the Committee urges the state party to take a number of measures to address the particular plight of the Roma. For example:

The Committee urges the State party to intensify its efforts to reduce Roma unemployment through specifically targeted measures, including by enhancing professional training and sustainable employment opportunities in communities with significant Roma populations and increasing the number of Roma in the central and local governments. It also recommends that the State party ensure the strict application of anti-discrimination legislation by the courts, local governments and labour offices. The Committee further recommends that the State party take more effective measures to encourage the private sector to provide adequate employment opportunities for the Roma.[44]

IN RELATION TO COVENANT RIGHTS

This element of the definition of discrimination concerns the scope of application of the prohibition in Article 2(2). According to the definition in General Comment No. 20, discrimination occurs where differential treatment 'has the intention or effect of nullifying or impairing the recognition, enjoyment or exercise, on an equal footing, of Covenant rights'.[45] In other words, the scope of operation of Article 2(2) is limited to discrimination which affects the recognition, enjoyment or exercise of Covenant rights. Article 2(2) is not a free-standing non-discrimination provision, such as Article 26 of the ICCPR, but is rather subordinate to the substantive rights contained in the Covenant. This conclusion follows from the wording of Article 2(2) itself (under which states guarantee that 'the rights enunciated in the

[42] CECSR, General Comment No. 20, [39].

[43] CESCR, Concluding Observations: Hungary, E/C.12/HUN/CO/3 (16 January 2008), [22], [25], [27] and [28], [34], [41], [45], [48], [50] and [51].

[44] CESCR, Concluding Observations: Hungary, E/C.12/HUN/CO/3 (16 January 2008), [34].

[45] CECSR, General Comment No. 20, [7].

present Covenant will be exercised without discrimination'), and the fact that it is found in Part II of the Covenant, not in Part III, which contains the substantive rights protected by the ICESCR.

This raises the question of whether Article 2(2) in fact adds anything to the substantive rights contained in the Covenant, since discrimination under Article 2(2) will only occur where differential treatment has the effect of 'nullifying or impairing the recognition, enjoyment or exercise' of Covenant rights. This suggests that there must inevitably be a violation of the substantive Covenant right for there also to be a breach of the non-discrimination provision.

In practice, however, the Committee seems to give Article 2(2) a broader scope of application, commenting on discrimination in general terms, without tying it to the enjoyment of particular Covenant rights. So, for example, in relation to Zambia:

> 14. The Committee notes that the prevalence of customary law—certain traditions, customs and cultural practices—leads to substantial discrimination against girls and women, in particular widows, thereby preventing them from fully exercising their rights under the Covenant.
>
> …
>
> 23. The Committee is concerned about the large number of widows and orphans, a situation further exacerbated by the HIV/AIDS pandemic. It is also concerned about the harsh living conditions of widows and girl orphans due to, among other things, harmful traditional practices such as 'widow-cleansing', early marriages and denial of inheritance.[46]

Similarly, in relation to Uruguay:

> The Committee is concerned that despite the efforts and progress made by the State party to raise the standard of living, a high proportion of the population continues to live below the poverty line, in particular the black minority. Furthermore, the Committee is concerned about the surveys conducted among the population of the State party itself which tend to show that prejudice against the black minority continues to exist in the country.[47]

The Committee has also shown concern about particular issues which disproportionately affect certain groups, without tying its comments to violations of particular rights. So, for example, in relation to Brazil, the Committee 'is deeply concerned about the high incidence of trafficking in women for the purpose of sexual exploitation'.[48]

Craven has noted how, under the ECHR (where Article 14 similarly prohibits discrimination only with respect to the enjoyment of rights under that Convention), the European Court of Human Rights has found violations where states have gone beyond the strict scope of their obligations under a particular Article, but have done so in a discriminatory manner.[49] For example, in relation

[46] CESCR, Concluding Observations: Zambia, E/C.12/1/Add.106 (23 June 2005).
[47] CESCR, Concluding Observations: Uruguay, E/C.12/1994/3 (30 May 1994), [8].
[48] CESCR, Concluding Observations: Brazil, E/C.12/1/Add.87 (26 June 2003), [30].
[49] Craven, *The ICESCR*, 179.

to the right to education, in the case of *Ponomaryov v Bulgaria*,[50] the Court noted that Bulgaria did not need to provide free secondary education, under Article 2 of Protocol 1 to the ECHR. However, once it decided to do so, it could not do so on a discriminatory basis (in this case, requiring non-nationals to pay secondary school fees). The Court noted:

The Court would emphasize at the outset that its task in the present case is not to decide whether and to what extent it is permissible for the States to charge fees for secondary—or, indeed, any—education. It has in the past recognized that the right to education by its very nature calls for regulation by the State, and that this regulation may vary in time and place according to the needs and resources of the community... The Court must solely determine whether, once a state has voluntarily decided to provide such education free of charge, it may deny that benefit to a distinct group of people, for the notion of discrimination includes cases where a person or group is treated, without proper justification, less favourably than another, even though the more favourable treatment is not called for by the Convention...[51]

The European Court thus gives Article 14 a scope of operation which extends beyond the strict requirements of the substantive rights of the ECHR, such that it applies to any discrimination in the spheres regulated by those rights. The approach adopted by the Committee would seem to mirror this approach. According to Craven:

The approach of the Committee would seem to be close to that of the European Court. While it will not concern itself with matters that do not fall within the general scope of economic, social and cultural rights, it will not confine itself to combatting discrimination only in those areas where a violation of the substantive rights occurs.[52]

Prohibited Grounds of Discrimination

As noted above, the prohibited grounds of discrimination listed in Article 2(2) are not exhaustive. The following discussion first addresses some general issues regarding the prohibited grounds of discrimination, and then considers each of the grounds enumerated in Article 2(2), as well as other grounds of discrimination which have been considered in the Committee's work.

GENERAL ISSUES

Membership of a group

If discrimination is prohibited on grounds of membership of a group (ethnic, national, religious, political, etc), there is a question of how the Committee is to determine whether individuals belong to a particular group, for the purpose of determining whether discrimination against them is based on a prohibited ground.

[50] *Ponomaryov and Ponomaryov v Bulgaria* (App. 5335/05), 21 June 2011, IHRL 1655.
[51] *Ponomaryov and Ponomaryov v Bulgaria*, [53]. [52] Craven, *The ICESCR*, 180.

The Committee has made clear, in General Comment No. 20, that it will rely on self-identification by the individual concerned:

In determining whether a person is distinguished by one or more of the prohibited grounds, identification shall, if no justification exists to the contrary, be based upon self-identification by the individual concerned. Membership also includes association with a group characterized by one of the prohibited grounds (e.g. the parent of a child with a disability) or perception by others that an individual is part of such a group (e.g. a person has a similar skin colour or is a supporter of the rights of a particular group or a past member of a group).[53]

Multiple discrimination

Although the Covenant lists individual grounds on which discrimination is prohibited, some groups suffer from discrimination on more than one basis. In these cases, the interaction of different forms of discrimination can be particularly problematic. However, this is often overlooked, as indicated by the Committee, for example, in its General Comment on persons with disabilities, where it notes that:

Persons with disabilities are sometimes treated as genderless human beings. As a result the double discrimination suffered by women with disabilities is often neglected.[54]

The importance of considering the intersectionality of multiple forms of discrimination is specifically noted by the Committee in General Comment No. 20:

Some individuals or groups of individuals face discrimination on more than one of the prohibited grounds, for example women belonging to an ethnic or religious minority. Such cumulative discrimination has a unique and specific impact on individuals and merits particular consideration and remedying.[55]

And in its Concluding Observations, the Committee is sensitive to the particular, and heightened, disadvantage experienced by groups which suffer discrimination on multiple bases.[56]

ENUMERATED GROUNDS OF DISCRIMINATION

'Race and colour'

According to General Comment No. 20:

Discrimination on the basis of 'race and colour', which includes an individual's ethnic origin, is prohibited by the Covenant as well as by other treaties including the International Convention on the Elimination of Racial Discrimination. The use of the term 'race' in the

[53] CECSR, General Comment No. 20, [16].

[54] CESCR, General Comment No. 5, Persons with disabilities ('General Comment No. 5'), E/1994/22 (9 December 1994), [19].

[55] CECSR, General Comment No. 20, [17].

[56] See, eg, CESCR, Concluding Observations: Libyan Arab Jamahiriya, E/C.12/1/Add.15 (20 May 1997), [17] and [23]; France, E/C.12/FRA/CO/3 (9 June 2008), [13].

Covenant or the present general comment does not imply the acceptance of theories which attempt to determine the existence of separate human races.[57]

The Committee has consistently expressed concern regarding such discrimination in its Concluding Observations, and has particularly been concerned with discrimination against ethnic minorities and indigenous peoples.[58] So, for example, in relation to Bolivia:

The Committee is particularly concerned about the marginalization of, and discrimination against, indigenous communities in Bolivia, who constitute the majority of Bolivia's rural population and who suffer from inadequate access to basic education, adequate housing, and health services. Moreover, the Committee is concerned that the State party does not acknowledge the economic, social and cultural rights of indigenous populations as a distinct group.[59]

Similarly, in relation to Croatia:

The Committee notes with concern that many displaced ethnic Serbs continue to face legal and administrative difficulties in attempting to repossess their former home. The Committee is also concerned that while the process of repatriation and relocation of ethnic Serbs has begun showing signs of improvements, the results and the pace of their return and the settlement of their property and tenancy claims in relation to those of other displaced Croatians revealed that ethnic Serbs continue to face excessive obstacles to their return. The Committee is deeply disturbed that these obstacles have resulted in the violation of the rights of many Serbs under Articles 2 and 11 of the Covenant.[60]

And in relation to Kenya:

The Committee expresses its concern about the marginalization of ethnic minorities in Kenya, particularly of the nomadic pastoralists and the ethnic Somalis in the North Eastern Province.[61]

Sex

The equal right of men and women to the enjoyment of economic, social and cultural rights is not only protected under Article 2(2), but also under Article 3 of the Covenant. It has also been the subject of a specific General Comment (General Comment No. 16) of the Committee. According to General Comment No. 20:

The Covenant guarantees the equal right of men and women to the enjoyment of economic, social and cultural rights. Since the adoption of the Covenant, the notion of the prohibited ground 'sex' has evolved considerably to cover not only physiological characteristics but also the social construction of gender stereotypes, prejudices and expected roles, which have created obstacles to the equal fulfilment of economic, social and cultural rights. Thus, the refusal to hire a woman, on the ground that she might become pregnant, or the

[57] CESCR, General Comment No. 20, [19].

[58] See CESCR, General Comment No. 20, [18].

[59] CESCR, Concluding Observations: Bolivia, E/C.12/1/Add.60 (21 May 2001), [14]. See also, eg, Chile, E/C.12/1/Add.105 (1 December 2004), [13] and [33] and [34].

[60] CESCR, Concluding Observations: Croatia, E/C.12/1/Add.73 (5 December 2001), [10].

[61] CESCR, Concluding Observations: Kenya, E/C.12/1993/6 (3 June 1993), [21].

allocation of low-level or part-time jobs to women based on the stereotypical assumption that, for example, they are unwilling to commit as much time to their work as men, constitutes discrimination. Refusal to grant paternity leave may also amount to discrimination against men.[62]

The issues relating to this ground of discrimination are discussed in more detail in the chapter on Article 3, below.

Language

According to General Comment No. 20:

Discrimination on the basis of language or regional accent is often closely linked to unequal treatment on the basis of national or ethnic origin. Language barriers can hinder the enjoyment of many Covenant rights, including the right to participate in cultural life as guaranteed by article 15 of the Covenant. Therefore, information about public services and goods, for example, should also be available, as far as possible, in languages spoken by minorities, and States parties should ensure that any language requirements relating to employment and education are based on reasonable and objective criteria.[63]

The Committee has frequently expressed concern about discrimination on the basis of language, in particular in the context of rights to education and the right to participate in cultural life under Article 15. So, for example, in relation to Cambodia, the Committee has noted that:

[P]rimary education continues to be a problem for the various ethnic minorities in the north and east of the country, where there are 20 minority languages spoken by these groups as their mother tongue while the formal education curriculum has only used Khmer as the medium of instruction… The Committee recommends that the State party extend the coverage of the Education Law to ensure the right to education to all Cambodian children whose first language is not Khmer.[64]

Similarly, in relation to Article 15, the Committee has, for example, expressed concern regarding prohibitions on the use of the Amazigh language in Libya,[65] and has considered the position of the Russian language in 'culture, on television and in the cinema' in Belarus.[66]

Religion

According to General Comment No. 20:

This prohibited ground of discrimination covers the profession of religion or belief of one's choice (including the non-profession of any religion or belief), that may be publicly or privately manifested in worship, observance, practice and teaching. For instance, discrimination arises when persons belonging to a religious minority are denied equal access to universities, employment, or health services on the basis of their religion.

[62] CECSR, General Comment No. 20, [20]. [63] CECSR, General Comment No. 20, [21].
[64] CESCR, Concluding Observations: Cambodia, E/C.12/KHM/CO/1 (12 June 2009), [34].
[65] CESCR Concluding Observations on Libya (25 January 2006), E/C.12/LYB/CO/2, [23].
[66] CESCR, Report on the Seventh Session, E/1993/22 (23 November–11 December 1992), [63].

In its Concluding Observations, the Committee has expressed particular concern for the position of religious minorities. Thus, in its Concluding Observations on Iran:

The Committee regrets . . . the broad consensus that there has been practically no progress in ensuring . . . protection for rights of the non-Muslim religious communities in the Islamic Republic of Iran in general, and of the economic, social and cultural rights of persons belonging to those minority groups in particular.[67]

Similarly, in relation to Poland:

11. The Committee notes that under the new Constitution, Poland is a secular State with no formal role attributed to any religious denomination. The Committee is nevertheless concerned that policies and decisions of a social nature seem to be excessively influenced by particular religious considerations and do not take adequate account of the existence of minority religious groups.

. . .

19. The Committee recommends that special care be taken to ensure full respect for the rights of all religious groups, particularly concerning issues of national policy such as education, gender equality and healthcare.[68]

Political or other opinion

According to General Comment No. 20:

Political and other opinions are often grounds for discriminatory treatment and include both the holding and not-holding of opinions, as well as expression of views or membership within opinion-based associations, trade unions or political parties. Access to food assistance schemes, for example, must not be made conditional on an expression of allegiance to a particular political party.[69]

In practice, this ground of discrimination has given rise to very little comment in the Committee's Concluding Observations. However, it is clear that, in an appropriate case, the Committee would find any distinction in treatment based on opinion to be contrary to Article 2(2). Thus, in relation to Germany, the Committee:

. . . notes with alarm that only 12% of public servants in the science and technology sector of the former German Democratic Republic, including teachers, scientists and professionals, have been reemployed and that the rest remain without employment or adequate compensation or a satisfactory pension plan. The Committee fears that the majority of the affected people may have been dismissed from their positions for political rather than for professional or economic reasons, in violation of Article 2.2 of the Covenant.[70]

67 CESCR, Concluding Observations: Iran, E/C.12/1993/7 (9 June 1993), [5].
68 CESCR, Concluding Observations: Poland, E/C.12/1/Add.26 (16 June 1998), [11] and [19].
69 CECSR, General Comment No. 20, [23].
70 CESCR, Concluding Observations: Germany, E/C.12/1/Add.29 (4 December 1998), [16].

National or social origin

According to General Comment No. 20:

'National origin' refers to a person's State, nation, or place of origin. Due to such personal circumstances, individuals and groups of individuals may face systemic discrimination in both the public and private sphere in the exercise of their Covenant rights. 'Social origin' refers to a person's inherited social status.[71]

This ground of discrimination overlaps, to some extent, with 'race and colour', discussed above, and also the ground of nationality discussed below. The concept of 'social origin' also overlaps with discrimination on the basis of property status, birth, and economic and social status, all discussed below.

This ground of discrimination was addressed by the Committee, for example, in its Concluding Observations on Sri Lanka in 1998:

The Committee notes with concern the uncertain situation of 85,000 Tamils of Indian origin living in Sri Lanka. They possess neither Indian nor Sri Lankan citizenship, have no access to basic services such as education, and do not enjoy their economic, social and cultural rights.[72]

Similarly, in relation to Israel:

The Committee is deeply concerned about the continuing difference in treatment between Jews and non-Jews, in particular Arab and Bedouin communities, with regard to their enjoyment of economic, social and cultural rights in the State party's territory. The Committee reiterates its concern that the 'excessive emphasis upon the State as a "Jewish State" encourages discrimination and accords a second-class status to its non-Jewish citizens' ...[73]

Property

According to General Comment No. 20:

Property status, as a prohibited ground of discrimination, is a broad concept and includes real property (e.g. land ownership or tenure) and personal property (e.g. intellectual property, goods and chattels, and income), or the lack of it. The Committee has previously commented that Covenant rights, such as access to water services and protection from forced eviction, should not be made conditional on a person's land tenure status, such as living in an informal settlement.[74]

So, for example, the Committee has indicated, in its General Comment No. 4 on the right to adequate housing, that 'all persons should possess a degree of security of tenure which guarantees legal protection against forced eviction, harassment and other threats. States parties should consequently take immediate measures aimed at conferring legal security of tenure upon those persons and households currently lacking such protection, in genuine consultation with affected persons

[71] CECSR, General Comment No. 20, [24].
[72] CESCR, Concluding Observations: Sri Lanka, E/C.12/1/Add.24 (16 June 1998), [8].
[73] CESCR, Concluding Observations: Israel, E/C.12/1/Add.90 (26 June 2003), [16].
[74] CECSR, General Comment No. 20, [25].

and groups.'[75] Similarly, in its General Comment No. 15 on the right to water, the Committee has indicated that 'no household should be denied the right to water on the grounds of their housing or land status'.[76]

Birth

General Comment No. 20 makes the following observations on this ground of discrimination:

> Discrimination based on birth is prohibited and article 10, paragraph 3, of the Covenant specifically states, for example, that special measures should be taken on behalf of children and young persons 'without any discrimination for reasons of parentage'. Distinctions must therefore not be made against those who are born out of wedlock, born of stateless parents or are adopted or constitute the families of such persons. The prohibited ground of birth also includes descent, especially on the basis of caste and analogous systems of inherited status. States parties should take steps, for instance, to prevent, prohibit and eliminate discriminatory practices directed against members of descent-based communities and act against the dissemination of ideas of superiority and inferiority on the basis of descent.[77]

Thus, the Committee frequently expresses concern about discriminatory treatment of children born out of wedlock.[78] The Committee also considers caste-based discrimination, such as that identified in the context of Nepal:[79]

> The Committee notes with concern that, in spite of the provisions in the Interim Constitution prohibiting caste-based discrimination, such discrimination persists with impunity. The Committee is particularly concerned about the obstacles that victims of caste-based discrimination reportedly face in accessing justice.[80]

OTHER STATUS

The Committee has noted that what constitutes discrimination will vary over time, and it is therefore not possible to set out an exhaustive list of prohibited grounds of discrimination:

> The nature of discrimination varies according to context and evolves over time. A flexible approach to the ground of 'other status' is thus needed in order to capture other forms of differential treatment that cannot be reasonably and objectively justified and are of a comparable nature to the expressly recognized grounds in article 2, paragraph 2. These additional grounds are commonly recognized when they reflect the experience of social groups that

[75] CESCR, General Comment No. 4, The right to adequate housing (Art. 11(1)), E/1992/23 (13 December 1991), [8].

[76] CESCR, General Comment No. 15, The right to water ('General Comment No. 15'), E/C.12/2002/11 (20 January 2003), [16(c)].

[77] CECSR, General Comment No. 20, [26].

[78] See, eg, CESCR, Concluding Observations: Algeria, E/C.12/1995/17 (28 December 1995), [19]; Japan, E/C.12/1/Add.67 (24 September 2001), [14] and [41]; Benin, E/C.12/BEN/CO/2 (9 June 2008), [11] and [32].

[79] CESCR, Concluding Observations: Nepal, E/C.12/NPL/CO/2 (16 January 2008), [7].

[80] CESCR, Concluding Observations: Nepal, E/C.12/NPL/CO/2 (16 January 2008), [13]. See also India, E/C.12/IND/CO/5 (8 August 2008), [13] and [14].

are vulnerable and have suffered and continue to suffer marginalization. The Committee's general comments and concluding observations have recognized various other grounds and these are described in more detail below. However, this list is not intended to be exhaustive. Other possible prohibited grounds could include the denial of a person's legal capacity because he or she is in prison, or is involuntarily interned in a psychiatric institution, or the intersection of two prohibited grounds of discrimination, e.g. where access to a social service is denied on the basis of sex and disability.[81]

In its work, the Committee has identified a number of other grounds of discrimination which are contrary to Article 2(2).

Disability

The Committee recognized discrimination against persons with disabilities as contrary to the requirements of Article 2(2) of the Covenant in its General Comment No. 5 on persons with disabilities. In that General Comment, the Committee noted that:

> ...the requirement contained in Article 2(2) of the Covenant that the rights 'enunciated...will be exercised without discrimination of any kind' based on certain specified grounds 'or other status' clearly applied to discrimination on the grounds of disability.[82]

The Committee has defined discrimination against persons with disabilities as 'any distinction, exclusion, restriction or preference, or denial of reasonable accommodation based on disability which has the effect of nullifying or impairing the recognition, enjoyment or exercise of economic, social or cultural rights'.[83] According to General Comment No. 20, addressing such discrimination requires states to take the following measures:

> The denial of reasonable accommodation should be included in national legislation as a prohibited form of discrimination on the basis of disability. States parties should address discrimination, such as prohibitions on the right to education, and denial of reasonable accommodation in public places such as public health facilities and the workplace, as well as in private places, e.g. as long as spaces are designed and built in ways that make them inaccessible to wheelchairs, such users will be effectively denied their right to work.[84]

Further guidance as to the steps states should take to address discrimination against persons with disabilities is provided in General Comment No. 5. The Committee stresses, in particular, the importance of legislative measures to protect the rights of those with disabilities:

> In order to remedy past and present discrimination and to deter future discrimination, comprehensive anti-discrimination legislation in relation to disability would seem to be indispensable in virtually all States parties. Such legislation should not only provide persons with disabilities with judicial remedies as far as possible and appropriate, but also provide for social-policy programmes which enable persons with disabilities to live an integrated, self-determined and independent life.[85]

[81] CECSR, General Comment No. 20, [27].
[82] CESCR, General Comment No. 5, [5].
[83] CESCR, General Comment No. 5, [15].
[84] CECSR, General Comment No. 20, [28].
[85] CESCR, General Comment No. 5, [16].

In addition, the Committee has noted that:

The obligation of States parties to the Covenant to promote progressive realization of the relevant rights to the maximum of their available resources clearly requires Governments to do much more than merely abstain from taking measures which might have a negative impact on persons with disabilities. The obligation in the case of such a vulnerable and disadvantaged group is to take positive action to reduce structural disadvantages and to give appropriate preferential treatment to people with disabilities in order to achieve the objectives of full participation and equality within society for all persons with disabilities. This almost invariably means that additional resources will need to be made available for this purpose and that a wide range of specially tailored measures will be required.[86]

The importance of addressing discrimination against persons with disabilities is also repeatedly stressed by the Committee in its Concluding Observations.[87]

Age

According to General Comment No. 20:

Age is a prohibited ground of discrimination in several contexts. The Committee has highlighted the need to address discrimination against unemployed older persons in finding work, or accessing professional training or retraining, and against older persons living in poverty with unequal access to universal old-age pensions due to their place of residence. In relation to young persons, unequal access by adolescents to sexual and reproductive health information and services amounts to discrimination.[88]

The Committee specifically considered the issue of the economic, social and cultural rights of older persons in its General Comment No. 6 in 1995:[89]

12. …The Committee notes that while it may not yet be possible to conclude that discrimination on the grounds of age is comprehensively prohibited by the Covenant, the range of matters in relation to which such discrimination can be accepted is very limited. Moreover, it must be emphasized that the unacceptableness of discrimination against older persons is underlined in many international policy documents and is confirmed in the legislation of the vast majority of States. In the few areas in which discrimination continues to be tolerated, such as in relation to mandatory retirement ages or access to tertiary education, there is a clear trend towards the elimination of such barriers. The Committee is of the view that States parties should seek to expedite this trend to the greatest extent possible.

13. Accordingly, the Committee on Economic, Social and Cultural Rights is of the view that States parties to the Covenant are obligated to pay particular attention to promoting and protecting the economic, social and cultural rights of older persons. The

[86] CESCR, General Comment No. 5, [9].

[87] See, eg, CESCR, Concluding Observations: Hungary, E/C.12/HUN/CO/3 (16 January 2008), [12] and [35]; Benin, E/C.12/BEN/CO/2 (9 June 2008), [13]; Angola, E/C.12/AGO/CO/3 (1 December 2008), [16]; Brazil, E/C.12/BRA/CO/2 (12 June 2009), [13].

[88] CECSR, General Comment No. 20, [29].

[89] CESCR, General Comment No. 6, The economic, social and cultural rights of older persons ('General Comment No. 6'), E/1996/33 (12 August 1995).

Committee's own role in this regard is rendered all the more important by the fact that, unlike the case of other population groups such as women and children, no comprehensive international convention yet exists in relation to the rights of older persons and no binding supervisory arrangements attach to the various sets of United Nations principles in this area.

General Comment No. 6 offers some guidance on the measures states are required to take to address discrimination against older persons:

> The methods that States parties use to fulfil the obligations they have assumed under the Covenant in respect of older persons will be basically the same as those for the fulfilment of other obligations (see general comment No. 1 (1989)). They include the need to determine the nature and scope of problems within a State through regular monitoring, the need to adopt properly designed policies and programmes to meet requirements, the need to enact legislation when necessary and to eliminate any discriminatory legislation and the need to ensure the relevant budget support or, as appropriate, to request international cooperation. In the latter connection, international cooperation in accordance with articles 22 and 23 of the Covenant may be a particularly important way of enabling some developing countries to fulfil their obligations under the Covenant.[90]

Discrimination against older persons is frequently addressed in the Committee's Concluding Observations.[91]

Nationality

It is a well-established principle of international law that 'it is the sovereign right of every state to determine on what conditions non-nationals may enter, reside, and take up employment in its territory'.[92] It is clear from the *travaux préparatoires* that the drafters did not wish this sovereign right to be affected by Article 2(2). A number of representatives expressed concern that Article 2(2) might affect, in particular, the ability of states to restrict the rights of non-nationals to employment. Thus, the representative of Australia expressed concern not to create difficulties in respect of 'the quite legitimate restrictions which some States imposed on the employment of aliens',[93] while the representative of New Zealand argued against too 'categorical' an approach to Article 2(2), noting, for example, that:

> New Zealand had taken steps to facilitate the entry of tourists, but it did not treat them in the same way as it did its own nationals and in particular denied them the right to take up employment.[94]

[90] CESCR, General Comment No. 6, [18].

[91] See, eg, CESCR, Concluding Observations: China, E/C.12/1/Add.58 (21 May 2001), [21] and [31]; United Kingdom of Great Britain and Northern Ireland, the Crown Dependencies and the Overseas Dependent Territories, E/C.12/1/Add.79 (5 June 2002), [18]; Georgia, E/C.12/1/Add.83 (19 December 2002), [23] and [40].

[92] Emmanuel Victor Oware Dankwa, 'Working Paper on Article 2(3) of the International Covenant on Economic, Social and Cultural Rights' (1987) 9(2) *Human Rights Quarterly* 230, 246–7.

[93] UNGA Third Committee, A/C.3/SR.658 (9 November 1955), 173.

[94] UNGA Third Committee, A/C.3/SR.1181 (13 November 1962), 238.

The representative of Egypt specifically noted the 'international rule' regarding the treatment of aliens, and indicated that Article 2(2) should not be taken as altering this position:

As to the right to work, while no modern State passed laws forbidding the employment of aliens, international practice made it incumbent on the State to specify the terms under which aliens might work in its territory. It could, for example, stipulate that certain professions were reserved exclusively for its nationals or that a certain percentage of appointments in other professions was reserved for them. There being, therefore, an accepted 'international rule' in that field, Egypt could... subscribe without difficulty to the non-discrimination clause.[95]

Thus, not all distinctions on the basis of nationality will be contrary to Article 2(2). This position is confirmed in the 'interpretative declarations' issued by a number of States upon ratification of the Covenant, indicating that they did not interpret Article 2(2) as requiring States to treat foreigners in the same way as nationals in all matters. The interpretative declaration made by Belgium, for example, provides:

With respect to Article 2, paragraph 2, the Belgian Government interprets non-discrimination as to national origin as not necessarily implying an obligation on States automatically to guarantee to foreigners the same rights as to their nationals. The terms should be understood to refer to the elimination of any arbitrary behaviour but not of differences in treatment based on objective and reasonable considerations, in conformity with the principles prevailing in democratic societies.[96]

And the declaration made by France goes further, providing:

The Government of the Republic [of France] declares that Articles 6, 9, 11 and 13 are not to be interpreted as derogating from provisions governing the access of aliens to employment or establishing residence requirements for the allocation of certain social benefits.

It is therefore clear that states have the ability to maintain differential treatment of non-nationals in certain circumstances. In addition, Article 2(3) of the Covenant, discussed further below, specifically authorizes developing countries to limit the extent to which they guarantee economic rights to non-nationals.

Nonetheless, according to General Comment No. 20:

The ground of nationality should not bar access to Covenant rights, e.g. all children within a State, including those with an undocumented status, have a right to receive education and

[95] UNGA Third Committee, A/C.3/SR.658 (9 November 1955), 171.

[96] And the declaration of the United Kingdom indicates that the 'Government of the United Kingdom reserve the right to interpret Article 6 as not precluding the imposition of restrictions, based on place of birth or residence qualifications, on the taking of employment in any particular region or territory for the purpose of safeguarding the employment opportunities of workers in that region or territory'. Note that although the declaration refers to discrimination on the basis of national origin, it is clear that it treats this ground of discrimination as covering discrimination on the basis of nationality. Similarly, the declaration issued by Monaco indicates that that state 'interprets the principle of non-discrimination on the grounds of national origin, embodied in Article 2, paragraph 2, as not necessarily implying an automatic obligation on the part of States to guarantee foreigners the same rights as their nationals'.

access to adequate food and affordable health care. The Covenant rights apply to everyone including non-nationals, such as refugees, asylum-seekers, stateless persons, migrant workers and victims of international trafficking, regardless of legal status and documentation.[97]

Reconciling this statement in the General Comment with the intentions of the drafters of the Covenant, and with state practice, it would seem that what is prohibited is *arbitrary* distinctions in treatment based on nationality, that is, distinctions for which there is no 'objective and reasonable justification'. Restrictions on the rights of non-nationals to work and receive social security, for example, could be justified on reasonable and objective bases, particularly in view of the consistency of state practice in these areas, together with the express authorization in Article 2(3) for developing countries to limit these 'economic rights' in relation to non-nationals. On the other hand, there can be no reasonable justification for restrictions on the right of foreign children to receive school education, or restrictions on the right of non-nationals to access health care.

In practice, when considering this ground of discrimination, the Committee has focused, in particular, on the rights of refugees, asylum-seekers and migrant workers.[98] So, for example, in relation to Germany:

The Committee is concerned about the considerable length of time taken to process applications for asylum, resulting in the limitation of the enjoyment of the economic, social and cultural rights enshrined in the Covenant by asylum-seekers and their dependents.[99]

And in relation to Kazakhstan:

The Committee is deeply concerned at the precarious situation of migrant workers who are employed without contracts in tobacco plantations and are, together with their families, vulnerable to exploitation and abuse.[100]

Marital and family status

According to General Comment No. 20:

Marital and family status may differ between individuals because, inter alia, they are married or unmarried, married under a particular legal regime, in a de facto relationship or one not recognized by law, divorced or widowed, live in an extended family or kinship group or have differing kinds of responsibility for children and dependants or a particular number of children. Differential treatment in access to social security benefits on the basis of whether an individual is married must be justified on reasonable and objective criteria. In certain cases, discrimination can also occur when an individual is unable to exercise a right protected by the Covenant because of his or her family status or can only do so with spousal consent or a relative's concurrence or guarantee.[101]

[97] CESCR, General Comment No. 20, [30].

[98] See generally CESCR, Concluding Observations: Liechtenstein, E/C.12/LIE/CO/1 (9 June 2006), [11] and [25].

[99] CESCR, Concluding Observations: Germany, E/C.12/1/Add.68 (24 September 2001), [16] and [34].

[100] CESCR, Concluding Observations: Kazakhstan, E/C.12/KAZ/CO/1 (7 June 2010), [20]. See also, eg, Libyan Arab Jamahiriya, E/C.12/1/Add.15 (20 May 1997), [15], [17] and [23].

[101] CESCR, General Comment No. 20, [31].

The Committee, in its Concluding Observations, has expressed particular concern about discrimination against single-parent families. For example, in relation to Belgium:

In the light of Article 28 of the Covenant, the Committee is concerned about the significant shortage of social housing in Belgium, especially in Flanders. The Committee is also concerned that larger families, as well as single-parent and low-income families, are at a disadvantage in qualifying for such social housing.[102]

Similarly, in relation to Canada, the Committee is 'deeply concerned by the discriminatory impact of the National Child Benefit "clawback system" on the poorest families in Canada, in particular single-mother-led families'.[103] The Committee has also expressed concern about 'widespread discrimination in housing against people with children'.[104]

Discrimination on the basis of family status has also been considered in relation to the enjoyment of economic, social and cultural rights by the Human Rights Committee (HRC) in the context of claims under Article 26 of the ICCPR. In the case of *Broeks v Netherlands*, for example, the author of the communication complained about legislation which prevented her from claiming unemployment benefits because she was a woman and married at the time in question, whereas unmarried women—and men, married or unmarried—would be entitled to such benefits. The HRC ultimately characterized the distinction in that case as being based on sex rather than family status.[105] However, other cases have specifically considered allegations of discrimination on the basis of marital status. *Sprenger v Netherlands*, for example, also concerned differences in Dutch unemployment benefits between married and unmarried couples; *Danning v Netherlands*[106] related to insurance payments for injuries as a result of an automobile accident, which were higher for married individuals, but not for individuals living in de facto relationships; and *Hoofdman v Netherlands*[107] concerned differences in survivors' benefits as between married and unmarried couples. In each of those cases, the HRC found reasonable bases for the differentiation in treatment on the facts. However, it is clear that the HRC accepted that differential treatment on the basis of marital or family status could constitute a violation of Article 26.

Sexual orientation and gender identity

According to General Comment No. 20:

'Other status' as recognized in article 2, paragraph 2, includes sexual orientation. States parties should ensure that a person's sexual orientation is not a barrier to realizing Covenant rights, for example, in accessing survivor's pension rights. In addition, gender identity is

[102] CESCR, Concluding Observations: Belgium, E/C.12/1994/7 (31 May 1994), [14].
[103] CESCR, Concluding Observations: Canada, E/C.12/CAN/CO/4 (22 May 2006), [23].
[104] CESCR, Concluding Observations: Canada, E/C.12/1993/5 (10 June 1993), [18].
[105] *Broeks v Netherlands*, [14].
[106] HRC Communication No. 180/84 (9 April 1987).
[107] HRC Communication No. 602/94 (3 November 1998).

recognized as among the prohibited grounds of discrimination; for example, persons who are transgender, transsexual or intersex often face serious human rights violations, such as harassment in schools or in the workplace.[108]

The Committee has expressed concern regarding the treatment of such groups in its Concluding Observations.[109] The issue of discrimination against these groups in relation to economic, social and cultural rights has also been the subject of decisions by the Human Rights Committee under Article 26 of the ICCPR. In the case of *Young v Australia*,[110] for example, the HRC considered legislation which provided for payment of pensions to partners of war veterans only where those partners had been married to the veteran, or had been in a de facto relationship with a veteran of the opposite sex. The author, who had been in a same-sex relationship with the relevant veteran for thirty-eight years, complained that this discriminated against him on the grounds of his sexuality. The Human Rights Committee upheld his claim:

10.4 The Committee recalls its earlier jurisprudence that the prohibition against discrimination under article 26 comprises also discrimination based on sexual orientation. It recalls that in previous communications the Committee found that differences in the receipt of benefits between married couples and heterosexual unmarried couples were reasonable and objective, as the couples in question had the choice to marry with all the entailing consequences. It transpires from the contested sections of the VEA [Veterans' Entitlement Act] that individuals who are part of a married couple or of a heterosexual cohabiting couple (who can prove that they are in a 'marriage-like' relationship) fulfill the definition of 'member of a couple' and therefore of a 'dependant', for the purpose of receiving pension benefits. In the instant case, it is clear that the author, as a same-sex partner, did not have the possibility of entering into marriage. Neither was he recognized as a cohabiting partner of Mr. C, for the purpose of receiving pension benefits, because of his sex or sexual orientation. The Committee recalls its constant jurisprudence that not every distinction amounts to prohibited discrimination under the Covenant, as long as it is based on reasonable and objective criteria. The State party provides no arguments on how this distinction between same-sex partners, who are excluded from pension benefits under law, and unmarried heterosexual partners, who are granted such benefits, is reasonable and objective, and no evidence which would point to the existence of factors justifying such a distinction has been advanced. In this context, the Committee finds that the State party has violated article 26 of the Covenant by denying the author a pension on the basis of his sex or sexual orientation.[111]

Health status

The Committee has indicated that discrimination on the basis of a person's physical or mental health may be contrary to Article 2(2):

Health status refers to a person's physical or mental health. States parties should ensure that a person's actual or perceived health status is not a barrier to realizing the rights under the Covenant. The protection of public health is often cited by States as a basis for restricting

108 CESCR, General Comment No. 20, [32].

109 See, eg, CESCR, Concluding Observations: Poland, E/C.12/POL/CO/1 (2 December 2009), [12].

110 HRC Communication No. 941/00 (6 August 2003).

111 *Young v Australia*, [10.4].

human rights in the context of a person's health status. However, many such restrictions are discriminatory, for example, when HIV status is used as the basis for differential treatment with regard to access to education, employment, health care, travel, social security, housing and asylum. States parties should also adopt measures to address widespread stigmatization of persons on the basis of their health status, such as mental illness, diseases such as leprosy and women who have suffered obstetric fistula, which often undermines the ability of individuals to enjoy fully their Covenant rights. Denial of access to health insurance on the basis of health status will amount to discrimination if no reasonable or objective criteria can justify such differentiation.[112]

In this context, the Committee has expressed particular concern about discrimination against HIV positive individuals. So, for example, in relation to the Philippines:

The Committee notes with concern that, in the face of a rapidly growing population infected by HIV and AIDS, only several hundred of an affected population estimated by WHO to be in excess of 30,000 have been registered under the Government's program. This would seem to indicate that the program is either punitive of those who register or is not adequately publicized and made available to victims of the virus. In addition, the Committee was not provided with any information indicating that the Government is seeking to combat widespread discrimination against the victims of the virus.[113]

Place of residence

According to General Comment No. 20:

The exercise of Covenant rights should not be conditional on, or determined by, a person's current or former place of residence; e.g. whether an individual lives or is registered in an urban or a rural area, in a formal or an informal settlement, is internally displaced or leads a nomadic lifestyle. Disparities between localities and regions should be eliminated in practice by ensuring, for example, that there is even distribution in the availability and quality of primary, secondary and palliative health-care facilities.[114]

In this context, the Committee has expressed particular concern about disparities in enjoyment of economic, social and cultural rights between rural and urban areas; the position of immigrants; and the particular situation of internally displaced persons. So, for example, in relation to Benin:

The Committee notes with concern the disparities in living standards between urban and rural areas, given that people living in rural areas have considerably less access to drinking water, sanitation and electricity and that the privatization of water and electricity are leading to a rise in costs.[115]

[112] CESCR, General Comment No. 20, [33].

[113] CESCR, Concluding Observations: Philippines, E/C.12/1995/7 (7 June 1995), [22]. See also Libyan Arab Jamahiriya, E/C.12/1/Add.15 (20 May 1996), [15], [17] and [23]; India, E/C.12/IND/CO/5 (8 August 2008), [13]; Angola, E/C.12/AGO/CO/3 (1 December 2008), [15]; Mauritius, E/C.12/MUS/CO/4 (8 June 2010), [12].

[114] CESCR, General Comment No. 20, [34].

[115] CESCR, Concluding Observations: Benin, E/C.12/1/Add.78 (5 June 2002), [22]. See also, eg, Iraq, E/C.12/1/Add.17 (12 December 1997), [13]; Guatemala, E/C.12/1/Add.93 (12 December 2003), [24]; Greece, E/C.12/1/Add.97 (7 June 2004), [24].

And in relation to China:

The Committee notes with deep concern the de facto discrimination against internal migrants in the fields of employment, social security, health services, housing and education.[116]

In relation to internally displaced person, the Committee has commented, for example, in relation to Georgia:

The Committee expresses deep concern about the deplorable situation of internally displaced persons in the State party. The State party's efforts to provide basic services to this disadvantaged group and special legislation adopted to that end have succeeded only partially in meeting the most basic needs of internally displaced persons, particularly with regard to employment, social security, adequate housing and access to water, electricity, basic health services and education.[117]

More generally, the Committee has noted, for example, differences between the former West and East Germany:

The Committee is concerned that, despite the great efforts made by the State party to narrow the gap between the new and the old Länder, considerable differences continue to exist, particularly in terms of generally lower standards of living, a higher unemployment rate, and lower wages for civil servants in the new Länder.[118]

Economic and social situation

Discrimination on the basis of poverty, or economic and social situation, is frequently addressed by the Committee in its work. In relation to Hungary, for example:

22. The Committee is deeply concerned that…Roma are frequently denied access to social housing, e.g.… as a result of the distribution of social housing by local governments through public auction at high prices.

…

41. The Committee urges the State party to review its regulations on social assistance allowances and raise the amounts in order to better target the most disadvantaged and marginalized individuals, families and groups, such as the Roma, and provide them with a safety net that enables them to enjoy their economic social and cultural rights.[119]

Similarly, in relation to Belgium:

In view of information received by the Committee that not all social housing units are occupied by lower income groups, the Committee urges the government to undertake all

[116] CESCR, Concluding Observations: China, E/C.12/1/Add.107 (13 May 2005), [15].

[117] CESCR, Concluding Observations: Georgia, E/C.12/1/Add.83 (19 December 2002), [12]. See also, eg, Nepal, E/C.12/NPL/CO/2 (16 January 2008), [14].

[118] CESCR, Concluding Observations: Germany, E/C.12/1/Add.68 (24 September 2001), [17]. See also [35].

[119] CESCR, Concluding Observations: Hungary, E/C.12/HUN/CO/3 (16 January 2008), [22] and [41].

necessary measures to ensure that lower-income groups have access to social housing which is affordable.[120]

It is sometimes unclear, however, whether the Committee is concerned in these cases simply with a substantive violation of the right in question, or whether it is concerned with discrimination under Article 2(2). This is because, in most cases, if economic, social and cultural rights are enjoyed only by those who can afford to pay for them, this will constitute a violation by the state of its obligation to guarantee those rights. Thus, according to one commentator, the 'independent utility of the non-discrimination provision becomes apparent only when the State has gone further than it is obliged to under the provisions of the Covenant'.[121]

According to General Comment No. 20, however, the Committee will also be concerned with discrimination as a result of the stigma associated with certain economic and social situations, and the corresponding prejudice against, for example, those living in poverty:

Individuals and groups of individuals must not be arbitrarily treated on account of belonging to a certain economic or social group or strata within society. A person's social and economic situation when living in poverty or being homeless may result in pervasive discrimination, stigmatization and negative stereotyping which can lead to the refusal of, or unequal access to, the same quality of education and health care as others, as well as the denial of or unequal access to public places.[122]

State Obligations

IMMEDIATE OR PROGRESSIVE IMPLEMENTATION?

Whereas the obligations under Article 2(1) of the Covenant are based on the notion of 'progressive realization', Article 2(2) of the Covenant appears to impose an immediate obligation on state parties to 'guarantee' that the rights under the Covenant will be enjoyed without discrimination. This interpretation of Article 2(2) is confirmed by the drafting history. An amendment, introducing the concept of progressive realization, was suggested to make clear that states would not be expected to 'guarantee that when the Covenant was ratified the limited resources available to them, which according to law would be open to all, would in fact be utilized equally by the various groups of the population':

63. The amendment was withdrawn, however, after a number of representatives had stressed that, in their view, to apply the notion of progressive realization to the principle of equality was contrary to the Charter of the United Nations and might give rise to serious abuse, particularly in territories which were not yet independent.

[120] CESCR, Concluding Observations: Belgium, E/C.12/1994/7 (31 May 1994), [14]. See also, eg, Benin, E/C.12/1/Add.78 (5 June 2002), [29].

[121] Craven, *The ICESCR*, 175.

[122] CESCR, General Comment No. 20, [35].

64. If it was understood that the realization of the rights proclaimed in the Covenant must of necessity be progressive, it should be equally clear that there that there must be no discrimination during the process of progressive implementation of those rights.[123]

Thus, as stated by the Committee in its General Comment No. 3:

[W]hile the Covenant provides for progressive realization and acknowledges the constraints due to the limits of available resources, it also imposes various obligations which are of immediate effect. Of these, two are of particular importance in understanding the precise nature of State parties obligations. One of these, which is dealt with in a separate General Comment, and which is to be considered by the Committee at its sixth session, is the 'undertaking to guarantee' that relevant rights 'will be exercised without discrimination…'.[124]

This position is confirmed by the Committee in General Comment No. 20, which notes that '[n]on-discrimination is an immediate and cross-cutting obligation in the Covenant',[125] and highlighted in the Limburg Principles on the Implementation of the International Covenant on Economic, Social and Cultural Rights, which indicate that 'Article 2(2) calls for immediate application'.[126]

The Limburg Principles go on to note, however:

37. Upon becoming a party to the Covenant, states shall eliminate *de jure* discrimination by abolishing without delay any discriminatory laws, regulations and practices (including acts of omission as well as commission) affecting the enjoyment of economic, social and cultural rights.

38. *De facto* discrimination occurring as a result of the unequal enjoyment of economic, social and cultural rights, or on account of a lack of resources or otherwise, should be brought to an end as speedily as possible.

It therefore appears that, although the obligations in Article 2(2) are of immediate effect, states are only under an obligation to bring de facto discrimination to an end 'as speedily as possible'. Although de jure discrimination must be removed immediately, there would seem to be some element of progressive realization, or at least acknowledgement of the fact that a lack of resources may prevent the immediate realization of complete equality, in relation to de facto discrimination. This is implicitly acknowledged in General Comment No. 20, although the Committee indicates that this will only be the case in exceptional circumstances:

A failure to remove differential treatment on the basis of a lack of available resources is not an objective and reasonable justification [and therefore constitutes impermissible

[123] UNGA, Draft International Covenants on Human Rights: Report of the Third Committee (Rapporteur Mrs Marie Sivomey (Togo)), A/5365 (17 December 1962), 20. See also CESCR, Concluding Observations: Japan, E/C.12/1/Add.67 (24 September 2001), [12].

[124] CESCR, General Comment No. 3, The nature of States parties obligations (Art. 2, Para.1, of the Covenant) ('General Comment No. 3'), E/1991/23 (14 December 1990), [1].

[125] CESCR, General Comment No. 20, [7].

[126] Limburg Principles on the Implementation of the International Covenant on Economic, Social and Cultural Rights, as contained in Commission on Human Rights, Note Verbale dated 5 December 1986 from the Permanent Mission of the Netherlands to the United Nations Office at Geneva addressed to the Centre for Human Rights ('Limburg Principles'), E/CN.4/1987/17 (8 January 1987), [35].

discrimination] unless every effort has been made to use all resources that are at the State party's disposition in an effort to address and eliminate the discrimination, as a matter of priority.[127]

Thus, although the obligation in Article 2(2) is an immediate one, failure to achieve de facto equality immediately may, in exceptional cases, be justified on the basis of a lack of available resources.

SPECIFIC ACTION REQUIRED

According to General Comment No. 20, '[i]n addition to refraining from discriminatory actions, States parties should take concrete, deliberate and targeted measures to ensure the discrimination in the exercise of Covenant rights is eliminated'.[128]

As a first step in this process, states are required to identify disadvantaged groups within the population: 'the essential first step towards promoting the realization of economic, social and cultural rights is diagnosis and knowledge of the existing situation'.[129] This information is then to provide 'the basis for the elaboration of clearly stated and carefully targeted policies'.[130] According to General Comment No. 20, individuals from affected groups should be afforded the opportunity to participate in the development of such policies:

> Individuals and groups of individuals, who may be distinguished by one or more of the prohibited grounds, should be ensured the right to participate in decision-making processes over the selection of such measures.[131]

Further, 'States parties should regularly assess whether the measures chosen are effective in practice'.[132]

The Committee has indicated that there are certain measures, in particular, which states should be encouraged to take. These include, first and foremost, the adoption of legislation.

Legislation

According to General Comment No. 20:

> Adoption of legislation to address discrimination is indispensable in complying with article 2, paragraph 2. States parties are therefore encouraged to adopt specific legislation that prohibits discrimination in the field of economic, social and cultural rights. Such laws should aim at eliminating formal and substantive discrimination, attribute obligations to public and private actors and cover the prohibited grounds discussed above. Other laws should be regularly reviewed and, where necessary, amended in order to ensure that they do not discriminate or lead to discrimination, whether formally or substantively, in relation to the exercise and enjoyment of Covenant rights.[133]

[127] CESCR, General Comment No. 20, [13]. [128] CESCR, General Comment No. 20, [36].
[129] CESCR, General Comment No. 1, Reporting by States parties ('General Comment No. 1'), E/1989/22 (27 July 1981), [3].
[130] CESCR, General Comment No. 1, [4]. [131] CESCR, General Comment No. 20, [36].
[132] CESCR, General Comment No. 20, [36]. [133] CESCR, General Comment No. 20, [37].

Similar emphasis on the importance of legislation as a first step in addressing discrimination can be found elsewhere in the work of the Committee. For example, General Comment No. 5 on persons with disabilities provides:

In order to remedy past and present discrimination and to deter future discrimination, comprehensive anti-discrimination legislation in relation to disability would seem to be indispensable in virtually all States parties. Such legislation should not only provide persons with disabilities with judicial remedies as far as possible and appropriate, but also provide for social-policy programmes which enable persons which disabilities to live an integrated, self-determined and independent life.[134]

The Committee has also stressed the importance of legislation in its Concluding Observations.[135]

Policies, plans and strategies

According to General Comment No. 20:

States parties should ensure that strategies, policies, and plans of action are in place and implemented in order to address both formal and substantive discrimination by public and private actors in the area of Covenant rights. Such policies, plans and strategies should address all groups distinguished by the prohibited grounds and States parties are encouraged, among other possible steps, to adopt temporary special measures in order to accelerate the achievement of equality. Economic policies, such as budgetary allocations and measures to stimulate economic growth, should pay attention to the need to guarantee the effective enjoyment of the Covenant rights without discrimination. Public and private institutions should be required to develop plans of action to address non-discrimination and the State should conduct human rights education and training programmes for public officials and make such training available to judges and candidates for judicial appointments. Teaching on the principles of equality and non-discrimination should be integrated in formal and non-formal inclusive and multicultural education, with a view to dismantling notions of superiority or inferiority based on prohibited grounds and to promote dialogue and tolerance between different groups in society. States parties should also adopt appropriate preventive measures to avoid the emergence of new marginalized groups.[136]

The need for policies, plans and strategies, and the effectiveness of such policies adopted by states, have been considered by the Committee in its Concluding Observations.[137]

[134] CESCR, General Comment No. 5, [16].

[135] See, eg, CESCR, Concluding Observations: Austria, E/C.12/1994/16 (14 December 1994), [4]; Uruguay, E/C.12/1/Add.18 (22 December 1997), [19]; Algeria, E/C.12/1/Add.71 (30 November 2001), [39]; Uzbekistan, E/C.12/UZB/CO/1 (24 January 2006), [42] and [43]; Belgium, E/C.12/BEL/CO/3 (4 January 2008), [28]; Benin, E/C.12/BEN/CO/2 (9 June 2008), [32] and [34].

[136] CESCR, General Comment No. 20, [38].

[137] See, eg, CESCR, Concluding Observations: Ireland, E/C.12/1/Add.35 (14 May 1999), [14], [15], [24] and [26]; Republic of Korea, E/C.12/1995/3 (7 June 2005), [18]; Kosovo, E/C.12/UNK/CO/1 (1 December 2008), [13]; Afghanistan, E/C.12/AFG/CO/2-4 (7 June 2010), [7].

Remedies

Legislative and other measures alone will not be effective in combating discrimination unless there are mechanisms and institutions to enforce them and to provide remedies to the victims of discrimination. The Committee has thus emphasized the importance of the availability of remedies, and accountability for violations of the prohibition on discrimination. Thus, in General Comment No. 20, the Committee notes:

40. National legislation, strategies, policies and plans should provide for mechanisms and institutions that effectively address the individual and structural nature of the harm caused by discrimination in the field of economic, social and cultural rights. Institutions dealing with allegations of discrimination customarily include courts and tribunals, administrative authorities, national human rights institutions and/or ombudspersons, which should be accessible to everyone without discrimination. These institutions should adjudicate or investigate complaints promptly, impartially, and independently and address alleged violations relating to article 2, paragraph 2, including actions or omissions by private actors. Where the facts and events at issue lie wholly, or in part, within the exclusive knowledge of the authorities or other respondent, the burden of proof should be regarded as resting on the authorities, or the other respondent, respectively. These institutions should also be empowered to provide effective remedies, such as compensation, reparation, restitution, rehabilitation, guarantees of non-repetition and public apologies, and State parties should ensure that these measures are effectively implemented. Domestic legal guarantees of equality and non-discrimination should be interpreted by these institutions in ways which facilitate and promote the full protection of economic, social and cultural rights.[138]

The Committee has not hesitated to scrutinize the adequacy of remedies provided by state parties. Thus, in relation to Hungary:

The Committee is concerned that the shared burden of proof under the Equal Treatment Act, requiring the victim merely to establish a prima facie case of discrimination, whereupon the burden of proof shifts to the alleged discriminator, is reportedly rarely applied by the courts. It is also concerned that the low level of resources provided to the Equal Treatment Authority since its inception and the recent reduction in its funding and the number of staff may adversely affect its capacity to deal with an increasing caseload.[139]

Monitoring, indicators and benchmarks

According to the Committee, states should monitor the effect of measures taken to eliminate discrimination under Article 2(2). General Comment No. 20 provides:

States parties are obliged to monitor effectively the implementation of measures to comply with article 2, paragraph 2, of the Covenant. Monitoring should assess both the steps taken and the results achieved in the elimination of discrimination. National strategies, policies

[138] CESCR, General Comment No. 20, [40].

[139] CESCR, Concluding Observations: Hungary, E/C.12/HUN/CO/3 (16 January 2008), [8]. See also, eg, Jordan, E/C.12/1/Add.46 (1 September 2000), [31]; Ireland, E/C.12/1/Add.77 (5 June 2002), [14]; India, E/C.12/IND/CO/5 (8 August 2008), [14].

and plans should use appropriate indicators and benchmarks, disaggregated on the basis of the prohibited grounds of discrimination.[140]

In its Concluding Observations, the Committee frequently indicates that states should collect data to measure progress on eliminating discrimination. So, for example, in relation to Algeria:

The Committee also requests the Government to take all necessary measures to ensure that girls are fully able to exercise their right to education and to mental and physical health. Such measures should be accompanied by the setting up of a data collection system enabling their impact to be assessed.[141]

In addition, the Committee regularly asks states to provide statistics and indicators, disaggregated on the basis of grounds of discrimination.[142] Thus, the Guidelines on Treaty-Specific Documents to be Submitted by States Parties under Articles 16 and 17 of the International Covenant on Economic, Social and Cultural Rights indicate that states should:

[P]rovide disaggregated and comparative statistical data on the effectiveness of specific anti-discrimination measures and the progress achieved towards ensuring equal enjoyment of each of the Covenant rights by all, in particular the disadvantaged and marginalized individuals and groups.[143]

The Committee itself also relies on statistics and indicators to determine the existence of discrimination and assess whether states are complying with their obligations under the Covenant. The Committee's comments in relation to Bolivia exemplify its approach in this regard:

Notwithstanding the impressive number of legal instruments and policies adopted by the State party to ensure gender equality, the Committee expresses its concern about the de facto inequality between men and women… Such discrimination is particularly reflected in the low level of representation of women in public service, the high female illiteracy rate, unequal wages for work of equal value, and the high proportion of women working under inadequate conditions in the informal sector or as domestic workers.[144]

AFFIRMATIVE ACTION

A particular issue arises as to whether affirmative action, that is, the adoption of special measures aimed to improve the situation of disadvantaged groups, is allowed, or indeed required, under Article 2(2).

As noted above, the *travaux préparatoires* indicate that the word 'distinction' in the original draft of Article 2(2) was amended to 'discrimination' in order to

[140] CESCR, General Comment No. 20, [41].

[141] CESCR, Concluding Observations: Algeria, E/C.12/1995/17 (28 December 1995), [26].

[142] See, eg, CESCR, Concluding Observations: Azerbaijan, E/C.12/1/Add.104 (14 December 2004), [41]; Hungary, E/C.12/HUN/CO/3 (16 January 2008), [34].

[143] CESCR, Guidelines on Treaty-Specific Documents to be Submitted by States Parties under Articles 16 and 17 of the ICESCR, E/C.12/2008/2 (24 March 2009), [10].

[144] CESCR, Concluding Observations: Bolivia, E/C.12/1/Add.60 (21 May 2001), [15].

ensure that 'protective measures taken by various States for the benefit of certain socially and educationally backward groups of the population' could not constitute violations of Article 2(2). From the outset, then, it is clear that Article 2(2) was intended to allow certain measures of affirmative action.

This position is endorsed by the Committee in General Comment No. 20:

> In order to eliminate substantive discrimination, States parties may be, and in some cases are, under an obligation to adopt special measures to attenuate or suppress conditions that perpetuate discrimination. Such measures are legitimate to the extent that they represent reasonable, objective and proportional means to redress de facto discrimination and are discontinued when substantive equality has been sustainably achieved. Such positive measures may exceptionally, however, need to be of a permanent nature, such as interpretation services for linguistic minorities and reasonable accommodation of persons with sensory impairments in accessing health-care facilities.[145]

The need to adopt 'temporary special measures' to ensure equality was also acknowledged by the Committee in its General Comment No. 16 on the equal right of men and women to the enjoyment of all economic, social and cultural rights:

> The principles of equality and non-discrimination, by themselves, are not always sufficient to guarantee true equality. Temporary special measures may sometimes be needed in order to bring disadvantaged or marginalized persons or groups of persons to the same substantive level as others. Temporary special measures aim at realizing not only de jure or formal equality, but also de facto or substantive equality for men and women. However, the application of the principle of equality will sometimes require that States parties take measures in favour of women in order to attenuate or suppress conditions that perpetuate discrimination. As long as these measures are necessary to redress de facto discrimination and are terminated when de facto equality is achieved, such differentiation is legitimate.[146]

The necessity of affirmative action has also been affirmed in the Limburg Principles,[147] and by the Human Rights Committee in its General Comment No. 18 on Non-Discrimination.[148]

It is therefore clear that, in general terms, affirmative action is acceptable under international law, and in fact may be required in some situations in order to ensure substantive equality. However, a question arises as to exactly what forms of affirmative action will be considered legitimate or appropriate. As Joseph and others have noted, '"affirmative action" is not synonymous with "positive" or "reverse" discrimination'.[149] Measures which involve special assistance to disadvantaged groups, such as special treatment facilities for those suffering from

145 CESCR, General Comment No. 20, [9]. The Committee also encourages states to adopt temporary special measures 'in order to accelerate the achievement of equality' (at [38]) throughout the General Comment: see, eg, [38] and [39].

146 CESCR, General Comment No. 16, [15].

147 Limburg Principles, [39].

148 HRC, General Comment No. 18, Non-discrimination (10 November 1989), as contained in UN, Compilation of General Comments and General Recommendations Adopted by Human Rights Treaty Bodies, HRI/GEN/1/Rev.1 (29 July 1994), [10].

149 Joseph et al, *ICCPR Cases*, 728.

HIV/AIDS, or interpretation services for linguistic minorities, are obviously acceptable. Positive or reverse discrimination, for example through the imposition of quotas for positions in employment and education, is more controversial.

In addition to general objections which can be made to the imposition of quotas, the terms of some Articles of the Covenant would seem to prevent their use. Article 7(c), for example, requires equal opportunity for promotion 'subject to no considerations other than those of seniority and competence'. Similarly, Article 13(2)(c) requires higher education to be equally accessible to all 'on the basis of capacity'.[150] Nonetheless, the Committee, in its Concluding Observations, has recommended the use of quotas to address discriminatory situations and to achieve substantive equality. In relation to Uzbekistan, for example, the Committee has recommended that the state strengthen:

> …programs to reduce unemployment, targeting on a priority basis the most affected groups, including through the creation and stimulation of small and medium-sized enterprises, and the establishment of an obligatory quota for employment of disabled persons.[151]

Similarly, in its Concluding Observations on Costa Rica:

> The Committee urges the State party to intensify its efforts to reduce unemployment among marginalized and disadvantaged groups and individuals through specifically targeted measures, including by ensuring the strict application of anti-discrimination legislation by the judiciary, local government and labour offices; introducing and effectively enforcing legal provisions requiring an ethnically balanced workforce in the public and private sectors; and enhancing professional training and sustainable employment opportunities in the remote areas where the indigenous population resides.[152]

The acceptability of affirmative action in the form of quotas is supported by the fact that such measures have been upheld by other international bodies, including the Human Rights Committee. Thus, in *Stalla Costa v Uruguay*,[153] the Human Rights Committee found no violation of Article 26 of the ICCPR where a law gave preferential access to positions in the public service to those who had suffered from discrimination in the past, namely those who had been dismissed from the public service by the previous government for political reasons.

It therefore seems clear that a range of affirmative action measures, including the imposition of quotas, will be authorized, and may be required, under the ICESCR.[154]

[150] See Craven, *The ICESCR*, 187.

[151] CESCR, Concluding Observations: Uzbekistan, E/C.12/UZB/CO/1 (24 January 2006), [45].

[152] CESCR, Concluding Observations: Costa Rica, E/C.12/CRI/CO/4/Corr.1 (22 April 2008), [39]. See also, eg, Guatemala, E/C.12/1/Add.3 (28 May 1996), [27]; Denmark: E/C.12/1/Add.102 (14 December 2004), [25]; Costa Rica, E/C.12/CRI/CO/4/Corr.1 (22 April 2008), [36].

[153] HRC Communication No. 198/1985 (9 July 1987).

[154] This suggests that, in spite of the specific formulation of Articles 7(c) and 13(2)(c), it is nonetheless appropriate to consider the temporary imposition of quotas as part of the 'progressive realization' of a situation where promotion in employment and access to higher education are genuinely available to all on the basis of equality. See Craven, *The ICESCR*, 187.

PRIVATE ACTORS

Article 2(2) requires States not only to refrain from engaging in discrimination through public bodies, but also to address discrimination within the private sector. According to General Comment No. 20:

Discrimination is frequently encountered in families, workplaces, and other sectors of society. For example, actors in the private housing sector (e.g. private landlords, credit providers and public housing providers) may directly or indirectly deny access to housing or mortgages on the basis of ethnicity, marital status, disability or sexual orientation while some families may refuse to send girl children to school. States parties must therefore adopt measures, which should include legislation, to ensure that individuals and entities in the private sphere do not discriminate on prohibited grounds.[155]

The Limburg Principles similarly indicate that 'Article 2(2) demands from States parties that they prohibit private persons and bodies from practising discrimination in any field of public life'.[156]

The importance of addressing discrimination in the private sphere is also noted in the Committee's General Comment No. 5 on persons with disabilities:

Given the increasing commitment of Governments around the world to market-based policies, it is appropriate in that context to emphasize certain aspects of States parties' obligations. One is the need to ensure that not only the public sphere, but also the private sphere, are, within appropriate limits, subject to regulation to ensure the equitable treatment of persons with disabilities. In a context in which arrangements for the provision of public services are increasingly being privatized and in which the free market is being relied on to an ever greater extent, it is essential that private employers, private suppliers of goods and services, and other non-public entities be subject to both non-discrimination and equality norms in relation to persons with disabilities.[157]

The need for states to address discrimination in the private sector is emphasized in the Committee's Concluding Observations. In relation to China, for example:

It is the Committee's view that the failure by HKSAR [Hong Kong Special Administrative Region] to prohibit race discrimination in the private sector constitutes a breach of its obligations under Article 2 of the Covenant. The Committee calls upon HKSAR to extend its prohibition of race discrimination to the private sector.[158]

Similarly, in relation to Croatia:

The Committee notes with concern that measures to promote ethnic harmony appear to be inadequate and are impeded by continued application of discriminatory laws, policies and practices. It is concerned by reports that private acts of discrimination and ethnically-motivated violence are frequently not adequately addressed by the competent authorities.[159]

155 CESCR, General Comment No. 20, [11]. 156 Limburg Principles, [40].
157 CESCR, General Comment No. 5, [11].
158 CESCR, Concluding Observations: China, E/C.12/1/Add.58 (21 May 2001), [30].
159 CESCR, Concluding Observations: Croatia, E/C.12/1/Add.73 (5 December 2001), [9].

The difficulty associated with extending the obligations of states in relation to non-discrimination to the actions of private actors is determining what activities by private actors must be addressed by the state, and which fall within the exclusively private sphere and should not be subject to state regulation. In other words, there is a tension between individual freedom and privacy, protected under numerous provisions of international law, and the need to address discrimination. This issue has not been specifically addressed by the Committee. However, the Committee's comments in its Concluding Observations have generally been focused on private sector activity in 'quasi-public' fields, such as the provision of health and housing services, and employment. So, for example, in relation to France:

> 41. The Committee urges the State party to take all appropriate measures... in order to:
>
> ...
>
> (c) Ensure the effective implementation of existing legislation to combat discrimination in housing, including discriminatory practices carried out by private actors.[160]

And the majority of Concluding Observations addressing private sector discrimination focus on discrimination in relation to employment. Thus, in relation to Canada:

> The Committee recommends that legislation be adopted at the provincial and territorial levels, where necessary, to ensure equal remuneration for work of equal value in both the public and private sectors.[161]

Similarly, in relation to the Netherlands, the Committee has recommended that the government:

> ... should continue its endeavours to root out racial discrimination in the labour market with a view to facilitating the integration of immigrants and their families into the national life.[162]

And in relation to Hungary, the Committee has recommended 'that the State take more effective measures to encourage the private sector to provide adequate employment opportunities for the Roma'.[163]

This focus on 'quasi-public' activities reflects the approach to private sector discrimination taken by other international bodies, such as the Human Rights Committee. Thus, in *Nahlik v Austria*,[164] the Human Rights Committee noted that:

> ... under articles 2 and 26 of the Covenant the State party is under an obligation to ensure that all individuals within its territory and subject to its jurisdiction are free from discrimination, and consequently the courts of States parties are under an obligation to protect individuals against discrimination, whether this occurs within the public sphere or among private parties in the quasi-public sector of, for example, employment.[165]

[160] CESCR, Concluding Observations: France, E/C.12/FRA/CO/3 (9 June 2008), [41(c)].
[161] CESCR, Concluding Observations: Canada, E/C.12/CAN/CO/4 (22 May 2006), [50].
[162] CESCR, Concluding Observations: Netherlands, E/C.12/1/Add.25 (16 June 1998), [23].
[163] CESCR, Concluding Observations: Hungary, E/C.12/HUN/CO/3 (16 January 2008), [34].
[164] HRC Communication No. 608/95 (22 July 1996).
[165] *Nahlik v Austria*, [8.2].

At times, however, the CESCR seems to go further, and to concern itself with discrimination within the private sector generally. In relation to Togo, for example, the Committee noted:

> The occurrence of societal discrimination on the basis of ethnicity by all ethnic groups is a matter of grave concern to the Committee, in particular the discrimination between southerners and northerners, which is evident in private sector hiring, buying patterns, and the de facto ethnic segregation in urban neighbourhoods.[166]

Conclusion

Article 2(2) imposes concrete and immediate obligations on states to eliminate discrimination with respect to the rights contained in the Covenant. It is therefore central to the operation of the Covenant as whole and, as discussed further in the chapters below, affects the interpretation and application of each of the substantive rights in the ICESCR. Since the obligations which Article 2(2) creates are immediate and not subject to progressive realization, and should be justiciable,[167] Article 2(2) seems likely to provide a focus for complaints under the Optional Protocol to the ICESCR. In this context, it will be interesting to see whether complaints about discrimination in relation to the enjoyment of economic, social and cultural rights will in future be brought before the CESCR, rather than as complaints to the Human Rights Committee of violations of Article 26 of the ICCPR.

166 CESCR, Concluding Observations: Togo, E/C.12/1/Add.61 (21 May 2001), [13].
167 See, eg, Limburg Principles, [35].

5

Article 2(3): Non-Nationals in Developing States

Article 2(3)

Developing countries, with due regard to human rights and their national economy, may determine to what extent they would guarantee the economic rights recognized in the present Covenant to non-nationals.

Article 2(3) effectively authorizes developing countries to limit the extent to which they guarantee economic rights recognized in the Covenant to non-nationals. In practice, no developing country has sought to invoke this Article, and the provision has been the subject of very little attention by the Committee and in the literature. Nonetheless, an understanding of the provision and the rationale for its inclusion in the Covenant is useful for an understanding of the Covenant as a whole, and the operation of its non-discrimination provisions in particular.

Background and context

As noted above, Article 2(2) prohibits discrimination based on nationality. However, certain differences in the treatment of nationals and non-nationals can be justified on 'reasonable and objective bases' and were not intended to be covered by the prohibition in Article 2(2). In particular, it is accepted state practice that the rights of non-nationals to employment and social security will be limited. Against this background, Article 2(3) addresses one particular situation where states may wish to differentiate between foreigners and nationals, namely where the economies of developing countries are dominated by non-nationals, and states need to limit the economic rights of these non-nationals in order to promote more equitable access to economic opportunities.

Paragraph 3 was not included in the original text of Article 2 which was proposed by the Commission on Human Rights. Amendments to introduce the provision were first suggested by Indonesia and Burma. The purpose of doing so, according to the *travaux préparatoires*, was to allow former colonies which had recently gained independence, and whose economies were consequently dominated by the influence of non-nationals, to protect the position of their nationals. The intentions of those proposing the introduction of Article 2(3) is clear from their response to concerns that the provision would 'give rise to all kinds of discrimination alien to the intentions of the sponsors':[1]

> 68. Several other representatives endeavoured to dispel such misgivings, stressing that the sole aim of the proposals in question was to rectify situations which frequently existed in the developing countries, particularly those which had recently won their independence. In such countries, the influence of non-nationals on the national economy—a heritage of the colonial era—was often such that nationals were prevented from enjoying the economic rights set forth in the draft Covenant.
>
> 69. Far from opening the door to discrimination, the amendments were designed to restore the proper balance by enabling nationals to exercise their rights. In the developed countries which had not been subjected to colonial domination, on the other hand, immigration had always been controlled by the Government and non-nationals did not, as a rule, offer serious competition to the economic activities of nationals.[2]

Article 2(3) was therefore intended to allow developing countries to address structural inequalities in their economies which resulted from colonialism. It can be seen as a specific example of legitimate special measures involving differential treatment in order to bring about substantive equality: it is designed to allow developing states to implement systems of positive or reverse discrimination in favour of their own nationals, in fields such as employment, in order to ensure that their own nationals have equal access to, and representation in, the national economy.

Given that Article 2(2) would seem to allow differential treatment of foreigners and nationals in relation to certain rights, including, in particular, rights to employment, there is a question as to whether Article 2(3) provides developing countries with any additional rights over and above those retained by all states in relation to their treatment of non-nationals. It is certainly the view of some commentators that Article 2(3) 'creates no new right that developed countries do not have'.[3] However, the differential treatment of non-nationals envisaged by those proposing the addition of Article 2(3) was not simply the continuation of existing state practice, in the form of restrictions on immigration and employment rights, but the introduction of *new* measures designed to limit the rights which non-nationals had previously enjoyed under the relevant colonial regimes. In other words, the measures envisaged would be deliberately retrogressive, in

[1] UNGA, Third Committee, A/5365 (17 December 1962), 21.
[2] UNGA, Third Committee, A/5365 (17 December 1962), 20–21.
[3] Emmanuel Victor Oware Dankwa, 'Working Paper on Article 2(3) of the International Covenant on Economic, Social and Cultural Rights' (1987) 9(2) *Human Rights Quarterly* 230, 249.

terms of introducing discrimination against non-nationals which had not previously existed. As a result, Article 2(3) may well be necessary to protect developing states taking such measures from violating the prohibition on discrimination in Article 2(2).

Definitions

According to the Limburg Principles on the Implementation of the International Covenant on Economic, Social and Cultural Rights:

42. As a general rule, the Covenant applies equally to nationals and non-nationals.

43. The purpose of Article 2(3) was to end the domination of certain economic groups of non-nationals during colonial times. In the light of this the exception in Article 2(3) should be interpreted narrowly.

44. This narrow interpretation of Article 2(3) refers in particular to the notion of economic rights and to the notion of developing countries. The latter notion refers to those countries which have gained independence and which fall within the appropriate United Nations classifications of developing countries.[4]

'DEVELOPING COUNTRIES'

The term 'developing country' is not defined in the Covenant. However, it is clear that, in the context of Article 2(3), it was intended primarily to refer to those countries which had been in a relationship of economic dependence on other states—to quote the Limburg Principles, 'those countries which have gained independence'.[5] In particular, therefore, the provision was intended to cover states which had recently achieved independence from colonial rule.

The Limburg Principles also require countries to 'fall within the appropriate United Nations classifications of developing countries'. As Dankwa has noted, the classifications adopted by different United Nations agencies are often inconsistent and are problematic in a number of respects.[6] In essence, however, such classifications aim to identify states which are economically weak. The concept of 'developing countries' in Article 2(3) would therefore seem to refer to countries which are economically weak and which were formerly subject to colonial rule.

'ECONOMIC RIGHTS'

Since the intention of Article 2(3) was simply to address situations where non-nationals effectively controlled the national economy, it authorizes states

[4] Limburg Principles on the Implementation of the International Covenant on Economic, Social and Cultural Rights, as contained in Commission on Human Rights, Note Verbale dated 5 December 1986 from the Permanent Mission of the Netherlands to the United Nations Office at Geneva addressed to the Centre for Human Rights, E/CN.4/1987/17 (8 January 1987) ('Limburg Principles'), [42]–[44].

[5] Limburg Principles, [44].

[6] Dankwa, 'Working Paper on Article 2(3)', 236–8.

to limit only the 'economic rights' of non-nationals. 'Social and cultural rights' are therefore excluded from the scope of Article 2(3) and must be guaranteed to nationals and non-nationals alike. This raises the question of which rights under the Covenant are to be characterized as 'economic rights'.

The distinction between economic, social and cultural rights is not entirely clear. As the Committee has noted in relation to the right to education, for example:

> The right to education...has been variously classified as an economic right, a social right and a cultural right. It is all of these.[7]

It is clear from the *travaux préparatoires*, however, that Article 2(3) was primarily intended to cover rights to participate in economic activity. This would include, in particular, rights to work under Articles 6 and 7 of the Covenant. Dankwa, who has undertaken a detailed consideration of Article 2(3), has suggested that 'economic rights, in the context of the Covenant, are rights that enable a person to earn a living or that relate to that process'.[8] Examples would include not only rights to work under Articles 6 and 7, but also rights to form and join a trade union and to strike, under Articles 8(a) and (b), and rights to improved material conditions for teaching staff under Article 13(2)(e).

Conclusion

Although Article 2(3) has never been explicitly invoked by a developing country, it confirms the authority of developing states to address the legacies of colonialism and to assert control over their national economies. In this respect, Article 2(3) can be seen together with the right to self-determination under Article 1 of the Covenant, and the right 'of all peoples to enjoy and utilize fully and freely their natural wealth and resources' under Article 25, as protecting the rights of developing countries to control their national economies and to 'freely dispose of'[9] their natural resources. In providing an exception to the non-discrimination provision in Article 2(2), it allows for the achievement of substantive equality through measures to address the economic inequalities of the colonial era.

[7] CESCR, General Comment No. 11, Plans of action for primary education (Art. 14), E/C.12/1994/4 (10 May 1999), [2].

[8] Dankwa, 'Working Paper on Article 2(3)', 240.

[9] ICESCR, Article 1(2).

6

Article 3: Equal Rights of Men and Women

Article 3

The States Parties to the present Covenant undertake to ensure the equal right of men and women to the enjoyment of all economic, social and cultural rights set forth in the present Covenant.

Article 3 seeks to ensure equality between men and women in the enjoyment of economic, social and cultural rights. It is closely related to the general prohibition on discrimination in Article 2(2), which also prohibits discrimination on the basis of sex. As with the discussion of Article 2(2) above, this chapter will not consider the specifics of how this right to equality is interpreted and applied in the context of the substantive rights under the Covenant, as these issues are considered in the chapters on the substantive rights themselves. This chapter will concentrate instead on the theoretical basis of Article 3 and the general approach adopted by the Committee to issues of equality between men and women.

Background and Context

Although Article 3 is concerned with equality between men and women, and thus covers situations of discrimination against both men and women, the majority of the Committee's work in this area focuses on discrimination against women. As General Comment No. 16 on the equal right of men and women to the enjoyment of all economic, social and cultural rights notes, women 'are often denied equal enjoyment of their human rights, in particular by virtue of the lesser status ascribed to them by tradition and custom, or as a result of overt or covert discrimination'.[1]

The Montréal Principles on Women's Economic, Social and Cultural Rights[2]—principles which, like the Limburg Principles[3] and Maastricht Guidelines,[4] were developed by human rights experts to provide normative guidance regarding the interpretation and implementation of the Covenant—offer further insight into the background to this issue:

Sex or gender inequality is a problem experienced primarily by women. The systems and assumptions which cause women's inequality in the enjoyment of economic social and cultural rights are often invisible because they are deeply embedded in social relations, both public and private, within all States. Acknowledging this systemic and entrenched discrimination is an essential step in implementing guarantees of non-discrimination and equality.

…

Economic, social and cultural rights have a particular significance for women because as a group, women are disproportionately affected by poverty, and by social and cultural marginalization. Women's poverty is a central manifestation, and a direct result of women's lesser social, economic and political power. In turn, women's poverty reinforces their subordination, and constrains their enjoyment of every other right.

…

The inequality in the lives of women that is deeply embedded in history, tradition and culture affects women's access to and enjoyment of economic, social and cultural rights. To ensure women's enjoyment of these rights, they must be implemented in a way that takes into account the context in which women live. For example, the traditional assignment to women and girls of the role of primary care-giver for children, older persons and the sick restricts women's freedom of movement and consequently their access to paid employment and education. The economic and social devaluation of the work, paid and unpaid, that women traditionally do from a very young age, contributes further to fixing women in a position of economic and social inequality. These factors diminish women's earning capacity and their economic autonomy, and contribute to the high rates of poverty among women worldwide. Traditional, historical, religious or cultural attitudes are also used to justify and perpetuate discrimination against women in the delivery of economic, social and cultural rights, including health services and education, by public and private agencies.

[1] CESCR, General Comment No. 16, The equal right of men and women to the enjoyment of all economic, social and cultural rights (art. 3 of the International Covenant on Economic, Social and Cultural Rights), E/C.12/2005/3 (13 May 2005) ('General Comment No. 16'), [5].

[2] International Federation for Human Rights, Montréal Principles on Women's Economic, Social and Cultural Rights (December 2002), reproduced in (2004) 26 *Human Rights Quarterly* 760 ('Montréal Principles on Women's Economic, Social and Cultural Rights').

[3] Limburg Principles on the Implementation of the ICESCR, reproduced in UN Commission on Human Rights, Note Verbale dated 5 December 1986 from the Permanent Mission of the Netherlands to the UN Office at Geneva addressed to the Centre for Human Rights, E/CN.4/1987/17 (8 January 1987) ('Limburg Principles').

[4] CESCR, Substantive Issues Arising in the Implementation of the ICESCR: Maastricht Guidelines on Violations of Economic, Social and Cultural Rights, E/C.12/2000/13 (2 October 2000) ('Maastricht Guidelines').

Inequality in women's enjoyment of economic, social and cultural rights contributes to their economic dependence, denial of personal autonomy and lack of empowerment. These in turn limit still further women's ability to participate in public life, including fora for economic, social, political and legal policy and decision-making. As the Committee on the Elimination of Discrimination against Women has noted: 'Policies developed and decisions made by men alone reflect only part of human experience and potential.' Such policies and decisions are less likely to take account of gendered consequences, and the economic and social factors that affect women's lives.

Economic, social and cultural rights and civil and political rights are particularly indivisible and interconnected in the lives of women: inequality in economic, social and cultural rights undermines women's ability to enjoy their civil and political rights, which then limits their capacity to influence decision and policy-making in public life. Since '[a]ll human rights are universal, indivisible and interdependent and interrelated' equality in civil and political rights is undermined unless equality in the exercise and enjoyment of economic, social and cultural rights is secured.[5]

This issue of inequality as between men and women has been a central concern of the United Nations, and the principle of sexual equality is well recognized in contemporary international law. Article 1(3) of the United Nations Charter indicates that the purposes of the United Nations include 'promoting and encouraging respect for human rights and for fundamental freedoms for all without distinction as to... sex'. And international and regional human rights instruments include sex among the prohibited grounds of discrimination, both in free-standing non-discrimination provisions,[6] and in 'subordinate' provisions which prohibit discrimination in relation to the rights enjoyed under the relevant instrument.[7] More significantly, in 1979 the United Nations General Assembly adopted a convention specifically addressing the issue, namely the Convention on the Elimination of All Forms of Discrimination Against Women,[8] which entered into force in 1981. The issue of discrimination against women is also the subject of a number of specific mechanisms and institutions within the United Nations system.[9]

[5] Montréal Principles on Women's Economic, Social and Cultural Rights, 760–63.

[6] UNGA Res. 217 A (III), Universal Declaration of Human Rights, A/810 (10 December 1948) (UDHR), Article 7; International Covenant on Civil and Political Rights (adopted 16 December 1966, 999 UNTS 171, entered into force 23 March 1976) (ICCPR), Article 26; Protocol No. 12 to the European Convention for the Protection of Human Rights and Fundamental Freedoms (adopted 4 November 2000, ETS 177, entered into force 1 April 2005) (ECHR); American Convention on Human Rights (adopted 22 November 1969, 1144 UNTS 143, entered into force 18 July 1978), Article 4; African Charter on Human and Peoples' Rights (adopted 27 June 1981, 1520 UNTS 217, entered into force 21 October 1986), Article 3, and especially Article 18(3).

[7] UDHR, Article 2; ECHR, Article 14; American Convention on Human Rights, Article 1(1); and African Charter on Human and Peoples' Rights, Article 2.

[8] Convention on the Elimination of All Forms of Discrimination Against Women (adopted 18 December 1979, 1249 UNTS 13, entered into force 3 September 1981).

[9] In particular, the HRC has Special Rapporteurs on both violence against women and trafficking in persons, and also has a Working Group on the issue of discrimination against women in law and in practice. The Commission on the Status of Women is a commission of the UN Economic and Social Council, while UN Women is the general UN entity for gender equality and the empowerment of women. The Office of the UN High Commissioner for Human Rights also has a women's rights and gender section.

The specific issue of equality between men and women is addressed in Article 3 of both the ICESCR and the ICCPR, in identical terms. The inclusion of Article 3 was specifically requested by the General Assembly,[10] reflecting 'the preoccupation of the United Nations at the time of drafting with the issue of sexual equality'.[11] This raised questions as to how this provision would relate to the general prohibition on discrimination in Article 2(2), which also prohibits discrimination on the basis of sex. According to the *travaux préparatoires*:

84. Some representatives thought that article 3 duplicated article 2, paragraph 2, and that the adoption of a special article relating exclusively to the equality of men and women might cast doubt on the effect of the other anti-discrimination provisions contained in article 2…

85. On the other hand, many representatives thought it was essential to retain article 3. The Committee must respect the wish of the General Assembly, expressed in resolution 421(V), concerning the inclusion of such a provision. While article 2, paragraph 2, prohibited all discrimination based on sex, the same rights should be expressly recognized for men and women on an equal footing and suitable measures should be taken to ensure that women had the opportunity to exercise their rights; for example, it would be unrealistic to allow women to hold public office if they did not have the same opportunities as men to acquire the necessary training. Moreover, even if article 3 overlapped with article 2, paragraph 2, it was still necessary to reaffirm the equal rights of men and women. That fundamental principle, which was enshrined in the Charter of the United Nations, must be constantly emphasized, especially as there were still many prejudices preventing its full application.[12]

There is therefore some sense that Article 3 goes further than Article 2(2), requiring states to take positive measures to ensure equality between men and women, rather than simply prohibiting discrimination. However, the Committee, in General Comments No. 16 and No. 20, has interpreted both Article 2(2) and Article 3 as requiring states to take positive measures to ensure substantive equality. It is therefore doubtful whether Article 3 imposes any further obligations on states than Article 2(2), and it seems that Article 3 serves rather to underline the urgent need to address discrimination against women.

According to General Comment No. 20:

Article 2, paragraph 2, of ICESCR provides for a guarantee of non-discrimination on the basis of sex among other grounds. This provision, and the guarantee of equal enjoyment of rights by men and women in article 3, are integrally related and mutually reinforcing. Moreover, the elimination of discrimination is fundamental to the enjoyment of economic, social and cultural rights on a basis of equality.[13]

[10] In UNGA, Res. 421(V), 'Draft International Covenant on Human Rights and measures of implementation: future work of the Commission on Human Rights' (4 December 1950).

[11] Matthew Craven, *The International Covenant on Economic, Social and Cultural Rights: A Perspective on Its Development* (Clarendon Press, Oxford, 1998), 159.

[12] UNGA, Third Committee, A/5365 (17 December 1962), 23–4.

[13] CECSR, General Comment No. 20, Non-discrimination in economic, social and cultural rights (art. 2, para. 2, of the International Covenant on Economic, Social and Cultural Rights), E/C.12/GC/20 (2 July 2009) ('General Comment No. 20'), [3].

Definition

According to General Comment No. 16:

Discrimination against women is 'any distinction, exclusion or restriction made on the basis of sex which has the effect or purpose of impairing or nullifying the recognition, enjoyment or exercise by women, irrespective of their marital status, on a basis of equality of men and women, of human rights and fundamental freedoms in the political, economic, social, cultural, civil or any other field'. Discrimination on the basis of sex may be based on the differential treatment of women because of their biology, such as refusal to hire women because they could become pregnant; or stereotypical assumptions, such as tracking women into low-level jobs on the assumption that they are unwilling to commit as much time to their work as men.[14]

The Committee takes this definition from Article 1 of the Convention on the Elimination of All Forms of Discrimination Against Women and it is clear that the standards under this Convention, and the clarification and interpretation of those standards in the work of the Committee on the Elimination of Discrimination Against Women (CEDAW), will be relevant to the interpretation of Article 3. Thus, the Maastricht Guidelines provide as follows:

Discrimination against women in relation to the rights recognized in the Covenant is understood in light of the standard of equality for women under the Convention on the Elimination of All Forms of Discrimination Against Women. That standard requires the elimination of all forms of discrimination against women, including gender discrimination arising out of social, cultural and other structural disadvantages.[15]

In General Comment No. 16, the Committee makes clear that Article 3, like Article 2(2), requires both formal and substantive equality, and the removal of both direct and indirect discrimination:

6. The essence of article 3 of ICESCR is that the rights set forth in the Covenant are to be enjoyed by men and women on a basis of equality, a concept that carries substantive meaning. While expressions of formal equality may be found in constitutional provisions, legislation and policies of Governments, article 3 also mandates the equal enjoyment of the rights in the Covenant for men and women in practice.

7. The enjoyment of human rights on the basis of equality between men and women must be understood comprehensively. Guarantees of non-discrimination and equality in international human rights treaties mandate both de facto and de jure equality. De jure (or formal) equality and de facto (or substantive) equality are different but interconnected concepts. Formal equality assumes that equality is achieved if a law or policy treats men and women in a neutral manner. Substantive equality is concerned, in addition, with the effects of laws, policies and practices and with ensuring that they do not maintain, but rather alleviate, the inherent disadvantage that particular groups experience.

[14] CESCR, General Comment No. 16, [11].

[15] Maastricht Guidelines, [12].

8. Substantive equality for men and women will not be achieved simply through the enactment of laws or the adoption of policies that are, prima facie, gender-neutral. In implementing article 3, States parties should take into account that such laws, policies and practice can fail to address or even perpetuate inequality between men and women because they do not take account of existing economic, social and cultural inequalities, particularly those experienced by women.

9. According to article 3, States parties must respect the principle of equality in and before the law. The principle of equality in the law must be respected by the legislature when adopting laws, by ensuring that those laws further equal enjoyment of economic, social and cultural rights by men and women. The principle of equality before the law must be respected by administrative agencies, and courts and tribunals, and implies that those authorities must apply the law equally to men and women.

. . .

12. Direct discrimination occurs when a difference in treatment relies directly and explicitly on distinctions based exclusively on sex and characteristics of men or of women, which cannot be justified objectively.

13. Indirect discrimination occurs when a law, policy or programme does not appear to be discriminatory, but has a discriminatory effect when implemented. This can occur, for example, when women are disadvantaged compared to men with respect to the enjoyment of a particular opportunity or benefit due to pre-existing inequalities. Applying a gender-neutral law may leave the existing inequality in place, or exacerbate it.

State Obligations

The nature of state obligations under Article 3 is substantially the same as under Article 2(2).

In the first place, it is clear that the obligations of states under Article 3, like those under Article 2(2), are immediate and not subject to progressive realization:

The equal right of men and women to the enjoyment of economic, social and cultural rights is a mandatory and immediate obligation of States parties.[16]

The Committee goes on, in General Comment No. 16, to expand on the nature of state obligations under Article 3, in terms which largely mirror those found in General Comment No. 20 regarding Article 2(2), as follows:

18. The obligation to respect requires States parties to refrain from discriminatory actions that directly or indirectly result in the denial of the equal right of men and women to their enjoyment of economic, social and cultural rights. Respecting the right obliges States parties not to adopt, and to repeal laws and rescind, policies, administrative measures and programmes that do not conform with the right protected by article 3. In particular, it is incumbent upon States parties to take into account the effect

[16] CESCR, General Comment No. 16, [16].

of apparently gender-neutral laws, policies and programmes and to consider whether they could result in a negative impact on the ability of men and women to enjoy their human rights on a basis of equality.

19. The obligation to protect requires States parties to take steps aimed directly at the elimination of prejudices, customary and all other practices that perpetuate the notion of inferiority or superiority of either of the sexes, and stereotyped roles for men and women. States parties' obligation to protect under article 3 of ICESCR includes, inter alia, the respect and adoption of constitutional and legislative provisions on the equal right of men and women to enjoy all human rights and the prohibition of discrimination of any kind; the adoption of legislation to eliminate discrimination and to prevent third parties from interfering directly or indirectly with the enjoyment of this right; the adoption of administrative measures and programmes, as well as the establishment of public institutions, agencies and programmes to protect women against discrimination.

20. States parties have an obligation to monitor and regulate the conduct of non-State actors to ensure that they do not violate the equal right of men and women to enjoy economic, social and cultural rights. This obligation applies, for example, in cases where public services have been partially or fully privatized.

21. The obligation to fulfil requires States parties to take steps to ensure that in practice, men and women enjoy their economic, social and cultural rights on a basis of equality. Such steps should include:

- To make available and accessible appropriate remedies, such as compensation, reparation, restitution, rehabilitation, guarantees of non-repetition, declarations, public apologies, educational programmes and prevention programmes;
- To establish appropriate venues for redress such as courts and tribunals or administrative mechanisms that are accessible to all on the basis of equality, including the poorest and most disadvantaged and marginalized men and women;
- To develop monitoring mechanisms to ensure that the implementation of laws and policies aimed at promoting the equal enjoyment of economic, social and cultural rights by men and women do not have unintended adverse effects on disadvantaged or marginalized individuals or groups, particularly women and girls;
- To design and implement policies and programmes to give long-term effect to the economic, social and cultural rights of both men and women on the basis of equality. These may include the adoption of temporary special measures to accelerate women's equal enjoyment of their rights, gender audits, and gender-specific allocation of resources;
- To conduct human rights education and training programmes for judges and public officials;
- To conduct awareness-raising and training programmes on equality for workers involved in the realization of economic, social and cultural rights at the grass-roots level;
- To integrate, in formal and non-formal education, the principle of the equal right of men and women to the enjoyment of economic, social and cultural rights, and

to promote equal participation of men and women, boys and girls, in schools and other education programmes;

– To promote equal representation of men and women in public office and decision-making bodies;

– To promote equal participation of men and women in development planning, decision-making and in the benefits of development and all programmes related to the realization of economic, social and cultural rights.

As regards the formulation of national strategies to implement the equal right of men and women under Article 3, General Comment No. 16 further provides:

32. The most appropriate ways and means of implementing the right under article 3 of the Covenant will vary from one State party to another. Every State party has a margin of discretion in adopting appropriate measures in complying with its primary and immediate obligation to ensure the equal right of men and women to the enjoyment of all their economic, social and cultural rights. Among other things, States parties must, integrate into national plans of action for human rights appropriate strategies to ensure the equal right of men and women to the enjoyment of economic, social and cultural rights.

33. These strategies should be based on the systematic identification of policies, programmes and activities relevant to the situation and context within the State, as derived from the normative content of article 3 of the Covenant and spelled out in relation to the levels and nature of States parties' obligations referred to in paragraphs 16 to 21 above. The strategies should give particular attention to the elimination of discrimination in the enjoyment of economic, social and cultural rights.

34. States parties should periodically review existing legislation, policies, strategies and programmes in relation to economic, social and cultural rights, and adopt any necessary changes to ensure that they are consonant with their obligations under article 3 of the Covenant.

35. The adoption of temporary special measures may be necessary to accelerate the equal enjoyment by women of all economic, social and cultural rights and to improve the de facto position of women. Temporary special measures should be distinguished from permanent policies and strategies undertaken to achieve equality of men and women.

36. States parties are encouraged to adopt temporary special measures to accelerate the achievement of equality between men and women in the enjoyment of the rights under the Covenant. Such measures are not to be considered discriminatory in themselves as they are grounded in the State's obligation to eliminate disadvantage caused by past and current discriminatory laws, traditions and practices. The nature, duration and application of such measures should be designed with reference to the specific issue and context, and should be adjusted as circumstances require. The results of such measures should be monitored with a view to being discontinued when the objectives for which they are undertaken have been achieved.

37. The right of individuals and groups of individuals to participate in decision-making processes that may affect their development must be an integral component of any policy,

programme or activity developed to discharge governmental obligations under article 3 of the Covenant.

38. National policies and strategies should provide for the establishment of effective mechanisms and institutions where they do not exist, including administrative authorities, ombudsmen and other national human rights institutions, courts and tribunals. These institutions should investigate and address alleged violations relating to article 3 and provide remedies for such violations. States parties, for their part, should ensure that such remedies are effectively implemented.

39. National policies and strategies should identify appropriate indicators and benchmarks on the right to equal enjoyment by men and women of economic, social and cultural rights in order to effectively monitor the implementation by the State party of its obligations under the Covenant in this regard. Disaggregated statistics, provided within specific time frames, are necessary to measure the progressive realization of economic, social and cultural rights by men and women, where appropriate.

These extracts raise a number of issues, which reflect those issues identified in relation to Article 2(2) and discussed in more detail in that chapter. First, the measures required of States to implement Article 3 include the adoption of legislation; the formulation of policies, plans and strategies; the provision of remedies in the case of violations; and regular monitoring of the effectiveness of measures to eliminate discrimination, with the use of appropriate indicators and benchmarks.

Secondly, Article 3 may require States to adopt 'temporary special measures', including affirmative action, in order to achieve substantive equality between men and women. This is clear from paragraphs 35 and 36 of the General Comment, extracted above. More generally, General Comment No. 16 provides:

The principles of equality and non-discrimination, by themselves, are not always sufficient to guarantee true equality. Temporary special measures may sometimes be needed in order to bring disadvantaged or marginalized persons or groups of persons to the same substantive level as others. Temporary special measures aim at realizing not only de jure or formal equality, but also de facto or substantive equality for men and women. . . . [T]he application of the principle of equality will sometimes require that States parties take measures in favour of women in order to attenuate or suppress conditions that perpetuate discrimination. As long as these measures are necessary to redress de facto discrimination and are terminated when de facto equality is achieved, such differentiation is legitimate.[17]

In its Concluding Observations, the Committee not infrequently recommends that states adopt affirmative action in certain cases. For example, in relation to Angola:

The Committee recommends that the State party adopt special affirmative measures, such as guaranteed seats in Parliament and statutory minimum quotas for the appointment,

[17] CESCR, General Comment No. 16, [15]. See also CEDAW, General Recommendation No. 25, Temporary special measures (2004).

recruitment and promotion of women in Government positions and in the judiciary, including at senior levels and in the highest courts.[18]

Similarly, in relation to Latvia:

The Committee urges the State party to adopt a law on gender equality and take effective measures, including affirmative action measures where necessary, to ensure that women enjoy full and equal participation in the labour market and in political life.[19]

Thirdly, Article 3 not only requires states (through public bodies) to refrain from engaging in discrimination, but also to address discrimination within the private sector. So, for example, in its Concluding Observations in relation to France:

The Committee recommends that the State party take all appropriate measures—including temporary special measures, where needed—to promote equality between men and women, improve the employment rate of women, reduce wage differentials vis-à-vis men and increase the percentage of women in high-ranking posts, in the public as well as in the private sector.[20]

Similarly, in relation to Luxembourg:

The Committee recommends that the State party take all appropriate measures to ensure equal treatment of men and women in employment, especially in the private sector.[21]

Finally, women should be able to participate in decision-making which affects them.[22] According to the Montréal Principles on Women's Economic, Social and Cultural Rights:

States and inter-governmental bodies must ensure that women can and do participate fully in the formulation, development, implementation and monitoring of economic, social and cultural programs and policies. They must also ensure the full participation of women in the formulation, development, implementation and monitoring of specific strategies, plans and policies that aim to eliminate their gender specific disadvantages. This may require States and intergovernmental bodies to ensure women's participation in decision-making where non-State actors provide programs or services that are related to the enjoyment of economic, social and cultural rights.[23]

[18] CESCR, Concluding Observations: Angola, E/C.12/AGO/CO/3 (1 December 2008), [18].

[19] CESCR, Concluding Observations: Latvia, E/C.12/LVA/CO/1 (7 January 2008), [39]. See also CESCR, Concluding Observations: Chad, E/C.12/TCD/CO/3 (16 December 2009), [15]; Denmark, E/C.12/1/Add.102 (14 December 2004), [25]; Hungary, E/C.12/HUN/CO/3 (16 January 2008), [33]; Ukraine, E/C.12/UKR/CO/5 (4 January 2008), [35].

[20] CESCR, Concluding Observations: France, E/C.12/FRA/CO/3 (9 June 2008), [34].

[21] CESCR, Concluding Observations: Luxembourg, E/C.12/1/Add.22 (12 December 1997), [18]. See also Germany, E/C.12/1/Add.68 (24 September 2001), [19]; Ukraine, E/C.12/UKR/CO/5 (4 January 2008), [36]; Angola, E/C.12/AGO/CO/3 (1 December 2008), [17]. See also Montréal Principles on Women's Economic, Social and Cultural Rights, [22] and [23].

[22] See, eg, CESCR, General Comment No. 16, [21] and [37].

[23] Montréal Principles on Women's Economic, Social and Cultural Rights, [25].

The Approach of the CESCR

The Committee, in its work, stresses the importance of addressing discrimination against women, and has addressed the issue in a number of its General Comments.[24] The Committee seems particularly aware of the complexity of the issue of sex discrimination, and is sensitive to a number of factors which lead to discrimination against women. In particular, the Committee notes the systemic nature of discrimination against women, often resulting from customs and traditions which position women as having lesser status. Thus, General Comment No. 16 notes:

> Women are often denied equal enjoyment of their human rights, in particular by virtue of the lesser status ascribed to them by tradition and custom, or as a result of overt or covert discrimination.[25]

The Committee notes further the role of gender in creating systemic inequality:

> Gender affects the equal right of men and women to the enjoyment of their rights. Gender refers to cultural expectations and assumptions about the behaviour, attitudes, personality traits, and physical and intellectual capacities of men and women, based solely on their identity as men or women. Gender-based assumptions and expectations generally place women at a disadvantage with respect to substantive enjoyment of rights, such as freedom to act and to be recognized as autonomous, fully capable adults, to participate fully in economic, social and political development, and to make decisions concerning their circumstances and conditions. Gender-based assumptions about economic, social and cultural roles preclude the sharing of responsibility between men and women in all spheres that is necessary to equality.[26]

The Committee is also sensitive to the fact that discrimination on the basis of sex can intersect with discrimination on other bases, such as race, so as to leave certain groups of women particularly marginalized and disadvantaged. According to General Comment No. 16:

> Many women experience distinct forms of discrimination due to the intersection of sex with such factors as race, colour, language, religion, political and other opinion, national or social origin, property, birth, or other status, such as age, ethnicity, disability, marital, refugee or migrant status, resulting in compounded disadvantage.[27]

[24] See CESCR, General Comment No. 16, [4]. CESCR General Comments addressing factors which affect the equal right of men and women to enjoy economic, social and cultural rights include General Comment No. 4 on the right to adequate housing, E/1992 (13 December 1991), [6]; General Comment No. 7 on forced evictions, E/1998/22 (20 May 1997), [10]; General Comment No. 12 on the right to adequate food, E/C.12/1995/5 (12 May 1999), [26]; General Comment No. 11 on plans for primary education, E/1992/23 (10 May 1999), [3]; General Comment No. 13 on the right to education, E/C.12/1999/10 (8 December 1999), [6(b)], [31] and [32]; General Comment No. 14 on the right to health, E/C.12/2000/4 (11 August 2000), [18]–[22]; General Comment No. 15 on the right to water, E/C.12/2002/11 (20 January 2003), [13] and [14].

[25] CESCR, General Comment No. 16, [5].

[26] CESCR, General Comment No. 16, [14].

[27] CESCR, General Comment No. 16, [5]. This issue has also been identified in the work of the CEDAW: see, eg, CEDAW, General Recommendation No. 18, Disabled women (1991); CEDAW,

This awareness is also reflected in the Committee's Concluding Observations. For example, in relation to France:

The Committee notes with concern that women belonging to racial, ethnic and national minorities who live in ZUS areas, in particular single mothers, experience multiple forms of discrimination and encounter difficulties in access to employment, social security and social services, housing, health and education.[28]

In approaching the application of Article 3, the Committee has emphasized 'the fact that the Covenant is predicated on the principles of absolute non-discrimination against women and their full enjoyment of all the rights enjoyed by their male counterparts'.[29] As a result, the Committee has considered a range of issues affecting equality between men and women. A good example of the Committee's general approach is found in the Committee's Concluding Observations on the Dominican Republic in 1996:

The Committee is particularly concerned that the enjoyment by women of economic, social and cultural rights is undermined, inter alia by: a traditional and persistent male dominated society; the failure to ensure that single women heads of household benefit from the agrarian reform or the Government's housing programme; the absence of any administrative mechanism that allows women to file complaints in cases of discrimination by the Dominican Agrarian Institute; the failure of the Government to protect women workers from discrimination or arbitrary dismissal related to pregnancy, including failure to discourage employers from the practice of pregnancy testing; and failure to develop and promote family planning services. The Committee is also concerned that, despite the very high rate of hospital births in the Dominican Republic, the rate of maternal mortality is unacceptably high; common law marriages are not legally recognized, although 60% of all marriages are of this nature and, consequently, in cases of separation, abandonment or the death of the male bread-earner of the family a woman frequently loses everything and finds it difficult to acquire a cedula or collateral, without which she cannot obtain agricultural credit, housing or employment.[30]

Thus, in practice, the Committee's consideration of Article 3 leads it to consider and comment on a wide range of issues specifically affecting women. Interestingly, some of these do not appear to be directly related to women's enjoyment of economic, social and cultural rights. Thus, although Article 3, like Article 2(2), is formally limited in scope to cover only discrimination which affects enjoyment of economic, social and cultural rights, in practice the Committee appears to use Article 3 to conduct a more general consideration of measures affecting equality between the sexes within states. So, for example, in relation to Kuwait:

The Committee urges the State party to continue to take all necessary measures to grant women the right to vote. The Committee also urges that the State party harmonize its

General Recommendation No. 26, Women migrant workers (5 December 2008); and CEDAW, General Recommendation No. 27, Older women and protection of their human rights (19 October 2010). See also the Montréal Principles on Women's Economic, Social and Cultural Rights, [10].

[28] CESCR, Concluding Observations: France, E/C.12/FRA/CO/3 (9 June 2008), [13].

[29] CESCR, Concluding Observations: Libyan Arab Jamahiriya, E/C.12/1/Add.15 (20 May 1997), [13].

[30] CESCR, Concluding Observations: Dominican Republic, E/C.12/1/Add.6 (6 December 1996), [22].

domestic legislation with the principles and provisions of the Covenant with regard to the law of personal status and the Civil Code so as to abolish differences with regard to rights and responsibilities between women and men to achieve full gender equality.[31]

Similarly, as discussed further below, the Committee makes a number of observations on issues such as domestic violence and trafficking of women in general terms, without specifically relating these to the enjoyment of economic, social and cultural rights.

The discussion below considers a number of the key issues concerning discrimination against women which are raised by the Committee in its work.

STEREOTYPES

The Committee shows particular concern regarding stereotypes which negatively affect the position of women. So, for example, in relation to Algeria, the Committee has expressed concern regarding 'the persistence of stereotypes, attitudes and patriarchal traditions on family and societal roles of men and women'.[32]

Similarly, in relation to Chad:

The Committee requests the State party to take more stringent and effective legal and practical measures to counter inequality between the sexes and discrimination against women in the State party . . . The Committee encourages the State party to take effective measures, including through the use of the media and education, to eliminate traditional stereotypes regarding the status of women in the public and private spheres and to ensure effective gender equality in all fields . . .[33]

CULTURAL PRACTICES

Going beyond concerns about stereotypes, the Committee has expressed concern about a range of traditional cultural practices which affect the position of women. These include practices of female genital mutilation,[34] polygamy, and forced or arranged marriages.[35] A few examples will illustrate the Committee's general approach to these issues. For example, in relation to Nepal, the Committee has noted:

Although certain harmful traditional practices have been prohibited by law, the Committee expresses its continuing concern about the persistence of such practices that violate the rights of women and girls as deuki (dedicating girls to a god or goddess), badi

[31] CESCR, Concluding Observations: Kuwait, E/C.12/1/Add.98 (7 June 2004), [33].

[32] CESCR, Concluding Observations: Algeria, E/C.12/DZA/CO/4 (7 June 2010), [8].

[33] CESCR, Concluding Observations: Chad, E/C.12/TCD/CO/3 (16 December 2009), [14]; India, E/C.12/IND/CO/5 (8 August 2008), [16]; Kazakhstan, E/C.12/KAZ/CO/1 (7 June 2010), [15]; Uzbekistan, E/C.12/UZB/CO/1 (24 January 2006), [15].

[34] See, eg, CESCR, Concluding Observations: Cameroon, E/C.12/1/Add.40 (8 December 1999), [15]; Guinea, E/C.12/1/Add.5 (28 May 1996), [22]. On this issue, see also CEDAW, General Recommendation No. 14, Female circumcision (1990).

[35] See, eg, CESCR, Concluding Observations: Democratic Republic of Congo, E/C.12/COD/CO/4 (16 December 2009), [20]; Zimbabwe, E/C.12/1/Add.12 (20 May 1997), [10]. See also CEDAW, General Recommendation No. 21, Equality in marriage and family relations (1994).

(widespread practice of prostitution among the Badi caste), chaupadi (isolating a woman during menstruating because she is considered to be impure), marrying child brides, and witchcraft.[36]

In relation to Nigeria:

20. The Committee deplores the failure of the Government of Nigeria to abolish female genital mutilation, a practice which is incompatible with the human rights of women and in particular with the right to health.

…

22. The Committee notes with concern that polygamy, a practice which is very often incompatible with the economic, social and cultural rights of women, is widespread in Nigeria.[37]

And in relation to Benin:

8. The Committee notes that the prevalence of certain traditions, customs and cultural practices, including those set down in the 1931 Dahomey Code of Customary Law, leads to substantial discrimination against women and girls and prevents them from fully exercising their rights under the Covenant.

…

12. The Committee deplores the inadequate action taken by the State party to combat the persistent practice of female genital mutilation, generally of young women and girls.

13. The Committee deplores the State party's lack of progress in countering practices—in particular polygamy and the early and forced marriage of girls—which prevent women and girls from exercising the rights which the Covenant accords them.[38]

VIOLENCE AGAINST WOMEN

Violence against women, and particularly domestic violence, is a particular concern of the Committee. Such violence obviously affects women's ability to enjoy a wide range of economic, social and cultural rights, and in particular affects family rights under Article 10. In this context, the Committee has noted in General Comment No. 16:

Article 10, paragraph 1, of the Covenant requires that States parties recognize that the widest possible protection and assistance should be accorded to the family, and that marriage must be entered into with the free consent of the intending spouses. Implementing article 3, in relation to article 10, requires States parties, inter alia, to provide victims of domestic violence, who are primarily female, with access to safe housing, remedies and redress for physical, mental and emotional damage; to ensure that men and women have an equal right to choose if, whom and when to marry—in particular, the legal age of marriage for men and women should be the same, and boys and girls should be protected equally from practices

[36] CESCR, Concluding Observations: Nepal, E/C.12/NPL/CO/2 (16 January 2008), [15].
[37] CESCR, Concluding Observations: Nigeria, E/C.12/1/Add.23 (16 June 1998), [20] and [22].
[38] CESCR, Concluding Observations: Benin, E/C.12/1/Add.78 (5 June 2002), [8], [12] and [13].

that promote child marriage, marriage by proxy, or coercion; and to ensure that women have equal rights to marital property and inheritance upon their husband's death. Gender-based violence is a form of discrimination that inhibits the ability to enjoy rights and freedoms, including economic, social and cultural rights, on a basis of equality. States parties must take appropriate measures to eliminate violence against men and women and act with due diligence to prevent, investigate, mediate, punish and redress acts of violence against them by private actors.[39]

This approach is reflected in the Concluding Observations issued by the Committee: issues of gender-based violence and domestic violence are among the most common matters raised in the context of Article 3. So, for example, in relation to Bosnia and Herzegovina:

The Committee notes with concern that, despite the inclusion of specific provisions on the crime of domestic violence in the State Law on Gender Equality in the Criminal Codes of the Republika Srpska, of the Federation of Bosnia and Herzegovina, and of the Brčko District, the different laws of the Entities have not been harmonized with the State Law on Gender Equality. The Committee is also concerned that cases of domestic violence are rarely reported to and often not sufficiently investigated by the police, and that health-care services are inadequate to support women who are victims of domestic violence and fail to offer any type of treatment programmes.[40]

Similarly, in relation to Cambodia:

The Committee notes with grave concern that, despite the State party's efforts, the levels of violence against women and girls remain high and that the phenomenon tends to be correlated with high levels of general violence with significant gender inequalities. The Committee notes with concern that the incidence of gender-based violence and sexual assault is supported by gender-biased attitudes that blame the female victim and that redress for victims of violence against women is limited. The Committee further notes with concern that legal protection is constrained by ineffective enforcement of the Domestic Violence Law and that criminal prosecution in this regard remains rare.[41]

And in relation to Lithuania:

21. The Committee is concerned about the high incidence of domestic violence and the lack of shelters for battered women. The Committee is also concerned that victims of domestic violence are not adequately protected under existing legislation.

…

43. The Committee calls upon the State party to intensify its efforts to combat domestic violence. In particular the Committee encourages the State party to consider enacting specific legislation criminalizing domestic violence and affording effective protection to victims. The State party should also take effective measures to provide training for law enforcement personnel and judges regarding the criminal nature of domestic violence.

[39] CESCR, General Comment No. 16, [27]. On this issue see also CEDAW, General Recommendation No. 19, Violence against women (1992).

[40] CESCR, Concluding Observations: Bosnia and Herzegovina, E/C.12/BIH/CO/1 (24 January 2006), [21]. See also [43].

[41] CESCR, Concluding Observations: Cambodia, E/C.12/KHM/CO/1 (12 June 2009), [20].

Moreover, the Committee urges the State party to ensure the availability and accessibility of crisis centres where victims of domestic violence can find safe lodging and counselling.[42]

TRAFFICKING

The Committee has also expressed concern regarding the phenomenon of trafficking, which fundamentally violates a range of human rights, including a range of economic, social and cultural rights. Interestingly, in commenting on trafficking, an issue which disproportionately affects women, the Committee does not directly tie its comments to the effect of this practice on the enjoyment of economic, social and cultural rights, but considers the need to address the practice more generally. So, for example, in relation to Germany:

The Committee is concerned that the victims of trafficking in persons, and in particular women, are doubly victimized, owing to a lack of sensitization of police, judges and public prosecutors, a lack of appropriate care for victims, and the risks and dangers awaiting them upon deportation to their home countries.[43]

And in relation to Hungary:

The Committee is concerned that the number of women and girls trafficked to, from, and through the State party is not adequately documented and that the State party has not adopted a national action plan to combat trafficking.[44]

REPRODUCTIVE HEALTH

The Committee is concerned with issues of reproductive health, which affects the right to health of women, and also affects the status of women and their enjoyment of rights under the Covenant more generally. So, for example, in relation to Paraguay:

The Committee strongly encourages the State party to take the necessary legislative steps to address the problem of female mortality caused by clandestine abortions, and recommends that school curricula openly address the subjects of sex education and family planning in order to help prevent early pregnancies and the spread of sexually transmitted diseases. It also recommends that it adopt a law on sexual and reproductive health that is compatible with the provisions of the Covenant.[45]

In relation to Poland:

12. The Committee notes that restrictions have recently been imposed on abortions that exclude economic and social grounds for performing legal abortions. The Committee

[42] CESCR, Concluding Observations: Lithuania, E/C.12/1/Add.96 (7 June 2004), [21] and [43]. See also Nigeria, E/C.12/1/Add.23 (16 June 1998), [21]; Benin, E/C.12/BEN/CO/2 (9 June 2008), [4]; Brazil, E/C.12/1/Add.87 (26 June 2003), [28] and [29]; Canada, E/C.12/1/Add.31 (10 December 1998), [28].

[43] CESCR, Concluding Observations: Germany, E/C.12/1/Add.68 (24 September 2001), [25].

[44] CESCR, Concluding Observations: Hungary, E/C.12/HUN/CO/3 (16 January 2008), [20]. See also Kuwait, E/C.12/1/Add.98 (7 June 2004), [41]; Brazil, E/C.12/1/Add.87 (26 June 2003), [30]; Georgia, E/C.12/1/Add.83 (19 December 2002), [19]; India, E/C.12/IND/CO/5 (8 August 2008), [66].

[45] CESCR, Concluding Observations: Paraguay, E/C.12/PRY/CO/3 (4 January 2008), [32].

expresses its concern that because of this restriction, women in Poland are resorting to unscrupulous abortionists and risking their health in doing so. The Committee is also concerned that family planning services are not provided in the public healthcare system so that women have no access to affordable contraception.

. . .

20. The Committee recommends that every effort be made to ensure women's right to health, in particular reproductive health. It recommends that family planning services be made available to all persons, including counselling on safe alternatives to contraception and reliable and informative sex education for school-aged children.[46]

ACCESS TO RESOURCES

The Committee has also expressed concern regarding a cluster of laws and practices which treat women unequally and affect their access to resources, thus affecting their economic rights, in particular. The issues about which the Committee has expressed concern include women's access to employment, land and property, and credit, and inheritance laws which discriminate against women. So, for example, in relation to Cameroon:

The Committee is deeply concerned that the Government of Cameroon has not yet embarked on the necessary law reform to repeal laws which maintain the unequal legal status of women, particularly in aspects of the Civil Code and the Commercial Code relating to, inter alia, the right to own property and the laws regarding credit and bankruptcy, which restrict women's access to the means of production. They are in flagrant violation of the non-discrimination and equal treatment provisions of the Covenant and are inconsistent with the recently amended Constitution of Cameroon which upholds the equal rights of all citizens of Cameroon.[47]

Similarly, in relation to Benin, the Committee has expressed concern that 'women continue to face widespread discrimination, especially where access to employment, land and credit and inheritance rights are concerned'.[48]

WORK RIGHTS

According to General Comment No. 16:

23. Article 6, paragraph 1, of the Covenant requires States parties to safeguard the right of everyone to the opportunity to gain a living by work which is freely chosen or accepted and to take the necessary steps to achieve the full realization of this right. Implementing article 3, in relation to article 6, requires inter alia, that in law and in practice, men and women have equal access to jobs at all levels and all occupations and that vocational training

[46] CESCR, Concluding Observations: Poland, E/C.12/1/Add.26 (16 June 1998), [12] and [20]. See also Panama, E/C.12/1/Add.64 (24 September 2001), [20]; Mexico, E/C.12/1/Add.41 (8 December 1999 1998), [29].

[47] CESCR, Concluding Observations: Cameroon, E/C.12/1/Add.40 (8 December 1999), [13].

[48] CESCR, Concluding Observations: Benin, E/C.12/1/Add.78 (5 June 2002), [11]. See also Chad, E/C.12/TCD/CO/3 (16 December 2009), [14]; Guatemala, E/C.12/1/Add.93 (12 December 2003), [30]; Saint Vincent and the Grenadines, E/C.12/1/Add.21 (2 December 1997), [15].

and guidance programmes, in both the public and private sectors, provide men and women with the skills, information and knowledge necessary for them to benefit equally from the right to work.

24. Article 7(a) of the Covenant requires States parties to recognize the right of everyone to enjoy just and favourable conditions of work and to ensure, among other things, fair wages and equal pay for work of equal value. Article 3, in relation to article 7 requires, inter alia, that the State party identify and eliminate the underlying causes of pay differentials, such as gender-biased job evaluation or the perception that productivity differences between men and women exist. Furthermore, the State party should monitor compliance by the private sector with national legislation on working conditions through an effectively functioning labour inspectorate. The State party should adopt legislation that prescribes equal consideration in promotion, non-wage compensation and equal opportunity and support for vocational or professional development in the workplace. Finally, the State party should reduce the constraints faced by men and women in reconciling professional and family responsibilities by promoting adequate policies for childcare and care of dependent family members.

25. Article 8, paragraph 1(a), of the Covenant requires States parties to ensure the right of everyone to form and join trade unions of his or her choice. Article 3, in relation to article 8, requires allowing men and women to organize and join workers' associations that address their specific concerns. In this regard, particular attention should be given to domestic workers, rural women, women working in female-dominated industries and women working at home, who are often deprived of this right.

In practice, the Committee's comments, in its Concluding Observations, have concentrated on a few key issues concerning women's rights in relation to work. The first of these is the need for women to receive equal wages for work of equal value.[49] In this context, the Committee is not only concerned with the wages earned by women, but also with systemic inequalities, where fields in which women are employed tend to be those which are lower paid. For example, in relation to Gambia:

[T]he Committee notes with concern that income levels of females generally remain below the government minimum wage scale, particularly those of the female labour force working in contract farming production.[50]

Similarly, in relation to Japan:

The Committee is also concerned about the continuing de facto inequality in wages between men and women for work of equal value, and in particular about the persisting practice in many enterprises of employing women primarily in the clerical services, with little or no chance of promotion to the professional ranks.[51]

[49] On this issue, see also CEDAW, Recommendation No. 13, Equal remuneration for work of equal value (1989).

[50] CESCR, Concluding Observations: Gambia, E/C.12/1994/9 (31 May 1994), [12].

[51] CESCR, Concluding Observations: Japan, E/C.12/1/Add.67 (24 September 2001), [17]. See also Poland, E/C.12/1/Add.26 (16 June 1998), [14]; Netherlands, E/C.12/1/Add.25 (16 June 1998), [12]; Switzerland, E/C.12/1/Add.30 (7 December 1998), [18]; Denmark, E/C.12/1/Add.102 (14 December 2004), [14]; Colombia, E/C.12/1995/12 (28 December 1995), [186].

Secondly, the Committee has expressed particular concern regarding the number of women in domestic work and work in the informal economy, where they have lower wages and lack other protections usually guaranteed to workers. So, for example, in relation to the Former Yugoslav Republic of Macedonia:

> The Committee notes with concern that women, in particular Roma women and women living in rural areas, only have limited economic opportunities and frequently work in the informal or low-paid sectors or are employed in lower positions and receive lower salaries than men, irrespective of their qualifications.[52]

And in relation to Paraguay:

> The Committee notes with concern that the wages paid to domestic workers, the majority of whom are women, represent only 40% of the minimum wage. While noting the explanation presented by the State party that such employees receive board and lodging from their employers, the Committee believes such a low percentage of the minimum wage is not sufficient to ensure a decent living for these workers. Furthermore, domestic workers work up to twelve hours a day often without social security or overtime pay.[53]

Issues also arise in relation to unremunerated work carried out by women.[54] According to the Montréal Principles on Women's Economic, Social and Cultural Rights:

> States must adopt specific measures to recognize the economic and social contribution of the women who carry out unremunerated activities. States must also ensure that women or particular groups of women do not carry out a disproportionately large part of the unremunerated and devalued workload of families and communities, including domestic labour and the care of children, sick, and older persons.[55]

Thirdly, the Committee has considered the issue of sexual harassment in the workplace as affecting women's right to work. So, for example, in relation to Cameroon:

> The Committee is concerned that the Government has not yet introduced legislation to prohibit sexual harassment in the workplace which, according to information received by the Committee, is a widespread practice in Cameroon.[56]

Finally, the Committee has raised issues regarding the availability of childcare. In relation to Italy, for example:

> The Committee strongly recommends that the State party extend the network of affordable, accessible and available childcare services.[57]

[52] CESCR, Concluding Observations: Former Yugoslav Republic of Macedonia, E/C.12/MCD/CO/1 (15 January 2008), [13].

[53] CESCR, Concluding Observations: Paraguay, E/C.12/PRY/CO/3 (4 January 2008), [15]; India, E/C.12/IND/CO/5 (8 August 2008), [18].

[54] On this issue, see also CEDAW, General Recommendation No. 16, Unpaid workers in rural and urban family enterprises (1991); and CEDAW, General Recommendation No. 17, Measurement and quantification of the unremunerated domestic activities of women and their recognition in the GNP (1991).

[55] Montréal Principles on Women's Economic, Social and Cultural Rights, [24].

[56] CESCR, Concluding Observations: Cameroon, E/C.12/1/Add.40 (8 December 1999), [18]. See also Croatia, E/C.12/1/Add.73 (5 December 2001), [13]; Georgia, E/C.12/1/Add.42 (17 May 2000), [15]; Guatemala, E/C.12/1/Add.93 (12 December 2003), [34].

[57] CESCR, Concluding Observations: Italy, E/C.12/1/Add.103 (14 December 2004), [44]. See also Chile, E/C.12/1/Add.105 (1 December 2004), [37]; Germany, E/C.12/1/Add.68 (24 September 2001), [26].

UNDER-REPRESENTATION OF WOMEN IN KEY POSITIONS

The Committee expresses concern wherever women are under-represented in key positions, for example in elected bodies, or in senior positions in employment or the public service. In doing so, the Committee focuses on substantive equality, by looking directly at outcomes and statistics regarding the representation of women. For example, in relation to Hungary:

The Committee recommends that the State party adopt temporary special measures, such as statutory quotas, to ensure the adequate representation of women in Parliament and in local elected bodies. The Committee also recommends that the State party undertake a study on the reasons for the under-representation of women in senior positions in the public service and that it take measures to increase their representation.[58]

And in relation to Brazil, the Committee has expressed concern that:

[A]lthough women in general have a higher educational level than men, they are still under-represented in elected office and administrative and managerial posts, are concentrated in less remunerative and/or part-time employment and receive lower average pay.[59]

Conclusion

Article 3 substantially overlaps with the prohibition on discrimination on the basis of sex under Article 2(2). There are two significant points which flow from this. The first is that the interpretation and application of Article 3 is informed by the interpretation and application of Article 2(2), and the issues discussed in more detail in relation to Article 2(2), above, must be taken into account in relation to Article 3.

Secondly, as a result, it is doubtful whether, in practice, Article 3 adds anything to the protection which exists under Article 2(2). However, the existence of a separate Article guaranteeing the equality of men and women serves to highlight the importance of this issue, which is central to much of the work of the United Nations as a whole. In this context, it is interesting to note the United Nations Guiding Principles on Extreme Poverty and Human Rights,[60] which mirror the approach of the Committee and offer a good summary of issues relating to equality between men and women in the context of the enjoyment of economic, social and cultural rights:

23. Women are disproportionately represented among the poor owing to the multifaceted and cumulative forms of discrimination that they endure. States are obliged to eliminate

[58] CESCR, Concluding Observations: Hungary, E/C.12/HUN/CO/3 (16 January 2008), [33].

[59] CESCR, Concluding Observations: Brazil, E/C.12/BRA/CO/2 (12 June 2009), [14]. See also Armenia, E/C.12/1/Add.39 (8 December 1999), [10]; Kenya, E/C.12/KEN/CO/1 (1 December 2008), [15].

[60] HRC, Final Draft of the Guiding Principles on Extreme Poverty and Human Rights, submitted by the Special Rapporteur on extreme poverty and human rights, A/HRC/21/39 (18 July 2012).

both de jure and de facto discrimination against women and put in place measures to achieve equality between men and women.

24. International human rights law also requires States to take measures to eliminate harmful cultural and traditional practices and all other practices that are based on the idea of the inferiority or the superiority of either sex, or on stereotyped roles for women and men. These practices increase the social exclusion of women and girls, impede their access to resources and education and perpetuate poverty and discrimination.

25. States must take forceful action to combat gender-based violence. Women living in poverty who are victims of gender-based violence face particular difficulties in accessing justice and in leaving abusive relationships.

26. Women must have equal access to economic opportunities. States must accord priority to expanding employment and entrepreneurship opportunities for women, promote decent and productive work and improve access to finance. Public policies and employment regulations must take into account women's time constraints and enable both women and men to care for their households.

27. States must ensure women's full and equal legal capacity to own, control and administer economic resources such as land, credit and inheritance.

28. Women must also enjoy equal access to decision-making power. States must develop mechanisms to enhance the involvement of women, including those living in poverty, in political life and decision-making bodies at all levels.

29. Policies must promote gender equality in marriage and family relations, and ensure that women's decision-making, including regarding the number and spacing of children, is free and unconstrained and that food and other resources are equally distributed within the household.

30. Women must be ensured equal access to public services, including health, education and social protection, and equality in the labour market, including equal wages, conditions of employment and social security benefits. In particular, sexual and reproductive health services and information, early childhood education and post-primary education must be made available to women and girls.

31. States must articulate gender equality as a goal in policies, strategies, budgets, programmes and projects. They must increase targeted national resources and official development assistance for gender equality, and pay attention to women's economic empowerment in the context of international trade.

7

Articles 4, 5, and 24: Limitations on ICESCR Rights and 'No Prejudice' Clauses

Article 4

The States Parties to the present Covenant recognize that, in the enjoyment of those rights provided by the State in conformity with the present Covenant, the State may subject such rights only to such limitations as are determined by law only in so far as this may be compatible with the nature of these rights and solely for the purpose of promoting the general welfare in a democratic society.

Article 5

1. Nothing in the present Covenant may be interpreted as implying for any State, group or person any right to engage in any activity or to perform any act aimed at the destruction of any of the rights or freedoms recognized herein, or at their limitation to a greater extent than is provided for in the present Covenant.

2. No restriction upon or derogation from any of the fundamental human rights recognized or existing in any country in virtue of law, conventions, regulations or custom shall be admitted on the pretext that the present Covenant does not recognize such rights or that it recognizes them to a lesser extent.

Article 24

Nothing in the present Covenant shall be interpreted as impairing the provisions of the Charter of the United Nations and of the constitutions of the specialized agencies which define the respective responsibilities of the various organs of the United Nations and of the specialized agencies in regard to the matters dealt with in the present Covenant.

Introduction

Article 4 allows for certain limitations on any ICESCR right, unlike the right-specific approach to limitations under the ICCPR, and in the absence of a derogation clause as found in the ICCPR. Article 5 is common to both the ICESCR and ICCPR. Article 5(1) prohibits the abuse of one right to destroy another, while Article 5(2) prevents the ICESCR from undermining higher rights protections in national law or other international law. Article 24 emphasizes that the ICESCR does not prejudice the UN Charter or the constitutions of UN organs or specialized agencies.

A number of other ICESCR provisions may be regarded as permitting limitations or requiring 'no prejudice', but are considered elsewhere. Article 2(3) allows developing states to restrict the rights of non-nationals and was considered in that earlier chapter. Article 25 prevents the ICESCR being interpreted to impair the inherent right of all peoples to freely and fully enjoy and utilize their natural wealth and resources, and was examined alongside the right of self-determination in Article 1.

Article 4

LIMITATIONS

Article 4 is a general limitation clause applicable to all ICESCR rights. It is additional to right-specific limitations provisions in the ICESCR, such as the right of developing countries to restrict the rights of non-citizens under Article 2(3), or the multiple restrictions on trade union rights under Article 8(1) to (2).

The ICESCR approach to limitations is different from that taken by the ICCPR. The ICCPR does not contain a general limitation clause and instead provides only for the specific limitation of some (but not all) rights. In addition, the ICCPR provides for the derogation from certain rights during declared public emergencies threatening the life of the nation (Article 4), whereas no derogation clause appears in the ICESCR. The ICESCR also departs from the limitations formula in Article 29(2) of the UDHR, which provides:

> In the exercise of his rights and freedoms, everyone shall be subject only to such limitations as are determined by law solely for the purpose of securing due recognition and respect for the rights and freedoms of others and of meeting the just requirements of morality, public order and the general welfare in a democratic society.

During the drafting, a general limitations clause was proposed for inclusion in the ICESCR in 1952,[1] following earlier debates about limitations in the context of what became the ICCPR, the Draft International Covenant on Human Rights. In those earlier discussions, there was debate about whether the Draft Covenant should contain a general limitations clause or specific limitations provisions applying to particular rights.

The United States, for instance, opposed specific limitations provisions because it thought they would be open to abuse and reduce the effectiveness of the Covenant.[2] It was conversely concerned that expressing specific limitations would imply the exclusion of others not mentioned, thus being under-inclusive. In contrast, the United Kingdom felt that the general clause proposed by the United States would be more open to abuse and thought it preferable to tightly prescribe the limitations permitted in respect of each right.[3] Lebanon too favoured specific exceptions, but noted that there may be difficulty in enumerating all limitations.[4]

While the ICCPR ultimately adopted right-specific limitations clauses, along with a general derogation clause, similar debates carried through into the drafting of the ICESCR, although different issues also arose. Some states were against including any limitations clauses, general or specific, because there was no need for them given the nature of each economic, social and cultural right.[5] In particular, 'the nature of the obligations and the manner of enunciating the rights made limitations generally unnecessary', with the exception of trade unions whose 'responsibility as an organization' had to be recognized.[6] Considerations of morality and public order were considered more relevant to civil and political rights.[7]

By contrast, some states favoured a general clause because economic, social and cultural rights 'were recognized in broad terms and a list of specific

[1] Article 32 was adopted by the Commission on Human Rights on 23 May 1952: Commission on Human Rights (CHR), Draft International Covenants on Human Rights and Measures of Implementation, E/CN.4/666/Add.14 (26 May 1952).

[2] CHR, Comments from Governments on the Draft International Declaration on Human Rights, Draft International Covenant on Human Rights and the Question of Implementation, E/CN.4/82/Rev.1 (22 April 1948), 21; CHR, Collation of the Comments of Governments on the Draft International Declaration on Human Rights, Draft International Covenant on Human Rights and the Question of Implementation, E/CN.4/85 (1 May 1948), 50–51.

[3] CHR, Report of the Commission on Human Rights, E/600 (17 December 1947), 30–31; UNGA Third Committee, A/C.3/SR.288 (18 October 1950), 109.

[4] UNGA Third Committee, A/C.3/SR.289 (19 October 1950).

[5] CHR, Report to ECOSOC, E/2256(SUPP) (1 January 1952), 24.

[6] CHR, Report to ECOSOC, 24.

[7] CHR, Report to ECOSOC, 24.

limitations would necessarily be incomplete',[8] while specific limitations were more relevant to ICCPR rights. There was also a danger that specific provisions might be regarded as exhaustive.[9] Others preferred specific limitations provisions to safeguard against abuse, or were concerned that a general clause would adversely impact on the right of self-determination[10] (a concern also addressed by Article 25).

Many technical objections to Article 4 focused on the vagueness and imprecision of terms such as 'compatible with the nature of these rights' and 'for the purpose of promoting the general welfare in a democratic society'. Such terms were thought to give rise to varying interpretations and to weaken the protection of rights.[11] Proposals to specify the grounds for limitation in more detail were not, however, accepted, such as by reference to the 'requirements of morality and public order'[12] (expressions found in various provisions of the ICCPR).

Few concrete examples were raised during the drafting as to what kinds of restrictions would be justified by the formulation under Article 4. Pakistan emphasized measures to ensure state or collective security.[13] Lebanon mentioned 'internal labour regulations' as potentially coming within Article 4.[14] It is unclear from the drafting records whether it was intended to extend to issues of morality or public order; some delegations supported it because it was broadly expressed; others because they interpreted it narrowly.

In the end the debate was settled in part because, as a result of the sequence of drafting the various articles, it was impractical at a late stage to reopen settled rights to reconsider whether specific limitations could be re-inserted into them.[15] Some states had supported rights already drafted on the assumption that a general limitation clause would come later.[16] The 'in principle' proposal for a general clause was narrowly adopted in the Commission on Human Rights by nine votes to eight, with one abstention,[17] with mainly Western states in favour (plus China and India) and mainly socialist and developing states against.

What emerges most clearly from the drafting is that the central purpose of Article 4 is to ensure that states must not *arbitrarily* limit ICESCR rights.[18] Article 4 was primarily intended to be protective of the rights of individuals rather than permissive of the imposition of limitations by the State.[19] It enables the balancing of public interests in human rights and other public needs. As the

[8] CHR, Report to ECOSOC, 24.
[9] UNGA Third Committee, A/C.3/SR.738 (23 January 1957), 291 (Ireland).
[10] CHR, Report to ECOSOC, E/2256(SUPP) (1 January 1952), 24.
[11] CHR, Report to ECOSOC, 24; UNGA Third Committee, A/5365 (17 December 1962), 24; UNGA Third Committee, A/C.3/SR.1184 (15 November 1962), 252 (Indonesia), 253 (Brazil); UNGA Third Committee, A/C.3/SR.1185 (16 November 1962), 257 (Uruguay).
[12] CHR, Report to ECOSOC, E/2256(SUPP) (1 January 1952), 24.
[13] UNGA Third Committee, A/C.3/SR.1185 (16 November 1962), 260 (Pakistan).
[14] UNGA Third Committee, A/C.3/SR.659 (11 November 1955), 178 (Lebanon).
[15] CHR, Report to ECOSOC, E/2256(SUPP) (1 January 1952), 24.
[16] UNGA Third Committee, A/C.3/SR.788 (23 October 1957), 135 (Mexico).
[17] CHR, Report to ECOSOC, E/2256(SUPP) (1 January 1952), 24.
[18] CHR, Report to ECOSOC, 24; UNGA Third Committee, A/5365 (17 December 1962), 24.
[19] Limburg Principles on the Implementation of the ICESCR, E/CN.4/1987/17 (8 January 1987), [46].

French delegate stated, Article 4 strikes 'a balance between the trend to exclude any derogation from the provisions of the Covenant and the trend to permit States to evade their obligations in an uncontrolled manner on the pretext, for example, of public danger'.[20]

Regional instruments also commonly contain limitations clauses. In the area of socio-economic rights, the European Social Charter includes right-specific clauses, a general limitations clause (Article 31),[21] and a derogation clause for emergencies (Article 30). Article 31 provides:

1. The rights and principles set forth in Part I when effectively realised, and their effective exercise as provided for in Part II, shall not be subject to any restrictions or limitations not specified in those parts, except such as are prescribed by law and are necessary in a democratic society for the protection of the rights and freedoms of others or for the protection of public interest, national security, public health, or morals.

2. The restrictions permitted under this Charter to the rights and obligations set forth herein shall not be applied for any purpose other than that for which they have been prescribed.

In other regional instruments, the European Convention on Human Rights includes right-specific clauses,[22] a derogation clause (Article 15), but no general limitations clause. The African Charter contains right-specific clauses,[23] a general clause,[24] but no derogation clause. The American Convention on Human Rights contains all three types: right-specific clauses,[25] a general limitations clause[26] and a derogation clause (Article 27). The application of these various formulas to socio-economic rights at the regional level sheds light on common and divergent approaches to limitations in this context.

RELATIONSHIP TO SPECIFIC LIMITATIONS PROVISIONS

As already noted, there are a number of specific limitation provisions in the ICESCR. These foremost include restrictions on the rights of non-nationals in developing states (Article 2(3)) and on trade union rights (Article 8). In addition, Article 13(3) and (4) allows states to lay down minimum educational standards governing non-public schools, thus affecting the freedom of parents, guardians and educational institutions to pursue their own educational choices. Further, in realizing the right to health, Article 12(2)(c) permits states to take steps for the 'prevention, treatment and control of epidemic, endemic, occupational and other

[20] UNGA Third Committee, A/C.3/SR.1182 (14 November 1962), 240 (France).

[21] European Social Charter 1961, Article 31.

[22] ECHR, Articles 8(2), 9(2), 10(2) and 11(2).

[23] African Charter, Articles 6, 8, 9, 11, 12 and 14.

[24] African Charter, Article 27(2): 'The rights and freedoms of each individual shall be exercised with due regard to the rights of others, collective security, morality and common interest'.

[25] ACHR, Articles 12(3), 13(2), 13(4), 13(5), 15, 16(2), 21(2) and 22(3)–(4).

[26] ACHR, Article 30: 'The restrictions that, pursuant to this Convention, may be placed on the enjoyment or exercise of the rights or freedoms recognized herein may not be applied except in accordance with laws enacted for reasons of general interest and in accordance with the purpose for which such restrictions have been established.'

diseases', which potentially includes certain restrictions (such as quarantine or compulsory treatment) on those suffering from those diseases to protect public health.

The drafting record is inconclusive on the legal relationship between these provisions and Article 4 and there was little discussion of the issue. It was suggested that trade union-specific limitations were unnecessary because Article 4 already covered such situations, but also noted that a 'general limitation did not... preclude specific limitations'.[27] Others felt that trade union-specific limitations were exclusive, following the ICCPR model of specific clauses.[28]

Logically, the adoption of specific limitations, which are tailored to the special circumstances of a particular subject area and expressed in greater detail, signifies that such provisions ordinarily apply in place of a more general provision. The more difficult question is whether the special provision applies exclusively, or only takes precedence or priority but allows a residual field of application for further restrictions not encompassed by the special provision.

The better view is that the specific limitation provisions should be treated as exclusively governing the field. Otherwise, a specific provision would be redundant, since it would be subsumed by the wider scope of the general clause in Article 4. This is obvious from examination of the specific limitations. The possibility to restrict non-nationals' rights in developing countries under Article 2(3) would be no protection at all if *developed* states could resort to Article 4 to also deny rights to non-nationals. Likewise, the carefully crafted limitations on trade unions under Article 8 could be circumvented if Article 4 allowed a wider range of restrictions in the purported public interest. In its practice, the CESCR has only ever assessed restrictions on trade unions according to the limitations permitted under Article 8.[29]

It should be noted that the CESCR has, however, looked outside the ICESCR for guidance on the limitation of certain rights. In relation to restrictions on the right to housing under the ICESCR, the CESCR has invoked Article 17 of the ICCPR (freedom from arbitrary interference in the home) in evaluating the lawfulness of (forced) evictions:[30]

15. In cases where eviction is considered to be justified, it should be carried out in strict compliance with the relevant provisions of international human rights law and in accordance with general principles of reasonableness and proportionality. In this regard it is especially pertinent to recall General Comment 16 by the Human Rights Committee, relating to Article 17 of the International Covenant on Civil and Political Rights, which states that interference with a person's home can only take place 'in cases envisaged by the law'. The Committee observed that the law 'should be in accordance with the provisions, aims and objectives of the Covenant and should be, in any event, reasonable in the particular

27 UNGA Third Committee, A/C.3/SR.723 (7 January 1957), 214 (Uruguay).

28 UNGA Third Committee, A/C.3/SR.721 (4 January 1957), 201 (Lebanon).

29 See, eg, CESCR, Concluding Observations: South Korea, E/C.12/1995/3 (7 June 1995), [8]; Ukraine, E/C.12/1/Add.65 (24 September 2001), [27]; and the chapter in this book on Article 8.

30 See the chapter on Article 11 (the right to an adequate standard of living, including housing) for the conditions that must be satisfied to justify a forced eviction.

circumstances'. The Committee also indicated that 'relevant legislation must specify in details the precise circumstances in which such interferences may be permitted'.[31]

The Human Rights Committee's (HRC's) comments were in the context of what is an 'arbitrary' interference in the home, which necessarily allows for interferences which are not arbitrary, although Article 17 is not expressed as a limitations clause as such. The CESCR has no strict legal mandate to apply ICCPR provisions in assessing ICESCR compliance. However, it is free to borrow appropriate legal concepts from elsewhere in developing its own jurisprudence, particularly to harmonize its own approach with that of its twin Covenant. In this case, the CESCR's invocation of an ICCPR standard served to raise, not diminish, human rights protection for affected persons.

While the CESCR does not mention it, one legal route by which to import such considerations into the evaluation of limitations on the right to housing under the ICESCR is by reference to Article 4 of the ICESCR. As discussed below, Article 4 involves similar evaluation of legality and non-arbitrariness. Depending on the right in question, additional requirements may govern limitations. Thus, in the evictions context, the CESCR has required certain due process or procedural protections (such as adequate notice, information and consultation).[32] Further general requirements will also apply to the limitation of any right, including a proportionality assessment (including consideration of less invasive alternatives) and the availability of effective remedies and adequate compensation.[33]

IMPLIED OR INHERENT LIMITATIONS

A number of ICESCR rights allow competing public interests to be accommodated without the need to resort to the express limitations provision in Article 4. The primary rules themselves govern the terrain of limitation, whether by their definition or interpretation. One example is non-discrimination under Article 2, where an 'objective and reasonable' basis for treating members of a protected group differently will not amount to discrimination. The legal test for differentiation is regarded as inherent or implicit in the non-discrimination standards themselves, and the CESCR has not sought to justify this test by reference to what is necessary for the 'general welfare' of society under Article 4. The CESCR has also resisted efforts by states to justify limitations on non-discrimination by reference to wider social values, such as traditional customary law or Sharia law.[34]

[31] CESCR, General Comment No. 7, E/1996/22 annex IV (20 May 1997), [15]. General Comment No. 4 of the CESCR also stated that 'instances of forced eviction are prima facie incompatible with the requirements of the Covenant and can only be justified in the most exceptional circumstances, and in accordance with the relevant principles of international law': CESCR, General Comment No. 4, E/1992/23 (13 December 1991), [18]. See also CESCR, Concluding Observations: Mexico, E/C.12/1993/16 (5 January 1994), [14]; Nicaragua, E/C.12/1993/14 (4 January 1994), [9].

[32] CESCR, General Comment No. 7, E/1996/22 (20 May 1997), annex IV [12]–[16].

[33] CESCR, General Comment No. 7, annex IV [12]–[16].

[34] See, eg, CESCR, Concluding Observations: Zambia, E/C.12/1/Add.106 (23 June 2005), [15]; Libya, E/C.12/1/Add.15 (20 May 1997), [13].

Likewise, in relation to the right to work in Article 6, an employer's stipulation of 'inherent requirements of a job' is not regarded as infringing an unqualified candidate's freedom to work. The requirement of certain job qualifications is not evaluated by reference to what is necessary 'for the general welfare' under Article 4. Indeed, job qualifications may be of concern only to the particular employer and have little to do with the 'general welfare', unless that concept is applied in a very broad and attenuated fashion. The same is true of grounds of lawful dismissal, which are justifiable reasons for interfering in a person's right to work, without reference to Article 4.

Further, certain work required of people on public interest grounds (such as military service, prison labour, or work in emergencies or as part of civic obligations) is not regarded as unlawful forced labour under Article 6. The permissible grounds for compelling labour are not articulated in Article 6 itself, but are implicitly accepted as permitted within it (corresponding to the exceptions permitted under Article 8(3)(c) of the ICCPR)—even though such grounds could alternatively be regarded as for the general welfare under Article 4. Likewise, it is well accepted that a person may be excluded from employment on national security grounds, based on ILO practice, within a breach of Article 6, and without any recourse to Article 4 justifications—even if Article 4 would likely accommodate such concerns.

In the area of social security rights, certain eligibility criteria or qualifying conditions for receipt of benefits may be imposed by states without infringing Article 9. Such conditions on the right to social security are generally not assessed by reference to what is necessary for the general welfare under Article 4, but are treated as inherent with the body of social security rights. This is the case even though Article 4 could often independently support such conditions, for instance a requirement on a job seeker to undertake skills training to increase her employability and thus hasten her transition off publicly funded benefits.

RELATIONSHIP TO PROGRESSIVE REALIZATION

During the drafting, some thought that Article 4 was 'superfluous' since the principle of progressive realization already covered such concerns.[35] Others supported the general clause because they viewed it as allowing for the progressive realization of broadly defined economic, social and cultural rights, and thus as relating only to 'the general attainment' of the rights, but not as grounds to otherwise limit rights.[36] It was further suggested that Article 4 'should be drafted in more general and less legal terms than the corresponding article' of the ICCPR, because the ICESCR is subject to progressive realization and not immediate application.[37] Specific limitations on trade union rights under Article 8 were thought necessary

[35] CHR, Report to ECOSOC, E/2256(SUPP) (1 January 1952), 24.
[36] CHR, Report to ECOSOC.
[37] UNGA Third Committee, A/C.3/SR.721 (4 January 1957), 201 (Lebanon).

only because 'their exercise was in no way connected with economic and social conditions in the country'.[38]

The drafting indicates some confusion about the concepts of, and relationship between, progressive realization and the limitation of rights. Progressive realization concerns the state's capacity to implement rights in the context of its maximum available resources. In a certain sense, the preservation or allocation of scarce resources for matters other than the fulfillment of ICESCR rights might be seen as a form of restriction on the application of ICESCR rights. However, the principle of progressive realization is expressed as a free-standing principle which is thus carved out of the sphere of limitations more generally.[39]

In contrast, limitations concern a state's power to restrict the provision or protection of a right in order to pursue some other, countervailing, weightier public interest. In theory, a right may be limited at any point on the spectrum along which that right is being progressively realized—that is, whether the right is being minimally provided due to resource limitations, or maximally provided where the state is flush with resources, or somewhere in between. The principles accordingly apply concurrently and on different conceptual planes. As discussed further below, however, limitations cannot lawfully reduce an ICESCR right beneath its 'minimum core', just as a lack of resources cannot do so.

In practice, it may be that the most common reason for 'restricting' a right (so to speak) is that the state lacks resources, but that is really referring to the state's progress in realizing the right. The CESCR has rarely addressed the application of Article 4 most likely because resource limitations, and thus the issue of progressive realization, are the most prevalent reason why ICESCR rights are not fulfilled. But its lack of attention does not suggest that the notion of limitations as such is subsumed within the broad concept of progressive realization, as some suggested during the drafting of Article 4.

THE REQUIREMENTS OF ARTICLE 4

As already noted, in many cases there is little residual room to apply Article 4 because some ICESCR rights already contain specific limitations, others are inherently defined or interpreted to embody their own limiting criteria, and the principle of progressive realization already addresses resource-based constraints. The zone of operation of Article 4 may therefore be relatively small.

It has seldom arisen in the CESCR's monitoring of state reports, though that may also be because the analysis of state reports is often at a macroscopic level rather than at the level of individual cases, confining the CESCR's capacity to consider more closely actual instances of limitation. Very occasionally the CESCR has invoked Article 4, as when it reminded Chinese Hong Kong, in relation to its policies on permanent residence and split families, that 'any limitations

[38] UNGA Third Committee, A/C.3/SR.721 (4 January 1957), 201 (Lebanon).

[39] See the chapter on Article 2(1) for the full examination of progressive realization under the ICESCR.

in connection with Article 10 [concerning the protection of the family] must be justified in relation to each element set out in article 4'.[40]

Some guidance can be drawn from limitations practice under the ICCPR and ECHR (to the extent that they are comparable and can be transposed to the ICESCR), as well as the expert (but non-binding) Limburg Principles on the Implementation of the ICESCR. Each of the elements of Article 4 is considered in turn.

'Determined by law'

First, Article 4 provides that any limitation must be 'determined by law', which may be interpreted to entail the following minimum elements:

48. No limitation on the exercise of economic, social and cultural rights shall be made unless provided for by national law of general application which is consistent with the Covenant and is in force at the time the limitation is applied.

49. Laws imposing limitations on the exercise of economic, social and cultural rights shall not be arbitrary or unreasonable or discriminatory.

50. Legal rules limiting the exercise of economic, social and cultural rights shall be clear and accessible to everyone.

51. Adequate safeguards and effective remedies shall be provided by law against illegal or abusive imposition on application of limitations on economic, social and cultural rights.[41]

The focus is accordingly not only on the formal existence of law, but also on its *quality*: non-retrospective, not arbitrary or discriminatory, accessible and forseeable, and subject to effective remedies. Such interpretation is supported by the jurisprudence on similar requirements for limitations under the ICCPR and ECHR.[42] The HRC has thus emphasized that 'law' must be 'formulated with sufficient precision to enable an individual to regulate his or her conduct accordingly',[43] accessible to the public, and must not confer an unfettered discretion in implementation.[44]

'Law' can be of various forms: constitutional, legislative, administrative, common law, or even international law or regional law,[45] as long as it is accessible

[40] CESCR, Concluding Observations: China (Hong Kong SAR), E/2002/22 (2001), [202].

[41] Limburg Principles on the Implementation of the ICESCR, E/CN.4/1987/17 (8 January 1987), [48]–[51].

[42] *Sunday Times v UK* (App. 6538/74), 26 April 1979, (1980) 2 EHRR 245, [49].

[43] See *de Groot v Netherlands*, HRC Communication CCPR/C/54/D/578/1994 (24 July 1995); HRC, General Comment No. 34, CCPR/C/G/34 (12 September 2011), [25].

[44] See HRC, General Comment No. 27, CCPR/C/21/Rev.1/Add.9 (2 November 1999); on discretion, see *Al-Nashif v Bulgaria* (App. 50963/99), 20 June 2002, (2002) 36 EHRR 655 [119]–[123]; *Gorzelik et al v Poland* (App. 44158/98), 17 February 2004, (2004) 40 EHRR 76, [74]–[79].

[45] Under the ECHR, see, eg, *Groppera Radio AG v Switzerland* (App. 10890/84), 28 March 1990, (1990) 12 EHRR 321, [68]; *Bosphorous Airways v Ireland* (App. 45036/98), 30 June 2005, (2006) 42 EHRR 1, [143]; *Slivenko v Latvia* (App. 48321/99), 9 October 2003, (2004) 39 EHRR 490, [104]–[109].

and precise. But the HRC has noted that a restriction cannot be 'enshrined in traditional, religious or other such customary law'.[46] In monitoring states, the CESCR appears to have adopted the same position in criticizing restrictions on ICESCR rights which derive from the imposition of a single religious tradition on society as a whole. It thus condemned provisions of Iran's Constitution which purported to qualify ICESCR-type rights by requirements of consistency with Islam:

4. … the Committee observes that various articles of the Constitution of Iran subject the enjoyment of universally recognized human rights, including economic, social and cultural rights, to such restrictions as: 'provided it is not against Islam' (art. 28); 'with due regard to Islamic standards' (art. 20); 'in conformity with the Islamic criteria' (art. 20); and 'except when it is detrimental to the fundamental principles of Islam' (art. 24). In that connection the Committee considers, in the light of the Covenant provisions and of all the information available to it, that such restrictive clauses negatively affect the application of the Covenant, in particular its articles 2 (2) (non-discrimination), article 3 (equality of rights of men and women), article 6 (right to work), article 12 (right to health), article 13 (right to education) and article 15 (right to take part in cultural life). It is apparent that the authorities in Iran are using the religion as a pretext in order to abuse these rights.[47]

Similarly, the CESCR found that the religious basis of Moroccan civil law impermissibly interfered with ICESCR rights:

9. Other difficulties noted by the Committee relate to the contradiction between the obligations set forth under the Covenant and various provisions relating to the civil law status governed by the Code of Personal Status (mudawana) which is partly based on religious precepts and falls within the King's competence. The Committee considers that when a State has ratified the Covenant without making any reservations, it is obliged to comply with all of the provisions of the Covenant. It may therefore not invoke any reasons or circumstances to justify the non-application of one or more articles of the Covenant, except in accordance with the provisions of the Covenant and the principles of general international law.[48]

While religious law may accord with majority sentiment in a particular society, the UN treaty bodies, like the ECHR, have been conscious that the state's legal entrenchment of religious values may impermissibly interfere with certain requirements of the ICESCR and ICCPR. Democracy is, therefore, not simply conceived of as a reflection of majoritarian preferences, but as protective of pluralism and respect for minority rights and individual autonomy. Under the ECHR jurisprudence, secularism is overtly regarded as a precondition of democracy and the protection of ECHR rights within it.[49]

[46] HRC, General Comment No. 34, CCPR/C/G/34 (12 September 2011), [24]; General Comment No. 32, CCPR/C/GC/32 (23 August 2007).

[47] CESCR, Concluding Observations: Iran, E/C.12/1993/7 (9 June 1993), [4].

[48] CESCR, Concluding Observations: Morocco, E/C.12/1994/5 (30 May 1994), [9].

[49] See, eg, *Leyla Sahin v Turkey* (App. 44774/98), 10 November 2005, (2007) 44 EHRR 5.

'Promoting the general welfare'

Secondly, under Article 4 the purpose of a limitation must be 'promoting the general welfare', which the Limburg Principles suggest means 'furthering the well-being of the people as a whole'.[50] The language of Article 4 departs from the more numerous grounds for limitations in the ICCPR, which permits certain rights to be limited on grounds such as 'national security, public order (*ordre public*), public health or morals or the rights and freedoms of others'.[51]

From the drafting, it is unclear whether the 'general welfare' was intended to be a generic ground which encompasses these more specific grounds, or establishes a higher or stricter threshold. Some states argued to include references to morality or public order, but others appeared to regard the 'general welfare' as sufficiently broad to capture such concerns.[52]

On an ordinary interpretation of the 'general welfare', matters of national security, public order, public health or public morals would seem to be species of the general welfare and within its ambit. As such, in the absence of much guidance on Article 4 from the CESCR thus far, reference to the grounds of limitation developed in the context of the ICCPR may be useful in understanding the permissibility of limitations under the ICESCR, at least to the extent that such grounds can relevantly apply to economic, social and cultural rights. For example, in relation to 'public morals' under the ICCPR, the HRC stated:

> 32. The Committee observed in general comment No. 22, that 'the concept of morals derives from many social, philosophical and religious traditions; consequently, limitations…for the purpose of protecting morals must be based on principles not deriving exclusively from a single tradition'. Any such limitations must be understood in the light of universality of human rights and the principle of non-discrimination.[53]

While the CESCR has rarely considered Article 4 specifically, in general it has been alert to bad faith or abusive justifications by the state for interfering in protected ICESCR rights. Thus, it criticized Libya for the arbitrary expulsion of lawful foreign workers on the basis that the state's purported justifications were not well founded:

> 16. The Committee also expresses its concern at reports that during the second half of 1995 thousands of foreign workers were arbitrarily expelled from the State party and were not given adequate compensation. It further regrets that there was no possibility for a legal or judicial remedy against those expulsions. The Committee is alarmed that the justification given by the delegation for this action was that foreign workers were the cause of many of the State party's social problems, such as violent crime, immoral activities, black market transactions, drug trafficking, trafficking in women and the spread of communicable diseases. Such a rationale is unacceptable to the Committee and a clear violation of the Covenant…[54]

[50] Limburg Principles on the Implementation of the ICESCR, E/CN.4/1987/17, 8 January 1987.

[51] ICCPR, Article 12; see also Articles 14(1), 18(3), 19(3), 21 and 22(2).

[52] UNGA, Annotations on the text of the draft International Covenants on Human Rights, A/2929 (1 July 1955), 27.

[53] HRC, General Comment No. 34, CCPR/C/G/34 (12 September 2011), [25].

[54] CESCR, Concluding Observations: Libya, E/C.12/1/Add.1 (20 May 1997), [16].

The African Commission has also been concerned where states have invoked the African Charter's limitations clause to justify deporting citizens based on vague public order grounds:

49. The Government of Zambia has relied on the 'claw-back' clause of Article 12(2): This right may only be subject to restrictions, provided for by law for the protection of national security, law or order, public health or morality . . .

50. The deportation order also stated that the deportees were considered 'a danger to peace and good order to Zambia'. The Commission is of the view that the 'claw-back' clauses must not be interpreted against the principles of the Charter. Recourse to these should not be used as a means of giving credence to violations of the express provisions of the Charter. Secondly, the rules of natural justice must apply. Among these are in the *audi alteram partem* rule, the right to be heard, the right of access to the Court. The Court in Zambia, in Banda's case failed to examine the basis of administrative action and as such, it has not been proved that the deportees were indeed a danger to law and order. In any event the suggestion that they were 'likely' to be a danger was vague and not proved. It is important for the Commission to caution against a too easy resort to the limitation clauses in the African Charter. The onus is on the state to prove that it is justified to resort to the limitation clause. The Commission should act bearing in mind the provisions of Articles 61 and 62 of the Charter.[55]

In supervising limitations under the ECHR, violations for failure to identify a legitimate ground of restriction have been rare.[56] In part this is because the grounds of possible limitation are broad and accommodate a wide range of state interests: 'the state can usually make a plausible case that it did have a good reason for interfering with the right'.[57] But it is also because the European analysis, and arguably that under the ICCPR, has focused instead on the legal implications of what is necessary 'in a democratic society'.

In principle, most ICESCR rights (bar Article 8) are susceptible to limitation to promote the general welfare under Article 4. For example, the CESCR has noted that forced evictions may be justified for 'persistent non-payment of rent or of damage to rented property without any reasonable cause',[58] and public infrastructure or development projects (such as dams, roads, agricultural projects or urban redevelopment) also commonly limit rights in state practice.

Other examples may be envisaged. Access to surplus water (that is, not essential to survival) might be restricted by rationing in times of scarcity or drought. Access to certain foods might be restricted by quarantine or bio-safety concerns. The availability of certain non-essential medicines might be restricted by intellectual property laws. The right to health may involve difficult choices of priority, as in the area of organ transplants. The key legal questions, discussed in the

[55] *Amnesty International v Zambia*, African Commission Communication No. 212/98 (1999).

[56] Pieter Van Dijk et al (eds), *Theory and Practice of the European Court of Human Rights* (4th edn, Intersentia, Antwerpen–Oxford, 2006), 340.

[57] David J Harris et al, *Law of the European Convention on Human Rights* (2nd edn, Oxford University Press, Oxford, 2009), 348.

[58] CESCR, General Comment No. 7, E/1996/22 (20 May 1997), annex IV [12].

next section, will be whether the measures adopted are necessary and proportionate 'in a democratic society', whether rights-respecting procedures are followed, whether minimum core rights are maintained, and whether effective remedies are available.

The right of peoples to economic self-determination under Article 1 is also not absolute but may be limited, for instance by requirements to respect environmental protection laws, or pay tax on commercial revenue. By analogy, in *Centre for Minority Rights Development v Kenya*,[59] the African Commission applied a limitations analysis to the right of peoples to freely dispose of their wealth and natural resources under Article 21 of the African Charter. That case, discussed in the chapter on Article 1 of the ICESCR, concerned the forcible removal of an indigenous group from their ancestral lands due to mining concessions. Influenced by the Inter-American Court of Human Rights, the African Commission found that limitations on group economic rights were not justified on the facts of the case:

263. The African Commission notes the opinion of the IActHR in the *Saramaka* case as regards the issue of permissible limitations. The State of Suriname had argued that, should the Court recognise a right of the members of the Saramaka people to the natural resources found within traditionally owned lands, this right must be limited to those resources traditionally used for their subsistence, cultural and religious activities. According to the State, the alleged land rights of the Saramakas would not include any interests on forests or minerals beyond what the tribe traditionally possesses and uses for subsistence (agriculture, hunting, fishing etc), and the religious and cultural needs of its people.
264. The Court opined that while it is true that all exploration and extraction activity in the Saramaka territory could affect, to a greater or lesser degree, the use and enjoyment of some natural resource traditionally used for the subsistence of the Saramakas, it is also true that Article 21 of the Convention should not be interpreted in a way that prevents the State from granting any type of concession for the exploration and extraction of natural resources within Saramaka territory. The Court observed that this natural resource is likely to be affected by extraction activities related to other natural resources that are not traditionally used by or essential for the survival of the Saramaka community and, consequently, their members. That is, the extraction of one natural resource is most likely to affect the use and enjoyment of other natural resources that are necessary for the survival of the Saramakas.

265. Nevertheless, the Court said that protection of the right to property under Article 21 of the Convention is not absolute and therefore does not allow for such a strict interpretation. The Court also recognised the interconnectedness between the right of members of indigenous and tribal peoples to the use and enjoyment of their lands and their right to those resources necessary for their survival but that these property rights, like many other rights recognised in the Convention, are subject to certain limitations and restrictions. In this sense, Article 21 of the Convention states that the 'law may subordinate [the] use and enjoyment [of property] to the interest of society.' *But the Court also said that it had previously held that, in accordance with Article 21 of the Convention, a State may restrict the use and enjoyment of the right to property*

[59] *Centre for Minority Rights Development (Kenya) and Minority Rights Group International on behalf of Endorois Welfare Council v Kenya*, African Commission on Human and Peoples' Rights Communication No. 276/2003, (2009) AHRLR 75, 4 February 2010, [211].

where the restrictions are: a) previously established by law; b) necessary; c) proportional, and d) with the aim of achieving a legitimate objective in a democratic society.

266. The Saramaka case is analogous to the instant case with respect to ruby mining. The IActHR analysed whether gold-mining concessions within traditional Saramaka territory have affected natural resources that have been traditionally used and are necessary for the survival of the members of the Saramaka community. According to the evidence submitted before the Court, the Saramaka community, traditionally, did not use gold as part of their cultural identity or economic system. Despite possible individual exceptions, the Saramaka community do not identify themselves with gold nor have demonstrated a particular relationship with this natural resource, other than claiming a general right to 'own everything, from the very top of the trees to the very deepest place that you could go under the ground.' Nevertheless, the Court stated that, because any gold mining activity within Saramaka territory will necessarily affect other natural resources necessary for the survival of the Saramakas, such as waterways, the State has a duty to consult with them, in conformity with their traditions and customs, regarding any proposed mining concession within Saramaka territory, as well as allow the members of the community to reasonably participate in the benefits derived from any such possible concession, and perform or supervise an assessment on the environmental and social impact prior to the commencement of the project. The same analysis would apply regarding concessions in the instant case of the Endorois.

267. In the instant case of the Endorois, the Respondent State has a duty to evaluate whether a restriction of these private property rights is necessary to preserve the survival of the Endorois community. The African Commission is aware that the Endorois do not have an attachment to ruby. Nevertheless, it is instructive to note that the African Commission decided in *The Ogoni case* that the right to natural resources contained within their traditional lands vested in the indigenous people. This decision made clear that a people inhabiting a specific region within a state can claim the protection of Article 21. Article 14 of the African Charter indicates that the two-pronged test of 'in the interest of public need or in the general interest of the community' and 'in accordance with appropriate laws' should be satisfied.

268. As far as the African Commission is aware, that has not been done by the Respondent State. The African Commission is of the view the Endorois have the right to freely dispose of their wealth and natural resources in consultation with the Respondent State. Article 21(2) also concerns the obligations of a State Party to the African Charter in cases of a violation by spoliation, through provision for restitution and compensation. *The Endorois have never received adequate compensation or restitution of their land. Accordingly, the Respondent State is found to have violated Article 21 of the Charter.*[60]

'In a democratic society'

Thirdly, Article 4 requires that a restrictive measure must be for the purpose of the general welfare 'in a democratic society'. In principle, economic, social and cultural rights enable a person's civil and political participation and democracy is accordingly threatened if ICESCR rights are too readily restricted.

[60] *Centre for Minority Rights Development (Kenya) and Minority Rights Group International on behalf of Endorois Welfare Council v Kenya*, [262–8] (emphasis in original).

There was little discussion of this phrase during the drafting, with only Pakistan mentioning that it had 'misgivings' about the reference to democracy and pleading that it should be 'given the widest possible interpretation'.[61] On this point, the Limburg Principles suggest that '[w]hile there is no single model of a democratic society, a society which recognizes and respects the human rights set forth in the United Nations Charter and the Universal Declaration of Human Rights may be viewed as meeting this definition'.[62]

The larger question is whether the phrase should be regarded as a substantive, autonomous requirement of Article 4, or as just a rhetorical gloss. Certainly, the Limburg Principles recommend that 'the expression "in a democratic society" [in the ICESCR] shall be interpreted as imposing a further restriction on the application of limitations' and that the 'burden is upon a State imposing limitations to demonstrate that the limitations do not impair the democratic functioning of the society'.[63]

This view is supported by the interpretation of similar references to what is necessary in a democratic society under the limitations provisions of the ICCPR[64] and ECHR.[65] The HRC has not elaborated on the meaning of the phrase in any general comments, but has occasionally addressed it in specific cases and given it an autonomous meaning. Thus, in the context of freedom of association under Article 22 of the ICCPR, the HRC stated:

> 7.2. ... The reference to a 'democratic society' indicates, in the Committee's view, that the existence and functioning of a plurality of associations, including those which peacefully promote ideas not favourably received by the government or the majority of the population, is one of the foundations of a democratic society. Therefore, the existence of any reasonable and objective justification for limiting the freedom of association is not sufficient. The State party must further demonstrate that the prohibition of the association and the criminal prosecution of individuals for membership in such organizations are in fact necessary to avert a real, and not only hypothetical danger to the national security or democratic order and that less intrusive measures would be insufficient to achieve this purpose.[66]

Under the ICCPR, therefore, the reference to 'democratic society' imports twin requirements of necessity and proportionality (in the requirement to demonstrate that less invasive measures would be insufficient). The HRC has not always expressly linked these twin principles to the requirements of 'democratic society',

[61] UNGA Third Committee, A/C.3/SR.1185 (16 November 1962), 260 (Pakistan).

[62] Limburg Principles on the Implementation of the ICESCR, E/CN.4/1987/17, 8 January 1987, [55].

[63] Limburg Principles on the Implementation of the ICESCR, [53] and [54].

[64] ICCPR, Articles 14(1), 21 and 22.

[65] ECHR, Articles 8(2)–11(2) and Protocol No. 4 to the Convention of 4 November 1950 for the Protection of Human Rights and Fundamental Freedoms, securing certain rights and freedoms other than those already included in the Convention and in the first Protocol thereto ('Protocol No. 4') (adopted 16 September 1963, 1496 UNTS 263, entered into force 2 May 1968), Article 2(3).

[66] *Lee v Republic of Korea*, HRC Communication CCPR/C/84/D/1119/2002 (23 August 2005), [7.2]. As already noted, trade union rights are not governed by the general limitations clause in Article 4 of the ICESCR, but are subject to a special regime under Article 8. Similar considerations apply, however, in the application of the Article 8 limitations, which expressly refer to limitations being 'necessary in a democratic society'.

and they have tended to evolve into free-standing general principles in the evaluation of the lawfulness of a limitation. The following is a typical expression of the principles by the HRC:

34. Restrictions must not be overbroad. The Committee observed in general comment No. 27 that 'restrictive measures must conform to the principle of proportionality; they must be appropriate to achieve their protective function; they must be the least intrusive instrument amongst those which might achieve their protective function; they must be proportionate to the interest to be protected…The principle of proportionality has to be respected not only in the law that frames the restrictions but also by the administrative and judicial authorities in applying the law' …[67]

35. When a State party invokes a legitimate ground for restriction…it must demonstrate in specific and individualized fashion the precise nature of the threat, and the necessity and proportionality of the specific action taken, in particular by establishing a direct and immediate connection between the… [right to be restricted] and the threat.[68]

The CESCR invokes similar standards for assessing limitations in its rare, explicit invocation of Article 4 in its General Comment on the right to take part in cultural life:

19. Applying limitations to the right of everyone to take part in cultural life may be necessary in certain circumstances, in particular in the case of negative practices, including those attributed to customs and traditions, that infringe upon other human rights. Such limitations must pursue a legitimate aim, be compatible with the nature of this right and be strictly necessary for the promotion of general welfare in a democratic society, in accordance with article 4 of the Covenant. Any limitations must therefore be proportionate, meaning that the least restrictive measures must be taken when several types of limitations may be imposed. The Committee also wishes to stress the need to take into consideration existing international human rights standards on limitations that can or cannot be legitimately imposed on rights that are intrinsically linked to the right to take part in cultural life, such as the rights to privacy, to freedom of thought, conscience and religion, to freedom of opinion and expression, to peaceful assembly and to freedom of association.[69]

In an example under the African Charter, also discussed in the next chapter, the African Commission found that there was no discrimination or unjustifiable infringement of freedom of religion due to restrictions on cannabis use which precluded the registration of a Rastafarian as a lawyer in South Africa. (By extension, such requirements may be permissible limitations on the right to work under Article 6 of the ICESCR.) The African Commission reasoned as follows:

43. The African Commission considers that the restrictions in the two South African legislations on the use and possession of cannabis are similarly reasonable as they serve a general purpose and that the Charter's protection of freedom of religion is not absolute.

[67] HRC, General Comment No. 34, CCPR/C/G/34 (12 September 2011), [34]; see also HRC General Comment No. 27, CCPR/C/21/Rev.1/Add.9 (2 November 1999), [14]; *Marques v Angola*, HRC Communication CCPR/C/83/D/1128/2002 (18 April 2005); *Coleman v Australia*, HRC Communication CCPR/C/87/D/1157/2003 (10 August 2005).

[68] See *Shin v Republic of Korea*, HRC Communication CCPR/C/80/D/926/2000 (19 March 2004).

[69] CESCR, General Comment No. 21: Article 15(1)(a), E/C.12/GC/21, 21 (21 December 2009), [4].

The only legitimate limitations to the rights and freedoms contained in the African Charter are found in article 27(2); i.e. that the rights in the African Charter 'shall be exercised with due regard to the rights of others, collective security, morality, and common interest'. The limitation is inspired by well-established principle that all human and peoples' rights are subject to the general rule that no one has the right to engage in any activity or perform any act aimed at the destruction of any of the rights and freedoms recognised elsewhere. The reasons for possible limitations must be founded in a legitimate state interest and the evils of limitations of rights must be strictly proportionate with and absolutely necessary for the advantages, which are to be obtained. It is noted that the respondent state's interest to do away with the use of cannabis and its abuse/trafficking stems from the fact that, and this is also admitted by the complainant, cannabis is an undesirable dependence-producing substance. For all intents and purposes, this constitutes a legitimate limitation on the exercise of the right to freedom of religion within the spirit of article 27(2) cum article 8.

44. Besides, the limitations so visited upon the complainant and his fellow Rastafari fall squarely under article 2 of the African Charter which requires states to ensure equal protection of the law. As the limitations are of general application, without singling out the complainant and his fellow Rastafari but applying to all across the board, they cannot be said discriminatory so as to curtail the complainant's free exercise of his religious rights.[70]

References in the ECHR's limitation provisions[71] to what is necessary in a democratic society have been interpreted to require a limitation to correspond to a 'pressing social need' and be 'proportionate to the legitimate aim pursued'.[72] The proportionality test also asks whether the state's reasons for the restriction are 'relevant' (to the legitimate aim) and 'sufficient' (requiring consideration of the nature, severity, effects and expected harm of the restriction).[73]

One aspect of the ECHR approach must, however, be distinguished from that under the twin Covenants. National authorities are accorded a 'margin of appreciation' under the ECHR in the assessment of whether a restriction is justified in a democratic society.[74] By contrast, the HRC has expressly stated that (for instance) freedom of expression under the ICCPR 'is not to be assessed by reference to a "margin of appreciation"'.[75] A stricter, more intense standard of scrutiny is thus applied by the HRC. It would seem appropriate for the CESCR to follow a similar approach to restrictions of ICESCR rights, particularly given that the nature of economic, social and cultural rights does not easily admit restrictions.

The requirement of what is necessary in a democratic society may pose particular challenges in reviewing the extraterritorial application of restrictive measures. In its *Israeli Wall Advisory Opinion*, the ICJ did not explain how the 'democratic society' requirement applied to measures taken by Israel (a democracy) in foreign occupied territory (under military rule and in the absence of local

[70] *Prince v South Africa*, African Commission Communication No. 255/2002 (December 2004), (2004) AHRLR 105.

[71] ECHR, Articles 8(2)–11(2) and Protocol No. 4, Article 2(3).

[72] See, eg, *Silver et al v UK* (Apps. 5947/72, 6205/73, 7052/75, 7061/75, 7107/75, 7113/75 and 7136/75), 25 March 1983, (1983) 5 EHRR 357, [97].

[73] See, eg, *Dudgeon v UK* (App. 7525/76), 22 October 1981, (1981) 4 EHRR 149, [54].

[74] *Handyside v UK* (App. 5493/72), 7 December 1976, (1976) 1 EHRR 737, [48] and [49].

[75] *Ilmari Länsman et al v Finland*, HRC Communication CCPR/C/52/D/511/1992 (8 November 1993).

democracy). A democracy occupying another state or foreign people will often view what are necessary and proportionate restrictions on its 'enemies' quite differently from the inhabitants of occupied territory, given the universal temptation to disproportionately value the safety of one's own people over the rights of others.

The requirement plainly cannot refer only to what restrictions would be acceptable to the occupying power's democratic polity, for that would give free reign to one democracy to decide which limitations may be lawfully imposed on another society which has been occupied and whose democratic institutions have been displaced.

The reference to democratic society must, therefore, comprise both subjective and objective elements. The subjective element refers to what a particular democracy believes is necessary in the context of that society, its values and people. The objective element involves a supervening consideration of what restrictions a hypothetical 'reasonable' democracy would accept, including if it were to place itself in the shoes of those it occupies, and thus better understand and weight the value of the rights of those subject to occupation. Such approach is also consistent with international humanitarian law, which regards an occupying power as a trustee administering territory for the benefit of the local inhabitants, and requires minimal impairment of existing laws, legal rights and institutions. It is further noted that in the European jurisprudence, values such as 'tolerance and broad-mindedness' are identified as 'hallmarks' of democracy.[76]

'Compatible with the nature of these rights'

There was little discussion of this phrase during the drafting. The Limburg Principles suggest this element 'requires that a limitation shall not be interpreted or applied so as to jeopardize the essence of the right concerned'.[77] It thus introduces and emphasizes a 'non-derogable' component to ICESCR rights which rules out certain extreme restrictions. To put it another way, minimum core ICESCR rights cannot be limited, just as progressive realization is not an excuse for their non-fulfilment: measures which render people homeless, starving, deprived of essential medical care or enslaved can never be justified. As the Limburg Principles declare, Article 4 'was not meant to introduce limitations on rights affecting the subsistence or survival of the individual or integrity of the person'.[78] Thus, in the context of the right to housing, the CESCR stated that even where evictions are justified, they cannot leave a person a homeless:

17. Evictions should not result in rendering individuals homeless or vulnerable to the violation of other human rights. Where those affected are unable to provide for themselves, the State party must take all appropriate measures, to the maximum of its available resources,

[76] *Dudgeon v UK* (App. 7525/76), 22 October 1981, (1981) 4 EHRR 149, [53].
[77] Limburg Principles on the Implementation of the ICESCR, E/CN.4/1987/17, 8 January 1987, [56].
[78] Limburg Principles on the Implementation of the ICESCR, [47].

to ensure that adequate alternative housing, resettlement or access to productive land, as the case may be, is available.[79]

The same result would likely be achieved on a proper application of the proportionality principle already inherent in the assessment of a limitation: no matter how significant the public interest, the destruction of core rights cannot easily be viewed as proportionate, and certainly not if core individual human dignity is accorded sufficient weight.

Also, Article 5(1) prohibits reliance on anything in the ICESCR to destroy any ICESCR right, further reinforcing this requirement. The limitation of minimum core subsistence rights, such as basic food, water, shelter, clothing, and health care, all essential to survival, would destroy those ICESCR rights, contrary to Article 5(1), and the elementary human dignity which those basic rights confer. The 'minimum core' level of such rights is already pegged at the low level of what is necessary to ensure survival or subsistence, so it is very difficult to envisage situations where restricting such rights could be necessary for 'promoting the general welfare'. Such argument would imply that it would be an acceptable trade off to impoverish some people in society to promote the welfare of others.

Survival rights are clearly of a different order of importance than certain civil and political rights (such as freedom of expression), the restriction of which does not necessarily endanger a person's very survival. The limitation of minimum core rights could also potentially result in inhuman or degrading treatment, where it leaves a person destitute, homeless or starving, and which would also be contrary to Article 7 of the ICCPR.[80]

PUBLIC EMERGENCIES

There is no express derogation clause in the ICESCR equivalent to Article 4 of the ICCPR. The CESCR has not explicitly addressed whether derogation from ICESCR rights is permitted in a public emergency and under what conditions or procedures. The drafting record sheds little light on the issue.

The absence of a derogation clause can only be understood to mean that the suspension of economic, social and cultural rights is not permitted. Derogation is an exceptional procedure which the drafters consciously and tightly circumscribed in substance and procedure under Article 4 of the ICCPR. The ICESCR was drafted alongside the ICCPR, yet no derogation clause was included. It cannot be presumed that the drafters intended to permit derogation *by implication* from the ICESCR, in the absence of an express provision and its strict safeguards—including the duties to publicly proclaim and internationally notify a derogation, and the express designation of certain rights as non-derogable. Further, Article 5(1) specifically provides that nothing in the ICESCR permits a

[79] CESCR, General Comment No. 7, E/1996/22 (20 May 1997), annex IV [17].

[80] *R v Secretary of State for the Home Department, ex parte Adam* [2006] 1 AC 396 (concerning inhuman treatment contrary to the comparable Article 3 of the ECHR).

state to limit rights 'to a greater extent than is provided for' in the Covenant, thus ruling out any doctrine of implied derogation.

Moreover, the HRC has observed that the specific limitations already permitted in particular ICCPR provisions are 'generally sufficient' to deal with emergency situations.[81] On that reasoning, the general limitations provision in Article 4 of the ICESCR is similarly capable of accommodating the exigencies of emergency situations, without further requiring the suspension of rights. Similarly under the African Charter, the African Commission has found that the absence of a derogation clause means that the limitations clause is the only permissible basis for restricting rights:

> 67. In contrast to other international human rights instruments, the African Charter does not contain a derogation clause. Therefore limitations on the rights and freedoms enshrined in the Charter cannot be justified by emergencies or special circumstances.
>
> 68. The only legitimate reasons for limitations to the rights and freedoms of the African Charter are found in Article 27.2, that is that the rights of the Charter 'shall be exercised with due regard to the rights of others, collective security, morality and common interest.'[82]

To some extent, the concepts of derogation and limitation entail a distinction without difference: both are governed by strict requirements of necessity and proportionality, perhaps with a wider deference or margin of appreciation accorded to derogating states. The HRC has admitted that 'the obligation to limit any derogations to those strictly required by the exigencies of the situation reflects the principle of proportionality which is common to derogation and limitation powers'.[83] The distinction can, however, make a difference in respect of certain civil and political rights, where, for example, certain safeguards on detention may be relaxed under a derogation regime where they could not normally be limited; or where it may be necessary to turn off telecommunications altogether to prevent the incitement of violence or civil unrest.

Yet, the distinction is often less meaningful in the context of economic, social and cultural rights, where it is hard to imagine how suspending rights to food, water, shelter or health care would be necessary in confronting any emergency.[84] Certainly, the CESCR has accepted that the minimum core of certain rights (such as health, food and water) are 'non-derogable'[85] (a term used in a non-technical sense) even during armed conflicts, emergencies or natural disasters. In such emergencies, the protection of such rights will ordinarily become more, not less, pressing.[86]

[81] HRC, General Comment No. 29, CCPR/C/21Rev.1/Add.11 (31 August 2001), [5].

[82] *Media Rights Agenda et al v Nigeria*, African Commission Communication Nos. 105/93, 128/94, 130/94 and 152/96 (1998), [67] and [68].

[83] HRC, General Comment No. 29, CCPR/C/21Rev.1/Add.11 (31 August 2001), [4].

[84] Manisuli Ssenyonjo, 'Economic, Social and Cultural Rights' in Mashood Baderin and Manisuli Ssenyonjo (eds), *International Human Rights Law: Six Decades after the UDHR and Beyond* (Ashgate, Aldershot, 2010), 49 and 77.

[85] CESCR, General Comment No. 14, E/C.12/2000/4 (11 August 2000), [47]; CESCR, General Comment No. 15, E/C.12/2005/4 (11 August 2005), [17].

[86] See Office of the UN High Commissioner for Human Rights, *The Right to Adequate Food*, Fact Sheet 34 (2010), 3: 'when people are not able to feed themselves with their own means, for instance because of an armed conflict, natural disaster or because they are in detention, the State must provide food directly'.

Looking beyond the core, where a public emergency necessitates special measures infringing on economic, social or cultural rights, such measures could usually already be justified by reference to the limitations inherent in existing rights, or by recourse to Article 4 of the ICESCR, but without any need for an overriding concept of derogation. Thus, a person's freedom to choose work is not violated where a person is required to work in an emergency, or where a person is called into military service in a time of war. National security concerns can lawfully preclude the employment of a person who presents a substantiated danger.

In relation to other rights, military requirements or public safety could be recognised under Article 4 as permitting forcible evacuation of civilians from their homes in an area of combat, or the suspension of health services in a hospital surrounded by hostilities. Education in schools might be justifiably closed for temporary periods during floods, earthquakes, disasters or civil unrest. Whether one characterizes such examples as a 'suspension' or 'limitation' of the rights in question is less important than the analysis of whether such measures are necessary and proportionate in the given situations. As noted in the chapter on Article 13, states must adapt education to emergency situations, such as by providing security for children to attend school during conflicts,[87] or to help children to return to school after natural disasters.[88] The Special Rapporteur on the right to education has observed that 'States have an obligation to respect, protect and fulfil the right to education, whether or not an emergency situation prevails'.[89]

In practice, courts and treaty bodies have not identified any legal lacuna in the ICESCR in its application to emergency situations, or developed any doctrine of implied derogation. Perhaps the most authoritative consideration of the issue thus far is the statement by the ICJ in the *Israeli Wall Advisory Opinion* that Israel's restrictive security measures in occupied territory must comply with Article 4 of the ICESCR:

> 136. … The Court would further observe that the restrictions on the enjoyment by the Palestinians living in the territory occupied by Israel of their economic, social and cultural rights, resulting from Israel's construction of the wall, fail to meet a condition laid down by Article 4 of the International Covenant on Economic, Social and Cultural Rights, that is to say that their implementation must be 'solely for the purpose of promoting the general welfare in a democratic society'.[90]

The ICJ accordingly accepted that Article 4 governs measures necessary in a paradigmatic emergency situation: the occupation of foreign territory in an

[87] CESCR, Concluding Observations: Afghanistan, E/C.12/AFG/CO/24 (7 June 2010), [43]; see also Sri Lanka, E/C.12/1/Add.24 (16 June 1998), [7].

[88] CESCR, Concluding Observations: Democratic People's Republic of Korea, E/C.12/1/Add.95 (12 December 2003), [40].

[89] Human Rights Council, Report of the Special Rapporteur on the right to education in emergency situations, A/HRC/8/10 (20 May 2008), [37].

[90] *Legal Consequences of the Construction of a Wall in Occupied Palestinian Territory (Advisory Opinion)* [2004] ICJ Rep 136, [136].

international armed conflict, in the face of a sustained campaign of terrorist suicide bombing against civilians; and where the state in question claimed to be acting under the international law on self-defence.

The CESCR too has repeatedly stated that the ICESCR continues to apply extraterritorially to the armed conflict in the Palestinian Occupied Territories,[91] notwithstanding the concurrent application of international humanitarian law and Israel's security concerns. While the CESCR has not mentioned Article 4 or derogation in this context, its insistence that the ICESCR continues to apply confirms that it has not accepted any doctrine of implied derogation:

31. The Committee recognizes that the State party has serious security concerns, which must be balanced with its efforts to comply with its obligations under international human rights law. However, the Committee reaffirms its view that the State party's obligations under the Covenant apply to all territories and populations under its effective control. The Committee repeats its position that even in a situation of armed conflict, fundamental human rights must be respected and that basic economic, social and cultural rights, as part of the minimum standards of human rights, are guaranteed under customary international law and are also prescribed by international humanitarian law. Moreover, the applicability of rules of humanitarian law does not by itself impede the application of the Covenant or the accountability of the State under article 2(1) for the actions of its authorities. The Committee therefore requests that the State party provide more extensive information on the enjoyment of economic, social and cultural rights enshrined in the Covenant by those living in the occupied territories in its next periodic report.

…

40. The Committee urges the State party to ensure that any security measure it adopts does not disproportionally limit or impede the enjoyment of economic, social and cultural rights enshrined in the Covenant, in particular access to land and water resources by Palestinians, and that adequate restitution and compensation are provided to those who have incurred damage to and loss of property and lands as a result of these security measures.[92]

The CESCR has also expressed concern about the impact of other armed conflicts on economic, social and cultural rights, as in Sudan:

25. The Committee is concerned at the bombardment of villages and camps of the civilian population, in the war zones in southern Sudan, including the bombing of schools and hospitals. In addition, the Committee expresses its concern about the reported resort to the weapon of deprivation of food and the creation of a man-made famine as an instrument of war, coupled with the diversion of humanitarian food aid supplies from groups of the population in need.[93]

In reviewing emergency measures adopted under national law which affect economic, social and cultural rights, the CESCR has cautioned against maintaining

[91] CESCR, Concluding Observations: Israel, E/C.12/1/Add.90 (26 June 2003), [31]; Israel, E/C.12/1/Add.69 (31 August 2001), [12]; Israel E/C.12/1/Add.27 (4 December 1998), [8].

[92] CESCR, Concluding Observations: Israel, E/C.12/1/Add.90 (26 June 2003), [31] and [40].

[93] CESCR, Concluding Observations: Sudan, E/C.12/1/Add.48 (1 September 2000), [25].

protracted emergency regimes which are no longer necessary and proportionate under Article 4, as in Algeria:

23. The Committee recommends that the State party consider, based on the principles of necessity and proportionality, lifting the protracted state of emergency, in place since 1992, insofar as it has a negative effect on the enjoyment of economic, social and cultural rights in the State party (arts. 4 and 5).[94]

Finally, the CESCR has emphasized that even when states are implementing measures to restore international peace and security, such as Security Council sanctions, they must 'do everything possible to protect at least the core content of the economic, social and cultural rights of the affected peoples':

7. The Committee considers that the provisions of the Covenant, virtually all of which are also reflected in a range of other human rights treaties as well as the Universal Declaration of Human Rights, cannot be considered to be inoperative, or in any way inapplicable, solely because a decision has been taken that considerations of international peace and security warrant the imposition of sanctions. Just as the international community insists that any targeted State must respect the civil and political rights of its citizens, so too must that State and the international community itself do everything possible to protect at least the core content of the economic, social and cultural rights of the affected peoples of that State (see also General Comment 3 (1990), paragraph 10).[95]

Thus, even an international 'emergency' situation, addressed by the Security Council, does not permit suspension or limitation of minimum core economic, social or cultural rights. The CESCR concedes that measures not affecting core rights may be permissible, but that does not imply a necessity of derogation as opposed to an extraterritorial application of Article 4.

Article 5(1)

Article 5(1) prohibits the abuse of rights to destroy other rights, while Article 5(2) prohibits states from invoking the ICESCR to lower existing protections in national law. Article 5 is common to the ICESCR and ICCPR. There was only a little discussion of it in the drafting of the ICESCR[96] and it has seldom been examined by the CESCR. A comparable provision is in Article 17 of the ECHR, in relation to which there has been occasional judicial consideration.

A further drafting proposal to exclude any restrictions on rights which would be incompatible with the purposes and principles of the UN Charter or the UDHR was not accepted.[97] That proposal aimed to prevent human rights treaties taking precedence over the Charter. It was rejected mainly because it was felt that human rights treaties 'could not possibly be in contradiction' with it.[98] Article 24

[94] CESCR, Concluding Observations: Algeria, E/C.12/DZA/CO/4 (7 June 2010), [23].
[95] CESCR, General Comment No. 8, E/C.12/1997/8 (12 December 1997), [7].
[96] UNGA Third Committee, A/5365 (17 December 1962), 25.
[97] UNGA, A/2929 (1 July 1955), 27.
[98] UNGA, A/2929 (1 July 1955), 27.

of the ICESCR, discussed below, instead requires that the ICESCR shall not be interpreted to impair the UN Charter or the constitutions of UN organs or specialized agencies.

'ANY ACT AIMED AT THE DESTRUCTION OF ANY OF THE RIGHTS OR FREEDOMS RECOGNIZED HEREIN'

Article 5(1) derived from Article 30 of the UDHR: 'Nothing in this Declaration may be interpreted as implying for any State, group or person any right to engage in any activity or to perform any act aimed at the destruction of any of the rights and freedoms set forth herein'. Both provisions are unusual in addressing the conduct not only of states, but groups and individuals, although there was some drafting debate concerning whether Article 5(1) should cover both states and non-state groups and individuals.[99] Article 5(1) will apply to restrict how an ICESCR right would otherwise apply; but it may only restrict the rights upon which the person seeks to rely to pursue their abusive activities[100] and does not disqualify the person from the enjoyment of other, unrelated rights.

The provision was justified in the drafting as providing 'protection against misinterpretation' of ICESCR rights.[101] More concretely, it 'aimed at checking the growth of nascent nazi, fascist or other totalitarian ideologies; groups with such tendencies could not invoke the covenants to justify their activities'.[102] In *MA v Italy*, for example, the HRC found that Article 5(1) of the ICCPR prevented the abuse of rights by a person seeking to reorganize a dissolved fascist party: 'it would appear to the Committee that the acts of which M.A. was convicted (reorganizing the dissolved fascist party) were of a kind which are removed from the protection of the Covenant by article 5 thereof'.[103] Article 5 has thus been used as an instrument of 'militant democracy'.[104]

Some states in the drafting opposed the provision because it was thought to be 'vague, unnecessary and open to abuse', potentially allowing states to excessively curtail freedom of expression.[105] It was further thought 'difficult to know exactly what actions could be considered as being aimed at the destruction of rights'.[106]

Since states are already empowered to limit rights under other ICESCR provisions, some states thought they should not be encouraged to restrict them further.[107] That argument has considerable force, given that hate speech and inciting violence can already be restricted under the limitations on freedom of expression

[99] Manfred Nowak, *UN Covenant on Civil and Political Rights: CCPR Commentary* (2nd edn, Clarendon, Oxford, 2005), 112.

[100] *Lawless v Ireland* (App. 332/57), 1 July 1961, (1961) 1 EHRR 15, [4]–[7].

[101] UNGA, A/2929 (1 July 1955), 26.

[102] UNGA, A/2929 (1 July 1955), 26.

[103] *MA v Italy*, HRC Communication No. 117/81, (21 September 1981), [13.3]. The complaint was found inadmissible, but could have been examined on the merits on the basis of the same reasons: Sarah Joseph, Jenny Schultz and Melissa Castan, *The International Covenant on Civil and Political Rights: Cases, Materials, and Commentary* (2nd edn, Oxford University Press, Oxford, 2004), 534.

[104] Nowak, *CCPR Commentary*, 115.

[105] UNGA, A/2929 (1 July 1955), 26.

[106] UNGA, A/2929 (1 July 1955), 26.

[107] UNGA, A/2929 (1 July 1955), 27.

in Article 19 of the ICCPR, in combination with Article 20's prohibition on propaganda for war or advocacy of group discrimination, hostility or violence.

In *MA v Italy*, for instance, the HRC found that fascist acts to which Article 5 applied 'were in any event justifiably prohibited by Italian law having regard to the limitations and restrictions applicable to the rights in question under the provisions of articles 18(3), 19(3), 22(2) and 25 of the Covenant'.[108] Likewise, regarding the similarly worded Article 17 of the ECHR, European institutions have declined to apply the provision and instead applied ordinary limitations, or relied on Article 17 in a subsidiary fashion to support a limitations analysis.[109]

One difference between Article 5 and other limitations clauses is that it concerns the 'intent' of the measure, namely to destroy rights,[110] whereas ordinary limitations clauses are concerned with restrictions on rights which may pursue legitimate aims, or illegitimate aims not intending the destruction of rights. One jurist in a HRC communication suggested that Article 5 may:

> …cover instances where formally rules under the Covenant [ICCPR] seem to legitimize actions which substantially run counter to its purposes and general spirit. Thus, Governments may never use the limitation clauses supplementing the protected rights and freedoms to such an extent that the very substance of those rights and freedoms would be annihilated; individuals are legally barred from availing themselves of the same rights and freedoms with a view to overthrowing the regime of the rule of law which constitutes the basic philosophy of the Covenant.[111]

It nonetheless remains the case that a measure intended to destroy rights would almost certainly be ruled out by a proper application of the ICESCR limitations clauses, whether as not promoting the general welfare, or as being unnecessary or disproportionate in a democratic society, or as being incompatible with the nature of the rights in question. Article 5(1) thus largely reinforces or complements the limitations clauses, including, for instance, where a military dictatorship seeks to suspend or restrict rights to preserve its own unlawful position.[112]

In ECHR practice, the prohibition on abuse of rights has been applied in cases involving a communist organization aiming to overthrow democracy by force;[113] the publication of Holocaust denials which incited hatred against Jews;[114] and the possession of racially discriminatory, anti-immigrant leaflets for public distribution.[115] Past activities (such as Nazi activities during a past war) will not be sufficient absent any present risk of totalitarian abuse of rights.[116] In contemporary times, violent,

[108] *MA v Italy*, HRC Communication No. 117/81, (21 September 1981), [13.3].

[109] Van Dijk et al, *Theory and Practice of the ECHR*, 1085–6.

[110] Nowak, *CCPR Commentary*, 114.

[111] *Lopez Burgos v Uruguay*, HRC Communication No. 52/1979, Individual Opinion of Christian Tomuschat.

[112] See the discussion of the military emergency in Chile in Nowak, *CCPR Commentary*, 114.

[113] *German Communist Party case, Yearbook I* (1956–7), 222.

[114] *Remer v Germany* (App. 25096/94), 6 September 1995, DR82 117.

[115] *Glimmerveen and Hagenbeek v Netherlands* (Apps. 8348/78 and 8406/78), 11 October 1979, (1982) 4 EHRR 260, 187.

[116] *De Becker v Belgium* (App. 214/05), 27 March 1962, (1962) 1 EHRR 43, 137–8.

extremist religious groups which seek to overthrow democracy or destroy human rights would also come within Article 5(1) of the ICESCR.

There has been some controversy surrounding whether the violent aims of an organization are sufficient to bring it within Article 17 of the ECHR,[117] or whether the focus should be on the actual activities it carries out[118] (thus providing more protection for political freedoms). There is a real risk, for example, that overbroad offences such as 'encouraging', 'praising', 'glorifying' or 'justifying' terrorism may unnecessarily or disproportionately interfere in freedom of expression,[119] and it would seem prudent to avoid applying Article 5 of the ICCPR/ ICESCR to sustain such excessive measures.

As is apparent, in practice the prohibition on abuse of rights has largely arisen in respect of abuses of key political rights, such as hate speech in the guise of free expression, or violent, anti-democratic activities organized under the cover of freedom of association.[120] Conceptually, it only rules out the abuse of rights which are capable of destroying other rights; under the ICCPR, for instance, it has no application to 'rights of existence' such as the rights to life, liberty, legal personality, privacy and freedom from torture or slavery.[121]

Many ICESCR rights are not as easily capable of being invoked to destroy the rights of others as some ICCPR rights. The CESCR has not yet spelled out all possible forms of abuse of ICESCR rights. One rare example is its statement that cultural rights may not be invoked to infringe upon other human rights, with an implied reference to Article 5(1):

> 18. The Committee wishes to recall that, while account must be taken of national and regional particularities and various historical, cultural and religious backgrounds, it is the duty of States, regardless of their political, economic or cultural systems, to promote and protect all human rights and fundamental freedoms. Thus, no one may invoke cultural diversity to infringe upon human rights guaranteed by international law, nor to limit their scope.[122]
>
> …
>
> 20. Article 15, paragraph 1(a) may not be interpreted as implying for any State, group or person any right to engage in any activity or perform any act aimed at the destruction of

[117] As in the prohibition of the German Communist Party in the 1950s: *German Communist Party case, Yearbook I* (1956–7); see also *United Communist Party of Turkey et al v Turkey* (App. 133/1996/752/951), 30 January 1998, (1998) 26 EHRR 121, [23], where Article 17 did not apply because there was no evidence of terrorist violence or undemocratic means in the aims or programmes of the party.

[118] As in *Refah Partisi (Welfare Party) et al v Turkey* (Apps. 41340/98, 41342/98, 41343/98 and 41344/98), 13 February 2003, (2003) 37 EHRR 1, [136] and [137], where the written aims and objectives of an organization were not sufficient to disqualify it from political participation.

[119] HRC, General Comment No. 34, CCPR/C/G/34 (12 September 2011).

[120] It will have most relevance to freedoms of religion, belief, expression, information, media, association, assembly, trade unions, self-determination and minority rights under the ICCPR: Nowak, *CCPR Commentary*, 116.

[121] Nowak, *CCPR Commentary*, 115–16.

[122] CESCR, General Comment No. 21, E/C.12/GC/21 (21 December 2009), [18].

any of the rights and freedoms recognized in the Covenant or at their limitation to a greater extent than is provided for therein.[123]

Problems of cultural relativism and extreme traditional cultural practices are considered in the chapter below on Article 15. However, as noted earlier, the CESCR also suggested in the same General Comment that the primary mechanism for limiting cultural rights to prevent infringements upon other rights is Article 4.[124] It is questionable whether Article 5(1) adds anything to that analysis and contains any autonomous content, or performs only a subsidiary role in augmenting the balancing exercise under Article 4.

The CESCR has not mentioned the application of Article 5 in any other context. Certain examples of one right being invoked to destroy another might be envisaged. For instance, the exercise of economic self-determination by one people in a manner which deprives another of its wealth or resources (for instance, through transboundary pollution, or exploitative resource concessions) might come within the ambit of Article 5. So too might large scale development projects which, for example, diverted the subsistence water supply of a minority group to supply a water-scarce urban population; or which demolished slums to make way for housing for others.

In other contexts, trade union rights under Article 9 of the ICESCR, like freedom of association generally under Article 22 of the ICCPR, may not be invoked to destroy the rights of others, whether employers, non-union workers or members of the public. Under Article 13, the right of parents to choose education for their children cannot be understood to permit them to choose forms of instruction (such as extreme religious schooling) which deny their children essential learning such as literacy, numeracy and social membership.

In relation to Article 12 of the ICESCR, parents' rights in respect of the medical treatment of their children cannot be understood to permit parents to refuse life-sustaining treatment such as blood transfusions. Likewise, parents' refusal to immunize children might be curtailed in order to protect the health of others who thereby become exposed to the transmission of preventable diseases. Parental rights in the family under Article 10 of the ICESCR cannot be invoked to place children in lethal danger from a violent or neglectful parent. Most of the examples would already be accommodated by the application of the ordinary limitations clauses.

As under the ICCPR, the prohibition on abuse of rights would seem to have no application to many ICESCR rights. It is difficult to envisage how subsistence or survival rights – such as the minimum core of the rights to food, water, housing, an adequate standard of living, work, social security or education – could be misused to destroy the rights of others. As such, the field of application of Article 5(1) under the ICESCR will be relatively small; the provision would seem to have a wider utility in respect of abusive political action under the ICCPR.

[123] Limburg Principles on the Implementation of the ICESCR, E/CN.4/1987/17 (8 January 1987), [17]–[20].

[124] CESCR, General Comment No. 21, E/C.12/GC/21 (21 December 2009), [19].

It has been suggested that Article 5(1) should not be deployed in militant defence of liberal democracy,[125] as Article 17 of the ECHR has been used, because the ICCPR (and by extension, the ICESCR) is a universal instrument applicable to a diversity of states.[126] However, it may be countered that ordinary limitations under Article 4 of the ICESCR themselves must be necessary 'in a democratic society', and that democracy is ultimately presupposed as a precondition of full and effective protection of human rights under the twin Covenants. In this light, it would seem appropriate for democratic systems to safeguard themselves against the abuse of rights by groups which seek to destroy the democratic foundations which sustain the protection of human rights.

'LIMITATION TO A GREATER EXTENT THAN IS PROVIDED FOR IN THE PRESENT COVENANT'

The only significant change in language between the UDHR provision of 1948 and the ICESCR was the addition of a prohibition on the 'limitation [of ICESCR rights] to a greater extent than is provided for in the present Covenant'. That further protection 'underlines the fact that there is no general, implied or residual right for a State to impose limitations beyond those which are specifically provided for in the law'.[127] It is a more general iteration of the specific rule in Article 25 that the ICESCR must not be interpreted to impair a people's right to utilize their national resources,[128] considered earlier in the context of self-determination (Article 1). While this provision may state an obvious point, it underscores the broader principle common in many national legal systems that human rights cannot be restricted by mere implication; overt or express grounds of limitation are required, thus appropriately weighting the value of rights.

Article 5(2)

Article 5(2) precludes states from relying on the ICESCR to restrict or derogate from 'any of the fundamental human rights recognized or existing…in virtue of law, conventions, regulations or custom'. During the drafting, various states were keen to ensure that the ICESCR would not affect laws or conventions affecting human rights which were 'more advanced' than in the ICESCR.[129] Article 5(2) accordingly provides that higher levels of human rights protection under national or other international law are not prejudiced by the ICESCR:

58. The purpose of Article 5(2) is to ensure that no provision in the Covenant shall be interpreted to prejudice the provisions of domestic law or any bilateral or multilateral treaties,

[125] Nowak, *CCPR Commentary*, 116. [126] Nowak, *CCPR Commentary*, 116.

[127] Limburg Principles on the Implementation of the ICESCR, E/CN.4/1987/17 (8 January 1987), [57].

[128] Limburg Principles on the Implementation of the ICESCR, [57].

[129] Commission on Human Rights, Report to ECOSOC, E/2256(SUPP) (1 January 1952), 23.

conventions or agreements which are already in force, or may come into force, under which more favourable treatment would be accorded to the persons protected. Neither shall Article 5(2) be interpreted to restrict the exercise of any human right protected to a greater extent by national or international obligations accepted by the State Party.[130]

In other words, the ICESCR provides minimum human rights standards, but does not require states to change their laws to mimic *only* what it provides and thus to undermine existing protections (or preclude the future development of stronger protections). Article 5(2) of the ICCPR is identical. Similar, but narrower, provisions are Article 53 (formerly Article 60) of the ECHR and Article 29(b) of the ACHR, which are limited to domestic laws and treaties to which the respective states are parties (but exclude, for instance, regulations or customs).

In the drafting, certain states had a number of examples in mind. The United States observed that the legal protection of human rights in the United States was 'more extensive' than in the Covenant, which could not be understood to reduce domestic rights.[131] Belgium wanted to maintain its affirmative action provisions for women.[132] The absence of a right to property was also mentioned.[133] In practice, the provision will have most significance in states where regional human rights systems, or national bills of rights, provide additional or stronger protections than under the ICESCR.

Some during the drafting opposed the provision because it was 'inconceivable' that a State ratifying the Covenant would use it as a pretext to abridge rights already enjoyed in its territory[134] (perhaps not anticipating adverse changes of government in the future). More importantly, others thought that Article 5(2) was 'superfluous' because its rule was already part of international law.[135] Since nothing in the ICESCR explicitly requires states to confine their human rights protections to what it provides, Article 5(2) may be an overly cautious provision.

However, human rights were still fairly 'new' at the time of the drafting and confusion was rife. Some thought Article 5(2) might create misunderstanding and allow states to avoid their ICESCR obligations[136]—even though it says the opposite. Perhaps most significantly, the ordinary principle of treaty interpretation that a later in time treaty prevails over an earlier one to the extent of the inconsistency[137] could conceivably result in the ICESCR displacing more generous earlier treaty provisions, but for the existence of Article 5(2).[138] Likewise, Article 5(2) ensures a

[130] Limburg Principles on the Implementation of the ICESCR, E/CN.4/1987/17 (8 January 1987), [57–8].

[131] UNGA Third Committee, A/C.3/SR.1455 (12 December 1966), 478 (United States).

[132] UNGA Third Committee, A/C.3/SR.1184 (15 November 1962), 253.

[133] UNGA Third Committee, A/C.3/SR.575 (5 November 1954), 165.

[134] Commission on Human Rights, Report to ECOSOC, E/2256(SUPP) (1 January 1952), 23.

[135] UNGA, A/2929 (1 July 1955), 27.

[136] UNGA, A/2929 (1 July 1955), 27.

[137] Vienna Convention on the Law of Treaties (adopted 23 May 1969, 1155 UNTS 331, entered into force 27 January 1980), Article 30(3); see also Nowak, *CCPR Commentary*, 118 ('*lex posterior derogat legi priori*').

[138] Vienna Convention, Article 30(2): 'When a treaty specifies that it is subject to, or that it is not to be considered as incompatible with, an earlier or later treaty, the provisions of that other treaty prevail.'

particular ICESCR provision is not to be characterized as the special law (*lex specialis*) in a given area where that would displace a more generous standard in another treaty.

Article 24

Article 24 provides that the ICESCR shall not be interpreted to impair the UN Charter or the constitutions of UN organs or specialized agencies dealing with ICESCR matters. It is identical to Article 46 of the ICCPR, and related to the differently worded Article 29(3) of the UDHR, which provides that 'rights and freedoms may in no case be exercised contrary to the purposes and principles of the United Nations'. It does not, however, preserve the competence of regional human rights bodies, or, for instance, other human rights instruments;[139] such obligations come instead within the ambit of Article 5(2).

There was little discussion of Article 24 in the drafting. It was suggested that the term 'impair' was problematic because neither the Charter nor the constitutions of specialized agencies could be impaired by the ICESCR: '[t]he question was rather to ensure that nothing in the Covenant would prejudice' the full application of those other instruments.[140] An amendment to that effect was withdrawn when other states objected that it would in turn create interpretive problems.

Article 24 is a somewhat cautious provision given that nothing in the ICESCR expressly authorizes states to rely on their ICESCR obligations to override or displace other UN obligations in the same field. Even if it sought to do so, Article 103 of the UN Charter provides that Charter obligations take precedence over all other commitments.

However, Article 24 still has a role in emphasizing that the ICESCR is not regarded as a 'later in time' or more 'special' treaty displacing the mandates of other UN bodies in the event of apparent conflicts; the ICESCR is an additional monitoring scheme, not a substitute one. In this regard, there was an apparently 'widespread' view among states that the adoption of the ICESCR scheme would gradually displace other UN mechanisms, 'such as the general reporting system, the confidential complaint system under ECOSOC Res. 1503 (XLVIII) or the various public procedures ... [such as] special working groups and Special Rapporteurs'.[141]

Given that human rights are among the UN purposes in Article 1(3) of the Charter, there would seem to be little scope for real conflicts of obligation to arise in any event. The preamble to the ICESCR expressly invokes both the UDHR and the Charter, and certain other provisions mention the Charter (such as Article 1(3) on non-self-governing and trust territories, and Article 18 on the role of ECOSOC). The substance of the ICESCR evidences an express intention

[139] Nowak, *CCPR Commentary*, 797 (in relation to the identical Article 46 of the ICCPR).
[140] UNGA Third Committee, A/2929 (1 July 1955), 17.
[141] Nowak, *CCPR Commentary*, 798 (concerning the identical Article 46 of the ICCPR).

to harmonize, not impliedly contradict, the UN Charter or its specialized bodies. A requirement to report to one human rights body or mechanism does not raise a 'conflict' as such with an obligation to report to another, unless the primary obligation itself expresses an intention to exclusively cover the field of reporting; none of the relevant UN instruments does so.

Nor does the ICESCR itself stipulate or imply that cooperation with the mandated treaty bodies (such as ECOSOC and the Commission on Human Rights) excludes cooperation with other UN bodies or mechanisms. The monitoring system established under the ICESCR, and by ECOSOC, is not expressed as an exhaustive or exclusive scheme. Rather, there are indications in the ICESCR that the competence of multiple actors is recognized, such as the ILO in Article 8; in monitoring states too, the CESCR has frequently invoked the practice of more specialized bodies. As a well-intentioned statement of principle, however, Article 24 is unobjectionable.

8

Article 6: The Right to Work

Article 6

1. The States Parties to the present Covenant recognize the right to work, which includes the right of everyone to the opportunity to gain his living by work which he freely chooses or accepts, and will take appropriate steps to safeguard this right.

2. The steps to be taken by a State Party to the present Covenant to achieve the full realization of this right shall include technical and vocational guidance and training programmes, policies and techniques to achieve steady economic, social and cultural development and full and productive employment under conditions safeguarding fundamental political and economic freedoms to the individual.

Introduction: Purpose, Origins and Drafting

Human rights law regards work as essential not only to human survival, but life with dignity. The CESCR explains the purpose of the right to work thus:

> 1. . . . The right to work is essential for realizing other human rights and forms an inseparable and inherent part of human dignity. Every individual has the right to be able to work, allowing him/her to live in dignity. The right to work contributes at the same time to the survival of the individual and to that of his/her family, and insofar as work is freely chosen or accepted, to his/her development and recognition within the community.[1]

During the drafting, Pakistan argued that the right to work 'was bound up with man's very existence and enabled him to contribute to the enrichment of the civilization to which he belonged and to the production of the goods and services which were essential to the life of his country'.[2] Afghanistan noted that the opportunity to work enabled people to fulfil the 'other purposes of human life'.[3] The Soviet Union opined that 'virtually all the other rights' in the ICESCR 'would be illusory without a real guarantee of the right to work'.[4]

The right to work brings dignity because it allows a person freedom to choose their work, but also because it enables 'personal development' and 'social and economic inclusion',[5] including through self-reliance, self-esteem and the sense of social worth that comes from an individual's contribution to the economy and society. The preamble to International Labour Organization (ILO) Convention No. 168 concerning Employment Promotion and Protection against Unemployment 1988 thus emphasizes:

> . . . the importance of work and productive employment in any society not only because of the resources which they create for the community, but also because of the income which

[1] CESCR, General Comment No. 18, Article 6 of the ICESCR, E/C.12/GC/18 (6 February 2006) ('General Comment No. 18'), [1].
[2] UNGA Third Committee, A/C.3/SR.709 (13 December 1956), 138 (Pakistan).
[3] UNGA Third Committee, A/C.3/SR.710 (13 December 1956), 141 (Afghanistan).
[4] UNGA Third Committee, A/C.3/SR.709 (13 December 1956), 142 (USSR).
[5] UNGA Third Committee, A/C.3/SR.709 (13 December 1956), 142 (USSR), [4].

they bring to workers, the social role which they confer and the feeling of self-esteem which workers derive from them.[6]

The income from work enables the realization of 'survival' rights, such as food, housing and health, and aids in achieving other socio-economic rights such as education and culture.[7] Where full employment is not available, the right to work may still enable a measure of dignity to the unemployed in that there is still a demand on states to adopt policies to address unemployment or to provide vocational training. It thus gives even unemployed individuals hope that their life opportunities may improve and that, in concert with the right to social security in Article 9 of the ICESCR, they will not be left destitute or forgotten. As noted by the CESCR, in extreme cases job insecurity can even lead to suicide.[8]

Article 6 states 'a principle clearly and simply', in part reflecting the view during the drafting that the detail of the right to work should be left to specialized agencies such as the ILO.[9] Rights 'in' work (that is, conditions of work) are separately the subject of Article 7 of the ICESCR, while the 'collective dimension' of the right to work is addressed by the trade union-related rights in Article 8.[10] The CESCR regards Articles 6, 7 and 8 as 'interdependent'.[11] For example, a failure to pay the minimum wage under Article 7 could be regarded as forced or compulsory labour under Article 6.[12]

The articulation of work as an explicit human right is a relatively modern development, although antecedents can be found in the earlier national origins of rights discourse.[13] Concerns about exploitative labour conditions as a result of industrialization grew during the nineteenth century.[14] At the international level, the ILO was established in 1919 through the Treaty of Versailles after the First World War. The ILO Constitution 1919 does not articulate a right to work, but its preamble states that unjust or inhumane labour conditions produce unrest and imperil peace.[15] As a result, the ILO Constitution links the attainment of peace to

[6] ILO Convention No. 168 concerning Employment Promotion and Protection against Unemployment (adopted 21 June 1988, 1654 UNTS 67, entered into force 17 October 1991).

[7] Matthew Craven, *The International Covenant on Economic, Social and Cultural Rights: A Perspective on Its Development* (Oxford, Clarendon Press, 1995), 194.

[8] CESCR, Concluding Observations: France, E/C.12/1/Add.72 (30 November 2001), [17] and [28].

[9] UNGA Third Committee, A/C.3/SR.709 (13 December 1956), 137 (UK, Canada), 138 (France).

[10] CESCR, General Comment No. 18, [2].

[11] General Comment No. 18, [8].

[12] See, eg, *People's Union for Democratic Rights v Union of India* (*'Asiad Workers case'*) (1982) 3 SCC 235, 259–60 (Supreme Court of India) (where a failure to pay the minimum wage was forced labour contrary to Article 23 of the Constitution of India).

[13] Angelika Nussberger, 'Work, Right to, International Protection', *Max Planck Encyclopedia of Public International Law*, online entry, <http://www.mpepil.com>, [1] and [2] (mentioning the ideas of John Locke, the American Declaration of Independence 1776 and the French Constitution 1793).

[14] Krzysztof Drzewicki, 'The Right to Work and Rights in Work' in Asbjorn Eide, Catarina Krause and Allan Rosas (eds), *Economic, Social and Cultural Rights: A Textbook* (2nd edn, Kluwer, The Hague, 2001), 223, 224.

[15] Constitution of the International Labour Organization (adopted 1 April 1919, 15 UNTS 40, entered into force 28 June 1919, as Part XIII of the Treaty of Versailles), preamble. The original ILO Constitution was modified by amendments of 1922 (in force 4 June 1934), 1945 (in force 26 September 1946), 1946 (in force 20 April 1948), 1953 (in force 20 May 1954), 1962 (in force 22 May 1963) and 1972 (in force 1 November 1974).

'social justice', including through the '[r]egulation of labour supply, prevention of unemployment and provision of an adequate living wage'. In 1937, the ILO urged that 'women should have the full opportunity to work and should receive remuneration without discrimination because of sex'.[16]

The high levels of unemployment during the Great Depression of the 1930s, consequent civil unrest and the rise of fascism in states such as Germany, and the spread of socialism, were all factors conducive to renewed concern for workers' rights (including during the drafting), albeit from different ideological standpoints.[17] One significant influence on the drafting of post-1945 international human rights instruments was the Constitution of the Soviet Union of Socialist Republics 1936, Article 118 of which guaranteed citizens 'the right to work' in the context of a socialist economy:

> Citizens of the USSR have the right to work, that is, are guaranteed the right to employment and payment for their work in accordance with its quantity and quality.
>
> The right to work is ensured by the socialist organization of the national economy, the steady growth of the productive forces of Soviet society, the elimination of the possibility of economic crises, and the abolition of unemployment.

In refreshing the aims and objectives of the ILO, the Declaration of Philadelphia in 1944 emphasized that 'labour is not a commodity'[18] and implied a rights-based approach to work:

> ...all human beings, irrespective of race, creed or sex, have the right to pursue both their material well-being and their spiritual development in conditions of freedom and dignity, of economic security and equal opportunity...[19]

The ILO also committed itself to promote among states programmes which would achieve:

> (a) full employment and the raising of standards of living;
>
> (b) the employment of workers in the occupations in which they can have the satisfaction of giving the fullest measure of their skill and attainments and make their greatest contribution to the common well-being...[20]

In 1946, the ILO was absorbed as a specialized agency of the newly established United Nations. The UN Charter 1945 does not specifically mention the right to work, but Article 55(a) relevantly refers to the creation of 'higher standards of living, full employment and conditions of economic and social progress and development'.[21] The reference to 'full employment' was controversial, with the

[16] ILO Conference (23rd session), Resolution 7 concerning Women Workers (21 June 1937), [2].
[17] UNGA Third Committee, A/C.3/SR.711 (14 December 1956), 148 (Czechoslovakia).
[18] ILO General Conference (26th Session), Declaration concerning the aims and purposes of the International Labour Organization (Declaration of Philadelphia) (10 May 1944), annexed to the ILO Constitution, [1](a).
[19] Declaration of Philadelphia, [2](a). [20] Declaration of Philadelphia, [3].
[21] See also the later UNGA Res. 2542 (XXIV), Declaration on Social Progress and Development (11 December 1969), Article 6: 'Social development requires the assurance to everyone of the right to work and the free choice of employment'.

United States proposing the alternative phrase 'adequate employment'.[22] The International Monetary Fund (IMF) Articles of Agreement 1944 also mention the IMF's purpose to promote 'high levels of employment and real income' through international trade.[23]

A Soviet proposal to entrench work as a right resulted in the adoption in 1948 of Article 23(1) of the UDHR, which provides that '[e]veryone has the right to work, to free choice of employment…'. Article 6 of the ICESCR is inspired by the UDHR provision. The inclusion of the right to work in the ICESCR was first suggested in 1950 during discussions in the General Assembly's Third Committee, with draft texts presented in the Commission on Human Rights in 1951 and finalized by the Third Committee in 1956.[24] There was broad support from socialist, capitalist and developing states for its inclusion, although there was much debate about its scope, degree of specificity, implementation and enforcement, as discussed below.[25]

Relationship between Article 6 and ILO Standards

In declaring a human right to work, the ICESCR broke with the ILO's traditionally non-rights based,[26] social justice-focused and policy-oriented approach to labour issues. At the same time, the scope and content of Article 6 is inextricably connected to specialized ILO standard setting as developed through subject-specific ILO conventions and recommendations over more than ninety years. ILO standards were often referred to during the drafting.[27] Because of the greater specificity of particular ILO conventions and the more specific consent of states to them, ILO standards can enable and inform the scope of Article 6.

Further, the ILO's Committee of Experts, established in 1926, reviews state compliance with ILO norms and issues 'observations' on states, which, along with 'commissions of inquiry' that investigate inter-state complaints, have produced a rich body of international jurisprudence on labour issues. In part because of ILO standards, labour rights are also among the most developed or juridified of socio-economic rights in domestic jurisprudence worldwide.[28] Because of its much wider mandate, and resource and expertise limitations, the CESCR cannot be expected to match the level of sophistication of the ILO system in reviewing labour standards even for the more limited purpose of Article 6 (or Article 7, 8 or 9).

In monitoring Article 6, the CESCR has frequently (and appropriately) drawn on ILO standards. It has sometimes identified states as being in breach of their

[22] Bruno Simma, Daniel-Erasmus Khan, Georg Nolte and Andreas Paulus (eds), *The Charter of the United Nations: A Commentary* (3rd edn, Oxford University Press, Oxford, 2012), vol. II, 1541–2.

[23] Articles of Agreement of the International Monetary Fund, UN Monetary and Financial Conference at Bretton Woods (adopted 22 July 1944, 2 UNTS 39, entered into force 27 December 1945), Article I(ii).

[24] Craven, *The ICESCR*, 195. [25] See Craven, *The ICESCR*, ch. 5; and further below.

[26] Nussberger, 'Work, Right to, International Protection', [12]. [27] Craven, *The ICESCR*, 200.

[28] Drzewicki, 'The Right to Work and Rights in Work', 225.

ILO treaty commitments[29] or the views of the ILO Committee of Experts,[30] and called for domestic legislative implementation of binding ILO treaties.[31] There is a standing arrangement whereby the ILO assists the CESCR by transmitting the comments of the ILO Committee of Experts on the application of various ILO conventions.[32]

However, the CESCR has not limited its analysis to duplication of the ILO's own monitoring of states' obligations under ILO treaties. Thus, the CESCR has occasionally criticized states for not being in conformity with ILO conventions to which they are not even parties.[33] Further, the CESCR has often called on individual states to ratify specific ILO treaties, usually where its consideration of a state's report has flagged issues pertinent to those conventions, including Convention: No. 2 on Unemployment 1919;[34] No. 29 on Forced or Compulsory Labour;[35] No. 81 on Labour Inspection;[36] No. 87 on Trade Unions;[37] No. 98 on the Right to Organize;[38] No. 105 on Forced Labour;[39] No. 111 on Discrimination (Employment and Occupation);[40] No. 122 on Employment Policy;[41] No. 138 on Minimum Age;[42] No. 158 on Termination of Employment;[43] No. 159 on Disabled Persons;[44] No. 169 on Indigenous and Tribal Peoples;[45]

29 CESCR, Concluding Observations: China, E/C.12/1/Add.107 (13 May 2005), [23] (ILO Convention No. 182 on Child Labour); Estonia, E/C.12/1/Add.85 (19 December 2002), [35] (ILO Convention No. 29 on Forced Labour); Luxembourg, E/C.12/1/Add.22 (12 December 1997), [10] (ILO Convention Nos. 77 and 78 on Medical Examination of Young Persons); Luxembourg, E/C.12/1/Add.86 (26 June 2003), [20]; Morocco, E/C.12/1/Add.55 (1 December 2000), [41].

30 CESCR, Concluding Observations: Democratic Republic of Congo, E/C.12/COD/CO/4 (16 December 2009), [21] (forced labour by detainees); Germany, E/C.12/1/Add.29 (4 December 1998), [16] (discrimination in the employment of teachers in the new Länder); Mauritius, E/C.12/1994/8 (31 May 1994), [8] (forced labour to discipline seamen).

31 CESCR, Concluding Observations: Luxembourg, E/C.12/1/Add.22 (12 December 1997), [19].

32 International Labour Conference (92nd session), *Promoting Employment: Policies, Skills, Enterprises*, Report III (Part 1B) (2004), 16.

33 CESCR, Concluding Observations: Morocco, E/C.12/1/Add.55 (1 December 2000), [17] (minimum age for labour and conditions of child labour not in conformity with ILO Convention Nos. 138 and 182).

34 CESCR, Concluding Observations: Azerbaijan, E/C.12/1/Add.104 (14 December 2004), [43]; China, E/C.12/1/Add.107 (13 May 2005), [50]; Guatemala, E/C.12/1/Add.93 (12 December 2003), [31]; Iraq, E/C.12/1/Add.17 (12 December 1997), [61]; Uzbekistan, E/C.12/UZB/CO/1 (24 January 2006), [46].

35 CESCR, Concluding Observations: China, E/C.12/1/Add.107 (13 May 2005), [51]; Kazakhstan, E/C.12/KAZ/CO/1 (7 June 2010), [16]; Nepal, E/C.12/1/Add.66 (24 September 2001), [50].

36 CESCR, Concluding Observations: Nepal, E/C.12/1/Add.66 (24 September 2001), [50].

37 CESCR, Concluding Observations: Morocco, E/C.12/1/Add.55 (1 December 2000), [41]; Nepal, E/C.12/1/Add.66 (24 September 2001), [50]; New Zealand, E/C.12/1/Add.88 (26 June 2003), [25]; Solomon Islands, E/C.12/1/Add.84 (19 December 2002), [21].

38 CESCR, Concluding Observations: Solomon Islands, E/C.12/1/Add.84 (19 December 2002), [21].

39 CESCR, Concluding Observations: Japan, E/C.12/1/Add.67 (24 September 2001), [45].

40 CESCR, Concluding Observations: Estonia, E/C.12/1/Add.85 (19 December 2002), [37]; India, E/C.12/IND/CO/5 (8 August 2008), [59]; Japan, E/C.12/1/Add.67 (24 September 2001), [45]; Luxembourg, E/C.12/1/Add.22 (12 December 1997), [18].

41 CESCR, Concluding Observations: Luxembourg, E/C.12/1/Add.86 (26 June 2003), [33].

42 CESCR, Concluding Observations: India, E/C.12/IND/CO/5 (8 August 2008), [59]; Morocco, E/C.12/1/Add.55 (1 December 2000), [41].

43 CESCR, Concluding Observations: Tunisia, E/C.12/1/Add.36 (14 May 1999), [25].

44 CESCR, Concluding Observations: Italy, E/C.12/1/Add.43 (23 May 2000), [26].

45 CESCR, Concluding Observations: Japan, E/C.12/1/Add.67 (24 September 2001), [45]; Morocco, E/C.12/1/Add.55 (1 December 2000), [41].

No. 174 on Prevention of Major Industrial Accidents; and No. 182 on Child Labour.[46] The CESCR has also expressed concern where a state was not a party to any or many ILO conventions,[47] and encouraged states to seek ILO assistance in dealing with specific issues.[48] (The CESCR has also encouraged states to accede to a related non-ILO instrument, the International Convention on the Protection of the Rights of All Migrant Workers and Members of Their Families (ICMW).[49])

All of this suggests that the CESCR regards at least certain key ILO treaties as basic standards informing the scope of states' obligations under Article 6, regardless of whether a state has specifically consented to the ILO treaty in question. The CESCR has thus already taken the right to work beyond the formally binding set of ILO norms (namely, ratified treaties) which governs the conduct of any particular state.

Authority for this approach can be partly drawn from the ILO framework. The ILO Declaration on Fundamental Principles and Rights at Work 1988 provides that, by virtue of their membership of the ILO, all states are obliged to respect, promote and realize certain fundamental labour rights, regardless of whether they have ratified specific conventions.[50] The fundamental rights relevant to Article 6 of the ICESCR include the elimination of forced or compulsory labour and child labour, and discrimination in employment; while freedom of association and collective bargaining are relevant to Article 8 of the ICESCR.

While the CESCR must necessarily 'borrow' from ILO standards in understanding the scope of Article 6, it is not limited to reproducing them. In accordance with principles of treaty interpretation, the ordinary textual meaning of Article 6, coupled with an appreciation of its context, object and purpose, justifies going beyond ILO norms. Expressed as a human right directed towards human dignity, rather than a list of technical standards, the right to work in Article 6 has a more open-ended character than the numerous but more closed ILO standards.

The ICESCR thus brings a certain flexibility and dynamism to the protection of work rights, allowing the underlying objective of furthering human dignity to be expanded beyond the more finite and technical conception embodied in ILO standards. It may also be capable of taking into account evolving, contemporary and complementary extra-legal normative frameworks for conceptualizing work,

[46] CESCR, Concluding Observations: India, E/C.12/IND/CO/5 (8 August 2008), [59]; Kyrgyzstan, E/C.12/1/Add.49 (1 September 2000), [31]; Morocco, E/C.12/1/Add.55 (1 December 2000), [41]; Nepal, E/C.12/1/Add.66 (24 September 2001), [52]; Solomon Islands, E/C.12/1/Add.84 (19 December 2002), [21].

[47] CESCR, Concluding Observations: Gambia, E/C.12/1994/9 (31 May 1994), [13]; Solomon Islands, E/C.12/1/Add.84 (19 December 2002), [8].

[48] CESCR, Concluding Observations: Nepal, E/C.12/NPL/CO/2 (16 January 2008), [38] (child labour); Russian Federation, E/C.12/1/Add.13 (20 May 1997), [34] (assisting the unemployed to find work and receive benefits).

[49] CESCR, Concluding Observations: Moldova, E/C.12/1/Add.91 (12 December 2003), [36]; Russian Federation, E/C.12/1/Add.94 (12 December 2003), [45].

[50] ILO, Declaration on Fundamental Principles and Rights at Work (June 1988), [2].

such as the ILO's 'decent work' agenda, or the human development discourse which views work as enabling freedom through the development of human capabilities, opportunity and achievement.[51]

Other International Human Rights Instruments

Article 6 is related to work-related protections in other human rights instruments. Article 8(3)(a) of the ICCPR prohibits forced or compulsory labour, that is, the absence of the freedom to choose work under Article 6 of the ICESCR. Article 26 of the ICCPR provides for equality of treatment generally, which may include certain areas of employment (such as state programmes). Article 25(c) provides for a person's equal access to public service in her or his own country, which includes employment. The non-discrimination protection in Article 2 of the ICCPR, which only applies in the provision of other ICCPR rights, does not apply directly because there is no right to work in the ICCPR as such.

By contrast, Article 5(e)(i) of the International Convention on the Elimination of All Forms of Racial Discrimination (ICERD) expressly prohibits racial discrimination in 'rights to work, to free choice of employment...to protection against unemployment'. Discrimination against women in employment is extensively prohibited by Article 11(1)(a) of the Convention on the Elimination of All Forms of Discrimination against Women (CEDAW). Qualified protections against exploitative child labour are found in Article 32 of the Convention on the Rights of the Child (CROC), while two CROC protocols contain more specific prohibitions on forced recruitment in armed conflict and sexual exploitation.

The Convention on the Rights of Persons with Disabilities (CRPD) recognizes the right to work of persons with disabilities and outlines extensive steps states may take to safeguard and promote it (Article 27). The CRPD also encourages awareness-raising about the contributions of persons with disabilities to the workplace and labour market, and promotes workplace accessibility.[52] The ICMW does not recognize a right to work as such, but establishes minimum conditions and entitlements for all foreign workers.[53]

In addition to the non-discrimination context, the right to work is also related to other civil and political rights under the ICCPR, such as non-imprisonment for inability to fulfil a contractual obligation (Article 11), which could cover the breach of an employment contract. The arbitrary expulsion of a foreign worker under Article 13 of the ICCPR may result in a violation of the right to work under Article 6 of the ICESCR. So too may arbitrary detention under Article 9 of the

[51] Guy Mundlak, 'The Right to Work—The Value of Work' in Daphne Barak-Erez and Aeyal Gross (eds), *Exploring Social Rights: Between Theory and Practice* (Hart, Oxford, 2011), 341, 348–51.

[52] Convention on the Rights of Persons with Disabilities (adopted 13 December 2006, 2515 UNTS 3, entered into force 3 May 2008), Articles 8(2)(a)(iii) and 9(1)(a) respectively.

[53] International Convention on the Protection of the Rights of All Migrant Workers and Members of Their Families (adopted 18 December 1990, 2220 UNTS 3, entered into force 1 July 2003) ('Convention on Migrant Workers'), Articles 11, 25, 26, 40, 52 and 54.

ICCPR interfere in employment. Minority language rights in employment and vocational training are engaged by Article 27, while the work of indigenous peoples may arise in connection with indigenous self-determination rights under common Article 1 of the ICCPR and ICESCR.

Where a person is prevented from working, denied social security and no other means of support are available, leaving a person destitute and homeless, there may be a violation of a person's freedom from inhuman or degrading treatment under Article 7 of the ICCPR. Such was the case where the United Kingdom treated certain asylum seekers in this manner, contrary to the prohibition on inhuman or degrading treatment in Article 3 of the European Convention on Human Rights.[54]

In certain national practice, as in India, a 'right to livelihood' has been implied into the constitutional right to life (under Article 21 of the Constitution of India), 'because no person can live without the means of living'.[55] It includes, for instance, the right of farmers to cultivation.[56] Just and humane conditions of work (relevant to Article 7 of the ICESCR) have also been read into the right to life, including through interpretive reliance on non-enforceable directive principles of state policy also contained in the Indian Constitution.[57] Further, a fair procedure has been implied into the right to life where a person's livelihood is jeopardized by dismissal from work.[58]

The Content of the Right to Work

Article 6 aims to recognize the broad principle of the right to work, but also to give it specific, albeit non-exhaustive, content, as the CESCR explains:

> 2. …When drafting article 6 of the Covenant, the Commission on Human Rights affirmed the need to recognize the right to work in a broad sense by laying down specific legal obligations rather than a simple philosophical principle. Article 6 defines the right to work in a general and non-exhaustive manner…[59]

[54] *R v Secretary of State for the Home Department, ex parte Adam* [2005] UKHL 66.

[55] *Olga Tellis v Bombay Municipal Corporation* (1983) 3 SCC 545, 572 (Supreme Court of India); cf *Baitsokoli and Another v Maseru City Council et al* (2004) AHRLR 195 (Lesotho) (the domestic court did not accept that the constitutional right to life should be interpreted to include a 'right to livelihood' in a case where food traders were forcibly moved to a new market location, resulting in a drastic loss of income). On labour rights under the Indian Constitution, see Ramapriya Gopalakrishnan, 'Enforcing Labour Rights through Human Rights Norms: The Approach of the Supreme Court of India' in Colin Fenwick and Tonia Novitz (eds), *Human Rights at Work: Perspectives on Law and Regulation* (Hart, Oxford, 2010) ('*Human Rights at Work*'), 195.

[56] See, eg, *Dalmia Cement (Bharat) Ltd v Union of India* (1996) 10 SCC 104; *Charan Singh v State of Punjab* (1997) 1 SCC 151.

[57] *Bandhua Mukti Morcha v Union of India* (1984) 3 SCC 161, 183.

[58] *DK Yadav v JMA Industries Ltd* (1993) 3 SCC 259, 269 (Supreme Court of India); *Delhi Transport Corporation v DTC Mazdoor Congress* (1991) Supp 1 SCC 600, 651.

[59] CESCR, General Comment No. 18, [2].

While Article 6 is fairly briefly expressed, in interpretation and practice it comprises a number of key constituent elements. To summarize, there is first a freedom to choose and accept work where it is available (but no correlative legal duty to work). There is no denial of the right where a person does not satisfy the inherent requirements of a job, or meet other objective criteria such as considerations of security. Secondly, there is a prohibition on discrimination in all aspects of employment, which would infringe the freedom to work, and additionally violate Articles 2(2) and 3 in combination with Article 6. Non-discrimination extends to all aspects of employment including recruitment, in the workplace, and termination; it may also demand positive measures to promote disadvantaged workers.

Thirdly, Article 6 implies a prohibition on forced or compulsory labour, which would infringe the right to freely choose work or the negative 'freedom' not to work. There are, however, some significant exceptions in the definition of what constitutes forced or compulsory labour. The freedom to work also implies a right not to be arbitrarily denied work through arbitrary recruitment or unjustified dismissal.

Fourthly, while there is no obligation on states to immediately guarantee full employment, states must adopt a national employment policy directed towards the progressive expansion over time of the quantity and quality of employment opportunities. Such policy must be implemented in accordance with the maximum of the state's available resources, in the shortest possible time, and by prioritizing the needs of the most vulnerable or disadvantaged groups. Policies must address employment creation and availability, but also accessibility, including through the provision of appropriate vocational guidance and training (as under Article 6(2)). States must also provide effective remedies for violations of the right to work, including by private employers, and adequately regulate non-state actors to ensure respect for the right.

As discussed in this chapter, some elements of Article 6 have immediate effect (such as non-discrimination, the prohibitions on forced labour and unjustified dismissal, and the obligations to formulate a national employment policy and provide effective remedies). Other aspects of Article 6 are subject to progressive realization, particularly the progressive expansion of employment opportunities. The right to work is thus 'a complex normative aggregate' involving 'classic freedoms and modern rights approaches as well as an obligations-oriented perspective made up of strictly legal obligations and political commitments'.[60] Before turning to each of the elements of the right, it is first necessary to define 'work'.

MEANING OF 'WORK'

The CESCR has interpreted 'work' to encompass 'all forms of work, whether independent work or dependent wage-paid work'.[61] The text of Article 6 does not

[60] Drzewicki, 'The Right to Work and Rights in Work', 227.
[61] CESCR, General Comment No. 18, [6].

clarify whether work is limited to remunerated work,[62] stating only that the right to work 'includes' (but may not be restricted to) 'the opportunity to gain his living by work'. During the drafting, some delegations suggested that work should not be limited to paid work.[63]

By suggesting that Article 6 requires 'decent' work which 'provides an income allowing workers to support themselves and their families as highlighted in Article 7', the CESCR seems to confine the notion of work to paid work:

7. Work as specified in article 6 of the Covenant must be *decent work*. This is work that respects the fundamental rights of the human person as well as the rights of workers in terms of conditions of work safety and remuneration. It also provides an income allowing workers to support themselves and their families as highlighted in article 7 of the Covenant. These fundamental rights also include respect for the physical and mental integrity of the worker in the exercise of his/her employment.[64]

Remuneration and conditions of work are separately addressed by Article 7, but the idea of decent, remunerated work also defines the scope of Article 6. Decent work need not, however, be 'interesting, stimulating or enjoyable work'.[65]

If Article 6 (and the cognate rights in Articles 7 and 8) is confined to paid work, it may give rise to troubling lacunae. It would exclude from protection those who undertake unpaid voluntary work, such as professional internships (or even unpaid apprenticeships), work for non-profit organizations (from community service organizations to human rights advocacy groups), assisting the elderly or persons with disabilities at home or in care facilities, or assisting religious or political organizations. It may also exclude other non-wage labour, such as subsistence farming, hunting/gathering and agricultural producers.[66]

Some of the above activities may be separately covered by other human rights, for instance the ICCPR freedoms of political participation, religion, expression and association. Certain limited carer responsibilities may also be expected in the ordinary course of family life, for instance for close relatives. Internships may be a recognized training component in certain professions and thus bring future career rewards. Non-waged subsistence agriculture comes partly within the right to an adequate standard of living and specifically the right to food.

However, if the purpose of Article 6 is to ensure that a person has a right to 'freely choose' their work, that rationale also holds true for unpaid work. Volunteers should be entitled not to be coerced into working for particular causes, for instance as a result of undue pressure from organizations. Volunteers could equally expect not to be discriminated against when they offer their services, and ought to enjoy safe conditions of work as under Article 7. In most states the

[62] Craven, *The ICESCR*, 219.
[63] Craven, *The ICESCR*, 196.
[64] CESCR, General Comment No. 18, [7].
[65] Sarah Joseph, 'UN Covenants and Labour Rights' in Fenwick and Novitz, *Human Rights at Work*, 331, 337.
[66] Philip Harvey, 'Benchmarking the Right to Work' in Shareen Hertel and Lanse Minkler (eds), *Economic Rights: Conceptual, Measurement and Policy Issues* (Cambridge University Press, Cambridge, 2007), 115, 124.

economic value of voluntary work and the number of volunteers are very substantial, and voluntary work is sometimes connected to private enterprise (as in the case of internships and apprenticeships), further supporting an argument to apply Article 6.

The reference to 'productive' work under Article 6(2) is arguably of little importance other than perhaps to distinguish it from 'social projects of little significance merely to draw in the unemployed for the purpose of maintaining full employment'.[67] The UN General Assembly Declaration of 1969 also refers to '[s]ocial progress and development' requiring the participation of all members of society in productive and socially useful labour'.[68] The notion of productive work could also (somewhat tenuously) relate to the satisfaction or dignity it brings to the worker her- or himself.

'THE RIGHT TO WORK, WHICH INCLUDES THE RIGHT OF EVERYONE TO THE OPPORTUNITY TO GAIN HIS LIVING BY WORK WHICH HE FREELY CHOOSES OR ACCEPTS'

The right to work foremost includes the right to freely choose a trade or profession, as well as a right to accept or refuse an offer of employment. The right to work is not 'an absolute and unconditional right to obtain employment'.[69] There is no strict duty on the state or the private sector to employ a person who wishes to work, or to provide a job suitable to a person's skills, needs or preferences.[70] The United Kingdom observed during the drafting that 'freedom of choice of occupation for everyone was an ideal, not a practical proposition'.[71] As discussed further below, states are, however, required to immediately adopt national employment policies or plans directed towards progressively realizing 'full employment'[72] in line with the maximum of their available resources.

By extension, Article 6 must include the right of a worker to terminate their employment. Such right is, however, subject to any lawful and reasonable contractual conditions voluntarily entered into, as well as a requirement to give reasonable notice (although there is no obligation to give a valid reason for resigning—unlike the requirement on an employer terminating a worker's contract, discussed below).[73]

Some national constitutions (particularly in socialist states) link a person's right to work with a correlative duty to work.[74] Certain regional conceptions of human rights also emphasize a duty to work. The non-binding American Declaration on

[67] Craven, *The ICESCR*, 202.

[68] UNGA Res. 2542 (XXIV), Declaration on Social Progress and Development (11 December 1969), Article 6(2).

[69] CESCR, General Comment No. 18, [6].

[70] Craven, *The ICESCR*, 204.

[71] UNGA Third Committee, A/C.3/SR.712 (14 December 1956), 154 (UK).

[72] The meaning of which is discussed below.

[73] ILO, *Protection against Unjustified Dismissal*, International Labour Conference (82nd session) (Geneva, 1995) ('ILO, *Protection against Unjustified Dismissal*'), 31; see also the discussion of forced labour below.

[74] See, eg, Constitution of the People's Republic of China (4 December 1982), Article 42.

the Rights and Duties of Man 1948 recognizes the 'duty of every person to work, as far as his capacity and possibilities permit in order to obtain the means of livelihood or to benefit his community' (Article XXXVII). Likewise, the African Charter on Human and Peoples' Rights 1981 acknowledges the duty of everyone 'to serve his national community by placing his physical and intellectual abilities at its service' and 'to work to the best of his abilities and competence' (Article 29).

By contrast, Article 6 of the ICESCR does not express or imply a duty to work, even if it may be a social or moral expectation in a given society.[75] Certainly, during the drafting some states were concerned that permitting people not to work would encourage 'social parasitism, idleness or laziness',[76] and were in favour of a duty to work.[77] But there was no general endorsement of a duty to work.[78] The text of Article 6 requires that work must be freely accepted, which is further understood to entail a prohibition on forced labour (discussed later in this chapter).

In monitoring states, the CESCR criticized North Korea for its 'system of compulsory State-allocated employment, which is contrary to the right of the individual to freely choose his/her career or his/her workplace'.[79] While there is no general duty to work, under certain conditions a person may be required to work as a criterion of eligibility to receive social security assistance, discussed below. There are also a number of recognized exceptions to the prohibition on forced labour, discussed subsequently.

A number of considerations affect (by enabling or qualifying) the freedom to choose or accept work, including: (a) the inherent requirements of a job; (b) security considerations; (c) the principle of non-discrimination; and (d) the availability of work, in light of the state's duty to take steps to progressively realize full employment. The first three considerations are addressed immediately below. The latter is examined later in this chapter in the context of state employment policy.

Inherent requirements of a job

Employers are not required to give a job to anybody. Particular qualifications, skills, experience or other necessary characteristics may be legitimately required of a person to perform certain work. So much is recognized by Article 1(2) of ILO Convention No. 111 on Discrimination in Respect of Employment and Occupation 1958, adopted prior to the ICESCR, which provides that '[a]ny distinction, exclusion or preference in respect of a particular job based on the inherent requirements thereof shall not be deemed to be discrimination'.[80] The CESCR has invoked the

[75] Mundlak, 'The Right to Work—The Value of Work', 356–8.
[76] UNGA Third Committee, A/C.3/SR.709 (13 December 1956), 137 (Spain).
[77] UNGA Third Committee, A/C.3/SR.709 (13 December 1956), 138 (Colombia).
[78] Craven, *The ICESCR*, 199.
[79] CESCR, Concluding Observations: DPR Korea, E/C.12/1/Add.95 (12 December 2003), [14].
[80] ILO Convention No. 111 concerning Discrimination in Respect of Employment and Occupation (adopted 25 June 1958, 362 UNTS 31, entered into force 15 June 1960) ('ILO Convention No. 111').

notion of 'inherent requirements' in assessing for employment discrimination,[81] and it may be characterized as an 'objective and reasonable' basis for differentiation under anti-discrimination law.

The 'inherent requirements' of a job are interpreted strictly by the ILO,[82] so as to ensure that the protection against discrimination is not unjustifiably eroded. An 'inherent' requirement is one that is 'essential' (rather than incidental or peripheral) to the performance of the job.[83] The requirements of a job should ordinarily be identified in advance of a person's employment and advertised as part of the recruitment process. They may, however, be deduced from the wider context of a person's employment, such as where a person is physically able to fly an aircraft but cannot fly it on international routes because international civil aviation rules (assuming they in turn are rationally based) prohibit pilots over the age of 60 from doing so.[84] An age limit is thus an inherent requirement of that job and not unlawful age discrimination.[85]

While the absence of a criminal record may be an inherent requirement of certain jobs, such a requirement will be tightly construed. Thus, an old conviction for minor theft of alcohol by a person who was then a minor would not be a sound basis for refusing to employ the person as a bar attendant, on the purported basis that the person is not honest or trustworthy, and where other evidence in her favour was not properly considered.[86] There must be a tight correlation between the requirement regarding a person's criminal record and the job and not merely some connection.[87] Likewise, 'moral' characteristics, such as a requirement on a solicitor to be a 'fit and proper' person, should be narrowly construed, such that past misconduct (even assaults) which are unrelated to practice as a lawyer are not grounds to refuse employment.[88]

Occupational health and safety considerations may be an inherent requirement of a job, as where a good driving record is necessary for a public transport driving position, or where pregnant women cannot be safely exposed to toxic substances. Likewise, a certain disease may pose special risks or liabilities in a

[81] CESCR, Revised guidelines regarding the form and content of reports to be submitted by states parties under Articles 16 and 17 of the ICESCR, UN ESCOR, Supp. No. 3, E/1991/23 (1991), Annex IV, 88, 91.

[82] ILO Committee of Experts on the Application of Conventions and Recommendations (CEACR), Direct Request: Czech Republic (2012); *Commonwealth v Bradley* (1999) 95 FCR 218, 235 per Black CJ [Federal Court of Australia]; *Commonwealth v Human Rights and Equal Opportunity Commission et al* (1998) 158 ALR 468 at 482 (Wilcox J) [Federal Court of Australia].

[83] *Qantas Airways Ltd v Christie* [1998] HCA 18 (19 March 1998) (Gaudron J) [High Court of Australia].

[84] *Qantas Airways Ltd v Christie*.

[85] As long as the medical and safety evidence supports such a conclusion: see further below.

[86] [Australian] Human Rights and Equal Opportunity Commission, *Ms Renai Christensen v Adelaide Casino Pty Ltd*, HREOC Report No. 20 (2002), 20–1.

[87] [Australian] Human Rights and Equal Opportunity Commission, *Mr Mark Hall v NSW Thoroughbred Racing Board*, HREOC Report No. 19, 34–5; *Commonwealth v Bradley* (1999) 95 FCR, 237 (Black CJ); *Wall v NT Police Services*, Anti-Discrimination Commission, 14 March 2005.

[88] *A Solicitor v The Council of the Law Society of New South Wales* [2004] HCA 1 (4 February 2004), 32.

particular context, as where bleeding on military operations may infect others,[89] or a diabetic cannot be deployed in a combat situation.[90] In relation to disability discrimination, however, careful attention must be given to whether reasonable accommodations or adjustments can be made to enable the person to perform the job rather than simply excluding the person from consideration altogether.

The inherent requirements of a job are context dependent. While it is permissible to require a minister of religion to possess that faith, religious belief is not inherent in an administrative position (such as the job of a statistician) working for a religious institution.[91] A language requirement is permissible where it is essential to a job (as in customer service roles), but not where it may be peripheral (as in a cleaner position) and thus result in impermissible discrimination on the basis of race, nationality, ethnicity or social origin. The reasonableness of such requirements may also be affected by cross-cutting considerations such as age, culture and religion.

Some typical examples of inherent job requirements which may not constitute sex or gender discrimination are given in an Australian statute, such as where:

> (a) the duties of the position can be performed only by a person having particular physical attributes (other than attributes of strength or stamina) that are not possessed by persons of the opposite sex to the relevant sex;
>
> (b) the duties of the position involve performing in a dramatic performance or other entertainment in a role that, for reasons of authenticity, aesthetics or tradition, is required to be performed by a person of the relevant sex;
>
> (c) the duties of the position need to be performed by a person of the relevant sex to preserve decency or privacy because they involve the fitting of clothing for persons of that sex;
>
> (d) the duties of the position include the conduct of searches of the clothing or bodies of persons of the relevant sex;
>
> (e) the occupant of the position is required to enter a lavatory ordinarily used by persons of the relevant sex while the lavatory is in use by persons of that sex;
>
> (f) the occupant of the position is required to live on premises provided by the employer or principal of the occupant of the position and—
>
> (i) the premises are not equipped with separate sleeping accommodation and sanitary facilities for persons of each sex;
>
> (ii) the premises are already occupied by a person or persons of the relevant sex and are not occupied by any person of the opposite sex to the relevant sex; and
>
> (iii) it is not reasonable to expect the employer or principal to provide separate sleeping accommodation and sanitary facilities for persons of each sex;

[89] *X v The Commonwealth* [1999] HCA 63 (2 December 1999) [High Court of Australia] (where an HIV-positive serviceman was discharged from the military).

[90] *Commonwealth v Williams* [2002] FCAFC 435 [Federal Court of Australia].

[91] *Jean-Louis Ramiaranjatovo v Fitsaboana Maso*, Antsirabe Labour Court Judgment No. 58, 7 June 2004 (Madagascar).

(g) the occupant of the position is required to enter areas ordinarily used only by persons of the relevant sex while those persons are in a state of undress…[92]

The ILO has found that legal provisions stipulating common height or athletic standards for admission to the police force may constitute indirect discrimination against women.[93] In cases of manual labour, there was sex or gender discrimination where female workers were dismissed on the basis that they could not perform 'very heavy' work or night-shift work, even though they were not actually required to lift heavy loads and were rarely required to work nights.[94]

Blanket exclusions are hard to defend, as where all women are barred from combat roles, regardless of whether they meet the physical requirements of combat or whether technological developments alter prior assumptions about the conditions of combat. In certain areas, however, strict gender segregation appears to be widely accepted, as in professional sporting competitions involving career athletes, where objective performance criteria are applicable.

Security considerations

Article 4 of Convention No. 111 further allows for security exceptions in employment:

Any measures affecting an individual who is justifiably suspected of, or engaged in, activities prejudicial to the security of the State shall not be deemed to be discrimination, provided that the individual concerned shall have the right to appeal to a competent body established in accordance with national practice.

The principle of refusal of employment on security grounds can be accommodated under Article 6 of the ICESCR by reference to Article 4 of the ICESCR (discussed in an earlier chapter of this book), which allows states to limit a right by law, where compatible with the nature of the right, for the sole purpose of promoting the general welfare in a democratic society. National security may be an objective and reasonable criterion on which to restrict work rights.

In monitoring states, the ILO has identified a number of principles to guide the application of the security exception in employment. First, the individual must be justifiably suspected of, or proven to be engaged in, acts which are prejudicial to the security of the state. While a criminal conviction or court finding is unnecessary, and no rigid standard of proof is required, a person must be 'justifiably' suspected of or 'engaged in' prejudicial activities. Mere suspicion, without some firm evidentiary foundation, is insufficient.

Secondly, the person must present a *current* risk. While past activities may indicate that a person is still a risk, past conduct alone is not determinative. This is particularly so where there is evidence that a person is no longer involved

[92] Sex Discrimination Act 1984 (Commonwealth of Australia), s. 30.

[93] International Labour Conference (101st Session), *Giving Globalization a Human Face*, Report III(1B) (General Survey on the Fundamental Conventions) (Geneva, 2 March 2012) ('*Giving Globalization a Human Face*'), 330.

[94] *Moatswi and Another v Fencing Center (Pty) Ltd*, Botswana Industrial Court BwIC 2002, 7 March 2002.

with dangerous persons, groups or ideologies; where underlying conditions have changed (such as where a dangerous foreign government disappears or a conflict ends); or where a person has expiated their guilt by serving a criminal sentence and shows that they have rehabilitated.

Thirdly, any risks posed by a person must be examined in the light of their impact on the actual performance of the job, task or occupation.[95] Thus, the CESCR noted that a duty of faithfulness to a free democratic order in Germany was not usually a necessary qualification for positions such as teaching.[96] An ILO Commission of Inquiry conceded, however, that in exceptional cases the German requirement may not constitute impermissible discrimination on the grounds of political opinion:

> ...the concern to ensure the functioning of the public service in times of crisis or conflict would permit the public authorities to consider political reliability to constitute an inherent requirement for employment in certain positions, having regard to the nature of the functions involved; such a condition should, however, not be extended to the employment of officials in the public service generally.[97]

The ILO elsewhere found that Lithuania's exclusion of former Soviet security or intelligence personnel from the entire civil service was unjustifiably broad because it was not tailored to specific jobs, functions or tasks. Instead, it applied to membership of a particular group or community without any assessment of whether the particular individual was a security risk in a particular position.[98] Similar findings were made in respect of the Lithuanian law by the European Court of Human Rights and the European Committee on Social Rights.[99]

Likewise, the Czech Republic's exclusion from public service and private sector employment of categories of people associated with the former communist regime constituted discrimination based on political opinion.[100] In its consideration of a later Czech law, the ILO acknowledged that exclusions from employment may arise 'from the perceived need and assumption that during the transition from the totalitarian State to a democratic society, it is necessary to ensure full credibility of persons called on to perform leading functions',[101] including where people had committed past human rights abuses. However, the ILO noted that even where a law applies only to the 'highest management levels', the level of a post 'may not be determinative and that what is required is a careful and objective consideration of the inherent requirements of a job on a case-by-case-basis'.[102]

95 ILO CEACR, Observations: Lithuania (2001) and (2009).

96 CESCR, Concluding Observations: Federal Republic of Germany, E/C.12/1987/SR.19 (1987), [45].

97 ILO, Report of the Commission of Inquiry appointed under Article 26 of the ILO Constitution to examine the observance of the Discrimination (Employment and Occupation) Convention, 1958 (No. 111), by the Federal Republic of Germany (Vol. LXX, 1987, Series B, Supplement 1), [573].

98 ILO CEACR, Observation: Lithuania (2001).

99 *Sidabras and Dziautas v Lithuania* (Apps. 55480/00, 59330/00), 27 July 2004, [2004] 42 EHRR 104, [59]; *Rainys and Gasparavicius v Lithuania* (Apps. 70665/01, 74345/01), 7 April 2005, [2005] ECtHR 226; European Committee on Social Rights (ECSR), Conclusions: Lithuania (2006).

100 ILO CEACR, Observation: Czech Republic (1992).

101 ILO CEACR, Observation: Czech Republic (1998).

102 ILO CEACR, Observation: Czech Republic (1998).

Fourthly, the mere expression of political, religious or philosophical beliefs will not suffice to exclude a person from employment on security grounds where the person does not resort to or incite violence. Thus, Egypt's exclusion from certain public sector employment of any person convicted of advocating the rejection of Islam was not permitted by the security exception where such persons did not incite or resort to violence.[103] This was the case even where the law only applied to positions which issued orders, affected public opinion or involved representation.

The ILO has conceded that criteria such as political opinion, national extraction and religion may be taken into account as inherent requirements of a job in certain cases. But Iran's exclusion from government employment of persons of the Bahá'í faith, on the basis that this group was not constitutionally recognized as a religion, involved discrimination not justified by the security exception.[104]

Finally, restrictive measures must be sufficiently well defined and delimited to ensure that they do not constitute impermissible discrimination.[105] Thus, a Turkish martial law which permitted dismissal of persons considered 'harmful or undesirable in respect of state security' was considered too broad, and needed to be defined and delimited so as not to discriminate on the basis of political opinion. So too would laws be overbroad if they excluded workers on the basis of, for example, lack of 'loyalty', 'the public interest', or 'anti-democratic' views.[106]

Ethiopia's mass deportation of Eritrean workers at the outbreak of a border conflict involved discrimination on the basis of nationality or political opinion which was not justified by security concerns.[107] There is no necessary correlation between a person's nationality and their home government's policies, and the indiscriminate exclusions of whole national groups from employment can never be justified by the security exception.

At the same time, a citizenship requirement for sensitive security jobs is fairly commonplace in state practice, predicated on the notion that citizenship implies a duty of loyalty or allegiance which safeguards against the greater potential risks presented by non-nationals. Such distinction is necessarily blunt—one can envisage a disloyal national and a loyal non-national—but it seems accepted at least in respect of sensitive positions. The legal issue remains, however, whether it is an inherent requirement of the particular job in question.

Wherever employment is affected by security grounds, ILO Convention No. 111 requires states to provide a 'right to appeal to a competent body established in accordance with national practice'. States are accorded flexibility in implementation ('in accordance with national practice'). A range of 'competent bodies' may be envisaged, from full judicial review, to merits review by relatively

[103] ILO CEACR, Observation: Egypt (1995).

[104] ILO CEACR, Observation: Iran (1990) and (1999).

[105] ILO CEACR, Observation: Sudan (1993).

[106] ILO, Report of the Commission of Inquiry appointed under Article 26 of the ILO Constitution to examine the observance of the Discrimination (Employment and Occupation) Convention, 1958 (No. 111), by the Federal Republic of Germany (Vol. LXX, 1987, Series B, Supplement 1), [93].

[107] ILO CEACR, Observation: Ethiopia (2002).

independent administrative tribunals, to internal departmental reconsideration. Impartiality would seem to be a minimum characteristic in all cases, thus tending to rule out internal departmental reviews.

The applicable procedure will also vary from state to state and context to context. The full protections of a fair criminal trial or a civil court hearing (such as those provided under Article 14 of the ICCPR) are not strictly required. But elementary due process or fair hearing protections, of the kind typically expected in administrative proceedings, would seem necessary. These relevantly include rights to know the essence of the case against oneself, and to defend oneself in a fair process.

Certain adjustments may be made to ensure the protected disclosure of security-sensitive or classified information, but such modifications may not deprive the affected person of a fair hearing. There is no reason why such procedures should vary as between citizens and non-citizens, if the concern is the protection of sensitive information from any person, citizen or foreigner, who may jeopardize intelligence sources.

Non-discrimination and equal opportunity

The 'right of everyone to the opportunity to gain his living by work' in Article 6 entails protection from discrimination and a guarantee of equal opportunity in employment, which the CESCR regards as a 'core obligation' of states:

31. In general comment No. 3 (1990) the Committee confirms that States parties have a core obligation to ensure the satisfaction of minimum essential levels of each of the rights covered by the Covenant. In the context of article 6, this 'core obligation' encompasses the obligation to ensure non-discrimination and equal protection of employment. Discrimination in the field of employment comprises a broad cluster of violations affecting all stages of life, from basic education to retirement, and can have a considerable impact on the work situation of individuals and groups…[108]

The guarantee of non-discrimination and equal opportunity in Article 6 is connected to the general prohibition on discrimination in Article 2(2) and the protection of gender equality in Article 3 of the ICESCR, which the CESCR refers to in approaching Article 6:

Under its article 2, paragraph 2, and article 3, the Covenant prohibits any discrimination in access to and maintenance of employment on the grounds of race, colour, sex, language, religion, political or other opinion, national or social origin, property, birth, physical or mental disability, health status (including HIV/AIDS), sexual orientation, or civil, political, social or other status, which has the intention or effect of impairing or nullifying exercise of the right to work on a basis of equality.[109]

Some of the grounds mentioned above are not found in the strict text of Articles 2(2) or 3,[110] but appear to be expansively interpreted by the CESCR as

[108] CESCR, General Comment No. 3, E/1991/23 (14 December 1990), [31].

[109] CESCR, General Comment No. 3, [12(b)(i)].

[110] Such as health status (including HIV/AIDS), disability, sexual orientation, and civil, political, social or other status: Joseph, 'UN Covenants and Labour Rights', 355.

falling within the more open-ended categories of 'other status' or 'social origin'. In monitoring states, the CESCR has identified many groups as vulnerable to discrimination and/or lack of equal opportunity, including: women (including single mothers), young people (including school leavers and recent graduates), the elderly, persons with disabilities, minorities, indigenous peoples, migrants, refugees, workers with family responsibilities, returnees, workers in the informal economy, rural residents and people without qualifications or low skills.

Mention should also be made of ILO Convention No. 111 concerning Discrimination (Employment and Occupation) of 1958, which defines discrimination as any distinction, exclusion or preference made on the basis of race, colour, sex, religion, political opinion, national extraction or social origin, which has the effect of nullifying or impairing equality of opportunity or treatment in employment or occupation.

Non-discrimination in work encompasses both direct and indirect discrimination, the latter occurring where the same condition, criterion or treatment has a disproportionately harsh impact on some people based on race, colour, sex, religion and so on. Non-discrimination also applies to all facets of the employment field, including vocational training, access to employment and to particular occupations, and terms and conditions of employment.[111]

Freedom from discrimination in work is subject to the usual test for permissible 'reasonable and objective', and proportionate, differential treatment under non-discrimination law, as set out by the CESCR in General Comment No. 20:

> Differential treatment based on prohibited grounds will be viewed as discriminatory unless the justification for differentiation is reasonable and objective. This will include an assessment as to whether the aim and effects of the measures or omissions are legitimate, compatible with the nature of the Covenant rights and solely for the purpose of promoting the general welfare in a democratic society. In addition, there must be a clear and reasonable relationship of proportionality between the aim sought to be realized and the measures or omissions and their effects. A failure to remove differential treatment on the basis of a lack of available resources is not an objective and reasonable justification unless every effort has been made to use all resources that are at the State party's disposition in an effort to address and eliminate the discrimination, as a matter of priority.[112]

The CESCR has stated that non-discrimination in Article 2(2) 'is immediately applicable and is neither subject to progressive implementation nor dependent on available resources. It is directly applicable to all aspects of the right to work.'[113] While national judicial decisions on the right to work generally are relatively rare,[114] non-discrimination in employment is among the most commonly litigated areas of work rights in national practice. According to the CESCR, the 'core

[111] See, eg, ILO Convention No. 111, Article 1(3).

[112] CESCR, General Comment No. 20, Non-discrimination in economic, social and cultural rights, E/C.12/GC/20 (2 July 2009), [13].

[113] CESCR, General Comment No. 20, [33].

[114] Nussberger, 'Work, Right to, International Protection', [26].

obligations' of states in respect of non-discrimination and equal opportunity in employment are threefold:

(a) To ensure the right of access to employment, especially for disadvantaged and marginalized individuals and groups, permitting them to live a life of dignity; (b) To avoid any measure that results in discrimination and unequal treatment in the private and public sectors of disadvantaged and marginalized individuals and groups or in weakening mechanisms for the protection of such individuals and groups; (c) To adopt and implement a national employment strategy and plan of action based on and addressing the concerns of all workers on the basis of a participatory and transparent process that includes employers' and workers' organizations. Such an employment strategy and plan of action should target disadvantaged and marginalized individuals and groups in particular and include indicators and benchmarks by which progress in relation to the right to work can be measured and periodically reviewed.[115]

Non-discriminatory, equal access to employment may require, for example, measures to ensure the physical accessibility of workplaces for persons with disabilities; as well as 'the right to seek, obtain and impart information on the means of gaining access to employment through the establishment of data networks on the employment market at the local, regional, national and international levels'.[116] Access to information may further require the provision of information in languages which minority or indigenous groups can understand.

In monitoring states, the CESCR has seldom identified specific measures which involve discrimination or unequal treatment and has instead tended to more generally urge the state to prevent discrimination and ensure equal treatment. In a rare example, in Poland it was concerned about 'discriminatory practices such as job advertisements specifying the preferred gender of the employees sought and women candidates for jobs being asked to take pregnancy tests'.[117]

The requirement to promote non-discrimination and equal opportunity as part of a national employment strategy and plan is drawn from Article 2 of ILO Convention No. 111.[118] The CESCR has highlighted that '[m]any measures...can be pursued with minimum resource implications through the adoption, modification or abrogation of legislation or the dissemination of information'.[119] The CESCR has further suggested that 'even in times of severe resource constraints, disadvantaged and marginalized individuals and groups must be protected by the adoption of relatively low-cost targeted programmes'.[120]

In this respect, Article 5(1) of ILO Convention No. 111 provides that 'special measures' of protection or assistance for vulnerable groups are not regarded as

115 CESCR, General Comment No. 20, [31].

116 CESCR, General Comment No. 20, [12]; see also CESCR, General Comment No. 5, Persons with disabilities, E/1995/22 (9 December 1994), [22].

117 CESCR, Concluding Observations: Poland, E/C.12/1/Add.26 (16 June 1998), [14].

118 ILO Convention No. 111, Article 2 (by which states must 'declare and pursue a national policy designed to promote, by methods appropriate to national conditions and practice, equality of opportunity and treatment in respect of employment and occupation, with a view to eliminating any discrimination in respect thereof').

119 CESCR, General Comment No. 18, [12(b)(i)].

120 CESCR, General Comment No. 18, [12(b)(i)].

unlawful discrimination. Thus, the CESCR has endorsed particular states' adoption of employment quotas for marginalized groups, particularly persons with disabilities[121] and ethnic minorities,[122] and called for 'affirmative action measures to promote active political participation of women' in respect of work-related decision-making.[123] Quotas can have a rapid and dramatic impact: the ILO noted that in Norway, a requirement on public companies to have equal representation on their boards lifted the rate of women from 7 to 40 per cent in one year.[124] The CESCR has also called for other special measures for persons with disabilities, such as training, the removal of physical barriers, and wage subsidies or other incentives for employers.[125]

In its practice the CESCR has been particularly concerned about the following groups: women, younger and older people, persons with disabilities, migrant workers, refugees, minorities and indigenous peoples. Each of these is briefly considered in turn.

Women

The CESCR has discussed women's right to work under Article 6 in conjunction with Article 3 (gender equality generally) and Article 2 (non-discrimination generally). In General Comment No. 18 it briefly emphasizes that pregnancy should not be a barrier to employment or a cause of dismissal, and that women's lesser access to education, and vulnerability to traditional cultural practices, compromise their work rights:

> 13. Article 3 of the Covenant prescribes that States parties undertake to 'ensure the equal right of men and women to the enjoyment of all economic, social and cultural rights'. The Committee underlines the need for a comprehensive system of protection to combat gender discrimination and to ensure equal opportunities and treatment between men and women in relation to their right to work by ensuring equal pay for work of equal value. In particular, pregnancies must not constitute an obstacle to employment and should not constitute justification for loss of employment. Lastly, emphasis should be placed on the link between the fact that women often have less access to education than men and certain traditional cultures which compromise the opportunities for the employment and advancement of women.[126]

In monitoring states, the CESCR has routinely expressed concern about the high or disproportionate level of unemployment affecting women; the prevalence of women in the informal economy,[127] other irregular employment[128] or part-time

[121] CESCR, Concluding Observations: China (including HK, Macao), E/C.12/1/Add.107 (13 May 2005), [21]; Latvia, E/C.12/LVA/CO/1 (7 January 2008), [41]; Lithuania, E/C.12/1/Add.96 (7 June 2004), [34]; Russian Federation, E/C.12/1/Add.94 (12 December 2003), [44]; Uzbekistan, E/C.12/UZB/CO/1 (24 January 2006), [45].

[122] CESCR, Concluding Observations: Sri Lanka, E/C.12/1/Add.24 (16 June 1998), [11].

[123] CESCR, Concluding Observations: India, E/C.12/IND/CO/5 (8 August 2008), [57].

[124] ILO, *Giving Globalization a Human Face*, 316.

[125] CESCR, Concluding Observations: Serbia and Montenegro, E/C.12/1/Add.108 (23 June 2005), [44].

[126] CESCR, General Comment No. 18, [13].

[127] CESCR, Concluding Observations: Nicaragua, E/C.12/NIC/CO/4 (28 November 2008), [14].

[128] CESCR, Concluding Observations: Republic of Korea, E/C.12/1/Add.59 (21 May 2001), [17].

work;[129] and employment discrimination (including dismissal for pregnancy[130]) and unequal pay, including in the private sector.[131] Occasionally, the CESCR has highlighted the disproportionate impact of redundancies on women.[132] It has also highlighted lower education or literacy rates and cultural practices which limit women's employment and promotion opportunities.[133] The issue of equal pay for equal work is more squarely addressed under Article 7 of the ICESCR concerning conditions of work, and is also the subject of ILO Convention No. 100.[134]

The CESCR has routinely criticized gender discrimination generally, and occasionally identified specific instances of it, as where laws required a husband's permission for a wife to work,[135] or where employers demanded medical certificates to prove that a prospective or current employee is not pregnant.[136]

The most common form of discrimination under Article 6 mentioned by the CESCR is sexual harassment,[137] and this issue also arises under Article 7 (conditions of work). The CESCR's 2009 reporting guidelines on Article 7 ask states to report on sexual harassment in the workplace and measures taken to prevent and remedy it:

> 22. Indicate whether the State party has adopted and effectively implemented legislation that specifically criminalizes sexual harassment in the workplace, and describe the mechanisms to monitor such implementation. Also indicate the number of registered cases, the sanctions imposed on perpetrators and the measures taken to compensate and assist victims of sexual harassment.[138]

In monitoring states, the CESCR has condemned the failure by states to legislate against[139] and criminalize[140] sexual harassment in the workplace. It was concerned at the lack of understanding about what constitutes harassment.[141] It has regularly

[129] CESCR, Concluding Observations: Netherlands, E/C.12/1/Add.25 (16 June 1998), [12]; Sweden, E/C.12/SWE/CO/5 (1 December 2008), [18].

[130] CESCR, Concluding Observations: Bulgaria, E/C.12/1/Add.37 (8 December 1999), [30]; Suriname, E/C.12/1995/6 (7 June 1995), [10]; Mexico, E/C.12/1/Add.41 (8 December 1999), [21].

[131] CESCR, Concluding Observations: Luxembourg, E/C.12/1/Add.22 (12 December 1997), [18].

[132] CESCR, Concluding Observations: China (including Hong Kong, Macao), E/C.12/1/Add.107 (13 May 2005), [21].

[133] CESCR, Concluding Observations: Senegal, E/C.12/1993/18 (5 January 1994), [6].

[134] ILO Convention No. 100 concerning Equal Remuneration for Men and Women Workers for Work of Equal Value (adopted 29 June 1951, 165 UNTS 303, entered into force 23 May 1953).

[135] CESCR, Concluding Observations: Zaire, E/C.12/1988/SR.17 (1988), [3]; Iran, E/C.12/1993/7 (9 June 1993), [6].

[136] CESCR, Concluding Observations: Mexico, E/C.12/1/Add.41 (8 December 1999), [21].

[137] CESCR, Concluding Observations: Georgia, E/C.12/1/Add.42 (17 May 2000), [15]; Macedonia, E/C.12/MKD/CO/1 (15 January 2008), [34]; Hungary, E/C.12/HUN/CO/3 (16 January 2008), [13]; Latvia, E/C.12/LVA/CO/1 (7 January 2008), [17]; Morocco, E/C.12/MAR/CO/3 (4 September 2008), [24]; Poland, E/C.12/1/Add.82 (19 December 2002), [18].

[138] CESCR, Guidelines on treaty specific documents to be submitted by states parties under Articles 16 and 17 of the ICESCR, E/C.12/2008/2 (24 March 2009), [22] (Article 7).

[139] CESCR, Concluding Observations: Cameroon, E/C.12/1/Add.40 (8 December 1999), [18]; China (including HK, Macao), E/C.12/1/Add.107 (13 May 2005), [110].

[140] CESCR, Concluding Observations: Republic of Korea, E/C.12/KOR/3 (17 December 2009), [17]; Slovenia, E/C.12/SVN/CO/1 (25 January 2006), [14].

[141] CESCR, Concluding Observations: Republic of Korea, E/C.12/KOR/3 (17 December 2009), [17].

expressed concern about underreporting,[142] including where women are afraid that they will lose their jobs[143] or jeopardize their immigration status.[144] It was also concerned that sexual harassment was covered up during legal proceedings;[145] and at its prevalence in special trading zones.[146]

In response, the CESCR has frequently recommended that states adopt laws prohibiting[147] or criminalizing[148] sexual harassment in the workplace, and strengthen the legal and institutional mechanisms for combating discrimination.[149] It has called on states to improve reporting mechanisms by ensuring a safe environment for women to report cases,[150] and to ensure that perpetrators of sexual harassment are sanctioned.[151] In one instance, the CESCR called for a state to provide consular assistance to nationals in other countries who have been subject to discrimination or abuse in the workplace by ensuring that reports are investigated by competent authorities in those countries.[152] The CESCR has also urged states to raise awareness about the problem.[153]

Like the CEDAW, ILO Convention No. 111 predates public awareness about sexual harassment and does not explicitly address it.[154] However, the ILO Committee of Experts has since confirmed in 1996 that it regards sexual harassment as a form of sex discrimination against women in employment and defines it as:

> [A]ny insult or inappropriate remark, joke, insinuation and comment on a person's dress, physique, age, family situation, etc; a condescending or paternalistic attitude with sexual implications undermining dignity; any unwelcome invitation or request, implicit or

[142] CESCR, Concluding Observations: Madagascar, E/C.12/MDG/CO/2 (16 December 2009), [22]; Republic of Korea, E/C.12/KOR/3 (17 December 2009), [17].

[143] CESCR, Concluding Observations: Mauritius, E/C.12/MUS/CO/4 (8 June 2010), [18]; Republic of Korea, E/C.12/KOR/3 (17 December 2009), [15].

[144] CESCR, Concluding Observations: Republic of Korea, E/C.12/KOR/3 (17 December 2009), [17].

[145] CESCR, Concluding Observations: Republic of Korea, E/C.12/KOR/3 (17 December 2009), [17].

[146] CESCR, Concluding Observations: Kenya, E/C.12/KEN/CO/1 (1 December 2008), [17]; Madagascar, E/C.12/MDG/CO/2 (16 December 2009), [22].

[147] CESCR, Concluding Observations: Madagascar, E/C.12/MDG/CO/2 (16 December 2009), [22]; Poland, E/C.12/1/Add.82 (19 December 2002), [40]; Cameroon, E/C.12/1/Add.40 (8 December 1999), [34].

[148] CESCR, Concluding Observations: China (including HK, Macao), E/C.12/1/Add.107 (13 May 2005), [120]; Latvia, E/C.12/LVA/CO/1 (7 January 2008), [43]; Republic of Korea, E/C.12/KOR/3 (17 December 2009), [17]; Russian Federation, E/C.12/1/Add.94 (12 December 2003), [48]; Slovenia, E/C.12/SVN/CO/1 (25 January 2006), [29].

[149] CESCR, Concluding Observations: Brazil, E/C.12/BRA/ZO/2 (12 June 2009), [16]; Mauritius, E/C.12/MUS/CO/4 (8 June 2010), [18]; Republic of Korea, E/C.12/KOR/3 (17 December 2009), [17].

[150] CESCR, Concluding Observations: Mauritius, E/C.12/MUS/CO/4 (8 June 2010), [18]; Madagascar, E/C.12/MDG/CO/2 (16 December 2009), [22].

[151] CESCR, Concluding Observations: Madagascar, E/C.12/MDG/CO/2 (16 December 2009), [22].

[152] CESCR, Concluding Observations: Philippines, E/C/12/PHL/CO/4 (1 December 2008), [21].

[153] CESCR, Concluding Observations: Madagascar, E/C.12/MDG/CO/2 (16 December 2009), [22]; Mauritius, E/C.12/MUS/CO/4 (8 June 2010), [18]; Republic of Korea, E/C.12/KOR/3 (17 December 2009), [17].

[154] ILO, *Sexual Harassment at Work: National and International Responses*, Conditions of Work and Employment Series No. 2 (Geneva, 2005), 13–14. ILO Convention No. 169 concerning Indigenous and Tribal Peoples in Independent Countries (adopted 27 June 1989, 1650 UNTS 383, entered into force 5 September 1991) ('ILO Convention No. 169'), Article 20(3)(d) expressly requires states to protect such peoples from sexual harassment.

explicit, whether or not accompanied by threats; any lascivious look or other gesture associated with sexuality; and any unnecessary physical contact such as touching, caresses, pinching or assault.[155]

It may also result from 'situations which are generally hostile to one sex or the other'. The above behaviour must also either 'be justly perceived as a condition of employment or precondition for employment or influence [employment] decisions' and/or 'affect job performance'.[156]

On quite a few occasions the CESCR has commented on the low representation of women in professional or management positions,[157] and the difficulties women face in being promoted to higher positions.[158] It has also specifically commented on the low representation of women in parliament;[159] government and the public service;[160] law enforcement, the legal profession and the judiciary;[161] and in academic institutions.[162] Notably, Article 25(c) of the ICCPR specifically confers upon citizens an equal right to work in the public service.[163]

The CESCR has frequently encouraged states to adopt and fund measures to assist women, or men and women, or parents 'to reconcile professional and family life'.[164] It has most commonly recommended providing or supporting adequate or affordable child care services,[165] but also called for flexible parental leave,[166] assistance for single mothers,[167] and training for women to re-enter the labour market after child-rearing and career breaks.[168]

It may be noted that ILO Convention No. 156 on Workers with Family Responsibilities of 1981 requires states to make it a goal of national policy to enable persons with family responsibilities who work or wish to work to do so without discrimination, and to minimize conflict between their employment and

[155] ILO, *Equality in Employment and Occupation: Special Survey on Equality in Employment and Occupation in Respect of Convention No. 111* (Geneva, 1996), [39].

[156] ILO, *Equality in Employment and Occupation*, [39].

[157] CESCR, Concluding Observations: Japan, E/C.12/1/Add.67 (24 September 2001), [17]; Malta, E/C.12/1/Add.101 (14 December 2004), [14]; Sweden, E/C.12/SWE/CO/5 (1 December 2008), [18].

[158] CESCR, Concluding Observations: Nigeria, E/C.12/1/Add.23 (16 June 1998), [14]; Japan, E/C.12/1/Add.67 (24 September 2001), [17].

[159] CESCR, Concluding Observations: Georgia, E/C.12/1/Add.42 (17 May 2000), [13].

[160] CESCR, Concluding Observations: Serbia and Montenegro, E/C.12/1/Add.108 (23 June 2005), [43].

[161] CESCR, Concluding Observations: Ukraine, E/C.12/1/Add.65 (24 September 2001), [24].

[162] CESCR, Concluding Observations: Germany, E/C.12/1/Add.68 (24 September 2001), [19].

[163] See HRC, General Comment No. 25, The right to participate in public affairs, voting rights, and the right of equal access to public service, CCPR/C/21/Rev.1/Add.7 (12 July 1996), [23].

[164] CESCR, Concluding Observations: Denmark, E/C.12/1/Add.102 (14 December 2004), [26]; Chile, E/C.12/1/Add.105 (1 December 2004), [37]; Canada, E/C.12/CAN/CO/4, E/C.12/CAN/CO/5 (22 May 2006), [46]; Spain, E/C.12/1/Add.99 (7 June 2004), [29].

[165] CESCR, Concluding Observations: Canada, E/C.12/CAN/CO/4, E/C.12/CAN/CO/5 (22 May 2006), [46]; Chile, E/C.12/1/Add.105 (1 December 2004), [37]; Italy, E/C.12/1/Add.103 (14 December 2004), [23]; Spain, E/C.12/1/Add.99 (7 June 2004), [29]; Malta, E/C.12/1/Add.101 (14 December 2004), [33].

[166] CESCR, Concluding Observations: Malta, E/C.12/1/Add.101 (14 December 2004), [15].

[167] CESCR, Concluding Observations: El Salvador, E/C.12/SLV/CO/2 (27 June 2007), [40].

[168] CESCR, Concluding Observations: Republic of Korea, E/C.12/KOR/CO/3 (17 December 2009), [14].

family responsibilities. States must consider their needs in community planning and in developing or promoting childcare, family services and facilities. Other ILO standards further suggest that special efforts should be made to facilitate the entry or re-entry into employment of older persons who have been out of work due to family responsibilities.[169]

The inadequacy of legal remedies for women has also been highlighted by the CESCR, including where non-discrimination mechanisms are lacking[170] or are available but rarely used.[171] The CESCR has urged amendments to existing sex discrimination laws, such as by including provisions on reinstatement or removing compensation caps.[172] It has encouraged better investigation or enforcement of existing laws, including regarding penalties and compensation;[173] the training of judges, labour inspectors and public servants in applying the law;[174] and raising awareness among employers, employees and the public.[175] The CESCR has also encouraged extraterritorial legal and consular assistance for overseas migrant workers in relation to discrimination or abuse (including sexual violence).[176] More generally, there must also be equality of opportunity in vocational training.[177]

Other international standards may also usefully inform the CESCR's future consideration of women's right to work under Article 6. Article 11(1)(a) of the Convention on the Elimination of All Forms of Discrimination against Women provides specifically for women's right to work and equal opportunity in work:

> 1. States Parties shall take all appropriate measures to eliminate discrimination against women in the field of employment in order to ensure, on a basis of equality of men and women, the same rights, in particular:
>
> (a) The right to work as an inalienable right of all human beings;
>
> (b) The right to the same employment opportunities, including the application of the same criteria for selection in matters of employment;
>
> (c) The right to free choice of profession and employment, the right to promotion, job security and all benefits and conditions of service and the right to receive vocational training and retraining, including apprenticeships, advanced vocational training and recurrent training…

The monitoring of women's work rights by the CEDAW Committee may assist the CESCR in identifying areas of concern and recommendations for state action.

169 ILO Recommendation No. 162 on Older Workers (23 June 1980), [19].
170 CESCR, Concluding Observations: Sri Lanka, E/C.12/1/Add.24 (16 June 1998), [11].
171 CESCR, Concluding Observations: Estonia, E/C.12/1/Add.85 (19 December 2002), [14].
172 CESCR, Concluding Observations: UK (Hong Kong), E/C.12/1/Add.10 (6 December 1996), [36].
173 CESCR, Concluding Observations: Philippines, E/C.12/PHL/CO/4 (1 December 2008), [21]; Ukraine, E/C.12/UKR/CO/5 (4 January 2008), [36].
174 CESCR, Concluding Observations: Ukraine, E/C.12/UKR/CO/5 (4 January 2008), [36].
175 CESCR, Concluding Observations: Ukraine, E/C.12/UKR/CO/5 (4 January 2008), [36].
176 CESCR, Concluding Observations: Philippines, E/C.12/PHL/CO/4 (1 December 2008), [21].
177 ILO Recommendation No. 150 on Human Resources Development (23 June 1975), [54]–[56].

Older people

While the CESCR has commonly been concerned about unemployment facing older people,[178] or particular age groups (such as those over 45 years, or between 55 and 65 years),[179] it has seldom made further comment on their work situation. General Comment No. 18 on Article 6 only emphasizes the need to prevent age discrimination in employment,[180] and refers back to the CESCR's earlier General Comment No. 6 on the rights of older workers. A few paragraphs of the latter are relevant to the right to work under Article 6:

22. Article 6 of the Covenant requires States parties to take appropriate steps to safeguard the right of everyone to the opportunity to gain a living by work which is freely chosen or accepted. In this regard, the Committee, bearing in mind that older workers who have not reached retirement age often encounter problems in finding and keeping jobs, stresses the need for measures to prevent discrimination on grounds of age in employment and occupation.

…

24. In the years preceding retirement, retirement preparation programmes should be implemented, with the participation of representative organizations of employers and workers and other bodies concerned, to prepare older workers to cope with their new situation. Such programmes should, in particular, provide older workers with information about: their rights and obligations as pensioners; the opportunities and conditions for continuing an occupational activity or undertaking voluntary work; means of combating detrimental effects of ageing; facilities for adult education and cultural activities, and the use of leisure time.[181]

Those recommendations are in turn influenced by ILO Recommendation No. 162 of 1980 concerning Older Workers, which encourages states to ensure equality of opportunity and non-discrimination in all aspects of employment (paragraphs 3 to 10); allows special measures of protection or assistance of older workers (paragraph 10); suggests numerous specific measures to enable older persons to continue working (paragraphs 11 to 19); and encourages measures to prepare workers for retirement, including in relation to pensions and social security (paragraphs 20 to 30).[182]

The ILO has not prohibited mandatory retirement ages nor stipulated a permissible minimum retirement age. Recommendation No. 162 instead encourages retirement to be regarded as voluntary and for pension eligibility to be flexible:

21. Wherever possible, measures should be taken with a view to—

(a) ensuring that, in a framework allowing for a gradual transition from working life to freedom of activity, retirement is voluntary;

(b) making the age qualifying for an old-age pension flexible.

[178] See, eg, CESCR, Concluding Observations: Netherlands, E/C.12/1/Add.25 (16 June 1998), [14].

[179] CESCR, Concluding Observations: Japan, E/C.12/1/Add.67 (24 September 2001), [20] and Netherlands, E/C.12/1/Add.25 (16 June 1998), [14] respectively.

[180] CESCR, General Comment No. 18, [16].

[181] CESCR, General Comment No. 6, The economic, social and cultural rights of older persons, E/1996/22 (8 December 1995) ('General Comment No. 6'), [22] and [24].

[182] On old-aged pensions and social security, see the chapter on Article 9 in this book.

It was noted earlier that age limits may be inherent requirements of a job, as where safety considerations apply to international civil aviation pilots. Otherwise, historically the establishment of a fixed retirement age and a right not to work was seen as a social achievement of the welfare state,[183] and a reward for or recognition of a lifetime of work. However, as life expectancy has lengthened, and the burdens of manual labour have lessened in many occupations, many workers may wish to continue in employment. There is also a risk that a compulsory retirement age may be used to push older people out of work and redistribute work to others,[184] thus rationing scarce employment opportunities on a potentially discriminatory basis unrelated to the requirements of a particular position.

The CESCR has been somewhat equivocal on mandatory retirement ages. In its General Comment on Older Persons, it observes that 65 would appear to be the most common retirement age, although the trend is towards later retirement.[185] It noted further that this is an area where discrimination 'continues to be tolerated', although there is a trend towards eliminating such barriers, which the CESCR supports:

> In the few areas in which discrimination continues to be tolerated, such as in relation to mandatory retirement ages or access to tertiary education, there is a clear trend towards the elimination of such barriers. The Committee is of the view that States parties should seek to expedite this trend to the greatest extent possible.[186]

In the related context of social security, the CESCR has also encouraged states to establish 'flexible' retirement ages 'depending on the occupations performed and the working ability of elderly persons, with due regard to demographic, economic and social factors'.[187] In monitoring states, the CESCR also criticized 'arbitrary' retirement criteria such as mandatory 'retirement in the public interest' in Trinidad and Tobago.[188] In addressing retirement ages in specific areas, the CESCR will presumably apply the usual test for permissible differentiation based on age, namely whether they are based on 'objective and reasonable' criteria.

Such is the approach already adopted by the Human Rights Committee (HRC) where mandatory retirement ages have been challenged in individual communications arising under Article 26 (the right to equal treatment) of the ICCPR. *Love v Australia* concerned airline pilots who were forced to retire at the age of 60.[189] The HRC found that a mandatory retirement age does not 'generally' constitute

[183] Nussberger, 'Work, Right to, International Protection', [38].
[184] Nussberger, 'Work, Right to, International Protection', [38].
[185] CESCR, General Comment No. 6, [9]. [186] CESCR, General Comment No. 6, [12].
[187] CESCR, General Comment No. 6, [28] (also invoking ILO conventions and ILO Recommendation No. 162).
[188] CESCR: Concluding Observations: Trinidad and Tobago, E/C.12/1989/SR.17 (1989), [89].
[189] *Love et al v Australia*, HRC Communication No. 983/2001 (25 March 2003), [4.9], [5.8], [5.11] and [6.12].

age discrimination, especially where it aims to protect workers, social security will support retirees, 'employment policy' considerations are involved, and the ILO does not prohibit it:

8.2. … While age as such is not mentioned as one of the enumerated grounds of prohibited discrimination in the second sentence of article 26, the Committee takes the view that a distinction related to age which is not based on reasonable and objective criteria may amount to discrimination on the ground of 'other status' under the clause in question, or to a denial of the equal protection of the law within the meaning of the first sentence of article 26. However, it is by no means clear that mandatory retirement age would generally constitute age discrimination. The Committee takes note of the fact that systems of mandatory retirement age may include a dimension of workers' protection by limiting the life-long working time, in particular when there are comprehensive social security schemes that secure the subsistence of persons who have reached such an age. Furthermore, reasons related to employment policy may be behind legislation or policy on mandatory retirement age. The Committee notes that while the International Labour Organisation has built up an elaborate regime of protection against discrimination in employment, mandatory retirement age does not appear to be prohibited in any of the ILO Conventions. These considerations will of course not absolve the Committee's task of assessing under article 26 of the Covenant whether any particular arrangement for mandatory retirement age is discriminatory.

In the case of the airline pilots, aircraft safety and International Civil Aviation Organization standards and practice supported a retirement age of 60 (even if a particular pilot was still physically or medically capable of flying):

8.3 In the present case, as the State party notes, the aim of maximising safety to passengers, crew and persons otherwise affected by flight travel was a legitimate aim under the Covenant. As to the reasonable and objective nature of the distinction made on the basis of age, the Committee takes into account the widespread national and international practice, at the time of the author's dismissals, of imposing a mandatory retirement age of 60. In order to justify the practice of dismissals maintained at the relevant time, the State party has referred to the ICAO regime which was aimed at, and understood as, maximising flight safety. In the circumstances, the Committee cannot conclude that the distinction made was not, at the time of Mr Love's dismissal, based on objective and reasonable considerations. Consequently, the Committee is of the view that it cannot establish a violation of article 26.

By the time the communication was considered, the state had abolished the retirement age of 60 years for domestic pilots, but maintained that such age was based on reasonable and objective criteria at the time of the dismissals. The abolition was based on evolving medical evidence about the safe flying age and new domestic age discrimination laws.

It is significant that the HRC mentioned 'employment policy' in considering whether mandatory retirement is permissible, perhaps implying that the rationing of scarce employment opportunities on the basis of age—for instance, to free up opportunities for young people—may be acceptable. The concurring individual opinion of HRC Member Ando sought to give even wider latitude to states in assessing the economic and social factors which are relevant in the limitation of a socio-economic right such as the right to work:

…in my opinion, the present case concerns 'the right to work' and its 'legitimate limitations' under the International Covenant on Economic, Social and Cultural Rights (article 6, paragraph 1, and article 4, respectively). Thus, at issue here is a proper balance between an economic or social right and its limitations. Of course, article 26 of the International Covenant on Civil and Political Rights prohibits discrimination in law or in fact in any field regulated and protected by public authorities, thus applying to economic or social rights as well. Nevertheless, as in the present case, the limitations of certain economic or social rights, in particular the right to work or to pension or to social security, require thorough scrutiny of various economic and social factors, of which the State party concerned is ordinarily in the best position to make objective and reasonable evaluation and adjustment. This means that the Human Rights Committee should respect the limitations of those rights set by the State party concerned unless they involve clearly unfair procedural irregularities or entail manifestly inequitable results.

The HRC avoided directly confronting a different legal issue raised by the parties, namely whether the 'inherent requirement' of a job test in domestic law (implementing the same ILO standard) was equivalent to or different from the HRC's 'objective and reasonable' test under Article 26 of the ICCPR. The state party had suggested that the 'inherent' requirement test was stricter than the ICCPR test and should not be followed, since it focused on job requirements that were 'necessary' as opposed to objective and reasonable.

A domestic human rights body had earlier found that a retirement age of 60 years was not an 'inherent requirement' of being a pilot and constituted age discrimination, but that finding was non-binding and had been rejected by the state party, precipitating the ICCPR complaint. By reiterating its 'objective and reasonable' standard, the HRC appeared to implicitly reject the 'inherent requirement' test which had produced a different result under domestic law.

There is, however, no necessary incompatibility between the two approaches. It is arguable that the 'inherent requirement' standard is better viewed as a specific manifestation of what is 'objective and reasonable' in the context of employment and the right to work. In other words, the 'inherent requirement' standard, founded in widespread ILO standards in the area of employment discrimination, is the more special law (*lex specialis*) which assists in qualifying or clarifying what is objective and reasonable in an employment context.

Further, that the two tests produced different results in *Love*—as between domestic and ICCPR law—does not necessarily prove that the tests are different. Rather, it may demonstrate only that the different decision-makers appreciated or weighted the facts differently. *Love* can be criticized for setting the bar too low for permissible differentiation on the basis of age, when the domestic human rights body was not satisfied on the evidence that there was a sufficiently robust basis for mandating retirement for domestic pilots at the age of 60. (As noted earlier, however, a subsequent Australian High Court case accepted that it was an inherent requirement of the job of an *international* pilot to be under the age of 60, because of the additional factor that flying international routes is governed by an international civil aviation rule mandating that age restriction, in contrast to the situation of domestic pilots. That still does not answer the question of whether the international standards themselves are justified.[190])

In another ICCPR case, the HRC accepted that a public servant could be dismissed for being older than 60 years, as part of a special decree restructuring the civil service, even though the normal retirement age under normal statutory law was 70 years. The complaint was brought under Article 25(c) of the ICCPR, which provides for equality of opportunity in public service employment. The HRC applied the 'objective and reasonable' test for permissible differentiation under Article 26 to Article 25(c):

6.4 In the present case the Committee notes that the author was not the only public servant who lost his job, but that other employees of the National Customs Authority were also dismissed because of restructuring of that entity. The State party indicates that the restructuring originated from the Supreme Decree of 8 January 1991, wherein the Executive announced a reorganization of all public entities. The criteria for selecting those employees to be dismissed were established following a general implementation plan. The Committee considers that the age limit used in the present case for continued post occupancy was an objective distinguishing criterion and that its implementation in the context of a general plan for the restructuring of the civil service was not unreasonable. Under the circumstances, the Committee considers that the author has not been the subject of a violation of article 25(c).[191]

The HRC provided no further explanation of why the age limit was objective and reasonable in the context of restructuring, compared with, for example, other possible dismissal criteria such as competency, length of service,[192] family responsibilities and the like. Four members of the HRC dissented, arguing that the HRC had departed from its own jurisprudence in *Love*:

1. In the present case, the majority of the Committee concluded that age as such 'was an objective distinguishing criterion' and 'that its implementation in the context of a general plan for the restructuring of the civil service was not unreasonable' (para. 6.4). In our view this is tantamount to saying that age as such is an objective and reasonable criteria for deciding who would have to leave public service. This reasoning cannot be reconciled with the approach taken by the Committee in the case of *Love v. Australia*. There, the Committee decided that while age as such is not mentioned as one of the enumerated grounds of prohibited discrimination in the second sentence of article 26, a distinction related to age which is not based on reasonable and objective criteria may amount to discrimination on the ground of 'other status' under the clause in question. It stressed that while a mandatory retirement age would generally not constitute age discrimination, it still would have the task under article 26 of the Covenant of assessing in the particular case whether any particular arrangement for mandatory retirement age departing from the general retirement age in a given country is discriminatory. As it did in the case of *Love v. Australia*, the Committee should have examined in the present case whether there were reasonable and objective grounds justifying the use of age as a distinguishing criterion. It did not do so and

[190] *Qantas Airways Ltd v Christie* [1998] HCA 18 (19 March 1998).

[191] *Rubén Santiago Hinostroza Solís v Peru*, HRC Communication No. 1016/2001 (27 March 2006).

[192] Although the common practice of 'last hired, first fired' can also produce unfairness.

thus departed from the approach taken in the case of *Love v. Australia* in a way that cannot be justified in our view.[193]

Applying the test from *Love*, the dissenting members found that the age criterion was not objective and reasonable; there were also certain legal irregularities in the restructuring:

2. In the present case, the State party has failed to demonstrate that the aims of the plan to restructure the National Customs Authority were legitimate. In this context, we note that the Committee in particular did not address the claims of the author that both the Constitution and laws adopted by Parliament guaranteed him security of employment and that these guarantees were not removed as a result of a democratic process of amending the relevant provisions but by decree issued by the then President of Peru. Furthermore, the use of the criterion of age as applied to the author is not objective and reasonable for several reasons. First, the case concerns a matter of dismissal and not retirement. Second, while age may justify dismissal in cases where age affects the ability of the person concerned to perform their functions or where the person concerned has worked long enough to have acquired full or at least substantial pension rights, the State party has not shown that in the case of the author who, notwithstanding his age, had been employed for just 11 years, any such reasons were present. It is therefore our view that the author has been the subject of a violation of article 25(c) of the Covenant.[194]

Three other members of the HRC observed further that 'the State has offered no reason for its discriminatory use of age in lay-offs'.[195] Although not at issue in the case, the same three members also observed that the restructuring criteria involved gender discrimination:

One thing remains clear, however: the Committee's decision in this case should not be understood as supporting Peru's use of gender discrimination in lay-offs and downsizing. The Peruvian National Customs Authority peculiarly requires women to leave public service five years earlier than men, based on age and length of service. There is no evident reason why women should be forced into retirement at an earlier stage than men, and it is hard to see how, if the issue had been litigated between the parties, such a practice could be regarded as consistent with either article 25 or article 26 of the Covenant.[196]

Young people

Along with women, young people are among the most common group highlighted by the CESCR in monitoring the right to work. The CESCR routinely expresses concern about high and/or disproportionate levels of unemployment among young people. As the ILO notes, youth unemployment or underemployment affects not only human dignity, but also brings economic costs (a point which should also be

[193] *Rubén Santiago Hinostroza Solís v Peru*, Individual Opinion of HRC members Walter Kälin, Edwin Johnson, Michael O'Flaherty and Hipólito Solari-Yrigoyen (dissenting).

[194] *Rubén Santiago Hinostroza Solís v Peru*, Individual Opinion of HRC members Walter Kälin, Edwin Johnson, Michael O'Flaherty and Hipólito Solari-Yrigoyen (dissenting).

[195] *Rubén Santiago Hinostroza Solís v Peru*, Individual Opinion of HRC members Sir Nigel Rodley, Mr Ivan Shearer and Ms Ruth Wedgwood (concurring).

[196] *Rubén Santiago Hinostroza Solís v Peru*, Individual Opinion of HRC members Sir Nigel Rodley, Mr Ivan Shearer and Ms Ruth Wedgwood (concurring).

borne in mind when the progressive realization of young people's right to work is being considered):

Youth unemployment and underemployment impose heavy social and economic costs, resulting in the loss of opportunities for economic growth, erosion of the tax base which undermines investment in infrastructure and public services, increased welfare costs, and unutilized investment in education and training, and may also be associated with social instability and conflict, increased levels of poverty, crime and substance abuse.[197]

The CESCR's concern has rarely been about age discrimination (which does occur), but often relates to lack of employment experience and/or education or training, which are barriers to young people's employment:

14. Access to a first job constitutes an opportunity for economic self-reliance and in many cases a means to escape poverty. Young persons, particularly young women, generally have great difficulties in finding initial employment. National policies relating to adequate education and vocational training should be adopted and implemented to promote and support access to employment opportunities for young persons, in particular young women.

The CESCR has tended to make very general recommendations to states in respect of young people, most commonly by encouraging states to create targeted employment opportunities (usually without specifying how), or develop vocational training opportunities. Occasionally, it has mentioned more specific measures, such as providing 'career guidance', tax incentives for companies hiring young people and limiting temporary employment contracts.[198] It has also urged states to adopt incentives for young persons to stay and work in their own regions to prevent regional emigration from places of high unemployment.[199] Occasionally, it has encouraged states to consult with workers' and employers' organizations, and local stakeholders, in formulating youth training and employment strategies.[200]

While there is no young person-specific ILO convention, general ILO standards encompass young people and occasionally contain youth-specific measures.[201] The issues of forced or compulsory child labour, and child labour generally, are separately considered below.[202] There are also particular ILO standards addressing vocational training and education for young people, including those who never went to school or left school early;[203] as well as measures to encourage entrepreneurship by young people.[204] The ILO has noted that measures to

[197] International Labour Conference (93rd session), Resolution concerning Youth Employment (15 June 2005), [11].

[198] CESCR, Concluding Observations: France, E/C.12/FRA/CO/3 (9 June 2008), [35] and [37].

[199] CESCR, Concluding Observations: Germany, E/C.12/1/Add.68 (24 September 2001), [36].

[200] CESCR, Concluding Observations: Cambodia, E/C.12/KHM/CO/1 (12 June 2009), [21].

[201] See the list of standards in the International Labour Conference (93rd session), Resolution concerning Youth Employment (15 June 2005), Appendix at 11–12.

[202] See the next chapter in this book on Article 7 of the ICESCR.

[203] ILO Recommendation No. 150 on Human Resources Development, [46]–[49]. Under [2(1)], vocational guidance and training means 'that guidance and training are directed to identifying and developing human capabilities for a productive and satisfying working life and, in conjunction with the different forms of education, to improve the ability of the individual to understand and, individually or collectively, to influence working conditions and the social environment.'

[204] ILO Recommendation No. 150, [24]–[26].

address youth unemployment in state practice can be grouped into four broad categories: school-to-work transition programmes; post-compulsory education skill training; subsidized temporary employment, training and work experience schemes; and business-creation schemes.[205]

The ILO has emphasized that certain categories of young people may be particularly vulnerable in relation to work, including those with disabilities, those affected by HIV/AIDS, indigenous youth, those involved in hazardous work, demobilized soldiers, ethnic minorities, migrants, socially disadvantaged youth and young women with children.[206] Gender, age, education, family background and health status also affect labour market prospects.[207]

Persons with disabilities

In General Comment No. 5 on Persons with Disabilities (1994), the CESCR emphasized that disability discrimination has been 'prominent and persistent' in the field of employment:

> 20. The field of employment is one in which disability-based discrimination has been prominent and persistent. In most countries the unemployment rate among persons with disabilities is two to three times higher than the unemployment rate for persons without disabilities. Where persons with disabilities are employed, they are mostly engaged in low-paid jobs with little social and legal security and are often segregated from the mainstream of the labour market. The integration of persons with disabilities into the regular labour market should be actively supported by States.

Employment discrimination is also expressly prohibited by Article 27(1)(a) of the Convention on the Rights of Persons with Disabilities (CRPD), which extends to 'all matters concerning all forms of employment, including conditions of recruitment, hiring and employment, continuance of employment, career advancement and safe and healthy working conditions'. The CESCR has, however, seldom addressed specific instances of disability discrimination in employment.

It is notable that the CRPD also requires states to pursue equal opportunity through effecting cultural change, specifically by promoting the 'recognition of the skills, merits and abilities of persons with disabilities, and their contributions to the workplace and the labour market' (Article 8(2)(a)(iii)). States must also take measures to promote the employment opportunities and career advancement of persons with disabilities, and assist them to find, obtain, maintain and return to employment (CRPD, Article 27(1)(e)).

In monitoring states under Article 6 of the ICESCR, the CESCR has frequently highlighted the high unemployment rate experienced by persons with disabilities (such as the 72 per cent unemployed in Israel[208]) and called for targeted

[205] International Labour Conference (92nd session), *Promoting Employment: Policies, Skills, Enterprises*, Report III (Part 1B) (2004), 49.

[206] International Labour Conference (93rd session), Resolution concerning Youth Employment (15 June 2005), [16].

[207] International Labour Conference (93rd session), [8].

[208] CESCR, Concluding Observations: Israel, E/C.12/1/Add.27 (4 December 1998), [15].

measures to improve the accessibility of employment (in both the open labour market and in sheltered facilities[209]) as well as educational, vocational and professional training. It has called on states to provide incentives for employers to employ persons with disabilities,[210] such as through wage subsidies,[211] and criticized states for removing prior tax benefits for hiring disabled persons.[212] It has even called on states to impose penalty payments for non-employment of persons with disabilities.[213]

The use of quotas in the employment of persons with disabilities has been particularly emphasized by the CESCR, whether in calling on states to meet existing quotas under national law[214] or in establishing them.[215] The CRPD Committee too supports 'affirmative action' and incentive measures in the public and private sectors,[216] although it has cautioned against offering employment 'only of symbolic value' and criticized Chinese companies and government bodies which 'frequently opt to pay the employment levy rather than employing persons with disabilities'.[217]

The CESCR has not nominated any particular figure in setting quotas, such as by reference to the rate of disability in the population (which is estimated at 15 per cent of the global population[218]). Where national laws establish quotas, the CESCR has simply called for more information on compliance (as for France's requirement on companies with more than twenty employees to recruit 6 per cent of their workforce from persons with disabilities) or better efforts to meet such quotas (as for South Korea's 2 per cent quota in enterprises with over 300 employees).[219] It has refrained from calling on existing quota levels to be raised to any particular level. In principle, two types of quotas are available.[220] Strict quotas accord preferential treatment to persons with disabilities regardless of whether she or he is as qualified as other candidates. Flexible quotas only give

209 CESCR, Concluding Observations: France, E/C.12/FRA/CO/3 (9 June 2008), [38].

210 CESCR, Concluding Observations: China (including HK, Macao), E/C.12/1/Add.107 (13 May 2005), [121]; Lithuania, E/C.12/1/Add.96 (7 June 2004), [12]; Malta, E/C.12/1/Add.101 (14 December 2004), [13].

211 CESCR, Concluding Observations: Serbia and Montenegro, E/C.12/1/Add.108 (23 July 2005), [44].

212 CESCR, Concluding Observations: Russian Federation, E/C.12/1/Add.94 (12 December 2003), [16].

213 CESCR, Concluding Observations: Russian Federation, E/C.12/1/Add.94 (12 December 2003), [44].

214 CESCR, Concluding Observations: France, E/C.12/FRA/CO/3 (9 June 2008), [38]; Republic of Korea, E/C.12/1/Add.59 (21 May 2001), [24].

215 CESCR, Concluding Observations: Uzbekistan, E/C.12/UZB/CO/1 (24 January 2006), [45]; Israel, E/C.12/1/Add.27 (4 December 1998), [15].

216 CRPD, Article 27(1)(g)–(h).

217 CRPD, Concluding Observations: China, CRPD/C/CHN/CO/1 (15 October 2012), [41].

218 Commission on Human Rights, 'Thematic Study on the Work and Employment of Persons with Disabilities', OHCHR Report, A/HRC/22/25 (17 December 2012) ('Thematic Study'), [7].

219 CESCR, Concluding Observations: France, E/C.12/FRA/CO/3 (9 June 2008), [38]; Republic of Korea, E/C.12/1/Add.59 (21 May 2001), [24]; see also CRPD, Concluding Observations: Argentina, CRPD/C/ARG/CO/1 (8 October 2012), [43] (calling for disaggregated data (by, inter alia, sex, age, type of disability and geographic location) about compliance with a 4 per cent public sector quota).

220 Commission on Human Rights, 'Thematic Study, [37].

preference if the person with a disability is equally qualified on merit, and are less common than strict quotas.

The confinement of persons with disabilities to 'sheltered' work facilities or categories may violate their right to freely choose or accept work, as the CESCR observes:

> 21. The 'right of everyone to the opportunity to gain his living by work which he freely chooses or accepts' (art. 6 (1)) is not realized where the only real opportunity open to disabled workers is to work in so-called 'sheltered' facilities under substandard conditions. Arrangements whereby persons with a certain category of disability are effectively confined to certain occupations or to the production of certain goods may violate this right. Similarly, in the light of principle 13 (3) of the Principles for the Protection of Persons with Mental Illness and for the Improvement of Mental Health Care ... "therapeutical treatment" in institutions which amounts to forced labour is also incompatible with the Covenant. In this regard, the prohibition on forced labour contained in the International Covenant on Civil and Political Rights is also of potential relevance.

This view is consistent with the obligation on states under Article 27(1)(j) of the CRPD to '[p]romote the acquisition by persons with disabilities of work experience in the open labour market', whether in the public service, private sector, or through self-employment or entrepreneurship.[221] The CRPD Committee criticized China, for example, for its 'practice of reserved employment (such as the field of "blind massage"), which discriminates against persons with disabilities in their vocational and career choices'.[222] The CRPD separately prohibits slavery, servitude and forced or compulsory labour in respect of persons with disabilities.[223]

The CESCR has emphasized the importance of making workplaces physically accessible for persons with disabilities, and the need to make 'reasonable accommodations' for particular workers:

> 22. According to the Standard Rules, persons with disabilities, whether in rural or urban areas, must have equal opportunities for productive and gainful employment in the labour market. Standard Rules (see note 6 above), Rule 7. For this to happen it is particularly important that artificial barriers to integration in general, and to employment in particular, be removed. As the International Labour Organisation has noted, it is very often the physical barriers that society has erected in areas such as transport, housing and the workplace which are then cited as the reason why persons with disabilities cannot be employed ... For example, as long as workplaces are designed and built in ways that make them inaccessible to wheelchairs, employers will be able to 'justify' their failure to employ wheelchair users. Governments should also develop policies which promote and regulate flexible and alternative work arrangements that reasonably accommodate the needs of disabled workers.

> 23. Similarly, the failure of Governments to ensure that modes of transportation are accessible to persons with disabilities greatly reduces the chances of such persons finding suitable, integrated jobs, taking advantage of educational and vocational training, or commuting

[221] CRPD, Article 27(1)(f)–(h).
[222] CRPD, Concluding Observations: China, CRPD/C/CHN/CO/1 (15 October 2012), [41].
[223] CRPD, Article 27(2).

to facilities of all types. Indeed, the provision of access to appropriate and, where necessary, specially tailored forms of transportation is crucial to the realization by persons with disabilities of virtually all the rights recognized in the Covenant.

States are also required to take appropriate measures to make workplaces accessible under Article 9(1)(a) of the CRPD. According to the ILO's Code of Practice on Managing Disability in the Workplace, accessibility should address physical matters such as workplace entrances, movement around the premises, and toilets and washroom facilities; informational issues such as signage, manuals, workplace instructions and electronic resources; and alternatives to sounds (such as bells, alarms, whistles or sirens) for the hearing impaired (such as the use of flashing lights); and emergency evacuation procedures.[224]

In monitoring states, the CESCR has not addressed particular instances of or the need for 'reasonable accommodations' in the workplace. Article 27(1)(i) of the CRPD specifically requires states to '[e]nsure that reasonable accommodation is provided to persons with disabilities in the workplace' and 'reasonable accommodation' is defined generally in Article 2 of the CRPD as:

> …necessary and appropriate modification and adjustments not imposing a disproportionate or undue burden, where needed in a particular case, to ensure to persons with disabilities the enjoyment or exercise on an equal basis with others of all human rights and fundamental freedoms…

Reasonable accommodations are measures required for particular individuals, in contrast to the more general requirement to make workplaces physically accessible to all.[225] Denial of a reasonable accommodation constitutes disability discrimination.

In the context of the right to work, the ILO Code of Practice suggests that 'adaptations' (that is, accommodations or adjustments) may be required to a person's workstation, tools and equipment, job description, work schedule or performance requirements.[226] In all cases workers and their representatives should be consulted. Examples of reasonable accommodations might include lowering a chair or providing wheelchair access to a desk; providing large print, braille or voice recognition software for the visually impaired; installing a hand control in place of a foot pedal on a sewing machine; or providing longer training or practice sessions for slower learners.

Accommodations must be 'reasonable' and not impose an undue or disproportionate burden. It may be noted, however, that many adjustments involve no cost, or a low cost, or the benefits of making the adjustments outweigh the costs. In some cases employers may also be eligible for government assistance to subsidize the cost of making more expensive adjustments. The assessment of proportionality is also not a purely economic quantification. Whether an adjustment would impose an undue burden must also be evaluated in the light of

224 ILO, *Managing Disability in the Workplace: ILO Code of Practice* (Geneva, 2002) ('*Managing Disability in the Workplace*'), [7.1].

225 Commission on Human Rights, 'Thematic Study', [32].

226 ILO, *Managing Disability in the Workplace*, [7.2].

the individual human dignity and wider social inclusion which the adjustment would bring.

It may also be noted that UN Human Rights Council Resolution 22/3 (2013) on '[t]he work and employment of persons with disabilities' has called for 'universal design' in the design of products, environments, programmes and services. Universal design 'requires the consideration of the needs of all members of society in order to avoid the need for any subsequent adaptation or specialized design'.[227]

The CESCR has further urged states to ensure that their obligation to provide vocational guidance and training under Article 6(2) of the ICESCR reflects 'the needs of all persons with disabilities':

24. The 'technical and vocational guidance and training programmes' required under article 6(2) of the Covenant should reflect the needs of all persons with disabilities, take place in integrated settings, and be planned and implemented with the full involvement of representatives of persons with disabilities.[228]

The CRPD also requires persons with disabilities to have 'effective access' to general technical and vocational guidance programmes, placement services and vocational and continuing training.[229] ILO Recommendation No. 150 on Human Resources Development 1975 also addresses vocational guidance and training access, the provision of specially adjusted programmes for the severely disabled, and awareness raising for the public, employers and workers on the need for persons with disabilities to receive training.[230] More generally, the CESCR has endorsed and encouraged states to ratify the 'valuable and comprehensive' ILO standards relating to the work rights of persons with disabilities.[231]

Indigenous peoples

The CESCR has occasionally drawn attention to the work rights of indigenous peoples, or groups assimilable to indigenous peoples (such as Afro-Colombians in Colombia),[232] but usually only by mentioning them in a list of other disadvantaged groups in a state (including where equal concern was expressed for Maori (indigenous) and Pacific Islander (non-indigenous) employment in New Zealand).[233] The CESCR's recommendations to states have also tended not to be indigenous-specific, but rather applicable to the range of disadvantaged groups mentioned in a particular

[227] Commission on Human Rights Resolution 22/3, Rights of persons with disabilities: work and employment, A/HRC/22/L.4 (March 2013), [12].

[228] CESCR, General Comment No. 5, [20]–[27]; see also CESCR, General Comment No. 18, [17].

[229] CRPD, Article 27(1)(d).

[230] ILO Recommendation No. 150 on Human Resources Development, [53]. See also ILO Recommendation No. 99 on Vocational Rehabilitation (Disabled) (22 June 1955) ('ILO Recommendation No. 99').

[231] CESCR, General Comment No. 5, [27] (including ILO Convention No. 159 on Vocational Rehabilitation and Employment of Persons with Disabilities 1983; ILO Recommendation No. 99; and ILO Recommendation No. 168 on Vocational Rehabilitation and Employment of Persons with Disabilities 1983).

[232] CESCR, Concluding Observations: Colombia, E/C.12/COL/CO/5 (7 June 2010), [11].

[233] CESCR, Concluding Observations: New Zealand, E/C.12/1993/13 (4 January 1994), [14] and [17].

state. A rare exception is its recommendation to Costa Rica to enhance professional training and sustainable employment opportunities in remote indigenous areas.[234] It also called on Morocco to ratify ILO Convention No. 169 on Indigenous and Tribal Peoples in Independent Countries 1989.[235]

While ILO Convention No. 169 only has twenty-two states parties,[236] its normative influence is far greater than that number suggests and it has shaped subsequent 'soft law' standards such as the UN General Assembly's Declaration on the Rights of Indigenous Peoples 2007. Convention No. 169 includes a general right of non-discrimination and gender equality for indigenous peoples (Article 3) as well as non-discrimination in citizenship (Article 4). Article 20 provides for non-discrimination and 'special measures' for indigenous workers:

1. Governments shall, within the framework of national laws and regulations, and in co-operation with the peoples concerned, adopt special measures to ensure the effective protection with regard to recruitment and conditions of employment of workers belonging to these peoples, to the extent that they are not effectively protected by laws applicable to workers in general.

2. Governments shall do everything possible to prevent any discrimination between workers belonging to the peoples concerned and other workers, in particular as regards:

(a) admission to employment, including skilled employment, as well as measures for promotion and advancement;

(b) equal remuneration for work of equal value;

(c) medical and social assistance, occupational safety and health, all social security benefits and any other occupationally related benefits, and housing;

(d) the right of association and freedom for all lawful trade union activities, and the right to conclude collective agreements with employers or employers' organisations.

3. The measures taken shall include measures to ensure:

(a) that workers belonging to the peoples concerned, including seasonal, casual and migrant workers in agricultural and other employment, as well as those employed by labour contractors, enjoy the protection afforded by national law and practice to other such workers in the same sectors, and that they are fully informed of their rights under labour legislation and of the means of redress available to them;

(b) that workers belonging to these peoples are not subjected to working conditions hazardous to their health, in particular through exposure to pesticides or other toxic substances;

(c) that workers belonging to these peoples are not subjected to coercive recruitment systems, including bonded labour and other forms of debt servitude;

[234] CESCR, Concluding Observations: Costa Rica, E/C.12/CRI/CO/4 (4 January 2008), [39].

[235] CESCR, Concluding Observations: Morocco, E/C.12/1/Add.55 (1 December 2000), [14]. See ILO Convention No. 169.

[236] Argentina, Bolivia, Brazil, Central African Republic, Chile, Colombia, Costa Rica, Denmark, Dominica, Ecuador, Fiji, Guatemala, Honduras, Mexico, Nepal, the Netherlands, Nicaragua, Norway, Paraguay, Peru, Spain and Venezuela.

(d) that workers belonging to these peoples enjoy equal opportunities and equal treatment in employment for men and women, and protection from sexual harassment.

4. Particular attention shall be paid to the establishment of adequate labour inspection services in areas where workers belonging to the peoples concerned undertake wage employment, in order to ensure compliance with the provisions of this Part of this Convention.

Convention No. 169 further provides for equal opportunities and special measures for indigenous peoples in vocational training (Articles 21 and 22), based on 'the economic environment, social and cultural conditions and practical needs' of indigenous peoples and in consultation with them. Special recognition is given to certain indigenous forms of economic activity in Article 23:

1. Handicrafts, rural and community-based industries, and subsistence economy and traditional activities of the peoples concerned, such as hunting, fishing, trapping and gathering, shall be recognised as important factors in the maintenance of their cultures and in their economic self-reliance and development. Governments shall, with the participation of these people and whenever appropriate, ensure that these activities are strengthened and promoted.

2. Upon the request of the peoples concerned, appropriate technical and financial assistance shall be provided wherever possible, taking into account the traditional technologies and cultural characteristics of these peoples, as well as the importance of sustainable and equitable development.[237]

Convention No. 169 aimed to revise the approach taken in an earlier ILO instrument, Convention No. 107 on Indigenous and Tribunal Populations 1957, ratified by twenty-seven countries, which by the 1980s was considered to take an obsolete, detrimental 'integrationist' approach. Convention No. 107 is closed for accession but remains in force, however, for eighteen states. It also contains significant safeguards for non-discrimination and special measures of protection in employment (Article 15), and provisions for vocational training, handicrafts and rural industries (Articles 16 to 18).

Other norms relevant to indigenous peoples in the context of Article 6 of the ICESCR are found in the UN Declaration on the Rights of Indigenous Peoples 2007, which has the widespread support of states. Article 2 of the Declaration is a general provision on non-discrimination, while Article 21 refers to non-discrimination in the indigenous right to 'the improvement of their economic and social conditions', including 'employment' and 'vocational training and retraining', including through states' adoption of 'special measures'. The Declaration also recognizes that indigenous 'individuals' and 'peoples' 'have the right to enjoy fully all rights established under applicable international and domestic labour law' (Article 17(1)) and 'the right not to be subjected to any discriminatory conditions of labour and, inter alia, employment or salary'

[237] See also ILO Convention No. 169, Article 5(c): 'policies aimed at mitigating the difficulties experienced by these peoples in facing new conditions of life and work shall be adopted, with the participation and co-operation of the peoples affected'.

(Article 17(3)). Recognition is also given to indigenous peoples' economic and subsistence rights, as in Article 20:

1. Indigenous peoples have the right to maintain and develop their political, economic and social systems or institutions, to be secure in the enjoyment of their own means of subsistence and development, and to engage freely in all their traditional and other economic activities.

2. Indigenous peoples deprived of their means of subsistence and development are entitled to just and fair redress.

This importantly includes the economic significance of indigenous rights in land, which is the subject of numerous provisions in the Declaration. The CESCR's relative lack of attention to the work rights of indigenous peoples may be partly explained by some indigenous peoples not depending on wage-earning employment in a market economy for their livelihoods, but instead depending on subsistence agriculture, hunting, fishing, forestry and the like. Yet, that too is 'work' and traditional occupations depend on access to those underlying resources.[238]

Minorities

The various prohibited grounds of discrimination in employment under the ICESCR cover minority groups, including the grounds of race, colour, language, religion, national origin, birth and social origin or 'other status' (which can also encompass certain social, cultural or economic stratifications such as caste or bonded labourers). The concept of 'national origin' can cover place of birth, ancestry or foreign origin,[239] as well as indigenous peoples. In Europe, additional protection against discrimination and guarantees of equality before the law and equal protection are accorded to the special legal category of 'national minorities'.[240]

In monitoring states, the CESCR has often expressed concern about high unemployment rates affecting minorities[241] or immigrant communities, whether in absolute terms (such as the 80 per cent of Roma unemployed in Slovakia)[242] or relative to the general population (such as where 16.6 per cent of minorities were unemployed compared to 9.9 per cent of the population in Estonia).[243] Sometimes it has attributed high unemployment to racial discrimination, at least 'to some

[238] ILO, *Giving Globalization a Human Face*, 321.

[239] ILO, *Giving Globalization a Human Face*, 319.

[240] Council of Europe, Framework Convention for the Protection of National Minorities (adopted 10 November 1994, ETS No. 157, entered into force 1 February 1998), Article 4(1).

[241] CESCR, Concluding Observations: Bosnia and Herzegovina, E/C.12/BIH/CO/1 (24 January 2006), [14]; Estonia, E/C.12/1/Add.85 (19 December 2002), [12]; Macedonia, E/C.12/MKD/CO/1 (15 January 2008), [15]; Hungary, E/C.12/HUN/CO/3 (16 January 2008), [11]; Poland, E/C.12/POL/CO/5 (2 December 2009), [16]; Republic of Moldova, E/C.12/1/Add.91 (12 December 2003), [14]; Serbia and Montenegro, E/C.12/1/Add.108 (23 June 2005), [16]; Slovakia, E/C.12/1/Add.81 (19 December 2002), [11]; Slovenia, E/C.12/SVN/CO/1 (25 January 2006), [13]; Spain, E/C.12/1/Add.99 (7 June 2004), [12]; United Kingdom, E/1995/22 (E/C.12/1194/20), (2–20 May 1994 and 21 November–9 December 1994), [273].

[242] CESCR, Concluding Observations: Slovakia, E/C.12/1/Add.81 (19 December 2002), [11].

[243] CESCR, Concluding Observations: Estonia, E/C.12/1/Add.85 (19 December 2002), [12].

extent',[244] including discrimination in recruitment.[245] It has also noted that some minorities are often relegated to low-skilled employment.[246]

The CESCR also expressed concern where high unemployment among Roma people prompted massive emigration from Moldova,[247] and where Roma faced difficulties in Russia in obtaining personal identification documents, including registration of residence, which were necessary for them to enjoy the right to work.[248] The special problems faced by Crimean Tartars repatriated to the Ukraine were also highlighted by the CESCR, particularly the need to regularize their civil status, reintegrate them and guarantee their work rights.[249]

In making recommendations, the CESCR has sometimes made vague calls to states to 'root out racial discrimination in the labour market'[250] or take 'effective measures' to that end, but without stipulating particular means. In many cases it has been more prescriptive. It has called for legislative reform, as when it asked Liechtenstein to broaden its law against racial discrimination beyond the termination of contractual employment to also cover recruitment, remuneration and promotion.[251] It has urged the strict application of anti-discrimination laws by the courts, governments and labour offices,[252] and the provision of better statistical data on discrimination complaints and prosecutions[253] or minority unemployment generally.[254]

The CESCR has encouraged states to increase the employment of minorities in central and local governments, as well as in the private sector,[255] including by providing 'specifically targeted measures' such as financial incentives for employers.[256] It has also encouraged assistance to minorities to open their own businesses.[257] The CESCR has not generally called for quotas for minority employment, but where quotas exist, as with ethnic recruitment in the Sri Lankan public service, the CESCR has urged them to be expanded to also cover promotions.[258] It may be recalled that affirmative action is not regarded as discrimination.[259] The CESCR has, however, called on states to set specific benchmarks for reducing the employment gap between minorities and others.

[244] CESCR, Concluding Observations: Netherlands, E/C.12/1/Add.25 (16 June 1998), [13].
[245] CESCR, Concluding Observations: Ukraine, E/C.12/UKR/CO/5 (4 January 2008), [14].
[246] CESCR, Concluding Observations: Ukraine, E/C.12/UKR/CO/5 (4 January 2008), [14].
[247] CESCR, Concluding Observations: Republic of Moldova, E/C.12/1/Add.91 (12 December 2003), [14].
[248] CESCR, Concluding Observations: Russian Federation, E/C.12/1/Add.94 (12 December 2003), [12].
[249] CESCR, Concluding Observations: Ukraine, E/C.12/1995/15 (28 December 1995), [24].
[250] CESCR, Concluding Observations: Netherlands, E/C.12/1/Add.25 (16 June 1998), [23].
[251] CESCR, Concluding Observations: Liechtenstein, E/C.12/LIE/CO/1 (9 June 2006), [14] and [29] (the law addressed discrimination on the basis of race, colour, descent, nationality or ethnic origin).
[252] CESCR, Concluding Observations: Hungary, E/C.12/HUN/CO/3 (16 January 2008), [34].
[253] CESCR, Concluding Observations: Sweden, E/C.12/SWE/CO/5 (1 December 2008), [16].
[254] CESCR, Concluding Observations: Hungary, E/C.12/HUN/CO/3 (16 January 2008), [34].
[255] CESCR, Concluding Observations: Hungary, E/C.12/HUN/CO/3 (16 January 2008), [34].
[256] CESCR, Concluding Observations: Ukraine, E/C.12/UKR/CO/5 (4 January 2008), [37].
[257] CESCR, Concluding Observations: Ukraine, E/C.12/UKR/CO/5 (4 January 2008), [37].
[258] CESCR, Concluding Observations: Sri Lanka, E/C.12/1/Add.24 (16 June 1998), [11].
[259] Council of Europe, Framework Convention for the Protection of National Minorities, Article 4(3).

The need for vocational or professional training for minorities has been frequently emphasized by the CESCR.[260] Notably, ILO Recommendation No. 150 on Human Resources Development calls on states to provide members of 'linguistic and other minority groups' with vocational guidance 'in a language with which they are familiar, or if necessary through interpreters', and with vocational training programmes in their own language 'if possible'.[261] While the CESCR has infrequently called for vocational training in minority languages,[262] it has said little about the recognition of minority languages in the workplace. According to the ILO, where the imposition of a state language for employment is excessive or disproportionate to its aim, it can amount to discrimination on the basis of national extraction.[263]

Occasionally, the CESCR has urged states to 'increase the resources allocated' to reducing unemployment among minorities,[264] and to make 'every effort' to obtain international assistance to guarantee the right to work of a repatriated minority.[265]

The CESCR does not appear to have addressed the issue of religion and the right to work. As noted earlier, a religious belief may be a requirement of certain religious positions, but only where objectively necessary.[266] In addition, a person's freedom to practise religion may intersect with the right to work, as where their religion requires special types of clothing, work conditions, holidays or practices (such as prayer times or fasting). According to the ILO, 'the worker's right to practise his or her faith or belief needs to be weighed against the need to meet the requirements inherent in the job', and 'at very least, the most important aspects of religious practice' must be respected and reconciled with work commitments.[267] In a case under Article 26 of the ICCPR, the HRC found that it was not discriminatory to terminate the employment of a Sikh railway electrician for failing to wear a hard hat because he insisted on wearing a turban:

> If the requirement that a hard hat be worn is seen as a discrimination de facto against persons of the Sikh religion under article 26, then, applying criteria now well established in the jurisprudence of the Committee, the legislation requiring that workers in federal employment be protected from injury and electric shock by wearing of hard hats is to be regarded as reasonable and directed towards objective purpose that are compatible with the Covenant.[268]

Invoking this case, the African Commission found that there was no discrimination or unjustifiable infringement of freedom of religion due to restrictions on

[260] CESCR, Concluding Observations: Hungary, E/C.12/HUN/CO/3 (16 January 2008), [34]; Ukraine, E/C.12/UKR/CO/5 (4 January 2008), [37]; Latvia, E/C.12/LVA/CO/1 (7 January 2008), [15].

[261] ILO Recommendation No. 150 on Human Resources Development, [51]–[52].

[262] CESCR, Concluding Observations: Latvia, E/C.12/LVA/CO/1 (7 January 2008), [15].

[263] ILO, *Giving Globalization a Human Face*, 319.

[264] CESCR, Concluding Observations: Slovakia, E/C.12/1/Add.81 (19 December 2002), [24].

[265] CESCR, Concluding Observations: Ukraine, E/C.12/1995/15 (28 December 1995), [24].

[266] *Jean-Louis Ramiaranjatovo v Fitsaboana Maso*, Antsirabe Labour Court Judgment No. 58, 7 June 2004 (Madagascar).

[267] ILO, *Giving Globalization a Human Face*, 334.

[268] *K Singh Bhinder v Canada*, HRC Communication No. 208/1986 (9 November 1989).

cannabis use which precluded the registration of a Rastafarian as a lawyer in South Africa:

> 43. The African Commission considers that the restrictions in the two South African legislations on the use and possession of cannabis are similarly reasonable as they serve a general purpose and that the Charter's protection of freedom of religion is not absolute. The only legitimate limitations to the rights and freedoms contained in the African Charter are found in article 27(2); ie that the rights in the African Charter 'shall be exercised with due regard to the rights of others, collective security, morality, and common interest'. The limitation is inspired by well-established principle that all human and peoples' rights are subject to the general rule that no one has the right to engage in any activity or perform any act aimed at the destruction of any of the rights and freedoms recognised elsewhere. The reasons for possible limitations must be founded in a legitimate state interest and the evils of limitations of rights must be strictly proportionate with and absolutely necessary for the advantages, which are to be obtained. It is noted that the respondent state's interest to do away with the use of cannabis and its abuse/trafficking stems from the fact that, and this is also admitted by the complainant, cannabis is an undesirable dependence-producing substance. For all intents and purposes, this constitutes a legitimate limitation on the exercise of the right to freedom of religion within the spirit of article 27(2) cum article 8.
>
> 44. Besides, the limitations so visited upon the complainant and his fellow Rastafari fall squarely under article 2 of the African Charter which requires states to ensure equal protection of the law. As the limitations are of general application, without singling out the complainant and his fellow Rastafari but applying to all across the board, they cannot be said discriminatory so as to curtail the complainant's free exercise of his religious rights.[269]

In other contexts, laws requiring religious clothing to be worn in public employment and universities (such as headscarves in Iran) have been criticized by the ILO as jeopardizing the employment or education of non-Muslims.[270] Conversely, laws forbidding the wearing of religious clothing or symbols in the public service or schools may give rise to concerns about religious discrimination, particularly in the absence of consultation. It depends, however, on the context. The European Court of Human Rights accepted, for instance, that a ban on the headscarf in Turkish universities was justified by the need to protect secular democracy, pluralism and the rights of women, in the face of Islamist pressures supposedly advanced by the emblem of the headscarf.[271]

[269] *Prince v South Africa* (2004) AHRLR 105.

[270] ILO CEACR, Observation on ILO Convention No. 11: Iran (2007), [11].

[271] *Şahin v Turkey* (App. 44774/98), [2005] ECtHR 819 (Grand Chamber, 10 November 2005) (the case concerned the right to education rather than the right to work). For criticism of the judgment, see Ben Saul, 'Wearing Thin: Restrictions on Headscarves and Other Religious Symbols' in Jane McAdam (ed), *Forced Migration and Human Rights* (Hart, Oxford, 2008), 181–212.

Migrant workers

The CESCR has applied the principle of non-discrimination to migrant workers:

18. The principle of non-discrimination as set out in article 2.2 of the Covenant and in article 7 of the International Convention on the Protection of the Rights of All Migrant Workers and Members of Their Families should apply in relation to employment opportunities for migrant workers and their families. In this regard the Committee underlines the need for national plans of action to be devised to respect and promote such principles by all appropriate measures, legislative or otherwise.

Foreign workers would normally fall within the protected grounds of 'race, colour, descent or national or ethnic origin' under the ICESCR or, where a state has made a reservation to such grounds, their citizenship may still bring them within the ground of 'other status'.[272]

In practice, the CESCR has provided little elucidation of the legal position of migrant workers. In monitoring states, it routinely comments on high levels of unemployment among 'immigrants', 'foreigners', 'foreign nationals', the 'foreign-born' or 'migrant workers', but does not explain whether its concern is limited to lawfully present foreigners or also encompasses 'illegal', irregular, unauthorized or undocumented migrants. At most, it has welcomed efforts by states to regularize the status of ('illegal') migrant workers.[273] One method of regularizing status is by granting amnesties to illegal workers.[274]

A distinction may be drawn between the work rights of non-citizens who are lawfully present in a foreign state and those who have entered without authorization. Under Article 6(1) 'everyone' has the right to work, on a non-discriminatory basis (including on grounds of nationality) under Article 2(2). However, as already noted, a measure will not be discriminatory where there is a reasonable and objective justification for differentiation.[275] In relation to the right to work of non-citizens, general international law provides an objective and reasonable basis for differentiating between citizens and non-citizens, on the basis that it permits states to restrict labour market access by foreigners (unless there are specific treaty commitments allowing access). In the alternative, labour restrictions on non-nationals may be justified by the general limitations clause in Article 4 of the ICESCR,[276] again on the basis of a permissive international rule.

Specifically, there is no general, unqualified right under international law of a foreign national to seek or obtain work in another state. States enjoy a sovereign discretion to control the admission, presence and expulsion of aliens, subject to any bilateral or multilateral agreements, and international refugee law. This

[272] As found by the HRC in assessing the same grounds under the ICCPR: see *Karakurt v Austria*, HRC Communication No. 965/2000, (4 April 2002), Individual Opinion of HRC members Sir Nigel Rodley and Mr Martin Scheinin (partly dissenting).

[273] CESCR, Concluding Observations: Italy, E/C.12/1/Add.103 (26 November 2004), [8].

[274] International Labour Conference (92nd session), *Promoting Employment: Policies, Skills, Enterprises*, Report III (Part 1B) (2004), 58.

[275] CESCR, General Comment No. 20, [13].

[276] Craven, *The ICSECR*, 214.

power includes the state's right to impose labour restrictions (whether partial or total) on foreign nationals,[277] whether they enter with or without the state's permission. Certain regional law also restricts work rights to those 'lawfully' in a state, as under Article 19 of the Revised European Social Charter.

While states enjoy a sovereign discretion whether to permit labour market access by foreigners, such choices may be regarded as 'objective and reasonable' differentiations on the basis of national origin or foreign citizenship status for various reasons. States are typically eager to preserve scarce employment opportunities for their own nationals. Where there are labour shortages, states may wish to select the most highly skilled or needed foreign workers rather than allowing open access. There are also reasons of political and social solidarity which drive the state's construction and composition of its own economic community. Singling out particular nationalities for exclusion is, however, generally suspect, compared with general restrictions on labour market access by any foreign national. On the other hand, according preferential labour market access to citizens of designated foreign states is commonly accepted (for instance, among EU states, or in bilateral arrangements).

Neither the drafting history nor subsequent state practice suggests that the ICESCR modifies the general position under international law. That Article 2(3) of the ICESCR allows developing countries to determine the extent to which they guarantee ICESCR rights to non-nationals does not necessarily imply that *developed* countries must guarantee the right to work to non-nationals,[278] where there is a specific international rule permitting states to control foreign access to their labour markets.

Some states have formally stated that Article 6 does not limit the state's right to impose birth or residence qualifications on employment (as in the case of the United Kingdom on ratification, and China in respect of Hong Kong in 2001) or to restrict access to employment by aliens (as in the case of France).[279] If reservations, such statements would ordinarily imply that such states believed that Article 6 guarantees non-nationals the right to work, necessitating a reservation to modify that obligation. If interpretive declarations, they would normally be evidence confirming that Article 6 does not provide foreigners with a right to work.

The UK statement is expressed as a reservation; the French statement as a declaration (although later seemingly viewed by France as a reservation);[280] and the Chinese statement does not self-characterize. No state has objected to any of the three statements. It has been suggested that the UK and French statements are not incompatible with the object and purpose of the ICESCR,[281] although that

[277] Robert Jennings and Arthur Watts, *Oppenheim's International Law* (9th edn, Pearson Education, London, 1996), vol. II: Peace, 905; Nussberger, 'Work, Right to, International Protection', [44]. Some constitutions expressly limit work rights to citizens rather than casting them as universal rights.

[278] As Craven suggests in *The ICSECR*, 213.

[279] See UN Treaty Series, ICESCR Status, <http://treaties.un.org/Pages/ViewDetails.aspx?src=TREATY&mtdsg_no=IV-3&chapter=4&lang=en>.

[280] Craven, *The ICSECR*, 214.

[281] Craven, *The ICSECR*, 214.

depends on the importance placed on non-discrimination on the basis of nationality in employment in effecting human dignity.

The effect or significance of these statements is somewhat inconclusive. Even a reservation may be expressed as such because of a state's abundant caution to avoid an otherwise uncertain obligation, rather being determinative of whether the provision does in fact impose the obligation sought to be clarified or qualified. More decisive is the concrete reality that most states impose labour market restrictions on foreigners; they do so because they believe international law entitles them to do so; and most states have not sought to formally interpret or reserve their Article 6 obligation because it is not understood as requiring them to guarantee the right to work to any non-citizen.

This legal position is confirmed by the practice of other UN human rights treaty bodies. For example, the CERD Committee reminded Denmark that '*although it is not obliged to provide work permits to foreign residents*, it should guarantee that foreigners who are entitled to a work permit are not discriminated against in their access to employment'.[282]

In this regard, restrictions on the right *to* work of non-nationals must be distinguished from the rights of non-citizens once *at or in* work (regardless of whether they entered work lawfully or unlawfully), including under Articles 7 and 8 of the ICESCR. Otherwise, a worker's 'illegal' status could be invoked as an excuse for failing to provide humane and dignified conditions of work, exposing illegal workers to exploitation and abuse. In a case under the ICCPR, the HRC found that where a state grants a work permit to a non-national, while differentiation on the basis of nationality may be permissible in some circumstances, it is not reasonable to deny a non-national the right to stand for election to a work council on the basis of nationality, since the purpose of the council was to promote staff interests and to supervize compliance with work conditions.[283]

The CESCR itself has encouraged various states to ratify the Migrant Workers Convention, implying that it accepts the bifurcated regime of rights applicable to documented and undocumented migrant workers. Under that regime, foreigners enjoy no right to work as such in a receiving state,[284] but once in work various labour protections apply.

All migrant workers enjoy certain basic rights under the Migrant Workers Convention, including freedom from slavery, servitude or forced compulsory labour (Article 11); pay and conditions equal to that of nationals (Article 25); the right to join trade unions (Article 26); equal treatment in social security (Article 27); and emergency health care (Article 28). *Documented or regular* migrant workers enjoy additional protections, including the right to form associations or trade unions (Article 40); equal national treatment concerning

[282] CERD, Concluding Observations: Denmark, A/57/18 (1 November 2002), [120] (emphasis added).

[283] *Karakurt v Austria*, HRC Communication No. 965/2000, (4 April 2002), [8.4].

[284] The Convention on Migrant Workers, Article 35, provides that nothing in the Convention 'shall be interpreted as implying the regularization of the situation of migrant workers or members of their families who are non-documented or in an irregular situation or any right to such regularization'.

protection against dismissal, unemployment benefits and access to alternative employment (Article 54); and the right to seek remedies for contractual violations by an employer.

Relatively few states have ratified the Migrant Workers Convention, and hardly any receiving states, limiting its practical significance. However, the CESCR's invocation of it to inform interpretation of Article 6 of the ICESCR gives it an independent normative authority which may shape the development of ICESCR standards in relation to migrant workers.

Regional human rights practice also supports the protection of migrant workers. In an advisory opinion, the Inter-American Court of Human Rights found that while the state is not required to offer work to foreigners, where an employment relationship is established a migrant worker is entitled to equality of treatment in rights in work:

> 133. Labor rights necessarily arise from the circumstance of being a worker, understood in the broadest sense. A person who is to be engaged, is engaged or has been engaged in a remunerated activity, immediately becomes a worker and, consequently, acquires the rights inherent in that condition. The right to work, whether regulated at the national or international level, is a protective system for workers; that is, it regulates the rights and obligations of the employee and the employer, regardless of any other consideration of an economic and social nature. A person who enters a State and assumes an employment relationship, acquires his labor human rights in the State of employment, irrespective of his migratory status, because respect and guarantee of the enjoyment and exercise of those rights must be made without any discrimination.
>
> 134. In this way, the migratory status of a person can never be a justification for depriving him of the enjoyment and exercise of his human rights, including those related to employment. On assuming an employment relationship, the migrant acquires rights as a worker, which must be recognized and guaranteed, irrespective of his regular or irregular status in the State of employment. These rights are a consequence of the employment relationship.
>
> 135. It is important to clarify that the State and the individuals in a State are not obliged to offer employment to undocumented migrants. The States and individuals, such as employers, can abstain from establishing an employment relationship with migrants in an irregular situation.
>
> 136. However, if undocumented migrants are engaged, they immediately become possessors of the labor rights corresponding to workers and may not be discriminated against because of their irregular situation. This is very important, because one of the principal problems that occurs in the context of immigration is that migrant workers who lack permission to work are engaged in unfavorable conditions compared to other workers.[285]

Often, the lawful presence of a foreign worker is conditional on certain visa conditions, such as employer sponsorship in a particular position. The ILO has stated that where an employment system 'places workers in a particularly vulnerable position and provides employers with the opportunity to exert disproportionate

[285] *Juridical Condition and Rights of Undocumented Migrants: Advisory Opinion*, IACHR, OC-18/03 (17 September 2003), [133]–[136].

power over them, this could result in discrimination'.[286] Severe restrictions on the possibility of workers changing workplaces, employers or sponsors may be incompatible with a person's freedom from discrimination. The state does not, therefore, enjoy a complete discretion as to the terms on which it permits foreign nationals to enter for employment.

The CESCR has criticized the arbitrary expulsion of foreign workers, the failure to provide them with 'adequate compensation' and the absence of remedies.[287] While it may be lawful to expel a foreign worker who may be in breach of domestic immigration or labour laws, arbitrary expulsion may constitute arbitrary interference in the work rights of foreign nationals.[288] Expulsion may be arbitrary where is it not in accordance with national law,[289] where the state fails to provide reasons[290] or a right of review, or where it is discriminatory. In this context, Article 13 of the ICCPR protects any alien 'lawfully' in a state's territory from arbitrary expulsion, and guarantees minimum procedural and review rights:

> An alien lawfully in the territory of a State Party to the present Covenant may be expelled therefrom only in pursuance of a decision reached in accordance with law and shall, except where compelling reasons of national security otherwise require, be allowed to submit the reasons against his expulsion and to have his case reviewed by, and be represented for the purpose before, the competent authority or a person or persons especially designated by the competent authority.[291]

The International Law Commission's draft articles on the expulsion of aliens also requires any expulsion to be 'in pursuance of a decision reached in accordance with law' (Article 4), prohibits the collective expulsion of aliens, including migrant workers and their families (Article 10), and prohibits discrimination in expulsion (Article 15).[292] The prohibition on mass expulsions is also found in Article 22 of the Migrant Workers Convention and in regional human rights treaties.[293]

It should also be noted that the CESCR has occasionally expressed concern about high levels of unemployment driving migration for work abroad, as with

[286] ILO, *Giving Globalization a Human Face*, 325.

[287] CESCR, Concluding Observations: Libya, E/C.12/1/Add.15 (20 May 1997), [15].

[288] Manisuli Ssenyonjo, *Economic, Social and Cultural Rights in International Law* (Hart, Oxford, 2009), 292.

[289] See also *Ahmadou Sadio Diallo (Republic of Guinea v Democratic Republic of the Congo) (Judgment)*, (2011) ICJ Rep 639, [65].

[290] *Ahmadou Sadio Diallo*, [81].

[291] See also African Charter on Human and People's Rights (adopted 27 June 1981, 1520 UNTS 217, entered into force 21 October 1986), Article 12.

[292] International Law Commission (64th Session), Report, A/67/10 (7 May–1 June and 2 July–3 August 2012), chapter 4, 12–14.

[293] American Convention on Human Rights (adopted 22 November 1969, 1144 UNTS 123, entered into force 18 July 1978), Article 22; Protocol No. 4 to the [European] Convention of 4 November 1950 for the Protection of Human Rights and Fundamental Freedoms, securing certain rights and freedoms other than those already included in the Convention and in the first Protocol thereto (adopted 16 September 1963, 1496 UNTS 263, entered into force 2 May 1968), Article 4; African Charter on Human and People's Rights, Article 12(5); Arab Charter on Human Rights (adopted 22 May 2004, entered into force 15 March 2008), Article 26(2).

'much of' the Bolivian population.[294] It has thus encouraged states to 'take the necessary measures to encourage the population to remain in the country'.[295]

In this regard, ILO Recommendation No. 169 concerning Employment Policy (Supplementary Provisions) 1984 encourages states to adopt policies 'to create more employment opportunities and better conditions of work in countries of emigration so as to reduce the need to migrate to find employment'.[296] Sending and receiving countries are also urged to cooperate in job creation and on conditions of work (paragraphs 40 to 44).

The situation of workers in occupied territory under international humanitarian law has been specifically addressed by the CESCR. It has expressed concern about high unemployment (over 50 per cent) as a result of military closures which prevented Palestinians from working in Israel, and recommended that Israel ensure that workers living in the occupied territories are permitted to continue to work in Israel.[297] The application of the ICESCR to occupied territory was discussed earlier in the context of Article 2 of the ICESCR.

The inhabitants of occupied territories generally do not enjoy an international legal right to work in the territory of the occupying power. The CESCR's position may, however, be explained by a number of factors. Where national law has permitted the inhabitants of occupied territory to work in the state's own territory, arbitrary interruptions of such rights—as by the unpredictable operation of the closures regime—may infringe Article 6, just as in the ordinary case of lawful foreign workers whose rights are arbitrarily infringed.

Certainly, legitimate security considerations may justify temporary interference in work rights (including pursuant to the limitations clause in Article 4 of the ICESCR, as understood in light of the special international law of occupation), but any such measures cannot be arbitrary, excessive or disproportionate. Further, where such interference prevents the ability of workers to survive and support their families, other measures of state support to compensate for such effects would be required, such as through income support, food supplies and so on. Where livelihoods and the economy of occupied territory are heavily dependent on access to the occupying power's labour market, sudden disruption of such access must be closely scrutinized.

Refugees

The CESCR has frequently expressed concern about high unemployment among refugees and called on states in very general terms to take measures to address it.[298] It has said little more than this, including in relation to refugees living in camp situations. Nor has it referred to asylum seekers (those not yet formally recognized as refugees) in the context of the right to work.

294 CESCR, Concluding Observations: Bolivia, E/C.12/BOL/CO/2 (8 August 2008), [17].

295 CESCR, Concluding Observations: El Salvador, E/C.12/SLV/CO/2 (27 June 2007), [40].

296 ILO Recommendation No. 169 on Employment Policy (Supplementary Provisions) (26 June 1984), [39(a)].

297 CESCR, Concluding Observations: Israel, E/C.12/1/Add.90 (26 June 2003), [20] and [36].

298 CESCR, Concluding Observations: Azerbaijan, E/C.12/1/Add.104 (14 December 2004), [17]; Denmark, E/C.12/1/Add.34 (14 May 1999), [18] and [26]; Denmark, E/C.12/1/Add.102 (14 December 2004), [15] and [26]; Finland, E/C.12/1/Add.8 (5 December 1996), [12].

The work rights recognized under Articles 17 to 19 of the Refugee Convention 1951 apply only to refugees 'lawfully staying' in a state's territory. They do not, therefore, apply to asylum seekers whose refugee claims have yet to be determined.[299] They are, however, obligations of immediate effect and are not subject to progressive realization,[300] thus raising the bar for implementation compared with the general position under the ICESCR. In this respect, the Refugee Convention standards arguably operate as the *lex specialis* in determining the right to work of refugees under Article 6 of the ICESCR, placing them in a more advantageous position than other foreign nationals in certain circumstances. Refugees are not entitled to the same rights as nationals, but nor are their rights as limited as those of foreigners generally.

Article 17(1) of the Refugee Convention 1951 requires states to give refugees and stateless persons 'lawfully staying' in their territory 'the most favourable treatment' accorded to foreign nationals as regards the right to 'wage-earning employment'. In addition, labour restrictions may not be imposed on a refugee who has lived in the state for three years, or is married to one of the state's nationals, or whose children are nationals (Article 17(2)). States are also exhorted to 'give sympathetic consideration to assimilating the rights of all refugees with regard to wage-earning employment to those of nationals' (Article 17(3)). Article 17 as a whole provides:

1. The Contracting States shall accord to refugees lawfully staying in their territory the most favourable treatment accorded to nationals of a foreign country in the same circumstances, as regards the right to engage in wage-earning employment.

2. In any case, restrictive measures imposed on aliens or the employment of aliens for the protection of the national labour market shall not be applied to a refugee who was already exempt from them at the date of entry into force of this Convention for the Contracting State concerned, or who fulfils one of the following conditions:

(a) He has completed three years' residence in the country.

(b) He has a spouse possessing the nationality of the country of residence. A refugee may not invoke the benefits of this provision if he has abandoned his spouse.

(c) He has one or more children possessing the nationality of the country of residence.

3. The Contracting States shall give sympathetic consideration to assimilating the rights of all refugees with regard to wage-earning employment to those of nationals, and in particular of those refugees who have entered their territory pursuant to programs of labour recruitment or under immigration schemes.

Article 18 of the Refugee Convention further provides for refugees in self-employment and engaging in their own businesses to be treated at least equally to other foreign nationals:

The Contracting States shall accord to a refugee lawfully in their territory treatment as favourable as possible and, in any event, not less favourable than that accorded to aliens generally

[299] James Hathaway, *The Rights of Refugees under International Law* (Cambridge University Press, Cambridge, 2011), 754–5; Nussberger, 'Work, Right to, International Protection', [45].

[300] Hathaway, *Rights of Refugees*, 741–2.

in the same circumstances, as regards the right to engage on his own account in agriculture, industry, handicrafts and commerce and to establish commercial and industrial companies.

Article 19 of the Refugee Convention also provides for qualified refugees practising in a 'liberal profession' to be treated at least as favourably as similarly situated foreigners:

1. Each Contracting State shall accord to refugees lawfully staying in their territory who hold diplomas recognized by the competent authorities of that State, and who are desirous of practising a liberal profession, treatment as favourable as possible and, in any event, not less favourable than that accorded to aliens generally in the same circumstances.

2. The Contracting States shall use their best endeavours consistently with their laws and constitutions to secure the settlement of such refugees in the territories, other than the metropolitan territory, for whose international relations they are responsible.

Prohibition on Forced Labour

According to the CESCR, the right to freely choose or accept work 'implies not being forced in any way whatsoever to exercise or engage in employment',[301] a point also made during the drafting of the ICESCR.[302] Article 10(3) of the ICESCR specifically addresses the issue of child labour and that aspect of Article 6 is considered in the chapter on Article 10.

The problem of forced labour is significant, complex and widespread. In 2012, the ILO estimated that 20.9 million people globally are victims of forced labour,[303] of whom 22 per cent were victims of sexual exploitation, 68 per cent were exploited in economic activities, and 10 per cent in state-imposed labour (such as prison labour or military work). Women and girls were 55 per cent of victims. Almost half (44 per cent) of victims had migrated internally or internationally (the latter most common among those subject to sexual exploitation), while the remainder worked in their place of origin or residence. The Asia-Pacific region accounted for around 56 per cent of forced labour, while Africa represented 18 per cent, Latin America and the Caribbean 9 per cent, and the developed economies 7 per cent.

DEFINITION OF FORCED LABOUR

In defining the scope of Article 6, the CESCR has invoked the external standards of the Slavery Convention 1926, ILO standards on forced labour and Article 8 of the ICCPR:

9. The International Labour Organization defines forced labour as 'all work or service which is exacted from any person under the menace of any penalty and for which the

[301] CESCR, General Comment No. 18, [6].

[302] UNGA Third Committee, A/C.3/SR.710 (13 December 1956), 144 (Syria); A/C.3/SR.711 (14 December 1956), 150 (Australia).

[303] ILO, 'ILO Global Estimate of Forced Labour 2012: Results and Methodology' (Geneva, 2012), <http://www.ilo.org/sapfl/Informationresources/ILOPublications/WCMS_182004/lang--en/index.htm>.

said person has not offered himself voluntarily' [in Article 2(1) of ILO Convention No. 29 of 1930]. The Committee reaffirms the need for States parties to abolish, forbid and counter all forms of forced labour as enunciated in article 4 of the Universal Declaration of Human Rights, article 5 of the Slavery Convention and article 8 of the ICCPR.[304]

The concept of forced labour is wider than the earlier, more restricted legal concept of slavery, which was prohibited by Article 1 of the Slavery Convention 1926 but confined to the powers attaching to the right of ownership,[305] albeit subject to expansive interpretation over time.[306] Article 5 of the Slavery Convention 1926 did not prohibit forced or compulsory labour, but only required states to take measures to 'progressively' end it, and then only when it was not exacted for ill-defined 'public purposes':

The High Contracting Parties recognise that recourse to compulsory or forced labour may have grave consequences and undertake, each in respect of the territories placed under its sovereignty, jurisdiction, protection, suzerainty or tutelage, to take all necessary measures to prevent compulsory or forced labour from developing into conditions analogous to slavery.

It is agreed that:

(1) Subject to the transitional provisions laid down in paragraph (2) below, compulsory or forced labour may only be exacted for public purposes.

(2) In territories in which compulsory or forced labour for other than public purposes still survives, the High Contracting Parties shall endeavour progressively and as soon as possible to put an end to the practice. So long as such forced or compulsory labour exists, this labour shall invariably be of an exceptional character, shall always receive adequate remuneration, and shall not involve the removal of the labourers from their usual place of residence.

(3) In all cases, the responsibility for any recourse to compulsory or forced labour shall rest with the competent central authorities of the territory concerned.[307]

The innovation of ILO Convention No. 29 concerning Forced or Compulsory Labour 1930[308] was to require states 'to suppress the use of forced or compulsory labour in all its forms within the shortest possible period' (Article 1(1)) and criminalize its unlawful use (Article 25). Article 2(1) defines forced or compulsory labour as 'all work or service which is exacted from any person under the menace

[304] CESCR, General Comment No. 18, [9].

[305] Slavery Convention (adopted 25 September 1926, 60 LNTS 253, entered into force 9 March 1927), Article 1(1): 'Slavery is the status or condition of a person over whom any or all of the powers attaching to the right of ownership are exercised'.

[306] See, eg, *R v Tang* (2008) 237 CLR 1 (High Court of Australia) (slavery is not limited to chattel slavery, but concerns the nature and extent of the enslaver's powers and/or reference to the victim's freedom of choice; thus foreign women recruited to work in a brothel and to pay off travel debts were enslaved, despite not being kept under lock and key).

[307] Slavery Convention, Article 5.

[308] ILO Convention No. 29 concerning Forced or Compulsory Labour, as modified by the Final Articles Revision Convention, 1946 (adopted 28 June 1930, 39 UNTS 55, entered into force 1 May 1932) ('ILO Convention No. 29').

of any penalty and for which the said person has not offered himself voluntarily'.[309] Article 2(2) sets out exceptions from the definition, considered further below. The CESCR has identified the definition in Convention No. 29 as an essential reference point in its understanding of forced labour in Article 6.

The notion of a 'penalty' in Convention No. 29 was intended to include not only 'penal sanctions', but 'a loss of rights or privileges',[310] which the CESCR has found to include refusal of early release from prison.[311] In the European cases it includes the risk to a lawyer of being struck off the roll of pupils or a refusal to be registered,[312] or otherwise disciplined.[313] According to the ILO, it covers loss of privileges or rights such as promotion, transfer, access to employment, acquisition of goods, housing benefits or university access.[314]

A penalty will plainly include arbitrary physical punishments outside the law, as an ILO Commission of Inquiry on forced labour in Myanmar found in 1998:

> 292. The information before the Commission was that the penalties for failing to comply with forced labour demands were harsh. Punishments included detention at the army camp, often in leg-stocks or in a pit in the ground, commonly accompanied by beatings and other forms of torture, as well as deprivation of food, water, medical attention and other basic rights. Women were subject to rape and other forms of sexual abuse at such times...[315]

Apart from physical violence, a penalty 'can also take subtler forms, of a psychological nature, such as threats to denounce victims to the police or immigration authorities when their employment status is illegal', or confiscation of identity documents.[316] The notion of a penalty was accordingly interpreted flexibly in a European case of a vulnerable, irregular migrant girl who was exploited as an unpaid domestic worker, and whose passport had been confiscated:

> 118. The Court notes that, in the instant case, although the applicant was not threatened by a 'penalty', the fact remains that she was in an equivalent situation in terms of the perceived seriousness of the threat.
>
> She was an adolescent girl in a foreign land, unlawfully present on French territory and in fear of arrest by the police. Indeed, Mr and Mrs B. nurtured that fear and led her to believe that her status would be regularised...

[309] Rather than the context and nature of the service demanded, the means by which it is obtained, or the identity of or relationship between the perpetrator and victim: Santiago M Villalpando, 'Forced/Slave Labour', *Max Planck Encyclopedia of Public International Law* online, <http://www.mpepil.com>, [1].

[310] International Labour Conference (CEACR) (65th Session), *General Survey of the reports relating to the Forced Labour Convention 1930 (No. 29) and the Abolition of Forced Labour Convention 1957 (No. 105)*, Report III (Part 4B) (Geneva, 1979), [21]; International Labour Conference (14th Session), Record of Proceedings (Geneva, 1930), 691.

[311] CESCR, Concluding Observations: Estonia, E/C.12/1/Add.85 (19 December 2002), [13].

[312] *Van der Mussele v Belgium* (App. 8919/80), 23 November 1983, (1983) 6 EHRR 163, [35].

[313] *Graziani-Weiss v Austria* (App. 31950/06), ECtHR 18 October 2011, [39].

[314] ILO, *Eradication of Forced Labour*, General Survey on ILO Conventions No. 29 and 105, Report III (Part 1B) (Geneva, 2007) ('*Eradication of Forced Labour*'), 20.

[315] ILO, *Forced Labour in Myanmar (Burma)*, Report of the Commission of Inquiry appointed under Article 26 of the Constitution of the ILO to examine the observance by Myanmar of the Forced Labour Convention 1930 (No. 29) (Geneva, 2 July 1998) ('*Forced Labour in Myanmar*'), [292].

[316] *CN and V v France* (App. 67724/09), ECtHR, 11 October 2012, [77].

Accordingly, the Court considers that the first criterion was met, especially since the applicant was a minor at the relevant time, a point which the Court emphasises.[317]

The 'menace' of a penalty referred to in Convention No. 29 can encompass overt or implied threats, again as the ILO found in respect of Myanmar:

289. The written orders to provide porters and labourers which were sent to village heads by the local military or civil administration typically contained some kind of overt or implied threat. Examples of overt threats included such statements as 'Anyone who refuses to come to build the road shall be punished according to the law', 'If you don't come because you are afraid of Mon rebels, we the Army must show you that we are worse than Mon rebels', 'I warn you that if you make excuses and fail to come, violent action will be taken against you' or 'If nobody comes this time [you] will be destroyed by an artillery attack'. In one case when two villagers ran away from portering, an order from the military column to the village head demanding their return stated: 'Should this happen in the future, we will take action and you will be charged with disturbing and causing delay to our military operations'. Examples of implied threats included statements such as 'If you fail to comply it will be your responsibility', which villagers knew from experience meant that they would face serious punishment, or 'If you fail to come we will not take any responsibility for [your] village', which the villagers knew was a threat to destroy their village. Another common form of threat was the inclusion with the order of some combination of a bullet, chilli and piece of charcoal, implying that the recipient would be shot, face problems, or have their house or village burned down if they failed to comply with the order.[318]

Work will not be 'forced' or 'compulsory' where a person offers themselves voluntarily, whether for specific tasks or all of the burdens entailed in accepting a particular position. Of course, this does not answer the Marxist critique that labour per se is exploitative in capitalist economies,[319] or acknowledge the economic realities which may fundamentally constrain the sphere within which a person may 'choose': 'what kind of consent lies at the basis of a woman's "choice" to prostitute herself, or a dwarf's to be thrown around, or a migrant worker's to leave her family for years?'.[320] Work is not forced simply because a person must earn a living.[321]

More direct threats or coercion of the kind mentioned above will vitiate a person's consent to work. The threat of sanctions for breach of a freely negotiated employment contract does not, however, constitute the menace of a penalty.[322] Special considerations apply to consent by a child, and in the context of human trafficking, both discussed further below.

Agreeing to join some professions may entail the performance of certain responsibilities which will not be regarded as 'forced' or 'compulsory' labour, but rather as part of the normal work of those professions. In European cases arising under the forced labour prohibition in Article 4 of the ECHR, it has been

[317] *Siliadin v France* (App. 73316/01), ECtHR 26 July 2005, [118].
[318] ILO, *Forced Labour in Myanmar*, [289].
[319] See, eg, Mundlak, 'The Right to Work—The Value of Work', 345–8.
[320] Mundlak, 'The Right to Work—The Value of Work', 341, 347.
[321] ILO, *Eradication of Forced Labour*, 20.
[322] *Van der Mussele v Belgium* (App. 8919/80), 23 November 1983, (1983) 6 EHRR 163, 37.

held that a person directed by law to perform certain work in the public interest—such as paid dental work in remote areas of need—was not 'forced' to work, because (among other things) joining the dental profession was understood to entail such responsibilities.[323]

Likewise, a requirement to provide legal assistance to poor clients did not inflict 'forced' labour on a law student who voluntarily sought to join the legal profession, knowing that this was a professional responsibility.[324] Similar findings have been made in respect of obligations on: practising lawyers required to be periodically on call, with pay, to assist detainees in police custody;[325] a doctor to provide emergency medical care;[326] a notary public to discount work done for churches (that is, non-profit groups);[327] or a restriction on a footballer from joining a different football club for a period after leaving another.[328]

However, consent in advance to a profession's normal work, by choosing to enter that profession, is an important consideration, but not 'decisive',[329] and all of the circumstances must be examined. Consent will be negated where the work imposed 'a burden which was so excessive or disproportionate to the advantages attached to the future exercise of [the] profession that the service could not be treated as having been voluntarily accepted'.[330]

Thus, in a case involving pro bono work required of a law student, the work was not considered forced due to a combination of factors: it was part of a lawyer's normal work; it helped the lawyer's training; membership of the profession brought compensatory advantages; it contributed to realizing the state's ECHR obligation to provide legal aid; it was a 'normal civic obligation' and grounded in 'social solidarity'; and the burden was not disproportionate (eighteen hours' work), still allowing for paid work.[331]

Where a person withdraws consent to work, it will not necessarily convert hitherto voluntary work into forced labour, as for instance when a person seeks to withdraw from a freely negotiated employment contract in breach of its terms.[332] Such was the case even where contractual commitments were lengthy (up to twelve years) and involved minors (15 to 16 years of age) who had joined

[323] *Iversen v Norway* (App. 1468/62), (1963) 6 Yearbook 278, 326–8.
[324] *X v Federal Republic of Germany* (App. 4653/70), 1 April 1974, (1974) 17 Yearbook 148, 172.
[325] *Doyen v France* (App. 39109/97), 9 September 1998, DR No. 94-B, 151.
[326] *Steindel v Germany* (App. 29878/07), ECtHR 14 September 2010.
[327] *X v Federal Republic of Germany* (App. 8410/78), 13 December 1979, D&R 18 (1980), 216, 219.
[328] *X v Netherlands*, (App. 9322/81), 3 May 1983, D&R 32 (1983), 180, 182–3.
[329] *Van der Mussele v Belgium* (App. 8919/80), 23 November 1983, (1983) 6 EHRR 163, [36].
[330] *Van der Mussele v Belgium*, [37]; see also [40].
[331] *Van der Mussele v Belgium*, [39]; see Pieter van Dijk, Fried van Hoof, Arjen van Rijn and Leo Zwaak (eds), *Theory and Practice of the European Convention on Human Rights* (4th edn, Intersentia, Antwerp, 2006) ('*Theory and Practice of the ECHR*'), 449–50. In Europe, it may no longer be necessary also to establish that, in order to be forced, work must also be unjust, oppressive or involve avoidable hardship, as in earlier Commission cases such as *X v Federal Republic of Germany* (App. 4653/70), (1974) 17 Yearbook 148, 172. See also *Graziani-Weiss v Austria* (App. 31950/06), ECtHR 18 October 2011, [38].
[332] See, eg, *Van der Mussele v Belgium* (App. 8919/80), 23 November 1983, (1983) 6 EHRR 163, [34].

the military with the consent of their parents.[333] In that case, there was, however, the possibility of compassionate discharge and a right to 'buy out' of service within the first three months. In other cases, however, lengthy but rigid contractual arrangements may impose undue burdens and interfere with a person's right to freely choose their employment where they change their mind, regardless of their original contractual consent.

Forced labour is distinguishable by the type and amount of work that is reasonably expected of family members or among persons living together.[334] Notably, the Commonwealth of Independent States (CIS) Human Rights Convention provides an additional, explicit exception for duties owed by parents to children and adult children to parents in need,[335] although practice varies on the extent to which familial duties are better treated as social responsibilities rather than legally enforceable ones.

Importantly, remuneration for work does not eliminate its forced or compulsory character, as the ILO Commission of Inquiry on forced labour in Myanmar explains:

> …the mere payment of wages for labour obtained through the call-up of local residents does not remove such labour from the scope of the definition of forced or compulsory labour in Article 2(1) of the Convention. Payment does not change the character of labour exacted compulsorily or by force; it merely becomes paid compulsory or forced labour.[336]

However, there is no forced labour where an employee is transferred to a less lucrative job absent any evidence that the work was performed involuntarily on threat of penalty.[337]

In response to changes in the prevailing forms of forced labour (including Stalin's punitive use of forced labour in the Soviet Union),[338] ILO Convention No. 105 concerning the Abolition of Forced Labour 1957,[339] ratified by 174 states, elaborates further forms of unlawful forced or compulsory labour where it is used:

(a) as a means of political coercion or education or as a punishment for holding or expressing political views or views ideologically opposed to the established political, social or economic system;

(b) as a method of mobilising and using labour for purposes of economic development;

[333] *W, X, Y and Z* (Apps. 3435/67, 3438/67), 28 CD 109 (1968) ('*Boy Soldiers*' cases).

[334] *CN and V v France* (App. 67724/09), ECtHR 11 October 2012, [74].

[335] Commonwealth of Independent States (CIS) Convention on Human Rights and Fundamental Freedoms (adopted 26 May 1995, entered into force 11 August 1998), Article 4(3)(e): 'the fulfilment by parents of their duty to create the necessary conditions for their children, and by children who have reached the age of majority of their duty to support parents unable to work and requiring assistance'.

[336] ILO, *Forced Labour in Myanmar*, [473].

[337] *Antonov v Russia* (App. 38020/03), 3 November 2005.

[338] Colin Fenwick, 'The International Labour Organization: An Integrated Approach to Economic and Social Rights' in Malcolm Langford (ed), *Social Rights Jurisprudence: Emerging Trends in International and Comparative Law* (Cambridge University Press, Cambridge, 2008), 591, 599.

[339] ILO Convention No. 105 concerning the Abolition of Forced Labour (adopted 25 June 1957, 320 UNTS 291, entered into force 17 January 1959).

(c) as a means of labour discipline;

(d) as a punishment for having participated in strikes;

(e) as a means of racial, social, national or religious discrimination.[340]

Each of these grounds has been drawn upon by the CESCR in monitoring states. Thus, the CESCR was concerned that Afghanistan used forced labour to punish people for 'holding or expressing political or ideological views' and urged review of the penal law to ensure that forced labour is not used as a penalty.[341] It was also concerned for North Koreans sent to labour camps for travelling abroad without a passport in quest of employment and better living conditions.[342] It feared that the majority of public servants in the former East Germany (including teachers, scientists and professionals) 'may have been dismissed from their positions for political rather than for professional or economic reasons'.[343]

As regards economic development, the CESCR criticized the Democratic Republic of Congo for maintaining a compulsory civic work programme known as 'Salongo',[344] which involved weekly compulsory labour on agricultural and development projects. The scope of the exception for civic obligations in Convention No. 29 is discussed separately below.

The infliction of forced labour as a means of labour discipline is one of the more common grounds on which the CESCR has criticized states. The problem has been particularly prevalent in the area of maritime labour, where breaches of discipline by seamen (including absenteeism) are punishable by an obligation to perform labour on board ships.[345] The CESCR has also criticized the punishment of foreign employees by imprisonment with compulsory labour for breaches of disciplinary rules.[346] In relation to the United Kingdom, the CESCR observed that excessive restrictions on the right to strike—such as the threat of loss of employment for taking strike action—may involve 'involuntary servitude' (and also violate Article 8).[347]

The prohibition on forced labour as a means of discrimination is reinforced by Article 5 of the International Convention on the Elimination of Racial Discrimination, which guarantees free choice of employment on a non-discriminatory basis. The International Convention on the Suppression and Punishment of the Crime of Apartheid further prohibits 'exploitation of the

[340] ILO Convention No. 105, Article 1.

[341] CESCR, Concluding Observations: Afghanistan, E/C.12/AFG/CO/2-4 (7 June 2010), [20].

[342] CESCR, Concluding Observations: DPR Korea, E/C.12/1/Add.95 (12 December 2003), [15] and [35].

[343] CESCR, Concluding Observations: Germany, E/C.12/1/Add.29 (4 December 1998), [16].

[344] CESCR, Concluding Observations: Democratic Republic of Congo, E/C.12/COD/CO/4 (16 September 2009), [21].

[345] CESCR, Concluding Observations: Mauritius, E/C.12/1994/8 (31 May 1994), [8]; Ireland, E/C.12/1/Add.35 (14 May 1999), [18].

[346] CESCR, Concluding Observations: Libyan Arab Jamahiriya, E/1998/22 (1997), [184]; see also Craven, *The ICESCR*, 220.

[347] CESCR, Concluding Observations: UK, E/1998/22 (1997), [306]; see also Craven, *The ICESCR*, 220.

labour of the members of a racial group or groups, in particular by submitting them to forced labour'.

The CESCR has not yet made much of the discrimination ground, although the ILO Commission of Inquiry on Myanmar observed that the 'burden of forced labour also appears to be particularly great for non-Burman ethnic groups, especially in areas where there is a strong military presence, and for the Muslim minority, including the Rohingyas'.[348] The CERD has also been alert to the burden of forced labour falling disproportionately on minority groups, such as the descendants of slaves in Madagascar and Mauritania, bonded agricultural labourers (*kamaiyas*) in Nepal, indigenous children in Venezuela, migrant women domestic workers in Bahrain, foreign trainees in South Korea, and females of the Ewe ethnic group (subject to a form of slavery called *Trokosi*).[349] The HRC has occasionally commented on the risks of forced labour for ethnic minorities and refugees, as in Thailand.[350]

The Supplementary Convention on the Abolition of Slavery, the Slave Trade, and Institutions and Practices Similar to Slavery 1956 further criminalizes slavery-like practices, including debt bondage, serfdom and the exploitation of child labour.[351] The CESCR has been influenced by these extended slavery-like concepts. It thus criticized debt bondage in the salt-mining communities north of Timbuktu in Mali, and the continuing difficulties faced by the *kamaiyas* in Nepal, notwithstanding the formal abolition of bonded labour there in 2000.[352]

Unlike the implicit prohibition on forced labour under Article 6 of the ICESCR, Article 8 of the ICCPR expressly prohibits slavery, servitude and forced or compulsory labour, broadly recognizing the extended forms of compulsion identified in the various ILO and other treaty standards already mentioned. Article 8 of the ICCPR provides that:

1. No one shall be held in slavery; slavery and the slave-trade in all their forms shall be prohibited.

2. No one shall be held in servitude.

3. (a) No one shall be required to perform forced or compulsory labour…

Significantly, in *Faure v Australia*, the HRC did not confine its conception of forced labour strictly to the text of particular ILO standards, but set out a more general formulation of the concept:

7.5 …the Committee observes that the Covenant does not spell out in further detail the meaning of the terms 'forced or compulsory labour'. While the definitions of the relevant ILO instruments may be of assistance in elucidating the meaning of the terms, it ultimately

[348] ILO, *Forced Labour in Myanmar*, [534].

[349] CERD, Concluding Observations: Madagascar, A/59/18 (2004), [320]; Mauritania, A/59/18 (2004), [342]; Nepal, A/59/18 (2004), [133]; Venezuela, A/60/18 (2005), [381]; Bahrain, A/60/18 (2005), [85]; Republic of Korea, A/51/18 (1996), [331]; Ghana, A/55/18 (2000), [379].

[350] HRC, Concluding Observations: Thailand, A/60/40 (2005), [95(20)] and [95(23)].

[351] Supplementary Convention on the Abolition of Slavery, the Slave Trade, and Institutions and Practices Similar to Slavery (adopted 7 September 1956, 266 UNTS 3, 30 April 1957).

[352] CESCR, Concluding Observations: Mali, E/C.12/1994/17 (21 December 1994), [8]; Nepal, E/2002/22 (2002), [525] and [538].

falls to the Committee to elaborate the indicia of prohibited conduct. In the Committee's view, the term 'forced or compulsory labour' covers a range of conduct extending from, on the one hand, labour imposed on an individual by way of criminal sanction, notably in particularly coercive, exploitative or otherwise egregious conditions, through, on the other hand, to lesser forms of labour in circumstances where punishment as a comparable sanction is threatened if the labour directed is not performed…[353]

Relatively few individual communications have arisen in respect of Article 8. The HRC did not accept an argument that an unexpected tax liability, outside an employment contract, resulting in employees working under conditions they had not agreed to, amounted to forced labour.[354] Its approach to prison labour is discussed further below.

The HRC's concluding observations have highlighted various issues under Article 8, including bonded labour in India; debt bondage in rural areas in Brazil; slave-like exploitation of Haitian workers in the Dominican Republic; hereditary servitude in Mali; forced labour on communal projects in Tanzania; and the existence of legal provisions allowing forced labour in Luxembourg and Tanzania.[355]

Overwhelmingly, however, under Article 8 the HRC has been most concerned about the trafficking of women and the exploitation of children, discussed below. The same is true of the CESCR's observations on states in relation to the forced labour aspect of Article 6 of the ICESCR. In that regard, further international standards are relevant to the CESCR's understanding of the scope of forced labour. Article 11 of the CEDAW provides for women's free choice of employment, while Article 6 seeks to suppress trafficking in women and exploitation of female prostitution. The Protocol to Prevent, Suppress and Punish Trafficking in Persons, Especially Women and Children 2000[356] defines forced labour and the like as among the 'purposes' of human trafficking, in Article 3(a):

(a) 'Trafficking in persons' shall mean the recruitment, transportation, transfer, harbouring or receipt of persons, by means of the threat or use of force or other forms of coercion, of abduction, of fraud, of deception, of the abuse of power or of a position of vulnerability or of the giving or receiving of payments or benefits to achieve the consent of a person having control over another person, for the purpose of exploitation. Exploitation shall include, at a minimum, the exploitation of the prostitution of others or other forms of sexual exploitation, forced labour or services, slavery or practices similar to slavery, servitude or the removal of organs…

[353] *Faure v Australia*, HRC Communication No. 1036/2001 (31 October 2005).
[354] *Silvia et al v Zambia*, HRC Communication No. 825-8/98 (28 October 1998).
[355] HRC, Concluding Observations: India, A/52/40 (1997), [444]; Brazil, A/51/40 (1996), [319]; Dominican Republic, A/48/40 (1993), [464]; Mali, A/58/40 (2003), [81(16)]; United Republic of Tanzania, A/53/40 (1998), [393]; Luxembourg, A/48/40 (1993), [143]; United Republic of Tanzania, A/48/40 (1993), [184].
[356] Protocol to Prevent, Suppress and Punish Trafficking in Persons, Especially Women and Children, Supplementing the United Nations Convention against Transnational Organized Crime (adopted 15 November 2000, 2237 UNTS 319, entered into force 25 December 2003).

A person's purported consent to exploitation is vitiated if any of the above means is used.[357] In monitoring states, the CESCR has frequently criticized the various forms of labour exploitation of women. One common form involves women exploited as domestic helpers or servants, typically 'underpaid and treated as virtual slaves',[358] enjoying little right to rest, and sometimes deprived of their freedom of movement (for instance, where their employers confiscate their passports).[359] Forced labour imposed on female domestic workers has also been criticized by the HRC under Article 8 of the ICCPR.[360]

Another common form of forced labour and the like criticized by the CESCR is human trafficking, particularly for the purpose of forced prostitution.[361] Sometimes it involves corrupt law enforcement officials, as in Serbia and Montenegro.[362] Victims have also been found to lack support, as in Greece, where victims are often deported to their countries of origin, without procedural safeguards, rather than being granted a residence permit.[363] Trafficking and sexual exploitation of women has also been much criticized by the HRC under Article 8 of the ICCPR,[364] including failures to provide witness protection, shelters or raise awareness among law enforcement officials.[365] The CEDAW Committee has described prostitution as 'one of the most heinous forms of slavery',[366] and also criticized conflict-related abduction and sexual slavery of women and girls.[367]

EXCEPTIONS TO THE PROHIBITION ON FORCED LABOUR

The general prohibition on forced labour in ILO Convention No. 29 is subject to public purpose exceptions in Article 2(2), although unlike in the Slavery Convention the permissible public purposes are precisely enumerated and subject to extensive regulation (in Articles 3 to 24). Private individuals or companies are also no longer

[357] Protocol to Prevent, Suppress and Punish Trafficking in Persons, Article 3(b).

[358] CESCR, Concluding Observations: Sri Lanka, E/1999/22 (1999), [77].

[359] CESCR, Concluding Observations: Kuwait, E/2005/22 (2005), [190] and [210].

[360] HRC, Concluding Observations: Mali, A/58/40 (2003), [81(16)]–[81(18)]; Russian Federation, A/59/40 (2004), [64(10)].

[361] CESCR: Concluding Observations: Togo, E/2002/22 (2002), [317]; Greece, E/2005/22 (2004), [138] and [159]; Serbia and Montenegro, E/2006/22 (2006), [285] and [312].

[362] CESCR: Concluding Observations: Serbia and Montenegro, E/2006/22 (2006), [285] and [312].

[363] CESCR: Concluding Observations: Greece, E/2005/22 (2005), [138] and [159].

[364] HRC, Concluding Observations: Ukraine, A/57/40 (2002), [74(18)]; Azerbaijan, A/57/40 (2002), [77(15)]; Georgia, A/57/40 (2002), [78(15)]; Republic of Moldova, A/57/40 (2002), [84(10)]; Mali, A/58/40 (2003), [81(18)]; Russian Federation, A/59/40 (2004), [64(10)]; Latvia, A/59/40 (2004), [65(12)]; Germany, A/59/40 (2004), [68(18)]; Serbia and Montenegro, A/59/40 (2004), [75(16)]; Thailand, A/60/40 (2005), [95(20)]; Philippines, A/59/40 (2004), [63(13)]; Israel, A/53/40 (1998), [312]; Italy, A/53/40 (1998), [333]; Japan, A/54/40 (1999), [171]; Venezuela, A/56/40 (2001), [77(16)]; Croatia, A/56/40 (2001), [80(12)]; Czech Republic, A/56/40 (2001), [83(13)]; Democratic People's Republic of Korea, A/56/40 (2001), [86(26)].

[365] HRC, Concluding Observations: Serbia and Montenegro, A/59/40 (2004), [75(16)].

[366] CEDAW, Concluding Observations: Bolivia, A/50/38 (1996), [102].

[367] CEDAW, Concluding Observations: Uganda, A/57/38 (2002), [155] and [156].

permitted to use forced labour for private purposes (Articles 5 and 6). Article 2(2) sets out the exceptions:

Nevertheless, for the purposes of this Convention, the term *forced or compulsory labour* shall not include—

(a) any work or service exacted in virtue of compulsory military service laws for work of a purely military character;

(b) any work or service which forms part of the normal civic obligations of the citizens of a fully self-governing country;

(c) any work or service exacted from any person as a consequence of a conviction in a court of law, provided that the said work or service is carried out under the supervision and control of a public authority and that the said person is not hired to or placed at the disposal of private individuals, companies or associations;

(d) any work or service exacted in cases of emergency, that is to say, in the event of war or of a calamity or threatened calamity, such as fire, flood, famine, earthquake, violent epidemic or epizootic diseases, invasion by animal, insect or vegetable pests, and in general any circumstance that would endanger the existence or the well-being of the whole or part of the population;

(e) minor communal services of a kind which, being performed by the members of the community in the direct interest of the said community, can therefore be considered as normal civic obligations incumbent upon the members of the community, provided that the members of the community or their direct representatives shall have the right to be consulted in regard to the need for such services.

Article 8(3) of the ICCPR imports similarly worded exceptions into its prohibition on slavery, servitude and forced or compulsory labour:

3. (b) Paragraph 3(a) shall not be held to preclude, in countries where imprisonment with hard labour may be imposed as a punishment for a crime, the performance of hard labour in pursuance of a sentence to such punishment by a competent court;

(c) For the purpose of this paragraph the term 'forced or compulsory labour' shall not include:

(i) Any work or service, not referred to in sub-paragraph (b), normally required of a person who is under detention in consequence of a lawful order of a court, or of a person during conditional release from such detention;

(ii) Any service of a military character and, in countries where conscientious objection is recognized, any national service required by law of conscientious objectors;

(iii) Any service exacted in cases of emergency or calamity threatening the life or well-being of the community;

(iv) Any work or service which forms part of normal civil obligations.

Similar exceptions appear in the American Convention on Human Rights (Article 6(2) to (3)) and the Commonwealth of Independent States Convention on Human Rights (Article 4(3)).

Given that the prohibition on forced labour in Article 6 of the ICESCR is implicit in the freedom to choose employment, any exceptions to forced labour are equally not expressly articulated in Article 6 itself. However, Article 4 of the ICESCR allows states to limit a right by law, where compatible with the nature of the right, for the sole purpose of promoting the general welfare in a democratic society. In this way, Article 6 is able to accommodate the various public interest grounds on which work may be compelled pursuant to ILO standards and the exceptions expressed in Article 8(3) of the ICCPR.

Indeed, the exceptions in ILO Convention No. 29 have shaped the CESCR's notion of forced labour under Article 6 of the ICESCR, just as they have influenced the HRC's approach to Article 6 of the ICCPR and the application of similar exceptions in Article 4(3) of the ECHR.[368] Most commonly, the CESCR has dealt with prison labour, but has seldom addressed the other possible exceptions. Each of the main grounds of exception will be considered in turn, in the wider context of the relevant ILO, ICCPR and ECHR standards.

Naturally, any of the exceptions considered below cannot be applied on unlawfully discriminatory grounds. Thus, for instance, the ECtHR found unlawful the subjection of a Jehovah's Witness leader to civil service (where he conscientiously objected to military service) when comparable ministers of other faiths were not liable to it.[369] In another case, the ECtHR identified unlawful sex discrimination where men but not women were required to undertake civil service in the fire brigade.[370] For the same reasons, it is unlawful to discriminatorily require jury service of men but not women.[371] In a communication brought under the ICCPR, an author was unable to substantiate his claim that he was discriminated against based on his status as a prisoner because his prison labour was not remunerated at the same level as on the general labour market.[372]

Compulsory military service

ILO Convention No. 29 excludes 'compulsory military service…for work purely of a military character' from being regarded as forced labour. There are, however, various limitations on a state's right to conscript. First, compulsory service must be authorized by law and not instituted arbitrarily or summarily. The ILO thus faulted Myanmar for forcibly recruiting people into the *Tatmadaw* and militia groups where this did not occur pursuant to any laws,[373] including where civilians were co-opted into 'portering' for the military.[374] However, where national conscription laws exist, but their scope is unknown and evidence of recruitment

[368] Van Dijk et al, *Theory and Practice of the ECHR*, 445.

[369] *Grandrath v Germany* (App. 2299/64), 23 April 1965, (1965) 8 Yearbook ECHR 324; (1966) 10 Yearbook ECHR 626.

[370] *Schmidt v Germany*, A 291-B (1994) 18 EHRR 513, [23]–[29].

[371] *Zarb Adami v Malta* (2006)-VIII; 44 EHRR 49.

[372] *Radosevic v Germany*, HRC Communication No. 1292/2004 (22 July 2005), [7.2].

[373] ILO, *Forced Labour in Myanmar*, [489]. [374] ILO, *Forced Labour in Myanmar*, [485].

practices lacking, the ILO has given the state the benefit of the doubt by refusing to find a violation.[375]

Secondly, those liable to military service but not presently enlisted cannot be forced to labour on public works, since the exception is necessarily limited by and to its purpose, namely military service, as an ILO Commission of Inquiry explains:

> 208. ...There was general agreement [in the drafting of Convention No. 29] that compulsory military service as such should remain beyond the purview of the Convention. Considerable discussion however took place with regard to systems existing at the time in various territories, whereby persons liable to military service but not in fact incorporated in the armed forces might be called up for public works. It was pointed out that to sanction this form of labour implicitly by excluding it from the scope of the Convention would be to sanction a system which ran counter to the avowed purpose of the Convention—namely the abolition of forced or compulsory labour in all its forms, for public purposes as well as for private employers. It was also stressed that the reason and justification for compulsory military service was the necessity for national defence, but that no such reason or justification existed for imposing compulsory service obligations for the execution of public works. The Conference accordingly decided that compulsory military service should be excluded from the Convention only if used for work of a purely military character.[376]

Thirdly, voluntary, serving military personnel can, however, be required to perform non-military work in the regular course of their employment:

> 209. The Committee of Experts also recalled that the provisions of the 1930 Convention relating to compulsory military service do not apply to career servicemen. Consequently... the Convention is not opposed to the performance of non-military work by persons who are serving in the armed forces on a voluntary basis...

Unlike ILO Convention No. 29, Article 8(3)(c)(ii) of the ICCPR is not confined to *compulsory* military service, but extends to '[a]ny service of a military character', and the same is true of Article 4(3)(b) of the ECHR. Thus, under the latter instruments, a person who voluntarily joins the military for a predefined period, but who later wishes to resign early, is not subject to forced labour.[377]

Fourthly, the exception for compulsory military service does not, however, justify precluding personnel who originally chose to join the military from leaving it (subject to certain qualifications), because a worker's free choice of employment is 'inalienable':

> 209. ...the fact that compulsory military service is not covered by the Convention cannot be invoked to justify denying career servicemen the right to leave the service either at certain reasonable intervals or by means of notice of reasonable length. Although, in such cases, employment is originally the result of a freely concluded agreement, the worker's

[375] ILO, *Forced Labour in Myanmar*, [490]–[491]. [376] ILO, *Forced Labour in Myanmar*, [208].

[377] *W, X, Y and Z v UK* (Apps. 3435/67, 3436/67, 3437/67, 3438/67), 19 July 1968, (1968) 28 CD 109 ('*Boy Soldiers*' cases). This wider coverage may, however, be preferably understood as confined to cases where a person 'chooses' to undertake military service in place of a liability to perform compulsory military service, and does not apply to those who freely join the military in the same way as any other form of employment: van Dijk et al, *Theory and Practice of the ECHR*, 451–2.

right to free choice of employment remains inalienable. The Committee has accordingly considered that the effect of statutory provisions preventing termination of employment of indefinite duration by means of notice of reasonable length is to turn a contractual relationship based on the will of the parties into service by compulsion of law, and is thus incompatible with the Conventions relating to forced labour. This is also the case when a worker is required to serve beyond the expiry of a contract of fixed duration.[378]

In a case under Article 1(2) of the European Social Charter, the European Committee on Social Rights found that a compulsory service period of fifteen years for career army officers was excessive and contrary to the freedom to choose and leave an occupation.[379]

Finally, a question arises about the legal position of conscientious objectors. Article 8(3)(c)(ii) of the ICCPR provides an exception for 'any national service required by law of conscientious objectors', but only in countries where conscientious objection is recognized. It does not thus provide the basis for a right to conscientious objection as such. To the contrary, in 1985 the HRC relied upon the military service exception under Article 8 of the ICCPR to preclude recognition of conscientious objection under Article 18 of the ICCPR (freedom of conscience).[380] Since General Comment No. 22 of 1993, however, the HRC accepts in principle that Article 18 supports conscientious objection.[381]

Under the ICESCR, where conscientious objection is permitted, a requirement to perform civil service in place of military service would not amount to forced labour. Civil service in lieu of military service is permissible under the ECHR and European Social Charter.[382] While the 'less onerous' nature of civil service may justify a longer period than of military service, it must still come within reasonable limits and not unduly infringe on the right to freely earn a living in a freely chosen occupation; eighteen more months is too long.[383]

Concerning the basis for conscientious objection itself, the ICESCR contains no provision on freedom of conscience equivalent to Article 18 of the ICCPR. However, Article 5(2) of the ICESCR provides that the fact that the ICESCR does not recognize a fundamental human right found elsewhere, including under other conventions, or recognizes it to a lesser extent, does not justify the restriction of that right. It is therefore open to the CESCR to recognize that conscientious objection, and the freedom of conscience it expresses, is a legitimate exception to any liability to military conscription permitted, as an exception to the prohibition on forced labour, under Article 6 of the ICESCR.

[378] ILO, *Forced Labour in Myanmar*, [209].

[379] *International Federation of Human Rights v Greece*, ECSR Complaint No. 7/2000 (15 December 2000), [5].

[380] *LTK v Finland*, HRC Communication No. 185/84 (9 July 1985), [5.2].

[381] HRC, General Comment No. 22, The right to freedom of thought, conscience and religion (Article 18), CCPR/C/21/Rev.1/Add.4 (30 July 1993), [11].

[382] ECHR, Article 4(3)(b); see, eg, *Johansen v Norway* (App. 10600/83), 14 October 1985, DR 44, 155; *Quaker Council for European Affairs v Greece*, ECSR Complaint No. 8/2000 (25 April 2001), [2]–[4].

[383] *Quaker Council for European Affairs v Greece*, [4].

Prison labour

Prison labour is the most common issue confronted by the CESCR in relation to the forced labour aspect of Article 6. As noted above, ILO Convention No. 29 allows work 'exacted from any person as a consequence of a conviction in a court of law' and as long as it is supervized by a public authority and not performed for private actors. These requirements of a conviction and work for public authorities are 'important guarantees against the administration of the penal system being diverted from its true course by coming to be considered as a means of meeting labour requirements'.[384]

Thus, work assignments given to prisoners soon before their release, but which would extend beyond the end of their sentence, can no longer be regarded as the consequence of a conviction.[385] The ILO's requirement of a conviction does not, however, presuppose that the sentence itself mandates labour, but envisages that work may be required as part of the state's penal policy within prisons.

Article 8 of the ICCPR refers more broadly to 'any detention in consequence of a lawful order of a court, or of a person during conditional release from such detention'. It is seemingly not limited to imprisonment following a criminal conviction, but may extend to other kinds of judicially authorized detention (such as administrative detention for mental health or immigration purposes) or conditional release (such as pre-trial bail or post-prison parole). Article 4 of the ECHR is similarly not limited to convicted persons, but extends to detainees generally, such as where vagrants are forced to work in vagrancy centres.[386]

Few situations in this regard have arisen under the twin covenants. The HRC found factually unsubstantiated a claim by a detainee awaiting sentencing that he was subjected to forced labour.[387] But it did not directly address the legal question of whether forced labour is unlawful if imposed on un-sentenced prisoners, or by extension, on other detainees involved in criminal or non-criminal processes, as long as detention is judicially authorized.

What is clear is that forced labour cannot be lawful in situations of administrative detention without judicial authorization or review. The CESCR was 'gravely concerned about the use of forced labour as a corrective measure, without charge, trial or review, under China's "Re-education through Labour" (*laodong jiaoyang*) programme' and called for it to be abolished.[388] A similar analysis could be applied to other forms of administrative detention which are not judicially authorized or controlled, such as summary immigration detention.

From a human rights perspective, by their nature most forms of administrative detention—even those which *are* judicially controlled—would not easily warrant the imposition of forced labour, whether for immigration or mental health purposes. For this reason, the ILO's restrictive approach—confining forced labour

[384] ILO, *Forced Labour in Myanmar*, [211]. [385] ILO, *Forced Labour in Myanmar*, [483].

[386] *De Wilde, Ooms and Versyp v Belgium* ('*Vagrancy*' cases), 18 June 1971, (1971) 1 EHRR 373, [89]–[90].

[387] *Wolf v Panama*, HRC Communication No. 289/88 (1992), [6.8].

[388] CESCR, Concluding Observations: China, E/C.12/1/Add.107 (13 May 2005), [22] and [51].

to the criminally convicted—is a preferable approach for the CESCR to follow than the wider possibilities permitted under the ECHR or (arguably) the ICCPR.

It is, however, apparent under the ICCPR and ECHR that any compulsory labour must be directed towards the rehabilitation of a detainee, whether as an incident of a criminal conviction or, for instance, where vagrants are required to work in a vagrancy centre.[389] The HRC stated as follows in *Radosevic v Germany*:

7.3. …article 8, paragraph 3(c)(i), read in conjunction with article 10, paragraph 3, of the Covenant requires that work performed by prisoners primarily aims at their social rehabilitation, as indicated by the word 'normally' in article 8, paragraph 3(c)(i), but does not specify whether such measures would include adequate remuneration for work performed by prisoners. While reiterating that, rather than being only retributory, penitentiary systems should seek the reformation and social rehabilitation of prisoners, the Committee notes that States may themselves choose the modalities for ensuring that treatment of prisoners, including any work or service normally required of them, is essentially directed at these aims…[390]

While the German courts had already found that adequate remuneration was essential to a prisoner's resocialization, the HRC inexplicably allowed the state a transitional period within which to increase wages.[391] Article 14 of ILO Convention No. 29 requires that 'forced or compulsory labour of all kinds shall be remunerated in cash at rates not less than those prevailing for similar kinds of work' elsewhere.

In the context of the range of standards above, a number of threads emerge from the practice of the CESCR in monitoring states. First, the CESCR has opposed the use of forced labour as a 'punitive measure for convicts' ordered by a court,[392] 'as a corrective measure or as a penal sentence against persons found guilty of a crime',[393] or as practice in prisons,[394] particularly for children or in respect of petty offences.[395] Related to this, secondly the CESCR has called on states to obtain the consent of prisoners to work.[396]

In these respects, while the CESCR has often invoked ILO standards, it appears to take a more restrictive approach to prison labour—opposing forced prison labour altogether, and generally calling for the prisoner's consent. This may also be contrasted with the more permissive approach under the American Convention

389 *De Wilde, Ooms and Versyp v Belgium* ('*Vagrancy*' cases), 18 June 1971, (1971) 1 EHRR 373, [89]–[90].

390 *Radosevic v Germany*, HRC Communication No. 1292/2004, (22 July 2005), [7.3].

391 See Joseph, 'UN Covenants and Labour Rights', 354.

392 CESCR, Concluding Observations: Kazakhstan, E/C.12/KAZ/CO/1 (7 June 2010), [16].

393 CESCR, Concluding Observations: Azerbaijan, E/C.12/1/Add.104 (14 December 2004), [19]; China (including HK, Macao), E/C.12/1/Add.107 (13 May 2005), [22]; Syrian Arab Republic, E/C.12/1/Add.63 (24 September 2001), [18].

394 CESCR, Concluding Observations: Syrian Arab Republic, E/2002/22 (2001), [408] and [424]; Estonia, E/C.12/1/Add.85 (19 December 2002), [13].

395 CESCR, Concluding Observations: Syrian Arab Republic, E/2002/22 (2001), 67, [408] and [424].

396 CESCR, Concluding Observations: Kazakhstan, E/C.12/KAZ/CO/1 (7 June 2010), [16]; Estonia, E/C.12/1/Add.85 (19 December 2002), [35].

on Human Rights, which allows forced labour as a penalty for a criminal conviction 'in those countries' where it is used (Article 6(2)).

Thirdly, the CESCR has criticized states for imposing forced labour for crimes of conscience, expressing political opinions or ideological opposition, participation in 'illegal' strikes, or as labour discipline.[397] This is consistent with the express prohibitions in ILO Convention No. 105. Fourthly, it has criticized compelling prisoners to work on national food production programmes or to levy taxes.[398] Certainly, such purposes would not appear to be directed towards a prisoner's rehabilitation, and national food production may be more properly considered under the separate exception for 'normal civic obligations'.

Fifthly, the CESCR has stated that prisoners may only work for private companies by prior consent and where the 'conditions of work (including wages and social security) must be close to those of a free employment relationship'.[399] In this regard, it has expressly invoked ILO Convention No. 29,[400] Article 2 of which prohibits prisoners from being 'hired to' or 'placed at the disposal of' private actors.[401] The American Convention on Human Rights likewise prohibits prison labour for private actors (Article 6(3)(e)). The CESCR, ILO and Inter-American position contrasts with that under the ECHR and the CIS Human Rights Convention, which do not prohibit compulsory labour of detainees for private actors.

Sixthly, given the contemporary reality of privatized prisons in some states, the CESCR has demanded that labour in private prisons is voluntarily undertaken and properly remunerated.[402] In this respect, the CESCR has taken a restrictive approach. It precludes altogether private prisons from compelling prisoners to work, even though states may have delegated their sovereign detention authority to private actors, and even if compulsory work would be beneficial to a prisoner's rehabilitation—just as it would be in a public facility.

Given that prisoners must be fairly remunerated regardless of whether the facility is public or private, the CESCR's position appears to be opposed to private companies profiting from prison labour, and/or to the state delegating its sovereign power to detain. It perhaps has less to do with a human rights rationale, for the prisoner's autonomy is equally infringed by a public prison compelling him or her to work as by a private facility authorized by law to exercise the public power to detain.

As noted earlier, however, given the CESCR's apparent departure from ILO standards even in respect of compulsory work in public prisons, the distinction

[397] CESCR, Concluding Observations: Tunisia, E/C.12/1/Add.36 (14 May 1999), [25]; Iraq, E/1998/22 (1997), [259] and [275].

[398] CESCR, Concluding Observations: Democratic Republic of Congo, E/C.12/COD/CO/4 (16 September 2009), [21].

[399] CESCR, Concluding Observations: Luxembourg, E/C.12/1/Add.86 (26 June 2003), [32]; see also Germany, E/C.12/1/Add.68 (24 September 2001), [21] and [39].

[400] CESCR, Concluding Observations: Luxembourg, E/C.12/1/Add.86 (26 June 2003), [20].

[401] On interpretation of these phrases, see ILO, *Eradication of Forced Labour*, 28–9.

[402] CESCR, Concluding Observations: Australia, E/2001/22 (2000), [395]; see also ILO, *Eradication of Forced Labour*, 58–67.

it has drawn here is one without difference: consent and fair pay are required in both cases. This approach contrasts with that under Article 4 of the ECHR, which is held not to address prisoners' remuneration.[403]

Emergencies

Thus far, the CESCR has not considered whether forced labour may be justified by an emergency. Work or service demanded 'in cases of emergency' is permitted under Article 2(2)(d) of ILO Convention No. 29. The ICCPR provides for a similar exception for '[a]ny service exacted in cases of emergency or calamity threatening the life or well-being of the community' (Article 8(3)(c)(iii)), and a comparable formula is found in Article 4(3)(c) of the ECHR ('emergency or calamity threatening the life or well-being of the community'). ILO Convention No. 29 provides illustrative examples of what is meant by an emergency:

> …that is to say, in the event of war or of a calamity or threatened calamity, such as fire, flood, famine, earthquake, violent epidemic or epizootic diseases, invasion by animal, insect or vegetable pests, and in general any circumstance that would endanger the existence or the well-being of the whole or part of the population…[404]

It would seem that the concept of an emergency in the context of forced labour is not co-extensive with the higher threshold of a 'public emergency threatening the life of the nation' which permits derogation from certain rights under Article 4 of the ICCPR. Rather, it is an exception which operates within the ordinary framework of rights, including where an emergency has more localized effects on the 'community' rather than the 'nation'. Thus, under the ECHR it was accepted that a person who held shooting rights over land could be compelled to participate in the gassing of foxholes to control the rabies disease.[405]

At the same time, the concept of emergency should not be stretched too far. In one ECHR case, it was suggested (by a minority) that even a shortage of dentists in a remote area of Norway could constitute an emergency so as to justify compelling dentists to serve there.[406] Critics have noted that 'structural inconveniences' such as these are not the stuff of an emergency,[407] which connotes a sudden, temporary, acute problem—and not merely the predictable prevalence of bad teeth. As an ILO Commission of Inquiry observed:

> 212. …the concept of emergency—as indicated by the enumeration of examples in the Convention—involves a sudden, unforeseen happening calling for instant counter-measures. To respect the limits of the exception provided for in the Convention, the power to call up labour should be confined to genuine cases of emergency. Moreover, the duration and

[403] *Twenty-one Detained Persons v Germany* (Apps. 3134/67, 3172/67, 3188-3206/67), ECtHR 6 April 1968.

[404] ILO Convention No. 29, Article 2(2)(d).

[405] *S v Federal Republic of Germany* (App. 9686/82), 39 DR 90 (1984).

[406] *Iversen v Norway* (App. 1468/62), 6 Yearbook 278 (1963).

[407] Van Dijk et al, *Theory and Practice of the ECHR*, 452.

extent of compulsory service, as well as the purpose for which it is used, should be limited to what is strictly required by the exigencies of the situation.[408]

In a case under Article 1(2) of the European Social Charter (concerning the right of workers to earn a living in a freely chosen occupation), the European Committee on Social Rights found that a decree mobilizing the civilian population 'in any unforseen situation causing disruption of the country's economy and society' was too general.[409]

In relation to Myanmar, the ILO Commission of Inquiry implied that a series of armed conflicts between the government and ethnic groups may no longer constitute an 'emergency' where the government stated it was 'no longer conducting military campaigns'.[410] Moreover, the ILO interpreted the forced labour exception restrictively even in armed conflict, finding that the requisition of civilians to perform tasks for the military (such as acting as porters, guides, human shields, minesweepers and sentries) was not 'in reaction to a case of emergency', but 'was merely the habitual way for the armed forces and paramilitary units to shift to the civilian population the burden of any labour they wished to be done and which otherwise would have to be performed by army personnel'.[411] Further, the ILO found that the danger posed by the emergency of an armed conflict was precisely

> …the kind of danger for which the exigencies of the situation would call on the military to protect the civilian population, while the forced labour exacted in Myanmar in such cases shifts the dangerous tasks from the military to the civilian population. This is contrary to the concept of 'emergency' expressed in the Convention. In Myanmar, the civilian population is forced to protect the military.[412]

Normal civic obligations and minor communal service

Article 8(3)(c)(iv) of the ICCPR excludes from the ambit of forced labour '[a]ny work or service which forms part of normal civil obligations'. It would appear to combine two related exceptions under ILO Convention No. 29, namely 'any work or service which forms part of the normal civic obligations of the citizens of a fully self-governing country' (Article 2(2)(b)) and 'minor communal services' under Article 2(2)(e):

> …minor communal services of a kind which, being performed by the members of the community in the direct interest of the said community, can therefore be considered as normal civic obligations incumbent upon the members of the community, provided that the members of the community or their direct representatives shall have the right to be consulted in regard to the need for such services.

[408] ILO, *Forced Labour in Myanmar*, [212].

[409] *International Federation of Human Rights v Greece*, ECSR Complaint No. 7/2000 (15 December 2000), [5].

[410] *International Federation of Human Rights v Greece*, [486]; see also [488].

[411] *International Federation of Human Rights v Greece*, [486] and [488].

[412] *International Federation of Human Rights v Greece*, [488].

Normal civic work can include categories already discussed above, such as compulsory military service or work in an emergency.[413] Otherwise, the appreciation of what are 'normal' civic obligations does not involve a rigid, universal standard, but is contextual and may vary from society to society, place to place or even sector by sector.

It has been found to include activities such as compulsory jury service, fire service and 'the duty to assist a person in danger or to assist in the enforcement of law and order'.[414] The exception has also sustained obligations on: a lessor to maintain a building;[415] a holder of shooting rights in land to gas foxholes to prevent a rabies epidemic;[416] and companies to calculate and deduct taxes and social security contributions from employees' salaries.[417]

As noted earlier, under Article 4 of the ECHR, civic obligations inherent in certain professions have been found not to involve 'forced' labour so that consideration of the civic obligation exception was unnecessary. However, in some cases it has been suggested that if such duties can be said to involve 'compulsory' work, they might still be supported by the civic obligations exception in the context of what is ordinarily required by members of those professions. Examples include the provision of legal aid by private lawyers[418] or an obligation on medical professionals to conduct free medical examinations.[419]

Further, the ILO acknowledged the potential relevance of Buddhist values in assessing labour contributions in Myanmar:

> 298. …there was information before the Commission regarding the relationship between Buddhist values and labour contribution. The information indicated that while various deeds, including contribution of labour for certain purposes, were considered noble and meritorious according to the values held by Buddhists in Myanmar, it was not the case that labour for roads or bridges, or forced labour of any kind, could be considered noble and meritorious in this way. According to the information received, Buddhism was clear as to which kinds of acts were meritorious, and such things as construction of roads and bridges could not be considered among them; Buddhism was also clear that merit came not from the act itself, but from the intentions of the person in carrying out the act, so that an act which was forced to be carried out could not be considered meritorious. Furthermore, since much of the forced labour in the country was exacted from non-Buddhist ethnic people, considerations of this kind were irrelevant in these cases.[420]

Cultural rights of minority groups or indigenous peoples may also be relevant in assessing whether work may be considered 'forced' in the context of those communities.[421]

[413] *International Federation of Human Rights v Greece*, [210].

[414] *International Federation of Human Rights v Greece*, [210]; see also *Zarb Adami v Malta* (2006)-VIII, 44 EHRR 49 (jury service); *Schmidt v Germany*, A 291-B, 18 July 1994, 18 EHRR 513, [22] (fire service).

[415] *X v Austria* (App. 5593/72), 11 December 1973, (1973) 45 CD 113.

[416] *S v Federal Republic of Germany* (App. 9686/82), 4 October 1984, (1984) 39 DR 90.

[417] *Four Companies v Austria* (App. 7427/76), 27 September 1976, 7 DR 148 (1976).

[418] *Van der Mussele v Belgium* (App. 8919/80), 23 November 1983, (1983) 6 EHRR 163.

[419] *Reitmayr v Austria* (App. 23866/94), 28 June 1995, (1995) 20 EHRR CD 89.

[420] ILO, *Forced Labour in Myanmar*, [298].

[421] See, eg, UNGA Res. 61/295, Declaration on the Rights of Indigenous Peoples (2 October 2007), Article 35: 'Indigenous peoples have the right to determine the responsibilities of individuals to their communities.'

According to the ILO Committee of Experts, minor communal services are subject to the following stringent criteria:

- the services must be 'minor services', i.e. relate primarily to maintenance work and, in exceptional cases, to the erection of certain buildings intended to improve the social conditions of the population of the community itself (a small school, a medical consultation and treatment room, etc.);
- the services must be 'communal services' performed 'in the direct interest of the community', and not relate to the execution of works intended to benefit a wider group;
- the 'members of the community' (i.e. the community which has to perform the services) or their 'direct' representatives (e.g. the village council) must 'have the right to be consulted in regard to the need for such services'.[422]

While the CESCR has not yet set out its general legal approach to civic obligations, in *Faure v Australia* the HRC outlined the legal parameters of the concept under the ICCPR:

> 7.5 ...In the Committee's view, to so qualify as a normal civil obligation, the labour in question must, at a minimum, not be an exceptional measure; it must not possess a punitive purpose or effect; and it must be provided for by law in order to serve a legitimate purpose under the Covenant.[423]

With scant reasoning, in that communication the HRC found that a 'Work for the Dole' programme, which required a person to undertake specified work to receive unemployment benefits (including, for instance, concreting), was not forced labour, including because the work was not 'degrading or dehumanizing'.[424] The state had argued that the programme aimed to enhance the person's skills, experience, self-esteem, employability and future self-sufficiency.[425] It was also said to be 'based on the concept of mutual obligation between an unemployed person and the community supporting him or her', whereby the work projects 'provide real tangible benefits to communities in the form of community facilities, infrastructure, care and assistance'.[426] The individual opinion of HRC member Ruth Wedgwood went further:

> In a world that is still replete with problems of caste, customary systems of peonage and indentured labor, forced labor in remote areas under conditions that often mimic slavery, and the disgrace of sexual trafficking in persons, it demeans the significance of the International Covenant on Civil and Political Rights to suppose that a reasonable work and training requirement for participation in national unemployment benefits in a modern welfare state could amount to 'forced or compulsory labor' within the meaning of Article 8(3)(a).[427]

[422] ILO, *Forced Labour in Myanmar*, [213].
[423] *Faure v Australia*, HRC Communication No. 1036/2001 (31 October 2005), [7.5].
[424] *Faure v Australia*, [7.5]. [425] *Faure v Australia*, [4.12] and [4.15].
[426] *Faure v Australia*, [4.15].
[427] *Faure v Australia*, Individual Opinion of HRC member Ruth Wedgwood.

The HRC's position has been criticized.[428] Depending on their design and implementation, such programmes may overstate the extent of mutual reciprocity or the problem of welfare abuse, and under-protect a person's freedom to choose suitable employment. They may also have a discriminatory gender impact, as where eligibility rules do not recognize a mother's 'work' (including childcare) at home.[429] Work assignments are particularly questionable where they have a punitive element, or do not align with a person's skills or career aspirations and have not been crafted in consultation with them.

Nonetheless, under Article 4 of the ECHR restrictions on the right to freely choose work have also been accepted in the social security context. In *Schuitemaker v Netherlands*, it did not involve forced labour to require a social security beneficiary to accept 'generally accepted' work rather than 'suitable' work to receive benefits:

> …it must in general be accepted that where a State has introduced a system of social security, it is fully entitled to lay down conditions which have to be met for a person to be eligible for benefits pursuant to that system. In particular a condition to the effect that a person must make demonstrable efforts in order to obtain and take up generally accepted employment cannot be considered unreasonable in this respect. This is the more so given that Dutch legislation provides that recipients of benefits pursuant to the Work and Social Assistance Act are not required to seek and take up employment which is not generally socially accepted or in respect of which they have conscientious objections. Therefore, the condition at issue cannot be equated with compelling a person to perform forced or compulsory labour within the meaning of Article 4 § 2 of the Convention.[430]

It is arguable that the ECHR has allowed states too much discretion in the design of social security (which is not a right recognized under the ECHR), at least from the perspective of Articles 6 (freedom to choose work) and 9 (social security rights) of the ICESCR. Indeed, the CESCR has taken a more restrictive approach to the permissibility of such programmes, implying that they may violate Articles 2, 6 and 9 of the ICESCR, although it has stopped short of stating that they constitute forced labour. The CESCR found that Canada's 'workfare' programmes cannot unlawfully undercut international labour protections, or discriminate based on age or social origin:

> 30. The Committee notes with concern that at least six provinces in Canada (including Quebec and Ontario) have adopted 'workfare' programmes that either tie the right to social assistance to compulsory employment schemes or reduce the level of benefits when recipients, who are usually young, assert their right to choose freely what type of work they wish to do. In many cases, these programmes constitute work without the protection of fundamental labour rights and labour standards legislation. The Committee further notes that in the case of the Province of Quebec, those workfare schemes are implemented despite the opinion of the Human Rights Commission and the decisions of the Human Rights Tribunal that those programmes constitute discrimination based on social status or age.[431]

[428] Joseph, 'UN Covenants and Labour Rights', 353.
[429] Mundlak, 'The Right to Work—The Value of Work', 352.
[430] *Schuitemaker v Netherlands* (App. 15906/08), ECtHR 4 May 2010.
[431] CESCR, Concluding Observations: Canada, E/C.12/1993/5 (10 June 1993), [30].

In other contexts, the CESCR has seldom considered whether a person can be compelled to work in the performance of normal civil obligations. One example is where the CESCR was concerned, without further explanation, that 'the obligatory civic work programme known as Salongo is still widely practised' in the Democratic Republic of Congo.[432] Salongo was a colonial 'adaptation and perversion of a traditional custom of communal labor in service of a local tribal leader or on public works', revived by the Mobutu regime in the 1970s for agriculture and development projects.[433] Recently, it has been imposed by military and rebel groups, which have required civilians to build houses, clean camps, transport goods, collect firewood or work in mines,[434] for one or even two days per week, and under threat of fines, arrest, beatings, torture or death.[435]

The CESCR's approach is consistent with that taken by the ILO. The concepts of normal civic obligations and minor community service cannot justify forced labour in pursuit of national development, public infrastructure or military objectives. ILO Convention No. 29 expressly prohibits forced labour on agricultural production, except in case of famine and then only for the benefit of those undertaking the work (Article 19(1)). Thus, it was unlawful for Myanmar to compel villagers to grow and harvest cash crops to profit the military.[436]

The ILO Commission of Inquiry on Mynamar further found that other activities required of civilians by military forces in Myanmar were not part of normal civic obligations or minor communal service. These included the construction, maintenance and repair of military camps; cooking, cleaning, washing clothes and collecting water or firewood; and acting as messengers, guides, human shields, minesweepers and sentries for the military.[437]

In relation to forced labour on public infrastructure, the ILO found that most such instances in Myanmar were also not justified by the civic obligations or communal service exceptions. These included work on roads, railways, bridges, dams, power stations, canals, irrigation projects, airports, electricity lines, museums, palaces, pagodas and monasteries, stadiums, fences, sport facilities, helipads, hotels, telecommunications, villages, schools, clinics, toilets and cleaning.[438]

A number of legal factors explain the ILO's conclusion.[439] First, the 'sheer size' of some projects demonstrates that they were designed to meet national or regional needs rather than local communal ones. Secondly, the various projects

[432] CESCR, Concluding Observations: Democratic Republic of Congo, E/C.12/COD/CO/4 (16 September 2009), [21].

[433] Free the Slaves, *The Congo Report: Slavery in Minerals* (June 2011), 13.

[434] See, eg, US Department of State, *2011 Human Rights Report: Democratic Republic of the Congo*, 24 May 2012, <http://www.state.gov/j/drl/rls/hrrpt/2011/af/186183.htm>; Human Rights Watch, *The Curse of Gold: Democratic Republic of Congo* (New York, 2005), 48; and Free the Slaves, *The Congo Report*, 13.

[435] Human Rights Watch, *The Curse of Gold*, 48; Free the Slaves, *The Congo Report*, 13.

[436] ILO, *Forced Labour in Myanmar*, [513].

[437] ILO, *Forced Labour in Myanmar*, [351]–[373], [374]–[388] and [487].

[438] ILO, *Forced Labour in Myanmar*, [493]–[502].

[439] ILO, *Forced Labour in Myanmar*, [495]–[499].

were often not 'minor', but involved large numbers of workers, a high number of workdays and a wide geographical spread. Thirdly, the projects often did not benefit the workers or local communities, but were for the benefit of the military, authorities or the wider national community. Fourthly, the work was imposed without consultation with affected communities. Finally, the labour demands were unduly burdensome because the work required was often far from the workers' villages, the volume of work demanded unreasonable and the conditions of work inadequate.

The ILO acknowledged that the building of a new primary school, clinic or public toilet in a village, or digging drainage ditches in a town could in principle be 'minor communal service' of benefit to those communities.[440] However, it found that such work 'must relate primarily to maintenance work and only in exceptional cases to the building of new facilities and should not normally exceed a few days per year'.[441] By contrast, Myanmarese were called up once a week or three times a month, for one or two days, 'far' exceeding what is permitted.[442] Some were also required to perform other forced labour while being required to build a local school. The ILO further criticized 'the authoritarian manner in which the villagers were ordered to do the work' and the lack of consultation with the community or their representatives.[443]

The ILO also accepts in principle that cleaning and beautifying public areas, roads, schools, hospitals or a lake shore could be minor communal service of local benefit (in contrast to cleaning or portering for military camps).[444] But it is excessive to call up one person per household for one day per weekend, particularly absent consultation.

AN OBLIGATION OF IMMEDIATE EFFECT

Most of Article 6 is subject to progressive realization by states. In General Comment No. 18, the CESCR identifies only non-discrimination and the duty 'to take steps' to fully realize the right to work as obligations of 'immediate effect'.[445] It apparently does not regard the prohibition on forced labour, implicit in the freedom to choose one's work, as an obligation of immediate effect. Whether a result of deliberation or omission, that position is unsupportable. A number of considerations powerfully indicate that the prohibition on forced labour is one of immediate effect.

As a civil right, the prohibition on forced labour under Article 8 of the ICCPR has immediate effect and as far as possible the ICESCR must be harmoniously interpreted in the 'context' of its sibling covenant. Further, ILO Convention No. 29 admittedly requires states to suppress forced labour 'within the shortest possible time'. However, that transitional qualification was primarily directed

440 ILO, *Forced Labour in Myanmar*, [501].
441 ILO, *Forced Labour in Myanmar*, [501].
442 ILO, *Forced Labour in Myanmar*, [501].
443 ILO, *Forced Labour in Myanmar*, [501].
444 ILO, *Forced Labour in Myanmar*, [501] and [502]; see also [486].
445 CESCR, General Comment No. 18, [19] and [33].

towards allowing leeway for colonizing states to totally suppress it.[446] In 1998, an ILO Commission of Inquiry confirmed that the provision—adopted in 1930—can no longer be understood to allow the persistence of forced labour pending its future progressive suppression,[447] but is rather to be understood as an obligation of immediate effect.

Moreover, the ILO regards the prohibition of forced labour as a fundamental right which all ILO member states must respect, regardless of whether they are parties to ILO conventions dealing with it.[448] A prohibition on forced labour is also found in most regional human rights systems, including the European, Inter-American, African, Arab and Commonwealth of Independent States treaties.[449] An ILO Commission of Inquiry even described the prohibition as a *jus cogens* (peremptory) norm, involving a fundamental interest of the international community:

> 203. The Commission concludes that there exists now in international law a peremptory norm prohibiting any recourse to forced labour and that the right not to be compelled to perform forced or compulsory labour is one of the basic human rights. A State which supports, instigates, accepts or tolerates forced labour on its territory commits a wrongful act for which it bears international responsibility; furthermore, this wrongful act results from a breach of an international obligation that is so essential for the protection of the fundamental interests of the international community that it could be qualified, if committed on a widespread scale, as an international crime under the terms of article 19 of the draft articles of the International Law Commission on state responsibility. Similarly, the International Court of Justice has qualified the obligation to protect the human person against slavery as an obligation *erga omnes* since, in view of the importance of this right, all States can be held to have a legal interest in its protection.[450]

Under international criminal law, individual criminal liability exists for certain types of forced labour in defined circumstances. Crimes against humanity under Article 7(1) of the Rome Statute of the International Criminal Court relevantly include enslavement, sexual slavery, enforced prostitution, persecution and other inhumane acts causing great suffering.[451] While enslavement is defined by reference to the traditional indicia of slavery (the powers attaching to the right of ownership, but expressly including human trafficking),[452] it is also interpreted to

[446] ILO, *Forced Labour in Myanmar*, [214]. [447] ILO, *Forced Labour in Myanmar*, [218].

[448] ILO Declaration on Fundamental Principles and Rights at Work (June 1988), [2].

[449] Council of Europe, Convention for the Protection of Human Rights and Fundamental Freedoms (adopted 4 November 1950, 213 UNTS 221, entered into force 3 September 1953) ('European Convention on Human Rights' or 'ECHR'), Article 4; Organization of American States, American Convention on Human Rights (adopted 22 November 1969, 1144 UNTS 123, entered into force 18 July 1978), Article 6 (slavery and forced labour); Organization of African Unity, African Charter on Human and Peoples' Rights (adopted 27 June 1981, 1520 UNTS 217, entered into force 21 October 1986), Articles 5 (prohibition on 'exploitation and degradation of man, including slavery') and 15 (right to work); League of Arab States, Arab Charter on Human Rights (adopted 22 May 2004, entered into force 15 March 2008), Article 31 (forced labour); Commonwealth of Independent States, Commonwealth of Independent States Convention on Human Rights and Fundamental Freedoms (adopted 26 May 1995, entered into force 11 August 1998), Article 4 (slavery and forced labour).

[450] ILO, *Forced Labour in Myanmar*, [203]–[204]. [451] See also the ICTY and ICTR Statutes.

[452] Rome Statute of the International Criminal Court (adopted 17 July 1998, 2187 UNTS 3, entered into force 1 July 2002) ('ICC Statute'), Article 7(2)(c).

extend to forced labour.[453] Such acts must be committed as part of a widespread or systematic attack on a civilian population or part thereof. The existence of war crimes liability for forced labour in armed conflicts, discussed below, also supports the view that the ICESCR prohibition on forced labour is of immediate effect.

INTERNATIONAL HUMANITARIAN LAW

In situations of armed conflict, the special norms of international humanitarian law (IHL) complement Article 6 of the ICESCR[454] and prohibit forced labour in certain contexts. In *international* conflicts,[455] prisoners of war (that is, captured combatants) cannot be forcibly conscripted to fight for the enemy or compelled to work on military preparations or operations,[456] although they can be required to work for various non-military purposes.[457] For example, Article 50 of Geneva Convention III of 1949 provides:

> Besides work connected with camp administration, installation or maintenance, prisoners of war may be compelled to do only such work as is included in the following classes:
>
> (a) agriculture;
>
> (b) industries connected with the production or the extraction of raw materials, and manufacturing industries, with the exception of metallurgical, machinery and chemical industries; public works and building operations which have no military character or purpose;
>
> (c) transport and handling of stores which are not military in character or purpose;
>
> (d) commercial business, and arts and crafts;

[453] ICC, Elements of Crimes: Article 7(1)(c), [1] and note 11; *Prosecutor v Kunarac (Judgment)*, IT-96-23-T and IT-96-23/1-T, ICTY Trial Chamber (22 February 2001), [541] and [542].

[454] *Armed Activities on the Territory of the Congo (Democratic Republic of the Congo v Uganda)* (2005) ICJ Rep 168, [216]; *Legal Consequences of the Construction of a Wall in Occupied Palestinian Territory (Advisory Opinion)* (2004) ICJ Rep 136, [106]–[113]; *Legality of the Threat or Use of Nuclear Weapons (Advisory Opinion)* (1996) ICJ Rep 226, [25].

[455] Defined by Common Article 2 of the four 1949 Geneva Conventions: Geneva Convention for the Amelioration of the Condition of the Wounded and Sick in Armed Forces in the Field (adopted 12 August 1949, 75 UNTS 31, entered into force 21 October 1951) ('GC I'); Geneva Convention for the Amelioration of the Condition of Wounded, Sick and Shipwrecked Members of Armed Forces at Sea (adopted 12 August 1949, 75 UNTS 85, entered into force 21 October 1950) ('GC II'); Geneva Convention Relative to the Treatment of Prisoners of War (adopted 12 August 1949, 75 UNTS 135, entered into force 21 October 1950) ('GC III'); Geneva Convention Relative to the Protection of Civilian Persons in Time of War (adopted 12 August 1949, 75 UNTS 287, entered into force 21 October 1950) ('GC IV').

[456] Regulations Respecting the Laws and Customs of War on Land ('Hague Regulations') annexed to the Convention Respecting the Laws and Customs of War on Land (adopted 18 October 1907, entered into force 26 January 1910), Article 23(2); Convention Relative to the Treatment of Prisoners of War, with Annex (adopted 27 July 1929, 118 LNTS 303, entered into force 19 June 1931), Article 31(1) ('it is forbidden to employ prisoners in the manufacture or transport of arms or munitions of any kind, or on the transport of material destined for combatant units').

[457] Hague Regulations, Article 6 (prisoners' work 'shall have no connection with the operations of the war'); Convention Relative to the Treatment of Prisoners of War 1929, Articles 27–34; GC III, Articles 49–57.

(e) domestic service;

(f) public utility services having no military character or purpose.

Should the above provisions be infringed, prisoners of war shall be allowed to exercise their right of complaint, in conformity with Article 78.

IHL likewise prohibits the conscription of civilians into the occupying power's military,[458] but permits them to be compelled to work in defined circumstances. An occupying power may 'only' compel civilians in occupied territory to perform work 'which is necessary either for the needs of the army of occupation, or for the public utility services, or for the feeding, sheltering, clothing, transportation or health of the population of the occupied country'.[459] Workers must be at least 18 years old and fair wages and work conditions must be provided.[460] Enforced prostitution is specifically forbidden.[461] In non-international armed conflict, slavery and the slave trade are also forbidden.[462]

To the extent that IHL authorizes prisoners of war and civilians to be compelled to work for certain non-military purposes, as the *lex specialis* IHL qualifies the application of Article 6 of the ICESCR. The relationship between the two sets of international rules can be understood in one of two ways. First, IHL may be understood to displace the ICESCR prohibition on forced labour *to the extent that* IHL authorizes certain forced labour in armed conflict.

Alternatively, if Article 6 of the ICESCR encompasses the well-accepted ILO exception for forced labour in an 'emergency', which in turn includes war, then IHL can be understood to supply the more specific rules for forced labour in the emergency situation of armed conflict. The latter approach harmonizes the IHL and ICESCR rules, without invoking the 'hard' form of the *lex specialis* principle (which would displace the ICESCR rule entirely). Given that forced conscription of POWs or civilians is prohibited by IHL, the question of conscientious objection under Article 18 of the ICCPR, and its relationship to IHL, does not arise.

It may be noted that the various IHL prohibitions on forced labour do not all attract explicit criminal responsibility. Certainly, aspects of forced labour are recognized as war crimes, including: conscripting a POW or civilian,[463] or a child;[464]

[458] GC IV, Article 51; and including children: GC IV, Article 50; Protocol I, Article 77(2).

[459] GC IV, Article 51; see also Hague Regulations 1907, Article 52. Similar provisions apply to aliens in occupied territory: GC IV, Article 40.

[460] GC IV, Article 51.

[461] Protocol Additional to the Geneva Conventions of 12 August 1949, and relating to the Protection of Victims of International Armed Conflicts (adopted 8 June 1977, 1125 UNTS 3, entered into force 7 December 1978) ('Protocol I'), Articles 72(2)(b) and 76(1).

[462] Protocol Additional to the Geneva Conventions of 12 August 1949, and relating to the Protection of Victims of Non-International Armed Conflicts (adopted 8 June 1977, 1125 UNTS 609, entered into force 7 December 1978) ('Protocol II'), Article 4(2)(f).

[463] GC III, Article 130; GC IV, Article 147; ICTY Statute, Article 2(e); ICC Statute, Articles 8(2)(a)(v) and 8(2)(b)(xv) (in international armed conflicts) and 8(2)(e)(vi) (in non-international armed conflicts).

[464] ICC Statute, Articles 8(2)(b)(xxvi) (in international conflicts) and 8(2)(e)(vii) (in non-international conflicts).

enforced prostitution;[465] and forced deportation (including where it involves forced labour).[466] It is also arguable that forced labour may be an instance of the war crime of inhuman or cruel treatment; and slavery generally is a violation of the laws and customs of war.[467] Forced labour per se is not, however, a war crime, even when in violation of IHL prohibitions which are not regarded as 'grave breach' provisions.

The Right Not to Be Arbitrarily Deprived of Work

The right to work is understood to include a right not to be arbitrarily deprived of work.[468] Arbitrariness may arise due to impermissible discrimination (discussed earlier) or where a person is unfairly deprived of employment.[469] In this context, the CESCR has expressly invoked ILO standards governing unfair dismissal from employment:

> 11. ILO Convention No. 158 concerning Termination of Employment (1982) defines the lawfulness of dismissal in its article 4 and in particular imposes the requirement to provide valid grounds for dismissal as well as the right to legal and other redress in the case of unjustified dismissal.

ILO Convention No. 158 has been ratified by only thirty-six states, but its principles on unfair dismissal have had a wider normative influence, not only on the practice of non-party states, but also in defining the scope of Article 6 of the ICESCR. The ILO Committee of Experts noted in 2008 that the Convention's basic principles—a valid reason for termination, notice and an opportunity to respond, and appeal to an independent body—are now common in most countries.[470] Each of these principles is considered below.

As a matter of economic policy, a purely contractual, laissez-faire view of the employment relationship would suggest that the will of the parties should be given maximum effect. Over time, however, many states have limited contractual freedom by imposing protections against unfair dismissal, including because of the often unequal bargaining power that employers enjoy over employees in defining the employment relationship. There remains economic debate about the costs and benefits of labour protections such as those against unfair dismissal.[471]

[465] ICC Statute, Article 8(2)(b)(xxii) (in international conflicts); Statute of the International Criminal Tribunal for Rwanda (ICTR), Article 4(e) (non-international conflicts); Statute of the Special Court for Sierra Leone, Article 3 (non-international conflicts).

[466] GC IV, Article 147; ICC Statute, Article 8(2)(a)(vii); Statute of the International Criminal Tribunal for the Former Yugoslavia (ICTY), Article 2(g).

[467] See, eg, *Prosecutor v Krnojelac (Judgment)*, ICTY Trial Chamber, IT-97-25-T, 15 March 2002, [351]–[356].

[468] Craven, *The ICESCR*, 197.

[469] CESCR, General Comment No. 18, [6].

[470] ILO, Note on Convention No. 158 and Recommendation No. 166 concerning termination of employment, NORMES-2009-02-0268-1-En.doc/v2 (9 March 2009), 14.

[471] ILO, Note on Convention No. 158 and Recommendation No. 166, 21–4.

The ILO standards reflect a balance between the need to ensure labour market flexibility and worker protection.[472] That flexibility is expressed most explicitly by provisions which allow certain categories of work or workers to be excluded from the application of Convention No. 158 at the election of the state.[473] A majority of states parties have availed themselves of such provisions to some extent,[474] which complicates reliance on ILO standards to inform a uniform understanding of the minimum requirements of Article 6 of the ICESCR.

UNFAIR DISMISSAL—GROUNDS OF TERMINATION

Article 4 of Convention No. 158 provides that there must be a valid reason for terminating employment:

> The employment of a worker shall not be terminated unless there is a valid reason for such termination connected with the capacity or conduct of the worker or based on the operational requirements of the undertaking, establishment or service.

According to the ILO, a valid dismissal based on the 'capacity' of a worker may occur where the worker lacks the necessary skills or qualities to perform certain tasks, or (non-temporary) illness or injury renders the worker incapable of performing required tasks.[475] The ILO suggests that a period of six months commonly defines 'temporary' illness or injury in national practice, within which a worker's position cannot be terminated, although it is common to suspend employment during that period[476] (once sickness benefits are exhausted). Illness or injury caused in the workplace is often subject to greater levels of protection.[477]

Dismissal connected with the 'conduct' of a worker includes where the worker has committed professional misconduct or behaved improperly. Professional misconduct encompasses neglect of duty, violation of work rules (including on occupational health and safety), disobeying legitimate orders and absence or lateness without cause.[478] Improper behaviour may include:

> …disorderly conduct, violence, assault, using insulting language, disturbing the peace and order of the workplace, [habitually] turning up for work in a state of intoxication or under

[472] ILO, Note on Convention No. 158 and Recommendation No. 166, 4.

[473] ILO Convention No. 158 concerning Termination of Employment at the Initiative of the Employer (adopted 22 June 1982, 1412 UNTS 159, entered into force 23 November 1985) ('ILO Convention No. 158'), Article 2(2), including: '(a) workers engaged under a contract of employment for a specified period of time or a specified task; (b) workers serving a period of probation or a qualifying period of employment, determined in advance and of reasonable duration; (c) workers engaged on a casual basis for a short period'. Contracts must not be designed to circumvent the protections of the Convention: ILO Convention No. 158, Article 2(3). Article 2(5) also allows exclusion where 'special problems of a substantial nature arise in the light of the particular conditions of employment of the workers concerned or the size or nature of the undertaking that employs them'.

[474] ILO, Note on Convention No. 158 and Recommendation No. 166, 6.

[475] ILO, *Protection against Unjustified Dismissal*, 38.

[476] ILO, *Protection against Unjustified Dismissal*, 59.

[477] ILO, *Protection against Unjustified Dismissal*, 60.

[478] ILO, *Protection against Unjustified Dismissal*, 37.

the influence of narcotic drugs, or the consumption of alcohol or drugs at the workplace, various acts displaying a lack of honesty and trustworthiness, such as fraud, deceit, breach of trust, theft and various disloyal activities (such as divulging trade secrets or undertaking activities in competition with the employer) or causing material damage to the property of the undertaking.[479]

Dismissal connected with 'operational requirements' typically concerns redundancies, workforce reductions or even closure due to economic or technical reasons, *force majeure* or accident.[480] It can also involve the restructuring of positions in response to technology or changes in production, including where workers are unable to be retrained for new roles.[481]

Article 5 of Convention No. 158 then enumerates reasons which 'shall not constitute valid reasons for termination':[482]

The following, inter alia, shall not constitute valid reasons for termination:

(a) union membership or participation in union activities outside working hours or, with the consent of the employer, within working hours;

(b) seeking office as, or acting or having acted in the capacity of, a workers' representative;

(c) the filing of a complaint or the participation in proceedings against an employer involving alleged violation of laws or regulations or recourse to competent administrative authorities;

(d) race, colour, sex, marital status, family responsibilities, pregnancy, religion, political opinion, national extraction or social origin;

(e) absence from work during maternity leave.

Nor is '[t]emporary absence from work because of illness or injury' a valid reason, subject to considerations concerning the definition of 'temporary' absence, requirements for medical certification and other limits (Articles 6 and 1).

ILO Recommendation No. 166 concerning Termination of Employment 1982 adds two further invalid reasons for terminating employment:

(a) age, subject to national law and practice regarding retirement;

(b) absence from work due to compulsory military service or other civic obligations, in accordance with national law and practice.

Since the Article 5 list is non-exhaustive ('inter alia'), states remain free to prohibit other grounds of dismissal in national law, for instance for: participation in strikes; non-membership of a trade union; health or disability status; citizenship status; sexual orientation; past criminal convictions; level of education; or refusal to take a lie-detector test[483] (although refusal to take a drug test may be a valid

[479] ILO, *Protection against Unjustified Dismissal*, 37.
[480] ILO, *Protection against Unjustified Dismissal*, 39.
[481] ILO, *Protection against Unjustified Dismissal*, 39.
[482] See generally ILO, *Protection against Unjustified Dismissal*, 42–54.
[483] ILO, *Protection against Unjustified Dismissal*, 41, 57.

ground of termination where it is necessary to ensure workplace safety, such as when driving vehicles or operating machinery).

In monitoring states, the CESCR has frequently criticized lack of protection against unfair dismissal,[484] including after privatization.[485] It has noted that certain workers are at greater risk, including migrant workers,[486] older workers,[487] 'non-regular' workers[488] and domestic workers.[489] It has often criticized employers for refusing to pay termination payments.[490] It has identified discriminatory dismissals, such as for pregnancy,[491] one of the grounds expressly prohibited under ILO Convention No. 158 (and which would also be covered by the ICESCR's non-discrimination protections (Article 2) and special protections for pregnant women (Article 10(2)). The CESCR was likewise concerned about dismissals involving discrimination on the basis of political opinion, where a political movement ('Charter 77') sought to peacefully (but not violently) change the social order.[492]

The CESCR also criticized a Nepalese law which permitted dismissal from the civil service based on 'moral turpitude', which was 'not defined with sufficient precision and which can lead to arbitrary interpretations'.[493] It has thus focused on notions of certainty and arbitrariness in examining infringements of the right to work as a result of dismissal.

In another example, the CESCR criticized Nigeria's dismissal by decree of 22,000 civil servants for going on strike.[494] Notably, Convention No. 158 does not expressly protect against dismissal for strike action, but only for 'union membership or participation in union activities outside working hours or, with the consent of the employer, within working hours'. Article 8(1)(d) of the ICESCR recognizes the 'right to strike', but only 'provided that it is exercised in conformity with the laws of the particular country'. Various states continue to permit dismissal of workers for striking.[495]

Other ILO instruments are, however, pertinent. ILO Convention No. 98 provides that 'workers shall enjoy adequate protection against acts of anti-union discrimination in respect of their employment' (Article 1(1)).[496] The ILO

[484] CESCR, Concluding Observations: UK (Hong Kong), E/C.12/Add.10 (6 December 1996), [21]; China (Hong Kong SAR), E/C.12/1/Add.58 (21 May 2001), [15].

[485] CESCR, Concluding Observations: Bosnia and Herzegovina, E/C.12/BIH/CO/1 (24 January 2006), [15].

[486] CESCR, Concluding Observations: Mauritius, E/C.12/MUS/CO/4 (8 June 2010), [19].

[487] CESCR, Concluding Observations: Japan, E/C.12/1/Add.67 (24 September 2001), [20].

[488] CESCR, Concluding Observations: Republic of Korea, E/C.12/KOR/CO/3 (17 December 2009), [15].

[489] CESCR, Concluding Observations: Bolivia, E/C.12/1/Add.60 (21 May 2001), [16].

[490] CESCR, Concluding Observations: Morocco, E/C.12/MAR/CO/3 (4 September 2006), [19]; Japan, E/C.12/1/Add.67 (24 September 2001), [20]; Republic of Korea, E/C.12/KOR/CO/3 (17 December 2009), [15].

[491] CESCR, Concluding Observations: Bulgaria, E/C.12/1/Add.37 (8 December 1999), [30]; Suriname, E/C.12/1995/6 (7 June 1995), [10]; Mexico, E/C.12/1/Add.41 (8 December 1999), [21].

[492] CESCR, Concluding Observations: E/C.12/1987/SR.13 (1987), [40].

[493] CESCR, Concluding Observations: Nepal, E/C.12/1/Add.66 (24 September 2001), [25] and [51].

[494] CESCR, Concluding Observations: Nigeria, E/C.12/1/Add.23 (16 June 1998), [18].

[495] ILO, *Protection against Unjustified Dismissal*, 45.

[496] Further, ILO Convention No. 135 concerning Protection and Facilities to be Afforded to Workers' Representatives in the Undertaking (adopted 23 June 1971, 883 UNTS 111, entered into

Committee on Freedom of Association has determined that dismissal of workers or trade union leaders because of a strike, which is a legitimate trade union activity, constitutes serious discrimination in employment and is contrary to Convention No. 98.[497] Workers must also not be threatened with dismissal or their re-employment refused for planned or previous strike participation.[498]

Moreover, the ILO Committee of Experts has declared that the protection of workers and trade union officials against anti-union discrimination is an essential aspect of freedom of association, the denial of which violates Convention No. 87 on Freedom of Association and Protection of the Right to Organise.[499] The ILO accepts, however, that:

> The protection of freedom of association does not cover abuses in the exercise of the right to strike involving failure to comply with reasonable requirements regarding lawfulness, or consisting of acts of a criminal nature...[500]

Even a criminal conviction, however, does not automatically provide a valid reason for dismissal.[501] Sanctions must be proportionate to the seriousness of the abuse.[502] The ILO encourages states to suspend rather than terminate a convicted worker's employment, so as to assist the worker to resume a normal life after prison.[503]

UNFAIR DISMISSAL—PROCEDURE GOVERNING TERMINATION

In its monitoring, the CESCR has often recommended that states take legislative and other measures to prevent unfair dismissals.[504] It has also suggested providing remedies for workers who have been unfairly dismissed and encouraged publicity campaigns to make workers aware of their rights[505] and ensure older workers have job security.[506]

force 30 June 1973), Article 1, protects workers' representatives from prejudicial acts, including dismissal, based on their status or activities as representatives, union members or for participating in union activities, 'in so far as they act in conformity with existing laws or collective agreements or other jointly agreed arrangements'. ILO Convention No. 151 concerning Protection of the Right to Organise and Procedures for Determining Conditions of Employment in the Public Service (adopted 27 June 1978, 1218 UNTS 87, entered into force 25 February 1981) protects public employees against 'acts of anti-union discrimination in respect of their employment' (Article 4(1)), including against dismissal for membership of participation in public employees' organizations (Article 4(2)(b)).

[497] Bernard Gernigon, Alberto Odero and Horacio Guido, *ILO Principles concerning the Right to Strike* (ILO, Geneva, 2000), 37–8.

[498] Gernigon et al, *ILO Principles Concerning the Right to Strike*, 37–8.

[499] Gernigon et al, *ILO Principles Concerning the Right to Strike*, 37.

[500] Gernigon et al, *ILO Principles Concerning the Right to Strike*, 56.

[501] ILO, *Protection against Unjustified Dismissal*, 38.

[502] Gernigon et al, *ILO Principles Concerning the Right to Strike*, 56.

[503] See, eg, ILO General Survey 1974 on Recommendation No. 119, in ILO, *Protection against Unjustified Dismissal*, 38.

[504] CESCR, Concluding Observations: UK (Hong Kong), E/C.12/Add.10 (6 December 1996), [38]; Venezuela, E/C.12/1/Add.56 (21 May 2001), [24]; Bolivia, E/C.12/1/Add.60 (21 May 2001), [33]; Bosnia and Herzegovina, E/C.12/BIH/CO/1 (24 January 2006), [36].

[505] CESCR, Concluding Observations: Morocco, E/C.12/MAR/CO/3 (4 September 2006), [42].

[506] CESCR, Concluding Observations: Japan, E/C.12/1/Add.67 (24 September 2001), [47].

ILO Convention No. 158 also sets out in more detail a minimum procedure governing dismissals. Article 7 provides that a worker must be given an opportunity to defend him- or herself before termination, unless this cannot be reasonably expected of an employer:

> The employment of a worker shall not be terminated for reasons related to the worker's conduct or performance before he is provided an opportunity to defend himself against the allegations made, unless the employer cannot reasonably be expected to provide this opportunity.

The right to defend oneself in Article 7 does not apply where terminations are due to 'operational requirements', which are subject to separate consultation procedures under Article 13 (see below). The purpose of Article 7 is to ensure that any decision to terminate is 'preceded by dialogue and reflection between the parties'.[507]

Article 7 does not provide further detail about the right to defend oneself. The drafting confirms that it allows flexibility in implementation and does not require an adversarial or quasi-judicial procedure,[508] although states are free to provide stronger guarantees. What matters is that 'the allegations are expressed and communicated to the worker without ambiguity and that the worker is give a real opportunity to defend himself'.[509]

ILO Recommendation No. 166 adds that a worker should also be 'entitled to be assisted by another person when defending himself' (paragraph 9), which in practice may be a staff delegate, trade union representative, friend or legal representative.[510] The recommendation also encourages states to notify a worker in writing of a termination decision (paragraph 12) and to provide written reasons on request (paragraph 13(1)). The recommendation is also more generous in suggesting that termination for misconduct should only result in case of a repeated infraction following an earlier written warning (paragraph 7); and termination for unsatisfactory performance only after the employee has been given a written warning, performance instructions, and has still failed to adequately perform after a reasonable period of time has elapsed (paragraph 8). An employer is also deemed to have waived the right to terminate a worker for known misconduct after the elapse of a reasonable period of time (paragraph 10).

Following termination, there must be a right of appeal to 'an impartial body' under Article 8 of ILO Convention No. 158:

> 1. A worker who considers that his employment has been unjustifiably terminated shall be entitled to appeal against that termination to an impartial body, such as a court, labour tribunal, arbitration committee or arbitrator.

[507] ILO, *Protection against Unjustified Dismissal*, 64.
[508] ILO, *Protection against Unjustified Dismissal*, 64.
[509] ILO, *Protection against Unjustified Dismissal*, 63.
[510] Paragraph 11 allows employers also to consult workers' representatives before termination, as defined in ILO Convention No. 135 concerning Protection and Facilities to be Afforded Workers Representatives in the Undertaking (adopted 23 June 1971, 883 UNTS 111, entered into force 30 June 1973).

2. Where termination has been authorised by a competent authority the application of paragraph 1 of this Article may be varied according to national law and practice.

3. A worker may be deemed to have waived his right to appeal against the termination of his employment if he has not exercised that right within a reasonable period of time after termination.

While states may choose the type of appeal body, it must be impartial and not part of the employment hierarchy.[511] Even within a state, different bodies may be appropriate depending on the category of worker, grounds of termination, legal basis of employment or rights involved. Labour tribunals of various kinds have developed in order to provide less formal, quicker and cheaper procedures than is typical of the courts.[512] Recommendation No. 166 encourages conciliation to be used 'before or during appeal' (paragraph 14) so as to promote the possibility of an agreed solution.[513]

Stronger institutional protection may be mandated by regional human rights systems. In the Americas, for example, the Inter-American Court of Human Rights found that mass dismissals of members of Congress under an emergency regime in Peru violated Article 8 of the American Convention on Human Rights (providing for a fair hearing, including in 'labour' decisions) and Article 25 (providing for an effective remedy for rights violations):

129. In conclusion, the Court observes that this case took place within the framework of practical and normative impediments to a real access to justice and a general situation of absence of guarantees and ineffectiveness of the judicial institutions to deal with facts such as those of the instant case. In this context and, in particular, the climate of legal uncertainty promoted by the norms that restricted complaints against the evaluation procedure and the eventual dismissal of the alleged victims, it is clear that the latter had no certainty about the proceeding they should or could use to claim the rights they considered violated, whether this was administrative, under administrative-law, or by an action for *amparo*.

130. In this regard, in *Akdivar v Turkey*, the European Court of Human Rights found, *inter alia*, that the existence of domestic recourses must be sufficiently guaranteed, not only in theory, but also in practice; to the contrary, they would not comply with the required accessibility and effectiveness. It also considered that the existence of formal recourses under the legal system of the State in question should be taken into account, and also the general political and legal context in which they operate as well as the personal circumstances of the petitioners or plaintiffs.

131. In this case, the existing domestic recourses were not effective, either individually or as a whole, to provide the alleged victims dismissed from the Peruvian Congress with an adequate and effective guarantee of the right of access to justice in the terms of the American Convention.[514]

[511] ILO, *Protection against Unjustified Dismissal*, 72.
[512] ILO, *Protection against Unjustified Dismissal*, 73.
[513] ILO, *Protection against Unjustified Dismissal*, 76.
[514] *Case of the Dismissed Congressional Employees (Aguado-Alfaro et al) v Peru (Preliminary Objections, Merits, Reparations and Costs)*, 24 November 2007, IACHR Ser C No. 158, [129]–[131].

Under ILO Convention No. 158, the right to appeal expires within a 'reasonable period of time' to recognize that the elapse of time makes proof of facts more difficult and to ensure finality and certainty of decisions.[515] The Convention does not specify what is a 'reasonable' period, but it must not be so limited that it prevents workers from ascertaining their rights, assessing the facts and seeking assistance where necessary, to make an informed decision about whether to seek review. While Convention No. 158 does not require workers to be notified of their right to appeal, Recommendation No. 166 urges that 'workers are fully informed of the possibilities of appeal' (paragraph 15), so as to make their right effective.

Impartial review bodies must be empowered to examine the reasons for termination and the circumstances, and to make a decision about whether termination was justified (Article 9(1)). Article 9(2) seeks to better protect workers by placing the burden of proof for establishing the validity of a termination on the employer, or allowing the review body to inquire for itself. It thus departs from the traditional position in contract law in common law countries, where the burden is on the complainant.[516] This is justified in part because proof of the real reasons for a dismissal will often be in the possession of the employer.[517] Article 9 provides:

1. The bodies referred to in Article 8 of this Convention shall be empowered to examine the reasons given for the termination and the other circumstances relating to the case and to render a decision on whether the termination was justified.

2. In order for the worker not to have to bear alone the burden of proving that the termination was not justified, the methods of implementation referred to in Article 1 of this Convention shall provide for one or the other or both of the following possibilities:

(a) the burden of proving the existence of a valid reason for the termination as defined in Article 4 of this Convention shall rest on the employer;

(b) the bodies referred to in Article 8 of this Convention shall be empowered to reach a conclusion on the reason for the termination having regard to the evidence provided by the parties and according to procedures provided for by national law and practice.

3. In cases of termination stated to be for reasons based on the operational requirements of the undertaking, establishment or service, the bodies referred to in Article 8 of this Convention shall be empowered to determine whether the termination was indeed for these reasons, but the extent to which they shall also be empowered to decide whether these reasons are sufficient to justify that termination shall be determined by the methods of implementation referred to in Article 1 of this Convention.

Under Article 9(3), states enjoy more flexibility in controlling the review procedure for terminations based on operational requirements.

[515] ILO, *Protection against Unjustified Dismissal*, 75.
[516] ILO, *Protection against Unjustified Dismissal*, 78.
[517] ILO, Note on ILO Convention No. 158 and Recommendation No. 166, 10.

Review bodies are empowered by Article 10 of the Convention to invalidate a termination and order reinstatement and/or 'adequate' compensation or other appropriate remedy:

If the bodies referred to in Article 8 of this Convention find that termination is unjustified and if they are not empowered or do not find it practicable, in accordance with national law and practice, to declare the termination invalid and/or order or propose reinstatement of the worker, they shall be empowered to order payment of adequate compensation or such other relief as may be deemed appropriate.

Factors affecting whether reinstatement is appropriate may include the length of time between the termination and the review decision, the nature of the employment relationship (resuming employment may be difficult in small undertakings with close personal working relationships) and the enforceability of reinstatement.[518] Where reinstatement is appropriate, a worker should also be entitled to wages lost between termination and reinstatement, as well as any acquired benefits (such as social insurance or qualifying periods for leave), less any wages received from other employment gained after termination.[519]

Where compensation is ordered in place of reinstatement, the quantum of compensation may be affected by a range of factors: the nature of employment, length of service, age, acquired rights, grounds of termination, future job or career prospects, personal circumstances (such as family status), and the nature and size of the employer.[520] Beyond financial loss, some states also provide for 'moral' damages[521] or even punitive damages, such as where the termination was malicious, discriminatory or affected fundamental rights.[522] The ILO recommends that compensation 'should be aimed at compensating fully, in financial and occupational terms, the prejudice suffered by the worker, the best solution generally being reinstatement of the worker in his job with payment of unpaid wages and maintenance of acquired rights'.[523]

Before termination, a worker is entitled under Article 11 to receive a 'reasonable period of notice or compensation in lieu thereof, unless he is guilty of serious misconduct'.[524] This protection operates regardless of whether a termination is valid or invalid and aims to assist the worker to adapt to losing employment and find a new job.[525] What is a 'reasonable' period varies in state practice and often by category of employment, length of service or salary amount, but is commonly two weeks to a month for workers paid on a monthly basis, or one to two weeks

[518] ILO, *Protection against Unjustified Dismissal*, 82.

[519] ILO, *Protection against Unjustified Dismissal*, 83.

[520] ILO, *Protection against Unjustified Dismissal*, 85.

[521] Moral damage may be defined as 'an injury inflicted resulting in mental suffering, injury to his feelings, humiliation, shame, degradation, loss of social position or injury to his credit or to his reputation': *Opinion in the Lusitania Cases*, 1 November 1923, (1923) 7 RIAA 32, 40.

[522] ILO, *Protection against Unjustified Dismissal*, 85–6.

[523] ILO, *Protection against Unjustified Dismissal*, 87.

[524] Defined as 'misconduct of such a nature that it would be unreasonable to require the employer to continue his employment during the notice period': ILO Convention No. 158, Article 11.

[525] ILO, *Protection against Unjustified Dismissal*, 89.

for workers paid on a daily, weekly or fortnightly basis.[526] Where notice is not provided, Article 11 requires compensation to be paid in lieu, which should correspond to the remuneration that would have been received during the notice period forgone.[527]

Notice or compensation in lieu may be dispensed with in cases of 'serious misconduct', a phrase which is not defined and varies in state practice. The ILO suggests that it includes:

> …theft, fraud or dishonesty; assaulting, threatening or insulting superiors or, sometimes, fellow workers; repeated violations of applicable rules (particularly those relating to safety); deliberate refusal to fulfil essential obligations…disobedience of legitimate orders; habitual negligence; acts causing serious damage to property; habitual absence without leave or unpunctuality; habitually being in a state of drunkenness or under the influence of narcotic drugs during working hours; and conviction of a crime involving moral turpitude.[528]

It may also extend to cases of breach of trust (including disclosure of trade secrets), misleading an employer during recruitment (such as by false information), or working for one's own benefit to the employer's detriment.[529]

Recommendation No. 166 suggests that during the notice period, workers should be entitled to 'a reasonable amount of time off without loss of pay, taken at times that are convenient to both parties' (paragraph 16), which aims to give the worker time to find a new job. Paragraph 17 further provides that a worker is entitled to request and receive a certificate from the employer specifying the term of his or her employment and the type of work performed. Only on the worker's request should the certificate provide an evaluation of the worker's conduct and performance or reasons for termination.

A worker whose employment has been terminated is entitled to a severance allowance and/or accrued social insurance benefits under Article 12 of ILO Convention No. 158:

> 1. A worker whose employment has been terminated shall be entitled, in accordance with national law and practice, to—
>
> (a) a severance allowance or other separation benefits, the amount of which shall be based inter alia on length of service and the level of wages, and paid directly by the employer or by a fund constituted by employers' contributions; or
>
> (b) benefits from unemployment insurance or assistance or other forms of social security, such as old-age or invalidity benefits, under the normal conditions to which such benefits are subject; or
>
> (c) a combination of such allowance and benefits.
>
> 2. A worker who does not fulfil the qualifying conditions for unemployment insurance or assistance under a scheme of general scope need not be paid any allowance or benefit

[526] ILO, *Protection against Unjustified Dismissal*, 90–1.
[527] ILO, *Protection against Unjustified Dismissal*, 92.
[528] ILO, *Protection against Unjustified Dismissal*, 94.
[529] ILO, *Protection against Unjustified Dismissal*, 94.

referred to in paragraph 1, subparagraph (a), of this Article solely because he is not receiving an unemployment benefit under paragraph 1, subparagraph (b).

3. Provision may be made by the methods of implementation referred to in Article 1 of this Convention for loss of entitlement to the allowance or benefits referred to in paragraph 1, subparagraph (a), of this Article in the event of termination for serious misconduct.

Severance or unemployment benefits are distinct from compensation for unlawful dismissal and compensation in lieu of notice, and aim to financially cushion the worker from the effects of termination and transition into new employment. A severance allowance is particularly important in states where there is no universal social security system; entitlement to the latter depends on national law and whatever qualifying conditions apply.[530] A severance allowance may be withheld in cases of serious misconduct or where minimum qualifying periods of employment have not been met. The amount of a severance allowance varies in state practice. It is most commonly a flat rate, or based on length of service or salary level; but is sometimes fixed at one or two months' wages, or subject to minimum or maximum limits.[531]

Special considerations apply where terminations are contemplated for economic, technological, structural or like reasons, when employers are required to consult with workers' representatives to discuss ways of averting or mitigating terminations. Article 13 accordingly provides:

1. When the employer contemplates terminations for reasons of an economic, technological, structural or similar nature, the employer shall:

(a) provide the workers' representatives concerned in good time with relevant information including the reasons for the terminations contemplated, the number and categories of workers likely to be affected and the period over which the terminations are intended to be carried out;

(b) give, in accordance with national law and practice, the workers' representatives concerned, as early as possible, an opportunity for consultation on measures to be taken to avert or to minimise the terminations and measures to mitigate the adverse effects of any terminations on the workers concerned such as finding alternative employment.

2. The applicability of paragraph 1 of this Article may be limited by the methods of implementation referred to in Article 1 of this Convention to cases in which the number of workers whose termination of employment is contemplated is at least a specified number or percentage of the workforce.

3. For the purposes of this Article the term *the workers' representatives concerned* means the workers' representatives recognised as such by national law or practice, in conformity with the Workers' Representatives Convention, 1971.

The consultation requirement is not merely a duty to provide information, but 'should be able to have some influence on the decision taken',[532] and should occur 'as early as possible'. While the Convention does not stipulate the means

[530] See Article 9 (social security) in this book; and 'forced labour' above in this chapter.
[531] ILO, *Protection against Unjustified Dismissal*, 100.
[532] ILO, *Protection against Unjustified Dismissal*, 105.

by which terminations may be averted or minimized, or their effects mitigated, Recommendation No. 166 illustrates some in paragraph 21, clustered around work sharing or voluntary workforce reductions:

> …restriction of hiring, spreading the workforce reduction over a certain period of time to permit natural reduction of the workforce, internal transfers, training and retraining, voluntary early retirement with appropriate income protection, restriction of overtime and reduction of normal hours of work.

It also envisages a more active role for the state: 'the competent authority should assist the parties in seeking solutions to the problems raised by the terminations contemplated' (paragraph 19). Such assistance may include, for example, job search assistance, retraining and financial assistance in this respect (paragraphs 25 and 26), which recognizes that 'workers who lose their employment for reasons beyond their control should not suffer unduly from the consequences and the community should bear part of the burden of avoiding this by sharing in the risks associated with economic change and the costs of redeploying workers'.[533]

Other ILO standards also recommend that special account should be taken of the needs of older workers,[534] and multinational enterprises should give early notice of major redundancies to governments and workers' organizations.[535] Other actors too have adopted standards in this area, such as the International Finance Corporation's guidelines on consultation in the development and implementation of retrenchment plans.[536]

The adoption of criteria for selecting whose employment is to be terminated is also suggested by Recommendation No. 166 (paragraph 23), so that the choice between workers is objectively and prospectively made rather than arbitrary. The weight and priority to be given to different criteria may also be set out, for instance relating to skills, length of service, family circumstances, the difficulty of finding new employment or vulnerability.[537] According priority of rehiring to workers made redundant is also recommended (paragraph 24).

In monitoring states, the CESCR has sometimes commented on inadequacies in a state's procedures or remedies concerning dismissals. It recommended simply that Venezuela provide protection against 'unwarranted dismissal' for workers.[538] In relation to pre-termination processes, the CESCR queried the Netherlands Antilles on the abolition of the obligation on industries to obtain dismissal permits, and the introduction of short-term employment contracts, in relation to their effects on employment.[539]

[533] ILO, *Protection against Unjustified Dismissal*, 126.

[534] ILO Recommendation No. 162 on Older Workers, [18].

[535] ILO, Tripartite Declaration of Principles concerning Multinational Enterprises and Social Policy, 92-2-119010-2 (1 January 2006), [26].

[536] International Finance Corporation, Good Practice Note No. 4: Managing Retrenchment (1 August 2005).

[537] ILO, *Protection against Unjustified Dismissal*, 121–2.

[538] CESCR, Concluding Observations: Venezuela, E/C.12/1/Add.56 (21 May 2001), [24].

[539] CESCR, Concluding Observations: Netherlands Antilles, E/C.12/NLD/CO/3/Add.1 (31 January 2008), [11].

In respect of post-termination processes, the CESCR was concerned about Nigeria's policy of retrenchment aimed at dismissing up to 200,000 employees in the public sector 'without adequate compensation'.[540] It was worried that there were insufficient 'social support measures' to deal with, or efforts to prevent, mass dismissals resulting from the privatization or liquidation of national enterprises in Benin.[541] Likewise, it was concerned by large-scale redundancies in China due to economic restructuring of state-owned enterprises, and asked the state for more information about 'measures taken to facilitate re-employment of women' who had been made redundant.[542]

Availability of Employment and Progressive Realization of Full Employment

The right to work is not an immediately enforceable individual right to obtain employment,[543] nor does it entail a correlative duty on the state to immediately provide full employment. It has been suggested that the right to work as a whole has received perhaps the least judicial attention of all human rights, and has been regarded as 'of inferior status even among the social rights themselves'.[544] Certain aspects of the right to work have, however, been heavily litigated, as in the area of non-discrimination law.

At the same time, the right to work is not merely promotional, aspirational or exhortatory, but involves an obligation on the state to progressively realize those aspects of the right which do not have immediate effect, as the CESCR explains:

19. The principal obligation of States parties is to ensure the progressive realization of the exercise of the right to work. States parties must therefore adopt, as quickly as possible, measures aiming at achieving full employment. While the Covenant provides for progressive realization and acknowledges the constraints due to the limits of available resources, it also imposes on States parties various obligations which are of immediate effect. States parties have immediate obligations in relation to the right to work, such as the obligation to 'guarantee' that it will be exercised 'without discrimination of any kind' (art. 2, para. 2) and the obligation 'to take steps' (art. 2, para. 1) towards the full realization of article 6. Such steps must be deliberate, concrete and targeted towards the full realization of the right to work.

20. The fact that realization of the right to work is progressive and takes place over a period of time should not be interpreted as depriving States parties' obligations of all meaningful content. It means that States parties have a specific and continuing obligation 'to move as expeditiously and effectively as possible' towards the full realization of article 6.[545]

540 CESCR, Concluding Observations: Nigeria, E/C.12/1/Add.23 (16 June 1998), [18].
541 CESCR, Concluding Observations: Benin, E/C.12/1/Add.78 (5 June 2002), [14] and [33].
542 CESCR, Concluding Observations: China (including Hong Kong and Macao), E/C.12/1/Add.107 (13 May 2005), [21] and [50].
543 Nussberger, 'Work, Right to, International Protection', [19].
544 Mundlak, 'The Right to Work—The Value of Work', 341–2.
545 CESCR, General Comment No. 18, [19]–[20].

A state will violate its obligation under Article 6 where it is 'unwilling' to use its maximum available resources to realize the right to work.[546] By contrast, there will be no violation where the state is 'unable' to fully guarantee the right to work after demonstrating that it has deployed all available resources as a matter of priority.[547] The 'steps' immediately required of states to fulfil the right to work are considered further below, but foremost include legal protections for the right to work and the adoption of a national employment strategy or plan.

The obligation to progressively realize the right to work reflects a compromise reached by capitalist, socialist and developing states during the drafting of Article 6, as Craven writes:

> Socialist States proposed that States should undertake to 'guarantee' or 'ensure' the right to work. In contrast, the Western States' proposals merely required States to 'promote conditions' under which the right to work might be realized. The main compromise formula was for the article to include a bold statement of the right to work while deferring a decision on whether or not the obligation should be progressive until the adoption of a general clause. It soon became apparent that many States would not accept an obligation to 'guarantee' the right to work in the sense of ensuring full employment or eliminating unemployment. In particular, it was feared that such a guarantee would bind States to a centralized system of government and require that all labour be under the direct control of the State.[548]

Article 6 thus 'recognize[s]' the right to work, but does not 'guarantee' it, at least in respect of full employment, although other aspects of the right (such as the implied prohibition of forced labour) are susceptible to immediate implementation.[549] Most states accepted that the available employment is limited by a state's social and economic development,[550] as well as national policy and international factors. As the United Kingdom observed during the drafting, there is also no obligation 'to subsidize work of no value whatever to the community'[551] in the name of full employment. Given the modern interdependence of national economies, the CESCR has acknowledged that the right to work is affected by factors outside the control of any individual state:

> 4. ... for millions of human beings throughout the world, full enjoyment of the right to freely chosen or accepted work remains a remote prospect. The Committee recognizes the existence of structural and other obstacles arising from international factors beyond the control of States which hinder the full enjoyment of article 6 in many States parties.[552]

In considering the resources available to the state in progressively realizing the right to work, the CESCR will take into account the assistance provided to the state by other actors:

> 53. ... When examining the reports of States parties and their ability to meet their obligations under article 6, the Committee will consider the effects of the assistance provided by actors other than States parties.[553]

[546] CESCR, General Comment No. 18, [32]. [547] CESCR, General Comment No. 18, [32].
[548] Craven, *CCPR Commentary*, 195. [549] Craven, *CCPR Commentary*, 196 and 203.
[550] Craven, *CCPR Commentary*, 197.
[551] UNGA Third Committee, A/C.3/SR.712 (14 December 1956), 154 (UK).
[552] CESCR, General Comment No. 18, [4]. [553] CESCR, General Comment No. 18, [53].

By extension, the willingness of a state to request assistance will also be relevant. The CESCR has occasionally called on individual states to request external assistance.

The CESCR has also stated that retrogressive measures in relation to the right to work are presumptively impermissible and would require strong justification:

21. As with all other rights in the Covenant, retrogressive measures should in principle not be taken in relation to the right to work. If any deliberately retrogressive steps are taken, States parties have the burden of proving that they have been introduced after consideration of all alternatives and that they are duly justified by reference to the totality of the rights provided for in the Covenant in the context of the full use of the States parties' maximum available resources.

…

34. …there is a strong presumption that retrogressive measures taken in relation to the right to work are not permissible. Such retrogressive measures include, inter alia, denial of access to employment to particular individuals or groups, whether such discrimination is based on legislation or practice, abrogation or suspension of the legislation necessary for the exercise of the right to work or the adoption of laws or policies that are manifestly incompatible with international legal obligations relating to the right to work. An example would be the institution of forced labour or the abrogation of legislation protecting the employee against unlawful dismissal. Such measures would constitute a violation of States parties' obligation to respect the right to work.[554]

The CESCR appears to use the term 'retrogressive' measures in different and somewhat confusing senses here. Ordinarily, retrogression relates to the obligation to progressively realize socio-economic rights (as it does in paragraph 21 above). However, it is odd that the CESCR mentions (in paragraph 34 above) reintroducing 'discrimination' as an example of a retrogressive measure. The CESCR has elsewhere stated that the obligation of non-discrimination, including in relation to the right to work, is immediately applicable and not subject to progressive realization. As such, discriminatory provisions have nothing to do with the field of progressive realization, but are properly characterized as simple violations of the immediate obligation not to discriminate.[555] If this analysis is correct, the CESCR is really using the notion of retrogression more loosely to describe backsliding on progress already made towards fulfilling the right to work, as distinct from the availability of resources.

In monitoring states, the CESCR seems to have adopted a relatively strict approach to the principle of progressive realization in the context of the right to work. It has seldom explicitly acknowledged resource limitations in assessing a state's performance. One rare instance was when it acknowledged the impact on employment of the extensive economic and climatic difficulties faced by Mongolia:

267. The Committee is aware that the State party is currently experiencing great difficulties in the process of transition to a market economy. These difficulties are due, *inter alia*, to the sudden interruption of economic links with the former Soviet Union, and the

[554] CESCR, General Comment No. 18, [21] and [34].

[555] To the extent that the prohibition on forced labour is also of immediate effect (as argued below), the same can be said of that example also used by the CESCR above.

discontinuance of various types of assistance previously received, which accounted for almost 30 per cent of GDP in 1990. This influenced the closure or downsizing of State enterprises and gave rise to great increases in unemployment and to a serious lowering of standards of living. The concurrent deterioration in the State party's terms of trade in international markets and the Asian economic crisis further aggravated Mongolia's economic situation. It is acknowledged that problems related to these matters seriously hamper the State party's ability to comply with its obligations under the Covenant.

268. It is acknowledged that the existing divergence between available resources and the needs of the people is further exacerbated by the recent extreme climatic conditions prevailing in Mongolia, which also constitute a serious impediment to the enjoyment of economic, social and cultural rights in the country.[556]

The CESCR nonetheless called on Mongolia to protect the most vulnerable groups from poverty 'even under severe resource constraints'.[557] In another instance, the CESCR stated that it was 'fully aware that Solomon Islands is severely affected by financial constraints caused by the current economic crisis', but it went on to 'nevertheless' recall that 'the recent downsizing of the public sector, which accounts for almost one third of wage employment, has had significant social repercussions'.[558] It further expressed concern about the rise in unemployment, 'which has played a major role in stirring up civil strife in the country', and highlighted the limited access to employment for disabled persons.[559] Thus, even in situations of severe economic constraints, the CESCR has conceded little to states. The CESCR did not, however, provide much guidance on how public service salaries could be funded in Solomon Islands or poverty alleviated in Mongolia.

More commonly, the CESCR has implicitly invoked progressive realization as a means of demanding more, not less, of states. Thus, it was concerned that 'despite an increase in the rate of economic growth in the last three years', the majority of workers in Angola remained unprotected in the informal economy.[560] It also recommended to Bolivia that 'the fruits of the State party's economic macroeconomic growth should be used also to create decent new jobs'.[561]

The CESCR has noted generally that 'insufficient expenditure or misallocation of public funds which results in the non-enjoyment of the right to work by individuals or groups' will constitute a violation of the state's obligation to fulfil the right to work.[562] Finding such a violation will, however, require the CESCR to make complex evaluative judgments. For instance, the CESCR may need to consider how far state resources should be expended on creating jobs instead of on other public goods; what priority should be given to work creation compared with other ICESCR rights; whether trade-offs between different work rights are

[556] CESCR, Concluding Observations: Mongolia, E/2001/22 (2000), 53, [267] and [268].
[557] CESCR, Concluding Observations: Mongolia, E/2001/22 (2000), 53, [280].
[558] CESCR, Concluding Observations: Solomon Islands, E/C.12/1/Add.33 (14 May 1999), [18].
[559] CESCR, Concluding Observations: Solomon Islands, E/C.12/1/Add.33 (14 May 1999), [17] and [18].
[560] CESCR, Concluding Observations: Angola, E/C.12/AGO/CO/3 (1 December 2008), [20].
[561] CESCR, Concluding Observations: Bolivia, E/C.12/BOL/CO/2 (8 August 2008), [30].
[562] CESCR, General Comment No. 18, [36].

permitted (as between full employment and work conditions);[563] and where funds for job creation should be sourced from.

Measures to Realize Article 6—Paragraphs 1 and 2

States are required to 'take appropriate steps to safeguard' the right to work under Article 6(1) and specific (but non-exhaustive) 'steps' to realize it are listed in Article 6(2), namely 'technical and vocational guidance and training programmes, policies and techniques to achieve steady economic, social and cultural development and full and productive employment'. States enjoy a 'margin of discretion' in implementing their obligations, although they remain obligations nonetheless, as the CESCR explains:

> ...Every State party has a margin of discretion in assessing which measures are most suitable to meet its specific circumstances. The Covenant, however, clearly imposes a duty on each State party to take whatever steps are necessary to ensure that everyone is protected from unemployment and insecurity in employment and can enjoy the right to work as soon as possible.[564]

In interpreting what is required of states under Article 6, the CESCR has invoked the tripartite typology of obligations common to all human rights:

> 22. Like all human rights, the right to work imposes three types or levels of obligations on States parties: the obligations to *respect, protect* and *fulfil*. The obligation to *respect* the right to work requires States parties to refrain from interfering directly or indirectly with the enjoyment of that right. The obligation to *protect* requires States parties to take measures that prevent third parties from interfering with the enjoyment of the right to work. The obligation to *fulfil* includes the obligations to provide, facilitate and promote that right. It implies that States parties should adopt appropriate legislative, administrative, budgetary, judicial and other measures to ensure its full realization.[565]

The obligation to respect the right to work primarily requires states to prohibit forced or compulsory labour and to guarantee non-discrimination and equal opportunity, as discussed earlier:

> 23. States parties are under the obligation to *respect* the right to work by, inter alia, prohibiting forced or compulsory labour and refraining from denying or limiting equal access to decent work for all persons, especially disadvantaged and marginalized individuals and groups, including prisoners or detainees, members of minorities and migrant workers. In particular, States parties are bound by the obligation to respect the right of women and young persons to have access to decent work and thus to take measures to combat discrimination and to promote equal access and opportunities.
>
> 24. With regard to the obligations of States parties relating to child labour as set out in article 10 of the Covenant, States parties must take effective measures, in particular legislative measures, to prohibit labour of children under the age of 16. Further, they have to

[563] Joseph, 'UN Covenants and Labour Rights', 340.
[564] CESCR, General Comment No. 18, [37].
[565] CESCR, General Comment No. 18, [22].

prohibit all forms of economic exploitation and forced labour of children. States parties must adopt effective measures to ensure that the prohibition of child labour will be fully respected.[566]

The obligation to protect the right to work requires states to ensure non-discrimination and equal opportunity particularly in the private sector, and to ensure that labour market reform does not reduce worker protection:

25. Obligations to *protect* the right to work include, inter alia, the duties of States parties to adopt legislation or to take other measures ensuring equal access to work and training and to ensure that privatization measures do not undermine workers' rights. Specific measures to increase the flexibility of labour markets must not render work less stable or reduce the social protection of the worker. The obligation to protect the right to work includes the responsibility of States parties to prohibit forced or compulsory labour by non-State actors.[567]

EMPLOYMENT POLICY

The obligation to fulfil foremost requires states to formulate a national policy on the right to work, which should address unemployment (particularly among vulnerable groups) and allocate resources where needed:

26. States parties are obliged to *fulfil (provide)* the right to work when individuals or groups are unable, for reasons beyond their control, to realize that right themselves by the means at their disposal. This obligation includes, inter alia, the obligation to recognize the right to work in national legal systems and to adopt a national policy on the right to work as well as a detailed plan for its realization. The right to work requires formulation and implementation by States parties of an employment policy with a view to 'stimulating economic growth and development, raising levels of living, meeting manpower requirements and overcoming unemployment and underemployment'. It is in this context that effective measures to increase the resources allocated to reducing the unemployment rate, in particular among women, the disadvantaged and marginalized, should be taken by States parties…[568]

The CESCR's reference to the need for a national employment policy is drawn directly from Article 1 of ILO Convention No. 122 concerning Employment Policy 1964:

1. With a view to stimulating economic growth and development, raising levels of living, meeting manpower requirements and overcoming unemployment and underemployment, each Member shall declare and pursue, as a major goal, an active policy designed to promote full, productive and freely chosen employment.

2. The said policy shall aim at ensuring that—

(a) there is work for all who are available for and seeking work;

(b) such work is as productive as possible;

[566] CESCR, General Comment No. 18, [23] and [24].
[567] CESCR, General Comment No. 18, [25].
[568] CESCR, General Comment No. 18, [26].

(c) there is freedom of choice of employment and the fullest possible opportunity for each worker to qualify for, and to use his skills and endowments in, a job for which he is well suited, irrespective of race, colour, sex, religion, political opinion, national extraction or social origin.

3. The said policy shall take due account of the stage and level of economic development and the mutual relationships between employment objectives and other economic and social objectives, and shall be pursued by methods that are appropriate to national conditions and practices.

Article 1(3) of Convention No. 122 is consistent with the principle of progressive realization underpinning the implementation of the employment aspect of Article 6 of the ICESCR. States are not required to immediately guarantee a job to everyone who wants one, but must take active steps to the maximum of their resources to reach the goal of 'full and productive employment' under Article 6(2).

The CESCR has not expounded on what a policy for 'full employment'[569] requires. The original and basic ideal of full employment is that 'there is work for all who are available for and seeking work' (ILO Convention No. 122, Article 1(2)(a)). Yet, full employment in a market economy cannot mean zero unemployment.[570] Some people will inevitably be out of work when entering the labour market for the first time and starting to look for work, or when moving between jobs ('frictional' unemployment).[571]

More problematic are forms of 'cyclical' or 'structural' unemployment.[572] The aspiration of full employment from the 1940s has been tempered over time in the light of changing economic conditions and what is now considered possible in a market economy. It is widely believed that some level of job shortage is 'inevitable' in a market economy.[573] Full employment is thus reconceived as 'the lowest level of unemployment considered prudent for the government of a market economy to try to maintain',[574] including in the light of other economic objectives (such as wage pressures, inflation or productivity)[575] and social goods (such as an adequate standard of living).[576]

Regionally, the European Social Charter makes such concession explicit in providing that the 'right to work' requires states 'to accept as one of their primary aims and responsibilities the achievement and maintenance of *as high and stable a level of employment as possible, with a view to the attainment of full employment*'.[577] In monitoring states, the ECSR has focused on the need for states to

[569] CESCR, General Comment No. 18, [41].
[570] Harvey, 'Benchmarking the Right to Work', 129.
[571] Craven, *CCPR Commentary*, 206.
[572] Craven, *CCPR Commentary*, 206.
[573] Harvey, 'Benchmarking the Right to Work', 115.
[574] Harvey, 'Benchmarking the Right to Work', 120.
[575] Richard Siegel, 'The Right to Work: Core Minimum Obligations' in Audrey Chapman and Sage Russell (eds), *Core Obligations: Building a Framework for Economic, Social and Cultural Rights* (Intersentia, Antwerp, 2002), 23.
[576] International Labour Conference (92nd session), *Promoting Employment: Policies, Skills, Enterprises*, Report III (Part 1B) (2004), 21.
[577] European Social Charter (adopted 18 October 1961, 529 UNTS 89, entered into force 26 February 1961), Article 1(1) (emphasis added).

pursue a 'coherent economic policy' rather than prescribing a particular result in terms of employment or unemployment.[578]

Thus, in 1996, the ILO reaffirmed the traditional definition of full employment as 'fundamentally valid', but observed that 'changes in the structure of employment in terms of what constitutes full, productive and freely chosen employment need to be taken into account'.[579] It also accepted that 'the concept may have to be interpreted differently for developing countries'.[580] The shift in the ILO's emphasis from full employment to a 'decent work' agenda[581] has also influenced national priorities and standard setting.

In monitoring states, the CESCR almost always expresses concern about the level of unemployment in a given state, but never stipulates any particular level which it believes the state should aim for or is capable of achieving given its circumstances. Its scrutiny is perhaps more intense the higher the rate of unemployment[582] or the more disproportionate the impact on vulnerable groups. Occasionally, the CESCR has acknowledged that states have reduced unemployment. But it is otherwise difficult to deduce what the CESCR would accept as constituting 'full employment' in a given situation; certainly, it has never suggested that any particular state has fully realized it; and it almost always asks states to do more.

The CESCR has given some guidance on the formulation of employment policies, although there is 'room for the Committee to expand further upon the type of policy it expects'.[583] It has been attentive to the *processes* of policy-making by calling for any national employment strategy and plan of action to address 'the concerns of workers on the basis of a participatory and transparent process that includes employers' and workers' organizations'.[584] It has thus endorsed the tripartite stakeholder approach of the ILO to labour issues. The CESCR has specifically noted that '[c]ollective bargaining is a tool of fundamental importance in the formulation of employment policies'.[585] Civil society engagement is also considered essential in the implementation of employment policy:

> 42. The formulation and implementation of a national employment strategy should involve full respect for the principles of accountability, transparency, and participation by interested groups. The right of individuals and groups to participate in decision-making should be an integral part of all policies, programmes and strategies intended to implement the obligations of States parties under article 6. The promotion of employment also requires effective involvement of the community and, more specifically, of associations for the protection and promotion of the rights of workers and trade unions in the definition of priorities, decision-making, planning, implementation and evaluation of the strategy to promote employment.

[578] Diamond Ashiagbor, 'The Right to Work' in Grainne de Burca and Bruno de Witte (eds), *Social Rights in Europe* (Oxford University Press, Oxford, 2005), 241, 244.

[579] ILO, Resolution concerning Employment Policies in a Global Context, GB.267/ESP/3/2 (19 June 1996), appendix [5].

[580] ILO, Resolution concerning Employment Policies in a Global Context.

[581] Harvey, 'Benchmarking the Right to Work', 121.

[582] Craven, *CCPR Commentary*, 209.

[583] Craven, *CCPR Commentary*, 208; see also Joseph, 'UN Covenants and Labour Rights', 340.

[584] CESCR, General Comment No. 18, [31(c)].

[585] CESCR, General Comment No. 18, [39].

As regards the substantive content of employment policies, the CESCR has provided some—but far from comprehensive—guidance. As noted already, states must specially target disadvantaged groups, ensure non-discrimination and equal opportunity generally, and prohibit forced or compulsory labour.

In recommending measures to promote access to employment, the CESCR has urged the establishment of employment services (public or private) at the national and local levels.[586] While such services were historically provided by public authorities, the proliferation of private providers is now accepted[587] under certain conditions. ILO Convention No. 181 concerning Private Employment Agencies 1997 requires private employment agencies (including temporary employment agencies) to respect non-discrimination and protect job seekers against unethical or inappropriate practices, and also protects workers under subcontracting arrangements and those recruited abroad. A range of other ILO and regional standards also address employment services.[588]

Additional considerations may apply under regional law. For example, under European competition law, a state's monopoly on job placement services may infringe the freedom of competition of private providers.[589] This is particularly the case where public services provide inadequate assistance to job seekers, thus failing to fulfil their legitimate purpose.

The provision of technical and vocational training has also been emphasized by the CESCR as part of the state's obligation to fulfil ('facilitate') access to employment.[590] Vocational training should be tailored to the needs of different groups (such as young people, older workers, workers transitioning between industries or those seeking to re-enter the labour market after periods of absence). Relevant ILO standards include Convention No. 142 on Human Resources Development 1975, which requires states to develop policies and programmes of vocational guidance and vocational training, including for young people, adults and persons with disabilities. The purpose of such training is to enable all people 'to develop and use their capabilities for work in their own best interests and in accordance with their own aspirations, account being taken of the needs of society' (Article 1(5)). Article 1 of the Convention provides as follows:

1. Each Member shall adopt and develop comprehensive and co-ordinated policies and programmes of vocational guidance and vocational training, closely linked with employment, in particular through public employment services.

[586] CESCR, General Comment No. 18, [12(a)] and [26].

[587] Drzewicki, 'The Right to Work and Rights in Work', 223, 235.

[588] See ILO Convention No. 2 concerning Unemployment (adopted 28 November 1919, 38 UNTS 41, entered into force 14 July 1921); ILO Convention No. 88 concerning the Organisation of the Employment Service (adopted 9 July 1948, 70 UNTS 85, entered into force 10 August 1950); ILO Convention No. 96 concerning Fee-Charging Employment Agencies (adopted 1 July 1949, 96 UNTS 237, entered into force 18 July 1951); and European Social Charter (adopted 18 October 1961, 529 UNTS 89, entered into force 26 February 1961), Article 1(3).

[589] *Job Centre Case*, 11 December 1997, [1997] ECR I-7119.

[590] CESCR, General Comment No. 18, [27].

2. These policies and programmes shall take due account of—

(a) employment needs, opportunities and problems, both regional and national;

(b) the stage and level of economic, social and cultural development; and

(c) the mutual relationships between human resources development and other economic, social and cultural objectives.

3. The policies and programmes shall be pursued by methods that are appropriate to national conditions.

4. The policies and programmes shall be designed to improve the ability of the individual to understand and, individually or collectively, to influence the working and social environment.

5. The policies and programmes shall encourage and enable all persons, on an equal basis and without any discrimination whatsoever, to develop and use their capabilities for work in their own best interests and in accordance with their own aspirations, account being taken of the needs of society.

In addition, ILO Convention No. 140 concerning Paid Educational Leave 1974 requires states to formulate and apply a policy to promote the granting of paid educational leave for the purpose of training at any level, general, social and civic education, and trade union education (in all cases, by methods appropriate to national conditions and practice and by stages as necessary). Subsidiary ILO standards are also relevant.[591]

The CESCR has also stated that the obligation to *fulfil* (*promote*) Article 6 requires states to undertake educational and informational programmes to instil public awareness on the right to work.[592] This also extends to awareness of the right to work in both the public and private sectors.[593]

A particular focus of the CESCR's scrutiny of national employment policies is the precarious situation of workers in the 'informal economy':

10. High unemployment and the lack of secure employment are causes that induce workers to seek employment in the informal sector of the economy. States parties must take the requisite measures, legislative or otherwise, to reduce to the fullest extent possible the number of workers outside the formal economy, workers who as a result of that situation have no protection. These measures would compel employers to respect labour legislation and declare their employees, thus enabling the latter to enjoy all the rights of workers, in particular those provided for in articles 6, 7 and 8 of the Covenant. These measures must reflect the fact that people living in an informal economy do so for the most part because of the need to survive, rather than as a matter of choice. Moreover, domestic and agricultural work must be properly regulated by national legislation so that domestic and agricultural workers enjoy the same level of protection as other workers.[594]

[591] ILO Recommendation No. 195 on Human Resources Development (17 June 2004); ILO Recommendation No. 136 on Special Youth Employment and Training Schemes for Development Purposes (23 June 1970); ILO Recommendation No. 148 on Paid Educational Leave (24 June 1974).

[592] CESCR, General Comment No. 18, [27] and [28].

[593] CESCR, General Comment No. 18, [43].

[594] CESCR, General Comment No. 18, [10].

In monitoring states, the CESCR routinely highlights the problem of informal work, which is as high as 95 per cent in some developing states.[594] It typically calls on states to provide better working conditions and social security access to such workers (matters also addressed under Articles 7 and 9 respectively), to reduce the size of the informal sector and to regularize their employment situation over time. The CESCR has cautioned, however, against state efforts to simply 'eradicate' the informal sector,[595] as opposed to moving people into regular work. Specific measures to address informal work in employment policy are also found in ILO Recommendation No. 169 concerning Employment Policy (Supplementary Provisions) 1984 (see, for example, paragraphs 27 to 29).

In terms of measures to *create* employment more generally, the CESCR has seldom provided detailed recommendations beyond generally calling for more effective or targeted measures. It has very occasionally called on states to provide Keynesian 'infrastructural' projects;[596] promote 'entrepreneurship';[597] facilitate 'investments' that create jobs;[598] create accessible credit schemes to encourage the establishment of small businesses;[599] or use macroeconomic growth to generate jobs.[600]

In criticizing high employment taxes which encourage informal employment,[601] the CESCR has implied that lowering high taxation (thus reducing state revenue) may create conditions for regular employment. Similarly, in suggesting that the excessive use of 'permissive' Dutch labour laws on overtime 'may give rise to a decline in the creation of further jobs',[602] the CESCR has implied that workers' benefits may need to be traded off against creating new jobs. The economic assumptions underlying these judgments are hard to ascertain from the brevity of the concluding observations themselves.

Apart from these sporadic suggestions, the CESCR has not elaborated a sophisticated or coherent economic vision of the range of minimum measures necessary to stimulate employment. In part, this is because national economic systems and conditions vary widely, and the CESCR has largely deferred to national authorities in the formulation of employment policies and strategies. It has thus tended to restrict its review to matters of process (ensuring consultation, accessibility and non-discrimination, social inclusion of disadvantaged groups,

594 CESCR, Concluding Observations: Benin, E/C.12/BEN/CO/2 (9 June 2008), [15].

595 CESCR, Concluding Observations: Azerbaijan, E/C.12/1/Add.20 (22 December 1997), [19].

596 CESCR, Concluding Observations: Angola, E/C.12/AGO/CO/3 (1 December 2008), [19]; Kenya, E/C.12/KEN/CO/1 (1 December 2008), [16].

597 CESCR, Concluding Observations: Croatia, E/C.12/1/Add.73 (5 December 2001), [23]. See also ILO Recommendation No. 189 on General Conditions to Stimulate Job Creation in Small and Medium-Sized Enterprises (17 June 1998); and ILO Recommendation No. 193 on Promotion of Cooperatives (20 June 2002).

598 CESCR, Concluding Observations: Guatemala, E/C.12/1/Add.93 (12 December 2003), [31].

599 CESCR, Concluding Observations: Solomon Islands, E/C.12/1/Add.84 (19 December 2002), [19].

600 CESCR, Concluding Observations: Angola, E/C.12/AGO/CO/3 (1 December 2008), [19]; Bolivia, E/C.12/BOL/CO/2 (8 August 2008), [30].

601 CESCR, Concluding Observations: Poland, E/C.12/1/Add.26 (16 June 1998), [15].

602 CESCR, Concluding Observations: Netherlands, E/C.12/1/Add.25 (16 June 1998), [15].

and the adoption of indicators and benchmarks to measure national progress). But it may also be that the CESCR is not sufficiently expert in the difficult economic policy issues which are necessary for it to make serious and robust interventions in employment policy.

Much of that work is being done elsewhere. For example, the ILO's Global Employment Agenda 2003 comprehensively addresses the wider spectrum of economic and labour market issues that can affect the goal of full employment:

The elements addressing the economic environment are:

1. Promoting trade and investment for productive employment and market access for developing countries.
2. Promoting technological change for higher productivity and job creation and improved standards of living.
3. Promoting sustainable development for sustainable livelihoods.
4. Macroeconomic policy for growth and employment: a call for policy integration.

Those addressing the labour market are:

5. Decent employment through entrepreneurship.
6. Employability by improving knowledge and skills.
7. Active labour market policies for employment, security in change, equity and poverty reduction.
8. Social protection as a productive factor.
9. Occupational safety and health: synergies between security and productivity.
10. Productive employment for poverty reduction and development.[603]

Creating employment thus requires a broad understanding of intersecting economic issues, including macroeconomic policy (such as monetary, fiscal, credit and exchange rate policies), taxation, trade, investment and technology. The CESCR could accordingly do more to supervise the economic policy choices made by states which bear upon employment, by reference to agreed global policy standards.

There are, of course, substantial challenges in doing so: the CESCR would need to acquire greater economic literacy; and it would have to be prepared to take and defend complex economic policy positions which may be contested, thus politicizing its hitherto relatively 'procedural' interest in the right to work. Yet, doing so is necessary to ensure that the CESCR remains relevant in the face of globalization[604]—and does not become dismissed as a body which simplistically criticizes unemployment without offering real solutions.

[603] ILO, Review of the Core Elements of the Global Employment Agenda, GB.286/ESP/1(Rev) (March 2003), 5; see also ILO, 'Implementing the Global Employment Agenda: Employment Strategies in Support of Decent Work—"Vision" Document' (Geneva, 2006).

[604] Joseph, 'UN Covenants and Labour Rights', 341.

INDICATORS, BENCHMARKS, MONITORING

The CESCR has, however, been more attentive to what is required of states in monitoring the employment policies that they adopt. States are required to include in their policies 'indicators and benchmarks by which progress in relation to the right to work can be measured and periodically reviewed'.[605] These should include numerical targets, time frames for implementation and mechanisms or means for ensuring compliance:

38. States parties should consider the adoption of specific legislative measures for the implementation of the right to work. Those measures should (a) establish national mechanisms to monitor implementation of employment strategies and national plans of action and (b) contain provisions on numerical targets and a time frame for implementation. They should also provide (c) means of ensuring compliance with the benchmarks established at the national level and (d) the involvement of civil society, including experts on labour issues, the private sector and international organizations. In monitoring progress on realization of the right to work, States parties should identify the factors and difficulties affecting the fulfilment of their obligations.[606]

They should also 'identify the resources available to States parties for achieving their objectives as well as the most cost-effective ways of using them'.[607] In monitoring states, however, while the CESCR frequently calls on states to do more to address unemployment, it seldom stipulates a particular level of resourcing which states should allocate to employment generation, or identifies where such resources should be sourced or diverted from.

The CESCR has encouraged states to define indicators on the right to work based on ILO indicators, and to set and monitor national benchmarks for each indicator:

46. A national employment strategy must define indicators on the right to work. The indicators should be designed to monitor effectively, at the national level, the compliance by States parties with their obligations under article 6 and should be based on ILO indicators such as the rate of unemployment, underemployment and the ratio of formal to informal work. Indicators developed by the ILO that apply to the preparation of labour statistics may be useful in the preparation of a national employment plan.

47. Having identified appropriate right to work indicators, States parties are invited to set appropriate national benchmarks in relation to each indicator. During the periodic reporting procedure the Committee will engage in a process of 'scoping' with the State party. Scoping involves the joint consideration by the State party and the Committee of the indicators and national benchmarks which will then provide the targets to be achieved during the next reporting period. During the following five years the State party will use these national benchmarks to help monitor its implementation of the right to work. Thereafter, in the subsequent reporting process, the State party and the Committee will consider whether or not the benchmarks have been achieved and the reasons for any difficulties that may have been encountered. Further, when setting benchmarks and preparing their reports States parties should utilize the extensive information and advisory services of specialized agencies with regard to data collection and disaggregation.[608]

[605] CESCR, General Comment No. 18, [31](c).
[606] CESCR, General Comment No. 18, [38].
[607] CESCR, General Comment No. 18, [41].
[608] CESCR, General Comment No. 18, [46]–[47].

The choice of employment indicators can affect whether employment policy fulfils the right to work, such as where its quantitative aspect (the level of unemployment) is neglected in favour of other dimensions (such as its distributive and qualitative aspects).[609] The ILO has published labour statistics since 1935 and its current *Key Indicators of the Labour Market* (7th edition, 2011) uses widely recognized methodologies to measure eighteen core indicators (which are relevant to work rights under both Articles 6 and 7 of the ICESCR):

1. Labour force participation rate
2. Employment-to-population ratio
3. Status in employment
4. Employment by sector
5. Employment by occupation
6. Part-time workers
7. Hours of work
8. Employment in the informal economy
9. Unemployment
10. Youth unemployment
11. Long-term unemployment
12. Time-related underemployment
13. Inactivity
14. Educational attainment and illiteracy
15. Average monthly wages
16. Hourly compensation costs
17. Labour productivity
18. Poverty, income distribution and the working poor

In 2008, a new Millennium Development Goal (MDG) Target (1B) was agreed as part of global efforts to address poverty and hunger: '[to a]chieve full and productive employment and decent work for all, including women and young people'. Four employment indicators were adopted to monitor (including at the national level) progress towards that target, and which were based on ILO standards, best practice and well-established data sources:[610]

1.4 Growth rate of labour productivity (GDP per person employed)

1.5 Employment-to-population ratio

[609] See Harvey, 'Benchmarking the Right to Work', 117.

[610] ILO, Guide to the New Millennium Development Goals Employment Indicators: Including the Full Set of Decent Work Indicators, 978-92-2-122304-7 (10 July 2009).

1.6 Proportion of employed people living below the poverty line (working poor)

1.7 Proportion of own-account and contributing family workers in total employment (vulnerable employment rate)

These indicators may be of special significance in the CESCR's monitoring of the performance of developing countries in implementing Article 6, including in the context of resource limitations, progressive realization and the availability of international assistance under the MDG regime.

The Office of the High Commission for Human Rights has also engaged in efforts to develop indicators on the right to work which align more closely with human rights objectives, as opposed to the ILO's economic emphasis or the MDG's developmental perspective. The OHCHR's 'illustrative indicators' are based on the work rights in Article 23 of the UDHR and focus on access to decent and productive work; training, skill upgrading and professional development; and protection from forced labour and unemployment; all are then assessed at the structural, process and outcome levels.[611]

Closely related to the setting of indicators is the need for states to maintain 'mechanisms' to monitor progress towards realizing the right to work, as the CESCR explains:

45. States parties should develop and maintain mechanisms to monitor progress towards the realization of the right to freely chosen or accepted employment, to identify the factors and difficulties affecting the degree of compliance with their obligations and to facilitate the adoption of corrective legislative and administrative measures, including measures to implement their obligations under articles 2.1 and 23 of the Covenant.[612]

The ILO reports that relatively few countries have reported to it on their monitoring mechanisms,[613] but these may include a range of processes: ministerial level consideration; inter-departmental committees; data collection and reporting; or parliamentary oversight. The CESCR has frequently noted, however, where states have not provided it with disaggregated data (such as by group, region or sector) on employment and labour statistics, and has called on states to establish data collection mechanisms[614] or to provide it with more or better data.[615] The CESCR has noted that the failure to monitor the right to work through indicators and benchmarks is a violation of the state's obligation to fulfil the right to work.[616]

[611] OHCHR, *Human Rights Indicators: A Guide to Measurement and Implementation*, HR/PUB/12/5 (2012), 95.

[612] CESCR, General Comment No. 18, [45].

[613] ILO, Promoting Employment: Policies, Skills, Enterprises, Report III (Part 1B), (2004), 32–4.

[614] CESCR, Concluding Observations: Angola, E/C.12/AGO/CO/3 (1 December 2008), [19]; Kenya, E/C.12/KEN/CO/1 (1 December 2008), [16].

[615] CESCR, Concluding Observations: Benin, E/C.12/BEN/CO/2 (9 June 2008), [36]; Macedonia, E/C.12/MKD/CO/1 (15 January 2008), [35]; Greece, E/C.12/1/Add.97 (7 June 2004), [35]; Hungary, E/C.12/HUN/CO/3 (18 January 2008), [34]; Iceland, E/C.12/1/Add.89 (26 June 2003), [22].

[616] CESCR, General Comment No. 18, [36].

Remedies for Violations of the Right to Work

Violations of the right to work are subject to the general principle that the state must provide effective remedies for violations. Article 6 does not stipulate any special remedies or remedial mechanisms for the right to work and the CESCR has invoked the usual suite of forums and remedies, while also noting the special role for trade unions:

48. Any person or group who is a victim of a violation of the right to work should have access to effective judicial or other appropriate remedies at the national level. At the national level trade unions and human rights commissions should play an important role in defending the right to work. All victims of such violations are entitled to adequate reparation, which may take the form of restitution, compensation, satisfaction or a guarantee of non-repetition.

Occasionally, the CESCR has identified the need for particular remedies in monitoring states, such as compensation for loss of employment.[617]

The most common mechanism addressed by the CESCR is the labour inspectorate. The CESCR has called on states to amend their laws to establish a system of labour inspectors, including with ILO technical assistance.[618] It has asked states to clarify the role of labour inspectors in monitoring the right to work.[619] It has urged states to ensure that labour inspectors act independently and effectively to combat violations of basic labour rights.[620] It has called on states to provide 'sufficient resources to the labour inspectorate to enable regular and independent inspections'.[621] It has also emphasized the need to train them.[622]

Various ILO standards are relevant. Convention No. 81 on Labour Inspection 1947 requires states to maintain a system of labour inspection for workplaces in industry and commerce, while allowing exceptions for mining and transport. It covers the functions, organization, powers and obligations of labour inspectors. Protocol No. 81 of 1995 extends Convention No. 81 to non-commercial workplaces (that is, neither industrial nor commercial), and allows for inspection of listed public services. There is also a specific convention governing agricultural labour inspection, which can also extend to tenants, sharecroppers, collective economic enterprises (such as cooperatives) and family farms.[623]

More broadly, the CESCR has encouraged judges and law enforcement authorities 'to pay greater attention to violations of the right to work in the exercise

[617] CESCR, General Comment No. 18, [26].

[618] CESCR, Concluding Observations: Chad, E/C.12/TCD/CO/3 (16 December 2009), [16].

[619] CESCR, Concluding Observations: Venezuela, E/C.12/1/Add.56 (21 May 2001), [23].

[620] CESCR, Concluding Observations: Angola, E/C.12/AGO/CO/3 (1 December 2008), [19]; Kenya, E/C.12/KEN/CO/1 (1 December 2008), [16].

[621] CESCR, Concluding Observations: India, E/C.12/IND/CO/5 (8 August 2008), [59].

[622] CESCR, Concluding Observations: Ukraine, E/C.12/UKR/CO/5 (4 January 2008), [36].

[623] ILO Convention No. 129 concerning Labour Inspection in Agriculture (adopted 25 June 1969, 812 UNTS 87, entered into force 19 January 1972).

of their functions',[624] perhaps reflecting the historical pattern of socio-economic rights being under-enforced or unenforceable.

In considering the establishment of enforcement mechanisms, the CESCR has suggested that ratifying, domestically incorporating or giving direct effect to international instruments recognizing the right to work 'significantly enhances the scope and effectiveness of remedial measures and is encouraged in all cases':

49. Incorporation of international instruments setting forth the right to work into the domestic legal order, in particular the relevant ILO conventions, should strengthen the effectiveness of measures taken to guarantee the right to work and is encouraged. The incorporation of international instruments recognizing the right to work into the domestic legal order, or the recognition of their direct applicability, significantly enhances the scope and effectiveness of remedial measures and is encouraged in all cases. Courts would then be empowered to adjudicate violations of the core content of the right to work by directly applying obligations under the Covenant.[625]

Various formulations of the right to work are found in numerous national constitutions,[626] although these are often aspirational directives of state policy[627] rather than justiciable rights. The ICESCR and ILO conventions can therefore provide an external legal basis on which states can legislate or judicially incorporate labour rights into domestic law. As already noted, the various ILO procedures also provide further means of internationally supervising and monitoring states.

Defenders of work rights have also been the focus of concern by the CESCR:

51. States parties should respect and protect the work of human rights defenders and other members of civil society, in particular the trade unions, who assist disadvantaged and marginalized individuals and groups in the realization of their right to work.

Violence or intimidation against trade unionists or workers' representatives is a particular problem arising under Article 8 of the ICESCR. Various cases in the Inter-American human rights system have particularly focused on attacks on trade unionists, typically as infringing civil and political rights such as those relating to life and freedom from torture or arbitrary detention.[628]

Obligations of Non-State Actors

The CESCR has specifically highlighted the role of business in enabling the right to work:

52. While only States are parties to the Covenant and are thus ultimately accountable for compliance with it, all members of society—individuals, local communities, trade

[624] CESCR, General Comment No. 18, [50]. [625] CESCR, General Comment No. 18, [49].

[626] Nussberger, 'Work, Right to, International Protection', [3]–[7].

[627] See, eg, Constitution of India (adopted 26 November 1949, entered into force 26 January 1950), Article 41.

[628] *Huilca-Tesce v Peru (Merits, Reparations and Costs)*, 3 March 2005, (2005) Ser C No. 121 (IACHR).

unions, civil society and private sector organizations—have responsibilities regarding the realization of the right to work. States parties should provide an environment facilitating the discharge of these obligations. Private enterprises—national and multinational—while not bound by the Covenant, have a particular role to play in job creation, hiring policies and non-discriminatory access to work. They should conduct their activities on the basis of legislation, administrative measures, codes of conduct and other appropriate measures promoting respect for the right to work, agreed between the government and civil society. Such measures should recognize the labour standards elaborated by the ILO and aim at increasing the awareness and responsibility of enterprises in the realization of the right to work.

The UN Guiding Principles on Business and Human Rights also specifically highlight that the responsibility of business enterprises to respect human rights includes the fundamental rights in the ILO's Declaration on Fundamental Principles and Rights at Work 1988.[629]

Some elements of Article 6 will be more relevant to private enterprise than others. Clearly, businesses must comply with national laws implementing Article 6 obligations, and are expected not to discriminate on impermissible grounds in recruitment; use forced or child labour;[630] or engage in unfair dismissals. The CESCR has emphasized to states, such as India, that they must raise awareness among employers of, for instance, child labour standards.[631] The CESCR has often been concerned to ensure greater state protection of those working in the informal economy in relation to Articles 6, 7 and 8.[632]

The imperatives on business may be more equivocal in respect of other aspects of Article 6. For example, the state must pursue employment and training policies directed towards full employment and businesses may certainly be encouraged to take part in such initiatives, for instance through job creation, hiring practices, or providing apprenticeships or other vocational training opportunities.

However, in market economies it would generally be considered unacceptable to mandate (as oppose to incentivize) businesses to undertake such activities, or to demand that businesses divert resources to them by sacrificing profits or their duties to shareholders or investors. In this regard, the CESCR has only encouraged states (such as India) to 'provide the necessary conditions to encourage private sector employers to create additional jobs in the process of economic growth';[633] or recommended states (such as Solomon Islands) to 'encourage the

[629] John Ruggie, Report of the Special Representative of the Secretary General: Guiding Principles on Business and Human Rights for implementing the UN 'Protect, Respect and Remedy' Framework, A/HRC/17/31 (21 March 2011), annex, Principle 12. The Guiding Principles were endorsed by the UN Human Rights Council on 16 June 2011.

[630] As noted earlier, private individuals or companies are not permitted to use forced labour for private purposes under Articles 5–6 of ILO Convention No. 29.

[631] CESCR, Concluding Observations: India, E/C.12/IND/CO/5 (8 August 2008), [19].

[632] See the relevant chapters in this book.

[633] CESCR, Concluding Observations: India, E/C.12/IND/CO/5 (8 August 2008), [60].

establishment of small businesses, including through the creation of accessible credit schemes'.[634]

In general, the CESCR has not addressed its observations on Article 6 specifically to business, but has urged states to better regulate business activities in various contexts. Its concern about non-consensual prison labour for private companies was noted earlier.[635] Most commonly, the CESCR has expressed concern about the status of women in the private sector, particularly regarding: equal treatment;[636] equal remuneration for work of equal value;[637] the lack of anti-discrimination mechanisms;[638] and the lack of flexible parental leave schemes and affordable childcare, making it difficult for women to balance employment and family responsibilities.[639] The CESCR has also urged states to adopt better preventive and remedial measures against discrimination in the private sector, as in its observations on the Ukraine:

> 36. The Committee recommends that the State party train judges, labour inspectors and officers of the State Employment Service to apply strictly the Law on Equal Rights and Opportunities for Men and Women and the amended Labour Code, with a view to combating gender discrimination in the public and private employment sectors, in particular at the recruitment stage, conduct awareness-raising campaigns for employers, employees and the general public, and ensure that fines or other appropriate sanctions are imposed on employers who discriminate against women, and that the victims of such discrimination have access to effective remedies, including compensation. It urges the State party to further enhance vocational training, job training and retraining opportunities for unemployed women and women employed in low-paid jobs.[640]

Employment opportunities for ethnic minorities in the private sector have also been of concern to the CESCR, including (as in the case of Sri Lanka) where there is a lack of anti-discrimination mechanisms, including in respect of promotions.[641] The CESCR urged Hungary to 'take more effective measures to encourage the private sector to provide adequate employment opportunities for the Roma',[642] although it stopped short of calling for quotas. To reduce unemployment among marginalized groups in Costa Rica, the CESCR called for the introduction of 'specifically targeted measures, including by…introducing and effectively enforcing legal provisions requiring an ethnically balanced workforce in the public and

[634] CESCR, Concluding Observations: Solomon Islands, E/C.12/1/Add.84 (19 December 2002), [19].

[635] CESCR, Concluding Observations: Germany, E/C.12/1/Add.68 (24 September 2001), [21] and [39]; Luxembourg, E/C.12/1/Add.86 (26 June 2003), [20] and [32].

[636] CESCR, Concluding Observations: Luxembourg, E/C.12/1/Add.22 (12 December 1997), [18].

[637] CESCR, Concluding Observations: Chad, E/C.12/TCD/CO/3 (16 December 2009), [17]; Sri Lanka, E/C.12/1/Add.24 (16 June 1998), [11]; India, E/C.12/IND/CO/5 (8 August 2008), [57].

[638] CESCR, Concluding Observations: Sri Lanka, E/C.12/1/Add.24 (16 June 1998), [11].

[639] CESCR, Concluding Observations: Malta, E/C.12/1/Add.101 (14 December 2004), [15] and [33].

[640] CESCR, Concluding Observations: Ukraine, E/C.12/UKR/CO/5 (4 January 2008), [36].

[641] CESCR, Concluding Observations: Sri Lanka, E/C.12/1/Add.24 (16 June 1998), [11].

[642] CESCR, Concluding Observations: Hungary, E/C.12/HUN/CO/3 (16 January 2008), [34].

private sectors'.[643] Such measures go beyond non-discrimination and seemingly envisage state-mandated measures of 'positive discrimination' in private sector employment, such as through quotas for minority groups.

The CESCR has also been concerned where privatization has risked undermining the existing employment of ethnic minorities. It thus faulted UNMIK in Kosovo for failing to provide adequate safeguards during the privatization of 'Socially Owned Enterprises', which were a socialist legal category in which entities were 'owned' by society (rather than the state):

18. The Committee notes with concern reports that UNMIK has failed to provide adequate safeguards during the privatization of former Socially Owned Enterprises aimed at preserving the pre-armed conflict ethnic composition of the workforce, and that it has set discriminatory deadlines precluding many internally displaced persons and returnees from applying for inclusion in the list of former employees eligible to participate in the distribution of the proceeds from the sale of such enterprises, and from appealing to the Special Chamber of the Supreme Court in case of their non-inclusion. (art. 6)[644]

Business practices also have critical effects on labour conditions under Article 7 of the ICESCR and trade union rights under Article 8, which are considered subsequently.

The CESCR has also emphasized the 'fundamental role' of trade unions in relation to Article 6:

54. Trade unions play a fundamental role in ensuring respect for the right to work at the local and national levels and in assisting States parties to comply with their obligations under article 6. The role of trade unions is fundamental and will continue to be considered by the Committee in its consideration of the reports of States parties.

However, the CESCR's concluding observations on states in relation to Article 6 seldom mention trade unions or elaborate upon their role in relation to the right to work. This is true of both the potential positive contributions of trade unions (in furthering the right to work by combating discrimination or unfair dismissal) and their negative effects (for instance, by making unreasonable demands for wage increases or better conditions, thus making labour unaffordable, business unprofitable, and reducing employment opportunities overall).

Mainly this is because trade unions are separately covered by Article 8, discussed later, including in the context of their right to confederate or associate internationally and thereby to campaign transnationally for workers' rights. It may also be noted that trade unions may have a role not only in partisan advocacy for workers, but in ensuring the right to work more generally (for instance, in arguing for wage restraint in difficult economic conditions),

[643] CESCR, Concluding Observations: Costa Rica, E/C.12/CRI/CO/4 (4 January 2008), [39].
[644] CESCR, Concluding Observations: UN Interim Administration Mission in Kosovo, E/C.12/UNK/CO/1 (1 December 2008), [18].

including where this may conflict with the sectoral interests of particular employees.

Naturally, where a state fails to take the necessary measures to protect workers' rights from infringements by private parties, there may be a violation of the state's own obligation to protect workers from such risks.[645] Violations may result from 'omissions such as the failure to regulate the activities of individuals, groups or corporations so as to prevent them from violating the right to work of others; or the failure to protect workers against unlawful dismissal'.[646]

International Cooperation and the Role of International Organizations

A state's capacity to fulfil the right to work will depend on domestic and international economic conditions, including those outside the control of the state.[647] As for other ICESCR rights, states are required to take steps individually and through international assistance and cooperation (ICESCR, Article 2(1)) to achieve the right to work, including by treaty action, soft law making, consultation, research and technical assistance (ICESCR, Article 23).[648]

These obligations of cooperation have a number of implications for the right to work. First, the CESCR encourages states 'to promote the right to work in other countries'.[649] The CESCR has not, however, elaborated on what this means in practice and has tended not to address the point in its concluding observations, which generally focus on a state's domestic protection of the right.

Secondly, the CESCR has stated that 'States parties should, through international agreements where appropriate, ensure that the right to work as set forth in articles 6, 7 and 8 of the Covenant is given due attention'.[650] This includes bilateral and multilateral agreements.[651] Again, in its practice the CESCR has not identified what this means with much particularity. As already noted, occasionally it has encouraged states to ratify the Migrant Workers' Convention,[652] or to otherwise 'conclude international agreements with a view to ensuring the social protection of migrant workers'.[653] Such agreements are particularly important in setting out the respective labour-related obligations of sending and receiving states.

[645] CESCR, General Comment No. 18, [35].
[646] CESCR, General Comment No. 18, [35].
[647] CESCR, General Comment No. 18, [4].
[648] CESCR, General Comment No. 18, [29].
[649] CESCR, General Comment No. 18, [30].
[650] CESCR, General Comment No. 18, [29].
[651] CESCR, General Comment No. 18, [30].
[652] CESCR, Concluding Observations: Moldova, E/C.12/1/Add.91 (12 December 2003), [36]; Russian Federation, E/C.12/1/Add.94 (12 December 2003), [45].
[653] CESCR, Concluding Observations: Moldova, E/C.12/1/Add.91 (12 December 2003), [36]; Russian Federation, E/C.12/1/Add.94 (12 December 2003), [45].

Beyond the areas identified by the CESCR, in principle various other areas of transnational regulation are ripe for labour rights cooperation. For example, bilateral investment treaties might recognize international labour rights. The Draft Model Norwegian Bilateral Investment Treaty 2007, although abandoned in 2008, sought to prevent states from driving down labour protections so as to attract investment. Article 11(1) provides:

The Parties recognize that it is inappropriate to encourage investment by relaxing domestic health, safety or environmental measures or core labour standards. Accordingly, a Party should not waive or otherwise derogate from, or offer to waive or otherwise derogate from, such measures as an encouragement for the establishment, acquisition, expansion or retention of an investment of an investor.

Likewise, free trade agreements can be drafted to include labour protections, as in the Revised Cotonou Agreement 2010[654] between the twenty-seven states of the European Union and seventy-nine states from Africa, the Caribbean and Pacific, which governs development, economic, trade and political cooperation. Article 50 refers to 'Trade and Labour Standards':

1. The Parties reaffirm their commitment to the internationally recognised core labour standards, as defined by the relevant International Labour Organisation (ILO) Conventions, and in particular the freedom of association and the right to collective bargaining, the abolition of forced labour, the elimination of worst forms of child labour and non-discrimination in respect to employment.

2. They agree to enhance cooperation in this area, in particular in the following fields:

— exchange of information on the respective legislation and work regulation;

— the formulation of national labour legislation and strengthening of existing legislation;

— educational and awareness raising programmes;

— enforcement of adherence to national legislation and work regulation;

3. The Parties agree that labour standards should not be used for protectionist purposes.[655]

The injunction against invoking labour standards for protectionist purposes did not appear in the original 2000 Agreement, but was added to the Revised Agreement of 2010, reflecting the tensions in the interaction of global trade and labour law regimes. Political dialogue is encouraged on child labour under Article 8(4), while Article 9 of the Agreement refers to human rights more generally.

Article 50 is principally hortatory and procedural—states 'reaffirm' existing commitments and 'agree to enhance cooperation', including in regulatory

[654] ACP-EC Partnership Agreement ('Cotonou Agreement') (adopted 23 June 2000, entered into force April 2003, revised in Luxembourg on 25 June 2005, revised in Ouagadougou on 22 June 2010, OJ L 287/3, 4 November 2010).

[655] Cotonou Agreement, Article 50; see also preamble (in which the parties express that they are '[a]nxious to respect basic labour rights, taking account of the principles laid down in the relevant conventions of the International Labour Organization').

enforcement. But the Agreement does not create new mechanisms or penalties as such for the enforcement of labour standards, other than the generally available dialogue and consultation procedures in respect of disputes arising under it.

The broad scope of the Agreement—development, trade, political cooperation—does, however, indicate the potential for including labour clauses outside the trade context, for instance in foreign aid and development assistance.

A third area for international cooperation on labour rights identified by the CESCR concerns states' role in relation to international financial institutions:

> …In negotiations with international financial institutions, States parties should ensure protection of the right to work of their population. States parties that are members of international financial institutions, in particular the International Monetary Fund, the World Bank and regional development banks, should pay greater attention to the protection of the right to work in influencing the lending policies, credit agreements, structural adjustment programmes and international measures of these institutions. The strategies, programmes and policies adopted by States parties under structural adjustment programmes should not interfere with their core obligations in relation to the right to work and impact negatively on the right to work of women, young persons and the disadvantaged and marginalized individuals and groups.[656]

In monitoring states, however, the CESCR has seldom commented on whether particular states have negotiated with international financial institutions either to protect their own population's work rights or influence institutions' policies in other states. One rare example is its comment on the Republic of Korea in its response to an economic crisis:

> 12. The Committee is concerned that the State party did not take into account its Covenant obligations when negotiating with international financial institutions to overcome its financial crisis and restructure its economy. The overreliance on macroeconomic policies has had profound negative effects on the enjoyment of economic, social and cultural rights in that there have been large-scale employee dismissals and lay-offs, a significant deterioration in employment stability, growing income inequalities, an increasing number of broken families and marginalization of a large number of persons.[657]

A fourth and final area of international cooperation identified by the CESCR concerns the role of international institutions, including the United Nations, International Labour Organization, World Bank, International Monetary Fund, World Trade Organization (WTO) and regional organizations:

> 53. The role of the United Nations agencies and programmes, and in particular the key function of the ILO in protecting and implementing the right to work at the international, regional and national levels, is of particular importance. Regional institutions and instruments, where they exist, also play an important role in ensuring the right to work…In conformity with articles 22 and 23 of the Covenant, the ILO and the other specialized agencies of the United Nations, the World Bank, regional development banks, the International

[656] CESCR, General Comment No. 18, [30]; see also [53]; CESCR, General Comment No. 2, E/1990/23 (2 February 1990), [9].

[657] CESCR, Concluding Observations: Republic of Korea, E/C.12/1/Add.59 (21 May 2001), [12].

Monetary Fund, the World Trade Organization and other relevant bodies within the United Nations system should cooperate effectively with States parties to implement the right to work at the national level, bearing in mind their own mandates . . .[658]

The CESCR has especially called for states to cooperate with the ILO on labour rights:

53. . . . When formulating and implementing their national employment strategies, States parties should avail themselves of the technical assistance and cooperation offered by the ILO. When preparing their reports, States parties should also use the extensive information and advisory services provided by the ILO for data collection and disaggregation as well as the development of indicators and benchmarks.[659]

The CESCR has specifically called on states to request international assistance in drafting and reviewing employment legislation:

40. United Nations agencies and programmes should, upon States parties' request, assist in drafting and reviewing relevant legislation. The ILO, for example, has considerable expertise and accumulated knowledge concerning legislation in the field of employment.[660]

Various specialized agencies may be relevant in the context of labour rights. In respect of displacement, UNHCR may be relevant to the work rights of refugees or even internally displaced persons, and the International Organization of Migration may also have a role to play. The CESCR pointed to the need for international assistance in the Ukraine's repatriation of Crimean Tartar minorities, including to guarantee their work rights:

24. The Committee recommends that the civil status of the repatriated members of minorities, especially the Crimean Tatars, be regularised as soon as possible. It recommends that steps be taken immediately to fully reintegrate them into the region and to guarantee their rights to work and to an adequate standard of living, as defined under article 11. The Committee recommends that every effort be made in order to obtain international assistance toward this end.[661]

The CESCR has acknowledged that in assessing states' compliance with Article 6, it 'will consider the effects of the assistance provided by actors other than States parties'.[662]

In relation to world trade law and labour rights, mention was made earlier of the possibility of including labour standards in free trade agreements. The issue is more complicated within the multilateral framework of the WTO. WTO members bear concurrent legal obligations under Article 6 of the ICESCR (and ILO standards) and the various WTO agreements to which they are parties. The question is whether those two sets of obligations may come into conflict and if so, what rules apply to resolve inconsistencies between the different regimes.

[658] CESCR, General Comment No. 18, [53].
[659] CESCR, General Comment No. 18, [53].
[660] CESCR, General Comment No. 18, [40].
[661] CESCR, Concluding Observations: Ukraine, E/C.12/1995/15 (12 December 1995), [24].
[662] CESCR, General Comment No. 18, [30]; see also [53].

For example, trade liberalization may produce structural unemployment[663] in areas of domestic economic activity which are no longer competitive once protectionist measures (such as subsidies or tariffs) are reduced or removed. In severe cases, it may even provoke civil unrest. The Preamble of the WTO Agreement provides that 'trade should be conducted with a view to raising standards of living, ensuring full employment…in accordance with the objective of sustainable development'.[664] WTO agreements otherwise scarcely mention labour standards,[665] although labour interests can be protected to some extent through both the interpretation of, and exceptions within, WTO law.[666]

For its part, the CESCR has not directly confronted the interaction between trade and labour commitments in monitoring states' compliance with Article 6, although it has criticized the impacts of export-oriented activities in relation to Articles 7 (work conditions) and 8 (trade unions).[667] Globalization brings certain risks for labour protection, although some suggest that it has not thus far produced a 'race to the bottom' in labour standards either in developing or developed countries.[668] Globalization is also double-edged: the spread of international labour protection standards and monitoring is also a manifestation of globalization. It may also be noted that much labour in any given state is local rather than in global competition, whether public service employment, school teachers, retail workers and so on.

Given that the binding dispute resolution mechanisms of the WTO provide an opportunity for the relationship to be elaborated in a trade-oriented legal environment, it is nonetheless important that the CESCR demarcates its own position on these issues and, where necessary, engages in a dialogue with WTO law.

It is true that the CESCR is not explicitly mandated to apply trade law, and UN human rights treaty bodies as a whole have tended to avoid grappling with specialized branches of international law outside their own limited, treaty-based mandates. However, to the extent that free trade stimulates structural or causal risks for work rights (such as unemployment or wage exploitation), or the application of trade law results in economic interests being prioritized over labour rights, the CESCR cannot avoid confronting these issues.

Regional competition law may also raise challenges for compliance with labour rights. The European Commission, for example, has indicated that state-supported employment training measures may raise EU competition law issues where it reduces costs that companies would normally bear themselves,

[663] Lorand Bartels, 'Trade and Human Rights' in Daniel Bethlehem, Donald McRae, Rodney Neufeld and Isabelle Van Damme (eds), *The Oxford Handbook of International Trade Law* (Oxford University Press, Oxford, 2009), 571, 579.

[664] Marrakesh Agreement establishing the World Trade Organization (adopted 15 April 1994, 1867 UNTS 154, 1 January 1994).

[665] Gabrielle Marceau, 'Trade and Labour' in Bethlehem et al, *The Oxford Handbook of International Trade Law*, 539, 541.

[666] Marceau, 'Trade and Labour', 542–3, 549–52 (eg, exceptions relating to public morals, health and prison labour).

[667] See Joseph, 'UN Covenants and Labour Rights', 344–5.

[668] Siegel, 'The Right to Work', 23, 26.

give them an advantage over others and distort competition.[669] An obligation under regional law does not relieve a state of its obligation to comply with international law. However, public interests in competition may be a legitimate basis for restricting this aspect of the right to work under the limitations clause in Article 4 of the ICESCR. Restrictive measures must, however, be necessary and proportionate and accord due weight to the importance of training in realizing the right to work and human dignity.

Where a state fails to take into account its legal obligations concerning the right to work in its bilateral or multilateral agreements with other states, international organizations and other entities (such as multinationals), the state violates its obligation to 'respect' the right to work.[670] The international dimensions of trade union rights are considered in the chapter on Article 8 of the ICESCR.

Regional Protection of the Right to Work

Express protection of the right to work is found in all major regional human rights systems except in Asia and the Pacific. In Europe, the right to work is expressed in terms similar to Article 6 of the ICESCR, both in the European Social Charter of 1961 (Part I, Article 1) and the Revised European Social Charter of 1996 (Part II, Article 1) ('Everyone shall have the opportunity to earn his living in an occupation freely entered upon') and the Charter of Fundamental Rights of the European Union 2000 ('a right to engage in work and to pursue a freely chosen or accepted occupation' in Article 15).

None of these instruments is directly enforceable. The system of state supervision and monitoring under the European Social Charter framework is, however, gradually interpreting the scope of work rights. The former Committee of Independent Experts (now the European Committee on Social Rights (ECSR)) authoritatively monitored state reports from 1991 onwards, and collective complaints have been possible since 1998. The relatively few individual cases have tended to concern trade union-related rights rather than the right to work proper. In monitoring state reporting, the ECSR has tended to focus on the need for states to pursue a 'coherent economic policy' rather than prescribing a particular result in terms of employment or unemployment.[671]

Work rights do not appear in the binding regime of the European Convention on Human Rights (ECHR), which focuses on civil and political rights. At most, the ECHR prohibits slavery and forced labour (Article 4) and guarantees freedom of association (Article 11). Work has, however, been tangentially protected under the rubric of other ECHR rights.[672] To give some examples, in the

[669] European Commission Communication, Framework on Training Aid, OJ C 343/7, 11 November 1998, [7].

[670] CESCR, General Comment No. 18, [33]. [671] Ashiagbor, 'The Right to Work', 244.

[672] See Tonia Novitz, 'Protection of Workers under Regional Human Rights Systems: An Assessment of Evolving and Divergent Practices' in Fenwick and Novitz, *Human Rights at Work*, 409, 425; Ida Elisabeth Koch, *Human Rights as Indivisible Rights: The Protection of Socio-Economic Demands*

non-discrimination field, freedom of expression was violated where a television director was fired for publicly criticizing his employer.[673] There was religious discrimination where a Jehovah's Witness was refused employment following a conviction for refusal to perform military service.[674] There was discrimination where Austria differentiated between nationals and non-nationals in the emergency advance payment of accrued pension entitlements.[675]

Further, some protection for work has come through the right to private life in Article 8 of the ECHR, which has been interpreted to encompass relationships of a 'professional or business nature' in the course of a person's working life.[676] Private life was infringed, for instance, where a sailor was discharged from the navy for homosexuality;[677] and where restrictions on the employment of former intelligence (KGB) officers long after the fall of communism were disproportionate.[678]

Proprietary interests related to work have been protected under the right to property in Article 1 of Protocol 1 to the ECHR. Examples include cases concerning: agricultural assets on which livelihoods depend; ancestral interests in land; interference in landlords' rights to use their properties; and remuneration owed.[679] At the procedural level, the right to a fair civil hearing in Article 6 of the ECHR has extended to private and certain public occupational disputes.[680]

In Africa, the right to work is bundled together with conditions of work in Article 15 of the African Charter on Human and Peoples' Rights 1981, which provides that '[e]very individual shall have the right to work under equitable and satisfactory conditions, and shall receive equal pay for equal work.' State reporting and complaints have been made to the African Commission on Human Rights since 1987, and complaints are possible before the reformed African Court of Justice and Human Rights since 2008.

A few African cases have involved work rights.[681] The African Commission found that Cameroon violated Article 15 by failing to reinstate a judge after his release from prison following a military trial, and where an amnesty had been granted to others in a similar situation.[682] A Gambian court incidentally noted that

under the European Convention on Human Rights (Martinus Nijhoff, Leiden, 2009), chapter 9 ('Work-Related Rights under the ECHR').

673 *Fuentes Bobo v Spain* (App. 39293/98), 29 February 2000, (2001) 31 EHRR 1115.

674 *Thlimmenos v Greece* (App. 34369/97), 6 April 2000, (2001) 31 EHRR 15.

675 *Gaygusuz v Austria* (App. 17371/90), 16 September 1996, (1997) 23 EHRR 364.

676 *Niemietz v Germany*, ECtHR 16 December 1992, [29].

677 *Lustig-Prean and Beckett v United Kingdom* (Apps. 31417/96 and 32377/96), 27 September 1999, (2000) 29 EHRR 548.

678 *Sidabras and Dziautas v Lithuania* (Apps. 55480/00, 59330/00), 27 July 2004, [2004] 42 EHRR 104, [59].

679 See the cases discussed in Koch, *Human Rights as Indivisible Rights*, 222–6.

680 Koch, *Human Rights as Indivisible Rights*, 226–33. See especially *Pellegrin v France*, ECtHR Judgment, 8 December 1999; *Vilho Eskelinen et al v Finland*, ECtHR 19 April 2007.

681 Novitz, 'Protection of Workers under Regional Human Rights Systems', 409, 425.

682 *Annette Pagnoulle (on behalf of Abdoulaye Mazou)*, African Commission on Human Rights Communication No. 39/90, (2000) AHRLR 57 (24 April 1997).

the unlawful detention of a person by security forces may also interfere in the right to work under Article 15 of the Charter.[683]

In another case, the African Commission found that the Zimbabwean Government's action to prohibit a newspaper from publishing and to seize its assets, which forced the business to close and prevented its employees from working, violated Article 15 of the Charter:

> 178. …the action of the State to stop the Complainants from publishing their newspapers, close their business premises and seize all their equipment cannot be supported by any genuine reasons. In a civilised and democratic society, respect for the rule of law is an obligation not only for the citizens but for the State and its agents as well. If the State considered the Complainants to be operating illegally, the logical and legal approach would have been to seek a court order to stop them. The State did not do that but decided to use force and in the process infringed on the rights of the Complainants.
>
> Holding
>
> 179. The action of the Respondent State to stop the Complainants from publishing their newspapers, close their business premises and seize their equipment resulted in them and their employees not being able to express themselves through their regular medium; and to disseminate information.… By closing their business premises and preventing the Complainants' and their employees to work *[sic]*, the Respondent State also violated Article 15 of the Charter…[684]

The Commission also observed that the 'confiscation of the complainants' equipment and depriving them of a source of income and livelihood is also a violation of their right to property guaranteed under Article 14',[685] which can thus be connected with work rights.

In the discrimination area, a South African court, applying domestic law, observed that the refusal of South African Airlines to employ an HIV-positive person as a cabin attendant also constituted unlawful discrimination under Article 2 of the African Charter,[686] although it did not mention Article 15.

However, there was no violation of the right to work in Article 15 (or freedom of religion under Article 8) where a South African Law Society refused to register as a lawyer a person who admitted to prior convictions for cannabis and indicated an intention to continue using it as a part of his Rastafarian religion.[687] Admission as a lawyer required the person to be 'fit and proper' and the African Commission accepted that the restriction was legitimate in the interests of society and given the nature of the employment:

> 46. One purpose of this Charter provision is to ensure that states respect and protect the right of everyone to have access to the labour market without discrimination. The protection

[683] *Denton v The Director-General, National Intelligence Agency et al*, 24 July 2006, (2006) AHRLR 241 (GaHC 2006), [31].

[684] *Zimbabwe Lawyers for Human Rights and Associated Newspapers of Zimbabwe*, African Commission Communication No. 284/03 (3 April 2009), (2009) AHRLR 235, [178] and [179].

[685] *Zimbabwe Lawyers for Human Rights*, [179].

[686] *Hoffmann v South African Airways* (Case CCT 17/00), 28 September 2000, (2001) AHRLR 186 (SACC 2000) (Constitutional Court of South Africa).

[687] *Prince v South Africa*, African Commission on Human Rights Communication No. 255/2002, December 2004, (2004) AHRLR 105.

should be construed to allow certain restrictions depending on the type of employment and the requirements thereof. Given the legitimate interest the state has in restricting the use and possession of cannabis as shown above, it is held that the complainant's occupational challenge can be done away with should he chose to accommodate these restrictions. Although he has the right to choose his occupational call, the Commission should not give him or any one a leeway to bypass restrictions legitimately laid down for the interest of the whole society. There is no violation, thus, of his right to choose his occupation as he himself chose instead to disqualify himself from inclusion by choosing to confront the legitimate restrictions.[688]

In relation to the expulsion of foreign workers, the African Commission found that the abrupt deportation of Gambians working legally in Angola, without due process or judicial review, violated the right to work under Article 15:

75. The Complainant alleges that the victims were in possession of official documents, including passports, visas, work and residence permits, allowing them to stay and work legally in Angola. The victims were required on a monthly basis to pay for their work permits that enabled them to continue working in the mines. Nevertheless, they were arrested on the grounds that foreigners were not permitted to engage in mining activities in Angola.

76. As indicated above, the Respondent State has regrettably not forwarded any arguments to refute any of the allegations made in this communications including the alleged violation under Article 15 of the African Charter. The facts indicate and the African Commission agrees that the abrupt expulsion without any possibility of due process or recourse to national courts to challenge the Respondent State's actions severely compromised the victims' right to continue working in Angola under equitable and satisfactory conditions. Accordingly, the African Commission holds that the Respondent States actions of arbitrary arrest, detention and subsequent deportation resulted in persons who were lawfully working in Angola losing their jobs in a manner that is in violation of Article 15 of the African Charter.[689]

In the Americas, the American Declaration on the Rights and Duties of Man 1948 recognizes a range of work rights, including the right to work and to fair remuneration (Article XIV), as well as the right to leisure time (Article XV) and freedom to associate in trade unions (Article XXII). The Declaration is, however, non-binding, although it may be of use in the interpretation of the American Convention on Human Rights 1969 (ACHR).

The binding ACHR focuses on civil and political rights and prohibits forced slavery and servitude (Article 6) and guarantees freedom of association for labour (Article 16), but does not recognize the right to work. Occasionally, ACHR rights have been successfully invoked to protect labour interests, as where the rights to a fair hearing and an effective remedy applied to mass dismissals,[690] or where

688 *Prince v South Africa*, [46].

689 *Institute for Human Rights and Development in Africa v Angola (Merits)*, African Commission on Human Rights Communication No. 292/2004 (May 2008), (2008) AHRLR 43, [75] and [76]. See also *Union Interafricaine des Droits de l'Homme et al v Angola*, African Commission on Human Rights Communication No. 159/96, November 1997, (2000) AHRLR 18 (where this kind of deportation 'calls into question' violations of Article 15, although on the facts the Commission did not specifically declare that the right to work had been violated).

690 *Case of the Dismissed Congressional Employees (Aguado-Alfaro et al) v Peru (Preliminary Objections, Merits, Reparations and Costs)*, 24 November 2007, Ser C No. 158 (IACHR), [129]–[131].

attacks on trade unionists infringed rights to life, freedom from torture and arbitrary detention, and freedom of association.[691]

However, the Additional Protocol to the ACHR in the Area of Economic, Social and Cultural Rights 1988 provides for the right to freely choose work (Article 6(1)). In Article 6(2) it also sets out measures states must take to fulfil it, including vocational training, assistance to the disabled and measures for families and women (thus crossing over with Article 10 of the ICESCR). Article 6 as a whole provides:

> 1. Everyone has the right to work, which includes the opportunity to secure the means for living a dignified and decent existence by performing a freely elected or accepted lawful activity.
>
> 2. The State Parties undertake to adopt measures that will make the right to work fully effective, especially with regard to the achievement of full employment, vocational guidance, and the development of technical and vocational training projects, in particular those directed to the disabled. The States Parties also undertake to implement and strengthen programs that help to ensure suitable family care, so that women may enjoy a real opportunity to exercise the right to work.

Conditions of work (Article 7) and trade union rights (Article 8) are also provided for. The Protocol has been ratified by sixteen states as of 2013.[692] While the right to form and join trade unions can be subject to individual petition to the Inter-American Commission and Court, other work rights are monitored by a state-reporting process determined in principle in 2007 and on the basis of progress indicators for some rights settled in 2012.[693] The first state reports are due by June 2014 on the rights to social security, health and education. Indicators and reporting deadlines for the right to work are yet to be developed and there is accordingly not yet any practice or jurisprudence arising under the Additional Protocol.

Another more elaborate formulation of the right to work appears in the Arab Charter on Human Rights 2004, which combines the rights to work and social security in Article 30; provides for free choice of work and a prohibition on forced labour in Article 31; and guarantees equal opportunity and fair work conditions in Article 32:

> Article 30
>
> The State guarantees every citizen's right to work in order to secure for himself a standard of living that meets the basic requirements of life. The State also guarantees every citizen's right to comprehensive social security.
>
> Article 31
>
> Free choice of work is guaranteed and forced labour is prohibited. Compelling a person to perform work under the terms of a court judgement shall not be deemed to constitute forced labour.

[691] *Huilca-Tesce v Peru (Merits, Reparations and Costs)*, 3 March 2005, (2005) Ser C No. 121 (IACHR).

[692] See OAS Department of International Law, Multilateral Treaties: Signatories and Ratifications, <http://www.oas.org/juridico/english/Sigs/a-52.html>.

[693] OAS General Assembly Resolution 2713 (XLII-O/12), OEA/Ser.P/XLII-O.2 (4 June 2012).

Article 32

The State shall ensure that its citizens enjoy equality of opportunity in regard to work, as well as a fair wage and equal remuneration for work of equal value.

The Arab Charter entered into force in 2008 and state reports under it are monitored by a Committee of Experts, which first met in 2009.[694] There is no provision for individual or inter-state complaints under the Charter, and as yet there is little practice or jurisprudence on the right to work or other rights under the Charter.

A combination of the right to work and rights in work is found in Article 14(1) of the Commonwealth of Independent States (CIS) Convention on Human Rights and Fundamental Freedoms 1995:

Everyone shall have the right to work and to protection from unemployment, as well as to equal remuneration for equal work, including work-related benefits, to identical conditions in respect of work of equal value and to equal treatment in the assessment of the quality of his work.[695]

While the CIS Human Rights Commission was proposed in 1993 to monitor CIS states' human rights performance, it has failed to become institutionalized in practice and there is accordingly little guidance available on the scope of the right to work in the CIS system. A CIS human rights court has also been proposed, but has not thus far gained support.

[694] Mervat Rishmawi, 'The Arab Charter on Human Rights and the League of Arab States: Update' (2010) 10 *Human Rights Law Review* 169, 172.

[695] CIS Convention on Human Rights and Fundamental Freedoms (adopted 26 May 1995, entered into force 11 August 1998), Article 14.

9

Article 7: Just and Favourable Conditions of Work

Article 7

The States Parties to the present Covenant recognize the right of everyone to the enjoyment of just and favourable conditions of work which ensure, in particular:

(a) Remuneration which provides all workers, as a minimum, with:

(i) Fair wages and equal remuneration for work of equal value without distinction of any kind, in particular women being guaranteed conditions of work not inferior to those enjoyed by men, with equal pay for equal work;

(ii) A decent living for themselves and their families in accordance with the provisions of the present Covenant;

(b) Safe and healthy working conditions;

(c) Equal opportunity for everyone to be promoted in his employment to an appropriate higher level, subject to no considerations other than those of seniority and competence;

(d) Rest, leisure and reasonable limitation of working hours and periodic holidays with pay, as well as remuneration for public holidays.

Introduction: Drafting History and Purpose

The right to just and favourable conditions of work in Article 7 serves a number of inter-related purposes. The requirement that remuneration ensures fair wages and a 'decent living' for workers and their families in Article 7(a)(ii) provides a vital means of achieving the right to an adequate standard of living in Article 11,[1] and the protection of the family in Article 10.

The broad concept of 'remuneration' in Article 7(a) connects it with the right to social insurance in Article 9 in calculating fair wages for a decent living, and, where necessary, making up the difference through universal social security benefits also under Article 9.[2]

The right to rest and leisure in Article 7(d) is also related to family rights under Article 10, as well as the right to health in Article 12. The requirement of safe and healthy working conditions in Article 7(b) likewise contributes to fulfilling the right to health. Other rights too may depend on a decent wage for their fulfilment, including education and culture.

The 'fairness' of wages also engages an autonomous notion of justice in duly rewarding workers for the fair socio-economic 'value' of the work performed,

[1] Matthew Craven, *The International Covenant on Economic, Social and Cultural Rights: A Perspective on Its Development* (Clarendon Press, Oxford, 1998), 235.

[2] See the chapter below on Article 9.

and to ensure that, as the Netherlands argued in the drafting, 'man could not be treated as a mere cog in the economic machine'.[3] A different sense of fairness is embedded in the explicit references to equal pay and conditions (Article 7(a)(i)), and equal opportunity in promotion (Article 7(c)), which reinforce and particularize the general guarantees of non-discrimination and equality in Articles 2(2) and 3 of the ICESCR.

Article 7 logically follows the right to work in Article 6 and precedes a particularly important means of advancing workers' rights, namely trade union-related rights in Article 8. A Uruguayan proposal for Article 7 to require respect for the 'moral and civic independence' of the worker's 'conscience' was not, however, adopted. Uruguay thought that the worker must have the right 'to express his philosophic or religious ideas, to civil independence, that is, to express his political opinions, and to belong to the party of his choice'.[4] While states did not object in principle, it was felt that the ICCPR already addressed civil and political rights.[5] Political expression and action for workers' interests are also protected by the individual and collective trade union rights in Article 8 of the ICESCR.

Conceptually, like certain other rights in the ICESCR (including trade unions under Article 8), Article 7 is vulnerable to the criticism that it presupposes the natural social existence of particular kinds of (constructed) economic relations: the wage-earner, paid in cash at a minimum rate, working for an employer in a workplace, and formally governed by requirements as to health and safety, promotion, hours and holidays. Thus, 'the "human" in human rights is the *homo oeconomicus*, the modern market being…whose attempt to realize his/her full potentialities are confined within the moral possibilities of the state and the material conditions of the global market'.[6]

As a result, informal work (including subsistence livelihoods outside the modern cash economy), or work in the family, risks exclusion,[7] as do those who do not work at all. In a different way, those who control the market are also partly outside of Article 7; managers and employers, and the self-employed, are not 'wage earners' either. Work for wages also has implicit or explicit gender implications: historical legal governance of wages was often based on a 'breadwinner' model (a male worker with a dependent family), and that residue still lingers in some contemporary standards or interpretations.

Article 7 thus prescribes a 'universal' right which is both partial and contingent, pegged to particular kinds of human economic experience and stages of human 'development', albeit critically affecting vast numbers of people in every

[3] UNGA Third Committee, A/C.3/SR.713 (17 December 1956), 158. In 1919, the Treaty of Versailles also stated the principle that 'labour should not be regarded merely as an article of commerce': Treaty of Peace between the Allied and Associated Powers and Germany (adopted 28 June 1919, HMSO 1920), Article 427.

[4] UNGA Third Committee, A/C.3/SR.713 (17 December 1956), 161 (Uruguay).

[5] UNGA Third Committee, A/C.3/SR.713 (17 December 1956), 160 (Egypt).

[6] Balakrishnan Rajagopal, *International Law from Below: Development, Social Movements and Third World Resistance* (Cambridge University Press, Cambridge, 2004), 199.

[7] Rajagopal, *International Law from Below*, 201.

state. In doing so, it potentially forecloses other (radical) non-market possibilities for arranging socio-economic life, such as collective arrangements or a universal social income not limited to work performed.

During the drafting,[8] two overarching challenges arose. The first lay in reaching agreement between states with very different labour markets. States with liberal, market-based economies typically had a 'tripartite system ... where employers, workers and the State all took part in fixing working conditions',[9] while states with planned or socialist economies allowed the state to play a greater role in determining wages and conditions.[10] This had implications for crafting obligations on states in relation to minimum wages and conditions and equal pay. The drafters were aware of the need to strike a balance between these two systems, and to word Article 7 generally to express 'universally accepted principles'.[11]

The second challenge was in situating the provision in relation to other international instruments. States wished Article 7 'to do more than merely repeat the principles proclaimed in the Charter of the United Nations and the Universal Declaration of Human Rights but to avoid reproducing detailed provisions embodied in the International Labour Conventions'.[12] The level of detail in the provision was accordingly formulated to allow it to 'serve as a link'[13] between general aspirations and more detailed labour instruments. For this reason, some provisions were opposed not because of substantive disagreements, but to avoid replicating ILO conventions.[14] The ILO itself advocated leaving to specialized bodies 'the detailed working out and application of precise and detailed provisions'.[15]

At the time of drafting the ICESCR, the ILO had already adopted Convention No. 26 on Minimum Wage-Fixing Machinery 1928,[16] which requires states to

[8] An early iteration of Article 7 was in Article 21 of the Draft International Covenant of Human Rights, produced by the Commission on Human Rights in its Seventh Session in 1951 (218th, 219th and 229th meetings). Of three proposals, the Commission adopted the text of an amended proposal submitted jointly by France and the United States, by thirteen votes to none, with four abstentions: Commission on Human Rights, Report to the Economic and Social Council on the seventh session of the Commission, E/1992 (16 April–19 May 1951), 9, 23. That text was discussed by the Commission on Human Rights at its 279th to 281st meetings in 1952, with amendments: Commission on Human Rights, Report to the Economic and Social Council on the eighth session of the Commission, E/2256 (14 April–14 June 1952), 15. The draft article as a whole was adopted at the 281st meeting (Commission on Human Rights, Report to the Economic and Social Council on the eighth session of the Commission, E/2256 (14 April–14 June 1952), 45; UNGA Third Committee, A/3525 (9 February 1957), 9) and was similar to the final provision as adopted, absent the reference to equal opportunity in promotion found in the final version of Article 7(c). The Commission draft finalized at its Tenth Session in 1954 was debated and amended in the Third Committee in its 713th to 718th meetings in December 1956: UNGA Res. 833 (IX), A/RES/833(IX) (4 December 1954). The article in its final form was adopted at the Third Committee's 718th meeting on 21 December 1956: UNGA Third Committee, A/C.3/SR.718 (21 December 1956), 187.

[9] UNGA Third Committee, A/C.3/SR.713 (17 December 1956), 159 (Chile).

[10] UNGA Third Committee, A/C.3/SR.715 (18 December 1956), 173 (France).

[11] UNGA Third Committee, A/C.3/SR.713 (17 December 1956), 159 (Chile).

[12] UNGA Third Committee, A/C.3/SR.713 (17 December 1956), 161 (Uruguay).

[13] UNGA Third Committee, A/C.3/SR.715 (18 December 1956), 173 (France).

[14] UNGA Third Committee, A/C.3/SR.713 (17 December 1956), 159 (Chile).

[15] UNGA Third Committee, A/C.3/SR.714 (17 December 1956), 164 (ILO).

[16] ILO Convention No. 26 concerning the Creation of Minimum Wage-Fixing Machinery (adopted 28 January 1928, entered into force 14 June 1930).

create or maintain minimum wage-fixing machinery where there is no effective wage regulation and wages are 'exceptionally low'. Convention No. 99 of 1951 extended similar arrangements to agriculture.[17] While Convention No. 26 does not stipulate any substantive criteria for determining the minimum wage, ILO Recommendation No. 30 on Minimum Wage-Fixing Machinery 1928 provides that the 'wage-fixing body should…take account of the necessity of enabling the workers concerned to maintain a suitable standard of living'.[18]

Soon after the adoption of the ICESCR in 1966, the ILO adopted Convention No. 131 on Minimum Wage Fixing 1970,[19] which extended minimum wage machinery to all wage earners and provided that wages should be fixed according to the needs of workers and in light of economic conditions. That Convention currently has only fifty-two ratifications. The accompanying ILO Recommendation No. 135 on Minimum Wage Fixing 1970 usefully identifies the purposes of minimum wage fixing, even if the minimum wage alone cannot cure poverty:[20]

> 1. Minimum wage fixing should constitute one element in a policy designed to overcome poverty and to ensure the satisfaction of the needs of all workers and their families.
>
> 2. The fundamental purpose of minimum wage fixing should be to give wage earners necessary social protection as regards minimum permissible levels of wages.[21]

Also of relevance is ILO Convention No. 94 concerning Labour Clauses (Public Contracts) 1949, which ensures respect for minimum labour standards in public contracts;[22] Convention No. 95 on the Protection of Wages 1949, which provides for the payment of wages at regular intervals;[23] and Convention No. 173 on the Protection of Workers' Claims (Employer's Insolvency), which protects wage claims in the event of insolvency or bankruptcy.[24] The ILO standards are discussed below where relevant to interpreting Article 7 of the ICESCR.

RELATED REGIONAL INSTRUMENTS

Subsequently, a number of regional instruments have reiterated some or all of the guarantees in Article 7. The simplest is Article 15 of the African Charter on

[17] ILO Convention No. 99 concerning Minimum Wage Fixing Machinery in Agriculture (adopted 28 June 1951, entered into force 23 August 1953). See also ILO Recommendation No. 89 on Minimum Wage-Fixing Machinery (Agriculture) 1951.

[18] ILO Recommendation No. 30 on Minimum Wage-Fixing Machinery 1928, [III]; see discussion below.

[19] ILO Convention No. 131 concerning Minimum Wage Fixing, with Special Reference to Developing Countries (adopted 22 June 1970, entered into force 29 April 1972); see also ILO Recommendation No. 135 on Minimum Wage Fixing 1970.

[20] ILO Committee of Experts on the Application of Conventions and Recommendations, *General Survey of the Reports on the Minimum Wage-Fixing Machinery Convention (No. 26)* et al ('*General Survey*'), International Labour Conference (79th session), Report III (Part 4B) (Geneva, 1992), 11.

[21] ILO Recommendation No. 135 on Minimum Wage Fixing 1970, [I(1) and (2)].

[22] See also ILO Recommendation No. 84 on Labour Clauses (Public Contracts) 1949.

[23] See also ILO Recommendation No. 85 on Protection of Wages 1949.

[24] See also ILO Recommendation No. 180 on Protection of Workers' Claims (Employer's Insolvency) 1992.

Human and Peoples' Rights 1981,[25] which provides that '[e]ach individual shall have the right to work under equitable and satisfactory conditions, and shall receive equal pay for equal work'. Also brief is Article 27(1) of the ASEAN Declaration on Human Rights 2012, which relevantly provides that '[e]very person has the right... to enjoy just, decent and favourable conditions of work'. Article 34(2) and (4) of the Arab Charter on Human Rights 2004 is more elaborate:

2. Every worker has the right to the enjoyment of just and favourable conditions of work which ensure appropriate remuneration to meet his essential needs and those of his family and regulate working hours, rest and holidays with pay, as well as the rules for the preservation of occupational health and safety and the protection of women, children and disabled persons in the place of work.

...

4. There shall be no discrimination between men and women in their enjoyment of the right to effectively benefit from training, employment and job protection and the right to receive equal remuneration for equal work.[26]

In the Americas, Article 7 of the Protocol of San Salvador 1988 sets out extensive rights to just, equitable and satisfactory conditions of work which are roughly similar to those in the ICESCR, including in relation to minimum and equal remuneration, promotion, safety and hygiene at work, reasonable limitation of working hours, and rest, leisure and paid holidays:

The States Parties to this Protocol recognize that the right to work to which the foregoing article refers presupposes that everyone shall enjoy that right under just, equitable, and satisfactory conditions, which the States Parties undertake to guarantee in their internal legislation, particularly with respect to:

(a) Remuneration which guarantees, as a minimum, to all workers dignified and decent living conditions for them and their families and fair and equal wages for equal work, without distinction;

(b) The right of every worker to follow his vocation and to devote himself to the activity that best fulfills his expectations and to change employment in accordance with the pertinent national regulations;

(c) The right of every worker to promotion or upward mobility in his employment, for which purpose account shall be taken of his qualifications, competence, integrity and seniority;

(d) Stability of employment, subject to the nature of each industry and occupation and the causes for just separation. In cases of unjustified dismissal, the worker shall have the right to indemnity or to reinstatement on the job or any other benefits provided by domestic legislation;

(e) Safety and hygiene at work;

[25] African Charter on Human and Peoples' Rights (adopted 27 June 1981, 1520 UNTS 217, entered into force 21 October 1986).

[26] Arab Charter on Human Rights (adopted 22 May 2004, entered into force 15 March 2008), Articles 2 and 4.

(f) The prohibition of night work or unhealthy or dangerous working conditions and, in general, of all work which jeopardizes health, safety, or morals, for persons under 18 years of age. As regards minors under the age of 16, the work day shall be subordinated to the provisions regarding compulsory education and in no case shall work constitute an impediment to school attendance or a limitation on benefiting from education received;

(g) A reasonable limitation of working hours, both daily and weekly. The days shall be shorter in the case of dangerous or unhealthy work or of night work;

(h) Rest, leisure and paid vacations as well as remuneration for national holidays.[27]

The most extensive regional guarantees are found in Articles 2 and 3 of the Revised European Social Charter 1996 (and almost identically in the same provisions of the original European Social Charter 1961). Article 2 provides for just conditions of work (including as to pay, holidays and dangerous work); Article 3 elaborates on the right to safe and healthy working conditions; and Article 4 concerns the right to fair remuneration:

Article 2—The right to just conditions of work

With a view to ensuring the effective exercise of the right to just conditions of work, the Parties undertake:

1. to provide for reasonable daily and weekly working hours, the working week to be progressively reduced to the extent that the increase of productivity and other relevant factors permit;

2. to provide for public holidays with pay;

3. to provide for a minimum of four weeks' annual holiday with pay;

4. to eliminate risks in inherently dangerous or unhealthy occupations, and where it has not yet been possible to eliminate or reduce sufficiently these risks, to provide for either a reduction of working hours or additional paid holidays for workers engaged in such occupations;

5. to ensure a weekly rest period which shall, as far as possible, coincide with the day recognised by tradition or custom in the country or region concerned as a day of rest;

6. to ensure that workers are informed in written form, as soon as possible, and in any event not later than two months after the date of commencing their employment, of the essential aspects of the contract or employment relationship;

7. to ensure that workers performing night work benefit from measures which take account of the special nature of the work.

Article 3—The right to safe and healthy working conditions

With a view to ensuring the effective exercise of the right to safe and healthy working conditions, the Parties undertake, in consultation with employers' and workers' organisations:

1. to formulate, implement and periodically review a coherent national policy on occupational safety, occupational health and the working environment. The primary

[27] Additional Protocol to the American Convention on Human Rights in the Area of Economic, Social and Cultural Rights (adopted 17 November 1988, OAS Treaty Series No. 69, entered into force 16 November 1999), Article 7.

aim of this policy shall be to improve occupational safety and health and to prevent accidents and injury to health arising out of, linked with or occurring in the course of work, particularly by minimising the causes of hazards inherent in the working environment;

2. to issue safety and health regulations;

3. to provide for the enforcement of such regulations by measures of supervision;

4. to promote the progressive development of occupational health services for all workers with essentially preventive and advisory functions.

Article 4—The right to a fair remuneration

With a view to ensuring the effective exercise of the right to a fair remuneration, the Parties undertake:

1. to recognise the right of workers to a remuneration such as will give them and their families a decent standard of living;

2. to recognise the right of workers to an increased rate of remuneration for overtime work, subject to exceptions in particular cases;

3. to recognise the right of men and women workers to equal pay for work of equal value;

4. to recognise the right of all workers to a reasonable period of notice for termination of employment;

5. to permit deductions from wages only under conditions and to the extent prescribed by national laws or regulations or fixed by collective agreements or arbitration awards. The exercise of these rights shall be achieved by freely concluded collective agreements, by statutory wage-fixing machinery, or by other means appropriate to national conditions.[28]

The interpretation of these provisions by the European Committee on Social Rights in particular will be drawn upon where relevant in this chapter. The European Union's Charter of Fundamental Rights also addresses conditions of work, albeit an 'idiosyncratic pick and mix' from other legal instruments:[29]

Article II-91

Fair and just working conditions

1. Every worker has the right to working conditions which respect his or her health, safety and dignity.

2. Every worker has the right to limitation of maximum working hours, to daily and weekly rest periods and to an annual period of paid leave.[30]

[28] Revised European Social Charter (adopted 3 May 1996, CETS 163, entered into force 1 July 1999), Articles 2–4.

[29] Jo Hunt, 'Fair and Just Working Conditions' in Tamara Hervey and Jeff Kremer (eds), *Economic and Social Rights under the EU Charter of Fundamental Rights: A Legal Perspective* (Hart, Oxford, 2003), 45, 52.

[30] Treaty establishing a Constitution for Europe (adopted 29 October 2004, OJ C 310, Vol. 47, 16 December 2004, not yet in force), Part II: Charter of Fundamental Rights and Freedoms.

Article 7(a): Remuneration

PERSONAL SCOPE OF APPLICATION

While the first sentence of Article 7 recognizes rights belonging to 'everyone', paragraph (a) is restricted to 'workers'. Debate arose as to the intended scope of the provision, on account of the different meanings of 'worker' when translated into languages other than English. Afghanistan proposed to replace the words 'all workers' by the word 'everyone',[31] and later by the phrase 'all those who work'.[32] This was supported by some states which felt that the term 'workers' might be interpreted as limited to physical labourers,[33] as its meaning was so confined in Persian, Arabic and Greek.[34] The proposed amendment in turn created difficulties in other languages, such as Spanish and Portuguese.[35] The ILO representative noted that the relevant terms in the ILO Constitution ('workers' or 'work-people' in English, or *travailleurs* in French) were used in 'a very broad sense, including agricultural workers, fishermen and industrial workers'.[36] Egypt wryly wondered how the Arab states had acceded to the ILO treaties if the language difficulties were indeed so pronounced.[37]

While various states agreed that the rights were not to be limited to physical labourers, some were concerned that the phrase 'all those who work' would extend rights to those not entitled to them.[38] It was also felt that the provision was appropriately limited to a specific group in need of special protection, just as specific protection was given to children, mothers or other groups in the Covenant.[39] Chile thought the word was 'technically synonymous with "wage-earner"',[40] and some states believed the provision did not cover the self-employed,[41] employers,[42] people living on investment income[43] or housewives.[44] These suggestions did not raise objections and it was resolved that Afghanistan's concerns be remedied in the various official languages of the text.[45] Unlike the wider scope of Article 6, this aspect of Article 7 evidently cannot apply to volunteers,[46] who do not draw wages or receive remuneration.

[31] UNGA Third Committee, A/3525 (9 February 1957), 11.
[32] UNGA Third Committee, A/3525 (9 February 1957), 12.
[33] UNGA Third Committee, A/C.3/SR.714 (17 December 1956), 166 (Yugoslavia).
[34] UNGA Third Committee, A/C.3/SR.717 (20 December 1956), 182–3 (Afghanistan; Iran; Saudi Arabia; Greece).
[35] UNGA Third Committee, A/C.3/SR.717 (20 December 1956), 183 (Spain; Portugal).
[36] UNGA Third Committee, A/C.3/SR.718 (21 December 1956), 185 (ILO).
[37] UNGA Third Committee, A/C.3/SR.717 (20 December 1956), 183 (Egypt; see also Chile).
[38] UNGA Third Committee, A/C.3/SR.717 (20 December 1956), 183 (Spain).
[39] UNGA Third Committee, A/C.3/SR.715 (18 December 1956), 171 (Chile).
[40] UNGA Third Committee, A/C.3/SR.717 (20 December 1956), 183 (Chile). This is consistent with the approach in ILO Convention No. 131 concerning Minimum Wage Fixing, with Special Reference to Developing Countries, Article 1.
[41] UNGA Third Committee, A/C.3/SR.715 (18 December 1956), 170 (China); cf Craven, *The ICESCR*, 229 (suggesting Article 7(a) covers the self-employed), but noting (at 235) that the CESCR has not addressed the point.
[42] UNGA Third Committee, A/C.3/SR.715 (18 December 1956), 170 (China).
[43] UNGA Third Committee, A/C.3/SR.716 (19 December 1956), 175 (Venezuela).
[44] UNGA Third Committee, A/C.3/SR.717 (20 December 1956), 183 (Chile).
[45] UNGA Third Committee, A/C.3/SR.718 (21 December 1956), 185.
[46] Craven, *The ICESCR*, 229.

In monitoring states, the CESCR has repeatedly stressed that the minimum wage should apply universally, irrespective of industry[47] or geographic area.[48] It has frequently noted that indigenous workers[49] and workers in the following sectors are at risk of inadequate wages: domestic work;[50] 'community mothers' (child carers);[51] public service;[52] health;[53] education;[54] shop assistants, nurses, clerks and nursery assistants;[55] the garment industry;[56] *maquilas* (assembly plants in which workers are primarily female, and the employers are transnational corporations);[57] rural work (including forest clearing, logging and harvesting of sugar cane);[58] and mining, chestnut and flower production, and poultry slaughtering.[59]

The CESCR has also observed that indigenous peoples[60] and migrant workers are at risk of inadequate wages.[61] In this regard, it may be noted that Article 25 of the Migrant Workers Convention provides that migrant workers, whether documented or irregular, shall enjoy no less favourable treatment than nationals in respect of remuneration (and overtime and holiday pay), and that such protections cannot be contracted out of:

1. Migrant workers shall enjoy treatment not less favourable than that which applies to nationals of the State of employment in respect of remuneration and:

   (a) Other conditions of work, that is to say, overtime, hours of work, weekly rest, holidays with pay, safety, health, termination of the employment relationship and any other conditions of work which, according to national law and practice, are covered by these terms;

   …

2. It shall not be lawful to derogate in private contracts of employment from the principle of equality of treatment referred to in paragraph 1 of the present article.

3. States Parties shall take all appropriate measures to ensure that migrant workers are not deprived of any rights derived from this principle by reason of any irregularity in their stay or employment. In particular, employers shall not be relieved of any legal or contractual obligations, nor shall their obligations be limited in any manner by reason of such irregularity.

47 CESCR, Concluding Observations: Dominican Republic, E/C.12/1/Add.16 (12 December 1997), [36]; Cambodia, E/C.12/KHM/CO/1 (12 June 2009), [23].

48 CESCR, Concluding Observations: Netherland Antilles, E/C.12/NLD/CO/3/Add.1 (31 January 2008), [31].

49 CESCR, Concluding Observations: Mexico, E/C.12/MEX/CO/4 (9 June 2006), [14].

50 CESCR, Concluding Observations: Chile, E/C.12/1/Add.105 (1 December 2004), [18]; Bolivia, E/C.12/1/Add.60 (21 May 2001), [16].

51 CESCR, Concluding Observations: Colombia, E/C.12/1/Add.74 (6 December 2001), [14].

52 CESCR, Concluding Observations: Angola, E/C.12/DZA/CO/4 (7 June 2010), [10].

53 CESCR, Concluding Observations: Angola, [10].

54 CESCR, Concluding Observations: Angola, [10].

55 CESCR, Concluding Observations: Cyprus, E/C.12/1/Add.28 (4 December 1998), [14].

56 CESCR, Concluding Observations: Cambodia, E/C.12/KHM/Co/1 (12 June 2009), [23].

57 CESCR, Concluding Observations: Honduras, E/C.12/Add.57 (21 May 2001), [15]; El Salvador, E/C.12/SLV/CO/2 (27 June 2007), [14] (maquiladoras, or in bond assembly and finishing plants).

58 CESCR, Concluding Observations: Brazil, E/C.12/1/Add.87 (26 June 2003), [23]; China (including HK, Macao), E/C.12/1/Add.107 (13 May 2005), [25]; Brazil, E/C.12/BRA/ZO/2 (12 June 2009), [15].

59 CESCR, Concluding Observations: Bolivia, E/C.12/BOL/CO/2 (8 August 2008), [14].

60 CESCR, Concluding Observations: Mexico, E/C.12/MEX/CO/4 (9 June 2006), [14].

61 CESCR, Concluding Observations: Kuwait, E/C.12/1/Add.98 (7 June 2004), [17]; Canada, E/C.12.CAN/CO/4 (22 May 2006), [49].

Regionally, the Inter-American Court of Human Rights has also confirmed that undocumented migrant workers are entitled to equal protection in fair wages.[62]

The universal coverage of Article 7 of the ICESCR sets it apart from the more restricted ILO standards. Convention No. 26 is limited to trades (meaning manufacture and commerce, including home working) (Article 1) and states parties are largely free to determine which trades are covered (Article 2).[63] The accompanying ILO Recommendation No. 30 suggests, however, that 'special regard might usefully be had to trades or parts of trades in which women are ordinarily employed', but '[w]ithout prejudice to the discretion left to Members by the Convention to decide in which trades or parts of trades in their respective countries it is expedient to apply minimum wage-fixing machinery' (paragraph I(2)). Convention No. 99 is limited to agriculture and related work, and even then permits the exclusion of certain workers such as members of a farmer's family (Article 1(3)).

Convention No. 131 applies to 'all groups of wage earners whose terms of employment are such that coverage would be appropriate' (Article 1(1)), signalling an aspiration of universal coverage. However, states may still 'determine the groups of wage earners to be covered' after tripartite consultations (Article 1(2)) and as long as excluded groups are reported, with reasons, to the ILO (Article 1(3)):

> 1. Each Member of the International Labour Organisation which ratifies this Convention undertakes to establish a system of minimum wages which covers all groups of wage earners whose terms of employment are such that coverage would be appropriate.
>
> 2. The competent authority in each country shall, in agreement or after full consultation with the representative organisations of employers and workers concerned, where such exist, determine the groups of wage earners to be covered.
>
> 3. Each Member which ratifies this Convention shall list in the first report on the application of the Convention submitted under Article 22 of the Constitution of the International Labour Organisation any groups of wage earners which may not have been covered in pursuance of this Article, giving the reasons for not covering them, and shall state in subsequent reports the positions of its law and practice in respect of the groups not covered, and the extent to which effect has been given or is proposed to be given to the Convention in respect of such groups.

Recommendation No. 135 on Minimum Wage Fixing 1970 further suggests that '[t]he number and groups of wage earners who are not covered in pursuance of Article 1.... should be kept to a minimum' (paragraph III(4)). In practice, minimum wage fixing applies to all workers in many countries.[64] A further ILO

[62] *Juridical Condition and Rights of Undocumented Migrants*, IACHR Advisory Opinion, 17 September 2003, OC-18/03, [157]–[160].

[63] Article 2 provides: 'Each Member which ratifies this Convention shall be free to decide, after consultation with the organisations, if any, of workers and employers in the trade or part of trade concerned, in which trades or parts of trades, and in particular in which home working trades or parts of such trades, the minimum wage-fixing machinery referred to in Article 1 shall be applied.'

[64] ILO, *General Survey*, 84.

convention requires public contracts to include clauses guaranteeing workers no less favourable wages than for 'work of the same character in the trade or industry concerned in the district where the work is carried on'.[65]

In principle, Article 7 of the ICESCR appears to be an advance on the ILO standards. However, a key reason why states choose to limit the sectoral coverage of minimum wage-fixing machinery under ILO instruments is for economic or developmental reasons. The principle of progressive realization under the ICESCR may similarly apply to restrict the universal application of Article 7 in various ways, to accommodate economic concerns about wage costs,[66] as discussed below.

For present purposes, it should be emphasized, however, that economic considerations cannot justify direct or indirect discrimination on impermissible grounds (such as those specified in Article 2 of the ICESCR) in the application of minimum wage coverage. This has implications, for instance, for wages in sectors involving predominantly female workers (such as domestic work), where indirect discrimination may arise from the withholding of minimum wage protections.

While the ILO instruments do not specifically provide for the fixing of minimum wages on the basis of sex, age or disability, other ILO standards are relevant. These include the principle of equal pay for equal work in Convention No. 100 on Equal Remuneration 1951, Recommendation No. 146 on Minimum Age 1973 (paragraph 13(1)(a)) and Recommendation No. 162 on Older Workers 1980 (paragraph 5).

While it is common for apprentices to be paid lower wages, such differentiation should relate to the training period during which they acquire skills and not be based simply on their (typically) young age. The CESCR was concerned where all young people aged 16 to 25 years were characterized as 'apprentices', resulting in their exclusion from wage protections,[67] and where young people (aged 18 to 22) received a smaller proportion of the minimum wage.[68]

The principle of equal opportunity in Convention No. 159 on Vocational Rehabilitation and Employment (Disabled Persons) 1983 is also relevant for workers with disabilities. However, earlier ILO standards are problematic from a human rights perspective, including the benevolent but anachronistic provision in Convention No. 99 for exceptions to the minimum wage for agricultural workers with physical or mental disabilities, where necessary 'to prevent curtailment of the opportunities of employment' (Article 3(5)). That overbroad, class-based exclusion potentially permits exploitation of cheap labour by workers with disabilities, and is contrary to the modern standards articulated in the ICESCR and the Convention on the Rights of Persons with Disabilities (CRPD). Relevantly, Article 27(1)(a) of the CRPD specifically prohibits any form of disability discrimination in work and Article 27(2) protects against slavery, servitude and forced or compulsory labour.

65 ILO Convention No. 94 concerning Labour Clauses in Public Contracts (adopted 29 June 1949, entered into force 20 September 1952), Article 2; see also ILO Recommendation No. 84 on Labour Clauses 1949.
66 Discussed further below.
67 CESCR, Concluding Observations: Peru, E/C.12/1/Add.14 (20 May 1997), [18].
68 CESCR, Concluding Observations: UK, E/C.12/1/Add.79 (5 June 2002), [15].

The groups sometimes excluded or restricted from minimum wage protections in state practice under ILO instruments indicate areas of special vulnerability or disadvantage to which the CESCR should be alert under Article 7. These include, for example, younger or older workers, persons with disabilities, non-profit organization workers (religious, philanthropic, political, patriotic, charitable), part-time workers, stand-by or on-call workers, domestic or home workers, carers, private drivers and students in training or seasonal work.[69] Occupations also excluded include those in sales, fishing, trapping, logging, agriculture, construction, oil rigging, small enterprises, or those paid by piece-work or commission.[70]

During the drafting, there was general support to refer to families in Article 7(a)(ii), in ensuring that wages provide a decent living, to recognize that a worker was a member of, and may be responsible for, a family.[71] Families are thus derivative beneficiaries of the right in Article 7. However, Greece noted that in some families several members may be employed, and thought that the requirement should be impliedly limited to workers responsible for the livelihood of other family members.[72] The reference to families is significant in the context of determining minimum wages, as discussed below, although it is in tension with the requirement of equal pay for equal work: in state practice, single workers without dependent families seldom receive lower wages than those with families.

MEANING OF 'REMUNERATION' AND 'WAGES'

Article 7(a) requires 'remuneration' which provides all workers with 'fair wages', 'equal remuneration' and a 'decent living'. A definitional debate arose during the drafting over the term 'remuneration'. Some states argued that the word 'remuneration' was more appropriate than 'wages' because it included supplementary pay received by workers[73] (such as bonuses and the like) and state support for their well-being.[74] Venezuela included non-monetary 'benefits such as cheap housing, hospital treatment, schools, health centres, profit-sharing and paid holidays'[75] within the term. Australia supported this interpretation because an 'alternative interpretation might imply that "a decent living" should be provided by earnings alone and that social security benefits might be regarded as superfluous'.[76] There was general support for remuneration going beyond monetary wages to include other benefits.[77]

In this respect there is a close relationship between Article 7(a) and the right to social security in Article 9, which includes social insurance (namely,

[69] ILO, *General Survey*, 28–9.
[70] ILO, *General Survey*, 29–30.
[71] UNGA Third Committee: A/C.3/SR.713 (17 December 1956), 161 (Uruguay); A/C.3/SR.714 (17 December 1956), 163 (Spain).
[72] UNGA Third Committee, A/C.3/SR.714 (17 December 1956), 167 (Greece).
[73] UNGA Third Committee, A/C.3/SR.713 (17 December 1956), 161 (Uruguay).
[74] UNGA Third Committee, A/C.3/SR.716 (19 December 1956), 175 (Venezuela).
[75] UNGA Third Committee, A/C.3/SR.716 (19 December 1956), 175 (Venezuela).
[76] UNGA Third Committee, A/C.3/SR.716 (19 December 1956), 176 (Australia).
[77] Craven, *The ICESCR*, 230.

co-contributions by employers to various insured worker benefits). There is also cross-over with Article 10 dealing with maternity, family and child benefits. In terms of the division of labour between these provisions, given the more specialized coverage of Articles 9 and 10, the focus of Article 7(a) is predominantly on wages rather than non-pecuniary benefits (except for holidays as provided for in Article 7(d)). In its practice, the CESCR has tended to narrowly focus on wages rather than on the broader ambit of remuneration.[78] Indeed, where minimum wage amounts have been discounted because of meals and accommodation provided to migrant workers, the CESCR has cautioned against disproportionate adverse impacts on that group.[79]

In ILO practice, Convention No. 100 on Equal Remuneration defines 'remuneration' in Article 1(a):

> …the term *remuneration* includes the ordinary, basic or minimum wage or salary and any additional emoluments whatsoever payable directly or indirectly, whether in cash or in kind, by the employer to the worker and arising out of the worker's employment…

It is distinguishable from the narrower concept of 'wages' as defined in Article 1 of ILO Convention No. 95 on the Protection of Wages:

> …the term *wages* means remuneration or earnings, however designated or calculated, capable of being expressed in terms of money and fixed by mutual agreement or by national laws or regulations, which are payable in virtue of a written or unwritten contract of employment by an employer to an employed person for work done or to be done or for services rendered or to be rendered.

In monitoring states, the CESCR has occasionally taken into account non-pecuniary benefits in assessing the adequacy of remuneration. Thus, it found that wages at 40 per cent of the minimum wage were still too low even taking into account that domestic workers received board and lodging from their employers.[80]

'FAIR WAGES' AND A 'DECENT LIVING'

During the drafting, there was broad support for a rights-based approach to wages, but more difficulty in determining how to express the concept or quantify the standard. In the Commission on Human Rights, an early draft provided everyone with a 'right to receive pay commensurate with his ability and skill', but South Africa protested that wages were determined by the law of supply and demand[81] and preferred the formula 'fair and reasonable' wages.[82] Other states also supported a move away from wages being 'commensurate' with performance and

[78] Craven, *The ICESCR*, 234.
[79] CESCR, Concluding Observations: Republic of Korea, E/C.12/KOR/CO/3 (17 December 2009), [16].
[80] CESCR, Concluding Observations: Paraguay, E/C.12/PRY/CO/3 (4 January 2008), [15].
[81] Commission on Human Rights, E/CN.4/85 (1 May 1948), 40 (Union of South Africa).
[82] Commission on Human Rights, E/CN.4/85 (1 May 1948), 40 (Union of South Africa).

instead believed that a worker's salary 'should be enough to ensure him and his family the means of living a decent human life'.[83]

In the Third Committee, Australia objected to the vagueness of reference to 'a decent living' and suggested its replacement with 'an adequate standard of living' as in Article 12.[84] Pakistan also suggested that wages would be fair if they gave the worker 'a standard of living that would enable him to take a constructive part in civil life', but noted the difficulties in identifying both workers' needs and the quantum of wages.[85] Pakistan also highlighted the redistributive aspect of minimum wages, observing a tension between 'private profit or the general interest' and arguing that 'there must be sufficiency for all before there was superfluity for some'.[86]

A proposal to determine wages according to both the cost of living and business profits was not adopted, in part because a profit-related formula would be problematic for state enterprises or businesses which did not make a profit in a given year (thus risking reduction of wages).[87] Such an approach might also be problematic, for instance, in relation to other entities which do not follow a corporate approach, such as the public service or non-profit organizations like charities.

The dual formula ultimately adopted refers to both 'fair wages' and a 'decent living' for workers and their families (the further procedural requirement of equal remuneration is considered separately below). In the drafting, some states thought that the idea of 'fair wages' already covered the notion of a 'decent living'[88] or that the notions were synonymous.

However, there is also evidence that other states thought the concepts were distinct,[89] even if in practice the CESCR has not made much of the difference. Whereas a 'decent living' implies the satisfaction of basic needs (including the minimum core of other rights), fairness suggests a higher distributive and/or qualitative standard. Fair wages are wages that are equitable or just, which in turn involves judgments about the social value of employment and the economic contribution of a worker,[90] but also concerns about economic inequality in society at large. Wages could provide a 'decent living', but still not be 'fair'. Among other things, fair pay 'should reflect the nature and circumstances of the work undertaken', such as by reference to skill, responsibility, impact on family or quality of life, economic value, and health and safety risks.[91]

In monitoring states, the CESCR has largely focused on whether remuneration secures a decent living rather than also involves 'fair' wages, either subsuming the latter within the former or treating it as an aspect of the further requirement

[83] Commission on Human Rights, E/CN.4/AC.1/SR.42 (27 May 1948), 8 (Chile); see also 10 (USSR).
[84] UNGA Third Committee, A/C.3/SR.716 (19 December 1956), 176 (Australia).
[85] UNGA Third Committee, A/C.3/SR.713 (17 December 1956), 160 (Pakistan).
[86] UNGA Third Committee, A/C.3/SR.713 (17 December 1956), 160 (Pakistan).
[87] Craven, *The ICESCR*, 229.
[88] Craven, *The ICESCR*, 230.
[89] Craven, *The ICESCR*, 232–6.
[90] Craven, *The ICESCR*, 233.
[91] Craven, *The ICESCR*, 233.

of equal pay for equal work (that is, as an aspect of 'fairness' between genders). The CESCR has expressed the requirement of a decent living in different ways. It has criticized wages that are too low to: enable people to live above the poverty line;[92] cover the subsistence costs of a household;[93] 'enable workers to meet their families' essential needs';[94] meet the 'minimum consumer budget';[95] 'allow a modest standard of living';[96] or secure a 'standard of living in dignity'.[97] Only occasionally has it looked beyond basic needs to a more relational or distributive concept of fairness, as when it criticized minimum wages which did not reach '50 per cent of the average net wage in the labour market'.[98]

The CESCR has repeatedly urged states to implement a 'minimum wage' which meets the essential needs of workers and their families.[99] It has regularly observed that the basic food basket should be taken into account when determining the minimum wage[100] and stated on one occasion that the minimum wage should cover 100 per cent of this basket.[101]

A basic needs approach to the minimum wage may be appropriate particularly in developing states where survival or subsistence is at stake, and coverage of the minimum wage is gradually expanded to encompass new occupational or sectoral groups of workers. However, the progressive realization principle applicable to Article 7 applies across the spectrum of states, including middle income and developed ones. In wealthier states, it is to be expected that the minimum wage will no longer be confined to subsistence levels, but will also be more capable of accommodating the redistributive or equity dimensions of fairness in wages. What is a 'decent' living, and what are 'fair wages', thus varies according to the economic and developmental context, and is not statically confined to satisfaction of basic needs. During the drafting, Pakistan argued that a 'minimum living wage' must be guaranteed even in developing states, which 'could only then progress to greater achievements'.[102]

A more sophisticated approach to the criteria for quantifying a 'minimum wage'[103] is found in the accretion of ILO standards on the issue. As noted earlier,

[92] CESCR, Concluding Observations: Mexico, E/C.12/1993/16 (5 January 1994), [6]; Ukraine, E/C.12/1995/15 (28 December 1995), [20].

[93] CESCR, Concluding Observations: El Salvador, E/C.12/1/Add.4 (28 May 1996), [18]; Hungary, E/C.12/HUN/CO/3 (16 January 2008), [14].

[94] CESCR, Concluding Observations: Benin, E/C.12/1/Add.78 (5 June 2002), [34].

[95] CESCR, Concluding Observations: Kyrgyzstan, E/C.12/1/Add.49 (1 September 2000), [14].

[96] CESCR, Concluding Observations: Kenya, E/C.12/1993/6 (3 June 1993), [12].

[97] CESCR, Concluding Observations: Bolivia, E/C.12/1/Add.60 (21 May 2001), [17].

[98] CESCR, Concluding Observations: Austria, E/C.12/AUT/CO/3 (25 January 2006), [11].

[99] CESCR, Concluding Observations: Canada, E/C.12/1/Add.31 (10 December 1998), [32]; Benin, E/C.12/1/Add.78 (5 June 2002), [34]; Afghanistan, E/C.12/AFG/CO/24 (7 June 2010), [23].

[100] CESCR, Concluding Observations: Colombia, E/C.12/1995/18 (1–19 May 1995, 20 November–8 December 1995), [187]; Mexico, E/C.12/1/Add.41 (8 December 1999), [36]; Chile, E/C.12/1/Add.105 (1 December 2004), [39].

[101] CESCR, Concluding Observations: Nicaragua, E/C.12/NIC/CO/4 (28 November 2008), [2].

[102] UNGA Third Committee, A/C.3/SR.716 (19 December 1956), 177 (Pakistan).

[103] According to a meeting of ILO experts, 'minimum wage' means 'the lowest level of remuneration permitted, in law or fact, whatever the method of remuneration or the qualification of the

the earliest instrument, Convention No. 26, did not set out the criteria for determining the minimum wage, but the related Recommendation No. 30 on Minimum Wage-Fixing Machinery 1928 urged states 'to take account of the necessity of enabling the workers concerned to maintain a suitable standard of living', with reference to pay rates in similar but organized trades or, failing that, general prevailing wages (paragraph III):

For the purpose of determining the minimum rates of wages to be fixed, the wage-fixing body should in any case take account of the necessity of enabling the workers concerned to maintain a suitable standard of living. For this purpose regard should primarily be had to the rates of wages being paid for similar work in trades where the workers are adequately organised and have concluded effective collective agreements, or, if no such standard of reference is available in the circumstances, to the general level of wages prevailing in the country or in the particular locality.

Provision should be made for the review of the minimum rates of wages fixed by the wage-fixing bodies when this is desired by the workers or employers who are members of such bodies.

A similar proposal to refer to a 'suitable standard of living' or 'subsistence' needs was discussed in the drafting of Convention No. 99 on agricultural workers, but was ultimately omitted.[104] Recommendation No. 89 does, however, incorporate that idea, along with more extensive criteria concerning the cost of living, value of the work, wages for comparable work and the general level of wages:

1. For the purpose of determining minimum rates of wages to be fixed it is desirable that the wage fixing body should in any case take account of the necessity of enabling the workers concerned to maintain a suitable standard of living.

2. Among the factors which should be taken into consideration in the fixing of minimum wage rates are the following: the cost of living, fair and reasonable value of services rendered, wages paid for similar or comparable work under collective bargaining agreements in agriculture, and the general level of wages for work of a comparable skill in other industries in the area where the workers are sufficiently organised.

By the time of ILO Convention No. 131 concerning Minimum Wage Fixing 1970, states agreed to make similarly extensive criteria binding in Article 3, including new elements of social security benefits and the relative living standards of other social groups:

The elements to be taken into consideration in determining the level of minimum wages shall, so far as possible and appropriate in relation to national practice and conditions, include—

(a) the needs of workers and their families, taking into account the general level of wages in the country, the cost of living, social security benefits, and the relative living standards of other social groups;

worker...which in each country has the force of law and which is enforceable under threat of penal or other appropriate sanctions... [and including where] fixed by collective agreements made binding by public authorities': ILO, *General Survey*, 10.

[104] ILO, *General Survey*, 11.

(b) economic factors, including the requirements of economic development, levels of productivity and the desirability of attaining and maintaining a high level of employment.[105]

The criteria accordingly combine considerations of basic needs with the relational or distributive aspect of fairness, all in the light of prevailing economic conditions and policies. Unlike Recommendation No. 89, however, Convention No. 131 does not mention the value of the services rendered or wages for comparable work under collective agreements.

An ILO expert meeting suggests that the 'needs' of workers and families include 'the vital necessities of food, clothing, housing, education and recreation'.[106] Needs are thus not limited to subsistence of survival needs, but include broader life opportunities such as education (and by extension, culture).

No priority or hierarchy is specified as between the criteria in Convention No. 131,[107] leaving considerable discretion to states in weighting, assessing and balancing the different and often competing interests. It is, to some extent, a subjective choice,[108] which is perhaps why the CESCR has minimally emphasized the fulfilment of a basic family food basket rather than more elaborately scrutinizing minimum wage levels. There is, however, scope for the CESCR to do more in supervising whether wages are 'fair' to ensure a 'decent' living, as opposed to merely providing a minimum, subsistence level.

The reference to 'economic factors' in Convention No. 131 relates in part to the general limitations clause in Article 4 of the ICESCR, by which it may be necessary to limit certain rights (the level of wages) to secure the rights of others (where, for instance, wage restraint is necessary to preserve the state's budgetary position and its capacity to pay wages, or to provide other basic rights such as work for the unemployed, health care, social security, education and the like).

The impact of wages on the total volume of employment and on inflation will be significant factors,[109] given that wage increases have the potential to increase unemployment or aggravate inflation in certain economic circumstances. The interdependency of the global economy is also important given its potential to affect commodity and stock prices, investment levels, currency rates, exports and imports, balance of payments, debt levels, consumer prices, national competitiveness and structural adjustment imposed by international institutions.

The reference to 'economic factors' includes the sub-criterion of 'economic development', which in turn relates Convention No. 131 also to the progressive realization principle in Article 2(1) of the ICESCR. ILO experts suggest that 'economic development' includes considerations of poverty, inequality and inadequate average incomes.[110] It intersects with related contexts of progressive

[105] See similarly Recommendation No. 135 on Minimum Wage Fixing 1970, [III(3)].
[106] ILO, *General Survey*, 11.
[107] Unlike in ILO Recommendation No. 30 on Minimum Wage-Fixing Machinery 1928, but like in ILO Recommendation No. 89 on Minimum Wage-Fixing Machinery (Agriculture) 1951.
[108] ILO, *General Survey*, 104. Some states also apply additional factors: 106.
[109] ILO, *General Survey*, 107.
[110] ILO, *General Survey*, 18.

realization in the ICESCR, such as employment policy in developing states under the right to work in Article 6.

In both cases—progressive realization or limitations—wage policy or measures must not: be applied in an impermissibly discriminatory way; prejudice vulnerable, marginalized or disadvantaged groups; or lower wages below the minimum level necessary to ensure subsistence, freedom from inhuman or degrading treatment, and basic dignity. At least, a subsistence wage must be part of the non-derogable minimum core of Article 7; only a higher level of fairness and decent living may be progressively realized over time. The CESCR has criticized states which have failed to raise the minimum wage despite economic growth,[111] and called on states to 'gradually' raise wages in taking into account economic growth.[112]

The determination of an adequate minimum wage alone is not sufficient to ensure the fairness of wages and/or a decent living for workers and their families. The CESCR has criticized states where minimum wages have not kept pace with the rate of inflation,[113] economic growth,[114] the devaluation of currency,[115] or where the negative impacts of free trade agreements have not been mitigated in calculation methods.[116]

There is thus an obligation of continuing vigilance or diligence in respect of wage rates in view of changing conditions. The CESCR has often suggested that states should apply a system of indexation[117] which adjusts the minimum wage to the cost of living[118] and inflation and economic growth.[119] It has often stressed that the minimum wage should be annually adjusted,[120] although it has also suggested that adjustment need only be from time to time.[121] The CESCR's approach is consistent with ILO standards. Recommendation No. 135 of 1970 addresses the adjustment of minimum wages (Part V) as follows:

> 11. Minimum wage rates should be adjusted from time to time to take account of changes in the cost of living and other economic conditions.
>
> 12. To this end a review might be carried out of minimum wage rates in relation to the cost of living and other economic conditions either at regular intervals or whenever such a review is considered appropriate in the light of variations in a cost-of-living index.

[111] CESCR, Concluding Observations: Mexico, E/C.12/1/Add.41 (8 December 1999), [20].

[112] CESCR, Concluding Observations: Portugal, E/C.12/1995/4 (7 June 1995), [13].

[113] CESCR, Concluding Observations: Kenya, E/C.12/1993/6 (3 June 1993), [12]; Mexico, E/C.12/1993/16 (5 January 1994), [11]; Ukraine, E/C.12/1995/15 (28 December 1995), [20].

[114] CESCR, Concluding Observations: Portugal, E/C.12/1995/4 (7 June 1995), [10].

[115] CESCR, Concluding Observations: Mali, E/C.12/1994/17 (21 December 1994), [10].

[116] CESCR, Concluding Observations: Mexico, E/C.12/1993/16 (5 January 1994), [11].

[117] CESCR, Concluding Observations: Azerbaijan, E/C.12/1/Add.10 (14 December 2004), [46]; Zambia, E/C.12/1/Add.106 (23 June 2005), [41]; Uzbekistan, E/C.12/UZB/CO/1 (24 January 2006), [49]; India, E/C.12/IND/CO/5 (8 August 2008), [62].

[118] CESCR, Concluding Observations: Azerbaijan, E/C.12/1/Add.104 (14 December 2004), [46]; Zambia, E/C.12/1/Add.106 (23 June 2005), [41]; Uzbekistan, E/C.12/UZB/CO/1 (24 January 2006), [49].

[119] CESCR, Concluding Observations: Portugal, E/C.12/1995/4 (7 June 1995), [13].

[120] CESCR, Concluding Observations: Finland, E/C.12/1/Add.8 (5 December 1996), [20]; Nepal, E/C.12/1/Add.66 (24 September 2001), [23]; Kenya, E/C.12/KEN/CO/1 (1 December 2008), [18].

[121] CESCR, Concluding Observations: Syrian Arab Republic, E/C.12/1/Add.63 (24 September 2001), [35].

13. (1) In order to assist in the application of Paragraph 11 of this Recommendation, periodical surveys of national economic conditions, including trends in income per head, in productivity and in employment, unemployment and underemployment, should be made to the extent that national resources permit.

(2) The frequency of such surveys should be determined in the light of national conditions.

A simplified formula or criteria may apply to adjustments compared to initial wage fixing.[122]

The European regional approach

At the regional level, Article 4(1) of the Revised European Social Charter recognizes 'the right of workers to a remuneration such as will give them and their families a decent standard of living', and thus embodies a partly similar standard to Article 7 of the ICESCR. As in ILO practice, over time the European Committee on Social Rights (ECSR) has come to define a 'decent standard of living' as going beyond mere material basic necessities:

As interpreted by the Committee, this provision which obliges Contracting States to take appropriate measures to ensure a decent standard of living for workers and their families, requires those states to make a continuous effort to achieve the objectives set by this provision of the Charter. This being so, account must be taken of the fact that the socio-economic status of the worker and his family changes and that his basic needs, which at first are centred on the provision of purely material basic necessities such as food and housing, subsequently move towards concerns of a more advanced and complex nature, such as educational facilities and cultural and social benefits.[123]

While noting the variability of what is a 'decent' standard of living between states and the early paucity of reliable national wage data,[124] in 1977 the ECSR nonetheless identified various approaches to assessing the minimum wage. Its earliest approach was to identify any excessive deviation from the wage paid to the largest number of workers in a state; later it adopted a more mathematical 'decency threshold' of 68 per cent of the national average wage (based on a Council of Europe study).[125] That rate was attractive for its simplicity, since it could be assessed based only on statistics on the national average wage and the lowest wages actually paid in different sectors. That very simplicity, however, led to objections from states which felt that various other wage indicators needed to be considered.[126] The ECSR further observed that other factors remained relevant, including social benefits, family and housing subsidies, educational and cultural subsidies, tax concessions, excessive income inequality and government assistance.[127]

[122] ILO, *General Survey*, 103, 109–17.

[123] ECSR, Statements of Interpretation: Article 4(1) (31 May 1969); see also (31 December 1977); (30 November 1998); (22 October 2010).

[124] ECSR, Statement of Interpretation: Article 4(1) (31 July 1971).

[125] ECSR, Statement of Interpretation: Article 4(1) (31 December 1977).

[126] ECSR, Statement of Interpretation: Article 4(1) (30 November 1995).

[127] ECSR, Statement of Interpretation: Article 4(1) (30 November 1995).

Criticisms of that formula have included that it focuses more on income distribution rather than adequacy, and may be too low in poorer states and too high in wealthier states.[128] The problem is aggravated by the enlargement of the Council of Europe through the inclusion of poorer, post-communist transition states in the 1990s and thus a greater diversity of economies. In 1998, the ECSR adjusted the threshold to 60 per cent of the national net average wage for a full-time wage earner,[129] as long as that was also above the poverty line:

> The Committee proceeds from the expectation that a wage amounting to at least 60% of the average wage (calculated net…) will provide the wage earner concerned—and not the family—with a decent living standard. It nevertheless underlines that a wage does not meet the requirements of the Charter, irrespective of the percentage, if it does not ensure a decent living standard in real terms for a worker, i.e. it must be clearly above the poverty line for a given country.[130]

In explaining the change, the ECSR highlighted the outdated assumption that a single wage earner should provide a decent living for a family, and that the original rate was based on early statistical studies when member states were more limited and homogenous; wage structures and dispersion were different in the newly admitted Central and Eastern European states.[131]

Given the even greater diversity of states parties to the ICESCR, even greater difficulty would be faced in attempting to identify a generally applicable minimum wage formula. This is particularly the case in developing states where national average or median wages may not necessarily provide a 'decent' living as required by Article 7 of the ICESCR. At the same time, pegging the minimum wage to very low indicators—such as global poverty line indicia—may also fail to capture the requirements of 'fair' wages and a decent living. The challenge for the CESCR lies in applying criteria which are both sensitive to national conditions but also generalizable across states, or groups of states (such as developing, middle income or developed states), so as to enable meaningful but expeditious supervision.

OBLIGATION TO ESTABLISH OR FACILITATE MINIMUM WAGE-FIXING MACHINERY

In order to ensure remuneration that provides all workers with fair wages and a decent living, it is implicitly necessary for states to establish or facilitate adequate minimum

[128] Craven, *The ICESCR*, 236.

[129] 'The Committee defines remuneration for the purposes of the assessment under Article 4 para. 1 as the net value, i.e. after deduction of social security contributions and taxes, of the total wages, in principle both monetary and in kind, paid regularly by an employer to a worker for work carried out. Account shall where applicable be taken of bonuses and gratuities not paid regularly with each pay packet. Social security contributions shall be calculated on the basis of employee contribution rates laid down by law or collective agreement. Taxes are all taxes on earned income. Indirect taxes are thus not taken into account. Social transfers or welfare benefits which are not directly linked to the wage will not be taken into consideration as Article 4 para. 1 concerns remuneration for work as such': ECSR, Statement of Interpretation: Article 4(1) (30 November 1998).

[130] ECSR, Statement of Interpretation: Article 4(1) (30 November 1998).

[131] ECSR, Statement of Interpretation: Article 4(1) (30 November 1998).

wage-fixing machinery. Article 7 is silent on the means, methods or mechanisms for determining wages that are adequate to meet its requirements, leaving to states a flexible and discretionary choice of means in achieving the necessary result.

During the drafting, Canada had objected to 'the imposition of State decisions' in determining whether wages were fair and what was the relative value of different kinds of work.[132] A Soviet proposal to expressly require states to guarantee just and favourable conditions of work either through law or collective agreements was rejected.[133] The drafting reflected the tensions between socialist/planned and market-based approaches to industrial relations, and over the respective roles of the state, market and organized labour.

In monitoring states, the CESCR has rarely paid attention to the means or methods of minimum wage determination. It has certainly criticized states where methods for determining minimum wages are non-existent[134] or arbitrary,[135] and urged states to enact legislation implementing a minimum wage where there is none.[136] It was concerned where minimum wages determined by industry-specific wage boards did not protect workers in the smaller industries which were not part of the wage board system.[137] It was also concerned where wages set by collective agreements were far below average wages (in some cases less than 50 per cent).[138] It has encouraged states to conduct labour market surveys[139] as an informational precursor to wage fixing, and been concerned to ensure worker participation[140] in wage fixing, instead of unilateral state action.

Perhaps the strongest indication of the CESCR's approach to wage fixing methods lies in its criticism of states for failing to ratify ILO Convention No. 131 on Minimum Wage-Fixing[141] and its calls for the ratification of it.[142] International standards on wage fixing pre-date the ICESCR. Convention No. 26 of 1926 requires states to create a minimum wage-fixing 'machinery' (Article 1), but leaves states free to determine its 'nature and form', subject to consulting and involving workers and employers (Article 3):

Article 1

1. Each Member of the International Labour Organisation which ratifies this Convention undertakes to create or maintain machinery whereby minimum rates of wages can be fixed for workers employed in certain of the trades or parts of trades (and in particular in home working trades) in which no arrangements exist for the

132 UNGA Third Committee, A/C.3/SR.714 (17 December 1956), 166 (Canada).

133 Craven, *The ICESCR*, 227.

134 CESCR, Concluding Observations: Portugal (Macau), E/C.12/1/Add.9 (6 December 1996), [15].

135 CESCR, Concluding Observations: Bolivia, E/C.12/1/Add.60 (21 May 2001), [17].

136 CESCR, Concluding Observations: Yemen, E/C.12/1/Add.92 (12 December 2003), [30].

137 CESCR, Concluding Observations: Sri Lanka, E/C.12/1/Add.24 (16 January 1998), [18].

138 CESCR, Concluding Observations: Austria, E/C.12/AUT/CO/3 (25 January 2006), [11].

139 CESCR, Concluding Observations: Dominican Republic, E/C.12/1/Add.16 (12 December 1997), [36].

140 Craven, *The ICESCR*, 235.

141 CESCR, Concluding Observations: Sweden, E/C.12/1/Add.70 (30 November 2001), [22].

142 CESCR, Concluding Observations: Uruguay, E/C.12/1994/3 (30 May 1994), [17]; Sweden, E/C.12/1/Add.70 (30 November 2001), [33]; Sweden, E/C.12/SWE/CO/5 (1 December 2008), [31].

effective regulation of wages by collective agreement or otherwise and wages are exceptionally low.

2. For the purpose of this Convention, the term trades includes manufacture and commerce.

…

Article 3

1. Each Member which ratifies this Convention shall be free to decide the nature and form of the minimum wage-fixing machinery, and the methods to be followed in its operation…

While the Convention does not define the meaning of wage-fixing machinery, the contemporaneous Recommendation No. 30 gives the illustrative examples of general or specific trade boards or compulsory arbitration (paragraph II(1)). Recommendation No. 135 of 1970 indicates an extensive range of possibilities in paragraph VI(6), notably including: statute; decisions of competent bodies, boards, councils, tribunals or courts; and collective agreements which have the force of law.

What is decisive is that the minimum wage resulting from the various processes must be legally enforceable, as Article 2 of Convention No. 131 of 1970 provides:

1. Minimum wages shall have the force of law and shall not be subject to abatement, and failure to apply them shall make the person or persons concerned liable to appropriate penal or other sanctions.

2. Subject to the provisions of paragraph 1 of this Article, the freedom of collective bargaining shall be fully respected.

Within these limits states enjoy considerable flexibility, in line with their economic and industrial conditions, in the choice of means in giving effect to the obligation to ensure fair wages and a decent living for all workers. Both centralized intervention and decentralized and voluntary collective bargaining between workers' and employers' organizations may qualify. National practice varies very significantly.[143]

States bear a direct obligation to determine and pay minimum wages to their own public employees. States must also ensure that private employers participate in minimum wage-fixing mechanisms (such as collective bargaining or voluntary arbitration)[144] or otherwise apply minimum wages determined through other processes (including those facilitated by the state, such as judicial determinations).

The state will have to intervene in the private sector where party autonomy (as exercised through collective bargaining) fails to ensure fair wages and a decent living as required by Article 7. This may occur in exceptional cases where

[143] See ILO, *General Survey*, 25–64.
[144] See the chapter on Article 8 (trade union-related rights).

workers are disorganized, unions are weak or unemployment is high, and employers thus enjoy disproportionate power to determine or suppress wage levels. The state may then be required to legislate or legally set a minimum wage beneath which bargaining may not lawfully occur.

It should also be noted that ILO standards envisage the possibility of a single minimum wage, but also multiple minimum wages across different sectors or regions, as Recommendation No. 135 of 1970 outlines (in paragraph 5). Different minimum wages are compatible with Article 7 as long as none of the minimum levels is unfair or fails to ensure a decent living for workers and their families, and the principles of non-discrimination and equal pay for equal work are applied.

Consultation and participation

Whatever the form of minimum wage-fixing machinery adopted, ILO standards place a considerable emphasis on consultation and participation by workers and employers, including their representative organizations, pursuant to the tripartite structure underlying the ILO. In the early Convention No. 26 of 1928, states' freedom to choose the nature and form of the wage machinery is subject to the provisos of *consultation* in respect of prospective trade coverage, and *participation* in the operation of machinery once adopted (Article 3(2)):

> (1) before the machinery is applied in a trade or part of trade, representatives of the employers and workers concerned, including representatives of their respective organisations, if any, shall be consulted as well as any other persons, being specially qualified for the purpose by their trade or functions, whom the competent authority deems it expedient to consult;
>
> (2) the employers and workers concerned shall be associated in the operation of the machinery, in such manner and to such extent, but in any case in equal numbers and on equal terms, as may be determined by national laws or regulations…

Recommendation No. 30 calls for workers and employers' organizations, and independent persons, to be consulted in, but also to directly participate in, decision-making, and for women to be included as far as possible (Part II).

The most contemporary binding standards are in Article 4 of Convention No. 131 of 1970, which requires consultation with representative bodies and, where 'appropriate', their direct participation in decision-making, as well as the involvement of independent experts:

> 1. Each Member which ratifies this Convention shall create and/or maintain machinery adapted to national conditions and requirements whereby minimum wages for groups of wage earners covered in pursuance of Article 1 thereof can be fixed and adjusted from time to time.
>
> 2. Provision shall be made, in connection with the establishment, operation and modification of such machinery, for full consultation with representative organisations of employers and workers concerned or, where no such organisations exist, representatives of employers and workers concerned.

3. Wherever it is appropriate to the nature of the minimum wage fixing machinery, provision shall also be made for the direct participation in its operation of—

(a) representatives of organisations of employers and workers concerned or, where no such organisations exist, representatives of employers and workers concerned, on a basis of equality;

(b) persons having recognised competence for representing the general interests of the country and appointed after full consultation with representative organisations of employers and workers concerned, where such organisations exist and such consultation is in accordance with national law or practice.

Recommendation No. 135 of 1970 elaborates on the range of matters for consultation, and expands on the participation and independent expert elements (in Part IV).

According to the ILO, consultation means more than mere information and less than co-determination or participation in decision-making, but that those consulted should be capable of having a real influence on decisions.[145] Participation 'implies direct collaboration with the responsible authorities' in wage fixing,[146] and it must be on an equal footing.[147] Considerable discretion is left to states as to the forms of consultation and participation,[148] and to workers and employers in the selection of their representatives.

LEGAL EFFECTS, IMPLEMENTATION AND ENFORCEMENT OF MINIMUM WAGE FIXING

As mentioned earlier, the minimum wage is defined in part by the requirement that it be legally enforceable, whether directly in law or through a binding collective agreement.[149] This in turn presupposes the availability of information about worker entitlements and employer responsibilities; adequate procedures for the payment of wages; effective supervision of payments; and remedies and dissuasive sanctions for breaches resulting from non-payment (whether by failure to pay at all, payment below the minimum amount or late payment). Each of these issues is considered in turn.

Information and publicity

An important means of ensuring the practical effectiveness of the minimum wage is through the provision and publicizing of information about wage rates, so that workers may know their rights and employers their responsibilities. This will be particularly important for certain kinds of vulnerable workers, including those who are not organized in unions, migrant workers (who may not well know the language, or lack protective networks), workers with certain disabilities, young people and isolated workers (such as home or domestic workers).

[145] ILO, *General Survey*, 66–7, 81.
[146] ILO, *General Survey*, 66–7, 81.
[147] ILO, *General Survey*, 82.
[148] ILO, *General Survey*, 65–99.
[149] ILO Convention No. 26 concerning the Creation of Minimum Wage-Fixing Machinery, Article 3(3).

ILO standards are useful in informing the potential scope of Article 7 of the ICESCR. Convention No. 26 requires states to take the necessary measures 'to ensure that the employers and workers concerned are informed of the minimum rates of wages in force' (Article 4) and a similar obligation exists in relation to agricultural workers under Convention No. 99 (Article 4(1)). Early Recommendation No. 30 encouraged states to provide 'arrangements for informing the employers and workers of the rates in force' (Part VI(a)) and required employers to inform workers by displaying rates in accessible places (Part IV(1)):

In order that the workers, who are less likely than the employers to have their own means of acquainting themselves with the wage-fixing body's decisions, may be kept informed of the minimum rates at which they are to be paid, employers might be required to display full statements of the rates in force in readily accessible positions on the premises where the workers are employed, or in the case of home workers on the premises where the work is given out or returned on completion or wages paid.

The obligation on states to take '[a]ppropriate measures' to protect the minimum wage, in Article 5 of Convention No. 131, is also interpreted by Recommendation No. 135 to encompass 'arrangements for giving publicity to minimum wage provisions in languages or dialects understood by workers who need protection, adapted where necessary to the needs of illiterate persons' (paragraph 14(a)).

In relation to wage protection more generally, Convention No. 95 of 1949 requires relevant laws to be publicized (Article 15(a)). Workers must also be informed 'in an appropriate and easily understandable manner' of wage conditions before entering employment, when changes take place, and upon payment of wages (Article 14):

Article 14

Where necessary, effective measures shall be taken to ensure that workers are informed, in an appropriate and easily understandable manner—

(a) before they enter employment and when any changes take place, of the conditions in respect of wages under which they are employed; and

(b) at the time of each payment of wages, of the particulars of their wages for the pay period concerned, in so far as such particulars may be subject to change.

Article 15

The laws or regulations giving effect to the provisions of this Convention shall—

(a) be made available for the information of persons concerned…

Recommendation No. 85 particularizes the kinds of wage information (Part III(6)) and payment records (Part IV(7)) which should be brought to workers' attention.

Wage payment and protection

In relation to the payment of the minimum wage, ILO standards on wage protection generally provide useful guidance. According to ILO Convention No. 95 on

Protection of Wages 1949, wages should normally be paid only in legal tender (Article 3),[150] with limited exceptions for part payment in kind on the basis of fair and reasonable value (Article 4):[151]

Article 3

1. Wages payable in money shall be paid only in legal tender, and payment in the form of promissory notes, vouchers or coupons, or in any other form alleged to represent legal tender, shall be prohibited.

2. The competent authority may permit or prescribe the payment of wages by bank cheque or postal cheque or money order in cases in which payment in this manner is customary or is necessary because of special circumstances, or where a collective agreement or arbitration award so provides, or, where not so provided, with the consent of the worker concerned.

Article 4

1. National laws or regulations, collective agreements or arbitration awards may authorise the partial payment of wages in the form of allowances in kind in industries or occupations in which payment in the form of such allowances is customary or desirable because of the nature of the industry or occupation concerned; the payment of wages in the form of liquor of high alcoholic content or of noxious drugs shall not be permitted in any circumstances.

2. In cases in which partial payment of wages in the form of allowances in kind is authorised, appropriate measures shall be taken to ensure that—

(a) such allowances are appropriate for the personal use and benefit of the worker and his family; and

(b) the value attributed to such allowances is fair and reasonable.

Convention No. 95 further provides that wages shall normally be paid directly to the worker (Article 5). Employers must not limit 'in any manner the freedom of the worker to dispose of his wages' (Article 6), including by coercing a worker to use work stores or services (Article 7). Any wage deductions must be in accordance with law and not for the purpose of securing employment (Articles 8 and 9). Recommendation No. 85 on Protection of Wages 1949 adds that deductions should be limited by the necessity of maintaining the worker and her or his family (paragraph 1).[152] Under the Convention, any attachment or assignment of wages must be in accordance with law and not deprive the worker and her or his family of maintenance (Article 10).

[150] See also ILO Convention No. 117 concerning Basic Aims and Standards of Social Policy (adopted 22 June 1962, entered into force 23 April 1964), Article 11(2).

[151] On the latter point, see also ILO Convention No. 99 concerning Minimum Wage Fixing Machinery in Agriculture, Article 2(1); ILO Convention No. 131 concerning Minimum Wage Fixing, with Special Reference to Developing Countries is silent on the point.

[152] The Recommendation also covers deductions for reimbursement of loss or damage to products, goods or installations of the employer where the worker is responsible ([2]), and for limited deductions for essential work tools, materials or equipment ([3]).

One problem that has commonly arisen in the CESCR's monitoring of states is the late payment of wages. The CESCR has criticized wage arrears[153] and noted that it exacerbates inadequacies in minimum wages,[154] and robs workers of the value of the money earned.[155] It has also been concerned where privatization has resulted in the non-payment of wages.[156] The CESCR has recommended that states take measures to prevent wage arrears,[157] including by imposing sanctions on employers who are late paying wages.[158]

In this regard, Article 12 of Convention No. 95 requires wages to be paid at regular intervals, which helps to ensure against the harmful accumulation of unpaid wages:

1. Wages shall be paid regularly. Except where other appropriate arrangements exist which ensure the payment of wages at regular intervals, the intervals for the payment of wages shall be prescribed by national laws or regulations or fixed by collective agreement or arbitration award.

2. Upon the termination of a contract of employment, a final settlement of all wages due shall be effected in accordance with national laws or regulations, collective agreement or arbitration award or, in the absence of any applicable law, regulation, agreement or award, within a reasonable period of time having regard to the terms of the contract.[159]

While the Convention does not specify the payment intervals, Recommendation No. 85 suggests that the maximum interval should be fortnightly for wages calculated by the hour, day or week; monthly for wages calculated by the month or annually; and fortnightly for those paid on a piece-work or output basis (paragraphs 4 to 5).

Unpaid wages may also arise where an employer becomes bankrupt. The CESCR has been concerned where workers have not received their wage settlements after the closure of an enterprise.[160] Article 11 of Convention No. 95

[153] CESCR, Concluding Observations: Russian Federation, E/C.12/1/Add.13 (20 May 1997), [18]; Georgia, E/C.12/1/Add.42 (17 May 2000), [11]; Kyrgyzstan, E/C.12/1/Add.49 (1 September 2000), [14]; Ukraine, E/C.12/1/Add.65 (24 September 2001), [14]; including Georgia, E/C.12/1/Add.83 (19 December 2002), [15]; Russian Federation, E/C.12/1/Add.94 (12 December 2003), [18]; China (including HK, Macao), E/C.12/1/Add.107 (13 May 2005), [25]; Bosnia and Herzegovina, E/C.12/BIH/CO/1 (24 January 2006), [15].

[154] CESCR, Concluding Observations: Russian Federation, E/C.12/1/Add.13 (20 May 1997), [18]; Ukraine, E/C.12/1/Add.65 (24 September 2001), [14]; Russian Federation, E/C.12/1/Add.94 (12 December 2003), [18]; China (including HK, Macao), E/C.12/1/Add.107 (13 May 2005), [25].

[155] CESCR, Concluding Observations: Russian Federation, E/C.12/1/Add.13 (20 May 1997), [18].

[156] CESCR, Concluding Observations: Bosnia and Herzegovina, E/C.12/BIH/CO/1 (24 January 2006), [15].

[157] CESCR, Concluding Observations: Georgia, E/C.12/1/Add.42 (17 May 2000), [24]; Ukraine, E/C.12/1/Add.65 (24 September 2001), [25]; Georgia, E/C.12/1/Add.83 (19 December 2002), [33]; Russian Federation, E/C.12/1/Add.94 (12 December 2003), [46]; Bosnia and Herzegovina, E/C.12/BIH/CO/1 (24 January 2006), [36].

[158] CESCR, Concluding Observations: China (including HK, Macao), E/C.12/1/Add.107 (13 May 2005), [54].

[159] Wages should also be paid on work days and at or near the workplace: ILO Convention No. 95 concerning the Protection of Wages (adopted 1 July 1949, entered into force 24 September 1952), Article 13.

[160] CESCR, Concluding Observations: Nicaragua, E/C.12/NIC/CO/4 (28 November 2008), [15].

requires workers to be treated as privileged creditors in the event of bankruptcy or liquidation, for wage periods or amounts prescribed by national law, and subject to national rules on priority between privileged creditors:

1. In the event of the bankruptcy or judicial liquidation of an undertaking, the workers employed therein shall be treated as privileged creditors either as regards wages due to them for service rendered during such a period prior to the bankruptcy or judicial liquidation as may be prescribed by national laws or regulations, or as regards wages up to a prescribed amount as may be determined by national laws or regulations.

2. Wages constituting a privileged debt shall be paid in full before ordinary creditors may establish any claim to a share of the assets.

3. The relative priority of wages constituting a privileged debt and other privileged debts shall be determined by national laws or regulations.

A higher level of protection is provided by ILO Convention No. 173 on Protection of Workers' Claims (Employer's Insolvency) 1992. It stipulates the periods of wages that are privileged (Article 6), subject only to prescribed amounts which must not be below a 'socially acceptable level' (Article 7); and prioritizes workers' wages higher than 'most other' privileged claims (Article 8):

Article 5

In the event of an employer's insolvency, workers' claims arising out of their employment shall be protected by a privilege so that they are paid out of the assets of the insolvent employer before non-privileged creditors can be paid their share.

Article 6

The privilege shall cover at least:

(a) the workers' claims for wages relating to a prescribed period, which shall not be less than three months, prior to the insolvency or prior to the termination of the employment;

(b) the workers' claims for holiday pay due as a result of work performed during the year in which the insolvency or the termination of the employment occurred, and in the preceding year;

(c) the workers' claims for amounts due in respect of other types of paid absence relating to a prescribed period, which shall not be less than three months, prior to the insolvency or prior to the termination of the employment;

(d) severance pay due to workers upon termination of their employment.

Article 7

1. National laws or regulations may limit the protection by privilege of workers' claims to a prescribed amount, which shall not be below a socially acceptable level.

Article 8

1. National laws or regulations shall give workers' claims a higher rank of privilege than most other privileged claims, and in particular those of the State and the social security system.

> 2. However, where workers' claims are protected by a guarantee institution in accordance with Part III of this Convention, the claims so protected may be given a lower rank of privilege than those of the State and the social security system.

Where workers' wages cannot be paid by an employer because of insolvency, Convention No. 173 requires states to guarantee their claims through a 'guarantee institution' (Article 9), and sets out (somewhat lower) minimum periods of protected wages (Article 12):

Article 9

The payment of workers' claims against their employer arising out of their employment shall be guaranteed through a guarantee institution when payment cannot be made by the employer because of insolvency.

. . .

Article 12

The workers' claims protected pursuant to this Part of the Convention shall include at least:

> (a) the workers' claims for wages relating to a prescribed period, which shall not be less than eight weeks, prior to the insolvency or prior to the termination of the employment;
>
> (b) the workers' claims for holiday pay due as a result of work performed during a prescribed period, which shall not be less than six months, prior to the insolvency or prior to the termination of the employment;
>
> (c) the workers' claims for amounts due in respect of other types of paid absence relating to a prescribed period, which shall not be less than eight weeks, prior to the insolvency or prior to the termination of employment;
>
> (d) severance pay due to workers upon termination of their employment.

A more extensive list of suggested protected claims (whether payable by an employer or guarantor) is set out Recommendation No. 180 on Protection of Workers' Claims (Employer's Insolvency) 1992 (paragraphs 3 and 9), importantly including occupational injury compensation and accrued social security or social insurance benefits. The Recommendation also provides for accelerated payment procedures where insolvency proceedings are protracted (paragraph 6). It makes further recommendations on operational principles for guarantee institutions (paragraph 8).

Supervision and enforcement

A range of private and public, and individual or collective, enforcement methods for guaranteeing the minimum wage may be envisaged within the ambit of Article 7 of the ICESCR. These include individual, private claims for breach of contract, as through the courts; union-initiated complaints for breaches of collective agreements and recourse to dispute settlement procedures in such agreements (such as conciliation or arbitration leading to binding awards); and public regulatory or administrative action, such as labour inspections, civil sanctions or criminal penalties.

Whatever the methods, enforcement action must be capable of restoring the worker's rights, namely the payment of the minimum wage, but also of remedying loss (in the form of unpaid or under-paid wages) and punishing and deterring violators (whether through exemplary or punitive compensatory damages, criminal fines or punishment, or appropriate civil or administrative penalties). However, there must be a strong and direct role for the state, given the importance of the minimum wage in securing a decent living (and thus other basic socio-economic rights), and the vulnerability of low-paid or disadvantaged workers (including the likely inaccessibility of pursuing private legal remedies for breach of contract).

In this regard, ILO standards provide considerable guidance. Under Convention No. 26, the minimum wage must be subject to state 'supervision and sanctions' for employers and remedies for employees (Article 4):

> 1. Each Member which ratifies this Convention shall take the necessary measures, by way of a system of supervision and sanctions, to ensure that the employers and workers concerned are informed of the minimum rates of wages in force and that wages are not paid at less than these rates in cases where they are applicable.
>
> 2. A worker to whom the minimum rates are applicable and who has been paid wages at less than these rates shall be entitled to recover, by judicial or other legalised proceedings, the amount by which he has been underpaid, subject to such limitation of time as may be determined by national laws or regulations.[161]

Recommendation No. 30 of 1928 suggests more extensive measures in Part IV, including: official supervision of the rates paid; penalties for infringements; a sufficient and adequately empowered labour inspectorate; a duty on employers to keep wage records; and effective remedies for workers not in a position to individually enforce their own claims.

Labour inspections are among the necessary measures states may take to ensure that the minimum wage is paid under Conventions No. 99 (Article 4(1), for agriculture) and No. 131 (Article 5, for all wage earners). In addition, there are a number of specialized ILO conventions on labour inspection generally (including wages, but also conditions) in particular sectors, such as industry, commerce and agriculture.[162] ILO Convention No. 81 on Labour Inspection 1947 is indicative of

[161] See also ILO Convention No. 99 concerning Minimum Wage Fixing Machinery in Agriculture, Article 4(1): 'Each Member which ratifies this Convention shall take the necessary measures to ensure that the employers and workers concerned are informed of the minimum rates of wages in force and that wages are not paid at less than these rates in cases where they are applicable; these measures shall include such provision for supervision, inspection, and sanctions as may be necessary and appropriate to the conditions obtaining in agriculture in the country concerned.'

[162] ILO Convention No. 81 concerning Labour Inspection in Industry and Commerce (adopted 11 July 1947, entered into force 7 April 1950), Article 3(1)(a); ILO Convention No. 129 concerning Labour Inspection in Agriculture (adopted 25 June 1969, entered into force 19 January 1972), Article 6(1)(a).

the powers of labour inspectors that are necessary to enable them to effectively enforce labour laws:

Article 12

1. Labour inspectors provided with proper credentials shall be empowered:

(a) to enter freely and without previous notice at any hour of the day or night any workplace liable to inspection;

(b) to enter by day any premises which they may have reasonable cause to believe to be liable to inspection; and

(c) to carry out any examination, test or enquiry which they may consider necessary in order to satisfy themselves that the legal provisions are being strictly observed, and in particular—

(i) to interrogate, alone or in the presence of witnesses, the employer or the staff of the undertaking on any matters concerning the application of the legal provisions;

(ii) to require the production of any books, registers or other documents the keeping of which is prescribed by national laws or regulations relating to conditions of work, in order to see that they are in conformity with the legal provisions, and to copy such documents or make extracts from them;

(iii) to enforce the posting of notices required by the legal provisions…

2. On the occasion of an inspection visit, inspectors shall notify the employer or his representative of their presence, unless they consider that such a notification may be prejudicial to the performance of their duties.

Article 13

1. Labour inspectors shall be empowered to take steps with a view to remedying defects observed in plant, layout or working methods which they may have reasonable cause to believe constitute a threat to the health or safety of the workers.

2. In order to enable inspectors to take such steps they shall be empowered, subject to any right of appeal to a judicial or administrative authority which may be provided by law, to make or to have made orders requiring—

(a) such alterations to the installation or plant, to be carried out within a specified time limit, as may be necessary to secure compliance with the legal provisions relating to the health or safety of the workers; or

(b) measures with immediate executory force in the event of imminent danger to the health or safety of the workers.

3. Where the procedure prescribed in paragraph 2 is not compatible with the administrative or judicial practice of the Member, inspectors shall have the right to apply to the competent authority for the issue of orders or for the initiation of measures with immediate executory force.

…

Article 16

Workplaces shall be inspected as often and as thoroughly as is necessary to ensure the effective application of the relevant legal provisions.

Article 17

1. Persons who violate or neglect to observe legal provisions enforceable by labour inspectors shall be liable to prompt legal proceedings without previous warning: Provided that exceptions may be made by national laws or regulations in respect of cases in which previous notice to carry out remedial or preventive measures is to be given.

2. It shall be left to the discretion of labour inspectors to give warning and advice instead of instituting or recommending proceedings.

Article 18

Adequate penalties for violations of the legal provisions enforceable by labour inspectors and for obstructing labour inspectors in the performance of their duties shall be provided for by national laws or regulations and effectively enforced.

In monitoring states, the CESCR has sometimes suggested that minimum wage laws should be better enforced through an increase in labour inspections and sanctions for employers.[163]

Convention No. 131 requires perpetrators to be liable to appropriate penal or other sanctions (Article 2(1)),[164] and states must generally provide 'adequate inspection reinforced by other necessary measures . . . to ensure effective application' of the Convention (Article 5):

Article 2

1. Minimum wages shall have the force of law and . . . failure to apply them shall make the person or persons concerned liable to appropriate penal or other sanctions.

. . .

Article 5

Appropriate measures, such as adequate inspection reinforced by other necessary measures, shall be taken to ensure the effective application of all provisions relating to minimum wages.

Recommendation No. 135 of 1970 details further measures to improve the accessibility and effectiveness of enforcement, and to protect against victimization (Part VI).

Mention should also be made of the enforcement provisions for wage protection generally in Convention No. 95, Article 15 of which requires laws to, inter alia, prescribe adequate penalties and remedies:

[163] CESCR, Concluding Observations: Philippines, E/C.12/PHL/CO/4 (1 December 2008), [11]; Republic of Korea, E/C.12/KOR/CO/3 (17 December 2009), [16].

[164] Some states objected to this during the drafting: ILO, *General Survey*, 23.

The laws or regulations giving effect to the provisions of this Convention shall—

(a) be made available for the information of persons concerned;

(b) define the persons responsible for compliance therewith;

(c) prescribe adequate penalties or other appropriate remedies for any violation thereof;

(d) provide for the maintenance, in all appropriate cases, of adequate records in an approved form and manner.

Further, Convention No. 117 on Social Policy (Basic Aims and Standards) 1962 provides that a worker who has been paid less than the minimum wage is entitled to recover, by judicial or other legal means, the amount owed, subject to prescribed time limits.

'EQUAL REMUNERATION FOR WORK OF EQUAL VALUE WITHOUT DISTINCTION OF ANY KIND, IN PARTICULAR WOMEN BEING GUARANTEED CONDITIONS OF WORK NOT INFERIOR TO THOSE ENJOYED BY MEN, WITH EQUAL PAY FOR EQUAL WORK'

While there was general support for the principle of equal remuneration in the drafting, some states objected that its inclusion in Article 7(a) unnecessarily duplicated the guarantees of non-discrimination in Article 2 and gender equality in Article 3 of the ICESCR,[165] or because women were already covered by the references to 'everyone' or 'workers' in Article 7.[166]

Some states noted that equal remuneration was already addressed by ILO Convention No. 100 on Equal Remuneration 1951,[167] adopted after a world war in which '[w]omen had been on the front line of production… and the myth that they could not do certain jobs or were not as productive as men could no longer be sustained'.[168] As early as 1919, the Treaty of Versailles, which includes the original ILO Constitution, laid down the principle of 'special and urgent importance' that 'men and women should receive equal remuneration for work of equal value'.[169] The principle is also mentioned in ILO Recommendation No. 30 of 1928 in the context of minimum wage fixing (Part B), while equal opportunity generally is enshrined in the Declaration of Philadelphia 1944 as part of the revised ILO Constitution.

[165] In the Commission on Human Rights: E/CN.4/85 (1 May 1948), 40 (Brazil); E/2256 (14 April–14 June 1952), 15; in the UNGA Third Committee: A/C.3/SR.713 (17 December 1956), 160 (Sweden), 158 (Netherlands); A/C.3/SR.714 (17 December 1956), 163 (Afghanistan), 165 (Finland); A/C.3/SR.716 (19 December 1956), 176 (Australia); A/C.3/SR.717 (20 December 1956), 181 (Canada).

[166] Craven, *The ICESCR*, 229.

[167] UNGA Third Committee, A/C.3/SR.713 (17 December 1956), 160 (Sweden).

[168] ILO, *Giving Globalization a Human Face: General Survey on the Fundamental Conventions concerning Rights at Work in light of the ILO Declaration on Social Justice for a Fair Globalization 2008* ('*Giving Globalization a Human Face*'), International Labour Conference (101st session) Report III(1B) (Geneva, 2012), 272; see also UNGA Third Committee, A/C.3/SR.714 (18 December 1956), 164 (Dominican Republic).

[169] Treaty of Versailles 1919, Article 427.

The Netherlands opposed the provision for the different reason that it feared requiring equality would preclude 'special' or differential treatment in favour of women, such as 'a prohibition of night-work for women only'.[170] That is not the prevailing understanding of non-discrimination guarantees in the ICESCR and ICCPR generally, or in ILO instruments,[171] which permit 'positive discrimination' or affirmative action to redress substantive disadvantage. There was also a suggestion that the clause implied that employing women was somehow disadvantageous.[172] At the other end of the spectrum of debate, the United Kingdom was concerned that the provision would limit its ability to control inflation by restricting equal pay claims,[173] a view not shared by others.

A clear majority of states supported the provision,[174] including to particularize non-discrimination in the specific context of rights in work,[175] to progress women's rights,[176] because of the prevalence of discrimination against women,[177] and since the General Assembly and Commission on the Status of Women had recommended its inclusion.[178] Some believed that more 'explicit legal protection'[179] would improve enforcement[180] and 'prevent States from merely proclaiming the principle of equality without attempting to apply it in practice'.[181] The Dominican Republic criticized the ILO's opposition on the basis that the ILO 'had always been somewhat conservative with regard to women's rights'.[182]

The provision remains relevant almost a century after it was articulated at Versailles. The ILO estimates that the current global gender pay gap is about 23 per cent—that is, women earn only 77 per cent of what men earn, and it may

[170] Commission on Human Rights, E/CN.4/85 (1 May 1948), 40 (Netherlands).

[171] See, eg, ILO Convention No. 111 concerning Discrimination in Respect of Employment and Occupation (adopted 25 June 1958, entered into force 15 June 1960), Article 3 (special measures are not discriminatory).

[172] Craven, *The ICESCR*, 229.

[173] Craven, *The ICESCR*, 230.

[174] An amendment by Afghanistan and the Netherlands to delete the provision was rejected by thirty-nine votes to eleven, with twelve abstentions: UNGA Third Committee, A/3525 (9 February 1957), 12.

[175] UNGA Third Committee, A/C.3/SR.713 (17 December 1956), 161 (Uruguay), 162 (Venezuela); A/C.3/SR.714 (17 December 1956), 165 (India).

[176] UNGA Third Committee, A/C.3/SR.714 (17 December 1956), 164 (Dominican Republic); Colombia expressed its full support: UNGA Third Committee, A/C.3/SR.715 (18 December 1956), 171.

[177] UNGA Third Committee, A/C.3/SR.716 (19 December 1956), 178 (Ukrainian Soviet Socialist Republic); A/C.3/SR.715 (18 December 1956), 171 (Chile).

[178] Craven, *The ICESCR*, 229; see UNGA Res. 421 (V): Draft International Covenant on Human Rights and Measures of Implementation: Future Work of the Commission on Human Rights (4 December 1950).

[179] UNGA Third Committee, A/C.3/SR.717 (20 December 1956), 182 (Guatemala).

[180] UNGA Third Committee, A/C.3/SR.715 (18 December 1956), 172 (Byelorussian Soviet Socialist Republic).

[181] UNGA Third Committee, A/C.3/SR.715 (18 December 1956), 170 (China); see also 172 (Byelorussian Soviet Socialist Republic).

[182] UNGA Third Committee, A/C.3/SR.714 (17 December 1956), 164–5 (Dominican Republic).

take seventy-five years to close the gap.[183] Even in the 117 states which now have equal pay laws,[184] challenges of application and result remain.

The principle has since been reaffirmed in Article 11(1)(d) of the Convention on the Elimination of All Forms of Discrimination against Women:

> 1. States Parties shall take all appropriate measures to eliminate discrimination against women in the field of employment in order to ensure, on a basis of equality of men and women, the same rights, in particular:
>
> ...
>
> (d) The right to equal remuneration, including benefits, and to equal treatment in respect of work of equal value, as well as equality of treatment in the evaluation of the quality of work...

It is also found in regional instruments, including Article 4(3) of the European Social Charter ('the right of men and women workers to equal pay for work of equal value'); Article 141 of the EC Treaty ('the principle of equal pay for male and female workers for equal work or work of equal value');[185] Article 7(a) of the Protocol of San Salvador 1988 ('equal wages for equal work, without distinction'); Article 15 of the African Charter ('equal pay for equal work'); and Article 34(4) of the Arab Charter on Human Rights 2004 ('[t]here shall be no discrimination between men and women in...the right to receive equal remuneration for equal work'). It is, however, absent from the brief work rights included in Article 27 of the ASEAN Declaration on Human Rights 2012.

'Without distinction of any kind'

It is unsurprising that gender has been the focus of equal remuneration protection given the special mention of women in Article 7(a), the fact that women compose roughly half of the population, and that ILO Convention No. 100 and Article 11(1)(d) of the CEDAW focus solely on women. However, the language of Article 7(a) makes clear that women are only one, non-exhaustive illustration ('in particular') of the principle that equal remuneration for work of equal value applies 'without distinction of any kind'.

In the drafting, there was little discussion of the potentially broader application of the provision. However, as already noted, some states thought a specific reference to women was unnecessary because the general non-discrimination guarantee in Article 2(2) of the ICESCR, including on the basis of 'sex', would apply to Article 7.

In that light, the meaning of equal remuneration 'without distinction of any kind' can be implicitly interpreted by reference to the prohibited grounds of discrimination

[183] ILO, *Giving Globalization a Human Face*, 280.

[184] UN Women, 'Equal Pay for Work of Equal Value', <http://progress.unwomen.org/equal-pay/>.

[185] Consolidated Version of the Treaty Establishing the European Community, as amended by the Treaty of Nice (adopted 26 February 2001, entered into force 1 February 2003), Article 141; formerly the Treaty of Maastricht (adopted 7 February 1992, entered into force 1 November 1993), Article 119.

in Article 2(2), namely 'race, colour, sex, language, religion, political or other opinion, national or social origin, property, birth or other status'. In the CESCR's practice, 'other status' can include disability, age, nationality, marital and family status, sexual orientation and gender identity, health status, place of residence, and economic and social situation, as discussed in the earlier chapter on Article 2 of the ICESCR. Other ILO instruments also support non-discrimination on various broad grounds.[186]

This view is supported by the drafting debate on an unsuccessful Uruguayan proposal to replace the phrase 'without distinction of any kind' with 'without distinctions based on sex or other considerations'.[187] The United Kingdom presumed that 'other considerations' referred to the distinctions listed in Article 2(2) of the draft Covenant,[188] and Uruguay explained that 'other considerations' in its proposal was intended to refer to the distinctions in Article 1(3) of the UN Charter[189] (namely, the more limited grounds of 'race, sex, language, or religion').

The amendment was opposed by the ILO, which felt that prohibiting 'other considerations' might preclude 'differential [pay] rates, established without regard to sex on the basis of an objective appraisal' of jobs, as provided for by ILO Convention No. 100 on Equal Remuneration 1951.[190] Of course, the same objection may technically be levelled at the phrase 'distinction of any kind' as adopted in Article 7(a). Plainly, the provision is not intended to eliminate differences in pay rates based on objective, non-biased criteria, as discussed below, and including, for instance, skill, effort, responsibility and working conditions,[191] or market competition for scarce skills.

Subsequent human rights instruments confirm that the principle of equal remuneration applies to groups other than women. Article 5(e)(i) of the Convention on the Elimination of Racial Discrimination requires states to 'undertake to prohibit and to eliminate racial discrimination', including in the enjoyment of the rights 'to just and favourable conditions of work…to equal pay for equal work, [and] to just and favourable remuneration'. Article 17(3) of the Declaration on the Rights of Indigenous Peoples 2007 recognizes that: 'Indigenous individuals have the right not to be subjected to any discriminatory conditions of labour and, inter alia, employment or salary'. Article 27(1)(b) of the Convention on the Rights of Persons with Disabilities requires states to '[p]rotect the rights of persons with disabilities, on an equal basis with others, to just and favourable conditions of work, including equal opportunities and equal remuneration for work of equal value…'.

[186] See, eg, ILO Convention No. 111 concerning Discrimination in Respect of Employment and Occupation, Article 1 ('race, colour, sex, religion, political opinion, national extraction or social origin').

[187] UNGA Third Committee, A/3525 (9 February 1957), 10.

[188] UNGA Third Committee, A/C.3/SR.715 (18 December 1956), 169 (UK).

[189] UNGA Third Committee, A/C.3/SR.715 (18 December 1956), 170 (Uruguay).

[190] UNGA Third Committee, A/C.3/SR.714 (17 December 1956), 164 (ILO).

[191] ILO, *Giving Globalization a Human Face*, 281–2.

In practice, the equal remuneration principle will be particularly important for certain vulnerable, marginalized or disadvantaged groups, and the CESCR has treated the equal pay guarantee as also applying to groups other than women.[192] These may include foreign or migrant workers, indigenous peoples, workers with disabilities, child or young labourers, agricultural workers, workers from lower socio-economic 'castes', casual and part-time workers, those in the informal economy (including domestic workers) and workers in precarious industries (such as garments and textiles, or manufacturing 'sweat-shops').

'Equal remuneration for work of equal value' and 'equal pay for equal work'

Article 7(a) refers both to 'equal remuneration for work of equal value' and 'equal pay for equal work' by women, with the latter expressed as an example ('in particular') of the former. ILO Convention No. 100 defines equal remuneration for work of equal value as 'rates of remuneration established without discrimination based on sex' (Article 1(b)). As discussed earlier, the concept of 'remuneration' in Article 7 was intended to include not only wages, but also allowances. This is also the understanding in ILO Convention No. 100, where remuneration 'includes the ordinary, basic or minimum wage or salary and any additional emoluments whatsoever payable directly or indirectly, whether in cash or in kind, by the employer to the worker and arising out of the worker's employment' (Article 1(a)).

The concept of equal pay for equal work is more restrictive than the notion of equal remuneration for work of equal value, since it compares pay rates between the same jobs and/or in the same enterprise,[193] and is concerned with direct discrimination. This includes the historical legacy in some states where 'the male basic wage was fixed as a family wage and…the female basic wage was fixed as a wage for a single woman without dependants'.[194]

By contrast, equal pay for work of equal value demands wider comparisons across different jobs, enterprises, employers, sectors and places,[195] and is the concept utilized in Article 1 of ILO Convention No. 100 and the European Social Charter.[196] It goes beyond direct discrimination to address the undervaluation of jobs perceived to be 'female' based on gender stereotypes about the abilities and aspirations of women, and the occupational segregation of women into such areas (for example, in carer roles or domestic work).[197] Thus, the CESCR has, for example, criticized states where women in agriculture are paid lower wages on the assumption that they are less productive in labour-intensive work.[198] It has also called on states 'to take measures to encourage women to choose

[192] Craven, *The ICESCR*, 238.
[193] Craven, *The ICESCR*, 237.
[194] *Equal Pay Cases*, 1969, 127 CAR 1142, 1152 (Australian Conciliation and Arbitration Commission).
[195] ILO, *Giving Globalization a Human Face*, 291.
[196] ILO, *Giving Globalization a Human Face*, 291.
[197] ILO, *Giving Globalization a Human Face*, 281; Craven, *The ICESCR*, 237.
[198] CESCR, Concluding Observations: Mauritius, E/C.12/1994.8 (31 May 1994), [9].

occupations and professions that are traditionally exercised by men and which are better remunerated'.[199]

In monitoring states, the CESCR has observed that women are disproportionately represented in poorly paid jobs[200] (including in agriculture, health and education),[201] part-time jobs,[202] and in unskilled[203] or informal labour.[204] It has also criticized the under-representation of women in high-ranking positions in professional fields,[205] public administration and universities,[206] which also produces gendered wage differentials. It has further identified wage gaps in the private[207] the public sectors.[208]

The principle of equal pay for work of equal value 'permits a broad scope of comparison, including, but going beyond equal remuneration for "equal", "the same" or "similar" work, and also encompasses work that is of an entirely different nature, which is nevertheless of equal value'.[209] The ILO Committee of Experts on the Application of Conventions and Recommendations (CEACR) explains in a General Observation:

1. The Committee notes that while equal remuneration for men and women for work of equal value is a principle that is widely accepted, the scope of the concept and its application in practice can be more difficult to grasp and apply. Unequal remuneration is often due to subtle, chronic problems that are difficult to overcome without a clear understanding of the concepts and their relevance to the workplace and society in general. The Committee notes that difficulties in applying the Convention in law and in practice result in particular from a lack of understanding of the scope and implications of the concept of 'work of equal value'. This concept is a cornerstone of the Convention and lies at the heart of the fundamental right of equal remuneration for men and women for work of equal value, and the promotion of equality. The Committee, therefore, considers it necessary to underscore the importance and clarify the meaning of 'work of equal value'.

2. The Committee notes that historical attitudes towards the role of women in society, along with stereotypical assumptions regarding women's aspirations, preferences, capabilities and 'suitability' for certain jobs, have contributed to occupational sex segregation in the labour market. As a result, certain jobs are held predominantly or exclusively by women and others by men. These views and attitudes also tend to result in the undervaluation of 'female jobs' in comparison with those of men who are performing different work and using different skills, when determining wage rates.

199 CESCR, Concluding Observations: Norway, E/C.12/1/Add.109 (23 June 2005), [30].

200 CESCR, Concluding Observations: Austria, E/C.12/AUT/CO/3 (25 January 2006), [10]; Kazakhstan, E/C.12/KAZ/CO/1 (7 June 2010), [19]; Mauritius, E/C.12/MUS/CO/4 (8 June 2010), [17].

201 CESCR, Concluding Observations: Kazakhstan, E/C.12/KAZ/CO/1 (7 June 2010), [19].

202 CESCR, Concluding Observations: Austria, E/C.12/AUT/CO/3 (25 January 2006), [10]; Sweden, E/C.12/SWE/CO/5 (1 December 2008), [18].

203 CESCR, Concluding Observations: Mauritius, E/C.12/MUS/CO/4 (8 June 2010), [17].

204 CESCR, Concluding Observations: Kazakhstan, E/C.12/KAZ/CO/1 (7 June 2010), [19].

205 CESCR, Concluding Observations: Sweden, E/C.12/SWE/CO/5 (1 December 2008), [18].

206 CESCR, Concluding Observations: Belgium, E/C.12/BEL/CO/3 (4 January 2008), [15].

207 CESCR, Concluding Observations: Australia, E/C.12/1/Add.50 (11 September 2000), [17]; Colombia, E/C.12/1/Add.74 (6 December 2001), [16]; Trinidad and Tobago, E/C.12/1/Add.80 (5 June 2002), [17].

208 CESCR, Concluding Observations: Poland, E/C.12/POL/CO/5 (2 December 2009), [17].

209 ILO, *Giving Globalization a Human Face*, 281.

3. In order to address such occupational segregation, where men and women often perform different jobs, under different conditions, and even in different establishments, the concept of 'work of equal value' is essential, as it permits a broad scope of comparison. 'Work of equal value' includes but goes beyond equal remuneration for 'equal', the 'same' or 'similar' work, and also encompasses work that is of an entirely different nature, which is nevertheless of equal value. Furthermore, the application of the Convention's principle is not limited to comparisons between men and women in the same establishment or enterprise. It allows for a much broader comparison to be made between jobs performed by men and women in different places or enterprises, or between different employers.[210]

According to Article 3(1) of Convention No. 100, an 'objective appraisal of jobs on the basis of the work to be performed' is required. In the practice of the ILO, an objective appraisal includes an overall assessment of factors such as skill, effort, responsibilities and working conditions.[211] It is not sufficient to confine the comparison to the same, equal or similar work, work conditions or work results; equal skills, ability, qualifications or effort; or work of equal complexity, difficulty or responsibility.[212] Nor is it sufficient to simply determine the market 'value' of the work performed, in view of the inherent gender bias in the market.[213]

Thus, to give some examples from ILO practice, work of equal value was found to be performed by (mainly female) wardens in sheltered accommodation for the elderly and (mainly male) security guards in offices; or by (mainly female) school meal supervisors and (mainly male) garden and park supervisors.[214] A female manager in a municipal social affairs department performed work of equal value to a male municipal engineer.[215] In the *Enderby* case, under Article 119 of the EC Treaty (Maastricht version)[216] on equal remuneration, the

[210] ILO CEACR, General Observation (adopted 2006, published 96th ILC session 2007), [1] and [2].
[211] ILO, *Giving Globalization a Human Face*, 281–2.
[212] ILO, *Giving Globalization a Human Face*, 283.
[213] ILO, *Giving Globalization a Human Face*, 281.
[214] ILO CEACR, General Observation (adopted 2006, published 96th ILC session 2007), [4].
[215] *Case No. 258/2004*, 20 January 2005 (Supreme Court of Iceland).
[216] Now the Consolidated Version of the Treaty Establishing the European Community, as amended by the Treaty of Nice (adopted 26 February 2001, entered into force 1 February 2003), Article 141 provides:

> 1. Each Member State shall ensure that the principle of equal pay for male and female workers for equal work or work of equal value is applied.
>
> 2. For the purpose of this article, 'pay' means the ordinary basic or minimum wage or salary and any other consideration, whether in cash or in kind, which the worker receives directly or indirectly, in respect of his employment, from his employer.
>
> Equal pay without discrimination based on sex means:
>
> (a) that pay for the same work at piece rates shall be calculated on the basis of the same unit of measurement;
>
> (b) that pay for work at time rates shall be the same for the same job.
>
> 3. The Council, acting in accordance with the procedure referred to in Article 251, and after consulting the Economic and Social Committee, shall adopt measures to ensure the application of the principle of equal opportunities and equal treatment of men and women in matters of employment and occupation, including the principle of equal pay for equal work or work of equal value.

European Court of Justice found that work performed by male pharmacists and female speech therapists was prima facie work of equal value:[217]

15. . . . First, it is not a question of de facto discrimination arising from a particular sort of arrangement such as may apply, for example, in the case of part-time workers. Secondly, there can be no complaint that the employer has applied a system of pay wholly lacking in transparency since the rates of pay of NHS speech therapists and pharmacists are decided by regular collective bargaining processes in which there is no evidence of discrimination as regards either of those two professions.

16. However, if the pay of speech therapists is significantly lower than that of pharmacists and if the former are almost exclusively women while the latter are predominantly men, there is a prima facie case of sex discrimination, at least where the two jobs in question are of equal value and the statistics describing that situation are valid.

. . .

18. Where there is a prima facie case of discrimination, it is for the employer to show that there are objective reasons for the difference in pay. Workers would be unable to enforce the principle of equal pay before national courts if evidence of a prima facie case of discrimination did not shift to the employer the onus of showing that the pay differential is not in fact discriminatory (see, by analogy, the judgment in Danfoss, cited above, at paragraph 13).

19. In these circumstances, the answer to the first question is that, where significant statistics disclose an appreciable difference in pay between two jobs of equal value, one of which is carried out almost exclusively by women and the other predominantly by men, Article 119 of the Treaty requires the employer to show that that difference is based on objectively justified factors unrelated to any discrimination on grounds of sex.

The Court further accepted that certain economic conditions, such as labour shortages, may be factors which justify pay differences in certain circumstances:

25. The Court has consistently held that it is for the national court, which has sole jurisdiction to make findings of fact, to determine whether and to what extent the grounds put forward by an employer to explain the adoption of a pay practice which applies independently of a worker's sex but in fact affects more women than men may be regarded as objectively justified economic grounds (Case 170/84 *Bilka-Kaufhaus*, cited above, at paragraph 36 and Case C-184/89 *Nimz*, cited above, at paragraph 14). Those grounds may include, if they can be attributed to the needs and objectives of the undertaking, different criteria such as the worker's flexibility or adaptability to hours and places of work, his training or his length of service (Case 109/88 *Danfoss*, cited above, at paragraphs 22 to 24).

26. The state of the employment market, which may lead an employer to increase the pay of a particular job in order to attract candidates, may constitute an objectively justified economic ground within the meaning of the case-law cited above. How it is to be applied

4. With a view to ensuring full equality in practice between men and women in working life, the principle of equal treatment shall not prevent any Member State from maintaining or adopting measures providing for specific advantages in order to make it easier for the underrepresented sex to pursue a vocational activity or to prevent or compensate for disadvantages in professional careers.

[217] *Enderby v Frenchay Health Authority*, ECJ Case No. C-127/92, 27 October 1993.

in the circumstances of each case depends on the facts and so falls within the jurisdiction of the national court.

27. If…the national court has been able to determine precisely what proportion of the increase in pay is attributable to market forces, it must necessarily accept that the pay differential is objectively justified to the extent of that proportion. When national authorities have to apply Community law, they must apply the principle of proportionality.

28. If that is not the case, it is for the national court to assess whether the role of market forces in determining the rate of pay was sufficiently significant to provide objective justification for part or all of the difference.

29. The answer to the third question therefore is that it is for the national court to determine, if necessary by applying the principle of proportionality, whether and to what extent the shortage of candidates for a job and the need to attract them by higher pay constitutes an objectively justified economic ground for the difference in pay between the jobs in question.

The Court's reference to 'objectively justified economic ground[s]' does, however, raise questions as to how far the principle of equal value should properly reach. For matters such as a worker's flexibility or adaptability to hours and places of work, or training or length of service, may themselves be affected by structural gender inequalities. These may include, for example, inadequate childcare services or subsidies for working mothers, which restrict their flexibility to work certain hours; inadequate training opportunities for women; or where periods of maternity leave affect length of service. The criteria may be 'objective' in a narrow sense, but the ability of women to fulfil them is deeply affected by structural inequalities.

Nature of state obligations

Under Article 7, states '*recognise* the right of everyone to the enjoyment of just and favourable conditions of work which ensure, in particular': (a) remuneration which provides workers with 'fair wages and equal remuneration' and 'in particular women being *guaranteed*…equal pay for equal work' (emphasis added).

During the drafting, there was controversy over the term 'guarantee'. Some states objected that they could not immediately 'guarantee' equal pay because they did not intervene in pay negotiations between workers and employers[218] and doing so would be 'incompatible with the complete liberty enjoyed by the parties in the…labour market'.[219] It was also argued that the word 'guarantee' created a more inflexible and absolute obligation than elsewhere in the Covenant,[220] namely pursuant to the progressive realization principle in Article 2.

[218] UNGA Third Committee, A/C.3/SR.713 (17 December 1956), 158 (Netherlands), 160 (Sweden); A/C.3/SR.715 (18 December 1956), 170 (UK), 172 (Chile); A/C.3/SR.717 (20 December 1956), (Denmark).

[219] UNGA Third Committee, A/C.3/SR.713 (17 December 1956), 160 (Sweden); A/C.3/SR.719 (3 January 1957), 190 (Australia).

[220] UNGA Third Committee, A/C.3/SR.715 (18 December 1956), 173 (France).

One commentator has suggested there is a distinction between the duty of states to 'recognize' the right to work conditions which 'ensure' minimum remuneration, and the separate 'guarantee' of equal pay.[221] The former is subject to progressive realization, whereas the latter implies immediate application.[222] The provision is nonetheless poorly expressed. It would be odd to immediately 'guarantee' only women 'equal pay for equal work', but to merely 'recognize' a progressive right to 'equal remuneration' of all other groups.

A more coherent approach is to interpret equal remuneration generally as of immediate application, and to confine progressive realization to the attainment of 'fair wages' affording a 'decent living' (subject to a minimum core obligation to ensure a subsistence wage). This would also make the provision consistent with the general non-discrimination guarantee in Article 2 of the ICESCR, of which Article 7(a) is a particular expression, and which the CESCR has interpreted as 'an immediate and cross-cutting obligation in the Covenant'.[223]

That equal pay for women specifically is not subject to progressive realization is supported by the CEDAW Committee's interpretation of states' general obligations under Article 2 of the CEDAW, which requires states 'to pursue by all appropriate means and without delay a policy of eliminating discrimination against women'. The Committee stated:

> 29. The words 'without delay' make it clear that the obligation of States parties to pursue their policy, by all appropriate means, is of an immediate nature. This language is unqualified, and does not allow for any delayed or purposely chosen incremental implementation of the obligations that States assume upon ratification of or accession to the Convention. It follows that a delay cannot be justified on any grounds, including political, social, cultural, religious, economic, resource or other considerations or constraints within the State. Where a State party is facing resource constraints or needs technical or other expertise to facilitate the implementation of its obligations under the Convention, it may be incumbent upon it to seek international cooperation in order to overcome these difficulties.[224]

The CEDAW Committee has also called on states to ratify ILO Convention No. 100 on Equal Remuneration '[i]n order to implement fully' the CEDAW.[225] Under Article 2 of Convention No. 100, states shall 'promote' and 'ensure' equal remuneration. The ILO accepts that the principle is to be achieved over time, but observes that equal remuneration is a right of 'fundamental' importance and must accordingly be achieved over the shortest possible time, with deadlines fixed for the attainment of specific objectives.[226] In this regard, it should be emphasized that any delay in securing equal pay is not justified by economic or developmental concerns (that is, by progressive realization), but by the need to adopt

[221] Craven, *The ICESCR*, 238 (including in the CESCR's reporting guidelines).
[222] Craven, *The ICESCR*, 238.
[223] CECSR, General Comment No. 20, Non-discrimination in economic, social and cultural rights (Article 2, para. 2, of the ICESCR), E/C.12/GC/20 (2 July 2009), [7].
[224] CEDAW, General Recommendation No. 28 (16 December 2010), [29].
[225] CEDAW, General Recommendation No. 13 (3 March 1989), [1].
[226] ILO, *Giving Globalization a Human Face*, 280.

and apply procedures to attain equality (such as comparative job evaluations, discussed below).[227]

If equalizing wages seems presently unaffordable, that does not justify the ongoing suppression of women's wages so much as a general and more equitable recalibration of wages, including male wage restraint or even the levelling down of male wages. The burden of economic difficulties must be equitably shared if equal remuneration is to be treated as an obligation of immediate effect. This is consistent with the approach to Articles 2 and 3 of the ICESCR; resource constraints do not justify the continued privileging of advantaged groups (whether men or ethnic majorities) at the expense of the disadvantaged (whether women or minorities): the poor cannot be kept poor to preserve the position of the wealthy.

Reservations to the equal remuneration provision would seem to be particularly problematic in view of their basis in the non-discrimination and equality principles which are fundamental to the object and purpose of the ICESCR. Both the United Kingdom and Barbados reserved the right to postpone the application of Article 7(1)(a) 'in so far as it concerns the provision of equal pay to men and women for equal work'.[228] While the United Kingdom further stated that it fully accepted the principle and pledged to work towards its complete application at the earliest possible time, 'the problems of implementation are such that complete application cannot be guaranteed at present'. That the United Kingdom felt it necessary make such reservation also supports the view that equal pay is a guarantee of immediate, not progressive, application.

Methods of implementation

Article 7(a) does not indicate the specific measures states must take to guarantee equal remuneration for women or other groups protected from discrimination. Some indication of the range of possibilities is given in ILO Convention No. 100.

Enabling legal frameworks

Article 2 of Convention No. 100 requires states to take measures 'appropriate to the methods in operation for determining rates of remuneration' and which may include laws, wage determination machinery, collective agreements or a combination of these:

> 1. Each Member shall, by means appropriate to the methods in operation for determining rates of remuneration, promote and, in so far as is consistent with such methods, ensure

[227] Note that ILO Recommendation No. 90 on Equal Remuneration 1951, [4] allows for the 'progressive application' of equal remuneration where 'it is not deemed feasible to implement immediately' after consultations with workers and employers. In such circumstances, progressive measures may include: '(a) decreasing the differentials between rates of remuneration for men and rates of remuneration for women for work of equal value; (b) where a system of increments is in force, providing equal increments for men and women workers performing work of equal value.'

[228] A further UK reservation applies to equal pay in the private sector in Jersey, Guernsey, the Isle of Man, Bermuda, (then) Hong Kong and the Solomon Islands: see Appendix II to this book.

the application to all workers of the principle of equal remuneration for men and women workers for work of equal value.

2. This principle may be applied by means of—
   (a) national laws or regulations;
   (b) legally established or recognised machinery for wage determination;
   (c) collective agreements between employers and workers; or
   (d) a combination of these various means.

Convention No. 100 leaves the choice of means to the state in achieving the result of equal pay; thus, legislation is not strictly necessary where collective agreements or other means suffice. In interpreting Article 4(3) of the European Social Charter, the European Committee on Social Rights has similarly indicated that states may implement equal pay by legislation, collective agreements or other means appropriate to national conditions.[229]

However, where collective agreements do not achieve equal pay, 'the state concerned must nevertheless intervene through legislation or any other methods',[230] including through wage-fixing machinery.[231] This is because equal pay is a right under the Charter, not a matter merely to be 'promoted' as under Convention No. 100.[232] Further, the ECSR has held that 'any clauses of collective agreements or individual contracts which contravene this principle must be declared null and void by law'.[233]

In monitoring states, the CESCR has frequently condemned states for failing to legislate to ensure equal pay[234] and often called for laws to mandate equal pay for work of equal value.[235] It has criticized states where they do not regard wage differentials as discriminatory;[236] or where laws compel earlier retirement by women, resulting in lower pensions.[237]

As noted earlier, during the drafting some states were reluctant for Article 7 to require intervention in the private labour market. Plainly, the state has greater direct leverage over wages in the public sector. Recommendation No. 90 on Equal Remuneration 1951 directs states' attention to equal remuneration in all areas of public employment, whether central or other departments and agencies,

[229] ECSR, Statements of Interpretation: Article 4(3) (31 December 1977) and (31 May 1969).

[230] ECSR, Statements of Interpretation: Article 4(3) (31 December 1977) and (31 May 1969); see also ECSR, Statement of Interpretation: Article 4(3) (31 July 1971).

[231] ECSR, Statement of Interpretation: Article 4(3) (31 July 1971).

[232] ECSR, Statement of Interpretation: Article 4(3) (31 July 1971).

[233] ECSR, Statement of Interpretation: Article 4(3) (31 January 1984).

[234] CESCR, Concluding Observations: Mauritius, E/C.12/MUS/CO/4 (8 June 2010), [17]; Netherlands Antilles, E/C.12/NLD/CO/3/Add.1 (31 January 2008), [13].

[235] CESCR, Concluding Observations: China (including Hong Kong SAR), E/C.12/1/Add.58 (21 May 2001), [35]; Netherlands Antilles, E/C.12/NLD/CO/3/Add.1 (31 January 2008), [32]; Paraguay, E/C.12/1/Add.1 (28 May 1996), [24]; Poland, E/C.12/POL/CO/5 (2 December 2009), [17]; Cambodia, E/C.12/KHM/Co/1 (12 June 2009), [22]; Trinidad and Tobago, E/C.12/1/Add.80 (5 June 2002), [40].

[236] CESCR, Concluding Observations: Netherlands Antilles, E/C.12/NLD/CO/3/Add.1 (31 January 2008), [31].

[237] CESCR, Concluding Observations: Poland, E/C.12/1/Add.82 (19 December 2002), [19].

public enterprises, in public contracts, or wherever wages are subject to statutory regulation or public control (paragraphs 1 and 2).

However, it is clear that Article 7(a) is not limited to guaranteeing equal remuneration in the public sector, and that national laws should also apply to the private sector, even if the modalities of implementing equal remuneration may differ. In this regard, Recommendation No. 90 also calls for legal enactment for the 'general application' of equal remuneration, along with measures to inform employers and workers:

3. (1) Where appropriate in the light of the methods in operation for the determination of rates of remuneration, provision should be made by legal enactment for the general application of the principle of equal remuneration for men and women workers for work of equal value.

(2) The competent public authority should take all necessary and appropriate measures to ensure that employers and workers are fully informed as to such legal requirements and, where appropriate, advised on their application.

Thus, even where private sector wages are determined by collective bargaining, a legislative requirement of equal remuneration is a permissible limitation on the autonomy of the parties to freely bargain, necessary to safeguard the rights of others (and also justified pursuant to the general limitations clause in Article 4 of the ICESCR). The CEDAW Committee has further urged states to encourage parties to collective agreements to respect the principle of equal remuneration under that Convention:

3. They should support, as far as practicable, the creation of implementation machinery and encourage the efforts of the parties to collective agreements, where they apply, to ensure the application of the principle of equal remuneration for work of equal value.[238]

Article 4 of Convention No. 100 also provides that states 'shall co-operate as appropriate with the employers' and workers' organizations concerned for the purpose of giving effect to' equal remuneration. In practice, for example, Singapore's Industrial Arbitration Court recommends a model clause on equal remuneration for inclusion in collective agreements:

(1) Both parties accept that the principle of equal remuneration for men and women for work of equal value shall apply. 'Remuneration' means salary (as defined in the Employment Act) and any other consideration, whether in cash or in kind, which the employee receives directly or indirectly, in respect of employment.

(2) The employer shall ensure that the principles of equal remuneration for men and women for work of equal value are adhered to. Regardless of their gender, employees will be paid and rewarded based on the value of job, performance and contribution.[239]

Under the EC Treaty provision on equal remuneration, the European Court of Justice in the above-mentioned *Enderby* case found that wage differences resulting from different collective bargaining processes cannot objectively justify unequal pay:

[238] CEDAW, General Recommendation No. 13 (13 March 1989), [3].

[239] Industrial Arbitration Court (Singapore), 'Collective Agreements Sample Clauses', <http://www.iac.gov.sg/Pages/SampleClauses.aspx#Part11>.

22. The fact that the rates of pay at issue are decided by collective bargaining processes conducted separately for each of the two professional groups concerned, without any discriminatory effect within each group, does not preclude a finding of prima facie discrimination where the results of those processes show that two groups with the same employer and the same trade union are treated differently. If the employer could rely on the absence of discrimination within each of the collective bargaining processes taken separately as sufficient justification for the difference in pay, he could, as the German Government pointed out, easily circumvent the principle of equal pay by using separate bargaining processes.

23. Accordingly…the fact that the respective rates of pay of two jobs of equal value, one carried out almost exclusively by women and the other predominantly by men, were arrived at by collective bargaining processes which, although carried out by the same parties, are distinct, and, taken separately, have in themselves no discriminatory effect, is not sufficient objective justification for the difference in pay between those two jobs.[240]

Job evaluation methods

As mentioned earlier, Article 3 of Convention No. 100 encourages states to 'promote objective appraisal of jobs on the basis of the work to be performed':

1. Where such action will assist in giving effect to the provisions of this Convention measures shall be taken to promote objective appraisal of jobs on the basis of the work to be performed.

2. The methods to be followed in this appraisal may be decided upon by the authorities responsible for the determination of rates of remuneration, or, where such rates are determined by collective agreements, by the parties thereto.

3. Differential rates between workers which correspond, without regard to sex, to differences, as determined by such objective appraisal, in the work to be performed shall not be considered as being contrary to the principle of equal remuneration for men and women workers for work of equal value.

Recommendation No. 90 on Equal Remuneration 1951 further calls for such job appraisal methods to be established in agreement with employers' and workers' organizations.[241] In relation to equal remuneration under the CEDAW too, the CEDAW Committee has encouraged states to adopt job evaluation systems based on gender-neutral criteria:

2. They should consider the study, development and adoption of job evaluation systems based on gender-neutral criteria that would facilitate the comparison of the value of those jobs of a different nature, in which women presently predominate, with those jobs in which men presently predominate, and they should include the results achieved in their reports to the Committee on the Elimination of Discrimination against Women…[242]

Job evaluation methods involve a formal procedure which gives a numerical value to each job assessed, and jobs receiving the same score are entitled

[240] *Enderby v Frenchay Health Authority*, ECJ Case No. C-127/92, 27 October 1993.
[241] See also ILO Recommendation No. 90 on Equal Remuneration 1951, [5].
[242] CEDAW, General Recommendation No. 13 (3 March 1989), [2].

to equal remuneration.[243] They thus systematically enable the kinds of 'value' comparisons mentioned earlier, that is, on the basis of objective factors such as skills, qualifications, effort, responsibilities and working conditions; as well as sub-factors such as physical, mental and emotional effort, or financial value alongside responsibilities for people and human resources.[244] The selection of criteria and their weighting should be free from gender bias, so as to not undervalue traditionally 'female' activities (such as caring) or overvalue 'male' work (like manual labour).[245] The ILO Committee of Experts on the Application of Conventions and Recommendations has discussed the parameters of methods for job evaluation, which should apply to the public and private sectors alike:

> 5. In order to establish whether different jobs are of equal value, there has to be an examination of the respective tasks involved. This examination must be undertaken on the basis of entirely objective and non-discriminatory criteria to avoid an assessment being tainted by gender bias. While the Convention does not prescribe any specific method for such an examination, it does presuppose the use of appropriate techniques for objective job evaluation (Article 3). For the purpose of ensuring gender equality in the determination of remuneration, analytical methods of job evaluation have been found to be the most effective. Such methods analyse and classify jobs on the basis of objective factors relating to the jobs to be compared such as skill, effort, and responsibilities or working conditions (see paragraph 141 of the 1986 General Survey on equal remuneration). Whatever methods are used for the objective evaluation of jobs, particular care must be taken to ensure that they are free from gender bias: it is important to ensure that the selection of factors for comparison, the weighting of such factors and the actual comparison carried out, are not inherently discriminatory. Often skills considered to be 'female', such as manual dexterity and those required in caring professions, are undervalued or even overlooked, in comparison with traditionally 'male' skills, such as heavy lifting.
>
> ...
>
> 7. The Committee urges governments, in cooperation with workers' and employers' organizations, to promote, develop and implement practical approaches and methods for the objective evaluation of jobs with a view to effectively applying the principle of equal remuneration for men and women for work of equal value in the public and private sectors. Measures for the objective evaluation of jobs can be taken at the enterprise, sectoral or national level, in the context of collective bargaining, as well as through national wage-fixing mechanisms. The Committee stresses the importance of training on this matter for government officials, as well as workers, employees and their organizations.[246]

In principle, job evaluation methods may compare work of equal value across jobs in the public and private sectors.[247] This does, however, raise certain economic difficulties given that the means available for, and the approach to,

[243] ILO, *Giving Globalization a Human Face*, 293.
[244] ILO, *Giving Globalization a Human Face*, 293.
[245] ILO, *Giving Globalization a Human Face*, 293.
[246] ILO CEACR, General Observation (adopted 2006, published 96th ILC session 2007), [5], [7].
[247] Craven, *The ICESCR*, 239.

funding wages in each sector is very different. Whereas private sector wages may be pegged to economic performance (leading to bonuses or higher wages in times of plenty, and lower wages in economic downturn), wages in the public sector tend to be less volatile, without the same peaks or troughs, and based in limited public finances. Thus, a lawyer in private practice may be paid vastly more than a lawyer in government service; and even if more private lawyers are male and more government lawyers are female, the capacity to equalize wages may be limited given the magnitude of the wage differential and constraints on the public purse.

Policies, plans, programmes, research and education

In addition to legislation and job evaluation measures, it may be necessary for states to adopt other proactive measures to guarantee equal remuneration. It will be particularly important for states to collect comprehensive and reliable survey data on pay differences,[248] so as to identify areas of need and priority, to facilitate action and to enable job evaluation processes. States may also empower bodies to monitor and promote equal remuneration, whether through tripartite bodies, pay equity councils or national human rights commissions.

In ILO practice, national plans or policies are regarded as one means of advancing equal pay, including through targets and time frames for public and private employers to measure progress.[249] A link can be drawn here to Article 2 of Convention No. 111 on Discrimination (Employment and Occupation) 1958:

> Each Member for which this Convention is in force undertakes to declare and pursue a national policy designed to promote, by methods appropriate to national conditions and practice, equality of opportunity and treatment in respect of employment and occupation, with a view to eliminating any discrimination in respect thereof.[250]

States and employers may also develop and utilize pay valuation guides, codes of conduct, wage guidelines or self-assessment tools,[251] in addition to modernizing their job classification schemes in the light of job evaluation or appraisal methods, discussed earlier.

The CESCR has suggested that temporary special measures may be necessary to reduce the wage gap under Article 7.[252] In ILO practice, compensatory pay equity benefits have been used to bridge the gap. In addition, incentives of various kinds may be offered to employers, such as grants, awards or employer

[248] See also ECSR, Statement of Interpretation: Article 4(3) (31 May 1969) (concerning job evaluation in respect for equal pay under Article 4(3) of the European Social Charter). States should also collect broader data 'to measure and value the unremunerated domestic activities of women': CEDAW, General Recommendation No. 17 (1991), [a]; and further data on the 'legal and social situation of unpaid women working in family enterprises': CEDAW, General Recommendation No. 16 (1991), [a].

[249] ILO, *Giving Globalization a Human Face*, 301.

[250] See also ILO Convention No. 156 concerning Equal Opportunities and Equal Treatment for Men and Women with Family Responsibilities (adopted 23 June 1981, entered into force 11 August 1983), Article 3(1).

[251] ILO, *Giving Globalization a Human Face*, 297, 303.

[252] CESCR, Concluding Observations: Kazakhstan, E/C.12/KAZ/CO/1 (7 June 2010), [19].

certification systems such as equality labels[253] (which may be attractive to employers also for their 'soft marketing' or good corporate citizen benefits).

Finally, both the CESCR and ILO have recommended awareness-raising campaigns and the provision of information about equal remuneration rights, whether for workers, employers, labour inspectors or the general public.[254]

Enforcement and remedies

The CESCR has frequently condemned states where unequal pay persists in practice despite the existence of legislation.[255] It has urged states to ensure the enforcement of relevant laws,[256] including by improving the responsible legal and institutional mechanisms.[257] In ILO practice also, there must be a legal and administrative framework enabling workers to claim equal remuneration and a right to redress where job evaluation is discriminatory.[258]

As in relation to the minimum wage, discussed earlier, remedies and enforcement may take different forms: private actions (whether informal, as by mediation or conciliation, or formal, as by arbitration or civil actions in the courts), collective or representative claims by unions, labour inspections and public regulatory or administrative action, or prosecutions. Whatever the methods, enforcement action must be capable of restoring the worker's rights, namely equal pay, but also of remedying loss (in the form of underpaid wages) and punishing and deterring violators (whether through exemplary or punitive compensatory damages, criminal fines or punishment, or appropriate civil or administrative penalties).

In addition, 'workers must enjoy effective protection from measures of retaliation arising from their claim for equal pay (notably protection against dismissal)', as the European Committee on Social Rights noted in relation to equal pay under Article 4(3) of the European Social Charter.[259]

The ILO Committee of Experts on the Application of Conventions and Recommendations has also suggested that training of judges and labour inspectors is important, given the specialized technical nature of standards on determining work of equal value:

8. The Committee underlines the important role of judges and labour inspectors in ensuring the application of the principle of equal remuneration for men and women for work of equal value. Noting that in a number of countries certain measures have been taken to assist

[253] ILO, *Giving Globalization a Human Face*, 304.

[254] ILO, *Giving Globalization a Human Face*, 304; CESCR, Concluding Observations: Afghanistan, E/C.12/AFG/CO/24 (7 June 2010), [24].

[255] CESCR, Concluding Observations: Austria, E/C.12/1994/20 (2–20 May 1994), [254]; Republic of Korea, E/C.12/1995/3 (7 June 1995), [11].

[256] CESCR, Concluding Observations: Portugal, E/C.12/1/Add.53 (1 December 2000), [20]; Slovakia, E/C.12/1/Add.81 (19 December 2002), [26]; Kenya, E/C.12/KEN/CO/1 (1 December 2008), [18]; Poland, E/C.12/POL/CO/5 (2 December 2009), [17].

[257] CESCR, Concluding Observations: Brazil, E/C.12/BRA/ZO/2 (12 June 2009), [16]; Afghanistan, E/C.12/AFG/CO/24 (7 June 2010), [24].

[258] ILO, *Giving Globalization a Human Face*, 293.

[259] ECSR, Statement of Interpretation: Article 4(3) (31 January 1984).

judges and labour inspectors to fulfil this role, including providing training regarding the concept of 'work of equal value' and how to apply it in practice, the Committee encourages all governments to consider taking such action.[260]

Measures to address structural inequalities

Simply legislating to protect equal pay, or inducing employers to implement it, remains insufficient to guarantee equal remuneration as long as underlying structural gender inequalities persist in the labour market. In monitoring states, the CESCR has been attentive to structural impediments to women's participation in the workforce and which confine them to segregated low-paid occupations, or underemployment,[261] including lower literacy rates and cultural practices.[262] It has thus called on states to promote women's access to all levels of the labour market,[263] including full-time work[264] and managerial positions,[265] and to eliminate occupational segregation.[266] It has recommended affirmative action[267] and qualification programmes for women who are unemployed or work in low-paid jobs.[268]

The ILO too has identified many structural causes of pay inequality, including: occupational segregation; inadequate career-oriented education, training and skills; household and family responsibilities; the perceived costs of employing women; pay structures; lack of promotion opportunities; and lack of transparency in pay and promotion.[269] Broader efforts to address social, political and cultural stereotyping of gender roles are accordingly necessary. In this respect, Recommendation No. 90 emphasizes the need for vocational guidance, counselling and training for women, welfare and social services for women with family responsibilities, and equality in promotion (paragraphs 6 and 7).

In relation to barriers to equal pay linked to family responsibilities, reference may also be made to Convention No. 156 on Workers with Family Responsibilities 1981, which requires states to address matters such as childcare and family services, public education and information about equality of opportunity for workers, and vocational guidance and training:

[260] ILO CEACR, General Observation (adopted 2006, published 96th ILC session 2007), [8].

[261] CESCR, Concluding Observations: Luxembourg, E/C.12/1/Add.86 (26 June 2003), [22]; Madagascar, E/C.12/MDG/CO/2 (16 December 2009), [18].

[262] CESCR, Concluding Observations: Senegal, E/C.12/1993/18 (5 January 1994), [6].

[263] CESCR, Concluding Observations: Belgium, E/C.12/1/Add.5 (1 December 2000), [23]; Uzbekistan, E/C.12/UZB/CO/1 (24 January 2006), [48].

[264] CESCR, Concluding Observations: Sweden, E/C.12/SWE/CO/5 (1 December 2008), [18].

[265] CESCR, Concluding Observations: Sweden, E/C.12/SWE/CO/5 (1 December 2008), [18]; Kazakhstan, E/C.12/KAZ/CO/1 (7 June 2010), [19].

[266] CESCR, Concluding Observations: Mauritius, E/C.12/MUS/CO/4 (8 June 2010), [17].

[267] CESCR, Concluding Observations: Paraguay, E/C.12/1/Add.1 (28 May 1996), [24]; Russian Federation, E/C.12/1/Add.94 (12 December 2003), [48].

[268] CESCR, Concluding Observations: Austria, E/C.12/AUT/CO/3 (25 January 2006), [22].

[269] ILO, *Giving Globalization a Human Face*, 297–8.

Article 5

All measures compatible with national conditions and possibilities shall further be taken—

(a) to take account of the needs of workers with family responsibilities in community planning; and

(b) to develop or promote community services, public or private, such as child-care and family services and facilities.

Article 6

The competent authorities and bodies in each country shall take appropriate measures to promote information and education which engender broader public understanding of the principle of equality of opportunity and treatment for men and women workers and of the problems of workers with family responsibilities, as well as a climate of opinion conducive to overcoming these problems.

Article 7

All measures compatible with national conditions and possibilities, including measures in the field of vocational guidance and training, shall be taken to enable workers with family responsibilities to become and remain integrated in the labour force, as well as to re-enter the labour force after an absence due to those responsibilities.[270]

Attention may also be drawn to the obligations on states to support working mothers and families under Article 10 of the ICESCR, and social security and social insurance measures targeted at workers and families under Article 9 of the ICESCR, discussed in later chapters.

Article 7(b): Safe and Healthy Working Conditions

In Article 7, states parties 'recognize the right of everyone to the enjoyment of just and favourable conditions of work which ensure, in particular… (b) [s]afe and healthy working conditions'. The protection in Article 7(b) may be understood as an aspect of 'the right to personal integrity, one of the fundamental principles of human rights'.[271] Efforts to regulate occupational health and safety originated during the industrial revolution in Europe in the nineteenth century and gradually internationalized through the work of the ILO after 1919, with the modern prevention, risk management and systems approaches stemming from the 1970s.[272]

Despite the proliferation of standards, the ILO estimates that globally there are still 2 million work-related fatalities and 330 million work-related accidents each

[270] ILO Convention No. 156 concerning Equal Opportunities and Equal Treatment for Men and Women with Family Responsibilities (adopted 23 June 1981, entered into force 11 August 1983).

[271] ECSR, Statement of Interpretation: Article 3 (31 May 1969) (referring to the comparable provision of the European Social Charter).

[272] ILO, *General Survey concerning the Occupational Safety and Health Convention, 1981 (No. 155), the Occupational Safety and Health Recommendation, 1981 (No. 164), and the Protocol of 2002 to the Occupational Safety and Health Convention, 1981*, ('*Survey on standards on health and safety*'), International Labour Conference (98th session) Report III (Part 1B) (Geneva, 2009), 4.

year.[273] There is also much technical work still to be done. For example, of the estimated 110,000 synthetic chemicals in industrial production, only 6,000 have adequate hazard assessment data and merely 600 have agreed occupational exposure limits.[274]

There was little discussion of Article 7(b) in the drafting.[275] The more specific problem of hazardous child labour is separately addressed in Article 10 of the ICESCR, as an aspect of the protection of children. Sexual harassment in the workplace is of concern to the CESCR under both Article 6 (the right to work, including non-discrimination and equal opportunity, and protection against unfair dismissal) and Article 7, and for present purposes was considered in the previous chapter on Article 6. Article 7(b) also crosses over with the right to social security in Article 9, which extends to workplace injuries. The right to health in Article 12 of the ICESCR pointedly requires states to improve all aspects of 'industrial hygiene' (paragraph (b)) and to prevent, treat and control 'occupational' diseases (paragraph (c)).[276]

As discussed below, there are also numerous specific ILO instruments in the field of occupational health and safety which can inform the scope of Article 7(b). While the utility of Article 7(b) has been questioned because of its broad and general terms compared with the many ILO standards,[277] it should be emphasized that the ICESCR has 160 states parties (more than three-quarters of all states), whereas most of the ILO instruments have less than fifty ratifications (that is, less than one-quarter of states), and many have less than thirty parties. There is accordingly potential for Article 7(b) to 'universalize' key ILO standards by importing them into the interpretation of what is 'safe and healthy' at work. This is also because despite their limited ratifications, the ILO instruments have still been influential in setting standards widely adopted by non-party states.[278]

The CESCR has often looked to the ILO instruments to help define its understanding of states' obligations under Article 7(b). It has called on states to implement relevant ILO treaties to which they are parties,[279] and its earlier Revised Reporting Guidelines 1991 asked states to report on implementation of ILO instruments binding on them.[280] More importantly, the CESCR has urged states

[273] ILO, *Survey on standards on health and safety*, xi.

[274] ILO, *Survey on standards on health and safety*, 44.

[275] Craven, *The ICESCR*, 230.

[276] On which, see ILO Convention No. 121 concerning Benefits in the Case of Employment Injury (adopted 8 July 1964, entered into force 28 July 1967), Schedule I; ILO Recommendation No. 194 on List of Occupational Diseases 2002.

[277] Craven, *The ICESCR*, 240.

[278] ILO, *Survey on standards on health and safety*, 93.

[279] CESCR, Concluding Observations: Kazakhstan, E/C.12/KAZ/CO/1 (7 June 2010), [21] (ILO Convention No. 167 concerning Safety and Health in Construction (adopted 20 June 1988, entered into force 11 January 1991)).

[280] CESCR, Revised general guidelines regarding the form and contents of reports to be submitted by states parties under Articles 16 and 17 of the ICESCR, E/C.12/1991/1 (17 June 1991), 4 (namely, ILO Convention No. 81 concerning Labour Inspection in Industry and Commerce, ILO Convention No. 129 concerning Labour Inspection in Agriculture, and ILO Convention No. 155 concerning Occupational Safety and Health and the Working Environment (adopted 22 June 1981, entered into

to ratify certain treaties, particularly Convention No. 174 on the Prevention of Major Industrial Accidents[281] (despite that treaty currently having only eighteen parties), but also Conventions No. 155 on Occupational Safety and Health and the Working Environment and No. 176 on Safety and Health in Mines.[282] Regional human rights bodies have also deferred to ILO standards along with the standards of regional bodies.[283]

There is a vast repository of ILO standards on occupational health and safety in many areas of work, the earliest adopted in 1919 (on white phosphorous).[284] Around 80 per cent of all ILO standards are estimated to address occupation and health and safety issues in some way.[285] Overarching framework conventions address the need for a national policy on occupational health and safety (Convention No. 155 on Occupational Health and Safety 1981, with sixty parties), occupational health services (Convention No. 161 on Occupational Health Services 1985, with thirty parties), and promotion of a preventive health and safety culture (Convention No. 187 on Promotional Framework for Occupational Safety and Health Convention 2006, with twenty-five parties).

Many ILO instruments then address substantive areas of health and safety. Some concern particular branches of economic activity, including commerce, dock work, construction, mining and agriculture.[286] However, the conventions

force 11 August 1983)). The simplified 2009 Guidelines replacing the 1991 Guidelines make no mention of the ILO standards: see CESCR, Guidelines on treaty specific documents to be submitted by states parties under Articles 16 and 17 of the ICESCR, E/C.12/2008/2 (24 March 2009) (see Appendix VIII of this book).

281 CESCR, Concluding Observations: Switzerland, E/C.12/1/Add.31 (7 December 1998), [14], [30]; Italy, E/C.12/1/Add.43 (23 May 2000), [12]; Iceland, E/C.12/1/Add.89 (26 June 2003), [23]; Kuwait, E/C.12/1/Add.98 (7 June 2004), [35]; Slovenia, E/C.12/SVN/CO/1 (25 January 2006), [20], [27]; Latvia, E/C.12/LVA/CO/1 (7 January 2008), [42].

282 CESCR, Concluding Observations: Democratic Republic of Congo, E/C.12/COD/CO/4 (16 December 2009), [22].

283 See, eg, ECSR, Statement of Interpretation: Article 3 (30 November 1998) (in interpreting Article 3(1) of the European Social Charter (and Article 3(2) of the Revised Charter), the ECSR 'has at its disposal a very complete set of international technical reference standards which can be of use for defining and listing the main risks and occupations concerning which regulations should provide for', as well as European Community law—particularly EC Framework Directive 89/391/EEC on Occupational Health and Safety (12 June 1989)): ECSR, Statement of Interpretation: Article 3 (30 November 1998).

284 ILO Recommendation No. 6 on White Phosphorus 1919.

285 ILO, *Survey on standards on health and safety*, 1.

286 ILO Conventions No. 120 concerning Hygiene in Commerce and Offices (adopted 8 July 1964, entered into force 29 March 1966); No. 152 concerning Occupational Safety and Health in Dock Work (adopted 25 June 1979, entered into force 5 December 1981); No. 167 concerning Safety and Health in Construction (adopted 20 June 1988, entered into force 11 January 1991); No. 176 concerning Safety and Health in Mines (adopted 22 June 1995, entered into force 5 June 1998); No. 184 concerning Safety and Health in Agriculture (adopted 21 June 2001, entered into force 20 September 2003); and No. 45 concerning the Employment of Women on Underground Work in Mines of all Kinds (adopted 21 June 1935, entered into force 30 May 1937). See also ILO Recommendation No. 31 on Prevention of Industrial Accidents 1929; ILO Recommendation No. 120 on Hygiene (Commerce and Offices) 1964; ILO Recommendation No. 175 on Safety and Health in Construction Recommendation 1988; ILO Recommendation No. 183 on Safety and Health in Mines 1995; and ILO Recommendation No. 192 on Safety and Health in Agriculture 2001.

do not have particularly widespread participation by states, with fifty-one, twenty-six, twenty-four, twenty-seven and fifteen ratifications respectively.

Other instruments protect against specific work risks such as: radiation (fifty ratifications); occupational cancer (thirty-nine parties); air pollution, noise and vibration (forty-five parties); asbestos (thirty-five parties); chemicals (seventeen parties); lead (sixty-three parties) and benzene (thirty-eight parties); anthrax (a Recommendation only); dangerous machines (fifty-two parties); heavy weights (twenty-nine parties); major accidents (such as emissions, fire or explosions) at major hazard installations (such as those involving substances with hazardous chemical, physical or toxicological properties) (eighteen parties); and other occupational diseases (a Recommendation only).[287]

The formal instruments are supplemented by forty ILO Codes of Practice which establish practical guidelines for public authorities, employers, workers, enterprises and specialized occupational safety and health protection bodies (such as enterprise safety committees). Substantively, the codes similarly cover health and safety in certain economic sectors[288] or involving particular hazards,[289] in addition to addressing wider issues.[290] Other ILO instruments on the periphery of health and safety are also relevant, such as on welfare facilities for workers (for example, workplace facilities for food, restrooms, rest and recreation).[291]

[287] ILO Conventions No. 115 concerning the Protection of Workers against Ionising Radiations (adopted 22 June 1960, entered into force 17 June 1962); No. 139 concerning Prevention and Control of Occupational Hazards caused by Carcinogenic Substances and Agents (adopted 24 June 1974, entered into force 10 June 1976); No. 148 concerning the Protection of Workers against Occupational Hazards in the Working Environment Due to Air Pollution, Noise and Vibration (adopted 20 June 1977, entered into force 11 July 1979); No. 162 concerning Safety in the Use of Asbestos (adopted 24 June 1986, entered into force 16 June 1989); No. 170 concerning Safety in the Use of Chemicals at Work (adopted 25 June 1990, entered into force 4 November 1993); No. 13 concerning the Use of White Lead in Painting (adopted 19 November 1921, entered into force 31 August 1923); No. 136 concerning Protection against Hazards of Poisoning Arising from Benzene (adopted 23 June 1971, entered into force 27 July 1973); No. 119 concerning the Guarding of Machinery (adopted 25 June 1963, entered into force 21 April 1965); No. 127 concerning the Maximum Permissible Weight to be Carried by One Worker (adopted 28 June 1967, entered into force 19 March 1970); and No. 174 concerning the Prevention of Major Industrial Accidents (adopted 22 June 1993, entered into force 3 January 1997). See also ILO Recommendations No. 3 on Anthrax Prevention 1919; No. 114 on Radiation Protection 1960; No. 147 on Occupational Cancer 1974; No. 156 on Working Environment (Air Pollution, Noise and Vibration) 1977; No. 172 on Asbestos 1986; No. 177 on Chemicals 1990; No. 181 on Prevention of Major Industrial Accidents 1993; No. 118 on Guarding of Machinery 1963; No. 128 on Maximum Weight 1967; No. 144 on Benzene 1971; No. 4 on Lead Poisoning (Women and Children) 1919; No. 6 on White Phosphorus 1919; No. 97 on Protection of Workers' Health 1953; and No. 194 on List of Occupational Diseases 2002.

[288] Such as construction, open-cast mines, coal mines, iron and steel industries, non-ferrous metals industries, agriculture, shipbuilding and ship repairing, and forestry.

[289] Such as radiation, lasers, visual display units, chemicals, asbestos and airborne substances.

[290] Eg, ILO Codes address management systems; ethical guidelines for workers' health surveillance; recording and notification of accidents and diseases; protection of workers' personal data; and transfer of technology to developing states: see <http://www.ilo.org/safework/info/standards-and-instruments/codes/lang--en/index.htm>. See also ILO Guidelines on occupational safety and health management systems (ILO-OSH 2001).

[291] ILO Recommendation No. 102 on Welfare Facilities 1956.

Beyond the ILO, there is a plethora of other relevant standard-setting bodies, including the World Health Organization, International Maritime Organization, International Civil Aviation Organization, International Atomic Energy Agency, UN Food and Agriculture Organization, UN Environment Programme and the OECD.[292] Regional and national technical bodies also play a role, as do private global standard setters such as the International Organization for Standardization (ISO) and International Ergonomics Association.[293]

In monitoring states, the CESCR has criticized unsafe working conditions or workplaces, including high rates of occupational accidents,[294] including fatal accidents[295] and increases in accidents.[296] It has sometimes attributed accidents to dangerous working conditions such as out-of-date technology[297] or a lack of protection for workers.[298]

The CESCR has also drawn attention to particularly hazardous industries or substances. It has highlighted the dangers in mines and the high number of mining accidents[299] and been concerned about inadequate clothing, equipment or training for workers.[300] It has called on states to protect workers from the use of toxic and other dangerous substances (such as cyanide) in mining[301] and to modernize mining infrastructure.[302]

Further, the CESCR has identified unsatisfactory working conditions in nuclear power stations,[303] including a lack of transparency in the disclosure of safety information, and a lack of advance nationwide and community prevention

[292] ILO, *Survey on standards on health and safety*, 55.

[293] ILO, *Survey on standards on health and safety*, 55.

[294] CESCR, Concluding Observations: Russian Federation, E/C.12/1/Add.94 (12 December 1994), [19]; Republic of Korea, E/C.12/1995/3 (7 June 1995), [12]; Russian Federation, E/C.12/1/Add.13 (20 May 1997), [18]; Italy, E/C.12/1/Add.43 (23 May 2000), [12]; Ukraine, E/C.12/1/Add.65 (24 September 2001), [15]; Poland, E/C.12/1/Add.82 (19 December 2002), [43]; Iceland, E/C.12/1/Add.89 (26 June 2003), [14]; Spain, E/C.12/1/Add.99 (7 June 2004), [14]; Malta, E/C.12/1/Add.101 (14 December 2004), [16]; Norway, E/C.12/1/Add.109 (23 June 2005), [13]; Ukraine, E/C.12/UKR/CO/5 (4 January 2008), [16]; Latvia, E/C.12/LVA/CO/1 (7 January 2008), [18]; Republic of Korea, E/C.12/KOR/CO/3 (17 December 2009), [18]; Kazakhstan, E/C.12/KAZ/CO/1 (7 June 2010), [21].

[295] CESCR, Concluding Observations: Russian Federation, E/C.12/1/Add.13 (20 May 1997), [18]; Ukraine, E/C.12/UKR/CO/5 (4 January 2008), [16]; Hungary, E/C.12/HUN/CO/3 (16 January 2008), [15].

[296] CESCR, Concluding Observations: Mauritius, E/C.12/1994/8 (31 May 1994), [9]; Uruguay, E/C.12/1/Add.1 (22 December 1997), [3]; Republic of Korea, E/C.12/1/Add.59 (21 May 2001), [18]; Lithuania, E/C.12/1Add.96 (7 June 2004), [14]; Spain, E/C.12/1/Add.99 (7 June 2004), [14].

[297] CESCR, Concluding Observations: Russian Federation, E/C.12/1/Add.13 (20 May 1997), [18]; Ukraine, E/C.12/1/Add.65 (24 September 2001), [15].

[298] CESCR, Concluding Observations: Russian Federation, E/C.12/1/Add.13 (20 May 1997), [18].

[299] CESCR, Concluding Observations: Ecuador, E/C.12/1/Add.100 (7 June 2004), [18]; China (including HK, Macao), E/C.12/1/Add.107 (13 May 2005), [23]; Ukraine, E/C.12/UKR/CO/5 (4 January 2008), [16].

[300] CESCR, Concluding Observations: Democratic Republic of Congo, E/C.12/COD/CO/4 (16 December 2009), [22].

[301] CESCR, Concluding Observations: Ecuador, E/C.12/1/Add.100 (7 June 2004), [41]; Honduras, E/C.12/1/Add.57 (21 May 2001), [38].

[302] CESCR, Concluding Observations: Ukraine, E/C.12/UKR/CO/5 (4 January 2008), [16].

[303] CESCR, Concluding Observations: Japan, E/C.12/1/Add.67 (24 September 2001), [22].

and safe handling of nuclear accidents.[304] The CESCR has also noted the high number of accidents in construction,[305] ports,[306] fishing,[307] offshore oil facilities,[308] transportation[309] and among workers employed on temporary contracts.[310] It has been concerned about the absence or restriction of health and safety laws in certain industries, such as banana plantations using pesticides,[311] export processing zones[312] or small businesses with a certain number of employees.[313]

As will be apparent from the discussion below, the CESCR's monitoring of Article 7(b) has not yet developed particularly elaborate standards. The CESCR's approach has been principally limited to identifying occupational health and safety concerns or breaches, calling for the adoption or strengthening of national laws, and urging stronger implementation and enforcement (particularly through labour inspections and sanctions for violators). It has not gone far beyond this.

To further explore the potential scope of Article 7(b), reference will be made to the key ILO principles in the area. In particular, ILO standards require states to adopt and continuously review a coherent national policy and maintain national institutional systems; to ensure processes for worker and employer consultation and participation; to demarcate the responsibilities of employers and workers; to undertake certain measures of training, education, information provision and incident reporting; and to protect workers from retaliation or prejudicial treatment in relation to complaints or self-protection.

PROGRESSIVE REALIZATION AND IMMEDIATE APPLICATION

In principle, Article 7(b) as a whole is subject to the principle of progressive realization in Article 2(1) of the ICESCR. It takes time and resources to eliminate or mitigate workplace hazards, including by conducting the necessary consultations with workers' and employers' organizations, formulating and adopting the necessary technical standards, and implementing the health and safety processes and modifications in workplaces. Further, a system of labour inspection requires the dedication of resources, as does workplace injury compensation (whether funded by employers at fault, or on the basis of a no-fault universal workplace injury scheme, as pursuant to the right to social security in Article 9 of the ICESCR).

The background ILO standards are also relevant. The ILO conventions contain various 'flexibility clauses' which permit states to: limit coverage by branches of economic activity or categories of workers; to formulate national policies or

[304] CESCR, Concluding Observations: Japan, [22].

[305] CESCR, Concluding Observations: Uruguay, E/C.12/1/Add.18 (22 December 1997), [11]; Hungary, E/C.12/HUN/CO/3 (16 January 2008), [15].

[306] CESCR, Concluding Observations: Italy, E/C.12/1/Add.43 (23 May 2000), [12].

[307] CESCR, Concluding Observations: Iceland, E/C.12/1/Add.89 (26 June 2003), [14].

[308] CESCR, Concluding Observations: Norway, E/C.12/1/Add.109 (23 June 2005), [13].

[309] CESCR, Concluding Observations: Hungary, E/C.12/HUN/CO/3 (16 January 2008), [15].

[310] CESCR, Concluding Observations: Spain, E/C.12/1/Add.99 (7 June 2004), [14].

[311] CESCR, Concluding Observations: Ecuador, E/C.12/1/Add.100 (7 June 2004), [18].

[312] CESCR, Concluding Observations: Kenya, E/C.12/KEN/CO/1 (1 December 2008), [17].

[313] CESCR, Concluding Observations: Republic of Korea, E/C.12/1995/3 (7 June 1995), [12].

implement certain measures in the light of national conditions and practice; to progressively achieve certain objectives; or to attain certain objectives 'as far as practicable'.[314] The purpose of such provisions is to accommodate the economic and developmental concerns of states, much in the same way as under Article 2(2) of the ICESCR.

At the same time, a number of factors should be understood to considerably confine the application of the progressive realization principle in respect of occupational health and safety. First, health and safety at work is a particularly fundamental or important right given its relationship to the right to life and the adverse consequences of its breach (including serious injury or death, and the potential destitution of dependent family members). The value of the right should be weighted accordingly when examining the scope for progressive realization and the potential for immediate application of certain of the right's elements.

Secondly, while workplace health and safety measures carry certain economic costs, their absence or inadequacy is also costly—perhaps even more so. The ILO observes that the 'economic costs [of workplace injury and disease] are colossal at the enterprise, national and global levels' and that 'taking into account compensation, lost working time, interruption of production, training and retraining, medical expenses, social assistance etc, these losses are estimated annually at 5 per cent of global gross domestic national product'.[315] The European Committee on Social Rights has also emphasized 'the cost to the community of each case of industrial injury, loss of capital in the form of knowledge, infrastructures required for the physical rehabilitation and social and economic reintegration of workers'.[316] The costs and affordability of occupational health and safety measures must consequently be assessed in the light of the costs of not implementing them, or implementing them too slowly; such measures may ultimately be a form of investment in productivity, not a burden on development. One difficulty is that the full costs of workplace injuries are too often borne by the community or the state rather than employers; the latter can be tempted to cut corners to make profits, and fail to account for the true socio-economic costs of injuries.

Thirdly, in relation to the ILO flexibility clauses, the ILO observes that such devices are intended to be temporary measures only and that coverage is expected to expand over time, particularly the further the distance from the date of adoption of the conventions. Such provisions 'should thus be used as enabling provisions and should not be used as a means of derogation'.[317] Fourthly, under Article 23 of the ICESCR, states should request international assistance in cases where they are unable to fulfil Article 7(b) within the limits of their own resources.

[314] ILO, *Survey on standards on health and safety*, 6–7.

[315] ILO, *Survey on standards on health and safety*, 2. Major industrial accidents alone cost US$5 billion per year and this is a low estimate given under-reporting: infra.

[316] ECSR, Statement of Interpretation: Article 3 (31 December 1977).

[317] ILO, *Survey on standards on health and safety*, 7.

Finally, even where there remains scope for progressive realization, certain aspects of Article 7(b) must be regarded as minimum core obligations which are immediately applicable. These include an obligation to adopt national occupational health and safety laws;[318] to establish a system of labour inspection and other means to enforce such laws; to provide dissuasive sanctions and compensatory remedies for breaches; to formulate a national policy with benchmarks and targets for the progressive elimination or mitigation of risks; to keep laws and policies under continuous review in the light of changing circumstances; and to take special measures of protection in relation to vulnerable groups (such as child labourers, pregnant women, workers with disabilities and undocumented migrant workers).

LEGISLATIVE FRAMEWORKS

In addressing health and safety at work, the CESCR has been concerned about the absence of occupational health and safety laws or regulations[319] and recommended their adoption.[320] Its Reporting Guidelines 2009 ask states to '[i]ndicate what legal, administrative or other provisions have been taken to ensure safety and healthy conditions at the workplace'.[321] It has also called for laws to address matters antecedent to workplace safety, such as by applying strict safety requirements for the granting of mining permits.[322]

Health and safety laws clearly must apply to all forms of employment, whether public or private, and regardless of the legal basis of the employment relationship. The CESCR was thus concerned where a state denied responsibility for worker safety on the grounds that workers can negotiate their own conditions with employers.[323] Statutory health and safety laws under Article 7(b) may thus be understood as a necessary limitation on the freedom of the parties to collectively bargain under Article 8 of the ICESCR (discussed in the next chapter).

ILO framework instruments require implementation of obligations 'by laws or regulations or any other method consistent with national conditions and practice and in consultation with the representative organizations of employers and workers concerned' (Convention No. 155, Article 8).[324] While a choice of means is permitted, where non-legislative measures (such as collective agreements) fail to ensure health and safety, states must intervene. Most states have adopted legislation in recognition of the fundamental importance of occupational health and safety, and the insufficiency of voluntary or self-regulatory approaches by

[318] See also Craven, *The ICESCR*, 241.

[319] CESCR, Concluding Observations: Morocco, E/C.12/1/Add.5 (28 May 1996), [15]; Kazakhstan, E/C.12/KAZ/CO/1 (7 June 2010), [21].

[320] CESCR, Concluding Observations: Italy, E/C.12/1/Add.43 (23 May 2000), [25].

[321] CESCR, Guidelines on treaty specific documents to be submitted by states parties under Articles 16 and 17 of the ICESCR, E/C.12/2008/2 (24 March 2009), [23].

[322] CESCR, Concluding Observations: Ukraine, E/C.12/UKR/CO/5 (4 January 2008), [39].

[323] CESCR, Concluding Observations: Cameroon, E/C.12/1/Add.40 (8 December 1999), [17].

[324] An obligation to legislate or otherwise effectively implement obligations is also common in the many ILO instruments addressing the various substantive areas of occupational health and safety.

industry. In ILO practice, legislation must also be kept under periodic review, in the light of experience, constant advances in science and technology[325] and changes in the workforce.

In regional law, the European Committee on Social Rights has been quite prescriptive in identifying the international technical standards which states must enact into domestic regulations under Article 3(1) of the European Social Charter (or 3(2) of the Revised Charter), providing a comparative guidepost for the CESCR under Article 7. These include measures in relation to the following:

Establishment, alterations and upkeep of workplaces—Work equipment

- Workplaces and equipment, in particular the protection of machines, manual handling of loads, work with display screen equipment
- Hygiene (Commerce and Offices)
- Maximum Weight
- Air Pollution, Noise and Vibration
- Personal protective equipment
- Safety and/or health signs at work.

Hazardous agents and substances

- Chemical, physical and biological agents in particular carcinogens, including: white lead (painting), benzene, asbestos, vinyl chloride monomer, metallic lead and its ionic compounds, ionizing radiation;
- Control of major accident hazards involving dangerous substances

Risks connected with certain sectors or activities

- Marking of weight (packages transported by vessels)
- Protection of dockers against accidents
- Dock Work
- Building Safety Provisions, temporary or mobile construction sites
- Mines, mineral through drilling and underground mineral extracting industries
- Ships and fishing vessels
- Prevention of Major Industrial Accidents[326]

As the ILO observes, occupational health and safety 'is an area where guidelines, codes of practice, and above all, technical standards play a very important role', and may be variously given direct legal effect or indirectly influence regulatory approaches.[327]

[325] ILO Recommendation No. 164 on Occupational Safety and Health 1981, [4].
[326] ECSR, Statement of Interpretation: Article 3 (30 November 1998).
[327] ILO, *Survey on standards on health and safety*, 30.

NATIONAL POLICIES

One important means of advancing occupational health and safety is through the formulation, adoption and implementation of national policies. While the CESCR has not thus far stipulated a requirement to formulate and implement a national policy under Article 7, it is a key aspect of both ILO standards and national practice in this area, and may provide a useful framework to structure obligations under Article 7. The requirement of a 'coherent national policy' is central to Convention No. 155, Article 4 of which provides:

1. Each Member shall, in the light of national conditions and practice, and in consultation with the most representative organisations of employers and workers, formulate, implement and periodically review a coherent national policy on occupational safety, occupational health and the working environment.

2. The aim of the policy shall be to prevent accidents and injury to health arising out of, linked with or occurring in the course of work, by minimising, so far as is reasonably practicable, the causes of hazards inherent in the working environment.[328]

The policy should address the material elements of work and their relationships to workers and employers; training; and communication and cooperation, as Article 5 stipulates:

The policy referred to in Article 4 of this Convention shall take account of the following main spheres of action in so far as they affect occupational safety and health and the working environment:

(a) design, testing, choice, substitution, installation, arrangement, use and maintenance of the material elements of work (workplaces, working environment, tools, machinery and equipment, chemical, physical and biological substances and agents, work processes);

(b) relationships between the material elements of work and the persons who carry out or supervise the work, and adaptation of machinery, equipment, working time, organisation of work and work processes to the physical and mental capacities of the workers;

(c) training, including necessary further training, qualifications and motivations of persons involved, in one capacity or another, in the achievement of adequate levels of safety and health;

(d) communication and co-operation at the levels of the working group and the undertaking and at all other appropriate levels up to and including the national level…

To implement their policy, states must ensure certain functions are carried out in relation to the design, construction and layout of workplaces, the determination of work processes and dealings with dangerous substances (Article 11):

[328] See also ILO Convention No. 187 concerning the promotional framework for occupational safety and health (adopted 15 June 2006, entered into force 20 February 2009), Article 3(1).

To give effect to the policy referred to in Article 4 of this Convention, the competent authority or authorities shall ensure that the following functions are progressively carried out:

(a) the determination, where the nature and degree of hazards so require, of conditions governing the design, construction and layout of undertakings, the commencement of their operations, major alterations affecting them and changes in their purposes, the safety of technical equipment used at work, as well as the application of procedures defined by the competent authorities;

(b) the determination of work processes and of substances and agents the exposure to which is to be prohibited, limited or made subject to authorisation or control by the competent authority or authorities; health hazards due to the simultaneous exposure to several substances or agents shall be taken into consideration;

...

(f) the introduction or extension of systems, taking into account national conditions and possibilities, to examine chemical, physical and biological agents in respect of the risk to the health of workers.

In addition, states must regulate those who design, manufacture, import, provide or transfer machinery, equipment or substances for occupational use (Article 12):

Measures shall be taken, in accordance with national law and practice, with a view to ensuring that those who design, manufacture, import, provide or transfer machinery, equipment or substances for occupational use—

(a) satisfy themselves that, so far as is reasonably practicable, the machinery, equipment or substance does not entail dangers for the safety and health of those using it correctly;

(b) make available information concerning the correct installation and use of machinery and equipment and the correct use of substances, and information on hazards of machinery and equipment and dangerous properties of chemical substances and physical and biological agents or products, as well as instructions on how known hazards are to be avoided;

(c) undertake studies and research or otherwise keep abreast of the scientific and technical knowledge necessary to comply with subparagraphs (a) and (b) of this Article.

Recommendation No. 164 on Occupational Health and Safety 1981 suggests more specific areas for national policy (under Article 4 of Convention No. 155) to focus on (paragraph 3):

3. As appropriate for different branches of economic activity and different types of work and taking into account the principle of giving priority to eliminating hazards at their source, measures should be taken in pursuance of the policy referred to in Article 4 of the Convention, in particular in the following fields:

(a) design, siting, structural features, installation, maintenance, repair and alteration of workplaces and means of access thereto and egress therefrom;

(b) lighting, ventilation, order and cleanliness of workplaces;

(c) temperature, humidity and movement of air in the workplace;

(d) design, construction, use, maintenance, testing and inspection of machinery and equipment liable to present hazards and, as appropriate, their approval and transfer;

(e) prevention of harmful physical or mental stress due to conditions of work;

(f) handling, stacking and storage of loads and materials, manually or mechanically;

(g) use of electricity;

(h) manufacture, packing, labelling, transport, storage and use of dangerous substances and agents, disposal of their wastes and residues, and, as appropriate, their replacement by other substances or agents which are not dangerous or which are less dangerous;

(i) radiation protection;

(j) prevention and control of, and protection against, occupational hazards due to noise and vibration;

(k) control of the atmosphere and other ambient factors of workplaces;

(l) prevention and control of hazards due to high and low barometric pressures;

(m) prevention of fires and explosions and measures to be taken in case of fire or explosion;

(n) design, manufacture, supply, use, maintenance and testing of personal protective equipment and protective clothing;

(o) sanitary installations, washing facilities, facilities for changing and storing clothes, supply of drinking water, and any other welfare facilities connected with occupational safety and health;

(p) first-aid treatment;

(q) establishment of emergency plans;

(r) supervision of the health of workers.

It also makes further detailed recommendations in relation to the range of actions that may be taken at the national (Part III) and undertaking (Part IV) levels.

Convention No. 187 on Promotional Framework for Occupational Safety and Health 2006 adds that national policy (under Article 4 of Convention No. 155) 'shall promote basic principles such as assessing occupational risks or hazards; combating occupational risks or hazards at source; and developing a national preventative safety and health culture that includes information, consultation and training' (Article 3(3)). The latter reference introduces the new concept of a 'preventative safety and health culture', which in turn is defined (in Article 1(d)) as:

. . . a culture in which the right to a safe and healthy working environment is respected at all levels, where government, employers and workers actively participate in securing a safe and healthy working environment through a system of defined rights, responsibilities and duties, and where the principle of prevention is accorded the highest priority.

More broadly, under Convention No. 155 national policy must indicate the respective, albeit complementary, 'functions and responsibilities' for work health and safety as between public authorities, employers, workers and others (Article 6). It must also ensure the necessary coordination between various authorities and bodies responsible for health and safety, including the possibility of a central body (Article 15). This in turn leads to consideration of the nature of the bodies or systems that may be necessary to fulfil a state's obligations under Article 7(b) of the ICESCR, discussed in the next section.

The requirement of a national policy is also found in regional law. Article 3(1) of the Revised European Social Charter 1996 requires states, in consultation with employers' and workers' organizations:

> ...to formulate, implement and periodically review a coherent national policy on occupational safety, occupational health and the working environment. The primary aim of this policy shall be to improve occupational safety and health and to prevent accidents and injury to health arising out of, linked with or occurring in the course of work, particularly by minimising the causes of hazards inherent in the working environment...[329]

Consistent with the CESCR's concerns in relation to other ICESCR rights, any national policy required under Article 7 should be attentive to particularly vulnerable, disadvantaged or marginalized groups. The ILO observes that in national practice, the coverage of occupational health and safety measures is sometimes non-existent or limited in certain sectors or for certain categories of workers. These have included, for example, in shipping, fishing, mining, agriculture, aviation and the oil industry; police, military or security personnel; firefighters; and traditional industries, domestic workers and homeworkers.[330] Workers in the informal economy can be particularly vulnerable, as in India, where 94 per cent of workers are in the informal sector and not covered by health and safety protections.[331] Certain types of insecure employment brought by economic changes have also raised concerns in regional practice, including temporary and fixed-term employment.[332]

The self-employed raise additional considerations. As noted at the outset of this chapter, during the drafting it was suggested that Article 7 as a whole may not cover the self-employed, as not being workers. In relation to occupational health and safety specifically, in the ILO context some states have highlighted the difficulties of extending such protections to the self-employed, given that they are both employers and workers and that their workplaces may not be so easily supervized. However, in interpreting Article 3(1) of the European Social Charter (or Article 3(2) of the Revised Charter), the European Committee on Social Rights has indicated that there are good reasons for applying occupational health and safety protections to the self-employed, albeit with necessary adjustments:

> Contrary to the view of the Governmental Committee, there is no impossibility in imposing a duty of self-protection on a self-employed worker, if this is necessary to secure effective

[329] No such requirement was found in the original European Social Charter: European Social Charter (adopted 18 October 1961, ETS 35, entered into force 26 February 1965).

[330] ILO, *Survey on standards on health and safety*, 12–14.

[331] ILO, *Survey on standards on health and safety*, 12–14.

[332] ECSR, Statement of Interpretation: Article 3 (30 November 1998).

regulation and inspection of a dangerous workplace. The question of sanctions is separate and subsidiary; no one would suggest the punishing of workers for injuring themselves. The Committee considers that self-employed (and other non-employed) workers are, in a modern economy usually nodes in a complex web of economic, technical, social and therefore legal relationships at their places of work for the purposes of safety and health as for others; and it will normally be in their own interests to have their position defined by regulations.

However, this may be, the activities of the self-employed also affect both the personal health and safety, and the duties in this regard, of other people; these therefore have an interest in effective regulation and inspection. We can point to:

- the use of the same workplace by other workers (not being employees of the workers in question)—family workers—unpaid helpers—employees of contractors—maintenance men, etc.;
- risks to children (see Article 7, paragraph 10 of the Charter) or third parties generally (Article 11, paragraph 1);
- legal duties owed by landlords, manufacturers, contractors, public utilities, etc., as well as by other workers mentioned above, affecting the health and safety of the workplace.

These considerations lead to the assumption that Article 3, paragraph 1 implies a system of workplace regulation and inspection for non-employed workers as well as the employed with, of course, derogations for practical reasons, such as to the low risk of certain economic sectors, the difficulty of inspection, lack of cooperation with inspection and so on. It is also clear that as regards more specifically agriculture there is no presumption that there is a case warranting such derogations: rather the opposite. In the case of certain countries, the fatal accident rate in manufacturing industry is much lower than that in the agricultural sector.[333]

NATIONAL SYSTEMS

In order to effectively implement national policy on occupational health and safety, Convention No. 187 requires states to adopt a national system (Part IV) and a national programme (Part V) on health and safety. A 'national system' is 'the infrastructure which provides the main framework for implementing the national policy and national programmes' (Article 1(b)). It should include, for example, laws and regulations, authorities or bodies, compliance mechanisms including systems of inspection, and arrangements at the level of undertakings. Article 4 outlines the required elements:

1. Each Member shall establish, maintain, progressively develop and periodically review a national system for occupational safety and health, in consultation with the most representative organizations of employers and workers.

[333] ECSR, Statement of Interpretation: Article 3 (30 November 1975); see also ECSR, Statements of Interpretation: Article 3 (31 July 1973); and (30 November 1998).

2. The national system for occupational safety and health shall include among others:

(a) laws and regulations, collective agreements where appropriate, and any other relevant instruments on occupational safety and health;

(b) an authority or body, or authorities or bodies, responsible for occupational safety and health, designated in accordance with national law and practice;

(c) mechanisms for ensuring compliance with national laws and regulations, including systems of inspection; and

(d) arrangements to promote, at the level of the undertaking, cooperation between management, workers and their representatives as an essential element of workplace-related prevention measures.

3. The national system for occupational safety and health shall include, where appropriate:

(a) a national tripartite advisory body, or bodies, addressing occupational safety and health issues;

(b) information and advisory services on occupational safety and health;

(c) the provision of occupational safety and health training;

(d) occupational health services in accordance with national law and practice;

(e) research on occupational safety and health;

(f) a mechanism for the collection and analysis of data on occupational injuries and diseases, taking into account relevant ILO instruments;

(g) provisions for collaboration with relevant insurance or social security schemes covering occupational injuries and diseases; and

(h) support mechanisms for a progressive improvement of occupational safety and health conditions in micro-enterprises, in small and medium-sized enterprises and in the informal economy.

National systems should cover all workers, particularly in high-risk sectors, and vulnerable workers (such as those in the informal economy or migrant and young workers), be attentive to reproductive health, and take into account the constraints on smaller enterprises.[334]

One specialized component of a national system is the establishment of occupational health services at the enterprise level, which is common on most continents.[335] The CESCR has been concerned at the inadequate provision of occupational medical care, including in private companies.[336] Under a further ILO instrument, Convention No. 161 on Occupational Health Services 1985,[337]

[334] ILO Recommendation No. 197 on the Promotional Framework for Occupational Safety and Health 2006, [3], [4] and [5(g)] respectively.

[335] ILO, *Survey on standards on health and safety*, 64.

[336] CESCR, Concluding Observations: Morocco, E/C.12/MAR/CO/3 (4 September 2006), [20].

[337] See also ILO Recommendations No. 171 on Occupational Health Services 1985; No. 164 on Occupational Safety and Health 1981, [13].

states are required by Article 2 to 'formulate, implement and periodically review a coherent national policy on occupational health services'. The purpose of such services is explained in Article 1:

...

(a) the term *occupational health services* means services entrusted with essentially preventive functions and responsible for advising the employer, the workers and their representatives in the undertaking on—

(i) the requirements for establishing and maintaining a safe and healthy working environment which will facilitate optimal physical and mental health in relation to work;

(ii) the adaptation of work to the capabilities of workers in the light of their state of physical and mental health...

Health services should be established in consultation with the most representative organizations of employers and workers (Article 4), based in law or regulations, collective agreements or another approved manner (Article 6), and may be shared across a number of enterprises (Article 7). Services should be multidisciplinary and enjoy full professional independence (Articles 9 to 10). They should operate at no cost to workers (Article 12), inform workers of any health hazards (Article 13), and workers and employers should report hazards or injuries or illnesses to them (Articles 14 to 15). The broad functions of occupational health services are set out in Article 5:

(a) identification and assessment of the risks from health hazards in the workplace;

(b) surveillance of the factors in the working environment and working practices which may affect workers' health, including sanitary installations, canteens and housing where these facilities are provided by the employer;

(c) advice on planning and organisation of work, including the design of workplaces, on the choice, maintenance and condition of machinery and other equipment and on substances used in work;

(d) participation in the development of programmes for the improvement of working practices as well as testing and evaluation of health aspects of new equipment;

(e) advice on occupational health, safety and hygiene and on ergonomics and individual and collective protective equipment;

(f) surveillance of workers' health in relation to work;

(g) promoting the adaptation of work to the worker;

(h) contribution to measures of vocational rehabilitation;

(i) collaboration in providing information, training and education in the fields of occupational health and hygiene and ergonomics;

(j) organising of first aid and emergency treatment;

(k) participation in analysis of occupational accidents and occupational diseases.

At the regional level also, Article 3(4) of the Revised European Social Charter 1996 requires states 'to promote the progressive development of occupational health services for all workers with essentially preventive and advisory functions'.

NATIONAL PROGRAMMES

A 'national programme' under Convention No. 187 means any national programme 'that includes objectives to be achieved in a predetermined time frame, priorities and means of action formulated to improve occupational safety and health, and means to assess progress' (Article 1(c)). Article 5 indicates the content of such programmes:

1. Each Member shall formulate, implement, monitor, evaluate and periodically review a national programme on occupational safety and health in consultation with the most representative organizations of employers and workers.

2. The national programme shall:

(a) promote the development of a national preventative safety and health culture;

(b) contribute to the protection of workers by eliminating or minimizing, so far as is reasonably practicable, work-related hazards and risks, in accordance with national law and practice, in order to prevent occupational injuries, diseases and deaths and promote safety and health in the workplace;

(c) be formulated and reviewed on the basis of analysis of the national situation regarding occupational safety and health, including analysis of the national system for occupational safety and health;

(d) include objectives, targets and indicators of progress; and

(e) be supported, where possible, by other complementary national programmes and plans which will assist in achieving progressively a safe and healthy working environment.

3. The national programme shall be widely publicized and, to the extent possible, endorsed and launched by the highest national authorities.

Again, while it is unrealistic to expect the immediate elimination or mitigation of all workplace risks, national policies, systems and programmes can be immediately adopted, including benchmarks and indicators for the progressive reduction of workplace risks in accordance with maximum available resources.

A national programme should be based on principles of risk and hazard assessment and management, identify priorities for action, be periodically reviewed and updated, and be coordinated with related programmes on public health and economic development.[338] A useful technical tool for formulating and reviewing the national programme is the preparation of a 'national profile' which summarizes the situation of and progress on health and safety.[339]

[338] ILO Recommendation No. 197 on the Promotional Framework for Occupational Safety and Health 2006, [7]–[8], [11].

[339] ILO Recommendation No. 197, [13].

A national profile collates information on issues such as: laws, regulations and collective agreements; responsible bodies; compliance mechanisms (including inspectors); technical standards, codes of practice and guidelines; advisory bodies; technical experts; preventive measures, information and advice; training and education; research and research institutions; data on diseases and injury; health services; social insurance and social security; coordination and collaboration; employers' policies and programmes; financial and budgetary resources; and data on demography, literacy, the economy and development.[340]

In relation to data collection more generally, Article 11(e) of Convention No. 155 requires states to annually publish information on occupational accidents, diseases and injuries, as well as measures taken in pursuance of national policy. The 2002 Protocol to Convention No. 155 further provides for the establishment and periodic review of procedures for detailed recording (Articles 2 to 3) and notifying (Articles 4 to 5) of occupational accidents and diseases and dangerous occurrences, as well as the publication of annual statistics, following ILO classifications (Articles 6 to 7).[341]

INFORMATION, EDUCATION AND TRAINING

The provision of information and training about occupational health and safety risks is a particularly important means of ensuring safe and healthy working conditions under Article 7(b). In monitoring states, the CESCR has expressed concern about low levels of awareness of labour safety protection measures among employers.[342] To address this, the CESCR has recommended training and awareness-raising programmes for employers, employees and inspectors,[343] including in highly specific areas such as training to seamen in vessel stability and the use and treatment of hoisting equipment[344] to prevent accidents in ports.[345] The CESCR has also recommended increased transparency and disclosure of all information on the safety of nuclear power installations, and plans for prevention of and early reaction to accidents.[346]

In ILO practice, Convention No. 155 requires states to 'provide guidance to employers and workers so as to help them to comply with legal obligations' (Article 10) and to include occupational health and safety 'at all levels of education and training, including higher technical, medical and professional education' (Article 14). Recommendation No. 197 on the Promotion Framework for Occupational Health and Safety 2006 further suggests that states should conduct national campaigns to raise workplace and public awareness; promote

340 ILO Recommendation No. 197, [14]. 341 Thus far the Protocol has nine ratifications.
342 CESCR, Concluding Observations: Latvia, E/C.12/LVA/CO/1 (7 January 2008), [18].
343 CESCR, Concluding Observations: Iceland, E/C.12/1/Add.89 (26 June 2003), [14]; Hungary, E/C.12/HUN/CO/3 (16 January 2008), [38]; Republic of Korea, E/C.12/KOR/CO/3 (17 December 2009), [18].
344 CESCR, Concluding Observations: Iceland, E/C.12/1/Add.89 (26 June 2003), [14].
345 CESCR, Concluding Observations: Italy, E/C.12/1/Add.43 (23 May 2000), [25].
346 CESCR, Concluding Observations: Japan, E/C.12/1/Add.67 (24 September 2001), [49].

mechanisms for training at all levels; and provide information and advice to employers and workers (paragraph 5).

RESPONSIBILITIES OF EMPLOYERS

National laws and policies should impose direct obligations on employers to ensure safe and healthy working conditions under Article 7(b). Some guidance is given by Article 16 of Convention No. 155, which requires employers to ensure the safety of workplaces, machinery, equipment, processes and substances under their control, and to provide adequate protective clothing where necessary:

1. Employers shall be required to ensure that, so far as is reasonably practicable, the workplaces, machinery, equipment and processes under their control are safe and without risk to health.

2. Employers shall be required to ensure that, so far as is reasonably practicable, the chemical, physical and biological substances and agents under their control are without risk to health when the appropriate measures of protection are taken.

3. Employers shall be required to provide, where necessary, adequate protective clothing and protective equipment to prevent, so far as is reasonably practicable, risk of accidents or of adverse effects on health.

Recommendation No. 164 elaborates on the means of fulfilling the obligations in Article 16:

10. The obligations placed upon employers with a view to achieving the objective set forth in Article 16 of the Convention might include, as appropriate for different branches of economic activity and different types of work, the following:

(a) to provide and maintain workplaces, machinery and equipment, and use work methods, which are as safe and without risk to health as is reasonably practicable;

(b) to give necessary instructions and training, taking account of the functions and capacities of different categories of workers;

(c) to provide adequate supervision of work, of work practices and of application and use of occupational safety and health measures;

(d) to institute organisational arrangements regarding occupational safety and health and the working environment adapted to the size of the undertaking and the nature of its activities;

(e) to provide, without any cost to the worker, adequate personal protective clothing and equipment which are reasonably necessary when hazards cannot be otherwise prevented or controlled;

(f) to ensure that work organisation, particularly with respect to hours of work and rest breaks, does not adversely affect occupational safety and health;

(g) to take all reasonably practicable measures with a view to eliminating excessive physical and mental fatigue;

(h) to undertake studies and research or otherwise keep abreast of the scientific and technical knowledge necessary to comply with the foregoing clauses.

The Recommendation also calls on employers to 'set out in writing their policy and arrangements' and those responsible, and 'bring this information to the notice of every worker, in a language or medium the worker readily understands' (paragraph 14). It further suggests that employers should be required to verify implementation (such as through environmental monitoring) and undertake periodic safety audits; and keep relevant records (such as of accidents and injuries and exposure to dangerous substances) (paragraph 15).

Under Convention No. 155, employers must also provide measures to deal with emergencies and accidents, including adequate first-aid arrangements (Article 18). In monitoring states, the CESCR has occasionally expressed concern about the inadequate provision of occupational medical care,[347] and recommended that states ensure companies have occupational medical officers available.[348] Occupational health and safety measures must also not involve any costs to workers (Convention No. 155, Article 21).

RESPONSIBILITIES OF WORKERS

Workers also bear responsibilities for ensuring health and safety in the workplace. Convention No. 155 is indicative. Under Article 19, workers and their representatives should cooperate with employers in fulfilling health and safety obligations:

There shall be arrangements at the level of the undertaking under which—

(a) workers, in the course of performing their work, co-operate in the fulfilment by their employer of the obligations placed upon him;

(b) representatives of workers in the undertaking co-operate with the employer in the field of occupational safety and health…

To that end, Article 19 further provides that workers should be given adequate information and training on health and safety, and be consulted on all aspects of it:

(c) representatives of workers in an undertaking are given adequate information on measures taken by the employer to secure occupational safety and health and may consult their representative organisations about such information provided they do not disclose commercial secrets;

(d) workers and their representatives in the undertaking are given appropriate training in occupational safety and health;

(e) workers or their representatives and, as the case may be, their representative organisations in an undertaking, in accordance with national law and practice, are enabled to enquire into, and are consulted by the employer on, all aspects of occupational safety and health associated with their work; for this purpose technical advisers may, by mutual agreement, be brought in from outside the undertaking…

More specific directives to workers are set out in Recommendation No. 164:

[347] CESCR, Concluding Observations: Morocco, E/C.12/MAR/CO/3 (4 September 2006), [20].
[348] CESCR, Concluding Observations: Morocco, [43].

16. The arrangements provided for in Article 19 of the Convention should aim at ensuring that workers—

(a) take reasonable care for their own safety and that of other persons who may be affected by their acts or omissions at work;

(b) comply with instructions given for their own safety and health and those of others and with safety and health procedures;

(c) use safety devices and protective equipment correctly and do not render them inoperative;

(d) report forthwith to their immediate supervisor any situation which they have reason to believe could present a hazard and which they cannot themselves correct;

(e) report any accident or injury to health which arises in the course of or in connection with work.

A broader obligation of cooperation between employers and workers is established in Article 20 of Convention No. 155:

Co-operation between management and workers and/or their representatives within the undertaking shall be an essential element of organisational and other measures taken in pursuance of Articles 16 to 19 of this Convention.

Examples of cooperative measures are given in Recommendation No. 164, most prominently including the appointment of workers' safety delegates, workers' safety and health committees and/or joint safety and health committees (paragraph 12), and the provision of information to, and consultation with, them.[349]

ENFORCEMENT, SANCTIONS, REMEDIES

In monitoring states, the CESCR has been concerned about the inadequate enforcement of laws and regulations[350] and its Reporting Guidelines 2009 ask states to address the 'enforcement in practice' of laws and administrative measures.[351] It has sometimes expressed concern about inadequate systems for reporting unsafe conditions and accidents,[352] and has suggested independent investigations of all reported cases of deaths and injuries in mines.[353]

The CESCR has repeatedly called on states to ensure that employers who violate safety standards are duly sanctioned,[354] and that judicial remedies are

[349] On the establishment of joint safety and health committees and the designation of workers' health and safety representatives, see also ILO Recommendation No. 197 on the Promotional Framework for Occupational Safety and Health 2006, [5(f)].

[350] CESCR, Concluding Observations: Ecuador, E/C.12/1/Add.100 (7 June 2004), [18].

[351] CESCR, Guidelines on treaty specific documents to be submitted by states parties under Articles 16 and 17 of the ICESCR, E/C.12/2008/2 (24 March 2009), [23].

[352] CESCR, Concluding Observations: Russian Federation, E/C.12/1/Add.13 (20 May 1997), [18]; Saint Vincent and the Grenadines, E/C.12/1/Add.21 (2 December 1997), [17].

[353] CESCR, Concluding Observations: Democratic Republic of Congo, E/C.12/COD/CO/4 (16 December 2009), [22].

[354] Including CESCR, Concluding Observations: Morocco, E/C.12/1994/5 (30 May 1994), [21]; Russian Federation, E/C.12/1/Add.94 (12 December 1994), [19]; Poland, E/C.12/1/Add.82

available for victims of violations of labour safety regulations.[355] It was also concerned at the refusal of employers to compensate workers for work injuries.[356] In this respect, it may be recalled that the right to social security under Article 9 of the ICESCR encompasses workplace injury benefits.

Guidance on enforcement and remedies is also found in Convention No. 155. Article 9 requires enforcement by 'an adequate and appropriate system of inspection and adequate penalties for violations', while Article 11 requires the establishment for procedures to notify occupational accidents and diseases, and to hold inquiries on 'serious' situations:

Article 9

> 1. The enforcement of laws and regulations concerning occupational safety and health and the working environment shall be secured by an adequate and appropriate system of inspection.
>
> 2. The enforcement system shall provide for adequate penalties for violations of the laws and regulations.
>
> …

Article 11

> …
>
> (c) the establishment and application of procedures for the notification of occupational accidents and diseases, by employers and, when appropriate, insurance institutions and others directly concerned, and the production of annual statistics on occupational accidents and diseases;
>
> (d) the holding of inquiries, where cases of occupational accidents, occupational diseases or any other injuries to health which arise in the course of or in connection with work appear to reflect situations which are serious…

That Convention does not prescribe the nature of 'adequate penalties'. A similar requirement for the 'enforcement' of health and safety laws under Article 3(2) of the European Social Charter (or Article 3(3) of the Revised Charter) has been interpreted to encompass 'civil and criminal sanctions'.[357]

In ILO practice, a range of other possibilities for dealing with offenders is apparent, including adverse publicity ('shaming'), prohibitions on tendering for public contracts, the maintenance of a 'warnings' register, increasing insurance premiums, suspending or revoking operating licences, or issuing 'improvement' notices.[358] Forms of 'cooperative' compliance, including for instance

(19 December 2002), [43]; Kuwait, E/C.12/1/Add.98 (7 June 2004), [35]; Lithuania, E/C.12/1/Add.96 (7 June 2004), [36]; Spain, E/C.12/1/Add.99 (7 June 2004), [31]; China (including HK, Macao), E/C.12/1/Add.107 (13 May 2005), [53]; Ukraine, E/C.12/UKR/CO/5 (4 January 2008), [39]; Latvia, E/C.12/LVA/CO/1 (7 January 2008), [42]; Hungary, E/C.12/HUN/CO/3 (16 January 2008), [38].

355 CESCR, Concluding Observations: Morocco, E/C.12/1994/5 (30 May 1994), [21].

356 CESCR, Concluding Observations: Russian Federation, E/C.12/1/Add.13 (20 May 1997), [18].

357 ECSR, Statement of Interpretation: Article 3 (31 May 1969).

358 ILO, *Survey on standards on health and safety*, 34–5.

accreditation schemes, will be as important as traditional sanctions and deterrence in this area, which involves complex technical standards and collaborative, consultative implementation processes.

In monitoring states, the CESCR has criticized the absence of labour inspection systems.[359] It has also been concerned about restrictions on their functions,[360] including limited powers,[361] restricted access to certain workplaces[362] or the inability to make unscheduled inspections.[363] It has criticized external influence on inspectorates which impairs their ability to independently monitor work conditions.[364] It was also concerned where inspectors focused on workers' migration status rather than on health and safety.[365] Coordination problems have also arisen where inspection functions were transferred to decentralized bodies.[366] The CESCR has encouraged states to extend inspectorates' powers,[367] ensure their independence,[368] remove restrictions on unscheduled inspections[369] and improve transparency.[370]

The CESCR has also been concerned where labour inspectorates are under-resourced,[371] including where inspections are irregular,[372] or infrequent or absent in rural areas[373] or the private sector.[374] It has recommended strengthening them with further resources, funding and staff,[375] and increasing the number

[359] CESCR, Concluding Observations: Colombia, E/C.12/1995/18 (1–19 May 1995, 20 November–8 December 1995), [190]; Chad, E/C.12/TCD/CO/3 (16 December 2009), [16].

[360] CESCR, Concluding Observations: Jordan, E/C.12/1/Add.4 (1 September 2000), [20]; Honduras, E/C.12/1/Add.5 (21 May 2001), [16]; Kazakhstan, E/C.12/KAZ/CO/1 (7 June 2010), [21].

[361] CESCR, Concluding Observations: Georgia, E/C.12/1/Add.83 (19 December 2002), [16].

[362] CESCR, Concluding Observations: Morocco, E/C.12/1994/5 (30 May 1994), [14]; Jordan, E/C.12/1/Add.46 (1 September 2000), [20]; Honduras, E/C.12/1/Add.57 (21 May 2001), [16]; Georgia, E/C.12/1/Add.83 (19 December 2002), [16].

[363] CESCR, Concluding Observations: Kazakhstan, E/C.12/KAZ/CO/1 (7 June 2010), [21].

[364] CESCR, Concluding Observations: Democratic Republic of Congo, E/C.12/COD/CO/4 (16 December 2009), [22] (in the mining sector).

[365] CESCR, Concluding Observations: Republic of Korea, E/C.12/KOR/CO/3 (17 December 2009), [18].

[366] CESCR, Concluding Observations: Italy, E/C.12/1/Add.43 (23 May 2000), [12].

[367] CESCR, Concluding Observations: Honduras, E/C.12/1/Add.57 (21 May 2001), [37]; Ukraine, E/C.12/1/Add.65 (24 September 2001), [26].

[368] CESCR, Concluding Observations: China (including HK, Macao), E/C.12/1/Add.107 (13 May 2005), [53].

[369] CESCR, Concluding Observations: Kazakhstan, E/C.12/KAZ/CO/1 (7 June 2010), [21].

[370] CESCR, Concluding Observations: Ukraine, E/C.12/UKR/CO/5 (4 January 2008), [39].

[371] CESCR, Concluding Observations: Russian Federation, E/C.12/1/Add.13 (20 May 1997), [18]; Honduras, E/C.12/1/Add.57 (21 May 2001), [16]; Republic of Korea, E/C.12/1Add.59 (21 May 2001), [18]; Georgia, E.C.12/1/Add.83 (19 December 2002), [16]; Democratic Republic of Congo, E/C.12/COD/CO/4 (16 December 2009), [22]; Republic of Korea, E/C.12/KOR/CO/3 (17 December 2009), [18].

[372] CESCR, Concluding Observations: Saint Vincent and the Grenadines, E/C.12/1/Add.21 (2 December 1997), [17]; Guatemala, E/C.12/1/Add.93 (12 December 2003), [15]; Ecuador, E/C.12/1/Add.100 (7 June 2004), [18].

[373] CESCR, Concluding Observations: Guatemala, E/C.12/1Add.93 (12 December 2003), [15]; Ecuador, E/C.12/1/Add.100 (7 June 2004), [18].

[374] CESCR, Concluding Observations: Georgia, E/C.12/1/Add.83 (19 December 2002), [16].

[375] Including CESCR, Concluding Observations: Russian Federation, E/C.12/1/Add.94 (12 December 1994), [19]; El Salvador, E/C.12/1/Add.4 (28 May 1996), [31]; Russian Federation, E/C.12/1/Add.13

or regularity of inspections.[376] The CESCR has called for inspectors to be adequately trained,[377] including through technical assistance from the ILO.[378]

In urging states to ratify ILO Convention No. 81 on Labour Inspection in Industry and Commerce 1947,[379] the CESCR has invoked ILO standards as a guiding framework on labour inspections. Labour inspection under Convention No. 155 too is understood by reference to Convention No. 81.[380] States are required under Convention No. 81 to maintain a system of labour inspection (Article 1) under the 'supervision and control of a central authority' (Article 4), and staffed by 'public officials whose status and conditions of service are such that they are assured of stability of employment and are independent of changes of government and of improper external influences' (Article 6).[381] The functions of labour inspection are set out in Article 3 and include health and safety:

1. The functions of the system of labour inspection shall be:

(a) to secure the enforcement of the legal provisions relating to conditions of work and the protection of workers while engaged in their work, such as provisions relating to hours, wages, safety, health and welfare, the employment of children and young persons, and other connected matters, in so far as such provisions are enforceable by labour inspectors;

(b) to supply technical information and advice to employers and workers concerning the most effective means of complying with the legal provisions;

(c) to bring to the notice of the competent authority defects or abuses not specifically covered by existing legal provisions.

2. Any further duties which may be entrusted to labour inspectors shall not be such as to interfere with the effective discharge of their primary duties or to prejudice in any way the authority and impartiality which are necessary to inspectors in their relations with employers and workers.

(20 May 1997), [18]; Honduras, E/C.12/1/Add.57 (21 May 2001), [37]; Ukraine, E/C.12/1Add.65 (24 September 2001), [26]; Georgia, E/C.12/1/Add.83 (19 December 2002), [34]; Poland, E/C.12/1/Add.82 (19 December 2002), [43]; Kuwait, E/C.12/1/Add.98 (7 June 2004), [35]; China (including HK, Macao), E/C.12/1/Add.107 (13 May 2005), [53]; Bosnia and Herzegovina, E/C.12/BIH/CO/1 (24 January 2006), [15]; Republic of Korea, E/C.12/KOR/CO/3 (17 December 2009), [18].

376 CESCR, Concluding Observations: Guatemala, E/C.12/1/Add.93 (12 December 2003), [33]; Lithuania, E/C.12/1/Add.96 (7 June 2004), [36]; including Spain, E/C.12/1/Add.99 (7 June 2004), [31]; China (including HK, Macao), E/C.12/1/Add.107 (13 May 2005), [53]; El Salvador, E/C.12/SLV/CO/2 (27 June 2007), [32]; Hungary, E/C.12/HUN/CO/3 (16 January 2008), [38].

377 CESCR, Concluding Observations: Republic of Korea, E/C.12/KOR/CO/3 (17 December 2009), [18].

378 CESCR, Concluding Observations: Chad, E/C.12/TCD/CO/3 (16 December 2009), [16]. ILO Recommendation No. 197 on the Promotional Framework for Occupational Safety and Health 2006, [15], calls for international cooperation and exchange of information on preventive occupational health and safety.

379 CESCR, Concluding Observations: Ukraine, E/C.12/1/Add.65 (24 September 2001), [26]; Iceland, E/C.12/1/Add.89 (26 June 2003), [23]; Chile, E/C.12/1/Add.105 (1 December 2004), [41]; China: Hong Kong SAR, E/C.12/1/Add.107 (13 May 2005), [53]. See also ILO Convention No. 129 concerning Labour Inspection in Agriculture.

380 ILO Recommendation No. 164 on Occupational Safety and Health 1981, [5] (and also by ILO Convention No. 129 concerning Labour Inspection in Agriculture).

381 Staff must also be qualified and adequately trained—Article 7; technical experts should also be involved where necessary—Article 9.

Inspectorates must be adequately resourced with staff (Article 10) and facilities (Article 11). Their powers of inspection (Articles 12 and 16) and to take remedial action (Article 13) are set out in detail:

Article 12

1. Labour inspectors provided with proper credentials shall be empowered:

(a) to enter freely and without previous notice at any hour of the day or night any workplace liable to inspection;

(b) to enter by day any premises which they may have reasonable cause to believe to be liable to inspection; and

(c) to carry out any examination, test or enquiry which they may consider necessary in order to satisfy themselves that the legal provisions are being strictly observed, and in particular—

(i) to interrogate, alone or in the presence of witnesses, the employer or the staff of the undertaking on any matters concerning the application of the legal provisions;

(ii) to require the production of any books, registers or other documents the keeping of which is prescribed by national laws or regulations relating to conditions of work, in order to see that they are in conformity with the legal provisions, and to copy such documents or make extracts from them;

(iii) to enforce the posting of notices required by the legal provisions;

(iv) to take or remove for purposes of analysis samples of materials and substances used or handled, subject to the employer or his representative being notified of any samples or substances taken or removed for such purpose.

2. On the occasion of an inspection visit, inspectors shall notify the employer or his representative of their presence, unless they consider that such a notification may be prejudicial to the performance of their duties.

Article 13

1. Labour inspectors shall be empowered to take steps with a view to remedying defects observed in plant, layout or working methods which they may have reasonable cause to believe constitute a threat to the health or safety of the workers.

2. In order to enable inspectors to take such steps they shall be empowered, subject to any right of appeal to a judicial or administrative authority which may be provided by law, to make or to have made orders requiring—

(a) such alterations to the installation or plant, to be carried out within a specified time limit, as may be necessary to secure compliance with the legal provisions relating to the health or safety of the workers; or

(b) measures with immediate executory force in the event of imminent danger to the health or safety of the workers.

3. Where the procedure prescribed in paragraph 2 is not compatible with the administrative or judicial practice of the Member, inspectors shall have the right to apply to

the competent authority for the issue of orders or for the initiation of measures with immediate executory force.

…

Article 16

Workplaces shall be inspected as often and as thoroughly as is necessary to ensure the effective application of the relevant legal provisions.

Inspectorates must be notified of industrial accidents and occupational diseases (Article 14) and states must promote collaboration between inspectorates and employers and workers (Article 5). There must also be prompt legal proceedings against those who violate laws enforceable by labour inspectors (Article 17) with adequate penalties (Article 18):

Article 17

1. Persons who violate or neglect to observe legal provisions enforceable by labour inspectors shall be liable to prompt legal proceedings without previous warning: Provided that exceptions may be made by national laws or regulations in respect of cases in which previous notice to carry out remedial or preventive measures is to be given.

2. It shall be left to the discretion of labour inspectors to give warning and advice instead of instituting or recommending proceedings.

Article 18

Adequate penalties for violations of the legal provisions enforceable by labour inspectors and for obstructing labour inspectors in the performance of their duties shall be provided for by national laws or regulations and effectively enforced.

Finally, inspectorates must publish annual reports detailing their operations and statistics on, inter alia, the number of inspections, industrial accidents and occupational diseases, and violations and penalties imposed (Articles 19 to 21). In this respect, the CESCR's earlier 1991 reporting guidelines requested states to provide information on 'how the number, nature and frequency of occupational accidents (particularly with fatal results) and diseases have developed over time (10 years ago, 5 years as compared with the present)'.[382]

Workers must also be protected against retaliation for reporting occupational health and safety incidents or concerns. The CESCR has sometimes recommended that states develop a framework to protect and encourage workers who report inadequate conditions of work.[383] Under ILO Convention No. 155, states must ensure 'the protection of workers and their representatives from disciplinary measures as a result of actions properly taken by them in conformity with'

[382] CESCR, Revised general guidelines regarding the form and contents of reports to be submitted by states parties under Articles 16 and 17 of the ICESCR, E/C.12/1991/1 (17 June 1991), 4.

[383] CESCR, Concluding Observations: Russian Federation, E/C.12/1/Add.13 (20 May 1997), [33]; El Salvador, E/C.12/SLV/VO/2 (27 June 2007), [32].

national occupational health and safety policy under the Convention (Article 5(e)). Nor should any other 'prejudicial' measure be taken against a worker.[384]

Further, Article 13 of the same Convention requires the workers to be 'protected from undue consequences' for removing him- or herself 'from a work situation which he has reasonable justification to believe presents an imminent and serious danger to his life or health'. Under Article 19(f), where a worker has reported such a situation to his or her supervisor, until the employer has taken remedial action the employer cannot require the worker to return to a work situation where there is a 'continuing imminent and serious danger to life or health'.

It is obvious that all occupational health and safety risks cannot be eliminated, even with a strong culture of prevention and effective legislation, inspection and enforcement. Certain work is innately dangerous, whether policing, fire-fighting, mining, nuclear power generation, fighting in the armed forces and so on. In this respect, Article 2(4) of the Revised European Social Charter provides that 'where it has not yet been possible to eliminate or reduce sufficiently' the risks of 'inherently dangerous or unhealthy occupations', states must compensate workers by providing 'for either a reduction of working hours or additional paid holidays for workers engaged in such occupations'. The European Committee on Social Rights considered the provision in *Marangopoulos Foundation for Human Rights v Greece*:

> …The Committee points out that Article 2§4 of the Charter requires states to grant workers exposed to occupational health risks compensatory measures.
>
> 222. The Committee notes that for a number of years Greece, like the other states party to the Charter, has been pursuing a policy of occupational risk prevention and elimination rather than one of compensation. It considers that this development needs to be taken into account in interpreting Article 2§4 of the Charter, to ensure consistency with Articles 3 (right to safe and healthy working conditions) and 11 (right to protection of health). A literal reading of Article 2§4, without taking other factors into consideration, would point to the conclusion that there had been a violation of the Charter.
>
> 223. It follows from the newer interpretation that states' obligation under Article 2§4 of the Charter consists in measures to compensate for residual risks. By this, the Committee means situations in which workers are exposed to risks that it is not possible or has not yet been possible to eliminate or sufficiently reduce despite the application of the preventive and protective measures referred to in Articles 3 and 11 or in the absence of their application…
>
> 224. Article 2§4 mentions two forms of compensation, namely reduced daily working hours and additional paid holidays. In its examination of reports under the revised Charter, the Committee has stated that other means of reducing the length of exposure to risks may be considered acceptable (Conclusions 2003, Bulgaria, Article 2§4 of the revised Charter, pp. 24–27). It states that under no circumstances can financial compensation be considered an appropriate response under Article 2§4. Apart from this particular situation, the Committee will rule on the suitability of other approaches not in the abstract but case by

[384] Recommendation No. 164 on Occupational Safety and Health 1981, [17].

case. For example, in a situation where a measure of this type was contemplated as a general solution, making no distinction according to the type and nature of the risk involved, it ruled that a reduction in the number of years of exposure was not an appropriate measure in all cases (ibid).[385]

Pecuniary compensation alone for dangerous work may therefore be insufficient. The ECSR has observed that reduced working hours and additional holidays are necessary because 'they allow for a reduced accumulation of physical and mental fatigue and a reduction in the exposure to risk, whilst at the same time granting workers longer periods of rest'.[386]

Article 7(c): Equal Opportunity for Promotion

Article 7(c) guarantees '[e]qual opportunity for everyone to be promoted in his employment to an appropriate higher level, subject to no considerations other than those of seniority and competence'. It was introduced by Guatemala in the Third Committee[387] and had no equivalent in the earlier text proposed by the Commission on Human Rights. It aimed to address 'discrimination in matters of promotion, based, for instance, on sex or political opinions'.[388]

A number of states thought that the reference to seniority and competence alone was too restrictive because there were other criteria on which promotion could be based,[389] or because seniority could be a problematic basis for promotion.[390] Guatemala replied that the word 'seniority' in the English text did not convey the meaning intended by the Spanish language amendment[391] ('tiempo de servicio'—literally, length of service) and suggested that the English text be amended. However, the word 'seniority' appears in the English text as adopted.[392] There is a certain difference in meaning here: the Spanish formula concerns duration of employment, whereas the English can convey that idea or refer instead to a person's employment level within the hierarchy of an organization.

The central thrust of the provision is, however, tolerably clear: promotion must not be based on or impeded by impermissible discrimination. In monitoring states

[385] *Marangopoulos Foundation for Human Rights (MFRH) v Greece (Decision on the Merits)*, ECSR Complaint No. 30/2005 (6 December 2006), [222]–[224]; see also ECSR, Statement of Interpretation: Article 2(4) (30 June 2006), [9].

[386] ECSR, Statement of Interpretation: Article 2(4) (31 December 1977). See, eg, *STTK ry and Tehy ry v Finland*, ECSR Complaint No. 10/2000 (17 October 2001) (where Finland refused to reduce working hours or provide additional paid holidays for workers exposed to low level ionizing radiation).

[387] UNGA Third Committee, A/3525 (9 February 1957), 12.

[388] UNGA Third Committee, A/C.3/SR.715 (18 December 1956), 169 (Guatemala).

[389] UNGA Third Committee, A/C.3/SR.715 (18 December 1956), 171 (Philippines), 174 (Syria); UNGA Third Committee, A/C.3/SR.716 (19 December 1956), 179 (Israel).

[390] UNGA Third Committee, A/C.3/SR.716 (19 December 1956), 177 (Pakistsan).

[391] UNGA Third Committee, A/C.3/SR.717 (20 December 1956), 182 (Guatemala).

[392] By thirty votes to thirteen, with eighteen abstentions: UNGA Third Committee, A/3525 (9 February 1957), 17.

under Article 7, the CESCR has raised concern about inequality in promotion opportunities for women,[393] and for workers in special trading zones.[394] It recommended that states implement laws to guarantee equal opportunity for promotion subject to no considerations other than seniority and competence,[395] and encourage promotion opportunities for workers in export zones.[396]

As mentioned in the previous chapter, the CESCR has also been concerned about equal opportunity in promotion as an aspect of the right of 'everyone' to work in Article 6 of the ICESCR. This includes where lower education or literacy rates and cultural practices limit women's promotion opportunities,[397] or where national laws against racial discrimination in aspects of employment failed to also cover promotion.[398]

A literal interpretation of Article 7(c) might suggest that if seniority and competence are the only permissible considerations for promotion, affirmative action or positive discrimination in promotion to assist disadvantaged groups is not permitted.[399] However, it is also necessary to consider the provision in the light of the general limitations clause in Article 4 of the ICESCR, which permits rights to be restricted to protect the rights of others.

While the CESCR has not explicitly addressed the legal issue, this view appears consistent with its observations on states. Where ethnic quotas in public service recruitment existed in Sri Lanka, for example, the CESCR called for them to be expanded to also cover promotions.[400] The CESCR's superseded reporting guidelines of 1991 also required states to report on steps taken to eliminate inequality in promotion among disadvantaged groups,[401] thereby obliquely implying that positive measures may be required.

It may be recalled that affirmative action is not unlawful discrimination, as provided, for instance, in the form of 'special measures' under Article 1(4) of the International Convention on the Elimination of All Forms of Racial Discrimination (ICERD):

> Special measures taken for the sole purpose of securing adequate advancement of certain racial or ethnic groups or individuals requiring such protection as may be necessary in order to ensure such groups or individuals equal enjoyment or exercise of human rights and fundamental freedoms shall not be deemed racial discrimination, provided, however, that such measures do not, as a consequence, lead to the maintenance of separate rights for

393 CESCR, Concluding Observations: Japan, E/C.12/1/Add.67 (24 September 2001), [17]; Austria, E/C.12/1994/20 (2–20 May 1994), [254].

394 CESCR, Concluding Observations: Kenya, E/C.12/KEN/CO/1 (1 December 2008), [17].

395 CESCR, Concluding Observations: Poland, E/C.12/1/Add.82 (19 December 2002), [39].

396 CESCR, Concluding Observations: Kenya, E/C.12/KEN/CO/1 (1 December 2008), [17].

397 CESCR, Concluding Observations: Senegal, E/C.12/1993/18 (5 January 1994), [6].

398 CESCR, Concluding Observations: Liechtenstein, E/C.12/LIE/CO/1 (9 June 2006), [14], [29] (the law addressed discrimination on the basis of race, colour, descent, nationality or ethnic origin).

399 Craven, *The ICESCR*, 243.

400 CESCR, Concluding Observations: Sri Lanka, E/C.12/1/Add.24 (16 June 1998), [11].

401 CESCR, Revised general guidelines regarding the form and contents of reports to be submitted by states parties under Articles 16 and 17 of the ICESCR, E/C.12/1991/1 (17 June 1991), 4. The simplified 2009 reporting guidelines make no mention of promotion.

different racial groups and that they shall not be continued after the objectives for which they were taken have been achieved.[402]

A similar provision in found in the CEDAW (Article 4). The CEDAW further requires states to take all appropriate measures to eliminate discrimination against women in 'the right to promotion' (Article 11(1)(c)). The ICERD provides for non-discrimination in various work rights (Article 5(e)(i)), but does not directly mention promotion. Most explicit is ILO Convention No. 169, which provides for 'special measures' for the 'promotion and advancement' of indigenous workers (Article 20(2)).

Support for the permissibility of affirmative action in promotion can be found in India's declaration concerning Article 7(c), which states that the provision 'shall be so applied as to be in conformity with the provisions of article 16(4) of the Constitution of India'. The constitutional provision ensures that 'special provision for the advancement of any socially and educationally backward classes of citizens or for the Scheduled Castes and the Scheduled Tribes' is not regarded as unlawful discrimination under the Constitution. The Indian statement may be properly understood as an interpretive declaration for the purposes of certainty, rather than as a disguised reservation signalling a belief that Article 7(c) would not otherwise permit special measures.

Article 7(d): Rest, Leisure, Reasonable Hours and Paid Holidays

Under Article 7(d), states recognize the right of everyone to the enjoyment of just and favourable conditions of work which ensure, in particular, '[r]est, leisure and reasonable limitation of working hours and periodic holidays with pay, as well as remuneration for public holidays'.

The provision is the culmination of a historical struggle by the labour movement since the mid-nineteenth century to reduce working hours and secure the iconic eight-hour day, in response to working hours of up to sixteen hours per day during early industrialization.[403] A ten-hour day was still common even in Europe until the First World War.[404] The Treaty of Versailles in 1919 recognized the urgent objective to establish a maximum working day of eight hours or a forty-eight-hour working week,[405] and influenced the formulation of the very first ILO instrument, Convention No. 1 on Hours of Work (Industry) 1919, discussed below.

As will be seen, the continuing historical changes in labour relations raise certain problems for prescriptive attempts to regulate working hours in particular. The maximum working hours fixed in ILO instruments, and which influence the

[402] See also the Council of Europe Framework Convention for the Protection of National Minorities (adopted 10 November 1994, ETS 57, entered into force 1 February 1998), Article 4(3).

[403] ILO, *Survey on standards on health and safety*, 2.

[404] ILO, *Survey on standards on health and safety*, 2.

[405] Treaty of Versailles 1919, Article 427.

interpretation of (the more flexibly worded) Article 7(d), are responses to the prevailing patterns of, or aspirations as to, work, family and social life at the time of their adoption. As the ILO itself has noted, changes in the workforce, economy and family raise legitimate questions about the ongoing relevance or legitimacy of certain aspects of the ILO standards, at least for some workers. There may be nothing inherent in the human condition which implies that, for instance, human dignity is infringed by a requirement to work in excess of forty (or forty-eight) hours per week, or some other particular number; such standards are imperfect attempts to express an important underlying ideal rather than definitive in themselves.

While the ILO instruments are more rigidly prescriptive, there is greater capacity for Article 7(d) to dynamically respond to such changes because of the flexibility in the concept of 'reasonable' hours of work. At the same time, the standard must be interpreted to maintain a sense of the minimum core of rights necessary to ensure the dignity of the worker and to preserve the freedom to pursue and enjoy life opportunities outside of work.

REST AND LEISURE

In the CESCR's monitoring of states, and in the relevant ILO instruments, the focus has been principally on hours of work and holidays, and less on independent requirements of rest and leisure. In one sense, rest and leisure are the natural consequences of limiting work hours and providing holidays; the latter is the means to achieve the ends of the former. The provision conflates the purpose of the right with the means of attaining it, which led to confusion in the drafting and lingering questions about the scope of obligations under Article 7(d). One commentator has even queried whether rest and leisure are 'sufficiently important' to qualify as a human right;[406] one's perspective may change if one is deprived of it.

During the drafting, some states thought that the reasonable limitation of hours and the provision of periodic holidays were sufficient and implied rest and leisure.[407] Uruguay argued to omit mention of rest and leisure for the different reason that it feared that planned economies 'might be paternalistic and take steps to regulate the leisure of workers instead of merely providing them with the means of making the best use of time they did not spend at work'.[408]

Others states were not so concerned,[409] although Chile somewhat proved Uruguay's point by insisting that 'workers ought to use their leisure in self-improvement rather than spend it in harmful idleness'.[410] Pakistan defended the right to leisure since without it 'men might have no time to think and might have no share in the intellectual heritage handed down to them'.[411] In this respect

406 Craven, *The ICESCR*, 226.

407 Craven, *The ICESCR*, 231.

408 UNGA Third Committee, A/C.3/SR.713 (17 December 1956), 161 (Uruguay).

409 UNGA Third Committee, A/C.3/SR.713 (17 December 1956), 162 (Venezuela); UNGA Third Committee, A/C.3/SR.715 (18 December 1956), 169 (Italy).

410 UNGA Third Committee, A/C.3/SR.714 (18 December 1956), 171 (Chile).

411 UNGA Third Committee, A/C.3/SR.713 (17 December 1956), 160 (Pakistan).

there is a connection with rights to education and culture elsewhere in the ICESCR. There was majority support for the phrase.[412]

It is clear that rest and leisure are partly achieved and/or subsumed by the limitation of working hours and the provision of holidays. They are not, however, thereby deprived of any autonomous content. First, in ILO and regional practice at least, as discussed below, holidays are characterized not only as the right of the worker, but as involving a quasi-duty on the worker to take them. Thus, paid holidays may not be waived by a worker, and states may also restrict workers from undertaking activities incompatible with holidays (such as other work when on holiday from a principal occupation). While such approach is somewhat paternalistic—a 'duty to relax', even if at odds with the worker's autonomy to choose more work—it suggests that rest and leisure are values distinct from, and served by, the simple limitation of working hours or the provision of holidays.

Secondly, the right involves positive obligations on the state to facilitate rest and leisure, for instance by providing opportunities through basic public recreational facilities (including parks, sports fields, swimming pools, enabling cultural activities and so on). During the drafting, for example, Chile noted that some governments provided 'sports fields, clubs and other recreational facilities',[413] while Bulgaria observed that '[r]estaurants, rest-homes and other facilities' were provided by it or trade unions.[414] Such opportunities may be particularly important for disadvantaged groups who may not be able to privately fund the kinds of recreational activities available to the wealthy.

Thirdly, the right to rest and leisure may also demand the imposition of direct obligations on employers in specific contexts. For example, certain workplaces are located in remote areas, such as mining operations in the desert, construction camps in the mountains, logging operations in forests, oil platforms at sea and merchant shipping on the high seas. In such circumstances, workers are often forced to live on worksites for protracted periods, and may not easily or affordably be able to leave work for recreational or family activities. It may thus be necessary for employers to provide rest and leisure opportunities on-site (as is common, for instance, in mining camps, from televisions to sports fields), or to provide periodic free or subsidized transport to distant cities or towns to enable recreational activities or family reunion.

REASONABLE LIMITATION OF WORKING HOURS

During the drafting, some states thought the reference to 'reasonable' hours of work to be too vague, susceptible to discretion, too difficult to enforce in certain sectors or too disruptive of the freedom of trade unions to negotiate conditions.[415] In seeking to give content to the phrase, the ILO representative referred to Convention

[412] UNGA Third Committee, A/3525 (9 February 1957), 17.
[413] UNGA Third Committee, A/C.3/SR.713 (17 December 1956), 159.
[414] UNGA Third Committee, A/C.3/SR.716 (19 December 1956), 178 (Bulgaria).
[415] Craven, *The ICESCR*, 231.

No. 47 on the Forty-Hour Week 1935, which was scheduled to come into force in 1957.[416] As noted earlier, the concept of reasonable hours entails a certain flexibility to accommodate dynamic changes in the labour market and variability across sectors and types of work, but also demands a minimum core content so as to ensure that all workers enjoy dignity and protection from unduly burdensome work hours.

The CESCR has thus far not set out any detailed interpretation of reasonable hours under Article 7(d). In monitoring states, it has criticized excessive working hours,[417] such as over eight hours a day,[418] up to twelve hours a day[419] or a fifty-four-hour week.[420] The CESCR has also criticized overtime work without pay.[421] It observed that the private sector may be less likely to conform to legal limits on the working day and weekly rest,[422] and highlighted that certain workers are at particular risk of excessive hours, such as domestic workers,[423] prostitutes at risk of employer retaliation[424] or workers in special trading zones.[425] The CESCR has recommended that states take measures to reduce working hours in all sectors;[426] investigate allegations of excessive working hours;[427] review overtime pay rates[428] and paid weekly rest time;[429] and withdraw reservations to Article 7(d).[430]

Relevant ILO instruments can provide further guidance. In accordance with such practice, the 'reasonable limitation' of working hours can be understood to regulate both the maximum duration of daily work, but also the spacing of work during the week and the intervals of rest in between. The starting point is Convention No. 1 on Hours of Work (Industry), and Convention No. 30 on Hours of Work (Commerce and Offices) 1930, both of which establish the general maximums of the eight-hour work day and forty-eight-hour work week.[431]

416 UNGA Third Committee, A/C.3/SR.714 (18 December 1956), 164 (ILO).

417 CESCR, Concluding Observations: Cyprus, E/C.12/1/Add.28 (4 December 1998), [13]; Japan, E/C.12/1/Add.67 (24 September 2001), [19]; Kuwait, E/C.12/1/Add.98 (7 June 2004), [17]; China (including HK, Macao), E/C.12/1/Add.107 (13 May 2005), [24].

418 CESCR, Concluding Observations: Costa Rica, E/C.12/CRI/CO/4 (4 January 2008), [18].

419 CESCR, Concluding Observations: Paraguay, E/C.12/PRY/CO/3 (4 January 2008), [15].

420 Craven, *The ICESCR*, 245.

421 CESCR, Concluding Observations: Paraguay, E/C.12/PRY/CO/3 (4 January 2008), [15].

422 CESCR, Concluding Observations: Austria, E/C.12/1994/20 (2–20 May 1994), [255].

423 CESCR, Concluding Observations: Cyprus, E/C.12/1/Add.28 (4 December 1998), [13]; Bolivia, E/C.12/1/Add.60 (21 May 2001), [16]; Kuwait, E/C.12/1/Add.98 (7 June 2004), [17]; Costa Rica, E/C.12/CRI/CO/4 (4 January 2008), [18]; Paraguay, E/C.12/PRY/CO/3 (4 January 2008), [15].

424 CESCR, Concluding Observations: Cyprus, E/C.12/1/Add.28 (4 December 1998), [13].

425 CESCR, Concluding Observations: Mauritius, E/C.12/1994/8 (31 May 1994), [9]; Kenya, E/C.12/KEN/CO/1 (1 December 2008), [17].

426 CESCR, Concluding Observations: Japan, E/C.12/1/Add.67 (24 September 2001), [46].

427 CESCR, Concluding Observations: Poland, E/C.12/POL/CO/5 (2 December 2009), [18].

428 CESCR, Concluding Observations: UK (Hong Kong), E/C.12/1/Add.10 (6 December 1996), [38].

429 CESCR, Concluding Observations: China: Hong Kong SAR, E/C.12/1/Add.58 (21 May 2001), [34].

430 CESCR, Concluding Observations: Sweden, E/C.12/1/Add.70 (30 November 2001), [32].

431 ILO Conventions No. 1 Limiting the Hours of Work in Industrial Undertakings to Eight in the Day and Forty-eight in the Week (adopted 28 November 1919, entered into force 13 June 1921) ('Convention No. 1'), Article 2; No. 30 concerning the Regulation of Hours of Work in Commerce and Offices (adopted 28 June 1930, entered into force 29 August 1933) ('Convention No. 30'), Article 3. See also ILO Convention No. 153 concerning Hours of Work and Rest Periods in Road Transport (adopted 27 June 1979, entered into force 10 February 1983).

Convention No. 47 on the Forty-Hour Week 1935 establishes the more generous principle of a forty-hour week, 'applied in such a manner that the standard of living is not reduced in consequence'.[432] 'Hours of work' means 'the time during which the persons employed are at the disposal of the employer; it does not include rest periods during which the persons employed are not at the disposal of the employer'.[433]

While these instruments have attracted modest ratifications,[434] and apply only to particular work sectors[435] and exclude certain workers,[436] their basic principles are reflected in wider state practice. An ILO survey in 2005 found that the forty-eight-hour week limit is applied in sixty-one states and lower limits in 107 states, with a trend towards decreased hours in about a quarter of states over the past two decades.[437] This suggests that 'reasonable' hours under Article 7(d) of the ICESCR should normally be no more than forty hours per week, and certainly no more than forty-eight hours per week.

The ILO instruments are not merely intended to set hourly limits excess of which triggers liability to pay overtime. Rather, such instruments share in the ICESCR's human rights purpose by establishing maximum limits on work 'to provide against undue fatigue, or ensure reasonable leisure and opportunities for recreation and social life'.[438] To that end they are not merely aspirational standards, but require states to enforce the standards through measures such as notification of work hours and rest intervals, record-keeping of hours of work, and ultimately the application of criminal penalties for breaches.[439]

The concepts of an eight-hour day and forty-eight- (or forty-) hour week are, however, deceptively simple. Within the maximum limits on hours, the ILO conventions allow flexibility to accommodate different types of work, the needs of employers and workers, and exceptional circumstances. Thus, under Convention No. 1, a maximum nine-hour day is permissible if hours are correspondingly reduced on another day of the week (Article 2(b)); under Convention No. 30,

[432] ILO Convention No. 47 concerning the Reduction of Hours of Work to Forty a Week (adopted 22 June 1935, entered into force 23 June 1957) ('Convention No. 47'), Article 1. See also ILO Recommendation No. 116 on Reduction of Hours of Work 1962.

[433] ILO Convention No. 30, Article 2. On the difficulties in characterizing 'on call' or 'stand by' requirements on workers, see ILO, *Survey on standards on health and safety*, 18–19.

[434] ILO Convention No. 1 has fifty-two parties; ILO Convention No. 30 has thirty parties; ILO Convention No. 47 has fifteen parties.

[435] ILO Convention No. 1 applies to 'industry', which includes, inter alia, mining, manufacturing, energy, utilities and some transport: Article 1. ILO Convention No. 30 applies to commerce and office work. Workers not covered by either Convention include, for example, those in agriculture, maritime or inland navigation, fisheries and domestic service: ILO, *Survey on standards on health and safety*, 5.

[436] ILO Convention No. 1 does not apply to family members employed in family business; supervisors and managers; or persons employed in a confidential capacity: Article 2. ILO Convention No. 30 does not apply to workers in health care, hospitality, entertainment, family business, public administration, management, travellers and representatives, or those employed in confidence: Article 1(2)–(3). Convention No. 1 also recognizes special regimes for certain states, such as a sixty-hour week in (then) British India (Article 10) and up to sixty hours in certain industries in Japan (Article 9).

[437] ILO, *Survey on standards on health and safety*, 22.

[438] ILO, *Survey on standards on health and safety*, 4.

[439] ILO Convention No. 1, Article 8; Convention No. 30, Articles 11–12.

a ten-hour day is permissible in the same circumstances (Article 4). Further, in exceptional cases, hours of work may be distributed over a period longer than a week, provided that the average hours per week do not exceed forty-eight hours[440] and that no more than ten hours are worked per day.[441] Averaging is also permitted for shift work.[442] Additional ILO instruments address the schedules and protection of night workers, including women.[443]

Both Convention Nos. 1 and 30 also allow states to declare permanent or temporary exceptions to the general rules. Temporary exceptions are permitted to deal with exceptional work pressure,[444] or in case of accident, force majeure, urgent work, to prevent loss of perishable goods, to avoid endangering technical results, or for special work (such as stocktaking and preparing balance sheets, settlement days, liquidations, and accounting).[445] Permanent exceptions are permitted for intermittent workers (such as caretakers) and preparatory or complementary work,[446] or for shops and other establishments where the nature of the work, the size of the population or the number of workers render the normal limits inapplicable.[447] Workers and employers' organizations must be consulted in advance,[448] and overtime must be paid at a rate of at least one and one-quarter times the regular rate.[449] Problematically, the exceptions are not subject to any maximum limits on the additional hours worked, although the ILO has suggested states must consider the object of the conventions and take into account the consequences of fatigue on workers and the public.[450]

Finally, the ILO instruments also permit hours in excess of the normal limits to be worked in case of certain emergencies, such as (under Convention No. 1) accident, urgent repair work or force majeure, 'but only so far as may be necessary to avoid serious interference with the ordinary working of the undertaking'.[451] Convention No. 30 takes a stricter approach, allowing increased work hours to make up for hours lost to local holidays or accidents or force majeure,[452] but only as long as hours are not: increased by more than one additional hour per day, beyond ten hours per day, imposed on more than thirty days per year, and

[440] ILO Convention No. 1, Article 5; Convention No. 30, Article 6.

[441] ILO Convention No. 30, Article 6.

[442] ILO Convention No. 1, Articles 2(c) and 4 (hours worked may be averaged over a three-week period so as not to exceed the eight-hour-day and forty-eight-hour week limits overall, and subject to a maximum of fifty-six hours in any week).

[443] ILO Convention No. 89 concerning Night Work of Women Employed in Industry (Revised) (adopted 9 July 1948, entered into force 27 February 1951); ILO Convention No. 171 concerning Night Work (adopted 26 June 1990, entered into force 4 January 1995) (eleven ratifications); ILO Recommendation No. 178 on Night Work 1990.

[444] ILO Convention No. 1, Article 6(1)(b); Convention No. 30, Article 7(2)(d).

[445] ILO Convention No. 30, Article 7(2)(a)–(c).

[446] ILO Convention No. 1, Article 6(a); Convention No. 30, Article 7(1)(a)–(b).

[447] ILO Convention No. 30, Article 7(1)(c).

[448] ILO Convention No. 1, Article 6(2); Convention No. 30, Article 8.

[449] ILO Convention No. 1, Article 6(2); Convention No. 30, Article 7(4).

[450] ILO, *Survey on standards on health and safety*, 61.

[451] ILO Convention No. 1, Article 3.

[452] Defined as 'accidents to plant, interruption of power, light, heating or water, or occurrences causing serious material damage to the establishments': ILO Convention No. 30, Article 5(1).

imposed after an unreasonable lapse of time.[453] On the other hand, conventions may be suspended in 'war or other emergency endangering national safety'[454] (but not, for example, mere economic crisis). The general limitations provision in Article 4 of the ICESCR is capable of accommodating the above limitations to the extent that any measures taken are necessary and proportionate.

The obligation in Article 7(d) concerning reasonable limitation of work hours is subject to the ordinary principle of progressive realization in Article 2 of the ICESCR. However, there is widespread state practice broadly consistent with the standard of a maximum forty-eight-hour week, suggesting that this outer limit should be regarded as a minimum core obligation of states that is of immediate application.

This view is supported by ILO Recommendation No. 116 on Reduction of Hours of Work, which encourages states to adopt a national policy to progressively achieve a forty-hour week (paragraph 1). Paragraph 5 of the Recommendation provides that where the working week presently exceeds forty-eight hours, 'immediate steps should be taken to bring it down' to that level. By contrast, where the working week is forty-eight hours or less, the Recommendation provides for the 'progressive reduction' of work hours to ultimately reach forty hours (paragraph 6). Such measures should take into account economic considerations (paragraph 7) as follows:

> (a) the level of economic development attained and the extent to which the country is in a position to bring about a reduction in hours of work without reducing total production or productivity, endangering its economic growth, the development of new industries or its competitive position in international trade, and without creating inflationary pressures which would ultimately reduce the real income of the workers;
>
> (b) the progress achieved and which it is possible to achieve in raising productivity by the application of modern technology, automation and management techniques;
>
> (c) the need in the case of countries still in the process of development for improving the standards of living of their peoples; and
>
> (d) the preferences of employers' and workers' organisations in the different branches of activity concerned as to the manner in which the reduction in working hours might be brought about.

Progressive reductions may proceed in temporal phases or by branch or sector, or both (paragraph 8). Priority should be given to 'industries and occupations which involve a particularly heavy physical or mental strain or health risks for the workers concerned, particularly where these consist mainly of women and young persons' (paragraph 9).

Progressive realization in this area is also acknowledged in regional law. Article 2(4) of the Revised European Social Charter 1996 (and similarly Article 2(1) of the original European Social Charter 1961) requires states 'to provide for reasonable

[453] ILO Convention No. 30, Article 5(1).
[454] ILO Convention No. 1, Article 14; Convention No. 30, Article 9.

daily and weekly working hours, the working week to be progressively reduced to the extent that the increase of productivity and other relevant factors permit'. For that reason, the European Committee on Social Rights has refused to set an 'absolute' standard for 'reasonable' working hours, which varies 'from place to place and from time to time, depending on productivity and other factors'.[455] It has allowed, for example, the averaging of work hours over periods as long as six months in ordinary cases, and up to a maximum of one year in exceptional circumstances.[456]

Instead of stipulating a fixed number of daily or weekly work hours, the European Committee on Social Rights examines a range of factors to assess conformity with Article 2(4), in the light of the underlying purpose of the provision to protect workers' health and safety, and their private and family life.[457] States must make legal provision for reasonable daily and weekly working hours (including to regulate minimum requirements for collective agreements where necessary, and to regulate labour flexibility measures); laws must not be too general; and laws must be adequately enforced (such as through labour inspection).[458]

Further, the ECSR considers the nature of the work and risks to workers' safety and health (particularly from prolonged working periods);[459] the nature and extent of an employer's right to require overtime; and economic matters such as the level of unemployment. Where labour flexibility measures are at issue, the ECSR is attentive to the effects of workers being part-time, 'on call'[460] or working discontinuous hours; and has demanded more safeguards in collective agreements.[461] The ECSR has also been concerned that limiting hours may cause workers to do overtime or seek a second job, rendering 'futile' the intended protection unless measures are taken to offset the adverse effects.[462] The ESCR has also rather cryptically suggested that 'the current tendency for the 5-day, 40-hour week to become general is already giving rise to new social problems, such as those of the use of leisure time'.[463]

The European approach is more dynamic than the prescriptive ILO approach to daily and weekly work hours. In reviewing the key ILO instruments in 2005, the ILO itself recognized that Convention Nos. 1 and 30 are perhaps too rigid to accommodate contemporary demands for more flexible work.[464] In many states,

[455] ECSR, Statement of Interpretation: Article 2 (31 May 1969); see also ECSR, Statement of Interpretation: Article 2 (30 November 1998).

[456] ECSR, Statement of Interpretation: Article 2 (30 November 1998).

[457] ECSR, Statement of Interpretation: Article 2 (30 November 1998).

[458] ECSR, Statement of Interpretation: Article 2 (30 November 1998).

[459] ECSR, Statement of Interpretation: Article 2 (30 November 1998).

[460] See, eg, *Confédération français de l'Encadrement v France*, ECSR Complaint No. 16/2003 (12 October 2004) and *Confédération générale du travail v France*, ECSR Complaint No. 22/2003 (7 December 2004) ('on call' legislative provisions violated the Charter's reasonable work and rest hours safeguards).

[461] ECSR, Statement of Interpretation: Article 2 (30 November 1998).

[462] ECSR, Statement of Interpretation: Article 2 (30 November 1975).

[463] ECSR, Statement of Interpretation: Article 2 (31 May 1969).

[464] ILO, *General Survey of the reports concerning the Hours of Work (Industry) Convention, 1919 (No. 1), and the Hours of Work (Commerce and Offices) Convention, 1930 (No. 30)* ('*Survey on hours of work*'), International Labour Conference (93rd session) Report III (Part 1B) (Geneva, 2005), 98.

work is no longer organized on a regular daily, weekly or annual basis, as a result of various factors: the diversification, decentralization and individualization of work hours; the multiplicity of different types of work; globalization, competition and productivity considerations; and concerns about family responsibilities, gender equality, and worker choice and control over their working hours.[465] There are also substantial differences in the stage of development of developing and developed states.

For its part, the ILO believes that 'it remains important and relevant, to provide for minimum standards of working hours' because 'the "human rights" dimension of the limitation of hours of work transcends existing distinctions between working-time patterns in the various sectors of economic activity and between the various categories of workers'.[466] At the same time, it acknowledges that 'the changes that have taken place since these two instruments were adopted, warrant their revision'.[467]

The ILO has accordingly suggested to states that it is desirable to consolidate in a single comprehensive instrument the standards on working hours, weekly rest and annual leave without pay, which are currently spread across different instruments from different times. It argues further that more flexibility in working hours and periods may be needed, as well as the co-regulation of work hours and rest periods, in order to address the increased use of 'part-time work, compressed work weeks, staggered hours, variable daily shift lengths, annualized working hours, flexitime and on-call work'.[468] At the same time, gaps also need to be filled, such as by confining the scope of some of the broad exceptions in the current instruments.

WEEKLY REST

A further aspect of the 'reasonable limitation' of working hours under Article 7(d) of the ICESCR, and the connected requirement of rest and leisure, is the provision of weekly rest intervals between periods of work. As noted earlier, the CESCR has occasionally mentioned the need for weekly rest periods, without elaborating further. Reference may be made to ILO standards. Convention No. 14 on Weekly Rest (Industry) 1921 and Convention No. 106 on Weekly Rest (Commerce and Offices) 1957 establish the general rule that workers shall enjoy a rest period of at least twenty-four consecutive hours every seven days.[469]

Wherever possible, the period of rest should be granted simultaneously to the whole staff of the employer and coincide with the days already established by the traditions or customs of the country or district[470] (and the traditions and customs

[465] ILO, *Survey on hours of work*, 8–9, 12.

[466] ILO, *Survey on hours of work*, 105, 106.

[467] ILO, *Survey on hours of work*, 105.

[468] ILO, *Survey on hours of work*, 107.

[469] ILO Convention No. 14 concerning the Application of the Weekly Rest in Industrial Undertakings (adopted 17 November 1921, entered into force 19 June 1923) ('Convention No. 14'), Article 2; ILO Convention No. 106 concerning Weekly Rest in Commerce and Offices (adopted 26 June 1957, entered into force 4 March 1959) ('Convention No. 106'), Article 6.

[470] ILO Convention No. 14, Article 2; Convention No. 106, Article 6.

of religious minorities shall be respected where possible[471]). The latter requirement indicates that weekly rest is important not only to the physical well-being of the worker, but also to her or his social life and cultural identity. Rest periods must also be duly notified to workers.[472] Convention No. 106 also requires labour inspections and penalties to enforce its provisions.[473] In the manner typical of many ILO instruments, certain restrictions or exceptions may be applied.[474]

The ILO instruments have achieved significant levels of ratification.[475] A weekly rest period is also recognized in regional law. Under Article 2(1) of the Revised European Social Charter 1996,[476] states must 'ensure a weekly rest period which shall, as far as possible, coincide with the day recognised by tradition or custom in the country or region concerned as a day of rest'. According to the European Committee on Social Rights, the traditional day of rest in Europe is Sunday, but it may be taken on a different day 'where the type of activity so requires or for reasons of an economic nature'.[477] A weekly rest day may be postponed as long as two days' rest are provided after a (maximum) twelve consecutive work days.[478] However, workers have no right to waive their weekly rest periods,[479] such are their importance to a worker's well-being.

PERIODIC HOLIDAYS WITH PAY

In addition to limiting the duration and periodization of 'reasonable' work hours, Article 7(d) separately requires 'periodic holidays with pay', without defining their frequency or duration or any associated procedural matters. The CESCR has not given much attention to paid holidays, aside from occasionally criticizing inadequate pay for rest periods[480] or vacations.[481]

During the drafting, Uruguay proposed changing the phrase 'periodic holidays with pay' to 'annual holidays with pay'.[482] However, other states were concerned that this would unduly restrict workers' rights to take holidays at more frequent intervals.[483] The ILO noted that under (then and non-binding) ILO standards, paid holidays should be available for a few days at a time at various periods during the year.[484] In response, Uruguay clarified its intention that workers should be given

[471] ILO Convention No. 106, Article 6(4).
[472] ILO Convention No. 14, Article 7.
[473] ILO Convention No. 106, Article 10.
[474] See, eg, ILO Convention No. 14, Articles 3–6; Convention No. 106, Articles 5 and 7–8.
[475] There are 119 parties to Convention No. 14 and sixty-three parties to ILO Convention No. 106.
[476] Also similarly under Article 2(5) of the European Social Charter.
[477] ECSR, Statement of Interpretation: Article 2 (30 November 1998).
[478] ECSR, Statement of Interpretation: Article 2 (30 November 1998).
[479] ECSR, Statements of Interpretation: Article 2 (31 May 1969) and (30 November 1998).
[480] CESCR, Concluding Observations: Costa Rica, E/C.12/CRI/CO/4 (4 January 2008), [18]; United Kingdom of Great Britain and Northern Ireland (Hong Kong), E/C.12/1/Add.10 (6 December 1996), [21]; China (Hong Kong SAR), E/C.12/1/Add.58 (21 May 2001), [34].
[481] CESCR, Concluding Observations: Costa Rica, E/C.12/CRI/CO/4 (4 January 2008), [18].
[482] UNGA Third Committee, A/3525 (9 February 1957), 10.
[483] UNGA Third Committee, A/C.3/SR.713 (17 December 1956), 160 (Egypt).
[484] UNGA Third Committee, A/C.3/SR.714 (17 December 1956), 164 (ILO) (citing ILO Recommendation No. 98 on Holidays with Pay 1954).

consecutive holidays of not less than two weeks' duration at least once a year,[485] and the suggestion was not opposed, although its amendment referring to 'annual holidays' was withdrawn.[486]

Subsequent to the adoption of the ICESCR, ILO Convention No. 132 on Holidays with Pay 1970[487] establishes a general rule that 'all employed persons'[488] are entitled to a paid annual holiday of at least 'three working weeks for one year of service' (Article 3),[489] paid at the worker's 'normal or average remuneration' and in advance of the holiday (Article 7). While the Convention only has thirty-six ratifications, it is indicative of standard development in this area.

While the holiday may be divided into parts, there must normally be a consecutive period of 'at least two uninterrupted working weeks' taken in each work year (Articles 8 to 9), at times fixed by the employer in consultation with the worker (or by law or collective agreement), taking into account work requirements and opportunities for rest and relaxation (Article 10). Public holidays or sick leave periods are not to be counted as part of annual holidays (Article 6). Accrued holidays must be paid out on termination of employment (Article 11).

The importance of paid annual holidays is such that the right cannot be waived (Article 12) and states may regulate workers who engage 'in a gainful activity conflicting with the purpose of the holiday' (Article 13). Effective measures must be taken to implement and enforce the Convention as a whole, such as by inspection or other means (Article 14). It may also be noted that part-time workers are entitled to enjoy equivalent conditions of paid annual leave (and paid public holidays) under Convention No. 175 on Part-Time Work 1994.[490]

Higher protection is found in certain regional law. Article 2(3) of the Revised European Social Charter provides for 'a minimum of four weeks' annual holiday with pay'. The ECSR has interpreted that provision to require 'at least two weeks uninterrupted annual holidays during the year the holidays were due', while '[a]nnual holidays exceeding two weeks may be postponed in particular circumstances defined by domestic law, the nature of which should justify the postponement'.[491] Annual holidays are considered so fundamentally important by the ECSR that they cannot be waived even if compensation is offered:

> ... the Committee interpreted the provisions of this paragraph as laying down the principle that workers must not be able to waive their right to annual holidays, even in consideration of an extra payment by the employer. The Committee considered that the need to protect the workers as fully as possible made such a waiver incompatible with the Charter, even with the free consent of the workers concerned. The Committee recognised, however, that

[485] UNGA Third Committee, A/C.3/SR.716 (19 December 1956), 177 (Uruguay); see also Craven, *The ICESCR*, 245.

[486] UNGA Third Committee, A/3525 (9 February 1957), 10.

[487] See earlier ILO Recommendation No. 98 on Holidays with Pay 1954.

[488] Except seafarers, and subject to limited restrictions in special cases: Article 2.

[489] Paid holidays of a proportionate duration for a shorter length of service (Article 4 permits paid holidays apportioned to a shorter length of service). Article 5 permits minimum qualifying periods.

[490] Article 7. See also ILO Recommendation No. 182 on Part-Time Work 1994.

[491] ECSR, Statement of Interpretation: Article 2 (31 October 2007).

this principle does not prevent the payment of a lump sum to an employee at the end of his employment in compensation for the paid holiday to which he was entitled but which he had not taken.[492]

Annual holidays also cannot be discounted by periods of illness or injury occurring during the same period.[493] Certain conditions are, however, permissible, such as the expiration of a twelve-month qualifying working period before holidays may be taken.[494]

REMUNERATION FOR PUBLIC HOLIDAYS

During the drafting, Spain proposed 'remuneration for public holidays' in the belief that the right to 'periodic holidays with pay' did not extend to public holidays, since 'workers who were paid by the hour or the day did not receive pay for their weekly day or rest or for days declared public holidays by the State'.[495] Thus, Spain argued that 'men who worked hard all week were expected to go hungry on days of enforced leisure'.[496] While some states thought the amendment unnecessary,[497] or privileged paid public holidays over other considerations,[498] it was adopted by a large majority, albeit with numerous abstentions.[499]

The CESCR has seldom addressed the provision or duration of paid public holidays in monitoring states and there is no ILO convention on paid public holidays.[500] The CESCR did criticize Sweden's reservation to remunerated public holidays.[501] The same criticism is apposite to Japan's similar reservation to Article 7(d). A Danish reservation made upon ratification was later withdrawn.[502] The CESCR's position indicates that it considers paid public holidays as significant to the object and purpose of the ICESCR.

All work cannot and does not stop on public holidays, particularly in essential services and utilities, but also with the liberalization of commercial trading hours in many states, sometimes linked to a decline in the importance of universal religious holidays. Article 2(2) of the Revised European Social Charter (and the same provision of the original European Social Charter) provides for 'public holidays with pay'. The European Committee on Social Rights has interpreted that right to require at least double pay, or time off of double the days worked, for work done on public holidays:

492 ECSR, Statement of Interpretation: Article 2 (31 May 1969); see also ECSR, Statement of Interpretation: Article 2 (30 November 1992).

493 ECSR, Statement of Interpretation: Article 2 (30 November 1992).

494 ECSR, Statement of Interpretation: Article 2 (31 May 1969).

495 UNGA Third Committee, A/C.3/SR.714 (17 December 1956), 164 (Spain).

496 UNGA Third Committee, A/C.3/SR.714 (17 December 1956), 164 (Spain).

497 UNGA Third Committee, A/C.3/SR.715 (18 December 1956), 170 (UK), 173 (Indonesia).

498 Craven, *The ICESCR*, 231–2.

499 By twenty-two votes to eight, with twenty-nine abstentions.

500 Craven, *The ICESCR*, 244.

501 CESCR, Concluding Observations: Sweden, E/C.12/1/Add.70 (30 November 2001), [21].

502 Denmark, Notification to the UN Secretary-General, 14 January 1976: see Appendix II of this book.

The Committee considers that work performed on a public holiday requires a constraint on the part of the worker, who should be compensated with a higher remuneration than that usually paid. Accordingly, in addition to the paid public holiday, work carried out on that holiday must be paid at least double the usual wage. The remuneration may also be provided as compensatory time-off, in which case it should be at least double the days worked.[503]

That compensatory approach does not give workers a choice in whether or not they wish to work on public holidays. Article 7(d) provides workers with a right to 'remuneration for public holidays', but neither requires states to declare public holidays nor to guarantee workers a choice whether they wish to take such holidays or work and receive compensation in lieu. In practice, collective agreements or national law may address the ancillary issue as to whether workers enjoy any choice, or a certain degree of choice, in working on public holidays. The position in respect of paid public holidays may thus be different from that in relation to paid annual leave. The ECSR has found that the latter cannot be waived even by the worker, let alone overridden by an employer; whereas the former may be subject to an employer's needs and/or the waiver of time off by the worker, as long as due compensation is provided.

[503] ECSR, Statement of Interpretation: Article 2(2) (22 October 2010).

10

Article 8: Trade Union-Related Rights

Article 8

1. The States Parties to the present Covenant undertake to ensure:

(a) The right of everyone to form trade unions and join the trade union of his choice, subject only to the rules of the organization concerned, for the promotion and protection of his economic and social interests. No restrictions may be placed on the exercise of this right other than those prescribed by law and which are necessary in a democratic society in the interests of national security or public order or for the protection of the rights and freedoms of others;

(b) The right of trade unions to establish national federations or confederations and the right of the latter to form or join international trade-union organizations;

(c) The right of trade unions to function freely subject to no limitations other than those prescribed by law and which are necessary in a democratic society in the interests of national security or public order or for the protection of the rights and freedoms of others;

(d) The right to strike, provided that it is exercised in conformity with the laws of the particular country.

2. This article shall not prevent the imposition of lawful restrictions on the exercise of these rights by members of the armed forces or of the police or of the administration of the State.

3. Nothing in this article shall authorize States Parties to the International Labour Organisation Convention of 1948 concerning Freedom of Association and Protection of the Right to Organize to take legislative measures which would prejudice, or apply the law in such a manner as would prejudice, the guarantees provided for in that Convention.

Introduction: Drafting, Purpose, History

Trade union rights are both civil-political and socio-economic rights.[1] In drafting Article 8, states were aware that the rights to form and join a trade union were simply '[o]ne aspect of the freedom of association' already guaranteed in Article 22 of the ICCPR,[2] and the same view is taken of trade unions in relation to freedom of association under Article 11 of the ECHR.[3] Article 22 of the ICCPR explicitly recognizes trade unions and precludes prejudice to ILO standards:

1. Everyone shall have the right to freedom of association with others, including the right to form and join trade unions for the protection of his interests.

2. No restrictions may be placed on the exercise of this right other than those which are prescribed by law and which are necessary in a democratic society in the interests of national security or public safety, public order (*ordre public*), the protection of public health or morals or the protection of the rights and freedoms of others. This Article shall not prevent the imposition of lawful restrictions on members of the armed forces and of the police in their exercise of this right.

3. Nothing in this article shall authorize States Parties to the International Labour Organisation Convention of 1948 concerning Freedom of Association and Protection of the Right to Organize to take legislative measures which would prejudice, or to apply the law in such a manner as to prejudice, the guarantees provided for in that Convention.

Some states were opposed to providing special ICESCR protection for trade unions over others forms of association.[4] Others thought trade unions worthy of separate treatment because they had 'very important economic and social consequences',[5] and also for fear that unions might be unduly restricted under the general ICCPR provision.[6] In subsequent practice, the Human Rights Committee (HRC) has interpreted aspects of Article 22 of the ICCPR more narrowly in relation to trade unionism than Article 8 of the ICESCR requires, such as by denying the existence of a right to strike on the basis that it is covered by the ICESCR.[7]

[1] Manfred Nowak, *UN Covenant on Civil and Political Rights: CCPR Commentary* (2nd edn, Clarendon, Oxford, 2005), 500–501.

[2] UNGA Third Committee, A/C.3/SR.721 (4 January 1957), 200 (Canada).

[3] *Sigurdur A Sigurjónsson v Iceland* ('*Sigurjónsson v Iceland*') (App. 16130/90), 30 June 1993, (1993) 16 EHRR 462, [32].

[4] Matthew Craven, *The International Covenant on Economic, Social and Cultural Rights: A Perspective on its Development* (Clarendon, Oxford, 1995), 250.

[5] UNGA Third Committee, A/C.3/SR.721 (4 January 1957), 200 (Canada).

[6] Craven, *The ICESCR*, 250.

[7] *JB v Canada*, HRC Communication No. 118/1982 (18 July 1986), discussed below in the context of the right to strike.

At the same time, the CESCR has sometimes referred to HRC findings in relation to the freedom of association of trade unions to inform its own assessment under the ICESCR.[8]

The original proposal for Article 8 in the Commission on Human Rights was limited to the right to form and join trade unions. Following a 'three power amendment' by Bolivia, Peru and Uruguay,[9] however, by the end of the drafting in the Third Committee the provision had expanded to guarantee a bundle of further rights. The right to strike and the right of trade unions to function freely, and various limitations on those rights, were thus recognized. The resulting provision is 'a hybrid of individual and collective rights',[10] protecting individuals in relation to trade unions, but also certain operational 'rights' of unions themselves.

During the drafting, Pakistan emphasized the importance of trade unionism, invoking Keynes to support the view that 'men could exert their influence only by joining forces with others',[11] since 'the worker, as an individual, was too weak economically to discuss working conditions with his employer on a footing of equality'.[12] Pakistan also discussed the problem whereby 'unassociated workers competed with one another' and so 'formed a kind of reserve on which management could call for cheap labour'.[13]

As was recognized throughout the drafting, trade unionism was 'a form of organization closely linked with other economic and political ideas',[14] including Marxist or socialist approaches to economic and social life. Many states emphasized the importance of trade unionism. The Soviet Union, for example, described it as 'a great victory for the workers of all countries',[15] and Peru considered it 'one of the most important factors in developing democracy and promoting social progress'.[16]

Historically, during industrialization, national law was often 'used as a tool to limit workers' rights to unionize', whether through the banning of labour organization through the common law doctrine of criminal conspiracy, statutory restrictions, economic torts or anti-trust law.[17] National struggles for the recognition of trade union rights gradually spilled over into the development of international standards. ILO norms on trade unions formed the immediate legal background to the drafting of Article 8.

[8] CESCR, Concluding Observations: Germany, E/C.12/1/Add.68 (24 September 2001), [22] (citing the opinions of the HRC and the ILO Committee of Experts on strikes by public servants such as judges and teachers).

[9] UNGA Third Committee, A/3525 (9 February 1957), 20, 26–9.

[10] Craven, *The ICESCR*, 249.

[11] UNGA Third Committee, A/C.3/SR.719 (3 January 1957), 190 (Pakistan).

[12] UNGA Third Committee, A/C.3/SR.719 (3 January 1957), 190 (Pakistan).

[13] UNGA Third Committee, A/C.3/SR.719 (3 January 1957), 190 (Pakistan).

[14] UNGA Third Committee, A/C.3/SR.720 (3 January 1957), 195 (Chile).

[15] UNGA Third Committee, A/C.3/SR.719 (3 January 1957), 192 (USSR).

[16] UNGA Third Committee, A/C.3/SR.719 (3 January 1957), 192 (Peru).

[17] *Health Services and Support—Facilities Subsector Bargaining Association v British Columbia* ('*Health Services* case'), 8 June 2007, [2007] SCC 27 (Supreme Court of Canada), [47]–[49], [56] (discussing the position in the United Kingdom, Canada and the United States).

The Declaration of Philadelphia 1944, part of the ILO Constitution, recognizes that 'freedom of expression and association are essential to sustained progress' and are part of the 'fundamental principles' on which the ILO is based. Article 8(3) of the ICESCR explicitly requires states parties not to prejudice their obligations under ILO Convention No. 87 concerning Freedom of Association and Protection of the Right to Organize 1948. That Convention sets out the right of workers and employers to establish and join organizations of their own choosing without previous authorization (Article 2); to organize and function freely (Article 3); to federate, confederate or internationally affiliate (Article 5); and to be protected against administrative dissolution or suspension (Article 4).

It was soon followed by ILO Convention No. 98 concerning the Right to Organise and Collective Bargaining 1949, which protects workers against anti-union discrimination (Article 1); protects workers' and employers' organizations from interference by each other (Article 2); and recognizes collective bargaining (Article 4). There are also related ILO instruments.[18] Because freedom of association is a 'fundamental' ILO constitutional principle, the ILO Committee on Freedom of Association can review complaints against ILO member states even if a state has not ratified relevant conventions, thus generating wider practice adhering to the ILO treaty norms. Trade union rights are now found in many national constitutions,[19] either as distinct rights or as part of freedom of association generally.

The linkage between ILO standards and Article 8 of the ICESCR is evident in the CESCR's monitoring of states. The CESCR has often expressly or implicitly invoked ILO standards in interpreting and applying Article 8. It has called on states to implement or respect ILO treaties to which they are already parties;[20] to respect specific norms or interpretive views advanced by the ILO and its supervisory bodies;[21] to follow the views or decisions of ILO bodies made previously in relation to the particular state in question;[22] and to ratify key instruments such

[18] ILO Recommendation No. 91 on Collective Agreements (29 June 1951).

[19] ILO, *Giving Globalization a Human Face*, ILC.101/III/1B (2012), 18.

[20] CESCR, Concluding Observations: Belarus, E/C.12/1/Add.78 (5 June 2002), [37]; Benin, E/C.12/1/Add.78 (5 June 2002), [35]; Croatia, E/C.12/1/Add.73 (5 December 2001), [30]; Estonia, E/C.12/1/Add.85 (19 December 2002), [39]; Guinea, E/C.12/1/Add.5 (28 May 1996), [16].

[21] CESCR, Concluding Observations: Azerbaijan, E/C.12/1/Add.104 (14 December 2004), [21] (on the ILO definition of 'essential services' during strikes); Azerbaijan, E/C.12/1/Add.20 (22 December 1997), [32] (referring to the opinion of the ILO Committee of Experts on strike limitations); Benin, E/C.12/1/Add.78 (5 June 2002), [35]; Japan, E/C.12/1/Add.67 (24 September 2001), [21]; Kazakhstan, E/C.12/KAZ/CO/1 (7 June 2010), [22]; Zambia, E/C.12/1/Add.106 (23 June 2005), [42] (on the ILO definition of 'essential services' in relation to strikes). See also CESCR, Concluding Observations: Guinea, E/C.12/1/Add.5 (28 May 1996), [16] (complaint before the ILO Committee on Freedom of Association concerning strikes by teachers and researchers); Germany, E/C.12/1/Add.68 (24 September 2001), [22] (referring to the opinion of the ILO Committee of Experts on strikes by public servants such as judges and teachers); Japan, E/C.12/1/Add.67 (24 September 2001), [21]; Morocco, E/C.12/1/Add.55 (1 December 2000), [22].

[22] CESCR, Concluding Observations: Bulgaria, E/C.12/1/Add.37 (8 December 1999), [16] (ILO Committee of Experts on strike limitations); Germany, E/C.12/1/Add.68 (24 September 2001), [22] (ILO Committee of Experts on strikes by public servants such as judges and teachers); Nigeria, E/C.12/1/Add.23 (16 June 1998), [15] (state dissolution of or interference in unions, including

as ILO Convention No. 87 or 98.[23] On many occasions, the CESCR has implicitly invoked concepts from ILO treaties or interpretive practice, without expressly referencing the ILO sources.[24] It has further indicated that a principle of 'tripartism', on which the ILO is based, is also set forth in Article 8 of the ICESCR.[25] Further, the CESCR has encouraged states to seek the technical cooperation facilities of the ILO, for example in reinforcing institutional capacity, establishing labour courts and revising legislation.[26]

In one sense, a specific human right to form and join a trade union is perhaps not as fundamental to human dignity as certain 'survival' rights under the ICESCR, such as rights to food, water, housing, health care or social security; nor is it as formative of life chances or personal identity as rights to education or culture. Trade union rights do, however, play an indispensible ancillary role in securing the right to work and conditions in work (under Articles 6 and 7 of the ICESCR) and ultimately in attaining an adequate standard of living (Article 11) and the protection of the family (Article 10), which are all basic to dignity. They also have an autonomous value in enabling worker participation in decision-making and workplace democracy, thus enhancing the worker's dignity.

To describe trade union rights as innate to human dignity, or as a universal feature of the human condition, is however ahistorical. Trade unions were rare until the onset of industrialization in the eighteenth century, and their growth was a response to the economic conditions of capitalist and socialist modernization. As rights they are thus contingent on the existence of particular modes of economic organization, which—unlike food, water, housing and so on—are not themselves an integral or universal part of human existence or experience.

Even today, trade union rights are scarcely relevant to large parts of the working population. They may matter little to the human dignity of corporate executives, bankers, small business owners or subsistence farmers outside the formal economy—let alone to the human population prior to industrialization. In quite a few developed states, trade union membership as a proportion of all

international associations, and refusal of ILO visits); Poland, E/C.12/1/Add.82 (18 December 2002), [44] (ILO Committee of Experts and restrictions on public servants); Republic of Korea, E/C.12/KOR/CO/3 (17 December 2009), [19] (ILO Committee of Experts and strikes by public servants); Syrian Arab Republic, E/C.12/1/Add.63 (24 September 2001), [21] (strike restrictions); Venezuela, E/C.12/1/Add.56 (21 May 2001), [25] (interference in a union-related referendum); Mauritius, E/C.12/1994/8 (31 May 1994), [10] (ILO Committee on Experts on essential services and strikes).

[23] CESCR, Concluding Observations: India, E/C.12/IND/CO/5 (8 August 2008), [63]; Kenya, E/C.12/KEN/CO/1 (1 December 2008), [19]; Mexico, E/C.12/MEX/CO/4 (9 June 2006), [34]; Morocco, E/C.12/1/Add.55 (1 December 2000), [41]; Morocco, E/C.12/MAR/CO/3 (4 September 2006), [45]; New Zealand, E/C.12/1993/13 (4 January 1994), [20]; Republic of Korea, E/C.12/KOR/CO/3 (17 December 2009), [20]; Tunisia, E/C.12/1/Add.36 (14 May 1999), [25]; Zimbabwe, E/C.12/1/Add.12 (20 May 1997), [11].

[24] Including rules in relation to the formation of unions, elections, membership, dissolution, the right to strike, restrictions, 'essential services', rights of public servants, collective bargaining, compulsory arbitration, anti-union violence, federation and international association, among others.

[25] CESCR, Consideration of Report Submitted by State Party: Afghanistan, E/1992/23 (1991), [93].

[26] CESCR, Concluding Observations: Cambodia, E/C.12/KHM/CO/1 (12 June 2009), [24].

workers is now quite low (less than 20 per cent);[27] many workers elect not to unionize, yet labour protection overall may still be high, despite shrinking union power. Trade union membership rarely rises above half of the working population in most countries, with the exception of Scandinavia and a few socialist states.[28]

Yet, even in highly advanced economies with low union membership rates, unions were historically vital in raising labour standards. Further, despite low membership, unions still often lead collective bargaining and labour campaigns which secure better work rights and conditions for all workers, including those who choose not to join unions but reap the benefits obtained by them. For example, union density was only 9 per cent among French workers in 1995, but collective bargaining covered 90 per cent of workers, and a similar relationship (albeit not so stark) is evident in quite a few European states.[29] However, the converse can also occur: in Chile, 33 per cent of workers were unionized, but collective bargaining covered less than 13 per cent of workers.[30]

In developing countries, where 'modernization' is still in progress, unions may be especially important in raising labour protection during the trajectory of development, whether on minimum wages, workplace safety or child labour. In such countries, low union membership is often not due to choice or because worker protection is already high, but because of unlawful barriers to union formation, membership and activities.

Relevant Regional Standards

Trade union rights are widely recognized in regional human rights systems, whether as civil rights or socio-economic rights or both. As in the ICCPR, Article 11 of the ECHR 1950 explicitly mentions trade unions in the context of the general freedom of association:

> 1. Everyone has the right to freedom of peaceful assembly and to freedom of association with others, including the right to form and to join trade unions for the protection of his interests.
>
> 2. No restrictions shall be placed on the exercise of these rights other than such as are prescribed by law and are necessary in a democratic society in the interests of national security or public safety, for the prevention of disorder or crime, for the protection of health

[27] Eg: Australia (17.1 per cent), New Zealand (17.2 per cent), Japan (15.5 per cent), United States (10.7 per cent), France (8 per cent), Germany (17.5 per cent), Spain (11.9 per cent), the Netherlands (17.7 per cent) (Susan Hayter and Valentina Stoevska, *Social Dialogue Indicators: International Statistical Inquiry 2008–09—Technical Brief* (ILO, Geneva, 2011), 12).

[28] Hayter and Stoevska, *Social Dialogue Indicators*, 11–12: Denmark (71.5 per cent), Finland (63.5 per cent), Norway (65.5 per cent), Sweden (65.8 per cent), Belgium (79.2 per cent), Belarus (90.5 per cent) and Cuba (70.6 per cent).

[29] See Greg Bamber and Peter Sheldon, 'Collective Bargaining: An International Analysis' in Roger Blanpain (ed), *Comparative Labour Law and Industrial Relations in Industrialized Market Economies* (Kluwer, Netherlands, 2007), 585, Table 1: 'Collective bargaining coverage, union density and trends in collective bargaining levels in selected IMEs'. Union density means the proportion of salary and wage earners who are union members. The collective bargaining figures refer to the formal sector only.

[30] Bamber and Sheldon, 'Collective Bargaining', 585, Table 1.

or morals or for the protection of the rights and freedoms of others. This article shall not prevent the imposition of lawful restrictions on the exercise of these rights by members of the armed forces, of the police or of the administration of the State.

The Revised European Social Charter 1996 (and before it the original European Social Charter 1961) expressly protects both the right to organize (Article 5) and a right to collectively bargain (Article 6):

Article 5—The right to organise

With a view to ensuring or promoting the freedom of workers and employers to form local, national or international organisations for the protection of their economic and social interests and to join those organisations, the Parties undertake that national law shall not be such as to impair, nor shall it be so applied as to impair, this freedom. The extent to which the guarantees provided for in this article shall apply to the police shall be determined by national laws or regulations. The principle governing the application to the members of the armed forces of these guarantees and the extent to which they shall apply to persons in this category shall equally be determined by national laws or regulations.

Article 6—The right to bargain collectively

With a view to ensuring the effective exercise of the right to bargain collectively, the Parties undertake:

1. to promote joint consultation between workers and employers;

2. to promote, where necessary and appropriate, machinery for voluntary negotiations between employers or employers' organisations and workers' organisations, with a view to the regulation of terms and conditions of employment by means of collective agreements;

3. to promote the establishment and use of appropriate machinery for conciliation and voluntary arbitration for the settlement of labour disputes;

and recognise:

4. the right of workers and employers to collective action in cases of conflicts of interest, including the right to strike, subject to obligations that might arise out of collective agreements previously entered into.

The CESCR has also noted that aspects of trade union rights, such as the right to strike, have also been considered by other European bodies such as the European Court of Justice,[31] in adjudicating on EU law. The Charter of Fundamental Rights of the Constitution for Europe 2004[32] recognizes a general freedom of association but includes the specific right to form and join trade unions (Article II-72(1)), as well as the 'solidarity' rights of workers to information and consultation at work (Article II-87) and collective bargaining and action, including strikes

[31] CESCR, Concluding Observations: Germany, E/C.12/1/Add.68 (24 September 2001), [22] (referring to the opinion of the ILO Committee of Experts on strikes by public servants such as judges and teachers).

[32] Treaty establishing a Constitution for Europe (adopted 29 October 2004, OJ C 310, Vol. 47, 16 December 2004, not yet in force).

(Article II-88). These rights are fairly cautiously expressed and are likely to have only a fairly limited impact on EU law.[33]

In the Americas, Article 16 of the American Convention on Human Rights 1969 protects freedom of association generally:

1. Everyone has the right to associate freely for ideological, religious, political, economic, labor, social, cultural, sports, or other purposes.

2. The exercise of this right shall be subject only to such restrictions established by law as may be necessary in a democratic society, in the interest of national security, public safety or public order, or to protect public health or morals or the rights and freedoms of others.

3. The provisions of this article do not bar the imposition of legal restrictions, including even deprivation of the exercise of the right of association, on members of the armed forces and the police.

Article 8 of the Protocol of San Salvador 1988, concerning economic, social and cultural rights, specifically recognizes trade union rights:

1. The States Parties shall ensure:

(a) The right of workers to organize trade unions and to join the union of their choice for the purpose of protecting and promoting their interests. As an extension of that right, the States Parties shall permit trade unions to establish national federations or confederations, or to affiliate with those that already exist, as well as to form international trade union organizations and to affiliate with that of their choice. The States Parties shall also permit trade unions, federations and confederations to function freely;

(b) The right to strike.

2. The exercise of the rights set forth above may be subject only to restrictions established by law, provided that such restrictions are characteristic of a democratic society and necessary for safeguarding public order or for protecting public health or morals or the rights and freedoms of others. Members of the armed forces and the police and of other essential public services shall be subject to limitations and restrictions established by law.

3. No one may be compelled to belong to a trade union.[34]

In Africa, Article 10 of the African Charter on Human and Peoples' Rights 1981 protects freedom of association generally:

1. Every individual shall have the right to free association provided that he abides by the law.

[33] Bernard Ryan, 'The Charter and Collective Labour Law' in Tamara Hervey and Jeff Kremer (eds), *Economic and Social Rights under the EU Charter of Fundamental Rights: A Legal Perspective* (Hart, Oxford, 2003), 67.

[34] Additional Protocol to the American Convention on Human Rights in the Area of Economic, Social and Cultural Rights (adopted 17 November 1988, OAS Treaty Series No. 69, entered into force 16 November 1999).

2. Subject to the obligation of solidarity provided for in 29 no one may be compelled to join an association.[35]

Most African cases arising under Article 10 have concerned political parties rather than trade unions,[36] and some union specific complaints were inadmissible.[37] However, as discussed below, trade unions and their members have often been incidentally protected in the application of civil rights, particularly the right to life, freedom from arbitrary detention and freedom of expression.

Mention should also be made of Article 15 of the African Charter (the right to work),[38] in relation to which the Guidelines for National Periodic Reports request states to report on 'the right to form and belong to free and independent trade unions':

In relation to trade union rights, governments should provide information in their Initial Report on:

- Principal laws, regulations, collective agreements and court decisions designed to promote, safeguard or regulate trade union rights
- Right to form or join unions, and restrictions placed on that right
- Right of trade unions to function freely, and restrictions placed on that right
- Right to strike, and restrictions placed on that right.[39]

Other African regional initiatives have also emphasized trade union rights,[40] including the African Charter for Popular Participation in Development and Transformation 1990, adopted by the Economic Commission for Africa.[41]

[35] African Charter on Human and Peoples' Rights (adopted 27 June 1981, OAU Doc. CAB/LEG/67/3 rev. 5, entered into force 21 October 1986) ('African Charter').

[36] See, eg, *Tanganyika Law Society, Legal and Human Rights Centre and Reverend Christopher Mtikila v Tanzania*, 14 June 2003 (African Court on Human and Peoples' Rights). See also the many decisions of the African Commission on Human and Peoples' Rights: eg, *Lawyers of Human Rights v Swaziland*, Communication No. 251/02, 2 July 2005. See also Kolawole Olaniyan, 'Civil and Political Rights in the African Charter: Articles 8–14' in Malcolm Evans and Rachel Murray (eds), *The African Charter on Human and Peoples' Rights: The System in Practice 1986–2006* (2nd edn, Cambridge University Press, Cambridge, 2010), 213, 226–9.

[37] *Kenya Human Rights Commission v Kenya*, African Commission Communication No. 135/94 (October 1995), (2000) AHRLR 133 (a complaint about a refusal to register a trade union formed by four public universities, and arrest and detention of national union leaders, was inadmissible due to failure to exhaust domestic remedies); *Union Nationale des Syndicats Autonomes du Senegal v Senegal* (2000) AHRLR 290 (arrest of union delegates).

[38] 'Every individual shall have the right to work under equitable and satisfactory conditions, and shall receive equal pay for equal work.'

[39] Reproduced in Rachel Murray and Malcolm Evans (eds), *Documents of the African Commission on Human and Peoples' Rights: Volume 2* (Hart, Oregon, 2009), 53, 55.

[40] Such as the Africa Leadership Forum, Kampala Document of the Conference on Security, Stability, Development and Cooperation in Africa (19–22 May 1991): '*Trade union rights*: In order to ensure industrial peace and harmony, which is a prerequisite for economic growth and development, all governments should respect trade union rights in accordance with ILO conventions and recommendations'.

[41] African Charter for Popular Participation in Development and Transformation 1990, [23G] (outlining the nature and roles of organized labour). Trade unions are also identified as an indicator of popular participation: [32(b)].

Nature and Scope of State Obligations under Article 8

Article 8(1) requires states to 'undertake to ensure' trade union rights. In a General Comment, the CESCR stated that Article 8 is 'capable of immediate application by judicial and other organs'.[42] In monitoring states, too, the CESCR has observed, for example, that a 'lack of material resources does not explain why there is only one trade union in the State party',[43] and that the right to strike is considered 'self-executing' according to 'the great majority of observers'.[44]

The term 'ensure' in Article 8 indicates that trade union rights are immediately applicable[45] and not subject to progressive realization. This approach is supported by the coterminous character of trade union rights as socio-economic and civil/political freedoms of association, the latter being immediately applicable under Article 22 of the ICCPR. In ILO practice, too, developmental considerations are not regarded as justifying a failure to ensure union rights, and to the contrary indicate the need for strong protection of the right to organize:

> Development needs should not justify maintaining the entire trade union movement of a country in an irregular legal situation, thereby preventing the workers from exercising their trade union rights, as well as preventing organizations from carrying out their normal activities. Balanced economic and social development requires the existence of strong and independent organizations which can participate in this process.[46]

Article 8 has minimal resource implications because it foremost imposes a negative obligation on the state not to interfere in (that is, a duty to *respect*) the formation and free functioning of trade unions (although, as already noted, contested economic arguments have been made that unionism impairs economic efficiency). However, like all human rights, Article 8 also has a positive dimension[47] and may be understood to impose three types or levels of obligations on states: the obligations to *respect, protect* and *fulfil*.[48]

In addition to the obligation to respect just mentioned, the obligation to *protect* requires states to take measures that prevent third parties from interfering with trade union rights. Private interference in unions may emanate from other unions or employers, employers' associations, political organizations, strike-breakers (colloquially known as 'scabs' or 'blacklegs'), and even violent or armed groups.

[42] CESCR, General Comment No. 3, HRI/GEN/1/Rev.9 (Vol. I) at 7 (14 December 1990), [5].

[43] CESCR, Consideration of Report Submitted by State Party: Rwanda, E/1989/22 (1989), [190].

[44] CESCR, Consideration of Report Submitted by State Party: Luxembourg, E/1991/23 (1990), [129].

[45] Craven, *The ICESCR*, 261.

[46] ILO, Freedom of Association: Digest of Decisions and Principles of the Freedom of Association Committee of the Governing Body of the ILO (5th rev. edn, Geneva, 2006), [695].

[47] This is also consistent with regional practice, such as in the interpretation of freedom of association under Article 11 of the ECHR; see, eg, *Gustafsson v Sweden* (App. 15573/89), 25 April 1996, (1996) 22 EHRR 409, [45]: 'Although the essential object of Article 11 is to protect the individual against arbitrary interferences by the public authorities with his or her exercise of the rights protected, there may in addition be positive obligations to secure the effective enjoyment of these rights.'

[48] See, eg, CESCR, General Comment No. 18, E/C.12/GC/18 (6 February 2006), [22] (concerning the right to work in Article 6).

The obligation to *fulfil* includes the obligations to provide, facilitate and promote union rights. States should adopt appropriate legislative, administrative, budgetary, judicial and other measures to ensure the full realization of Article 8.[49] As discussed throughout this chapter, this may require legal or other measures to: recognize unions (and to establish relevant administrative authorities for registration and the like); protect them from interference and anti-union discrimination; enable their free functioning (including collective bargaining); permit unions to federate, confederate and internationally affiliate; protect the right to strike and strikers against dismissal; and facilitate union activities in the workplace. Article 8 may also require states to take positive action to actively promote trade unionism among workers.[50]

Legislative (or even constitutional) measures to protect trade union rights are a particularly important means of implementing the components of Article 8, although other means are evident in ILO practice: declarations, public programmes, policies, codes of conduct, self-regulatory measures and voluntary dispute settlement procedures.[51] In ILO practice, tripartite consultation should normally precede the adoption of legislation in this field.

The obligation to fulfil further requires states to provide an effective machinery of remedies and sanctions where violations of Article 8 occur. Measures to prevent violations are also appropriate, such as labour inspection authorities[52] or human rights commissions,[53] or public awareness raising and education for workers, employers, government bodies, the police and the public. During the drafting, Chile observed that promotional measures might include 'training trade-union leaders, promoting the trade-union movement, propagating trade-union techniques and awakening the workers' awareness of their own rights'.[54]

Obligations in relation to international cooperation are discussed at the end of this chapter.

Meaning of 'trade union' in Article 8

EMPLOYERS' ORGANIZATIONS

Significant disagreement arose during the drafting as to whether Article 8 of the ICESCR only applied to workers' organizations or also extended to employer organizations. The ambiguity arose from both the use of the word 'everyone' and

[49] See similarly in relation to Article 22 of the ICCPR: Nowak, *CCPR Commentary*, 498.

[50] Craven, *The ICESCR*, 251.

[51] Craven, *The ICESCR*, 251.

[52] ILO, *Giving Globalization a Human Face*, 19–20.

[53] CESCR, Concluding Observations: Mexico, E/C.12/MEX/CO/4 (9 June 2006), [34].

[54] UNGA Third Committee, A/C.3/SR.720 (3 January 1957), 195 (Chile); see also UNGA Third Committee, A/C.3/SR.721 (4 January 1957), 203 (Chile) (comments made in relation to a slightly differently worded draft Article 8, referring to measures to 'ensure the free exercise of the rights of everyone to form and join…trade unions': UNGA Third Committee, A/3525 (9 February 1957), 19. The phrase 'free exercise' was not adopted: infra, 20.

the different connotations of the idea of a 'trade union' as translated in various languages.[55] In originating the provision, the Commission on Human Rights had not intended it to govern the rights of employers.[56] Employers' organizations would, in any event, be protected by the general freedom of association in Article 22 of the ICCPR.

However, some states felt that the term should be broadly interpreted[57] and voted for the provision on the basis that it included employer organizations. Examples given of groups that needed the protection of collective representation included 'small farmers, most of whom employed hired help and themselves worked on the land',[58] and 'self-employed persons, artists, or employers who also exercised a trade'.[59] Chile argued that including employer organizations would enhance productivity and economic development.[60]

However, the Soviet Union countered that the provision should be limited to workers' associations to 'avoid confusing two different ideas'—the right of association in the ICCPR (which already covered employers) and the right to join a trade union (which was a distinctive economic and social right).[61] It reserved the right to formally object to a wider interpretation of Article 8.[62] It was supported by some states who voted for the text on the basis that it applied only to workers' organizations.[63]

By way of compromise, some states suggested that each state should interpret the term for itself,[64] although this was criticized on the basis that Covenant rights should be 'applicable everywhere in exactly the same way'.[65] A motion to take a separate vote on the intended scope of Article 8 was rejected.[66] Even after the adoption of the provision, it was clear that no consensus existed, since states had either voted on the basis of their own understanding of the phrase,[67] or abstained from voting because of its uncertain scope.[68]

Given the lack of consensus during the drafting, the specialized, background ILO standards may usefully inform interpretation of Article 8. While it does not

[55] See UNGA Third Committee, A/C.3/SR.724 (8 January 1957), 217 (Belgium, Union of Soviet Socialist Republics, Chile, Dominican Republic), 218 (Australia, Colombia, Uruguay).

[56] UNGA Third Committee, A/C.3/SR.723 (7 January 1957), 211 (Secretariat).

[57] UNGA Third Committee, A/C.3/SR.722 (7 January 1957), 208 (Belgium, Chile); UNGA Third Committee, A/C.3/SR.724 (8 January 1957), 217 (Belgium, Dominican Republic), 219 (Greece).

[58] UNGA Third Committee, A/C.3/SR.724 (8 January 1957), 220 (France).

[59] UNGA Third Committee, A/C.3/SR.725 (9 January 1957), 221 (Ecuador).

[60] UNGA Third Committee, A/C.3/SR.725 (9 January 1957), 222 (Chile).

[61] UNGA Third Committee, A/C.3/SR.724 (8 January 1957), 219 (Union of Soviet Socialist Republics); UNGA Third Committee, A/C.3/SR.725 (9 January 1957), 222 (Union of Soviet Socialist Republics).

[62] UNGA Third Committee, A/C.3/SR.724 (8 January 1957), 219 (Union of Soviet Socialist Republics).

[63] UNGA Third Committee, A/C.3/SR.725 (9 January 1957), 221 (Norway), 222 (China, Israel).

[64] UNGA Third Committee, A/C.3/SR.725 (9 January 1957), 221 (Ecuador).

[65] UNGA Third Committee, A/C.3/SR.725 (9 January 1957), 222 (Chile).

[66] UNGA Third Committee, A/C.3/SR.725 (9 January 1957), 222 (Chile).

[67] UNGA Third Committee, A/C.3/SR.726 (9 January 1957), 225 (Denmark), 226 (Syria, Guatemala, Czechoslovakia).

[68] UNGA Third Committee, A/C.3/SR.726 (9 January 1957), 226 (Colombia, El Salvador).

use the language of 'trade unions', ILO Convention No. 87 concerning Freedom of Association and Protection of the Right to Organise 1948 recognizes the right of '[w]orkers and employers, without distinction whatsoever', to establish and join organizations of their own choosing, and states may not confine the equal protections for workers and employers:[69]

Article 2

Workers and employers, without distinction whatsoever, shall have the right to establish and, subject only to the rules of the organisation concerned, to join organisations of their own choosing without previous authorisation.

Article 3

1. Workers' and employers' organisations shall have the right to draw up their constitutions and rules, to elect their representatives in full freedom, to organise their administration and activities and to formulate their programmes.

2. The public authorities shall refrain from any interference which would restrict this right or impede the lawful exercise thereof.

…

Article 6

The provisions of Articles 2, 3 and 4 hereof apply to federations and confederations of workers' and employers' organisations.

Article 7

The acquisition of legal personality by workers' and employers' organisations, federations and confederations shall not be made subject to conditions of such a character as to restrict the application of the provisions of Articles 2, 3 and 4 hereof.

…

Article 10

In this Convention the term organisation means any organisation of workers or of employers for furthering and defending the interests of workers or of employers.

Employers' organizations can be particularly important in protecting the interests of small enterprises,[70] over which unions may have some influence or advantage. If employer organizations are covered by Article 8, this will have implications for the reconciliation of competing group rights in relation to Article 8 matters such as collective bargaining, as well as in the imposition of restrictions to safeguard one group's rights from interference by another's. In monitoring states, the CESCR has almost exclusively focused on the protection of workers' unions, not employer organizations, which may be explained by the typical imbalance of economic power between those groups.

[69] ILO Convention No. 87 concerning Freedom of Association and Protection of the Right to Organise (adopted 9 July 1948, entered into force 4 July 1950) ('ILO Convention No. 87 concerning Freedom of Association').

[70] ILO, *Giving Globalization a Human Face*, 18.

PRIVATE OR PUBLIC CHARACTER

A different question arises regarding whether trade unions include 'professional associations established by public law that fulfil a legal duty or form part of a public institution'.[71] In European practice under Article 11 of the ECHR (freedom of association, specifically including trade union rights), the answer is no. In *Le Compte, Van Leuven and De Meyere v Netherlands*, the European Court of Human Rights found that a statutory, state-controlled college of physicians, which regulated the practice of medicine, was not an 'association' under Article 11, and did not inhibit the freedom of association of health professionals, who remained free to form and join their own voluntary organizations:

64. The Court notes firstly that the Belgian Ordre des médecins is a public-law institution. It was founded not by individuals but by the legislature; it remains integrated within the structures of the State and judges are appointed to most of its organs by the Crown. It pursues an aim which is in the general interest, namely the protection of health, by exercising under the relevant legislation a form of public control over the practice of medicine. Within the context of this latter function, the Ordre is required in particular to keep the register of medical practitioners. For the performance of the tasks conferred on it by the Belgian State, it is legally invested with administrative as well as rule-making and disciplinary prerogatives out of the orbit of the ordinary law (prerogatives exorbitantes du droit commun) and, in this capacity, employs processes of a public authority (see paragraphs 20–34 above).

65. Having regard to these various factors taken together, the Ordre cannot be considered as an association within the meaning of Article 11 (art. 11). However, there is a further requirement: if there is not to be a violation, the setting up of the Ordre by the Belgian State must not prevent practitioners from forming together or joining professional associations. Totalitarian régimes have resorted—and resort—to the compulsory regimentation of the professions by means of closed and exclusive organisations taking the place of the professional associations and the traditional trade unions. The authors of the Convention intended to prevent such abuses (see the Collected Edition of the Travaux Préparatoires, vol. II, pp. 116–118).

The Court notes that in Belgium there are several associations formed to protect the professional interests of medical practitioners and which they are completely free to join or not (see paragraph 22 above). In these circumstances, the existence of the Ordre and its attendant consequence—that is to say, the obligation on practitioners to be entered on the register of the Ordre and to be subject to the authority of its organs—clearly have neither the object nor the effect of limiting, even less suppressing, the right guaranteed by Article 11 par. 1 (art. 11-1).[72]

By contrast, there will be a violation of freedom of association where a person is forced, on pain of penalty or detriment, to join a predominantly private industry association that performs only minor public regulatory functions. In *Sigurjonsson v Iceland*, the European Court of Human Rights found a violation of Article 11 where a taxi driver was forced to be a paid-up member of a private taxi industry

[71] Craven, *The ICESCR*, 263.

[72] *Le Compte, Van Leuven and De Meyere v Netherlands* (Apps. 6878/75, 7238/75), 18 October 1982, (1982) 4 EHRR 1, [64] and [65].

association (Frami) or face losing his taxi licence.[73] The Court found that Frami was largely independent of the state and primarily pursued the interests of its members. It was unnecessary to determine whether it was a trade union since unions were considered one aspect of the wider right to freedom of association:

31. The Court agrees with the applicant and the Commission that the above-mentioned elements are not sufficient for Frami to be regarded as a public-law association outside the ambit of Article 11 (art. 11). Admittedly, Frami performed certain functions which were to some extent provided for in the applicable legislation and which served not only its members but also the public at large (see paragraphs 22–23 above). However, the role of supervision of the implementation of the relevant rules was entrusted primarily to another institution, namely the Committee, which in addition had the power to issue licences and to decide on their suspension and revocation (see paragraphs 20 and 25 above). Frami was established under private law and enjoyed full autonomy in determining its own aims, organisation and procedure. According to its Articles, admittedly old and currently under revision, the purpose of Frami was to protect the professional interests of its members and promote solidarity among professional taxicab drivers; to determine, negotiate and present demands relating to the working hours, wages and rates of its members; to seek to maintain limitations on the number of taxicabs and to represent its members before the public authorities (see paragraph 21 above). Frami was therefore predominantly a private-law organisation and must thus be considered an 'association' for the purposes of Article 11 (art. 11).

32. It is not necessary to decide whether Frami can also be regarded as a trade union within the meaning of Article 11 (art. 11), since the right to form and join trade unions in that provision is an aspect of the wider right to freedom of association, rather than a separate right (see, amongst other authorities, the Schmidt and Dahlström v. Sweden judgment of 6 February 1976, Series A no. 21, p. 15, para. 34).

Where an organization performs mixed public and private functions, the issues are which characteristics are predominant and how proximate is the relationship to the state.[74]

Where an existing private body performs regulatory functions, and a state seeks to subordinate that arrangement to public control, there may be unlawful interference in freedom of association. In *Civil Liberties Organization v Nigeria*, a decree established a new governing body of the Nigerian Bar Association, filled with mainly government appointees and only a small proportion from the Bar Association itself. The new body assumed responsibility for regulating practising fees and disciplining lawyers, and excluded judicial review. The African Commission found a violation of Article 10 of the African Charter:

15. …Freedom of association is enunciated as an individual right and is first and foremost a duty for the State to abstain from interfering with the free formation of associations.

[73] *Sigurjónsson v Iceland.*

[74] See, eg, *Chassagnou et al v France* (Apps. 25088/94, 28331/95, 28443/95), 29 April 1999, (1999) 29 EHRR 615, [98]–[101] (hunters' associations established by law and supervised by the state were nonetheless associations of private individuals pursuing their interests).

There must always be a general capacity for citizens to join, without State interference, in associations in order to attain various ends.

16. In regulating the use of this right, the competent authorities should not enact provisions which would limit the exercise of this freedom. The competent authorities should not override constitutional provisions or undermine fundamental rights guaranteed by the Constitution and international human rights standards.

17. The Body of Benchers is dominated by representatives of the government and has wide discretionary powers. This interference with the free association of the Nigerian Bar Association is inconsistent with the preamble of the African Charter in conjunction with *UN Basic Principles on the Independence of the Judiciary* and thereby constitutes a violation of Article 10 of the African Charter.[75]

Where states establish public consultative bodies which affect or concern workers' interests, trade unions may seek to be represented on such bodies in protecting members' interests. In European practice, states are accorded a wide margin of appreciation in the composition of such bodies where they are not concerned with essential trade union prerogatives (such as collective bargaining). Thus, in *SAGES v France*, there was no violation of Article 5 of the Revised European Social Charter where the union had no standing to challenge elections to the French National Council for higher education and research.[76] The European Committee on Social Rights stated:

37. While collective bargaining is the primary means to protect the economic and social interests of a trade union and its members in the meaning of Article 5, the Committee holds that being or seeking to be represented on public law bodies, whether consultative, judicial or administrative, may be an additional means among many for the pursuit by a trade union of such interest protection. The Committee therefore considers that the issue of trade union participation in such bodies falls within the scope of Article 5 when read in conjunction with Article 6§1 (joint consultation). The information adduced by the Government on the specific mandate and functions of the CNESER and the fact that its membership is not confined to representatives of staff do not lead the Committee to take any other view in the case before it.

38. Nevertheless, the Committee holds that where States Parties establish various consultation bodies that are not directly concerned with the essential trade union prerogatives, such as collective bargaining, they have a wide margin of appreciation in determining the composition of the bodies in question. This applies *a fortiori* to any modalities, such as elections, which may be used to determine the composition of these bodies as long as said modalities do not arbitrarily benefit certain trade unions at the expense of others or effectively prevent certain trade unions from enjoying the essential trade union prerogatives. In the present case, the Committee notes that trade unions may present lists for election of representatives to the CNESER. The Committee further notes that any individual voter and

[75] *Civil Liberties Organisation (in respect of the Nigerian Bar Association) v Nigeria*, 22 March 1995, African Commission on Human Rights Communication No. 101/93, 22 March 1995, [15]–[17].

[76] *Syndicat des Agrégés de l'Enseignement Supérieur (SAGES) v France*, 15 June 2005, ECSR Complaint No. 26/2004.

candidate may challenge the lawfulness of the CNESER elections, although there is no collective remedy in this respect.

39. Having considered all these issues, the Committee concludes that the regulations applicable to the CNESER do not exceed the margin of appreciation of the national authorities and it therefore finds that there is no violation of Article 5 of the Revised Charter.

OTHER FORMS OF ASSOCIATION

There is no 'association' in the mere relationship between employees of the same employer, which is based on a contractual connection, not voluntary association.[77]

The ILO has also distinguished 'solidarist' organizations from trade unions, which are mutual benefit societies involving workers and employers, partly funded by employers, which provide socio-economic welfare support (such as savings and credit, housing, education and so on).[78] Workers typically comprise the deliberative organs of such bodies, with employers represented *ex officio*. Such cooperation is not prohibited by ILO standards, but must not interfere or engage in the roles and activities of trade unions (including collective bargaining where unions exist), in view of their limited independence from employers.

PROTECTED PURPOSES OF TRADE UNIONS AND 'POLITICAL' ORGANIZATIONS

The text of Article 8(1)(a) confines a person's rights to form and join trade unions 'for the promotion and protection of his economic and social interests'. During the drafting, Belgium unsuccessfully objected that trade union rights 'should be absolute, and independent of the purpose sought by the individual'.[79] Others were concerned that trade unions should not be prevented from being involved in debates about social and economic policies and laws.[80] The phrase was, however, strongly supported in a separate vote.[81]

At the same time, the three-power amendment which introduced the phrase emphasized that trade unions were intended to promote, not merely protect, their members' economic and social rights.[82] It was thus designed to expand, not limit, trade union rights. This suggests that 'economic and social interests' cover a wide spectrum of purposes and activities related to the protection of workers' interests. Only organizations pursuing 'purely political' issues,[83] detached from workers'

[77] *Young, James and Webster v United Kingdom* ('*Young v UK*'), Report of 14 December 1979, B.39 (1984) (European Commission on Human Rights), 47.

[78] ILO, Freedom of Association: Digest of Decisions and Principles, [869]–[879].

[79] By forty-seven votes to one, with nineteen abstentions: UNGA Third Committee, A/C.3/SR.722 (7 January 1957), 208 (Belgium).

[80] Craven, *The ICESCR*, 253.

[81] UNGA Third Committee, A/3525 (9 February 1957), 26.

[82] UNGA Third Committee, A/C.3/SR.719 (3 January 1957), 192 (Peru).

[83] Craven, *The ICESCR*, 253.

interests, would fall outside the scope of Article 8, in which case it would be an artifice to characterize them as trade unions in any case.

To the extent that otherwise legitimate trade unions stray beyond their mandate and intrude on extraneous political issues, that is not a basis for denying them legal personality or protection as trade unions per se. Rather, it may be a ground for (cautiously) regulating their 'free functioning' under Article 8(1)(c) through the application of the limitations provisions, as discussed below. ILO practice under Convention No. 87 confirms that a state should not refuse to register an organization simply because it could exceed ordinary union activities:[84]

> 305. Normal control of the activities of trade unions should be effected a posteriori and by the judicial authorities; and the fact that an organization which seeks to enjoy the status of an occupational organization might in certain cases engage in activities unconnected with trade union activities would not appear to constitute a sufficient reason for subjecting trade union organizations a priori to control with respect to their composition and with respect to the composition of their management committees. The refusal to register a union because the authorities, in advance and in their own judgement, consider that this would be politically undesirable, would be tantamount to submitting the compulsory registration of trade unions to previous authorization on the part of the authorities, which is not compatible with the principles of freedom of association.[85]

Article 8(1)(a): Right to Form and Join Trade Unions

A RIGHT OF 'EVERYONE'

Article 8(1)(a) recognizes the 'right of everyone to form trade unions and join the trade union of his choice, subject only to the rules of the organization concerned'. It partly borrows from the language of Article 2 of ILO Convention No. 87.[86] The reference to the right of 'everyone' is subject only to the specific limitation in Article 8(2) that states may impose 'lawful restrictions on the exercise of these rights by members of the armed forces or of the police or of the administration of the State', discussed below.

It may also be recalled that Article 2(3) of the ICESCR provides that developing countries may limit the extent to which they guarantee rights to non-nationals. However, no state party has made a reservation or lodged an interpretive declaration to the effect that the trade union rights of non-nationals under Article 8 are restricted by virtue of Article 2(3).

Moreover, Article 2(3) refers to the restriction of 'economic' rights of non-nationals in view of the state of the national economy of the developing country. Given that trade union rights share a civil and political character as well

[84] ILO, Freedom of Association: Digest of Decisions and Principles, [297].

[85] ILO, Freedom of Association: Digest of Decisions and Principles, [305].

[86] ILO Convention No. 87, Article 2: 'Workers and employers, without distinction whatsoever, shall have the right to establish and, subject only to the rules of the organisation concerned, to join organisations of their own choosing without previous authorisation.'

as being socio-economic, and are obligations of immediate effect rather than subject to progressive realization, in principle it is difficult to see why a country's state of development or economic circumstances would necessitate the deprivation or restriction of trade union rights in respect of non-nationals. Sacrificing the trade union rights of foreigners for domestic economic gain would hardly be compatible with the purpose of the ICESCR in protecting the dignity of 'everyone'. It would also render already vulnerable migrant workers more susceptible to exploitation.

In this regard, under Convention No. 87, the ILO has explicitly rejected 'economic arguments' that workers in export processing zones (EPZs) can be denied trade union rights, or that foreign investment incentives may include limitations on freedom of association or the right to organize.[87] The ILO notes that there are 66 million people employed in 3,500 EPZs in 120 states, often subject to lesser labour protections in contravention of ILO standards.[88]

In monitoring states, the CESCR has frequently criticized restrictions on the ability of non-nationals or migrant workers to join trade unions[89] or be involved in union leadership,[90] as not being compatible with Article 8. This includes inhabitants of occupied territory working in the territory of the occupying power.[91] It has called on states to take steps to extend these rights to all workers including non-nationals,[92] and to amend national legislation to permit foreign workers to hold trade union office.[93] Occasionally, it has invoked the Migrant Workers' Convention, as well as ILO Convention No. 143 concerning Migrants in Abusive Conditions 1975, in the context of migrants' trade union rights.[94]

This approach is consistent with that of the ILO, which has emphasized that all workers, including foreigners, enjoy the right to organize under Article 2 of ILO Convention No. 87, with the sole possible exceptions of armed forces and police (under Article 9).[95] Conditioning the trade union rights of foreigners on the basis of reciprocity is also not acceptable.[96] In regional practice, too, the Inter-American Court of Human Rights has confirmed that even undocumented migrant workers enjoy trade union and association rights.[97]

[87] ILO, Freedom of Association: Digest of Decisions and Principles, [264]–[266].

[88] ILO, *Giving Globalization a Human Face*, 27–8.

[89] CESCR, Consideration of Report Submitted by State Party: Costa Rica, E/1991/23 (1990), [194]; CESCR, Concluding Observations: Costa Rica, E/C.12/CRI/CO/4 (4 January 2008), [20]; Jordan, E/C.12/1/Add.46 (1 September 2000), [19]; Kuwait, E/C.12/1/Add.98 (7 June 2004), [18].

[90] CESCR, Consideration of Report Submitted by State Party: Panama, E/1992/23 (1991), [138]; CESCR, Concluding Observations: El Salvador, E/C.12/1/Add.4 (28 May 1996), [19]; Senegal, E/C.12/1993/18 (5 January 1994), [8]; Senegal, E/C.12/1/Add.62 (24 September 2001), [22].

[91] CESCR, Concluding Observations: Israel, E/C.12/1/Add.90 (26 June 2003), [22].

[92] CESCR, Concluding Observations: Kuwait, E/C.12/1/Add.98 (7 June 2004), [38].

[93] CESCR, Consideration of Report Submitted by State Party: Senegal, E/1994/23 (1993), [266].

[94] CESCR, Concluding Observations: Mauritius, E/C.12/MUS/CO/4 (8 June 2010), [19].

[95] ILO, Freedom of Association: Digest of Decisions and Principles, [214].

[96] ILO, Freedom of Association: Digest of Decisions and Principles, [215].

[97] *Juridical Condition and Rights of the Undocumented Migrants (Advisory Opinion)*, 17 September 2003, Series A No. 18, [157].

The ILO has further indicated that Convention No. 87 'is applicable to locally recruited personnel in embassies' and also protects workers in international airlines.[98] This raises the wider and separate question of whether a state's obligations under Article 8 of the ICESCR apply extraterritorially. Generally, the ICESCR applies to a state's territory or wherever it exercises jurisdiction.[99] A narrow view of jurisdiction would confine it to situations where the state exercises physical control over foreign territory or persons (such as in custody).

However, a wider view of jurisdiction might encompass employees working for the state or even its corporations abroad. Evidently, trade union rights abroad are primarily governed by the foreign state's law, not the law of another state employing persons there. However, Article 8 may require the employer state not to impose contractual or legislative impediments to the right of state employees in foreign territory to unionize, and to ensure that its corporate law does not permit companies of its nationality to bar the union rights of employees abroad.

The CESCR has occasionally expressed concern that certain categories of workers may face obstacles in exercising their trade union rights, such as temporary or contract workers.[100] It has accordingly recommended that states take steps to ensure that temporary contracts are not used to circumvent the enjoyment of rights.[101]

ILO practice has identified many unlawful situations (under Convention No. 87) where it could be said that the trade union rights of 'everyone' under Article 8 of the ICESCR would also not be protected. Discrimination in the provision of trade union rights would violate Article 8 (and Article 2) of the ICESCR, such as on the basis of race or political opinion (including where a person opposes the state's socio-economic or political model).[102] Very occasionally, the CESCR has been alert to the low levels of union participation by women, such as the 6 per cent of women workers who are unionized in Nicaragua.[103]

Further, the ILO has found that workers in any occupation (or sector or industry) have the right to establish and join organizations of their choosing[104] (subject to the possible exceptions for armed forces and police). Such rights cannot be restricted by law on the basis of the type, nature or character of employment (whether probationary, in training, temporary or permanent; salaried or self-employed (including those in cooperatives), dismissed or retired; casual, part-time or full-time; or by reference to the legal basis of the work relationship (such as by contract or other arrangement)).

[98] ILO, Freedom of Association: Digest of Decisions and Principles, [238], [244], respectively.

[99] *Legal Consequences of the Construction of a Wall in the Occupied Palestinian Territory (Advisory Opinion)* [1996] ICJ Rep 240, [112].

[100] CESCR, Concluding Observations: Ecuador, E/C.12/1/Add.100 (7 June 2004), [19]; Finland, E/C.12/FIN/CO/5 (16 January 2008), [15].

[101] CESCR, Concluding Observations: Finland, E/C.12/FIN/CO/5 (16 January 2008), [15].

[102] ILO, Freedom of Association: Digest of Decisions and Principles, [210]–[213].

[103] CESCR, Concluding Observations: Nicaragua, E/C.12/NIC/CO/4 (28 November 2008), [15].

[104] ILO, Freedom of Association: Digest of Decisions and Principles, [209]–[271].

The ILO has also recognized that unpaid workers may enjoy such rights, as where a person is working in a community participation programme. The CESCR thus criticized a Canadian law which denied 'workfare' participants the right to join unions.[105] For a similar reason, in principle there is no reason why those engaged in lawful compulsory labour (including in prisons) should be denied union rights.

While public and private employees enjoy equal rights under ILO Convention No. 87, those working in 'the administration of the State' are subject to potential limitations under Article 8(2) of the ICESCR, thus diverging from the ILO standards. The scope and operation of the limitation in Article 8(2) is considered separately below.

RIGHT TO FORM TRADE UNIONS

limitations

The right to form trade unions under Article 8(1)(a) is subject solely to limitations 'prescribed by law and which are necessary in a democratic society in the interests of national security or public order or for the protection of the rights and freedoms of others'. The same limitations formula is used in Article 8(1)(c) in relation to the right of trade unions to function freely.

In the drafting it was originally proposed that Article 8 as a whole would be subject to the same restrictions as in Article 22 of the ICCPR, which similarly refers to the grounds of national security, public order and the rights of others, but also to public health or morals. Some thought specific limitations were unnecessary in view of the general clause in Article 4 of the ICESCR. Others were concerned that the limitations would conflict with ILO Convention No. 87. The language of the provision as adopted leaves no room for the concurrent application of the general clause in Article 4 of the ICESCR.

The non-binding Limburg Principles on the Implementation of the ICESCR suggest the manner in which the limitations clauses in Article 8 should be interpreted:

'prescribed by law'[106]

59. See the interpretative principles under the synonymous term 'determined by law' in Article 4.

[105] CESCR, Concluding Observations: Canada, E/C.12/1/Add.31 (10 December 1998), [31].

[106] Note that the Inter-American Court of Human Rights has interpreted a comparable requirement of restrictions by 'law' in Article 16 (freedom of association) of the American Convention on Human Rights as follows: 'one cannot interpret the word *laws*, used in Article 30 [of the Convention], as a synonym for just any legal norm, since that would be tantamount to admitting that fundamental rights can be restricted at the sole discretion of governmental authorities... [and] to recognize in those who govern virtually absolute power over their subjects... [T]he word "laws" acquires all of its logical and historical meaning if it is regarded as a requirement of the necessary restriction of governmental interference in the area of individual rights and freedoms': *Baena-Ricardo et al v Panama*, 2 February 2001, IACHR Series C No. 72, [169] (emphasis added).

[48. No limitation on the exercise of economic, social and cultural rights shall be made unless provided for by national law of general application which is consistent with the Covenant and is in force at the time the limitation is applied.

49. Laws imposing limitations on the exercise of economic, social and cultural rights shall not be arbitrary or unreasonable or discriminatory.

50. Legal rules limiting the exercise of economic, social and cultural rights shall be clear and accessible to everyone.[107]

51. Adequate safeguards and effective remedies shall be provided by law against illegal or abusive imposition on application of limitations on economic, social and cultural rights.]

'necessary in a democratic society'

60. In addition to the interpretative principles listed under Article 4 concerning the phrase 'in a democratic society', Article 8 imposes a greater restraint upon a State Party which is exercising limitations on trade union rights. It requires that such a limitation is indeed necessary. The term 'necessary' implies that the limitation:

(a) responds to a pressing public or social need;[108]

(b) pursues a legitimate aim; and

(c) is proportional to that aim.

61. Any assessment as to the necessity of a limitation shall be based upon objective considerations.

'national security'

62. National security may be invoked to justify measures limiting certain rights only when they are taken to protect the existence of the nation or its territorial integrity or political independence against force or threat of force.

63. National security cannot be invoked as a reason for imposing limitations to prevent merely local or relatively isolated threats to law and order.

64. National security cannot be used as a pretext for imposing vague or arbitrary limitations and may be invoked only when there exist adequate safeguards and effective remedies against abuse.

65. The systematic violation of economic, social and cultural rights undermines true national security and may jeopardize international peace and security. A State responsible for such violation shall not invoke national security as a justification for measures aimed at suppressing opposition to such violation or at perpetrating repressive practices against its population.

'public order (ordre public)'

66. The expression 'public order (*ordre public*)' as used in the Covenant may be defined as the sum of rules which ensures the functioning of society or the set of fundamental

[107] The focus is accordingly not only on the existence of law, but also its quality. Such interpretation is supported by the jurisprudence on limitations under the ICCPR and ECHR: see, eg, *Sunday Times v United Kingdom* (App. 6538/74), 26 April 1979, (1979) 2 EHRR 245, [49].

[108] See, eg, *Handyside v United Kingdom* (App. 5493/72), 7 December 1976, (1979–80) 1 EHRR 737.

principles on which a society is founded. Respect for economic, social and cultural rights is part of public order (*ordre public*).

67. Public order (*ordre public*) shall be interpreted in the context of the purpose of the particular economic, social and cultural rights which are limited on this ground.

68. State organs or agents responsible for the maintenance of public order (*ordre public*) shall be subject to controls in the exercise of their power through the parliament, courts, or other competent independent bodies.

'rights and freedoms of others'

69. The scope of the rights and freedoms of others that may act as a limitation upon rights in the Covenant extends beyond the rights and freedoms recognized in the Covenant.[109]

In monitoring states, the CESCR has often been concerned about restrictions on the right to form trade unions. For example, it has drawn attention to requirements of prior authorization to form new independent unions,[110] unduly narrow legal criteria,[111] and delays in registration.[112] The HRC, too, has expressed concern under Article 22 of the ICCPR where unions have been subject to unduly onerous registration procedures.[113]

The CESCR has also expressed concern about the imposition of monopolistic, centralized, hierarchical or government-controlled union structures which restrict the ability to form or join independent trade unions,[114] as well as the creation of 'sham unions'.[115] It has recommended that obstacles to the creation of independent trade unions be removed,[116] and called on states to respect the right to establish free and independent trade unions.[117]

The issues of concern to the CESCR have arisen in more detail in the extensive ILO practice in the area, along with other circumstances in which unions may be permissibly regulated. ILO practice can thus help to illuminate interpretation of

[109] Limburg Principles on the Implementation of the International Covenant on Economic, Social and Cultural Rights, E/CN.4/1987/17 (8 January 1987), [59]–[69] (reincorporating [48]–[51]).

[110] CESCR, Concluding Observations: Algeria, E/C.12/1/Add.71 (30 November 2001), [16]; Angola, E/C.12/DZA/CO/4 (7 June 2010), [11]; Democratic People's Republic of Korea, E/C.12/1/Add.95 (12 December 2003), [16]; Senegal, E/C.12/1/Add.62 (24 September 2001), [22]; Serbia and Montenegro, E/C.12/1/Add.108 (23 June 2005), [18].

[111] CESCR, Concluding Observations: Croatia, E/C.12/1/Add.73 (5 December 2001), [16]; Serbia and Montenegro, E/C.12/1/Add.108 (23 June 2005), [18].

[112] CESCR, Concluding Observations: Kenya, E/C.12/KEN/CO/1 (1 December 2008), [19]; Morocco, E/C.12/1/Add.55 (1 December 2000), [46].

[113] HRC, Concluding Observations: Belarus, CCPR/C/79/Add.86 (19 November 1997), [19]; Lithuania, CCPR/C/79/Add.87 (19 November 1997), [20].

[114] CESCR, Concluding Observations: Democratic People's Republic of Korea, E/C.12/1/Add.95 (12 December 2003), [16]; Iraq, E/C.12/1/Add.17 (12 December 1997), [16]; Kenya, E/C.12/1993/6 (3 June 1993), [13]; Syrian Arab Republic, E/C.12/1/Add.63 (24 September 2001), [20]; Ukraine, E/C.12/UKR/CO/5 (4 January 2008), [17]; Honduras, E/C.12/1/Add.57 (21 May 2001), [18]; Mexico, E/C.12/MEX/CO/4 (9 June 2006), [16].

[115] CESCR, Concluding Observations: Democratic Republic of the Congo, E/C.12/COD/CO/4 (16 December 2009), [23].

[116] CESCR, Concluding Observations: Algeria, E/C.12/1/Add.71 (30 November 2001), [32].

[117] CESCR, Concluding Observations: Syrian Arab Republic, E/C.12/1/Add.63 (24 September 2001), [38].

the scope and application of the Article 8(1) limitations clauses in the contexts discussed below.

Approval, formalities, registration

In the first place, the ILO has found that the principle of freedom of association would remain a 'dead letter' if prior state authorization to establish an organization or to obtain approval of its constitution or rules was required.[118] Organizations are, however, required to observe any legal or procedural formalities for their establishment and which are necessary to ensure their normal functioning, as long as such formalities do not constitute de facto prior authorization or an obstacle to establishment.[119] Article 7 of ILO Convention No. 87 provides that:

> The acquisition of legal personality by workers' and employers' organisations, federations and confederations shall not be made subject to conditions of such a character as to restrict the application of the provisions of Articles 2, 3 and 4 hereof.

Permissible formalities may include, for example, a legal requirement to register, to maintain a registered office, or to deposit and publicize the organization's rules.[120] Registration confers official recognition on an organization, which 'is an essential facet of the right to organize since that is the first step that workers' or employers' organizations must take in order to be able to function efficiently, and represent their members adequately'.[121] Under national law it may also confer various advantages, such as special taxation status or exemptions and recognition in collective bargaining.[122]

The ILO has, however, taken a strict approach to formalities which otherwise restrict the right to organize. Unfettered or excessive state discretion in approving the registration of organizations will not conform to Convention No. 87, nor will excessive procedural complexities or undue delay in registration.[123] A statutory period of one month for the registration of an organization is reasonable.[124] A suspicion that a union could exceed normal union activities or be unable to function is not sufficient to deny registration.[125] Establishment cannot be conditioned on approval from a central trade union; nor can a union be required to include in its constitution provisions which are inconsistent with the freedom to organize.[126]

Further, suspicion that union leaders have committed criminal acts, even if they are detained prior to conviction, is not sufficient to deny registration to an

[118] ILO, Freedom of Association: Digest of Decisions and Principles, [272].

[119] ILO, Freedom of Association: Digest of Decisions and Principles, [272]–[282], [294]–[307]. See ILO Convention No. 87 concerning Freedom of Association, Article 8 (organizations shall respect the law of the land, without prejudice to their Convention rights).

[120] See also Nowak, *CCPR Commentary*, 506–7, commenting on permissible public order limitations on the right of association under Article 22 of the ICCPR.

[121] ILO, Freedom of Association: Digest of Decisions and Principles, [295].

[122] ILO, Freedom of Association: Digest of Decisions and Principles, [306].

[123] ILO, Freedom of Association: Digest of Decisions and Principles, [296].

[124] ILO, Freedom of Association: Digest of Decisions and Principles, [308].

[125] ILO, Freedom of Association: Digest of Decisions and Principles, [278].

[126] ILO, Freedom of Association: Digest of Decisions and Principles, [299] and [280], respectively.

organization.[127] Nor is a mere suspicion that a union 'is about to engage' in activities prejudicial to public safety or order enough, and such risks should be cautiously appraised.[128] In both cases, suspected criminals or security risks should be dealt with through ordinary judicial processes.

In ILO practice, any administrative decision to refuse registration must be subject to judicial review; a right of appeal is a 'necessary safeguard against unlawful or ill-founded decisions'.[129] Appeal is not, however, sufficient to cure excessive administrative discretion under ill-defined laws on registration. Rather, registration criteria must be clearly defined, and the courts must be 'able to deal with the substance of a case' to determine whether there is a violation of protected rights to organize.[130]

Legally required membership conditions

In monitoring states, the CESCR has been concerned about restrictive minimum membership requirements for establishing or registering trade unions.[131] It found minimum requirements of thirty and 100 workers too high,[132] as well as 10 per cent of the workforce.[133] In ILO practice, it is accepted that a minimum membership requirement is not in itself incompatible with Convention No. 87, but the number should be fixed 'in a reasonable manner so that the establishment of organizations is not hindered'.[134] What is reasonable varies according to the circumstances.

In terms of raw numbers, the ILO has found, for instance, that a minimum requirement of twenty members is not 'excessive', but fifty members is 'obviously too high'.[135] The number of thirty workers might normally be acceptable for sectoral unions, but was found to be too high for works councils in a country with a very large proportion of small enterprises and where the trade union structure was based on enterprise unions.[136] Where the required number is too high (such as 100 members), the ILO has called for its reduction by consultation with workers' and employers' organizations.[137] A requirement of 10,000 workers for federal registration of a union was also too high.[138]

Where membership requirements are expressed as a proportion of workers in a given sector, the ILO has found minimum conditions of 50 per cent and

[127] ILO, Freedom of Association: Digest of Decisions and Principles, [297].
[128] ILO, Freedom of Association: Digest of Decisions and Principles, [298].
[129] ILO, Freedom of Association: Digest of Decisions and Principles, [300].
[130] ILO, Freedom of Association: Digest of Decisions and Principles, [302]–[304].
[131] CESCR, Concluding Observations: Croatia, E/C.12/1/Add.73 (5 December 2001), [16]; Ecuador, E/C.12/1/Add.100 (7 June 2004), [19]; Panama, E/C.12/1/Add.64 (24 September 2001), [15].
[132] CESCR, Concluding Observations: Ecuador, E/C.12/1/Add.100 (7 June 2004), [19]; India, E/C.12/IND/CO/5 (8 August 2008), [23].
[133] CESCR, Concluding Observations: India, E/C.12/IND/CO/5 (8 August 2008), [23].
[134] ILO, Freedom of Association: Digest of Decisions and Principles, [287].
[135] ILO, Freedom of Association: Digest of Decisions and Principles, [292] and [284], respectively.
[136] ILO, Freedom of Association: Digest of Decisions and Principles, [285].
[137] ILO, Freedom of Association: Digest of Decisions and Principles, [283].
[138] ILO, Freedom of Association: Digest of Decisions and Principles, [291].

also 30 per cent of the workers concerned to be too high.[139] The ILO has also faulted minimum membership requirements for employers' organizations, such as a provision requiring ten or more employers in the same sector to establish an employers' association.[140]

Minimum membership requirements are sometimes coupled with qualitative requirements. The ILO thus criticized a law which required 60 per cent of a union's members to be literate;[141] under the ICESCR, such a condition could also amount to prohibited discrimination on the basis of 'other status'. Qualitative conditions alone may also infringe the freedom of association. It is not permissible to require that workers be employees of only one employer to establish a union,[142] or have attained the age of majority.[143]

National security and/or destruction of others' rights

A Soviet proposal to explicitly exclude fascist or anti-democratic associations from the protection of Article 22 of the ICCPR was not adopted during the drafting.[144] However, the prohibition of such groups may be a justifiable restriction to protect the rights of others under Article 22(2) of the ICCPR and Article 8(1) of the ICESCR, as well as under common Article 5(1) of the ICCPR/ICESCR, which prohibits the abuse of rights.[145] In addition, the national security exception in Article 22 of the ICCPR and Article 8 of the ICESCR would likely permit their prohibition or restriction in cases where they present a grave threat.

Thus far, there is little interpretive practice on the non-registration, prohibition or dissolution of trade unions which aim at the destruction of the rights of others, or otherwise threaten national security. Most of the international and regional cases concern political organizations, although aspects of the limitations analysis applied in such cases may apply to trade unions. In *MA v Italy*, the HRC found that the protection of Article 22 did not extend to a person convicted of reorganizing a dissolved Italian fascist party:

13.3 The execution of a sentence of imprisonment imposed prior to the entry into force of the Covenant is not in itself a violation of the Covenant. Moreover, it would appear to the Committee that the acts of which M.A. was convicted (reorganizing the dissolved fascist party) were of a kind which are removed from the protection of the Covenant by article 5 thereof and which were in any event justifiably prohibited by Italian law having regard to the limitations and restrictions applicable to the rights in question under the provisions of articles 18 (3), 19 (3), 22 (2) and 25 of the Covenant. In these respects therefore the

139 ILO, Freedom of Association: Digest of Decisions and Principles, [290] and [288], respectively.
140 ILO, Freedom of Association: Digest of Decisions and Principles, [293].
141 ILO, Freedom of Association: Digest of Decisions and Principles, [242].
142 ILO, Freedom of Association: Digest of Decisions and Principles, [271].
143 ILO, *Giving Globalization a Human Face*, 41. 144 Nowak, *CCPR Commentary*, 505.
145 It may also be justified by prohibition on propaganda for war and advocacy of hatred in Article 20 of the ICCPR: Nowak, *CCPR Commentary*, 505.

communication is inadmissible under article 3 of the Optional Protocol, as incompatible with the provisions of the Covenant, *ratione materiae*.[146]

In the ECHR case of *United Communist Party of Turkey v Turkey*,[147] a Kurdish communist party was dissolved by the state for its alleged involvement in terrorism and the threat it posed to Turkey's existence. Turkey claimed this was a necessary restriction on freedom of association under Article 11 of the ECHR, to ensure national security, public safety, territorial integrity, and the rights and freedoms of others.[148] The ECtHR accepted that the measure was taken in pursuit of at least the legitimate aim of national security.[149] The Court found, however, that the ban was disproportionate to that aim and unnecessary in a democratic society, given the importance of political pluralism to democracy and the lack of evidence that the party was involved in terrorism or threatened the rights and freedoms of others:

51. The Court notes at the outset that the TBKP was dissolved even before it had been able to start its activities and that the dissolution was therefore ordered solely on the basis of the TBKP's constitution and programme, which however—as is for that matter apparent from the Constitutional Court's decision—contain nothing to suggest that they did not reflect the party's true objectives and its leaders' true intentions (see paragraph 58 below). Like the national authorities, the Court will therefore take those documents as a basis for assessing whether the interference in question was necessary.

...

53. In the first... [submission accepted by the Turkish court] it was alleged that the TBKP had included the word 'communist' in its name, contrary to section 96(3) of Law no. 2820 (see paragraph 12 above). The Constitutional Court held, in particular, that that provision prohibited the formation of political parties on a purely formal ground: the mere fact of using a name proscribed in that section sufficed to trigger its application and consequently to entail the dissolution of any political party that, like the TBKP, had contravened it (see paragraph 10 above).

54. The Court considers that a political party's choice of name cannot in principle justify a measure as drastic as dissolution, in the absence of other relevant and sufficient circumstances.

In this connection, it must be noted, firstly, that on 12 April 1991 the provisions of the Criminal Code making it a criminal offence to carry on political activities inspired, in particular, by communist ideology were repealed by Law no. 3713 on the prevention of terrorism. The Court also attaches much weight to the Constitutional Court's finding that the TBKP was not seeking, in spite of its name, to establish the domination of one social

[146] *MA v Italy*, HRC Communication No. 117/81 (21 September 1981), [13.3]. The complaint was found inadmissible, but could have been examined on the merits on the basis of the same reasons: Sarah Joseph, Jenny Schultz and Melissa Castan, *The International Covenant on Civil and Political Rights: Cases, Materials, and Commentary* (2nd edn, Oxford University Press, Oxford, 2004), 534.

[147] *United Communist Party of Turkey et al v Turkey* (App. 133/1996/752/951), 30 January 1998, (1998) 26 EHRR 121.

[148] *United Communist Party of Turkey*, [39].

[149] *United Communist Party of Turkey*, [41].

class over the others, and that, on the contrary, it satisfied the requirements of democracy, including political pluralism, universal suffrage and freedom to take part in politics (see paragraph 10 above). In that respect, the TBKP was clearly different from the German Communist Party, which was dissolved on 17 August 1956 by the German Constitutional Court (see the Commission's decision cited above in the German Communist Party case).

Accordingly, in the absence of any concrete evidence to show that in choosing to call itself 'communist', the TBKP had opted for a policy that represented a real threat to Turkish society or the Turkish State, the Court cannot accept that the submission based on the party's name may, by itself, entail the party's dissolution.

55. The second submission accepted by the Constitutional Court was that the TBKP sought to promote separatism and the division of the Turkish nation. By drawing a distinction in its constitution and programme between the Kurdish and Turkish nations, the TBKP had revealed its intention of working to achieve the creation of minorities which—with the exception of those referred to in the Treaty of Lausanne and the treaty with Bulgaria—posed a threat to the State's territorial integrity. It was for that reason that self-determination and regional autonomy were both proscribed by the Constitution (see paragraph 10 above).

56. The Court notes that although the TBKP refers in its programme (see paragraph 9 above) to the Kurdish 'people' and 'nation' and Kurdish 'citizens', it neither describes them as a 'minority' nor makes any claim—other than for recognition of their existence—for them to enjoy special treatment or rights, still less a right to secede from the rest of the Turkish population. On the contrary, the programme states: 'The TBKP will strive for a peaceful, democratic and fair solution of the Kurdish problem, so that the Kurdish and Turkish peoples may live together of their free will within the borders of the Turkish Republic, on the basis of equal rights and with a view to democratic restructuring founded on their common interests.' With regard to the right to self-determination, the TBKP does no more in its programme than deplore the fact that because of the use of violence, it was not 'exercised jointly, but separately and unilaterally', adding that 'the remedy for this problem is political' and that '[i]f the oppression of the Kurdish people and discrimination against them are to end, Turks and Kurds must unite'.

The TBKP also said in its programme: 'A solution to the Kurdish problem will only be found if the parties concerned are able to express their opinions freely, if they agree not to resort to violence in any form in order to resolve the problem and if they are able to take part in politics with their own national identity.'

57. The Court considers one of the principal characteristics of democracy to be the possibility it offers of resolving a country's problems through dialogue, without recourse to violence, even when they are irksome. Democracy thrives on freedom of expression. From that point of view, there can be no justification for hindering a political group solely because it seeks to debate in public the situation of part of the State's population and to take part in the nation's political life in order to find, according to democratic rules, solutions capable of satisfying everyone concerned. To judge by its programme, that was indeed the TBKP's objective in this area. That distinguishes the present case from those referred to by the Government (see paragraph 49 above).

58. Admittedly, it cannot be ruled out that a party's political programme may conceal objectives and intentions different from the ones it proclaims. To verify that it does not, the content of the programme must be compared with the party's actions and the positions it

defends. In the present case, the TBKP's programme could hardly have been belied by any practical action it took, since it was dissolved immediately after being formed and accordingly did not even have time to take any action. It was thus penalised for conduct relating solely to the exercise of freedom of expression.

59. The Court is also prepared to take into account the background of cases before it, in particular the difficulties associated with the fight against terrorism (see, among other authorities, the Ireland v. the United Kingdom judgment cited above, pp. 9 et seq., §§ 11 et seq., and the Aksoy v. Turkey judgment of 18 December 1996, Reports 1996-VI, pp. 2281 and 2284, §§ 70 and 84). In the present case, however, it finds no evidence to enable it to conclude, in the absence of any activity by the TBKP, that the party bore any responsibility for the problems which terrorism poses in Turkey.

60. Nor is there any need to bring Article 17 into play as nothing in the constitution and programme of the TBKP warrants the conclusion that it relied on the Convention to engage in activity or perform acts aimed at the destruction of any of the rights and freedoms set forth in it (see, mutatis mutandis, the Lawless v. Ireland judgment of 1 July 1961 (merits), Series A no. 3, pp. 45–46, § 7).

61. Regard being had to all the above, a measure as drastic as the immediate and permanent dissolution of the TBKP, ordered before its activities had even started and coupled with a ban barring its leaders from discharging any other political responsibility, is disproportionate to the aim pursued and consequently unnecessary in a democratic society. It follows that the measure infringed Article 11 of the Convention.

In another ECtHR case, *Sidiropoulos v Greece*, the Greek courts refused to register a minority Macedonian organization alleged to endanger national security, public order, and Greece's cultural traditions and historical and cultural symbols.[150] This was because of the organization's alleged intention to dispute the Greek identity and population in the Macedonian region and to undermine Greece's territorial integrity. The ECtHR found that only the security and order aims were legitimate grounds for restrictions under Article 11 of the ECHR, but not the concern about undermining cultural considerations. The Court thus stated that: '[e]xceptions to freedom of association must be narrowly interpreted, such that the enumeration of them is strictly exhaustive and the definition of them necessarily restrictive'.[151] The Court found that the permissible grounds of restriction were 'prescribed by law'[152] before discussing the requirement that the restrictions be 'necessary in a democratic society', in the context of freedom of association:

40. The Court points out that the right to form an association is an inherent part of the right set forth in Article 11, even if that Article only makes express reference to the right to form trade unions. That citizens should be able to form a legal entity in order to act collectively in a field of mutual interest is one of the most important aspects of the right to freedom of association, without which that right would be deprived of any meaning. The way in which national legislation enshrines this freedom and its practical application by the authorities

[150] *Sidiropoulos et al v Greece* (App. 57/1997/841/1047), 10 July 1998, (1998-IV) 27 EHRR 633, [37].

[151] *Sidiropoulos v Greece*, [38].

[152] *Sidiropoulos v Greece*, [39].

reveal the state of democracy in the country concerned. Certainly States have a right to satisfy themselves that an association's aim and activities are in conformity with the rules laid down in legislation, but they must do so in a manner compatible with their obligations under the Convention and subject to review by the Convention institutions.

Consequently, the exceptions set out in Article 11 are to be construed strictly; only convincing and compelling reasons can justify restrictions on freedom of association. In determining whether a necessity within the meaning of Article 11 § 2 exists, the States have only a limited margin of appreciation, which goes hand in hand with rigorous European supervision embracing both the law and the decisions applying it, including those given by independent courts.

When the Court carries out its scrutiny, its task is not to substitute its own view for that of the relevant national authorities but rather to review under Article 11 the decisions they delivered in the exercise of their discretion. This does not mean that it has to confine itself to ascertaining whether the respondent State exercised its discretion reasonably, carefully and in good faith; it must look at the interference complained of in the light of the case as a whole and determine whether it was 'proportionate to the legitimate aim pursued' and whether the reasons adduced by the national authorities to justify it are 'relevant and sufficient'. In so doing, the Court has to satisfy itself that the national authorities applied standards which were in conformity with the principles embodied in Article 11 and, moreover, that they based their decisions on an acceptable assessment of the relevant facts (see, the United Communist Party of Turkey and Others judgment cited above, p. 22, §§ 46 and 47).

On the facts, the Court found that the measures were disproportionate and violated Article 11. This was because the organization's memorandum of association indicated that it was devoted to the peaceful pursuit of minority cultural and spiritual heritage, and there was no other evidence that the organization posed a danger to Greece's territorial integrity:

44. The Court notes, in the first place, that the aims of the association called 'Home of Macedonian Civilisation', as set out in its memorandum of association, were exclusively to preserve and develop the traditions and folk culture of the Florina region (see paragraph 8 above). Such aims appear to the Court to be perfectly clear and legitimate; the inhabitants of a region in a country are entitled to form associations in order to promote the region's special characteristics, for historical as well as economic reasons. Even supposing that the founders of an association like the one in the instant case assert a minority consciousness, the Document of the Copenhagen Meeting of the Conference on the Human Dimension of the CSCE (Section IV) of 29 June 1990 and the Charter of Paris for a New Europe of 21 November 1990—which Greece has signed—allow them to form associations to protect their cultural and spiritual heritage.

In the second place, in justifying its refusal of the application for registration, the Salonika Court of Appeal decided that it had 'good reasons... to believe that the purpose of using the term "Macedonian" [was] to dispute the Greek identity of Macedonia and its inhabitants by indirect and therefore underhand means, and discern[ed] in it an intention on the part of the founders to undermine Greece's territorial integrity'.

In reaching that decision, the Court of Appeal, of its own motion, took into consideration as evidence material which the applicants maintained they had not been able to challenge during the proceedings as it had not been placed in the case file.

45. The Court reiterates that the taking of evidence is governed primarily by the rules of domestic law and that it is in principle for the national courts to assess the evidence before them (see, among many other authorities, the Saïdi v. France judgment of 20 September 1993, Series A no. 261-C, p. 56, § 43).

However, careful study of the press articles in question (see paragraphs 14 and 15 above), which had a decisive influence on the outcome of the proceedings, shows that they reported matters some of which were unconnected with the applicants and drew inferences derived from a subjective assessment by the authors of the articles. Relying on those articles and having regard to the political dispute that then dominated relations between Greece and the FYROM (the latter of which had not yet even proclaimed its independence at the material time), the national courts held that the applicants and the association they wished to found represented a danger to Greece's territorial integrity.

That statement, however, was based on a mere suspicion as to the true intentions of the association's founders and the activities it might have engaged in once it had begun to function.

The Court also takes into account in this context the fact that Greek law does not lay down a system of preventive review for setting up non-profit-making associations. Article 12 of the Constitution provides that the forming of associations cannot be made subject to prior authorisation (see paragraph 17 above); Article 81 of the Civil Code allows the courts merely to review lawfulness and not to review desirability (see paragraph 18 above).

46. In the United Communist Party of Turkey and Others judgment cited above (p. 35, § 58) the Court held that it could not rule out that a political party's programme might conceal objectives and intentions different from the ones it proclaimed. To verify that it did not, the content of the programme had to be compared with the party's actions and the positions it defended.

Similarly, in the instant case the Court does not rule out that, once founded, the association might, under cover of the aims mentioned in its memorandum of association, have engaged in activities incompatible with those aims. Such a possibility, which the national courts saw as a certainty, could hardly have been belied by any practical action as, having never existed, the association did not have time to take any action. If the possibility had become a reality, the authorities would not have been powerless; under Article 105 of the Civil Code, the Court of First Instance could order that the association should be dissolved if it subsequently pursued an aim different from the one laid down in its memorandum of association or if its functioning proved to be contrary to law, morality or public order (see paragraph 18 above).

47. In the light of the foregoing, the Court concludes that the refusal to register the applicants' association was disproportionate to the objectives pursued. That being so, there has been a violation of Article 11.

In view of the above jurisprudence in relation to political associations, restrictions on the right to form trade unions, or on their continued existence, should not be lightly presumed under Article 8(1) of the ICESCR, even where national security or the rights of others is invoked. Trade unions may be vulnerable to abusive prohibition because of their political sympathies (including links with communism), their international affiliations (bringing perceptions of external interference in national sovereignty), the potentially damaging effects of strikes on the national economy or employers, or fears of public disorder ensuing from protests and demonstrations. Unions are less likely to engage state concerns on issues of territorial integrity or racial hatred.

RIGHT TO 'JOIN THE TRADE UNION OF HIS CHOICE, SUBJECT ONLY TO THE RULES OF THE ORGANIZATION'

During the drafting, some states were concerned that by simply protecting the right of everyone to join the union 'of his choice', an earlier draft of Article 8 would deprive unions 'of the right to determine their own organization in certain particulars, such as conditions of membership'.[153] It would further imply that states had a duty to ensure that even those who did not fulfil the conditions of membership were able to join.[154] In consequence, Canada proposed adding the phrase 'subject only to the rules of the organization concerned'.[155] The Philippines was concerned that this might protect union rules which would otherwise be 'contrary to the general policies or laws of a particular country',[156] but the amendment was adopted.[157]

Unions thus enjoy a right to regulate the terms and conditions of their own membership. The state must accordingly refrain from legally mandating membership conditions. In practice, restrictions on membership eligibility which raise concerns under Article 8 most commonly arise due to legal interferences by the state (or by employers exercising statutory powers[158]) rather than because of abusive or arbitrary criteria for membership imposed by unions. Whereas states may not limit membership by reference to trade, occupation or enterprise, unions are free to specify and confine their membership in these ways.

While membership is subject 'only' to the organization's rules, in practice it is accepted that the limitations clause within the same provision (Article 8(1)(a)) still applies. Thus, the state may lawfully interfere in union rules which infringe the rights of others, such as membership conditions which involve discrimination (such as on the basis of race, ethnicity, religion, gender, age, nationality and so on) or impair other trade union rights.[159]

It may also be permissible for states to prevent managerial or supervisory employees (who represent the employer's interests) from being members of the same unions as their workers, as long as: (a) the former can form and join unions of their own; and (b) members of the former categories are not defined so broadly

153 UNGA Third Committee, A/C.3/SR.719 (3 January 1957), 191 (Pakistan).
154 UNGA Third Committee, A/C.3/SR.721 (4 January 1957), 201 (Canada).
155 UNGA Third Committee, A/C.3/SR.721 (4 January 1957), 201 (Canada).
156 UNGA Third Committee, A/C.3/SR.722 (7 January 1957), 207 (Philippines).
157 By twenty-five votes to nine, with thirty-five abstentions.
158 ILO, Freedom of Association: Digest of Decisions and Principles, [237] (where a law allowed universities to determine who could join staff associations).
159 See also Craven, *The ICESCR*, 253 and 266.

as to substantially weaken membership of the unions of the latter.[160] Managers and supervisors are generally those who can appoint or dismiss staff, but it is too expansive to include anyone who exercises disciplinary control.[161] Artificial promotions to deplete union strength are also out of order.

Implications of the 'choice' to join a union—trade union diversity

The ILO has noted that the freedom to form and join a union must be respected 'in law and in fact'.[162] The degree of factual freedom to join a union of one's choice will partly depend on the number of unions that exist and the ability of a person to choose one they prefer. As noted earlier, in monitoring states, the CESCR has been concerned about trade union monopolies,[163] prohibitions on multiple unions in a single enterprise[164] (or by extension, occupational category[165]) and centralized or politicized trade union structures (including single central federations or confederations[166]) controlled by a government.[167] It was concerned where a military government in Nigeria decreased the number of unions from forty-two to twenty-nine, dissolving some unions and appointing military administrators to them.[168] The CESCR has thus emphasized independence from government and pluralism in trade unionism.[169]

ILO Convention No. 87 (Articles 2 and 11) supports neither union diversity nor unity; it requires only that workers must be free to choose diversity and that states must not mandate unity.[170] The ILO notes that it 'may be generally to the advantage of workers to avoid a multiplicity of trade union organizations'[171] because of the stronger bargaining power unity brings. Even if a state is genuinely concerned for workers, it still must not institutionalize monopolies and must leave it to workers to voluntarily unify their representative structures.[172]

States must also refrain from treating some unions more favourably and discriminating against others, which can influence workers' choice of union[173] and impair

[160] ILO, Freedom of Association: Digest of Decisions and Principles, [247].
[161] ILO, Freedom of Association: Digest of Decisions and Principles, [249] and [250].
[162] ILO, Freedom of Association: Digest of Decisions and Principles, [309].
[163] CESCR, Concluding Observations: Mexico, E/C.12/MEX/CO/4 (9 June 2006), [16]; see also Craven, *The ICESCR*, 267.
[164] CESCR, Concluding Observations: Honduras, E/C.12/1/Add.57 (21 May 2001) and [18].
[165] ILO, Freedom of Association: Digest of Decisions and Principles, [313], [315]–[317].
[166] CESCR, Concluding Observations: Syrian Arab Republic, E/C.12/1/Add.63 (24 September 2001), [20]; Ukraine, E/C.12/UKR/CO/5 (4 January 2008), [17]; Tunisia, E/C.12/1/Add.36 (14 May 1999), [15].
[167] CESCR, Concluding Observations: Democratic People's Republic of Korea, E/C.12/1/Add.95 (12 December 2003), [16]; Iraq, E/C.12/1/Add.17 (12 December 1997), [16]; Kenya, E/C.12/1993/6 (3 June 1993), [13]; China, E/C.12/1/Add.107 (13 May 2005), [26], [55]; Syrian Arab Republic, E/C.12/1/Add.63 (24 September 2001), [20].
[168] CESCR, Concluding Observations: Nigeria, E/C.12/1/Add.23 (16 June 1998), [15].
[169] CESCR, Consideration of Report Submitted by State Party: Vietnam, E/1994/23 (1993), [139]; see also ILO, Freedom of Association: Digest of Decisions and Principles, [311].
[170] ILO, Freedom of Association: Digest of Decisions and Principles, [323].
[171] ILO, Freedom of Association: Digest of Decisions and Principles, [319]; see also [320]–[332].
[172] ILO, Freedom of Association: Digest of Decisions and Principles, [329].
[173] ILO, Freedom of Association: Digest of Decisions and Principles, [339].

their free choice. Favouritism may occur, for example, by governments making public statements supporting one union or denigrating another; unequally distributing union subsidies; offering premises or facilities to some but not others, or arbitrarily evicting a union; refusing to recognize the leaders of a union; establishing an alternative union; or offering unfair inducements to join a different union.[174]

In is accepted, however, that states may permissibly privilege certain unions in some circumstances. Reference may be made to Article 3(5) of the ILO Constitution:

> The Members undertake to nominate non-Government delegates and advisers chosen in agreement with the industrial organisations, if such organisations exist, which are most representative of employers or workpeople, as the case may be, in their respective countries.

Thus, a 'most representative' union may be given 'priority in representation, on the ground of their having the largest membership, for such purposes as collective bargaining or consultation by governments, or for the purpose of nominating delegates to international bodies'.[175] Privileges should generally not influence workers' choice of union; the ILO found, for instance, that a right to sit on ECOSOC would not do so.[176] Such influence may, however, be inevitable where the privilege is the right to collective bargaining, which necessarily gives the most representative union greater power to protect its workers.

Other (minority) unions cannot be deprived of their rights to defend the social and economic interests of their members. They 'should be permitted to perform their activities and at least to speak on behalf of their members and represent them in the case of an individual claim'.[177]

Where such distinctions are drawn, they must be based on pre-established, precise and objective criteria for determining representivity, and not left to state discretion, so as to avoid partiality and abuse.[178] Where it is necessary to verify membership numbers, such procedures must ensure confidentiality (to protect union members' privacy and freedom from the risk of anti-union discrimination) and impartiality and independence (to prevent political abuse).[179] Normally anonymized evidence of membership dues should be sufficient to establish the union's strength and the state should not be given lists of members' names or details.

The 'right' not to join a union

While Article 20(2) of the UDHR provides that '[n]o one may be compelled to belong to an association', no such express provision is found in Article 8 of the ICESCR, Article 22 of the ICCPR or Article 11 of the ECHR. The question arises

[174] ILO, Freedom of Association: Digest of Decisions and Principles, [342] and [344].
[175] ILO, Freedom of Association: Digest of Decisions and Principles, [346].
[176] ILO, Freedom of Association: Digest of Decisions and Principles, [355].
[177] ILO, Freedom of Association: Digest of Decisions and Principles, [359].
[178] ILO, Freedom of Association: Digest of Decisions and Principles, [347] and [348].
[179] ILO, Freedom of Association: Digest of Decisions and Principles, [350]–[353].

as to whether the freedom to join a union also implies a negative right not to join a union, and if so, what is the extent of such freedom and what kinds of restrictions may be placed upon it? Conceptually, it is difficult to see how there can exist the freedom to join a union of one's choice if one may be compelled to join a union one does not wish to choose.

In relation to the ICCPR, in *Gauthier v Canada*, a majority of the HRC found no violation of Article 22 where a journalist complained that he was compelled to acquire membership of a parliamentary press association in order to access parliamentary press facilities.[180] This was despite finding that there was a violation of freedom of expression under Article 19 because, while accreditation requirements may be legitimate in principle, the restrictions on his access were neither necessary nor proportionate to ensure the effective operation of Parliament and the safety of its members, and risked the arbitrary exclusion of individuals.[181] A minority of four HRC members also found a violation of Article 22 for violating the author's right not to join an association:

In regard to article 22, the author's claim is that requiring membership in the Press Gallery Association as a condition of access to the Parliamentary press facilities violated his rights under article 22. The right to freedom of association implies that in general no one may be forced by the State to join an association. When membership of an association is a requirement to engage in a particular profession or calling, or when sanctions exist on the failure to be a member of an association, the State party should be called on to show that compulsory membership is necessary in a democratic society in pursuit of an interest authorised by the Covenant. In this matter, the Committee's deliberations in paragraph 13.6 of the Views make it clear that the State party has failed to show that the requirement to be a member of a particular organisation is a necessary restriction under paragraph 2 of article 22 in order to limit access to the press gallery in Parliament for the purposes mentioned. The restrictions imposed on the author are therefore in violation of article 22 of the Covenant.[182]

Under Article 11 of the ECHR, in the *Young* case, concerning 'closed shop' arrangements (discussed further below), the European Court of Human Rights refrained from deciding whether freedom of association encompassed an equal negative right not to be compelled to join a union.[183] However, the Court found that at least some of the negative aspect was protected, where compulsion 'would strike at the very substance of the freedom':

52. …The Court recalls, however, that the right to form and to join trade unions is a special aspect of freedom of association (see the National Union of Belgian Police judgment of 27 October 1975, Series A no. 19, p. 17, par. 38); it adds that the notion of a freedom implies some measure of freedom of choice as to its exercise.

[180] *Gauthier v Canada*, HRC Communication No. 633/1995 (5 May 1999), [13.2].

[181] *Gauthier v Canada*, [13.6].

[182] *Gauthier v Canada*, Individual Opinion by members Lord Colville, Elizabeth Evatt, Cecilia Medina Quiroga and Mr Hipólito Solari Yrigoyen (partly dissenting).

[183] *Young v UK*, [51] and [52].

Assuming for the sake of argument that, for the reasons given in the above-cited passage from the travaux préparatoires, a general rule such as that in Article 20 par. 2 of the Universal Declaration of Human Rights was deliberately omitted from, and so cannot be regarded as itself enshrined in, the Convention, it does not follow that the negative aspect of a person's freedom of association falls completely outside the ambit of Article 11 (art. 11) and that each and every compulsion to join a particular trade union is compatible with the intention of that provision. To construe Article 11 (art. 11) as permitting every kind of compulsion in the field of trade union membership would strike at the very substance of the freedom it is designed to guarantee…

On the facts, the Court found that a threat of dismissal for not joining, involving loss of livelihood, was a serious form of compulsion. Where directed against a person employed before the imposition of any obligation to join a particular union, it also struck at the very substance of the freedom guaranteed by Article 11:

55. The situation facing the applicants clearly runs counter to the concept of freedom of association in its negative sense.

Assuming that Article 11 (art. 11) does not guarantee the negative aspect of that freedom on the same footing as the positive aspect, compulsion to join a particular trade union may not always be contrary to the Convention.

However, a threat of dismissal involving loss of livelihood is a most serious form of compulsion and, in the present instance, it was directed against persons engaged by British Rail before the introduction of any obligation to join a particular trade union.

In the Court's opinion, such a form of compulsion, in the circumstances of the case, strikes at the very substance of the freedom guaranteed by Article 11 (art. 11). For this reason alone, there has been an interference with that freedom as regards each of the three applicants.

The compulsion was not cured by the possibility of joining other organizations:

56. Another facet of this case concerns the restriction of the applicants' choice as regards the trade unions which they could join of their own volition. An individual does not enjoy the right to freedom of association if in reality the freedom of action or choice which remains available to him is either non-existent or so reduced as to be of no practical value (see, mutatis mutandis, the Airey judgment of 9 October 1979, Series A no. 32, p. 12, par. 24).

The Government submitted that the relevant legislation (see paragraph 26 above) not only did not restrict but also expressly protected freedom of action or choice in this area; in particular, it would have been open to the applicants to form or to join a trade union in addition to one of the specified unions. The applicants, on the other hand, claimed that this was not the case in practice, since such a step would have been precluded by British Rail's agreement with the railway unions and by the Bridlington Principles (see paragraph 27 above); in their view, joining and taking part in the activities of a competing union would, if attempted, have led to expulsion from one of the specified unions. These submissions were, however, contested by the Government.

Be that as it may, such freedom of action or choice as might have been left to the applicants in this respect would not in any way have altered the compulsion to which they were subjected since they would in any event have been dismissed if they had not become members of one of the specified unions.

The Court also considered freedom of association in the light of the related freedoms of thought, conscience and expression, which are 'purposes' of free association, given that the applicants objected to the trade unions' policies, activities and political affiliations.[184]

Whether the Court thought the above interference was justified by the rationale for closed shop arrangements is considered in the next section. A separate concurring opinion of eight judges found that compulsory membership alone violates Article 11, even absent the additional factors of dismissal or infringements of freedom of thought and the like (which tipped the balance for the majority):

> We voted in favour of the operative provisions of the judgment, but the reasons which it contains do not appear to us to reflect properly the scope of freedom of association as guaranteed by Article 11 (art. 11) of the Convention.
>
> By confining itself strictly to what it calls the "substance" of the right, the Court's judgment leaves outside the protection of the Convention numerous situations entailed by legislation permitting the closed shop.
>
> In fact, as we understand Article 11 (art. 11), the negative aspect of freedom of association is necessarily complementary to, a correlative of and inseparable from its positive aspect. Protection of freedom of association would be incomplete if it extended to no more than the positive aspect. It is one and the same right that is involved.
>
> The 'travaux préparatoires' of the Convention—which anyway are not conclusive—speak only of 'undesirability' and so do not enable one to conclude that the negative aspect of trade union freedom was intended to be excluded from the ambit of Article 11 (art. 11).
>
> In its judgment, the Court rightly states that, in the present case, Article 11 (art. 11) has implications in the area covered by Articles 9 and 10 (art. 9, art. 10) of the Convention. We should like to point out that it is not necessary, for there to be a violation of Article 11 (art. 11), that the refusal to join an association was justified by considerations, connected with freedom of thought, of conscience or of religion, or with freedom of expression. In our view, the mere fact of being obliged to give the reasons for one's refusal constitutes a violation of freedom of association.
>
> Trade union freedom, a form of freedom of association, involves freedom of choice: it implies that a person has a choice as to whether he will belong to an association or not and that, in the former case, he is able to choose the association. However, the possibility of choice, an indispensable component of freedom of association, is in reality non-existent where there is a trade union monopoly of the kind encountered in the present case.
>
> Here, the sanction—be it the giving of notice or dismissal—which was a consequence of the system instituted by the law, did not give rise to but simply aggravated the violation. The violation, already constituted by compulsion in the shape of obligatory membership, is irreconcilable with the freedom of choice that is inherent in freedom of association.[185]

[184] *Young v UK*, [57].

[185] *Young v UK*, Concurring Opinion of Judges Ganshof van der Meersch, Bindschedler-Robert, Liesch, Gölcüklü, Matscher, Pinheiro Farinha and Pettiti.

Some have argued that this more protective approach should also apply in the context of Article 22 of the ICCPR.[186]

In *Sigurjonsson v Iceland*, the European Court of Human Rights found a violation of Article 11 where a taxi driver was forced to be a paid-up member of a private taxi industry association (Frami) or face losing his taxi licence.[187] Following *Young*, and in light of international practice, the Court found that Article 11 recognized a negative right of association, although it was unnecessary to decide if it was equal to the positive right:

35. As to the question of the general scope of the right in issue, the Court notes, in the first place, that although the aforementioned judgment [*Young*] took account of the travaux préparatoires, it did not attach decisive importance to them; rather it used them as a working hypothesis... Moreover, whereas the membership obligation concerning Mr Young, Mr James and Mr Webster was based on an agreement between their employer and the trade unions, that of Mr Sigurdur A. Sigurjónsson was imposed by law. Under Articles 5 and 8 of the 1989 Law and Article 8 of the 1989 Regulation, he had to be a member of a specified association—Frami—in order to satisfy the licence conditions and it was not possible for him to join or form another association for that purpose. It was further provided that a failure to meet this condition could entail revocation of the licence and liability to pay a fine. Compulsory membership of this nature, which, it may be recalled, concerned a private-law association, does not exist under the laws of the great majority of the Contracting States. On the contrary, a large number of domestic systems contain safeguards which, in one way or another, guarantee the negative aspect of the freedom of association, that is the freedom not to join or to withdraw from an association.

A growing measure of common ground has emerged in this area also at the international level... Even in the absence of an express provision, the Committee of Independent Experts set up to supervise the implementation of the [European Social] Charter considers that a negative right is covered by this instrument and it has in several instances disapproved of closed-shop practices found in certain States Parties, including Iceland...

Furthermore, according to the practice of the Freedom of Association Committee of the Governing Body of the International Labour Office (ILO), union security measures imposed by law, notably by making union membership compulsory, would be incompatible with Conventions Nos. 87 and 98 (the first concerning freedom of association and the right to organise and the second the application of the principles of the right to organise and to bargain collectively; see Digest of decisions and principles of the said committee, 1985, paragraph 248).

In this connection, it should be recalled that the Convention is a living instrument which must be interpreted in the light of present-day conditions (see, amongst other authorities, the Soering v. the United Kingdom judgment of 7 July 1989, Series A no. 161, p. 40, para. 102). Accordingly, Article 11 (art. 11) must be viewed as encompassing a negative right of association. It is not necessary for the Court to determine in this instance whether this right is to be considered on an equal footing with the positive right.

The Court also considered Article 11 in the light of Articles 9 and 10 of the ECHR (freedom of opinion and expression), given that the applicant disagreed with the

[186] Nowak, *CCPR Commentary*, 502.

[187] *Sigurjónsson v Iceland*.

association's policies. In examining whether the interference was justified under the limitations clause in Article 11(2), the Court accepted that the membership requirement was 'prescribed by law' and pursued the legitimate aim of protecting the rights and freedoms of others,[188] namely by regulating the taxi industry in the public interest. It found, however, that although the state's reasons for imposing the restrictions were relevant, they were neither necessary nor proportionate in a democratic society:

41. In the first place, the Court recalls that the impugned membership obligation was one imposed by law, the breach of which was likely to bring about the revocation of the applicant's licence. He was thus subjected to a form of compulsion which, as already stated, is rare within the community of Contracting States and which, on the face of it, must be considered incompatible with Article 11 (art. 11) (see, mutatis mutandis, the Le Compte, Van Leuven and De Meyere v. Belgium judgment of 23 June 1981, Series A no. 43, p. 27, para. 65).

The Court does not doubt that Frami had a role that served not only the occupational interests of its members but also the public interest, and that its performance of the supervisory functions in question must have been facilitated by the obligation of every licence-holder within the association's area to be a member. However, the Court is not convinced that compulsory membership of Frami was required in order to perform those functions. Firstly, the main responsibility for the supervision of the implementation of the relevant rules lay with the Committee (see paragraph 20 above). Secondly, membership was by no means the only conceivable way of compelling the licence-holders to carry out such duties and responsibilities as might be necessary for the relevant functions; for instance, some of those provided for in the applicable legislation (see paragraph 22 above) could be effectively enforced without the necessity of membership. Lastly, it has not been established that there was any other reason that would have prevented Frami from protecting its members' occupational interests in the absence of the compulsory membership imposed on the applicant despite his opinions (see, inter alia, the above-mentioned Schmidt and Dahlström judgment, p. 16, para. 36, and the above-mentioned Young, James and Webster judgment, pp. 25–26, para. 64).

Having regard to the foregoing, the reasons adduced by the Government, although they can be considered relevant, are not sufficient to show that it was 'necessary' to compel the applicant to be a member of Frami, on pain of losing his licence and contrary to his own opinions. In particular, notwithstanding Iceland's margin of appreciation, the measures complained of were disproportionate to the legitimate aim pursued. Consequently, there has been a violation of Article 11 (art. 11).

In the Americas, the Inter-American Court of Human Rights has found that Article 16 of the American Convention on Human Rights and Article 8(3) of the Protocol of San Salvador protect the negative right not to join or belong to a union:

159. In labour matters, and pursuant to the terms of Article 16 of the American Convention, freedom of association includes a right and a freedom, to wit: the right to form associations without restrictions other than those permitted according to sections 2 and 3 of that conventional precept, and the freedom of all persons not to be compelled or forced to join the association. The November 17, 1988, San Salvador Protocol, in its Article 8(3), contains

[188] *Sigurjónsson v Iceland*, [39].

the same idea, and specifies that, in trade union matters '[n]o one may be obliged to belong to a labour union.'[189]

The 'right' not to join a union—'union security' clauses

On one view, 'closed shop' arrangements (or 'union security clauses') which require a worker to join a union as a condition of employment might be seen as a permissible limitation on the individual's negative freedom not to join a union, justified to secure the rights of others (namely, the union as a collective or the individual interests of the union's members).[190] The CESCR, however, has indicated that the right to form and join a union under Article 8(1) will be compromised by such requirements.[191]

A similar position has been adopted under Article 5 of the Revised European Social Charter, which guarantees the freedom to form and join organizations, but does not also mention an explicit right not to join. A complaint before the European Committee on Social Rights, *The Confederation of Swedish Enterprise v Sweden*, concerned clauses in collective agreements between trade unions and employers which required employers to give priority to union members in recruitment.[192] While Swedish law protected workers against dismissal for refusal to join a union or if they wished to withdraw from a union, it did not prohibit pre-entry closed shop clauses.

The Swedish Confederation, a business and industry body, argued that such clauses violated the right not to join a union, which it said came within the protection of Article 5. It was supported by the International Organisation of Employers. Sweden disagreed, as did the European Trade Union Confederation, which argued that the negative aspect of the right to organize should be interpreted restrictively so as not to weaken the content of the positive right to organize. The Committee found that the clauses infringed a worker's right to freely join a union, somewhat ironically ruling in favour of a complainant which was a business confederation, not a worker or worker's organization:

> 29. …the freedom guaranteed by Article 5 of the Charter implies that the exercise of a worker's right to join a trade union is the result of a choice and that, consequently, it is not to be decided by the worker under the influence of constraints that rule out the exercise of this freedom.
>
> 30. The clauses at issue set out in the collective agreements in question which reserve in practice employment for members of a certain union are clearly contrary to the freedom guaranteed by Article 5. They restrict workers' free choice as to whether or not to join one or other of the existing trade unions or to set up separate organisations of this type. Accordingly, the Committee considers that an obligation of this nature strikes at the very substance of the freedom enshrined in Article 5 and therefore constitutes an interference with that freedom.

[189] *Baena-Ricardo v Panama*, [156].

[190] See, eg, Nowak, *CCPR Commentary*, 507, commenting on possible limitations on the right of association under Article 22 of the ICCPR in the context of securing the rights of others.

[191] Craven, *The ICESCR*, 268–9.

[192] *Confederation of Swedish Enterprise v Sweden*, 15 May 2003, ECSR Complaint No. 12/2002.

The ECSR has thus weighted individual rights in relation to unions more heavily than the collective interests of workers exercised through the choices made by unions (and which may be inconsistent with the choices of certain individual workers). In the same case, the ECSR further accepted that non-union members could be forced to accept compulsory deductions provided to unions for wage monitoring, but not for other purposes.[193]

Under the ECHR, the European Court of Human Rights has refrained from determining whether closed shop arrangements as such *always* violate Article 11 and has instead confined itself to assessing the degree and justification of compulsion imposed in a given case.[194] In *Young*, mentioned above, the applicants faced dismissal for refusing to join a union as required by a law adopted after they had already been employed for some time (a 'post-entry' closed shop arrangement). While the state did not seek to justify the arrangement under the restrictions clause in Article 11(2), the Court assumed that the restrictions were 'prescribed by law' and aimed to protect the rights and freedoms of others.[195] It skirted whether the closed shop arrangement per se may be justified, noting only its purported justification in stable industrial relations:

> 61. In connection with the last point, the Court's attention has been drawn to a number of advantages said to flow from the closed shop system in general, such as the fostering of orderly collective bargaining, leading to greater stability in industrial relations; the avoidance of a proliferation of unions and the resultant trade union anarchy; the counteracting of inequality of bargaining power; meeting the need of some employers to negotiate with a body fully representative of the workforce; satisfying the wish of some trade unionists not to work alongside non-union employees; ensuring that trade union activities do not benefit those who make no financial contribution thereto.
>
> Any comment on these arguments would be out of place in the present case since the closed shop system as such is not under review…

Instead, the Court focused on whether the particular restrictions were necessary in a democratic society, which required that the measures be more than advantageous; respect pluralism, tolerance and broadmindedness, and not simply equate 'democracy' with majority decisions overriding minority interests or views; and be proportionate.[196] On the facts, the Court found that the unions could have protected their members' interests without the law compelling union membership, such that the restrictions were excessive:

> 64. The Court has noted in this connection that a majority of the Royal Commission on Trade Unions and Employers' Associations, which reported in 1968, considered that the position of existing employees in a newly-introduced closed shop was one area in which special safeguards were desirable (see paragraph 14 above). Again, recent surveys suggest that, even prior to the entry into force of the Employment Act 1980 (see paragraph 24 above), many closed shop arrangements did not require existing non-union employees to join a specified union (see paragraph 13 above); the Court has not been informed of any

[193] *Confederation of Swedish Enterprise v Sweden*, [40]. [194] *Young v UK*, [53] and [61].
[195] *Young v UK*, [60]. [196] *Young v UK*, [63].

special reasons justifying the imposition of such a requirement in the case of British Rail. Besides, according to statistics furnished by the applicants, which were not contested, a substantial majority even of union members themselves disagreed with the proposition that persons refusing to join a union for strong reasons should be dismissed from employment. Finally, in 1975 more than 95 per cent of British Rail employees were already members of NUR, TSSA or ASLEF (see paragraph 31 above).

All these factors suggest that the railway unions would in no way have been prevented from striving for the protection of their members' interests (see the above-mentioned National Union of Belgian Police judgment, p. 18, par. 39) through the operation of the agreement with British Rail even if the legislation in force had not made it permissible to compel non-union employees having objections like the applicants to join a specified union.

65. Having regard to all the circumstances of the case, the detriment suffered by Mr. Young, Mr. James and Mr. Webster went further than was required to achieve a proper balance between the conflicting interests of those involved and cannot be regarded as proportionate to the aims being pursued. Even making due allowance for a State's 'margin of appreciation' (see, inter alia, the above-mentioned Sunday Times judgment, p. 36, par. 59), the Court thus finds that the restrictions complained of were not 'necessary in a democratic society', as required by paragraph 2 of Article 11 (art. 11-2).

More recently, the European Court has been even less willing to tolerate interference with the negative right not to join unions. In *Sørensen and Rasmussen v Denmark*, the Court found that pre-entry closed shop agreements which required two new employees to join a union as a condition of employment violated Article 11.[197] The Court reiterated its previous jurisprudence that Article 11 includes a negative right of association, and added that 'personal autonomy is an important principle underlying the interpretation' of the ECHR as a whole.[198] It also extended the negative freedom to pre-entry closed shop agreements (beyond the more limited post-entry arrangement in *Young*), and closed much of the gap in the scope of protection of the positive and negative aspects of freedom of association:

56. The Court does not in principle exclude that the negative and the positive aspects of the Article 11 right should be afforded the same level of protection in the area under consideration. However, it is difficult to decide this issue in the abstract since it is a matter that can only be properly addressed in the circumstances of a given case. At the same time, an individual cannot be considered to have renounced his negative right to freedom of association in situations where, in the knowledge that trade union membership is a precondition of securing a job, he accepts an offer of employment notwithstanding his opposition to the condition imposed. Accordingly, the distinction made between pre-entry closed-shop agreements and post-entry closed-shop agreements in terms of the scope of the protection guaranteed by Article 11 is not tenable. At most, this distinction is to be seen as a consideration which will form part of the Court's assessment of the surrounding circumstances and the issue of their Convention compatibility.

[197] *Sørensen and Rasmussen v Denmark* ('*Sørensen v Denmark*') (Apps. 52562/99, 52620/99), 11 January 2006, (2008) 46 EHRR 29, [75].

[198] *Sørensen v Denmark*, [54], citing *Sigurjónsson v Iceland*, [35], [37]; *Gustafsson v Sweden*, [45]; *Young v UK*, [55] and [57]; *Chassagnou v France*, [103].

...

58. The boundaries between the State's positive and negative obligations under Article 11 of the Convention do not lend themselves to precise definition. The applicable principles are nonetheless similar. Whether the case is analysed in terms of a positive duty on the State or in terms of interference by a public authority which needs to be justified, the criteria to be applied do not differ in substance. In both contexts regard must be had to the fair balance to be struck between the competing interests of the individual and of the community as a whole...

... where the domestic law of a Contracting State permits the conclusion of closed-shop agreements between unions and employers which run counter to the freedom of choice of the individual inherent in Article 11, the margin of appreciation [normally afforded on labour issues] must be considered reduced. The Court reiterates in this connection that, although individual interests must on occasion be subordinated to those of a group, democracy does not simply mean that the views of a majority must always prevail: a balance must be achieved which ensures the fair and proper treatment of minorities and avoids any abuse of a dominant position (see Young, James and Webster, cited above, § 63, and Chassagnou and Others, cited above, §§ 112–13). In assessing whether a Contracting State has remained within its margin of appreciation in tolerating the existence of closed-shop agreements, particular weight must be attached to the justifications advanced by the authorities for them and, in any given case, the extent to which they impinge on the rights and interests protected by Article 11. Account must also be taken of changing perceptions of the relevance of closed-shop agreements for securing the effective enjoyment of trade union freedom.

The Court sees no reason not to extend these considerations to both pre-entry and post-entry closed-shop agreements.

On the facts, the Court found that the jobseekers were compelled to join the union and that this struck at the very substance of freedom of association where the requirement was unrelated to their capacity to perform the jobs and contrary to their political beliefs.[199] This was the case even though they could have sought employment elsewhere in the 90 per cent of the Danish labour market which did not involve closed shops. The Court noted that while closed shop arrangements were a long-standing practice in Denmark, given modern developments they no longer struck a fair balance between the applicants' interests and the need to ensure that trade unions can protect their members' interests:[200]

66. ... Closed-shop agreements thus presently affect only approximately 220,000 wage earners, which is equivalent to less than 10% of all Danish employees on the labour market.

67. Furthermore... the general developments in society and the labour market could no longer justify, to the same extent as before, the need for closed-shop agreements, since strong and representative trade unions and organisations had now been established on the labour market. Moreover, since closed-shop agreements merely covered a small part of the labour market, a change in the law would have only a marginal impact on union density rates...

[199] *Sørensen v Denmark*, [59]–[64].

[200] *Sørensen v Denmark*, [65]–[76].

70. …legislative attempts [in Denmark between 2003 and 2005] to eliminate entirely the use of closed-shop agreements in Denmark [though unsuccessful] would appear to reflect the trend which has emerged in the Contracting Parties, namely that such agreements are not an essential means for securing the interests of trade unions and their members and that due weight must be given to the right of individuals to join a union of their own choosing without fear of prejudice to their livelihood. In fact, only a very limited number of Contracting States, including Denmark and Iceland, continue to permit the conclusion of closed-shop agreements…

71. It is true that in the context of the Danish debate on this topic LO has voiced its opposition to the attempts to eliminate the remaining areas where pre-entry closed-shop agreements continue to be applied. LO has pointed to the severe consequences which the prohibition of closed-shop clauses would entail, and in particular its view that it would become difficult or impossible to enforce collective agreements vis-à-vis small non-affiliated employers (see paragraph 51 above). However, the Court considers that these concerns have been adequately addressed by the Minister for Employment in his reply to question no. 7 put by the parliamentary committee, namely that an annulment of a closed-shop provision in a collective-bargaining agreement with a non-organised employer would not change the fact that the collective-bargaining agreement is still valid and must be complied with (see paragraph 29 above). Furthermore, the Court has not been informed that the concerns expressed by LO have materialised in any of the very many Contracting Parties which have abolished closed-shop agreements entirely.

72. The Court also observes that the desire of the Danish legislature to bring an end to the use of closed-shop agreements in the private sector is consistent with the manner in which the 1961 Social Charter has been applied to the issue of pre-entry closed-shop agreements…

73. Reference should also be made to the Community Charter of the Fundamental Social Rights of Workers, adopted by the heads of State or government of eleven member States of the European Communities on 9 December 1989. [and to]

74. Article 12 of the Charter of Fundamental Rights of the European Union, proclaimed in Nice on 7 December 2000…

75. In view of the above, it appears that there is little support in the Contracting States for the maintenance of closed-shop agreements and that the European instruments referred to above clearly indicate that their use in the labour market is not an indispensable tool for the effective enjoyment of trade union freedoms.

In thus interpreting the ECHR as a 'living instrument', the ECtHR has adapted the requirements of Article 11 in the light of changing labour practices in ECHR member states. In doing so, it has entrenched stronger protection of the negative individual freedom not to join a union at the expense of the collective rights of unions to pursue their interests by adversely affecting non-unionized workers. Freedom of association accordingly does not have a static or innate content in the labour field, but is pegged to prevailing or dominant labour market conditions.

This approach may be appropriate in the highly integrated European regional human rights community. However, it may present difficulties if transposed to the ICESCR, since national labour regulation worldwide varies much more and it would be more difficult to identify a global consensus. Regardless, given that the CESCR has prioritized the right of individual workers not to join unions over collective union rights, the recent ECtHR approach brings European states closer into line with ICESCR practice, even if the CESCR's approach would not appear to be based on the greater diversity of national practice globally.

ILO practice is less strict about protecting individual rights over collective ones in this context. Conventions No. 87 and No. 98 neither require nor prohibit either a negative individual right not to join a union or a collective right to compel others to join. Instead, states remain free to choose whether to guarantee a right not to join a union or conversely to permit union security clauses (in the interests of solidarity).[201] Where the latter is permitted, it must, however, result from voluntary negotiation between unions and employers.

In a given state, the rights of a union may thus be prioritized over the rights of individual workers (or minority unions where a 'representative' union is privileged in bargaining). Such clauses may even require non-union members to pay dues to a union, although this should not be imposed by law.[202] Where union membership is a condition of employment, however, there may be discrimination if unreasonable or arbitrary conditions are imposed on a person seeking to join.[203]

Three dissenting judges of the European Court of Human Rights in *Young* preferred the ILO approach, on the basis of the drafting history of the ECHR (and the European Social Charter) and a 'logical' analysis of the relationship between the positive and negative aspects of freedom of association. Judges Sørensen, Thór Vilhálmsson and Lagergren found that union security arrangements and 'closed shops' are neither prohibited nor authorized by Article 11, but left to national discretion.[204]

A different consideration arises at the regional level under Article 10(2) of the African Charter, which expressly provides that 'no one may be compelled to join an association', but then subjects that protection to the multi-faceted 'obligation of solidarity' in Article 29 of the Charter. In practice, 'duties' under the African Charter have been interpreted reasonably restrictively, and there is little evidence thus far that Article 29 has provided a legal basis for compelling workers to join unions.

Article 8(1)(b): Right of Unions to Federate, Confederate or Internationally Associate

Notwithstanding the importance of union diversity in realizing the freedom to join a union of one's choice, workers also benefit from the coordination or

[201] ILO, *Giving Globalization a Human Face*, 37; ILO, Freedom of Association: Digest of Decisions and Principles, [363]–[366].
[202] ILO, *Giving Globalization a Human Face*, 37.
[203] ILO, Freedom of Association: Digest of Decisions and Principles, [368].
[204] *Young v UK*, Dissent of Judges Sørensen, Thór Vilhálmsson and Lagergren, [2]–[7].

harmonization of efforts to advance their interests (including, for instance, in relation to collective bargaining at a centralized national or sectoral, rather than solely enterprise, level). The right of unions under Article 8(1)(b) to establish national federations or confederations, and the right of the latter to form or join international union organizations, mirrors Article 5 of ILO Convention No. 87 of 1948:

> Workers' and employers' organisations shall have the right to establish and join federations and confederations and any such organisation, federation or confederation shall have the right to affiliate with international organisations of workers and employers.

Article 8(1)(b) is expressed as a collective right of unions, to which some objections were raised during the drafting by those who thought that the focus should be on individual rights. In general, however, the legal ability of unions to act was seen as necessary precisely so as to guarantee the related right to form and join trade unions,[205] and to most effectively represent workers' interests through the solidarity of unions.

The CESCR has occasionally expressed concern about prohibitions[206] or restrictions[207] on the establishment of national federations or confederations, or on affiliation with international trade union organizations.[208] The CESCR has recommended that such restrictions be lifted,[209] and that states take measures to ensure that the right of trade unions to establish national federations or confederations is facilitated and respected in practice.[210]

ILO practice confirms that federations or confederations of unions enjoy many of the same rights and freedom to function as the individual unions constituting them, since this is necessary to defend and promote the economic and social interests of their members. Thus, such organizations (and their component unions) are generally entitled to determine their own rules, operations, activities and programmes.[211]

Further, freedom to organize or associate will be infringed by laws: requiring prior authorization; imposing substantive restrictions as opposed to reasonable procedural formalities; predicating legal personality on state discretion; demanding an excessively high number of minimum unions to federate or confederate; limiting the right to unions of the same trade, occupation or enterprise types; prohibiting membership of certain persons; or imposing geographical restrictions on unions.[212]

The inclusion of a right to form or join international trade union organizations raised sensitivities during the drafting about international interference in

[205] Craven, *The ICESCR*, 255.

[206] CESCR, Concluding Observations: Brazil, E/C.12/BRA/CO/2 (12 June 2009), [17]; UK (Hong Kong), E/C.12/1/Add.10 (6 December 1996), [22].

[207] CESCR, Concluding Observations: Mexico, E/C.12/MEX/CO/4 (9 June 2006), [16].

[208] CESCR, Concluding Observations: UK (Hong Kong), E/C.12/1/Add.10 (6 December 1996), [22]; Nigeria, E/C.12/1/Add.23 (16 June 1998), [15].

[209] CESCR, Concluding Observations: UK (Hong Kong), E/C.12/1/Add.10 (6 December 1996), [37].

[210] CESCR, Concluding Observations: Angola, E/C.12/DZA/CO/4 (7 June 2010), [11].

[211] ILO, Freedom of Association: Digest of Decisions and Principles, [730] and [731].

[212] ILO, Freedom of Association: Digest of Decisions and Principles, [710]–[721], [725], [726] and [728].

sovereignty and domestic affairs,[213] particularly against the ideological background of socialist internationalism and revolutionary struggle. But it is generally accepted (even in market economies) that, as the ILO observes, '[i]nternational trade union solidarity constitutes one of the fundamental objectives of any trade union movement'.[214] The ILO and the United Nations also recognize the principle. To that end, unions enjoy the right to affiliate internationally (and by implication, to disaffiliate[215]). Such right is protected even when international assistance or support to unions conflicts with the social, economic or political 'tendencies' in a country.[216]

Accordingly, states must not interfere either in the establishment of or affiliation with international union organizations, or the relationship between and activities of such organisations and their affiliated unions. Unions in a particular industry or undertaking must not be prevented from affiliating with international organizations encompassing wider sectoral interests.[217] An international organization cannot be banned from receiving external financial assistance from affiliated unions, nor can affiliated unions be prevented from receiving support from the international organization.[218]

The protected relationship between international organizations and affiliated unions extends to the maintenance of contacts and communications, the exchange of information and publications, the giving and receiving of advice, support and funding, and participation in and travel to meetings. It may even extend to the embryonic possibility of multinational collective bargaining.[219]

In relation to visits, a state should not deny a trade unionist permission to exit his or her own country to attend an international meeting, or require prior authorization to do so, including to participate in meetings of the ILO.[220] Entry to a state by non-citizen trade unionists (whether of international organizations or affiliated unions) is subject to ordinary sovereign immigration law controls.[221] Article 8(1)(b) does not confer an international right of a trade unionist to enter a foreign state. However, entry (and related procedures such as visas or travel documents) must not be refused or tainted by anti-union discrimination. So too must any restrictions on national security or public order grounds be based on objective criteria (such as the risk of 'real repercussions' if entry is granted).[222] An example might be where there is strong evidence that a foreign trade union leader's presence would incite violence or serious unlawful activities.

A number of reservations to Article 8(1)(b) raise potential problems of compatibility with the object and purpose of the ICESCR. On signing the ICESCR,

[213] Craven, *The ICESCR*, 255.
[214] ILO, Freedom of Association: Digest of Decisions and Principles, [732].
[215] ILO, Freedom of Association: Digest of Decisions and Principles, [736].
[216] ILO, Freedom of Association: Digest of Decisions and Principles, [739].
[217] ILO, Freedom of Association: Digest of Decisions and Principles, [734].
[218] ILO, Freedom of Association: Digest of Decisions and Principles, [740], [742]–[744].
[219] Bamber and Sheldon, 'Collective Bargaining', 596.
[220] ILO, Freedom of Association: Digest of Decisions and Principles, [760]–[768].
[221] ILO, Freedom of Association: Digest of Decisions and Principles, [750]–[753].
[222] ILO, Freedom of Association: Digest of Decisions and Principles, [759].

the UK reserved the right not to apply Article 8(1)(b) in British Hong Kong to allow 'trade unions not engaged in the same trade or industry to establish federations or confederations'. On ratifying the ICESCR, the United Kingdom reserved the right not to apply Article 8(1)(b) at all in Hong Kong. After the handover of Hong Kong to China, China declared in 2001 that Article 8(1)(b) 'does not imply the right of trade union federations or confederations to form or join political organizations or bodies established outside' Hong Kong.[223] While no state has formally objected to the reservations of either the United Kingdom or China, in 1996 the CESCR found that the United Kingdom's then restrictions on affiliation by trade unions in Hong Kong with international trade union organizations were 'incompatible' with the ICESCR.[224] The same would apply to China's current reservation, which follows Britain's lead in restricting human rights.

In relation to international affiliation in practice, the International Trade Union Confederation (ITUC) was established in 2006 following the dissolution of two earlier but divided organizations (the International Confederation of Free Trade Unions (ICFTU) and the World Confederation of Labour (WCL)).[225] The ITUC represents 175 million workers in 156 countries and territories and has 315 national affiliates, and observer status in the ECOSOC. It also provides the Secretariat of the Workers' Group within the ILO's tripartite structure, and coordinates with regional trade union organizations (which is another level of international association protected under Article 8). Membership of the ITUC is open to '[a]ll democratic, independent and representative national trade union centres adhering to the Constitution of the Confederation'.[226] Its constitutional 'aims' are as follows:

> It shall be the permanent responsibility of the Confederation:
>
> To defend and promote the rights and interests of all working people, without distinction, and to obtain, in particular, a fair return for their labour in conditions of dignity, justice, and safety at work and in society in general.
>
> …
>
> To promote the growth and strength of the independent and democratic trade union movement.
>
> …
>
> To be a countervailing force in the global economy, committed to securing a fair distribution of wealth and income within and between countries, protection of the environment,

[223] China, Communication to the UN Secretary-General, 20 April 2001. The Chinese declaration also limits national level unionism to Hong Kong, not China: '"National federations or confederations" in Article 8.1(b) of the Covenant shall be interpreted, in this case, as "federations or confederations in the HKSAR"'.

[224] CESCR, Concluding Observations: United Kingdom, E/C.12/1/Add.10 (6 December 1996), [22].

[225] International Trade Union Confederation Constitution (adopted November 2006, amended June 2010).

[226] International Trade Union Confederation Constitution, Article I(a).

universal access to public goods and services, comprehensive social protection, life-long learning and decent work opportunities for all.

…

To make the trade union movement inclusive, and responsive to the views and needs of all sectors of the global workforce.

…

To mobilise the strength, energy, resources, commitment, and talent of its affiliates and their members in the achievement of these goals, making trade union internationalism an integral part of their daily work.

…

The Confederation pledges to pursue these goals with determination, and in accordance with the enduring trade union values of solidarity, democracy and justice. It will not desist from their achievement nor be deterred by the enemies of progress, sure in the conviction that it lies in the hands of working people to determine their own future.

Another level of international cooperation is through global union federations (GUFs), which are autonomous and self-governing bodies which unite workers in the same or related trades, industries, occupations or crafts.[227] Further, a Council of Global Unions was created in 2007 between ten GUFs, the ITUC and the Trade Union Advisory Committee to the OECD (TUAC), to more actively promote trade unions' rights.

In some cases, GUFs have negotiated with multilateral enterprises (particularly European entities) to adopt international framework agreements (IFMs) which include trade union standards, including freedom of association and collective bargaining, and reference to ILO Conventions No. 87 and No. 98.[228] IFMs aim to secure core labour rights across transnational corporations' global supply chains and have increased in number since the 1980s and 1990s.[229]

If Article 8(1)(b) also includes employers' organizations within the concept of trade unions, mention may also be made of relevant international associations[230] such as the International Organization of Employers (IOE),[231] established in 1920 and representing business in the area of labour and social policy. The IOE is comprised of 150 independent national business or employers' federations from 143 states. Membership is open to any independent and voluntary national federation which

[227] ILO, *Giving Globalization a Human Face*, 31. Global unions exist in the areas of education; chemicals, energy and mining; building and wood working; journalism; metal working; transport; textile, garment and leather working; public services; and food, agricultural, hotel, restaurant, catering and tobacco working.

[228] ILO, *Giving Globalization a Human Face*, 32.

[229] See Nikolaus Hammer, 'International Framework Agreements: Global Industrial Relations between Rights and Bargaining' (2005) 11 *Transfer* 511; ILO, 'International Framework Agreements and Global Social Dialogue: Parameters and Prospects', Employment Working Paper No. 47 (2010).

[230] See generally Gary Rynhart, 'International Employers' Organizations' in Blanpain, *Comparative Labour Law and Industrial Relations*, 41.

[231] See International Organisation of Employers (IOE), 'Home' (2011) <http://www.ioe-emp.org>.

'stands for and defends the principles of free enterprise and the market economy'.[232] The IOE acts as the Secretariat for the Employers' Group of the ILO Governing Body. It also partners with regional and global sectoral employers' organizations.[233] The IOE's aims are set out in Article 2 of its Statutes:

The objectives of the IOE are:

1. To promote the economic, employment and social policy environment necessary to sustain and develop free enterprise and the market economy.

2. To provide an international forum to bring together, represent and promote the interests of national employers' organizations and their members throughout the world in all labour and socio-economic policy issues.

3. To assist, advise, represent and provide relevant services and information to members, to establish and maintain permanent contact among them and to coordinate the interests of employers at the international level, particularly within the ILO and other international institutions.

4. To promote and support the advancement and strengthening of independent and autonomous employers' organizations and to enhance their capabilities and services to members.

5. To inform public opinion and promote understanding of employers' points of view.

6. To facilitate and promote the exchange and transfer of information, experience and good practice amongst members.

Article 8(1)(c): Right of Trade Unions to Function Freely

The USSR proposed that Article 8 guarantee 'the right of all trade unions to the free exercise of their functions',[234] because otherwise 'trade-union rights were meaningless'.[235] The proposal was incorporated into the three-power amendment which became the basis of Article 8. A Uruguayan proposal to also protect union members and leaders from 'reprisals' was not adopted, although such protection is implicit in the broad scope of Article 8.[236] Union members are also equally entitled to the enjoyment of civil and political rights, including the right to life, freedom from ill-treatment or arbitrary detention and non-discrimination.

A conceptual disagreement arose in the drafting over whether it was appropriate for the Covenant to go beyond individual rights to recognize the rights of groups or associations,[237] which the Commission on Human Rights had 'deliberately omitted to deal with' and which was claimed to risk the 'eclipse'

[232] IOE Statutes, 1 June 2010, Article 3(1)(a).

[233] For examples, see ILO, *Giving Globalization a Human Face*, 30–31.

[234] UNGA Third Committee, A/3525 (9 February 1957), 19.

[235] UNGA Third Committee, A/C.3/SR.719 (3 January 1957), 192 (Union of Soviet Socialist Republics); see also UNGA Third Committee, A/C.3/SR.720 (3 January 1957), 196 (Poland).

[236] UNGA Third Committee, A/3525 (9 February 1957), 19; UNGA Third Committee, A/C.3/SR.722 (7 January 1957), 205 (Bulgaria).

[237] UNGA Third Committee, A/C.3/SR.720 (3 January 1957), 197 (United Kingdom); A/C.3/SR.721 (4 January 1957), 201 (Canada); A/C.3/SR.722 (7 January 1957), 206 (Iran).

of individual rights.[238] In response, Pakistan argued that '[w]hile the Covenant was principally concerned with the individual, the individual could not protect his rights and interest by himself but only in association with others'.[239] A clear majority agreed.[240]

States were nonetheless concerned that the provision would be too broad unless accompanied by restrictions,[241] including to protect other organizations.[242] On the initiative of the United Kingdom and the Netherlands,[243] Article 8(1)(c) replicates the limitations clause in Article 8(1)(a).

While there was also concern about what constituted legitimate trade union activities,[244] the provision does not attempt to define the scope of permissible activities. Other paragraphs in Article 8 expressly protect certain aspects of the free functioning of unions, such as the right to strike (Article 8(1)(d)) and the right to federate, confederate or internationally associate (Article 8(1)(b)).[245] Otherwise, reference may be made back to Article 8(1)(a), which broadly describes the purpose of unions in promoting and protecting the economic and social interests of workers. The scope of union activities is considered further below in the light of the practice of the CESCR and the ILO (principally under Article 2 of Convention No. 98).

In monitoring states, the CESCR has often expressed concern about interference with the right of trade unions to function freely. It has criticized state interference in the management and operation of unions,[246] and the legal or practical obstruction of union activities,[247] including peaceful campaigns[248] and in Export Processing Zones.[249] The CESCR has also condemned interference by employers[250] and recommended that states apply all legal means to put an end to private interference.[251]

[238] UNGA Third Committee, A/C.3/SR.721 (4 January 1957), 201 (Lebanon).

[239] UNGA Third Committee, A/C.3/SR.723 (7 January 1957), 212 (Pakistan); see also A/C.3/SR.722 (7 January 1957), 205 (Bulgaria).

[240] By forty votes to two, with twenty-seven abstentions.

[241] UNGA Third Committee, A/C.3/SR.719 (3 January 1957), 191 (Pakistan); A/C.3/SR.720 (3 January 1957), 198 (United Kingdom); A/C.3/SR.722 (7 January 1957), 206 (Iran).

[242] UNGA Third Committee, A/C.3/SR.720 (3 January 1957), 197 (United Kingdom).

[243] UNGA Third Committee, A/3525 (9 February 1957), 21, 27; adopted by twenty-eight votes to nine, with thirty abstentions.

[244] UNGA Third Committee, A/C.3/SR.723 (7 January 1957), 213 (Australia); A/C.3/SR.720 (3 January 1957), 198 (United Kingdom).

[245] Craven, *The ICESCR*, 256.

[246] CESCR, Concluding Observations: Egypt, E/C.12/1/Add.44 (23 May 2000), [19]; Kenya, E/C.12/KEN/CO/1 (1 December 2008), [19]; Nigeria, E/C.12/1/Add.23 (16 June 1998), [15].

[247] CESCR, Concluding Observations: Democratic Republic of the Congo, E/C.12/COD/CO/4 (16 December 2009), [23]; Angola, E/C.12/DZA/CO/4 (7 June 2010), [11].

[248] CESCR, Concluding Observations: China: Hong Kong Special Administrative Region, E/C.12/1/Add.58 (21 May 2001), [26]; Azerbaijan, E/C.12/1/Add.104 (14 December 2004), [21].

[249] CESCR, Concluding Observations: El Salvador, E/C.12/1/Add.4 (28 May 1996), [19]; India, E/C.12/IND/CO/5 (8 August 2008), [23]; Kenya, E/C.12/KEN/CO/1 (1 December 2008), [19].

[250] CESCR, Concluding Observations: Kyrgyzstan, E/C.12/1/Add.49 (1 September 2000), [15].

[251] CESCR, Concluding Observations: Kyrgyzstan, E/C.12/1/Add.49 (1 September 2000), [28].

In categorizing the range of matters protected within the free functioning of unions, reference may be made to the much more extensive ILO practice in the area. A starting point is some key provisions of ILO Convention No. 87, which sets out certain freedoms of trade unions (Article 3) and their responsibility to respect the law (Article 8):

Article 3

1. Workers' and employers' organisations shall have the right to draw up their constitutions and rules, to elect their representatives in full freedom, to organise their administration and activities and to formulate their programmes.

2. The public authorities shall refrain from any interference which would restrict this right or impede the lawful exercise thereof.

…

Article 8

1. In exercising the rights provided for in this Convention workers and employers and their respective organisations, like other persons or organised collectivities, shall respect the law of the land.

2. The law of the land shall not be such as to impair, nor shall it be so applied as to impair, the guarantees provided for in this Convention.

Further, Article 2 of ILO Convention No. 98 guarantees to workers' and employers' organizations protection from interference by each other in their establishment, functioning and administration:

1. Workers' and employers' organisations shall enjoy adequate protection against any acts of interference by each other or each other's agents or members in their establishment, functioning or administration.

2. In particular, acts which are designed to promote the establishment of workers' organisations under the domination of employers or employers' organisations, or to support workers' organisations by financial or other means, with the object of placing such organisations under the control of employers or employers' organisations, shall be deemed to constitute acts of interference within the meaning of this Article.

In broad terms, issues commonly arising in ILO practice, and considered below, include the freedom of unions to: (a) establish internal rules, organize their internal administration and enjoy financial independence; (b) conduct elections; (c) pursue lawful activities in defence of workers' interests and union rights; (d) engage in collective bargaining; (e) be protected from arbitrary suspension or dissolution; and (f) be free from anti-union discrimination, intimidation or violence.

States are obliged to take measures to protect these freedoms, as provided by Article 11 of Convention No. 87 and Article 3 of Convention No. 98:

Convention No. 87, Article 11

Each Member of the International Labour Organisation for which this Convention is in force undertakes to take all necessary and appropriate measures to ensure that workers and employers may exercise freely the right to organise.

Convention No. 98, Article 3

Machinery appropriate to national conditions shall be established, where necessary, for the purpose of ensuring respect for the right to organise as defined in the preceding Articles.

INTERNAL RULES, ADMINISTRATION AND FINANCE

In ILO practice, unions must be generally free to establish their own internal rules, including as regards their constitution, structure, composition, leadership and membership. Such freedom extends to matters such as the geographical coverage of a union;[252] whether it covers workers from different trades, occupations or enterprises;[253] its relationship to federations or confederations, including central unions;[254] and its use of experts, advisers, lawyers or agents.[255] States should not draft union constitutions themselves, require state approval of them[256] or mandate the aims and functions of a union[257] (including vague duties to subscribe to 'socialist' or 'democratic' ideologies).[258]

While legislative regulation of unions brings risks of impermissible interference, the mere existence of regulatory laws is not unlawful.[259] While laws should leave 'the greatest possible autonomy' to unions in their functioning and organization,[260] laws may require unions to comply with the general law and formalities,[261] such as registration or annual reporting. Any reporting requirements must not be excessive or compromise union members' privacy, such as by a requirement to disclose members' names and details,[262] thereby risking discrimination.

Legal intervention should otherwise be limited to what is necessary to protect members' interests and the democratic functioning of unions,[263] such as certain election rules (see below), or by prohibiting racial or other discrimination in membership or procedures (such as segregated meetings of workers).[264] A union member cannot rely on the state to interfere in legitimate union rules with which the member disagrees.[265]

The free functioning of unions further requires financial independence from state control, including in raising, administering, investing and using funds. The

[252] ILO, Freedom of Association: Digest of Decisions and Principles, [372].
[253] ILO, Freedom of Association: Digest of Decisions and Principles, [333]–[335].
[254] ILO, Freedom of Association: Digest of Decisions and Principles, [387].
[255] ILO, Freedom of Association: Digest of Decisions and Principles, [457]–[459].
[256] ILO, Freedom of Association: Digest of Decisions and Principles, [374] and [375].
[257] ILO, Freedom of Association: Digest of Decisions and Principles, [380].
[258] ILO, Freedom of Association: Digest of Decisions and Principles, [506] and [507].
[259] ILO, Freedom of Association: Digest of Decisions and Principles, [370].
[260] ILO, Freedom of Association: Digest of Decisions and Principles, [369].
[261] ILO, Freedom of Association: Digest of Decisions and Principles, [371].
[262] ILO, Freedom of Association: Digest of Decisions and Principles, [383].
[263] ILO, Freedom of Association: Digest of Decisions and Principles, [369].
[264] ILO, Freedom of Association: Digest of Decisions and Principles, [385].
[265] See, eg, *Cheall v United Kingdom* (App. 10550/83), 13 May 1985, (1985) 42 DR 178 (where a member contested his expulsion from a union due to violating reasonable union rules in a case under Article 11 of the ECHR).

CESCR was concerned, for example, at a law imposing government control over unions seeking external funding.[266] State laws must not prohibit the deduction of union dues from wages, and any procedural requirements (such as a permissible requirement for deductions to be authorized in writing) must not interfere in union members' privacy (by disclosing their details to the state).[267] The law must not prohibit or regulate remuneration of union leaders or officials.[268] The ILO has encouraged developing states to take positive measures to assist unions, such as tax deductions for union dues,[269] but subsidies should not compromise the autonomy of unions[270] or favour some unions over others.

Unions may be required by law to present annual financial statements, but any auditing or supervision requirements, permissible solely to prevent mismanagement of members' funds, should be undertaken by qualified independent professionals, not the state.[271] The law should not provide a right of the state to inspect or compel production of records on demand.[272] Investigation procedures must instead be subject to independent, impartial and substantive (not merely procedural) judicial supervision to avoid excessive or arbitrary interference in the free functioning of unions.[273]

UNION ELECTIONS

States must generally refrain from interfering in union elections, including in election rules, the eligibility of candidates to stand, whether voting is voluntary or compulsory, the conduct of elections and election disputes.[274] State laws accordingly should not impose eligibility conditions such as a minimum length of employment or union membership,[275] or continuing employment,[276] or be involved in the nomination or approval of candidates.[277] States must not prohibit candidates on political grounds (such as anti-communism),[278] impose a background check on candidates,[279] or disqualify a candidate on the basis of a criminal record where the conduct does not affect the integrity required of union office.[280] A state should also not express support for or oppose particular candidates.[281]

[266] CESCR, Concluding Observations: Egypt, E/C.12/1/Add.44 (23 May 2000), [19].
[267] ILO, Freedom of Association: Digest of Decisions and Principles, [473]–[484].
[268] ILO, Freedom of Association: Digest of Decisions and Principles, [457]–[459].
[269] ILO, Freedom of Association: Digest of Decisions and Principles, [484].
[270] ILO, Freedom of Association: Digest of Decisions and Principles, [466]–[472].
[271] ILO, Freedom of Association: Digest of Decisions and Principles, [487].
[272] ILO, Freedom of Association: Digest of Decisions and Principles, [489] and [490].
[273] ILO, Freedom of Association: Digest of Decisions and Principles, [369].
[274] ILO, Freedom of Association: Digest of Decisions and Principles, [391], [407] and [408], [427]–[428].
[275] ILO, Freedom of Association: Digest of Decisions and Principles, [410], [413] and [414].
[276] ILO, Freedom of Association: Digest of Decisions and Principles, [411] and [412].
[277] ILO, Freedom of Association: Digest of Decisions and Principles, [433]–[438].
[278] ILO, Freedom of Association: Digest of Decisions and Principles, [415]–[418].
[279] ILO, Freedom of Association: Digest of Decisions and Principles, [419].
[280] ILO, Freedom of Association: Digest of Decisions and Principles, [421]–[424] (including for 'any' offence of fraud, dishonesty or extortion, or violation of press laws).
[281] ILO, Freedom of Association: Digest of Decisions and Principles, [433]–[438].

Some state regulation of union elections is permissible to promote the rights of others,[282] including by democratic principles, and to avoid disputes, although any laws should not be 'excessively meticulous and detailed' or give broad discretionary powers to the state.[283] It may be permissible, for example, for the law to require a universal secret ballot and majority voting,[284] specify the frequency of elections and maximum periods of terms of office, prohibit discrimination[285] or impose (reasonable) minimum residency requirements on foreigners.[286] The combination of legal restrictions may, however, become excessive, as where laws fix maximum terms for leaders and limit their re-election.[287] Another example is where an exclusion from union leadership of workers from other occupations or enterprises does not exempt former workers or a reasonable proportion of the total leadership from such requirement.[288]

Where elections are disputed, the ILO has found that judicial supervision is necessary to ensure the impartiality and objectivity of dispute settlement procedures. Such procedures should also not prevent the continued operation of the union or suspend the election result until a final decision is made.[289] State authorities themselves should not intervene to remove leaders or settle disputes, and even in cases of corruption the state should not directly appoint an administrator, but leave such procedures to independent entities under judicial supervision.[290] Where exceptional reasons exist for state intervention, any takeover of a union must be temporary and aimed solely at permitting the organizing of free elections.[291]

In relation to inter-union disputes more generally, whether election related or otherwise, states should refrain from interfering in the resolution of such disputes, which should be resolved internally or with the assistance of an independent arbitrator or court.[292]

ACTIVITIES IN DEFENCE OF WORKERS' INTERESTS AND UNION RIGHTS

The free functioning of unions extends to the activities and programmes they undertake in the interests of their members, such as meetings, conferences, campaigns, and the representation of individual workers in disputes with employers.[293]

[282] See also Nowak, *CCPR Commentary*, 507, commenting on permissible limitations on the right of association under Article 22 of the ICCPR to secure the rights of others.

[283] ILO, Freedom of Association: Digest of Decisions and Principles, [393]–[395].

[284] ILO, Freedom of Association: Digest of Decisions and Principles, [378], [382].

[285] ILO, Freedom of Association: Digest of Decisions and Principles, [396]–[400], [406].

[286] ILO, Freedom of Association: Digest of Decisions and Principles, [420].

[287] ILO, Freedom of Association: Digest of Decisions and Principles, [426].

[288] ILO, Freedom of Association: Digest of Decisions and Principles, [409].

[289] ILO, Freedom of Association: Digest of Decisions and Principles, [431], [440]–[443].

[290] ILO, Freedom of Association: Digest of Decisions and Principles, [445] and [446]. In cases of central unions, administrators appointed on behalf of affiliate unions should limit their activities to coordinating the affiliate unions to reorganize the central body.

[291] ILO, Freedom of Association: Digest of Decisions and Principles, [451].

[292] ILO, Freedom of Association: Digest of Decisions and Principles, [1118], [1120]–[1122].

[293] ILO, Freedom of Association: Digest of Decisions and Principles, [517].

States should also not interfere in the premises, property, correspondence and communications of a union, without a judicial warrant issued on legitimate grounds (such as public order or law enforcement), and where the execution of the warrant is strictly limited to the authorized interference.[294]

Various forms of protest action short of strikes are protected, such as presenting petitions or grievances, submitting claims to employers, minimum wage campaigns, and demonstrations or action against anti-union discrimination, intimidation or violence.[295] The issue of 'secondary boycotts' or 'sympathy strikes' by unions not directly involved in a workplace dispute is considered below in the context of the right to strike under Article 8(1)(d).[296]

Difficulty arises in distinguishing (protected) union activities (in pursuit of the economic and social interests of workers) from broader (and unprotected) political activities. The ILO has observed that '[i]t is only in so far as trade union organizations do not allow their occupational demands to assume a clearly political aspect that they can legitimately claim that there should be no interference in their activities'.[297] Thus, unions generally 'should not engage in political activities in an abusive manner and go beyond their true functions by promoting essentially political interests'.[298]

Craven suggests, for example, that it would be 'difficult to justify . . . trade union action being taken to protest against a government's commitment to nuclear weapons or its maintenance of diplomatic relations with certain other States'.[299] This perhaps depends on the context, and also how restrictively or broadly one interprets the 'economic and social interests' of workers. On a wide view, workers may genuinely believe their interests are threatened by nuclear annihilation, or by their state's recognition of a foreign state which tolerates slavery or child labour, or their state's refusal to recognize a foreign state for being socialist (and thus disrupting the possibilities for international labour solidarity).

In other cases, too, it may simply be that workers are genuinely concerned to save urban heritage buildings at risk of demolition (as in the case of 'green bans' in the construction industry), because they want to live in a historical city; or to donate union funds by way of foreign aid to assist the poor in developing countries; or to oppose their government's harsh policies on refugees. In one sense, these are all 'social' interests workers may wish to promote and protect, illustrating the difficulties in legally circumscribing the fields of the 'political' and non-political.

While unions must exercise restraint in their political activities (not least so as to avoid inviting state repression), states are not permitted to impose a general prohibition on unions engaging in any political activities, since this would be incompatible with freedom of association and 'unrealistic in practice'. [300] The ILO has

[294] ILO, *Giving Globalization a Human Face*, 45.
[295] ILO, Freedom of Association: Digest of Decisions and Principles, [508]–[519].
[296] ILO, Freedom of Association: Digest of Decisions and Principles, [518].
[297] ILO, Freedom of Association: Digest of Decisions and Principles, [505]; see also [497] and [502].
[298] ILO, Freedom of Association: Digest of Decisions and Principles, [502].
[299] Craven, *The ICESCR*, 275.
[300] ILO, Freedom of Association: Digest of Decisions and Principles, [503].

noted that '[i]t is difficult to draw a clear distinction between what is political and what is, properly speaking, trade union in character. These two notions overlap'.[301] State interpretation of what is 'political' is also subjective and varies over time.[302]

In reality, the protection of workers' interests may require unions to express opinions or take action on a government's broad economic and social policies.[303] These may include inter-related issues relevant to workers such as taxation, inflation, the cost of living, housing affordability, education and training policy, immigration policy, social security, gender equality, family policy, and law enforcement and remedies for anti-union violence or discrimination, among others.

In practice, the ILO accepts that unions are permitted to affiliate with or support political parties,[304] and in many states there is a close historical association between labour unions and labour-oriented political parties. Such links are a legitimate expression of the freedom of opinion of union members, also protected under the ICCPR, and further the aims of unions to promote and protect workers' interests. Such links should not, however, 'compromise the continuance of the trade union movement or its social or economic functions'.[305] There may be controversy, for instance, where unions expend members' funds on donations to political parties' campaigns in national elections.

According to the ILO, any abusive political activities by unions should be dealt with by judicial authorities, not the state itself.[306] The personal political activities of individual union members, acting outside their union functions, should not be attributed to the union or be regarded as a basis to penalize it.[307]

FACILITIES AND ACCESS TO WORKPLACES

The effective functioning of trade unions depends on their access to and ability to organize in workplaces. Article 2 of ILO Convention No. 135 concerning Workers' Representatives 1971 provides for the provision of facilities to union leaders in a workplace to enable them to carry out their functions:

1. Such facilities in the undertaking shall be afforded to workers' representatives as may be appropriate in order to enable them to carry out their functions promptly and efficiently.

2. In this connection account shall be taken of the characteristics of the industrial relations system of the country and the needs, size and capabilities of the undertaking concerned.

3. The granting of such facilities shall not impair the efficient operation of the undertaking concerned.[308]

[301] ILO, Freedom of Association: Digest of Decisions and Principles, [505].
[302] ILO, Freedom of Association: Digest of Decisions and Principles, [501].
[303] ILO, Freedom of Association: Digest of Decisions and Principles, [503].
[304] ILO, Freedom of Association: Digest of Decisions and Principles, [498] and [499].
[305] ILO, Freedom of Association: Digest of Decisions and Principles, [498].
[306] ILO, Freedom of Association: Digest of Decisions and Principles, [501].
[307] ILO, Freedom of Association: Digest of Decisions and Principles, [504].
[308] ILO Convention No. 135 concerning Protection and Facilities to be Afforded to Workers' Representatives in the Undertaking (adopted 23 June 1971, entered into force 30 June 1973) ('ILO Convention No. 135 concerning Workers' Representatives').

ILO Recommendation No. 143 concerning Workers' Representatives 1971 makes further suggestions to facilitate time off work for union representatives (paragraphs 10 and 11), access to the workplace and management (paragraphs 12 and 13), the collection of dues (paragraph 14), the posting of union information (paragraph 15), facilities (paragraph 16) and access by external union leaders (paragraph 17).

COLLECTIVE BARGAINING

While it is not specifically mentioned in Article 8 of the ICESCR, during the drafting states were concerned to protect collective bargaining as a legitimate function of trade unions.[309] In General Comment No. 18 on the right to work (under Article 6 of the ICESCR), the CESCR observed that '[c]ollective bargaining is a tool of fundamental importance in the formulation of employment policies'.[310]

International protection for collective bargaining stems from Article 4 of ILO Convention No. 98 concerning the Right to Organise and Collective Bargaining 1949, which requires states to 'encourage and promote' collective bargaining, defined as voluntary negotiation between workers and employers on the terms and conditions of employment:

> Measures appropriate to national conditions shall be taken, where necessary, to encourage and promote the full development and utilisation of machinery for voluntary negotiation between employers or employers' organisations and workers' organisations, with a view to the regulation of terms and conditions of employment by means of collective agreements.

A similar obligation exists in respect of the public service under Article 7 of ILO Convention No. 151 concerning Labour Relations (Public Service) 1978. The most elaborate instrument is ILO Convention No. 154 on Collective Bargaining 1981, which requires states to take measures, including by law (Article 2), to promote collective bargaining (Articles 5 to 8):

> Article 5
>
> 1. Measures adapted to national conditions shall be taken to promote collective bargaining.
>
> 2. The aims of the measures referred to in paragraph 1 of this Article shall be the following:
>
> (a) collective bargaining should be made possible for all employers and all groups of workers in the branches of activity covered by this Convention;
>
> (b) collective bargaining should be progressively extended to all matters covered by subparagraphs (a), (b) and (c) of Article 2 of this Convention;
>
> (c) the establishment of rules of procedure agreed between employers' and workers' organisations should be encouraged;

[309] Craven, *The ICESCR*, 275.

[310] CESCR, General Comment No. 18, [39].

(d) collective bargaining should not be hampered by the absence of rules governing the procedure to be used or by the inadequacy or inappropriateness of such rules;

(e) bodies and procedures for the settlement of labour disputes should be so conceived as to contribute to the promotion of collective bargaining.

Article 6

The provisions of this Convention do not preclude the operation of industrial relations systems in which collective bargaining takes place within the framework of conciliation and/or arbitration machinery or institutions, in which machinery or institutions the parties to the collective bargaining process voluntarily participate.

Article 7

Measures taken by public authorities to encourage and promote the development of collective bargaining shall be the subject of prior consultation and, whenever possible, agreement between public authorities and employers' and workers' organisations.

Article 8

The measures taken with a view to promoting collective bargaining shall not be so conceived or applied as to hamper the freedom of collective bargaining.

To this may be added ILO Recommendation No. 163, which suggests further measures to states as to the levels of bargaining, training for bargaining, the mandate of negotiators, access to necessary information, and the settlement of disputes (paragraphs 4 to 8 respectively). Even for states that are not parties to the ILO instruments, the ILO Declaration on Fundamental Principles and Rights at Work 1998 declares that all ILO members must recognize collective bargaining:

2. . . . all Members, even if they have not ratified the Conventions in question, have an obligation arising from the very fact of membership in the Organization to respect, to promote and to realize, in good faith and in accordance with the Constitution, the principles concerning the fundamental rights which are the subject of those Conventions, namely:

(a) freedom of association and the effective recognition of the right to collective bargaining . . .

Historically, the right to collective bargaining developed at a later phase in the overall development of trade union rights. The liberalization of laws on trade unions in the late nineteenth and early twentieth centuries (as in the United Kingdom, United States and Canada) first focused on the right of unions to exist and to strike, but did not extend to protection for collective bargaining.[311] The powerful 'economic weapon' of the strike was thus often directed towards encouraging an employer to collectively bargain with a union, but employers remained free to ignore union demands or refuse to hire union members.[312] From the 1930s, however, this 'old laissez-faire model' gave way to statutory intervention in the United States and elsewhere to protect or even to require collective bargaining.[313]

[311] *Health Services* case, [53]–[63].
[312] *Health Services* case, [53]–[63].
[313] *Health Services* case, [56].

In the *Health Services* case (discussed below), in 2007 the Canadian Supreme Court found that collective bargaining is part of international law in interpreting freedom of association under section 2(d) of the Canadian Charter of Rights and Freedoms:

72. The *ICESCR*, the *ICCPR* and *Convention No. 87* extend protection to the functioning of trade unions in a manner suggesting that a right to collective bargaining is part of freedom of association. The interpretation of these conventions, in Canada and internationally, not only supports the proposition that there is a right to collective bargaining in international law, but also suggests that such a right should be recognized in the Canadian context under s. 2(*d*).

73. Article 8, para. (1)(*c*) of the *ICESCR* guarantees the 'right of trade unions to function freely subject to no limitations other than those prescribed by law and which are necessary in a democratic society in the interests of national security or public order or for the protection of the rights and freedoms of others.' This Article allows the 'free functioning' of trade unions to be regulated, but not legislatively abrogated (*per* Dickson C.J., *Alberta Reference*, at p. 351). Since collective bargaining is a primary function of a trade union, it follows that Article 8 protects a union's freedom to pursue this function freely.

74. Similarly, Article 22, para. 1 of the *ICCPR*...has been interpreted to suggest that it encompasses both the right to form a union and the right to collective bargaining: *Concluding Observations of the Human Rights Committee Canada*, U.N. Doc. CCPR/C/79/Add.105 (1999).

...

79. In summary, international conventions to which Canada is a party recognize the right of the members of unions to engage in collective bargaining, as part of the protection for freedom of association. It is reasonable to infer that s. 2(*d*) of the *Charter* should be interpreted as recognizing at least the same level of protection: *Alberta Reference*.[314]

In monitoring states, the CESCR has been alert to the protection of the existence and integrity of collective bargaining.[315] It has drawn attention to procedural barriers to unions collectively bargaining, such as licence requirements.[316] It criticized one state for insufficiently protecting unions which sought to negotiate with foreign employers.[317] It was concerned where national law favoured individual negotiation with employers over collective bargaining, thereby reducing the role of an independent industrial relations commission.[318] The CESCR has recommended that states remove, in law and practice, obstacles to trade unions participating freely in collective bargaining.[319] The wider freedom of association under Article 22 of the

[314] *Health Services* case, [72]–[74], [79].

[315] CESCR, Consideration of Report Submitted by State Party: Afghanistan, E/1992/23 (1991), [93]; Concluding Observations: Egypt, E/C.12/1/Add.44 (23 May 2000), [18]; Jamaica, E/1990/23 (1990), [168].

[316] CESCR, Concluding Observations: Egypt, E/C.12/1/Add.44 (23 May 2000), [18]; Ireland, E/C.12/1/Add.35 (14 May 1999), [19]; Ireland, E/C.12/1/Add.77 (5 June 2002), [18]; India, E/C.12/IND/CO/5 (8 August 2008), [23].

[317] CESCR, Concluding Observations: Honduras, E/C.12/1/Add.57 (21 May 2001), [18].

[318] CESCR, Concluding Observations: Australia, E/C.12/1/Add.50 (11 September 2000), [17].

[319] CESCR, Concluding Observations: India, E/C.12/IND/CO/5 (8 August 2008), [23]; Ireland, E/C.12/1/Add.77 (5 June 2002), [29]; France, E/C.12/1/Add.72 (30 November 2001), [29].

ICCPR has also been interpreted by the HRC to encompass collective bargaining by trade unions.[320]

While the broad concept and principles of collective bargaining may be part of international law, there is enormous diversity in collective bargaining in practice between states, regions and employment sectors. This includes in relation to worker coverage, subject matter, the bargaining unit, the level of bargaining, processes, negotiation techniques, dispute settlement, and the duration and legal consequences of agreements.[321] The mix of such factors can also affect the efficiency and effectiveness of bargaining. The ILO standards themselves are a hybrid product of different national approaches:

The continental European model induced most of the provisions on effects, interpretation and extension of agreements included in Recommendation 92 on Collective Agreements 1951. The British influence inspired the reference to 'machinery for voluntary negotiations' in one of the key provisions of Convention 98 on the Right to Organise and to Bargain Collectively 1949. Some elements of the American penchant for regulating collective bargaining procedures appear in Recommendation 130 concerning the Examination of Grievances within Undertakings, as well as in Convention 154 and Recommendation 163 concerning the Promotion of Collective Bargaining, 1981.[322]

Purpose

Collective bargaining fulfils a number of inter-related purposes. Narrowly conceived, its primary aim is to provide a means by which to improve the working conditions and living standards of workers.[323] It does so by providing a procedure for negotiation and 'interest accommodation'[324] to that end, structuring what might otherwise escalate into damaging conflict between the parties (such as strikes, lockouts or lay-offs). It is a procedural right, but does not mandate substantive outcomes, as the Canadian Supreme Court observed in the *Health Services* case:

89. …collective bargaining concerns the protection of the ability of workers to engage in associational activities, and their capacity to act in common to reach shared goals related to workplace issues and terms of employment. In brief, the protected activity might be described as employees banding together to achieve particular work-related objectives…. [It] does not guarantee the particular objectives sought through this associational activity. However, it guarantees the process through which those goals are pursued. It means that employees have the right to unite, to present demands to…employers collectively and to engage in discussions in an attempt to achieve workplace-related goals…[It] imposes corresponding duties on government employers to agree to meet and discuss with them. It also puts constraints on the exercise of legislative powers in respect of the right to collective bargaining…

[320] HRC, Concluding Observations: Canada, CCPR/C/79/Add.105 (7 April 1999), [17].
[321] See generally Bamber and Sheldon, 'Collective Bargaining'.
[322] Bamber and Sheldon, 'Collective Bargaining', 592.
[323] ILO, Freedom of Association: Digest of Decisions and Principles, [880].
[324] Bamber and Sheldon, 'Collective Bargaining', 589.

91. The right to collective bargaining thus conceived is a limited right. First, as the right is to a process, it does not guarantee a certain substantive or economic outcome. Moreover, the right is to a general process of collective bargaining, not to a particular model of labour relations, nor to a specific bargaining method.[325]

The process of dialogue and the exchange of different perspectives can help to build ongoing confidence between workers and employers. The voluntary commitment to be bound by resulting collective agreements makes them more likely to 'stick' and less likely to produce disputes later. It is thus a labour market governance tool which can promote harmonious industrial relations and assist business performance and efficiency.

Collective bargaining also has wider dignity-enhancing goals, such as increasing democratic participation by workers in decisions materially affecting their lives. In the *Health Services* case, the Canadian Supreme Court elaborated on the ways in which it reaffirms the values of dignity, personal autonomy, equality and democracy underlying human rights generally:

82. The right to bargain collectively with an employer enhances the human dignity, liberty and autonomy of workers by giving them the opportunity to influence the establishment of workplace rules and thereby gain some control over a major aspect of their lives, namely their work…

84. Collective bargaining also enhances the *Charter* value of equality. One of the fundamental achievements of collective bargaining is to palliate the historical inequality between employers and employees…

85. Finally, a constitutional right to collective bargaining is supported by the *Charter* value of enhancing democracy. Collective bargaining permits workers to achieve a form of workplace democracy and to ensure the rule of law in the workplace. Workers gain a voice to influence the establishment of rules that control a major aspect of their lives…

86. We conclude that the protection of collective bargaining under s. 2(*d*) of the *Charter* is consistent with and supportive of the values underlying the *Charter* and the purposes of the *Charter* as a whole. Recognizing that workers have the right to bargain collectively as part of their freedom to associate reaffirms the values of dignity, personal autonomy, equality and democracy that are inherent in the *Charter*.[326]

There is debate about the economic costs and benefits of collective bargaining, as well as about how to define costs and benefits. Discussion has focused on the labour-cost effects of collective bargaining more than on the non-labour-cost effects.[327] According to the ILO, there is little evidence that it adversely affects the global competitiveness of employers.[328] There is, however, evidence that it has beneficial non-labour-cost effects, including on social stability, economic performance and global competitiveness. It produces such effects by encouraging more predictable long-term growth, enhancing the ability to handle shocks, lowering

[325] *Health Services* case, [91].

[326] *Health Services* case, [82]–[86].

[327] International Labour Conference, Freedom of Association in Practice: Lessons Learned, Report of the Director General, Report I(B) (2008), 20.

[328] International Labour Conference, Freedom of Association in Practice, 21.

credit risk, increasing foreign investment and exports, producing more sustainable development and generating employment through the higher demand resulting from higher wages.[329]

Scope of bargaining

A reference point for understanding the scope of collective bargaining under Article 8 of the ICESCR is Article 2 of ILO Convention No. 154 on Collective Bargaining 1981:

For the purpose of this Convention the term *collective bargaining* extends to all negotiations which take place between an employer, a group of employers or one or more employers' organisations, on the one hand, and one or more workers' organisations, on the other, for—

(a) determining working conditions and terms of employment; and/or

(b) regulating relations between employers and workers; and/or

(c) regulating relations between employers or their organisations and a workers' organisation or workers' organisations.

In ILO practice, states should not unilaterally restrict the scope or subject matter of collective bargaining, which typically concerns wages and working conditions, including worker coverage, benefits and allowances, working time, leave, occupational health and safety, gender equality and non-discrimination, training and education, promotion and dismissal, restructuring and redundancy, dispute settlement and union-related matters (such as facilities, access to the workplace and collection of dues).[330]

In light of the changing nature of work, a variety of new issues is emerging: telework, personal data protection, new employment relationships (including arising from privatization, outsourcing and sub-contracting, and casualisation), career development, leisure time, bankruptcy, compensation, performance management, bonuses, family responsibilities, pensions, profit sharing, further education, harassment and medical coverage.[331]

It is broadly within the autonomy of the parties to determine the issues on which to negotiate. However, the ILO's Fact-Finding and Conciliation Commission on Freedom of Association has found that 'there are certain matters which clearly appertain primarily or essentially to the management and operation of government business; these can reasonably be regarded as outside the scope of negotiation'.[332] These may include business operations, policy issues and staffing levels, but not broader job security issues (such as dismissal rights or redundancy).

[329] International Labour Conference, Freedom of Association in Practice, 20.

[330] ILO, Freedom of Association: Digest of Decisions and Principles, [912], [913] and [916]; International Labour Conference, Freedom of Association in Practice, 23.

[331] International Labour Conference, Freedom of Association in Practice, 23–4.

[332] ILO, Freedom of Association: Digest of Decisions and Principles, [920].

The Canadian Supreme Court imposed a further restriction in the *Health Services* case, in finding that freedom of association does not protect against minor or insubstantial interferences in collective bargaining:

96. ... Laws or state actions that prevent or deny meaningful discussion and consultation about working conditions between employees and their employer may substantially interfere with the activity of collective bargaining, as may laws that unilaterally nullify significant negotiated terms in existing collective agreements. By contrast, measures affecting less important matters such as the design of uniform, the lay out and organization of cafeterias, or the location or availability of parking lots, may be far less likely to constitute significant interference with the ... right of freedom of association. This is because it is difficult to see how interfering with collective bargaining over these matters undermines the capacity of union members to pursue shared goals in concert.[333]

That view does not necessarily reflect the international law position under the ICESCR.

As regards eligibility for bargaining, 'everyone' enjoys Article 8 rights, with 'restrictions' (but not absolute exclusion) permitted under Article 8(2) in relation to the armed forces, police and those engaged in the administration of the state (but not public servants generally). The scope of these restrictions is considered separately below in relation to trade union rights as a whole under Article 8.

ILO Convention No. 154 on Collective Bargaining 1981 also applies to 'all branches of economic activity' (Article 1(1)), with the possibility to restrict its application to armed forces and police. While Convention No. 154 does not also permit restriction of those involved in the administration of the state (unlike Article 8(2)), it allows states to fix 'special modalities of application' for the 'public service', discussed further below.

Representative unions

As noted earlier, in ILO practice it is generally permitted to privilege the 'most representative' union for certain purposes,[334] including for exclusive or preferential participation in collective bargaining, and to the exclusion or disadvantage of minority unions. While neither ILO Conventions No. 98 nor No. 154 specifically provides for recognition of representativeness in collective bargaining, ILO Recommendation No. 163 on Collective Bargaining 1981 encourages states to do so (paragraph 3(a)):

3. As appropriate and necessary, measures adapted to national conditions should be taken so that—

(a) representative employers' and workers' organisations are recognised for the purposes of collective bargaining;

(b) in countries in which the competent authorities apply procedures for recognition with a view to determining the organisations to be granted the right to bargain

[333] *Health Services* case, [96].

[334] ILO Constitution (adopted 1919, amended 4 June 1934, 26 September 1946, 20 April 1948, 20 May 1954, 22 May 1963, 1 November 1974), Article 3(5).

collectively, such determination is based on pre-established and objective criteria with regard to the organisations' representative character, established in consultation with representative employers' and workers' organisations.

A most representative union may negotiate on behalf of all workers (such that any resulting collective agreement will cover the members of minority unions as well as non-unionized workers), or only on behalf of its own members; both situations are potentially compatible with ILO standards.[335] In the former situation, minority union members will thus benefit from the greater bargaining power of a majority union, even if the latter may not be as responsive to their particular interests as their own union.

In the latter situation, a minority union must not be deprived of its capacity to represent the interests of its members.[336] A 'representivity' approach should not go beyond according priority or preference in collective bargaining, and should not exclude minority unions altogether,[337] especially where majority unions negotiate only on behalf of their own members.

While the CESCR has not ruled out the ILO's 'representivity' approach in supervizing Article 8 of the ICESCR, in monitoring states it has found that criteria of 'representativity' can operate to exclude smaller and newer trade unions, jeopardizing their right to function freely.[338] In addition to the impact on the collective right of minority unions to function freely, it may ultimately impact on an individual's right to freely choose which union to join, where minority union interests are so affected that their members are induced to join a majority union to be heard, even where it may not reflect their true preferences.

ILO practice has been attentive to the criteria and procedures for determining the most representative unions entitled to negotiate. Decisions about the most representative union must be made according to objective and pre-established criteria to avoid abuse,[339] and the union must be not only representative, but also independent.[340] A branch-level union negotiating at the enterprise level should also be sufficiently representative at the enterprise level.[341]

Criteria should not, however, be too strict, such as by requiring a union to: represent an absolute majority of all workers;[342] satisfy a double majority of workers and enterprises;[343] or demonstrate a minimum membership number that is too high in the light of the small size of bargaining units or the geographical dispersal of workers.[344]

[335] ILO, *Giving Globalization a Human Face*, 92.
[336] ILO, Freedom of Association: Digest of Decisions and Principles, [974].
[337] ILO, *Giving Globalization a Human Face*, 92.
[338] CESCR, Concluding Observations: France, E/C.12/1/Add.72 (30 November 2001), [18].
[339] ILO, Freedom of Association: Digest of Decisions and Principles, [962].
[340] ILO, Freedom of Association: Digest of Decisions and Principles, [967].
[341] ILO, Freedom of Association: Digest of Decisions and Principles, [957].
[342] ILO, Freedom of Association: Digest of Decisions and Principles, [978].
[343] ILO, Freedom of Association: Digest of Decisions and Principles, [956].
[344] ILO, Freedom of Association: Digest of Decisions and Principles, [968].

States must have the power to objectively verify claims that a union is representative, such as through a certification process by an independent body, involving a membership count or the holding of a poll and a majority vote. A minority union should also have a right to request a new election after a reasonable period of time has elapsed.[345] The state should also encourage conciliatory measures to secure employers' recognition of a majority union.[346]

Where collective bargaining includes not only unions (whether majority or minority), but other elected 'workers' representatives',[347] Article 3(2) of ILO Convention No. 154 provides that negotiating with the latter should not be used to undermine the former:

2. Where, in pursuance of paragraph 1 of this Article, the term *collective bargaining* also includes negotiations with the workers' representatives referred to in that paragraph, appropriate measures shall be taken, wherever necessary, to ensure that the existence of these representatives is not used to undermine the position of the workers' organizations concerned.

Nor should employers bypass unions altogether by directly negotiating with employees;[348] that should occur only where no unions exist.[349]

Bargaining principles among the parties

The idea of collective bargaining involves voluntary negotiation between the parties,[350] which in turn implies that it is based on the autonomy of the parties.[351] The parties should thus be free to choose not only the subject matter, but the modalities of bargaining, including the level at which negotiation takes place.[352] One party is thus permitted to refuse to bargain at a particular level. The parties are further entitled to choose their own delegates and advisers for participation in negotiations.[353]

In international practice, the principle of negotiating in good faith is central to collective bargaining and derives, inter alia, from Article 4 of ILO Convention No. 98. The parties should accordingly recognize representative organizations entitled to bargain; make every effort to reach agreement; engage in genuine and constructive negotiations; compromise and 'give and take'; and establish and maintain confidence between one another.[354] They should refrain from deliberate or unjustified delays and hostile, uncompromising or unilateral attitudes.

[345] ILO, Freedom of Association: Digest of Decisions and Principles, [961] and [969].
[346] ILO, Freedom of Association: Digest of Decisions and Principles, [959].
[347] See ILO Convention No. 135 concerning Workers' Representatives.
[348] ILO, Freedom of Association: Digest of Decisions and Principles, [945].
[349] ILO Recommendation No. 91 on Collective Agreements.
[350] ILO Convention No. 98 concerning the Right to Organise and Collective Bargaining (adopted 1 July 1949, entered into force 18 July 1951), Article 4.
[351] ILO, *Giving Globalization a Human Face*, 82.
[352] ILO, Freedom of Association: Digest of Decisions and Principles, [988]–[991].
[353] ILO, Freedom of Association: Digest of Decisions and Principles, [984]–[987].
[354] ILO, Freedom of Association: Digest of Decisions and Principles, [935]–[943]; see also ILO, *Giving Globalization a Human Face*, 85.

Any agreement reached should also be mutually respected as binding and implemented. The Canadian Supreme Court in the *Health Services* case discussed at length the nature of 'the fundamental precept of collective bargaining—the duty to consult and negotiate in good faith':[355]

100. A basic element of the duty to bargain in good faith is the obligation to actually meet and to commit time to the process…

101. The parties have a duty to engage in meaningful dialogue and they must be willing to exchange and explain their positions. They must make a reasonable effort to arrive at an acceptable contract…

102. Nevertheless, the efforts that must be invested to attain an agreement are not boundless.

'[T]he parties may reach a point in the bargaining process where further discussions are no longer fruitful. Once such a point is reached, a breaking off of negotiations or the adoption of a "take it or leave it" position is not likely to be regarded as a failure to bargain in good faith' (Carter et al., at p. 302).

103. The duty to bargain in good faith does not impose on the parties an obligation to conclude a collective agreement, nor does it include a duty to accept any particular contractual provisions (Gagnon, LeBel and Verge, at pp. 499–500). Nor does the duty to bargain in good faith preclude hard bargaining. The parties are free to adopt a 'tough position in the hope and expectation of being able to force the other side to agree to one's terms'…

104. In principle, the duty to bargain in good faith does not inquire into the nature of the proposals made in the course of collective bargaining; the content is left to the bargaining forces of the parties (Carter et al., at p. 300). However, when the examination of the content of the bargaining shows hostility from one party toward the collective bargaining process, this will constitute a breach of the duty to bargain in good faith. In some circumstances, even though a party is participating in the bargaining, that party's proposals and positions may be 'inflexible and intransigent to the point of endangering the very existence of collective bargaining' (*Royal Oak Mines*, at para. 46). This inflexible approach is often referred to as 'surface bargaining'. This Court has explained the distinction between hard bargaining, which is legal, and surface bargaining, which is a breach of the duty to bargain in good faith…

105. Even though the employer participates in all steps of the bargaining process, if the nature of its proposals and positions is aimed at avoiding the conclusion of a collective agreement or at destroying the collective bargaining relationship, the duty to bargain in good faith will be breached…

107. In considering whether the legislative provisions impinge on the collective right to good faith negotiations and consultation, regard must be had for the circumstances surrounding their adoption. Situations of exigency and urgency may affect the content and the modalities of the duty to bargain in good faith. Different situations may demand different processes and timelines. Moreover, failure to comply with the duty to consult and bargain in good faith should not be lightly found, and should be clearly supported on the record…[356]

[355] *Health Services* case, [97].

[356] *Health Services* case, [100]–[105] and [107].

Role of the state in promoting, regulating or restricting collective bargaining

Non-interference

Given the voluntary character of collective bargaining, states should generally refrain from interfering[357] in recourse to it, its conduct or its outcomes. States should not, for example, require administrative approval of bargaining delegates, the level of bargaining, the bargaining rules (including time limits for reaching agreement) or any agreements reached.[358] Nor should the state intervene by stipulating the contents of an agreement, requiring its revision, or mandating its duration or extension. The ILO regards repeated state interventions in collective bargaining as harmful since they destabilize labour relations over time and may discourage union membership.[359]

Promotion

While there is no duty on the state to mandate or enter into collective bargaining,[360] Article 4 of ILO Convention No. 98 does, however, require states 'to encourage and promote the full development and utilisation of machinery for voluntary negotiation'. To that end, states may adopt laws, practices, procedures and mechanisms which facilitate collective bargaining. Articles 5 to 8 of ILO Convention No. 154 set out a range of measures which states must take to promote collective bargaining:

Article 5

1. Measures adapted to national conditions shall be taken to promote collective bargaining.

2. The aims of the measures referred to in paragraph 1 of this Article shall be the following:

(a) collective bargaining should be made possible for all employers and all groups of workers in the branches of activity covered by this Convention;

(b) collective bargaining should be progressively extended to all matters covered by subparagraphs (a), (b) and (c) of Article 2 of this Convention;

(c) the establishment of rules of procedure agreed between employers' and workers' organisations should be encouraged;

(d) collective bargaining should not be hampered by the absence of rules governing the procedure to be used or by the inadequacy or inappropriateness of such rules;

(e) bodies and procedures for the settlement of labour disputes should be so conceived as to contribute to the promotion of collective bargaining.

Article 6

The provisions of this Convention do not preclude the operation of industrial relations systems in which collective bargaining takes place within the framework of conciliation and/

[357] ILO, Freedom of Association: Digest of Decisions and Principles, [881].
[358] ILO, Freedom of Association: Digest of Decisions and Principles, [1012]–[1018].
[359] ILO, Freedom of Association: Digest of Decisions and Principles, [1000] and [1019].
[360] ILO, Freedom of Association: Digest of Decisions and Principles, [925]–[929].

or arbitration machinery or institutions, in which machinery or institutions the parties to the collective bargaining process voluntarily participate.

Article 7

Measures taken by public authorities to encourage and promote the development of collective bargaining shall be the subject of prior consultation and, whenever possible, agreement between public authorities and employers' and workers' organisations.

Article 8

The measures taken with a view to promoting collective bargaining shall not be so conceived or applied as to hamper the freedom of collective bargaining.[361]

Further, ILO Recommendation No. 163 encourages states to enable bargaining at all levels (paragraph 4), provide training opportunities for negotiators (paragraph 5), ensure the parties have access to essential information (paragraph 7)[362] and facilitate dispute settlement mechanisms (paragraph 8). ILO Recommendation No. 92 on Voluntary Conciliation and Arbitration 1951 also encourages states to develop voluntary dispute settlement mechanisms with certain minimum characteristics, and without limiting the right to strike:

I. Voluntary Conciliation

1. Voluntary conciliation machinery, appropriate to national conditions, should be made available to assist in the prevention and settlement of industrial disputes between employers and workers.

2. Where voluntary conciliation machinery is constituted on a joint basis, it should include equal representation of employers and workers.

3(1) The procedure should be free of charge and expeditious; such time limits for the proceedings as may be prescribed by national laws or regulations should be fixed in advance and kept to a minimum.

(2) Provision should be made to enable the procedure to be set in motion, either on the initiative of any of the parties to the dispute or ex officio by the voluntary conciliation authority.

4. If a dispute has been submitted to conciliation procedure with the consent of all the parties concerned, the latter should be encouraged to abstain from strikes and lockouts while conciliation is in progress.

5. All agreements which the parties may reach during conciliation procedure or as a result thereof should be drawn up in writing and be regarded as equivalent to agreements concluded in the usual manner.

[361] See also ILO, Freedom of Association: Digest of Decisions and Principles, [929], [932] and [933].

[362] On disclosure, see also Organisation for Economic Cooperation and Development, Guidelines for Multinational Enterprises (5th edn, 2011) 27–30; ILO Tripartite Declaration of Principles concerning Multinational Enterprises and Social Policy (4th edn, 2006); ILO Recommendation No. 163 concerning the Promotion of Collective Bargaining (19 June 1981); Council of Europe Council Directive 94/45/EC of 22 September 1994 on the establishment of a European Works Council.

II. Voluntary Arbitration

6. If a dispute has been submitted to arbitration for final settlement with the consent of all parties concerned, the latter should be encouraged to abstain from strikes and lockouts while the arbitration is in progress and to accept the arbitration award.

III. General

7. No provision of this Recommendation may be interpreted as limiting, in any way whatsoever, the right to strike.

Further, ILO Recommendation No. 130 concerning the Examination of Grievances within Undertakings 1967 suggests general principles and procedures for addressing grievances arising between workers and employers, including in relation to the interpretation and application of existing collective agreements. It also encourages parties to include grievance procedures within collective agreements when negotiating them, and to abstain from any action which might impede the effectiveness of such procedures (paragraph 5).

No duty on the state to collectively bargain

While states must promote and encourage collective bargaining, there is no duty on the state as employer to collectively bargain or enter into collective agreements. This follows from the principle that collective bargaining must be voluntary, and because collective bargaining is not the only means by which workers' interests may be pursued in the interaction between trade unions and the state. In *Swedish Engine Drivers' Union v Sweden*, the state agreed to bargain only with some state railway workers' federations, not others, leading to a decline in membership of an excluded union.[363] The European Court of Human Rights found no violation of Article 11 of the ECHR. The Court found that the right of unions to protect members' interests required that the union be heard and consulted, but states were free to choose the means to that end:

38. The majority of the Commission has expressed the opinion that included amongst the elements of the right protected by Article 11 para. 1 (art. 11-1) of the Convention are the right for trade unions to engage in collective bargaining and the legal capacity to conclude collective agreements in the interest of their members.

The Court finds that neither this right nor this capacity are at issue: both are granted to the applicant union under Swedish law (the 1928 Collective Agreements Act and the 1936 Act on the Right to Organise and Negotiate, read in conjunction with the 1965 State Officials Act), and the union does not claim to have been denied either of them.

39. On the other hand, it has to be ascertained whether Article 11 para. 1 (art. 11-1) requires the 'State as employer' to enter into any given collective agreement with a trade union representing certain of its employees whenever the parties are in accord on the substantive issues negotiated upon.

[363] *Swedish Engine Drivers' Union v Sweden* (App. 5614/72), 6 February 1976, (1976) 1 EHRR 617.

The Court notes in this connection that while Article 11 para. 1 (art. 11-1) presents trade union freedom as one form or a special aspect of freedom of association, the Article (art. 11) does not secure any particular treatment of trade unions, or their members, by the State, such as the right that the State should conclude any given collective agreement with them. Not only is this latter right not mentioned in Article 11 para. 1 (art. 11-1), but neither can it be said that all the Contracting States incorporate it in their national law or practice, or that it is indispensable for the effective enjoyment of trade union freedom. It is thus not an element necessarily inherent in a right guaranteed by the Convention.

In addition, trade union matters are dealt with in detail in another Convention, also drawn up within the framework of the Council of Europe, namely the Social Charter of 18 October 1961. Under Article 6 para. 2 of the Charter, the Contracting States 'undertake…to promote, where necessary and appropriate, machinery for voluntary negotiations between employers or employers' organisations and workers' organisations, with a view to the regulation of terms and conditions of employment by means of collective agreements'. As the Government and the Commission rightly emphasised, the Charter thus affirms the voluntary nature of collective bargaining and collective agreements. The prudence of the wording of Article 6 para. 2 demonstrates that the Charter does not provide for a real right to have any such agreement concluded, even assuming that the negotiations disclose no disagreement on the issue to be settled. Besides, Article 20 permits a ratifying State not to accept the undertaking in Article 6 para. 2. Thus, it cannot be supposed that such a right derives by implication from Article 11 para. 1 (art. 11-1) of the 1950 Convention, which incidentally would amount to admitting that the 1961 Charter took a retrograde step in this domain (cf. mutatis mutandis, paragraph 38 of the National Union of Belgian Police judgment of 27 October 1975, Series A no. 19, pp. 17–18).

40. The Court does not, however, accept the view expressed by the minority in the Commission who describe the phrase 'for the protection of his interests' as redundant. These words, clearly denoting purpose, show that the Convention safeguards freedom to protect the occupational interests of trade union members by trade union action, the conduct and development of which the Contracting States must both permit and make possible. In the opinion of the Court, it follows that the members of a trade union have a right, in order to protect their interests, that the trade union should be heard. Article 11 para. 1 (art. 11-1) certainly leaves each State a free choice of the means to be used towards this end. While the concluding of collective agreements is one of these means, there are others. What the Convention requires is that under national law trade unions should be enabled, in conditions not at variance with Article 11 (art. 11), to strive for the protection of their members' interests (paragraph 39 of the above-cited judgment of 27 October 1975, Series A no. 19, p. 18).

41. No-one disputes the fact that the applicant union can engage in various kinds of activity vis-à-vis the Government. It is open to it, for instance, to present claims, to make representations for the protection of the interests of its members or certain of them, and to negotiate with the Office. Nor does the applicant union in any way allege that the steps it takes are ignored by the Government. In these circumstances and in the light of the two foregoing paragraphs, the fact alone that the Office has in principle refused during the past few years to enter into collective agreements with the applicant union does not constitute a breach of Article 11 para. 1 (art. 11-1) considered on its own.

42. As concerns the alleged infringement of personal freedom to join or remain a member of the applicant union, the Court notes that the employees in question of the Swedish State

Railways retain this freedom as of right, notwithstanding the conduct of the Office. It may be the fact that the stagnation or fall in the membership of the Swedish Engine Drivers' Union is to be explained at least in part, as the applicant contends, by the disadvantage the applicant is placed at compared with trade unions enjoying a more favourable position. It may be the fact too that this state of affairs is capable of diminishing the usefulness and practical value of belonging to the applicant union. However, it is brought about by the Office's general policy of restricting the number of organisations with which collective agreements are to be concluded. This policy is not on its own incompatible with trade union freedom; the steps taken to implement it escape supervision by the Court provided that they do not contravene Articles 11 and 14 (art. 14+11) read in conjunction.[364]

Restrictions on bargaining freedom

The freedom of unions and employer organizations to collectively bargain is subject to limitations under Article 8(1)(c) of the ICESCR that are 'prescribed by law and which are necessary in a democratic society in the interests of national security or public order or for the protection of the rights and freedoms of others' (the latter including, for instance, provisions which involve unlawful discrimination[365]). There is also the possibility of restricting the rights of armed forces, police and those in state administration under Article 8(2). In ILO practice, common areas raising restrictions include essential services the interruption of which would endanger life, personal safety or health; national crises (particularly economic or financial); and cases of obvious and fruitless deadlock.[366]

In case of the latter, deadlock alone is not sufficient for state intervention, such as the imposition of compulsory arbitration.[367] There is, however, a role for the state in encouraging the parties to resolve disputes: 'there comes a time in bargaining where, after protracted and fruitless negotiations, the authorities might be justified in stepping in when it is obvious that the deadlock in bargaining will not be broken without some initiative on their part'.[368] Any recourse to dispute settlement must, however, remain voluntary, except in an acute national crisis.[369] Arbitration must be independent, involve freedom to choose the rules and arbitrators, and the outcomes must not be predetermined by law. A state might also be justified in imposing a reasonable temporary duration for an agreement where the parties cannot agree.

Even where limitations imposed by a state might be in pursuit of a legitimate aim and rationally connected to that aim, they must still be necessary. In the *Health Services* case, the Canadian Supreme Court struck down a federal law which gave health care employers greater labour flexibility by invalidating certain provisions of collective agreements already in force, and precluding bargaining

[364] *Swedish Engine Drivers' Union v Sweden*, [38]–[42].
[365] ILO, *Giving Globalization a Human Face*, 85.
[366] See also *Health Services* case, [108]: interference may be permitted in collective bargaining 'on an exceptional and typically temporary basis, in situations, for example, involving essential services, vital state administration, clear deadlocks and national crisis'.
[367] ILO, Freedom of Association: Digest of Decisions and Principles, [992]–[997].
[368] ILO, Freedom of Association: Digest of Decisions and Principles, [1003].
[369] ILO, Freedom of Association: Digest of Decisions and Principles, [1004].

on other issues. While the minor modifications raised no issues for the Court (such as transferring and reassigning employees, but with protections remaining in place), others substantially interfered in collective agreements and freedom of association (such as contracting out and provisions on lay-offs and 'bumping').

The Court accepted that the law aimed to address a pressing and substantial objective, namely a crisis in health services, and was rationally connected to that end.[370] However, it found that the measures adopted did not 'minimally impair' protected collective bargaining rights, since there was a range of 'reasonable alternatives' available to meet the objective (even if the least invasive means need not be adopted), and the state had not considered or consulted on these:

156. ... The record discloses no consideration by the government of whether it could reach its goal by less intrusive measures, and virtually no consultation with unions on the matter. ...

158. In this case, the only evidence presented by the government, including the sealed evidence, confirmed that a range of options were on the table. One was chosen. The government presented no evidence as to why this particular solution was chosen and why there was no consultation with the unions about the range of options open to it.

159. The evidence establishes that there was no meaningful consultation prior to passing the Act on the part of either the government or the HEABC (as employer)...

160. This was an important and significant piece of labour legislation. It had the potential to affect the rights of employees dramatically and unusually. Yet it was adopted with full knowledge that the unions were strongly opposed to many of the provisions, and without consideration of alternative ways to achieve the government objective, and without explanation of the government's choices.[371]

The Court found it unnecessary to consider whether the measures were proportionate given that they were not minimal impairments and thus failed the requirement of necessity.

Public finance and budgetary considerations

States must not normally intervene in collective bargaining to subordinate negotiations to their economic objectives, including, for example, stabilization or wage restraint policies, or productivity aims.[372] Nonetheless, some flexibility may be warranted in relation to the public service, since agreements depend on the state budgetary position and the budget cycle may not coincide with the duration of agreements. In such cases, there may be a need to balance the interests in party autonomy and the state's finances. This may be the case in bargaining on future agreements, but also in the implementation and revision of existing agreements.

In these circumstances, states should still not unilaterally impose wage rates and should still give priority to bargaining and the free conclusion of agreements.

[370] *Health Services* case, [142]–[149].
[371] *Health Services* case, [156], [158] and [159]–[160]; see as a whole [150]–[161].
[372] ILO, Freedom of Association: Digest of Decisions and Principles, [1029]–[1032].

However, there may be a role for the state in consulting with the parties, or even a right of the state to participate in negotiations, as long as a 'significant role' remains for bargaining and the parties can participate 'fully and meaningfully', including with access to all relevant information.[373] There are examples of negotiated tripartite agreements addressing matters such as wage restraint and inflation, such as Britain's former 'Social Contract' or Australia's 'Accord'.[374]

Particularly in periods of serious financial difficulty or economic stagnation, it may be permissible for laws to set upper and lower limits for wage negotiations, or outline the overall budgetary limits within which choices are permitted.[375] In emergency stabilization situations, restrictions on wages (amounts, indexation or productivity) in future agreements should only be imposed, after consultation, as an exceptional measure, where necessary, without exceeding a reasonable period, and with adequate safeguards to protect workers' living standards.[376] The non-wage aspects of bargaining should not, however, be curtailed.

Delaying the entry into force of an agreement may be permissible to allow further consultation on its economic implications.[377] If implementing an existing agreement becomes impossible over time because of lack of state funds, and all good faith efforts to implement it have failed, the state may become involved in efforts to renegotiate the agreement to the satisfaction of the parties.[378] Agreements in force should normally be respected and any modification secured through renegotiation by persuasion and consent.[379]

Positive obligations to protect unions or employers

Aside from safeguarding state or public interests, restrictions on collective bargaining may also be necessary to protect the rights of one party from interference by another, including by subordinating the latter's rights to protect the former's. The state has a positive obligation to intervene to protect such rights. The rights of minority unions or individual union members may also require protection from majority unions; it may thus be permissible to restrict the very long duration of a collective agreement where otherwise a borderline 'most representative' union could consolidate its position to the detriment of workers.[380]

A number of cases have arisen before regional bodies where actions of unions or employers have had adverse impacts on another party, requiring an assessment of competing rights. In *Gustafsson*, a trade union boycott put pressure on an employer to enter into a collective agreement and brought economic loss. The European Court of Human Rights observed that the state has a positive obligation

373 ILO, Freedom of Association: Digest of Decisions and Principles, [1038].
374 Bamber and Sheldon, 'Collective Bargaining', 624.
375 ILO, Freedom of Association: Digest of Decisions and Principles, [1033]–[1043].
376 ILO, Freedom of Association: Digest of Decisions and Principles, [1024]–[1029] and [1038]; ILO, *Giving Globalization a Human Face*, 90.
377 ILO, Freedom of Association: Digest of Decisions and Principles, [1017].
378 ILO, Freedom of Association: Digest of Decisions and Principles, [1022].
379 ILO, Freedom of Association: Digest of Decisions and Principles, [1005]–[1011].
380 ILO, Freedom of Association: Digest of Decisions and Principles, [1047]–[1049].

to protect the negative right of party (including an employer) not to join an association, but also a discretion in allowing collective agreements as a way of pursuing the rights of unions and their members:

45. The matters complained of by the applicant, although they were made possible by national law, did not involve a direct intervention by the State. The responsibility of Sweden would nevertheless be engaged if those matters resulted from a failure on its part to secure to him under domestic law the rights set forth in Article 11 (art. 11) of the Convention (see, amongst others, the *Sibson v. the United Kingdom* judgment of 20 April 1993, Series A no. 258-A, p. 13, para. 27). Although the essential object of Article 11 (art. 11) is to protect the individual against arbitrary interferences by the public authorities with his or her exercise of the rights protected, there may in addition be positive obligations to secure the effective enjoyment of these rights.

…Article 11 (art. 11) of the Convention has been interpreted to encompass not only a positive right to form and join an association, but also the negative aspect of that freedom, namely the right not to join or to withdraw from an association (see the above-mentioned *Sigurdur A. Sigurjónsson* judgment, pp. 15–16, para. 35). Whilst leaving open whether the negative right is to be considered on an equal footing with the positive right, the Court has held that, although compulsion to join a particular trade union may not always be contrary to the Convention, a form of such compulsion which, in the circumstances of the case, strikes at the very substance of the freedom of association guaranteed by Article 11 (art. 11) will constitute an interference with that freedom (see, for instance, the above-mentioned *Sibson* judgment, p. 14, para. 29).

It follows that national authorities may, in certain circumstances, be obliged to intervene in the relationships between private individuals by taking reasonable and appropriate measures to secure the effective enjoyment of the negative right to freedom of association (see, mutatis mutandis, the *Plattform "Ärzte für das Leben" v. Austria* judgment of 21 June 1988, Series A no. 139, p. 12, paras. 32–34).

At the same time it should be recalled that, although Article 11 (art. 11) does not secure any particular treatment of the trade unions, or their members, by the State, such as a right to conclude any given collective agreement, the words 'for the protection of [their] interests' in Article 11 para. 1 (art. 11-1) show that the Convention safeguards freedom to protect the occupational interests of trade-union members by trade-union action. In this respect the State has a choice as to the means to be used and the Court has recognised that the concluding of collective agreements may be one of these (see, for instance, the *Swedish Engine Drivers' Union v. Sweden* judgment of 6 February 1976, Series A no. 20, pp. 15–16, paras. 39–40).

In view of the sensitive character of the social and political issues involved in achieving a proper balance between the competing interests and, in particular, in assessing the appropriateness of State intervention to restrict union action aimed at extending a system of collective bargaining, and the wide degree of divergence between the domestic systems in the particular area under consideration, the Contracting States should enjoy a wide margin of appreciation in their choice of the means to be employed.[381]

On the facts the Court found that the union action, which restricted an employer's negative freedom not to bargain, did not violate Article 11 of the ECHR since it

[381] *Gustafsson v Sweden*, [45].

did not strike at the very substance of the negative right of the employer and in the light of the special importance accorded to collective agreements in Sweden:

52. …the union action must have entailed a considerable pressure on the applicant to meet the union's demand that he accept to be bound by a collective agreement, either by joining an employers' association or by signing a substitute agreement. However, only the first alternative involved membership of an association. It is true that, had the applicant opted for the second alternative, he might have had less opportunity to influence the contents of future collective agreements than as a member of an employers' association. On the other hand, a substitute agreement offered the advantage that it would have been possible to include in it individual clauses tailored to the special character of the applicant's business. In any event, it does not appear, nor has it been contended, that the applicant was compelled to opt for membership of an employers' association because of economic disadvantages attached to the substitute agreement.

In reality the applicant's principal objection to the second alternative was, as in relation to the first alternative, of a political nature, namely his disagreement with the collective-bargaining system in Sweden. However, Article 11 (art. 11) of the Convention does not as such guarantee a right not to enter into a collective agreement (see the above-mentioned *Swedish Engine Drivers' Union* judgment, pp. 15–16, paras. 40–41). The positive obligation incumbent on the State under Article 11 (art. 11), including the aspect of protection of personal opinion, may well extend to treatment connected with the operation of a collective-bargaining system, but only where such treatment impinges on freedom of association. Compulsion which, as here, does not significantly affect the enjoyment of that freedom, even if it causes economic damage, cannot give rise to any positive obligation under Article 11 (art. 11).

53. Furthermore, the applicant has not substantiated his submission to the effect that the terms of employment which he offered were more favourable than those required under a collective agreement. Bearing in mind the special role and importance of collective agreements in the regulation of labour relations in Sweden, the Court sees no reason to doubt that the union action pursued legitimate interests consistent with Article 11 (art. 11) of the Convention (see, for instance, the above-mentioned *Swedish Engine Drivers' Union* judgment, pp. 15–16, para. 40; and the *Schmidt and Dahlström v. Sweden* judgment of 6 February 1976, Series A no. 21, p. 16, para. 36). It should also be recalled in this context that the legitimate character of collective bargaining is recognised by a number of international instruments, in particular Article 6 of the European Social Charter, Article 8 of the 1966 International Covenant on Economic, Social and Cultural Rights and Conventions nos. 87 and 98 of the International Labour Organisation (the first concerning freedom of association and the right to organise and the second the application of the principles of the right to organise and to bargain collectively).

54. In the light of the foregoing, having regard to the margin of appreciation to be accorded to the respondent State in the area under consideration, the Court does not find that Sweden failed to secure the applicant's rights under Article 11 (art. 11) of the Convention.[382]

A similar position has arisen under Article 5 (the right to organize) of the Revised European Social Charter. *Federation of Finnish Enterprises v Finland* concerned a Finnish law that allowed employers who are members of national employer organizations to derogate from labour laws in local collective agreements, disadvantaging employers who were not members. The European Committee on Social

[382] *Gustafsson v Sweden*, [52]–[54].

Rights found that collective bargaining is a legitimate means to protect working conditions and may lawfully result in employers being treated differently:

28. In order to determine whether the rules relating to the effects of collective agreements are compatible with Article 5 of the Charter it is essential to interpret the provisions of Article 5 taking into account Article 6 of the Charter. It follows from this that it is legitimate in principle that the legal rules applicable to working conditions be the result of collective bargaining. Such a system implies that employers may be treated differently depending on whether or not they are members of an organisation.

29. Such a conclusion may of course lead to an incompatibility with Article 5 but only if it were to affect the very substance of the freedom of association (see judgment of the European Court of Human Rights in *Gustafsson v Sweden* of 25 April 1998).

30. The complainant organisation has not however demonstrated nor does the Committee find that the impugned provisions are in conflict with the substance of the freedom of association not [sic] has it been demonstrated that this freedom is affected in a manner that is more serious than what is necessary for the effectiveness and coherence of a system of collective bargaining.[383]

One dissenting member argued, however, that the matter should have been considered under Article 6 of the Revised European Social Charter (the right to collectively bargain), in relation to which the matter raised questions about the compatibility of giving priority to representativeness over voluntariness in collective bargaining:

However, although the complaint is unfounded under Article 5, it should be considered closely from the standpoint of Article 6. The majority acknowledge in paragraph 28 that to determine whether the rules relating to the effects of collective agreements are compatible with the Charter account must be taken of Article 6. Yet, instead of developing this line of reasoning they conclude that the differentiation made by the legislation between affiliated and non-affiliated employers is a logical consequence of the system.

Although it is not made explicit, this argument gives priority to the notion of representativeness. However, consideration needs to be given to the meaning and scope of representativeness, which in this case embodies significant powers to claim exemption from the law.

Such a privilege based on the notion of representativeness may not be consistent with the promotion of collective bargaining, as specified in Article 6 paragraph 2, and the same may apply to paragraph 3. In dismissing this aspect of the complaint, the majority appear not to have responded to the complainant organisation's allegations in their entirety.

I find that in this case, Finnish legislation and practice are incompatible with the spirit of Article 6 paragraphs 2 and 3.[384]

While there is no obligation under the ECHR on employers to collectively bargain, the state must not permit employers to undermine protected union rights. In *Wilson, National Union of Journalists et al*,[385] the ECHR found a

[383] *Federation of Finnish Enterprises v Finland*, 16 October 2007, ECSR Complaint No. 35/2006.

[384] *Federation of Finnish Enterprises v Finland*, Dissenting Opinion of Mr Tekin Akillioglu.

[385] *Wilson, National Union of Journalists et al v United Kingdom* (Apps. 30668/96; 30671/96; 30678/96), 2 July 2002, (2002) 35 EHRR 20, [48].

violation of Article 11 where a state allowed employers to de-recognize unions for collective bargaining purposes and offer more favourable conditions to employees who agreed not to be represented by the unions. The Court observed that collective bargaining is not 'indispensible' for the effective enjoyment of trade union freedoms and that other means of protecting such rights are possible, such that the absence of a legal obligation on employers to collectively bargain does not violate Article 11.[386] However, the Court also found that unions must be able to take action to persuade employers to collectively bargain, and that by permitting employers to use financial incentives to induce employees to surrender important union rights, the state had failed in its positive obligation to secure the enjoyment of these rights:

46. The Court agrees with the Government that the essence of a voluntary system of collective bargaining is that it must be possible for a trade union which is not recognised by an employer to take steps including, if necessary, organising industrial action, with a view to persuading the employer to enter into collective bargaining with it on those issues which the union believes are important for its members' interests. Furthermore, it is of the essence of the right to join a trade union for the protection of their interests that employees should be free to instruct or permit the union to make representations to their employer or to take action in support of their interests on their behalf. If workers are prevented from so doing, their freedom to belong to a trade union, for the protection of their interests, becomes illusory. It is the role of the State to ensure that trade union members are not prevented or restrained from using their union to represent them in attempts to regulate their relations with their employers.

47. In the present case, it was open to the employers to seek to pre-empt any protest on the part of the unions or their members against the imposition of limits on voluntary collective bargaining, by offering those employees who acquiesced in the termination of collective bargaining substantial pay rises, which were not provided to those who refused to sign contracts accepting the end of union representation. The corollary of this was that United Kingdom law permitted employers to treat less favourably employees who were not prepared to renounce a freedom that was an essential feature of union membership. Such conduct constituted a disincentive or restraint on the use by employees of union membership to protect their interests. However, as the House of Lords' judgment made clear, domestic law did not prohibit the employer from offering an inducement to employees who relinquished the right to union representation, even if the aim and outcome of the exercise was to bring an end to collective bargaining and thus substantially to reduce the authority of the union, as long as the employer did not act with the purpose of preventing or deterring the individual employee simply from being a member of a trade union.

48. Under United Kingdom law at the relevant time it was, therefore, possible for an employer effectively to undermine or frustrate a trade union's ability to strive for the protection of its members' interests. The Court notes that this aspect of domestic law

[386] *Wilson et al v United Kingdom*, [43]–[45]. See also *National Union of Belgian Police v Belgium* (App. 4464/70), 27 October 1975, (1975) 1 EHRR 578 (where there was no violation of Article 11 where the state chose to consult with some police unions but not others, leading to a decline in membership of an affected union).

has been the subject of criticism by the Social Charter's Committee of Independent Experts and the ILO's Committee on Freedom of Association (see paragraphs 32–33 and 37 above). It considers that, by permitting employers to use financial incentives to induce employees to surrender important union rights, the respondent State has failed in its positive obligation to secure the enjoyment of the rights under Article 11 of the Convention. This failure amounted to a violation of Article 11, as regards both the applicant trade unions and the individual applicants.[387]

Minimum core obligations and collective bargaining

It will be evident that various issues that may come within the ambit of collective bargaining are also addressed by particular ICESCR rights, such as the rights to work (Article 6), equal remuneration and just conditions of work (Article 7), social security (Article 9), an adequate standard of living (Article 11), and the rights of families, working mothers and children (Article 10). Core obligations on states in relation to these rights impose minimum, intransgressible parameters on the autonomy of the parties to negotiate.

It is thus permissible for the state to legislate a minimum wage to maintain adequate living standards for workers, and which the parties may not contract beneath. The same is true of minimum legislative standards on occupational health and safety, minimum maternity leave entitlements, gender equality and non-discrimination, unfair dismissal and so on, where the minimum floor in the relevant area is pegged to a state's core obligations. Collective agreements generally also should not undermine national law or public policy.

In practice, given that the purpose of collective bargaining is to establish more favourable conditions than those provided for in national law, there will usually be little reason to negotiate lower standards.[388] But two situations may be highlighted. One is where national law does not reflect the state's minimum core obligations, raising issues where parties are permitted to negotiate above national law, but still lower than the ICESCR requires. The second is where the bargaining power of unions is weak relative to an employer, such that, for example, unemployed or vulnerable workers may be tempted to undercut minimum national or ICESCR standards in order to secure employment.

In addition, since states are required to progressively realize the ICESCR beyond minimum core obligations, a more difficult question arises where state legislative intervention mandates worker rights which exceed the minimum core, but which the state believes are necessary to further progressively realize the right in question. State intervention is more invasive of party autonomy in such cases. A state may seek to justify such intervention by reference to the limitations clauses in Article 8, pursuant to which intervention in trade union rights may be considered a necessary and proportionate restriction to secure the rights of others.

[387] *Wilson, National Union of Journalists et al v UK*, [46]–[48].

[388] ILO, *Giving Globalization a Human Face*, 82.

Relationship to individual employment contracts

With the changing nature of the labour market and business efforts to bring about greater labour 'flexibility', individual employment contracts have been introduced alongside collective agreements in some workplaces. The ILO has found no issue with such contracts where they are a result of an agreement between unions and employers,[389] that is, where they are an expression of the collective will (even if they paradoxically undermine unions in the longer term, by offering better conditions and thus inducing workers to leave unions).

By contrast, where individual contracts are unilaterally offered by employers, or promoted by states, the ILO has been concerned that they may undermine the negotiating capacity of unions, discriminate in favour of non-union staff and undermine union membership.[390] The ILO has thus observed that it is:

> ... difficult to reconcile the equal status given in the law to individual and collective contracts with the ILO principles on collective bargaining, according to which the full development and utilization of machinery for voluntary negotiation between employers or employers' organizations and workers' organizations should be encouraged and promoted, with a view to the regulation of terms and conditions of employment by means of collective agreements.[391]

States should encourage and promote collective bargaining over other alternatives. In this sense, the ILO privileges the collective rights of unions over the freedom of individual workers not to join a union or not to be collectively represented in bargaining by a union, and thus to choose an individual contract over a collective agreement. The ILO has also been alert to 'disguised employment relationships' by which contractual or cooperative arrangements deprive workers of their entitlements.[392]

ILO Recommendation No. 91 on Collective Agreements 1951 specifically urges states (at paragraph 3) to ensure that employers and workers covered by collective agreements cannot enter into employment contracts which deviate from collective agreements, unless the former provide more favourable conditions than the latter.

If Article 8 of the ICESCR is interpreted to give greater weight to individual rights, the approach might be different from that adopted by the ILO. An individual's negative right not to join a union, and thus to remain free to bargain individually (through a contract), not collectively (through an agreement), would prevail in assessing whether union rights (under Article 8) may be restricted (under the limitations clauses in Article 8) to ensure the rights of others, namely individuals (also arising under Article 8).

389 ILO, Freedom of Association: Digest of Decisions and Principles, [1056].
390 ILO, Freedom of Association: Digest of Decisions and Principles, [1054].
391 ILO, Freedom of Association: Digest of Decisions and Principles, [1057].
392 ILO, *Giving Globalization a Human Face*, 29.

PROTECTION FROM ANTI-UNION DISCRIMINATION

The CESCR has routinely criticized discrimination against union members, such as dismissals,[393] harassment,[394] black-listing[395] and allowing employers to differentiate between union and non-union members in awarding pay rises.[396] The CESCR has recommended that states take effective measures to ensure workers are protected from such actions.[397]

Protection against anti-union discrimination is implicit in the right to form and join unions under Article 8(1)(a), the right of unions to function freely under Article 8(1)(c), and the right to enjoy ICESCR rights (including Article 8) without discrimination under Article 2(2) of the ICESCR, whether on the basis of 'political or other opinion' or 'other status'.

Article 1 of ILO Convention No. 98 explicitly requires states to protect workers against anti-union discrimination in employment, including in hiring and dismissal:

1. Workers shall enjoy adequate protection against acts of anti-union discrimination in respect of their employment.
2. Such protection shall apply more particularly in respect of acts calculated to—

   (a) make the employment of a worker subject to the condition that he shall not join a union or shall relinquish trade union membership;

   (b) cause the dismissal of or otherwise prejudice a worker by reason of union membership or because of participation in union activities outside working hours or, with the consent of the employer, within working hours.

ILO bodies have described anti-union discrimination as 'one of the most serious violations of freedom of association, as it may jeopardize the very existence of trade unions'.[398] The protection applies to trade union members and officials, current or former, future members intending to join, and majority or minority unions.[399] Even in emergency situations such as civil war, measures to prevent sabotage in public utilities must not involve discrimination.[400]

Discrimination may take various forms. In hiring, the 'black-listing' of union members is pernicious and difficult to challenge because of its secrecy.[401] During

[393] CESCR, Concluding Observations: Costa Rica, E/C.12/CRI/CO/4 (4 January 2008), [20]; Morocco, E/C.12/1994/5 (30 May 1994), [15]; Paraguay, E/C.12/1/Add.1 (28 May 1996), [12]; Poland, E/C.12/POL/CO/5 (2 December 2009), [20].

[394] CESCR, Concluding Observations, Costa Rica, E/C.12/CRI/CO/4 (4 January 2008), [20]; Poland, E/C.12/POL/CO/5 (2 December 2009), [20].

[395] CESCR, Concluding Observations: Brazil, E/C.12/BRA/CO/2 (12 June 2009), [18]; Costa Rica, E/C.12/CRI/CO/4 (4 January 2008), [20].

[396] CESCR, Concluding Observations: United Kingdom, E/C.12/1/Add.19 (12 December 1997), [11].

[397] CESCR, Concluding Observations: Brazil, E/C.12/BRA/CO/2 (12 June 2009), [18]; Poland, E/C.12/POL/CO/5 (2 December 2009), [20].

[398] ILO, Freedom of Association: Digest of Decisions and Principles, [769].

[399] ILO, Freedom of Association: Digest of Decisions and Principles, [775]–[777].

[400] ILO, Freedom of Association: Digest of Decisions and Principles, [777].

[401] ILO, Freedom of Association: Digest of Decisions and Principles, [782]–[784].

employment, discrimination may include: the withdrawal or restriction of benefits; demotion; frequent transfer; harassment and intimidation; preferential treatment of non-union members; or removal of union rights (such as collective bargaining) due to proprietorial changes.[402]

Discriminatory dismissals for union membership or activity can be overt (such as dismissals following strikes) or take disguised forms such as non-renewal of contracts, compulsory retirement, economic pretexts (including redundancies or restructuring), for 'workplace disharmony', or when public appointees serve at the executive's discretion or 'pleasure'. In *Baena-Ricardo et al v Panama*, the Inter-American Court of Human Rights found that a retrospective law dismissing 270 workers for trade union activities (including strikes) violated their freedom of association under Article 16 of the American Convention:

160. The entirety of the evidence in the instant case shows that, in dismissing the State workers, labour union leaders who were working on a number of claims were dismissed. In addition, the members or workers organisations were dismissed for acts that were not causes for dismissal according to the legislation in force at the time of the events. This proves that the intention in making Law 25 retroactive in compliance with orders from the Executive Branch, was to provide a basis for the massive dismissal of public sector trade union leaders and workers, such actions doubtlessly limiting the possibilities for action of the trade union organisations in the cited sector.

…

171. In order to arrive at conclusions on whether or not the State violated the right to freedom of association, the Court takes particularly into account… the following [uncontested] facts: (a) that Law 25 was issued 15 days after the events that gave rise to the instant case; (b) that the rules relative to the trade union domain were not observed in relationship to the dismissal of the workers; (c) that the workers unions' premises were blocked and that their banking accounts were intervened; and (d) that numerous dismissed workers were leaders of trade union organizations.

172. No evidence has been provided to the Court to prove that the measures adopted by the State were necessary to safeguard the public order in the context of the events, nor that they maintained a relationship to the principle of proportionality; in sum, the Court feels that such measures did not meet the requirement of being 'necessary in a democratic society' enshrined in Article 16(2) of the Convention.[403]

Trade union leaders are especially vulnerable to discrimination, the effects of which can chill union activity more broadly. Article 1 of ILO Convention No. 135 concerning Workers' Representatives relevantly provides:

Workers' representatives in the undertaking shall enjoy effective protection against any act prejudicial to them, including dismissal, based on their status or activities as a workers' representative or on union membership or participation in union activities, in so far as they act in conformity with existing laws or collective agreements or other jointly agreed arrangements.[404]

[402] ILO, Freedom of Association: Digest of Decisions and Principles, [785]–[789].
[403] *Baena-Ricardo v Panama*, [160] and [171]–[172].
[404] See also ILO Recommendation No. 143 concerning Workers' Representatives (23 June 1971), [1].

Leaders should not be adversely treated for performing their functions, including presenting grievances, representing members, during strikes or bargaining, or by dismissal followed by reinstatement to intimidate them. Elected workplace representatives should also not be used to undermine the position of trade unions and their leaders.[405] The state too must not intimidate leaders to surrender their posts.[406] The protection of union leaders does not, however, equate to immunity against dismissal for infringements such as serious misconduct, absence from work without permission, or misusing their employer's business position and personnel to undertake union activities.[407]

Various measures of protection against union discrimination are available, although the state enjoys some degree of discretion. Article 3 of ILO Convention No. 98 provides simply that '[m]achinery appropriate to national conditions shall be established, where necessary, for the purpose of ensuring respect for the right to organise'. Measures drawn from ILO practice can inform the nature of a state's obligations to protect under the ICESCR.

First, the law should set out clear prohibitions on anti-union discrimination in all of its forms. Secondly, clear and specific civil, administrative and criminal remedies and dissuasive sanctions[408] should be available and applied where it occurs. Remedial procedures must be impartial, fair, inexpensive and effective. They must also be prompt, since protracted delay can make infringements irreversible (particularly as regards reinstatement after dismissal).

While criminal penalties may be applied, in practice they may be less effective because of the high standard of proof and difficulty in evidencing anti-union discrimination. Often remedies will take the form of full and adequate compensation, not only for the material damage suffered (such as loss of wages), but also to punish perpetrators and prevent repetition. The latter requires adjusting the quantum of compensation to the size of the undertaking in order to ensure deterrence; awards may be higher in cases of dismissal, given its seriousness. In dismissal cases, reinstatement without loss of pay may be appropriate.

Special difficulty arises in proving discrimination at the hiring stage,[409] as well as in dismissals, given the secrecy which may attend such decisions. The ILO suggests that reasons should be available for decisions about both hiring and firing, and this is also required under Article 6 of the ICESCR in relation to protection of the right to work, discussed in an earlier chapter. It may be appropriate to adjust the burden of proof in such cases, such as by reversing the burden once discrimination is alleged, or once a prima facie case is established.

[405] ILO Convention No. 135 concerning Workers' Representatives, Article 5.

[406] *X v Ireland* (App. 4125/69), 1 January 1971, (1971) 14 Yearbook of the European Commission on Human Rights 198, 222 (dealing with Article 11 of the ECHR).

[407] ILO, Freedom of Association: Digest of Decisions and Principles, [799]–[812].

[408] ILO, Freedom of Association: Digest of Decisions and Principles, [813]–[836]; see also ILO, *Giving Globalization a Human Face*, 75–6 and 79.

[409] ILO, *Giving Globalization a Human Face*, 73, 78–9.

In relation to union leaders, ILO Recommendation No. 143 on Workers' Representatives of 1971 encourages states to adopt special measures to protect against discriminatory dismissals of union leaders (paragraph 6). These may include providing reasons for termination, protective procedures prior to and review after dismissal, effective remedies for unjustified dismissal (including reinstatement and/or compensation), reversing the burden of proof where unjustified dismissal is alleged, and priority retention in workforce reductions.

Finally, the state should also take measures to prevent anti-union discrimination. For example, labour inspectors should be able to freely enter enterprises without prior notice. A state could also require prior authorization or approval where an employer seeks to dismiss a union leader.[410] Measures to educate employers about their responsibilities, and to promote awareness and the accessibility of remedies, should also be taken. The state should also refrain from provoking employers to discriminate,[411] including through their public comments about unions, their discussions with employers or in the shaping of economic policy.

PROTECTION FROM VIOLENCE, INTIMIDATION AND VIOLATIONS OF CIVIL LIBERTIES

On many occasions, the CESCR has been concerned about actions directed at union leaders which infringe the right of unions to function freely and/or the right of members to join unions. It has expressed grave concern over the murder of or violence against union leaders,[412] sometimes on a massive scale, such as the killing of 1,500 union members in Colombia between 1991 and 2001.[413] In some instances, somewhat unusually at the level of state monitoring rather than in deciding individual complaints, it has named particular victims, such as the 'assassination' of union leaders Chea Vichea, Ros Savannareth and Hy Vuthy in Cambodia, and miscarriages of justice in convicting innocent suspects, all contributing to a 'climate of impunity'.[414]

The CESCR has also criticized the arbitrary arrest and detention of trade union officials or activists,[415] and intimidation, harassment or threats directed against them.[416] Again, it has occasionally identified victims, such as the disappearance (in the 1960s and 1970s) of Abdelhaq Rouissi and Houcine El Manouzi in

[410] ILO, *Giving Globalization a Human Face*, 74.

[411] ILO, Freedom of Association: Digest of Decisions and Principles, [815].

[412] CESCR, Concluding Observations: Brazil, E/C.12/BRA/CO/2 (12 June 2009), [17]; Cambodia, E/C.12/KHM/CO/1 (12 June 2009), [24]; Colombia, E/C.12/1/Add.74 (6 December 2001), [17]; Colombia, E/C.12/COL/CO/5 (7 June 2010), [12].

[413] CESCR, Concluding Observations: Colombia, E/C.12/1/Add.74 (6 December 2001), [17].

[414] CESCR, Concluding Observations: Cambodia, E/C.12/KHM/CO/1 (12 June 2009), [24].

[415] CESCR, Concluding Observations: Democratic Republic of the Congo, E/C.12/COD/CO/4 (16 December 2009), [23]; Morocco, E/C.12/1994/5 (30 May 1994), [15]; Nigeria, E/C.12/1/Add.23 (16 June 1998), [16].

[416] CESCR, Concluding Observations: Ukraine, E/C.12/1/Add.65 (24 September 2001), [16]; Ukraine, E/C.12/UKR/CO/5 (4 January 2008), [17].

Morrocco, and their suspected secret detention ever since—for more than thirty years.[417] It also criticized the detention without charge or trial for some years of union leaders Frank Kokori and Milton Dabibi in Nigeria.[418]

The CESCR has recommended that states take adequate steps to protect trade union leaders, investigate acts of violence, ensure there are effective sanctions[419] and provide compensation to victims' families.[420] It has emphasized that the rights under Article 8 'can only be exercised in a climate free from violence, pressure or threats of any kind',[421] echoing ILO standards. Where inter-union rivalry involves violence, the state's police may be required to intervene to protect the free exercise of trade union rights by those affected.[422]

The inclusion of trade union rights in both the ICESCR and ICCPR (Article 22(1)) indicates the dual nature of such rights as socio-economic and civil-political.[423] The ILO has repeatedly emphasized the interdependence of union rights with civil and political rights,[424] most prominently in its Resolution concerning Trade Union Rights and Their Relation to Civil Liberties 1970, which states, inter alia:

> ...the rights conferred upon workers' and employers' organizations must be based on respect for those civil liberties which have been enunciated in particular in the Universal Declaration of Human Rights and in the International Covenant on Civil and Political Rights, and that the absence of these civil liberties removes all meaning from the concept of trade union rights.

The ILO has been attentive to the full gamut of civil and political rights which affect trade unions, especially: the right to life of trade unionists;[425] the right to security of person and freedom from arbitrary arrest or detention (including preventive detention, forced labour or psychiatric internment);[426] freedom of movement (including freedom from exile or house arrest);[427] humane conditions of detention and freedom from torture or ill-treatment; the right to a fair trial in accordance with Article 14 of the ICCPR;[428] and the right to protection of union and members' property, premises and correspondence (except by judicial warrant).[429]

[417] CESCR, Concluding Observations: Morocco, E/C.12/1994/5 (30 May 1994), [15].

[418] CESCR, Concluding Observations: Nigeria, E/C.12/1/Add.23 (16 June 1998), [16].

[419] CESCR, Concluding Observations: Brazil, E/C.12/BRA/CO/2 (12 June 2009), [17]; Democratic Republic of the Congo, E/C.12/COD/CO/4 (16 December 2009), [23]; Morocco, E/C.12/1994/5 (30 May 1994), [21]; Ukraine, E/C.12/UKR/CO/5 (4 January 2008), [17].

[420] CESCR, Concluding Observations: Colombia, E/C.12/1/Add.74 (6 December 2001), [12].

[421] CESCR, Concluding Observations: Cambodia, E/C.12/KHM/CO/1 (12 June 2009), [24]; Democratic Republic of the Congo, E/C.12/COD/CO/4 (16 December 2009), [23].

[422] ILO, Freedom of Association: Digest of Decisions and Principles, [1125].

[423] Nowak, *CCPR Commentary*, 500–501.

[424] ILO, *Giving Globalization a Human Face*, 22.

[425] ILO, Freedom of Association: Digest of Decisions and Principles, [42]–[60].

[426] ILO, Freedom of Association: Digest of Decisions and Principles, [61]–[86].

[427] ILO, Freedom of Association: Digest of Decisions and Principles, [121]–[129].

[428] ILO, Freedom of Association: Digest of Decisions and Principles, [41] and [92]–[120].

[429] ILO, Freedom of Association: Digest of Decisions and Principles, [59] and [178]–[192] (including protection from the closure, occupation, sealing or ransacking of premises, or the unlawful confiscation of property).

The ILO has also been concerned about key expressive civil and political freedoms that are essential to the work of trade unions. Freedoms of assembly and demonstration[430] require that unions may hold meetings in their own premises without prior authorization, as well as strikes or demonstrations subject only to necessary public order considerations and procedural formalities (such as notification of the place, time and manner of a protest).

Further, freedom of opinion and expression,[431] including the right to seek, receive and impart information and ideas through any media and across frontiers,[432] is vital to union activity. Unions must thus be permitted to express their views in the media or in their own publications (whether newspapers, journals, leaflets or posters) without prior authorization, censorship or arbitrary licensing restrictions. They also enjoy the freedom to choose and display their own insignia and flags.

The ILO has suggested, however, that unions should 'respect propriety and refrain from the use of insulting language' or 'language of extravagance',[433] or publishing 'obviously political or anti-national' publications.[434] This does not necessarily imply that such excesses would justify restrictions on expression under Article 19 of the ICCPR; there may be a gap between what is proper and what is illegal. Yet, unions must still comply with necessary and proportionate legal restrictions designed to secure the right of others (including honour and reputation), such as laws relating to defamation, but also laws on hate speech[435] or incitement.

The ILO has found that respect for these fundamental civil and political rights is necessary for a 'climate free of violence, pressure, fear and threats of any kind'.[436] It has further observed that democracy is fundamental to the free exercise of union rights.[437] Unions are accordingly entitled to demand respect for civil and political rights,[438] which are not 'political' matters outside the proper purposes or activities of unions.

Two legal implications flow from the above considerations. First, the protection of trade unions (including their formation and free functioning) under Article 8 of the ICESCR implicitly requires states to guarantee relevant civil and political rights, defined by reference to the ICCPR. Civil and political rights thus provide indispensible further 'content' to Article 8.

Secondly, the protection of civil and political rights under the ICCPR is a further means of safeguarding trade unions and their members, independently of the ICESCR. In regional practice, too, there are numerous cases where trade

[430] ILO, Freedom of Association: Digest of Decisions and Principles, [130]–[151].
[431] ILO, Freedom of Association: Digest of Decisions and Principles, [154]–[173].
[432] ILO, Freedom of Association: Digest of Decisions and Principles, [154]–[173].
[433] ILO, Freedom of Association: Digest of Decisions and Principles, [154], [170].
[434] ILO, Freedom of Association: Digest of Decisions and Principles, [171].
[435] See also Nowak, *CCPR Commentary*, 507, commenting on permissible limitations on the right of association under Article 22 of the ICCPR to secure the rights of others.
[436] ILO, Freedom of Association: Digest of Decisions and Principles, [34].
[437] ILO, Freedom of Association: Digest of Decisions and Principles, [32].
[438] ILO, Freedom of Association: Digest of Decisions and Principles, [36].

unionists have found protection in the application of civil and political rights, as in cases of arbitrary arrests[439] or where the right to an effective remedy is invoked where national judicial decisions have not been enforced.[440]

Thirdly, a violation of the civil and political rights of unionists may supply the legal basis for finding a consequent violation of trade union rights. Thus, in *Ouko v Kenya*, the African Commission found that the political persecution of a student union leader, including detention without trial for ten months and torture in poor conditions in a 'notorious' secret police cell, after which he was forced to flee abroad, grounded a separate violation of his freedom of association under Article 10 of the African Charter.[441]

Likewise, in *Huilca Tecse v Peru*, the Inter-American Court of Human Rights found that Peru's violation of the right to life of a prominent trade union leader (under Article 4 of the American Convention) infringed not only his individual freedom of association (under Article 16), but also the freedom of union members generally, given its intimidatory effects:

67. . . . the extrajudicial execution of Pedro Huilca Tecse, in the context of this case, constitutes a violation of the contents of the right to freedom of association, in relation to trade union rights.

68. As established above (*supra* para. 64), the murder of the alleged victim was motivated by his being a trade union leader who opposed and criticized the policies of the Government at that time.

69. Article 16(1) of the Convention includes the 'right to associate freely for ideological, religious, political, economic, labor, social, cultural, sports, or other purposes.' These words establish literally that those who are protected by the Convention not only have the right and freedom to associate freely with other persons, without the interference of the public authorities limiting or obstructing the exercise of the respective right, which thus represents a right of each individual; but they also enjoy the right and freedom to seek the common achievement of a licit goal, without pressure or interference that could alter or change their purpose. Therefore, the execution of a trade union leader, in a context such as that of this case, not only restricts the freedom of association of an individual, but also the right and freedom of a determined group to associate freely, without fear; consequently, the right protected by Article 16 has a special scope and nature, and this illustrates the two dimensions of freedom of association.

70. In its individual dimension, labor-related freedom of association is not exhausted by the theoretical recognition of the right to form trade unions, but also corresponds, inseparably,

[439] *Krishna Achuthan (on behalf of Aleke Banda), Amnesty International (on behalf of Orton and Vera Chirwa) v Malawi*, 27 April 1994, African Commission on Human and Peoples' Rights Communication No. 64/92-68/92-78/92 8AR (violation of Article 6 of the African Charter).

[440] *Acevedo-Jaramillo et al v Peru*, 7 February 2006, IACHR Series C No. 144 (where national judgments, requiring the reinstatement, compensation and remuneration of unionized workers who were dismissed for striking, were not enforced, and the IACHR found violations of the right to judicial protection in Articles 25(1) and 25(2) of the American Convention on Human Rights (adopted 22 November 1969, OAS Treaty Series No. 36, entered into force 18 July 1978). It was thus unnecessary to separately consider whether Article 16 (freedom of association) had been violated).

[441] *Ouko v Kenya*, 6 November 2000, African Commission on Human and Peoples' Rights Communication No. 232/99, [29]–[30].

to the right to use any appropriate means to exercise this freedom. When the Convention proclaims that freedom of association includes the right to freely associate 'for [... any] other purposes,' it is emphasizing that the freedom to associate and to pursue certain collective goals are indivisible, so that a limitation of the possibilities of association represents directly, and to the same extent, a limitation of the right of the collectivity to achieve its proposed purposes. Hence the importance of adapting to the Convention the legal regime applicable to trade unions and the State's actions, or those that occur with its tolerance, that could render this right inoperative in practice.

71. In its social dimension, freedom of association is a mechanism that allows the members of a labor collectivity or group to achieve certain objectives together and to obtain benefits for themselves.

72. The two above-mentioned dimensions (*supra* paras. 69, 70 and 71) of freedom of association must be guaranteed simultaneously...

77. The Court considers that the content of freedom of association implies the power to choose how to exercise it. In this regard, an individual does not enjoy the full exercise of the freedom of association, if, in reality, this power is inexistent or is limited so that it cannot be implemented. The State must ensure that people can freely exercise their freedom of association without fear of being subjected to some kind of violence; otherwise, the ability of groups to organize themselves to protect their interests could be limited.

78. In view of the foregoing, the Court considers that, in this case, the legitimate exercise that Pedro Huilca Tecse made of the right to freedom of association, (in trade union matters), resulted in a lethal reprisal, which, in turn, constituted a violation of Article 16 of the American Convention. The Court also considers that the execution of Pedro Huilca Tecse had an intimidating effect on the workers of the Peruvian trade union movement and thereby reduced the freedom of a specific group to exercise this right.[442]

The Inter-American Court found similarly in *Cantoral Huamani and Garcia Santa Cruz v Peru*, where two union leaders in the mining industry were arrested and extrajudicially executed in the context of Peru's civil war:[443]

144. Article 16(1) of the Convention establishes that those who are subject to the jurisdiction of the States Parties have the right to associate freely with other persons, without the intervention of the public authorities limiting or obstructing the exercise of this right. In addition, they have the right and the freedom to associate in order to seek together a lawful purpose, without pressure or interference that can alter or denature this purpose. In addition to these negative obligations, freedom of association also gives rise to positive obligations, such as to prevent attacks on it, to protect those who exercise it, and to investigate violations. These positive obligations must be adopted, even in the sphere of relations between individuals, if the case merits it. As it has determined in other cases, the Court considers that the sphere of protection of Article 16(1) includes the exercise of the right to organize trade unions.

145. The ILO Committee on Freedom of Association has stated that some trade union rights cannot be exercised when impunity exists in situations of trade union violence characterized, *inter alia*, by extrajudicial executions.

[442] *Huilca Tecse v Peru*, 3 March 2005, IACHR Series C No. 121.

[443] *Cantoral Huamani and Garcia Santa Cruz v Peru*, 10 July 2007, IACHR Series C No. 167, [144]–[146].

146. The State must guarantee that people can freely exercise their freedom of association without fear that they will be subjected to any violence; otherwise, the ability of groups to organize themselves to protect their interests could be reduced. It is worth noting that when examining a complaint against Peru (*supra* para. 57), which included the report on the execution of Saúl Cantoral-Huamaní and Consuelo García-Santa Cruz, the ILO Committee on Freedom of Association considered that an environment of violence constituted a grave obstacle for the exercise of freedom of association. Freedom of association can only be exercised in a situation in which the fundamental human rights are fully respected and guaranteed, in particular the right to life and safety. The Court underscores the State's obligation to investigate crimes against union leaders effectively and with due diligence, bearing in mind that the failure to investigate such facts has an intimidating effect, which prevents the free exercise of trade union rights. The said due diligence is accentuated in contexts of violence against the trade union sector.

147. Based on the facts acknowledged and proven in the instant case, the Court finds that the legitimate exercise of the right to freedom of association in relation to trade unions by Saúl Cantoral-Huamaní was the motive for the attacks on his personal integrity and life (*supra* paras. 60 to 67), which, in turn, gave rise to a violation of Article 16 of the American Convention. With regard to the social leader, Consuelo García-Santa Cruz, the Court observes that her activities designed to promote the 'mining wives' committees' were directly connected to the mining strikes. In particular, during the two strikes, Consuelo García was providing support to the mining women and families who were on strike (supra paras. 52 and 143).

148. The Court also finds that the execution of Saúl Cantoral-Huamaní and Consuelo García-Santa Cruz had an intimidating effect on the workers of the Peruvian mining trade union movement. In a context such as that of the instant case, executions like these not only restricted the freedom of association of an individual, but also the right and the freedom of a specific group to associate freely without fear; in other words, the freedom of the mining workers to exercise this right was affected. In addition, this intimidating effect was accentuated and made more severe by the context of impunity that surrounds the case.

149. Consequently, the Court considers that the State is responsible for the violation of the right to freedom of association established in Article 16 of the American Convention…

DISSOLUTION OR SUSPENSION

The right of unions to freely function also requires their protection from arbitrary or unlawful suspension or dissolution. Voluntary dissolution is permissible in accordance with a union's internal procedures.

Any suspension or dissolution by the state must conform with the limitation clause in Article 8(1)(c), namely that it is necessary and proportionate in pursuit of national security, public order or the protection of the rights of others.[444] It should thus be a last resort, after less invasive alternatives have been exhausted.[445] As noted earlier in relation to such restrictions, exceptional circumstances might

[444] Craven, *The ICESCR*, 277.
[445] ILO, Freedom of Association: Digest of Decisions and Principles, [678].

include where an organization is 'state threatening' or seeks to destroy the rights of others.[446]

In ILO practice, dissolution may also be permissible where a union has failed to maintain a (reasonable) legislative minimum membership level[447] (assuming falling membership is not due to anti-union discrimination or intimidation). State intervention could also be warranted to re-establish respect for union rights, such as to restore democratic rules within a union, or in response to serious violations of internal rules.[448]

A state may not, however, suspend or dissolve a union at its discretion,[449] and the CESCR has recommended the repeal of such provisions.[450] A union must also not be dissolved because of the illegal activities of some leaders or members[451] or financial irregularities,[452] in relation to which ordinary legal sanctions on individuals should be applied. Economic or development reasons are an insufficient basis for interference,[453] as is the fact that a union strike or picket has disrupted public events or transport.

Where intervention is justified, legal guarantees on winding up must be applied (including in the disposition of assets to a successor entity or the workers themselves). Decisions must also be subject to suspensive and substantive judicial appeal, respecting due process, to avoid the appearance of arbitrary administrative interference.[454]

Article 8(1)(d): The Right to Strike

The right to strike was introduced into Article 8 by the three-power amendment.[455] While it is not explicitly mentioned in the UDHR, as with Article 8(1)(c) (concerning the free functioning of unions), various states saw the right to strike as 'an essential corollary of freedom of association'[456] and felt that recognizing a right to form trade unions without a right to strike would be 'to proclaim a purely theoretical right'.[457] It is both an individual and collective right.[458] The provision was

[446] Nowak, *CCPR Commentary*, 506 (in relation to Article 22 of the ICCPR); see above on restrictions generally.
[447] ILO, Freedom of Association: Digest of Decisions and Principles, [680].
[448] ILO, Freedom of Association: Digest of Decisions and Principles, [462]–[464].
[449] ILO Convention No. 87 concerning Freedom of Association, Article 4: 'Workers' and employers' organisations shall not be liable to be dissolved or suspended by administrative authority.' See similarly in respect of Article 22 of the ICCPR.
[450] CESCR, Concluding Observations: Senegal, E/C.12/1/Add.62 (24 September 2001), [22].
[451] ILO, Freedom of Association: Digest of Decisions and Principles, [692].
[452] ILO, Freedom of Association: Digest of Decisions and Principles, [694].
[453] ILO, Freedom of Association: Digest of Decisions and Principles, [677], [695].
[454] ILO, Freedom of Association: Digest of Decisions and Principles, [462]–[464], [680], [699]–[705].
[455] UNGA Third Committee, A/3525 (9 February 1957), 20.
[456] UNGA Third Committee, A/C.3/SR.719 (3 January 1957), 191 (Uruguay).
[457] UNGA Third Committee, A/C.3/SR.719 (3 January 1957), 193 (Peru); see also 191 (Uruguay).
[458] Craven, *The ICESCR*, 278.

adopted by a large majority,[459] although the drafting also reveals some emphatic differences of opinion.

Some states disliked strikes per se, not least because of their economic impacts. The Netherlands stated that strikes could 'only be exercised at a less advanced stage of human society... and could only be accepted at a certain stage of social evolution'.[460] It thought that strikes were 'both unnatural and undesirable', and that in modern societies 'associations of employers and employees had become instruments of co-operation working principally for the welfare of society as a whole'.[461] Brazil also described strikes as 'an anti-social and harmful practice incompatible with the higher interests of the community'.[462] The United Kingdom criticized strikes as 'a rather primitive approach to trade-union rights',[463] to be exercised only 'as a last resort, when the machinery of negotiation had failed'.[464]

Australia was concerned that the provision would 'distort the true concept of trade unionism' by giving undue prominence to the right to strike.[465] Others preferred to leave the matter to national law; or viewed strikes as a means to secure union rights but not a right in itself; or objected that, as a collective right, it was out of place in the ICESCR.[466] Iran was less critical of strikes, but was concerned that infant industries in under-developed countries may need to be protected from 'the effects of irresponsible trade-union action'.[467] Iran also highlighted the difficulty in distinguishing 'between strikes engineered by political intriguers and those started to promote the real economic and social interests of the workers'.[468]

Various states defended the importance of the right to strike. Pakistan disagreed with the characterization of strikes as a 'primitive device', arguing that '[t]he methods used by employers were... sometimes crude and ugly, and the workers must be given some means of self-defence'.[469] Peru recognized that strikes were not desirable, emphasizing that '[i]n an ideal society, strikes would have no *raison d'être*', but thought that in many societies it was still necessary to legally confirm the right.[470] Finally, Mexico made the argument that 'the value of the machinery for preserving peace depended on the effectiveness of that last resort',[471] and drew an analogy with the inclusion of sanctions in the UN

[459] By forty-one votes to two, with twenty-six abstentions: UNGA Third Committee, A/3525 (9 February 1957), 28.
[460] UNGA Third Committee, A/C.3/SR.721 (4 January 1957), 202 (Netherlands).
[461] UNGA Third Committee, A/C.3/SR.721 (4 January 1957), 202 (Netherlands).
[462] UNGA Third Committee, A/C.3/SR.723 (7 January 1957), 211 (Brazil).
[463] UNGA Third Committee, A/C.3/SR.720 (3 January 1957), 197 (United Kingdom).
[464] UNGA Third Committee, A/C.3/SR.720 (3 January 1957), 198 (United Kingdom).
[465] UNGA Third Committee, A/C.3/SR.723 (7 January 1957), 214 (Australia); see also A/C.3/SR.720 (3 January 1957), 198 (United Kingdom, Yugoslavia); A/C.3/SR.722, 205 (Sweden), 206 (Iran).
[466] Craven, *The ICESCR*, 257.
[467] UNGA Third Committee, A/C.3/SR.722 (7 January 1957), 206 (Iran).
[468] UNGA Third Committee, A/C.3/SR.722 (7 January 1957), 206 (Iran).
[469] UNGA Third Committee, A/C.3/SR.723 (7 January 1957), 212 (Pakistan).
[470] UNGA Third Committee, A/C.3/SR.721 (4 January 1957), 202 (Peru).
[471] UNGA Third Committee, A/C.3/SR.723 (7 January 1957), 211 (Mexico).

Charter.[472] That is, possessing the 'weapon' of a strike was necessary for workers to 'exercise any real influence' on employers.[473] Any potential abuse of the right is tempered by the economic consequences for workers themselves, who typically forgo their income during strikes.[474]

The explicit recognition of the right to strike in Article 8(1)(d) stands in contrast to its absence in ILO treaties. The Employers' Group at the ILO has long argued and still maintains that the text, drafting record and history of ILO Convention No. 87 on the Right to Organize does not support a right to strike.[475] The ILO bodies conversely regard it as a corollary of the right to organize under Convention No. 87.[476] Thus, Article 3 of the Convention recognizes the right of unions to organize their activities and formulate their programmes, while Article 10 provides that the objective of unions is to further and defend the interests of workers.[477]

The ILO Committee on the Application of Standards regards the absence of an express provision or drafting intention as not dispositive, given that a right to strike is supported by subsequent practice over fifty years and the object and purpose of Convention No. 87, both relevant considerations in the law of treaty interpretation.[478] Most national laws, many constitutions, and other international and regional instruments also recognize the right to strike.[479] ILO bodies frequently apply the right to strike to concrete situations in many countries every year, usually without protest by states against the basic principle.[480]

There is no such uncertainty in the explicit right to strike in Article 8(1)(d), which may also be regarded as a specific manifestation of the right of unions to freely function under Article 8(1)(c) of the ICESCR. The right to strike is also regarded as fundamental to the ICESCR as a whole. In response to Kuwait's reservation, that it 'reserves the right not to apply' Article 8(1)(d), four states formally objected on the basis that it is 'problematic' in view of the object and purpose of the ICESCR.[481]

While there is no international legal definition of a 'strike' as such, in ILO practice the concept encompasses 'any work stoppage'[482] for 'furthering and defending the interests of workers'[483] by exerting pressure on employers. It includes activities such as the work stoppage, tools-down, go-slow, working to

[472] UNGA Third Committee, A/C.3/SR.723 (7 January 1957), 211 (Mexico).
[473] UNGA Third Committee, A/C.3/SR.723 (7 January 1957), 214 (Uruguay).
[474] Craven, *The ICESCR*, 258. [475] ILO, *Giving Globalization a Human Face*, 47.
[476] ILO, Freedom of Association: Digest of Decisions and Principles, [523].
[477] ILO, *Giving Globalization a Human Face*, 46.
[478] ILO, *Giving Globalization a Human Face*, 48.
[479] ILO, *Giving Globalization a Human Face*, 49.
[480] ILO, *Giving Globalization a Human Face*, 49.
[481] Finland, Communication to the UN Secretary-General, 25 July 1997; Germany, Communication to the UN Secretary-General, 10 July 1997; Norway, Communication to the UN Secretary-General, 22 July 1997; Sweden, Communication to the UN Secretary-General, 23 July 1997. See Appendix III in this book.
[482] ILO, *Giving Globalization a Human Face*, 51.
[483] ILO Principles Concerning the Right to Strike (Geneva, 1998), 13. The phrase invoked is drawn from ILO Convention No. 87 concerning Freedom of Association, Article 10.

rule, sit-down, wild-cat strike (an action not authorized by the union itself), and sympathy strike (where a union not involved in a lawful workplace dispute strikes in support of the other union), as long as they are peaceful.[484]

Article 8(1)(d) does not define the purposes of protected strikes, but logically they must relate back to the *raison d'etre* of trade union rights in Article 8 as a whole, namely the protection of the social and economic interests of workers,[485] a view shared in ILO practice.[486] The right thus engages the distinction discussed earlier between legitimate trade union purposes and extraneous political activities, as well as the difficulty of drawing a bright line between them.

Strikes are accordingly legitimate to narrowly pursue better working conditions and occupational claims, including in respect of disputes about existing collective agreements, collective bargaining on future agreements, or disputes about the recognition of unions.[487] Sympathy strikes in aid of strikes by other unions should also not be generally prohibited, as long as the initial strike they support is lawful.[488]

More broadly, strikes are also permissible to promote solutions to economic and social policy questions of concern to workers or employers.[489] Given the inter-relationship between trade union rights and civil liberties, strikes are also legitimate to protect and promote fundamental rights,[490] such as to protest against the murder or arbitrary detention of unionists. Strikes of a 'purely' political nature are not, however, protected, nor are strikes which have unlawful or criminal objectives, or pre-emptive strikes prior to collective negotiations.[491]

STATE OBLIGATIONS

The CESCR has observed that the right to strike is considered 'self-executing' according to 'the great majority of observers'[492] and is thus not contingent on progressive realization. Under Article 8, states are firstly obliged to remove legal impediments to the right to strike. In monitoring states, the CESCR has criticized the characterization of strikes, or certain forms of strike, as criminal offences,[493] including disguised anti-union general offences such as 'obstruction of business',[494] which should be repealed. In a similar vein, unions should not

[484] ILO, Freedom of Association: Digest of Decisions and Principles, [545].

[485] Craven, *The ICESCR*, 278.

[486] ILO, Freedom of Association: Digest of Decisions and Principles, [520]–[522].

[487] ILO, Freedom of Association: Digest of Decisions and Principles, [536].

[488] ILO, Freedom of Association: Digest of Decisions and Principles, [534]. They may, however, be subject to restrictions such as prior notification or workplace security guarantees: ILO Principles Concerning the Right to Strike, 16.

[489] ILO, Freedom of Association: Digest of Decisions and Principles, [526].

[490] ILO, *Giving Globalization a Human Face*, 51.

[491] ILO, Freedom of Association: Digest of Decisions and Principles, [528]–[529] and [546].

[492] CESCR, Consideration of Report Submitted by State Party: Luxembourg, E/1991/23 (1990), [129].

[493] CESCR, Concluding Observations: Egypt, E/C.12/1/Add.44 (23 May 2000), [18]; Iraq, E/C.12/1/Add.17 (12 December 1997), [16]; Morocco, E/C.12/1/Add.55 (1 December 2000), [46]; Tunisia, E/C.12/1/Add.36 (14 May 1999), [25].

[494] ILO, *Giving Globalization a Human Face*, 64.

be dissolved, suspended or deregistered, their premises closed or their property seized for taking strike action.

The CESCR has frequently criticized the lack of legal recognition of the right to strike[495] and has recommended that it be explicitly inscribed in legislation.[496] The quality of laws is also important, with the CESCR criticizing the lack of clear and specific rules in some cases.[497] Recognizing a mere 'freedom' to strike (the mere 'illegality of being submitted to involuntary servitude') is not sufficient where striking still amounts to a breach of contract justifying dismissal, and where employees are forced to challenge such dismissal post facto. Rather, those 'participating in a lawful strike should not ipso facto be regarded as having committed a breach of an employment contract'.[498]

Consistent with the coverage of Article 8, laws should guarantee the right of 'everyone' to strike, subject to the permissible categories of restriction under Article 8(2). While certain procedural and substantive restrictions may be imposed on the right to strike, discussed below, such restrictions must not go beyond what is necessary to secure legitimate aims.

Workers and unions must enjoy legal protection for taking part in legitimate strikes. They must not be arbitrarily arrested (including without charge, in order to disable a strike or intimidate strikers), arbitrarily detained, banished or exiled, or subject to penalties or sanctions imposed by the state. In this respect it may be noted that ILO Convention No. 105 on the Abolition of Forced Labour 1957 expressly prohibits the use of forced or compulsory labour as a punishment for participating in strikes.

In addition, the state must protect strikers and unions from sanctions or penalties imposed by employers. The CECSR has also frequently expressed concern that workers may be dismissed as a result of participation in a strike[499] or unauthorized strike,[500] or be temporarily released.[501] It has also highlighted the inadequate protection of trade union officers engaged in the defence of employees

[495] CESCR, Concluding Observations: Afghanistan, E/C.12/AFG/CO/2-4 (7 June 2010), [25]; Democratic People's Republic of Korea, E/C.12/1/Add.95 (12 December 2003), [16]; Liechtenstein, E/C.12/LIE/CO/1 (9 June 2006), [16]; Saint Vincent and the Grenadines, E/C.12/1/Add.21 (2 December 1997), [18]; United Nations Interim Administration in Kosovo, E/C.12/UNK/CO/1 (1 December 2008), [20]; Sri Lanka, E/C.12/1/Add.24 (16 June 1998), [17]; United Kingdom, E/C.12/1/Add.19 (12 December 1997), [11]; Uzbekistan, E/C.12/UZB/CO/1 (24 January 2006), [51].

[496] CESCR, Concluding Observations: Belgium, E/C.12/1994/7 (31 May 1994), [12]; Democratic People's Republic of Korea, E/C.12/1/Add.95 (12 December 2003), [36].

[497] CESCR, Consideration of Report Submitted by State Party: Vietnam, E/1994/23 (1993), [139].

[498] CESCR, Concluding Observations: United Kingdom, E/C.12/1/Add.19 (12 December 1997), [11] and [23].

[499] CESCR, Concluding Observations: Belgium, E/C.12/CO/3 (4 January 2008), [17]; Chile, E/C.12/1/Add.105 (1 December 2004), [19]; Republic of Korea, E/C.12/1995/3 (7 June 1995), [8]; United Kingdom (Hong Kong), E/C.12/1/Add.10 (6 December 1996), [22]; United Kingdom, E/C.12/1/Add.79 (5 June 2002), [23]; Zimbabwe, E/C.12/1/Add.12 (20 May 1997), [11].

[500] CESCR, Concluding Observations: Ireland, E/C.12/1/Add.77 (5 June 2002), [18]; Mauritius, E/C.12/1994/8 (31 May 1994), [10].

[501] CESCR, Concluding Observations: Former Yugoslav Republic of Macedonia, E/C.12/MKD/CO/1 (15 January 2008), [17].

who have been dismissed.[502] The CESCR has recommended that the possibility of dismissal for involvement in a strike be removed.[503] In this respect, Article 6 of the ICESCR (the right to work) would also protect against unfair dismissal on the basis of anti-union discrimination. Employers also may not, for example, pay bonuses to those who do not go on strike and thereby discriminate on the basis of union activity.[504]

The CESCR has also criticized employers for suspending the wages of those who go on strike.[505] Otherwise, it is well accepted in ILO practice that employers may deduct wages for strike days, that is, for work not performed, but may not impose financial penalties as such. Equally, the state may not compel employers to pay wages, including, for instance, where an employer is deemed 'responsible' for causing the strike.[506]

In addition to adopting a legal framework recognizing the right to strike and protecting it from unlawful interference, states must also provide effective machinery for the protection of the right and the determination of disputes over it. In ILO practice, independent, impartial bodies must be available to settle disputes, including judicial safeguards where appropriate, discussed further below. The CESCR has also recommended that states take measures to increase the awareness of employers, labour judges and the police to guarantee the implementation of the right.[507]

RESTRICTIONS ON STRIKES

Article 8(1)(d) recognizes the right to strike 'provided that it is exercised in conformity with the laws of the particular country'. The CESCR has nonetheless frequently expressed concern about overly extensive national legal limitations on the right to strike.[508] The reference to national law cannot be understood as according states an unfettered discretion to unilaterally define the lawful limits of strikes. Otherwise, the right to strike could be deprived of any minimum content by national fiat. Certainly, the conduct of strikes must comply with ordinary national criminal laws and the right to strike does not immunize trade unionists for violence against people or property.

[502] CESCR, Concluding Observations: Hungary, E/C.12/HUN/CO/3 (16 January 2008), [16].

[503] CESCR, Concluding Observations: Former Yugoslav Republic of Macedonia, E/C.12/MKD/CO/1 (15 January 2008), [37].

[504] ILO, Freedom of Association: Digest of Decisions and Principles, [658]–[666].

[505] CESCR, Concluding Observations: Serbia and Montenegro, E/C.12/1/Add.108 (23 June 2005), [19].

[506] ILO, Freedom of Association: Digest of Decisions and Principles, [654]–[657].

[507] CESCR, Concluding Observations: Paraguay, E/C.12/1/Add.1 (28 May 1996), [25]; Peru, E/C.12/1/Add.14 (20 May 1997), [33].

[508] CESCR, Concluding Observations: El Salvador, E/C.12/1/Add.4 (28 May 1996), [19]; Ecuador, E/C.12/1/Add.100 (7 June 2004), [19]; Former Yugoslav Republic of Macedonia, E/C.12/MKD/CO/1 (15 January 2008), [17]; Kazakhstan, E/C.12/KAZ/CO/1 (7 June 2010), [22]; Paraguay, E/C.12/1/Add.1 (28 May 1996), [12]; Serbia and Montenegro, E/C.12/1/Add.108 (23 June 2005), [19]; Slovakia, E/C.12/1/Add.81 (19 December 2002), [14].

Other than the reference to national law, Article 8(1)(d) does not expressly specify the range of acceptable limitations on the right to strike. In its 'interpretive declarations and reservations', Monaco declared that in implementing Article 8(1)(d):

...it will take into account the requirements, conditions, limitations and restrictions which are prescribed by law and which are necessary in a democratic society in order to guarantee the rights and freedoms of others or to protect public order (*ordre public*), national security, public health or morals.

It thus invoked the limitations clause commonly found in the ICCPR, including in Article 22 on freedom of association, and which adds the grounds of 'public health or morals' to the more limited grounds found elsewhere in Article 8 of the ICESCR. No state objected to this declaration and the CESCR has made no adverse comment on it.

Further, France lodged a declaration that 'it will implement' the right to strike in conformity with Article 6(4) of the European Social Charter 'according to the interpretation thereof given in the annex [sic] to that Charter'. The Appendix to the Charter indicates that states may restrict the right to strike in accordance with Article 31 of the Charter, namely by law and where 'necessary in a democratic society for the protection of the rights and freedoms of others or for the protection of [the] public interest, national security, public health, or morals'. It thus replicates the limitations models of the ICCPR and ECHR.

The CESCR has only rarely indicated the applicable limitations test. The most overt instance is in its concluding observations on Canada in 2006, where it stated:

...restrictions should be eliminated where they are not strictly necessary for the promotion of the general welfare in a democratic society, for the protection of the interests of national security or public safety, public order, public health, or the protection of the rights and freedoms of others, and where no other alternative can be found.[509]

Oddly, the form of words used there corresponds more closely to the general limitations clause in Article 29(2) of the UDHR than the clauses in either the ICESCR (including elsewhere in Article 8(1)) or the ICCPR, including by mentioning the 'general welfare'.

Otherwise, one commentator has suggested that restrictions on the right to strike may be governed by the limitations clause in Article 8(1)(c).[510] That approach makes most sense given that the right to strike is a specific iteration of the right of unions to freely function, albeit that the latter right is expressed as a collective right of unions, while the right to strike is enjoyed by both individuals and unions. It would make restrictions on strikes consistent with the approach in the rest of Article 8, and not as broad as those permitted under the UDHR.

In its practice, the ILO has set out minimum objective international standards regulating the right to strike, indicating that the matter is not left to national law

[509] CESCR, Concluding Observations: Canada, E/C.12/CAN-CO/4-5 (22 May 2006), [51].
[510] Craven, *The ICESCR*, 258.

alone; and the ILO has frequently identified excessive national restrictions.[511] By virtue of the savings clause in Article 8(3) of the ICESCR, states parties to both the ICESCR and ILO Convention No. 87 must not lower the ILO standards in giving effect to Article 8.[512] As noted earlier, the CESCR has frequently called on states to ratify the ILO instruments.

More importantly, as discussed earlier, the ILO has routinely invoked concepts and interpretations concerning the right to strike which are drawn from ILO standards and practice, even where states are not parties to the ILO instruments. The CESCR thus accepts that ILO standards supply relevant guidance on the right to strike, and that its content is not left to national discretion. The ILO standards have tended to loosely operate as an informal *lex specialis* in defining the application of Article 8 limitations. Accordingly, in both ILO and the CESCR's practice, certain restrictions on strikes of a procedural and substantive nature are permissible.

Procedural restrictions

The CESCR has objected to requiring prior authorization from the state to go on strike[513] and has urged states to remove administrative obstacles to the right to strike.[514] Nonetheless, in ILO practice, it is accepted that national law may impose certain procedural or formal prerequisites for lawful strikes.

The law may, for instance, impose a reasonable voting requirement for the approval of strikes by union members, although voting should be left to unions as far as possible. The CESCR has criticized overly high voting requirements (such as a two-thirds majority of union members in Egypt),[515] since this may excessively impede the right to strike. Likewise, it criticized Russia's dual requirement of a two-thirds quorum of all workers and half of the workers present.[516]

In ILO practice, any voting rules should not be overly burdensome, such as by requiring a supra-majority, double majority, or even a majority of all workers, since these may be difficult to obtain in larger or dispersed workforces (and particularly where voting is voluntary). The state should also not impose a requirement of prior approval by a higher level or central union.[517] It is, however, acceptable to impose reasonable quorum and secret ballot requirements, and to require a bare majority of the quorum present (but not of all workers).[518] Wildcat strikes, namely those not approved by the union, may be prohibited.[519]

[511] ILO Principles Concerning the Right to Strike, 49–54 (identifying problematic laws).

[512] Craven, *The ICESCR*, 281.

[513] CESCR, Concluding Observations: Angola, E/C.12/DZA/CO/4 (7 June 2010), [11].

[514] CESCR, Concluding Observations: El Slavador, E/C.12/SLV/CO/2 (27 June 2007), [31]; Russian Federation, E/C.12/1/Add.94 (12 December 2003), [49].

[515] CESCR, Concluding Observations: Egypt, E/C.12/1/Add.44 (23 May 2000), [18]; Russian Federation, E/C.12/1/Add.94 (12 December 2003), [21].

[516] CESCR, Concluding Observations: Russian Federation, E/C.12/1/Add.94 (12 December 2003), [21].

[517] ILO, *Giving Globalization a Human Face*, 59.

[518] ILO, Freedom of Association: Digest of Decisions and Principles, [555]–[561]; ILO, *Giving Globalization a Human Face*, 59.

[519] ILO, *Giving Globalization a Human Face*, 50.

Where strike action is approved by members, a requirement of reasonable prior notice to an employer is acceptable. An ordinary notice period of sixty days is excessive,[520] although long periods (such as twenty or even forty days) may be permissible in essential services.[521] A reasonable 'cooling-off' period is also permissible where it aims to encourage the parties to negotiate and settle their difference before strike action is taken.[522]

Many states require recourse to prior mediation, conciliation or voluntary arbitration before a strike may be called.[523] ILO Recommendation No. 92 on Voluntary Conciliation and Arbitration 1951 encourages the parties to abstain from strikes when voluntary conciliation or arbitration is underway; strikes should also not be used to resolve legal disputes where judicial proceedings are on foot.[524]

Conciliation or arbitration requirements are permissible where they are solely designed to facilitate negotiated settlement of disputes, are impartial, and are not so slow or complex as to impede the right to strike.[525] As the CESCR also observed, '[c]onsultation and cooperation are no substitute for the right to strike'.[526] The CESCR has thus criticized procedures which set excessive time periods for negotiation.[527] The CESCR also found that a twenty-one-day cooling off period coupled with a ministerial discretion to require compulsory arbitration, enforceable by penalties of compulsory labour, violated Article 8.[528]

According to the CESCR and ILO, compulsory arbitration procedures (that is, producing binding decisions) should not usually be made obligatory or imposed unilaterally at the election of one party.[529] They are only acceptable at the request of both parties, or in the exceptional circumstances where a strike could otherwise be lawfully restricted or banned (for example, involving essential services, emergencies, or the armed forces, police or those in the administration of the state).[530]

Norway's reservation states that 'the current Norwegian practice of referring labour conflicts to the State Wages Board (a permanent tripartite arbitral commission in matters of wages) by Act of Parliament for the particular conflict shall not be considered incompatible with the right to strike, this right being fully recognised in Norway'. To the extent that the tripartite arbitral commission enjoys the voluntary consent of the parties, there is no issue under Article 8(1)(d). However, the fact

[520] ILO, *Giving Globalization a Human Face*, 58.
[521] ILO, Freedom of Association: Digest of Decisions and Principles, [547]–[549] and [552]–[554].
[522] ILO, *Giving Globalization a Human Face*, 57.
[523] ILO, *Giving Globalization a Human Face*, 58.
[524] ILO, Freedom of Association: Digest of Decisions and Principles, [532].
[525] ILO, Freedom of Association: Digest of Decisions and Principles, [550] and [551]; ILO, *Giving Globalization a Human Face*, 57.
[526] CESCR, Consideration of Report Submitted by State Party: Rwanda, E/1989/22 (1989), [192].
[527] CESCR, Concluding Observations: Bolivia, E/C.12/1/Add.60 (21 May 2001), [18].
[528] CESCR, Concluding Observations: Mauritius, E/C.12/1994/8 (31 May 1994), [10].
[529] CESCR, Concluding Observations: Libyan Arab Jamahiriya, E/C.12/LYB/CO/2 (25 January 2006), [16]; Malta, E/C.12/1/Add.101 (14 December 2004), [17]; Mauritius, E/C.12/1994/8 (31 May 1994), [10]; Norway, E/C.12/1995/13 (28 December 1995), [22]; Senegal, E/C.12/1993/18 (5 January 1994), [8].
[530] ILO, Freedom of Association: Digest of Decisions and Principles, [564]–[569].

that Norway felt it necessary to make a reservation indicates that there may be concerns in relation to involuntary compulsory arbitration.

The state must not impose time limits on the duration of strikes,[531] which should be free to continue indefinitely if a union so chooses. A practical limit on the duration of a strike is the capacity of union members to support themselves and their families while not receiving wages during the strike period. There is thus normally a strong financial incentive for union members not to engage in unnecessary or excessively long strikes. Indeed, there is a risk that legitimate strikes may fail precisely because some employers have deeper pockets than some unions.

Collective agreements voluntarily entered into by the parties may legitimately provide for the prohibition of strikes during the term of the agreement. In such cases, the ILO has found that there must still be the possibility of recourse to impartial and timely dispute settlement mechanisms concerning the interpretation or application of the agreement.[532] Also, any such 'social peace treaty'[533] does not preclude wider strikes by the same workers outside the workplace, for instance in relation to the economic or social policy of the state or the defence of unions from violence or fundamental rights violations.

Substantive restrictions

In ILO practice, there are four broad circumstances in which substantive restrictions may be placed on the right to strike: (a) acute national or local emergencies; (b) essential services, the interruption of which could endanger the life, personal safety or health of the whole or part of the population; (c) where a minimum operational service is necessary; and (d) where members of armed forces, police or those in the administration of the state, are involved.

Emergencies

As regards the first category, emergencies may include conflict, insurrection or disasters (natural, health or sanitary, or humanitarian), where the normal conditions for the functioning of society are absent.[534] The existence of an emergency necessitating restrictions on strikes should be determined or reviewable by an independent body, and not determined purely at the discretion of the state. In accordance with limitations generally, any restrictions must be prescribed by law and necessary and proportionate in a democratic society.

It may be recalled that the ICESCR does not contain a general derogation clause for public emergencies such as that in Article 4 of the ICCPR. The ILO

531 ILO, *Giving Globalization a Human Face*, 59.

532 ILO, Freedom of Association: Digest of Decisions and Principles, [533].

533 ILO, *Giving Globalization a Human Face*, 57.

534 ILO, *Giving Globalization a Human Face*, 57; ILO, Freedom of Association: Digest of Decisions and Principles, [570] and [571].

conventions on freedom of association also contain no derogation clauses.[535] Nonetheless, reference to the jurisprudence on identifying public emergencies may assist in informing the scope of this restriction, subject to the caveat that Article 4 is limited to emergencies threatening the life of the nation, whereas local emergencies may also justify strike restrictions.

The ILO has accepted, for example, that restrictions may be placed on the right to strike and freedom of expression during an attempted coup against a constitutional government; and other exceptional circumstances, such as civil war or revolution, will also be taken into account.[536] However, ordinary law rather than exceptional measures should be applied as far as possible, including in response to terrorism.

Essential services

In relation to the second category, strikes may be restricted in 'essential services' where the latter's disruption would present 'a clear and imminent threat to the life, personal safety or health of the whole or part of the population'.[537] Essential services are strictly interpreted in ILO practice.[538] It is not an absolute concept and depends on the circumstances; something inessential can become essential over the duration of a strike (as where the non-collection of garbage, or non-distribution of food, over time endangers public health).[539] The scope of essential services must be precisely defined by law and not left to broad state discretion, or subject to vague notions of public order or the national interest.[540] Disputes should be subject to effective, impartial and speedy conciliation or voluntary arbitration.[541]

Examples of essential services in ILO practice include: hospitals, electricity and water supplies, telecommunications, fire-fighting, prisons, food in schools and air traffic control.[542] It may be noted, however, that not all workers in essential services are necessarily 'essential' to those services, such as labourers or gardeners in a hospital.

The list of non-essential services is much longer: radio and television, petrol, ports, banking, excise duty collection, department stores, pleasure parks, metal and mining sectors, transport, pilots, garbage collection, refrigeration businesses, hotels, construction, car manufacturing, agriculture, food distribution, minting, state printing, state drug/salt/alcohol monopolies, education, water bottling, municipal services, animal loading facilities and road cleaning.[543]

[535] ILO, Freedom of Association: Digest of Decisions and Principles, [193]; see generally [194]–[204].

[536] ILO, Freedom of Association: Digest of Decisions and Principles, [194]–[204].

[537] ILO, Freedom of Association: Digest of Decisions and Principles, [541], [572] and [581].

[538] ILO, Freedom of Association: Digest of Decisions and Principles, [581]–[594].

[539] ILO, Freedom of Association: Digest of Decisions and Principles, [591].

[540] ILO, *Giving Globalization a Human Face*, 53.

[541] ILO, Freedom of Association: Digest of Decisions and Principles, [595]–[603].

[542] ILO, Freedom of Association: Digest of Decisions and Principles, [585].

[543] ILO, Freedom of Association: Digest of Decisions and Principles, [557]; ILO, *Giving Globalization a Human Face*, 55.

Essential services cannot be defined by the fact that strikes adversely affect trade, commerce or the economy. The ILO has recently expressed concern at decisions by the European Court of Justice that the right to strike may be restricted where it disproportionately impedes an employer's freedom of establishment or freedom to provide services.[544] On the ILO's stricter and more rights-protective approach, there is no room to 'balance' the right to strike against others' economic interests.

The CESCR has largely followed the ILO's approach, repeatedly stating that restrictions on the right to strike must be limited to those performing essential services,[545] 'the interruption of which is likely to endanger the life, personal health or safety of the whole or part of the population'.[546] It has criticized definitions of 'essential services' that are overly broad.[547] It has considered that the right to strike should not be denied to the following workers or sectors: teachers;[548] health services;[549] communications or postal workers;[550] energy production;[551] public corporations;[552] members of political parties;[553] and fire-fighting, sewerage and mining operations.[554]

It may be noted that Bahrain's 'declaration' on Article 8(1)(d) states that the provision 'shall not prejudice its right to prohibit strikes at essential utilities'. Similarly, by its 'reservation', Trinidad and Tobago 'reserves the right to impose lawful and/or reasonable restrictions on the exercise of the aforementioned rights by personnel engaged in essential services' under national law. Neither statement attracted formal objections from other states or adverse comment from the CESCR, and would appear largely in conformity with accepted interpretive practice. However, Trinidad and Tobago's reservation may be problematic to the extent that it purports to assert that national law may 'self-judge' the scope of

[544] ILO, *Giving Globalization a Human Face*, 52, citing *International Transport Workers' Federation and Finnish Seaman's Union v Viking Line ABP*, 11 December 2007, Case C-438/05 (ECJ) and *Laval un Partneri v Svenska Byggnadsarbetareforbundet*, 19 December 2007, Case C-341/05 (ECJ).

[545] CESCR, Concluding Observations: Benin, E/C.12/1/Add.78 (5 June 2002), [35]; Germany, E/C.12/1/Add.68 (24 September 2001), [22]; Japan, E/C.12/1/Add.67 (24 September 2001), [48].

[546] CESCR, Concluding Observations: Mauritius, E/C.12/1994/8 (31 May 1994), [10].

[547] CESCR, Concluding Observations: Lithuania, E/C.12/1/Add.96 (7 June 2004), [15]; Serbia and Montenegro, E/C.12/1/Add.108 (23 June 2005), [19]; Zambia, E/C.12/1/Add.106 (23 June 2005), [20].

[548] CESCR, Concluding Observations: Canada, E/C.12/CAN/CO/4 (22 May 2006), [19]; Republic of Korea, E/C.12/1/Add.59 (21 May 2001), [19]; Serbia and Montenegro, E/C.12/1/Add.108 (23 June 2005), [19].

[549] CESCR, Concluding Observations: Bulgaria, E/C.12/1/Add.37 (8 December 1999), [16]; Jordan, E/C.12/1/Add.46 (1 September 2000), [21].

[550] CESCR, Concluding Observations: Azerbaijan, E/C.12/1/Add.20 (22 December 1997), [20]; Bulgaria, E/C.12/1/Add.37 (8 December 1999), [16]; Ukraine, E/C.12/1995/15 (28 December 1995), [17]; Serbia and Montenegro, E/C.12/1/Add.108 (23 June 2005), [19].

[551] CESCR, Concluding Observations: Bulgaria, E/C.12/1/Add.37 (8 December 1999), [16].

[552] CESCR, Concluding Observations: Canada, E/C.12/CAN/CO/4 (22 May 2006), [19].

[553] CESCR, Concluding Observations: Chile, E/C.12/1/Add.105 (1 December 2004), [19].

[554] CESCR, Concluding Observations: Zambia, E/C.12/1/Add.106 (23 June 2005), [20].

'essential services',[555] which is an objective legal category subject to the ILO and CESCR jurisprudence mentioned above.

Minimum operational service

ILO practice accepts that a minimum safety or operational service may be instituted in certain circumstances and where a total prohibition or substantial restriction of strike action would not necessarily be justified.[556] The first situation is where strikes would disrupt essential services and endanger the life, personal safety or health of the whole or part of the population, as discussed above. A second situation is where services are not strictly essential, but the extent and duration of a strike results in an acute national crisis endangering normal living conditions. The third situation concerns public services of fundamental (but not 'essential') importance,[557] such as: ports, ferries to inhabited islands, railways, the transport of passengers and goods, postal services, refuse collection, banking, petrol and education.[558]

Provision for minimum service must be established clearly, applied strictly and publicized in advance. The scope of the service must not be overly generous so as to undermine the strike's effectiveness. It should be defined in consultation with the affected unions and employers, and not imposed unilaterally. A minimum service may be staffed by union members who agree to work (often with the agreement of their union), or in exceptional cases by requisitioned labour (such as police or army personnel, public servants or contractors). A minimum service must itself avoid endangering public health or safety, including by ensuring that any replacement staff are qualified to perform the necessary functions. Disagreements about minimum service should be settled by an independent body.

Armed forces, police and state administration

The right to strike is subject to the category restrictions on members of the armed forces, police or administration of the state under Article 8(2), discussed in the next section. The underlying rationale is to prevent those special categories from being perceived as 'political', but also to avoid the more serious inference that the police or military are somehow defying the state and its civilian leadership. As noted in the discussion of Article 8(2), that provision does not require the prohibition of strikes by these groups, but permits restrictions; restrictions still require a justification of their necessity and proportionality.

As also discussed later, members of the state administration do not automatically include all public servants or public employees. In monitoring states, the

[555] In this regard, the reservation states that 'essential services' may be defined 'under the Industrial Relations Act or under any Statute replacing same which has been passed in accordance with the provisions of the Trinidad and Tobago Constitution'.

[556] ILO, Freedom of Association: Digest of Decisions and Principles, [606]–[627].

[557] ILO, Freedom of Association: Digest of Decisions and Principles, [606].

[558] ILO, Freedom of Association: Digest of Decisions and Principles, [615]–[625].

CESCR has consistently expressed concern about limitations on the right to strike of civil servants,[559] including teachers,[560] university professors[561] and the judiciary,[562] and has called for the restrictions to be limited 'to those responsible for keeping order'.[563] It also criticized restrictions on the employees of state corporations.[564]

The ILO has found that restrictions on the right to strike of public servants should only apply to those in the state administration, or in essential services strictly interpreted (namely whose interruption could endanger the life, personal safety or health of the whole or part of the population). Public servants whose right to strike is restricted should still enjoy sufficient guarantees to protect their interests, including impartial and prompt conciliation and arbitration procedures, the decisions of which should bind the parties and be effective.[565]

The Netherlands' reservation that the right to strike does not apply to the 'central and local government bodies' of the Netherlands Antilles may therefore be overbroad, if not limited to members of the state administration or essential services. While no state has formally objected, the CESCR 'regrets that the State party has not clarified the reasons for maintaining its reservation'.[566]

Japan's reservation 'reserves the right not to be bound by' Article 8(1)(d) 'except in relation to the sectors in which the right... is accorded in accordance with the laws and regulations of Japan at the time of ratification'. While no state has objected, it is arguable that the unilateral restriction of the sectors entitled to strike is contrary to the object and purpose of the ICESCR. The CESCR criticized Japan's 'general prohibition of strikes for all public employees and civil servants, even those not working in essential government services, including teachers', and asserted that this violated Article 8(2).[567]

[559] CESCR, Concluding Observations: Azerbaijan, E/C.12/1/Add.20 (22 December 1997), [20]; Canada, E/C.12/CAN/CO/4 (22 May 2006), [19]; Estonia, E/C.12/1/Add.85 (19 December 2002), [16]; Germany, E/C.12/1/Add.29 (4 December 1998), [19]; Germany, E/C.12/1/Add.68 (24 September 2001), [22]; India, E/C.12/IND/CO/5 (8 August 2008), [23]; Japan, E/C.12/1/Add.67 (24 September 2001), [21]; Jordan, E/C.12/1/Add.46 (1 September 2000), [21]; Lebanon, E/C.12/1993/10 (9 June 1993), [14]; Liechtenstein, E/C.12/LIE/CO/1 (9 June 2006), [31]; Poland, E/C,12/1/Add.82 (19 December 2002), [22]; Republic of Korea, E/C.12/1995/3 (7 June 1995), [8]; Switzerland, E/C.12/1/Add.30 (7 December 1998), [13].

[560] CESCR, Concluding Observations: Germany, E/C.12/1/Add.68 (24 September 2001), [22]; Japan, E/C.12/1/Add.67 (24 September 2001), [21]; Jordan, E/C.12/1/Add.46 (1 September 2000), [21]; Canada, E/C.12/CAN/CO/4-5 (22 May 2006), [19].

[561] CESCR, Concluding Observations: Canada, E/C.12/CAN/CO/4-5 (22 May 2006), [19].

[562] CESCR, Concluding Observations: Chile, E/C.12/1/Add.105 (1 December 2004), [19]; Germany, E/C.12/1/Add.68 (24 September 2001), [22]. Note, however, that the ILO accepts that those in law enforcement, including the judiciary, may have their right to strike restricted: ILO Principles Concerning the Right to Strike, 18.

[563] CESCR, Concluding Observations: Benin, E/C.12/1/Add.78 (5 June 2002), [35].

[564] CESCR, Concluding Observations: Canada, E/C.12/CAN/CO/4-5 (22 May 2006), [19].

[565] ILO Principles Concerning the Right to Strike, 17–18.

[566] CESCR, Concluding Observations: Netherlands (Antilles), E/C.12/NLD/CO/3/Add.1 (31 January 2008), [14].

[567] CESCR, Concluding Observations: Japan, E/C.12/1/Add.67 (24 September 2001), [21].

IMPLEMENTATION OF STRIKES

In monitoring states, the CESCR has expressed concern about police attacks on strikers,[568] governments intimidating or arresting strikers[569] and abusive prosecutions.[570] It has also recommended that states refrain from using force unless absolutely necessary to maintain public order.[571] The ILO observes that any use of force must also be proportionate and taken only in response to serious public order threats or violence; the use of the army is not conducive to a climate free from violence, pressure or threats.[572]

At the same time, strikes or pickets must be peaceful, not violent (including by damaging property)[573] or coercive, and respect the freedom to work of non-union members and the right of employers to access their premises.[574] Strikers must also not endanger public safety, such as where air traffic controllers changed the passwords necessary to operate flight radars.[575] Any criminal penalties for illegal acts, imposed following a fair trial, must be proportionate;[576] and dismissals must follow due process.[577] Any power to determine the legality of a strike more generally must be exercised by an independent body, not the executive authorities.[578]

As noted earlier, it is permissible to requisition workers to maintain a minimum essential service in cases where such services are justified. However, it is otherwise forbidden to hire outside workers to break a strike, even where the strike disturbs ordinary life.[579] The CESCR has criticized legal provisions which permit the replacement of striking workers.[580] The CESCR has also condemned the deportation of migrant workers for 'breach of contract' after going on strike.[581]

RELATIONSHIP TO ARTICLE 22 OF THE ICCPR

The explicit recognition of the right to strike in the ICESCR contrasts with its absence in Article 22 of the ICCPR, concerning freedom of association generally.

568 CESCR, Concluding Observations: Republic of Korea, E/C.12/KOR/CO/3 (17 December 2009), [20]; Republic of Korea, E/C.12/1995/3 (7 June 1995), [9]; Republic of Korea, E/C.12/1/Add.59 (21 May 2001), [20].

569 CESCR, Concluding Observations: Guinea, E/C.12/1/Add.5 (28 May 1996), [16]; Nigeria, E/C.12/1/Add.23 (16 June 1998), [17].

570 CESCR, Concluding Observations: Republic of Korea, E/C.12/1/Add.59 (21 May 2001), [39]; Republic of Korea, E/C.12/KOR/CO/3 (17 December 2009), [20].

571 CESCR, Concluding Observations: Republic of Korea, E/C.12/1/Add.59 (21 May 2001), [39]; Republic of Korea, E/C.12/KOR/CO/3 (17 December 2009), [20].

572 ILO, Freedom of Association: Digest of Decisions and Principles, [641]–[647].

573 ILO Principles Concerning the Right to Strike, 42.

574 ILO, Freedom of Association: Digest of Decisions and Principles, [648]–[653].

575 ILO Principles Concerning the Right to Strike, 42.

576 ILO, Freedom of Association: Digest of Decisions and Principles, [667]–[673].

577 See the discussion in the chapter on Article 6 of the ICESCR.

578 ILO, Freedom of Association: Digest of Decisions and Principles, [628]–[631].

579 ILO, Freedom of Association: Digest of Decisions and Principles, [632]–[639].

580 CESCR, Concluding Observations: Chile, E/C.12/1/Add.105 (1 December 2004), [19].

581 CESCR, Concluding Observations: Mauritius, E/C.12/MUS/CO/4 (8 June 2010), [19].

In *JB v Canada*, the HRC held that Article 22 does not protect the right to strike, in part because such protection was instead allocated during the drafting to the ICESCR:[582]

6.2 . . . Since the right to strike is not *expressis verbis* included in article 22, the Committee must interpret whether the right to freedom of association necessarily implies the right to strike, as contended by the authors of the communication. The authors have argued that such a conclusion is supported by decisions of organs of the International Labour Organisation in interpreting the scope and the meaning of labour law treaties enacted under the auspices of ILO. The Human Rights Committee has no qualms about accepting as correct and just the interpretation of those treaties by the organs concerned. However, each international treaty, including the International Covenant on Civil and Political Rights, has a life of its own and must be interpreted in a fair and just manner, if so provided, by the body entrusted with the monitoring of its provisions.

6.3 In interpreting the scope of article 22, the Committee has given attention to the 'ordinary meaning' of each element of the article in its context and in the light of its object and purpose (article 31 of the Vienna Convention on the Law of Treaties). The Committee has also had recourse to supplementary means of interpretation (article 32 of the Vienna Convention on the Law of Treaties) and perused the *travaux préparatoires* of the Covenant on Civil and Political Rights, in particular the discussions in the Commission on Human Rights and in the Third Committee of the General Assembly. The Committee notes that in the course of drafting the Covenant on Civil and political Rights and the Covenant on Economic, Social and Cultural Rights, the Commission on Human Rights based itself on the Universal Declaration of Human Rights. The Universal Declaration, however, does not refer to the right to strike. At its seventh session in 1951 the Commission adopted the text of a single 'draft covenant on human rights' comprising 73 articles (E/1992, annex). The relevant draft articles 16 ('the right of association') and 27 ('the right of everyone, in conformity with article 16, to form and join local, national and international trade unions') did not provide for the right to strike. In the course of the discussions of these articles at the Commission's eighth session in 1952, article 27 was dealt with first. An amendment to article 27 providing for the inclusion of the right to strike was rejected by 11 votes to 6, with 1 abstention. Three weeks later the Commission discussed article 16 and adopted it with minor amendments, without, however, any proposal or amendment being tabled with a view to including the right to strike in that Article. Pursuant to General Assembly resolution A/543 (VI), the single draft Covenant on human rights was split into a draft covenant on civil and political rights and a draft covenant on economic, social and cultural rights. Article 16 is assigned to the draft covenant on civil and political rights, eventually being numbered as article 22. Article 27, on the other hand, was assigned to the draft covenant on economic, social and cultural rights, eventually being renumbered as Article 8. Five years after the adoption of draft articles 16 and 27 by the Commission on Human Rights, the Third Committee of the General Assembly again discussed the draft covenants. Whereas an amendment to the new draft article 8 of the Covenant on Economic, Social and Cultural Rights was adopted, including 'the right to strike, provided that it is exercised in conformity with the laws of the particular country', no similar amendment was introduced or discussed with respect the draft covenant on civil and political rights. Thus the Committee

[582] Discussed below in the context of the right to strike.

cannot deduce from the *travaux préparatoires* that the drafters of the Covenant on Civil and Political Rights intended to guarantee the right to strike.

6.4 The conclusions to be drawn from the drafting history are corroborated by a comparative analysis of the International Covenant on Civil and Political Rights of the International Covenant on Economic, Social and Cultural Rights, Article 8, paragraph 1(d), of the International Covenant on Economic, Social and Cultural Rights recognizes the right to strike, in addition to the right of everyone to form and join trade unions for the promotion and protection of his economic and social interests, thereby making it clear that the right to strike cannot be considered as implicit component of the right to form and join trade unions. Consequently, the fact that the International Covenant on Civil and Political Rights does not similarly provide expressly for the right to strike in article 22, paragraph 1, shows that this right is not included in the scope of this article, while it enjoys protection under the procedures and mechanisms of the International Covenant on Economic, Social and Cultural rights subject to the specific restrictions mentioned article 8 of that instrument.[583]

Five HRC members dissented on this point, finding the drafting history not determinative and instead emphasizing the textual and contextual scope of Article 22, thus finding that the right to strike is protected by Article 22 of the ICCPR:

3. Article 22 provides that 'Everyone shall have the right to freedom of association with others, including the right to form and join trade unions for the protection of his interests.' The right to form and join trade unions is thus an example of the more general right to freedom of association. It is further specified that the right to join trade unions is for the purpose of protection of one's interests. In this context we note that there is no comma after 'trade unions', and as a matter of grammar 'for the protection of his interests' pertains to 'the right to form and join trade unions' and not to freedom of association as a whole. It is, of course, manifest that there is no mention of the right to strike in article 22, just as there is no mention of the various other activities, such as holding meetings, or collective bargaining, that a trade-unionist may engage in to protect his interests. We do not find that surprising, because it is the broad right of freedom of association which is guaranteed by article 22. However, the exercise of this right requires that some measure of concerted activities be allowed; otherwise it could not serve its purposes. To us, this is an inherent aspect of the right Granted by article 22, paragraph 1. Which activities are essential to the exercise of this right cannot be listed a priori and must be examined in their social context in the light of the other paragraphs of this article.

4. The drafting history clearly shows that the right of association was dealt with separately from the right to form and join trade unions. The *travaux préparatoires* indicate that in 1952 the right to strike was proposed only for the draft article on trade unions. This is what we would have expected. It was at that time rejected. They show also that in 1957, when the right to strike (subject to certain limitations) was accepted as an amendment to the draft article on the right to form and join trade unions, such an amendment was neither introduced nor discussed with respect to the draft covenant on civil and political rights. The reason seems to us both clear and correct—namely, that because what is now article 22 of the Covenant on Civil and Political Rights deals with the right of association as a whole, concerning clubs and societies as well as trade unions, mentioning particular activities such as strike action would have been inappropriate.

[583] *JB v Canada*, [6.3] and [6.4].

5. We therefore find that the *travaux préparatoires* are not determinative of the issue before the Committee. Where the intentions of the drafters are not absolutely clear in relation to the point at hand, article 31 of the Vienna Convention also directs us to the object and purpose of the treaty. This seems to us especially important in a treaty for the promotion of human rights, where limitation of the exercise of rights, or upon the competence of the Committee to review a prohibition by a State of a given activity, are not readily to be presumed.

6. We note that article 8 of the International Covenant on Economic, Social and Cultural Rights, having spoken of the right of everyone to form trade unions and join the union of his choice, goes on to speak of 'the right to strike, provided that it is exercised in conformity with the laws of the particular country'. Which this latter phrase gives rise to some complex legal issues, it suffices for our present purpose that the specific aspect of freedom of association which is touched on as an individual right in article 22 of the Covenant on Civil and political Rights, but dealt with as a set of distinctive rights in article 8, does not necessarily exclude the right to strike in all circumstances. We see no reason for interpreting this common matter differently in the two Covenants.

7. We are also aware that the ILO Committee on Freedom of Association, a body singularly well placed to pronounce authoritatively on such matters, has held that the general prohibition of strikes for public employees contained in the Alberta Public Service Employees Relations Act was not in harmony with article 10 of ILO Convention No. 87 '… since it constituted a considerable restriction on the opportunities open to trade unions to further and defend the interests of their members.' While we do not at this stage purport to comment on the merits, we cannot fail to notice that the ILO finding is based on the furtherance and defence of interests of trade-union members; and article 22 also requires us to consider that the purpose of joining a trade union is to protect one's interests. Again, we see no reason to interpret article 22 in a manner different from ILO when addressing a comparable consideration. In this regard we note that article 22, paragraph 3, provides that nothing in that article authorizes a State party to ILO Convention No. 87 to take legislative measures which would prejudice, or to apply the law in such a manner as to prejudice, the guarantees provided for in that Convention.

8. We cannot see that a manner of exercising a right which has, under certain leading and widely ratified international instruments, been declared to be in principle lawful, should be declared to be incompatible with the Covenant on Civil and Political Rights.

9. Whereas article 22, paragraph 1, deals with the right of freedom of association as such, paragraph 2 deals with the extent of the exercise of the right which necessarily includes the means which may be resorted to by a member of a trade union for the protection of his interests.

10. Whether the right to strike is a necessary element in the protection of the interests of the authors, and if so whether it has been unduly restricted, is a question on the merits, that is to say, whether the restrictions imposed in Canada are or are not justifiable under article 22, paragraph 2. But we do not find the communication inadmissible on this ground.[584]

[584] *JB v Canada*, Individual Opinion of Mrs Higgins and Messrs Lallah, Mavrommatis, Opsahl and Wako, [3]–[10].

The majority has been criticized for drawing an unduly sharp distinction between the scope of protection of the ICCPR and ICESCR.[585] This is particularly apposite in view of the clear awareness during the drafting that trade union rights are both civil-political and socio-economic rights. Restrictions on the associational rights of police and armed forces in Article 22(2) were in part directed precisely to limiting strikes by such groups.[586] The '*minority opinion* corresponds more to the wording, object, purpose and historical background of this provision'.[587] The HRC itself has subsequently expressed concern about the right to strike under Article 22 of the ICCPR,[588] although there is as yet no relevant General Comment. Practice is also equivocal under regional instruments which subsume trade union rights within the general freedom of association. For instance, strikes have been interpreted as only one among various means of protecting collective interests under Article 11 of the ECHR and states thus enjoy a choice of means in realizing freedom of association.[589]

Article 8(2): Restrictions on Armed Forces, Police or the State Administration

During the drafting, the United Kingdom and the Netherlands argued for a specific restrictions clause for members of the armed forces, police and administration of the state.[590] While some states objected that the general limitations clauses (in Articles 2(1) and 4) were sufficient,[591] others doubted their adequacy in the context of Article 8.[592] In particular, some states noted that Article 8 created obligations that were more 'definite and immediate'[593] and entailed a rare exception to the general principle that ICESCR rights are progressively realizable.[594] As such, more precision or caution was thought necessary in enumerating restrictions. In addition, some states desired consistency with the similar exception that had already been drafted in Article 22(2) of the ICCPR.[595]

However, Article 8(3) goes further than the ICCPR, which only enables restrictions on the armed forces and police, by also permitting restrictions on members of 'the administration of the State'. In this respect, it also went beyond certain ILO

[585] Joseph et al, *ICCPR Cases*, 581. [586] Nowak, *CCPR Commentary*, 503.

[587] Nowak, *CCPR Commentary*, 503. [588] Joseph et al, *ICCPR Cases*, 582.

[589] *Schmidt and Dahlström v Sweden* (App. 5589/72), 6 February 1976, [36].

[590] It was first submitted as an amendment to the original text of the Commission on Human Rights (UNGA Third Committee, A/3525 (9 February 1957), 19) and then resubmitted as an amendment to the three-power proposal (at 22).

[591] UNGA Third Committee, A/C.3/SR.720 (3 January 1957), 196 (Poland), 198 (Yugoslavia); A/C.3/SR.721 (4 January 1957), 199 (Greece).

[592] UNGA Third Committee, A/C.3/SR.721 (4 January 1957), 201 (Lebanon); A/C.3/SR.722 (7 January 1957), 209 (United Kingdom).

[593] UNGA Third Committee, A/C.3/SR.720 (3 January 1957), 197 (United Kingdom); cf 198 (Denmark).

[594] UNGA Third Committee, A/C.3/SR.721 (4 January 1957), 201 (Lebanon).

[595] UNGA Third Committee, A/C.3/SR.719 (3 January 1957), 191 (United Kingdom); A/C.3/SR.720 (3 January 1957), 197 (United Kingdom); A/C.3/SR.721 (4 January 1957), 200 (France).

instruments already then in force.[596] The United Kingdom and the Netherlands believed the addition to be justified on the same grounds as the restriction on the armed forces and the police.[597] In this respect, Ceylon argued that 'civil servants…should not take an active part in political organizations' and 'it was essential to sound administration that their trade unions should remain non-political'.[598]

Some other states considered this, however, to be a dangerous limitation on civil servants' rights. Uruguay and the USSR argued that this was inconsistent with states' obligations under ILO instruments.[599] Article 9(1) of ILO Convention No. 87, and Article 5(1) of Convention No. 98, permit restrictions only on the armed forces and the police,[600] although the latter instrument neither covers nor affects the position of public servants engaged in the administration of the state (Article 6).[601]

Numerous states also expressed serious concern that 'in countries where socialism had reached an advanced stage, and where most of the population were in the employ of the State, such a provision might have effects prejudicial to the development of free trade-union rights'.[602] Sweden objected on the different ground that any restriction should be based on 'the degree of danger to society' by the exercise of rights, rather than on broad occupational groups:

> In matters of national security, the functions of certain technicians and workers might be just as important as, if not more important than, those of armed forces…a strike by power-station engineers might be more serious than a strike by the police…the rapid growth of mechanization might eventually lead to situations where a strike by a handful of key workers could paralyse the life of a nation.[603]

The phrase 'or of the administration of the State' was voted on separately and narrowly adopted.[604] Paragraph 2 as a whole was passed by a wider margin.[605]

The restriction for those engaged in the administration of the state has been described as a 'significant loophole' in international standards[606] and open to abuse given the potential breadth of the public service.[607] Article 8(3) does not, however, operate as an automatic exemption from Article 8 rights for the listed groups. Rather, the provision is expressed so that it 'shall not prevent

596 ILO Convention No. 87, Article 9; ILO Convention No. 98, Article 5.

597 UNGA Third Committee, A/C.3/SR.719 (3 January 1957), 191 (United Kingdom).

598 UNGA Third Committee, A/C.3/SR.720 (3 January 1957), 198 (Ceylon).

599 UNGA Third Committee, A/C.3/SR.719 (3 January 1957), 191 (Uruguay), 192 (USSR).

600 'The extent to which the guarantees provided for in this Convention shall apply to the armed forces and the police shall be determined by national laws or regulations.'

601 ILO Convention No. 87 concerning Freedom of Association, Article 6.

602 UNGA Third Committee, A/C.3/SR.720 (3 January 1957), 196 (Chile); see also A/C.3/SR.721 (4 January 1957), 200 (Greece); A/C.3/SR.722 (7 January 1957), 207 (Philippines); A/C.3/SR.723 (7 January 1957), 213 (Australia).

603 UNGA Third Committee, A/C.3/SR.722 (7 January 1957), 205 (Sweden).

604 By twenty votes to eighteen, with thirty-one abstentions: UNGA Third Committee, A/C.3/SR.725 (9 January 1957), 223.

605 By twenty-one votes to ten, with thirty-four abstentions: UNGA Third Committee, A/C.3/SR.725 (9 January 1957), 223.

606 Craven, *The ICESCR*, 264.

607 Craven, *The ICESCR*, 259.

the imposition of lawful restrictions' on those groups. A state may accordingly choose not to impose special restrictions on all or any of those groups.

Where a state wishes to impose restrictions, they must be 'lawful', that is, at the very least *prescribed by law*. The law must define to whom the law applies (namely, the extent of membership of the designated groups), as well as the scope and nature of the restrictions.

ARMED FORCES AND POLICE

Identifying membership of the armed forces and police will often be fairly straightforward. It is foremost a question of national law as to who falls within the 'armed forces' or 'police'. However, those concepts are also treaty terms which bear an objective meaning. States thus may not abusively or in bad faith define such categories in an overly expansive manner to restrict legitimate trade union rights. In ILO practice in relation to Article 9 of Convention No. 87, the ILO has found that armed forces and police 'should be defined in a restrictive manner'.[608]

As regards 'police', there is potentially a wide range of public officials exercising elements of law enforcement authority, some at the core and others more peripherally. In the context of the similar ground of restriction in Article 22 of the ICCPR, one commentator mentions the quasi-policing functions of 'customs or justice officials, labour and tax inspectors, fire brigades, mountain rangers, [and] field and forestry officials'.[609] However, Japan's reservation that 'police' is to be interpreted to include Japan's 'fire service' indicates that the term is ordinarily understood narrowly, thus necessitating the reservation.[610] This is consistent with the ILO's strict approach. Police are ordinarily those who directly enforce the criminal law and maintain public order.

In relation to armed forces, the ILO has observed that civilian workers associated with armed forces still enjoy the right to form and join their own unions, including civilians working in military factories and military banks and civilians performing services for the military.[611] Likewise, civilian intelligence officers or civilian defence personnel (working, for example, for the executive or parliament) are neither members of the armed forces nor the police.[612] Workers that may be penumbrally associated with the armed forces or police cannot be assimilated to the latter groups, such as aviation security personnel, fire service workers, judges and prosecutors or prison staff.[613] In cases of doubt, 'workers should be considered as civilians'.[614]

More difficult cases include paramilitaries or irregular 'civilian' militias, as well as private military or security contractors. One legal indicator is whether such groups are formally incorporated into the armed forces under national law

[608] ILO, Freedom of Association: Digest of Decisions and Principles, [223].
[609] Nowak, *CCPR Commentary*, 510.
[610] Nowak, *CCPR Commentary*, 510.
[611] ILO, Freedom of Association: Digest of Decisions and Principles, [227]–[229].
[612] ILO, *Giving Globalization a Human Face*, 25.
[613] ILO, *Giving Globalization a Human Face*, 25.
[614] ILO, Freedom of Association: Digest of Decisions and Principles, [226].

or pursuant to international humanitarian law,[615] and are performing 'military' type functions. In other cases, it is a question of fact whether such groups both (a) perform military (or police) like functions, and (b) are effectively controlled by the state under the international law of state responsibility.[616]

'MEMBERS . . . OF THE ADMINISTRATION OF THE STATE'

Membership of the 'administration of the State' is more complicated. The provision should not be understood as permitting restrictions on all public servants, broadly defined. Again, reference may be made to ILO standards. As noted earlier, while the ILO instruments do not permit restrictions on public servants per se, Article 4 of Convention No. 98 excludes from its application, without prejudice to their rights, public servants in the administration of the state. The ILO has considered the meaning of this category in its monitoring of states.

In ILO practice, those engaged in the state administration include public servants employed in government ministries or departments and comparable public bodies,[617] including intelligence services.[618] Given the divergence of terminology and classification of public servants under domestic law in different states,[619] the category cannot be determined subjectively or unilaterally, but relates to the objective functions performed; it concerns those exercising authority in the name of the state.[620]

However, the category should not be interpreted widely to include all persons employed by the government or all 'white collar' employees.[621] It excludes those working in autonomous public institutions (such as statutory or regulatory bodies); public undertakings (such as state-owned enterprises); public utilities (banking, postal, telecommunications, radio and television) or transport (such as flight controllers or aviation workers); essential services (such as teachers or hospital staff); and private contractors; and irrespective of whether employees are permanent or temporary.

The ILO's approach accordingly utilizes a kind of proximity criterion to differentiate between those more intimately involved in the political administration

[615] Eg, where irregular forces 'belong' to a state under Article 4 of the Geneva Convention Relative to the Treatment of Prisoners of War (opened for signature 12 August 1949, 75 UNTS 135, entered into force 21 October 1950) ('Third Geneva Convention'), or are guerilla forces in occupied territory under Article 43 of Protocol Additional to the Geneva Conventions of 12 August 1949, and relating to the Protection of Victims of International Armed Conflicts (opened for signature 8 June 1977, 1125 UNTS 3, entered into force 7 December 1979) ('Protocol I').

[616] International Law Commission, Articles on Responsibility of States for Internationally Wrongful Acts, UNGA Resolution 56/83 (12 December 2001), Annex, Article 8.

[617] ILO, Freedom of Association: Digest of Decisions and Principles, [886]–[887] and [893].

[618] See, eg, *Council of Civil Service Unions v United Kingdom* (App. 11603), 20 January 1987, (1987) 50 DR 228, 229 (concerning lawful restrictions on GCHQ personnel under Article 11(2) of the ECHR).

[619] ILO Principles Concerning the Right to Strike, 18.

[620] ILO Principles Concerning the Right to Strike, 18.

[621] ILO, Freedom of Association: Digest of Decisions and Principles, [886]–[887], [892]–[893] and [894]–[904].

of the state (including its law and policies) and those more peripheral to the exercise of core governmental or executive authority. This is consistent with the narrow purpose of the restrictions in Article 8(3) of the ICESCR, which aim to prevent the paralysis of core government activity, while balancing respect for the widest possible operation of trade union rights by the broader field of public employees.

As discussed earlier, the CESCR has often criticized expansive restrictions on public servants in the context of the right to strike, but also in collective bargaining. In relation to South Korea's ban on teachers forming trade unions, the CESCR rejected as 'wholly unacceptable' the state's justification based on 'cultural traditions' and the 'high esteem in which teachers are held'.[622] Monaco's apparent reservation that Article 8(2) 'should be interpreted as applying to…agents of the State, the Commune and public enterprises' encompasses public servants beyond those strictly engaged in state administration, but has met with no objections.

It should be emphasized that by virtue of the savings clause for ILO Convention No. 87 in Article 8(3) of the ICESCR, states that are parties to both instruments may not restrict the rights of those involved in the state administration, since the ILO treaty only permits restrictions on members of the armed forces and police.[623]

THE SCOPE AND NATURE OF RESTRICTIONS

Even where a state has properly identified by law those to whom Article 8(2) restrictions apply, the provision does not give *carte blanche* to states to exclude Article 8 rights altogether. The provision refers to the imposition of 'lawful restrictions' rather than using stronger language allowing the 'exclusion' or 'exemption' of the said categories. States are also equally free not to impose restrictions; in the ILO treaties also, the rights of armed forces and police under other laws are not affected.[624]

In the drafting, there was a suggestion that the provision was primarily intended to permit the prohibition or restriction of the right to strike, but not the freedom to form and join unions or the right of unions to freely function[625] (including, for instance, to collectively bargain). This is consistent with the CESCR's approach in monitoring states. The CESCR has criticized prohibitions on forming and joining trade unions for those in the public service,[626] and stated that '[g]overnment

[622] CESCR, Concluding Observations: Republic of Korea, E/C.12/1995/3 (7 June 1995), [8]; see also Republic of Korea E/C.12/1/Add.59 (21 May 2001), [19].

[623] Craven, *The ICESCR*, 263.

[624] ILO Convention No. 87 concerning Freedom of Association, Article 9(2) provides: 'In accordance with the principle set forth in paragraph 8 of Article 19 of the Constitution of the International Labour Organization the ratification of this Convention by any Member shall not be deemed to affect any existing law, award, custom or agreement in virtue of which members of the armed forces or the police enjoy any right guaranteed by this Convention.' See similarly ILO Convention No. 98 concerning the Right to Organise, Article 5(2).

[625] Craven, *The ICESCR*, 265.

[626] CESCR, Concluding Observations: India, E/C.12/IND/CO/5 (8 August 2008), [23]; Iraq, E/C.12/1/Add.17 (12 December 1997), [16]; Republic of Korea, E/C.12/1995/3 (7 June 1995), [8]; Zimbabwe, E/C.12/1/Add.12 (20 May 1997), [11].

employees should be accorded the right to form and join trade unions in accordance with the provisions of the Covenant'.[627]

The requirement in Article 8(2) that restrictions be 'lawful' implies not only the existence of a national law authorizing interference, but a certain minimum quality to the law. Laws authorizing restrictions must accordingly be clear, foreseeable and accessible, to transpose criteria from similar contexts in which the European Court of Human Rights has interpreted requirements of lawfulness in respect of restrictions on rights under the ECHR.[628]

A more unsettled question is whether reference to 'lawful restrictions' also imports the substantive test for restrictions found elsewhere in Article 8 (in paragraphs 1(a) and (c)),[629] namely that restrictions must not only be prescribed by law, but also 'necessary in a democratic society in the interests of national security or public order or for the protection of the rights and freedoms of others'. Neither Article 8(2) (concerning restrictions on the designated groups) nor Article 8(1)(d) (the right to strike) includes this more elaborate (and protective) limitations test, suggesting that 'lawfulness' (including its qualitative aspect) is the only intended constraint on the rights therein.

This view is textually supported by the separate existence and placement of Article 8(2) immediately following the rights in Article 8(1). If Article 8(2) were also subject to the limitations in Article 8(1), there would be no need to include an independent provision specially restricting the rights of armed forces, police and state administrators: the same result could be achieved through the application of the ordinary limitations provisions.

While reading the Article 8(1) limitations test into Article 8(2) is attractive for rights-maximizing reasons, it would render Article 8(2) redundant and would thus not seem consistent with an ordinary approach to treaty interpretation. It is, however, open to states to progressively interpret Article 8(2) of the ICESCR more narrowly in light of changing state practice, even to a vanishing point.

The similar category restrictions in Article 22 of the ICCPR are also understood not to impose requirements of a legitimate purpose, necessity or proportionality,[630] only that they be prescribed by law. The underlying assumption is that the restriction is justified by the need to preserve political neutrality, a rationale which is strong in relation to armed forces and police (given their centrality to maintaining public order and fidelity to constitutionalism), but less so (in relation to the ICESCR) for public servants. That Article 22 authorizes 'restrictions' on the 'exercise' of rights by these groups, not prohibitions on the existence or enjoyment of such rights, indicates that any limitations must not violate the 'essence' of the right.[631]

Such approach finds support in regional practice concerning restrictions on the union rights of police. Article 11(2) of the ECHR permits 'lawful restrictions on the exercise' of freedom of association by members of the police, armed forces or

[627] CESCR, Consideration of Report Submitted by State Party: Lebanon, E/1994/23 (1993), [176].
[628] See the discussion in the chapter on limitations under Article 4 of the ICESCR.
[629] Craven, *The ICESCR*, 265.
[630] Nowak, *CCPR Commentary*, 509; Joseph et al, *ICCPR Cases*, 576.
[631] Nowak, *CCPR Commentary*, 509.

administration of the state. The European Court of Human Rights has interpreted 'lawful restrictions' as requiring conformity with domestic law, but also 'qualitative requirements in the domestic law such as foreseeability and, generally, an absence of arbitrariness'.[632] It was permissible, for instance, to impose restrictions on political membership or activities by police or armed forces in pursuit of the legitimate aim of depoliticizing those forces and consolidating pluralistic democracy in the light of the totalitarian history of a post-communist state.[633]

Article 5 of the Revised European Social Charter provides that '[t]he extent to which the guarantees provided for in this article [concerning the right of workers and employers to organize] shall apply to the police shall be determined by national laws or regulations'. In *European Council of Police Trade Unions v Portugal*, the European Committee on Social Rights considered a complaint against a law which restricted the right to organize of the Public Security Police,[634] who could join professional associations, but not unions. In assessing the restrictions, instead of applying a general test for limitations, the ECSR outlined the minimum content of rights which restrictions must not impair:

25. The Committee recalls that Article 5 permits states to restrict but not to completely deny police officers' right to organise.

26. It follows, firstly, that police personnel must be able to form or join genuine organisations for the protection of their material and moral interests and secondly, that such organisations must be able to benefit from most trade union prerogatives.

27. …police personnel…[must be] given basic guarantees with regard to (i) the constitution of their professional associations; (ii) the trade union prerogatives that may be used by these associations; and (iii) the protection of their representatives…

(i) Constitution of professional organizations of the PSP

28. The Committee considers that the right to constitute trade unions can be effectively implemented only if the creation itself, the accession to an existing association, its hypothetical affiliation to other organizations and its internal organisation and internal operation are protected by appropriate guarantees…

(ii) Basic trade union prerogatives

40. The Committee points out that basic trade union prerogatives means the right to express demands with regard to working conditions and pay, the right of access to the working place as well as the right of assembly and speech…

(iii) Protection of trade union representatives

49. The Committee notes that the legislation and regulations…do not contain any provisions that are discriminatory or are such as to restrict representatives' freedom to exercise their prerogatives…

[632] *Rekvenyi v Hungary* (App. 253909/94), ECtHR (Grand Chamber), 20 May 1999, [59].
[633] *Rekvenyi v Hungary*, [59].
[634] *European Council of Police Trade Unions v Portugal*, 21 May 2013, ECSR Complaint No. 11/2000.

With regard to the constitution of organizations, the ECSR observed that law or practice must not impair the freedom of police to form or join organizations, although compulsory registration is permitted as long as there is adequate protection against abuse of any power to refuse registration.[635] The Portuguese police enjoyed such protections.[636] Article 5 was also found to permit national law to preclude police from joining trade unions where they could join professional police associations in which their organization and operation was freely determined by members without state interference.[637]

The associations were further found to enjoy basic trade union prerogatives, including the right to make demands on working conditions and pay (by participating directly in negotiations with the state), access to the workplace, and freedom of assembly and speech.[638] Restrictions on assembly found to be 'reasonable' included that meetings: could be held during work time but must guarantee the effective operation of the service; must not take place in premises accessible to the public; must be notified four days in advance; and could not consume more than fifteen working hours per person per year.[639] Importantly, employees in general were subject to similar restrictions.

In relation to expression and petition, the ECSR accepted the legitimacy of restrictions which obliged staff to refrain from making statements on matters about which they acquired knowledge in the performance of their duties or which were state secrets.[640] However, the ESCR found excessive a prohibition on police petitioning fundamental rights bodies before exhausting hierarchical (that is, 'chain of command') remedies. Also problematic for protected union rights were prohibitions on any statements that violated the principle of force discipline or any actions which might impair the proper performance of police duties.[641]

Finally, the ECSR found that the laws did not discriminate against the representatives of police associations or restrict their freedom to exercise their prerogatives, and indeed gave them time off work for union matters.[642] In this respect, a requirement that an association must obtain 10 per cent of the vote at the national professional elections (a representativity criterion) to enjoy their prerogatives was in conformity with Article 5.

The ECSR's approach has the advantage of establishing a minimum floor for the trade union rights of police which cannot be subject to restriction, even were it to be shown (for example) that restrictions were necessary in a democratic society in pursuit of a legitimate aim (as per the limitations test in Article 8(1) of the ICESCR). It is thus more protective of the rights of the designated groups, which would appear contrary to the drafting intention in the different context of Article 8(2) of the ICESCR.

635 *Police Trade Unions v Portugal*, [29] and [30].

636 *Police Trade Unions v Portugal*, [32]–[34].

637 *Police Trade Unions v Portugal*, [35]–[36] and [39].

638 *Police Trade Unions v Portugal*, [40]–[48], [58] and [66]–[67].

639 *Police Trade Unions v Portugal*, [44].

640 *Police Trade Unions v Portugal*, [45].

641 *Police Trade Unions v Portugal*, [46].

642 *Police Trade Unions v Portugal*, [49] and [50].

On a separate but related point, it should be noted that the ILO has been critical of national laws which only authorize public servants to join certain organizations, or to establish professional 'associations', but not real trade unions, even if such associations are recognized de facto by the state for the purposes of work negotiations.[643]

Article 8(3): No Prejudice to ILO Convention No. 87

Article 8(3) provides that Article 8 does not permit states to prejudice the guarantees in ILO Convention No. 87 concerning Freedom of Association and Protection of the Right to Organize 1948. The clause was proposed by the Netherlands and the United Kingdom[644] and intended to replicate a provision in the draft ICCPR on freedom of association (now Article 22(3)).[645]

During the drafting, a number of states felt that it was inappropriate or unnecessary to refer to a particular ILO treaty within the ICESCR,[646] particularly as the twin covenants 'should eventually become the code on which international conventions on specific subjects would be based'.[647] No comparable reference to ILO standards is found in Articles 6 or 7 of the ICESCR.[648] It was, however, narrowly adopted.[649]

In view of the general savings clause in Article 5(2) common to the ICESCR and ICCPR, the reference is also arguably superfluous[650] and adds 'hardly any legal significance'.[651] It does not purport to extend the ILO instrument to ICESCR parties which are not parties to it, although that has not hindered the CESCR from calling on states to ratify ILO instruments.

Nonetheless, writing of the comparable provision in the ICCPR, Nowak suggests that such provision recognizes the significance of the ILO's standard setting, and could even 'be understood as calling for an interpretation…in line with ILO Convention No. 87'.[652] A minority of the HRC in the *Alberta Unions* case invoked Article 22(3) and stressed an interpretation consistent with the ILO instrument.[653]

As noted earlier, Article 8(3) also has the savings effect of preventing states that are parties to the ILO Convention from restricting the rights of those involved in the administration of the state pursuant to Article 8(2), since only armed forces and police may be subject to restriction under the ILO instrument.

Commentators perhaps underestimate the potential legal significance of Article 8(3). For states that are parties to both the ICESCR and ILO Convention

[643] ILO, *Giving Globalization a Human Face*, 24.
[644] UNGA Third Committee, A/3525 (9 February 1957), 19.
[645] UNGA Third Committee, A/C.3/SR.719 (3 January 1957), 191 (United Kingdom).
[646] UNGA Third Committee, A/C.3/SR.720 (3 January 1957), 196 (Poland, Chile). A similar concern was expressed in the drafting of the ICCPR: Nowak, *CCPR Commentary*, 510.
[647] UNGA Third Committee, A/C.3/SR.722 (7 January 1957), 206 (Iran).
[648] Craven, *The ICESCR*, 260.
[649] By nineteen votes to fourteen, with thirty-five abstentions.
[650] Nowak, *CCPR Commentary*, 510.
[651] Nowak, *CCPR Commentary*, 511.
[652] Nowak, *CCPR* Commentary, 511.
[653] Nowak, *CCPR Commentary*, 512.

No. 87, the provision may be significant in resolving any conflict of obligations that may arise between the different treaty regimes, particularly if the CESCR interprets Article 8 differently from the ILO bodies. Article 8(3) may thus displace ordinary conflict resolution principles under international law, such as the rule that a later-in-time treaty prevails (pursuant to which the ICESCR 1966 might permit deviation from Convention No. 87 of 1948), or that the special law takes precedence over the general law (if the view were taken that Article 8, not ILO Convention No. 87, is the 'special' law on trade unions). Article 8(3) may thus mandate a different conflict resolution rule which preserves the primacy of ILO Convention No. 87 for those states that are parties to both instruments.

International Cooperation

As discussed earlier, Article 8(1)(c) of the ICESCR requires states to enable unions to internationally affiliate. In addition, as for other ICESCR rights, states are required to take steps individually and through international assistance and cooperation (ICESCR, Article 2(1)) to achieve trade union rights including by treaty action, soft law making, consultation, research and technical assistance (ICESCR, Article 23). International cooperation was discussed in relation to the right to work in Article 6 and many of those developments are apposite to Article 8.

To briefly reiterate, states should: (a) promote trade union rights in other states; (b) ensure that such rights are duly considered in international agreements; and (c) respect and promote trade union rights in dealings with international financial institutions. For example, some bilateral and multilateral trade agreements specifically address union rights, including the North American Agreement on Labor Cooperation 1994 and recent US bilateral free trade agreements.[654]

In addition, international organizations themselves should give due attention to trade union rights, including, for example, the United Nations and its agencies, World Bank, IMF, WTO and regional organizations. For instance, some international financial institutions, including development banks, have required borrowers to meet minimum labour standards on unions.[655] The International Finance Corporation's Performance Standard 2 (on labour and working conditions) addresses collective bargaining and workers' organizations:

Working Conditions and Terms of Employment

10. Where the client is a party to a collective bargaining agreement with a workers' organization, such agreement will be respected. Where such agreements do not exist, or do not

[654] North American Agreement on Labor Cooperation (adopted 13 September 1993, entered into force 1 January 1994) (concluded between the United States, Canada and Mexico, and including freedom of association, the right to collectively bargain and the right to strike); see also ILO, *Giving Globalization a Human Face*, 39; Cleopatra Doumbia-Henry and Eric Gravel, 'Free Trade Agreements and Labour Rights: Recent Developments' (2006) 145 *International Labour Review* 185.

[655] ILO, *Giving Globalization a Human Face*, 33.

address working conditions and terms of employment, the client will provide reasonable working conditions and terms of employment.

...

Workers' Organizations

13. In countries where national law recognizes workers' rights to form and to join workers' organizations of their choosing without interference and to bargain collectively, the client will comply with national law. Where national law substantially restricts workers' organizations, the client will not restrict workers from developing alternative mechanisms to express their grievances and protect their rights regarding working conditions and terms of employment. The client should not seek to influence or control these mechanisms.

14. In either case described in paragraph 13 of this Performance Standard, and where national law is silent, the client will not discourage workers from electing worker representatives, forming or joining workers' organizations of their choosing, or from bargaining collectively, and will not discriminate or retaliate against workers who participate, or seek to participate, in such organizations and collective bargaining. The client will engage with such workers' representatives and workers' organizations, and provide them with information needed for meaningful negotiation in a timely manner. Workers' organizations are expected to fairly represent the workers in the workforce.[656]

The IFC's Performance Standard 2 has influenced regional practice (such as the European Bank for Reconstruction and Development).[657] In addition, since 2007, the World Bank's procurement rules have included requirements on freedom of association and collective bargaining.[658] The Asian Development Bank's 'Core Labour Standards' also include freedom of association and the right to collective bargaining, on the basis of ILO standards, although subject to certain caveats:

The core standards on freedom of association and the effective recognition of the right to collective bargaining have often been considered by international financial institutions to be more controversial than other CLS. The reason for this in ADB comes from its Charter: Article 36 says '... shall not interfere in the political affairs of any member...' However, at the same time, ADB is committed to comply with all CLS in its lending activities based on sound economic considerations. ADB can attach conditions of CLS/ILS to individual loans, but only to the extent that lack of compliance with the standard undermines the economic development objective of its programs. Additionally, such conditions must not interfere in the domestic political affairs of the borrowing country.

While acknowledging that the relationship between collective bargaining and economic development is complex, ADB encourages the development of a positive role for labor market actors, especially workers' and employers' organizations, in its DMCs. Supported by research and training activities, dialogue with trade unions and tripartite arrangements are encouraged by ADB at the national level. ADB is introducing a number of initiatives, including this handbook, to ensure that staff better understand unions and

[656] International Finance Corporation, Performance Standard 2: Labour and Working Conditions (originally adopted 2006, revised 1 January 2012) (referencing ILO Convention No. 87 concerning Freedom of Association and ILO Convention No. 98 concerning the Right to Organise).

[657] ILO, *Giving Globalization a Human Face*, 36.

[658] ILO, *Giving Globalization a Human Face*, 36.

management and their role in supporting CLS, are able to have effective discussions with social partners to meet development goals, and understand that organized labor supports strong, independent unions and employers' organizations. Even where they do not yet exist, ADB should take no action that would make organization and collective bargaining more difficult.[659]

Finally, states should also encourage private actors to respect rights, including where they operate abroad (such as banks, investors or multinational enterprises). The IFC's Performance Standard 2 has influenced private banks which, through the Equator Principles, apply the IFC standards in larger project financing.[660] Socially responsible private investment funds (including pension funds) are also taking labour issues into account.[661]

For multinational enterprises, apart from the United Nations' Business and Human Rights Principles discussed in relation to Article 6, it should be added that trade union rights and collective bargaining are addressed by the ILO's Tripartite Declaration of Principles Concerning Multinational Enterprises and Social Policy (revised 2006):

Industrial relations

41. Multinational enterprises should observe standards of industrial relations not less favourable than those observed by comparable employers in the country concerned.

Freedom of association and the right to organize

42. Workers employed by multinational enterprises as well as those employed by national enterprises should, without distinction whatsoever, have the right to establish and, subject only to the rules of the organization concerned, to join organizations of their own choosing without previous authorisation. They should also enjoy adequate protection against acts of anti-union discrimination in respect of their employment.

43. Organizations representing multinational enterprises or the workers in their employment should enjoy adequate protection against any acts of interference by each other or each other's agents or members in their establishment, functioning or administration.

44. Where appropriate, in the local circumstances, multinational enterprises should support representative employers' organizations.

45. Governments, where they do not already do so, are urged to apply the principles of Convention No. 87, Article 5, in view of the importance, in relation to multinational enterprises, of permitting organizations representing such enterprises or the workers in their employment to affiliate with international organizations of employers and workers of their own choosing.

46. Where governments of host countries offer special incentives to attract foreign investment, these incentives should not include any limitation of the workers' freedom of association or the right to organize and bargain collectively.

[659] Asian Development Bank (ADB), *Core Labour Standards Handbook* (October 2006), 51–2; see also ADB, *Social Protection Strategy* (July 2003), 15.

[660] ILO, *Giving Globalization a Human Face*, 36.

[661] ILO, *Giving Globalization a Human Face*, 36.

47. Representatives of the workers in multinational enterprises should not be hindered from meeting for consultation and exchange of views among themselves, provided that the functioning of the operations of the enterprise and the normal procedures which govern relationships with representatives of the workers and their organizations are not thereby prejudiced.

48. Governments should not restrict the entry of representatives of employers' and workers' organizations who come from other countries at the invitation of the local or national organizations concerned for the purpose of consultation on matters of mutual concern, solely on the grounds that they seek entry in that capacity.

Collective bargaining

49. Workers employed by multinational enterprises should have the right, in accordance with national law and practice, to have representative organizations of their own choosing recognized for the purpose of collective bargaining.

50. Measures appropriate to national conditions should be taken, where necessary, to encourage and promote the full development and utilization of machinery for voluntary negotiation between employers or employers' organizations and workers' organizations, with a view to the regulation of terms and conditions of employment by means of collective agreements.

51. Multinational enterprises, as well as national enterprises, should provide workers' representatives with such facilities as may be necessary to assist in the development of effective collective agreements.

52. Multinational enterprises should enable duly authorized representatives of the workers in their employment in each of the countries in which they operate to conduct negotiations with representatives of management who are authorized to take decisions on the matters under negotiation.

53. Multinational enterprises, in the context of bona fide negotiations with the workers' representatives on conditions of employment, or while workers are exercising the right to organize, should not threaten to utilize a capacity to transfer the whole or part of an operating unit from the country concerned in order to influence unfairly those negotiations or to hinder the exercise of the right to organize; nor should they transfer workers from affiliates in foreign countries with a view to undermining bona fide negotiations with the workers' representatives or the workers' exercise of their right to organize.

54. Collective agreements should include provisions for the settlement of disputes arising over their interpretation and application and for ensuring mutually respected rights and responsibilities.

55. Multinational enterprises should provide workers' representatives with information required for meaningful negotiations with the entity involved and, where this accords with local law and practices, should also provide information to enable them to obtain a true and fair view of the performance of the entity or, where appropriate, of the enterprise as a whole.

56. Governments should supply to the representatives of workers' organizations on request, where law and practice so permit, information on the industries in which the enterprise operates, which would help in laying down objective criteria in the collective bargaining

process. In this context, multinational as well as national enterprises should respond constructively to requests by governments for relevant information on their operations.[662]

Reservations or Interpretive Declarations on Article 8

Reservations or declarations concerning the right to strike in Article 8(1)(d) and the exceptional categories of workers under Article 8(2) were discussed above. A number of states have also lodged problematic reservations or interpretive declarations concerning Article 8 more generally. China declared that 'the application' of Article 8(1)(a) 'shall be consistent with' China's Constitution and trade union and labour laws. Three states (the Netherlands, Norway and Sweden) objected on the basis that the reservation makes the provision subject to national law, a state may not invoke internal law to justify inconsistencies with a treaty, and that trade union rights are 'fundamental' and the reservation is incompatible with the object and purpose of the ICESCR.[663] The CESCR has since called on China to consider removing its reservation.[664]

Mexico's 'interpretive statement' is problematic for the same reasons, since Mexico's accession comes 'with the understanding that article 8 of the Covenant shall be applied ... under the conditions and in conformity with the procedure established in' Mexico's Constitution and implementing legislation. On multiple occasions, the CESCR has called on Mexico to consider withdrawing its interpretive statement.[665]

Algeria's 'interpretive declaration' similarly interprets Article 8 'as making the law the framework for action by the State with respect to the organization and exercise of the right to organize'. Germany responded that it interprets Algeria's declaration as 'not intended to eliminate the obligation of Algeria to ensure that the rights guaranteed in article 8, paragraph 1 ... may be restricted only for the reasons mentioned in the said articles and that such restrictions shall be prescribed by law'.[666]

Monaco declared that it considers Article 8(1)(a)–(c) 'to be compatible with the appropriate legislative provisions regarding the formalities, conditions and procedures designed to ensure effective trade union representation and to promote harmonious labour relations'. No other state or the CESCR has thus far commented on Monaco's position. However, a state's own interpretive view that its law already complies with Article 8 is not legally dispositive of whether such law objectively conforms to Article 8.

662 ILO Tripartite Declaration.

663 The Netherlands, Communication to the UN Secretary-General, 23 April 2002; Norway, Communication to the UN Secretary-General, 22 July 1997; Sweden, Communication to the UN Secretary-General, 2 April 2002. See Appendix III in this book.

664 CESCR, Concluding Observations: China, E/C.12/1/Add.107 (13 May 2005), [26] and [55].

665 CESCR, Concluding Observations: Mexico, E/C.12/MEX/CO/4 (9 June 2006), [34].

666 Government of Germany, Communication to the UN Secretary-General, 25 October 1990.

New Zealand's reservation has also not attracted adverse comment, despite reserving 'the right not [to] apply article 8 to the extent that existing legislative measures, enacted to ensure effective trade union representation and encourage orderly industrial relations, may not be fully compatible with that article'. Its reservation would nonetheless appear to subordinate Article 8 to its own domestic law and may be contrary to the object and purpose of the ICESCR for reasons similar to the objections made in respect of China's statement.

11

Article 9: The Right to Social Security

Article 9

The States Parties to the present Covenant recognize the right of everyone to social security, including social insurance.

Origins of Social Security

Various European states developed social security protections in the nineteenth century, followed by many Latin American states in the early twentieth century. The earliest modern form of social security was social insurance, by which workers and employers paid co-contributions with employers to finance sickness insurance and workers' compensation,[1] occasionally supplemented by the state. Social insurance was thus originally linked to labour force participation and insurance-based funding. This model was reflected at the international level in the earliest conventions adopted by the International Labour Organization (ILO) between the First and Second World Wars, covering issues such as maternity protection, sickness, old age, invalidity, workers' compensation, workplace diseases, survivors of workers killed at work, and unemployment of certain workers (later including foreigners).

The nature and availability of social security gradually widened over time to include needs-based social welfare or social assistance, such as old age pensions and unemployment benefits, which were decoupled from employment or insurance and funded by general taxation. Philosophically, this was linked to the growing human rights movement, including the call in the Atlantic Charter 1941 (by US President Roosevelt) to guarantee 'freedom from want'. In 1944, the ILO

[1] Martin Scheinin, 'The Right to Social Security' in Asbjorn Eide, Catarina Krause and Allan Rosas (eds), *Economic, Social and Cultural Rights: A Textbook* (2nd edn, Kluwer, The Hague, 2001), 211.

redefined its aims to place human rights at the centre of social policy and called for the 'extension of social security measures to provide a basic income to all in need of such protection and comprehensive medical care'.[2] Two ILO recommendations of 1944 seeking to widen the coverage of social security preceded its articulation as a human right from 1948 onwards.[3]

The conceptual change in and substantive expansion of social security was recognized in the Universal Declaration of Human Rights 1948. Article 22 provides that '[e]veryone, as a member of society, has the right to social security'. Article 25(1) states more specifically that '[e]veryone ... has the right to security in the event of unemployment, sickness, disability, widowhood, old age or other lack of livelihood in circumstances beyond his control'. Article 25(2) recognizes that '[m]otherhood and childhood are entitled to special care and assistance' and that '[a]ll children ... shall enjoy the same social protection'.

Against this background, during the drafting of Article 9 of the ICESCR, some states drew attention to other normative frameworks which supported the formulation of a universal right of social security. Despite the historical perception that socio-economic rights were non-justiciable, even in the 1950s various states had already made constitutional provision for social security, as in Latin America, Pakistan, Indonesia, Czechoslovakia and Albania (although these were not necessarily directly enforceable).

In addition, the drafting record evidences that there was considerable transnational legal borrowing or horizontal legal transplantation in the area of social security. Thus, France acknowledged that it, like others, had been influenced by Sir William Beveridge,[4] whose 1942 report on social insurance had sown the seeds for Britain's post-war welfare state. The new state of Israel also noted that its 1953 social security law had been influenced by the Beveridge Report, as well as laws in Scandinavia, New Zealand and Australia.[5] In the United States, President Roosevelt's 'New Deal' in the 1930s also included social security measures.

Non-legal, cross-cultural norms too were invoked during the drafting in support of a universal right of social security, with Saudi Arabia stating that '[i]n the Arab world, the tribes had taken care of all their members; and since the coming of Islam the community chests, supported by generous voluntary taxes on capital, had carried on the tradition'.[6] Religious and charitable conceptions of welfare did not, however, generally involve enforceable legal rights and obligations.[7] There

[2] CESCR, General Comment No. 19, E/C.12/GC/19 (4 February 2008), [6]; International Labour Organization (ILO), Declaration concerning the Aims and Purposes of the International Labour Organization (10 May 1944).

[3] ILO Recommendation No. 67 concerning Income Security (12 May 1944); ILO Recommendation No. 69 concerning Medical Care (12 May 1944). See also ILO, Social Security for Social Justice and a Fair Globalization, Report VI (8 March 2011) ('Report VI'), 12.

[4] UNGA Third Committee, A/C.3/SR.729 (14 January 1957), 242.

[5] UNGA Third Committee, A/C.3/SR.728 (11 January 1957), 235. See also William Beveridge, 'Social Insurance and Allied Services', presented to the UK Parliament (November 1942).

[6] UNGA Third Committee, A/C.3/SR.728 (11 January 1957), 238.

[7] Angelika Nussberger, 'Social Security, Right to, International Protection', *Max Planck Encyclopedia of Public International Law* (online), [6].

remains a belief in certain societies (including in the West) that assistance to economically 'inactive' people is more a moral or family duty rather than a right of individuals to make a claim on the state.[8]

Purpose of Social Security

The CESCR describes the purpose of the right to social security in General Comment No. 19:

> 1. ... The right to social security is of central importance in guaranteeing human dignity for all persons when they are faced with circumstances that deprive them of their capacity to fully realize their Covenant rights.
>
> ...
>
> 3. Social security, through its redistributive character, plays an important role in poverty reduction and alleviation, preventing social exclusion and promoting social inclusion.[9]

The ILO General Conference similarly concluded in 2001 that:

> 2. Social security is very important for the well-being of workers, their families and the entire community. It is a basic human right and a fundamental means for creating social cohesion, thereby helping to ensure social peace and social inclusion. It is an indispensable part of government social policy and an important tool to prevent and alleviate poverty. It can, through national solidarity and fair burden sharing, contribute to human dignity, equity and social justice. It is also important for political inclusion, empowerment and the development of democracy.[10]

Like the right to work in Article 6, the right to social security is a vital means of ensuring an individual's subsistence and securing their basic socio-economic rights under the ICESCR. Article 9 is thus intimately linked to realizing the rights to an adequate standard of living (Article 11), health (Article 12), education (Article 13) and culture (Article 15). In addition, social security furthers the independent values of reducing inequality and promoting fairness, equality, social justice and social cohesion.

Given the interdependence of all human rights, social security also enables individuals to realize their civil and political rights, including political participation. As the Pakistani delegate stated during the drafting of Article 9:

> ... political freedom was not possible without economic security, in which social security played a very important part. Workers must be free from the threat of want, unemployment and insecurity, or they became will-less nonentities, little better than slaves.[11]

[8] Scheinin, 'The Right to Social Security', 213.

[9] CESCR, General Comment No. 19, [1], [3]. Social security in the European Union is estimated to reduce the risk of poverty by almost 9 per cent: ILO, Report VI, 22.

[10] ILO, Conclusions concerning Social Security, ILC89-PR16-312-En.Doc (2001), 16, [2].

[11] UNGA Third Committee, A/C.3/SR.727 (10 January 1957), 232.

The ILO has also recognized that social security is 'important for political inclusion, empowerment and the development of democracy'.[12] At the same time, it can encourage social and political stability,[13] for example by preventing, mitigating or redressing the tensions which can arise from mass unemployment or acute inequality. As discussed further below (in the section on progressive realization), social security can also have ancillary economic benefits.

The Drafting of Article 9

The final text of Article 9 was settled by January 1957 after extensive debate.[14] Three key issues arose in the drafting. First, there was disagreement about how generally or specifically to articulate the right.[15] Some states wanted greater specification and suggested being guided by Articles 22 and 25 of the UDHR.[16] Israel argued for an explicit reference to ILO Convention No. 102 concerning Minimum Standards of Social Security.[17]

Others wished to list the grounds on which individuals would be granted social security. Thus, Italy proposed providing social security 'particularly in the case of accident, sickness, disability, old-age and involuntary unemployment'.[18] A proposal by Uruguay and Yugoslavia non-exhaustively mentioned infirmity, disability, old age, unemployment, family pensions in the event of death and where unforeseen circumstances make it impossible to acquire the necessary means of livelihood.[19] An Australian proposal instead prescribed a minimum content of social security, namely that the state assure 'to every person at least the means of subsistence', whether in cash or in kind:

> Everyone shall have the right to social security which shall be guaranteed by the provision of social benefits, either in cash or in kind, assuring to every person at least the means of subsistence and, when necessary, adequate treatment in any common contingency occasioning the involuntary loss of income or its insufficiency to meet family necessities. The State may prescribe that all or any of such benefits may be provided under a general contributory system.[20]

Others thought it difficult or undesirable to define social security, noting the difficulties in drafting ILO Convention No. 102, which deliberately omits any

[12] ILO, Conclusions concerning Social Security, [2].

[13] Scheinin, 'The Right to Social Security', 211.

[14] The final text of Article 9 was adopted by fifty-one votes to seven, with sixteen abstentions: UNGA Third Committee, A/3525 (9 February 1957), 32.

[15] Commission on Human Rights, E/CN.4/669 (14 April–14 June 1952), 17.

[16] UNGA Third Committee, A/3525 (9 February 1957), 30; A/C.3/SR.728 (11 January 1957), 238 (Romania).

[17] UNGA Third Committee, A/C.3/SR.728 (11 January 1957), 235 (Israel).

[18] UNGA Third Committee, A/C.3/SR.726 (9 January 1957), 228.

[19] Commission on Human Rights, E/CN.4/581 (1 May 1951).

[20] Commission on Human Rights, E/CN.4/507 (27 March–19 May 1950), 26.

definition.[21] It was noted that 'the concept of social security was continually developing and a rigid definition could only have a limiting effect'.[22] The expert role of the ILO in developing standards was noted in this context. The ILO representative observed that the 1952 ILO conference had recognized that many states would not ratify Convention No. 102 if it required them to cover all social risks.[23] A majority of states ultimately preferred a statement of general principle which was more spartan than the UDHR provisions, but allowed them the freedom to develop its scope.[24]

Such generality, however, allowed states to evade being bound by any minimum content of the right, leading Czecholovakia to fear that the right had been 'reduced to a universally acceptable lowest common denominator' instead of laying down as a model the standards in the most advanced countries.[25] This tension remains today in the interplay between Article 9 and ILO Convention No. 102, with the former casting social security as a universal human right and the latter confining it to specific measures which states opt into implementing.

Secondly, and partly as a result of the lack of definition, there was confusion about the meanings of the terms 'social security' and 'social insurance'. Some states thought social security excluded the separate category of social insurance,[26] with the former concerning state assistance to retirees and the unemployed and the latter assistance to workers.[27] Others thought that the historically limited scope of social insurance was changing to encompass wider or universal assistance.[28] Italy thought that social security referred to the replacement of lost wages (which other states described as social insurance), but not broader state assistance to ensure an adequate standard of living.[29]

Yet others thought that social security was a universal term encompassing the many different kinds of support[30] and this legal understanding was prevalent in Latin America.[31] The ILO representative endorsed this approach and sought to clarify the matter:

> The term 'social security', he explained, had originated in the United States of America, had been adopted in Europe and had gradually made its way into international terminology. In that connexion, he referred to the International Labour Convention (No. 102) concerning Minimum Standards of Social Security, which had been adopted in 1952. The replacement of the term 'social insurance' by the term 'social security' reflected, as the Yugoslav representative had noted, a broadening of the notion itself.[32]

21 UNGA Third Committee, A/3525 (9 February 1957), 31.
22 UNGA Third Committee, A/3525 (9 February 1957), 31.
23 UNGA Third Committee, A/C.3/SR.726 (9 January 1957), 229 (ILO).
24 UNGA Third Committee, A/C.3/SR.726 (9 January 1957), 228 (Chile), 229 (Syria).
25 UNGA Third Committee, A/C.3/SR.728 (11 January 1957), 236.
26 UNGA Third Committee, A/3525 (9 February 1957), 31.
27 UNGA Third Committee, A/C.3/SR.726 (9 January 1957), 228 (USSR).
28 UNGA Third Committee, A/C.3/SR.726 (9 January 1957), 228 (Yugoslavia).
29 UNGA Third Committee, A/C.3/SR.726 (9 January 1957), 228 (Italy).
30 UNGA Third Committee, A/C.3/SR.726 (9 January 1957), 228 (El Salvador); A/C.3/SR.728 (11 January 1957), 235 (Israel).
31 UNGA Third Committee, A/C.3/SR.726 (9 January 1957), 229 (Venezuela).
32 UNGA Third Committee, A/C.3/SR.726 (9 January 1957), 229 (ILO).

A compromise was adopted, with Article 9 referring primarily to the right to 'social security', but 'including' social assistance as a sub-category.[33] The terminological confusion led to a related disagreement over the identity of the right-holder. A few states sought to limit the right to 'workers'[34] (reflecting the traditional approach to social insurance), whereas a majority preferred to extend it to 'everyone'[35] (reflecting the universal ideal of social security for all in need). Earlier proposals to also mention 'the family' thus became redundant (although a similar reference to dependent family survives in relation to the adequacy of a worker's wages under Article 7 of the ICESCR).

Even today, there remain differences in the terminology used by different states and actors to describe the components of social security. The ILO provides the following guidance on some of the concepts in current use:

Social security

The notion of social security adopted here covers all measures providing benefits, whether in cash or in kind, to secure protection, inter alia, from:

- lack of work-related income (or insufficient income) caused by sickness, disability, maternity, employment injury, unemployment, old age, or death of a family member;
- lack of access or unaffordable access to health care;
- insufficient family support, particularly for children and adult dependants;
- general poverty and social exclusion.

Social security schemes can be of a contributory (social insurance) or non-contributory nature.

Social assistance

Social security benefits that are conditional on the level of income of recipient, i.e. are means-tested or based on similar forms of targeting (e.g. proxy means test, geographical targeting), are generally called social assistance. They are generally a device to alleviate/reduce poverty. Benefits can be delivered in cash or in kind.

'Conditional' social assistance schemes require beneficiaries (and/or their relatives or families), in addition to other conditions, to participate in prescribed public programmes (e.g. specified health or educational programmes). In recent years, schemes of this type have become known as *conditional cash transfer (CCT)* schemes.

Social assistance schemes are usually tax-financed and do not require a direct contribution from beneficiaries or their employers as a condition of entitlement to receive relevant benefits.[36]

Thirdly, drafting opinion was divided over whether the provision should specify the means of financing social security. The Soviet Union proposed that the state

[33] The USSR proposal to refer to 'including social insurance' was adopted by twenty-six votes to thirteen, with twenty-eight abstentions: UNGA Third Committee, A/3525 (9 February 1957), 32.

[34] UNGA Third Committee, A/C.3/SR.726 (9 January 1957), 228 (Italy).

[35] UNGA Third Committee, A/3525 (9 February 1957), 32.

[36] ILO, Report VI, 11.

or the employer should bear the cost,[37] a view supported by many socialist states.[38] Such states believed that it was not in the best interests of workers for them to be burdened with funding their own social security, which should instead be funded out of the capital profits of employers. Albania also noted that worker contributions favoured those who were well off.[39] It was further mentioned that the principle of progressive realization in Article 2(1) of the ICESCR would not require states to fund social security immediately,[40] which was a longer-term aspiration.

The Soviet proposal was decisively defeated[41] because most states (especially capitalist ones) were not opposed to workers making financial contributions. Many countries already utilized a 'tripartite' model to fund social security, in which contributions were made by workers, the state and employers, with the balance between contributions varying from state to state. The proposal was thus thought 'too mandatory', ignored the diversity among states, and interfered in the freedom of each state to determine the system best suited to its needs and resources.[42]

Further, many states did not believe that worker contributions were out of date or unjust. To the contrary, (fair and reasonable) worker contributions were seen to emphasize a 'principle of social solidarity' and entitled workers to participate on an equal basis with employers and the state in the establishment and functioning of social security.[43] Guatemala said it gave workers 'strength and dignity and educated them in their social responsibilities'.[44] Greece noted that it cultivated 'thrift' in workers and made them not feel a burden on society.[45] Portugal and the United Kingdom highlighted the 'psychological advantage' of worker participation.[46]

Requiring employers or states to wholly fund social security was also seen as economically unviable. Chile, for instance, noted that capital was scarce in Latin America, governments could not afford to fund it by themselves, and requiring employers to fund social security would risk provoking an economic downturn.[47] It would thus be 'unprogessive…to launch schemes which would bankrupt the State without achieving their purposes'.[48] Also, the Soviet approach could rebound on the worker if governments had to raise taxes, or businesses

[37] Commission on Human Rights, E/CN.4/507 (27 March–19 May 1950), Supplement No. 5, 26; E/CN.4/AC.14/2/Add.3, section IV; E/CN.4/640 (16 April–19 May 1951), Supplement No. 9, 9.

[38] UNGA Third Committee, A/C.3/SR.727 (10 January 1957), 234 (Ukraine); A/C.3/SR.728 (11 January 1957), 235 (Byelorussia), 237 (Czechoslovakia, Romania), 238 (Bulgaria); A/C.3/SR.729 (14 January 1957), 241 (Albania).

[39] UNGA Third Committee, A/C.3/SR.729 (14 January 1957), 241.

[40] UNGA Third Committee, A/3525 (9 February 1957), 31.

[41] The USSR proposal on financing was rejected by forty-one to nine, with seventeen abstentions: UNGA Third Committee, A/3525 (9 February 1957), 32.

[42] UNGA Third Committee, A/3525 (9 February 1957), 31.

[43] UNGA Third Committee, A/3525 (9 February 1957), 31.

[44] UNGA Third Committee, A/C.3/SR.728 (11 January 1957), 236.

[45] UNGA Third Committee, A/C.3/SR.729 (14 January 1957), 242.

[46] UNGA Third Committee, A/C.3/SR.729 (14 January 1957), 243.

[47] UNGA Third Committee, A/C.3/SR.727 (10 January 1957), 232.

[48] UNGA Third Committee, A/C.3/SR.727 (10 January 1957), 232.

raise consumer prices, to pay for social security.[49] Denmark presciently noted that it had taken 'about a hundred years' for it to a develop a modern, universal social security system and requiring under-developed states to fund it would retard their development.[50]

The ILO representative observed that Article 71 of ILO Convention No. 102 deals with financing[51] and requires social security costs to 'be borne collectively by way of insurance contributions or taxation or both', while avoiding hardship to poorer individuals and imposing a maximum 50 per cent individual contribution:

1. The cost of the benefits provided in compliance with this Convention and the cost of the administration of such benefits shall be borne collectively by way of insurance contributions or taxation or both in a manner which avoids hardship to persons of small means and takes into account the economic situation of the Member and of the classes of persons protected.

2. The total of the insurance contributions borne by the employees protected shall not exceed 50 per cent of the total of the financial resources allocated to the protection of employees and their wives and children. For the purpose of ascertaining whether this condition is fulfilled, all the benefits provided by the Member in compliance with this Convention, except family benefit and, if provided by a special branch, employment injury benefit, may be taken together.

As France noted, the question of financing is bound up in the very concept of social security: 'either as a system of protection against social risks or as a means of transforming social structures through the redistribution of income'.[52] France believed its essential purpose was non-economic.

While the right to social security does not presuppose a particular economic system, it does require some form of redistribution (whether from the state, employers or wealthier workers), demands more than mere self-insurance by employees, and requires state intervention and regulation. It thus presents an ideological challenge to extreme proponents of a free market, who may oppose government intervention in the economy or taxation for welfare redistribution, believe that individuals are responsible for their own welfare, or disagree that welfare is an appropriate means of addressing poverty or under-development.

As noted earlier, it also ideologically challenges socialist conceptions of economic life, since it allows for capitalist approaches to social security (such as worker contributions) and pursues limited redistribution to enable dignity, but not to even out inequality generally. Indeed, architects of social security such as William Beveridge believed that welfare is good for business because it shifts certain labour costs (such as pensions or health care) from companies to the state and supports workers to be more financially secure and healthier, thus making them more productive workers and more liberal consumers.

[49] UNGA Third Committee, A/C.3/SR.728 (11 January 1957), 239 (Saudi Arabia).
[50] UNGA Third Committee, A/C.3/SR.727 (10 January 1957), 233.
[51] UNGA Third Committee, A/C.3/SR.726 (9 January 1957), 229 (ILO).
[52] UNGA Third Committee, A/C.3/SR.729 (14 January 1957), 242.

DIFFERENT METHODS OF PROVIDING SOCIAL SECURITY

In view of the drafting history, the CESCR has recognized that Article 9 contemplates a range of different methods of providing social security, including contributory or insurance-based schemes, non-contributory schemes and community-based schemes:

> 4. …(a) Contributory or insurance-based schemes such as social insurance, which is expressly mentioned in article 9. These generally involve compulsory contributions from beneficiaries, employers and, sometimes, the State, in conjunction with the payment of benefits and administrative expenses from a common fund;
>
> (b) Non-contributory schemes such as universal schemes (which provide the relevant benefit in principle to everyone who experiences a particular risk or contingency) or targeted social assistance schemes (where benefits are received by those in a situation of need). In almost all States parties, non-contributory schemes will be required since it is unlikely that every person can be adequately covered through an insurance-based system.
>
> 5. Other forms of social security are also acceptable, including (a) privately run schemes, and (b) self-help or other measures, such as community-based or mutual schemes. Whichever system is chosen, it must conform to the essential elements of the right to social security and to that extent should be viewed as contributing to the right to social security and be protected by States parties in accordance with this general comment.[53]

In practice, there is considerable diversity in the variety and mix of schemes in different states. The ILO estimates that globally (excluding low-income states) about 40 per cent of health expenditure is financed by contributory social insurance schemes, whereas in low-income countries it is only about 7 per cent, with foreign aid financing, for instance, 46 per cent of health spending[54] (which is the dominant kind of social assistance in such states). Worldwide, most health spending is funded by general taxation. For non-health-related social security there are no global statistics. In the European Union, states finance 47 per cent of social security, while employers pay 30 per cent and households 21 per cent.[55] There are also numerous examples of hybrid schemes, including innovative ones such as the Bamako Initiative in the 1980s and 1990s, which involved state and community co-financing of more accessible, available and affordable drugs and health care in Africa.

Interpretation of Article 9

ILO STANDARDS

As is already apparent, many states accorded a prominent place to ILO standards in the drafting of Article 9. France noted that Convention No. 102 'stated at length what the international community considered minimum standards of

[53] CESCR, General Comment No. 19, [13].
[54] ILO, Report VI, 41.
[55] ILO, Report VI, 42.

social security', so that it was unnecessary for Article 9 to go into detail and risk 'a deeply regrettable conflict' with it.[56] Iran noted that detailed provisions should be left to other treaties.[57] The United Kingdom warned against encroaching on the ILO's sphere of action,[58] while Canada was concerned that defining the content of the right in Article 9 might create difficulties for the ILO.[59] Deference to the ILO's standard setting expertise in the area is a significant factor in explaining state support for Article 9 of the ICESCR.

There is accordingly some evidence of a drafting intention for ILO standards to operate, at least to some extent, as the special law (*lex specialis*) in respect of the content of the right to social security under Article 9 of the ICESCR. Convention No. 102 requires states parties to comply with certain general obligations and a minimum of three of the following nine areas of social security:

- medical care (Part II);
- sickness benefit (Part III);
- unemployment benefit (Part IV);
- old-age benefit (Part V);
- employment injury benefit (Part VI);
- family benefit (Part VII);
- maternity benefit (Part VIII);
- invalidity benefit (Part IX); and
- survivors' benefit (Part X).

In practice, the CESCR commonly invokes ILO conventions when assessing a state's compliance with Article 9. Its superseded 1991 reporting guidelines for states on Article 9 mirror the categories of assistance in ILO Convention No. 102,[60] while in general states are required to append reports already submitted to the ILO and other relevant UN bodies in relation to any relevant conventions of those organizations to which they are parties.[61]

While the invocation of ILO standards as *lex specialis* appears to offer a theoretically neat solution, it brings immediate problems. As of August 2013, the ICESCR had 160 states parties and ILO Convention No. 102 had forty-eight parties (all also ICESCR parties). Accordingly, only around one-third of the parties to the ICESCR formally accept the ILO standards (and the parties to the ILO Convention represent only about one-quarter of all states). As already noted, Convention No. 102

[56] UNGA Third Committee, A/C.3/SR.729 (14 January 1957), 242.
[57] UNGA Third Committee, A/C.3/SR.729 (14 January 1957), 242.
[58] UNGA Third Committee, A/C.3/SR.729 (14 January 1957), 243.
[59] UNGA Third Committee, A/C.3/SR.728 (11 January 1957), 237.
[60] CESCR, Revised General Guidelines Regarding the Form and Content of Reports to be Submitted by States Parties under Articles 16 and 17 of the ICESCR, E/C.12/1991/1 (17 June 1991), [27].
[61] CESCR, Revised General Guidelines, [5].

further only requires compliance with three of nine areas of assistance, although it aims to induce states to extend their coverage over time.

If a strict approach is taken to applying the ILO Convention as the special law under Article 9, some ICESCR parties (that is, those also party to the ILO Convention) will be held to different standards from others (both non-parties to the ILO Convention, as well as parties to the ILO Convention which have selected different fields of social protection). Similar patterns of variegated obligations are replicated in respect of other ILO conventions on social security to which ICESCR parties are or are not parties. Even fewer states have ratified ILO social security treaties subsequent to Convention No. 102; for instance, No. 121 has twenty-four states parties, No. 128 has twelve, No. 130 has fifteen, No. 168 has seven and No. 183 has thirteen.

Certainly, the CESCR has invoked particular ILO conventions that bind a state when assessing the state's compliance with Article 9. But the CESCR also routinely looks beyond the ILO commitments formally binding a given state. For instance, it has often called on states to ratify ILO Convention No. 102[62] and sometimes called for ratification of other ILO treaties such as Conventions No. 103 on maternity protection,[63] No. 117 concerning the basic aims and standards of social policy,[64] No. 118 concerning equality of treatment in social security[65] and No. 174 on major industrial accidents.[66] It has also expressed 'concern' where a state has not ratified any ILO Convention.[67] The CESCR has further observed that the incorporation into domestic law of international social security instruments is a means of enhancing the scope and effectiveness of remedies for violations of the right:

> 79. The incorporation in the domestic legal order of international instruments recognizing the right to social security can significantly enhance the scope and effectiveness of

[62] CESCR, Concluding Observations: Azerbaijan, E/C.12/1/Add.104 (14 December 2004), [48]; Angola, E/C.12/AGO/CO/3 (1 December 2008), [23]; Colombia, E/C.12/1/Add.74 (6 December 2001), [39]; Guatemala, E/C.12/1/Add.93 (12 December 2003), [35]; Honduras, E/C.12/1/Add.57 (21 May 2001), [39]; India, E/C.12/IND/CO/5 (8 August 2008), [64]; Kenya, E/C.12/KEN/CO/1 (1 December 2008), [21]; Kuwait, E/C.12/1/Add.98 (7 June 2004), [40]; Latvia, E/C.12/LVA/CO/1 (7 January 2008), [45]; Lithuania, E/C.12/1/Add.96 (7 June 2004), [38]; Morocco, E/C.12/MAR/CO/3 (4 September 2006), [46]; Nicaragua, E/C.12/NIC/CO/4 (28 November 2008), [18]; Yemen, E/C.12/1/Add.92 (12 December 2003), [32].

[63] CESCR, Concluding Observations: Australia, E/C.12/1/Add.50 (11 September 2000), [19]; Costa Rica, E/C.12/CRI/CO/4 (4 January 2008), [42].

[64] CESCR, Concluding Observations: Azerbaijan, E/C.12/1/Add.104 (14 December 2004), [48]; Honduras, E/C.12/1/Add.57 (21 May 2001), [39]; Iceland, E/C.12/1/Add.89 (23 May 2003), [24]; Luxembourg, E/C.12/1/Add.86 (23 May 2003), [33]; New Zealand, E/C.12/1/Add.88 (26 June 2003), [25].

[65] CESCR, Concluding Observations: Azerbaijan, E/C.12/1/Add.104 (14 December 2004), [48]; Costa Rica, E/C.12/CRI/CO/4 (4 January 2008), [42]; Honduras, E/C.12/1/Add.57 (21 May 2001), [39]; Iceland, E/C.12/1/Add.89 (23 May 2003), [24]; Lithuania, E/C.12/1/Add.96 (7 June 2004), [38]; Luxembourg, E/C.12/1/Add.86 (23 May 2003), [33]; Morocco, E/C.12/MAR/CO/3 (4 September 2006), [46]; Slovenia, E/C.12/SVN/CO/1 (25 January 2006), [27]; New Zealand, E/C.12/1/Add.88 (26 June 2003), [25].

[66] CESCR, Concluding Observations: Slovenia, E/C.12/SVN/CO/1 (25 January 2006), [27].

[67] CESCR, Concluding Observations: Gambia, E/C.12/1994/9 (31 May 1994), [13].

remedial measures and should be encouraged. Incorporation enables courts to adjudicate violations of the right to social security by direct reference to the Covenant.[68]

The ILO's Social Security Department lists various specialized ILO standards,[69] most of which are considered later in this chapter. In commenting on particular states, the CESCR has also sometimes identified areas of concern based on the ILO Committee of Experts' review of states' performance in relation to ILO convention standards binding on those states,[70] or other ILO information.[71]

Wider ILO standards—whether treaties or recommendations—are relevant in interpreting Article 9 because of the widely recognized expertise of the ILO, which predates the UN human rights instruments and bodies (being established in 1919, and becoming the first UN specialized agency in 1946). Institutionally, the ILO has had 'primary responsibility' for the realization of the right to social security since 1919.[72] ILO standards have also influenced the practice of non-party states on all continents[73] and seek to influence international law, as the following ILO statement suggests:

435. While providing for the right to social security, the international human rights instruments and their supervisory mechanisms have remained mostly silent on the definition and specific content of this right. In the absence of such definition and given the ILO's mandate, it has been left to the ILO to establish the parameters and substantive provisions of the right to social security. In this respect, ILO social security standards, and more particularly Convention No. 102, have constituted the main reference for the interpretation and definition of this right, while providing guidance for its implementation in a very detailed way. As mentioned previously, they have always been regarded as playing a key role by providing substantive content to the right to social security; moreover, on several occasions over the last ten years the Committee on Economic, Social and Cultural Rights (CESCR) has recommended to countries to ratify Convention No. 102 as a means of fulfilling their obligations under the International Covenant on Economic, Social and Cultural Rights (ICESCR).

436. Moreover, international experience shows that the ILO social security Conventions, and particularly Convention No. 102, are a means of preventing the levelling-down of social security systems worldwide, as they constitute benchmarks to assess whether their requirements have been met and contribute to the creation of a level playing-field for social conditions across the world.

…

438. Convention No. 102, the ILO's flagship Convention on social security, embodies an internationally accepted definition of the principles of social security and has been

[68] CESCR, General Comment No. 19, [79].

[69] ILO, 'Up to date ILO Social Security Conventions', <http://www.ilo.org/public/english/protection/secsoc/areas/legal/standard.htm>.

[70] CESCR, Concluding Observations: Iraq, E/C.12/1/Add.17 (12 December 1997), [17] (concerning ILO Convention Nos. 19 and 118).

[71] CESCR, Concluding Observations: Peru, E/C.12/1/Add.14 (16 May 1997), [21].

[72] ILO, Report VI, 11.

[73] ILO, Report VI, 15 (mentioning China, Latvia, Lebanon, Tunisia, Morocco, South Korea, Japan, pension systems in thirty African states, and generally in Europe, Latin America, the Caribbean, and in regional efforts by the Southern African Development Community).

recognized as a symbol of social progress. It plays a key role in defining the right to social security under international human rights instruments and to date has been ratified by 47 countries (32 in Europe, nine in the Americas, including the very recent ratifications by Brazil and Uruguay, five in Africa and one in Asia (Japan)). This and other up-to-date social security Conventions have had (and continue to have) a positive impact on the development of social security schemes in most countries worldwide and serve as models for regional instruments and national laws…[74]

Domestic courts have also looked to ILO standards to inform interpretation of social security rights under national law. For example, Taiwan's constitutional court held that a law denying recently adopted children the benefits of a parent's death insurance should be amended to take into account 'relevant international labour and social security Conventions'. ILO standards (particularly Convention No. 102, which Taiwan had ratified but only partly implemented in domestic law) were found to be relevant in interpreting the constitutional guarantee of social insurance as a part of 'fundamental national policy'.[75] A separate opinion by Judge Yueh-Chin Huang elaborated:

There are hundreds of conventions or legislative recommendations made by ILO, which plays the critical role in the worldwide value to protect human rights. In this Interpretation, the international conventions are used as a legal source. This is a very pleasing phenomenon for the growth of our constitutional interpretation system…

If we take the stand from the international viewpoint, because the worldwide value is to implement the aims or purposes of the conventions, the member states of the conventions have the duty to faithfully express the intents of the conventions, therefore the room for legislative discretion is very limited. In order to ensure the proper application of the legislative discretion, the Constitutional Interpretation Agency shall use the conventions as the legal sources to review the laws passed by Legislative Agency. This is the expression of faithfully interpreting the constitutional principles.[76]

Further, the ILO itself now takes a rights-based approach to social security and is increasingly concerned with widening its coverage:

The universal need for social security has been recognized by the world community as a human right. Since the ILO was first set up in 1919, pursuing the achievement of social security has consistently been at the core of its mandate. The Organization's approach to social security reflects both the status of social security in international law and its own constitutional mandate. The approach is rights-based: i.e. in order to realize the right to social security, the ILO uses international legal instruments as the starting point, the main reference and the legal basis for the recognition of the existence of this right, and seeks to anchor all assistance and policy advice in international social security standards.[77]

[74] ILO, Report VI, 148.

[75] Constitution of Taiwan, Articles 155 (concerning social insurance) and 153 (concerning labour protection).

[76] Judicial Yuan, Case No. 549, 2 August 2002 (Taiwan), <http://compendium.itcilo.org/en/compendium-decisions/judicial-yuan-2-august-2002-no.-549>, 12–14.

[77] ILO, Report VI, 10.

To do its legal work, however, Article 9 necessarily has a normative content independent of and wider than technical ILO standards, even if it refers back to such standards in elaborating the universal right of social security. Otherwise, the content of the right to social security would be dictated by an external authority (the ILO), in a normative field of different emphasis (labour rights) covering limited groups (not 'everyone'), and subject to the vagaries of state ratification of ILO treaties (including the selective, limited buy-in to Convention No. 102). Some of the technical standards are also expressed in antiquated or exclusionary language, such as references to a male breadwinner's earnings (even if that can paradoxically raise benefits for women).[78] The ILO itself has openly acknowledged the limitations of the ILO standards:

> [T]he up-to-date social security Conventions, including Convention No. 102, have their limitations when it comes to ensuring a defined minimum benefit package. Notably, they neither define priority benefits nor require universal coverage. Consideration should therefore be given to elaborating a mechanism for 'horizontal coverage extension' to provide further guidance to countries on how to establish a social protection floor comprising basic guarantees, in line with the ILO's constitutional mandate.[79]

While they aim to incrementally expand coverage over time, the ILO conventions allow states to select at any given time the limits of their social security commitments, thus inhibiting immediate universal coverage.[80]

The ILO's own proposals for a more comprehensive instrument are extracted at the end of this chapter. In general, a human rights approach to social security emphasizes universal coverage and greater social inclusion than ILO standards still grounded in employment contexts.[81] Article 9 also engages the much larger number of states that are parties to the ICESCR than any of the ILO instruments, although it remains subject to progressive realization in accordance with available state resources under Article 2(1) of the ICESCR.

OTHER ICESCR RIGHTS

As noted earlier, the interpretation of Article 9 is also intimately connected with the application of other ICESCR rights. The close connection between social insurance and labour rights (in Articles 6 to 8 of the ICESCR) has already been observed in relation to ILO standards, particularly as regards sickness benefits, employment injuries, maternity leave and unemployment assistance.

In addition, social security cash payments or services are often the means of securing aspects of family, mothers' and children's rights under Article 10,[82]

[78] ILO, Report VI, 14.

[79] ILO, Report VI, 149.

[80] Lucie Lamarche, 'The Right to Social Security in the International Covenant on Economic, Social and Cultural Rights' in Audrey Chapman and Sage Russell (eds), *Core Obligations: Building a Framework for Economic, Social and Cultural Rights* (Intersentia, Antwerp, 2002), 95.

[81] Malcolm Langford, 'The Right to Social Security and Implications for Law, Policy and Practice' in Eibe Riedel (ed), *Social Security as a Human Right: Drafting a General Comment on Article 9 ICESCR—Some Challenges* (SpringerVerlag, Berlin, 2007), 30.

[82] CESCR, General Comment No. 19, [18]–[19].

the right to an adequate standard of living (including food and housing) under Article 11 and the right to health (including disability care) under Article 12. In General Comment No. 19, the CESCR declares that 'States parties have immediate obligations in relation to the right to social security, such as…the obligation to take steps (article 2, paragraph 1) towards the full realization of articles 11, paragraph 1, and 12'.

It is clear that state action or omission in a given area may often be assessable under both Article 9 and other relevant ICESCR rights and the CESCR's examination of state reports may accordingly bundle together its assessment of related rights. At the same time, as the passage below suggests, there may be certain measures which remain specific to Article 9 or to other ICESCR rights. The CESCR has observed, however, that while social security-like measures may be required under the auspices of other ICESCR rights, that does not excuse states from their overarching obligation to create a wider social security system under Article 9:

28. The right to social security plays an important role in supporting the realization of many of the rights in the Covenant, but other measures are necessary to complement the right to social security. For example, States parties should provide social services for rehabilitation of the injured and persons with disabilities in accordance with article 6 of the Covenant, provide child care and welfare, advice and assistance with family planning and the provision of special facilities for persons with disabilities and older persons (article 10); take measures to combat poverty and social exclusion and provide supporting social services (article 11); and adopt measures to prevent disease and improve health facilities, goods and services (article 12). States parties should also consider schemes that provide social protection to individuals belonging to disadvantaged and marginalized groups, for example crop or natural disaster insurance for small farmers or livelihood protection for self-employed persons in the informal economy. However, the adoption of measures to realize other rights in the Covenant will not in itself act as a substitute for the creation of social security schemes.[83]

OTHER INTERNATIONAL HUMAN RIGHTS TREATIES

A number of other international human rights treaties make reference to social security and these may be applied as the relevant special law (*lex specialis*) in respect of their specialized subject matter. These include the International Convention on the Elimination of All Forms of Racial Discrimination (ICERD),[84] International Convention on the Elimination of All Forms of Discrimination against Women (CEDAW),[85] Convention on the Rights of the Child (CRC),[86] Convention on the

[83] CESCR, General Comment No. 19, [28].

[84] International Convention on the Elimination of All Forms of Racial Discrimination (adopted 7 March 1966, 660 UNTS 195, entered into force 4 January 1969), Article 5(e)(iv).

[85] International Convention on the Elimination of All Forms of Discrimination Against Women (adopted 18 December 1979, 1249 UNTS 13, entered into force 3 September 1981), Articles 11(1)(e), 11(2)(b), 13(a) and 14(2)(c).

[86] Convention on the Rights of the Child (adopted 20 November 1989, 1577 UNTS 3, entered into force 2 September 1990), Articles 26 and 27(3).

Rights of Persons with Disabilities (CRPD),[87] International Convention on the Rights of All Migrant Workers and Members of Their Families ('Migrant Workers Convention'),[88] and International Convention for the Protection of All Persons from Enforced Disappearance.[89] The UN General Assembly's non-binding Declaration on the Rights of Indigenous Peoples also contains social security provisions.[90]

Thus far, the CESCR has not had occasion to refer to the other specialized conventions in applying Article 9. Other UN treaty bodies have occasionally dealt with social security under their respective treaty regimes. As noted later, a denial of social security may also implicate civil and political rights under the ICCPR, particularly non-discrimination and freedom from inhuman or degrading treatment.

OTHER INTERNATIONAL STANDARDS

The CESCR has recognized the expertise of other international bodies in social security in informing state implementation of Article 9. Thus, states have been encouraged to obtain guidance in identifying social security 'indicators', for the purpose of monitoring their compliance under Article 9, from the ILO, World Health Organization (WHO) and International Social Security Association (ISSA).[91] The ILO has a dedicated Social Security Department responsible for the area. The ISSA was founded in 1927 and is headquartered at the ILO in Geneva. It brings together social security administrators, with 336 member organizations in 157 countries, and provides information, advice, standards and guidelines to members to improve social security administration.

The CESCR has further urged various international bodies to cooperate with states, 'building on their respective expertise', in implementing social security, namely the ILO, WHO, ISSA, UN Food and Agriculture Organization (FAO), the UN Children's Fund, the UN Human Settlements Programme, UN Development Programme and World Trade Organization.[92] The United Nations' 'Social Protection Floor' concept, discussed later, also deserves mention. The CESCR has called on international financial institutions, the World Bank and International Monetary Fund to take into account social security,[93] which may engage particular institutional standards and policies in that context.[94]

[87] Convention on the Rights of Persons with Disabilities (adopted 30 March 2007, 2515 UNTS 3, entered into force 3 May 2008), Articles 16(4), 26(1) and 28(2).

[88] International Convention on the Protection of Rights of Migrant Workers and their Families (adopted 18 December 1990, 2220 UNTS 3, entered into force 1 July 2003), Articles 27, 43, 45(1) and 54(1).

[89] International Convention for the Protection of All Persons from Enforced Disappearance (adopted 20 December 2006, UN Doc A/61/488, entered into force 23 December 2010), Article 24(6).

[90] UNGA Res. 61/295, Declaration on the Rights of Indigenous Peoples (13 September 2007), Articles 21, 23 and 24.

[91] CESCR, General Comment No. 19, [75].

[92] CESCR, General Comment No. 19, [82].

[93] CESCR, General Comment No. 19, [83].

[94] See further below.

REGIONAL STANDARDS

The CESCR has noted that the right to social security is found in some regional human rights systems,[95] although it is absent from the European Convention on Human Rights, the American Convention on Human Rights and the African Charter on Human and Peoples' Rights. Article 36 of the Arab Charter on Human Rights briefly recognizes that 'States parties shall ensure the right of every citizen to social security, including social insurance'. The right to social security is acknowledged in greater detail in Article 30 of the non-binding ASEAN Human Rights Declaration 2012, which mirrors elements of both Articles 9 and 10 of the ICESCR:

30. (1) Every person shall have the right to social security, including social insurance where available, which assists him or her to secure the means for a dignified and decent existence.

(2) Special protection should be accorded to mothers during a reasonable period as determined by national laws and regulations before and after childbirth. During such period, working mothers should be accorded paid leave or leave with adequate social security benefits.

(3) Motherhood and childhood are entitled to special care and assistance. Every child, whether born in or out of wedlock, shall enjoy the same social protection.

The most elaborate recognition of social security is found in the Americas and Europe. The earliest instrument of the Inter-American system, the American Declaration of the Rights and Duties of Man 1948, provides in Article 16 that:

Every person has the right to social security which will protect him from the consequences of unemployment, old age, and any disabilities arising from causes beyond his control that make it physically or mentally impossible for him to earn a living.

Social security is not mentioned in the subsequent American Convention on Human Rights 1978, which is primarily devoted to civil and political rights. At most, the Inter-American Court of Human Rights has indirectly protected social security by recognizing that public sector retirement pensions are acquired property rights and thus protected, under the right to property in Article 21 of the American Convention,[96] from arbitrary retrospective reductions.[97] The Court has not found it necessary to decide whether arbitrary reductions may also violate Article 26 of the Convention,[98] which requires states to progressively realize

[95] CESCR, General Comment No. 19, [6].

[96] American Convention on Human Rights (ACHR) (adopted 22 November 1969, OAS Treaty Series No. 36, entered into force 18 July 1978), Article 21 provides: '1. Everyone has the right to the use and enjoyment of his property. The law may subordinate such use and enjoyment to the interest of society. 2. No one shall be deprived of his property except upon payment of just compensation, for reasons of public utility or social interest, and in the cases and according to the forms established by law. 3. Usury and any other form of exploitation of man by man shall be prohibited by law.'

[97] *Case of the Five Pensioners v Peru* ('*Five Pensioners v Peru*'), 28 February 2003, IACHR Series C No. 98, [102]–[121].

[98] *Acevedo Buendia et al [Discharged and Retired Employees of the Comptroller] v Peru*, 1 July 2009, IACHR Series C No. 198 (IACHR), [106]–[107]. The Court found that arbitrary pension

economic, social and cultural rights in general[99] (without specifically mentioning social security).

The right to social security is, however, expressly protected in a later Inter-American instrument, Article 9 of the Additional Protocol to the American Convention on Human Rights in the Area of Economic Social and Cultural Rights 1988 (Protocol of San Salvador):

1. Everyone shall have the right to social security protecting him from the consequences of old age and of disability which prevents him, physically or mentally, from securing the means for a dignified and decent existence. In the event of the death of a beneficiary, social security benefits shall be applied to his dependents.

2. In the case of persons who are employed, the right to social security shall cover at least medical care and an allowance or retirement benefit in the case of work accidents or occupational disease and, in the case of women, paid maternity leave before and after childbirth.

It mentions some of the branches of social security common in ILO instruments, as well as aspects covered separately by Article 10(2) of the ICESCR (paid maternity leave).

While there is no right to social security in the ECHR,[100] which does not guarantee socio-economic rights,[101] the application of other ECHR rights has indirectly protected aspects of social security.[102] At the procedural level, the right to a fair 'civil' hearing (in Article 6) may apply to decisions involving domestic social security rights.[103] Substantively, as in the Inter-American system, domestic rights to social security have been protected through the right to property (as 'possessions'[104]) under Article 1 of the First Protocol to the ECHR.[105] Such protection has applied to contributory, employment-based benefits[106] and where an employer

reductions by Peru violated the right to property (Article 21) and the right to judicial protection (Article 25), including because the reductions were unlawful according to domestic court decisions.

[99] ACHR, Article 26.

[100] *Jazvinsky v Slovakia* (Apps. 33088/96, 52236/99, 52451/99-52453/99, 52455/99, 52457–52459/99), ECtHR 7 September 2000.

[101] *Panceno v Latvia*, 29 October 1999, ECtHR (Admissibility), [2].

[102] See generally Klaus Kapuy, Danny Pieters and Bernhard Zaglmayer, *Social Security Cases in Europe: The European Court of Human Rights* (Intersentia, Antwerp, 2007); Ida Elisabeth Koch, *Human Rights as Indivisible Rights: The Protection of Socio-Economic Rights under the European Convention on Human Rights* (Martinus Nijhoff, Leiden, 2009), 179–207; Ana Gómez Heredero, *Social Security as a Human Right: The Protection Afforded by the European Convention on Human Rights* (Council of Europe, 2007).

[103] *Feldbrugge v Netherlands* (App. 8562/79), 29 May 1986, (1986) 8 EHRR 425; *Lombardo v Italy* (App. 11519/85), 26 November 1992, (1992) 21 EHRR 188; *Salesi v Italy* (App. 13023/87), ECtHR 26 February 1993; *Schouten and Meldrum v Netherlands* (App. 19005/91), 9 December 1994, (1994) 19 EHRR 432.

[104] *Burdov v Russia* (App. 59498/00), 7 May 2002, (2002) 58 EHRR 29, [40]; *Teteriny v Russia* (App. 11931/03), ECtHR 30 June 2005.

[105] Protocol to the European Convention for the Protection of Human Rights and Fundamental Freedoms (adopted 20 March 1952, ETS No. 9, entered into force 18 May 1954), Article 1.

[106] *Gaygusuz v Austria* (App. 17371/90), 16 September 1996, (1996) 23 EHRR 364; *Azinas v Cyprus* (App. 56679/00), 20 June 2002, (2004) 40 EHRR 8, [34]; and also to contributions to a fund created by the state for the purpose of paying pensions: *Van Raalte v Netherlands* (App. 20060/92), 21 February 1997, (1997) 24 EHRR 503.

has a contractual obligation to pay a benefit.[107] More recently, it has also applied to non-contributory entitlements under domestic law.[108]

Further, social security entitlements have engaged the protection of the right to respect for private life or family life under Article 8, including in relation to discrimination in the provision of parental leave,[109] child benefits[110] or retirement pensions.[111] Finally, the European Court indicated in *Larioshina v Russia* that entirely inadequate social benefits 'may, in principle, raise an issue under Article 3 [of the ECHR]...which prohibits inhuman or degrading treatment', although on the facts of that case the low benefit amount provided to the applicant was not found to have 'caused such damage to her physical or mental health capable of attaining the minimum level of severity falling within the ambit of Article 3'.[112] In a different case, *R v Secretary of State for the Home Department, ex parte Adam*, the House of Lords in the United Kingdom found that the removal of subsistence support from asylum seekers exposed them to destitution and thus violated the prohibition on inhuman or degrading treatment under the ECHR.[113]

The most elaborate direct protection of social security is in the European Social Charter. The European Social Charter 1961 recognizes the rights to social security (Article 12), social and medical assistance (Article 13), and social welfare services (Article 14). Near-identical protections are found in the Revised European Social Charter 1996:

Article 12—The right to social security

With a view to ensuring the effective exercise of the right to social security, the Parties undertake:

1. to establish or maintain a system of social security;
2. to maintain the social security system at a satisfactory level at least equal to that necessary for the ratification of the European Code of Social Security;
3. to endeavour to raise progressively the system of social security to a higher level;
4. to take steps, by the conclusion of appropriate bilateral and multilateral agreements or by other means, and subject to the conditions laid down in such agreements, in order to ensure:
    (a) equal treatment with their own nationals of the nationals of other Parties in respect of social security rights, including the retention of benefits arising out of social security legislation, whatever movements the persons protected may undertake between the territories of the Parties;

[107] *Sture Stigson v Sweden* (App. 12264/86), 13 July 1988, Decisions and Reports 57 (European Commission on Human Rights), 131; *Azinas v Cyprus*, [34].

[108] *Stec et al v United Kingdom* (Apps. 65731/01, 65900/01), 6 July 2005, (2006) 43 EHRR 47, [54].

[109] *Petrovic v Austria* (App. 20458/92), 5 July 1995, (2001) 33 EHRR 14 (where only mothers, not fathers, were entitled to parental leave).

[110] *Niedzwiecki v Germany* (App. 58453/00), 25 October 2005 (2006) 42 EHRR 33 (where migrants were excluded).

[111] *Grant v United Kingdom* (App. 32570/03), 23 May 2006, (2007) 44 EHRR 1 (where a male to female transsexual was denied the female pension despite meeting the age requirement).

[112] *Larioshina v Russia* (App. 56869/00), 23 April 2002, (2002) 35 EHRR CD36, [3].

[113] *R v Secretary of State for the Home Department, ex parte Adam* [2005] UKHL 66, [7]–[9] (Lord Bingham).

(b) the granting, maintenance and resumption of social security rights by such means as the accumulation of insurance or employment periods completed under the legislation of each of the Parties.

Article 13—The right to social and medical assistance

With a view to ensuring the effective exercise of the right to social and medical assistance, the Parties undertake:

1. to ensure that any person who is without adequate resources and who is unable to secure such resources either by his own efforts or from other sources, in particular by benefits under a social security scheme, be granted adequate assistance, and, in case of sickness, the care necessitated by his condition;

2. to ensure that persons receiving such assistance shall not, for that reason, suffer from a diminution of their political or social rights;

3. to provide that everyone may receive by appropriate public or private services such advice and personal help as may be required to prevent, to remove, or to alleviate personal or family want;

4. to apply the provisions referred to in paragraphs 1, 2 and 3 of this article on an equal footing with their nationals to nationals of other Parties lawfully within their territories, in accordance with their obligations under the European Convention on Social and Medical Assistance, signed at Paris on 11 December 1953.

Article 14—The right to benefit from social welfare services

With a view to ensuring the effective exercise of the right to benefit from social welfare services, the Parties undertake:

1. to promote or provide services which, by using methods of social work, would contribute to the welfare and development of both individuals and groups in the community, and to their adjustment to the social environment;

2. to encourage the participation of individuals and voluntary or other organisations in the establishment and maintenance of such services.

While the European Social Charter and Revised Charter do not specify minimum benefit amounts, they require states to meet minimum external standards, work to progressively raise protection and treat foreigners as equal to their own nationals. Thus, the 1961 Charter requires states to establish and maintain a social security system 'at least equal to that required for ratification of' ILO Convention No. 102 (Article 12(2)). The key difference in the 1996 Revised Charter is that it requires states to maintain social security systems at a level at least equal to the European Code of Social Security (Article 12(2)).

The European Code of Social Security 1964 establishes higher minimum standards than ILO Convention No. 102[114] and has twenty-one ratifications (from forty-seven Council of Europe member states). It defines both minimum coverage

[114] European Code of Social Security ('European Code of Social Security 1964') (adopted 16 April 1964, ETS No. 48, entered into force 17 March 1968), preamble. See also Protocol to the European Code of Social Security (adopted 16 April 1964, ETS No. 48A, entered into force 17 March 1968).

and levels of protection in specified areas, and contains extensive provisions (running to eighty-three articles). Compared with the ILO instruments, it expands the categories of recipients, enhances the level and duration of benefits, and guarantees periodic payments.[115] Like the ILO instrument, however, it permits states discretion in selecting the branches of social security coverage and the classes of beneficiaries; is weighted towards the economically active;[116] and is based on gendered assumptions (such as 'man with wife and two children' as the baseline for calculating benefits).[117]

The Revised European Code of Social Security 1990 updates and improves the original Code, but has only one ratification and is not yet in force.[118] It further increases the rates of cover, extends the level and duration of benefits, includes new benefits, relaxes conditions for entitlements, and includes preventive and anti-discrimination measures. Both the Charter and Code are now subject to an integrated supervision mechanism.[119]

Finally, it may be briefly noted that Article 34 of the Charter of Fundamental Rights and Freedoms of the European Union also recognizes the 'entitlement' to social security:

> Social security and social assistance
>
> 1. The Union recognises and respects the entitlement to social security benefits and social services providing protection in cases such as maternity, illness, industrial accidents, dependency or old age, and in the case of loss of employment, in accordance with the rules laid down by Union law and national laws and practices.
>
> 2. Everyone residing and moving legally within the European Union is entitled to social security benefits and social advantages in accordance with Union law and national laws and practices.

Thus far, the European Union has not played an extensive role in social security, aside from its equality dimension and in the free movement of EU nationals.[120] The provision is likely to be interpreted in the light of the jurisprudence on Article 12 of the European Social Charter and ILO Convention No. 102.[121]

The Scope of State Obligations

In General Comment No. 19, the CESCR observes that, in the usual manner of socio-economic rights, the right to social security involves negative and positive

115 Lamarche, 'The Right to Social Security', 91.
116 Scheinin, 'The Right to Social Security', 218.
117 European Code of Social Security 1964, Part XI, Schedule.
118 European Code of Social Security (Revised) (adopted 6 November 1991, ETS No. 139, not yet in force).
119 In 2012, the supervision mechanisms for the European Social Charter and the European Code of Social Security were consolidated into a renamed entity, the Governmental Committee of the European Social Charter and the European Code of Social Security, which also considers the relevant ILO conclusions in monitoring states' compliance.
120 Jennifer Tooze, 'Social Security and Social Assistance' in Tamara Hervey and Jeff Kenner (eds), *Economic and Social Rights under the EU Charter of Fundamental Rights* (Hart, Oxford, 2003), 164.
121 Tooze, 'Social Security and Social Assistance', 161, 167.

dimensions and comprises obligations on the state to respect, protect and fulfil the right.[122]

THE OBLIGATION TO RESPECT

According to General Comment No. 19:

44. The obligation to respect requires that States parties refrain from interfering directly or indirectly with the enjoyment of the right to social security. The obligation includes, inter alia, refraining from engaging in any practice or activity that, for example, denies or limits equal access to adequate social security; arbitrarily or unreasonably interferes with self-help or customary or traditional arrangements for social security; arbitrarily or unreasonably interferes with institutions that have been established by individuals or corporate bodies to provide social security.[123]

In monitoring states, the CESCR has given scarce attention to any instances where states may have interfered in the provision of social security by private actors, cooperative or collective bodies, or traditional or customary institutions. In part, this is because most of the CESCR's attention has been focused instead on encouraging states to establish or promote social security, and to impose more (not less) regulation on private schemes.

It is not difficult, however, to envisage potential examples of interference, such as where a state imposes arbitrary, excessive or disproportionate taxation on social insurance schemes; imposes unreasonable regulatory burdens on charitable or religious organizations providing social assistance; arbitrarily withholds charitable status or tax privileges for organizations entitled to them; or expropriates without fair process or compensation the funds of a community scheme. Discriminatory state laws or practices which prohibit or restrict particular groups from participating in non-state arrangements, without an objective and legitimate basis, would also be incompatible with the duty to respect social security under Article 9.

THE OBLIGATION TO PROTECT

The state is also required to prevent third parties from interfering in the right to social security, as the CESCR explains:

45. The obligation to protect requires that State parties prevent third parties from interfering in any way with the enjoyment of the right to social security. Third parties include individuals, groups, corporations and other entities, as well as agents acting under their authority. The obligation includes, inter alia, adopting the necessary and effective legislative and other measures, for example, to restrain third parties from denying equal access to social security schemes operated by them or by others and imposing unreasonable eligibility conditions; arbitrarily or unreasonably interfering with self-help or customary or traditional arrangements for social security that are consistent with the right to social security; and failing to pay legally required contributions for employees or other beneficiaries into the social security system.

[122] CESCR, General Comment No. 19, [43].

[123] CESCR, General Comment No. 19, [44].

46. Where social security schemes, whether contributory or non-contributory, are operated or controlled by third parties, States parties retain the responsibility of administering the national social security system and ensuring that private actors do not compromise equal, adequate, affordable, and accessible social security. To prevent such abuses an effective regulatory system must be established which includes framework legislation, independent monitoring, genuine public participation and imposition of penalties for non-compliance.[124]

Article 9 leaves a choice of means to the state to decide whether to provide social security through a universal, publicly funded scheme, obligations on employers to administer contributory insurance schemes, other community methods, or a combination of the above. However, where a non-state scheme is provided by employers, or required by law, there is then an obligation on the state to regulate such schemes to ensure that they provide adequate, non-discriminatory, affordable and accessible social security.

In monitoring states, the CESCR criticized a government which did not interfere at all in the private sector, which employed most workers and where 'social security benefits are voluntary, depending on employers' whims'.[125] The CESCR was also concerned where states failed to ensure that employers register their workers with a national insurance scheme or send required information to the scheme;[126] or pay the legally required contributions for workers.[127] It has consequently called on states to strengthen the role of social security inspections to combat employer fraud.[128]

The CESCR has been concerned to ensure the accessibility and affordability of contributory social insurance schemes. It emphasized that contributions should be stipulated in advance and all direct and indirect costs and charges associated with making contributions must be affordable and not compromise the realization of other ICESCR rights.[129]

Where social security has been privatized, the CESCR has sometimes expressed concern about the inaccessibility of private schemes to certain vulnerable groups of workers, including agricultural or domestic workers and women,[130] and those who cannot contribute, such as the unemployed, underemployed, lower-paid workers and those in the informal sector.[131] It has also been concerned where privatized systems are financially unsustainable, leading to inadequate protection,[132]

124 CESCR, General Comment No. 19, [46].

125 CESCR, Concluding Observations: Nigeria, E/C.12/1/Add.23 (13 May 1998), [19].

126 CESCR, Concluding Observations: Saint Vincent and the Grenadines, E/C.12/1/Add.21 (2 December 1997), [19].

127 CESCR, Concluding Observations: Russia, E/C.12/1/Add.13 (15 May 1997), [22]; Saint Vincent and the Grenadines, E/C.12/1/Add.21 (2 December 1997), [19]; Ecuador, E/C.12/1/Add.100 (7 June 2004), [43].

128 CESCR, Concluding Observations: Ecuador, E/C.12/1/Add.100 (7 June 2004), [43].

129 CESCR, General Comment No. 19, [25].

130 CESCR, Concluding Observations: El Salvador, E/C.12/SLV/CO/2 (27 June 2007), [15].

131 CESCR, Concluding Observations: Mexico, E/C.12/1/Add.41 (8 December 1999), [24]; CESCR, Consideration of Report Submitted by State Party: Argentina, E/C.12/1994/20 (1994), [233].

132 CESCR, Concluding Observations: Zambia, E/C.12/1/Add.106 (23 June 2005), [22].

and has called for the safeguarding of pensioners' acquired rights.[133] The CESCR has also called on states to report on how they monitor private organizations using public funds,[134] and urged stronger monitoring.[135]

Privatization raises special difficulties for the accessibility and comprehensiveness of social security protection. Commercial private entities (as opposed to private non-profit organizations) are understandably concerned to profit from their business. To that end, they will instinctively prefer to selectively cover those workers from whom they are able to make money, and to avoid those who are either unprofitable or potentially loss-making. State intervention may be necessary to ensure that their profit imperative is balanced with social obligations to ensure the accessibility and affordability of social security, without imposing such burdensome requirements that the private schemes are no longer financially viable.

Given that private providers may also be restricted to the social insurance of workers, they may play no role at all in assisting those out of the workforce, including the unemployed, young people or family members. Thus, even adequate regulation of private entities may still require the state to provide complementary universal public social security, in order to fill the gaps left by private arrangements.

The obligation to protect may also require states to intervene in traditional or customary social security systems in certain circumstances. For example, a state would be justified in regulating a traditional or customary system which involved impermissible discrimination, such as sex or age discrimination in entitlements;[136] involved arbitrary exclusions; or which was tainted by fraud. Thus, the CESCR asked Uzbekistan to ensure that the powerful *Makhallas* (traditional citizens' organizations), which were responsible for social assistance payments, complied with criteria of equal treatment and transparency,[137] to ensure that all disadvantaged and marginalized persons were assisted.

THE OBLIGATION TO FULFIL

Perhaps the most challenging area for the CESCR's supervision of Article 9 concerns the obligation to fulfil, that is, the obligation on states to establish and implement a social security scheme, including by adopting the necessary laws and policies and allocating sufficient funding. In General Comment No. 19, the CESCR divides the obligation to fulfil into the obligations to facilitate, promote and provide social security:

47. The obligation to fulfil requires States parties to adopt the necessary measures, including the implementation of a social security scheme, directed towards the full realization of

[133] CESCR, Consideration of Report Submitted by State Party: Peru, E/1998/22 (1997), [161].

[134] CESCR, Concluding Observations: Luxembourg, E/C.12/1/Add.86 (23 May 2003), [35].

[135] CESCR, Concluding Observations: Zambia, E/C.12/1/Add.106 (23 June 2005), [44].

[136] See similarly Langford, 'The Right to Social Security', 39 (concerning resource and inheritance rights).

[137] CESCR, Concluding Observations: Uzbekistan, E/C.12/UZB/CO/1 (24 January 2006), [23] and [54].

the right to social security. The obligation to fulfil can be subdivided into the obligations to facilitate, promote and provide.

48. The obligation to facilitate requires States parties to take positive measures to assist individuals and communities to enjoy the right to social security. The obligation includes, inter alia, according sufficient recognition of this right within the national political and legal systems, preferably by way of legislative implementation; adopting a national social security strategy and plan of action to realize this right; ensuring that the social security system will be adequate, accessible for everyone and will cover social risks and contingencies.

49. The obligation to promote obliges the State party to take steps to ensure that there is appropriate education and public awareness concerning access to social security schemes, particularly in rural and deprived urban areas, or amongst linguistic and other minorities.

50. States parties are also obliged to provide the right to social security when individuals or a group are unable, on grounds reasonably considered to be beyond their control, to realize that right themselves, within the existing social security system with the means at their disposal. States parties will need to establish non-contributory schemes or other social assistance measures to provide support to those individuals and groups who are unable to make sufficient contributions for their own protection. Special attention should be given to ensuring that the social security system can respond in times of emergency, for example during and after natural disasters, armed conflict and crop failure.

51. It is important that social security schemes cover disadvantaged and marginalized groups, even where there is limited capacity to finance social security, either from tax revenues and/or contributions from beneficiaries. Low-cost and alternative schemes could be developed to cover immediately those without access to social security, although the aim should be to integrate them into regular social security schemes. Policies and a legislative framework could be adopted for the progressive inclusion of those in the informal economy or who are otherwise excluded from access to social security.[138]

Social security is accordingly not a right to be supported by the state in all circumstances. Rather, the state plays a role subsidiary or complementary to efforts by individuals and groups to provide for their own social security (such as through contributory, private or community schemes). The state steps in to provide it directly where a person is unable, on grounds reasonably beyond her or his control, to realize it him- or herself, within the means at her or his disposal. This includes where other methods of social security are inadequate.

Thus, in monitoring states, the CESCR has called for the state to provide assistance where traditional social support mechanisms, such as the *wantok* system in the Solomon Islands, have been eroded.[139] Community schemes may also be unable to cope with large communal risks, such as natural disasters or large-scale forced evictions,[140] or impoverishment resulting from industrialization.[141]

[138] CESCR, General Comment No. 19, [47]–[51].

[139] CESCR, Concluding Observations: Solomon Islands, E/C.12/1/Add.84 (19 December 2002), [9] and [22].

[140] Langford, 'The Right to Social Security', 42.

[141] Nussberger, 'Social Security, Right to, International Protection', [10].

Similarly, where private insurance schemes exclude those who are unable to contribute, the CESCR has urged states to establish targeted or universal non-contributory schemes to cover such persons.[142] The vulnerable or disadvantaged groups mentioned include seasonal and temporary workers, workers in the informal economy, casual workers, the self-employed, the unemployed, persons with disabilities, domestic workers, housewives, single parents, older persons, the homeless, victims of trafficking, street children, children in conflict with the law, and poor people and households.

The formulation and adoption of a national strategy, policy or plan on social security is an important step in ensuring that a state comprehensively addresses its Article 9 obligations. The CESCR has also been attentive to the procedural aspects of national policy:

69. The formulation and implementation of national social security strategies and plans of action should respect, inter alia, the principles of non-discrimination, gender equality and people's participation. The right of individuals and groups to participate in decision-making processes that may affect their exercise of the right to social security should be an integral part of any policy, programme or strategy concerning social security.

70. The national social security strategy and plan of action and its implementation should also be based on the principles of accountability and transparency. The independence of the judiciary and good governance are also essential to the effective implementation of all human rights.[143]

Indeed, a key advantage of a human-rights-based approach to social security is the focus on participation and accountability,[144] including in the administration of social security and the provision of information about it:

26. Beneficiaries of social security schemes must be able to participate in the administration of the social security system. The system should be established under national law and ensure the right of individuals and organizations to seek, receive and impart information on all social security entitlements in a clear and transparent manner.

The ILO has similarly observed that '[s]uccessful and sustainable social security systems are based on good governance, full accountability and participation of society at large in general, and workers' and employers' organizations in particular'.[145]

[142] CESCR, Concluding Observations: Chile, E/C.12/1/Add.105 (1 December 2004), [20] and [43]; Kenya, E/C.12/KEN/CO/1 (1 December 2008), [21]; Angola, E/C.12/AGO/CO/3 (1 December 2008), [23]; Brazil, E/C.12/BRA/CO/2 (12 June 2009), [19]; Cambodia, E/C.12/KHM/CO/1 (12 June 2009), [40]; Canada, E/C.12/CAN/CO/4, E/C.12/CAN/CO/5 (22 May 2006), [40]; Chad, E/C.12/TCD/CO/3 (16 December 2009), [18]; China: Hong Kong SAR, E/C.12/1/Add.58 (21 May 2001), [21] and [36]; Dominican Republic, E/C.12/1/Add.16 (12 December 1997), [38]; Jamaica, E/C.12/1/Add.75 (6 December 2001), [10] and [23].

[143] CESCR, General Comment No. 19, [69]–[70].

[144] Langford, 'The Right to Social Security', 31.

[145] ILO, Report VI, 26.

Implementation

OBLIGATIONS OF IMMEDIATE EFFECT

In fulfilling the right to social security, states bear certain obligations of immediate effect, while other measures are subject to progressive realization. According to the CESCR, non-discrimination and equality are obligations of immediate effect:

40. While the Covenant provides for progressive realization and acknowledges the constraints owing to the limits of available resources, the Covenant also imposes on States parties various obligations which are of immediate effect. States parties have immediate obligations in relation to the right to social security, such as the guarantee that the right will be exercised without discrimination of any kind (article 2, paragraph 2), ensuring the equal rights of men and women (article 3), and the obligation to take steps (article 2, paragraph 1) towards the full realization of articles 11, paragraph 1, and 12. Such steps must be deliberate, concrete and targeted towards the full realization of the right to social security.[146]

The non-discrimination requirement is considered further below, while Articles 11 and 12 are examined in subsequent chapters. Under Article 2(1), states enjoy some discretion in choosing the appropriate means, including legislation, for implementing Article 9:

66. In the implementation of their Covenant obligations, and in accordance with article 2, paragraph 1, of the Covenant, States parties are required to utilize 'all appropriate means, including particularly the adoption of legislative measures.' Every State party has a margin of discretion in assessing which measures are most suitable to meet its specific circumstances. The Covenant, however, clearly imposes a duty on each State party to take whatever steps are necessary to ensure that everyone enjoys the right to social security, as soon as possible.[147]

As a minimum, those steps require that a system be put in place, under domestic law, and supervised by the state, along with a reasonable national strategy and plan of action, to realize social security:

11. The right to social security requires, for its implementation, that a system, whether composed of a single scheme or variety of schemes, is available and in place to ensure that benefits are provided for the relevant social risks and contingencies. The system should be established under domestic law, and public authorities must take responsibility for the effective administration or supervision of the system.

…

67. States parties are obliged to adopt all appropriate measures such as legislation, strategies, policies and programmes to ensure that the specific obligations with regard to the right to social security will be implemented. Existing legislation, strategies and policies should be reviewed to ensure that they are compatible with obligations arising from the

[146] CESCR, General Comment No. 19, [40]. [147] CESCR, General Comment No. 19, [66].

right to social security, and should be repealed, amended or changed if inconsistent with Covenant requirements. Social security systems should also regularly be monitored to ensure their sustainability.

68. The duty to take steps clearly imposes on States parties an obligation to adopt a national strategy and plan of action to realize the right to social security, unless the State party can clearly show that it has a comprehensive social security system in place and that it reviews it regularly to ensure that it is consistent with the right to social security. The strategy and action plan should be reasonably conceived in the circumstances; take into account the equal rights of men and women and the rights of the most disadvantaged and marginalized groups; be based upon human rights law and principles; cover all aspects of the right to social security; set targets or goals to be achieved and the time-frame for their achievement, together with corresponding benchmarks and indicators, against which they should be continuously monitored; and contain mechanisms for obtaining financial and human resources. When formulating and implementing national strategies on the right to social security, States parties should avail themselves, if necessary, of the technical assistance and cooperation of the United Nations specialized agencies (see Part VI below).

…

72. States parties may find it advantageous to adopt framework legislation to implement the right to social security. Such legislation might include: (a) targets or goals to be attained and the time frame for their achievement; (b) the means by which the purpose could be achieved; (c) the intended collaboration with civil society, the private sector and international organizations; (d) institutional responsibility for the process; (e) national mechanisms for its monitoring; and (f) remedies and recourse procedures.

In its practice, the CESCR criticized a number of states for failing to establish basic social security systems, including Afghanistan:

26. The Committee notes with concern that the State party has not yet put into place a basic social security system and that therefore a large number of disadvantaged and marginalized individuals and groups, including older persons, self-employed persons, women, in particular single mothers, IDPs, returnees and refugees are not entitled to any protection (art. 9).

The Committee recommends that the State party design a national plan for social security and progressively supplement a social security scheme to ensure the protection of disadvantaged and marginalized groups. In this regard, the Committee encourages the State party to explore the possibilities of international cooperation in line with article 2, paragraph 1, of the Covenant and the Committee's general comment No. 19 (2008) on the right to social security.[148]

Likewise, the CESCR noted that the Democratic Republic of the Congo had been too slow to adopt a social security code:

24. The Committee notes with concern that although the State party recognizes the malfunctioning and extremely limited coverage of the social security system, insufficient measures have been taken to address the situation, as reflected in the very slow

[148] CESCR, Concluding Observations: Afghanistan, E/C.12/AFG/CO/2-4 (7 June 2010), [26].

process of adoption of a social security code and the lack of concrete measures taken to provide protection and assistance to the most disadvantaged and marginalized groups. (article 9)

> The Committee, while recognizing the difficulties of the State party, considers that budgetary constraints should not be invoked as the only justification for the lack of progress towards the establishment of a social security system. The Committee urges the State party to speed up the process of adoption of a social security code and the establishment of a sustainable social security system…[149]

The requirement to establish a national policy or plan, with appropriate indicators and benchmarks, will first require the collection of accurate data about poverty, as well as current social security expenditure. The CESCR has criticized states for failing to establish a national definition or threshold of poverty,[150] in relation to an adequate standard of living. Other bodies, such as the UN High Commissioner for Human Rights, have also developed model technical indicators on the right to social security, dealing with income security for workers, affordable health care access, family, child and dependent-adult support, and targeted social assistance schemes, each at the structural, process and outcome levels.[151]

The CESCR notes that over 80 per cent of the world's population lacks access to social security, of which 20 per cent live in extreme poverty.[152] Similarly, the ILO estimates that only about 20 per cent of the world's working-age population and their families have effective access to comprehensive social security; further, if 60 per cent of the world's population lives above the international poverty line of US$2 per day (thus presumptively enjoying basic social protection), then between 40 and 80 per cent of the world's population enjoys less than basic social protection.[153]

While some social security exists in all states, only a few provide it comprehensively across all nine ILO-defined 'branches' of assistance, at adequate levels, and to the whole population,[154] and most of those are high income states. Only between 1 and 2 per cent of the unemployed in Africa, Asia and the Middle East receive benefits. Even where social security is available, it is often limited to wage earners in the formal economy, excluding the majority in developing states: 'in a large part of the world where extreme poverty is high, the very

[149] CESCR, Concluding Observations: Democratic Republic of the Congo, E/C.12/COD/CO/4 (20 November 2009), [24].

[150] CESCR, Consideration of Report Submitted by State Party: Germany, E/2002/22 (2001), [669].

[151] OHCHR, Human Rights Indicators: A Guide to Measurement and Implementation (2012), 96 (based on the right to social security in Article 22 of the UDHR).

[152] CESCR, General Comment No. 19, [7]; see also ILO, Report VI, 32 ('Taking into account the non-economically active, only about 20 per cent of the world's working-age population (and their families) are estimated to have effective access to such comprehensive social security systems').

[153] ILO, World Social Security Report 2010/11: Providing Coverage in Times of Crisis ('World Social Security Report') (Geneva, 2010), 33.

[154] ILO, Report VI, 30; ILO, World Social Security Report, Executive Summary ('Only one-third of countries globally (inhabited by 28 per cent of the global population) have comprehensive social protection systems covering all branches of social security as defined in ILO Convention No. 102').

concept of "unemployment" seems to be irrelevant, as everybody has to work in order to survive'.[155] While 85 per cent of all those employed in developed states are employees, only around 20 per cent are in South Asia and sub-Saharan Africa, less than 40 per cent are in South East Asia and the Pacific, 40 per cent are in East Asia, and around 60 per cent are in North Africa, the Middle East, Latin America and the Caribbean.[156]

Unsurprisingly, the two most common criticisms that the CESCR has made of states under Article 9 are firstly that the coverage of social security is too restricted (both as regards the branches of assistance provided, and/or the groups that benefit), and secondly that the amount of benefits provided is inadequate. Before turning to these issues, it is first necessary to consider how the principles of 'progressive realization' and 'minimum core' obligations, discussed in the chapter on Article 2(1), apply to the right of social security.

PROGRESSIVE REALIZATION

The principle of progressive realization of socio-economic rights generally, and the concept of a minimum core of socio-economic rights, was considered in the earlier chapter on Article 2(1). The CESCR has applied these principles to social security, which raises its own issues:

> 4. In accordance with article 2(1), States parties to the Covenant must take effective measures, and periodically revise them when necessary, within their maximum available resources, to fully realize the right of all persons without any discrimination to social security, including social insurance. The wording of article 9 of the Covenant indicates that the measures that are to be used to provide social security benefits cannot be defined narrowly and, in any event, must guarantee all peoples a minimum enjoyment of this human right…
>
> …
>
> 41. The Committee acknowledges that the realization of the right to social security carries significant financial implications for States parties, but notes that the fundamental importance of social security for human dignity and the legal recognition of this right by States parties mean that the right should be given appropriate priority in law and policy. States parties should develop a national strategy for the full implementation of the right to social security, and should allocate adequate fiscal and other resources at the national level. If necessary, they should avail themselves of international cooperation and technical assistance in line with article 2, paragraph 1, of the Covenant.[157]

Under ILO Convention No. 102 on Social Security (Minimum Standards), resource constraints are accommodated by according states a choice in the number and combination of minimum branches of social security to be covered, as well as a choice in the scope of beneficiaries (typically 50 per cent of workers or 20 per cent of all residents). Minimum population coverage is further reduced

[155] ILO, World Social Security Report, Executive Summary.
[156] ILO, World Social Security Report, 27.
[157] CESCR, General Comment No. 19, [4] and [41].

for less developed states (Articles 15(d) and 27(d)). A state's obligations in financing social security are also to take into account its economic situation (Article 71).

In monitoring states, the CESCR has occasionally acknowledged the resource limitations facing states, as when it noted 'the decrease in the resources available' to Kyrgyzstan 'to fund social insurance, due to the need to reduce the national budget deficit'.[158] In relation to raising pensions to the minimum subsistence level in Russia, the CESCR observed that 'the realization of this goal may take time, owing to limited resources', but still urged the state to 'give priority to raising the minimum pension levels and to ensuring that social benefits are targeted to the families most in need'.[159] The CESCR acknowledged the budgetary difficulties facing the Democratic Republic of the Congo, but did not accept that they entirely justified the state's 'lack of progress towards the establishment of a social security system'.[160]

The CESCR has frequently called on states to increase funding to social security,[161] often without reference to the economic situation of the state. It sometimes qualifies its call on states by asking them to take all necessary measures to the maximum of their available resources,[162] or to 'progressively' increase social security funding or extend coverage.[163] It criticized one state for failing to restore social security to the level of a decade earlier 'in spite of the sustained economic growth in the State party during these last years'.[164] However, the CESCR has rarely directed states as to precisely how much they should spend on social security, for instance as a proportion of gross domestic product (GDP). As discussed later, however, the principle of progressive realization cannot justify impermissible discrimination in the provision of social security where it does exist.

As with other ICESCR rights, the principle of progressive realization also contains a presumption against retrogressive measures in social security, as the CESCR observes:

> 42. There is a strong presumption that retrogressive measures taken in relation to the right to social security are prohibited under the Covenant. If any deliberately retrogressive measures are taken, the State party has the burden of proving that they have been introduced

[158] CESCR, Concluding Observations: Kyrgyzstan, E/C.12/1/Add.49 (1 September 2000), [20].

[159] CESCR, Concluding Observations: Russia, E/C.12/1/Add.94 (12 December 2003), [50].

[160] CESCR, Concluding Observations: Democratic Republic of the Congo, E/C.12/COD/CO/4 (20 November 2009), [24].

[161] CESCR, Concluding Observations: Iceland, E/C.12/1/Add.32 (12 May 1999), [20]; Bosnia and Herzegovina, E/C.12/BIH/CO/1 (24 January 2006), [38]; Macedonia, E/C.12/MKD/CO/1 (15 January 2008), [38]; Russia, E/C.12/1/Add.13 (15 May 1997), [36]; Hungary, E/C.12/HUN/CO/3 (16 January 2008), [41].

[162] CESCR, Concluding Observations: Syria, E/C.12/1/Add.63 (24 September 2001), [39]; Ukraine, E/C.12/UKR/CO/5 (4 January 2008), [41].

[163] CESCR, Concluding Observations: Angola, E/C.12/AGO/CO/3 (1 December 2008), [23]; Kenya, E/C.12/KEN/CO/1 (1 December 2008), [20]–[21]; Afghanistan, E/C.12/AFG/CO/2-4 (7 June 2010), [26].

[164] CESCR, Concluding Observations: Canada, E/C.12/CAN/CO/4-5 (22 May 2006), [20].

after the most careful consideration of all alternatives and that they are duly justified by reference to the totality of the rights provided for in the Covenant, in the context of the full use of the maximum available resources of the State party. The Committee will look carefully at whether: (a) there was reasonable justification for the action; (b) alternatives were comprehensively examined; (c) there was genuine participation of affected groups in examining the proposed measures and alternatives; (d) the measures were directly or indirectly discriminatory; (e) the measures will have a sustained impact on the realization of the right to social security, an unreasonable impact on acquired social security rights or whether an individual or group is deprived of access to the minimum essential level of social security; and (f) whether there was an independent review of the measures at the national level.[165]

Thus, the CESCR criticized Canada's restriction of eligibility criteria and benefit amounts:

20. The Committee is concerned that newly-introduced successive restrictions on unemployment insurance benefits have resulted in a dramatic drop in the proportion of unemployed workers receiving benefits to approximately half of previous coverage, in the lowering of benefit rates, in reductions in the length of time for which benefits are paid and in increasingly restricted access to benefits for part-time workers. While the new programme is said to provide better benefits for low-income families with children, the fact is that fewer low-income families are eligible to receive any benefits at all. Part-time, young, marginal, temporary and seasonal workers face more restrictions and are frequently denied benefits, although they contribute significantly to the fund.

21. The Committee received information to the effect that cuts of about 10 per cent in social assistance rates for single people have been introduced in Manitoba; 35 per cent in those for single people in Nova Scotia; and 21.6 per cent in those for both families and single people in Ontario. These cuts appear to have had a significantly adverse impact on vulnerable groups, causing increases in already high levels of homelessness and hunger.[166]

The CESCR was also concerned by the reduction in social security as a result of Sweden's financial difficulties:

9. The Committee notes that many of the Government's social welfare programmes have been curtailed in response to the changed economic conditions. In this regard, the Committee notes with concern the adverse impact of the economic recession on the living conditions of the most vulnerable groups.

12. The Committee encourages the Government to continue to take adequate measures to ensure that the reduction of the Government's social welfare programmes do not result in a violation of the State party's obligations under the Covenant.[167]

The provision of a comprehensive, adequate and universal social security system evidently requires the mobilization of considerable resources. Over 17 per cent of global GDP is already allocated to social security (and more in developed states, such as 25 per cent in the European Union).[168] Most of that is concentrated in high

[165] CESCR, General Comment No. 19, [42].
[166] CESCR, Concluding Observations: Canada, E/C.12/1/Add.31 (10 December 1998), [20]–[21].
[167] CESCR, Concluding Observations: Sweden, E/C.12/1995/5 (7 June 1995), [9] and [12].
[168] ILO, World Social Security Report, 3.

income states (for instance, Europe spends 25 per cent of GDP on social security), with inadequate levels of assistance and gaps in coverage elsewhere (for example, African states spend less than 6 per cent of GDP, and most of that is on health care rather than social assistance).[169] Low-income countries spend on average under 4 per cent of GDP, middle-income countries 7 to 10 per cent, and high-income countries 20 per cent.[170] Most is spent on health care in low-income countries, and old age pensions in other countries.[171]

Even countries with the same level of overall government spending allocate quite different proportions of their resources to social security, which is the result of 'different, often historically influenced societal preferences' and the prevailing political and social will of governments, taxpayers and voters.[172] Such disparities suggest that the full and global realization of social security requires substantial additional investments, even if global spending has gradually increased over time.[173]

The affordability of social security, and thus the capacity of states to progressively realize it, must be assessed in the light of a number of relevant factors. First, the burden of funding social security does not fall on public finances alone, and indeed the state's burden may be proportionately small. In developed states where social security is most comprehensive, most of it is funded by contributory social insurance schemes rather than by public social assistance, as in the European Union, where means-tested benefits amount to less than 3 per cent of GDP, while total social protection is over 25 per cent.[174] Thus, a well-functioning social security system need not unduly burden public finances, but can play a subsidiary role in filling gaps where vulnerable individuals are unable to self-insure or otherwise support themselves.

Secondly, even in developing states where finances are limited, the ILO argues that 'a minimum package of social security is affordable even in the poorest countries', as in low-income African states, where the initial annual cost of such protection (excluding health care) would be 2.2 to 5.7 per cent of GDP.[175] If those economics are right, a minimum core of social security (discussed further below) is always affordable and the principle of progressive realization cannot justify a state's choice not to provide it. Globally, the ILO estimated in 2010 that a basic global Social Floor Protection package would cost US$46 billion per year, lifting 442 million people out of severe poverty, and representing 38 per cent of Official Development Assistance in 2009.[176]

Thirdly, the capacity to fund social security is sometimes not limited by an absolute scarcity of resources, but by a failure to prioritize social security spending or to mobilize resources that are available. Thus, the CESCR regretted that Senegal spent more on its military and servicing its debt than on basic social services;[177]

[169] ILO, Report VI, 36.
[170] ILO, Report VI, 37.
[171] ILO, Report VI, 38.
[172] ILO, Report VI, 40.
[173] Such as Argentina, Brazil, Chile, India, Indonesia, Mexico, South Africa, Uruguay, Botswana, Mauritius, Namibia, South Korea, Thailand: ILO, Report VI, 25.
[174] ILO, Report VI, 2.
[175] ILO, Report VI, 96.
[176] ILO, Report VI, 100.
[177] CESCR, Concluding Observations: Senegal, E/C.12/1/Add.62 (24 September 2001), [23].

called on Morocco to introduce direct, progressive taxation to fund social security;[178] and welcomed Guatemala's intention to reform its fiscal and monetary policy as a means of promoting social and economic development and resourcing social welfare.[179] International assistance to provide social security is another potential source of funding; as is broadening the revenue base and better enforcing taxation collection and strengthening good governance (to reduce corruption and enhance efficiency).[180] The CESCR also observed that the lack of adequate financial resources to pay pensioners in Russia was due to the serious failure of enterprises to make their legal contributions.[181]

Fourthly, while the right to social security is not chiefly designed as an instrument of economic policy, but aims to secure human dignity, a well-functioning social security system may also produce ancillary economic dividends. As such, social security should not be simplistically understood as a drain on state resources, but as potentially contributing to economic productivity, which in turn has implications for assessing progressive realization. As the ILO General Conference concluded in 2001:

> 3. Social security, if properly managed, enhances productivity by providing health care, income security and social services. In conjunction with a growing economy and active labour market policies, it is an instrument for sustainable social and economic development. It facilitates structural and technological changes which require an adaptable and mobile labour force. It is noted that while social security is a cost for enterprises, it is also an investment in, or support for, people. With globalization and structural adjustment policies, social security becomes more necessary than ever.[182]

The positive economic effects of social security arise in a range of ways. According to the ILO, social security benefits can boost consumer demand; promote investment, competition, jobs and growth; improve trade imbalances; reduce the social and health costs of poverty; assist the recovery of ill or injured workers; facilitate workforce renewal and productivity through retirement; improve vocational education, training and skills; and mitigate the transaction costs of economic and labour market adjustments, or stabilize economic and social crises.[183] Targeted measures can also improve women's participation in the labour force and empower women workers, including by assisting workers with family responsibilities to attain a better work/life balance, and increasing the affordability of essential services such as child care.[184] If benefits are well designed, they need not undermine employment or labour market participation, or foster welfare dependency.[185]

[178] CESCR, Concluding Observations: Morocco, E/C.12/1994/5 (30 May 1994), [19].
[179] CESCR, Concluding Observations: Guatemala, E/C.12/1/Add.3 (28 May 1996), [25].
[180] ILO, Report VI, 97–104, 109.
[181] CESCR, Consideration of Report Submitted by State Party: Russian Federation, E/1998/22 (1997), [108].
[182] ILO, Conclusions concerning Social Security, [3]; see also ILO, Social Security: A New Consensus (Geneva, 2001), chapter 2.
[183] ILO, Report VI, 16–21; ILO, Social Security: A New Consensus, 45–6.
[184] ILO, Report VI, 16–21; ILO, Social Security: A New Consensus, 45–6.
[185] ILO, Report VI, 19.

The OECD, too, has noted that social protection 'stimulates the involvement of poor women and men in economic growth…helps build human capital, manage risks, promote investment and entrepreneurship and improve participation in labour markets'.[186] The G20 has also supported the role of social security in good economic management.[187] Social security can be conducive to development even in low-income states.[188]

There is, however, a lack of strong empirical evidence of a causal link between social security and positive economic performance.[189] There is certainly a correlation between extensive social security systems, low poverty levels, and successful economies in certain industrialized states (particularly in Scandinavia).[190] But policy disagreement remains: the World Bank, for instance, has not endorsed social security as a human right and has instead approached it as a matter of discretionary policy or charity.[191]

The over-extension of unaffordable social security systems can itself have negative impacts on social security protection over time and/or on the realization of other human rights. For this reason, an important aspect of the affordability of a social security system is its sustainability over time, as the CESCR observes:

> 11. …The schemes should also be sustainable, including those concerning provision of pensions, in order to ensure that the right can be realized for present and future generations to take steps to the 'maximum of available resources' under an optional protocol to the Covenant (E/C.12/2007/1).

The integrity of social security systems also matters to its sustainability. The ILO explains:

> 92. …Benefits are considered adequate if they are neither too low nor too high…Cash benefits may be considered too high if they result in expenditure levels or behaviour detrimental to the common good or to acceptance by the public of the scheme itself.
>
> …
>
> 102. If benefit levels lead to expenditure that is not acceptable to the active generation financing them, the scheme itself is in jeopardy. *Economic adequacy* of benefits thus requires levels and entitlement conditions to be acceptable to contributors and taxpayers. Affordability and financial sustainability are always a concern, along with adequacy of coverage and of benefit levels: achieving minimum standards should happen 'as soon as possible' and 'as rapidly as national conditions allow'. Actually, it is quite clear that financial affordability and sustainability, on the one hand, and adequacy of benefit provision (in terms of amounts paid and of people effectively reached and protected), on the other, are two sides of the same coin. Only meaningful benefits effectively covering those in need can create a willingness among contributors and/or taxpayers to finance the various policies; inadequacy (and/or bad governance)—as too many examples in the history of social security show—undermine

[186] OECD Development Assistance Committee, The Role of Employment and Social Protection: Making Economic Growth More Pro-Poor—Policy Statement (Development Assistance Committee High-Level Meeting, Paris, 27–28 May 2009), 11.

[187] ILO, Report VI, 16.

[188] ILO, Report VI, 39; ILO, Social Security: A New Consensus, 53.

[189] ILO, Report VI, 109.

[190] ILO, Report VI, 22–3.

[191] Lamarche, 'The Right to Social Security', 97.

sustainability, as willingness to finance such programmes quickly erodes. Furthermore, the financing of benefits, by whatever means, should be equitable and affordable to all protected persons; in particular, the need to pay taxes or contributions to finance future benefits should not be a cause of 'hardship' for people on low incomes.[192]

The CESCR has not prescribed minimum percentages of GDP which individual states or particular groups of states should spend on social security. Certainly, a universal number would not be feasible given the diverse mix of public and private, and contributory and non-contributory, methods for financing it. The CESCR has, however, called on states to report to it on the GDP percentage they allocate to social security.[193]

MINIMUM CORE OBLIGATIONS

Given the potential importance of social security to a person's subsistence and, in extreme cases of destitution, to freedom from inhuman or degrading treatment and the right to life, the CESCR has identified a 'minimum core' to the right to social security, the non-fulfilment of which cannot be excused by a plea of resource limitations. The CESCR thus notes:

59. States parties have a core obligation to ensure the satisfaction of, at the very least, minimum essential levels of each of the rights enunciated in the Covenant. This requires the State party:

(a) To ensure access to a social security scheme that provides a minimum essential level of benefits to all individuals and families that will enable them to acquire at least essential health care, basic shelter and housing, water and sanitation, foodstuffs, and the most basic forms of education. If a State party cannot provide this minimum level for all risks and contingencies within its maximum available resources, the Committee recommends that the State party, after a wide process of consultation, select a core group of social risks and contingencies;

(b) To ensure the right of access to social security systems or schemes on a non-discriminatory basis, especially for disadvantaged and marginalized individuals and groups;

(c) To respect existing social security schemes and protect them from unreasonable interference;

(d) To adopt and implement a national social security strategy and plan of action;

(e) To take targeted steps to implement social security schemes, particularly those that protect disadvantaged and marginalized individuals and groups;

(f) To monitor the extent of the realization of the right to social security.

60. In order for a State party to be able to attribute its failure to meet at least its minimum core obligations to a lack of available resources, it must demonstrate that every effort has

[192] ILO, Report VI, 35.

[193] CESCR, Concluding Observations: Zambia, E/C.12/1/Add.106 (23 June 2005), [21].

been made to use all resources that are at its disposal in an effort to satisfy, as a matter of priority, these minimum obligations.[194]

The core obligations so identified nonetheless remain slippery. On the one hand, the CESCR requires states to provide the benefits necessary to guarantee basic subsistence rights (at paragraph 59(a) above), but in the next sentence allows for states which cannot provide a 'minimum essential level of benefits' to 'select a core group of social risks and contingencies' after consulting widely. There is thus an ill-defined lower minimum within a better defined higher minimum—even though the higher minimum itself is pegged at a very low level, namely the provision of subsistence rights (plus basic education).

This approach replicates the selectivity embedded in the ILO regime, which enables a state to select which treaties, and often which provisions within treaties, it wishes to be bound by. The ILO regime also builds in explicit concessions for resource scarcity. For example, Article 3 of Convention No. 102 allows a state to temporarily follow less stringent conditions concerning the duration of benefits and categories of protected persons where the state has insufficient economic or medical capacity.

The CESCR's indication that poor states may choose a narrow group of core risks and contingencies raises problems in a human rights instrument. The CESCR does not provide further guidance on whether particular social risks and contingencies must always be provided for (for instance, can housing be dispensed with as long as food is provided?), or whether a certain combination of risks must always be addressed (water and food, but not water and housing without food?). The choice is seemingly left to states, although admittedly subject to the requirements of other ICESCR rights (especially Articles 11 and 12) and ICCPR rights (particularly the right to life and freedom from inhuman or degrading treatment), which are presumably autonomous rights not subject to financing by social security under Article 9.

The selection or prioritization of a core group of social risks and contingencies also brings tension with the CESCR's wide approach to non-discrimination in social security. Prioritization involves picking winners and losers, and some of the losers may include groups prima facie protected against discrimination under the ICESCR and ICCPR. According to the jurisprudence of the UN treaty bodies, a measure which differentiates will not be impermissibly discriminatory if it is based on reasonable, legitimate and objective grounds.[195] The question is whether resource scarcity can provide the state with a legitimate justification for discriminating between different groups in prioritizing social security.

For instance, if funds are limited, is it lawful to deny aged care pensions to fund adequate disability insurance, or deny maternity leave to fund adequate workers' compensation? Or should the state spread around its resources so that all groups receive some—but perhaps then terribly inadequate—assistance? The CESCR's requirement of 'wide' consultation may socially legitimize particular choices, but

[194] CESCR, General Comment No. 19, [59]–[60].

[195] See the earlier chapter on non-discrimination under Article 2(2) of the ICESCR.

that does not necessarily mean that such choices are rights-based as opposed to political ones. Issues concerning states' coverage of the nine branches of social security, and the groups entitled to assistance, are considered subsequently.

In practice, however, the CESCR has seldom expressly accepted claims by particular states that they are unable to afford to fund basic social security. Instead, it has tended to routinely call on states to expand their areas of coverage, the groups entitled to assistance, and the amount of benefits provided. It has not lightly accepted claims of resource scarcity.

ADEQUACY OF BENEFITS

The adequacy of the amount of benefits is critically related to a state's minimum core obligations, the principle of progressive realization, and the affordability and accessibility of social security. Benefits that are too low may fail to provide a minimum subsistence or dignified standard of living; benefits that are too high may be unaffordable and thus compromise the accessibility of social security to a wider range of beneficiaries.

The CESCR has emphasized that benefits (in cash or kind) must be 'adequate in amount and duration' to realize the other ICESCR rights which may depend on social security. There is also a procedural requirement to continually monitor the adequacy of benefits:

> 22. Benefits, whether in cash or in kind, must be adequate in amount and duration in order that everyone may realize his or her rights to family protection and assistance, an adequate standard of living and adequate access to health care, as contained in articles 10, 11 and 12 of the Covenant. States parties must also pay full respect to the principle of human dignity contained in the preamble of the Covenant, and the principle of non-discrimination, so as to avoid any adverse effect on the levels of benefits and the form in which they are provided. Methods applied should ensure the adequacy of benefits. The adequacy criteria should be monitored regularly to ensure that beneficiaries are able to afford the goods and services they require to realize their Covenant rights. When a person makes contributions to a social security scheme that provides benefits to cover lack of income, there should be a reasonable relationship between earnings, paid contributions, and the amount of relevant benefit.[196]

In assessing states, the CESCR has frequently called to ensure that recipients receive benefits which provide them with an 'adequate',[197] 'reasonable'[198] or 'decent'[199] standard of living, or a standard of living consistent with Articles 9

[196] CESCR, General Comment No. 19, [22].

[197] CESCR, Concluding Observations: Italy, E/C.12/1/Add.103 (14 December 2004), [52]; Kazakhstan, E/C.12/KAZ/CO/1 (7 June 2010), [24]; Lithuania, E/C/12/1/Add.96 (7 June 2004), [16]; Morocco, E/C.12/MAR/CO/3 (4 September 2006), [22]; Netherlands Antilles, E/C.12/NLD/CO/3/Add.1 (31 January 2008), [16]; Serbia and Montenegro, E/C.12/1/Add.108 (23 June 2005), [47].

[198] CESCR, Concluding Observations: Hong Kong SAR, E/C.12/1/Add.58 (21 May 2001), [39]; Latvia, E/C.12/LVA/CO/1 (7 January 2008), [20].

[199] CESCR, Concluding Observations: China, E/C.12/1/Add.107 (13 May 2005), [84]; Latvia, E/C.12/LVA/CO/1 (7 January 2008), [20]; San Marino, E/C.12/SMR/CO/4 (4 January 2008), [14] and [26].

and 11 of the ICESCR.[200] Sometimes the CESCR has referred to the need for benefits not to fall below 'the minimum income poverty line'[201] or to be sufficient 'to enable the recipients to combat poverty'.[202] The CESCR has also criticized benefits which are 'far below the minimum level of subsistence'[203] and called for benefits not to fall below subsistence level[204] or to be raised 'to a level closer to the subsistence minimum'.[205] It has occasionally referred to benefit levels which are not sufficient to enable a family 'to acquire the basic food basket',[206] a concept it commonly utilizes in respect of the fair minimum wage under Article 7 of the ICESCR.[207] The CESCR has also challenged a state's own definition of the minimum subsistence level, as when it declared it too low in Suriname and called for it to be redefined to ensure recipients receive an adequate level of assistance.[208]

The CESCR has occasionally addressed the adequacy of benefits in special areas. Thus, childcare benefits must be sufficient 'to cover the cost of bringing up a child'.[209] Where benefits are victims compensation for past wrongs, the CESCR has invoked a more subjective standard. Thus, compensation from a private fund to 'comfort women' forced into prostitution by Japan during the Second World War was not 'deemed an acceptable measure by the women concerned' and the CESCR urged compensation which would 'meet their expectations'.[210]

While the CESCR frequently criticizes the inadequacy of benefits, it rarely stipulates a particular level of benefit that a given state should provide. But there are some examples. The CESCR stated that unemployment benefits in Estonia, which were calculated at 50 per cent of the amount earned in a previous job, 'may in some cases be inadequate to secure a decent standard of living for a worker and his/her family'.[211] That would particularly be the case for those whose wages when working were low. The CESCR accordingly called on the state 'to ensure that the lowest level of unemployment benefit is sufficient to secure a decent standard of living'.[212] In another instance, benefits amounting to 50 per cent of the minimum subsistence level in Ukraine did not enable an adequate standard of living.[213] Elsewhere, the CESCR found that a retirement pension of 500 dirhams was inadequate in Morocco.[214]

[200] CESCR, Concluding Observations: Latvia, E/C.12/LVA/CO/1 (7 January 2008), [20].

[201] CESCR, Concluding Observations: Ireland, E/C.12/1/Add.35 (14 May 1999), [13].

[202] CESCR, Concluding Observations: Netherlands Antilles, E/C.12/NLD/CO/3/Add.1 (31 January 2008), [16].

[203] CESCR, Concluding Observations: Georgia, E/C.12/1/Add.83 (19 December 2002), [17].

[204] CESCR, Concluding Observations: Latvia, E/C.12/LVA/CO/1 (7 January 2008), [45]; Azerbaijan, E/C.12/1/Add.104 (14 December 2004), [48].

[205] CESCR, Concluding Observations: Georgia, E/C.12/1/Add.83 (19 December 2002), [35].

[206] CESCR, Concluding Observations: El Salvador, E/C.12/SLV/CO/2 (27 June 2007), [16].

[207] See the earlier chapter on Article 7.

[208] CESCR, Concluding Observations: Suriname, E/C.12/1995/6 (7 June 1995), [19].

[209] CESCR, Concluding Observations: Ireland, E/C.12/1/Add.35 (14 May 1999), [13].

[210] CESCR, Concluding Observations: Japan, E/C.12/1/Add.67 (24 September 2001), [26] and [53].

[211] CESCR, Concluding Observations: Estonia, E/C.12/1/Add.85 (29 November 2002), [17].

[212] CESCR, Concluding Observations: Estonia, E/C.12/1/Add.85 (29 November 2002), [40].

[213] CESCR, Concluding Observations: Ukraine, E/C.12/UKR/CO/5 (4 January 2008), [18] and [41].

[214] CESCR, Concluding Observations: Morocco, E/C.12/MAR/CO/3 (4 September 2006), [22].

Otherwise, the CESCR tends to indicate certain factors which result in inadequacy. Thus, in Lithuania it was concerned about the 'absence of a system of indexing basic pensions to the consumer price index' and called for indexing to be introduced and to reflect 'changes in the cost of living'.[215] It was likewise concerned that high inflation in Azerbaijan destroyed the purchasing power of pensions and social insurance.[216]

ADEQUACY AND ILO AND UN STANDARDS

As noted earlier, the CESCR has often called on states to ratify ILO Convention No. 102 and other ILO conventions. However, in monitoring states' implementation of Article 9, the CESCR has generally not invoked the technical standards in those conventions for determining benefit amounts.

In general, the ILO conventions set minimum benefit levels as a proportion of previous earnings (for an employee) or the average national wage for unqualified male labour (for non-earnings-related benefits), and aim to 'be sufficient to maintain the family of the beneficiary in health and decency'.[217] The proportions required vary between 40 and 60 per cent across different conventions and different branches of social security, with rates lower under Convention No. 102 and higher in later conventions. The advantage of the ILO approach is that it locks in 'a long term and stable legal commitment that Member States must respect'[218] and is less vulnerable to 'political interference over the definition of appropriateness'.[219]

However, the ILO rates do not necessarily enable a state to meet its obligation under Article 9 of the ICESCR to provide a level of social security that ensures an adequate standard of living. The ILO model assumes that wages already fulfil or exceed basic needs[220] and is designed to preserve a worker's standard of living relative to their previous standard of living.[221] Yet, for earnings-based benefits, the ILO rates may be inadequate where a person's wages were too low. Similarly, where average national wages are low relative to the cost of living, then benefits based on a proportion of such wages will be even lower. In both situations, the ILO standards may leave a person in poverty or below subsistence levels;[222] in other cases, the ILO rates may keep a person alive, but not able to lead a dignified life.[223]

The ILO is aware of these limitations and is taking them into account in proposals for future standard-setting on social security, discussed below. More

[215] CESCR, Concluding Observations: Lithuania, E/C/12/1/Add.96 (7 June 2004), [16] and [38]; see also Latvia, E/C.12/LVA/CO/1 (7 January 2008), [45].
[216] CESCR, Concluding Observations: Azerbaijan, E/C.12/1/Add.20 (22 December 1997), [21].
[217] ILO Convention No. 102 concerning Social Security, Article 67.
[218] Lamarche, 'The Right to Social Security', 94.
[219] Lamarche, 'The Right to Social Security', 94.
[220] Lamarche, 'The Right to Social Security', 94. [221] ILO, Report VI, 35.
[222] ILO, Report VI, 35. [223] Langford, 'The Right to Social Security', 33–4.

broadly, the ILO recognizes the relative and context-dependent nature of what is adequate in a given situation:

94. A variety of reference variables may be used to assess adequacy of a given benefit, depending on the policy objectives being pursued. These variables include poverty lines, earnings or overall income levels (individual or average). Clearly, the choice of benchmark depends on the type of programme and on the country's socio-economic context. The notion of adequacy can have a different meaning for social insurance benefits financed from contributions and giving rise to acquired rights, or for basic, universal or social assistance schemes largely financed through general taxation or donor sources.[224]

In relation to the right to social security in Article 12 of the European Social Charter 1961, the European Committee on Social Rights has stated that:

To be considered as adequate, the level of benefit should in cases of wage substitution, whether temporary or permanent, always stand in a reasonable relation to the wage in question and should in any event exceed the minimum subsistence level. In particular, the income of the elderly should not be one of minimum assistance.[225]

Rather than stipulating minimum technical standards, the CESCR has required states, as part of their national framework for implementing Article 9, to develop social security 'indicators' against which they and the CESCR can assess their performance, and further to cooperatively develop performance targets. Indicators are not limited to the question of adequacy of benefits, but are an obvious context in which it arises:

74. States parties are obliged to monitor effectively the realization of the right to social security and should establish the necessary mechanisms or institutions for such a purpose. In monitoring progress towards the realization of the right to social security, States parties should identify the factors and difficulties affecting implementation of their obligations.

75. To assist the monitoring process, right to social security indicators should be identified in national strategies or plans of action in order that the State party's obligations under article 9 can be monitored at the national and international levels. Indicators should address the different elements of social security (such as adequacy, coverage of social risks and contingencies, affordability and accessibility), be disaggregated on the prohibited grounds of discrimination, and cover all persons residing in the territorial jurisdiction of the State party or under its control. States parties may obtain guidance on appropriate indicators from the ongoing work of the International Labour Organization (ILO), World Health Organization (WHO) and International Social Security Association (ISSA).

76. Having identified appropriate indicators for the right to social security, States parties are invited to set appropriate national benchmarks. During the periodic reporting procedure, the Committee will engage in a process of 'scoping' with States parties. Scoping involves the joint consideration by States parties and the Committee of the indicators and national benchmarks which will then provide the targets to be achieved during the next reporting period. In the following five years, the States parties will use these national benchmarks to help monitor their implementation of the right to social security. Thereafter, in

[224] ILO, Report VI, 35.

[225] European Committee of Social Rights (ECSR), Statement of Interpretation: Article 12, Conclusions XVI-1 vol. 1 (30 May 2003).

the subsequent reporting process, States parties and the Committee will consider whether or not the benchmarks have been achieved, and the reasons for any difficulties that may have been encountered. When setting benchmarks and preparing their reports, States parties should utilize the extensive information and advisory services of the United Nations specialized agencies and programmes.[226]

The CESCR refers to the technical work of the ILO, WHO and ISSA. It should also be noted that the ILO has invoked the UN-led concept of a 'Social Protection Floor' (SPF) in the context of socio-economic rights generally and social security specifically. The SPF was developed by the UN Chief Executives Board for Coordination in collaboration with other international organizations (including the ILO and WHO) and endorsed by the UN Summit on the Millennium Development Goals in 2010 as a contribution to development:[227]

The term 'social floor' or 'Social Protection Floor' (SPF) is used to describe a basic set of social rights, services and facilities that every person should enjoy. The term 'social floor' corresponds in many ways to the existing notion of 'core obligations', to ensure the realization of minimum essential levels of rights embodied in human rights treaties.

The United Nations suggests that a social protection floor could consist of two main elements that help to realize human rights:

– services: geographical and financial access to essential services such as water and sanitation, health, and education;

– transfers: a basic set of essential social transfers, in cash or in kind, to provide minimum income security and access to essential services, including health care.[228]

The 'transfer' component of the SPF correlates with social security[229] and articulation of the SPF in practice may assist in further defining the scope of Article 9 over time.

INHUMAN OR DEGRADING TREATMENT

In an extreme case, the denial of the minimum core of social security may violate civil and political rights such as the right to life or to freedom from inhuman or degrading treatment. In *R v Secretary of State for the Home Department, ex parte Adam*, the House of Lords in the United Kingdom found that the removal of subsistence support from asylum seekers exposed them to destitution and thus violated the prohibition on inhuman or degrading treatment (under Article 3 of the ECHR). Lord Bingham explained:

7. …Treatment is inhuman or degrading if, to a seriously detrimental extent, it denies the most basic needs of any human being. As in all article 3 cases, the treatment, to be proscribed, must achieve a minimum standard of severity, and I would accept that in a context such as this, not involving the deliberate infliction of pain or suffering, the threshold is a

[226] CESCR, General Comment No. 19, [74]–[76].

[227] UNGA Draft Resolution, Keeping the promise: United to achieve the Millennium Development Goals, A/65/L.1 (22 September 2010), [51].

[228] ILO, Report VI, 11–12.

[229] ILO, Report VI, 2.

high one. A general public duty to house the homeless or provide for the destitute cannot be spelled out of article 3. But I have no doubt that the threshold may be crossed if a late applicant with no means and no alternative sources of support, unable to support himself, is, by the deliberate action of the state, denied shelter, food or the most basic necessities of life…

8. When does the Secretary of State's duty under section 55(5)(a) arise? The answer must in my opinion be: when it appears on a fair and objective assessment of all relevant facts and circumstances that an individual applicant faces an imminent prospect of serious suffering caused or materially aggravated by denial of shelter, food or the most basic necessities of life. Many factors may affect that judgment, including age, gender, mental and physical health and condition, any facilities or sources of support available to the applicant, the weather and time of year and the period for which the applicant has already suffered or is likely to continue to suffer privation.

9. It is not in my opinion possible to formulate any simple test applicable in all cases. But if there were persuasive evidence that a late applicant was obliged to sleep in the street, save perhaps for a short and foreseeably finite period, or was seriously hungry, or unable to satisfy the most basic requirements of hygiene, the threshold would, in the ordinary way, be crossed.[230]

Lord Scott noted further:

71. …Not only did they have to face up to the physical discomfort of sleeping rough, with a gradual but inexorable deterioration in their cleanliness, their appearance and their health, but they had also to face up to the prospect of that state of affairs continuing indefinitely. People can put up with a good deal of discomfort and privation if they know its duration is reasonably short-lived and finite. Asylum seekers caught by section 55(1) do not have that comfort. Growing despair and a loss of self-respect are the likely consequences of the privation to which destitute asylum seekers, with no money of their own, no ability to seek state support and barred from providing for themselves by their own labour are exposed.[231]

The prohibition on inhuman or degrading treatment (under Article 7 of the ICCPR or its equivalents in regional law) is not susceptible to progressive realization and, as such, resource scarcity cannot excuse such conduct even when it comes about as a result of the state's resource incapacity.

However, such cases will be rare. In the *Adam* case, treatment was inhuman not only because the state denied all social security, but also because it prohibited asylum seekers from working to support themselves. Such prohibition would not normally apply to citizens or residents bereft of social security, including in developing countries. In *Singh v Canada*, the Human Rights Committee (HRC) found inadmissible a complaint by a Canadian citizen that Canada's failure to provide social security after his forced withdrawal from university left him unable to sustain his family, thus amounting to inhuman and degrading treatment.[232]

[230] *R v Secretary of State for the Home Department, ex parte Adam* [2005] UKHL 66, [7]–[9] (Lord Bingham).

[231] *R v Secretary of State for the Home Department, ex parte Adam*, [71] (Lord Scott).

[232] *Singh v Canada*, HRC Communication No. 761/1997, (29 July 1997), [3.5], [4.3], [5].

The HRC simply found that the case 'raises no issues under Article 7' of the ICCPR.[233] The author had to withdraw from university because of his own misconduct and poor grades, and there was no discrimination on account of his Sikh ethnic origin.

An Article 7 issue may still arise in the different circumstance where employment is so scarce that the prospects of obtaining work are remote, thus exposing a person to inhuman treatment if the state fails to provide subsistence support. In *Larioshina v Russia*, the ECtHR remarked that entirely inadequate social benefits 'may, in principle, raise an issue under Article 3 [of the ECHR]... which prohibits inhuman or degrading treatment'.[234] However, on the facts, the amount of the applicant's pension and benefits did not suggest that it had 'caused such damage to her physical or mental health capable of attaining the minimum level of severity falling within the ambit of Article 3'.[235] This was despite the amount of support being insufficient to lift her above the poverty line in Russia.

LIMITATIONS ON ARTICLE 9

In monitoring states, the CESCR has not explicitly discussed the general limitations clause in Article 4 of the ICESCR in relation to Article 9. However, like other rights, Article 9 is in principle subject to the general limitations clause, which allows social security to be limited by law solely for the purpose of promoting the general welfare in a democratic society.[236] Such ground is additional to the operation of the principle of progressive realization. In that context, Article 4 should not be understood as an additional basis on which to address a state's economic concerns, but rather serves to accommodate other public interests.

For example, reasonable procedural requirements to apply for a social benefit may be imposed to ensure the integrity of the social security system, combat fraud and maintain public confidence. These could include, for instance, requirements to verify one's identity, or provide evidence of one's needs, means or the birth of a child.

Such requirements must, however, comply with other protected rights. For example, the HRC found that identification techniques, such as fingerprinting and retinal scanning of people relying on social assistance, were intrusive measures adversely affecting the right to privacy under the ICCPR and should be eliminated.[237] The CESCR found too onerous a requirement to obtain a court declaration as to the death of a disappeared relative to qualify for benefits.[238] The failure of a state to register residency and identity documents was found to restrict access to social security,[239] as did the erasure of former nationals from a post-war

[233] *Singh v Canada*, [4.3]. [234] *Larioshina v Russia*, [3].
[235] *Larioshina v Russia*, [3].
[236] Similarly, the limitations clause in Article 5 of the Protocol of San Salvador would apply to the right to social security under the Protocol: see obiter in *Five Pensioners v Peru*, [116].
[237] HRC, Concluding Observations: Canada, A/54/40 vol. I at 40 (1999), [238].
[238] CESCR, Concluding Observations: Angola, E/C.12/DZA/CO/4 (7 June 2010), [13].
[239] CESCR, Concluding Observations: Russia, E/C.12/1/Add.94 (12 December 2003), [12].

population register[240] and the failure to conclude post-war inter-entity agreements on pension rights.[241]

In General Comment No. 19, the CESCR acknowledged that qualifying conditions may be imposed for eligibility for social security assistance: 'Qualifying conditions for benefits must be reasonable, proportionate and transparent'.[242] The CESCR thus objected where social security was administered on a 'discretionary basis', risking unequal protection of the poor, and called on the state to establish 'definite criteria'.[243] Unduly lengthy qualifying periods to obtain benefits may also raise concerns where the person is left without other means. The imposition of residency or other requirements on migrants is considered separately below.

The CESCR has also held that '[t]he withdrawal, reduction or suspension of benefits should be circumscribed, based on grounds that are reasonable, subject to due process, and provided for in national law',[244] and further that '[t]he right to social security includes the right not to be subject to arbitrary and unreasonable restrictions of existing social security coverage'.[245] The CESCR thus criticized states where pensions were unilaterally reduced or deferred,[246] or reduced without notice or reasons.[247] By extrapolation, the ECtHR found that proprietary social security rights[248] were disproportionately impaired where a long-term disability pensioner, who relied on the pension for one-third of his income, was among a small minority of disability pensioners who lost their pensions entirely after legislative changes:

> …as an individual, the applicant was made to bear an excessive and disproportionate burden which, even having regard to the wide margin of appreciation to be enjoyed by the State in the area of social legislation, cannot be justified by the legitimate community interests relied on by the authorities. It would have been otherwise had the applicant been obliged to endure a reasonable and commensurate reduction rather than the total deprivation of his entitlements.[249]

The reduction or withdrawal of a disability benefit will not necessarily be problematic, however, where other social security entitlements remain available to meet basic needs.[250]

The CESCR has further required due process to be afforded:

> 78. Before any action is carried out by the State party, or by any other third party, that interferes with the right of an individual to social security the relevant authorities must

[240] CESCR, Concluding Observations: Slovenia, E/C.12/SVN/CO/1 (25 January 2006), [16] and [32].
[241] CESCR, Concluding Observations: Bosnia and Herzegovina, E/C.12/BIH/CO/1 (24 January 2006), [20] and [42].
[242] CESCR, General Comment No. 19, [24].
[243] CESCR, Concluding Observations: Suriname, E/C.12/1995/6 (7 June 1995), [12] and [19].
[244] CESCR, General Comment No. 19, [24].
[245] CESCR, General Comment No. 19, [9].
[246] CESCR, Concluding Observations: Argentina, E/C.12/1/Add.38 (8 December 1999), [18] and [33].
[247] CESCR, Concluding Observations: Republic of Korea, E/C.12/1/Add.59 (21 May 2001), [23].
[248] Arising under Article 1 of the First Protocol to the ECHR, discussed earlier in this chapter.
[249] *Asmundsson v Iceland* (App. 60669/00), 12 October 2004, (2004) 41 EHRR 42.
[250] See, eg, *Hoogendijk v Netherlands* (App. 58641/00), 6 January 2005 (2005) 40 EHRR SE 22.

ensure that such actions are performed in a manner warranted by law, compatible with the Covenant, and include: (a) an opportunity for genuine consultation with those affected; (b) timely and full disclosure of information on the proposed measures; (c) reasonable notice of proposed actions; (d) legal recourse and remedies for those affected; and (e) legal assistance for obtaining legal remedies. Where such action is based on the ability of a person to contribute to a social security scheme, their capacity to pay must be taken into account. Under no circumstances should an individual be deprived of a benefit on discriminatory grounds or of the minimum essential level of benefits as defined in paragraph 59(a).[251]

In this regard, it has occasionally called on states to be less restrictive in providing free legal aid to facilitate access to social security.[252]

Some states impose participation or other requirements as a condition of eligibility for social security, such as training or work experience (for example, 'workfare' in Canada, 'work for the dole' in Australia or 'WorkFirst' in the Netherlands). Some of these were mentioned earlier in the chapter on the right to work under Article 6 (concerning whether they constitute forced labour). A related example is where family benefits are conditioned on a child's regular attendance at school,[253] or where benefits may only be spent on certain kinds of healthy food or drink.

Such requirements are ostensibly justified to improve the recipient's job prospects, as a form of 'reciprocal obligation' on the part of beneficiaries to contribute back to society, or to secure other public interests such as reducing truancy or improving public health. As noted in relation to Article 6, the CESCR objected to Canada's 'workfare' programmes on the basis that they did not conform to international labour standards, but also because they discriminated on the basis of age or social status in unfairly targeting young people.[254] As discussed below in the context of 'income quarantining' measures applied to indigenous peoples in Australia, such measures must also not be racially discriminatory.

Some states also impose restrictions on the duration of benefits: ILO treaty standards in particular branches specifically provide for this, as discussed below. Often these are related to particular events or circumstances, such as: the period of paid maternity leave around the birth of a child; family benefits while the child is dependent; disability pensions for the duration of a disability; or old age pensions for the duration of one's life. Other benefits are often more limited, such as unemployment, sickness or injury benefits for a defined period, regardless of whether one is still unemployed, or sick or injured.

Non-Discrimination in Social Security

As noted above, the CESCR has also treated non-discrimination as a 'core' obligation of states under Article 9. While Article 9 does not expressly refer to

[251] CESCR, General Comment No. 19, [78].
[252] CESCR, Concluding Observations: United Kingdom, E/C.12/1/Add.19 (12 December 1997), [22].
[253] ILO, World Social Security Report, 16.
[254] CESCR, Concluding Observations: Canada, E/C.12/1993/5 (10 June 1993), [30].

non-discrimination in the provision of social security, it refers to the right of 'everyone' to social security and thus declares its universal application. In addition, the CESCR observes in General Comment No. 19 that, like other socio-economic rights, Article 9 must be provided on a non-discriminatory basis under Articles 2(2) and 3 of the ICESCR:

29. The obligation of States parties to guarantee that the right to social security is enjoyed without discrimination (article 2, paragraph 2, of the Covenant), and equally between men and women (article 3), pervades all of the obligations under Part III of the Covenant. The Covenant thus prohibits any discrimination, whether in law or in fact, whether direct or indirect, on the grounds of race, colour, sex, age, language, religion, political or other opinion, national or social origin, property, birth, physical or mental disability, health status (including HIV/AIDS), sexual orientation, and civil, political, social or other status, which has the intention or effect of nullifying or impairing the equal enjoyment or exercise of the right to social security.

30. States parties should also remove de facto discrimination on prohibited grounds, where individuals are unable to access adequate social security. States parties should ensure that legislation, policies, programmes and the allocation of resources facilitate access to social security for all members of society in accordance with Part III. Restrictions on access to social security schemes should also be reviewed to ensure that they do not discriminate in law or in fact.[255]

As is the case under the ICESCR and ICCPR generally, the scope of non-discrimination in social security has been interpreted widely by the CESCR to encompass not only the expressly enumerated grounds under Articles 2(2) and 3 (which are dealt with generally in earlier chapters of this book), but also groups that are especially vulnerable:

31. Whereas everyone has the right to social security, States parties should give special attention to those individuals and groups who traditionally face difficulties in exercising this right, in particular women, the unemployed, workers inadequately protected by social security, persons working in the informal economy, sick or injured workers, people with disabilities, older persons, children and adult dependents, domestic workers, homeworkers, minority groups, refugees, asylum-seekers, internally displaced persons, returnees, non-nationals, prisoners and detainees.[256]

Formally, some such groups may come within the ambit of the express grounds of 'social origin' or 'other status' under Article 2(2), while others (such as workers in the informal economy) may also fall within the ambit of indirect gender discrimination under Article 3. Specific attention is given to particular groups below. First, it is necessary to consider how the principle of progressive realization affects protection against discrimination, and discuss certain other legal implications of non-discrimination.

NON-DISCRIMINATION AND PROGRESSIVE REALIZATION

Non-discrimination in social security is a 'core obligation' of states and is capable of being immediately enforced. In numerous views of the UN Human Rights

[255] CESCR, General Comment No. 19, [29]–[30]. [256] CESCR, General Comment No. 19, [31].

Committee, discussed later, the right to equality before the law under Article 26 of the ICCPR has been applied to ensure non-discriminatory access to social security schemes that are already provided by states. Article 2 of the ICCPR does not apply in such cases because it guarantees non-discrimination only in relation to other ICCPR rights, of which social security is not one. In *Broeks v Netherlands*, the HRC accordingly found that the question at issue in that context is not one of progressive realization, but rather of discriminatory legislation:

12.5. The Committee observes in this connection that what is at issue is not whether or not social security should be progressively established in the Netherlands, but whether the legislation providing for social security violates the prohibition against discrimination contained in article 26 of the International Covenant on Civil and Political Rights and the guarantee given therein to all persons regarding equal and effective protection against discrimination.[257]

In the different context of the ICESCR, however, a question arises about whether non-discrimination (under Articles 2(2) and 3) in the application of the right to social security under Article 9 is affected by claims of resource scarcity pursuant to the principle of progressive realization. In other words, while states must not discriminate under any social security schemes that they have already established, a different issue is whether states may refuse to provide further social security schemes for particular groups on account of resource limitations. An individual opinion by three members of the HRC in *Sprenger v Netherlands*, again involving Article 26 of the ICCPR, asserts that 'absolute equality or non-discrimination' is not required at all times in matters of social security:

While it is clear that article 26 of the Covenant postulates an autonomous right to non-discrimination, we believe that the implementation of this right may take different forms, depending on the nature of the right to which the principle of non-discrimination is applied.

We note, firstly, that the determination whether prohibited discrimination within the meaning of article 26 has occurred depends on complex considerations, particularly in the field of economic, social and cultural rights. Social security legislation, which is intended to achieve aims of social justice, necessarily must make distinctions. While the aims of social justice vary from country to country, they must be compatible with the Covenant. Moreover, whatever distinctions are made must be based on reasonable and objective criteria. For instance, a system of progressive taxation, under which persons with higher incomes fall into a higher tax bracket and pay a greater percentage of their income for taxes, does not entail a violation of article 26 of the Covenant, since the distinction between higher and lower incomes is objective and the purpose of more equitable distribution of wealth is reasonable and compatible with the aims of the Covenant.

Surely, it is also necessary to take into account the reality that the socio-economic and cultural needs of society are constantly evolving, so that legislation—in particular in the field of social security—may well, and often does, lag behind developments. Accordingly, article 26 of the Covenant should not be interpreted as requiring absolute equality or

[257] *Broeks v Netherlands*, HRC Communication No. 172/1984, (1990), 196.

non-discrimination in that field at all times; instead, it should be seen as a general undertaking on the part of States parties to the Covenant regularly to review their legislation in order to ensure that it corresponds to the changing needs of society. In the field of civil and political rights, a State party is required to respect Covenant rights such as the right to a fair trial, freedom of expression and freedom of religion immediately from the date of entry into force of the Covenant, and to do so without discrimination. On the other hand, with regard to rights enshrined in the International Covenant on Economic, Social and Cultural Rights, it is generally understood that States parties may need time for the progressive implementation of these rights and to adapt relevant legislation in stages; moreover, constant efforts are needed to ensure that distinctions that were reasonable and objective at the time of enactment of a social security provision are not unreasonable and discriminatory by the socio-economic evolution of society. Finally, we recognize that legislative review is a complex process entailing consideration of many factors, including limited financial resources, and the potential effects of amendments on other existing legislation…[258]

The individual opinion is undoubtedly correct to draw attention to the point that the notion of what is unreasonable and discriminatory changes over time and must be kept under review. However, the opinion appears to subordinate non-discrimination to progressive realization, thus potentially allowing protected groups to be denied or limited in the right to social security in order to ration scarce resources available to other privileged groups.

Such a view is inconsistent with the position taken by the CESCR on the relationship between progressive realization and the obligation to immediately 'guarantee' non-discrimination.[259] Thus, social security may be progressively realized, but not in a discriminatory manner. The burden of resource scarcity must be equitably distributed across different groups, rather than by arbitrarily picking winners and losers on the basis of prevailing social prejudices or political dynamics. In monitoring states, the CESCR has shown a preference for wider coverage over higher payments to fewer beneficiaries; it objected to Azerbaijan's plan to increase the volume of social security benefits by decreasing the number of beneficiaries.[260]

In another ICCPR case, *Oulajin and Kaiss v Netherlands*, again three members of the HRC expounded on the relationship between progressive realization and non-discrimination, ruling out 'manifestly discriminatory or arbitrary' distinctions, but accepting that the state need not provide child benefits for an author's extended family members in the light of the state's budgetary position:

We concur in the Committee's finding that the facts do not reveal a violation of article 26 of the Covenant…[W]e consider it proper to briefly expand on the Committee's rationale…

[258] *Sprenger v Netherlands*, HRC Communication No. 395/1990, (31 March 1992), Appendix (Individual Opinion by Mr Nisuko Ando, Mr Kurt Herndl and Mr Birama Ndiaya).

[259] CESCR, General Comment No. 3, HRI/GEN/1/Rev.9 (vol. I) at 7 (14 December 1990), [2]; CESCR, General Comment No. 20, E/C.12/GC/20 (2 July 2009), [7]; see the chapter of this book on Article 2(2).

[260] CESCR, Concluding Observations: Azerbaijan, E/C.12/1/Add.104 (14 December 2004), [22].

It is obvious that while article 26 of the Covenant postulates an autonomous right to non-discrimination, the implementation of this right may take different forms, depending on the nature of the right to which the principle of non-discrimination is applied.

With regard to the application of article 26 of the Covenant in the field of economic and social rights, it is evident that social security legislation, which is intended to achieve aims of social justice, necessarily must make distinctions. It is for the legislature of each country, which best knows the socio-economic needs of the society concerned, to try to achieve social justice in the concrete context. Unless the distinctions made are manifestly discriminatory or arbitrary, it is not for the Committee to reevaluate the complex socio-economic data and substitute its judgment for that of the legislatures of States parties.

Furthermore it would seem to us that it is essential to keep one's sense of proportion. With respect to the present cases, we note that the authors are asking for child benefits not only for their own children—to which they are entitled under the legislation of the Netherlands—but also for siblings, nephews and nieces, for whom they claim to have accepted responsibility and hence consider them as dependents. On the basis of the information before the Committee, such demands appear to run counter to a general sense of proportion, and their denial by the government concerned cannot be considered unreasonable in view of the budget limitations which exist in any social security system. While States parties to the Covenant may wish to extend benefits to such wide-ranging categories of dependents, article 26 of the Covenant does not require them to do so.[261]

OTHER LEGAL IMPLICATIONS OF NON-DISCRIMINATION

The obligation of non-discrimination has other implications for the design and implementation of the right to social security. In ensuring the accessibility of social security, the CESCR has called on all persons to be covered without discrimination. This also implies that non-contributory schemes will be necessary to include those outside traditional employment relationships:

23. All persons should be covered by the social security system, especially individuals belonging to the most disadvantaged and marginalized groups, without discrimination on any of the grounds prohibited under article 2, paragraph 2, of the Covenant. In order to ensure universal coverage, non-contributory schemes will be necessary.[262]

Further, social security must be physically accessible:

27. Benefits should be provided in a timely manner and beneficiaries should have physical access to the social security services in order to access benefits and information, and make contributions where relevant. Particular attention should be paid in this regard to persons with disabilities, migrants, and persons living in remote or disaster-prone areas, as well as areas experiencing armed conflict, so that they, too, can have access to these services.

In reviewing states' performance, the CESCR has identified various barriers to access. As noted above, it criticized the UN Interim Administration Mission in

[261] *Oulajin and Kaiss v Netherlands* ('*Oulajin v Netherlands*'), HRC Communication Nos. 406/1990, 426/1990 (23 October 1992), Appendix (Individual Opinion by Messrs. Kurt Herndl, Rein Mullerson, Birame N'Diaye and Waleed Sadi).

[262] CESCR, General Comment No. 19, [23].

Kosovo's (UNMIK) failure to provide application forms in the Serbian language in Kosovo and the requirement for UNMIK personnel to witness death certificates.[263] In relation to Russia, the CESCR was concerned about the lack of registration of place of residence and other identity documents, which prejudiced the ability to obtain social security:

> 12. The Committee is concerned about reports of cases where the lack of registration of place of residence and other identity documents in practice places limitations on the enjoyment of rights, including work, social security, health services and education. The Committee is also concerned about reports that some groups of people, including the homeless and the Roma, face particular difficulties in obtaining personal identification documents, including registration of residence.[264]

Commenting on Angola, the CESCR was concerned about a requirement on families of the disappeared to first obtain a court order before receiving benefits:

> 13. The Committee is concerned that the access of families of disappeared persons to social security benefits, including pension and child education benefits, is made conditional upon the family obtaining a court declaration that the disappeared relative has died (art. 9).
>
> The Committee recommends that the State party take measures to ensure that families of disappeared persons have unconditional access to social security, in particular pension and survivor benefits and child benefits. It draws the attention of the State party to its general comment No. 19 on the right to social security, which refers to the core obligation of a State party to ensure the right of access to social security systems or schemes on a non-discriminatory basis, especially for disadvantaged and marginalized individuals and groups.[265]

PARTICULAR GROUNDS OF NON-DISCRIMINATION

The CESCR has paid special attention to articulating the content of non-discrimination in relation to a number of particular protected groups, including women, indigenous peoples and minorities, non-nationals, internal migrants and vulnerable workers. In addition, its practice in assessing states reveals its further concern for victims of conflict and those affected by changes in nationality or statehood. Each of these groups is considered here. Other groups which come within the scope of non-discrimination are considered elsewhere in this chapter, where specialized branches of social security correspond with a relevant group (for example, persons with disabilities in relation to disability assistance).

Gender

The CESCR has given special attention to gender equality in social security. Non-discrimination requires not only that women's rights to social security are not impeded by the state or third parties, but that the state may need to take

[263] CESCR, Concluding Observations: UNMIK, E/C.12/UNK/CO/1 (1 December 2008), [22].
[264] CESCR, Concluding Observations: Russia, E/C.12/1/Add.94 (12 December 2003), [12].
[265] CESCR, Concluding Observations: Angola, E/C.12/DZA/CO/4 (7 June 2010), [13].

special gender-sensitive or gender-specific measures to bring about substantive equality. This is because gender inequality in the workplace reproduces inequality in women's social security, for instance because the income gap reduces their insurance contributions.[266] Women may also be over-represented in insecure or informal employment, bringing special social security problems. Women also often disproportionately bear the burden of certain family activities which may require social support (such as childcare). Women also typically live longer, requiring more aged pensions or aged care over time. In General Comment No. 19, the CESCR states:

> 32. In general comment No. 16 (2005) on the equal right of men and women to the enjoyment of all economic, social and cultural rights (art. 3), the Committee noted that implementation of article 3 in relation to article 9 requires, inter alia, equalization of the compulsory retirement age for both men and women; ensuring that women receive equal benefits in both public and private pension schemes; and guaranteeing adequate maternity leave for women, paternity leave for men, and parental leave for both men and women. In social security schemes that link benefits with contributions, States parties should take steps to eliminate the factors that prevent women from making equal contributions to such schemes (for example, intermittent participation in the workforce on account of family responsibilities and unequal wage outcomes) or ensure that schemes take account of such factors in the design of benefit formulas (for example by considering child rearing periods or periods to take care of adult dependents in relation to pension entitlements). Differences in the average life expectancy of men and women can also lead directly or indirectly to discrimination in provision of benefits (particularly in the case of pensions) and thus need to be taken into account in the design of schemes. Non-contributory schemes must also take account of the fact that women are more likely to live in poverty than men and often have sole responsibility for the care of children.

In its observations on states, the CESCR has frequently called for social security measures to be expanded to cover women or to more adequately meet their social needs,[267] including particular groups such as rural women.[268] It has highlighted the disproportionate poverty experienced by women, including the elderly and single mothers.[269] It noted the disproportionate or 'particularly harsh' impacts on women of welfare cuts in Canada.[270] The lack of funding and qualified personnel at Bosnian welfare centres responsible for the social protection of female heads of households and female victims of trafficking was criticized.[271] Social assistance

[266] Langford, 'The Right to Social Security', 45.

[267] CESCR, Concluding Observations: Afghanistan, E/C.12/AFG/CO/2-4 (7 June 2010), [26]; Ecuador, E/C.12/1/Add.100 (7 June 2004), [44]; Germany, E/C.12/1/Add.68 (24 September 2001), [23].

[268] CESCR, Concluding Observations: Madagascar, E/C.12/MDG/CO/2 (16 December 2009), [20].

[269] CESCR, Concluding Observations: Ireland, E/C.12/1/Add.35 (14 May 1999), [13]; see also United Kingdom, E/C.12/1/Add.19 (12 December 1997), [22] (over-representation of women in poverty statistics).

[270] CESCR, Concluding Observations: Canada, E/C.12/1993/5 (10 June 1993), [23].

[271] CESCR, Concluding Observations: Bosnia and Herzegovina, E/C.12/BIH/CO/1 (24 January 2006), [17] and [39].

for women victims of domestic violence has also been promoted by the CESCR, most prominently in the case of Canada:

28. The Committee is concerned that the significant reductions in provincial social assistance programmes, the unavailability of affordable and appropriate housing and widespread discrimination with respect to housing create obstacles to women escaping domestic violence. Many women are forced, as a result of those obstacles, to choose between returning to or staying in a violent situation, on the one hand, or homelessness and inadequate food and clothing for themselves and their children, on the other.[272]

In relation to employment-related social security, the CESCR has focused on the inequality arising out of insurance-based schemes, such as lack of coverage for non-contributors like housewives or homemakers,[273] who are predominantly women, and thus receive less than the minimum wage[274] or no pension at all.[275] It criticized Japan's 'persistent de facto gender inequality in the pension system which perpetuates the income gap between men and women' and called for a minimum pension for women.[276] It has also criticized indirect discrimination against women in access to privatized social security,[277] or due to their inability to obtain employment insurance.[278] It has also raised concerns about social security for women jobseekers.[279] The inability of married women in Kenya to participate in national health insurance if their husbands are employed was a further cause for concern.[280]

On a number of occasions, the CESCR was concerned about discrimination arising from differences in the retirement age for men and women, affecting pension benefits. It thus criticized the retirement age for women in Chile, which was five years earlier than for men, leaving working women with a 'much lower' average pension than men.[281] Likewise, it was concerned that Polish pension reforms had not implemented the CESCR's earlier recommendation to correct the difference in retirement age, 'which is not only discriminatory but also denies women senior positions and reduces the amount of their pension'.[282]

There are also gender-specific provisions on social security in the International Convention on the Elimination of All Forms of Discrimination against Women (CEDAW), which are separately assessed by the CEDAW Committee. Article 11(1)(e) of the CEDAW requires state to eliminate discrimination against women in the provision of social security, 'particularly in cases of retirement, unemployment, sickness, invalidity and old age and other incapacity

[272] CESCR, Concluding Observations: Canada, E/C.12/1993/5 (10 June 1993), [28].
[273] CESCR, Concluding Observations: Hong Kong SAR, E/C.12/1/Add.58 (21 May 2001), [36].
[274] CESCR, Concluding Observations: Australia, E/C.12/1/Add.50 (11 September 2000), [18].
[275] CESCR, Concluding Observations: Chile, E/C.12/1/Add.105 (1 December 2004), [20].
[276] CESCR, Concluding Observations: Japan, E/C.12/1/Add.67 (24 September 2001), [24] and [51].
[277] CESCR, Concluding Observations: El Salvador, E/C.12/SLV/CO/2 (27 June 2007), [15] and [33].
[278] CESCR, Concluding Observations: Mauritius, E/C.12/1994/8 (31 May 1994), [11].
[279] CESCR, Concluding Observations: Democratic People's Republic of Korea, E/C.12/1/Add.95 (12 December 2003), [38].
[280] CESCR, Concluding Observations: Kenya, E/C.12/1993/6 (3 June 1993), [14].
[281] CESCR, Concluding Observations: Chile, E/C.12/1/Add.105 (1 December 2004), [20] and [43].
[282] CESCR, Concluding Observations: Poland, E/C.12/POL/CO/5 (2 December 2009), [21].

to work, as well as the right to paid leave'. Article 13(a) of the CEDAW guarantees women the 'right to family benefits' so as to eliminate discrimination against women. Article 14(2)(c) of the CEDAW recognizes the right of rural women '[t]o benefit directly from social security programmes', so as to eliminate discrimination against rural women, and this would include social security for women who work without pay in family enterprises.[283] Article 11(2)(b) of the CEDAW requires states to guarantee paid maternity leave, an issue which is separately recognized in Article 10 of the ICESCR, considered in the next chapter.[284]

Children

Social assistance to children, whether as part of family benefits or maternity provisions or where children are in alternative care, is more specifically addressed in the chapter of this book on Article 10 of the ICESCR, which concerns the protection of families, mothers and children. In national social security practice, children tend to be treated as incidental beneficiaries of social security assistance to families or mothers or as part of institutional care, rather as rights-holders in themselves. In monitoring states, the CESCR has rarely addressed situations where children are social security claimants in their own right.

Despite this, in certain contexts children may be direct claimants of social security rights, such as when children are in the workforce, but unemployed and not dependent on families or parents, or when they are homeless. Under Article 26 of CROC, every child's right to social security is emphasized, taking into account the resources and circumstances of the child and their carers:

1. States Parties shall recognize for every child the right to benefit from social security, including social insurance, and shall take the necessary measures to achieve the full realization of this right in accordance with their national law.

2. The benefits should, where appropriate, be granted, taking into account the resources and the circumstances of the child and persons having responsibility for the maintenance of the child, as well as any other consideration relevant to an application for benefits made by or on behalf of the child.

Direct or indirect discrimination in social security for children often arises in situations involving cross-cutting grounds of discrimination, as in the case of foreign, minority or indigenous children; girls; or children with disabilities. But it may also arise on account of a child's socio-economic status, such as where a working child is accorded lesser protection (for instance, in social insurance, or workplace injury compensation); or where a child is unemployed, homeless, from a broken family or a member of a lower caste.

283 CEDAW Committee, General Recommendation No. 16, A/46/38 (1991), 1, [(c)].

284 See also ILO Convention No. 103 concerning Maternity Protection (Revised) (adopted 28 June 1952, entered into force 7 September 1955).

Minority groups and indigenous peoples

The CESCR has observed that:

35. States parties should take particular care that indigenous peoples and ethnic and linguistic minorities are not excluded from social security systems through direct or indirect discrimination, particularly through the imposition of unreasonable eligibility conditions or lack of adequate access to information.[285]

In practice, problems that will be encountered by minorities and indigenous peoples may include: physical barriers to access (such as a lack of forms in their own language, an absence of interpreters in their interaction with public authorities, or geographical remoteness); culturally inappropriate forms of social assistance (such as housing arrangements which are ill-suited to cultural preferences, family structures or climatic conditions, or economic assumptions inconsistent with indigenous subsistence livelihoods); and indirect discrimination (for instance, due to low participation rates or disproportionately high unemployment in the formal economy covered by contributory schemes).

Minorities

In assessing state performance, in relation to minorities the CESCR called on the United Kingdom to better target social assistance to alleviate poverty among those disproportionately suffering from long-term unemployment, low revenue or inability to work, which were found to include 'ethnic minorities' and Catholics in Northern Ireland, among others.[286] It also called on Vietnam to take special measures to protect minorities from the adverse impacts of structural economic change:

12. …Effective measures should also be adopted…to compensate for the effects on minorities and less privileged social groups of economic adjustments to promote the change to a free market society.[287]

The CESCR was further concerned by the lack of access to social security by Roma people in Greece, and the inadequacy of social assistance levels for Roma in Hungary, which it urged the state to increase.[288] It was also concerned that the Roma faced particular difficulties in obtaining personal identification documents, including registration of residence, in Russia.[289] Other minorities in the context of conflict or changes in statehood are considered below, particularly in the context of the disintegration of the former Yugoslavia.

Ensuring the accessibility of social security systems will be particularly important for minorities. The CESCR has noted that the obligation to fulfil (promote) social security requires the state to ensure that there is appropriate education and

[285] CESCR, General Comment No. 19, [35].

[286] CESCR, Concluding Observations: United Kingdom, E/C.12/1/Add.19 (12 December 1997), [22].

[287] CESCR, Concluding Observations: Vietnam, E/C.12/1993/8 (9 June 1993), [12].

[288] CESCR, Concluding Observations: Greece, E/C.12/1/Add.97 (7 June 2004), [15]; Hungary, E/C.12/HUN/CO/3 (16 January 2008), [17].

[289] CESCR, Concluding Observations: Russia, E/C.12/1/Add.94 (12 December 2003), [12].

public awareness concerning access to social security schemes among linguistic and other minorities.[290] In monitoring states, it has called for states to disseminate targeted accessible information on social security to overcome language, educational or cultural difficulties.[291]

Other treaty bodies, such as the HRC and CERD, have also expressed concern about discrimination against particular minorities in social security, including the Roma,[292] Irish Travellers,[293] ethnic Serbs,[294] Maori and Pacific Islanders[295] and Shia.[296]

Indigenous peoples

The CESCR has seldom mentioned indigenous peoples in the context of social security, although it called on Brazil to provide targeted assistance to them and requested Venezuela to provide more information about them.[297] Other UN human rights bodies have commented on indigenous peoples and social security. Article 5(e)(iv) of the International Convention on the Elimination of All Forms of Racial Discrimination (ICERD) likewise requires states to eliminate race discrimination in the right to social security and social services.

One example arising under the ICERD concerns a package of laws adopted by Australia in 2007 in response to concerns about child welfare in remote indigenous communities in northern Australia, known as the Northern Territory Emergency Response or 'Intervention'. The Intervention included measures to quarantine the social security income of residents of those communities, purportedly to prevent income being spent on drugs and gambling, to ensure that income was spent on the welfare of families (such as on fresh food), and to promote 'socially responsible' behaviour.[298]

The original Intervention also suspended the operation of Australia's racial anti-discrimination legislation, although it was subsequently reinstated and the measures were then sought to be justified as 'special measures' for the benefit of indigenous peoples. In its Concluding Observations on Australia in 2010, the CERD stated that the Intervention laws remained racially discriminatory and

[290] CESCR, General Comment No. 19, [49].

[291] CESCR, Concluding Observations: New Zealand, E/C.12/1/Add.88 (26 June 2003), [29].

[292] HRC, Consideration of Report Submitted by State Party: Hungary, A/57/40 (2002), [80(7)]; Serbia and Montenegro, A/59/40 (2004), [75(24)]; Albania, A/60/40 (2004) [82(21)]; CERD, Consideration of Report Submitted by State Party: Bulgaria, A/52/18 (1997), [282].

[293] CERD, Consideration of Report Submitted by State Party: United Kingdom, A/51/18 (1996), [234].

[294] CERD, Consideration of Report Submitted by State Party: Croatia, A/53/18 (1998), [316].

[295] CERD, Consideration of Report Submitted by State Party: New Zealand, A/57/18 (2002), [422].

[296] CERD, Consideration of Report Submitted by State Party: Bahrain, A/60/18 (2002), [86].

[297] CESCR, Concluding Observations: Brazil, E/C.12/BRA/CO/2 (12 June 2009), [20(b)]; Venezuela, E/C.12/1/Add.56 (21 May 2001), [20].

[298] Social Security and Other Legislation Amendment (Welfare Payment Reform) Act 2007 (Commonwealth of Australia).

doubted their lawfulness as special measures, even after the reinstatement of Australia's general racial anti-discrimination laws:

16. The Committee expresses its concern that the package of legislation under the Northern Territory Emergency Response (NTER) continues to discriminate on the basis of race as well as the use of so called 'special measures' by the State party. The Committee regrets the discriminatory impact this intervention has had on affected communities including restrictions on Aboriginal rights to land, property, social security, adequate standards of living, cultural development, work, and remedies (arts. 1, 2, and 5).

The Committee takes notes the State party will complete the reinstatement of the Racial Discrimination Act in December 2010, but is concerned by the continuing difficulties in using the Act to challenge and provide remedies for racially discriminatory NTER measures. It also urges the State party to guarantee that all special measures in Australian law, in particular those regarding the NTER, are in accordance with the Committee's general recommendation No. 32 on Special Measures (2009). It encourages the State party to strengthen its efforts to implement the NTER Review Board recommendations, namely that: it continue to address the unacceptably high level of disadvantage and social dislocation being experienced by Aboriginal Australians living in remote communities throughout the Northern Territory; that it reset the relationship with Aboriginal people based on genuine consultation, engagement and partnership; and that Government actions affecting the Aboriginal communities respect Australia's human rights obligations and conform with the Racial Discrimination Act.[299]

The UN Special Rapporteur on poverty (Magdalena Sepulveda Carmona) and the UN Special Rapporteur on indigenous rights (James Anaya) also informed Australia in March 2012 that they believed the Intervention may infringe equality and non-discrimination rights, stigmatize indigenous peoples and undermine efforts to improve their situation.[300] The Special Rapporteurs noted that there was no evidence that measures which stopped parents' welfare payments if their children did not attend school had improved school attendance rates over an earlier three-year trial period, suggesting that they could not be justified as necessary. Also, Australia had failed to adequately consult indigenous peoples, and had even failed to translate essential discussion documents into indigenous languages.

While the CERD did not further explain its reasoning as regards the discriminatory impact of the Australian laws on indigenous social security rights, the Australian Human Rights Commission, an independent national statutory authority, considered the impact of the welfare quarantining measures in 2007, finding:

- The blanket application of the income management regime in the 73 prescribed communities in the [Northern Territory] means that the measures are applied to individuals

[299] CERD, Concluding Observations: Australia, CERD/C/AUS/CO/15-17 (27 August 2010), [16].
[300] Lisa Martin, 'UN concerned about NT intervention', *Sydney Morning Herald* (29 August 2012), <http://news.smh.com.au/breaking-news-national/un-concerned-about-nt-intervention-20120829-250kk.html>.

that are not responsible for the care of children, do not gamble, and do not abuse alcohol or other substances. The criteria for being subject to the income management provisions is therefore solely on the basis of the race of the welfare recipient instead of being on the basis of need.

…

- As the income management measures are so broadly applied, there is a tenuous connection between the operation of the scheme and the object of addressing family violence and abuse. When coupled with the lack of participation and consultation with Indigenous communities, this renders it very difficult to support the view that these measures are appropriately characterised as a special measure.
- If the measures were targeted solely to parents or families in need of assistance to prevent neglect or abuse of children…then some form of income management may be capable of being seen as an appropriate exercise of the governments 'margin of discretion' to ensure that families benefit from welfare and receive the minimum essentials for survival.
- It is difficult, however, to see how the quarantining of 100% of welfare entitlements can be characterised as an adapted and appropriate response, given the impact that benefits are being provided in a form that is onerous and potentially undignified.
- …the limitations on reviewing decision making in relation to the income management regime, and especially the denial of external merits review processes, significantly undermines the ability to characterise the income management regime as an adapted and appropriate response. This is a clear denial of justice, is discriminatory in its impact and does not meet the requirement for the provision of effective judicial or other appropriate remedies that is integral to the right to social security. The absence of access to complaints processes such as under the RDA [Racial Discrimination Act] also breaches the right to social security.[301]

In addition to the ICESCR and ICERD, the 'soft law' of the UN General Assembly's 2007 Declaration on the Rights of Indigenous Peoples also relevantly provides for indigenous rights to social security on a non-discriminatory basis:

Article 21

1. Indigenous peoples have the right, without discrimination, to the improvement of their economic and social conditions, including, inter alia, in the areas of education, employment, vocational training and retraining, housing, sanitation, health and social security.

2. States shall take effective measures and, where appropriate, special measures to ensure continuing improvement of their economic and social conditions. Particular attention shall be paid to the rights and special needs of indigenous elders, women, youth, children and persons with disabilities.

…

[301] Human Rights and Equal Opportunity Commission (Australia), 'Social Justice Report 2007', Chapter 3: 'The Northern Territory "Emergency Response" Intervention—A Human Rights Analysis' (2008).

Article 24

1. ... Indigenous individuals also have the right to access, without any discrimination, to all social and health services.

Significantly, Article 23 of the 2007 Declaration recognizes a right of indigenous peoples to determine their own developmental priorities and strategies, which includes a further right to be actively involved in developing and administering social programmes:

Indigenous peoples have the right to determine and develop priorities and strategies for exercising their right to development. In particular, indigenous peoples have the right to be actively involved in developing and determining health, housing and other economic and social programmes affecting them and, as far as possible, to administer such programmes through their own institutions.

Such rights are connected with the underlying principle of indigenous self-determination, discussed in chapter 1, which recognizes the economic autonomy of indigenous peoples. In quite a few countries, welfare assistance to indigenous peoples was often provided in a paternalistic, top-down or centralist model, with little involvement by indigenous peoples in the design, implementation and 'ownership' of social security. For this reason, the Australian Human Rights Commission criticized Australia's 'Intervention' policy, mentioned above, for fostering a 'passive' welfare system:

... a system that divests Aboriginal people of any power to make choices to govern their own financial affairs is severely out of step with principles of both self-determination, and self-responsibility.[302]

Non-nationals (including migrant workers, refugees, asylum-seekers and stateless persons)

Article 9 of the ICESCR is not explicit on the rights of non-citizens and a number of questions arise in determining the scope of application to them. Under Article 12(4) of the European Social Charter, for instance, states must treat the nationals of other states parties equally to their own under national law in respect of social security, and make adequate efforts to conclude and implement international agreements to maintain or restore migrants' rights.[303] But the Charter does not assist nationals of non-party states.

Non-contributory schemes—migrants

The CESCR has found that non-nationals are in principle entitled to access non-contributory social security schemes, subject only to 'proportionate and reasonable' restrictions on social security (other than basic health care):

37. Non-nationals should be able to access non-contributory schemes for income support, affordable access to health care and family support. Any restrictions, including a

[302] Human Rights and Equal Opportunity Commission, 'Social Justice Report 2007', Chapter 3.
[303] ECSR, Statement of Interpretation: Article 12(4), Conclusions III (31 July 1973).

qualification period, must be proportionate and reasonable. All persons, irrespective of their nationality, residency or immigration status, are entitled to primary and emergency medical care.[304]

In monitoring states, the CESCR has occasionally criticised states for failing to equally protect migrant workers,[305] whether permanent residents[306] or undocumented migrants and their families.[307] Its comments were most extensive on foreign domestic workers in Chinese Hong Kong:

83. The Committee expresses its concern about the particularly precarious situation of foreign domestic workers, a majority of whom are from South-East Asia, who are underpaid and are not entitled to social security.

...

95. The Committee urges the State party to review the existing 'two-week rule' [which requires workers to leave Hong Kong within two weeks of the termination of a contract], with a view to eliminating discriminatory practices and abuse arising from it, and to improving the legal protection and benefits for foreign domestic workers so that they are in line with those afforded to local workers, particularly with regard to wages and retirement benefits. The Committee recommends that HKSAR enable domestic helpers to acquire pension rights through their inclusion in the Mandatory Provident Fund.

96. The Committee urges HKSAR to review the eligibility criteria for the CSSA so as to ensure that all those in need, including low-income persons and families, older persons and new migrants are adequately covered by the scheme to enable them to enjoy a decent standard of living.

... 114. The Committee is seriously concerned that migrant workers, who account for a significant proportion of the working population of MSAR, are excluded from the social welfare system.

...

124. The Committee recommends that MSAR take effective measures to ensure that all workers are entitled to adequate social security benefits, including migrant workers. The Committee requests MSAR to provide detailed information in its next periodic report on the extent of the coverage of its social security system, including protection for migrant workers and other disadvantaged and marginalized groups.[308]

The CESCR accepts that qualifying periods for new migrants may be lawful. The policy idea behind qualifying periods is that newly arrived migrants should not benefit immediately from full social security benefits until they have 'earned' the

[304] CESCR, General Comment No. 19, [37].

[305] CESCR, Concluding Observations: Costa Rica, E/C.12/CRI/CO/4 (4 January 2008), [21] and [42]; Mauritius, E/C.12/1995/14 (28 December 1995), [11]; Mauritius, E/C.12/MUS/CO/4 (8 June 2010), [20]; Kazakhstan, E/C.12/KAZ/CO/1 (7 June 2010), [23]; Jordan, E/C.12/1/Add.46 (1 September 2000), [19].

[306] CESCR, Concluding Observations: San Marino, E/C.12/SMR/CO/4 (4 January 2008), [13].

[307] CESCR, Concluding Observations: Greece, E/C.12/1/Add.97 (7 June 2004), [15].

[308] CESCR, Concluding Observations: China, E/C.12/1/Add.107 (13 May 2005), [83], [95]–[96], [114] and [124].

right to do so, such as by working and contributing to general taxation or otherwise contributing to the social life of their new country. It may also be designed to remove incentives for migrants to enter a country to obtain welfare instead of to work, thus becoming a drain on public finances. It can also exclude claims by temporary entrants such as tourists or short-term visitors, or deter irregular migrants from entering in the knowledge that they might face destitution.

The lawfulness of such periods will depend on their duration and the consequences for those affected, as well as on the resources available to the state in question. In relation to Chinese Hong Kong, the CESCR was concerned that a seven-year residence requirement prevented new migrants from applying for social security.[309] Article 36 of Hong Kong's Basic Law provides a right of social welfare to residents 'in accordance with law', while Article 39 of the Basic Law provides for the implementation of the ICESCR in Hong Kong law.

The CESCR was also concerned where a retroactive Israeli requirement to show that East Jerusalem was a person's 'centre of life' for the past seven years, in order to obtain social services, impeded the rights of Palestinians from elsewhere in Jerusalem, the West Bank or abroad.[310] It was also discriminatory because it did not apply to Israeli or foreign Jews. The scheme also separated Arab families and infringed the right to the protection of the family under Article 10, as discussed in the next chapter.

Shorter qualifying periods also raise issues. The CESCR found that a five-year residency requirement in Monaco should be reduced.[311] Also, in relation to a high-income state, the CESCR was concerned about a shorter waiting period of two years and called on Australia to ensure that it 'does not infringe upon their right to an adequate standard of living'.[312]

There are also countervailing policy considerations which weigh in favour of minimizing qualifying periods for the availability of social security to migrants, and these reasons bear on the calculation of whether a particular restriction may be considered proportionate and reasonable. First, a state's immigration law already determines the entry criteria for lawful migrant workers, such that a lack of means can be addressed at that point, whether by requiring evidence of a job, assurances of support or precluding entry altogether.

Secondly, it is hard to see why states should be entitled to admit foreign workers but refuse to support them if they later experience financial difficulty, such as where their employment is unexpectedly terminated. Such an asymmetrical relationship of advantage and exploitation can be appropriately corrected by human rights law.

Thirdly, withholding social security can impair the ability of a migrant to settle into and become established in a new community (and thus potentially lead to

[309] CESCR, Concluding Observations: China, E/C.12/1/Add.107 (13 May 2005), [84].

[310] CESCR, Consideration of Report Submitted by State Party: Israel, E/1999/22 (1998), [246], [266].

[311] CESCR, Concluding Observations: Monaco, E/C.12/MCO/CO/1 (13 June 2006), [18].

[312] CESCR, Concluding Observations: Australia, E/C.12/1/Add.50 (11 September 2000), [32].

social alienation, poverty, family disintegration and even crime). This was recognized by the CESCR when it encouraged Sweden to use its social security system as a means of speeding up the 'social integration' of immigrants.[313]

Some of the above issues arose in the South African Constitutional Court decision of *Khosa v Minister for Social Development*.[314] Permanent resident non-citizens were statutorily excluded from certain social security benefits. The Court held that the right of 'everyone' to social security and social assistance in Article 27(1) of the South African Constitution does not permit the right to be limited to citizens.[315] While some differentiation between different classes of non-citizens (such as permanent and non-permanent residents) would be 'reasonable' (the domestic constitutional standard), the exclusion of all permanent residents on the facts was not, even taking into account financial considerations:

[52] The right of access to social security, including social assistance, for those unable to support themselves and their dependants is entrenched because as a society we value human beings and want to ensure that people are afforded their basic needs. A society must seek to ensure that the basic necessities of life are accessible to all if it is to be a society in which human dignity, freedom and equality are foundational.

The reasonableness of citizenship as a criterion of differentiation

[53] It is necessary to differentiate between people and groups of people in society by classification in order for the state to allocate rights, duties, immunities, privileges, benefits or even disadvantages and to provide efficient and effective delivery of social services. However, those classifications must satisfy the constitutional requirement of 'reasonableness' in section 27(2). In this case, the state has chosen to differentiate between citizens and non-citizens. That differentiation, if it is to pass constitutional muster, must not be arbitrary or irrational nor must it manifest a naked preference. There must be a rational connection between that differentiating law and the legitimate government purpose it is designed to achieve. A differentiating law or action which does not meet these standards will be in violation of section 9(1) and section 27(2) of the Constitution.

[54] The respondents averred that citizenship is a requirement for social benefits in 'almost all developed countries'. That may be so in respect of certain benefits. But unlike ours, those countries do not have constitutions that entitle 'everyone' to have access to social security, nor are their immigration and welfare laws necessarily the same as ours.

[55] The respondents contended that immigrants, before entering the country, are required to show self-sufficiency in order to qualify for permanent residence status. They are only restricted from accessing the right in question for a temporary period of five years, after which they can apply for citizenship by reason of naturalisation. On receipt of citizenship, they would have a right to social security. In their submission, any infringement of the right was therefore only of a temporary nature. They did not, however, offer any justification for denying the right to permanent residents during this five-year period.

[313] CESCR, Concluding Observations: Sweden, E/C.12/1995/5 (7 June 1995), [12].

[314] *Khosa v Minister for Social Development* ('*Khosa v Minister*') [2004] ZACC 11 (South African Constitutional Court).

[315] *Khosa v Minister*, [47].

[56] In essence, the Constitution properly interpreted provides that a permanent resident need not be a citizen in order to qualify for access to social security…

[57] The respondents argued that the state has an obligation toward its own citizens first, and that preserving welfare grants for citizens only creates an incentive for permanent residents to naturalise. This argument, commonly found in American jurisprudence, is based on the social contract assumption that non-citizens are not entitled to the full benefits available to citizens. The argument, however, does not accord with the stated legislative intention in the Immigration Act…

Financial considerations

[58] I accept that the concern that non-citizens may become a financial burden on the country is a legitimate one and I accept that there are compelling reasons why social benefits should not be made available to all who are in South Africa irrespective of their immigration status. The exclusion of all non-citizens who are destitute, however, irrespective of their immigration status, fails to distinguish between those who have become part of our society and have made their homes in South Africa, and those who have not. It also fails to distinguish between those who are being supported by sponsors who arranged their immigration and those who acquired permanent residence status without having sponsors to whom they could turn in case of need.

[59] It may be reasonable to exclude from the legislative scheme workers who are citizens of other countries, visitors and illegal residents, who have only a tenuous link with this country. The position of permanent residents is, however, quite different to that of temporary or illegal residents. They reside legally in the country and may have done so for a considerable length of time. Like citizens, they have made South Africa their home. While citizens may leave the country indefinitely without forfeiting their citizenship, permanent residents are compelled to return to the country (except in certain circumstances) at least once every three years. While they do not have the rights tied to citizenship, such as political rights and the right to a South African passport, they are, for all other purposes mentioned above, in much the same position as citizens. Once admitted as permanent residents they can enter and leave the country. Their homes, and no doubt in most cases their families too, are in South Africa. Some will have children born in South Africa. They have the right to work in South Africa, and even owe a duty of allegiance to the state. For these reasons, I exclude temporary residents and it would have been appropriate for the High Court to have done so.

[60] The respondents also sought to deny the benefit to permanent residents on the grounds that this would impose an impermissibly high financial burden on the state…

[61] …The respondents were unable, however, to furnish this Court with information relating to the numbers who hold permanent resident status, or who would qualify for social assistance if the citizenship barrier were to be removed.

[62] There is thus no clear evidence to show what the additional cost of providing social grants to aged and disabled permanent residents would be. Taking into account certain assumptions relating to the composition of the groups and numbers of dependents, Mr Kruger concludes that the additional annual cost of including permanent residents in grants in terms of sections 3, 4 and 4B could range between R243 million and R672 million. The possible range demonstrates the speculative nature of the calculations, but even if they are taken as providing the best guide of what the cost may be, they do not support

the contention that there will be a huge cost in making provision for permanent residents. Approximately one fifth of the projected expenditure is in respect of child grants and the unconstitutionality of the citizenship requirement in that section of the Act has already been conceded by the respondents. The remainder reflects an increase of less than 2% on the present cost of social grants (currently R26.2 billion) even on the higher estimate. Bearing in mind that it is anticipated that the expenditure on grants will, in any event, increase by a further R18.4 billion over the next three years without making provision for permanent residents, the cost of including permanent residents in the system will be only a small proportion of the total cost.

Self-sufficiency

[63] Another reason given for excluding permanent residents from the scheme was the promotion of the immigration policy of the state, which seeks to exclude persons who may become a burden on the state and thereby to encourage self-sufficiency among foreign nationals.

[64] Limiting the cost of social welfare is a legitimate government concern. If it is considered necessary to control applications for permanent residence by excluding those who may become a burden on the state, that too is permissible, but it must be done in accordance with the Constitution and its values. The state can protect itself against persons becoming financial burdens by thorough, careful consideration in the admission of immigrants, or by taking adequate security from those admitted, or by demanding such security or guarantees from their sponsors at the time the immigrants are allowed into the country or are permitted to stay as permanent residents. It would not necessarily be unreasonable in such circumstances to require a permanent resident to look in the first instance to his or her sponsor for support, and to permit a claim on the security system only if, notwithstanding the security or guarantee, that fails.

[65] At the time the immigrant applies for admission to take up permanent residence the state has a choice. If it chooses to allow immigrants to make their homes here it is because it sees some advantage to the state in doing so. Through careful immigration policies it can ensure that those admitted for the purpose of becoming permanent residents are persons who will profit, and not be a burden to, the state. If a mistake is made in this regard, and the permanent resident becomes a burden, that may be a cost we have to pay for the constitutional commitment to developing a caring society, and granting access to socio-economic rights to all who make their homes here. Immigration can be controlled in ways other than allowing immigrants to make their permanent homes here, and then abandoning them to destitution if they fall upon hard times. The category of permanent residents who are before us are children and the aged, all of whom are destitute and in need of social assistance. They are unlikely to earn a living for themselves. While the self-sufficiency argument may hold in the case of immigrants who are viable in the job market and who are still in the process of applying for permanent resident status, the argument is seemingly not valid in the case of children and the aged who are already settled permanent residents and part of South African society.

The Court emphasized the vulnerability of non-citizens and the impact of their exclusion from social security on them and others:

[74] There can be no doubt that the applicants are part of a vulnerable group in society and, in the circumstances of the present case, are worthy of constitutional protection. We

are dealing, here, with intentional, statutorily sanctioned unequal treatment of part of the South African community. This has a strong stigmatising effect. Because both permanent residents and citizens contribute to the welfare system through the payment of taxes, the lack of congruence between benefits and burdens created by a law that denies benefits to permanent residents almost inevitably creates the impression that permanent residents are in some way inferior to citizens and less worthy of social assistance. Sharing responsibility for the problems and consequences of poverty equally as a community represents the extent to which wealthier members of the community view the minimal well-being of the poor as connected with their personal well-being and the well-being of the community as a whole. In other words, decisions about the allocation of public benefits represent the extent to which poor people are treated as equal members of society.

...

The impact of the exclusion

[76] The exclusion of permanent residents in need of social-security programmes forces them into relationships of dependency upon families, friends and the community in which they live, none of whom may have agreed to sponsor the immigration of such persons to South Africa. These families or dependants, who may be in need of social assistance themselves, are asked to shoulder burdens not asked of other citizens. The denial of the welfare benefits therefore impacts not only on permanent residents without other means of support, but also on the families, friends and communities with whom they have contact. Apart from the undue burden that this places on those who take on this responsibility, it is likely to have a serious impact on the dignity of the permanent residents concerned who are cast in the role of supplicants.

[77] As far as the applicants are concerned, the denial of the right is total and the consequences of the denial are grave. They are relegated to the margins of society and are deprived of what may be essential to enable them to enjoy other rights vested in them under the Constitution. Denying them their right under section 27(1) therefore affects them in a most fundamental way. In my view this denial is unfair.

...

[82] In my view the importance of providing access to social assistance to all who live permanently in South Africa and the impact upon life and dignity that a denial of such access has, far outweighs the financial and immigration considerations on which the state relies. For the same reasons, I am satisfied that the denial of access to social grants to permanent residents who, but for their citizenship, would qualify for such assistance does not constitute a reasonable legislative measure as contemplated by section 27(2) of the Constitution.[316]

Because the legislative exclusion was constitutionally 'unreasonable', the Court found it unnecessary to consider whether the measures were further 'reasonable… within its [the state's] available resources, to achieve the progressive realisation of each of these rights', as provided under Article 27(2) of the Constitution.[317] While the decision turned on the domestic constitutional standard of 'reasonableness', it suggests that where 'everyone' has a right of social security, and

[316] *Khosa v Minister*, [52]–[82].

[317] *Khosa v Minister*, [83]–[84].

discrimination is prohibited, progressive realization should be invoked in a blanket fashion to override these considerations.

Non-contributory schemes—refugees and asylum seekers

The above policy considerations are even more apposite in the case of refugees, stateless persons and asylum seekers, who do not choose to migrate for work, but are forced to flee from their countries of origin. The CESCR does not subject these special categories to the same express potential restrictions that apply in the case of regular migrants, in recognition of their particular vulnerability. In General Comment No. 19, the CESCR stated that:

> 38. Refugees, stateless persons and asylum-seekers, and other disadvantaged and marginalized individuals and groups, should enjoy equal treatment in access to non-contributory social security schemes, including reasonable access to health care and family support, consistent with international standards.[318]

In monitoring states, the CESCR has highlighted the right to social security of refugees, in both developed and developing states,[319] and including asylum seekers awaiting a decision.[320] Other treaty bodies have similarly expressed concern about discrimination in or restrictions on access to social security by refugees,[321] including where they are undocumented.[322]

In part, this higher level of protection stems from the 'special' international law (*lex specialis*) which applies to these groups. Under the ICERD, for example, the CERD has called on states to lift reservations to the 1951 Refugee Convention which reduce social security for refugees.[323] Article 23 of the 1951 Refugee Convention requires states to treat refugees equal to nationals in relation to 'public relief and assistance', a term which refers to the full spectrum of social security rather than more limited social insurance:

> The Contracting States shall accord to refugees lawfully staying in their territory the same treatment with respect to public relief and assistance as is accorded to their nationals.

There is considerable state practice in accordance with this equal national treatment requirement.[324] The provision is designed to assimilate refugees with citizens as far as possible because of their lack of protection and assistance elsewhere.[325] The

[318] CESCR, General Comment No. 19, [38].

[319] CESCR, Concluding Observations: Azerbaijan, E/C.12/1/Add.104 (14 December 2004), [48]; Afghanistan, E/C.12/AFG/CO/2-4 (7 June 2010), [26]; Finland, E/C.12/1/Add.8 (5 December 1996), [21]; Syria, E/C.12/1/Add.63 (24 September 2001), [23]; Uzbekistan, E/C.12/UZB/CO/1 (24 January 2006), [23].

[320] CESCR, Consideration of Report Submitted by State Party: Senegal, E/2002/22 (2001), [359].

[321] CERD, Consideration of Report Submitted by State Party: United Kingdom, A/51/18 (1996), [235]; Australia, A/60/18 (2005), [44].

[322] CERD, Consideration of Report Submitted by State Party: Austria, A/57/18 (2002), [33].

[323] CERD, Consideration of Report Submitted by State Party: Malawi, A/58/18 (2003), [559].

[324] James Hathaway, *The Rights of Refugees under International Law* (Cambridge University Press, Cambridge, 2011), 806.

[325] Hathaway, *The Rights of Refugees*, 813.

strength of the equal protection standard in Article 23 is also its limitation: where states provide little social security to their nationals (as in various developing states), even lawfully resident refugees may share equally in nothing.[326]

The protection under Article 23 of the Refugee Convention is limited to refugees who are 'lawfully staying' in the country of refuge, with asylum seekers entitled only to 'the necessities of life' (including adequate food, shelter, health care and education, including as protected under the ICESCR) pending determination of their refugee claims.[327] Few states appear to give equal access to their full social security entitlements to newly arrived asylum seekers until their status is regularized, although often states provide special measures of support during refugee processing which render regular social security inappropriate or unnecessary.

Article 24 of the 1951 Refugee Convention provides further equality of treatment in relation to specific elements of social security, focusing on contribution-based employment benefits. It was based on ILO Convention No. 97 on Migration for Employment 1949.[328] Article 24 provides:

1. The Contracting States shall accord to refugees lawfully staying in their territory the same treatment as is accorded to nationals in respect of the following matters:

. . .

(b) Social security (legal provisions in respect of employment injury, occupational diseases, maternity, sickness, disability, old age, death, unemployment, family responsibilities and any other contingency which, according to national laws or regulations, is covered by a social security scheme), subject to the following limitations:

(i) There may be appropriate arrangements for the maintenance of acquired rights and rights in course of acquisition;

(ii) National laws or regulations of the country of residence may prescribe special arrangements concerning benefits or portions of benefits which are payable wholly out of public funds, and concerning allowances paid to persons who do not fulfil the contribution conditions prescribed for the award of a normal pension.

2. The right to compensation for the death of a refugee resulting from employment injury or from occupational disease shall not be affected by the fact that the residence of the beneficiary is outside the territory of the Contracting State.

3. The Contracting States shall extend to refugees the benefits of agreements concluded between them, or which may be concluded between them in the future, concerning the maintenance of acquired rights and rights in the process of acquisition in regard to social security, subject only to the conditions which apply to nationals of the States signatory to the agreements in question.

4. The Contracting States will give sympathetic consideration to extending to refugees so far as possible the benefits of similar agreements which may at any time be in force between such Contracting States and non-contracting States.

[326] Hathaway, *The Rights of Refugees*, 808–9.
[327] Hathaway, *The Rights of Refugees*, 460–514, 807.
[328] Hathaway, *The Rights of Refugees*, 775.

In some respects, the provision may provide greater protection for refugees than nationals, as it is an absolute (not relative) requirement to pay a survivor's benefit even to non-resident family members.[329] On the other hand, a refugee may not receive the full benefit of social security contributions they made in a country of origin where there is no cost-sharing agreement between the country of origin and the country of asylum.[330]

The position of stateless persons is more precarious in view of the less developed international treaty regime protecting them,[331] which does not include any specific right to social security. At best, stateless persons enjoy a right to be treated the same as other aliens.[332] Article 9 of the ICESCR will therefore be particularly important in ensuring the right to social security of stateless persons who are otherwise scarcely protected.

In monitoring states, the CESCR was concerned about disparities between Syrian nationals and stateless persons in respect of social benefits and accident compensation.[333] Other UN treaty bodies have also addressed social security and statelessness. The CERD was concerned by delays in Croatia's processing of citizenship applications by stateless persons, affecting social benefits for minority communities.[334] The CRC criticized a Slovenian court decision which unlawfully rendered stateless many minority children born in Slovenia and thus deprived them of their rights to social assistance and family benefits.[335]

It is also recalled that a failure by the state to provide social security, where the person has no other means of support, rendering them destitute, may constitute a violation of the freedom from inhuman or degrading treatment under Article 7 of the ICCPR, the Convention against Torture and regional human rights instruments.[336]

Contributory schemes

The CESCR requires states not to discriminate against non-nationals by denying benefits to those who have contributed to an insurance-based scheme, but leave the country:

36. Article 2, paragraph 2, prohibits discrimination on grounds of nationality and the Committee notes that the Covenant contains no express jurisdictional limitation. Where non-nationals, including migrant workers, have contributed to a social security scheme, they should be able to benefit from that contribution or retrieve their contributions if they

[329] Hathaway, *The Rights of Refugees*, 776–7.

[330] Hathaway, *The Rights of* Refugees, 778–85.

[331] Convention relating to the Status of Stateless Persons ('1954 Convention on the Status of Stateless Persons') (adopted 26 April 1954, 360 UNTS 117, entered into force 6 June 1960); Convention on the Reduction of Statelessness (opened for signature 30 August 1961, 989 UNTS 175, entered into force 13 December 1975).

[332] 1954 Convention on the Status of Stateless Persons, Article 7(1).

[333] CESCR, Concluding Observations: Syria, E/C.12/1/Add.63 (24 September 2001), [23].

[334] CERD, Consideration of Report Submitted by State Party: Croatia, A/48/18 (1993), [497].

[335] CRC, Concluding Observations: Slovenia, CRC/C/137 (2004), [557].

[336] *R v Secretary of State for the Home Department, ex parte Adam* [2005] UKHL 66, [7]–[9] (Lord Bingham).

leave the country. A migrant worker's entitlement should also not be affected by a change in workplace.[337]

In monitoring states, the CESCR was concerned at discriminatory restrictions on the ability of foreign nationals to be paid their accrued benefits after leaving Iraq:

Concern is expressed that the payment of benefits abroad to a citizen of another country is ensured only if he returns to his country of origin at the end of his insured period of service. This precludes workers who leave the State party before their contract period has expired or who settle in a country other than their country of origin from receiving benefits. Furthermore, payment of benefits is made outside the State party only under reciprocity agreements or international labour conventions, and is subject to authorization. It is noted with concern that due to the current situation in the State party, all such payments have been suspended.[338]

In *Gueye et al v France*, the HRC found a violation of Article 26 of the ICCPR where amendments to French law (in 1974, 1979 and 1981) treated retired soldiers of Senegalese nationality, who had served in the French Army prior to Senegal's independence in 1960, less favourably than retired soldiers of French nationality, despite the law previously treating them equally (between 1951 and 1974).[339] Article 26 does not preclude discrimination on the basis of nationality as such, but the HRC found that it relevantly prohibited discrimination on the ground of 'other status':

9.4 The Committee has noted the authors claim that they have been discriminated against on racial grounds, that is, one of the grounds specifically enumerated in article 26. It finds that there is no evidence to support the allegation that the State party has engaged in racially discriminatory practices vis-à-vis the authors. It remains, however, to be determined whether the situation encountered by the authors falls within the purview of article 26. The Committee recalls that the authors are not generally subject to French jurisdiction, except that they rely on French legislation in relation to the amount of their pension rights. It notes that nationality as such does not figure among the prohibited grounds of discrimination listed in article 26, and that the Covenant does not protect the right to a pension, as such. Under article 26, discrimination in the equal protection of the law is prohibited on any grounds such as race, colour, sex, language, religion, political or other opinion, national or social origin, property, birth or other status. There has been a differentiation by reference to nationality acquired upon independence. In the Committee's opinion, this falls within the reference to 'other status' in the second sentence of article 26. The Committee takes into account, as it did in communication No. 182/1984, that 'the right to equality before the law and to equal protection of the law without any discrimination does not make all differences of treatment discriminatory. A differentiation based on reasonable and objective criteria does not amount to prohibited discrimination within the meaning of article 26'.

[337] CESCR, General Comment No. 19, [36].

[338] CESCR, Consideration of Report Submitted by State Party: Iraq, E/1998/22 (1997), [261], [267].

[339] *Ibrahima Gueye et al v France* ('*Gueye v France*'), HRC Communication No. 196/1985 (6 April 1989).

The HRC also rejected France's justifications for the different treatment, namely the soldiers' change of nationality, the different social and economic conditions in Senegal, and the heightened risk of abuse of pensions by those outside France:

9.5 In determining whether the treatment of the authors is based on reasonable and objective criteria, the Committee notes that it was not the question of nationality which determined the granting of pensions to the authors but the services rendered by them in the past. They had served in the French Armed Forces under the same conditions as French citizens; for 14 years subsequent to the independence of Senegal they were treated in the same way as their French counterparts for the purpose of pension rights, although their nationality was not French but Senegalese. A subsequent change in nationality cannot by itself be considered as a sufficient justification for different treatment, since the basis for the grant of the pension was the same service which both they and the soldiers who remained French had provided. Nor can differences in the economic, financial and social conditions as between France and Senegal be invoked as a legitimate justification. If one compared the case of retired soldiers of Senegalese nationality living in Senegal with that of retired soldiers of French nationality in Senegal, it would appear that they enjoy the same economic and social conditions. Yet, their treatment for the purpose of pension entitlements would differ. Finally, the fact that the State party claims that it can no longer carry out checks of identity and family situation, so as to prevent abuses in the administration of pension schemes cannot justify a difference in treatment. In the Committee's opinion, mere administrative inconvenience or the possibility of some abuse of pension rights cannot be invoked to justify unequal treatment. The Committee concludes that the difference in treatment of the authors is not based on reasonable and objective criteria and constitutes discrimination prohibited by the Covenant.

10. The Human Rights Committee, acting under article 5, paragraph 4, of the Optional Protocol to the International Covenant on Civil and Political Rights, is of the view that the events in this case, in so far as they produced effects after 17 May 1984 (the date of entry into force of the Optional Protocol for France), disclose a violation of article 26 of the Covenant.

11. The Committee, accordingly, is of the view that the State party is under an obligation, in accordance with the provisions of article 2 of the Covenant, to take effective measures to remedy the violations suffered by the victims.

The decision is also significant because it extended the protection of non-discrimination in social security under the ICCPR to persons living outside France and, but for their pension entitlement, otherwise beyond the jurisdiction of French law. The same analysis in this case would apply under Articles 2(2) and 9 of the ICESCR.

Concessions for developing countries

As discussed in Chapter 2, Article 2(3) of the ICESCR allows developing countries to limit rights provided to non-nationals:

Developing countries, with due regard to human rights and their national economy, may determine to what extent they would guarantee the economic rights recognized in the present Covenant to non-nationals.

On the one hand, this provision may seem unnecessary given that such states can largely rely on the principle of progressive realization to attain the same end—that is, conserving scarce resources. However, the existence of an explicit carve-out for non-nationals may indicate that Article 2(3) is designed to excuse what would otherwise be a breach of the non-discrimination provisions of the ICESCR, which cannot otherwise by undermined by reliance on progressive realization. The provision sits oddly in an instrument of universal application. There is little evidence in its practice that the CESCR has endorsed or tolerated its invocation in concrete cases, although some states may be tempted to invoke it.

Relevant ILO standards on migrant workers and social security

Other international standards are relevant in defining the contours of the right of migrant workers to social security under Article 9. There are numerous ILO instruments which address the rights of migrant workers generally.[340] Four 'up-to-date' ILO instruments specifically address their social security rights: two conventions (neither of which is widely ratified) and two recommendations.

The earliest, ILO Convention No. 97 on Migration for Employment 1949, has forty-nine parties. Article 6 provides migrant workers with non-discriminatory equivalent national treatment in social security, subject to certain express limitations:

> 1. Each Member for which this Convention is in force undertakes to apply, without discrimination in respect of nationality, race, religion or sex, to immigrants lawfully within its territory, treatment no less favourable than that which it applies to its own nationals in respect of the following matters:
>
> …
>
> (b) social security (that is to say, legal provision in respect of employment injury, maternity, sickness, invalidity, old age, death, unemployment and family responsibilities, and any other contingency which, according to national laws or regulations, is covered by a social security scheme), subject to the following limitations:
>
> (i) there may be appropriate arrangements for the maintenance of acquired rights and rights in course of acquisition;
>
> (ii) national laws or regulations of immigration countries may prescribe special arrangements concerning benefits or portions of benefits which are payable wholly out of public funds, and concerning allowances paid to persons who do not fulfil the contribution conditions prescribed for the award of a normal pension…

340 ILO Convention No. 97 concerning Migration for Employment (Revised) (adopted 1 July 1949, entered into force 22 January 1952); ILO Recommendation No. 86 concerning Migration for Employment (Revised) (1 July 1949) ('Recommendation No. 86 concerning Migration for Employment'); ILO Convention No. 143 concerning Migrant Workers (Supplementary Provisions) (adopted 24 June 1975, entered into force 9 December 1978); ILO Recommendation No. 151 concerning Migrant Workers (24 June 1975).

Adopted in the same year, the ILO's Migration for Employment Recommendation (Revised) No. 86 of 1949 further encourages information exchange (paragraph 1) and the validation of documents (paragraph 4) between states on social security, and in paragraph 21 provides for inter-state agreements on migrant social security on the basis of equivalent national treatment (subject to possible residency requirements and the maintenance of acquired rights).

ILO Convention No. 118 concerning Equality of Treatment of Nationals and Non-Nationals in Social Security 1962 more specifically provides for equivalent national treatment, in all accepted branches of social security, of the citizens of other states parties, on a reciprocal basis, and without residency conditions. In addition, ILO Convention No. 157 on Maintenance of Social Security Rights 1982 provides for the maintenance of acquired social security rights, and those in the course of acquisition, by foreign citizens who are nationals of state parties, or refugees or stateless persons.

ILO Convention No. 143 on Migrant Workers (Supplementary Provisions) 1975 builds on the 1949 Convention, but has only twenty-three ratifications. Article 9 extends equal protection to migrant workers in social security arising from past employment, even where their immigration status is irregular:

1. Without prejudice to measures designed to control movements of migrants for employment by ensuring that migrant workers enter national territory and are admitted to employment in conformity with the relevant laws and regulations, the migrant worker shall, in cases in which these laws and regulations have not been respected and in which his position cannot be regularised, enjoy equality of treatment for himself and his family in respect of rights arising out of past employment as regards remuneration, social security and other benefits.

2. In case of dispute about the rights referred to in the preceding paragraph, the worker shall have the possibility of presenting his case to a competent body, either himself or through a representative.

3. In case of expulsion of the worker or his family, the cost shall not be borne by them.

4. Nothing in this Convention shall prevent Members from giving persons who are illegally residing or working within the country the right to stay and to take up legal employment.

Article 10 requires states to pursue a policy to guarantee equal treatment in social security generally:

Each Member for which the Convention is in force undertakes to declare and pursue a national policy designed to promote and to guarantee, by methods appropriate to national conditions and practice, equality of opportunity and treatment in respect of employment and occupation, of social security, of trade union and cultural rights and of individual and collective freedoms for persons who as migrant workers or as members of their families are lawfully within its territory.

The ILO's Migrant Workers Recommendation No. 151 of 1975 provides for equal national treatment of lawful migrant workers and their families in social security, welfare facilities and benefits connected with employment (paragraph 2(f)), as well as equal treatment for irregular migrant workers in social security benefits arising from past and present employment (paragraph 8(3)). It also encourages prompt decision-making about the regularity or otherwise of a migrant's status (paragraph 8(1)). The Recommendation further provides for equal national treatment of migrant workers in a detailed range of social services (paragraphs 23 to 29). States are also encouraged to provide migrant workers who leave their country of employment with any workplace injury benefits and reimbursement of social security contributions (paragraph 34).

The migrant workers' convention and social security

The most recent relevant instrument is the Migrant Workers' Convention, which has forty-six parties, entered into force in 2003, and was adopted through the United Nations rather than the ILO. The CESCR has occasionally called on states to ratify the Migrant Workers' Convention.[341]

The Migrant Workers' Convention establishes core minimum rights for all migrant workers and their families, and additional rights for lawful or regular migrants. National implementation is monitored by the Committee on Migrant Workers (CMW), created by the Convention. All migrant workers are entitled to a minimum level of social protection under Article 27, although the provision is heavily qualified by reference to whatever is provided for by national law and treaties. Where benefits are unavailable, states are then merely required to 'examine the possibility' of reimbursing contributions made by workers to social insurance on an equivalent national treatment basis. Article 27 provides:

1. With respect to social security, migrant workers and members of their families shall enjoy in the State of employment the same treatment granted to nationals in so far as they fulfil the requirements provided for by the applicable legislation of that State and the applicable bilateral and multilateral treaties. The competent authorities of the State of origin and the State of employment can at any time establish the necessary arrangements to determine the modalities of application of this norm.
2. Where the applicable legislation does not allow migrant workers and members of their families a benefit, the States concerned shall examine the possibility of reimbursing interested persons the amount of contributions made by them with respect to that benefit on the basis of the treatment granted to nationals who are in similar circumstances.

Documented or regular migrant workers are entitled to the additional benefit of Article 43, which provides for full equality of national treatment in social security, housing and health:

1. Migrant workers shall enjoy equality of treatment with nationals of the State of employment in relation to:

…

(d) Access to housing, including social housing schemes, and protection against exploitation in respect of rents;

[341] CESCR, Consideration of Report Submitted by State Party: Russia, E/2004/22 (2003), [487].

(e) Access to social and health services, provided that the requirements for participation in the respective schemes are met;

…

Article 45(1) extends the same protections to migrant workers' families:

1. Members of the families of migrant workers shall, in the State of employment, enjoy equality of treatment with nationals of that State in relation to:

…

(c) Access to social and health services, provided that requirements for participation in the respective schemes are met…

Article 54(1) provides further equal national treatment to migrant workers in unemployment benefits:

1. Without prejudice to the terms of their authorization of residence or their permission to work and the rights provided for in articles 25 and 27 of the present Convention, migrant workers shall enjoy equality of treatment with nationals of the State of employment in respect of:

…

(b) Unemployment benefits;

(c) Access to public work schemes intended to combat unemployment…

In monitoring states, the CMW has often drawn attention to social security rights. It has been concerned about discrimination against migrant workers in social security[342] or their lack of access to it,[343] particularly for irregular migrant workers,[344] but also for those formally employed who were treated unequally in the payment of retirement pensions.[345] It recommended that Argentina review the required length of residence for non-contributory social benefits and consider extending those benefits to irregular migrant workers and their families 'in cases of extreme social vulnerability'.[346] It also criticized 'media coverage associating migrants with…abuse of social benefits' in Argentina.[347]

The CMW has expressed particular concern about the lack of 'full' social protection for the children of migrant workers,[348] including those forced to beg on the streets (such as *talibés*)[349] as well as those left behind in countries of origin while parents work abroad.[350] It has called for states to develop social protection policies for children[351] and provide psychosocial rehabilitation services.[352]

342 CMW, Concluding Observations: Albania, CMW/C/ALB/CO/1 (10 December 2010), [19].
343 CMW, Concluding Observations: Ecuador, CMW/C/ECU/CO/2 (15 December 2010), [27].
344 CMW, Concluding Observations: Algeria, CMW/C/DZA/CO/1 (19 May 2010), [19].
345 CMW, Concluding Observations: Senegal, CMW/C/SEN/CO/1 (10 December 2010), [14].
346 CMW, Concluding Observations: Argentina, CMW/C/ARG/CO/1 (2 November 2011), [30].
347 CMW, Concluding Observations: Argentina, CMW/C/ARG/CO/1 (2 November 2011), [17].
348 CMW, Concluding Observations: Albania, CMW/C/ALB/CO/1 (10 December 2010), [38].
349 CMW, Concluding Observations: Senegal, CMW/C/SEN/CO/1 (10 December 2010), [18].
350 CMW, Concluding Observations: Senegal, CMW/C/SEN/CO/1 (10 December 2010), [19].
351 CMW, Concluding Observations: Senegal, CMW/C/SEN/CO/1 (10 December 2010), [19].
352 CMW, Concluding Observations: Senegal, CMW/C/SEN/CO/1 (10 December 2010), [18].

Procedural barriers to social security for migrant workers and their families have also been criticized by the CMW, such as a lack of information about social security entitlements[353] or the availability of legal remedies (thus limiting their access to justice).[354] The CMW criticized a state's failure to register children at birth and issue them with identity documents to enable their access to assistance.[355] It also criticized a three-year residency requirement (for migrant worker parents and children) to qualify for a universal allowance for children from poor families, as well as a twenty-year residence requirement for non-contributory pensions for mothers with seven or more children.[356]

The CMW has frequently encouraged states to conclude bilateral or multilateral social security agreements with sending and receiving states, 'thus allowing migrant workers and members of their families to receive social security benefits from the country in which they worked when applicable'.[357] In this regard, the CMW has encouraged states to ratify ILO Convention No. 118 concerning Equality of Treatment of Nationals and Non-Nationals in Social Security 1962.[358]

Significantly, the CMW has drawn attention to states' extraterritorial obligations with respect to the social protection of migrant workers. It has thus urged states to improve the services provided by their embassies and consulates to their nationals working abroad, including 'psychosocial counselling' for victims of abuse and ill-treatment abroad.[359] It has also called on states to provide social assistance to their nationals working abroad and to develop policies that facilitate their return[360] and reintegration into society, including by addressing the psychosocial and economic needs of returnees and their families.[361]

Vulnerable workers

Aside from migrant workers, the CESCR has also highlighted the needs of other particularly vulnerable workers. Given that ILO instruments originally limited social security to formal employment relationships, the CESCR has been mindful of the need for Article 9 to specially protect irregular workers and workers in the informal economy:

> 3. Workers inadequately protected by social security (part-time, casual, self-employed and homeworkers)

[353] CMW, Concluding Observations: Paraguay, CMW/C/PRY/CO/1 (16 May 2012), [32]; Rwanda, CMW/C/RWA/CO/1 (10 October 2012), [35].

[354] CMW, Concluding Observations: Guatemala, CMW/C/GTM/CO/1 (18 October 2011), [20].

[355] CMW, Concluding Observations: Bosnia and Herzegovina, CMW/C/BIH/CO/2 (26 September 2012), [35].

[356] CMW, Concluding Observations: Argentina, CMW/C/ARG/CO/1 (2 November 2011), [29].

[357] CMW, Concluding Observations: Sri Lanka, CMW/C/LKA/CO/1 (14 December 2009), [42]; see also Albania, CMW/C/ALB/CO/1 (10 December 2010), [27], [28(c)]; Rwanda, CMW/C/RWA/CO/1 (10 October 2012), [32(b)]; Tajikistan, CMW/C/TJK/CO/1 (16 May 2012), [34]; Sri Lanka, CMW/C/LKA/CO/1 (14 December 2009), [41].

[358] CMW, Concluding Observations: Tajikistan, CMW/C/TJK/CO/1 (16 May 2012), [34].

[359] CMW, Concluding Observations: Sri Lanka, CMW/C/LKA/CO/1 (14 December 2009), [39]–[40]; see also Albania, CMW/C/ALB/CO/1 (10 December 2010), [28(a)].

[360] CMW, Concluding Observations: Senegal, CMW/C/SEN/CO/1 (10 December 2010), [8].

[361] CMW, Concluding Observations: Sri Lanka, CMW/C/LKA/CO/1 (14 December 2009), [45].

33. Steps must be taken by States parties to the maximum of their available resources to ensure that the social security systems cover workers inadequately protected by social security, including part-time workers, casual workers, the self-employed and homeworkers. Where social security schemes for such workers are based on occupational activity, they should be adapted so that they enjoy conditions equivalent to those of comparable full-time workers. Except in the case of employment injury, these conditions could be determined in proportion to hours of work, contributions or earnings, or through other appropriate methods. Where such occupation-based schemes do not provide adequate coverage to these workers, a State party will need to adopt complementary measures.

4. Informal economy

34. States parties must take steps to the maximum of their available resources to ensure that the social security systems cover those persons working in the informal economy. The informal economy has been defined by the International Labour Conference as 'all economic activities by workers and economic units that are—in law or in practice—not covered or insufficiently covered by formal arrangements.' This duty is particularly important where social security systems are based on a formal employment relationship, business unit or registered residence. Measures could include: (a) removing obstacles that prevent such persons from accessing informal social security schemes, such as community-based insurance; (b) ensuring a minimum level of coverage of risks and contingencies with progressive expansion over time; and (c) respecting and supporting social security schemes developed within the informal economy such as micro-insurance and other microcredit related schemes. The Committee notes that in a number of States parties with a large informal economy, programmes such as universal pension and health-care schemes that cover all persons have been adopted.[362]

The CESCR habitually draws attention to the exclusion of workers in the informal sector from social security, often noting that this excludes large sectors of the population where the informal sector accounts for a large share of a national economy.[363] It frequently calls on states to expand their social security systems to encompass the informal sector.[364] The CESCR has also been concerned about the impact of the privatization of social security on those in the informal sector, who may not be able to contribute to individual pensions.[365]

As noted already, a lack of coverage of irregular or informal workers can also give rise to indirect discrimination where particular groups are over-represented, such as women in homework, or migrants in domestic service. Other UN treaty bodies have been attentive to the impacts on vulnerable sub-categories of irregular or informal sector workers. The CEDAW Committee has frequently criticized the exclusion from social security of women who work in the

[362] CESCR, General Comment No. 19, [33]–[34].

[363] CESCR, Consideration of Report Submitted by State Party: Paraguay, E/1997/22 (1996), [76]; Peru, E/1998/22 (1997), [149] and [161]; Argentina, E/2000/22 (1999), [261]; Senegal, E/2002/22 (2001), [346]; Benin, E/2003/22 (2002), [171]; Russia, E/2004/22 (2003), [459]; Zambia, E/2006/22 (2005), [90].

[364] CESCR, Consideration of Report Submitted by State Party: Honduras, E/2002/22 (2001), [146]; Benin, E/2003/22 (2002), [190]; Russia, E/2004/22 (2003), [487]; Chile, E/2005/22 (2004), [569]; Zambia, E/2006/22 (2005), [112].

[365] CESCR, Consideration of Report Submitted by State Party: Mexico, E/2000/22 (1999), [386].

informal sector,[366] including those in domestic work or in the *maquila* industry (export-oriented factories in Mexico).[367] It has called on states to adopt legislative, administrative and other measures guaranteeing access to social security.[368]

Rural and agricultural workers have also been of concern to the CESCR, since they are often outside the formal economy, and social security may also be far less accessible outside urban areas.

Internally displaced persons and internal migrants

The CESCR has paid special attention to the often precarious situation of internally displaced persons (IDPs) and internal migrants. In General Comment No. 19, the CESCR stated:

> 39. Internally displaced persons should not suffer from any discrimination in the enjoyment of their right to social security and States parties should take proactive measures to ensure equal access to schemes, for example by waiving, where applicable, residence requirements and making allowance for provision of benefits or other related services at the place of displacement. Internal migrants should be able to access social security from their place of residence, and residence registration systems should not restrict access to social security for individuals who move to another district where they are not registered.

These groups are normally already entitled to full legal protection as citizens or residents under national law. As such, there are no 'hard' international law rules providing special protection to these groups in relation to social security rights.

However, the forced or voluntary movement of such groups may render them uniquely vulnerable and make it more difficult for them to access social security. The 'soft' law UN Guiding Principles on Internal Displacement accordingly provide that '[w]hen necessary, internally displaced persons shall have access to psychological and social services'.[369]

On a number of occasions, the CESCR has exposed difficulties faced by IDPs in relation to social security. It was concerned that IDPs from Kosovo in Serbia had not received their pensions for years, in part because their work booklets had been destroyed during the hostilities in Kosovo.[370] It was also concerned for IDPs in Azerbaijan.[371] Other treaty bodies have also expressed concern about social security for IDPs.[372]

[366] CEDAW, Consideration of Report Submitted by State Party: Saint Kitts and Nevis, A/57/38 part III (2002), [100]; Peru, A/57/38 part III (2002), [478]; Congo, A/58/38 part I (2003), [172]; Costa Rica, A/58/38 part II (2003), [63]; Argentina, A/59/38 part II (2004), [374].

[367] CEDAW, Consideration of Report Submitted by State Party: Mexico, A/57/38 part III (2002), [441].

[368] CEDAW, Consideration of Report Submitted by State Party: Dominican Republic, A/59/38 part II (2004), [303]; see also Republic of the Congo, A/58/38 part I (2003) [172].

[369] UN Guiding Principles on Internal Displacement, E/CN.4/1998/53/Add.2 (11 February 1998), Principle 19(1).

[370] CESCR, Concluding Observations: Serbia and Montenegro, E/C.12/1/Add.108 (23 June 2005), [22], [49].

[371] CESCR, Concluding Observations: Azerbaijan, E/C.12/1/Add.104 (14 December 2004), [48].

[372] CERD, Consideration of Report Submitted by State Party: Serbia and Montenegro, A/59/40 (2004), [75(18)]; CERD, Concluding Observations: Azerbaijan, E/C.12/1/Add.104 (14 December 2004), [48].

Issues that IDPs may commonly face in accessing social security include discrimination by local authorities outside their place of origin; inability to meet residency requirements; a lack of relevant documentation where they have fled suddenly; and language barriers. Since IDPs will have commonly lost their employment, homes, capital and support networks, their social security needs may be substantially greater than those of other citizens, and the law's allowances may not be tailored to their additional needs.

Where the administration of social security is decentralized to local or regional authorities, IDPs and internal migrants may also be at risk of falling through the cracks where there is inadequate coordination between different authorities. Such was the case for persons displaced by conflict in Bosnia-Herzegovina, where the lack of an inter-entity agreement prevented access to pensions and health care:

20. The [CESCR] Committee is concerned that the absence of an inter-Entity agreement on pension rights and the failure of the entities to implement the existing inter-Entity agreement on health insurance prevent many returnees moving from one Entity to the other from enjoying access to pension benefits and health care.

. . .

42. The Committee requests the State party to promote the adoption of an inter-Entity agreement on pension rights and to ensure the implementation of the inter-Entity agreement on health insurance with a view to guaranteeing access to pension benefits and health care by returnees who move from one Entity to the other.[373]

The above considerations also apply to internal migrants, many of whom may also be rural-urban migrant workers who are vulnerable to labour exploitation. But rural-urban migration also has implications for the rural areas experiencing rapid depopulation and ageing. The CESCR was mindful of the need to provide for the resulting special needs of rural areas left behind by economic transformation and urbanization in commenting on South Korea:

22. The Committee notes with concern the shifting population distribution from rural to urban areas, with most government programmes to develop infrastructure, education, health care and other essential facilities being highly concentrated in the urban areas. Urban migration of younger people has left many older persons to care for family farms in the countryside. The Committee regrets that the situation of persons living in rural areas has not been sufficiently dealt with during the present dialogue.[374]

Victims of conflict

In addition to the groups identified in General Comment No. 19, in its practice the CESCR has drawn attention to the needs of victims of conflict. In assessing Bosnia-Herzegovina's implementation of the ICESCR, the CESCR criticized a

[373] CESCR, Concluding Observations: Bosnia and Herzegovina, E/C.12/BIH/CO/1 (24 January 2006), [20] and [42].

[374] CESCR, Concluding Observations: Republic of Korea, E/C.12/1/Add.59 (21 May 2001), [22].

law which provided civilian victims of war with only 20 per cent of the pensions received by military victims of war:

18. The Committee notes with deep concern the extent of the discrepancy between the significant budget allocations for financing the pensions of military victims of war and the comparatively low resources allocated to social protection, as reflected by the fact that, under the Law on Amendments to the Law on Social Protection, Civilian War Victims, and Families with Children of the Federation of Bosnia and Herzegovina, civilian war victims will receive only 20 per cent of the pension benefits received by military victims of war.

39. The Committee urges the State party to ensure a more equitable allocation of existing funds to social protection, in particular of civilian war victims, with a view to reducing the discrepancy between, inter alia, the budgets for civilian and for military victims of war.

40. The Committee encourages the State party to promote the adoption of the proposed Law on Amendments to the Law on Social Protection, Civilian War Victims, and Families with Children, which is currently in the parliamentary procedure in the Federation of Bosnia and Herzegovina. It provides for the transfer of the budget for the social protection of civilian war victims and persons with disabilities not related to armed conflict from the cantons to the Federation, in order to eliminate inequalities resulting from the diverging availability of funds in the cantons. It also requests the State party to ensure that the authorities of the Federation of Bosnia and Herzegovina extend this budgetary transfer to other categories of social protection beneficiaries.[375]

The CESCR further criticized the absence of a coherent strategy by Bosnia-Herzegovina to support victims of sexual violence during the conflict:

19. The Committee is gravely concerned about the absence of a coherent strategy to support victims of sexual violence suffered during the armed conflict of 1992–1995 and that Entity laws pertaining to civilian war victims are gender-insensitive and provide inadequate social protection for victims of sexual violence.

…

41. The Committee recommends that the State party ensure that victims of sexual violence suffered during the armed conflict of 1992–1995 obtain the status of civilian war victims, to devise and implement a coherent strategy at State level to protect the economic, social and cultural rights of victims of sexual violence and their family members, and to ensure the participation of victims of sexual violence in any decision-making processes affecting them.[376]

In respect of Guatemala, the CESCR was concerned about the inattention to family reunion and children's rights in measures of reparation for victims of war:

19. The Committee also takes note of the efforts made by the State party towards the implementation of the National Reparation Programme for victims of war. However, the Committee expresses concern at the lack of effective measures to reunite families separated

[375] CESCR, Concluding Observations: Bosnia and Herzegovina, E/C.12/BIH/CO/1 (24 January 2006), [18], [39] and [40].

[376] CESCR, Concluding Observations: Bosnia and Herzegovina, E/C.12/BIH/CO/1 (24 January 2006), [19] and [41].

by the conflict, to establish the whereabouts of children who have disappeared and to safeguard the rights of children orphaned by the war.[377]

The CESCR also criticized the inadequate levels of pensions provided to war victims by UNMIK, as well as eligibility criteria which excluded from benefits returnees who formally owned land assets but could not access them because of the war. It further criticized a procedural failure to provide forms in a relevant language:

21. The Committee is concerned that the minimum levels of basic and contribution-based old-age pension benefits, disability pension benefits, war invalidity and survivor benefits and social assistance payments are insufficient to ensure an adequate standard of living to recipients and their families. The Committee is also concerned that the exclusion from such benefits of, inter alia, persons who own more than 0.5 hectares of arable land may have a discriminatory effect on returnees who are unable to repossess their lands because of illegal occupation or security concerns. (art. 9)

The Committee recommends that UNMIK, in cooperation with the Kosovo authorities, ensure that the minimum levels of basic and contribution-based old-age pension benefits, disability benefits, war invalidity and survivor benefits and social assistance payments are sufficient to ensure an adequate standard of living to recipients and their families. It also recommends that it review any discriminatory eligibility requirement for such benefits based on, inter alia, land ownership.

22. The Committee notes with concern reports about difficulties, such as the absence of application forms in Serbian prior to 2005 or the requirement that death certificates must be issued by UNMIK, which members of non-Albanian communities have been facing when applying for war invalidity and survivor benefits under UNMIK Regulation 2000/66. (art. 9)

The Committee recommends that UNMIK, in cooperation with the Kosovo authorities, ensure that members of non-Albanian communities enjoy equal access to war invalidity and survivor benefits, in law and in practice.[378]

Mention may also be made of Article 24(6) of the International Convention for the Protection of All Persons from Enforced Disappearance, which requires states to address the social welfare law considerations affecting disappeared persons and their families:

6. Without prejudice to the obligation to continue the investigation until the fate of the disappeared person has been clarified, each State Party shall take the appropriate steps with regard to the legal situation of disappeared persons whose fate has not been clarified and that of their relatives, in fields such as social welfare, financial matters, family law and property rights.

The right of compensation for victims of enforced disappearances is addressed by other rules of international law, although its payment may occur through social

[377] CESCR, Concluding Observations: Guatemala, E/C.12/1/Add.93 (12 December 2003), [19].
[378] CESCR, Concluding Observations: UNMIK, E/C.12/UNK/CO/1 (1 December 2008), [21]–[22].

security mechanisms. The right of social security under Article 9 itself does not impose an obligation on the state to compensate victims of human rights violations or international crimes.[379]

Other international standards are also relevant to the social assistance of victims of conflict, particularly international humanitarian law, which operates as the special law (*lex specialis*) in times of armed conflict. In occupied territory in international armed conflict, an Occupying Power must respect, 'unless absolutely prevented', the local law in force,[380] such that it would ordinarily be required to maintain the operation of local social security laws. Further, it must respect private property,[381] which arguably includes any accrued contributory social insurance benefits.[382] Further, the Fourth Geneva Convention of 1949,[383] on the protection of civilians, provides in Article 59 for emergency relief to populations in need, although such protection of basic necessities falls short of the wider range of protections conferred by social security law:

> If the whole or part of the population of an occupied territory is inadequately supplied, the Occupying Power shall agree to relief schemes on behalf of the said population, and shall facilitate them by all the means at its disposal.
>
> Such schemes, which may be undertaken either by States or by impartial humanitarian organizations such as the International Committee of the Red Cross, shall consist, in particular, of the provision of consignments of foodstuffs, medical supplies and clothing. All Contracting Parties shall permit the free passage of these consignments and shall guarantee their protection.
>
> A Power granting free passage to consignments on their way to territory occupied by an adverse Party to the conflict shall, however, have the right to search the consignments, to regulate their passage according to prescribed times and routes, and to be reasonably satisfied through the Protecting Power that these consignments are to be used for the relief of the needy population and are not to be used for the benefit of the Occupying Power.

There are also special measures of social protection for women and children, as under Article 50 of the Fourth Geneva Convention:

> . . . The Occupying Power shall not hinder the application of any preferential measures in regard to food, medical care and protection against the effects of war, which may have been adopted prior to the occupation in favour of children under fifteen years, expectant mothers, and mothers of children under seven years.

[379] See instead UNGA Res. 60/147, Basic Principles and Guidelines on the Right to a Remedy and Reparation for Victims of Gross Violations of International Human Rights Law and Serious Violations of International Humanitarian Law (21 March 2006) ('Van Boven Principles'), among others.

[380] Convention (IV) respecting the Laws and Customs of War on Land and its Annex: Regulations concerning the Laws and Customs of War on Land (adopted 18 October 1907, entered into force 26 January 1910), Article 43.

[381] Convention (IV), Article 46.

[382] As in the case under regional human rights law: see further below.

[383] Geneva Convention Relative to the Protection of Civilian Persons in Times of War (adopted 12 August 1949, 75 UNTS 287, entered into force 21 October 1950), Article 50.

Persons affected by changes in statehood

Related to conflict are situations involving the dissolution and creation of states. The CESCR commented on social security after the disintegration of the former Yugoslavia, in relation to newly independent states (such as Croatia and Bosnia-Herzegovina) and UNMIK in Kosovo. These situations concerned minorities who found themselves outside their former country of residence; minorities within a new federal state but outside the area where their benefits accrued; and minorities who were 'erased' from the official records upon which their social security entitlements were based. Thus, concerning Croatia:

33. The [CESCR] Committee recommends as a matter of urgency that the State party continue its negotiations with the relevant authorities to ensure that Croatians who made pension contributions prior to independence are able to benefit from their pensions.[384]

In relation to Bosnia-Herzegovina, it was noted earlier that the absence of an inter-entity agreement on pension rights, and the lack of implementation of an existing agreement on health insurance, risked depriving returnees of access to these rights if they returned home.[385] As regards the UNMIK:

16. The [CESCR] Committee is concerned that nationals of the former Yugoslavia have been 'erased' as their names were removed from the population registers in 1992. As a result of this, they have lost their Slovene nationality and their right to reside in the State party. The Committee observes that this situation entails violations of these persons' economic and social rights, including the rights to work, social security, health care and education. Moreover, the Committee regrets the lack of information on the actual situation with regard to the enjoyment by those individuals of the rights set out in the Covenant…

32. The Committee urges the State party to take the necessary legislative and other measures to remedy the situation of nationals of the States of former Yugoslavia who have been 'erased' as their names were removed from the population registers in 1992. While noting that bilateral agreements were concluded in this regard, the Committee strongly recommends that the State party should restore the status of permanent resident to all the individuals concerned, in accordance with the relevant decisions of the Constitutional Court. These measures should allow these individuals to reclaim their rights and regain access to health services, social security, education and employment. The Committee requests the State party to report to it, in its next periodic report, on progress in this regard.[386]

NON-DISCRIMINATION AND THE ICCPR

The UN Human Rights Committee has dealt with numerous communications under the ICCPR involving alleged discrimination in social security. Article 2 of the ICCPR, which prohibits discrimination in the provision of any ICCPR right, has no application in such cases because social security is not an ICCPR right.

[384] CESCR, Concluding Observations: Croatia, E/C.12/1/Add.73 (5 December 2001), [33].

[385] CESCR, Concluding Observations: Bosnia and Herzegovina, E/C.12/BIH/CO/1 (24 January 2006), [20] and [42].

[386] CESCR, Concluding Observations: Bosnia and Herzegovina, E/C.12/BIH/CO/1 (24 January 2006), [16], [32].

Article 26 of the ICCPR, however, entitles every person to equal protection before the law without discrimination. Thus, where a state chooses to provide social security, it must be offered on a non-discriminatory basis by virtue of Article 26.[387] The scope of protection is thus more extensive than under the ECHR, discussed earlier, which only protects against discrimination linked to another ECHR right (such as where a domestic social security entitlement can be assimilated to a property right under Article 21 of the ECHR).

The scope of non-discrimination in social security under the ICCPR is thus both more limited and more expansive than under the ICESCR. If states choose to do more than Article 9 of the ICESCR requires, they must do so in a non-discriminatory fashion pursuant to Article 26 of the ICCPR. But states cannot be compelled to provide social security under the ICCPR (subject to the extreme situation of not arbitrarily depriving a person of life, for instance by failing to provide subsistence where needed).

In the leading case of *Broeks v Netherlands*,[388] the HRC rejected the state's argument that Article 26 does not apply to socio-economic rights because they are separately dealt with by the ICESCR.[389] The case concerned a Dutch law which required a married woman to prove that she was a 'breadwinner' to qualify for unemployment benefits, but the same condition did not apply to married men:

12.1. The State party contends that there is considerable overlapping of the provisions of article 26 [of the ICCPR] with the provisions of article 2 of the International Covenant on Economic, Social and Cultural Rights. The Committee is of the view that the International Covenant on Civil and Political Rights would still apply even if a particular subject-matter is referred to or covered in other international instruments, for example, the International Convention on the Elimination of All Forms of Racial Discrimination, the Convention on the Elimination of All Forms of Discrimination against Women, or, as in the present case, the International Covenant on Economic, Social and Cultural Rights. Notwithstanding the interrelated drafting history of the two Covenants, it remains necessary for the Committee to apply fully the terms of the International Covenant on Civil and Political Rights. The Committee observes in this connection that the provisions of article 2 of the International Covenant on Economic, Social and Cultural Rights do not detract from the full application of article 26 of the International Covenant on Civil and Political Rights.

12.2. The Committee has also examined the contention of the State party that article 26 of the International Covenant on Civil and Political Rights cannot be invoked in respect of

[387] *Broeks v Netherlands*, [12.4]; see also *Zwaan-de Vries v Netherlands*, HRC Communication No. 182/1984 (1990), 209; *P P C v Netherlands*, HRC Communication No. 212/1985 (24 March 1988), 244, [6.2]; *Sprenger v Netherlands*, [7.2]; *Cavalcanti v Netherlands*, HRC Communication No. 418/1990 (8 November 1993), [7.3]; *J A M B-R v Netherlands*, HRC Communication No. 477/1991 (28 April 1994), [5.3]; *Neefs v Netherlands*, HRC Communiciation No. 425/1990 (15 July 1994), [7.2]; *Pepels v Netherlands*, HRC Communication No. 484/1991 (15 July 1994), [7.2]; *Pons v Spain*, HRC Communication No. 454/1991 (30 June 1994), [9.3]; *Danning v Netherlands*, HRC Communication No. 180/1984 at 205 (9 April 1987), [14]; *Gueye v France*, [9.4].

[388] *Broeks v Netherlands*.

[389] See also *Vos v Netherlands*, HRC Communication No. 218/1986 (29 March 1989), 232, [11.2].

a right which is specifically provided for under article 9 of the International Covenant on Economic, Social and Cultural Rights (social security, including social insurance). In so doing, the Committee has perused the relevant travaux preparatoires of the International Covenant on Civil and Political Rights, namely, the summary records of the discussions that took place in the Commission on Human Rights in 1948, 1949, 1950 and 1952 and in the Third Committee of the General Assembly in 1961, which provide a 'supplementary means of interpretation' (art. 32 of the Vienna Convention on the Law of Treaties) (see footnote 2). The discussions, at the time of drafting, concerning the question whether the scope of article 26 extended to rights not otherwise guaranteed by the Covenant, were inconclusive and cannot alter the conclusion arrived at by the ordinary means of interpretation referred to in paragraph 12.3 below.

12.3. For the purpose of determining the scope of article 26, the Committee has taken into account the 'ordinary meaning' of each element of the article in its context and in the light of its object and purpose (art. 31 of the Vienna Convention on the Law of Treaties). The Committee begins by noting that article 26 does not merely duplicate the guarantees already provided for in article 2. It derives from the principle of equal protection of the law without discrimination, as contained in article 7 of the Universal Declaration of Human Rights, which prohibits discrimination in law or in practice in any field regulated and protected by public authorities. Article 26 is thus concerned with the obligations imposed on States in regard to their legislation and the application thereof.

12.4. Although article 26 requires that legislation should prohibit discrimination, it does not of itself contain any obligation with respect to the matters that may be provided for by legislation. Thus it does not, for example, require any State to enact legislation to provide for social security. However, when such legislation is adopted in the exercise of a State's sovereign power, then such legislation must comply with article 26 of the Covenant.

The HRC further rejected an argument that the state's only obligation was to periodically examine national legislation to progressively eliminate discriminatory measures in accordance with the state's available resources:

12.5. The Committee observes in this connection that what is at issue is not whether or not social security should be progressively established in the Netherlands, but whether the legislation providing for social security violates the prohibition against discrimination contained in article 26 of the International Covenant on Civil and Political Rights and the guarantee given therein to all persons regarding equal and effective protection against discrimination.

13. The right to equality before the law and to equal protection of the law without any discrimination does not make all differences of treatment discriminatory. A differentiation based on reasonable and objective criteria does not amount to prohibited discrimination within the meaning of article 26.

On the facts, the Committee found that the law's differentiation was not based on reasonable and objective criteria and therefore amounted to prohibited discrimination on the basis of sex under Article 26:

14. It therefore remains for the Committee to determine whether the differentiation in Netherlands law at the time in question and as applied to Mrs. Broeks constituted

discrimination within the meaning of article 26. The Committee notes that in Netherlands law the provisions of articles 84 and 85 of the Netherlands Civil Code impose equal rights and obligations on both spouses with regard to their joint income. Under section 13, subsection 1(1), of the Unemployment Benefits Act (WWV), a married woman, in order to receive WWV benefits, had to prove that she was a 'breadwinner'—a condition that did not apply to married men. Thus a differentiation which appears on one level to be one of status is in fact one of sex, placing married women at a disadvantage compared with married men. Such a differentiation is not reasonable; and this seems to have been effectively acknowledged even by the State party by the enactment of a change in the law on 29 April 1985, with retroactive effect to 23 December 1984 (see para. 4.5 above).

15. The circumstances in which Mrs. Broeks found herself at the material time and the application of the then valid Netherlands law made her a victim of a violation, based on sex, of article 26 of the International Covenant on Civil and Political Rights, because she was denied a social security benefit on an equal footing with men.

16. The Committee notes that the State party had not intended to discriminate against women and further notes with appreciation that the discriminatory provisions in the law applied to Mrs. Broeks have, subsequently, been eliminated. Although the State party has thus taken the necessary measures to put an end to the kind of discrimination suffered by Mrs. Broeks at the time complained of, the Committee is of the view that the State party should offer Mrs. Broeks an appropriate remedy.

The HRC found similarly in *Zwaan-de Vries v Netherlands*.[390] Adverse treatment of men in social security has also been found discriminatory. In *Pauger v Austria*, a widower was denied a full pension if he had other sources of income, whereas a widow was not. The differentiation was not reasonable given that the social circumstances of both groups was similar and it was thus made purely on the basis of sex.[391]

As noted earlier, in *Gueye et al v France*, the HRC found a violation of Article 26 where the state paid lower pensions for equal work done by former Senegalese soldiers in the French Army, which involved discrimination on the basis of 'other status' (namely, nationality acquired upon independence).[392] In *Orihuela v Peru*, a dismissed civil servant who was denied his pension on politically motivated grounds did not enjoy non-discrimination and equal protection.[393] In *Derksen v Netherlands*, the denial of benefits where a child was born out of wedlock was not reasonable.[394] In *Young v Australia*, a law which excluded a same-sex partner from being a 'dependent' beneficiary of a deceased war veteran's pension involved discrimination on the basis of sexual orientation, where same-sex couples could not enter into marriage.[395]

[390] *F H Zwaan-de Vries v Netherlands*, HRC Communication No. 182/1984 (1990), 209, [11]–[16].
[391] *Pauger v Austria*, HRC Communication No. 415/1990 (30 March 1992), [7.4]–[7.6].
[392] *Gueye v France*, [9.4].
[393] *Orihuela v Peru*, HRC Communication No. 309/1988 (10 August 2003), [6.4].
[394] *Derksen v Netherlands*, HRC Communication No. 976/2001 (1 April 2004), [9.3].
[395] *Young v Australia*, HRC Communication No. 941/2000 (18 September 2003), [10.2]–[10.4].

A range of other social security complaints under Article 26 of the ICCPR have been less successful, in an area involving a high volume of complaints. These include cases involving unmarried couples,[396] same-sex couples,[397] marital status,[398] children living with parents[399] or foster parents,[400] refusal of retroactive benefits[401] and nationals living abroad treated differently due to bilateral treaties.[402] In many cases, complainants failed to meet reasonable, objective or uniform criteria or procedures for receipt of benefits.[403]

Branches of Social Security Assistance

In General Comment No. 19, the CESCR implicitly follows ILO Convention No. 102 in setting out the nine principal branches of social security that are covered by Article 9:

2. The right to social security encompasses the right to access and maintain benefits, whether in cash or in kind, without discrimination in order to secure protection, inter alia, from (a) lack of work-related income caused by sickness, disability, maternity, employment injury, unemployment, old age, or death of a family member; (b) unaffordable access to health care; (c) insufficient family support, particularly for children and adult dependents.

Reflecting the origins of the nine branches in ILO standards, the CESCR too has linked them to their original purpose in replacing or substituting lost work-related income. On the one hand, this ties in Article 9 to concrete, known and accepted ILO minimum standards. On the other hand, it has the drawback of seemingly limiting the general human right in Article 9 to the work-related contexts and limited sectoral coverage typical of ILO standards.

Some of these limitations are overcome by invoking the wider ICESCR rights also dealing with some of the issues covered by the nine branches under Article 9, including the right to health (Article 12), the rights of families, mothers and children (Article 10) and work rights (Article 6 to 8), although social security is one means by which such rights are realized.

[396] *Danning v Netherlands*, [14]; see also *Hoofdman v Netherlands*, HRC Communication No. 602/1994 (25 November 1998), [11.3], [11.4]; *Sprenger v Netherlands*, [7.2]–[7.4]; *Derksen v Netherlands*, [9.2].

[397] *Joslin et al v New Zealand*, HRC Communication No. 902/1999 (2002), 214, [8.2] (where marriage under Article 23(2) of the ICCPR was interpreted to exclude same-sex couples; by contrast, no such textual limitation is found in the ICESCR).

[398] *Snijders v Netherlands*, HRC Communication No. 651/1995 (27 July 1998), [8.2]–[8.5].

[399] *Neefs v Netherlands*, [7.2]–[7.4].

[400] *Oulajin v Netherlands*, [7.4]–[7.5].

[401] *J A M B-R v Netherlands*, [2.1]–[2.4], [5.3]–[5.5]; *Pepels v Netherlands*, [7.2], [7.5].

[402] *Van Oord v Netherlands*, HRC Communication No. 658/1995 (23 July 1997), [8.4]–[8.6].

[403] *Cavalcanti v Netherlands*, [7.3], [7.4]; *P P C v Netherlands*, [6.2]; *Hruska v Czech Republic*, HRC Communication No. 1191/2003 (30 October 2003), [4.2]; *Vos v Netherlands*, [11.3], [12]; *Althammer et al v Austria*, HRC Communication No. 998/2001 (22 September 2003), [10.2]; *Pons v Spain*, [9.3]–[9.5]; *Drake v New Zealand*, HRC Communication No. 601/1994 (3 April 1997), [8.4]–[8.6].

According to the ILO, some level of social security protection exists in all states, but only a few provide it across all nine areas of assistance or across all sectors of the population.[404] Health care assistance is the most common, followed by certain kinds of work-related assistance (contributory old age pensions, protection from employment injury, and paid sick leave, and paid maternity leave) which are often restricted to workers in the formal economy (or cover small sectors of) society.[405] In terms of formal legal protections, about one-third of states have comprehensive systems covering all nine branches (although often limited to those in formal employment), while half of states statutorily cover seven or eight branches.[406]

The nine branches can be clustered into a few broad groups: health-related assistance (health care, sickness, employment injury, disability, survivors and orphans); unemployment; old age; family and children; and maternity. The categories of health-related assistance tend to be fluid in practice and intersect depending on the type and progression of a health issue. The flexible language of Article 9 also does not limit it to the traditional nine branches of ILO coverage, but potentially accommodates the emergence of new forms of assistance.

In monitoring states, the CESCR has not tended to scrutinize each branch of social security in respect of every state, instead identifying either wider systemic issues or particular branches of concern where they arise. As such, the CESCR's practice does not provide much detail or elaboration about the content of each of the branches. Areas such as health, maternity and family support are addressed more fully in relation to the CESCR's monitoring of Articles 10 and 12. This section will briefly elaborate on the various branches by reference to the ILO standards in each area, and the limited CESCR practice where it exists.

HEALTH CARE

In General Comment No. 19, the CESCR highlights states' obligations to provide 'adequate access' to health services for all, either publicly or through affordable private or mixed plans:

> 13. States parties have an obligation to guarantee that health systems are established to provide adequate access to health services for all. In cases in which the health system foresees private or mixed plans, such plans should be affordable, in conformity with the essential elements enunciated in the present general comment. The Committee notes the particular importance of the right to social security in the context of endemic diseases such as HIV/AIDS, tuberculosis and malaria, and the need to provide access to preventive and curative measures.[407]

[404] ILO, Report VI, 30.
[405] ILO, Report VI, 30.
[406] ILO, Report VI, 31.
[407] CESCR, General Comment No. 19, [13].

Part II of ILO Convention No. 102 also sets out 'medical care' standards in a social security context, for any morbid condition and pregnancy and confinement and their consequences. Article 10(1) thus provides:

1. The benefit shall include at least—

   (a) in case of a morbid condition—

   (i) general practitioner care, including domiciliary visiting;

   (ii) specialist care at hospitals for in-patients and out-patients, and such specialist care as may be available outside hospitals;

   (iii) the essential pharmaceutical supplies as prescribed by medical or other qualified practitioners; and

   (iv) hospitalisation where necessary; and

   (b) in case of pregnancy and confinement and their consequences—

   (i) pre-natal, confinement and post-natal care either by medical practitioners or by qualified midwives; and

   (ii) hospitalisation where necessary.

The Convention allows states to select the categories of beneficiaries, in a manner typical of ILO social security standards, usually whether at least 50 per cent of prescribed classes of all employees, or at least 20 per cent of all economically active residents, or at least 50 per cent of all residents (Article 9). The state may also apply qualifying periods to prevent abuse (Article 11); confine the duration of benefits to twenty-six weeks (or in special cases, as low as thirteen weeks) (Article 12); and share the costs with beneficiaries (Article 10(2)). ILO Convention No. 130 on Medical Care and Sickness Benefits 1969 provides similar benefits, but extends assistance to dental care and medical rehabilitation.

The CESCR has occasionally commented on health care under Article 9. It has expressed concern about the impact of privatization on the accessibility of health care for vulnerable groups.[408] It called for health care to be included in a 'basic social protection package', alongside an old age pension and maternity benefit, for workers in the informal economy.[409] It was concerned at discrimination in health insurance where women married to working men were excluded from coverage.[410] It called for reimbursement of medicines to extend to traditional Chinese medicine.[411]

The CESCR has also recommended that one developing state immediately introduce a comprehensive compulsory health insurance scheme for everyone, including the unemployed, children, older persons, persons with disabilities and

[408] CESCR, Concluding Observations: Venezuela, E/C.12/1/Add.56 (21 May 2001), [29]; Republic of Korea, E/C.12/KOR/CO/3 (17 December 2009), [22].

[409] CESCR, Concluding Observations: Brazil, E/C.12/BRA/CO/2 (12 June 2009), [19].

[410] CESCR, Consideration of Report Submitted by State Party: Kenya, E/1994/23 (1993), [80].

[411] CESCR, Consideration of Report Submitted by State Party: United Kingdom (Hong Kong), E/1997/22 (1996), [346].

other disadvantaged and marginalized individuals and groups.[412] It called on the same state to progressively extend national hospital insurance to reimburse all hospitalization costs, in particular medical expenses; to cover all workers, including informal, casual, domestic and part-time workers and the self-employed, as well as persons without employment; and to remove any penalties imposed on those unable to pay their contributions on time.[413]

SICKNESS

According to the CESCR in General Comment No. 19, sickness benefits aim to replace income lost from inability to work due to illness; prolonged illness also crosses over into the separate branch of disability protection:

> 14. Cash benefits should be provided to those incapable of working due to ill-health to cover periods of loss of earnings. Persons suffering from long periods of sickness should qualify for disability benefits.

Disability is considered separately below. The CESCR has occasionally referred to sickness benefits, in criticizing their unavailability for most of the population[414] or unequal access to them between rural and urban areas.[415]

Part III of ILO Convention No. 102 sets out the notion of the 'sickness benefit' in international labour standards, covering 'incapacity for work resulting from a morbid condition and involving suspension of earnings, as defined by national laws or regulations' (Article 14). The benefit typically provides for periodical payments at 45 per cent of the reference wage (Article 16). ILO Convention No. 130 on Medical Care and Sickness Benefits 1969 increases the benefit to at least 60 per cent of the reference wage, and provides further assistance for funeral expenses in case of death of the beneficiary.

Under Convention No. 102, the benefit is normally payable for the duration of the incapacity, but states may choose to confine its duration in certain cases (including to as low as thirteen weeks) (Article 18). The Convention also allows states to select the categories of beneficiaries (Article 15), in a manner typical of ILO social security standards. Qualifying periods may be imposed to prevent abuse (Article 17).

EMPLOYMENT INJURY

Assistance for employment injury is one of the most common forms of social security, reflecting the concerns of organized labour in the area of occupational health and safety and the importance of replacement income in ensuring an adequate standard of living where a worker in no longer able to work. Most states provide some coverage of it, although globally less than 30 per cent of the working-age

[412] CESCR, Concluding Observations: Kenya, E/C.12/KEN/CO/1 (1 December 2008), [20].
[413] CESCR, Concluding Observations: Kenya, E/C.12/KEN/CO/1 (1 December 2008), [20].
[414] CESCR, Concluding Observations: Ecuador, E/C.12/1/Add.100 (7 June 2004), [21].
[415] CESCR, Concluding Observations: Morocco, E/C.12/MAR/CO/3 (4 September 2006), [46].

population, or less than 40 per cent of the economically active,[416] are covered. States' obligations to prevent workplace injury are additionally addressed by occupational health and safety measures required by Article 7(b) of the ICESCR (concerning safe and healthy working conditions).

The CESCR sets out states' obligations under Article 9 as follows:

> 17. States parties should also ensure the protection of workers who are injured in the course of employment or other productive work. The social security system should cover the costs and loss of earnings from the injury or morbid condition and the loss of support for spouses or dependents suffered as the result of the death of a breadwinner. Adequate benefits should be provided in the form of access to health care and cash benefits to ensure income security. Entitlement to benefits should not be made subject to the length of employment, to the duration of insurance or to the payment of contributions.[417]

In monitoring states, the CESCR has expressed concern where social insurance schemes do not cover work accidents and occupational diseases,[418] or where large parts of the population are excluded,[419] or where non-nationals, refugees and stateless persons are excluded.[420]

Part VI of ILO Convention No. 102 deals with 'employment injury' defined in Article 32:

> The contingencies covered shall include the following where due to accident or a prescribed disease resulting from employment:
>
> (a) a morbid condition;
>
> (b) incapacity for work resulting from such a condition and involving suspension of earnings, as defined by national laws or regulations;
>
> (c) total loss of earning capacity or partial loss thereof in excess of a prescribed degree, likely to be permanent, or corresponding loss of faculty; and
>
> (d) the loss of support suffered by the widow or child as the result of the death of the breadwinner; in the case of a widow, the right to benefit may be made conditional on her being presumed, in accordance with national laws or regulations, to be incapable of self-support.

The benefit provides for comprehensive medical care in Article 34(2), including:

> (a) general practitioner and specialist in-patient care and out-patient care, including domiciliary visiting;
>
> (b) dental care;
>
> (c) nursing care at home or in hospital or other medical institutions;
>
> (d) maintenance in hospitals, convalescent homes, sanatoria or other medical institutions;

[416] ILO, World Social Security Report, 2–3.

[417] CESCR, General Comment No. 19, [13].

[418] CESCR, Concluding Observations: Kuwait, E/C.12/1/Add.98 (7 June 2004), [19], [39]; Saint Vincent and the Grenadines, E/C.12/1/Add.21 (2 December 1997), [19].

[419] CESCR, Concluding Observations: India, E/C.12/IND/CO/5 (8 August 2008), [64].

[420] CESCR, Concluding Observations: Syria, E/C.12/1/Add.63 (24 September 2001), [23].

(e) dental, pharmaceutical and other medical or surgical supplies, including prosthetic appliances, kept in repair, and eyeglasses; and

(f) the care furnished by members of such other professions as may at any time be legally recognised as allied to the medical profession, under the supervision of a medical or dental practitioner.

It also provides for periodical payments of at least 50 per cent of the reference wage in cases of incapacity for work, total and likely permanent loss of earning capacity, normally as a periodical payment (Article 36) and for the duration of the incapacity (Article 38). It provides benefits to widows and dependent children in case of the death of breadwinner at a minimum of 40 per cent of the reference wage. Periodical payments must be revised where there are substantial changes in the cost of living; and may be converted into lump sums under certain conditions. There is also provision for vocational rehabilitation services and the re-establishment of disabled persons in suitable work (Article 35). In a manner typical of ILO social security standards, the Convention allows states to select the categories of beneficiaries (Article 33).

Convention No. 102 is supplemented by Convention No. 121 on Employment Injury Benefits 1964,[421] which increases the benefit to at least 60 per cent of the reference wage in cases of incapacity for work or invalidity; and to at least 50 per cent for widows, the disabled and dependent widower, and dependent children on the death of a breadwinner. There is also provision for care at the place of work, and supplementary benefits for disabled persons requiring constant care.

DISABILITY

While persons with disabilities are protected against discrimination in social security by Article 2(2) of the ICESCR, the needs of persons with disabilities call for additional measures. Disabilities may be connected to workplace sickness or injury, or arise independently of employment. In General Comment No. 19, the CESCR states:

20. In its general comment No. 5 (1994) on persons with disabilities, the Committee emphasized the importance of providing adequate income support to persons with disabilities who, owing to disability or disability-related factors, have temporarily lost, or received a reduction in, their income, have been denied employment opportunities or have a permanent disability. Such support should be provided in a dignified manner and reflect the special needs for assistance and other expenses often associated with disability. The support provided should cover family members and other informal carers.[422]

The relevant part of the CESCR's General Comment No. 5 states:

28. Social security and income-maintenance schemes are of particular importance for persons with disabilities. As stated in the Standard Rules, 'States should ensure the provision of adequate income support to persons with disabilities who, owing to disability or

[421] ILO Convention No. 121 concerning Benefits in the Case of Employment Injury (adopted 8 July 1964, entered into force 28 July 1967).

[422] CESCR, General Comment No. 19, [13].

disability-related factors, have temporarily lost or received a reduction in their income or have been denied employment opportunities'. Such support should reflect the special needs for assistance and other expenses often associated with disability. In addition, as far as possible, the support provided should also cover individuals (who are overwhelmingly female) who undertake the care of a person with disabilities. Such persons, including members of the families of persons with disabilities, are often in urgent need of financial support because of their assistance role.

29. Institutionalization of persons with disabilities, unless rendered necessary for other reasons, cannot be regarded as an adequate substitute for the social security and income-support rights of such persons.[423]

Protection and assistance in respect of disabilities also arises under the right to health in Article 12 of the ICESCR, discussed in a later chapter.

In monitoring states, the CESCR has expressed concern where persons with disabilities face discrimination in social security,[424] or are excluded from social security schemes,[425] including because they are unable to pay insurance contributions[426] or because of restricted eligibility requirements.[427] It has also drawn attention to the lack of funding or qualified personnel at social welfare centres for persons with disabilities;[428] and entirely inadequate programmes for those discharged from psychiatric institutions.[429]

In response, the CESCR has called on states to: establish comprehensive social security to assist persons with disabilities;[430] use all available resources to increase disability pensions, to the extent possible, to ensure an adequate standard of living;[431] better target assistance to reach persons with disabilities;[432] and expand community services.[433] The CESCR has also encouraged states to reintegrate persons with disabilities into the workplace to ease the financial burden on disability insurance.[434]

In ILO practice, Part IX of ILO Convention No. 102 deals with 'invalidity benefit' where a person is permanently unable to work or cannot work after a

[423] CESCR, General Comment No. 5, E/1995/22 at 19 (9 December 1994), [28]–[29].

[424] CESCR, Concluding Observations: Japan, E/C.12/1/Add.67 (24 September 2001), [25].

[425] CESCR, Concluding Observations: Hong Kong SAR, E/C.12/1/Add.58 (21 May 2001), [21]; Jamaica, E/C.12/1/Add.75 (6 December 2001), [10].

[426] CESCR, Concluding Observations: Angola, E/C.12/AGO/CO/3 (1 December 2008), [23]; China, E/C.12/1/Add.107 (13 May 2005), [56].

[427] CESCR, Concluding Observations: Serbia and Montenegro, E/C.12/1/Add.108 (23 June 2005), [21].

[428] CESCR, Concluding Observations: Bosnia and Herzegovina, E/C.12/BIH/CO/1 (24 January 2006), [17].

[429] CESCR, Consideration of Report Submitted by State Party: Canada, E/1999/22 (1998), [411].

[430] CESCR, Concluding Observations: Kenya, E/C.12/KEN/CO/1 (1 December 2008), [20].

[431] CESCR, Concluding Observations: Macedonia, E/C.12/MKD/CO/1 (15 January 2008), [38]; UNMIK, E/C.12/UNK/CO/1 (1 December 2008), [21]; Ukraine, E/C.12/UKR/CO/5 (4 January 2008), [41].

[432] CESCR, Concluding Observations: United Kingdom, E/C.12/1/Add.19 (12 December 1997), [22].

[433] CESCR, Concluding Observations: Japan, E/C.12/1/Add.67 (24 September 2001), [54].

[434] CESCR, Concluding Observations: Liechtenstein, E/C.12/LIE/CO/1 (9 June 2006), [2].

sickness benefit (also provided under Convention No. 102) has been exhausted (Article 54). The Convention provides for periodical payments of at least 40 per cent of the reference wage (Article 56). ILO Convention No. 128 on Invalidity, Old-Age and Survivors' Benefits 1967 increases payments to at least 50 per cent of the reference wage. The benefit is also subject to revision following substantial changes in the general level of earnings or the cost of living.

The benefit under Convention No. 102 is payable for the duration of the contingency or until the old age pension commences (Article 58). Qualifying periods or contributions may be imposed (Article 57). In a manner typical of ILO social security standards, the Convention allows states to select the categories of beneficiaries (Article 55).

The most comprehensive contemporary articulation of social security rights for persons with disabilities is in Article 28(2) of the CRPD, which uses the different terminology of 'social protection' in addressing the needs of such persons. Article 28 is not limited to social security in connection with an inability to work, but covers all situations of disabilities. Article 28(2) provides:

2. States Parties recognize the right of persons with disabilities to social protection and to the enjoyment of that right without discrimination on the basis of disability, and shall take appropriate steps to safeguard and promote the realization of this right, including measures:

(a) To ensure equal access by persons with disabilities to clean water services, and to ensure access to appropriate and affordable services, devices and other assistance for disability-related needs;

(b) To ensure access by persons with disabilities, in particular women and girls with disabilities and older persons with disabilities, to social protection programmes and poverty reduction programmes;

(c) To ensure access by persons with disabilities and their families living in situations of poverty to assistance from the State with disability-related expenses, including adequate training, counselling, financial assistance and respite care;

(d) To ensure access by persons with disabilities to public housing programmes;

(e) To ensure equal access by persons with disabilities to retirement benefits and programmes.

Article 16(4) of the CRPD also provides for the recovery, rehabilitation and social reintegration of persons with disabilities who become victims of any form of exploitation, violence or abuse, including through the provision of protection services:

4. States Parties shall take all appropriate measures to promote the physical, cognitive and psychological recovery, rehabilitation and social reintegration of persons with disabilities who become victims of any form of exploitation, violence or abuse, including through the provision of protection services. Such recovery and reintegration shall take place in an environment that fosters the health, welfare, self-respect, dignity and autonomy of the person and takes into account gender- and age-specific needs.

Article 26(1) of the CRPD provides for habilitation and rehabilitation services and programmes, including in the areas of employment and social services:

1. States Parties shall take effective and appropriate measures, including through peer support, to enable persons with disabilities to attain and maintain maximum independence, full physical, mental, social and vocational ability, and full inclusion and participation in all aspects of life. To that end, States Parties shall organize, strengthen and extend comprehensive habilitation and rehabilitation services and programmes, particularly in the areas of health, employment, education and social services…

SURVIVORS AND ORPHANS

The CESCR states in General Comment No. 19:

21. States parties must also ensure the provision of benefits to survivors and orphans on the death of a breadwinner who was covered by social security or had rights to a pension. Benefits should cover funeral costs, particularly in those States parties where funeral expenses are prohibitive. Survivors or orphans must not be excluded from social security schemes on the basis of prohibited grounds of discrimination and they should be given assistance in accessing social security schemes, particularly when endemic diseases, such as HIV/AIDS, tuberculosis and malaria, leave large numbers of children or older persons without family and community support.

In monitoring states, the CESCR has only rarely considered social security for survivors or orphans. It was concerned that survivor benefits were insufficient to ensure an adequate standard of living for recipients and their families under the UNMIK administration in Kosovo; and that certain land owners excluded from benefits suffered discrimination where they were unable to return to their lands because of illegal occupation or security concerns.[435] It accordingly called for benefits to be increased to ensure an adequate standard of living, and for discriminatory conditions to be reviewed.

The CESCR also objected to procedural obstacles to obtaining survivor benefits, such as the absence of application forms in the Serbian language or the requirement that UNMIK issue death certificates, which adversely affected non-Albanian communities.[436] Similarly, in Angola, the CESCR was concerned that pension and survivor benefits for the families of the disappeared were conditional on obtaining a court declaration that the disappeared relative had died.[437]

Orphans have been rarely mentioned under Article 9, although the CESCR was concerned at the lack of effective measures to safeguard the rights of children orphaned by the war in Guatemala.[438] Orphans arise more squarely under Article 10 on the protection of children, discussed in the next chapter, as well as under the CROC.

435 CESCR, Concluding Observations: UNMIK, E/C.12/UNK/CO/1 (1 December 2008), [21].
436 CESCR, Concluding Observations: UNMIK, E/C.12/UNK/CO/1 (1 December 2008), [22].
437 CESCR, Concluding Observations: Angola, E/C.12/DZA/CO/4 (7 June 2010), [13].
438 CESCR, Concluding Observations: Guatemala, E/C.12/1/Add.93 (12 December 2003), [19].

In ILO practice, Part X of Convention No. 102 provides for a 'survivor's benefit' for loss of support suffered by a 'widow or child' due to the death of a (presumptively male) 'breadwinner' (Article 60). The benefit is paid periodically at a minimum of 40 per cent of the reference wage for the duration of the contingency (Articles 62 and 64), subject to revision after substantial changes in general earnings and/or in the cost of living. Convention No. 128 on Invalidity, Old-Age and Survivors' Benefits 1967 increases the payment to at least 45 per cent of the reference wage.

The benefit under Convention No. 102 may be subject to qualifying periods or contributions, and even a minimum duration of marriage (Article 63), as well as restrictions where a beneficiary works or earns a certain amount (Article 60(2)). The Convention further allows states to select the categories of beneficiaries (Article 61).

OLD AGE

Globally, around 40 per cent of the working age population is covered by contributory old age pension schemes, with coverage as high as 75 per cent in high income states, but only 20 per cent in Asia, the Middle East and North Africa, and less than 5 per cent in sub-Saharan Africa.[439] The cost and adequacy of benefits also varies. High income states spend almost 7 per cent of GDP on old age pensions, middle income states around 2 per cent, and only 0.6 per cent is spent in low-income states.[440] Per person, the level of pensions is at about 56 per cent of GDP per capita in high income states, 33 per cent in middle income states, and 18 per cent in low-income states.[441] The variability in coverage is explained in part by the size of the informal work sector in less developed states, where pensions may not exist outside formal employment; and by moral expectations of family care for the elderly in some states.

In General Comment No. 19, the CESCR outlines states' obligations under Article 9 in respect of older persons:

15. States parties should take appropriate measures to establish social security schemes that provide benefits to older persons, starting at a specific age, to be prescribed by national law. The Committee stresses that States parties should establish a retirement age that is appropriate to national circumstances which take account of, inter alia, the nature of the occupation, in particular work in hazardous occupations and the working ability of older persons. States parties should, within the limits of available resources, provide non-contributory old-age benefits, social services and other assistance for all older persons who, when reaching the retirement age prescribed in national legislation, have not completed a qualifying period of contributions or are not otherwise entitled to an old-age insurance-based pension or other social security benefit or assistance, and have no other source of income.[442]

[439] ILO, World Social Security Report, 2.
[440] ILO, World Social Security Report, 55.
[441] ILO, World Social Security Report, 55.
[442] CESCR, General Comment No. 19, [13].

Retirement ages must also not be discriminatory, as discussed earlier in the chapter on the right to work under Article 6. As noted there, the CESCR has not stipulated a universal retirement age. In General Comment No. 6 on Older Persons, the CESCR encourages states to establish flexible retirement ages 'depending on the occupations performed and the working ability of elderly persons, with due regard to demographic, economic and social factors'.[443] Retirement ages must balance the right of a person to freely choose to work, non-discrimination on the basis of age, and the affordability of pensions, with factors such as the need to ensure employment opportunities for young people and productivity.

In General Comment No. 6, the CESCR also invokes relevant ILO standards in understanding the scope of social security for the elderly, and calls on states to establish universal non-contributory schemes for those not covered, or inadequately covered, by social insurance:

> 26. Article 9 of the Covenant provides generally that States parties 'recognize the right of everyone to social security', without specifying the type or level of protection to be guaranteed. However, the term 'social security' implicitly covers all the risks involved in the loss of means of subsistence for reasons beyond a person's control.
>
> 27. In accordance with article 9 of the Covenant and the provisions concerning implementation of the ILO social security conventions—Convention No. 102 concerning Social Security (Minimum Standards) (1952) and Convention No. 128 concerning Invalidity, Old-Age and Survivors' Benefits (1967)—States parties must take appropriate measures to establish general regimes of compulsory old-age insurance, starting at a particular age, to be prescribed by national law.
>
> 28. In keeping with the recommendations contained in the two ILO Conventions mentioned above and Recommendation No. 162, the Committee invites States parties to establish retirement age so that it is flexible, depending on the occupations performed and the working ability of elderly persons, with due regard to demographic, economic and social factors.
>
> 29. In order to give effect to the provisions of article 9 of the Covenant, States parties must guarantee the provision of survivors' and orphans' benefits on the death of the breadwinner who was covered by social security or receiving a pension.
>
> 30. Furthermore, as already observed in paragraphs 20 and 21, in order fully to implement the provisions of article 9 of the Covenant, States parties should, within the limits of available resources, provide non-contributory old-age benefits and other assistance for all older persons, who, when reaching the age prescribed in national legislation, have not completed a qualifying period of contribution and are not entitled to an old-age pension or other social security benefit or assistance and have no other source of income.

The key relevant ILO standards are in Part V of ILO Convention No. 102, which provides for an 'old age benefit' normally from 65 years of age unless a higher age is fixed by the state 'with due regard to the working ability of elderly persons in the country concerned' (Article 26). The benefit is paid periodically at a minimum of

[443] CESCR, General Comment No. 6, E/1996/22 at 20 (24 November 1995), [28].

40 per cent of the reference wage (Article 28) for the duration of old age (although the benefit may be suspended or reduced if the beneficiary continues to work and earns a prescribed amount (Article 26(3)). ILO Convention No. 128 on Invalidity, Old-Age and Survivors' Benefits 1967 increases payments to at least 45 per cent of the reference wage. Under Convention No. 102, the benefit may be subject to qualifying periods or contributions (Article 29). The Convention further allows states to select the categories of beneficiaries (Article 27).

In monitoring states, the CESCR has been concerned where older persons lack support because they were unable to pay contributions at all,[444] or for minimum or sufficient periods,[445] particularly in the informal sector[446] or by the self-employed,[447] unemployed, underemployed or low-paid.[448] It was concerned where employers failed to pay their legally required contributions to pensions,[449] and where pensions were not paid for over five years due to legal proceedings[450] or were otherwise in arrears.[451]

The CESCR has frequently criticized pension amounts which are insufficient to ensure an adequate standard of living,[452] including due to the absence of indexing[453] and where high inflation has destroyed their purchasing power.[454] It has been concerned at discriminatory differences in the retirement ages for men and women, which leave women with lower pensions[455] and perpetuate the income gap between men and women.[456]

Changes in retirement pensions have also attracted the CESCR's attention, including where pensions are adversely affected by privatization,[457] stricter eligibility requirements[458] or post-war changes in statehood affecting minorities.[459]

[444] CESCR, Concluding Observations: Angola, E/C.12/AGO/CO/3 (1 December 2008), [23].
[445] CESCR, Concluding Observations: Azerbaijan, E/C.12/1/Add.20 (22 December 1997), [21]; Republic of Korea, E/C.12/1/Add.59 (21 May 2001), [23].
[446] CESCR, Concluding Observations: Bolivia, E/C.12/BOL/CO/2 (8 August 2008), [18].
[447] CESCR, Concluding Observations: Republic of Korea, E/C.12/KOR/CO/3 (17 December 2009), [23].
[448] CESCR, Consideration of Report Submitted by State Party: Argentina, E/1995/22 (1994), [233].
[449] CESCR, Concluding Observations: Russia, E/C.12/1/Add.13 (15 May 1997), [22].
[450] CESCR, Concluding Observations: Peru, E/C.12/1/Add.14 (16 May 1997), [22].
[451] CESCR, Concluding Observations: Ukraine, E/C.12/1/Add.65 (24 September 2001), [14].
[452] CESCR, Concluding Observations: Macedonia, E/C.12/MKD/CO/1 (15 January 2008), [18]; Kazakhstan, E/C.12/KAZ/CO/1 (7 June 2010), [24]; Lithuania, E/C.12/1/Add.96 (7 June 2004), [16]; Morocco, E/C.12/MAR/CO/3 (4 September 2006), [22]; Russia, E/C.12/1/Add.94 (12 December 2003), [22]; San Marino, E/C.12/SMR/CO/4 (4 January 2008), [14]; UNMIK, E/C.12/UNK/CO/1 (1 December 2008), [21]; Ukraine, E/C.12/UKR/CO/5 (4 January 2008), [18].
[453] CESCR, Concluding Observations: Macedonia, E/C.12/MKD/CO/1 (15 January 2008), [18]; Kazakhstan, E/C.12/KAZ/CO/1 (7 June 2010), [24]; Lithuania, E/C.12/1/Add.96 (7 June 2004), [16].
[454] CESCR, Concluding Observations: Azerbaijan, E/C.12/1/Add.20 (22 December 1997), [21].
[455] CESCR, Concluding Observations: Chile, E/C.12/1/Add.105 (1 December 2004), [20]; Poland, E/C.12/POL/CO/5 (2 December 2009), [21].
[456] CESCR, Concluding Observations: Japan, E/C.12/1/Add.67 (24 September 2001), [24] and [51].
[457] CESCR, Concluding Observations: El Salvador, E/C.12/SLV/CO/2 (27 June 2007), [15]–[16].
[458] CESCR, Concluding Observations: Serbia and Montenegro, E/C.12/1/Add.108 (23 June 2005), [21].
[459] CESCR, Concluding Observations: Croatia, E/C.12/1/Add.73 (5 December 2001), [33]; Serbia and Montenegro, E/C.12/1/Add.108 (23 June 2005), [22] and [49].

The CESCR was also concerned where an increase in the pension age from 60 to 65 years potentially results in a transitional income gap where the retirement age and pension age do not coincide.[460]

Cultural barriers to social security have also been noted by the CESCR. In British Hong Kong, 60 per cent of the population were not covered by any public or private pension plan, but even those eligible often did not apply for it 'because they fear the cultural stigma attached to the concept of welfare assistance'.[461] The authorities also unlawfully discouraged applications.[462] Elsewhere, the CESCR has highlighted the difficult situation of older persons with no families or where their families are unable to support them.[463]

While the CESCR has predominantly focused on pensions in relation to the elderly, it should be noted that social security assistance may include services in addition to cash payments. For instance, the Protocol of San Salvador imposes express obligations on states to care for the elderly, including by providing 'suitable facilities, as well as food and specialized medical care, for elderly individuals who lack them and are unable to provide them for themselves'.[464] Aged care facilities are particularly important in those states where there is no longer a strong cultural tradition of families directly caring for elderly family members.

UNEMPLOYMENT

Statutory social security schemes for unemployment exist in only seventy-eight states and then often only covering a minority of workers (such as those in the formal sector), with coverage of less than 10 per cent of the unemployed in Africa, Asia and the Middle East.[465] Globally, it is estimated that about 30 per cent of the economically active are legally covered, with up to 80 per cent protected in developed states.[466] In General Comment No. 19, the CESCR sets out states' obligations in relation to unemployment:

> 16. In addition to promoting full, productive and freely chosen employment, States parties must endeavor to provide benefits to cover the loss or lack of earnings due to the inability to obtain or maintain suitable employment. In the case of loss of employment, benefits should be paid for an adequate period of time and at the expiry of the period, the social security system should ensure adequate protection of the unemployed worker, for example through social assistance. The social security system should also cover other workers, including part-time workers, casual workers, seasonal workers, and the self-employed, and those working in atypical forms of work in the informal economy. Benefits should be provided

[460] CESCR, Concluding Observations: Japan, E/C.12/1/Add.67 (24 September 2001), [23] and [50].

[461] CESCR, Concluding Observations: UK (Hong Kong), E/C.12/1/Add.10 (6 December 1996), [23]–[24].

[462] CESCR, Concluding Observations: UK (Hong Kong), E/C.12/1/Add.10 (6 December 1996), [23]–[24].

[463] CESCR, Concluding Observations: Afghanistan, E/C.12/AFG/CO/2-4 (7 June 2010), [27].

[464] Additional Protocol to the American Convention on Human Rights in the Area of Economic, Social and Cultural Rights ('Protocol of San Salvador') (adopted 17 November 1988, OAS Treaty Series No. 69, entered into force 16 November 1999), Article 17(a).

[465] ILO, World Social Security Report, 2.

[466] ILO, World Social Security Report, 60.

to cover periods of loss of earnings by persons who are requested not to report for work during a public health or other emergency.[467]

The CESCR does not specify minimum benefit amounts, other than that they should cover 'loss or lack of earnings'. It also does not specify minimum benefit periods, other than to suggest their duration must be 'adequate'.

Reference may be made to Part IV of ILO Convention No. 102, which requires periodic payment of an 'unemployment benefit' due to 'inability to obtain suitable employment in the case of a person protected who is capable of, and available for, work' (Article 20). Periodic benefits must be paid at a minimum of 45 per cent of the reference wage (Article 22). ILO Convention No. 168 on Employment Promotion and Protection against Unemployment 1988[468] raises the benefit level to at least 50 per cent of the reference wage, and requires that total benefits must guarantee healthy and reasonable living conditions.

Under Convention No. 102, the benefit may, however, be limited to thirteen weeks in a twelve-month period where states choose to cover classes of employees, or twenty-six weeks in twelve months where states choose to cover all residents (Article 24). Qualifying periods or contributions may also be imposed (Article 23). The Convention further allows states to select the categories of beneficiaries (Article 21) in a manner typical of ILO social security standards.

In monitoring states, the CESCR has given some attention to unemployment benefits. It found that the absence of unemployment benefits 'runs counter to the State party's obligation under the Covenant'.[469] Where benefits exist, the CESCR has been concerned at exclusionary eligibility requirements, such as regular employment for at least three years, and called for benefits to be extended to all unemployed persons.[470] It has been concerned where restrictions on unemployment insurance schemes reduced coverage and lowered benefit rates and duration,[471] including for part-time workers. It criticized excessive grounds for excluding people from benefits,[472] restrictions on coverage[473] and the exclusion of non-citizen permanent residents.[474] It has commonly criticized benefits levels which do not ensure an adequate standard of living.[475] The issue of participation requirements for receipt of unemployment benefits was discussed earlier. It called on one state to reconsider its system for detecting fraudulent benefits.[476]

[467] CESCR, General Comment No. 19, [13].

[468] ILO Convention No. 168 concerning Employment Promotion and Protection against Unemployment (adopted 21 June 1988, 1654 UNTS 67, entered into force 17 October 1991).

[469] CESCR, Concluding Observations: Syria, E/C.12/1/Add.63 (24 September 2001), [22].

[470] CESCR, Concluding Observations: Angola, E/C.12/DZA/CO/4 (7 June 2010), [12].

[471] CESCR, Concluding Observations: Canada, E/C.12/1/Add.31 (10 December 1998), [20].

[472] CESCR, Concluding Observations: Macedonia, E/C.12/MKD/CO/1 (15 January 2008), [38]; Lithuania, E/C.12/1/Add.96 (7 June 2004), [39]; Mexico, E/C.12/1/MEX/CO/4 (9 June 2006), [17].

[473] CESCR, Concluding Observations: Uzbekistan, E/C.12/UZB/CO/1 (24 January 2006), [53].

[474] CESCR, Concluding Observations: San Marino, E/C.12/SMR/CO/4 (4 January 2008), [13].

[475] CESCR, Concluding Observations: Macedonia, E/C.12/MKD/CO/1 (15 January 2008), [38]; Lithuania, E/C.12/1/Add.96 (7 June 2004), [39]; Serbia and Montenegro, E.C/12/1/Add.108 (23 June 2005), [47]; Ukraine, E/C.12/UKR/CO/5 (4 January 2008), [41]; Uzbekistan, E/C.12/UZB/CO/1 (24 January 2006), [22].

[476] CESCR, Consideration of Report Submitted by State Party: Russia, E/1998/22 (1997), [105].

MATERNITY

Maternity support is the third most common form of social assistance (after employment injury and retirement pensions), with some assistance (most commonly insurance-based) in 90 per cent of high-income states, 80 per cent of middle income states and 50 per cent of low-income states.[477] In General Comment No. 19 on Article 9, the CESCR points to Article 10 of the ICESCR for the more specific norms on maternity leave and benefits:

19. Article 10 of the Covenant expressly provides that 'working mothers should be accorded paid leave or leave with adequate social security benefits'. Paid maternity leave should be granted to all women, including those involved in atypical work, and benefits should be provided for an adequate period. Appropriate medical benefits should be provided for women and children, including perinatal, childbirth and postnatal care and care in hospital where necessary.

Accordingly, social security benefits in relation to maternity are considered in the next chapter on Article 10, although the general principles in relation to social security discussed in the present chapter also pertain, where relevant, to maternity benefits (including as regards periodic payment, remedies and accountability). Direct and indirect sex or gender discrimination in social security was discussed in an earlier section, including problems of accessibility and adequacy. As noted there, social security benefits for women are also addressed by other human rights instruments, such as the CEDAW.

In relation to maternity benefits and medical care, it may be briefly noted that Part VIII of ILO Convention No. 102 provides for maternity benefits for pregnancy, confinement and their consequences, and suspension of earnings (Article 47). Medical care provided must include at least prenatal, confinement and post-natal care either by medical practitioners or by qualified midwives and hospitalization where necessary (Article 49(2)).

There is also provision for periodical payments of at least 45 per cent of the reference wage (Article 50), for a minimum of twelve weeks (Article 52). Qualifying periods or contributions may be imposed (Article 51). The Convention also allows states to select the categories of beneficiaries (Article 48) in a manner typical of ILO social security standards.

ILO Convention No. 183 on Maternity Protection 2000[478] requires the benefit amount to ensure that the woman can maintain herself and her child in proper conditions of health and with a suitable standard of living. Where benefits are based on previous earnings, they must be paid at a minimum of two-thirds of previous earnings.

FAMILY AND CHILD SUPPORT

As will be apparent from the above discussion, the quantum in the various branches of social security assumes that benefits should be sufficient to ensure an adequate

[477] ILO, World Social Security Report, 71.

[478] ILO Convention No. 183 concerning the revision of the Maternity Protection Convention (Revised) (adopted 15 June 2000, entered into force 7 February 2002).

standard of living for the worker, but also for her or his family (based on a family 'breadwinner' model). Such assumptions are also inherent in a fair minimum wage under Article 7 of the ICESCR.

In addition, however, social security under Article 9 requires the further provision of family and child benefits. The CESCR states in General Comment No. 19 that family benefits and services are crucial for realizing the rights of children and dependents under Articles 9 and 10 of the ICESCR:

> 18. Benefits for families are crucial for realizing the rights of children and adult dependents to protection under articles 9 and 10 of the Covenant. In providing the benefits, the State party should take into account the resources and circumstances of the child and persons having responsibility for the maintenance of the child or adult dependent, as well as any other consideration relevant to an application for benefits made by or on behalf of the child or adult dependent. Family and child benefits, including cash benefits and social services, should be provided to families, without discrimination on prohibited grounds, and would ordinarily cover food, clothing, housing, water and sanitation, or other rights as appropriate.[479]

The protection of the family and children, including through benefits and services, is discussed in the next chapter on Article 10, given the more specialized focus of that provision, in conjunction with related standards in, and treaty body monitoring under, the ICCPR, the CEDAW and the CRC.

From time to time, the CESCR has nonetheless commented on families under Article 9. It was concerned where family benefits were confined to certain types of workers, such as civil servants and teachers;[480] or excluded certain workers, such as the self-employed.[481] It criticized the uneven coverage of family benefits between rural and urban areas and between regions.[482] Inadequate assistance to certain types of families was also of concern, including single parents (especially single mothers) or low-income families,[483] or families where parents are unemployed.[484] The CESCR was also concerned where pension reform discriminated against families,[485] or poverty reduction programmes excluded some of the poorest families.[486] It has called for childcare benefits to cover the cost of bringing up a child,[487] and for better reporting on family benefits.[488]

479 CESCR, General Comment No. 19, [13].

480 CESCR, Concluding Observations: Netherlands Antilles, E/C.12/NLD/CO/3/Add.1 (31 January 2008), [19].

481 CESCR, Concluding Observations: Monaco, E/C.12/MCO/CO/1 (13 June 2006), [12].

482 CESCR, Concluding Observations: Morocco, E/C.12/MAR/CO/3 (4 September 2006), [46].

483 CESCR, Concluding Observations: Cameroon, E/C.12/1/Add.40 (8 December 1999), [37]; Netherlands Antilles, E/C.12/NLD/CO/3/Add.1 (31 January 2008), [17]; Canada, E/C.12/1/Add.31 (10 December 1998), [20] and [22]–[23].

484 CESCR, Concluding Observations: Canada, E/C.12/1/Add.31 (10 December 1998), [20], [22]–[23].

485 CESCR, Concluding Observations: Germany, E/C.12/1/Add.68 (24 September 2001), [23].

486 CESCR, Concluding Observations: Afghanistan, E/C.12/AFG/CO/2-4 (7 June 2010), [27]; Brazil, E/C.12/BRA/CO/2 (12 June 2009), [20].

487 CESCR, Concluding Observations: Ireland, E/C.12/1/Add.35 (14 May 1999), [13].

488 CESCR, Concluding Observations: Hungary, E/C.12/HUN/CO/3 (16 January 2008), [40].

Provision for family benefits is made in Part VII of Convention No. 102 for the 'maintenance of children' (Article 40). The benefit involves periodical payments of at least 3 per cent of the reference wage per child if classes of employees are prescribed, or 1.5 per cent per child if all residents are covered (Article 43). Alternatively, in place of cash benefits, states may provide food, clothing, housing, holidays or domestic help, or a combination of these (Article 42). The benefits endure for as long as a person is responsible for the maintenance of a child. Qualifying periods may be imposed (Article 43), and states may select the extent of the population covered (Article 41) in the usual manner of ILO social security standards.

International Dimensions of Social Security

OBLIGATION OF STATES TO COOPERATE

As for all ICESCR rights, states should cooperate internationally in the realization of the right to social security, as the CESCR notes in General Comment No. 19:

> 52. Article 2, paragraph 1, and articles 11, paragraph 1, and 23 of the Covenant require that States parties recognize the essential role of international cooperation and assistance and take joint and separate action to achieve the full realization of the rights inscribed in the Covenant, including the right to social security.

In the first place, this means refraining from conduct which would impair social security elsewhere, as the CESCR observes:

> 53. To comply with their international obligations in relation to the right to social security, States parties have to respect the enjoyment of the right by refraining from actions that interfere, directly or indirectly, with the enjoyment of the right to social security in other countries.
>
> 54. States parties should extraterritorially protect the right to social security by preventing their own citizens and national entities from violating this right in other countries. Where States parties can take steps to influence third parties (non-State actors) within their jurisdiction to respect the right, through legal or political means, such steps should be taken in accordance with the Charter of the United Nations and applicable international law.

It would be appropriate, for instance, for a state to regulate their companies' operations abroad, such as to ensure compliance with contributory insurance rules in the foreign state, or to prohibit corrupt conduct by nationals in relation to foreign social security systems. The CESCR has also been alert to the adverse impacts on social security of trade liberalization agreements, or the measures taken by international institutions of which states are members (such as in lending policies or credit agreements):

> 57. With regard to the conclusion and implementation of international and regional agreements, States parties should take steps to ensure that these instruments do not adversely

impact upon the right to social security. Agreements concerning trade liberalization should not restrict the capacity of a State Party to ensure the full realization of the right to social security.

58. States parties should ensure that their actions as members of international organizations take due account of the right to social security. Accordingly, States parties that are members of international financial institutions, notably the International Monetary Fund, the World Bank, and regional development banks, should take steps to ensure that the right to social security is taken into account in their lending policies, credit agreements and other international measures. States parties should ensure that the policies and practices of international and regional financial institutions, in particular those concerning their role in structural adjustment and in the design and implementation of social security systems, promote and do not interfere with the right to social security.

As noted above, states should also take positive measures to facilitate the realization of social security abroad, not only through their participation in international organizations, but directly through their foreign aid programmes or by providing technical assistance:

55. Depending on the availability of resources, States parties should facilitate the realization of the right to social security in other countries, for example through provision of economic and technical assistance. International assistance should be provided in a manner that is consistent with the Covenant and other human rights standards, and sustainable and culturally appropriate. Economically developed States parties have a special responsibility for and interest in assisting the developing countries in this regard.

. . .

61. The Committee also wishes to emphasize that it is particularly incumbent on States parties, and other actors in a position to assist, to provide international assistance and cooperation, especially economic and technical, to enable developing countries to fulfil their core obligations.

In monitoring states, the CECSR has occasionally encouraged states to seek international assistance, for instance to establish a basic social security system and national plan of action.[489]

The CESCR found in General Comment No. 19 that adoption of bilateral or multilateral social security agreements, recognizing benefits of nationals on a reciprocal basis, is an important practical means of protecting social security:

56. States parties should ensure that the right to social security is given due attention in international agreements and, to that end, should consider the development of further legal instruments. The Committee notes the importance of establishing reciprocal bilateral and multilateral international agreements or other instruments for coordinating or harmonizing contributory social security schemes for migrant workers. Persons temporarily working in another country should be covered by the social security scheme of their home country.

[489] CESCR, Concluding Observations: Afghanistan, E/C.12/AFG/CO/2-4 (7 June 2010), [26].

As noted earlier, ILO instruments[490] and the CMW also encourage the adoption of reciprocal treaty arrangements. There are also regional arrangements,[491] such as the Ibero-American Multilateral Social Security Agreement 2010, which aims to preserve the social security rights (including through the portability of worker contributions) of around 5 million Ibero-American migrant workers, regardless of their migration status.[492]

As also mentioned earlier, the CESCR has called for agreements to be adopted in particular situations, as at the inter-entity level for minorities in the Balkans, and criticized the lack of implementation of existing agreements.[493] The CESCR also observed that agreements are no substitute for the restoration of permanent residency status (and consequent entitlements) where that is legally due.[494] It should be emphasized, however, that agreements do not discharge the state's obligation to provide social security for non-citizens, who must also be protected by non-contributory universal schemes where necessary.

OBLIGATIONS OF INTERNATIONAL ORGANIZATIONS

International organizations are not parties to the ICESCR and do not strictly bear legal obligations to respect it, unless provided for in their own constitutive instruments. In General Comment No. 19, the CESCR has nonetheless called on international organizations and institutions to 'cooperate effectively' with states in implementing the right to social security:

> 82. The United Nations specialized agencies and other international organizations concerned with social security, such as ILO, WHO, the United Nations Food and Agriculture Organization, the United Nations Children's Fund, the United Nations Human Settlements Programme, the United Nations Development Programme and ISSA, as well as international organizations concerned with trade such as the World Trade Organization, should cooperate effectively with States parties, building on their respective expertise, in relation to the implementation of the right to social security.

Assistance in social security should be developed and implemented in genuine cooperation with states, not pre-determined or imposed with little consultation by international organizations. An issue also arises as to the degree to which the state itself should be expected to provide social security, by prioritizing it over other national expenditure, so as to avoid undue reliance or dependency on foreign assistance where it is not essential. A sustainable social security system

[490] See, eg, ILO Convention No. 118 concerning Equality of Treatment of Nationals and Non-Nationals in Social Security (adopted 28 June 1962, entered into force 25 April 1964); ILO, Recommendation No. 86 concerning Migration for Employment, [21].

[491] European Social Charter 1961 (adopted 18 October 1961, ETS No. 35, entered into force 26 February 1965), Article 12(4) also encourages states to conclude 'appropriate bilateral and multilateral agreements'.

[492] Ibero-American Multilateral Social Security Agreement (adopted 10 November 2007, entered into force 1 May 2011).

[493] CESCR, Concluding Observations: Bosnia and Herzegovina, E/C.12/BIH/CO/1 (24 January 2006), [13], [20], [34] and [42].

[494] CESCR, Concluding Observations: Slovenia, E/C.12/SVN/CO/1 (25 January 2006), [32].

ultimately relies on national ownership of it and its recurrent inclusion in annual national budgeting.

The CESCR has also urged international financial institutions to 'take into account' the right to social security in their programmes and projects, and to promote not compromise it:

83. The international financial institutions, notably the International Monetary Fund and the World Bank, should take into account the right to social security in their lending policies, credit agreements, structural adjustment programmes and similar projects, so that the enjoyment of the right to social security, particularly by disadvantaged and marginalized individuals and groups, is promoted and not compromised.[495]

As noted earlier, existing social security systems, and the potential to develop or expand future systems, can be undermined by external pressure for certain economic policies. The CESCR has indicated that external actors should not only 'do no harm' to the prospects for social security, but should also actively promote it.

In assessing states' compliance with Article 9, the CESCR will take into account the effects of assistance provided by others:

84. When examining the reports of States parties and their ability to meet the obligations to realize the right to social security, the Committee will consider the effects of the assistance provided by all other actors. The incorporation of human rights law and principles in the programmes and policies of international organizations will greatly facilitate the implementation of the right to social security.[496]

Violations and Remedies

In General Comment No. 19, the CESCR synthesizes the various obligations of states under Article 9 by identifying where violations may occur, including by acts or omissions. In doing so, it introduces the more general meta-principles of good faith, reasonableness, proportionality and accountability in implementing the right to social security:

62. To demonstrate compliance with their general and specific obligations, States parties must show that they have taken the necessary steps towards the realization of the right to social security within their maximum available resources, and have guaranteed that the right is enjoyed without discrimination and equally by men and women (articles 2 and 3 of the Covenant). Under international law, a failure to act in good faith to take such steps amounts to a violation of the Covenant.

63. In assessing whether States parties have complied with obligations to take action, the Committee looks at whether implementation is reasonable or proportionate with respect to the attainment of the relevant rights, complies with human rights and democratic principles and whether it is subject to an adequate framework of monitoring and accountability.

64. Violations of the right to social security can occur through acts of commission, i.e. the direct actions of States parties or other entities insufficiently regulated by States. Violations

[495] CESCR, General Comment No. 19, [83].

[496] CESCR, General Comment No. 19, [84].

include, for example, the adoption of deliberately retrogressive measures incompatible with the core obligations outlined in paragraph 42 above; the formal repeal or suspension of legislation necessary for the continued enjoyment of the right to social security; active support for measures adopted by third parties which are inconsistent with the right to social security; the establishment of different eligibility conditions for social assistance benefits for disadvantaged and marginalized individuals depending on the place of residence; active denial of the rights of women or particular individuals or groups.

65. Violations through acts of omission can occur when the State party fails to take sufficient and appropriate action to realize the right to social security. In the context of social security, examples of such violations include the failure to take appropriate steps towards the full realization of everyone's right to social security; the failure to enforce relevant laws or put into effect policies designed to implement the right to social security; the failure to ensure the financial sustainability of State pension schemes; the failure to reform or repeal legislation which is manifestly inconsistent with the right to social security; the failure to regulate the activities of individuals or groups so as to prevent them from violating the right to social security; the failure to remove promptly obstacles which the State party is under a duty to remove in order to permit the immediate fulfilment of a right guaranteed by the Covenant; the failure to meet the core obligations (see paragraph 59 above); the failure of a State party to take into account its Covenant obligations when entering into bilateral or multilateral agreements with other States, international organizations or multinational corporations.[497]

The CESCR has further noted that states are responsible for violations by their component parts at the regional or local levels, and must supervise them accordingly:

73. Where responsibility for the implementation of the right to social security has been delegated to regional or local authorities or is under the constitutional authority of a federal body, the State party retains the obligation to comply with the Covenant, and therefore should ensure that these regional or local authorities effectively monitor the necessary social security services and facilities, as well as the effective implementation of the system. The States parties must further ensure that such authorities do not deny access to benefits and services on a discriminatory basis, whether directly or indirectly.[498]

Remedies must be available for violations of the right to social security, including effective procedures and adequate reparation:

77. Any persons or groups who have experienced violations of their right to social security should have access to effective judicial or other appropriate remedies at both national and international levels. All victims of violations of the right to social security should be entitled to adequate reparation, including restitution, compensation, satisfaction or guarantees of non-repetition. National ombudspersons, human rights commissions, and similar national human rights institutions should be permitted to address violations of the right. Legal assistance for obtaining remedies should be provided within maximum available resources.[499]

As noted earlier, the CESCR has also encouraged states to domestically incorporate international instruments so as to enable court adjudication of social security rights.[500] It has further called for judges, adjudicators and lawyers to be more

[497] CESCR, General Comment No. 19, [62]–[65].
[498] CESCR, General Comment No. 19, [73].
[499] CESCR, General Comment No. 19, [77].
[500] CESCR, General Comment No. 19, [79].

attentive to violations of social security rights.[501] States should further respect and enable human rights advocates and civil society to realize the right to social security:

81. States parties should respect, protect, facilitate and promote the work of human rights advocates and other members of civil society, with a view to assisting disadvantaged and marginalized individuals and groups in the realization of their right to social security.[502]

In monitoring states, the CESCR has not tended to give much attention to the procedures or mechanisms for vindicating violations of the right to social security, although it has occasionally commented on the non-enforcement of domestic decisions. A judicial remedy is not strictly required as long as other remedies are effective, for instance through the commonly used mechanism of the social security administrative tribunal.

Under ILO Convention No. 102, the basic procedural protection in social security cases is that '[e]very claimant shall have a right of appeal in case of refusal of the benefit or complaint as to its quality or quantity' (Article 70(1)) or, in the case of medical care, a right to have a complaint investigated by the appropriate authority (Article 70(2)). No right of appeal is required '[w]here a claim is settled by a special tribunal established to deal with social security questions and on which the persons protected are represented' (Article 70(3)).

Social security decisions are typically administrative decisions and courts are seldom entrusted with primary decision-making on the facts or merits. A question arises as to the nature and quality of procedural protections in social security decision-making, including the extent of a fair hearing. Article 9 of the ICESCR does not address the point. The CESCR's General Comment No. 9 on domestic implementation of the ICESCR notes that administrative remedies 'should be accessible, affordable, timely and effective':

9. The right to an effective remedy need not be interpreted as always requiring a judicial remedy. Administrative remedies will, in many cases, be adequate and those living within the jurisdiction of a State party have a legitimate expectation, based on the principle of good faith, that all administrative authorities will take account of the requirements of the Covenant in their decision-making. Any such administrative remedies should be accessible, affordable, timely and effective. An ultimate right of judicial appeal from administrative procedures of this type would also often be appropriate…[503]

Under Article 14 of the ICCPR, '[i]n the determination of…rights and obligations in a suit at law, everyone shall be entitled to a fair and public hearing by a competent, independent and impartial tribunal established by law'. A question arises whether a social security decision, whether at the administrative or judicial level, amounts to a 'suit at law' attracting the procedural guarantees of Article 14. Article 9 of the ICESCR does not resolve the issue, and Article 14 of the ICCPR does not in terms extend to administrative decisions. In certain circumstances, the

[501] CESCR, General Comment No. 19, [80]. [502] CESCR, General Comment No. 19, [81].
[503] CESCR, General Comment No. 9, E/C.12/1998/24 (3 December 1998), [9].

HRC has interpreted Article 14 to apply to the determination of social security benefits, as noted in General Comment No. 32 on Article 14 of the ICCPR:

16. The concept of determination of rights and obligations 'in a suit at law' (*de caractère civil/de carácter civil*) is more complex. It is formulated differently in the various languages of the Covenant that, according to article 53 of the Covenant, are equally authentic, and the *travaux préparatoires* do not resolve the discrepancies in the various language texts. The Committee notes that the concept of a 'suit at law' or its equivalents in other language texts is based on the nature of the right in question rather than on the status of one of the parties or the particular forum provided by domestic legal systems for the determination of particular rights. The concept encompasses (a) judicial procedures aimed at determining rights and obligations pertaining to the areas of contract, property and torts in the area of private law, as well as (b) equivalent notions in the area of administrative law such as the termination of employment of civil servants for other than disciplinary reasons, *the determination of social security benefits or the pension rights of soldiers*, or procedures regarding the use of public land or the taking of private property. In addition, it may (c) cover other procedures which, however, must be assessed on a case by case basis in the light of the nature of the right in question.[504]

Thus, in *Garcia Pons v Spain*, the HRC applied Article 14 in finding that a judge who was refused unemployment benefits was not denied a fair hearing:

9.6 With regard to the author's allegations concerning article 14, the Committee has carefully studied the various judicial proceedings engaged by the author in Spain as well as their disposition and concludes that the evidence submitted does not support a finding that he has been denied a fair hearing within the meaning of article 14, paragraph 1, of the Covenant.[505]

The HRC did not provide any further reasoning as to why Article 14 applied. On the facts, the Spanish Constitutional Tribunal had earlier rejected the author's complaint, and the author had not substantiated any procedural defects in such proceedings in his communication to the HRC. Spanish law thus provided for judicial review of social security decisions, and the HRC appeared to accept that the minimum procedural protections of Article 14 were applied in those judicial proceedings. Social security cases before the courts are thus seemingly 'suits at law' to which Article 14 applies.

The HRC did not, however, further determine whether Article 14 also applies to purely administrative social security decisions, where the state chooses not to provide for judicial review (which, as noted earlier, is not strictly required by Article 9 or the ICESCR). One question is then whether Article 14 applies to administrative tribunals empowered to review social security decisions. If so, a further question is whether the absence of such administrative tribunal also engages Article 14, so as to require a tribunal to be provided.

In another ICCPR case, *Y L v Canada*, a discharged soldier was refused a disability benefit by the Pension Review Board and argued that such tribunal

[504] HRC, General Comment No. 32, CCPR/C/GC/32 (23 August 2007), [16] (emphasis added).
[505] *Pons v Spain*, [9.6].

violated his Article 14 rights because it was made up of civil servants of the executive branch of government and was thus not independent and impartial.[506] The HRC found that the author was not denied a fair hearing because the Canadian legal system ultimately provided for judicial review of pension decisions (which the author had not pursued):

9.1 With regard to the alleged violation of the guarantees of 'a fair and public hearing by a competent, independent and impartial tribunal established by law,' contained in article 14, paragraph 1, of the Covenant, it is correct to state that those guarantees are limited to criminal proceedings and to any 'suit at law.' The latter expression is formulated differently in the various language texts of the Covenant and each and every one of those texts is, under article 53, equally authentic.

9.2 The *travaux préparatoires* do not resolve the apparent discrepancy in the various language texts. In the view of the Committee the concept of a 'suit at law' or its equivalent in other language texts is based on the nature of the right in question rather than on the status of one of the parties (governmental, parastatal or autonomous statutory entities), or else on the particular forum in which individual legal systems may provide that the right in question is to be adjudicated upon, especially in common law systems where there is no inherent difference between public law and private law and where the courts normally exercise control over the proceedings either at first instance or on appeal specifically provided by statute or else by way of judicial review. In this regard, each communication must be examined in the light of its particular features.

9.3 In the present communication, the right to a fair hearing in relation to the claim for a pension by the author must be looked at globally, irrespective of the different steps which the author had to take in order to have his claim for a pension finally adjudicated.

9.4 The Committee notes that the author pursued his claim successively before the Canadian Pension Commission, an Entitlement Board of the Commission and, finally, the Pension Review Board. It is clear from the observations made by the State party on the author's communication that the Canadian legal system subjects the proceedings in those various bodies to judicial supervision and control, because the Federal Court Act does provide the possibility of judicial review in unsuccessful claims of this nature. It would be hazardous to speculate on whether that Court would or would not have, first, quashed the decision of the Board on the grounds advanced by the author and, secondly, directed the Board to give the author a fair hearing on his claim. The fact that the author was not advised that he could have resorted to judicial review is irrelevant in determining the question whether the claim of the author was of a kind subject to judicial supervision and control. It has not been claimed by the author that this remedy would not have complied with the guarantees provided in article 14, paragraph 1, of the Covenant. Nor has he claimed that this remedy would not have availed in correcting whatever deficiencies may have marked the hearing of his case before the lower jurisdictions, including any grievance that he may have had regarding the denial of access to his medical file.

9.5 In the view of the Committee, therefore, it would appear that the Canadian legal system does contain provisions in the Federal Court Act to ensure to the author the right to a fair hearing in the situation. Consequently, his basic allegations do not reveal the possibility of any breach of the Covenant.

[506] *Y L v Canada*, HRC Communication No. 112/1981 (1986), [9.1]–[9.5] and [10].

The majority again emphasized the availability of judicial remedies in assessing whether Article 14 was satisfied. It thus avoided answering whether the various levels of administrative tribunal review were sufficiently independent and impartial to satisfy Article 14. Three HRC members dissented, arguing that pension decisions are administrative decisions of the executive and are therefore not 'civil' or criminal cases attracting the protections of Article 14 at all:

1. We concur in the view expressed by the majority of the Committee that the communication is inadmissible. But we do not share the reasons on which that view is based.

2. The majority view stresses in paragraph 9.4 that the Canadian legal system, in accordance with article 14, paragraph 1, of the Covenant, provides sufficient protection for a claim of the kind pursued by the author, because an appeal could be made to the Federal Court of Appeal. However, the availability of this legal remedy cannot be held against the author. In the letter by which the Pension Review Board informed the author of its decision as being final and enforceable, no mention was made of the possibility of such an appeal to a judicial body. Moreover, the lawyers who acted for the author and who are civil servants specifically appointed to represent claimants before the Pension Review Board did not advise the author accordingly. Under these circumstances, Canada is estopped from asserting that either, procedurally, the author has failed to exhaust local remedies or that, substantively, the requisite guarantees under article 14, paragraph 1, of the Covenant have been complied with.

3. However, the dispute between the author and Canada does not come within the purview of article 14, paragraph 1, of the Covenant. The guarantees therein contained apply to the determination both of any criminal charge and of rights and obligations in a suit at law. Whereas this phrase in its English and Russian versions refers to proceedings, the French and the Spanish texts rely on the nature of the right or obligation which constitutes the subject-matter of the proceedings concerned. In the circumstances of the present case, there is no need to clarify the common meaning to be given to the different terms used in the various language: which, under article 53 of the Covenant, are equally authentic. It is quite clear from the submissions of both the State party and the author that in Canada the relationship between a soldier, whether in active service or retired, and the Crown has many specific features, differing essentially from a labour contract under Canadian law. In addition, it has emerged that the Pension Review Board is an administrative body functioning within the executive branch of the Government of Canada, lacking the quality of a court. Thus, in the present case, neither of the two criteria which would appear to determine conjunctively the scope of article 14, paragraph 1, of the Covenant is met. It must be concluded, therefore, that proceedings before the Pension Review Board, initiated with a view to claiming pension rights, cannot be challenged by contending that the requirements of a fair hearing as laid down in article 14, paragraph 1, of the Covenant have been violated.[507]

The above passage is a dissenting opinion. The HRC as a whole has not yet determined whether, in the absence of domestic provision for judicial remedies, Article 14 applies to: (a) social security decisions by administrative tribunals, so as to require minimum procedural protections to be accorded; and (b) social

[507] *Y L v Canada*, [2], [3] (Individual Opinion by Messrs. Bernhard Graefrath, Fausto Pocar and Christian Tomuschat).

security decisions by primary administrative decision-makers, so as to require the availability of an administrative review tribunal.

Some observations may be made in the light of the CESCR's General Comment Nos. 9 and 19 on remedies, quoted earlier. The ICESCR does not require the provision of judicial remedies for violations of the right to social security, but it does require effective remedies to be available. Effective remedies will be absent where a primary administrative decision about a person's right to social security is final and no provision is made for either review by a court or a (well designed and sufficiently fair and independent) administrative tribunal.

Where judicial remedies are provided, they must conform to the fair hearing requirements of Article 14 of the ICCPR, which the HRC has accepted applies 'wherever domestic law entrusts a judicial body with a judicial task'.[508] Where administrative tribunals are provided, it is arguable that they should also conform to the requirements of Article 14, both to ensure the effectiveness of that remedy and to recognize the importance of the interests at stake. Such proceedings may be progressively interpreted as involving the determination of a 'suit at law', including because such tribunals often embody quasi-judicial characteristics.

As noted earlier, in regional practice, the right to a fair 'civil' hearing in Article 6 of the ECHR has been applied to decisions involving certain domestic social security rights. The earlier cases turned on whether the social security right in question had a predominantly private or public law character; only the former was recognized as a 'civil' right (for instance, contributory social insurance).[509] However, subsequent cases accept that statutory welfare rights (as opposed to administrative discretions), despite their public law character, also attract fair hearing rights under Article 6.[510] Given that social security can be vitally important in ensuring a person's subsistence or an adequate standard of living, it seems appropriate to extend procedural guarantees commensurate with the importance of the interests at stake.

Future International Standard Setting

In 2011, the ILO proposed eleven 'basic principles' to frame a possible new ILO instrument on the social security component of the Social Protection Floor (mentioned earlier), that is, for a 'new generic guiding mechanism for the extension of population coverage to all'.[511] Some of the key principles are as follows:

(1) *Universality*: Universal coverage of all residents by a defined set of essential social security guarantees should be achieved as quickly as possible.

(2) *Gradual target-oriented implementation*: The set of basic guarantees can be gradually implemented, in line with an overall development plan seeking ultimately to implement all

[508] HRC, General Comment No. 32, [7].
[509] See, eg, *Feldbrugge v Netherlands*.
[510] *Salesi v Italy*, [19].
[511] ILO, Report VI, 147, 150–51.

essential guarantees over a defined period, while ensuring immediate protection against discrimination.

(3) *Consensual and rational priority setting*: In the case of gradual implementation, the priorities should be identified through national social dialogue and rational procedures seeking to close a country's aggregate poverty gap as fast as possible.

(4) *Financial and fiscal sustainability*: The scope of the basic set of guarantees embodying the national SPF should be commensurate with the current and likely future fiscal space available to finance the social transfers required; the size of the fiscal space available should be determined by societal consensus.

(5) *Adequacy of guarantee levels*: The levels of guarantee should be defined so as to ascertain that people of all ages would be able to purchase all essential goods and services enabling them to live decently; this means that their income should be lifted above a poverty level to be defined through a transparent national process.

(6) *Core components*: The set of essential guarantees should aim to achieve a situation in which:

– all residents have sufficient financial protection to afford and have access to a nationally defined set of essential health-care services, in relation to which the State accepts general responsibility for ensuring the adequacy of the (usually) pluralistic financing and delivery systems;

– all children have income security, at least at the level of the nationally defined poverty line, through family/child benefits aimed at facilitating access to nutrition, education and care;

– all persons of active working age who cannot earn sufficient income through employment should have access to minimum income security through social assistance or social transfer schemes (such as income transfer schemes for women during the last weeks of pregnancy and the first weeks after delivery) or through employment guarantee schemes; and

– all residents in old age or with disabilities should have income security at least at the level of the nationally defined poverty line, through old-age pensions or disability pensions.

…

(10) *A rights-based approach*: The guarantees should be defined by law and every eligible man, woman or child should have the right to claim his/her respective benefits and, if necessary, to appeal against an administration's decision in court…

Existing ILO standards provide significant normative guidance on the content of Article 9 of the ICESCR, but are limited in their coverage and scope of protection. The suggested principles for a new ILO instrument are more reflective of the universal, rights-based approach of Article 9, and have the potential to bring greater harmony between the regimes and to reinforce the ICESCR's approach.

12

Article 10: The Rights of Families, Mothers and Children

Article 10

The States Parties to the present Covenant recognize that:

1. The widest possible protection and assistance should be accorded to the family, which is the natural and fundamental group unit of society, particularly for its establishment and while it is responsible for the care and education of dependent children. Marriage must be entered into with the free consent of the intending spouses.

2. Special protection should be accorded to mothers during a reasonable period before and after childbirth. During such period working mothers should be accorded paid leave or leave with adequate social security benefits.

3. Special measures of protection and assistance should be taken on behalf of all children and young persons without any discrimination for reasons of parentage or other conditions. Children and young persons should be protected from economic and social exploitation. Their employment in work harmful to their morals or health or dangerous to life or likely to hamper their normal development should be punishable by law. States should also set age limits below which the paid employment of child labour should be prohibited and punishable by law.

Introduction: Origins, Purpose, Drafting

Article 10(1) protects the family, including children, and requires free consent to marriage; Article 10(2) protects mothers, including workers; and Article 10(3) protects children, including in work. The provision establishes autonomous rights and does not merely particularize the application of other ICESCR rights to families, mothers or children.

At the same time, it clearly crosses over into the same or similar subject matter of some other ICESCR rights, namely rights to work, social security, non-discrimination and equality. Some of the sub-paragraphs of Article 10 also blur into each other, such as the obligation to protect and assist children in the family in Article 10(1) and all children in Article 10(3). During the drafting,[1] the French delegate objected to its composite and unwieldy quality:

> ... the attempt that had been made to express too many ideas in a single article ... [I]t contained a philosophical affirmation, a provision of civil law, a provision regarding social security benefits in the particular case of childbirth, provisions derived from labour law such as that concerning child labour and, finally, general principles regarding assistance.[2]

Delegates recognized that Article 10 overlapped with other ICESCR provisions, particularly work rights (Articles 6 to 8)[3] and social security (Article 9).[4] It was nonetheless seen as important to focus attention on the family, mothers and children, since certain economic and social rights manifest uniquely in family and parental relationships. In relation to similar obligations to protect the family in Article 16 of the European Social Charter, the European Committee on Social

[1] The original text of Article 10 was proposed by the Commission on Human Rights in 1954 (E/2573), then referred by the General Assembly to the Third Committee (A/RES/833(IX)), which discussed it in its 730th to 738th meetings in January 1957, in light of revisions by a Working Party (UNGA Third Committee, A/C.3/SR.733 (16 January 1957), 268), and adopted the final text at its 737th meeting (UNGA Third Committee, A/C.3/SR.737 (22 January 1957), 286–7).

[2] UNGA Third Committee, A/C.3/SR.737 (22 January 1957), 283 (France).

[3] UNGA Third Committee, A/C.3/SR.731 (15 January 1957), 256 (Chile).

[4] UNGA Third Committee, A/C.3/SR.571 (2 November 1954), 143 (Sweden).

Rights (ECSR) has emphasized that historical shifts necessitate a greater role for the state in the protection of the family:

> ...since the industrial revolution and the social upheavals it produced, the modern state has had to take on certain new tasks and, in particular...to create the living conditions necessary to give the family its full scope. The traditional affirmation of the family as the fundamental unit of society is maintained...[but to it is added] the idea that family welfare cannot henceforth be left to individual effort, as in the liberal epoch.[5]

Article 10 also overlaps with ICCPR rights. Article 23(1) of the ICCPR recognizes that the 'family is the natural and fundamental group unit of society and is entitled to protection by society and the State' and partly corresponds with Article 10(1) of the ICESCR. Article 24(1) of the ICCPR recognizes the right of every child, on a non-discriminatory basis, 'to such measures of protection as are required by his status as a minor, on the part of his family, society and the State', and thus overlaps in part with Article 10(3) of the ICESCR.

Also relevant is Article 17 of the ICCPR, which prohibits 'arbitrary or unlawful interference' in, inter alia, the 'family' and 'home'. In practice, that provision has mainly been interpreted by the Human Rights Committee (HRC) as a 'negative' obligation to protect families from 'interference' in the family, rather than as a duty to take positive or proactive measures of assistance.[6] By contrast, the text of Article 10 of the ICESCR is not limited to cases of 'interference' and its wider ambit encompasses 'the widest possible measures of assistance'.

In addition, the HRC has often combined consideration of family issues under Articles 17 and 23, according Article 23 a subsidiary role to Article 17 in its analysis and by focusing its assessment on interference rather than measures of assistance.[7] Commentators suggest that Article 23 should be interpreted more broadly than Article 17 to encompass positive measures to protect the existence of the family.[8] Positive measures might include 'financial assistance, protection of mothers, tax privileges, relief in setting up a household, etc'.[9] Given that positive assistance has been the focus of the CESCR under Article 10 of the ICESCR, as discussed below, there is room for the ICESCR to influence ICCPR practice.

As regards marriage, Article 23(3) of the ICCPR provides that '[n]o marriage shall be entered into without the free and full consent of the intending spouses', thus mirroring the second sentence of Article 10(1) of the ICESCR. The ICCPR goes further, however, in expressly recognizing the civil right to marry and found a family (Article 23(2)), which is not mentioned in the ICESCR,

[5] European Committee of Social Rights (ECSR), Statement of Interpretation on Article 16 of the European Social Charter (31 May 1969).

[6] Manfred Nowak, *UN Covenant on Civil and Political Rights: CCPR Commentary* (2nd edn, NP Engel, Kehl, 2005) ('*CCPR Commentary*'), 520.

[7] Sarah Joseph, Jenny Schultz and Melissa Castan, *The International Covenant on Civil and Political Rights: Cases, Materials and Commentary* (Oxford University Press, Oxford, 2004) ('*ICCPR Cases*'), 586.

[8] Nowak, *CCPR Commentary*, 519.

[9] Nowak, *CCPR Commentary*, 520.

and in guaranteeing equality and non-discrimination in marriage and upon its dissolution.[10]

To the extent that certain concepts, such as the 'family', 'marriage' and 'protection', are shared between Article 10 of the ICESCR and the various ICCPR provisions, it makes sense for such concepts to be interpreted consistently or harmoniously across both Covenants. As discussed below, some of the ICCPR jurisprudence may be usefully drawn on to inform the scope of Article 10 of the ICESCR, while CESCR practice can also inform under-developed dimensions of the ICCPR (such as measures of positive protection).

Families, mothers and children are also protected in various ways in regional human rights instruments, often influenced by international standards in the ICCPR and ICESCR. The African Charter on Human and Peoples' Rights requires the state to protect the family (Article 18), while children's rights are comprehensively elaborated in the specialized African Charter on the Rights and Welfare of the Child.

In Europe, the European Convention on Human Rights (ECHR) requires respect for family life (Article 8), while the European Social Charter 1961 recognizes the right to protection of children and young persons (Article 7) and employed women (Article 8), and the right to social, legal and economic protection of the family (Article 16) and mothers and children (Article 17). The Revised European Social Charter 1996 adds protection and assistance for migrant workers and their families (Article 19).

In the Inter-American system, the American Convention on Human Rights recognizes family rights (Article 17) and the rights of the child (Article 19), with related rights to a name (Article 18) and nationality (Article 20). The Protocol of San Salvador in the Area of Economic, Social and Cultural Rights gives further protection to families, including their formation (Article 15) and the rights of children (Article 16). Aspects of these regional standards will be discussed where they reinforce or otherwise shed light upon the ICESCR standards. The regional standards are also extracted in full at the end of this chapter.

Immediate Implementation and Progressive Realization

The CESCR has not yet adopted a General Comment on Article 10 or specifically addressed the content of any minimum core obligations or the application of the progressive realization principle. Like other ICESCR rights, Article 10 is subject to the principle of progressive realization under Article 2(1), including its

[10] See, eg, HRC, General Comment No. 19, Protection of the family, the right to marriage and equality of the spouses (Article 23), 27 July 1990, [6]–[8]; see further below. The HRC has also addressed matters such as polygamy, designating the husband as head of the family, and discriminatory customary laws relating to marriage, divorce, property, inheritance and succession: HRC, Concluding Observations: Togo, A/58/40 (2002), [78(21)]; see also Mali, A/58/40 (2003), [81(10)].

presumption against retrogressive measures (for instance, where a state decides to abolish or curtail existing family or child benefits).

However, certain obligations in respect of Article 10 plainly may have immediate effect. These include the general prohibition on discrimination under Article 2(2) of the ICESCR and the obligations concerning gender equality in Article 3. Most significantly, however, specific language in Article 10 indicates that certain obligations have immediate effect. Thus, Article 10(3) specifically prohibits discrimination on the basis of parentage in the provision of measures of protection to children.

In addition, under Article 10(1), marriage 'must' be entered into with free consent. Such safeguard is capable of immediate application through the adoption of legislative measures and the ordinary enforcement of the law. So much is further indicated by the identical protection in Article 23(3) of the ICCPR, which is not subject to progressive realization (even though the enforcement of any law, including civil rights, involves some resource allocation for the investigation of breaches and the taking of punitive or remedial action).

Similarly, legislative protection of the right to 'establish' a family under Article 10(1), and for recognition of its continuing existence, is largely not dependent on resources (beyond the usual costs associated with legislative enactment and law enforcement). Article 10(3) also requires states to make 'punishable by law' work that is harmful or dangerous to children or breaches of minimum age labour laws, again signifying obligations of immediate effect.

Beyond these areas, Article 10 conceivably encompasses a wide range of measures of 'protection' or 'assistance' which may have substantial resource implications and come within the ambit of progressive realization. These may include the extent of paid leave or social security benefits for maternity, as well as assistance (such as social security support, including childcare) for families, mothers and children generally.

In the related context of Article 23 of the ICCPR, even the HRC allowed for a version of progressive realization in relation to family protection, in *Aumeeruddy-Cziffra et al v Mauritius*:

> The Committee is of the opinion that the legal protection or measures a society or a State can afford to the family may vary from country to country and depend on different social, economic, political or cultural conditions and traditions.[11]

That statement was not dispositive or relevant on the facts of the case at hand. It also conflates the quite separate issues of resource constraints and other 'social', 'political' or 'cultural conditions and practices'. As discussed below, elsewhere the HRC has made allowance for different social and cultural conceptions of the family, and thus also appears to accept that similar considerations can affect the kind or degree of protection available.

[11] *Aumeeruddy-Cziffra et al v Mauritius*, HRC Communication No. 35/1978 (9 April 1981), [9.2(b)].

The aspects of Article 10 subject to progressive realization still require a state to immediately adopt a national policy or plan directed towards realizing them over time. A state must also demonstrate that special attention is given to particularly vulnerable, disadvantaged and marginalized families, mothers and children. These issues are discussed further below in the light of the CESCR's practice.

Limitations

Article 10 does not contain internal, specific limitations clauses. While it requires the 'widest possible protection and assistance' of the family, it is not expressed as an absolute right and is subject to the general limitations clause in Article 4 of the ICESCR. In this regard, the 'negative' aspect of Article 17 of the ICCPR may be relevant in understanding limitations on the scope of Article 10 of the ICESCR. In General Comment No. 16, the HRC set out the requirements of legality and specificity, and non-arbitrariness or reasonableness, which are necessary for an 'interference' in the family to be lawful under Article 17:

> 3. The term 'unlawful' means that no interference can take place except in cases envisaged by the law. Interference authorized by States can only take place on the basis of law, which itself must comply with the provisions, aims and objectives of the Covenant.
>
> 4. The expression 'arbitrary interference' is also relevant to the protection of the right provided for in article 17. In the Committee's view the expression 'arbitrary interference' can also extend to interference provided for under the law. The introduction of the concept of arbitrariness is intended to guarantee that even interference provided for by law should be in accordance with the provisions, aims and objectives of the Covenant and should be, in any event, reasonable in the particular circumstances.
>
> …
>
> 8. Even with regard to interferences that conform to the Covenant, relevant legislation must specify in detail the precise circumstances in which such interferences may be permitted. A decision to make use of such authorized interference must be made only by the authority designated under the law, and on a case-by-case basis.[12]

As discussed below, there are a range of circumstances in which the protections under Article 10 may need to be limited, including interference in the family to protect child welfare, or in pursuit of legitimate public interests such as immigration control or imprisonment for crime; to prevent child marriage, polygamy or harmful cultural practices in the family, and so on.

[12] HRC, General Comment No. 16, The right to respect of privacy, family, home and correspondence, and protection of honour and reputation (Article 17), 8 April 1988, [3]–[4] and [8].

Article 10(1): The Family

Article 10 deliberately begins with the central idea that the family is entitled to 'the widest possible protection',[13] from which the more specialized protections for mothers and children logically follow. This core principle is supplemented by the description of the family as 'the natural and fundamental group unit of society'.[14] Throughout the drafting, states frequently emphasized the important role of the family in economic, social and cultural life[15] and 'as the natural protector of young children'.[16] The provision is underpinned by various social, cultural and moral assumptions about the 'natural' role of the family in social order, although in its interpretation there is substantial flexibility and relativity in the notion of the family.

MEANING OF 'FAMILY' AND SCOPE OF PROTECTION

The original draft of Article 10 restricted the family to those 'based on marriage'.[17] Italy argued that marriage 'alone enabled parents to given children the protection they needed',[18] while Greece considered it to be a 'universally admitted' fact that family was based on marriage.[19] Other states in favour also believed that marriage 'was a social act of the highest importance'[20] and that 'the moral obligation of marriage must be stressed'.[21]

However, the limiting phrase was not included in the final text, in part to make Article 10 consistent with Article 23 of the ICCPR.[22] Some states were concerned that the earlier draft would exclude from protection family units other than those based on marriage.[23] Sweden, for example, argued that 'unmarried mothers with children and divorced or widowed persons with children should also be recognized as family units'.[24]

[13] The order of the provisions in Article 10 was amended by the Working Group following the recommendations of a number of states: see UNGA Third Committee Report, A/3525 (9 February 1957), 33 (Bulgaria), 34 (Ecuador and Greece), 36; UNGA Third Committee, A/C.3/SR.730 (14 January 1957), 247 (Philippines); cf UNGA Third Committee, A/C.3/SR.736 (21 January 1957), 280 (Pakistan).

[14] Introduced by Ecuador and Greece, A/C.3/L.563; adopted by fifty votes to five, with eight abstentions: UNGA Third Committee Report, A/3525 (9 February 1957), 42.

[15] UNGA Third Committee, A/C.3/SR.731 (15 January 1957), 257 (Italy).

[16] UNGA Third Committee, A/C.3/SR.735 (21 January 1957), 273 (Sweden).

[17] UNGA Third Committee Report, A/3525 (9 February 1957), 33.

[18] UNGA Third Committee, A/C.3/SR.731 (15 January 1957), 257 (Italy).

[19] UNGA Third Committee, A/C.3/SR.732 (16 January 1957), 261 (Greece); see also A/C.3/SR.735 (21 January 1957), 272 (Belgium).

[20] UNGA Third Committee, A/C.3/SR.735 (21 January 1957), 272 (Belgium).

[21] UNGA Third Committee, A/C.3/SR.733 (16 January 1957), 268 (Venezuela).

[22] See the proposal by Ecuador and Greece: UNGA Third Committee Report, A/3525 (9 February 1957), 34; UNGA Third Committee, A/C.3/SR.732 (16 January 1957), 261 (Greece).

[23] UNGA Third Committee, A/C.3/SR.732 (16 January 1957), 260 (Sweden); see also A/C.3/SR.732 (16 January 1957), 261 (Greece).

[24] UNGA Third Committee, A/C.3/SR.735 (21 January 1957), 273 (Sweden).

Article 10 is also not limited to families with children. In the drafting China queried 'whether a family with no children was also entitled to protection by the State'.[25] As adopted, Article 10 requires states to protect and assist the family generally, and 'particularly'—that is, non-exhaustively—'while it is responsible for the care and education of dependent children'. The qualifying phrase was voted on separately and adopted by a large majority.[26] Where a family includes children, the obligations of protection will simply be different and more extensive.

There is otherwise little more in either the drafting record or subsequent CESCR practice to indicate how the 'family' is defined for the purposes of Article 10. The HRC's interpretation of the ICCPR provisions is instructive. In respect of Article 17, the HRC called for a 'broad interpretation to include all those comprising the family as understood in the society of the State party concerned':

> 5. Regarding the term 'family', the objectives of the Covenant require that for purposes of article 17 this term be given a broad interpretation to include all those comprising the family as understood in the society of the State party concerned…[27]

In relation to Article 23 of the ICCPR, the HRC recognizes the relativity and diversity of the concept of the family:

> 2. The Committee notes that the concept of the family may differ in some respects from State to State, and even from region to region within a State, and that it is therefore not possible to give the concept a standard definition. However, the Committee emphasizes that, when a group of persons is regarded as a family under the legislation and practice of a State, it must be given the protection referred to in article 23. Consequently, States parties should report on how the concept and scope of the family is construed or defined in their own society and legal system. Where diverse concepts of the family, 'nuclear' and 'extended', exist within a State, this should be indicated with an explanation of the degree of protection afforded to each. In view of the existence of various forms of family, such as unmarried couples and their children or single parents and their children, States parties should also indicate whether and to what extent such types of family and their members are recognized and protected by domestic law and practice.[28]

While in the above passage the HRC accords a discretion to states to define at law their own conception of the family, it has not permitted unbounded relativity. In its subsequent practice, the HRC has recognized certain minimum characteristics of family life, beyond archetypal married heterosexual couples with children or whatever national law provides. First, 'the absence of formal marriage bonds, especially where there is a local practice of customary or common law marriage', will not preclude the existence of a family.[29] Local cultural considerations are therefore significant.

[25] UNGA Third Committee, A/C.3/SR.736 (21 January 1957), 278 (China).

[26] By forty-six votes to five, with twelve abstentions: UNGA Third Committee Report, A/3525 (9 February 1957), 42.

[27] HRC, General Comment No. 16 (1988), [5].

[28] HRC, General Comment No. 19 (1990), [2].

[29] *Ngambi v France*, HRC Communication No. 1179/2003 (9 July 2004), [6.4].

Secondly, the dissolution of marriage does not destroy family relationships involving children. The HRC accepts that the family 'does not refer solely to the family home as it exists during the marriage' and survives divorce to encompass relations between parents and child.[30] Such bonds 'do not depend on the continuation of the parents' marriage'.[31] This is consistent with view expressed in the drafting of Article 10 of the ICESCR, mentioned above.

Thirdly, marriage itself is not essential to the notion of family. The HRC has recognized that a family may arise from 'cohabitation'.[32] Thus, de facto couples may qualify, which are sometimes defined under national laws by reference to minimum time periods spent living together (such as twelve months) or other indicia of a shared life. Those traditions which recognize a family only based on marriage, such as certain Islamic legal views,[33] are incompatible with Article 10(1). Children outside marriage can thus still be part of a family, whether with biological parents, step parents, adoptive parents[34] or single parents.

Under the ICCPR, marriage has thus far been interpreted as restricted to that between a man and woman,[35] although the ICCPR does not forbid national law from recognizing same-sex marriages.[36] But in principle, same-sex couples can still constitute an unmarried 'family'[37] given that the latter concept is delinked from marriage. The HRC has not expressly confined its mention of 'cohabitants' to opposite genders and the implication that a same-sex couple could be a family was not contested in *Joslin v New Zealand* (where same-sex marriage was not recognized under Article 23(3) of the ICCPR).[38] While the legal recognition of same-sex unions may not be a 'core obligation' under Article 10(1),[39] the existence of a 'family' entitled to protection turns on the characteristics of the relationship rather than a 'legal' marriage, the gender of partners or majority social attitudes.

[30] *Hendriks v Netherlands*, HRC Communication No. 201/85 (12 August 1988), [10.3].

[31] *Hendriks v Netherlands*, [10.3].

[32] *Balaguer Santacana v Spain*, HRC Communication No. 417/90 (29 July 1994), [10.2]; see also *Kroon v Netherlands*, 27 October 1994, (1995) 19 EHRR 263, [30] (de facto family relationships recognized under Article 8 of the ECHR).

[33] Organisation of the Islamic Conference, Cairo Declaration on Human Rights in Islam (adopted 5 August 1990), Article 5: 'The family is the foundation of society, and marriage is the basis of its foundation'. See Mashood Baderin, *International Human Rights and Islam* (Oxford University Press, Oxford, 2005) ('*IHR and Islam*'), 195–6.

[34] *A S v Canada*, HRC Communication No. 68/1980 (31 March 1981), [5.1] (involving an adopted child, where there was no objection to the adoption relationship as a family in principle, although the family was not recognized for other reasons).

[35] *Joslin v New Zealand*, HRC Communication No. 902/1999 (17 July 2002), [8.3].

[36] *Minister of Home Affairs and Director-General of Home Affairs v Fourie and Bonthuys, Lesbian and Gay Equality Project and 18 ors v Minister of Home Affairs and ors*, 1 December 2005, [2005] ZACC 19 (South Africa Constitutional Court), [99]–[105].

[37] Cf *X and Y v UK* (App. 9369/81), 3 May 1983, (1983) 32 DR 220.

[38] *Joslin v New Zealand*; Nowak, *CCPR Commentary*, 394.

[39] Maja Kirilova Eriksson, 'Family Rights and the United Nations Covenant on Economic, Social and Cultural Rights: Article 10(1)' in Audrey Chapman and Sage Russell (eds), *Core Obligations: Building a Framework for Economic, Social and Cultural Rights* (Intersentia, Antwerp, 2001) ('Family Rights'), 127.

Certainly, national law is free to recognize such families, whether de facto or through civil unions or same-sex marriage (which is recognized in an increasing number of states). It may be noted in this respect that marriage or other recognition of same-sex couples serves not only equality and non-discrimination purposes, but also promotes the stability and reciprocity of relationships[40] and families which conventional marriage purports to encourage. Under the ECHR, the European Court of Human Rights has also found that there is 'no justification' for barring a transsexual from the right to marry 'under any circumstances'.[41]

Fourthly, social and cultural conceptions of the family are crucial in defining it (excluding harmful traditional marriage practices which are contrary to human rights, discussed further below). In *Hopu and Bessert v France*, the HRC found that the building of a hotel on the ancestral burial grounds of Polynesian Tahitians violated Article 23(1) of the ICCPR because their relationship to ancestors generally (not necessarily members of their own kinship group buried there) played an important role in their family life:

> [T]he objectives of the Covenant require that the term 'family' be given a broad interpretation so as to include all those comprising the family as understood in the society in question. It follows that cultural traditions should be taken into account when defining the term 'family' in a specific situation.[42]

Four members of the HRC dissented on the basis that there was no evidence that the complainants' own family members were among those in the burial ground.[43] They also thought that the issues more appropriately arose in relation to cultural rights in Article 27 of the ICCPR, the application of which was precluded by a French reservation. Regardless, cultural considerations concerning families will be particularly important in relation to indigenous peoples and minority groups, whose family relationships may not be adequately reflected in majoritarian preferences embedded in national laws.

It should be noted, however, that harmful cultural conceptions of family may be incompatible with the non-discrimination and equality requirements of international law, such as families based on polygamy, forced marriage, child marriage and the like. As noted by the CEDAW Committee, 'whatever the legal system, religion, custom or tradition within the country, the treatment of women in the family both at law and in private must accord with the principles of equality and justice for all people'.[44]

Fifthly, while recognizing the diversity of family types, the HRC has stated that '[s]ome minimal requirements for the existence of a family are, however, necessary, such as life together, economic ties, a regular and intense relationship, etc'.[45] In part,

[40] Eriksson, 'Family Rights', 127.

[41] *Goodwin v United Kingdom* (App. 17488/90), 11 July 2002, (1996) 22 EHRR 123, [103].

[42] *Hopu and Bessert v France*, HRC Communication No. 549/1993 (29 July 1997), [10.3].

[43] *Hopu and Bessert*, Individual Opinion of Kretzmer, Buergenthal, Ando and Colville, [4]–[5].

[44] CEDAW Committee, General Recommendation No. 21: Equality in marriage and family relations (1994), [13].

[45] *Balaguer Santacana v Spain*, [10.2].

this is to draw a line between families and other relationships, such as flatmates, friends sharing a residence, or tenants in a boarding house.

At the same time, the HRC has highlighted that there are no prescriptive minima given the diversity of different relationships and the array of potentially relevant indicia. Thus, the existence of a family is not 'necessarily displaced by geographical separation, infidelity, or the absence of conjugal relations'.[46] There must, however, 'first be a family bond to protect' (and not one that is fraudulent).[47]

In other words, 'protection requires *a priori* that an effective family life between the members of the family must have existed'.[48] The HRC thus found that there was no family entitled to protection where a mother and her adopted daughter had not lived together as a family for seventeen years and before that had lived together for a brief period of two years.[49] A formal legal link (such as marriage or adoption) alone may thus not be sufficient. Nor may a blood connection alone be enough without more indicia of a relationship.[50] As already noted, however, there may still be a family absent blood ties (as in the case of adoption).[51] Where paternity is contested, the state may be required to provide procedures to determine it.[52]

There is a risk, however, that the effectiveness requirement might be applied so as to doubly penalize or victimize families which have been separated by no fault of their own. For example, family members separated for protracted periods by conflict, refugee or internal displacement, state disintegration or succession, ethnic cleansing, racist child removal policies, child abduction, slavery, trafficking and so on may have suffered serious disruption or destruction of family life, but through no fault or choice of their own. In relation to Article 23 of the ICCPR, for example, the HRC stated that states must take measures to ensure the unity or reunification of families in certain circumstances:

> …the possibility to live together implies the adoption of appropriate measures, both at the internal level and as the case may be, in cooperation with other States, to ensure the unity or reunification of families, particularly when their members are separated for political, economic or similar reasons. [53]

Under Article 12 of the ECHR, the European Court of Human Rights has been more conscious of the need to positively enable family life where it may not thus far be wholly effective. In *Keegan v Ireland*, a biological father's child was adopted out by his former girlfriend. The father's application for guardianship under national law was unsuccessful, largely because the elapse of time (including due to legal proceedings) had strengthened the child's attachment to the adoptive parents and removing the child would traumatize her. The European Court found that the fact of a child's birth established 'family' life under

[46] *Ngambi v France*, [6.4].
[47] *Ngambi v France*, [6.4].
[48] *A S v Canada*, [5.1].
[49] *A S v Canada*, [8.2(b)].
[50] *Lebbink v Netherlands* (App. 45582/99), 1 June 2004, (2005) 40 EHRR 18.
[51] *X and Y v United Kingdom* (App. 7229/75), (1978) 12 DR 32, 34; *Söderback v Sweden* (App. 24484/94), 28 October 1998, (1998) 29 EHRR 95, [24].
[52] *Rasmussen v Denmark* (App. 8777/79), 28 November 1984, (1985) 7 EHRR 352, [33].
[53] HRC, General Comment No. 19 (1990), [5].

Article 8 of the ECHR, regardless of the brevity or instability of actual family relationships:

44. The Court recalls that the notion of the 'family' in this provision is not confined solely to marriage-based relationships and may encompass other de facto 'family' ties where the parties are living together outside of marriage (see, inter alia, the *Johnston and Others v. Ireland* judgment of 18 December 1986, Series A no. 112, p. 25, para. 55). A child born out of such a relationship is ipso iure part of that 'family' unit from the moment of his birth and by the very fact of it. There thus exists between the child and his parents a bond amounting to family life even if at the time of his or her birth the parents are no longer co-habiting or if their relationship has then ended (see, mutatis mutandis, the *Berrehab v. the Netherlands* judgment of 21 June 1988, Series A no. 138, p. 14, para. 21).

45. In the present case, the relationship between the applicant and the child's mother lasted for two years during one of which they co-habited. Moreover, the conception of their child was the result of a deliberate decision and they had also planned to get married (see paragraph 6 above). Their relationship at this time had thus the hallmark of family life for the purposes of Article 8 (art. 8). The fact that it subsequently broke down does not alter this conclusion any more than it would for a couple who were lawfully married and in a similar situation. It follows that from the moment of the child's birth there existed between the applicant and his daughter a bond amounting to family life.[54]

In another European case, a family life was found to exist between parents and two children living in the Netherlands and a 9-year-old child being raised by other relatives in Turkey.[55] Family ties also do not end automatically upon a child becoming an adult or starting their own family.[56]

More generally, the HRC has not indicated that children are an indispensible element of a family, although most of the cases have involved children, not childless couples or extended relatives (such as relations between adult siblings, grandparents and the like). It may be little burden on the state to recognize couples as families, given that in general, resource-intensive measures of protection will usually be those involving families with children.

Even so, examples of appropriate support for childless couples may include, for instance, relationship counselling, family planning, household skills or budgeting, joint income tax rules and the like. Further, once adult children leave the family home, the demands on the state will dissipate, even if the family relationship continues in a different, less intense form.

PROTECTION ISSUES ARISING UNDER ARTICLE 10(1)

In monitoring states, the CESCR has identified a number of issues which repeatedly arise within the ambit of Article 10(1), including: domestic violence; sexual violence, exploitation and trafficking; violence by harmful traditional practices;

[54] *Keegan v Ireland* (App. 16969/90), 26 May 1994, (1994) 18 EHRR 342, [44]–[45]; see also *Kroon v Netherlands* (App. 18535/91), 27 October 1994, (1995) 19 EHRR 263, [30].

[55] *Sen v Netherlands* (App. 31465/96), 21 December 2001, (2001) 36 EHRR 81.

[56] See Pieter van Dijk, Fried van Hoof, Arjen van Rijn and Leo Zwaak (eds), *Theory and Practice of the European Convention on Human Rights* (4th edn, Intersentia, Antwerp, 2006), 694–5.

family distintegration; and family separation. Its conception of protection under Article 10(1) is thus not limited to economic concerns, but embraces 'social' protection more broadly.

Domestic violence

The CESCR has frequently expressed concern under Article 10(1) at the high prevalence of domestic violence, particularly against women,[57] as well as its under-reporting[58] and its persistence in indigenous communities.[59] By contrast, the HRC has often dealt with domestic violence not in the context of family rights, but under other ICCPR rights, such as non-discrimination, equality and freedom from inhuman or degrading treatment.[60]

In responding to domestic violence, the CESCR has foremost recommended legislative reform, including: creating a specific offence of domestic violence;[61] broadening the definition of rape to include marital rape;[62] abolishing laws that permit the 'chastisement' of wives by husbands,[63] allow wives to 'forgive' husbands for marital rape[64] or take into account 'victim behaviour';[65] and reforming procedural rules that hinder rape prosecutions.[66]

To deal with domestic violence, the CESCR has encouraged states to ensure that cases are prosecuted without delay;[67] that police, law enforcement officials

[57] See, eg, CESCR, Concluding Observations: Afghanistan, E/C.12/AFG/CO/2-4 (7 June 2010), [31]: Algeria, E/C.12/1995/17 (28 December 1995), [19]; Algeria, E/C.12/1/Add.71 (30 November 2001), [17]; Angola, E/C.12/DZA/CO/4 (7 June 2010), [15]; Angola, E/C.12/AGO/CO/3 (1 December 2008), [24]; Argentina, E/C.12/1/Add.38 (8 December 1999), [25]: Belgium, E/C.12/BEL/CO/3 (4 January 2008), [18]; Benin, E/C.12/BEN/CO/2 (9 June 2008), [17]; Bolivia, E/C.12/1/Add.60 (21 May 2001), [37]; Bolivia, E/C.12/BOL/CO/2 (8 August 2008), [20]; Bosnia and Herzegovina, E/C.12/BIH/CO/1 (24 January 2006), [21]; Brazil, E/C.12/BRA/CO/2 (12 June 2009), [21]; Cambodia, E/C.12/KHM/CO/1 (12 June 2009), [20]; Canada, E/C.12/CAN/CO/4, E/C.12/CAN/CO/5 (22 May 2006), [25]; Chad, E/C.12/TCD/CO/3 (16 December 2009), [19]; Chile, E/C.12/1/Add.105 (1 December 2004), [44]; China (including Hong Kong and Macao), E/C.12/1/Add.107 (13 May 2005), [28] and [112]; Costa Rica, E/C.12/CRI/CO/4 (4 January 2008), [22]; Cyprus, E/C.12/1/Add.28 (4 December 1998), [15]; Czech Republic, E/C.12/1/Add.76 (5 June 2002), [17]; Democratic People's Republic of Korea, E/C.12/1/Add.95 (12 December 2003), [19]; Denmark, E/C.12/1/Add.102 (14 December 2004), [17].

[58] CESCR, Concluding Observations: France, E/C.12.FRA/CO/3 (9 June 2008), [19].

[59] CESCR, Concluding Observations: New Zealand, E/C.12/1/Add.88 (26 June 2003), [15].

[60] Including Articles 2 (Albania, A/60/40 (2004), [82(10)]), 3 (Albania, A/60/40 (2004), [82(10)]; Lithuania, A/59/40 (2004), [71(9)]; Slovakia, A/58/40 (2003), [82(9)]), 7 (Lithuania, A/59/40 (2004), [71(9)]) and 26 (Slovakia, A/58/40 (2003), [82(9)]).

[61] CESCR, Concluding Observations: Benin, E/C.12/BEN/CO/2 (9 June 2008), [17]; Bolivia, E/C.12/BOL/CO/2 (8 August 2008), [33]; Canada, E/C.12/CAN/CO/4, E/C.12/CAN/CO/5 (22 May 2006), [58]; China, E/C.12/1/Add.107 (13 May 2005), [122]; Czech Republic, E/C.12/1/Add.76 (5 June 2002), [36]; Democratic People's Republic of Korea, E/C.12/1/Add.95 (12 December 2003), [39]; Denmark, E/C.12/1/Add.102 (14 December 2004), [30].

[62] CESCR, Concluding Observations: Angola, E/C.12/DZA/CO/4 (7 June 2010), [15]; Angola, E/C.12/AGO/CO/3 (1 December 2008), [24]; Benin, E/C.12/BEN/CO/2 (9 June 2008), [17].

[63] CESCR, Concluding Observations: Nigeria, E/C.12/1/Add.23 (16 June 1998), [21].

[64] CESCR, Concluding Observations: Philippines, E/C.12.PHL/CO/4 (1 December 2008), [25].

[65] CESCR, Concluding Observations: Ukraine, E/C.12/UKR/CO/5 (4 January 2008), [42].

[66] CESCR, Concluding Observations: Macedonia, E/C.12/MKD/CO/1 (15 January 2008), [39].

[67] CESCR, Concluding Observations: Afghanistan, E/C.12/AFG/CO/2-4 (7 June 2010), [31]; Bosnia and Herzegovina, E/C.12/BIH/CO/1 (24 January 2006), [21]; Cambodia, E/C.12/KHM/CO/1

and judges are properly trained on its serious and criminal nature[68] and sensitized to victims' needs;[69] and that health workers are educated on the need to report it.[70] However, the CESCR has noted that even states with appropriate laws may fail to effectively reduce domestic violence if victims are reluctant to report it,[71] whether because of a woman's dependency on her spouse[72] or gender-biased attitudes that blame the victim.[73]

To protect victims, the CESCR has recommended that states should: establish crisis centres or shelters where victims can obtain safe lodging and assistance;[74] strictly enforce protection orders;[75] and provide remedies[76] and compensation[77] to victims. The CESCR has encouraged counselling and support to be provided to perpetrators, particularly those suffering trauma related to armed conflict.[78]

The CESCR has also recommended wider measures to prevent domestic violence, such as awareness-raising campaigns.[79] It has also urged states to address underlying stressors leading to domestic violence, such as unemployment or conflict-related trauma.[80]

Sexual violence, exploitation and trafficking

Under Article 10(1), the CESCR has expressed serious concern at sexual violence, especially when the violence is perpetrated by armed groups,[81] is ethnically

(12 June 2009), [20]; UNMIK, E/C.12/UNK/CO/1 (1 December 2008), [23(c)] (time limits for issuing protection orders).

[68] CESCR, Concluding Observations: Azerbaijan, E/C.12/1/Add.104 (14 December 2004), [49]; Algeria, E/C.12/1/Add.71 (30 November 2001), [33]; Angola, E/C.12/AGO/CO/3 (1 December 2008), [24]; Bolivia, E/C.12/BOL/CO/2 (8 August 2008), [33]; Bosnia and Herzegovina, E/C.12/BIH/CO/1 (24 January 2006), [43]; China, E/C.12/1/Add.107 (13 May 2005), [122]; Denmark, E/C.12/1/Add.102 (14 December 2004), [30].

[69] CESCR, Concluding Observations: Greece, E/C.12/1/Add.97 (7 June 2004), [37].

[70] CESCR, Concluding Observations: UNMIK, E/C.12/UNK/CO/1 (1 December 2008), [23(c)].

[71] CESCR, Concluding Observations: Macedonia, E/C.12/MKD/CO/1 (15 January 2008), [19].

[72] CESCR, Concluding Observations: Denmark, E/C.12/1/Add.102 (14 December 2004), [31] (fear of deportation); Greece, E/C.12/1/Add.97 (7 June 2004), [16] (economic dependency).

[73] CESCR, Concluding Observations: Cambodia, E/C.12/KHM/CO/1 (12 June 2009), [20].

[74] CESCR, Concluding Observations: Azerbaijan, E/C.12/1/Add.104 (14 December 2004), [49]; Bolivia, E/C.12/BOL/CO/2 (8 August 2008), [33]; China, E/C.12/1/Add.107 (13 May 2005), [122]; Cyprus, E/C.12/1/Add.28 (4 December 1998), [23].

[75] CESCR, Concluding Observations: Ukraine, E/C.12/UKR/CO/5 (4 January 2008), [42].

[76] CESCR, Concluding Observations: Azerbaijan, E/C.12/1/Add.104 (14 December 2004), [49]; Algeria, E/C.12/1995/17 (28 December 1995), [24] (right to compensation); Belgium, E/C.12/BEL/CO/3 (4 January 2008), [32]; Bosnia and Herzegovina, E/C.12/BIH/CO/1 (24 January 2006), [21] (health care); Brazil, E/C.12/BRA/CO/2 (12 June 2009), [21]; Cambodia, E/C.12/KHM/CO/1 (12 June 2009), [20]; Canada, E/C.12/CAN/CO/4, E/C.12/CAN/CO/5 (22 May 2006), [26].

[77] CESCR, Concluding Observations: Algeria, E/C.12/1995/17 (28 December 1995), [24]; Mexico, E/C.12/MEX/CO/4 (9 June 2006), [38].

[78] CESCR, Concluding Observations: Serbia and Montenegro, E/C.12/1/Add.108 (23 June 2005), [23], [50].

[79] CESCR, Concluding Observations: Afghanistan, E/C.12/AFG/CO/2-4 (7 June 2010), [31]; Algeria, E/C.12/1995/17 (28 December 1995), [19]; Algeria, E/C.12/1/Add.71 (30 November 2001), [33]; Angola, E/C.12/AGO/CO/3 (1 December 2008), [24]; Brazil, E/C.12/BRA/CO/2 (12 June 2009), [21].

[80] CESCR, Concluding Observations: Serbia and Montenegro, E/C.12/1/Add.108 (23 June 2005), [23].

[81] CESCR, Concluding Observations: Angola, E/C.12/DZA/CO/4 (7 June 2010), [16]; Colombia, E/C.12/COL/CO/5 (7 June 2010), [15].

motivated,[82] or takes place in camps for refugees or internally displaced persons.[83] A related concern has been the sexual exploitation of women through practices such as prostitution,[84] sex tourism,[85] sexual slavery,[86] marriage trafficking[87] and human trafficking generally.[88]

In response, the CESCR has recommended: an increase in police presence in situations of vulnerability;[89] the prosecution and sentencing of perpetrators;[90] the medical, psychological and social rehabilitation of victims;[91] and the provision of compensation to victims.[92] It has repeatedly emphasized the need for trafficking to be specifically criminalized[93] (but not the victims[94]) and for corrupt law enforcement officials involved in it to be prosecuted.[95] To promote effective enforcement, the CESCR has recommended implementing restrictive licensing policies and effective inspection regimes for tourist and marriage agencies.[96]

Policies that provide protection and assistance to victims have also been recommended,[97] including witness protection programmes[98] and crisis centres.[99]

82 CESCR, Concluding Observations: Democratic Republic of Congo, E/C.12/COD/CO/4 (16 December 2009), [25].

83 CESCR, Concluding Observations: Chad, E/C.12/TCD/CO/3 (16 December 2009), [20]; Colombia, E/C.12/COL/CO/5 (7 June 2010), [15].

84 CESCR, Concluding Observations: China (including Hong Kong and Macao), E/C.12/1/Add.107 (13 May 2005), [29]; Costa Rica, E/C.12/CRI/CO/4 (4 January 2008), [24].

85 CESCR, Concluding Observations: Costa Rica, E/C.12/CRI/CO/4 (4 January 2008), [17]; Jamaica, E/C.12/1/Add.75 (6 December 2001), [13]; Madagascar, E/C.12/MDG/CO/2 (6 December 2009), [24]; Colombia, E/C.12/COL/CO/5 (7 June 2010), [17].

86 CESCR, Concluding Observations: Democratic Republic of Congo, E/C.12/COD/CO/4 (16 December 2009), [26].

87 CESCR, Concluding Observations: Germany, E/C.12/1/Add.29 (4 December 1998), [20].

88 CESCR, Concluding Observations: Azerbaijan, E/C.12/1/Add.104 (14 December 2004), [24]; Afghanistan, E/C.12/AFG/CO/2-4 (7 June 2010), [32]; Benin, E/C.12/BEN/CO/2 (9 June 2008), [18]; Bosnia and Herzegovina, E/C.12/BIH/CO/1 (24 January 2006), [22]; Cambodia, E/C.12/KHM/CO/1 (12 June 2009), [26]; China (including Hong Kong and Macao), E/C.12/1/Add.107 (13 May 2005), [19], [29] and [113]; Costa Rica, E/C.12/CRI/CO/4 (4 January 2008), [24]; Croatia, E/C.12/1/Add.73 (5 December 2001), [14]; Czech Republic, E/C.12/1/Add.76 (5 June 2002), [18]; Denmark, E/C.12/1/Add.102 (14 December 2004), [19].

89 CESCR, Concluding Observations: Chad, E/C.12/TCD/CO/3 (16 December 2009), [20].

90 CESCR, Concluding Observations: Colombia, E/C.12/COL/CO/5 (7 June 2010), [15]; Democratic Republic of Congo, E/C.12/COD/CO/4 (16 December 2009), [25].

91 CESCR, Concluding Observations: Angola, E/C.12/DZA/CO/4 (7 June 2010), [15].

92 CESCR, Concluding Observations: Colombia, E/C.12/COL/CO/5 (7 June 2010), [15].

93 CESCR, Concluding Observations: Azerbaijan, E/C.12/1/Add.104 (14 December 2004), [50]; Afghanistan, E/C.12/AFG/CO/2-4 (7 June 2010), [32]; Benin, E/C.12/BEN/CO/2 (9 June 2008), [39]; Cambodia, E/C.12/KHM/CO/1 (12 June 2009), [26]; China (including Hong Kong and Macao), E/C.12/1/Add.107 (13 May 2005), [58].

94 CESCR, Concluding Observations: India, E/C.12/IND/CO/5 (8 August 2008), [27] and [66].

95 CESCR, Concluding Observations: Bosnia and Herzegovina, E/C.12/BIH/CO/1 (24 January 2006), [44]; Serbia and Montenegro, E/C.12/1/Add.108 (23 June 2005), [25] and [52].

96 CESCR, Concluding Observations: Ukraine, E/C.12/UKR/CO/5 (4 January 2008), [43].

97 CESCR, Concluding Observations: Azerbaijan, E/C.12/1/Add.104 (14 December 2004), [50]; Cambodia, E/C.12/KHM/CO/1 (12 June 2009), [26]; China (including Hong Kong and Macao), E/C.12/1/Add.107 (13 May 2005), [97].

98 CESCR, Concluding Observations: Benin, E/C.12/BEN/CO/2 (9 June 2008), [18].

99 CESCR, Concluding Observations: China (including Hong Kong and Macao), E/C.12/1/Add.107 (13 May 2005), [123].

The CESCR has also called for mechanisms to enable victims to complain irrespective of their immigration status[100] and without fear of deportation,[101] and for proper safeguards to apply when deporting victims to minimize the risks they may face on return.[102]

Reflecting the transnational character of the problem, the CESCR has encouraged regional and international cooperation,[103] and the ratification of the UN Protocol to Prevent, Suppress and Punish Trafficking in Persons, Especially Women and Children,[104] and the Council of Europe Convention against Trafficking Human Beings (No. 197).[105]

Harmful traditional practices

The CESCR has commented on the harmfulness to women of some traditional or customary practices, many of them violent, that continue to be practised in some states. Some of these involve cultural practices surrounding marriage, such as dowry deaths;[106] widow-cleansing[107] (an expectation of widows to have sex with another man after the death of their husband); widow burning (sati);[108] and polygamy.[109] Others relate to wider cultural expectations of women's sexual or gender relationships, whether within marriage or outside of it, such as honour killings,[110] whether by husbands or relatives. Yet others concern cultural or spiritual superstitions, such as witch-hunting[111] or devadasi[112] (where a girl is 'married' to a deity and lives in a temple, but often involving prostitution). As noted earlier in this book, Article 4 of the ICESCR permits limitations to be imposed on cultural or other rights or freedoms to prevent practices which harm others.

Family disintegration

The CESCR has expressed concern about various social trends in states which undermine the family unit and its ability to care for dependent children under Article 10(1). These include high incidence of: child abandonment and neglect,[113]

[100] CESCR, Concluding Observations: Republic of Korea, E/C.12/KOR/CO/3 (17 December 2009), [25].

[101] CESCR, Concluding Observations: Denmark, E/C.12/1/Add.102 (14 December 2004), [31].

[102] CESCR, Concluding Observations: China (including Hong Kong and Macao), E/C.12/1/Add.107 (13 May 2005), [97]; Germany, E/C.12/1/Add.68 (24 September 2001), [25].

[103] CESCR, Concluding Observations: Republic of Moldova, E/C.12/1/Add.91 (12 December 2003), [41].

[104] CESCR, Concluding Observations: Poland, E/C.12/1/Add.82 (19 December 2002), [46].

[105] CESCR, Concluding Observations: Slovenia, E/C.12/SVN/CO/1 (25 January 2006), [33].

[106] CESCR, Concluding Observations: India, E/C.12/IND/CO/5 (8 August 2008), [25].

[107] CESCR, Concluding Observations: Zambia, E/C.12/1/Add.106 (23 June 2005), [23].

[108] CESCR, Concluding Observations: India, E/C.12.IND/CO/5 (8 August 2008), [25].

[109] CESCR, Concluding Observations: Angola, E/C.12/DZA/CO/4 (7 June 2010), [14]; Gambia, E/C.12/1994/9 (31 May 1994), [14]; Nigeria, E/C.12/1/Add.23 (16 June 1998), [22].

[110] CESCR, Concluding Observations: Afghanistan, E/C.12/AFG/CO/2-4 (7 June 2010), [31]; India, E/C.12/IND/CO/5 (8 August 2008), [25].

[111] CESCR, Concluding Observations: India, E/C.12/IND/CO/5 (8 August 2008), [25].

[112] CESCR, Concluding Observations: India, E/C.12/IND/CO/5 (8 August 2008), [25].

[113] CESCR, Concluding Observations: Russian Federation, E/C.12/1/Add.94 (12 December 2003), [54]; Mexico, E/C.12/1993/16 (5 January 1994), [7].

particularly of those with mental disabilities;[114] desertion of families by fathers;[115] the prevalence of children in care institutions or foster homes,[116] particularly from disadvantaged families;[117] teenage pregnancies;[118] inadequately supported single-parent families;[119] youth delinquency[120] and gangs;[121] abuse of drugs and alcohol by young people;[122] and youth suicide.[123]

In response, the CESCR has recommended financial[124] and other support to assist parents in exercising their parental role and responsibility,[125] maintaining links with their children,[126] and preventing family disintegration which separates children. It has also encouraged integration and development measures for children from broken families.[127]

The CESCR has also recommended increasing and strengthening family-based alternative care so that children are only placed in institutions as a 'last resort'.[128] At the same time, concerns have arisen about the abuse of children in foster homes in the United Kingdom, leading the CESCR to urge the United Kingdom to reconsider what is in the best interests of children.[129]

Measures to protect children outside the family are considered below under Article 10(3) of the ICESCR, which provides that '[s]pecial measures of protection and assistance should be taken on behalf of all children and young persons without any discrimination for reasons of parentage or other reasons'.

An adequate and effective system of family law to regulate the legal consequences of family disintegration will be necessary to protect the family and its members under Article 10(1). Such laws should address core matters such as the division of family property on a non-discriminatory basis (measures concerning the protection of children, and child custody and access, are separately

[114] CESCR, Concluding Observations: Republic of Moldova, E/C.12/1/Add.91 (12 December 2003), [21]; Ukraine, E/C.12/1/Add.65 (24 September 2001), [13].

[115] CESCR, Concluding Observations: Paraguay, E/C.12/1/Add.1 (28 May 1996), [26].

[116] CESCR, Concluding Observations: Afghanistan, E/C.12/AFG/CO/2-4 (7 June 2010), [28]; Finland, E/C.12/FIN/CO/5 (16 January 2008), [29]; Norway, E/C.12/1/Add.109 (23 June 2005), [14].

[117] CESCR, Concluding Observations: Canada, E/C.12/CAN/CO/4, E/C.12/CAN/CO/5 (22 May 2006), [24].

[118] CESCR, Concluding Observations: Mauritius, E/C.12/1995/14 (28 December 1995), [13]; Netherlands Antilles, E/C.12/NLD/CO/3/Add.1 (31 January 2008), [20].

[119] CESCR, Concluding Observations: Iceland, E/C.12/1/Add.89 (26 June 2003), [16]; San Marino, E/C.12/SMR/CO/4 (4 January 2008), [16].

[120] CESCR, Concluding Observations: Iceland, E/C.12/1/Add.32 (12 May 1999), [15].

[121] CESCR, Concluding Observations: El Salvador, E/C.12/SLV/CO/2 (27 June 2007), [22].

[122] CESCR, Concluding Observations: Finland, E/C.12/1/Add.8 (5 December 1996), [16].

[123] CESCR, Concluding Observations: China (Hong Kong), E/C.12/1/Add.58 (21 May 2001), [23]; Finland, E/C.12/1/Add.8 (5 December 1996), [16]; Sri Lanka, E/C.12/1/Add.24 (16 June 1998), [14].

[124] CESCR, Concluding Observations: Canada, E/C.12/CAN/CO/4, E/C.12/CAN/CO/5 (22 May 2006), [56]; Iceland, E/C.12/1/Add.89 (26 June 2003), [26].

[125] CESCR, Concluding Observations: Norway, E/C.12/1/Add.109 (23 June 2005), [32]; Ukraine, E/C.12/1/Add.65 (24 September 2001), [30].

[126] CESCR, Concluding Observations: Finland, E/C.12/FIN/CO/5 (16 January 2008), [29].

[127] CESCR, Concluding Observations: El Salvador, E/C.12/SLV/CO/2 (27 June 2007), [41].

[128] CESCR, Concluding Observations: Ukraine, E/C.12/1/Add.65 (24 September 2001), [30].

[129] CESCR, Concluding Observations: UK, E/C.12/1/Add.19 (12 December 1997), [25].

considered below). Under European regional law, states are further specifically required to provide accessible and effective family mediation services.[130]

Family separation

In addition to cases where the family disintegrates, a range of state measures may result in the separation of children from their parents, such as child welfare and immigration policies. Many instances of child separation have arisen under the Convention on the Rights of the Child (CROC) and ICCPR, which have a more developed jurisprudence in this area and which may inform Article 10 of the ICESCR.

Broadly speaking, there will be no violation of the duty to protect the family in Article 10 where it is necessary to separate the child from her or his parents to protect the child, where less invasive measures would not be sufficient, and where the measures taken are proportionate (including preserving parental access rights where feasible).

Laws, procedures and practices concerning the separation of children from family members must not be discriminatory, as the HRC has observed in relation to family rights under Article 23 of the ICCPR:

> 9. Thus, any discriminatory treatment in regard to the grounds and procedures for separation or divorce, child custody, maintenance or alimony, visiting rights or the loss or recovery of parental authority must be prohibited, bearing in mind the paramount interest of the children in this connection. States parties should, in particular, include information in their reports concerning the provision made for the necessary protection of any children at the dissolution of a marriage or on the separation of the spouses.[131]

Child abuse or neglect

As a general principle, Article 9(1) of the CROC provides that children should not be separated from their parents against their will except when 'necessary in the best interests of the child',[132] such as for certain child welfare reasons, and only if minimum procedural protections are observed:

> 1. States Parties shall ensure that a child shall not be separated from his or her parents against their will, except when competent authorities subject to judicial review determine, in accordance with applicable law and procedures, that such separation is necessary for the best interests of the child. Such determination may be necessary in a particular case such as one involving abuse or neglect of the child by the parents, or one where the parents are living separately and a decision must be made as to the child's place of residence.
>
> 2. In any proceedings pursuant to paragraph 1 of the present article, all interested parties shall be given an opportunity to participate in the proceedings and make their views known.

[130] ECSR, Statement of Interpretation on Article 16 of the European Social Charter (31 October 2006), 14.

[131] HRC, General Comment No. 19 (1990).

[132] Convention on the Rights of the Child (CROC) (adopted 20 November 1989, 1577 UNTS 3, entered into force 2 September 1990), Article 9(1); see Committee on the Rights of Child (CRC), General Comment No. 14, Right of the child to have his or her best interests taken as a primary consideration (Article 3(1)) (29 May 2013).

3. States Parties shall respect the right of the child who is separated from one or both parents to maintain personal relations and direct contact with both parents on a regular basis, except if it is contrary to the child's best interests.

4. Where such separation results from any action initiated by a State Party, such as the detention, imprisonment, exile, deportation or death (including death arising from any cause while the person is in the custody of the State) of one or both parents or of the child, that State Party shall, upon request, provide the parents, the child or, if appropriate, another member of the family with the essential information concerning the whereabouts of the absent member(s) of the family unless the provision of the information would be detrimental to the well-being of the child. States Parties shall further ensure that the submission of such a request shall of itself entail no adverse consequences for the person(s) concerned.

Another important reference point is Article 19 of the CROC, which specifically requires states to protect children from harm when in the care of parents, guardians or carers:

1. States Parties shall take all appropriate legislative, administrative, social and educational measures to protect the child from all forms of physical or mental violence, injury or abuse, neglect or negligent treatment, maltreatment or exploitation, including sexual abuse, while in the care of parent(s), legal guardian(s) or any other person who has the care of the child.

2. Such protective measures should, as appropriate, include effective procedures for the establishment of social programmes to provide necessary support for the child and for those who have the care of the child, as well as for other forms of prevention and for identification, reporting, referral, investigation, treatment and follow-up of instances of child maltreatment described heretofore, and, as appropriate, for judicial involvement.

The HRC has also interpreted Article 24 of the ICCPR to require states to protect children at risk:

…in cases where the parents and the family seriously fail in their duties, ill-treat or neglect the child, the State should intervene to restrict parental authority and the child may be separated from his family when circumstances so require.[133]

A General Comment of the Committee on the Rights of the Child (CRC) defines what is covered by the forms of harm prohibited under Article 19,[134] and provides a useful reference point for understanding the protection of children under Article 10. The forms of violence extensively outlined by the CRC include neglect or negligent treatment; mental violence; physical violence; corporal punishment; sexual abuse and exploitation; torture and inhuman or degrading treatment or punishment; violence among children; self-harm; harmful practices;[135] violence in the mass media; and violence through information and communications technologies.

[133] HRC, General Comment No. 17, Rights of the child (Article 24) (7 April 1989), [6].

[134] CRC, General Comment No. 13, The right of the child to freedom from all forms of violence (18 April 2011), [19]–[31].

[135] Including: (a) corporal punishment and other cruel or degrading forms of punishment; (b) female genital mutilation; (c) amputations, binding, scarring, burning and branding; (d) violent and degrading initiation rites; force-feeding of girls; fattening; virginity testing (inspecting girls' genitalia);

The CESCR, for instance, has consistently condemned all forms of abuse of and violence against children, including corporal punishment within families, including where it is confined by national law to 'reasonable chastisement'.[136]

In an appropriate case, such forms of harm may justify a child's removal from their family in their best interests, without violating Article 10(1) of the ICESCR. There must, however, be strong justification for child removals; the CESCR criticized Norway, for instance, for the high number of children removed from families and placed in institutions or foster care.[137]

In one case, the HRC upheld the removal of children under the ICCPR where a mother was unable to adequately care for her children.[138] The HRC acknowledged the 'weighty nature' of forced removal, but found that it was in the children's best interests, and the state had carefully considered the evidence, followed extensive procedures (including judicial supervision), kept the matter under regular review and given the mother an opportunity to access her children. In addition, the state's submissions indicated that the grounds for removal were specified by law, less invasive measures had been unsuccessfully applied and removal was a last resort.

In a case under the right to family life in Article 8 of the ECHR, *Olsson v Sweden*, the European Court of Human Rights required 'sufficiently sound and weighty considerations in the interests of the child' to justify separation from a parent:

> . . . it is an interference of a very serious order to split up a family. Such a step must be supported by sufficiently sound and weighty considerations in the interests of the child; as the Commission rightly observed, it is not enough that the child would be better off if placed in care.[139]

In that case, there was sufficient evidence of serious impairment of three children's development, including language skills, and the parents' inability to adequately care for them. Taking into account the Swedish authorities' 'margin of appreciation', the Court accepted that taking the children into care was necessary. However, the implementation of the decision was disproportionate, and thus not 'necessary' in a democratic society, because the children were separated, and two of them were placed at a long distance from the parents, making visits and access

(e) forced marriage and early marriage; (f) 'honour' crimes; 'retribution' acts of violence (where disputes between different groups are taken out on children of the parties involved); dowry-related death and violence; (g) accusations of 'witchcraft' and related harmful practices such as 'exorcism'; and (h) uvulectomy and teeth extraction.

136 CESCR, Concluding Observations: Malta, E/C.12/1/Add.101 (14 December 2004), [22]. In regional law, see *World Organization against Torture v Greece*, ECSR Complaint No. 17/2003 (7 December 2004) (Greek law failed to protect children from corporal punishment at home or at school, contrary to the protection of children under Article 17 of the European Social Charter); see similarly *World Organization against Torture v Ireland*, ECSR Complaint No. 18/2003 (7 December 2004); *World Organization against Torture v Belgium*, ECSR Complaint No. 21/2003 (7 December 2004).

137 CESCR, Concluding Observations: Norway, E/C.12/1/Add.109 (23 June 2005), [14].

138 *Buckle v New Zealand*, HRC Communication No. 858/99 (25 October 2000).

139 *Olsson v Sweden* (App. 10465/83), 24 March 1988, (1989) 11 EHRR 259, [72].

difficult and impeding the ultimate aim of family reunification. The reasons for doing so were partly related to the state's administrative considerations rather than the interests of the children or the family.

Ordinarily, 'the financial circumstances of the family should not be the sole reason' for removing a child from their family;[140] instead, the family should be supported to enable it to care adequately for the child. Further, removal of a child should ordinarily be considered a temporary measure, 'during which the continuity of the relationship with the family should be maintained', and where the child's re-integration with the family is the ultimate aim.[141] Normally, a child separated from a parent 'shall have the right to maintain personal relations and direct contact with both parents on a regular basis'.[142]

Racially discriminatory child removal policies will not comply with Article 10, read in conjunction with the prohibition on discrimination in Article 2(2) of the ICESCR. The CESCR was concerned, for example, at the over-representation of Aboriginal and African Canadian children taken into foster care.[143] To extrapolate an example from another treaty body, the HRC criticized Australia's past policy of removing indigenous children from their families (known as the 'Stolen Generations').[144] The CERD found similarly:

> 13. The Committee notes the conclusions of the 'National Inquiry into the Separation of Aboriginal and Torres Strait Islander Children from their Families' and acknowledges the measures taken to facilitate family reunion and to improve counselling and family support services for the victims. Concern is expressed that the Commonwealth Government does not support a formal national apology and that it considers inappropriate the provision of monetary compensation for those forcibly and unjustifiably separated from their families, on the grounds that such practices were sanctioned by law at the time and were intended to 'assist the people whom they affected'. The Committee recommends that the State party consider the need to address appropriately the extraordinary harm inflicted by these racially discriminatory practices.[145]

The national inquiry by the Australian Human Rights and Equal Opportunity Commission in 1997 found that such removals were racially discriminatory and even amounted to genocide.[146] Nationally, between one in three and one

[140] ECSR, Statement of Interpretation on Article 16 of the European Social Charter (9 December 2011) (Article 16 concerns the right of the family to protection).

[141] ECSR, Statement of Interpretation on Article 16; see also ECSR, General Observation regarding Article 17 of the Revised European Social Charter (Article 16 of the European Social Charter 1961) (31 December 2001).

[142] African Charter on Human and Peoples' Rights (adopted 27 June 1981, 1520 UNTS 217, entered into force 21 October 1986), Article 19(2).

[143] CESCR, Concluding Observations: Canada, E/C.12/CAN/CO/4-5 (22 May 2006), [24].

[144] HRC, Concluding Observations: Australia, A/55/40 (28 July 2000), [512]–[513].

[145] CERD, Concluding Observations: Australia, CERD/C/304/Add.101 (19 April 2000), [13].

[146] Australian Human Rights and Equal Opportunity Commission, *Bringing Them Home: Report of the National Inquiry into the Separation of Aboriginal and Torres Strait Islander Children from Their Families* (April 1997), chapter 13. Genocide was not enacted as a crime in Australian law until 2002: see International Criminal Court (Consequential Amendments) Act 2002 (Cth). The Australian Federal Court declined to recognize genocide as a domestic crime on the basis of customary international law: *Nulyarimma v Thompson* [1999] FCA 1192; see Ben Saul, 'The International Crime

in ten indigenous children was forcibly removed from their families between 1910 and 1970. While the removals were ostensibly justified at the time as being in the best interests of the children, such conclusions proceeded from paternalistic, assimilationist, racist premises that a 'white' upbringing is preferable to a 'black' one. Under the ICESCR, the assessment of what is in the 'best interests' of a child is not a subjective one applied at the discretion of the state, but includes, among other things, objective requirements that removals must not be discriminatory and must take into account the child's own views.

Where a child is lawfully removed from his or her family, Article 20 of the CROC then requires the state to provide 'special care and assistance' where a child is so removed, mirroring the requirement in Article 10(3) of the ICESCR to assist all children, including those who now find themselves outside their family. Article 20 thus provides:

1. A child temporarily or permanently deprived of his or her family environment, or in whose own best interests cannot be allowed to remain in that environment, shall be entitled to special protection and assistance provided by the State.

2. States Parties shall in accordance with their national laws ensure alternative care for such a child.

3. Such care could include, inter alia, foster placement, kafalah of Islamic law, adoption or if necessary placement in suitable institutions for the care of children. When considering solutions, due regard shall be paid to the desirability of continuity in a child's upbringing and to the child's ethnic, religious, cultural and linguistic background.

Immigration policies

The scope of protection owed to the family under Article 10(1) is affected by a state's right to regulate the immigration of non-citizens, including those with non-citizen or citizen children. Article 10 is not limited to the protection of families which possess the nationality of the state in which they live, nor to non-citizen families who are lawfully resident in the state. Its protection applies to every 'family', regardless of citizenship or lawful immigration status.

While Article 10 obliges states to provide the 'widest possible protection and assistance', it is not an absolute freedom from interference or absolute right to family unity. The CESCR has seldom addressed the protection of the family in an immigration context. Reference may be made instead to the HRC's practice under Articles 17 (freedom from interference in the family), 23 (protection of the family) and 13 (expulsion of aliens) of the ICCPR, provisions of the CROC and principles of general international law. A number of principles emerge from the HRC's family rights jurisprudence which can inform the scope of protection under Article 10 of the ICESCR.

of Genocide in Australian Law' (2000) 22 *Sydney Law Review* 527. The High Court of Australia did not accept that a child removal ordinance in the Northern Territory evidenced an intent to destroy the group: *Kruger v Commonwealth* (1997) 190 CLR 1.

Removal of family members

In general, the expulsion of a non-national must be authorized by law, not arbitrary, not discriminatory,[147] in accordance with applicable procedures, and properly consider the interests of the family and the best interests of any child. The HRC upheld the deportation of a foreigner who had committed serious crimes in *Stewart v Canada*, notwithstanding that it would result in the separation of family members:

12.10 The deportation of Mr. Stewart will undoubtedly interfere with his family relations in Canada. The question is, however, whether the said interference can be considered either unlawful or arbitrary. Canada's Immigration Law expressly provides that the permanent residency status of a non-national may be revoked and that that person may then be expelled from Canada if he or she is convicted of serious offences. In the appeal process the Immigration Appeal Division is empowered to revoke the deportation order 'having regard to all the circumstances of the case'. In the deportation proceedings in the present case, Mr. Stewart was given ample opportunity to present evidence of his family connections to the Immigration Appeal Division. In its reasoned decision the Immigration Appeal Division considered the evidence presented but it came to the conclusion that Mr. Stewart's family connections in Canada did not justify revoking the deportation order. The Committee is of the opinion that the interference with Mr. Stewart's family relations that will be the inevitable outcome of his deportation cannot be regarded as either unlawful or arbitrary when the deportation order was made under law in furtherance of a legitimate state interest and due consideration was given in the deportation proceedings to the deportee's family connections. There is therefore no violation of articles 17 and 23 of the Covenant.[148]

An important issue is the weight to be accorded the interests of the family. In *Stewart*, the HRC appeared to accept Canada's arguments that 'his age and lack of dependents, suggest that the nature and quality of his family relationships could be adequately maintained through correspondence, telephone calls, and visits to Canada'.[149] In the case of *Canepa*, there was no violation in deporting a repeat criminal offender who had no spouse or children in Canada, where no financial dependence in the family was involved, his separation from the remaining family in Canada would not 'irreparably sever' those ties, and he had extended family in Italy, the state to which he was deported.[150]

Where children are involved, the weighting of interests is affected. In *Winata v Australia*, the HRC found that there may be 'interference' in the family under Article 17 of the ICCPR not only where the state forcibly separates family members, but where an expulsion produces 'substantial changes to long-settled family life', even if the family remains united:

7.2 …the Committee considers that a decision of the State party to deport two parents and to compel the family to choose whether a 13-year old child, who has attained citizenship

[147] Such as by not targeting people for removal on the basis of HIV/AIDS status: see, eg, *Constitutional Review*, No. 155-O (12 May 2006) (Constitutional Court of Russia) (considering Article 8 of the ECHR).

[148] *Stewart v Canada*, HRC Communication No. 538/1993 (16 December 1996), [12.10]; see also *Canepa v Canada*, HRC Communication No. 558/93 (13 October 1994).

[149] *Stewart v Canada*, [9.4].

[150] *Canepa v Canada*, [11.5].

of the State party after living there 10 years, either remains alone in the State party or accompanies his parents is to be considered 'interference' with the family, at least in circumstances where, as here, substantial changes to long-settled family life would follow in either case. The issue thus arises whether or not such interference would be arbitrary and contrary to article 17 of the Covenant.[151]

Four members of the HRC dissented on this point, arguing that '[i]t is not at all evident that actions of a State party that result in changes to long-settled family life involve interference in the family, when there is no obstacle to maintaining the family's unity'.[152] (Even if there is no interference in the family, there may be a separate interference in 'privacy' under Article 17 of the ICCPR, which may encompass 'moral and physical integrity', including mental condition and stability, which is disrupted by removing a family.[153])

However, the majority's more protective view is to be preferred for textual and purposive reasons. The family is described as the 'natural and fundamental group unit of society' in Article 23(1) of the ICCPR and Article 10(1) of the ICESCR. Disruption of the family is accordingly not to be lightly presumed under the twin Covenants. The language of Article 17 is not limited to safeguarding the family against 'separation' or 'disunity', but against 'interference', which on an ordinary interpretation connotes a wide spectrum of measures that may impede or obstruct the ordinary course of family life. Article 10 of the ICESCR calls for the 'widest possible' protection of the family, and not only of its unity. The approach under the ECHR supports this view, where a central feature of 'respect' for family life is the right to live together so that family relationships may 'develop normally'[154] and so that family members can 'enjoy each other's company'.[155]

The majority also found the interference in the family was arbitrary and in breach of Articles 17, 23 and 24, while recognizing the breadth of a state's discretion in immigration control:

7.3 It is certainly unobjectionable under the Covenant that a State party may require, under its laws, the departure of persons who remain in its territory beyond limited duration permits. Nor is the fact that a child is born, or that by operation of law such a child receives citizenship either at birth or at a later time, sufficient of itself to make a proposed deportation of one or both parents arbitrary. Accordingly, there is significant scope for States parties to enforce their immigration policy and to require departure of unlawfully present persons. That discretion is, however, not unlimited and may come to be exercised arbitrarily in certain circumstances. In the present case, both authors have been in Australia for

[151] *Winata v Australia*, HRC Communication No. 930/2000 (26 July 2001), [7.2].

[152] *Winata v Australia*, Individual Opinion by four Committee members (Prafullachandra Natwarlal Bhagwati, Tawfik Khalil, David Kretzmer and Max Yalden), [3].

[153] *Agbonlahor v Minister for Justice, Equality and Law Reform*, 3 March 2006, (2007) IEHC 166 (High Court of Ireland), [3.1]–[3.2] and [3.5] (concerning the right to 'private life' in Article 8 of the ECHR).

[154] *Marckx v Belgium* (App. 6833/74), 13 June 1979, (1979) 2 EHHR 330, [31] and [34] (concerning the protection against arbitrary interference in family life under Article 8 of the ECHR).

[155] *Olsson v Sweden* (App. 10465/83), 24 March 1988, (1989) 11 EHRR 259, [59].

over fourteen years. The authors' son has grown in Australia from his birth 13 years ago, attending Australian schools as an ordinary child would and developing the social relationships inherent in that. In view of this duration of time, it is incumbent on the State party to demonstrate additional factors justifying the removal of both parents that go beyond a simple enforcement of its immigration law in order to avoid a characterisation of arbitrariness. In the particular circumstances, therefore, the Committee considers that the removal by the State party of the authors would constitute, if implemented, arbitrary interference with the family, contrary to article 17, paragraph 1, in conjunction with article 23, of the Covenant in respect of all of the alleged victims, and, additionally, a violation of article 24, paragraph 1, in relation to Barry Winata due to a failure to provide him with the necessary measures of protection as a minor.[156]

The dissenting HRC members disagreed that the interference was arbitrary, finding that the state's decision did not force family separation and that the son's difficulties in adjusting to life in Indonesia would not be disproportionate to the state's immigration interests.[157] While acknowledging that expulsion may be disproportionate and arbitrary in exceptional cases, they disagreed that the state in question had to demonstrate an interest more than the simple enforcement of immigration law:

4. The Committee provides no support or reasoning for its statement that in order to avoid characterization of its decision as arbitrary the State party is duty-bound to provide additional factors besides simple enforcement of its immigration laws. There may indeed be exceptional cases in which the interference with the family is so strong that requiring a family member who is unlawfully in its territory to leave would be disproportionate to the interest of the State party in maintaining respect for its immigration laws. In such cases it may be possible to characterize a decision requiring the family member to leave as arbitrary. However, we cannot accept that the mere fact that the persons unlawfully in the State party's territory have established family life there requires a State party to 'demonstrate additional factors justifying the removal of both parents that go beyond a simple enforcement of its immigration law in order to avoid a characterisation of arbitrariness.' The implications of this interpretation, adopted by the Committee, are that if persons who are unlawfully in a State party's territory establish a family and manage to escape detection for a long enough period they in effect acquire a right to remain there. It seems to us that such an interpretation ignores prevailing standards of international law, which allow states to regulate the entry and residence of aliens in their territory.

The majority view prevails in subsequent HRC decisions.[158] Importantly, the reasons for expelling a family member must not be disproportionate to the harm to the family, as the HRC explains in *Maddaferi v Australia*:

...in cases where one part of a family must leave the territory of the State party while the other part would be entitled to remain, the relevant criteria for assessing whether or not

[156] *Olsson v Sweden*, [7.3]. [157] *Winata*, Individual Opinion, [5].

[158] *Madafferi v Australia*, HRC Communication No. 1011/2001 (26 August 2004); *Bakhtiyari v Australia*, HRC Communication No. 1069/2002 (29 October 2003), [9.6] ('to separate a spouse and children arriving in a State from a spouse validly resident in a State may give rise to issues under articles 17 and 23 of the Covenant'. That case involved the removal from Australia of a mother and child, separating them from a lawfully resident husband and father, pending final determination of

the specific interference with family life can be objectively justified must be considered, on the one hand, in light of the significance of the State party's reasons for the removal of the person concerned and, on the other, the degree of hardship the family and its members would encounter as a consequence of such removal.[159]

In that case, the HRC found that the removal would be disproportionate and violate Articles 17, 23(1) and 24(1), for the following reasons:

In the present case, the Committee notes that the State party justifies the removal of Mr. Madafferi by his illegal presence in Australia, his alleged dishonesty in his relations with the Department of Immigration and Multicultural Affairs, and his 'bad character' stemming from criminal acts committed in Italy twenty years ago. The Committee also notes that Mr. Madafferi's outstanding sentences in Italy have been extinguished and that there is no outstanding warrant for his arrest. At the same time, it notes the considerable hardship that would be imposed on a family that has been in existence for 14 years. If Mrs. Madafferi and the children were to decide to emigrate to Italy in order to avoid separation of the family, they would not only have to live in a country they do not know and whose language the children (two of whom are already 13 and 11 years old) do not speak, but would also have to take care, in an environment alien to them, of a husband and father whose mental health has been seriously troubled, in part by acts that can be ascribed to the State party. In these very specific circumstances, the Committee considers that the reasons advanced by the State party for the decision of the Minister overruling the Administrative Appeals Tribunal, to remove Mr. Madafferi from Australia are not pressing enough to justify, in the present case, interference to this extent with the family and infringement of the right of the children to such measures of protection as are required by their status as minors.[160]

The HRC's approach is broadly consistent with the European jurisprudence on the right to family life under Article 8 of the ECHR, under which long-established residence and family life in a country of immigration, and weak ties to a country of nationality, are relevant proportionality considerations even in cases involving criminal deportations,[161] and even where the crimes may be serious.[162] Some

the father's status); also *Sahid v New Zealand*, HRC Communication No. 893/99, [8.2] (no violation of Article 23 where a grandfather was expelled, leaving his citizen grandson behind in the care of the child's mother and father); *Rajan and Rajan v New Zealand*, HRC Communication No. 820/98 (6 August 2003), [7.3] (no violation of Articles 17, 23 or 24 where there was a failure to substantiate the adverse impact on the family, including a citizen child, of parents removed for immigration fraud); *Leghaei v Australia (Interim Measures)*, HRC Communication No. 1937/2010 (21 April 2010) (interim measures issued where the pending expulsion of two lawfully resident Iranian parents, on undisclosed security grounds, would force their fourteen-year-old daughter, by then an Australian citizen and in school, to choose whether to stay in Australia without her parents or follow them to Iran, where she had never lived and did not speak the language. Australia responded by granting the mother a visa to remain, while expelling the father).

[159] *Madafferi v Australia*, [9.8]; see also *Byahuranga v Denmark*, HRC Communication No. 1222/2003 (1 November 2004), [11.7]–[11.8].

[160] *Madafferi v Australia*, [9.8].

[161] See, eg, *Moustaquim v Belgium* (App. 12313/86), 18 February 1991, (1991) 13 EHRR 802; *Beldjoudi v France* (App. 12083/86), 26 March 1992, (1992) 14 EHRR 801.

[162] *Mehemi v France* (App. 25017/94), 26 September 1997, (2000) 30 EHRR 739; *Radovanovic v Austria* (App. 42703/98), 22 April 2004, (2005) 41 EHRR 6; *Amrollahi v Denmark* (App. 56811/00), ECtHR 11 July 2002.

general considerations were set out by the European Court of Human Rights in *Boultif v Switzerland*:

48. The Court has only a limited number of decided cases where the main obstacle to expulsion was that it would entail difficulties for the spouses to stay together and, in particular, for one of them and/or the children to live in the other's country of origin. It is therefore called upon to establish guiding principles in order to examine whether the measure in question was necessary in a democratic society.

In assessing the relevant criteria in such a case, the Court will consider the nature and seriousness of the offence committed by the applicant; the duration of the applicant's stay in the country from which he is going to be expelled; the time which has elapsed since the commission of the offence and the applicant's conduct during that period; the nationalities of the various persons concerned; the applicant's family situation, such as the length of the marriage; other factors revealing whether the couple lead a real and genuine family life; whether the spouse knew about the offence at the time when he or she entered into a family relationship; and whether there are children in the marriage and, if so, their age. Not least, the Court will also consider the seriousness of the difficulties which the spouse would be likely to encounter in the applicant's country of origin, although the mere fact that a person might face certain difficulties in accompanying her or his spouse cannot in itself preclude expulsion.[163]

While adults (such as elderly parents) who do not belong to the 'core' family may not come within the protection of family life under Article 8, connections to extended family members may amount to protected 'private life' under Article 8 ('the network of personal, social and economic relations that make up the private life of every human being').[164]

The general principle that a state is required to make the 'best interests' of a child a 'primary' consideration in all decisions affecting them extends to migration decisions, as the CRC explains:

States should conduct individual assessments and evaluations of the best interests of the child at all stages of and decisions on any migration process affecting children, and with the involvement of child protection professionals, the judiciary as well as children themselves. In particular, primary consideration should be given to the best interests of the child in any proceeding resulting in the child's or their parents' detention, return or deportation.[165]

While the 'best interests' principle is expressly articulated in Article 3(1) of the CRC, it is implicit in decisions affecting the protection of families and children under Article 10 of the ICESCR, as well as in Articles 17, 23(1) and 24(1) of the ICCPR.

Admission and reunification of family members abroad

Non-citizens resident in another state do not enjoy an automatic right to reunification with close family members (including children) living abroad, given the

[163] *Boultif v Switzerland* (App. 54273/00), 2 August 2001, (2001) 33 EHRR 1179, [48].

[164] *Slivenko v Latvia* (App. 48321/99), 9 October 2003, (2004) 39 EHRR 24, [96].

[165] CRC, 'The Rights of All Children in the Context of International Migration: Report of the 2012 Day of General Discussion' (28 September 2012), [72].

state's right to control immigration. Even the specialized provision in the CROC, Article 10, provides only that requests by family members to enter or leave a state must be processed 'in a positive, humane and expeditious manner', and that a child must be able to maintain contact with parents:

1. In accordance with the obligation of States Parties under article 9, paragraph 1, applications by a child or his or her parents to enter or leave a State Party for the purpose of family reunification shall be dealt with by States Parties in a positive, humane and expeditious manner. States Parties shall further ensure that the submission of such a request shall entail no adverse consequences for the applicants and for the members of their family.

2. A child whose parents reside in different States shall have the right to maintain on a regular basis, save in exceptional circumstances personal relations and direct contacts with both parents. Towards that end and in accordance with the obligation of States Parties under article 9, paragraph 1, States Parties shall respect the right of the child and his or her parents to leave any country, including their own, and to enter their own country. The right to leave any country shall be subject only to such restrictions as are prescribed by law and which are necessary to protect the national security, public order (ordre public), public health or morals or the rights and freedoms of others and are consistent with the other rights recognized in the present Convention.

Under the ICCPR, the HRC has nonetheless suggested in particular contexts that denying citizens or permanent residents family reunification with foreign spouses will breach Articles 17 and 23 of the ICCPR.[166] So too will gender (or other) discrimination in the residency rights of foreign spouses violate Article 23(1).[167] Other impermissible 'obstacles' to family reunion for foreign spouses include protracted waiting periods (such as eighteen months),[168] or a five-year probation to ensure marriage is genuine, followed by a further waiting period for citizenship.[169] The CESCR was concerned where Denmark raised the age for foreign spousal reunification to 25 years, impeding the right to family life.[170] Neither the HRC nor the CESCR have otherwise set out general principles on the reunification of close family members where national law prevents it.

In regional law, the European Court of Human Rights outlined some general principles in the *Abdulaziz* case, in relation to the right to family life under Article 8 of the ECHR:[171]

67. …the extent of a State's obligation to admit to its territory relatives of settled immigrants will vary according to the particular circumstances of the persons involved. Moreover, the Court cannot ignore that the present case is concerned not only with family

[166] HRC, Concluding Observations: Zimbabwe, CCPR/C/79/Add.89 (6 April 1998), [19].

[167] *Aumeeruddy-Cziffra et al v Mauritius*, HRC Communication No. 35/1978 (9 April 1981), [9.2(b)].

[168] HRC, Concluding Observations: Switzerland, CCPR/C/79/Add.70 (8 November 1996), [18]; see generally Denmark, A/52/40 (1999), [73]; Switzerland, A/52/50 (1997), [103]; Israel, A/53/40 (1998), [319]; Israel, A/58/40 (2003), [85(21)].

[169] HRC, Concluding Observations: Israel, CCPR/C/79/Add.93 (18 August 1998), [26].

[170] CESCR, Concluding Observations: Denmark, E/C.12/1/Add.102 (14 December 2004), [16].

[171] *Abdulaziz, Cabales and Balkandali v UK* (Apps. 9214/80; 9473/81; 9474/81), 28 May 1985, (1985) 7 EHRR 471, [67]–[68].

life but also with immigration and that, as a matter of well-established international law and subject to its treaty obligations, a State has the right to control the entry of non-nationals into its territory.

68. The Court observes that the present proceedings do not relate to immigrants who already had a family which they left behind in another country until they had achieved settled status in the United Kingdom. It was only after becoming settled in the United Kingdom, as single persons, that the applicants contracted marriage (see paragraphs 39–40, 44–45 and 50–52 above). The duty imposed by Article 8 (art. 8) cannot be considered as extending to a general obligation on the part of a Contracting State to respect the choice by married couples of the country of their matrimonial residence and to accept the non-national spouses for settlement in that country.

In the present case, the applicants have not shown that there were obstacles to establishing family life in their own or their husbands' home countries or that there were special reasons why that could not be expected of them.

Obstacles to establishing family life in another country, or special reasons why that cannot be expected, may include: lack of permission to enter and remain in the other country; where the national has no ties to the country of the foreign spouse's nationality and cannot speak the language there;[172] or a risk of torture or inhuman or degrading treatment there (contrary to Article 7 of the ICCPR). A state must 'strike a fair balance' between the applicant's interests and the state's interest in immigration control.[173]

Where children are involved, relevant factors will include 'the age of the children concerned, their situation in their country of origin and the degree of dependence on parents'.[174] There may be no violation of family rights where parents consciously choose to separate from a child by moving to another country, where the child has lived all its life elsewhere and has strong links to the culture, language and other family members in that foreign state, and where there are no obstacles to a parent joining the child elsewhere.[175] The right to family life 'does not guarantee a right to choose the most suitable place to develop family life'.[176]

However, even in such circumstances, where parents have been lawfully resident in a country for many years, with two children integrated into that country with few links elsewhere, there is a failure to strike a fair balance where a state refuses to permit a third child to join them there from abroad.[177] In such a case, the earlier separation from the child should not be regarded as an 'irrevocable' decision to abandon family reunification. Reunifying the family in the country of immigration will be the most appropriate way to develop family life, particularly given the young age of the third child, and outweighs the state's immigration interest.

172 See, eg, *Boultif v Switzerland* (App. 54273/00), 2 August 2005, (2001) 33 EHRR 50, [53]–[55].
173 *Ahmut v Netherlands* (App. 21702/93), 28 November 1996, (1997) 24 EHRR 62, [73].
174 *Sen v Netherlands* (App. 31465/96), ECtHR 21 December 2001.
175 *Ahmut v Netherlands* (App. 21702/93), ECtHR 28 November 1996.
176 *Ahmut v Netherlands*, [71].
177 *Sen v Netherlands*, [40]–[41].

Various national decisions which have considered the international right to found a family or to family life have accepted that such rights are subject to limitations in the immigration context, such as on national security grounds, or where a person has a choice to return to a country of origin or other country to reunite with his or her family.[178]

The CESCR has been specifically concerned where states have adopted a restrictive approach to family reunification of refugees, or the denial of reunification to those authorized to stay on the basis of 'subsidiary protection'[179] (that is, extended forms of protection against return to serious human rights violations, such as inhuman or degrading treatment) or on humanitarian grounds.[180] While the Refugee Convention 1951 does not expressly require states to enable family reunion, the Final Act of the UN Conference of Plenipotentiaries on that Convention recommends that states:

> ...take the necessary measures for the protection of the refugee's family, especially with a view to...[e]nsuring that the unity of the refugee's family is maintained particularly in cases where the head of the family has fulfilled the necessary conditions for admission to a particular country.[181]

Numerous UNHCR Executive Committee Conclusions also reiterate the importance of family unity and reunification,[182] which also assists in the social integration of refugees. State practice broadly indicates respect for the principle of refugee family reunification,[183] including on account of Articles 17, 23 and 24 in the ICCPR, and Article 10 of the ICESCR.

Detention; juvenile justice

The detention of a child can result in her or his separation from parents and family. Children are entitled to the general protection against unlawful or arbitrary detention under Article 9 of the ICCPR, humane treatment in detention under Article 10 of the ICCPR, and freedom from torture or inhuman or degrading treatment or punishment under Article 7 of the ICCPR. Child-specific standards on detention are found in Article 37 of the CROC:

> States Parties shall ensure that:
>
> (a) No child shall be subjected to torture or other cruel, inhuman or degrading treatment or punishment. Neither capital punishment nor life imprisonment without

178 *Kenya v Minister For Home Affairs and ors, ex p Leonard Sitamze*, 18 April 2007, [2008] eKLR (High Court of Kenya), [79].

179 CESCR, Concluding Observations: Hungary, E/C.12/HUN/CO/3 (16 January 2008), [21].

180 CESCR, Concluding Observations: Norway, E/C.12/1/Add.109 (23 June 2005), [16].

181 UN Conference of Plenipotentiaries on the Status of Refugees and Stateless Persons, Final Act, A/CONF.2/108/Rev.1 (25 July 1951).

182 ExCom Conclusions: No. 9 (XXVIII) Family Reunion, 1977; No. 24 (XXXII) Family Reunification, 1981; No. 84 (XLVIII) Refugee Children and Adolescents, 1997; No. 88 (L) Protection of the Refugee's Family, 1999; No. 104 (LVI) Local Reintegration, 2005.

183 See James Hathaway, *The Rights of Refugees under International Law* (Cambridge University Press, Cambridge, 2011), 533–60.

possibility of release shall be imposed for offences committed by persons below eighteen years of age;

(b) No child shall be deprived of his or her liberty unlawfully or arbitrarily. The arrest, detention or imprisonment of a child shall be in conformity with the law and shall be used only as a measure of last resort and for the shortest appropriate period of time;

(c) Every child deprived of liberty shall be treated with humanity and respect for the inherent dignity of the human person, and in a manner which takes into account the needs of persons of his or her age. In particular, every child deprived of liberty shall be separated from adults unless it is considered in the child's best interest not to do so and shall have the right to maintain contact with his or her family through correspondence and visits, save in exceptional circumstances;

(d) Every child deprived of his or her liberty shall have the right to prompt access to legal and other appropriate assistance, as well as the right to challenge the legality of the deprivation of his or her liberty before a court or other competent, independent and impartial authority, and to a prompt decision on any such action.

In addition, Article 9(4) of the CROC provides that the state must normally inform parents, on their request, of the whereabouts of a detained child, unless doing so would harm the child:

Where such separation results from any action initiated by a State Party, such as the detention, imprisonment, exile, deportation or death (including death arising from any cause while the person is in the custody of the State) of one or both parents or of the child, that State Party shall, upon request, provide the parents, the child or, if appropriate, another member of the family with the essential information concerning the whereabouts of the absent member(s) of the family unless the provision of the information would be detrimental to the well-being of the child. States Parties shall further ensure that the submission of such a request shall of itself entail no adverse consequences for the person(s) concerned.[184]

Children are also protected from prison labour under Articles 6 and 10(3) of the ICESCR.

Where children are detained in relation to criminal proceedings, the child is also entitled to due process and a fair trial under Article 40 of the CROC and Article 14 of the ICCPR. Importantly, Article 40(3) to (4) of the CROC requires states to divert juvenile offenders from the formal criminal justice and prison systems, and such considerations will be relevant in assessing whether a state has adequately protected the family under Article 10(1) and the child under Article 10(3) of the ICESCR:

3. States Parties shall seek to promote the establishment of laws, procedures, authorities and institutions specifically applicable to children alleged as, accused of, or recognized as having infringed the penal law, and, in particular:

(a) The establishment of a minimum age below which children shall be presumed not to have the capacity to infringe the penal law;

[184] See also African Charter on the Rights and Welfare of the Child (adopted 11 July 1990, OAU Doc. CAB/LEG/24.9/49(1990), entered into force 29 November 1999), Article 19(4): 'Where a child is apprehended by a State Party, his parents or guardians shall, as soon as possible, be notified of such apprehension by that State Party'; UNGA Res. 40/33, UN Standard Minimum Rules for the Administration of Juvenile Justice (29 November 1985), Rule 10.1.

(b) Whenever appropriate and desirable, measures for dealing with such children without resorting to judicial proceedings, providing that human rights and legal safeguards are fully respected.

4. A variety of dispositions, such as care, guidance and supervision orders; counselling; probation; foster care; education and vocational training programmes and other alternatives to institutional care shall be available to ensure that children are dealt with in a manner appropriate to their well-being and proportionate both to their circumstances and the offence.

Soft law standards are also relevant to juvenile justice and detention, such as the UN Standard Minimum Rules for the Administration of Juvenile Justice (the Beijing Rules). A significant number of the Beijing Rules address the relationship between parent and child or the role of parents in criminal processes involving children.[185]

Where detention is lawful and non-arbitrary, and in accordance with applicable safeguards, there will ordinarily be no failure by the state to protect the family under Article 10(1) or the child under Article 10(3).[186] As the European Court of Human Rights has observed in relation to Article 8 of the ECHR, separation from family and consequent distress are inherent in detention;[187] lawful, necessary and proportionate detention either does not interfere in family life or can be justified in pursuit of a legitimate aim.[188]

Even if detention is lawful, excessive or disproportionate restrictions on communication with or visits by family members may, however, constitute a failure by the state to protect the family and/or the child under Article 10(1) and (3) of the ICESCR. Certain restrictions may be permissible, such as to protect a child where she or he is at risk from a parent, or to prevent the child from misusing communications (such as to plan further offences, or to destroy evidence or interfere with witnesses).

In relation to prisoners serving sentences abroad, the HRC has recommended that long-term prisoners be allowed to serve their sentences in the person's home territory to enable the protection of the family under Article 23 of the ICCPR.[189] Prisoner transfer arrangements are in part intended to achieve this humanitarian purpose within wider rehabilitation objectives, whether bilaterally or pursuant to multilateral agreements such as the Council of Europe Convention on the Transfer of Sentenced Persons.[190] There are, however, limits

[185] UN Standard Minimum Rules, especially Rules 1.1, 1.3, 7.1, 11.3, 13.2, 15.2, 18.2, 25.1 and 26.5.

[186] Similarly, in relation to the ICCPR, where detention is in accordance with Article 9 of the ICCPR, there will normally be no unlawful or arbitrary interference in the family under Article 17, or failure to protect the family under Article 23 or the child under Article 24 of the ICCPR.

[187] *X v Austria* (App. 2676/65), ECtHR 3 April 1967.

[188] *DG v Ireland* (App. 39474/98), 16 May 2002, (2002) EHRR 33, [104]–[110].

[189] HRC, Concluding Observations: United Kingdom (Overseas Territories), A/57/40 (2002), [75(33)].

[190] Convention on the Transfer of Sentenced Persons (adopted 21 March 1983, CETS 112, entered into force 1 July 1985).

on prisoner transfers: convictions based on flagrant denials of justice should not be recognized.[191]

Regionally, the Inter-American Court of Human Rights emphasized the special vulnerability of child detainees and the need for special measures of protection and assistance under the American Convention on Human Rights and other international instruments.[192] In *Bulacio v Argentina*, the Court found violations of Articles 4, 5, 7, 8, 19 and 25 of the American Convention in a case involving the mass arbitrary detention of young people after a rock concert. The police beat one detainee to death. The Court observed:

133. …[T]he Court points out that the instant case is especially grave because the victim is a child, whose rights are protected not only by the American Convention, but also by numerous international instruments, widely accepted by the international community, prominently including the Convention on the Rights of the Child. These instruments establish the duty of the State to adopt special protection and assistance measures in favor of children under their jurisdiction.

134. With respect to protection of the rights of children and adopting measures to attain said protection, the ruling principle is that of the highest interest of the child, based on 'the very dignity of the human being, on the characteristics of children themselves, and on the need to foster their development, making full use of their potential.'

135. In this regard, several specific considerations have been made regarding detention of children, which as this Court has stated and is recognized in various international instruments, must be exceptional and for the briefest time possible.

136. To safeguard the rights of children detainees, and especially their right to humane treatment, it is indispensable for them to be separated from adult detainees. In addition, as this Court has established, those in charge of detention centers for children who are offenders or accused must be duly trained for the performance of their tasks. Finally, the right of detainees to communicate with third parties, who provide or will provide assistance and defense, goes together with the obligation of the State agents to immediately communicate to said persons the minor's detention, even if the minor has not requested it…[193]

In another case, *Juvenile Re-education Institute v Paraguay*, the Inter-American Court found that the state had failed to protect children where the conditions of detention involved overcrowding, lack of sanitation and adequate infrastructure, insufficient guards, a lack of trained personnel, no separation of unconvicted and convicted detainees, and inhumane treatment of detainees. As the Court noted, 'the inmates were forced to live permanently in inhuman and degrading conditions, exposed to an atmosphere of violence, danger, abuse,

[191] *Drozd and Janousek v France and Spain* (App. 12747/87), 26 June 1992, (1992) 14 EHRR 745, [110] ('The Contracting States are, however, obliged to refuse their cooperation if it emerges that the conviction is the result of a flagrant denial of justice').

[192] See generally Inter-American Commission on Human Rights, Rapporteurship on the Rights of the Child, *Juvenile Justice and Human Rights in the Americas*, OEA/Ser.L/V/II, Doc. 78 (13 July 2011).

[193] *Bulacio v Argentina*, 18 September 2003, IACHR (Ser. C) No. 100, [133]–[136].

corruption, mistrust and promiscuity, where the rule that prevailed was survival of the fittest'.[194] The health care and education of children was inadequate, and children were detained with adults.[195] The Court stated that Article 19 of the American Convention requires special measures of protection for detained children:

160. In the case of the right to life, when the person the State deprives of his or her liberty is a child, which the majority of the alleged victims in the instant case were, it has the same obligations it has regarding to any person, yet compounded by the added obligation established in Article 19 of the American Convention. On the one hand, it must be all the more diligent and responsible in its role as guarantor and must take special measures based on the principle of the best interests of the child. On the other hand, to protect a child's life, the State must be particularly attentive to that child's living conditions while deprived of his or her liberty, as the child's detention or imprisonment does not deny the child his or her right to life or restrict that right (supra para. 159).

161. Articles 6 and 27 of the Convention on the Rights of the Child include within the right to life the State's obligation to 'ensure to the maximum extent possible the survival and development of the child.' The Committee on the Rights of the Child has interpreted the word 'development' in its broadest sense as a holistic concept, embracing the child's physical, mental, spiritual, moral, psychological and social development. Regarding to children deprived of their liberty and thus in the custody of the State, the latter's obligations include that of providing them with health care and education, so as to ensure to them that their detention will not destroy their life plans. The United Nations Rules for the Protection of Juveniles Deprived of Their Liberty provide that:

13. Juveniles deprived of their liberty shall not for any reason related to their status be denied the civil, economic, political, social or cultural rights to which they are entitled under national or international law, and which are compatible with the deprivation of liberty.

162. In the case of the right to humane treatment of a child deprived of his or her liberty, the State's obligations are intimately related to quality of life. The standard applied to classify treatment or punishment as cruel, inhuman or degrading must be higher in the case of children.

163. In keeping with the foregoing, the United Nations' Standard Minimum Rules for the Administration of Juvenile Justice (Beijing Rules) provide that:

Juveniles in institutions shall receive care, protection and all necessary assistance-social, educational, vocational, psychological, medical and physical-that they may require because of their age, sex, and personality and in the interest of their wholesome development.[196]

The CESCR too has been concerned at the detention of juveniles among adults, which is 'in contravention of international standards'.[197]

[194] *Bulacio v Argentina*, [170].

[195] *Bulacio v Argentina*, [173]–[175].

[196] *Bulacio v Argentina*, [160]–[163].

[197] CESCR, Concluding Observations: Philippines, E/C.12/1995/7 (7 June 1995), [13].

Immigration detention

The requirement to consider the best interests of children and the interests of families is especially relevant in the context of immigration detention. Detention can interfere in families by separating children from detained parents, or detained children from parents in the community. As a general principle, the incidental detention of children based on their parents' migration status is not in the best interests of the children, as the CRC observes:

Children should not be criminalized or subject to punitive measures because of their or their parents' migration status. The detention of a child because of their or their parent's migration status constitutes a child rights violation and always contravenes the principle of the best interests of the child. In this light, States should expeditiously and completely cease the detention of children on the basis of their immigration status.[198]

At the same time, children should never be separated from their parents against their will except when 'necessary in the best interests of the child';[199] the views of children must also be taken into account.

A state is not required to prioritize the child's best interests above all other factors, but must regard it as a 'primary' consideration in balancing the competing interests. There may be individual cases where the security or criminal threat posed by a parent is so grave that her or his detention is warranted and some interference in the family is justified, as long as adequate steps are taken to mitigate the adverse effects of the interference.

Importantly, however, the child's interests in not being detained, and not being separated from her or his parents, affect the necessity and proportionality of detaining the parents. The state must consider whether it is possible to simultaneously *not* detain a child *and* preserve family unity, such as by releasing the whole family into the community, where necessary subject to security, reporting or surety conditions. The assessment cannot be limited only to whether the whole family should be detained based on a parent's adverse assessment, or whether some family members can be released while one or more remains detained.

In a domestic case applying international human rights law, *Sri Lankan Refugees v Australia*, the President of the Australian Human Rights Commission accordingly found that the state's failure to consider releasing the whole family from detention, including on security conditions, constituted a failure to consider the best interests of the children detained with parents who were suspected of being risks to security:

I consider that it is in the best interests of Atputha, Abinyan and Vahisan Rahavan to be released with their parents into the community pursuant to a visa or a residence determination, potentially with conditions attached. It may be that these interests are outweighed by other considerations. However, it does not appear that the Commonwealth has given any separate or specific consideration to whether the children could be released with their parents into the community. In particular, it does not appear that there has been any assessment

[198] CESCR, Concluding Observations: Philippines, [78].

[199] CROC, Article 9(1).

of the specific security risk of alternatives to closed detention for the family and how any risk could be mitigated. Rather, it appears that the Commonwealth made a decision about the detention of the adult complainants based on advice from ASIO that they not be granted a permanent visa which resulted in the consequential detention of the children.

I find that there has been a failure fully to consider available alternatives to closed detention for the whole family in a way that would be consistent with the best interests of each of the children. As a result, I find that the detention of the children has also been arbitrary in breach of article 37(b) of the CRC.[200]

While that finding related to Article 37(b) of the CRC, similar reasoning applies to the requirements under Articles 9, 17(1), 23(1) and 24(1) of the ICCPR, and Article 10 of the ICESCR, to consider the best interests of the child in decision-making on detention.

In weighting the relative interests of the children, family and the state, the development and mental health impacts of detention on children are particularly important considerations. It is well accepted that protracted detention of children brings a 'high risk of serious mental harm'[201] and long-term negative effects on child development and psychological and emotional health.[202] Such impacts arise from the 'multiple stressors' of detention on children, including exposure to behavioural and psychological distress in adults; dislocation from protective social groups and structures; witnessing violence and self-harm; separation from attachment figures; and particularly separation from parents or carers.[203] These stressors may combine with a refugee child's earlier exposure to conflict, community breakdown and cultural dislocation to bring risks of post-traumatic stress disorder.[204]

More generally, lawfully resident non-citizens enjoy greater procedural protections than those 'unlawfully' present in a state's territory, by virtue of Article 13 of the ICCPR:

An alien lawfully in the territory of a State Party to the present Covenant may be expelled therefrom only in pursuance of a decision reached in accordance with law and shall, except where compelling reasons of national security otherwise require, be allowed to submit the reasons against his expulsion and to have his case reviewed by, and be represented for the purpose before, the competent authority or a person or persons especially designated by the competent authority.

[200] *Sri Lankan Refugees v Commonwealth of Australia* (2012) AusHRC 56. In that case the parents' security assessments were rescinded the following year and the whole family was released from detention. See also UNICEF Australia, Submission to the National Inquiry into Children in Immigration Detention (April 2002).

[201] Australian Human Rights Commission, *Immigration Detention at Villawood 2011*, 31; see also Human Rights and Equal Opportunity Commission, *A Last Resort? Report of the National Inquiry into Children in Immigration Detention* (13 May 2004).

[202] Alliance of Health Professionals concerned about the Health of Asylum Seekers and their Children, Submission to the Human Rights and Equal Opportunity Commission (May 2002) (Australia), vii.

[203] Alliance of Health Professionals, Submission to the Human Rights and Equal Opportunity Commission, vii.

[204] Alliance of Health Professionals, Submission to the Human Rights and Equal Opportunity Commission, vii.

Whether a state has provided adequate 'protection' to the family under Article 10 of the ICESCR may therefore require an assessment of whether the procedural guarantees of Article 13 of the ICCPR have been met, including due process and independent review.

According to the HRC, there is no 'interference' in family life (at least under Article 17 of the ICCPR) where family members are detained together and the state takes special measures to assist the family in detention.[205] This is despite the very fact of detention disrupting the family's ability to determine its own place of residence, living conditions, choice of co-habitants, family activities outside the home and relationships with the community. The better view is that detention may potentially 'interfere' in the family, but the more decisive legal question is then whether such interference is justified. On either approach, detention conditions must still be appropriate for families and children, and not involve cruel, inhuman or degrading treatment.[206]

Child custody, access, abduction

Where the relationship between parents has irretrievably broken down, manifesting in separation or divorce, the protection owed to the 'family' under Article 10 of the ICESCR survives the disunity of its members. A particularly important issue then becomes the protection of the family relationships between a child and each parent.

The HRC has found that Article 17 of the ICCPR requires 'effective protection to the right of a parent to regular contact with his or her minor children',[207] absent exceptional circumstances for denying contact in the interests of the child. Article 23 requires similarly.[208] The HRC has also required states to protect the child's relationship with separated parents under Article 24 of the ICCPR:

> If the marriage is dissolved, steps should be taken, keeping in view the paramount interest of the children, to give them necessary protection and, so far as is possible, to guarantee personal relations with both parents.[209]

In *Patera v Czech Republic*, the complainant was a father whose son had been in the exclusive care of his ex-wife (the son's mother) since their separation. The father was repeatedly denied access to his son, despite national court orders granting him periodic access, which had not been effectively enforced. The HRC found as follows in relation to Article 17 of the ICCPR:

> 7.3 The Committee considers that article 17 generally includes effective protection to the right of a parent to regular contact with his or her minor children. While there may be

[205] *F K A G et al v Australia*, HRC Communication No. 2094/2011 (26 July 2013), [8.7].

[206] *F K A G et al v Australia*, [9.8].

[207] *Patera v Czech Republic*, HRC Communication No. 946/2000 (25 July 2002), [7.3]; *LP v Czech Republic*, HRC Communication No. 946/00 (19 August 2002), [7.3].

[208] *Hendriks v Netherlands*, HRC Communication No. 201/85 (12 August 1988), [10.4]; *Fei v Colombia*, HRC Communication No. 514/92 (26 April 1995), [8.9]; *Balaguer Santacana v Spain*, HRC Communication No. 417/90 (29 July 1994).

[209] HRC, General Comment No. 17 (1989), [6].

exceptional circumstances in which denying contact is required in the interests of the child and cannot be deemed unlawful or arbitrary, in the present case the domestic courts of the State party have ruled that such contact should be maintained. Consequently, the issue before the Committee is whether the State party has afforded effective protection to the author's right to meet his son in accordance with the court decisions of the State party.

7.4 Although the courts repeatedly fined the author's wife for failure to respect their preliminary orders regulating the author's access to his son, these fines were neither fully enforced nor replaced with other measures aimed at ensuring the author's rights. In these circumstances and taking into account the considerable delays at various stages of the proceedings, the Committee takes the view that the author's rights under article 17 of the Covenant, in conjunction with article 2, paragraphs 1 and 2 of the Covenant, did not receive effective protection. Consequently, the Committee is of the view that the facts before it disclose a violation of article 17, in conjunction with article 2 of the Covenant.[210]

The remedies indicated by the HRC—the prompt implementation of contact between the father and his son, and the prevention of recurring violations[211]—would similarly be appropriate measures of protection under Article 10 of the ICESCR where a child is unlawfully or arbitrarily withheld from a parent. Excessive procedural delays in determining custody or access cases may impair the effective protection of family life.[212]

While the above case concerned the non-enforcement of access orders under domestic law, in an appropriate case both the domestic legal framework itself, and decisions made under it, are reviewable for inconsistency with Article 10. This might be the case if granting custody to a particular parent would endanger the child's safety, or withholding access or visitation rights would be arbitrary, unreasonable, disproportionate (excessive) or discriminatory. A law or decision will be problematic if, for example, it presumptively awards custody to fathers, as under some Islamic systems;[213] refuses to award custody to a parent because of her religion;[214] or where it is assumed that it would not be in a child's interest to give custody to a transsexual[215] or homosexual[216] parent.

The HRC has found no inconsistency with Article 23 of the ICCPR where a father lost custody of and access to his children after killing their mother and being imprisoned,[217] a decision which has nonetheless been criticized for failing to adequately balance the competing interests.[218] Hard cases may involve finely balanced judgments, such as where a parent moves away and distance prevents the ready accommodation of competing interests. The illness (mental or

[210] *Patera v Czech Republic*, [7.3]–[7.4]. [211] *Patera v Czech Republic*, [8].

[212] *H v United Kingdom* (App. 9580/81), 8 July 1987, (1988) 19 EHRR 95, [89]; *Mikulic v Croatia* (App. 53176/99), ECtHR 7 February 2002.

[213] Eriksson, 'Family Rights', 139.

[214] *Hoffmann v Austria* (App. 12875/87), 23 June 1993, (1994) 17 EHRR 293, [36].

[215] *P V v Q F*, 22 December 2008, Constitutional Appeal (Spain), ILDC 1416 (ES 2008).

[216] Cf *Frette v France* (App. 36515/97), 26 February 2002, (2004) 38 EHRR 21, [41] (invoking the state's 'margin of appreciation').

[217] *A J v G v Netherlands*, HRC Communication No. 1142/2002 (14 April 2003).

[218] Nowak, *CCPR Commentary*, 521, also criticizing *Drbal v Czech Republic*, HRC Communication No. 498/1992 (2 August 1994).

physical) of a parent may, however, impair their capacity to care for children in exceptional cases.

National laws which permit excessive discretion in decisions about custody or access may need to be structured by more specific criteria, to ensure that the interests of the parent seeking custody or access are given adequate weight.[219] In *Keegan v Ireland*, the European Court of Human Rights found that a law which authorized the adopting out of a child without the father's knowledge or consent could not be justified as necessary in a democratic society, even if it otherwise pursued a legitimate aim and was in accordance with domestic law:[220]

55. The Court notes that the applicant was afforded an opportunity under Irish law to claim the guardianship and custody of his daughter and that his interests were fairly weighed in the balance by the High Court in its evaluation of her welfare. However, the essential problem in the present case is not with this assessment but rather with the fact that Irish law permitted the applicant's child to have been placed for adoption shortly after her birth without his knowledge or consent. As has been observed in a similar context, where a child is placed with alternative carers he or she may in the course of time establish with them new bonds which it might not be in his or her interests to disturb or interrupt by reversing a previous decision as to care (see, inter alia, the *W. v. the United Kingdom* judgment of 8 July 1987, Series A no. 121, p. 28, para. 62). Such a state of affairs not only jeopardised the proper development of the applicant's ties with the child but also set in motion a process which was likely to prove to be irreversible, thereby putting the applicant at a significant disadvantage in his contest with the prospective adopters for the custody of the child.

The Government have advanced no reasons relevant to the welfare of the applicant's daughter to justify such a departure from the principles that govern respect for family ties. That being so, the Court cannot consider that the interference which it has found with the applicant's right to respect for family life, encompassing the full scope of the State's obligations, was necessary in a democratic society. There has thus been a violation of Article 8 (art. 8).[221]

Decisions about custody and access must adequately take into account the views of the parents to ensure the protection of the family or the necessity of any interference in it.[222] There is also a practical imperative to do so: research suggests that compliance with payment of child support by fathers 'is closely linked to custody and visitation rights as well as to the way by which the support was decided'.[223] The involvement of parents in decision-making will ordinarily

[219] In *Hendriks v Netherlands*, HRC Communication No. 201/85 (12 August 1988), a number of HRC members were concerned that a mother's fear that allowing the father any supervised contact with his child would create tensions was a sufficient basis on which to deprive the father of access, absent any adverse evidence as to the father's behaviour: Individual Opinion (concurring) of Dimitrijevic, El Shafei, Zielinski and Higgins, [3]–[4]; see also Individual Opinion of Wako, [5]–[6].

[220] *Keegan v Ireland* (App. 16969/90), 26 May 1994, (1994) 18 EHRR 342), [53]–[55].

[221] *Keegan v Ireland*, [55].

[222] *W v United Kingdom* (App. 9749/82), 8 July 1987, (1988) 10 EHRR 29, [63]–[65]; *B v United Kingdom* (App. 9840/82), 8 July 1987, (1988) 10 EHRR 29, [64]–[66]; *R v United Kingdom* (App. 10496/83), 8 July 1987, (1988) 10 EHRR 74, [68]–[70].

[223] Ilona Ostner, Michael Reif and Hannu Turba, 'Family Policies in Germany', Third Report for the Project 'Welfare Policies and Employment in the Context of Family Change' (8–9 October 2003), 11 ('Family Policies in Germany').

require due process to be observed, such as by the disclosure to them of information or evidence essential to the decision.[224] The decision should also be based on sufficient information, including expert psychological reports where necessary.[225]

It may be emphasized, however, that the best interests of the child may override the parents' views, as the European Court of Human Rights has observed:

> ... a fair balance must be struck between the interests of the child and those of the parent... and that in doing so particular importance must be attached to the best interests of the child which, depending on their nature and seriousness, may override those of the parent. In particular, the parent cannot be entitled... to have such measures taken as would harm the child's health and development...[226]

There may be urgent situations where it is not possible to involve parents in decision-making, including where a parent is a threat to a child and cannot be forewarned of a decision without risk to the child.[227] The views of the child, consistent with the child's maturity, must be duly taken into account where feasible.[228]

Restrictions on access or custody by parent must be carefully scrutinized to ensure that they are proportionate and not excessive. Thus, for example, strict limitations on written or telephone communications between a child (justifiably) in foster care and his mother, in place for a protracted period, did more than was necessary to protect the child and impeded the ultimate aim of family reunification.[229] The removal of a newborn baby in hospital from its mother and father would require very heavy justification.[230]

Under Article 8 of the ECHR, the ECtHR has accorded a 'wide margin of appreciation' to national authorities in decisions about taking children into care and separating them from one or more parents.[231] At the same time, it has applied 'stricter scrutiny' to any further limitations, such as those imposed on parental access rights.[232] It may be emphasized, however, that neither the HRC nor the CESCR has endorsed the margin of appreciation doctrine generally or specifically in relation to family rights. Under Article 10 of the ICESCR, the legal question is whether any restrictions are necessary and proportionate, which requires an objective assessment of the grounds and effects of any restrictions.

224 *McMichael v United Kingdom* (App. 16424/90), 24 February 1995, (1995) 20 EHRR 205, [91].

225 See, eg, *Sahin v Germany* (App. 30943/96), ECtHR 8 July 2003; *Sommerfeld v Germany* (App. 31871/96), 8 July 2003, (2004) 38 EHRR 35, [70]–[74].

226 *Elsholz v Germany* (App. 25735/94), 13 July 2000, (2002) 34 EHRR 58, [49]–[50].

227 *K and T v Finland* (App. 25702/94), 12 July 2001, (2001) 36 EHRR 18.

228 CROC, Article 9.

229 *Margareta and Roger Andersson v Sweden* (App. 12963/87), 25 February 1992, (1992) 14 EHRR 615, [97].

230 *Haase v Germany* (App. 11057/02), 8 April 2004, (2005) 40 EHRR 19.

231 See *Elsholz v Germany* (App. 25735/94), 13 July 2000, (2002) 34 EHRR 58, [49]–[50]: 'the authorities enjoy a wide margin of appreciation, in particular when assessing the necessity of taking a child into care'.

232 *Elsholz v Germany*, [49]–[50].

In the exceptional circumstances of transnational child abductions, reference may be made to the other relevant standards in determining the application of Article 10. Relevantly, Article 11 of the CROC provides:

1. States Parties shall take measures to combat the illicit transfer and non-return of children abroad.

2. To this end, States Parties shall promote the conclusion of bilateral or multilateral agreements or accession to existing agreements.

A key multilateral agreement is the [Hague] Convention on the Civil Aspects of International Child Abduction 1980, which aims 'to secure the prompt return of children wrongfully removed to or retained in any Contracting State' and 'to ensure that rights of custody and of access under the law of one Contracting State are effectively respected in the other Contracting States'.[233] The Convention defines when the removal or retention of a child is 'wrongful':

Article 3

The removal or the retention of a child is to be considered wrongful where—

(a) it is in breach of rights of custody attributed to a person, an institution or any other body, either jointly or alone, under the law of the State in which the child was habitually resident immediately before the removal or retention; and

(b) at the time of removal or retention those rights were actually exercised, either jointly or alone, or would have been so exercised but for the removal or retention.

The rights of custody mentioned in sub-paragraph a) above, may arise in particular by operation of law or by reason of a judicial or administrative decision, or by reason of an agreement having legal effect under the law of that State.

Article 4

The Convention shall apply to any child who was habitually resident in a Contracting State immediately before any breach of custody or access rights. The Convention shall cease to apply when the child attains the age of 16 years.

Article 5

For the purposes of this Convention—

(a) 'rights of custody' shall include rights relating to the care of the person of the child and, in particular, the right to determine the child's place of residence;

(b) 'rights of access' shall include the right to take a child for a limited period of time to a place other than the child's habitual residence.

Articles 12 and 13 of the Hague Convention then set out the obligations on states to return wrongfully removed children, subject to safeguards for preventing harm

[233] Convention on the Civil Aspects of International Child Abduction 1980 (adopted 25 October 1980, 1343 UNTS 89, entered into force 1 July 1983), Article 1(a)–(b).

to the child. A range of other international[234] and regional[235] standards deal with the transnational dimensions of disputes involving custody, access or adoption of children.

Guardianship rights of extended family members may also be appropriate for protection under Article 10 of the ICESCR. The ICCPR case of *Mónaco v Argentina* concerned a child whose parents were 'disappeared' by a military dictatorship and was thereupon abducted by a nurse. The child's grandmother later discovered her whereabouts and sought guardianship through domestic legal proceedings, which were ultimately delayed or stymied for largely procedural reasons. The HRC could not apply Articles 17, 23(1) and 24(1) to the abduction and other conduct which occurred prior to the entry into force of the ICCPR and Optional Protocol, but did consider the 'continuing effects' of earlier violations.[236] The HRC found that the state violated Article 24(1) by failing to grant the child 'prompt and effective relief':

> 10.5 ... Bearing in mind the suffering already endured by Ms. Vicario, who lost both of her parents under tragic circumstances imputable to the State party, the Committee finds that the special measures required under article 24, paragraph 1, of the Covenant were not expeditiously applied by Argentina, and that the failure to recognize the standing of Mrs. Mónaco in the guardianship and visitation proceedings and the delay in legally establishing Ms. Vicario's real name and issuing identity papers also entailed a violation of article 24, paragraph 2, of the Covenant, which is designed to promote recognition of the child's legal personality.[237]

A failure to remedy a child abduction may similarly found a breach of Article 10 of the ICCPR and warrant measures to protect the child and her or his family relationships.

Protection of the family in armed conflict

The ICESCR does not cease to apply during armed conflicts regulated by international humanitarian law (IHL). The obligation to protect the family under Article 10(1) of the ICESCR may be defined during conflicts by the special law

[234] Convention on Jurisdiction, Applicable Law, Recognition, Enforcement and Co-operation in respect of Parental Responsibility and Measures for the Protection of the Children (adopted 19 October 1996, 35 ILM 1391, entered into force 1 January 2002); Convention on Protection of Children and Co-operation in respect of Intercountry Adoption (adopted 29 May 1993, 32 ILM 1134, entered into force 1 May 1995).

[235] (Revised) European Convention on the Adoption of Children (adopted 27 November 2008, CETS No. 202, entered into force 1 September 2011); European Convention on the Adoption of Children (adopted 24 April 1967, CETS No. 58, entered into force 26 April 1968); European Convention on Recognition and Enforcement of Decisions concerning Custody of Children and on Restoration of Custody of Children (adopted 20 May 1980, CETS No. 105, entered into force 1 September 1983); European Convention on the Exercise of Children's Rights (adopted 25 January 1996, CETS No. 160, entered into force 1 July 2000); European Convention on Contact Concerning Children (adopted 15 May 2003, CETS No. 192, entered into force 1 September 2005).

[236] *Mónaco de Gallicchio, on her behalf and on behalf of her granddaughter Ximena Vicario v Argentina*, HRC Communication No. 400/1990 (3 April 1995), [10.4].

[237] *Mónaco de Gallicchio*, [10.5].

(*lex specialis*) of IHL. In international armed conflicts, for instance, the Fourth Geneva Convention requires states to take special measures to protect families, including to enable communication between family members (Article 25) and re-establish contact between dispersed family members (Article 26). Article 26 was adopted in the light of the large numbers of people displaced during the Second World War, through flight, evacuation, transfer, deportation and the like. According to the Commentary on the Geneva Conventions, the obligation on states to facilitate inquiries may be implemented by means such as:

> ...the organization of official information bureaux and centres; notification by postal authorities of changes of address and possible places of evacuation, the arranging of broadcasts; the granting of facilities for forwarding requests for information and the replies; and, as a precautionary measure, the provision of identity discs for children under twelve years of age...free postage for correspondence dealing with family enquiries.[238]

Organizations typically involved in family reunification include the International Committee of the Red Cross and national Red Cross and Red Crescent Societies and their family 'tracing' services.

Other IHL provisions separately address the needs of families and children in detention.[239] Where it is necessary to transfer or evacuate civilians in occupied territory, Article 49 of the Fourth Geneva Convention provides for the protection of family unity:

> The Occupying Power undertaking such transfers or evacuations shall ensure, to the greatest practicable extent, that proper accommodation is provided to receive the protected persons, that the removals are effected in satisfactory conditions of hygiene, health, safety and nutrition, and that members of the same family are not separated.

Security measures taken by an occupying power may impact on the right to family life of those under occupation as well as its own citizens in family relationships with them. In 1998, the CESCR criticized retroactive and discriminatory residency laws which could result in Palestinians losing their right to live in East Jerusalem, thus separating Arab families and children from parents, and denying social services and health care rights (including maternity care for Arab women).[240] In 2003, the CESCR further criticized 'the practice of restrictive family reunification with regard to Palestinians, which has been adopted for reasons of national security'.[241]

Some such practices were considered by the Israeli Supreme Court in 2006. In *Adalah—The Legal Center for Arab Minority Rights in Israel v Minister of Interior*,[242] the Israeli Supreme Court considered whether the right to family life

[238] Jean Pictet (ed), *Commentary: IV Geneva Convention Relative to the Protection of Civilian Persons in Time of War* (ICRC, Geneva, 1958), 196–7 (Article 26).

[239] Geneva Convention Relative to the Protection of Civilian Persons in Time of War (adopted 12 August 1949, 75 UNTS 287, entered into force 21 October 1950), Article 82.

[240] CESCR, Concluding Observations: Israel, E/C.12/1/Add.27 (4 December 1998), [20].

[241] CESCR, Concluding Observations: Israel, E/C.12/1/Add.90 (26 June 2003), [18].

[242] *Adalah—The Legal Center for Arab Minority Rights in Israel v Minister of Interior* (14 May 2006), HCJ 7052/03 (Israeli Supreme Court).

was violated by an Israeli law which prohibited the entry into Israel of 'enemy nationals', namely Palestinian residents of the West Bank and Gaza, and which impacted most heavily on Palestinians married to Israeli Arabs living in Israel. By a narrow six to five majority, the Court found that a state may prevent 'enemy nationals' from entering its territory even if this prevents family reunification by a citizen with a foreign spouse. The right to life of Israelis was found to outweigh the right to family life of those affected by the law. There was evidence that some Palestinians previously admitted to Israel for family reasons had participated in terrorism, and the Court held that all 'hostile nationals' in times of war were 'presumed to endanger national security and public security' because of their stronger 'natural' ties and loyalty to their place of birth.[243] The majority also found the law to be proportionate, including because it was temporary and allowed for certain exceptions.

By contrast, Chief Justice Barak argued in dissent that while the law pursued a legitimate national security purpose, it was excessive because it did not require individual screening of Palestinians requesting entry to Israel. The 'blanket prohibition' was 'not proportionate in comparison with the additional damage caused to the family life and equality of the Israeli spouses'.[244] It thus unlawfully interfered in the right to family life, which protects the 'human dignity' of an Israeli to live with his or her spouse.[245] Chief Justice Barak rejected the majority's comparison between the rights to life and family and sacrificing of the latter for the former, since 'democracy and human rights cannot be maintained without taking risks':[246]

> 110. … we do not weigh life against the quality of life. In doing so, life always takes precedence and the result is to refrain from any act that endangers human life. Society cannot operate in this way, either in times of peace (such as with regard to road accident victims) or in times of war (such as with regard to victims of enemy attacks). The proper way of posing the question is by means of the level of the risks and the likelihood that they will occur, and their effect on the life of society as a whole. The questions that should be asked in our case are questions of probability. The question is what is the probability that human life will be harmed if we continue the individual check as compared with the likelihood that human life will be harmed if we change over to a blanket prohibition, and whether this additional likelihood is comparable to the certainty of the increase caused thereby to the violation of the rights of spouses who are citizens of the state.

Another dissenting judge substantially agreed,[247] while two other judges found that the law may have also had an impermissible 'demographic motive' unrelated to security.[248] The minority approach to the assessment of proportionality is more consistent with what Article 10 of the ICESCR requires, in contrast to the majority's blunt extinguishment of family rights by invoking an absolutist conception of what the right to life requires, based on group-based risk profiling.

[243] *Adalah v Minister of Interior*, [57] and [76]–[79].
[244] *Adalah v Minister of Interior*, [109].
[245] *Adalah v Minister of Interior*, [103].
[246] *Adalah v Minister of Interior*, [111].
[247] *Adalah v Minister of Interior*, [9] (Justice Levy).
[248] *Adalah v Minister of Interior*, [13]–[14] and [24] (Justices Proccacia and Jubran).

Even so, in 2007 the law was broadened to also exclude nationals of Iran, Iraq, Syria and Lebanon.

OTHER MEASURES OF PROTECTION

Article 10(1) requires that the 'widest possible protection and assistance be accorded to the family... particularly for its establishment and while it is responsible for the care and education of dependent children'. The provision does not specify the measures which states are required to adopt and there is a considerable discretion in implementation, just as there is concerning the protection of the family under Article 23 of the ICCPR, as the HRC notes:

3. Ensuring the protection provided for under article 23 of the Covenant requires that States parties should adopt legislative, administrative or other measures. States parties should provide detailed information concerning the nature of such measures and the means whereby their effective implementation is assured. In fact, since the Covenant also recognizes the right of the family to protection by society, States parties' reports should indicate how the necessary protection is granted to the family by the State and other social institutions, whether and to what extent the State gives financial or other support to the activities of such institutions, and how it ensures that these activities are compatible with the Covenant.[249]

Article 10(1) requires states to protect the family generally, and 'particularly' for its establishment and in the care and education of children.

Protection and assistance 'for its establishment'

The obligation on states to provide protection and assistance for the 'establishment' of the family first implies that the state must not interfere in its establishment, or permit non-state actors to so interfere. States must thus eliminate any barriers to the right to found a family, including arbitrary, unreasonable, disproportionate or discriminatory restrictions on marriage[250] or cohabitation, or the choice of parents to have children.

Examples might include laws prohibiting couples from cohabiting,[251] citizens from marrying or cohabiting with non-citizens, or members of one religious faith from marrying another. Children born outside of marriage must also enjoy legal recognition as part of a family. National laws should also permit adoption to enable families to be founded by that method.[252] Arbitrary restrictions on access to family services, such as public housing or social security, or limitations which discriminate against certain family types, may infringe Article 10.

Crucially, the state must prohibit, and not itself engage in, practices which would prevent or impede people from having children and thereby inhibiting the

[249] HRC, General Comment No. 19 (1990), [3].

[250] Discussed further below.

[251] *Abdulaziz, Cabales and Balkandali v United Kingdom* (Apps. 9214/90, 9473/81, 9474/81), 28 May 1985, (1985) 7 EHRR 471, [62].

[252] Nowak, *CCPR Commentary*, 533. Cf *X and Y v United Kingdom* (App. 7229/75), 15 December 1977, (1978) 12 D&R 32, 34 (Article 8 of the ECHR does not guarantee a right to adopt).

'establishment' of a family. Thus, practices such as compulsory birth control, forced sterilization,[253] forced abortion, female infanticide (including by parents themselves), prenatal sex selection or compulsory family planning measures are inconsistent with Article 10(1). Many of these measures are also forbidden as acts of violence against women.[254] National law should also not prohibit the use of reproductive technologies, subject to limitations necessary to protect the rights of others.[255]

While states may have legitimate interests in utilizing family planning to meet population policy objectives, such measures must respect certain minimum conditions. First, family planning measures cannot involve violence to children, as the CRC observed in criticizing China's one child policy:

> 36. It is the Committee's view that family planning policy must be designed to avoid any threat to the life of children, particularly girls. The Committee recommends in this regard that clear guidance be given to the population and the personnel involved in the family planning policy to ensure that the aims it promotes are in accordance with principles and provisions of the Convention, including those of its article 24. The State party is urged to take further action for the maintenance of strong and comprehensive measures to combat the abandonment and infanticide of girls as well as the trafficking, sale and kidnapping or abduction of girls.[256]

Secondly, family planning measures cannot discriminate, such as where China's one child policy produces de facto gender discrimination through female infanticide, or where Chinese families having a child with disabilities are permitted to have a second child.[257] Certain disadvantaged groups have also tended to suffer adversely from family planning measures, including persons with disabilities and minorities (such as 'gypsies'), sometimes subjected to forced sterilization or other measures impairing the establishment of family life.

Thirdly, population policy goals should ordinarily be met through non-coercive measures, as the HRC notes in respect of the family protections in Article 23 of the ICCPR:

> 5. The right to found a family implies, in principle, the possibility to procreate and live together. When States parties adopt family planning policies, they should be compatible with the provisions of the Covenant and should, in particular, not be discriminatory or compulsory...[258]

[253] Which can also amount to genocide under the Convention on the Prevention and Punishment of the Crime of Genocide (adopted 9 December 1948, 78 UNTS 277, entered into force 12 January 1951), Article 2(d).

[254] Fourth UN World Conference on Women, Beijing Declaration and Platform for Action, A/CONF.177/20 (15 September 1995), [115]: 'Acts of violence against women also include forced sterilization and forced abortion, coercive/forced use of contraceptives, female infanticide and prenatal sex selection.'

[255] Nowak, *CCPR Commentary*, 533, suggesting that permissible limitations may include 'the prohibition of paid surrogate motherhood...the total anonymity of sperm and ovum donors...reproductive cloning and all forms of genetic manipulation and experiments with embryo in the womb or *in vitro*'.

[256] CRC, Concluding Observations: China, CRC/C/15/Add.56 (7 June 1996), [36].

[257] CRC, Concluding Observations: China, CRC/C/CHN/CO/2 (24 November 2005), [60(d)].

[258] HRC, General Comment No. 19 (1990).

Thus, China's constitutional 'duty' on parents 'to practice family planning' is not compatible with Article 10.[259] Instead, population goals should be met by empowering individuals through the provision of information and education about family planning and contraception options. The CEDAW accordingly provides that states shall ensure, 'on a basis of equality of men and women',

> [t]he same rights to decide freely and responsibly on the number and spacing of their children and to have access to the information, education and means to enable them to exercise these rights.[260]

The reference to making decisions 'responsibly' is not, however, understood to mean that the state can terminate 'irresponsible' pregnancies against the parents' or mother's wishes. In addition, the 'equal' rights of fathers do not extend to compelling a woman to have a child,[261] or conversely to securing the abortion of a child that the father does not want. This is because fathers and mothers are not similarly situated as regards parentage; the mother possesses additional rights to her own physical and mental health, bodily integrity and life, which may be understood as taking precedence over a father's less extensive interests.

In this regard, the CEDAW Committee has observed that '[d]ecisions to have children or not, while preferably made in consultation with spouse or partner, must not nevertheless be limited by spouse, parent, partner or Government'.[262] Voluntary family planning measures not only improve general population health, but also population policy and environmental and sustainable development objectives.[263] The Beijing Platform of Action further elaborates on the obligations of states in relation to non-coercive family planning.[264]

The CESCR has called on states to educate families and young people about sexual and reproductive health services.[265] It has expressed alarm where high abortion rates are the most common form of family planning due to inadequate education and the high cost of contraceptives.[266] The CESCR has emphasized, however, that abortion must not be absolutely criminalized and should be available where a

[259] Constitution of the People's Republic of China (adopted 4 December 1982), Article 49(2).

[260] Convention on the Elimination of All Forms of Discrimination against Women (CEDAW) (adopted 18 December 1979, 1249 UNTS 13, entered into force 3 September 1981), Article 16(1)(e); see also Articles 10(h), 12(1) and 14(2)(b); CEDAW Committee, General Recommendation No. 21: Equality in marriage and family relations (1994), [21]–[23]; International Conference on Human Rights Res. XVIII, Human Rights Aspects of Family Planning, A/CONF.32/41 (12 May 1968); UNGA Res. 2542 (XXIV), Declaration on Social Progress and Development (11 December 1969), Article 4; CROC, Article 24(2); World Conference on Human Rights, Vienna Declaration and Programme of Action, A/ CONF.157/23 (25 June 1993), [41]; International Conference on Population and Development, Programme of Action, A/CONF.171/13/Rev.1 (1994), Principle 8; Beijing Declaration and Platform for Action, [223]; UNGA Res. 65/1, Keeping the Promise (19 October 2010), [75].

[261] See, eg, *Paton v United Kingdom* (App. 1416/78), 13 May 1980, (1981) 3 EHRR 408.

[262] CEDAW Committee, General Recommendation No. 21 (1994), [22].

[263] CEDAW Committee, General Recommendation No. 21, [23].

[264] Beijing Declaration and Platform for Action, [95].

[265] CESCR, Concluding Observations: Kazakhstan, E/C.12/KAZ/CO/1 (7 June 2010), [33].

[266] CESCR, Concluding Observations: Armenia, E/C.12/1/Add.39 (8 December 1999), [15].

mother's life is at risk and when the pregnancy is a result of rape or incest.[267] It has also referred to providing for 'therapeutic' abortions,[268] without defining the concept. Medically, the notion foremost refers to cases where a mother's life is at risk, but it can also encompass a variety of other situations: to prevent harm to a woman's physical or mental health; where there would be fatal foetal abnormalities; or where the child would be at significant risk of serious disability. State practice is variable. At a minimum, abortion must always be available where the mother's life or health is at risk, or in cases of rape or incest. The CESCR has noted that the criminalization of abortion results in life-threatening illegal or unsafe abortions; it has also called on states not to penalize medical professionals 'in the exercise of their professional responsibilities'.[269]

In the related context of the right to health, the CESCR has interpreted the requirement in Article 12(2)(a) of the ICESCR to reduce stillbirths and infant mortality and improve the health of children as:

> …requiring measures to improve child and maternal health, sexual and reproductive health services, including access to *family planning*, pre- and postnatal care, emergency obstetric services and access to information, as well as to resources necessary to act on that information.[270]

While a 'core' obligation on states may be to refrain from coercive family planning measures and to provide essential information, it has been suggested that there is unlikely to exist a positive obligation on the state to assist people to procreate by funding reproductive technologies (such as fertility treatment).[271]

There is no reason, however, why such measures may not be progressively provided as a state's resources allow, as within the elastic ambit of the state's duty to provide the 'widest possible' protection for the establishment of families. Otherwise, fertility treatment may be available only to the wealthy who can afford it. The state could always impose reasonable restrictions on access to state-funded fertility treatment, such as means-testing or age limits which correlate with rates of effectiveness or risks of abnormalities.

Protection for the 'establishment' of a family requires states to refrain from or prevent actions which would arbitrarily interfere in the unity of the family's members, as the HRC explains in relation to the similar right to 'found' a family in Article 23(2) of the ICCPR:

> …the possibility to live together implies the adoption of appropriate measures, both at the internal level and as the case may be, in cooperation with other States, to ensure the unity or reunification of families, particularly when their members are separated for political, economic or similar reasons.[272]

[267] CESCR, Concluding Observations: Mauritius, E/C.12.MUS/CO/4 (8 June 2010), [25]; Nicaragua, E/C.12/NIC/CO/4 (28 November 2008), [26].

[268] CESCR, Concluding Observations: Mauritius, E/C.12.MUS/CO/4 (8 June 2010), [25].

[269] CESCR, Concluding Observations: Nicaragua, E/C.12/NIC/CO/4 (28 November 2008), [26].

[270] CESCR, General Comment No. 14 (2000), [14].

[271] Eriksson, 'Family Rights', 128.

[272] HRC, General Comment No. 19 (1990), [5].

Common grounds for separating families were discussed earlier, including laws concerning child welfare and immigration. If such measures are discriminatory, arbitrary or disproportionate, they may involve unlawful interference in, or a failure to protect, the right to establish a family.

Likewise, arbitrary or unlawful detention (for example, contrary to Article 9 of the ICCPR) which separates family members may also violate Article 10(1). Even where detention is lawful, as in the case of prisoners, the arbitrary denial of family life, including even 'conjugal visits' by spouses,[273] may interfere with Article 10.

Equality in marriage

The issue of equality *within* marriage is addressed by Article 23(4) of the ICCPR, which has no direct equivalent in Article 10 of the ICESCR. However, the 'widest possible' protection of the family may be understood to guarantee minimum rights *within* the family, including equality between couples. Article 23(4) is limited to equality in *marriage*, but similar considerations apply to families under Article 10 of the ICESCR, whether founded by marriage or assuming other family forms (such as de facto relationships).[274] The HRC has said of equality in marriage:

6. Article 23, paragraph 4, of the Covenant provides that States parties shall take appropriate steps to ensure equality of rights and responsibilities of spouses as to marriage, during marriage and at its dissolution.

7. With regard to equality as to marriage, the Committee wishes to note in particular that no sex-based discrimination should occur in respect of the acquisition or loss of nationality by reason of marriage. Likewise, the right of each spouse to retain the use of his or her original family name or to participate on an equal basis in the choice of a new family name should be safeguarded.

8. During marriage, the spouses should have equal rights and responsibilities in the family. This equality extends to all matters arising from their relationship, such as choice of residence, running of the household, education of the children and administration of assets. Such equality continues to be applicable to arrangements regarding legal separation or dissolution of the marriage.[275]

Article 16(1) of the CEDAW similarly provides for equality of rights and responsibilities in marriage and the family, including in relation to children, choice of family name and work, and property:

. . .

(c) The same rights and responsibilities during marriage and at its dissolution;

[273] Cf Eriksson, 'Family Rights', 132.
[274] CEDAW Committee, General Recommendation No. 21 (1994), [18].
[275] HRC, General Comment No. 19 (1990), [7]–[8]; see also HRC, General Comment No. 28, Equality of Rights between Men and Women (Article 3) (29 March 2000), [25]–[26].

(d) The same rights and responsibilities as parents, irrespective of their marital status, in matters relating to their children; in all cases the interests of the children shall be paramount;

…

(g) The same personal rights as husband and wife, including the right to choose a family name, a profession and an occupation;

(h) The same rights for both spouses in respect of the ownership, acquisition, management, administration, enjoyment and disposition of property, whether free of charge or for a valuable consideration.

States must ensure that women are not forced to adopt their husband's name, nationality or domicile, or impose impediments to women making such choices on an equal basis.

Equality in relation to family property is particularly important to the position of women, their financial security and ability to provide for themselves and their family.[276] Women have the right to own an equal share of property within a marriage or de facto relationship, as well the equal right to manage such property.[277] Financial equality must be similarly guaranteed in de facto relationships.[278] Children in the same degree of relationship to a deceased must also enjoy equal rights in inheritance.[279] Children born out of wedlock are entitled to equal recognition.[280]

The above standards are designed to correct patriarchal hierarchies within families, including where the father is regarded as the 'head' of the family with decision-making authority over it, and which have often been embedded in national, religious or customary law.[281] Article 5 of the CEDAW directs states to modify such structures, including through the education of children about the common responsibilities of parents:

States Parties shall take all appropriate measures:

(a) To modify the social and cultural patterns of conduct of men and women, with a view to achieving the elimination of prejudices and customary and all other practices which are based on the idea of the inferiority or the superiority of either of the sexes or on stereotyped roles for men and women;

(b) To ensure that family education includes a proper understanding of maternity as a social function and the recognition of the common responsibility of men and women in the upbringing and development of their children, it being understood that the interest of the children is the primordial consideration in all cases.

[276] CEDAW Committee, General Recommendation No. 21 (1994), [26].
[277] CEDAW Committee, General Recommendation No. 21, [30]–[31] and [18].
[278] CEDAW Committee, General Recommendation No. 21, [18].
[279] CEDAW Committee, General Recommendation No. 21, [34].
[280] CEDAW, Article 16(1); CEDAW Committee, General Recommendation No. 21, [19].
[281] CEDAW Committee, General Recommendation No. 21 (1994), [17]; International Conference on Population and Development, Programme of Action, A/CONF.171/13/Rev.1 (1994), [4(27)]. Islam, for instance, explicitly requires gender 'role differentiation' in marriage: Baderin, *IHR and Islam*, 134–6.

Protection and assistance 'for the care and education of dependent children'

Article 10(1) requires states to take measures to support the family while it is responsible 'for the care and education of dependent children'. It thus focuses on protection of children within the family, as distinct from the wider protection of all children, including outside the family, under Article 10(3), which is also concerned with economic and other forms of exploitation of children.

The provision does not define what is meant by 'dependent' children, although the obligation expressly relates to the period 'while it [the family] is responsible for' the care and education of children. On the one hand, this could be interpreted as confining the obligation to the period in which the family is *actually* responsible for caring for the child, thus precluding the state's obligations where a family abandons a child. The better view, however, is that it concerns the period for which the family is *legally* responsible for the child.

Article 10 itself does not specify any criteria of child dependency or family responsibility. Different indicia will give different answers to when a child could be considered dependent. For example, it may be defined by reference to: custody or adoption; the age of economic maturity (as defined by international standards on lawful child labour, and which varies by sector); the end of compulsory schooling (such as that defined by the right to education in the ICESCR); adulthood (18 years under the CROC); social or national expectations about the duration of parental responsibilities (which may persist beyond 18 years, or in some cases fall beneath it); when a child actually leaves home (which again may be well into adulthood); or a combination of different indicia.

In national law, notions of 'dependency' vary, including for different purposes (such as social security, education, immigration and so on). Sometimes the concept is defined flexibly, such as where an adult is legally responsible, alone or jointly, 'for the day-to-day care, welfare and development' of a minor under a particular age,[282] and even if there are temporary absences from the adult's home. Some states define dependency more expansively, such as until a child becomes independent and self-reliant. In Germany, child benefits persist until a child reaches the age of 27 or 28.[283] In Switzerland, parents are obliged to support a child's education until the completion of a first higher educational qualification (vocational training or a university programme after school),[284] which could be well into the child's 20s.

At a minimum, given that the age of maturity of a child under international law is 18 years, it may be presumed that a child is 'dependent' at least until she or he turns 18, unless the child has voluntarily left the parents' care at an earlier time, for instance, to commence lawful and safe work, and is also able to adequately support him- or herself through such work.

[282] Social Security Act 1991 (Australia), section 5(2)(a).

[283] Ostner et al, 'Family Policies in Germany', 18.

[284] Swiss Civil Code, Articles 276–7.

It may be noted, however, that in urging states to provide family benefits, the CESCR has also been concerned for 'adult dependents',[285] suggesting that the age of maturity should not be viewed as automatically terminating dependency and family support. The continuation of state support for adult dependents may be particularly important where, for instance, unemployed young people are transitioning from school to work, or where adult children with disabilities require support for family-based carers (persons with disabilities also enjoy their own autonomous entitlements to social security support). Since Article 10(1) also refers to state support while the family is responsible for the child's education, it may also be linked to national laws which require parents to support a child's tertiary education even as adults.

Article 10(1) does not specify the measures which states should take to protect and assist families for the care and education of dependent children. A wide range of measures is possible and what is necessary in a given society will depend not only on resource availability, but social conceptions of the respective responsibilities of the family, the state and non-state actors. Article 10(1) recognizes that the family is 'responsible' for the care and education of children, and the state is thus called on to play a subsidiary role, albeit to take the 'widest possible' measures to protect and assist the family in discharging its functions. In discussing states' related obligation to protect children under Article 24 of the ICCPR, the HRC discusses the division of responsibilities between the family and the state:

> 6. Responsibility for guaranteeing children the necessary protection lies with the family, society and the State. Although the Covenant does not indicate how such responsibility is to be apportioned, it is primarily incumbent on the family, which is interpreted broadly to include all persons composing it in the society of the State party concerned, and particularly on the parents, to create conditions to promote the harmonious development of the child's personality and his enjoyment of the rights recognized in the Covenant. However, since it is quite common for the father and mother to be gainfully employed outside the home, reports by States parties should indicate how society, social institutions and the State are discharging their responsibility to assist the family in ensuring the protection of the child.[286]

Social conceptions of the respective responsibilities of the family and the state for the welfare of the family vary considerably between and within states. Even in relatively integrated communities such as Europe, there are marked differences in approach. In the Scandinavian countries, the state is expected to provide support to individuals in need, and the care of the elderly is not regarded as a family obligation.[287] In Southern European countries, notions of dependency and responsibility between extended family members are the norm, and state intervention is more limited. In Western European states, welfare is oriented around the status and

[285] CESCR, General Comment No. 19, The right to social security (Article 9), E/C.12/GC/19 (4 February 2008), [13].

[286] HRC, General Comment No. 17 (1989), [6].

[287] Jane Miller, 'Family Obligations in Europe', *Findings*, Social Policy Research 107 (Joseph Rowntree Foundation, New York, November 1996), 2.

relations[288] within the private nuclear family rather than conceived as individual entitlements as in Scandinavia;[289] as late as 2001, children in Germany were still required by law to look after needy parents. Previously, 'providential' socialist states (such as East Germany) 'took command of essential family interests, assuming a parental role and to some extent that of the breadwinner-husband',[290] and attempted to re-engineer family life to promote goals such as emancipation and gender equality.

In Europe, regional efforts have nonetheless been made to articulate the responsibilities of parents in the family, which in turn can help to define the role of the state in assisting parents in their responsibilities. Thus, a Council of Europe Recommendation of 1984 states that:

> . . . parental responsibilities are a collection of duties and powers which aim at ensuring the moral and material welfare of the child, in particular by taking care of the person of the child, by maintaining personal relationships with him and by providing for his education, his maintenance, his legal representation and the administration of his property . . .[291]

A Council of Europe Draft Recommendation on the Rights and Legal Status of Children and Parental Responsibilities of 2011 also seeks to define parental responsibilities:

> Parental responsibilities are a collection of duties, rights and powers, which aim to promote and safeguard the rights and welfare of the child in accordance with the child's evolving capacities, including:
>
> – health and development;
> – care and protection;
> – enjoyment and maintenance of personal relationships;
> – provision of education;
> – legal representation;
> – determination of residence;
> – administration of property.[292]

The Draft Recommendation lists the 'care, protection and education' responsibilities of parents, which are also to be exercised equally between parents, as follows:

> 1. The holders of parental responsibilities should provide the child with care, protection and education in order to promote the child's psychological, emotional, intellectual and social development in a manner consistent with his or her evolving capacities.

[288] Ostner et al, 'Family Policies in Germany', 5.

[289] Jane Miller, 'Family Obligations in Europe', *Findings*, Social Policy Research 107, Joseph Rowntree Foundation, November 1996, 2.

[290] Ostner et al, 'Family Policies in Germany', 4.

[291] Council of Europe, Recommendation No. R(84)4 of the Committee of Ministers to Member States on Parental Responsibilities, 28 February 1984, Principle I(a).

[292] Council of Europe Committee of Experts on Family Law, Draft Recommendation on the Rights and Legal Status of Children and Parental Responsibilities, CDCJ (2011) 15 (19 October 2011), Principle 20.

2. The child should not be subjected to violence or in any other way be treated so as to harm or endanger his or her mental or physical health.[293]

Beyond Europe, there is even greater pluralism and diversity in certain states and traditions in Africa, Asia, Latin America and the Middle East. In the African Charter, for instance, while the state has a 'duty' to assist the family (Article 18(2)), individuals have a duty 'to preserve the harmonious development of the family and to work for the cohesion and respect of the family; to respect his parents at all times, to maintain them in case of need' (Article 29(1)). Similar duties of children towards parents are found in national constitutions in all continents.[294] Obligations within families are also emphasized by Confucian traditions in parts of Asia, and the privacy of the family, and minimal state intervention, are expected (just as they are in conservative traditions in certain Western societies, such as the United States).

Under the African Charter on the Rights and Welfare of the Child 1999, the responsibilities of both parents and children are extensively elaborated in Articles 20 and 31:

Article 20: Parental Responsibilities

1. Parents or other persons responsible for the child shall have the primary responsibility of the upbringing and development the child and shall have the duty:

(a) to ensure that the best interests of the child are their basic concern at all times;

(b) to secure, within their abilities and financial capacities, conditions of living necessary to the child's development; and

(c) to ensure that domestic discipline is administered with humanity and in a manner consistent with the inherent dignity of the child.

2. States Parties to the present Charter shall in accordance with their means and national conditions the all appropriate measures:

(a) to assist parents and other persons responsible for the child and in case of need provide material assistance and support programmes particularly with regard to nutrition, health, education, clothing and housing;

(b) to assist parents and others responsible for the child in the performance of child-rearing and ensure the development of institutions responsible for providing care of children; and

(c) to ensure that the children of working parents are provided with care services and facilities.

...

[293] Draft Recommendation on the Rights and Legal Status of Children and Parental Responsibilities, Principle 30.

[294] Algeria Constitution 1967, Article 65; Brazil Constitution 1993, Article 229; Cambodia Constitution 1993, Article 47(2); Republic of Congo Constitution 1992, Article 40; Croatia Constitution 2004, Article 63(4); Cuba Constitution 2002, Article 38(2); Draft Eritrea Constitution 1996, Article 22(3); Lithuania Constitution 1992, Article 38(7); Paraguay Constitution 1992, Article 53(2); Russia Constitution 1993, Article 38(3).

Article 31: Responsibility of the Child

Every child shall have responsibilities towards his family and society, the State and other legally recognized communities and the international community. The child, subject to his age and ability, and such limitations as may be contained in the present Charter, shall have the duty:

(a) to work for the cohesion of the family, to respect his parents, superiors and elders at all times and to assist them in case of need;

(b) to serve his national community by placing his physical and intellectual abilities at its service;

(c) to preserve and strengthen social and national solidarity;

(d) to preserve and strengthen African cultural values in his relations with other members of the society, in the spirit of tolerance, dialogue and consultation and to contribute to the moral well-being of society;

(e) to preserve and strengthen the independence and the integrity of his country;

(f) to contribute to the best of his abilities, at all times and at all levels, to the promotion and achievement of African Unity.

Given the global diversity surrounding concepts of family responsibilities and the proper role of state intervention, it is difficult to prescribe a universal template for the kinds of measures of state support which must be taken in all circumstances under Article 10(1). Nonetheless, state measures of support for the 'care' of children will most commonly involve financial support (such as cash benefits or tax breaks), services (such as child care), and other assistance to maintain the balance between family and work life (such as paternity, parental and adoption leave; maternity leave is separately guaranteed by Article 10(2)). It should be mentioned that Article 18(3) of the CROC specifically requires states to 'take all appropriate measures to ensure that children of working parents have the right to benefit from child-care services and facilities for which they are eligible'.

Benefits and services

In relation to financial support for families, in its General Comment on social security (Article 9 of the ICESCR), the CESCR emphasizes that the provision of family benefits (cash or services) is 'crucial for realizing the rights of children and adult dependents to protection under articles 9 and 10':

18. Benefits for families are crucial for realizing the rights of children and adult dependents to protection under articles 9 and 10 of the Covenant. In providing the benefits, the State party should take into account the resources and circumstances of the child and persons having responsibility for the maintenance of the child or adult dependent, as well as any other consideration relevant to an application for benefits made by or on behalf of the child or adult dependent. Family and child benefits, including cash benefits and social services, should be provided to families, without discrimination on prohibited grounds,

and would ordinarily cover food, clothing, housing, water and sanitation, or other rights as appropriate.[295]

It is uncertain whether states must provide both cash benefits *and* services to families, or whether they enjoy a discretion in the choice of means for assisting the family. It is conceivable, for instance, that the provision of goods or services in kind, such as food 'stamps', clothing, free or subsidized water or sanitation, public housing or childcare, may suffice in a given situation, such that cash benefits may be unnecessary. This may be particularly the case in some less developed states, where cash economies are less established and state cash transfers are less common.

However, in many market economies, cash benefits may be a preferred strategy, since they reduce the administrative burden on states (compared with micro-managing a family's necessities by providing particular goods or services in kind). They also empower and dignify families by enabling them to exercise autonomy and make choices as to how they wish to allocate family expenditure and manage family needs. The privatization of essential services or utilities in many market economies may have also limited states' capacity to direct such utilities to provide free or subsidized services, thus rendering cash transfers more feasible.

Regardless of whether assistance takes the form of cash, services or in-kind contributions, the CESCR's General Comment indicates the underlying purpose of assistance: to ensure an adequate standard of living for the family and children.[296] Any measures taken must therefore be suitable to and capable of achieving that end, even if the CESCR has not thus far nominated specific benefit amounts or formulas. In monitoring states, the CESCR has, however, criticized childcare benefits which are 'not sufficient to cover the cost of bringing up a child'.[297] Article 27(3) of the CROC also requires the state to assist parents or carers of children, through social assistance and support, to realize a child's right to an adequate standard of living:

3. States Parties, in accordance with national conditions and within their means, shall take appropriate measures to assist parents and others responsible for the child to implement this right and shall in case of need provide material assistance and support programmes, particularly with regard to nutrition, clothing and housing.

While benefits are typically paid to parents, in principle they are intended to benefit the children and the family as a whole, not individual interests or needs of the parents; it cannot be assumed that all parents use benefits in the interests of their children all of the time. There is a trustee/beneficiary relationship of sorts, even if payments are not normally legally structured as such. More radical approaches are, of course, conceivable under Article 10, such as the payment of a 'childhood

[295] CESCR, General Comment No. 19 (2008), [13].
[296] Such purpose is explicitly expressed in Article 27(3) of the CROC.
[297] CESCR, Concluding Observations: Ireland, E/C.12/1/Add.35 (14 May 1999), [13].

pension' which accrues to the child not the parents, including in relation to the funding of childcare or other basic services. In any case, children remain independently entitled to whatever social security benefits are available to them under Article 9 of the ICESCR, considered in another chapter.

Historically, family benefits derive from the evolution of ILO standards on social protection. Part VII (Articles 39 to 45) of ILO Convention No. 102 concerning social security establishes a 'family benefit' for child maintenance, either on a contributory insurance or universal, means-tested social security basis, and involving either cash payments and/or direct support for children (for food, clothing, housing, holidays or domestic help). The state may determine qualifying periods, but the Convention establishes minimum benefits formulas at either 3 per cent of the average male wage per child (for prescribed classes of workers) or 1.5 per cent of the average wage per child where all residents are covered.

As with many ILO standards, Convention No. 102 permits states to limit coverage, but it has the advantage of specifying minimum benefit formulas and thus concretizing standards. An autonomous right of social security for all children, not limited to children in families, or to 'prescribed classes' or employment situations, is found in Article 26 of the CROC, discussed below in the context of Article 10(3) of the ICESCR.

An attempt has also been made in European regional standards to define minimum family benefits amounts. Article 16 of the European Social Charter has been interpreted to require family benefits to constitute an 'adequate' income supplement. Adequacy means a significant percentage of monthly 'median equivalised income', as defined by Eurostat.[298] A household's income is established by adding up all monetary income received from any source by each member of the household. To reflect differences in household size and composition, this total is divided by the number of 'equivalent adults' (using a modified OECD equivalence scale): the resulting figure is attributed to each member of the household. Benefit levels are also adjusted for inflation. Other forms of protection under European standards include birth grants, additional payments to large families and tax relief for children.

An important question is what 'limitations' may be placed on a family's right to benefits or services under Article 10(1), whether by the operation of the general limitations clause in Article 4 of the ICESCR or considerations of progressive realization under Article 2(2). While some states provide benefits to all families, the means-testing of family benefits is common in many countries, typically to ration scarce public resources.

In one sense, this may be viewed as an instance of progressive realization. However, if the purpose of family benefits is to ensure an adequate standard of living, wealthy families whose rights are already secure have no need for assistance from the state. Moreover, poorly targeted benefits which redistribute revenue to the wealthy—'middle class welfare'—ultimately reduce the

[298] ECSR, Conclusions 2006: General Introduction (2006), 14; Estonia, 215; Bulgaria, 130.

resources to fund social security for those in genuine need (even if they may be electorially popular). In part, the answer depends on whether family benefits are viewed through a social security lens (addressing the needy) or some other prism (such as social solidarity or as an expression of support for the value of the family per se).

In relation to Article 4 limitations proper, in national practice restrictions arise on various grounds. Residency or citizenship requirements are sometimes imposed, but risk impoverishing families who are already vulnerable precisely because of their precarious immigration status as 'illegal' workers or asylum seekers. A more justifiable restriction may be to condition family benefits on, for instance, a duty on parents to immunize their child against communicable diseases (which in turn is provided by free public health programmes).

More complicated are 'income quarantining' measures, discussed earlier in relation to social security generally under Article 9, which specify how cash benefits are to be spent (for example, on fresh food, not alcohol, ostensibly to protect child health and safety). Such restrictions necessarily interfere in the dignity and autonomy of families to decide how to manage their own affairs, and require strong justification (such as child protection). They must also be proportionate to the risk faced (rather than excessively doing more than is necessary) and cannot be imposed on a racially discriminatory basis.[299]

Childcare

Assistance for childcare may be a particularly important measure of protection for the family under Article 10. In monitoring states, the CESCR has been concerned about the shortage of child day care institutions, 'which constitutes an obstacle to women's equal participation in the labour market' and 'efforts to promote gender equality'.[300] It has recommended that states extend affordable, accessible and available childcare services.[301]

Childcare performs a bundle of functions: aiding the education, socialization and development of the child; enabling parents to work and thus contributing to labour market participation policies; and aiding gender equality objectives. The state can support childcare in a variety of ways: directly providing it in state facilities; subsidizing private providers; or paying social security benefits or giving tax relief to subsidize its cost to families.

In Europe, the European Committee on Social Rights has interpreted the family rights provision (Article 16) of the European Social Charter to require states to ensure that childcare facilities are available, affordable and of good quality (in relation to coverage with respect to the number of children aged 0 to 6, ratio of staff to children, staff training, suitable premises and cost of childcare

[299] As was the case for Australian measures directed exclusively at indigenous families under the Northern Territory National Emergency Response Act 2007 (Australia).

[300] CESCR, Concluding Observations: Germany, E/C.12/1/Add.68 (24 September 2001), [26].

[301] CESCR, Concluding Observations: Italy, E/C.12/1/Add.103 (14 December 2004), [44].

to parents).[302] The ECSR found 'manifestly inadequate' the situation in Turkey, where only some tens of thousands of childcare places were available in public and private facilities for 3.2 million children aged 0 to 4 years.[303]

Housing assistance

Housing assistance for families may be an important measure under Article 10(1). While a right to housing already comes within the right to an adequate standard of living under Article 11 of the ICESCR, Article 10(1) directs attention to the need for housing to be adapted to the requirements of families. The provision of family housing is otherwise subject to the modalities for fulfilling the right to housing generally under Article 11.

Regionally, family rights under both the ECHR (Article 8) and European Social Charter (Article 16) have addressed the housing dimensions of family rights, particularly in the context of the needs of minority families. While there is no right to housing under the ECHR,[304] the ECtHR has emphasized the obligation on states to take cultural differences into account in housing policies affecting family rights:

> The vulnerable position of gypsies as a minority means that some special consideration should be given to their needs and their different lifestyle both in the relevant regulatory planning framework and in arriving at the decisions in particular cases. To this extent there is thus a positive obligation imposed on the Contracting States by virtue of Article 8 to facilitate the Gypsy way of life.[305]

The original European Social Charter 1961 contains no right to housing, but 'family housing' is mentioned under the right of the family to social, legal and economic protection in Article 16:

> With a view to ensuring the necessary conditions for the full development of the family, which is a fundamental unit of society, the Contracting Parties undertake to promote the economic, legal and social protection of family life by such means as social and family benefits, fiscal arrangements, provision of family housing, benefits for the newly married, and other appropriate means.[306]

In contrast to the position under the ECHR, the European Social Charter requires states to take positive measures to protect families in respect of housing, and is thus assimilable to the positive obligations under Article 10(1) of the ICESCR, understood in conjunction with the right to housing under Article 11 of the ICESCR. According to the European Committee of Social Rights (ECSR), the

[302] ECSR, Conclusions XVII-1: Turkey (2004), 490.

[303] ECSR, Conclusions XVII-1: Turkey (2004), 490.

[304] *Doherty and Doherty v South Dublin County Council et al*, 22 January 2007, (2007) IEHC 4 (High Court of Ireland), [42]–[45].

[305] *Chapman v United Kingdom*, 18 January 2001, (2001) 33 EHRR 18, [96]–[99]; see also *Connors v United Kingdom*, 27 May 2004, (2005) 40 EHRR 9, [84].

[306] European Social Charter (adopted 18 October 1961, 529 UNTS 89, entered into force 26 February 1965), Article 16; see similarly European Social Charter (Revised) (adopted 3 May 1996, ETS 163, entered into force 1 July 1999), Article 16.

state must promote the provision of an adequate supply of housing for families, of a sufficient quality or standard and including essential services:

24. …in order satisfy Article 16 states must promote the provision of an adequate supply of housing for families, take the needs of families into account in housing policies and ensure that existing housing be of an adequate standard and include essential services (such as heating and electricity). The Committee has stated that adequate housing refers not only to a dwelling which must not be sub-standard and must have essential amenities, but also to a dwelling of suitable size considering the composition of the family in residence. Furthermore the obligation to promote and provide housing extends to security from unlawful eviction.[307]

The cultural needs of vulnerable minorities, such as Roma, gypsies or travellers, must also be taken into account: 'social housing offered to Roma should be, as far as possible, culturally suited to them'.[308] Equal treatment and non-discrimination requires the particular circumstances of the minority group to be taken into account[309] and 'differentiated treatment for these families and tailored measures to improve their housing conditions'.[310] There is similar scope for any family housing measures under Article 10(1) of the ICESCR to be read in conjunction with the non-discrimination protection in Article 2(1) of the ICESCR, and the cultural rights in Article 15 of the ICESCR and Article 27 of the ICCPR.

The ECSR accepts that the state enjoys a 'margin of appreciation' in taking positive measures, particularly as regards the balance to be struck between the general interest and the interest of a specific group, and in choices regarding priorities and resources: 'it is not the task of the Committee to substitute itself in determining the policy best adapted to the situation'.[311]

In assessing state implementation of policies, the ECSR considers whether a housing measure: (i) is implemented in a reasonable time frame; (ii) results in measurable progress; and (iii) is financed consistent with the maximum use of available resources.[312] A period as long as eight years has been found not to exceed the state's margin of appreciation, where measurable progress had been made and adequate resources applied.[313] Implementation must also not be discriminatory, as where Croatia differentially assisted Croatian returnees displaced

[307] *European Roma Rights Center v Greece*, ECSR Complaint No. 15/2003, 8 December 2004, [24]; see also *Centre on Housing Rights and Evictions v Italy*, ECSR Complaint No. 58/2009, 25 June 2010, [54].

[308] *European Roma Rights Centre v Portugal*, ECSR Complaint No. 61/2010, 30 June 2011, [49]; see also *European Roma Rights Center v Greece*, ECSR Complaint No. 15/2003, 8 December 2004, [25].

[309] *European Roma Rights Centre v Italy*, ECSR Complaint No. 27/2005, 7 December 2005, [21].

[310] *International Federation of Human Rights v Belgium*, ECSR Complaint No. 62/2010, 21 March 2012, [120].

[311] *European Roma Rights Centre v Bulgaria*, ECSR Complaint No. 31/2005, 18 October 2006, [35] and [37].

[312] *Centre on Housing Rights and Evictions v Croatia*, ECSR Complaint No. 52/2008, 22 June 2008, [81].

[313] *European Roma and Travellers Forum v France*, ECSR Complaint No. 64/2011, 24 January 2012, [105] (although there was discrimination in failing to take into account the needs of traveller families).

by conflict, but failed to adequately assist the bulk of returnees who were ethnic Serbs;[314] or where Roma settlements were physically segregated from others by a wall.[315] Arbitrary selection between families for housing support will also be problematic.[316]

The ECSR has decided numerous complaints involving the failure of states to adequately provide or protect family housing under Article 16, many involving Roma, gypsy or traveller minorities, as well as families displaced by conflict.[317] The ECSR has found family housing not to be culturally adequate where, for example, the state failed to provide an adequate quantity and/or quality (including infrastructure) of camping sites for the mobile homes (caravans) of Roma minorities.[318] It also criticized states where the law failed to recognize caravans as 'housing' entitled to state support,[319] or accorded lesser recognition (such as temporary rather than permanent approval of residences).[320] States have also failed to adequately take into account family size in resettling Roma.[321] The ECSR has also criticized the re-housing of Roma in apartment blocks:

> 49. …Re-housing of Roma families in apartment blocks has often prevented family and casual gatherings, given that their means of existence as a community and bonds of solidarity are broken. Moreover, they are also faced with hostile attitudes of neighbours in apartment blocks. Therefore, the Committee considers that attention should be paid to these problems in policy planning.[322]

Under the Revised European Social Charter 1996, there is now an autonomous right to housing in Article 31, but Article 16 still includes family housing as an aspect of the right of the family to protection. The ECSR has confirmed that the concepts of adequate housing under Articles 16 and 31 are identical.[323] In a similar way, it is arguable that housing measures to protect the family under Article 10(1) of the ICESCR should be harmonized with the scope of the right to housing under Article 11 of the ICESCR.

314 *Centre on Housing Rights and Evictions v Croatia*, ECSR Complaint No. 52/2008, 22 June 2008, [90].

315 *European Roma Rights Centre v Portugal*, ECSR Complaint No. 61/2010, 30 June 2011, [48].

316 *Médecins du Monde—International v France*, ECSR Complaint No. 67/2011, 11 September 2012, [63].

317 *Centre on Housing Rights and Evictions v Croatia*, ECSR Complaint No. 52/2008, 22 June 2008, [73] (noting that Article 16 does not provide a right of restitution or compensation for lost property).

318 *European Roma Rights Centre v Portugal*, ECSR Complaint No. 61/2010, 30 June 2011, [49]–[53]; *European Roma and Travellers Forum v France*, ECSR Complaint No. 64/2011, 24 January 2012, [109].

319 *European Roma Rights Centre v France*, ECSR Complaint No. 51/2008 (19 October 2009), [80]; *International Federation of Human Rights v Belgium*, ECSR Complaint No. 62/2010, 21 March 2012, [73] ('any place in which a family resides legally or illegally, whether a building or a movable piece of property such as a caravan, must be regarded as housing within the meaning of the Charter').

320 *International Federation of Human Rights v Belgium*, ECSR Complaint No. 62/2010, 21 March 2012, [137]–[138].

321 *European Roma Rights Centre v Portugal*, ECSR Complaint No. 61/2010, 30 June 2011, [50].

322 *European Roma Rights Centre v Portugal*, ECSR Complaint No. 61/2010, 30 June 2011, [49].

323 *European Roma Rights Centre v Bulgaria*, ECSR Complaint No. 31/2005, 18 October 2006, [17].

Leave to support family/work balance

As regards leave from work to assist in maintaining a balance between family life and work responsibilities, and which complements maternity leave under Article 10(2) (discussed below), no ILO standards have been adopted on paternity leave, parental leave or adoption leave.[324] These types of leave are, however, increasingly found in state practice, and may be justified as measures of protection for the family under Article 10(1) or children under Article 10(3), or as social security measures more broadly under Article 9.

In monitoring states, the CESCR has not generally called on states to provide paternity leave. Where national law already provides it, however, the CESCR has called for it to be available on a non-discriminatory basis, so that it is not confined to fathers married to mothers, but applied regardless of marital status.[325]

Regional standards are also emerging in some of these areas. The European Union, for example, recommends periods of non-transferable paid paternity leave to (flexibly) coincide with maternity leave.[326] Its duration varies in practice from one day to three months. Adoption leave is likewise increasingly available, although (as with paternity leave) it is often for shorter periods than for biological mothers given the absence of prenatal or post-natal health needs.[327]

While parenting leave pursues wider policy objectives[328] than maternity/paternity/adoption leave (which is limited to the period around childbirth or the time of adoption), it is part of the continuum of support for the family from childbirth into the child's early life. It is often available to be taken at any time during the child's early life (for instance, up to the age of 8 years in the European Union), to support the family/work balance. It may also mitigate the need for childcare support, although it can also shift the funding burden on the state from one area to another. The gender equality aims of parenting leave are not necessarily achieved in practice; there is a very low take-up rate by men even when it is available, reflecting gender disparities in earnings in the labour market, which encourage men in families to stay at work,[329] as well as persistent cultural attitudes about gender roles.

Measures of support for the 'education' of children

Some of the forms of support to families mentioned by the CESCR or other treaty bodies, such as assistance in relation to housing, food, clothing and water, fall more squarely within other ICESCR rights. These especially include the rights to an adequate standard of living in Article 11 and health in Article 12. The residual value of Article 10(1) may be to focus attention on the special needs of families

[324] ILO, *Maternity at Work: A Review of National Legislation* (2nd edn, Geneva, 2010) ('*Maternity at Work*'), 43–57.

[325] CESCR, Concluding Observations: Mauritius, E/C.12/MUS/CO/4 (8 June 2010), [21].

[326] ILO, *Maternity at Work*, 44.

[327] ILO, *Maternity at Work*, 56.

[328] ILO, *Maternity at Work*, 49.

[329] ILO, *Maternity at Work*, 53–4.

in relation to those rights, even if the specific modalities for addressing such concerns are found elsewhere in the ICESCR.

While Article 10(1) of the ICESCR expressly requires state support while the family is responsible for the 'education' of children, the right to education at all levels is already extensively provided for in Articles 13 and 14 of the ICESCR, including parents' rights in choosing the type of their child's education. The question arises whether the reference to 'education' in Article 10(1) adds anything to what is already addressed elsewhere in the ICESCR. There was little discussion in the drafting.

Three points may be made. First, Articles 13 and 14 mainly concern formal schooling in primary, secondary and tertiary institutions, or other fundamental education where a person cannot complete primary school. The reference to education in Article 10(1) can conceivably cover education outside these contexts, such as the child's early learning from time of birth until she or he starts primary school. States should accordingly take measures to support learning in infancy and early childhood; there is evidence that early learning (as in preschool) improves children's cognitive outcomes later in life.[330]

This could include measures to enable working parents to spend more time at home with their children (such as parental leave); support for childcare services (to encourage the socialization of children); and support for more structured learning in pre-primary institutions (such as preschool, nursery school or kindergarten). Under the Brazilian Constitution, for example, the state must provide free assistance to children from birth to 6 years for day care centres and kindergartens;[331] while day care centres and facilities are also mandated by the Portuguese Constitution.[332] The CRC has paid particular attention to the need for a positive agenda for early childhood:

> The Committee encourages States parties to construct a positive agenda for rights in early childhood. A shift away from traditional beliefs that regard early childhood mainly as a period for the socialization of the immature human being towards mature adult status is required. The Convention requires that children, including the very youngest children, be respected as persons in their own right. Young children should be recognized as active members of families, communities and societies, with their own concerns, interests and points of view. For the exercise of their rights, young children have particular requirements for physical nurturance, emotional care and sensitive guidance, as well as for time and space for social play, exploration and learning. These requirements can best be planned for within a framework of laws, policies and programmes for early childhood, including a plan for implementation and independent monitoring, for example through the appointment of a children's rights commissioner, and through assessments of the impact of laws and policies on children...[333]

[330] Patricia Apps, Silvia Mendolia and Ian Walker, 'The Impact of Pre-school on Adolescents' Outcomes', Institute for the Study of Labour, IZA Discussion Paper No. 6971, October 2012.

[331] Brazil Constitution 1993, Article 7(XXV).

[332] Portugal Constitution 1976, Article 67(2)(b).

[333] CRC, General Comment No. 7 (2005), Implementing child rights in early childhood (20 September 2006), [5].

Reference may be made here to Article 31 of the CROC, which guarantees the right of children to rest, leisure, play and recreation:

1. States Parties recognize the right of the child to rest and leisure, to engage in play and recreational activities appropriate to the age of the child and to participate freely in cultural life and the arts.

2. States Parties shall respect and promote the right of the child to participate fully in cultural and artistic life and shall encourage the provision of appropriate and equal opportunities for cultural, artistic, recreational and leisure activity.

Such activities promote children's development, resilience, creativity, motivation, health and well-being, belonging and cultural identity.[334] The state can assist by creating child-friendly urban and rural environments and supporting facilities and services for children, including, for instance, parks, community centres, sports and playgrounds, and cultural activities.[335]

Secondly, Article 10(1) requires states to support families while they are responsible for a child's education. Economic necessity may drive young children into work to support their families and thus deprive them of education. It is therefore appropriate for the state to provide financial assistance to families to prevent recourse to child labour and to enable children to go to school, reinforcing the further protections against child labour in Article 10(3) and in the implicit freedom from forced labour in Article 6 of the ICESCR. Moreover, the education and learning of children within the family will be impaired if the family suffers serious financial stress or overworked parents, necessitating financial payments to support the family and alleviate some of the pressure.

Thirdly, the state may assist families in relation to informal types of education for children of any age, outside the school framework, for instance related to social, cultural or health matters. Thus, there is a role for the state in educating young people about the risks of drugs or alcohol,[336] gambling,[337] sexually transmitted diseases or other harmful substances or activities. More positively, the state can provide public education about cultural, historical, civic and political matters, as well as promoting healthy lifestyles, sports[338] and so on.

The education of children, and state support for it, is also subject to other considerations. The state cannot unreasonably interfere in the family's autonomy to choose the child's early preschool educational path. Thus, constitutions which impose ideological or political requirements on a child's education may be suspect, as where the family is 'founded on religion, ethics and patriotism',[339] or where parents and the state must educate children in 'the socialist ideal' so they can contribute to 'national defence'.[340]

[334] CRC, General Comment No. 17 (2013): The right of the child to rest, leisure, play, recreational activities, cultural life and the arts (17 April 2013), [8]–[13].

[335] CRC, General Comment No. 17, [58].

[336] Ecuador Constitution 2008, Article 46(5).

[337] Turkey Constitution 1982, Article 58(2).

[338] Romania Constitution 1991, Article 45(5).

[339] Qatar Constitution 2003, Article 21.

[340] Vietnam Constitution 1992, Article 66.

At the same time, nor can parents unreasonably impair the child's education through harmful educational choices, such as by cultivating racial or religious hatred, violence or crime in children. Such abuse of parental authority also amounts to child neglect or abuse; some constitutions even sanction parents for 'insufficiencies' in the education of their children.[341]

Institutions relevant to Article 10

In order to ensure the protection of children and families, the state must establish, maintain, fund and supervise the necessary state institutions for fulfilling its obligations under Article 10. The nature and form of such institutions varies from state to state, with some states even according constitutional recognition to institutions for the protection of mothers and children.[342]

At a minimum, a state will need to establish: birth and marriage registries; child welfare authorities, supported by law enforcement where necessary, to deal with child abuse or neglect; a system of family law and judicial supervision to deal with family dissolution, separation and child custody and access disputes; authorities for regulating foster care and adoptions; institutions for the care of orphans; social security mechanisms for the payment of family benefits; childcare centres and authorities to regulate them; labour inspectorates to address issues of maternity protection and child labour; juvenile justice systems; and mechanisms which provide effective legal remedies for violations of Article 10.

FREE CONSENT TO MARRIAGE

The second sentence of Article 10(1), that marriage must be entered into with 'free consent', caused considerable debate in the drafting. Those in favour were concerned about practices such as child marriages,[343] arranged marriages[344] or women being 'considered as mere objects'[345] and 'married off like slaves'.[346]

Many were opposed, however, largely on the basis that the same safeguard was already found in the draft ICCPR (now Article 23(3)) and thought to be more appropriately located there.[347] Others were concerned that the protection did not go far enough, with Spain suggesting that free consent was only one of several equally important elements of a legally valid marriage.[348]

Thailand queried the legal consequences of distinguishing between consensual and non-consensual marriages, since a marriage entered into without free consent

[341] Republic of Congo Constitution 1992, Article 45.

[342] Costa Rica Constitution 2005, Article 55 (protection of mothers and children is entrusted to an autonomous institution, the National Infancy Foundation, and other state institutions).

[343] UNGA Third Committee, A/C.3/SR.730 (14 January 1957), 249 (Dominican Republic).

[344] UNGA Third Committee, A/C.3/SR.730 (14 January 1957), 250 (Lebanon).

[345] UNGA Third Committee, A/C.3/SR.732 (16 January 1957), 262 (Cuba).

[346] UNGA Third Committee, A/C.3/SR.730 (14 January 1957), 249 (Dominican Republic).

[347] UNGA Third Committee, A/C.3/SR.733 (16 January 1957), 266 (Canada).

[348] UNGA Third Committee, A/C.3/SR.730 (14 January 1957), 250 (Spain).

was not entitled to the same protection under the Covenant and thus the position of second wives in some states could be adversely affected.[349]

On this issue, Article 10(1) does not specify the legal consequences where marriage involves coercion and thus violates the ICESCR. Presumably, the marriage is void and should be annulled, since divorce presupposes an initially valid marriage. While this would result in the release of a coerced wife from an invalid marriage, there is a risk that she may suffer legal prejudice in the division of matrimonial property and the like. It is important, therefore, that any dissolution of marriage, whether by divorce or annulment, is subject to the same guarantee of equality in the settlement of rights or interests acquired in the marriage, particularly where it endures for a period of time and produces deep connections.

During the drafting, Saudi Arabia thought the provision was unsatisfactory because it made 'no clear distinction between genuinely free consent and consent which was the result of persuasion'.[350] Although agreeing in principle that a woman should not be coerced into marriage against her will, it stated that 'customs varied…[and] [t]he text should apply to the greatest possible number of countries, whatever the divergences in their customs'.[351] The idea of 'persuasion' is, however, highly problematic in traditions where social, cultural, religious or patriarchal expectations of women deprive them of any meaningful choice to resist a suitor or an arranged marriage which parents have 'persuaded' them to enter.

There was little discussion in the drafting of who is entitled to marry, probably because of the assumption that marriage was a union between a man and woman. Article 23(2) of the ICCPR refers to the 'right of men and women of marriageable age to marry' and the HRC interpreted this, in *Joslin v New Zealand*, as confining marriage to a man and a woman:

> Given the existence of a specific provision in the Covenant on the right to marriage, any claim that this right has been violated must be considered in the light of this provision. Article 23, paragraph 2, of the Covenant is the only substantive provision in the Covenant which defines a right by using the term 'men and women', rather than 'every human being', 'everyone' and 'all persons'. Use of the term 'men and women', rather than the general terms used elsewhere in Part III of the Covenant, has been consistently and uniformly understood as indicating that the treaty obligation of States parties stemming from article 23, paragraph 2, of the Covenant is to recognize as marriage only the union between a man and a woman wishing to marry each other.[352]

That view has been criticized, not least because the text of Article 23(3) does not refer to the right of men and women to marry 'each other', 'one another' or 'only each other', but could equally be interpreted as a right to marry whomever a person of either gender wishes.

[349] UNGA Third Committee, A/C.3/SR.731 (15 January 1957), 253 (Thailand).
[350] UNGA Third Committee, A/C.3/SR.730 (14 January 1957), 249 (Saudi Arabia).
[351] UNGA Third Committee, A/C.3/SR.730 (14 January 1957), 249 (Saudi Arabia).
[352] *Joslin v New Zealand*, HRC Communication No. 902/1999 (30 July 2002), [8.2].

Significantly, Article 10(1) of the ICESCR refers to the free consent of 'intending spouses' and is not textually limited in the same way as the gender-specific language of the ICCPR. It is therefore open to a more liberal interpretation, so as to protect free consent to marriage by same-sex couples, although at the expense of consistency with its twin Covenant. All other protections in Article 10 as a whole do not turn, however, on the existence of a marriage, but rather a 'family', so whether or not same-sex partnerships (or de facto partnership) are recognized as marriage, or something lesser (like 'civil unions'), or not at all will be immaterial if a 'family' relationship still exists.

Ultimately, the protection of free consent to marriage in Article 10(1) of the ICESCR was very narrowly adopted.[353] It reinforces, but adds little, to the same protection in Article 23(3) of the ICCPR, the latter embedded in a suite of more comprehensive protections for marriage (including the right to marry in Article 23(2), and equality in marriage and during its dissolution in Article 23(4)).

Most pertinently, the socio-economic protections for the family, mothers and children in Article 10 of the ICESCR as a whole are not contingent on the existence of marriage, but turn instead on the concept of 'family', which (as discussed earlier) is not limited to marriage. Accordingly, the requirement of consent to marriage is largely decoupled from the substantive socio-economic rights arising under Article 10 and is somewhat redundant.

Perhaps for these reasons, the CESCR has seldom paid attention to this aspect of Article 10(1) in monitoring state reports, only occasionally criticizing arranged or forced child marriages.[354] Forced marriage can also interfere in a person's freedom to pursue other ICESCR rights, such as education and employment, where a wife is forced to stay at home.

The issue of forced marriage has been given more attention by the HRC under Article 23(3) of the ICCPR, and such practice may inform the approach by the CESCR in future. Key issues that have arisen include consent in the context of the minimum age for marriage; arranged marriages; victims of violence coerced into marriage; certain cultural or religious practices (including decision-making by guardians, wife inheritance, polygamy and religious restrictions on the freedom to marry); and the freedom to end a marriage.

Before turning to those issues, four other factors should be mentioned. First, consent is vitiated where a person is incapable of making an informed decision. While age is discussed separately below, other reasons may include mental incapacity, intoxication or narcosis.[355]

Secondly, false pretexts or fraud will vitiate consent to marriage, such as where one party makes misrepresentations as to their identity or other essential characteristics. This may include cases where a person is already married but refuses to

[353] By twenty-four votes to twenty-three, with eighteen abstentions: UNGA Third Committee Report, A/3525 (9 February 1957), 42.

[354] CESCR, Concluding Observation: Afghanistan, E/C.12/AFG/CO/2-4 (7 June 2010), [28]; see also Chad, E/C.12/TCD/CO/3 (16 December 2009), [19]; Colombia, E/C.12/COL/CO/5 (7 June 2010), [17].

[355] Eriksson, 'Family Rights', 119.

inform the new spouse, thus also entering into the new marriage in violation of national law.

Thirdly, other public interests may justify restrictions, such as public health-related prohibitions on the ability of close blood relatives ('consanguinity'[356]) to marry, or enforcement of laws against polygamy. However, health concerns cannot justify, for example, prohibiting people with certain diseases or disabilities from marrying, which would involve impermissible discrimination on the basis of disability or health (ie, 'other') status.

Fourthly, concepts of coercion and free consent—as in the context of the freedom to choose work discussed in an earlier chapter—are not generally assessed by reference to economic imperatives to marry. Particularly in developing states, an impoverished woman's 'choice' to marry can be overwhelmingly driven by the imperative to escape poverty, since marriage may bring relative economic security. The same imperative often drives child marriage. Coercion of circumstances, however—the fear of destitution—does not feature in a conventional analysis of 'free consent'. Only overt economic exploitation by marriage—such as the pledging of girls for economic gain[357]—has been condemned by the HRC.

Minimum age

Whether valid consent to marry can be given is affected by age. The ICESCR does not set a minimum age for marriage. In monitoring states, the CESCR was concerned, for example, that children can marry at 14 years with parental consent in Colombia (even though the legal minimum age is 18 years), which negatively impacts on children's rights to health and education.[358] It also noted the inconsistency between the age of maturity in Suriname (21 years) and the ages of marriage (15 for males and 13 for females), as well as the gender discrimination in the ages of marriage, which it held to infringe Articles 2(2) and 10 of the ICESCR and Articles 2 and 3 of the CROC.[359]

On minimum age, the HRC has observed in relation to Article 23 of the ICCPR:

> The Covenant does not establish a specific marriageable age either for men or for women, but that age should be such as to enable each of the intending spouses to give his or her free and full personal consent in a form and under conditions prescribed by law.[360]

The HRC has further called on states to set a minimum age for marriage 'on the basis of equal criteria for men and women' and which ensures 'women's capacity to make an informed and uncoerced decision'.[361] It has not, however, stipulated a

[356] CEDAW, General Recommendation No. 21: Equality in marriage and family relations (1994), [16].

[357] HRC, Concluding Observations: Zimbabwe, A/53/40 (1998), [214].

[358] CESCR, Concluding Observations: Colombia, E/C.12/COL/CO/5 (7 June 2010), [18].

[359] CESCR, Concluding Observations: Suriname, E/C.12/1995/6 (7 June 1995), [11].

[360] HRC, General Comment No. 19 (1990).

[361] HRC, General Comment No. 28 (2000), [24]; see also: HRC, Concluding Observations: Suriname, A/59/40 (2004), [69(18)]; Chile, A/54/50 (1999) 44, [217]; Syrian Arab Republic, A/56/40 (2001) 70, [81(20)].

universal minimum age, which varies in practice between states and among different religions and cultures.

Neither the CROC nor the CEDAW sets a minimum age for marriage. Article 16(1)(b) of the CEDAW provides only that states must guarantee the 'same right' as men to women to 'freely to choose a spouse and to enter into marriage only with their free and full consent'. The CROC nominates below the age of 18 years as the general meaning of 'child', 'unless under the law applicable to the child, majority is attained earlier' (Article 1), but in any case it does not prohibit 'child' marriage. The CROC requires that the child's views be taken into account in decisions affecting her or him, but also recognizes the general capacity of parents to give consent on behalf of the child in many areas.

The Convention on Consent to Marriage, Minimum Age for Marriage and Registration of Marriages 1964 requires 'full and free consent of both parties' to marriage (Article 1) and requires states to provide a minimum age in Article 2:

> States Parties to the present Convention shall take legislative action to specify a minimum age for marriage. No marriage shall be legally entered into by any person under this age, except where a competent authority has granted a dispensation as to age, for serious reasons, in the interest of the intending spouses.[362]

It does not, however, nominate the minimum age, and the Convention has only fifty-five parties. A General Assembly Recommendation on Consent to Marriage, Minimum Age for Marriage and Registration of Marriages of 1965 provides that the minimum age for marriage is 15 years,[363] but allows states 'dispensation as to age for serious reasons' and it is in any event a non-binding resolution. The strongest statement comes from the CEDAW Committee, which recommends 18 years as the minimum age for men and women to marry:

> 36. . . . the Committee considers that the minimum age for marriage should be 18 years for both man and woman. When men and women marry, they assume important responsibilities. Consequently, marriage should not be permitted before they have attained full maturity and capacity to act. According to the World Health Organization, when minors, particularly girls, marry and have children, their health can be adversely affected and their education is impeded. As a result their economic autonomy is restricted.
>
> 37. This not only affects women personally but also limits the development of their skills and independence and reduces access to employment, thereby detrimentally affecting their families and communities.[364]

[362] Convention on Consent to Marriage, Minimum Age for Marriage and Registration of Marriages (adopted 7 November 1962, 521 UNTS 231, entered into force 9 December 1964).

[363] UNGA Res. 2018 (XX) (1 November 1965), Principle II.

[364] CEDAW, General Recommendation No. 21: Equality in marriage and family relations (1994), [36].

Only in African regional law is 18 years stipulated as the legal minimum age of marriage, under Article 22(2) of the African Charter on the Rights and Welfare of the Child:

> Child marriage and the betrothal of girls and boys shall be prohibited and effective action, including legislation, shall be taken to specify the minimum age of marriage to be 18 years and make registration of all marriages in an official registry compulsory.[365]

The reluctance of the HRC or CESCR to stipulate a minimum age for marriage seems driven by both fidelity to the strict text (and drafting intention) of the twin Covenants, and a concern to accommodate cultural and developmental differences among states. However, there is arguably legal scope for more intensive and less 'gentle' supervision of states, following the CEDAW Committee's lead.

Child marriage is destructive of the coerced spouse's basic life chances and developmental opportunities, including numerous ICESCR rights. Not only are child brides often at risk of marital violence and abuse, but they are typically unable to exercise their rights to education and employment, which enable the fullest realization of human dignity. Gender stereotyping of girls as destined for a life in the home is perpetuated. A precautionary approach may thus be warranted in considering whether a child under 18 can genuinely 'consent' to marriage.

In terms of the scale of the problem, the United Nations estimates that 10 million girls under 18 years are married each year.[366] In South Asia, 46 per cent of girls under 18 are married, 38 per cent in sub-Saharan Africa, 29 per cent in Latin America and the Caribbean, and 18 per cent in the Middle East and North Africa.

Discrimination in the establishment of minimum ages to marriage is prohibited. The CEDAW Committee states that different minimum ages 'assume incorrectly that women have a different rate of intellectual development from men, or that their stage of physical and intellectual development at marriage is immaterial'.[367]

Arranged marriages

As noted above, in the drafting of Article 10 arranged marriage was criticized and both the CESCR and HRC have expressed concern about it.[368] It was, however, apparently accepted that a requirement of parental consent to the marriage of minors was permissible.[369] As noted above, the full and free personal consent of the intending spouse must always be given to marriage, even where a child below 18 years is involved. This rules out parental consent alone as the basis of a child's

[365] African Charter on the Rights and Welfare of the Child (adopted 11 July 1990, OAU Doc. CAB/LEG/24.9/49(1990), entered into force 29 November 1999), Article 21(2).

[366] Joint Statement by a Group of UN Human Rights Experts to Mark the First International Day of the Girl Child, Geneva, 11 October 2012; see also UNICEF, *Early Marriage: A Harmful Traditional Practice*, April 2005, 4.

[367] CEDAW Committee, General Recommendation No. 21 (1994), [38].

[368] HRC, Concluding Observations: Suriname, A/59/40 (2004), [69(18)]; see also Uganda, A/59/40 (2004), [70(23)]; Nigeria, A/51/40 (1996) 37, [291].

[369] Nowak, *CCPR Commentary*, 534–5.

consent. This is supported by Article 16(2) of the CEDAW, which provides that '[t]he betrothal and the marriage of a child shall have no legal effect'. The HRC has additionally criticized laws which give a male guardian a right to consent to an (adult) woman's marriage.[370] Such prohibition is also consistent with major religious traditions, including Islam.[371]

While arranged marriages will immediately raise issues of consent, it cannot be ruled out that some arranged marriages may comply with Article 10(1) of the ICESCR: a person may, for example, willingly agree to marry someone chosen by their parents, and as long as the person is free to decline without penalty, this may comply. This could be because the person is genuinely interested in the chosen spouse, or (culturally) values respect for the parents' decision more highly than their freedom to instead choose a 'love' marriage. A critical determinant will be whether the person is truly free to decline the arrangement without adverse consequences. As noted by a UN Special Rapporteur:

> A marriage imposed on a woman not by explicit force, but by subjecting her to relentless pressure and/or manipulation, often by telling her that her refusal of a suitor will harm her family's standing in the community, can also be understood as forced.[372]

A more difficult issue arises where a marriage originally entered into without consent can be 'cured' or rectified by subsequent consent *during* the marriage. Thus, an arranged marriage may initially be lacking consent, but the spouses later form the view over time that they wish to remain together. Technically, the marriage is invalid until such time as consent forms, but it may produce unnecessary hardship to legally annul the marriage prior to that time and require it to be reconstituted. Genuine subsequent consent may still be difficult to disentangle from considerations of convenience in remaining together, or cultural pressures to remain together, so as not to 'dishonour' parents or families.

Cultural practices surrounding arranged marriages may raise additional legal issues. Thus, the practice of 'dowry', which ascribes a proprietary value to women, involves impermissible gender discrimination.[373] Where an arranged marriage is forced, it may also breach international legal prohibitions on slavery, servitude and sexual violence.[374]

Victims of violence

The HRC has also criticized overt violent coercion to marry, such as the kidnapping of young women.[375] In addition, it has expressed concern about social

[370] HRC, General Comment No. 28 (2000), [23]; HRC, Concluding Observations: Yemen, A/60/40 (2005) 65, [91(21)]; Sudan, A/53/40 (1998) 22, [122]; Algeria, A/53/40 (1998) 52, [361].

[371] *Chaudhury and Kendra v Bangladesh et al*, 19 January 2009, Writ Petition No. 7977 of 2008, 29 BLD (HCD) 2009 (Supreme Court of Bangladesh, High Court Division), [34] ('in Islam marriage lacking in consent of the bride is not valid').

[372] Human Rights Council, Report on the Human Rights Aspects of the Victims of Trafficking in Persons, Especially Women and Children (Special Rapporteur Sigma Huda), A/HRC/4/23 (24 January 2007).

[373] Eriksson, 'Family Rights', 119.

[374] Eriksson, 'Family Rights', 120.

[375] HRC, Concluding Observations: Uzbekistan, A/60/40 (2005) 56, [89(24)].

attitudes that discriminate against victims of rape and put pressure on them to marry their rapist, or laws which extinguish or mitigate a rapist's criminal responsibility if he marries the victim:

24. Another factor that may affect women's right to marry only when they have given free and full consent is the existence of social attitudes which tend to marginalize women victims of rape and put pressure on them to agree to marriage. A woman's free and full consent to marriage may also be undermined by laws which allow the rapist to have his criminal responsibility extinguished or mitigated if he marries the victim. States parties should indicate whether marrying the victim extinguishes or mitigates criminal responsibility and, in the case in which the victim is a minor, whether the rape reduces the marriageable age of the victim, particularly in societies where rape victims have to endure marginalization from society.[376]

Other cultural or religious practices

A range of cultural or religious practices affects the freedom to marry or consent to it. The HRC has criticized 'wife inheritance', such as where a widow is inherited by the deceased husband's brother or cousin,[377] either automatically (a 'levirate' marriage) or on the decision of the family. For similar reasons, the Yemeni practice of 'swap marriage', where the brother of the bride marries the sister of the groom, to avoid paying expensive bride prices, may raise issues of consent and family or social coercion.

Discriminatory restrictions on a woman's right to remarry, which are not imposed on men, have been criticized by the HRC[378] and may raise issues under Article 10 of the ICESCR. An example is a Japanese legal prohibition on the right of women to remarry for six months following the dissolution or annulment of her marriage.[379]

Religious or cultural restrictions may impair a person's freedom to choose who they marry, such as where a woman of a particular religion is not permitted to marry an atheist or a person of another religion.[380] Such was the case with Islam as applied in Morocco,[381] but a similar rule exists in some Orthodox Jewish practice. In such cases, religious rights cannot be invoked to destroy the freedom to choose whom to marry.[382]

The HRC has also held that polygamy, as is still practised under certain customary or religious laws,[383] is 'incompatible' with the principle of equality of treatment in the right to marry and should be abolished: 'Polygamy violates the

[376] HRC, General Comment No. 28 (2000), [24]; see also HRC, Concluding Observations: Guatemala, A/56/40 (2001) 93, [85(24)].

[377] HRC, Concluding Observations: Kenya, A/60/40 (2005) 44, [86(10)]; see also Mali, A/58/40 (2003), [81(10)].

[378] HRC, General Comment No. 28 (2000), [24].

[379] HRC, Concluding Observations: Japan, A/54/40 (1999) 36, [147].

[380] HRC, General Comment No. 28 (2000), [24].

[381] HRC, Concluding Observations: Morocco, A/60/40 (2004), [84(27)]. Such restriction applies in Islam generally: see Baderin, *IHR and Islam*, 144–6.

[382] See the prohibition on abuse of rights in ICESCR, Article 5(1).

[383] In Islam, see Baderin, *IHR and Islam*, 138–44.

dignity of women. It is an inadmissible discrimination against women.'[384] The CEDAW Committee also sees polygamy as contrary to gender equality:

> 14. States parties' reports also disclose that polygamy is practised in a number of countries. Polygamous marriage contravenes a woman's right to equality with men, and can have such serious emotional and financial consequences for her and her dependents that such marriages ought to be discouraged and prohibited. The Committee notes with concern that some States parties, whose constitutions guarantee equal rights, permit polygamous marriage in accordance with personal or customary law. This violates the constitutional rights of women, and breaches the provisions of article 5(a) of the [CEDAW] Convention.[385]

In practice, polygamy involves a man with multiple wives; there appear to be few cases where a woman is permitted to take multiple husbands. The treaty bodies oppose it on the basis of gender discrimination rather than an absence of free consent; the assumption appears to be that a woman's consent is vitiated by the discriminatory effect of the practice, even if she 'freely' enters into it in the absence of coercion.

In principle, if polygamy were available without discrimination—so that a woman could take multiple husbands (polyandry)—the problem of direct discrimination and indignity disappears. There may still arise indirect discrimination against women in practice if mainly men take up multiple spouses or social pressure vitiates the consent of women.

FREEDOM TO END MARRIAGE

While marriage must be 'entered into' based on free consent, Article 10 does not explicitly provide that free consent must persist throughout the duration of the marriage for it to remain valid. Strictly speaking, the right to freely marry does not imply a right to withdraw consent and thereby to terminate the marriage; there is no automatic 'right to divorce' as such. The right to marry is also not a right to remarry at the expense of an existing marriage.

At a minimum, however, *absolute* legal prohibitions on divorce, based on the 'dogma' of the indissolubility of marriage (after initial consent to it), are regarded as incompatible with Articles 17 and 23 of the ICCPR[386] and by extension Article 10 of the ICESCR. This contrasts with the right to marry under Article 12 of the ECHR, the different language of which has been interpreted as permitting a state to forbid divorce by law.[387]

If, however, a state permits divorce, it cannot impose unreasonable restrictions upon it under the ECHR, such as where a prohibition on remarriage for up to three years by the spouse 'at fault' in a divorce (because of adultery) is disproportionate to the aim of protecting marriage and the rights of others.[388] The CESCR

[384] HRC, General Comment No. 28 (2000), [24].
[385] CEDAW Committee, General Recommendation No. 21 (1994), [14].
[386] Nowak, *CCPR Commentary*, 531.
[387] *Johnston v Ireland* (App. 9697/82), 18 December 1986, (1987) 9 EHRR 203, [52].
[388] *F v Switzerland* (App. 11329/85), 18 December 1987, (1987) 10 EHRR 411.

criticized discrimination in Philippine divorce laws as between Muslim provinces (subject to Sharia law) and other parts of the country (where divorce is legally forbidden), and stated that civil marriage and divorce should leave to individuals the duties that their religion imposes.[389]

Beyond the terrain of absolute prohibitions on divorce, it is unclear what restrictions on the availability of divorce are permissible under the ICESCR or ICCPR. It has been suggested, for example, that restrictions may be necessary to protect a spouse or child.[390] Religious laws which permitted the dissolution of a marriage solely on the basis that a woman is infertile, or not a virgin, would involve gender discrimination and be incompatible with Article 10.

However, in many cases, it is difficult to see how forcing a person to remain in a marriage which they wish to leave is in the interests of that person, their children, the spouse who wishes to preserve a loveless or dysfunctional marriage, or the marriage itself. Coercion is hardly a basis for a happy marriage or family life. It is also inconsistent with the underlying purpose of human rights to respect the autonomy and dignity of the individual. A marriage is the sum of its human parts and has little value independent of the spouses' mutual interests. The marriage itself enjoys no 'right' of indissolubility or absolute state duty of protection, particularly since the 'family' is decoupled from marriage under Article 10.

A better approach is to regard the right to enter into marriage based on free consent as including a right to give continuing consent to the marriage; when consent is withdrawn, a correlative right to divorce arises. This approach also has the advantage of avoiding acrimonious and emotionally damaging legal disputes surrounding 'fault-based divorce', which pits spouses against each other, unnecessarily publicizes private difficulties, invites evidentiary contestation about highly personal behaviour, and stigmatizes marriage 'failure'.

Restrictions on the substantive grounds of divorce may be distinguished from procedural restrictions. Many states impose requirements on couples contemplating divorce to verify the certainty of their decision, such as through marriage counselling or mediation, or waiting periods, prior to the legal finalization of the divorce. Such procedures may temporarily restrict a person's freedom to immediately end a marriage, but ultimately serve the purpose of discerning a person's true choice while ensuring they give due consideration to whether the marriage is salvageable.

Importantly, a state must guarantee equality and non-discrimination upon the dissolution of a marriage under Article 23(4) of the ICCPR, and such protections are implicit in the duty of states under Article 10(1) and (3) of the ICESCR to protect any 'family' or 'children' after the marriage's dissolution. According to the HRC:

> 9. Thus, any discriminatory treatment in regard to the grounds and procedures for separation or divorce, child custody, maintenance or alimony, visiting rights or the loss or

[389] CESCR, Concluding Observations: Philippines, E/C.12/1995 (7 June 1995), [11].
[390] Nowak, *CCPR Commentary*, 531.

recovery of parental authority must be prohibited, bearing in mind the paramount interest of the children in this connection. States parties should, in particular, include information in their reports concerning the provision made for the necessary protection of any children at the dissolution of a marriage or on the separation of the spouses.[391]

The HRC has also addressed discriminatory customary laws relating to divorce, property, inheritance and succession.[392]

Article 10(2): Protection of Mothers relating to Childbirth

Article 10(2) as a whole provides that:

Special protection should be accorded to mothers during a reasonable period before and after childbirth. During such period working mothers should be accorded paid leave or leave with adequate social security benefits.

PROTECTION OF MOTHERS GENERALLY

The first sentence of Article 10(2) provides that '[s]pecial protection should be accorded to mothers during a reasonable period before and after childbirth'. In the drafting there was some discussion about the object of protection. The original text required protection for 'motherhood' and 'maternity',[393] but this was rejected for a less 'abstract'[394] requirement to protect 'mothers'.[395] The choice of the term 'mothers' indicates that protection was not strictly limited to the period of physical maternity narrowly defined (that is, carrying a child).

At the same time, the textual reference to 'childbirth' appears to confine the protection to 'natural' mothers, in the orthodox sense of those who physically give birth. Indonesia mentioned, for instance, that 'biological differences' justify certain distinctions.[396] It thus appears to exclude not only other parents (such as fathers or same-sex female partners who did not give birth), but also *social* 'mothers'. Adopted mothers, foster mothers, those who mother children arising from surrogacy or same-sex male parents are examples of different parenting and family relationships which seem to be excluded by the strict language of Article 10(2), unless the connection to 'childbirth' is interpreted liberally, or practice evolves to de-emphasize the necessity of that connection.

Plainly, the physical act of carrying a child and giving birth differentiates 'social' mothers from 'birth' mothers. The provision does not require the protection of 'parents' (ie, including fathers) and was thus deliberately aimed at the distinctive

391 HRC, General Comment No. 19 (1990), [9].

392 HRC, Concluding Observations: Togo, A/58/40 (2002), [78(21)]); Mali, A/58/40 (2003), [81(10)].

393 UNGA Third Committee Report, A/3525 (9 February 1957), 32.

394 UNGA Third Committee, A/C.3/SR.563, 99 (25 October 1954) (Saudi Arabia).

395 As recommended by Saudi Arabia and Uruguay: UNGA Third Committee Report, A/3525 (9 February 1957), 33–4.

396 UNGA Third Committee, A/C.3/SR.731 (15 January 1957), 266 (Indonesia).

physical experience and needs of those who give birth. However, it can also be argued that at least some of the human rights rationale of the provision should extend to other 'mothers' or primary carers (of any gender), who may require assistance in establishing a new child within a family, whether in the form of financial assistance, information and education, or measures of social support.

As alluded to already, there was considerable debate in the drafting about the duration of protection. Some states proposed that it should cover the extensive period that mothers are 'responsible for the care and education of dependent children'.[397] By contrast, other states preferred that protection be 'limited to a period around childbirth'.[398] Saudi Arabia was concerned that a mother 'might continue to receive social security benefits until she was eligible for an old-age pension' if 'assistance' was required until the youngest child was no longer 'dependent'.[399] Some states argued that women should not receive 'undue' protection, but only what is necessary to ensure equal protection with men.[400]

The more significant debate centred on the nature of protection required. States advocating wide protection thought that 'mothers should be accorded special rights, to enable them to provide for the proper physical care, upbringing and education of their children'.[401] There was a tendency to assume that it was the primary role of the mother to care for her child, evident in Yugoslavia's view that 'women had a very special part to play… in the home', [402] and Czechoslovakia's view that 'the mother's care of her child was as important socially as the father's professional activity'.[403]

However, the contrary view expressed was that affording women an 'undue measure of protection'[404] may 'paradoxically'[405] be counterproductive to the advancement of women, and 'detrimental to her status in society as an equal to men'.[406] It was felt that the care and education of children should not be assumed to be the sole responsibility of the mother.[407] France forcefully advocated for a narrower scope of protection, arguing that:

> … by discarding the vague idea of long-term protection and confining itself to the technical problem of pre-natal and post-natal benefits, it was based on a proper understanding of the role of women, who were not so much interested in receiving condescending protection as in enjoying rights equal to those enjoyed by men.[408]

[397] UNGA Third Committee Report, A/3525 (9 February 1957), 36; see, eg, UNGA Third Committee, A/C.3/SR.736 (21 January 1957), 277 (Chile); A/C.3/SR.735 (21 January 1957), 275 (Romania).
[398] UNGA Third Committee, A/C.3/SR.737 (22 January 1957), 283 (Sweden).
[399] UNGA Third Committee, A/C.3/SR.735 (21 January 1957), 273 (Saudi Arabia).
[400] UNGA Third Committee, A/C.3/SR.736 (21 January 1957), 277 (El Salvador).
[401] UNGA Third Committee, A/C.3/SR.735 (21 January 1957), 275 (Romania).
[402] UNGA Third Committee, A/C.3/SR.731 (15 January 1957), 255 (Yugoslavia).
[403] UNGA Third Committee, A/C.3/SR.736 (21 January 1957), 278 (Czechoslovakia).
[404] UNGA Third Committee, A/C.3/SR.736 (21 January 1957), 277 (El Salvador).
[405] UNGA Third Committee, A/C.3/SR.575 (5 November 1954), 164 (Dominican Republic).
[406] UNGA Third Committee, A/C.3/SR.738 (23 January 1957), 291 (Sweden).
[407] UNGA Third Committee Report, A/3525 (9 February 1957), 38.
[408] UNGA Third Committee, A/C.3/SR.737 (22 January 1957), 283 (France).

The Dominican Republic likewise argued that broader protection may 'place women under a system of permanent protection which would be detrimental to their family life and would limit their employment opportunities'.[409] The protection of Article 10(2) was ultimately confined to 'a reasonable period before and after childbirth'.[410]

The CESCR has not thus far addressed what is a 'reasonable' period. The period before childbirth is necessarily confined by the natural duration of gestation, typically around nine months. A 'reasonable' period after childbirth is far more open ended, and could be defined in various ways: the duration of maternity leave (at least twelve weeks and preferably fourteen weeks) under international law;[411] by the child's age (say, until 1, 2 or 3 years, and so on); or by other common markers of the child's social maturity (such as the commencement of primary school at age 5 or 6 years, high school at 12 or 13 years, or adulthood at 18 years).

Given that the text of the provision pegs protection to a period around 'childbirth', rather than mentioning broader parenting or family responsibilities, it is unlikely that Article 10(2) requires states to provide special protection for longer or ongoing periods. In addition, it may be that the further the distance from childbirth, the lesser protection is owed. It should be emphasized, however, even after a 'reasonable' period mothers will still enjoy the same autonomous right as others to social security under Article 9 of the ICESCR, and the special protection of children and young persons under Article 10(3) of the ICESCR is ongoing and not confined by the period surrounding their birth.

In monitoring states, the CESCR has seldom addressed the obligation on states to provide special protection for mothers in the first sentence of Article 10(2), and has instead focused on the protection of *working* mothers under the second sentence. One issue it has addressed, however, is abortion. The CESCR has expressed concern at the high rates of abortion in some states,[412] which it suggested arises from inadequate sexual and reproductive health services[413] and family planning programmes.[414] It also disapproved of the criminalization of abortions when a mother's life is at risk or when the pregnancy was the result of rape or incest,[415] noting in particular the risk of death by clandestine abortions.[416]

[409] UNGA Third Committee, A/C.3/SR.738 (23 January 1957), 292 (Dominican Republic).

[410] By fifty-one votes to eight, with six abstentions: UNGA Third Committee Report, A/3525 (9 February 1957), 43.

[411] ILO Convention No. 3 concerning the Employment of Women before and after Childbirth (adopted 29 November 1919, entered into force 13 June 1921).

[412] CESCR, Concluding Observations: Armenia, E/C.12/1/Add.39 (8 December 1999), [15]; China (including Hong Kong and Macao), E/C.12/1/Add.107 (13 May 2005), [18] (particularly of girls); Netherlands Antilles, E/C.12/NLD/CO/3/Add.1 (31 January 2008), [20].

[413] CESCR, Concluding Observations: Kazakhstan, E/C.12/KAZ/CO/1 (7 June 2010), [33].

[414] CESCR, Concluding Observations: Armenia, E/C.12/1/Add.39 (8 December 1999), [15]; Nicaragua, E/C.12/NIC/CO/4 (28 November 2008), [26].

[415] CESCR, Concluding Observations: Mauritius, E/C.12/MUS/CO/4 (8 June 2010), [25]; Nicaragua, E/C.12/NIC/CO/4 (28 November 2008), [26].

[416] CESCR, Concluding Observations: Nicaragua, E/C.12/NIC/CO/4 (28 November 2008), [27]; Poland, E/C.12/POL/CO/5 (2 December 2009), [28].

The right to health under Article 12 of the ICESCR already provides a comprehensive legal basis for the health needs of women before, during and after childbirth.[417] In addition, Article 12(2) of the CEDAW specifically requires states to provide 'appropriate services in connection with pregnancy, confinement and the post-natal period, granting free services where necessary, as well as adequate nutrition during pregnancy and lactation', which in turn may help to define the scope of Article 12 of the ICESCR in respect of mothers.

Given that Article 12 already covers the field of women's health (including the medical, psycho-social and legal aspects of abortion, or the practices of forced sterilization or forced pregnancies), the residual protection of Article 10 may be better understood as addressing the social and economic needs of mothers. Further, since Article 10(2) focuses on the protection of mothers in relation to children born or soon to be born, it does not extend to the antecedent issue (separately covered by Article 10(1)) of family planning and reproductive choice, which concerns a woman's right to decide whether and when to have children.[418]

A range of measures of protection may be envisaged under Article 10(2). First, where a non-working mother faces financial need, income support payments may be necessary. Such needs may arise, for instance, where a mother was not previously working and receives no work-related maternity benefits (which is separately addressed by the second sentence of Article 10(2)); is a single mother; or is otherwise in a low income family.

Universal income support is ordinarily provided through the right to social security in Article 9 of the ICESCR. However, where universal support is not yet available for resource reasons under Article 9, the effect of Article 10, in requiring states to give 'special protection' to mothers, may be to prioritize them for social security assistance which would not otherwise be provided.

Secondly, Article 10(2) read in conjunction with Articles 2(2) and 3 of the ICESCR ensures that mothers are entitled to equality in decision-making and responsibilities concerning children, parenting and the family, such as all aspects of how to care for and raise a child. Reference may be made here to the principle in Article 5(b) of the CEDAW, which requires that 'family education' measures must include:

> ...a proper understanding of maternity as a social function and the recognition of the common responsibility of men and women in the upbringing and development of their children, it being understood that the interest of the children is the primordial consideration in all cases.

[417] Article 12(2)(b) also requires states to provide 'for the reduction of the stillbirth-rate and of infant mortality and for the healthy development of the child', although it does not mention the special needs of mothers themselves.

[418] Family planning is an element of health rights under Article 12 of the ICESCR; and various provisions of the CEDAW specify the right of women to access information about family planning: Articles 10(h), 14(2)(b) and 16(1)(e); see also General Recommendation No. 21: Equality in marriage and family relations (1994), [21]–[23].

Thirdly, various forms of social support for mothers can be provided by the state. This could include information and education about parenting skills in caring for children (not limited to the health aspects covered by Article 12), telephone helplines or internet services, 'mothers' groups' (or parents' groups) for meeting other new mothers or other initiatives which address the social dimensions of adjusting to new motherhood.

There are many innovative measures evident in state practice, including the post-war Finnish 'baby box' given to new mothers and containing items such as bodysuits, a sleeping bag, outdoor wear, bathing products, nappies, bedding and a mattress, and the cardboard box itself can serve as a bed.[419] In Australia, a 'baby bonus' was paid to assist families with the cost of a new child, although it was criticized for being both excessively large and not means-tested. While childcare is normally related to a parent's working needs, it may be appropriate for non-working mothers in some cases, for instance where a single mother needs a periodic rest.

Regionally, under Article 30 of the African Charter on the Rights and Welfare of the Child, states are required to take special measures to protect mothers who have been accused of or found guilty of crimes, to preserve relationships with their children:

1. States Parties to the present Charter shall undertake to provide special treatment to expectant mothers and to mothers of infants and young children who have been accused or found guilty of infringing the penal law and shall in particular:

   (a) ensure that a non-custodial sentence will always be first considered when sentencing such mothers;

   (b) establish and promote measures alternative to institutional confinement for the treatment of such mothers;

   (c) establish special alternative institutions for holding such mothers;

   (d) ensure that a mother shall not be imprisoned with her child;

   (e) ensure that a death sentence shall not be imposed on such mothers;

   (f) the essential aim of the penitentiary system will be the reformation, the integration of the mother to the family and social rehabilitation.

As will be apparent, while the biological aspect of giving birth is unique, many measures of social support could apply equally to new parents regardless of gender or physical motherhood. Other forms of state support, such as family tax benefits or social security support, typically address the needs of the family as a whole, particularly as social safety nets progressively expand. The special needs of women around birth remain, however, distinctive.

PROTECTION OF WORKING MOTHERS

The second sentence of Article 10(2) provides that working mothers should be accorded paid leave or leave with adequate social security benefits, during the

419 Helen Lee, 'Why Finnish Babies Sleep in Cardboard Boxes', BBC News, 4 June 2013.

period mentioned in the first sentence ('a reasonable period before and after childbirth'). This aspect of Article 10(2) has been the primary focus of the CESCR's attention. The protection contributes to the health and well-being of mothers and children and helps to reconcile work and family life. It would appear, however, to exclude social assistance for 'housewives'.[420]

The work rights in the ICESCR (Articles 6 to 8) do not specifically mention maternity, although aspects of it arise in the areas of non-discrimination and unfair dismissal (Article 6)[421] and suitable conditions of work (Article 7). Likewise, the right to social security does not explicitly refer to maternity, but by virtue of state practice, ILO standards and the CESCR's approach, it is understood to incorporate paid maternity leave and benefits.[422] This aspect of Article 10(2) may be properly understood as a specific iteration of the general right under Article 9.

The provision generated considerable debate during the drafting. Most states agreed that financial assistance should be provided to working mothers. However, there was disagreement on whether the mechanism to achieve it (particularly paid leave) should be specified or whether 'the solution... should be left to be determined in the manner appropriate to the circumstances in each state'.[423]

Opposition emanated mainly from states that provided protection for mothers through social security or insurance schemes,[424] rather than by obligations on employers. The USSR sought to specify that 'paid leave' was to be 'at the expense of the State or the employer'.[425] Two objections were raised. First, as the method of financing maternity leave varied between states,[426] it was inappropriate to require states to alter existing schemes.[427] Many states supported 'tripartite' funding,[428] which includes worker contributions. The debate thus mirrored the concerns relating to social security in Article 9 of the ICESCR.

Secondly, some states argued that if employers were made to pay a larger share of the costs of maternity benefits they may be reluctant to employ female staff, ultimately prejudicing, not advancing, women's interests.[429] The ILO agreed.[430] It was noted that ILO Convention No. 103 on Maternity Protection recognized that employers should not be liable for paying it.[431] The Soviet amendment was rejected.[432]

420 UNGA Third Committee, A/C.3/SR.737 (22 January 1957), 290 (Sweden).
421 See also CEDAW, Article 11(2)(a).
422 CESCR, General Comment No. 19 (2008), [19].
423 UNGA Third Committee, A/C.3/SR.733 (16 January 1957), 265 (Canada).
424 Eg, UNGA Third Committee, A/C.3/SR.730 (14 January 1957), 248 (United Kingdom); A/C.3/SR.735 (21 January 1957), 273 (Sweden); A/C.3/SR.735 (21 January 1957), 273 (New Zealand); A/C.3/SR.735 (21 January 1957), 274 (Denmark).
425 UNGA Third Committee Report, A/3525 (9 February 1957), 44.
426 UNGA Third Committee, A/C.3/SR.731 (15 January 1957), 254 (El Salvador); A/C.3/SR.731 (15 January 1957), 255 (Yugoslavia).
427 UNGA Third Committee, A/C.3/SR.733 (16 January 1957), 265 (Brazil).
428 UNGA Third Committee, A/C.3/SR.732 (16 January 1957), 260 (Pakistan).
429 UNGA Third Committee, A/C.3/SR.730 (14 January 1957), 251 (Uruguay); A/C.3/SR.732 (16 January 1957), 260 (Sweden); A/C.3/SR.735 (21 January 1957), 271 (Israel).
430 UNGA Third Committee, A/C.3/SR.733 (16 January 1957), 265 (ILO).
431 UNGA Third Committee Report, A/3525 (9 February 1957), 39.
432 By thirty-seven votes to ten, with fourteen abstentions: UNGA Third Committee Report, A/3525 (9 February 1957), 44.

The other key debate in the drafting was whether the more extensive protections for working mothers should be expressly articulated. Thus, the '[m]ention of paid leave alone without any reference to other maternity benefits might not serve the Committee's purpose'.[433] Forms of protection suggested included: childcare;[434] guarantees against dismissal;[435] non-penalization in calculating retirement benefits;[436] prohibition of night work;[437] lighter work at the same pay;[438] nursing breaks;[439] and medical care (including antenatal care, hospitalization and medical care during confinement, and post-natal care).[440]

The compromise was to include 'leave with adequate social security benefits' as an alternative to 'paid leave',[441] which could encompass a variety of measures. Many of the above-mentioned measures are, in any case, covered by other ICESCR provisions. Thus, unfair dismissal comes within the right to work in Article 6 and equality guarantees in Articles 2(2) and 3; and conditions of work are governed by Article 7. Aside from maternity leave and benefits, however, other forms of state support for working mothers may be envisaged, such as adjusting school hours to enable mothers to work full-time.

In monitoring states, the CESCR has occasionally commented on the inadequacy of paid maternity leave schemes under Article 10(2).[442] Concern was expressed about schemes which make benefits dependent on marital status.[443] The CESCR has also advocated: broader policy outcomes to assist men and women to reconcile professional and family life,[444] including by increasing the capacity of childcare facilities;[445] funding training measures to facilitate the re-entry of women into the labour market following parental leave;[446] and creating incentives for the use of parental leave by fathers.[447]

In this regard, the CESCR appears to have been influenced by Article 11(2)(c) of the CEDAW, which widens the issue of maternity protection by asking states

[433] UNGA Third Committee, A/C.3/SR.735 (21 January 1957), 272 (Iraq); see also A/C.3/SR.736 (21 January 1957), 279 (United Kingdom).

[434] UNGA Third Committee, A/C.3/SR.731 (15 January 1957), 255 (Yugoslavia).

[435] UNGA Third Committee, A/C.3/SR.731 (15 January 1957), 255 (Yugoslavia).

[436] UNGA Third Committee, A/C.3/SR.736 (21 January 1957), 278 (Czechoslovakia).

[437] UNGA Third Committee, A/C.3/SR.731 (15 January 1957), 256 (Byelorussian Soviet Socialist Republic).

[438] UNGA Third Committee, A/C.3/SR.731 (15 January 1957), 256 (Byelorussian Soviet Socialist Republic).

[439] UNGA Third Committee, A/C.3/SR.731 (15 January 1957), 256 (Byelorussian Soviet Socialist Republic).

[440] UNGA Third Committee, A/C.3/SR.730 (14 January 1957), 248 (United Kingdom); A/C.3/SR.733 (16 January 1957), 265 (ILO).

[441] Proposed by Denmark: UNGA Third Committee Report, A/3525 (9 February 1957), 44. The amendment was adopted by twenty-eight votes to twelve, with twenty-two abstentions.

[442] CESCR, Concluding Observations: Mauritius, E/C.12/MUS/CO/4 (8 June 2010), [21]; Saint Vincent and the Grenadines, E/C.12/1/Add.21 (2 December 1997), [21].

[443] CESCR, Concluding Observations: Mauritius, E/C.12/MUS/CO/4 (8 June 2010), [23].

[444] CESCR, Concluding Observations: Austria, E/C.12/AUT/CO/3 (25 January 2006), [26].

[445] CESCR, Concluding Observations: Austria, E/C.12/AUT/CO/3 (25 January 2006), [26]; Germany, E/C.12/1/Add.68 (24 September 2001), [44].

[446] CESCR, Concluding Observations: Austria, E/C.12/AUT/CO/3 (25 January 2006), [26].

[447] CESCR, Concluding Observations: Austria, E/C.12/AUT/CO/3 (25 January 2006), [26].

to take measures to address broader concerns about equality in the family and in work:

> To encourage the provision of the necessary supporting social services to enable parents to combine family obligations with work responsibilities and participation in public life, in particular through promoting the establishment and development of a network of child-care facilities…

As noted above, the CESCR has also defined the scope of the right to social security in Article 9 by reference to the maternity requirements of Article 10(2):

> 19. Article 10 of the Covenant expressly provides that 'working mothers should be accorded paid leave or leave with adequate social security benefits'. Paid maternity leave should be granted to all women, including those involved in atypical work, and benefits should be provided for an adequate period. Appropriate medical benefits should be provided for women and children, including perinatal, childbirth and postnatal care and care in hospital where necessary.[448]

The health dimensions of maternity are already addressed by Article 12 of the ICESCR, although the linkage to Articles 9 and 10 emphasizes the state's duty to finance such measures.

The free-standing position of maternity rights in Article 10(2) of the ICESCR also points to the underlying conceptual tension surrounding whether maternity leave is a work right, a social security entitlement or a hybrid of both. Its characterization has implications for both the quantum of benefits and who pays for them. The purpose of paid maternity leave is to enable women to have children without prejudicing their employment position, but it also enables the social benefit of maintaining society's demographic renewal.

If maternity benefit is a work right, a woman may expect to be paid at her full wage for the period of leave. This will be more advantageous to women on high incomes compared with low incomes, particularly if the latter are below average wage levels. It may be less appealing to employers who must recruit a replacement worker for the period of maternity and thus pay two wages for one position. It will also be more costly to the state if it bears responsibility for funding it. There are, however, economic dividends in paying maternity leave at a true wage replacement rate, such as the retention of skilled workers. It also accords full value to the woman's forgone wages and thus does not discourage wealthier women from having children.

If maternity benefit is instead regarded as a social security benefit, it will often be pegged to average wage levels and thus advantage women on lower incomes and disadvantage women on higher incomes. Social security is typically designed as a safety net for the poor rather than as a system to subsidize high earners. It may be attractive to employers, however, because governments then commonly subsidize worker benefits, which is precisely why it can be less attractive to governments. For these reasons, funding of maternity leave is often shared between

[448] CESCR, General Comment No. 19 (2008), [19].

insurance contributions and publicly-funded social security, reflecting its hybrid purposes and a balancing of burdens between the worker, the state and sometimes the employer.

ILO standards on maternity protection

Historically, maternity leave has bridged work and social security rights. As early as 1919, the ILO adopted Convention No. 3 on Maternity Protection,[449] followed by Convention No. 103 on Maternity Protection of 1952[450] and Convention No. 183 of 2000.[451] Convention No. 102 on Social Security (Minimum Standards) of 1952 also addresses maternity benefits.[452] The key legal issues concern the duration, amount and nature of benefits, and the funding of benefits, each discussed below.

The ILO standards may assist in identifying minimum standards for maternity leave and benefits under Article 10(2) of the ICESCR. While the level of ratification of the ILO conventions is admittedly low (comprising less than one-quarter of states), their standards have influenced wider state practice, even if there remains diversity between states in their consistency with ILO standards and in respect of different indicators. Forms of leave which are complementary to maternity leave, also assisting in family/work balance, were discussed earlier, including paternity, parental and adoption leave.

Duration of maternity leave

Convention No. 3 provided for a total claimable period of twelve weeks' maternity leave (six weeks before 'confinement' and six afterwards).[453] The period was increased to a *minimum* of twelve weeks' paid leave in Convention Nos. 103 and 102, and fourteen weeks under the most recent Convention, No. 183.[454] The European Social Charter 1961 likewise establishes a minimum of twelve weeks, raised to fourteen weeks under the Revised European Social Charter 1996.[455] The non-binding ILO Recommendation No. 191 of 2000 suggests a minimum of eighteen weeks.[456]

It may be expected that the minimum duration of maternity leave may increase in line with progressive economic development, although there inevitably comes

[449] ILO Convention No. 3 concerning the Employment of Women before and after Childbirth (adopted 29 November 1919, entered into force 13 June 1921).

[450] ILO Convention No. 103 concerning Maternity Protection (Revised) (adopted 28 June 1952, entered into force 7 September 1955) (forty-one ratifications, seventeen denunciations).

[451] ILO Convention No. 183 concerning the revision of the Maternity Protection Convention (Revised) (adopted 15 June 2000, entered into force 7 February 2002) (twenty-eight ratifications).

[452] ILO Convention No. 102 on Social Security (Minimum Standards) (adopted 28 June 1952, entered into force 27 April 1955) (forty-nine ratifications).

[453] Article 3(a) and (b).

[454] ILO Convention No. 103, Article 3(2); No. 102, Article 52; No. 183, Article 4(1).

[455] Article 8(1) of both Charters.

[456] ILO Recommendation No. 191 concerning the revision of the Maternity Protection Recommendation 1952 (adopted 15 June 2000), [1].

a point where maternity leave (namely, leave related to childbirth or a new child) ends and other forms of subsequent support begin (such as family benefits, child support, parental leave and so on).

Amount and nature of benefits

Maternity benefits typically take the form of cash payments and health services. In early ILO Convention No. 3, there was no minimum rate of benefit specified other than that the payment to the mother had to be 'sufficient for the full and healthy maintenance of herself and her child, provided either out of public funds or by means of a system of insurance, the exact amount of which shall be determined by the competent authority in each country'.[457] A similar approach was adopted in Convention No. 103.

By contrast, Convention No. 102 on Social Security provided for a minimum payment corresponding to 45 per cent of the reference wage (usually, the average male breadwinner).[458] This was increased by Convention No. 183, which requires cash benefits to be paid at a minimum of two-thirds of the woman's previous earnings, and always 'at a level which ensures that the woman can maintain herself and her child in proper conditions of health and with a suitable standard of living' (Article 6(3) and (2)). Any qualifying periods must be capable of being satisfied by a large majority of women to whom the Convention applies (Article 6(5)). Women who do not qualify must remain entitled to receive ordinary social assistance (Article 6(6)). Recommendation No. 191 encourages states to pay higher benefits at the full rate of the woman's previous earnings (paragraph 2).

The Convention also provides for health benefits for mother and child, including prenatal, childbirth and post-natal care, as well as hospitalization care when necessary (Article 6(7)). Similar protection for maternal health is found in Article 49 of ILO Convention No. 102 on Social Security, for the purpose of 'maintaining, restoring or improving the health of the woman protected and her ability to work and to attend to her personal needs'. Maternal and child health are in any event separately covered by the right to health under the ICESCR.

Funding of benefits

Under Article 6(8) of Convention No. 183, benefits are to be funded by compulsory social insurance or public funds, and employers are not liable to fund benefits unless provided for by national law prior to the adoption of the Convention, or by tripartite agreement. The presumption against employer liability for the costs of maternity benefits is designed to remove an incentive for gender discrimination on the basis of maternity. If employers are required to pay the costs of maternity leave, discrimination against women is more likely.[459]

457 ILO Convention No. 3, Article 3(c).
458 ILO Convention No. 102, Articles 50 and 65 or 66.
459 ILO, *Maternity at Work*, 23.

In developed economies, including in the European Union, maternity benefits were paid by social security in 84 per cent of states by 2010.[460] This means that 'social security' is not conceived of as limited to assisting the poor, but encompasses redistribution of general revenue also to women on high incomes (and regardless of means), in pursuit of the different public interest in gender equity and non-discrimination. Employer liability is still the most common source of funding in Africa, Asia, the Pacific and the Middle East.[461]

Coverage

The coverage of ILO standards has gradually expanded over time. Convention No. 3 only covers women working in public or private industrial or commercial undertakings, while Convention No. 103 extends coverage to non-industrial and agricultural occupations. Convention No. 183 now applies maternity leave to all employed women. Convention No. 102 on Social Security permits states to choose a preferred approach to coverage from a number of alternatives set out in Article 48:

The persons protected shall comprise—

(a) all women in prescribed classes of employees, which classes constitute not less than 50 per cent of all employees and, for maternity medical benefit, also the wives of men in these classes; or

(b) all women in prescribed classes of the economically active population, which classes constitute not less than 20 per cent of all residents, and, for maternity medical benefit, also the wives of men in these classes; or

(c) where a declaration made in virtue of Article 3 is in force, all women in prescribed classes of employees, which classes constitute not less than 50 per cent of all employees in industrial workplaces employing 20 persons or more, and, for maternity medical benefit, also the wives of men in these classes.

In practice, groups of women 'frequently' excluded from maternity leave under national law include: domestic workers; casual or temporary workers; agricultural workers; members of an employer's family or those working in family businesses; those working in small businesses with less than a specified number of employees; armed forces or police personnel; some civil servants; managers and business executives; and high income earners.[462] As it has done in relation to many other ICESCR rights, it may be expected that the CESCR will ask states to pay special attention to disadvantaged or marginalized women who lack effective maternity protection, and to adopt targeted measures to assist them.

The coverage of maternity leave under national law is also often affected by eligibility conditions, such as minimum qualifying periods[463] (such as time already employed or hours routinely worked), citizenship or prior contributions to social insurance. The ILO Committee of Experts accepts that certain eligibility

[460] ILO, *Maternity at Work*, 26.
[461] ILO, *Maternity at Work*, 26.
[462] ILO, *Maternity at Work*, 36.
[463] See, eg, ILO Convention No. 102, Article 51.

conditions may be acceptable as long as they are reasonable and alternative social security measures are available to women in need.[464] There is thus a role for the CESCR in supervizing whether restrictions are arbitrary or discriminatory.

Summary of global practice

As noted earlier, ILO standards have influenced maternity protection worldwide and not only in states which are formally parties to the relevant conventions. In its global survey of maternity protection in 2010, the ILO found that 51 per cent of states now provide at least fourteen weeks' leave; 97 per cent of states provide paid leave of some kind, and 42 per cent do so at the two-thirds rate of pay for fourteen weeks; and only 26 per cent of states still require employers to fund it.[465] Attainment of the ILO standards was lowest in Africa, Asia and the Middle East,[466] reflecting the prevalence of developing economies and the progressive realization of social security systems there generally. Reference to ILO standards assists in giving a minimum content to the requirements of Article 10(2), and identifying issues of concern (such as lack of coverage of vulnerable groups, or unduly restrictive eligibility conditions).

It should also be noted that maternity protection alone is not sufficient to secure the equal rights of women in work. Even with maternity protection, mothers' participation in the labour force can decline for other reasons, such as the unaffordability of childcare, even taking account of childcare benefits or subsidies (thus discouraging women from returning to work), or the tax treatment of the second earner's income.[467]

Maternal health at work

While maternal health falls within the general protection of the right to health in Article 12 of the ICESCR, brief mention may be made of relevant international standards related to pregnant workers and mothers who work. ILO Convention No. 183 protects pregnant or breastfeeding mothers from being required to perform work that is prejudicial to the health of the mother or child, as determined by the competent authority or where so assessed (Article 3). It also provides for medical leave in the case of illness, complications or risk of complications arising out of pregnancy or childbirth (Article 5). Mothers are further entitled to daily breaks or reduced working hours to enable breastfeeding, which are to be counted as remunerated working time (Article 10).

ILO Recommendation No. 191 on Maternity Protection 2000 suggests stronger procedures and protections, including in identifying types of dangerous work and the various steps which employers can take to mitigate such risks (paragraph 6).

[464] ILO, *Maternity at Work*, 42.

[465] ILO, *Maternity at Work*, ix–x, 6 and 17. Maternity leave was unpaid, paid at less than the two-thirds rate, or for less than fourteen weeks, in 59 per cent of states: ILO, *Maternity at Work*, 20.

[466] ILO, *Maternity at Work*, 29.

[467] Patricia Apps and Ray Rees, 'Gender, Time Use, and Public Policy over the Life Cycle' (2005) 21 *Oxford Review of Economic Policy* 439.

Particular mention is made of: arduous work (such as manual lifting, carrying, pushing or pulling of loads); exposure to substances endangering reproductive health; work requiring special equilibrium; strenuous sitting, standing, temperatures or vibrations; and night work. Recommendation No. 191 also suggests greater flexibility in breastfeeding arrangements, as well as the provision of hygienic nursing facilities (paragraphs 7 to 9).

Article 10(3): Protection of Children and Young Persons

Article 10(3) requires states to take '[s]pecial measures of protection and assistance... on behalf of all young persons' and to protect them from 'economic and social exploitation', including harmful child labour. ICESCR rights in general apply to all people, including children. A child's rights to health, education, work, social security and an adequate standard of living are thus already covered by the respective ICESCR provisions (and other chapters of this book).

Article 10(3) should not, therefore, be understood as a miniature 'bill of rights' for children, sweeping up all other ICESCR rights within its ambit. Nor is Article 10(3) necessarily co-extensive with the Convention on the Rights of the Child, although it may be given shape and form by some of the CROC's key provisions. Regionally, there are sometimes more extensive guarantees for children, as in the African Charter on the Rights and Welfare of the Child 1999.

Article 10(3) is not redundant, but performs a number of distinctive functions. First, it particularizes aspects of certain ICESCR rights. Thus, the protection of children from economic exploitation is a more specific application of the work-related rights in Articles 6 to 8.

Secondly, by directing states to provide 'special measures of protection and assistance' to children, Article 10(3) prioritizes the needs of children. It may thus be understood to condition the manner in which states are required to progressively realize other ICESCR rights relevant to children, elevating the needs of children in resource allocation decisions.

Thirdly, Article 10(3) has autonomous content in requiring states to provide the enabling conditions necessary for children to enjoy their economic, social and cultural rights. Thus, it may be interpreted to require birth registration and the right to a name, recognition of a child's nationality, and non-discrimination in relation to matters such as inheritance (which may assist a child's economic security).

Further, where a child has no family or is separated from her or his family, states are required to provide special measures of protection and assistance. Such measures may include foster care, adoption, orphanages, guardianship and the like, that is, substitute state protection for children, whether they are nationals or foreigners (including unaccompanied refugee or stateless children). Protection against 'social exploitation' may include measures addressing the sexual exploitation and trafficking of children, and child abductions, matters also addressed by the CROC (Articles 33 to 35).

Article 10(3) is also related to the right of children to special measures of protection under Article 24 of the ICCPR and the numerous specialized provisions of the CROC. Even under Article 24 of the ICCPR, the HRC has observed that measures to protect children may necessarily be economic, social and cultural in nature:

> 3. …The Committee notes in this regard that such measures, although intended primarily to ensure that children fully enjoy the other rights enunciated in the Covenant, may also be economic, social and cultural. For example, every possible economic and social measure should be taken to reduce infant mortality and to eradicate malnutrition among children and to prevent them from being subjected to acts of violence and cruel and inhuman treatment or from being exploited by means of forced labour or prostitution, or by their use in the illicit trafficking of narcotic drugs, or by any other means. In the cultural field, every possible measure should be taken to foster the development of their personality and to provide them with a level of education that will enable them to enjoy the rights recognized in the Covenant, particularly the right to freedom of opinion and expression. Moreover, the Committee wishes to draw the attention of States parties to the need to include in their reports information on measures adopted to ensure that children do not take a direct part in armed conflicts.[468]

Special measures of protection for children under Article 10(3) of the ICESCR could conceivably extend to a range of matters covered by specific provisions of the ICCPR, such as the grounds and conditions of detention (Articles 9 and 10) and juvenile justice in criminal processes (Article 14).[469] Article 37 of the CROC also covers detention and juvenile justice.

Those issues are not, however, addressed in any great detail in this chapter, given that they fall more squarely within the ambit of the more specialized ICCPR and CROC provisions, and are comprehensively addressed by other commentators.[470] For present purposes, it is simply noted that the CESCR has occasionally addressed juvenile justice under Article 10(3), for instance by recommending to states that they: detain juvenile offenders separately from adults;[471] prohibit forced labour by minors in prisons;[472] prohibit corporal punishment in the penal system;[473] and raise the age of criminal responsibility.[474]

MEANING OF 'CHILDREN AND YOUNG PERSONS' AND SCOPE OF PROTECTION

During the drafting of Article 10(3), it was debated whether the provision should protect 'young persons', 'minors' or 'adolescents'. Some states preferred the terms

[468] HRC, General Comment No. 17 (1989), [3].

[469] HRC, General Comment No. 17 (1989), [2].

[470] Nowak, *CCPR Commentary*; Joseph, *ICCPR Cases*.

[471] CESCR, Concluding Observations: Philippines, E/C.12/1995/7 (7 June 1995), [13].

[472] CESCR, Concluding Observations: Syrian Arab Republic, E/C.12/1/Add.63 (24 September 2001), [18].

[473] CESCR, Concluding Observations: Mauritius, E/C.12/MUS/CO/4 (8 June 2010), [23]; Jamaica, E/C.12/1/Add.75 (6 December 2001), [14].

[474] China (Hong Kong Special Administrative Region), E/C.12/1/Add.58 (21 May 2001), [43].

'minors' and 'adolescents' as being more legally precise,[475] including because 'minors' are referred to in ILO instruments.[476] Other states rejected those terms for being too vague, and wanted a term that could capture differences between states and between fields of law.[477] New Zealand was concerned that the term 'minors' differed between states and would thus prevent 'uniformity of obligations' under the Covenant and exclude young people who had attained the age of majority but still needed protection.[478]

A United Kingdom proposal to refer to 'children and young persons' was ultimately accepted,[479] seemingly on the basis that this would protect children 'while they were still dependent on their families'.[480] Yet Article 10(3) applies to 'all' children and is not limited to children in families (see below) or 'dependants' (as is the case under Article 10(1)). Given the variety of views expressed, the drafting record is not determinative of the meaning of 'children and young persons' and there is no explicit age limit fixed for the application of Article 10(3). Some modern United Nations definitions of 'youth' mean people even up to the age of 24 years.[481]

Given the evolution of international standards in relation to children since the adoption of the ICESCR, the coverage of Article 10(3) should be interpreted dynamically and purposively. A key reference point is the presumptive age of majority of 18 years under the near-universally ratified CROC, unless defined as earlier by national law. In relation to the measures of protection similarly required by Article 24 of the ICCPR, the HRC has called on states to identify the ages of majority used for various purposes under national law, and a similar consideration should apply under Article 10(3) of the ICESCR:

> 4. The right to special measures of protection belongs to every child because of his status as a minor. Nevertheless, the Covenant does not indicate the age at which he attains his majority. This is to be determined by each State party in the light of the relevant social and cultural conditions. In this respect, States should indicate in their reports the age at which the child attains his majority in civil matters and assumes criminal responsibility... However, the Committee notes that the age for the above purposes should not be set unreasonably low and that in any case a State party cannot absolve itself from its obligations under the Covenant regarding persons under the age of 18, notwithstanding that they have reached the age of majority under domestic law.[482]

[475] UNGA Third Committee, A/C.3/SR.733 (16 January 1957), 267 (Indonesia).

[476] UNGA Third Committee Report, A/3525 (9 February 1957), 39.

[477] UNGA Third Committee, A/C.3/SR.736 (21 January 1957), 279 (United Kingdom); A/C.3/SR.736 (21 January 1957), 278 (Japan).

[478] UNGA Third Committee, A/C.3/SR.735 (21 January 1957), 273 (New Zealand).

[479] By forty-three votes to seven, with twelve abstentions: UNGA Third Committee Report, A/3525 (9 February 1957), 44.

[480] UNGA Third Committee Report, A/3525 (9 February 1957), 39.

[481] Geraldine van Bueren, 'The Minimum Core Obligations of States under Article 10(3) of the International Covenant on Civil and Political Rights' in Audrey Chapman and Sage Russell (eds), *Core Obligations: Building a Framework for Economic, Social and Cultural Rights* (Intersentia, Antwerp, 2002), 147, 158 ('Minimum Core Obligations').

[482] HRC, General Comment No. 17 (1989), [4]; see also Nowak, *CCPR Commentary*, 550–51.

Special legal considerations apply to the minimum ages for child labour, discussed below. Some regional instruments fix a higher minimum age of maturity, such as 18 years under the African Charter. While the term 'child' is not expressly defined in the American Convention on Human Rights, the Inter-American Court of Human Rights has interpreted it by reference to the CROC to mean any person who has not yet turned 18, unless he or she has attained majority, by legal mandate, before that age.[483] Where national law stipulates a higher minimum age for a particular purpose, however, a state may be required to guarantee the international human rights of the child, as when the Inter-American Court invoked Paraguay's age of majority of 20 years.[484]

NON-DISCRIMINATION AND VULNERABLE GROUPS

An early draft of Article 10(3) required measures of protection to be taken 'within and with the help of the family', while an early proposal for Article 10(1) described the 'family' as 'based on' marriage. Many states were concerned that children outside the family would not be adequately protected, especially illegitimate children and orphans[485] (particularly after the Second World War[486]), although others suggested it simply encouraged the support of children within families where that was appropriate,[487] but did not exclude other children.

In seeking clarity, Bulgaria and Uruguay proposed language to explicitly protect orphans and children born out of wedlock.[488] Most states supported the sentiment,[489] but thought it unnecessary and inappropriate to single out two categories of children for special consideration,[490] since this would risk excluding others such as 'the handicapped, the disabled, the blind, etc'.[491] The result was that the qualifying phrase 'within and with the help of the family' was deleted[492] and replaced with a requirement to provide protection 'without any discrimination for reasons of parentage or other conditions'.[493]

483 *Juridical Status and Human Rights of the Child*, 28 August 2002, IACHR (Ser. A) No. 17, [38]–[42] and [137].

484 *Juvenile Re-education Institute v Paraguay (Preliminary Objections, Merits, Reparations and Costs)*, 2 September 2004, IACHR (Ser. C) No 112, [181].

485 UNGA Third Committee, A/C.3/SR.730 (14 January 1957), 250 (Spain); see also A/C.3/SR.731 (15 January 1957), 256 (Chile).

486 UNGA Third Committee, A/C.3/SR.730 (14 January 1957), 247 (Bulgaria).

487 UNGA Third Committee Report, A/3525 (9 February 1957), 40.

488 UNGA Third Committee Report, A/3525 (9 February 1957), 33–4; UNGA Third Committee, A/C.3/SR.730 (14 January 1957), 247–8 (Bulgaria).

489 UNGA Third Committee, A/C.3/SR.731 (15 January 1957), 255 (Poland); A/C.3/SR.731 (15 January 1957), 257 (Byelorussian Soviet Socialist Republic).

490 UNGA Third Committee, A/C.3/SR.730 (14 January 1957), 248 (United Kingdom), 249 (Saudi Arabia); A/C.3/SR.732 (16 January 1957), 260 (Sweden); A/C.3/SR.733 (16 January 1957), 267 (Venezuela).

491 UNGA Third Committee Report, A/3525 (9 February 1957), 39.

492 The words were not included in the text submitted by the Working Party for further consideration.

493 The phrase 'without any discrimination' was adopted by forty-seven votes to seven, with ten abstentions. The phrase 'for reasons of parentage or other conditions' was adopted by thirty-six votes to seventeen, with ten abstentions. See UNGA Third Committee Report, A/3525 (9 February 1957), 44.

The unambiguous protection under Article 10(3) of children born outside wedlock contrasts with the related provision of the ICCPR, Article 24(1), over which there has been a debate whether its stipulated non-discrimination on the basis of 'birth' requires equal treatment of 'illegitimate' children.[494] The HRC has requested states to remove discrimination 'between legitimate children and children born out of wedlock', including in inheritance.[495] Non-discrimination on the basis of parentage is also found in the CROC and some regional instruments.[496] In monitoring states, the CESCR has recommended the abolition of any legal distinction drawn between 'legitimate' children and children born out of wedlock.[497]

Beyond parentage, Article 10(3) requires non-discrimination more generally and reference may be made back to the prohibited grounds of discrimination in Article 2(2) of the ICESCR: 'race, colour, sex, language, religion, political or other opinion, national or social origin, property, birth or other status'. While measures of protection for children under Article 10(3) are subject to progressive realization, where a state does provide protection or assistance it must do so on a non-discriminatory basis. Further, it is arguably a core obligation of states to identify vulnerable groups of children in need of special protection and assistance.[498]

Street children

One group to which the CESCR has drawn attention under Article 10(3) in monitoring states is street children, including the risks to homeless young girls of violence and rape.[499] It has recommended that states provide them with access to education, shelter and health care,[500] to assist them to reintegrate into society and the school system,[501] and establish or fund day centres for street students.[502] Children working on the streets are also of concern in relation to child labour (see below).

Regionally, the Inter-American Court of Human Rights has found that the precarious situation of street children can engage the state's duty to protect children under Article 19 of the American Convention on Human Rights, in conjunction with the right to life. In the *Street Children* case, the Court found that Guatemala

[494] Nowak, *CCPR Commentary*, 551–4 (concluding that children out of wedlock are entitled to be treated as equal to legitimate children).

[495] HRC, General Comment No. 17 (1989), [5].

[496] CROC, Article 2(1); American Convention on Human Rights (adopted 21 November 1969, 1144 UNTS 123, entered into force 18 July 1978), Article 17(5); European Convention on Human Rights (adopted 4 November 1950, 213 UNTS 222, entered into force 3 September 1953), Article 8; European Convention on the Legal Status of Children Born Out of Wedlock (adopted 15 October 1975, CETS No. 85, entered into force 11 August 1978).

[497] CESCR, Concluding Observations: Algeria, E/C.12/1995/17 (28 December 1995), [19]; Japan, E/C.12/1/Add.67 (24 September 2001), [41]; Malta, E/C.12/1/Add.101 (14 December 2004), [20].

[498] van Bueren, 'Minimum Core Obligations', 151.

[499] CESCR, Concluding Observations: Nigeria, E/C.12/1/Add.23 (16 June 1998), [23].

[500] CESCR, Concluding Observations: Brazil, E/C.12/BRA/CO/2 (12 June 2009), [24].

[501] CESCR, Concluding Observations: Benin, E/C.12/1/Add.78 (5 June 2002), [39]; Brazil, E/C.12/BRA/CO/2 (12 June 2009), [24].

[502] CESCR, Concluding Observations: Macedonia, E/C.12/MKD/CO/1 (15 January 2008), [41].

had failed to protect street children from grave risks of violence and to provide them with conditions that guarantee a dignified existence:

191. In the light of Article 19 of the American Convention, the Court wishes to record the particular gravity of the fact that a State Party to this Convention can be charged with having applied or tolerated a systematic practice of violence against at risk children in its territory. When States violate the rights of at-risk children, such as 'street children', in this way, it makes them victims of a double aggression. First, such States do not prevent them from living in misery, thus depriving them of the minimum conditions for a dignified life and preventing them from the 'full and harmonious development of their personality', even though every child has the right to harbor a project of life that should be tended and encouraged by the public authorities so that it may develop this project for its personal benefit and that of the society to which it belongs. Second, they violate their physical, mental and moral integrity and even their lives.

…

196. These provisions allow us to define the scope of the 'measures of protection' referred to in Article 19 of the American Convention, from different angles. Among them, we should emphasize those that refer to non-discrimination, special assistance for children deprived of their family environment, the guarantee of survival and development of the child, the right to an adequate standard of living, and the social rehabilitation of all children who are abandoned or exploited. It is clear to the Court that the acts perpetrated against the victims in this case, in which State agents were involved, violate these provisions.[503]

The Court invoked Articles 2, 3, 6, 20, 27 and 37 of the CROC to help define the measures of protection owed to children by the state under Article 19 of the American Convention, which has a comparable tenor to Article 10(3) of the ICESCR.

Children with disabilities

As noted earlier, children with disabilities were mentioned during the drafting of Article 10(3). The CESCR has thus far not given special attention to their protection, at least outside the specific contexts covered by other ICESCR rights (such as health, education and work). Useful reference may be made to Article 23 of the CROC, which recognizes the rights of children with disabilities:

1. States Parties recognize that a mentally or physically disabled child should enjoy a full and decent life, in conditions which ensure dignity, promote self-reliance and facilitate the child's active participation in the community.
2. States Parties recognize the right of the disabled child to special care and shall encourage and ensure the extension, subject to available resources, to the eligible child and those responsible for his or her care, of assistance for which application is made and which is appropriate to the child's condition and to the circumstances of the parents or others caring for the child.

[503] *Villagran Morales et al v Guatemala*, 19 November 1999, IACHR (Ser. C) No. 63.

3. Recognizing the special needs of a disabled child, assistance extended in accordance with paragraph 2 of the present article shall be provided free of charge, whenever possible, taking into account the financial resources of the parents or others caring for the child, and shall be designed to ensure that the disabled child has effective access to and receives education, training, health care services, rehabilitation services, preparation for employment and recreation opportunities in a manner conducive to the child's achieving the fullest possible social integration and individual development, including his or her cultural and spiritual development.

4. States Parties shall promote, in the spirit of international cooperation, the exchange of appropriate information in the field of preventive health care and of medical, psychological and functional treatment of disabled children, including dissemination of and access to information concerning methods of rehabilitation, education and vocational services, with the aim of enabling States Parties to improve their capabilities and skills and to widen their experience in these areas. In this regard, particular account shall be taken of the needs of developing countries.

The CRC has also interpreted Article 23 to require states to develop a comprehensive policy and plan of action on the rights of children with disabilities, which may also be an appropriate approach under Article 10(3) of the ICESCR:

10. In order to meet the requirements of article 23 it is necessary that States parties develop and effectively implement a comprehensive policy by means of a plan of action which not only aims at the full enjoyment of the rights enshrined in the Convention without discrimination but which also ensures that a child with disability and her or his parents and/or others caring for the child do receive the special care and assistance they are entitled to under the Convention.

...

18. ...Plans of action must be comprehensive, including plans and strategies for children with disabilities, and should have measurable outcomes... It is also essential that all programmes be adequately supplied with financial and human resources and equipped with built-in monitoring mechanisms, for example, indicators allowing accurate outcome measurements...[504]

The CRC further notes that special attention should be given to the needs of children with disabilities in the family (which may need support), alternative care and institutions.[505] The CRC has been particularly concerned by the high rate of institutionalization of children with disabilities and the often poor quality of institutional care. It has urged states to ensure that the placement of children in institutions is a measure of last resort, when absolutely necessary, involving the child in decision-making, and only where it is in the best interests of the child.[506]

Aside from measures taken in the context of other ICESCR rights (such as health, education, work, housing and so on), special measures for children with

[504] CRC, General Comment No. 9 (2006), The rights of children with disabilities (27 February 2007), [13] and [18].

[505] CRC, General Comment No. 9 (2006), [41]–[50].

[506] CRC, General Comment No. 9 (2006), [47]–[48].

disabilities may also be needed to prevent disabilities (whether acquired from inherited diseases, communicable diseases, poor nutrition, domestic and road traffic accidents, hazardous environmental toxins or armed conflicts).[507] Further, special measures may be needed to build the self-esteem and self-reliance of children with disabilities, and to enable their participation in recreation and cultural activities and sports.[508] Special attention should also be given to public transport and other facilities, as the CRC observes:

39. The physical inaccessibility of public transportation and other facilities, including governmental buildings, shopping areas, recreational facilities among others, is a major factor in the marginalization and exclusion of children with disabilities and markedly compromises their access to services, including health and education. Although this provision may be mostly realized in developed countries, it remains largely un-addressed in the developing world. All States parties are urged to set out appropriate policies and procedures to make public transportation safe, easily accessible to children with disabilities, and free of charge, whenever possible, taking into account the financial resources of the parents or others caring for the child.

40. All new public buildings should comply with international specifications for access of persons with disabilities and existing public buildings, including schools, health facilities, governmental buildings, shopping areas, undergo necessary alterations that make them as accessible as possible. [509]

The most contemporary standards on children with disabilities are found in the Convention on the Rights of Persons with Disabilities (CRPD), Article 7 of which provides:

1. States Parties shall take all necessary measures to ensure the full enjoyment by children with disabilities of all human rights and fundamental freedoms on an equal basis with other children.

2. In all actions concerning children with disabilities, the best interests of the child shall be a primary consideration.

3. States Parties shall ensure that children with disabilities have the right to express their views freely on all matters affecting them, their views being given due weight in accordance with their age and maturity, on an equal basis with other children, and to be provided with disability and age-appropriate assistance to realize that right.

In addition, Article 23(3) to (5) of the CRPD addresses children in the context of the right to respect for home and family life:

3. States Parties shall ensure that children with disabilities have equal rights with respect to family life. With a view to realizing these rights, and to prevent concealment, abandonment, neglect and segregation of children with disabilities, States Parties shall undertake to provide early and comprehensive information, services and support to children with disabilities and their families.

[507] CRC, General Comment No. 9 (2007), [53]–[55].
[508] CRC, General Comment No. 9 (2007), [64] and [70]–[72].
[509] CRC, General Comment No. 9 (2007), [39]–[40].

4. States Parties shall ensure that a child shall not be separated from his or her parents against their will, except when competent authorities subject to judicial review determine, in accordance with applicable law and procedures, that such separation is necessary for the best interests of the child. In no case shall a child be separated from parents on the basis of a disability of either the child or one or both of the parents.

5. States Parties shall, where the immediate family is unable to care for a child with disabilities, undertake every effort to provide alternative care within the wider family, and failing that, within the community in a family setting.

Article 23(1)(c) further recognizes the right of children with disabilities to 'retain their fertility on an equal basis with others'.

Minority and indigenous children

Special measures of protection may be necessary for minority and indigenous children, including to eliminate the conditions that cause discrimination[510] or impair life opportunities. Article 30 of the CROC recognizes the special needs of children from ethnic, religious or linguistic minorities or of indigenous origin:

In those States in which ethnic, religious or linguistic minorities or persons of indigenous origin exist, a child belonging to such a minority or who is indigenous shall not be denied the right, in community with other members of his or her group, to enjoy his or her own culture, to profess and practise his or her own religion, or to use his or her own language.

Measures may be required in many areas covered by ICESCR or ICCPR rights, including in health, nutrition, education, recreation and sports, social services, housing, sanitation and juvenile justice.[511] Data collection and public information and education about the needs of indigenous children will also be important.[512] Special measures may be needed in relation to the protection of children in the family environment and in alternative care, as the CRC explains:

46. …States parties should ensure effective measures are implemented to safeguard the integrity of indigenous families and communities by assisting them in their child-rearing responsibilities in accordance with articles 3, 5, 18, 25 and 27 (3) of the Convention.[513]

47. States parties should, in cooperation with indigenous families and communities, collect data on the family situation of indigenous children, including children in foster care and adoption processes. Such information should be used to design policies relating to the family environment and alternative care of indigenous children in a culturally sensitive way. Maintaining the best interests of the child and the integrity of indigenous families and

[510] CRC, General Comment No. 11 (2009), Indigenous children and their rights under the Convention (12 February 2009), [25].

[511] CRC, General Comment No. 11 (2009).

[512] CRC, General Comment No. 11 (2009), [26]–[27].

[513] CRC Day of General Discussion (34th Session), Recommendations on the Rights of Indigenous Children, 3 October 2003, [17].

communities should be primary considerations in development, social services, health and education programmes affecting indigenous children.[514]

48. Furthermore, States should always ensure that the principle of the best interests of the child is the paramount consideration in any alternative care placement of indigenous children and in accordance with article 20(3) of the Convention pay due regard to the desirability of continuity in the child's upbringing and to the child's ethnic, religious, cultural and linguistic background. In States parties where indigenous children are overrepresented among children separated from their family environment, specially targeted policy measures should be developed in consultation with indigenous communities in order to reduce the number of indigenous children in alternative care and prevent the loss of their cultural identity. Specifically, if an indigenous child is placed in care outside their community, the State party should take special measures to ensure that the child can maintain his or her cultural identity.[515]

The UN General Assembly's Declaration on the Rights of Indigenous Peoples 2007 encourages states to protect indigenous children from genocide by forced removals (Article 7(2)), take special measures to improve the economic and social conditions of youth and children (Article 21(2)), and address the special needs of indigenous youth and children, including protection against discrimination and violence (Article 22):[516]

Article 7(2)

Indigenous peoples have the collective right to live in freedom, peace and security as distinct peoples and shall not be subjected to any act of genocide or any other act of violence, including forcibly removing children of the group to another group.

Article 21(2)

States shall take effective measures and, where appropriate, special measures to ensure continuing improvement of their economic and social conditions. Particular attention shall be paid to the rights and special needs of indigenous elders, women, youth, children and persons with disabilities.

Article 22

1. Particular attention shall be paid to the rights and special needs of indigenous elders, women, youth, children and persons with disabilities in the implementation of this Declaration.

2. States shall take measures, in conjunction with indigenous peoples, to ensure that indigenous women and children enjoy the full protection and guarantees against all forms of violence and discrimination.

[514] CRC Day of General Discussion (34th Session), Recommendations on the Rights of Indigenous Children, [17].

[515] CRC, General Comment No. 11 (2009), [46]–[48].

[516] The Declaration also addresses the education of children (Article 14(2)–(3)) and the exploitation of children (Article 17).

Refugee children

Another particularly vulnerable group of children is refugee children. Article 22 of the CROC provides for the protection of refugee children, whether unaccompanied or accompanied by their parents:

1. States Parties shall take appropriate measures to ensure that a child who is seeking refugee status or who is considered a refugee in accordance with applicable international or domestic law and procedures shall, whether unaccompanied or accompanied by his or her parents or by any other person, receive appropriate protection and humanitarian assistance in the enjoyment of applicable rights set forth in the present Convention and in other international human rights or humanitarian instruments to which the said States are Parties.

2. For this purpose, States Parties shall provide, as they consider appropriate, co-operation in any efforts by the United Nations and other competent intergovernmental organizations or non-governmental organizations co-operating with the United Nations to protect and assist such a child and to trace the parents or other members of the family of any refugee child in order to obtain information necessary for reunification with his or her family. In cases where no parents or other members of the family can be found, the child shall be accorded the same protection as any other child permanently or temporarily deprived of his or her family environment for any reason, as set forth in the present Convention.

A range of 'soft law' standards also address refugee children, including in decision-making about refugee status[517] and detention. UNHCR's Executive Committee's (EXCOM) Conclusion on Children at Risk provides that refugee children should be among the first to receive protection and assistance and urges states to identify risk factors, such as:

Wider environmental risk factors including, but not limited to: an insecure environment; lack of access to child-sensitive asylum procedures; situations of displacement, particularly protracted situations; statelessness; lack of sustainable solutions; poverty and families' lack of self-reliance opportunities; inadequate access to and use of services such as education and health care; disruption of family and community support structures; prevalence of traditional practices that are harmful to children; discrimination, intolerance, xenophobia, and gender inequality; and lack of documentation of the parent-child relationship through birth registrations and issuance of birth certificates; and

Individual risk factors, including, but not limited to: unaccompanied and separated children, particularly those in child-headed households as well as those accompanied by abusive or exploitative adults; stateless children; adolescents, in particular girl mothers and their children; child victims of trafficking and sexual abuse, including pornography, pedophilia and prostitution; survivors of torture; survivors of violence, in particular sexual and gender-based violence and other forms of abuse and exploitation; children who get married under the age specified in national laws and/or children in forced marriages; children who are or have been associated with armed forces or groups; children in detention; children

[517] UNHCR, Guidelines on Determining the Best Interests of the Child (May 2008); UNGA, Report of the Secretary-General: Protection and Assistance to Unaccompanied and Separated Refugee Children, A/56/333 (7 September 2001).

who suffer from social discrimination; children with mental or physical disabilities; children living with or affected by HIV and AIDS and children suffering from other serious diseases; and children out of school…

The EXCOM Conclusion suggests a wide range of measures of prevention, response, protection and solutions,[518] while respecting the best interests of refugee children, maintaining family unity and promoting durable solutions.

Refugee children are also protected under Article 23 of the African Charter on the Rights and Welfare of the Child, which extends equal protection to internally displaced children:

1. States Parties to the present Charter shall take all appropriate measures to ensure that a child who is seeking refugee status or who is considered a refugee in accordance with applicable international or domestic law shall, whether unaccompanied or accompanied by parents, legal guardians or close relatives, receive appropriate protection and humanitarian assistance in the enjoyment of the rights set out in this Charter and other international human rights and humanitarian instruments to which the States are Parties.

2. States Parties shall undertake to cooperate with existing international organizations which protect and assist refugees in their efforts to protect and assist such a child and to trace the parents or other close relatives or an unaccompanied refugee child in order to obtain information necessary for reunification with the family.

3. Where no parents, legal guardians or close relatives can be found, the child shall be accorded the same protection as any other child permanently or temporarily deprived of his family environment for any reason.

4. The provisions of this Article apply mutatis mutandis to internally displaced children whether through natural disaster, internal armed conflicts, civil strife, breakdown of economic and social order or howsoever caused.

The CESCR too has occasionally expressed concern about the risk of violence to girls in communities of internally displaced persons, and urged states to provide better camp security, including by cooperating with UN peacekeeping missions and agencies.[519]

Migrant children

Relevantly, the CRC has issued a General Comment (No. 6) on the 'treatment of unaccompanied and separated children outside their country of origin', which calls on states to protect the rights of all children within their jurisdiction, 'including asylum-seeking, refugee and migrant children—irrespective of their nationality, immigration status or statelessness'.[520] It explicitly distinguishes the

[518] UNHCR, EXCOM Conclusion on Children at Risk, No. 107 (LVIII) (5 October 2007), [g(i)–(xiii)]–[h(i)–(xix)].

[519] CESCR, Concluding Observations: Chad, E/C.12/TCD/CO/3 (16 December 2009), [20] (such as the UN Mission in the Central African Republic and Chad (MINURCAT)).

[520] CRC, General Comment No. 6, Treatment of unaccompanied and separated children outside their country of origin (1 September 2005), [12].

position under the CROC of non-citizen children in developing states from the exclusion permitted under Article 2(3) of the ICESCR:

16. In view of the absolute nature of obligations deriving from the Convention and their *lex specialis* character, article 2 paragraph 3 of the *International Covenant on Economic Social and Cultural Rights* would not apply with regard to unaccompanied and separated children.[521]

The CRC observes that 'unaccompanied and separated children face greater risks', including of violence, sexual exploitation and abuse, military recruitment, child labour, detention and discrimination in or denial of access to food, shelter, housing, health services and education.[522] Such children may also lack access to proper and appropriate identification, registration, age assessment, documentation, family tracing, guardianship systems or legal advice. They are also frequently subject to arbitrary, restrictive or insensitive immigration practices, and limited in opportunities for family reunion. The CRC accordingly outlines the obligations of states in relation to such children under the CROC, which may relevantly inform the protection and assistance provided under Article 10(3) of the ICESCR:

13. Obligations deriving from the Convention *vis-à-vis* unaccompanied and separated children apply to all branches of government (executive, legislative and judicial). They include the obligation to establish national legislation; administrative structures; and the necessary research, information, data compilation and comprehensive training activities to support such measures. Such legal obligations are both negative and positive in nature, requiring States not only to refrain from measures infringing on such children's rights, but also to take measures to ensure the enjoyment of these rights without discrimination. Such responsibilities are not only limited to the provision of protection and assistance to children who are already unaccompanied or separated, but include measures to prevent separation (including the implementation of safeguards in case of evacuation). The positive aspect of these protection obligations also extend to requiring States to take all necessary measures to identify children as being unaccompanied or separated at the earliest possible stage, including at the border, to carry out tracing activities and, where possible and if in the child's best interest, to reunify separated and unaccompanied children with their families as soon as possible.[523]

Particular measures that may be required include: identification, registration and assessment of unaccompanied or separated children; appointment of a guardian or adviser and legal representative; and care and accommodation arrangements.[524]

The Convention on Migrant Workers also mentions the special needs of children in a number of contexts: detention of migrant parents (Article 17(6)), family reunification (Article 44(2)) and education (Article 45(2) to (4)):

Article 17

6. Whenever a migrant worker is deprived of his or her liberty, the competent authorities of the State concerned shall pay attention to the problems that may be posed for members of his or her family, in particular for spouses and minor children.

[521] CRC, General Comment No. 6, [16]. [522] CRC, General Comment No. 6, [3].
[523] CRC, General Comment No. 6, [13]. [524] CRC, General Comment No. 6, [31]–[40].

Article 44

2. States Parties shall take measures that they deem appropriate and that fall within their competence to facilitate the reunification of migrant workers with their spouses or persons who have with the migrant worker a relationship that, according to applicable law, produces effects equivalent to marriage, as well as with their minor dependent unmarried children.

Article 45

2. States of employment shall pursue a policy, where appropriate in collaboration with the States of origin, aimed at facilitating the integration of children of migrant workers in the local school system, particularly in respect of teaching them the local language.

3. States of employment shall endeavour to facilitate for the children of migrant workers the teaching of their mother tongue and culture and, in this regard, States of origin shall collaborate whenever appropriate.

4. States of employment may provide special schemes of education in the mother tongue of children of migrant workers, if necessary in collaboration with the States of origin.

BIRTH REGISTRATION, NAME AND NATIONALITY

In monitoring states, the CESCR has expressed concern that children may have difficulty accessing their rights under the ICESCR because their births were not registered, a problem which disproportionately affects marginalized groups such as people in remote areas, indigenous peoples, minorities and internally displaced persons.[525] In this regard, the CESCR has recommended the modernization of states' civil registry systems.[526] The UN Children's Fund (UNICEF) is also heavily involved in this issue, including by encouraging innovative approaches such as the use of mobile phones to register births.[527] The CESCR has also been concerned where children have been deprived of a nationality, such as where children born to a citizen mother and a non-citizen father cannot acquire the nationality of their mother and country of birth.[528]

Article 10 of the ICESCR does not expressly mention birth registration, the right to a name or nationality, unlike the Article 24 of the ICCPR, which also protects children. The CESCR thus appears to regard issues concerning the civil and political recognition of the legal status of children as implicit preconditions for the enjoyment of ICESCR rights. The HRC explains the requirement and purpose of birth registration under the ICCPR as follows:

7. Under article 24, paragraph 2, every child has the right to be registered immediately after birth and to have a name. In the Committee's opinion, this provision should be interpreted as being closely linked to the provision concerning the right to special measures of protection and it is designed to promote recognition of the child's legal personality. Providing for the right to have a name is of special importance in the case of children

[525] CESCR, Concluding Observations: Colombia, E/C.12/COL/CO/5 (7 June 2010), [19].

[526] CESCR, Concluding Observations: Colombia, E/C.12/COL/CO/5 (7 June 2010), [19].

[527] UNICEF, Thematic Report 2011: Child Protection from Violence, Exploitation and Abuse (2011), 3.

[528] CESCR, Concluding Observations: Madagascar, E/C.12/MDG/CO/2 (16 December 2009), [14].

born out of wedlock. The main purpose of the obligation to register children after birth is to reduce the danger of abduction, sale of or traffic in children, or of other types of treatment that are incompatible with the enjoyment of the rights provided for in the Covenant. Reports by States parties should indicate in detail the measures that ensure the immediate registration of children born in their territory.[529]

Article 7 of the CROC likewise recognizes the right of a child to be registered and to have a name from birth, but also the right to acquire a nationality:

1. The child shall be registered immediately after birth and shall have the right from birth to a name, the right to acquire a nationality and, as far as possible, the right to know and be cared for by his or her parents.

2. States Parties shall ensure the implementation of these rights in accordance with their national law and their obligations under the relevant international instruments in this field, in particular where the child would otherwise be stateless.

Similar protections are in Article 18 of the CRPD in relation to children with disabilities.

Regionally, the Inter-American Court of Human Rights has considered a number of cases involving state failure to protect the right of children to a name under Article 18 of the American Convention on Human Rights. In the *Las Dos Erres Massacre* case, the Court found a violation of Article 18 where a child was separated from his parents as a result of abduction and illegal retention during an armed conflict in Guatemala, and where the state had failed to guarantee the child's right to live with his biological family and to bear the name given to him by his parents:

192. In relation to the right to a name, the Court notes that it has established in its jurisprudence that the 'right to a name, recognized in Article 18 of the American Convention, constitutes a basic and indispensable element of each person's identity.' In this regard, the Court has indicated that 'the States should guarantee that a person is registered with the name chosen by that person or his/her parents, depending on the time of the registration, without any sort of restriction on the right nor interference with the decision to choose a name. Once the person is registered, their possibility to preserve and re-establish their name and surname should be guaranteed. The names and surnames are essential to formally establish a link between the various members of the family.'

…

194. …Ramiro Osorio Cristales was separated from his family, living under another name and identity, and with a family that was not his own. The separation from his family persisted until 1999, when Ramiro Osorio Cristales reunited with his biological family. Likewise, the name change, based on his abduction and illegal retention by the kaibil Santos Lopez Alonso, was maintained until 2002, when he recovered the name given to him by his parents.

195. The Court considers that the State had the obligation to adopt all positive measures necessary to guarantee that Ramiro Osorio Cristales could fully enjoy the right to live with his biological family, as well as his right to the name given to him by his parents.

[529] HRC, General Comment No. 17 (1989), [7]; see also Nowak, *CCPR Commentary*, 559–60.

The situation caused psychological damage and lasting suffering to the child, compounding the suffering from the prolonged lack of justice and impunity in the case.[530] In another case, *Yean and Bosico Children*, the Dominican state registry office refused to issue birth certificates to two girls of Haitian descent born in the Dominican Republic to Dominican citizen mothers. The Inter-American Court found that the state violated the children's right to a name under Article 18 of the American Convention in denying citizenship from birth:

183. Under Article 18 of the Convention, States are obliged not only to protect the right to a name, but also to provide the necessary measures to facilitate the registration of an individual, immediately after birth.

184. The State must also ensure that the individual is registered under the name that he or his parents have chosen, according to the moment when registration occurs, without any type of restriction to the right or interference in the decision of choosing the name. Once an individual is registered, the possibility of preserving and re-establishing the given name and surname must be ensured. The given name and surname are essential to establish formally the connection that exists between the different members of the family with society and with the State, and this was not ensured to the Yean and Bosico children by the Dominican Republic.[531]

The denial of birth certificates led to a further violation of the children's right to a nationality under Article 20 of the American Convention. The denial of registration also impaired socio-economic rights, since the lack of juridical personality and nationality prevented one girl from accessing appropriate schooling, forcing her to enrol among adults and exacerbating her vulnerability as a minor.[532] The Court thus found that the state had failed to provide the necessary special measures of protection to the child under Article 19 of the American Convention, namely 'free primary education to all children in an appropriate environment and in the conditions necessary to ensure their full intellectual development'.[533]

Nationality is also protected in limited terms by Article 8 of the CROC:

1. States Parties undertake to respect the right of the child to preserve his or her identity, including nationality, name and family relations as recognized by law without unlawful interference.

2. Where a child is illegally deprived of some or all of the elements of his or her identity, States Parties shall provide appropriate assistance and protection, with a view to re-establishing speedily his or her identity.

The right of a child to acquire a nationality originally stems from Article 24(3) of the ICCPR. It is not a right to a nationality as such,[534] and states are afforded some

[530] *Las Dos Erres Massacre case (Preliminary Objections, Merits, Reparations and Costs)*, 24 November 2009, IACHR (Ser. C) No. 211, [215].

[531] *Yean and Bosico Children v The Dominican Republic*, 8 September 2005, IACHR (Ser. C) No. 130, [183]–[184].

[532] *Yean and Bosico Children v Dominican Republic*, [185].

[533] *Yean and Bosico Children v Dominican Republic*, [185].

[534] Nowak, *CCPR Commentary*, 560–62.

discretion in formulating national laws on nationality, although states should avoid leaving children stateless. The HRC has interpreted states' obligations under Article 24(3) thus:

8. Special attention should also be paid, in the context of the protection to be granted to children, to the right of every child to acquire a nationality, as provided for in article 24, paragraph 3. While the purpose of this provision is to prevent a child from being afforded less protection by society and the State because he is stateless, it does not necessarily make it an obligation for States to give their nationality to every child born in their territory. However, States are required to adopt every appropriate measure, both internally and in cooperation with other States, to ensure that every child has a nationality when he is born. In this connection, no discrimination with regard to the acquisition of nationality should be admissible under internal law as between legitimate children and children born out of wedlock or of stateless parents or based on the nationality status of one or both of the parents. The measures adopted to ensure that children have a nationality should always be referred to in reports by States parties.[535]

The African Charter on the Rights and Welfare of the Child similarly recognizes that every child has a right to acquire a nationality (Article 6(3)). In the *Nubian Children* case, the African Children's Rights Committee found that Kenya's failure to grant nationality to children of Nubian descent (stemming from former colonial conscription of Sudanese men) violated their right to acquire a nationality.[536] The Committee interpreted the right to acquire a nationality expansively as a right to have a nationality from birth, by reference to related international standards:

42. …the African Committee is of the view that there is a strong and direct link between birth registration and nationality. This link is further reinforced by the fact that both rights are provided for in the same Article under the African Children's Charter (as well as the UN Convention on the Rights of the Child). The African Committee notes that Article 6(3) does not explicitly read, unlike the right to a name in Article 6(1), that 'every child has the right *from his birth* to acquire a nationality'. It only says that 'every child has the right to acquire a nationality'. Nonetheless, a purposive reading and interpretation of the relevant provision strongly suggests that, as much as possible, children should have a nationality beginning from birth. This interpretation is also in tandem with Article 4 of the African Children's Charter that requires that 'in all actions concerning the child undertaken by any person or authority the best interests of the child shall be the primary consideration'. Moreover, this interpretation is further supported by the UN Human Rights Committee that indicated: 'States are required to adopt every appropriate measure, both internally and in cooperation with other States, *to ensure that every child has a nationality when he is born*' (African Committee's emphasis). Moreover, by definition, a child is a person *below* the age of 18 (Article 2 of the African Children's Charter), and the practice of making children wait until they turn 18 years of age to apply to acquire a nationality cannot be seen as an effort on the part of the State Party to comply with its children's rights obligations. Therefore,

[535] HRC, General Comment No. 17 (1989), [8].

[536] *Institute for Human Rights and Development in Africa and Open Society Justice Initiative on behalf of Children of Nubian Descent in Kenya v Kenya*, Decision No. 2/Com/002/2009 (African Committee of Experts on the Rights and Welfare of the Child) (22 March 2011).

the seemingly routine practice (which is applied more of as rule than in highly exceptional instances) of the State Party that leaves children of Nubian descent without acquiring a nationality for a very long period of 18 years is neither in line with the spirit and purpose of Article 6, nor promotes children's best interests, and therefore constitutes a violation of the African Children's Charter.[537]

Article 20(2) of the American Convention on Human Rights confers a more explicit higher protection than the ICESCR or ICCPR: 'Every person has the right to the nationality of the state in whose territory he was born if he does not have the right to any other nationality.'

CHILDREN IN ALTERNATIVE CARE AND INSTITUTIONS

The grounds for separating children from abusive parents or families were discussed in relation to Article 10(1), as well as issues of access and custody. By contrast, Article 10(3) may be regarded as more concerned with the treatment of children once they are placed into alternative care (such as foster families) or institutions. It is also concerned not only with children separated from their families, but children who have no families (orphans).

The CROC contains some key principles which can inform interpretation of Article 10(3) of the ICESCR. First, as in all decisions affecting children, the best interests of the child must be a primary consideration in decisions about their placement and care; and care institutions must meet minimum health and safety standards. Article 3 of the CROC provides:

1. In all actions concerning children, whether undertaken by public or private social welfare institutions, courts of law, administrative authorities or legislative bodies, the best interests of the child shall be a primary consideration.

2. States Parties undertake to ensure the child such protection and care as is necessary for his or her well-being, taking into account the rights and duties of his or her parents, legal guardians, or other individuals legally responsible for him or her, and, to this end, shall take all appropriate legislative and administrative measures.

3. States Parties shall ensure that the institutions, services and facilities responsible for the care or protection of children shall conform with the standards established by competent authorities, particularly in the areas of safety, health, in the number and suitability of their staff, as well as competent supervision.

Under Article 20 of the CROC, children outside the family are entitled to 'special protection and assistance' by the state, including through suitable alternative care:

1. A child temporarily or permanently deprived of his or her family environment, or in whose own best interests cannot be allowed to remain in that environment, shall be entitled to special protection and assistance provided by the State.

2. States Parties shall in accordance with their national laws ensure alternative care for such a child.

[537] *Children of Nubian Descent in Kenya*, [42].

3. Such care could include, inter alia, foster placement, kafalah of Islamic law, adoption or if necessary placement in suitable institutions for the care of children. When considering solutions, due regard shall be paid to the desirability of continuity in a child's upbringing and to the child's ethnic, religious, cultural and linguistic background.

Similar standards are provided in the African Charter on the Rights and Welfare of the Child (Article 25). Generally, as suggested in the European regional jurisprudence, 'placement in a foster family or in a family-type environment should have preference over placement in an institution'.[538] Siblings should be kept together as far as possible.[539] An institution should protect the child's dignity, rights and satisfy their developmental needs and well-being.[540] It should also provide 'the nearest possible approximation to a normal home environment'.[541]

Institutions must be adequately supervised by the state.[542] Under the CROC, the situation of children in care must also be periodically reviewed under Article 25:

States Parties recognize the right of a child who has been placed by the competent authorities for the purposes of care, protection or treatment of his or her physical or mental health, to a periodic review of the treatment provided to the child and all other circumstances relevant to his or her placement.

The CESCR has noted that poor management of state care institutions (such as orphanages) may result in young people leaving and becoming homeless.[543]

ABDUCTION AND ADOPTION

Measures to prohibit abductions and regulate adoptions of children come within Article 10(3) of the ICESCR. Reference may be made to Articles 11 and 21 of the CROC, which respectively require states to combat the illicit transfer and non-return of children, and to impose safeguards on lawful adoptions:

Article 11

1. States Parties shall take measures to combat the illicit transfer and non-return of children abroad.

2. To this end, States Parties shall promote the conclusion of bilateral or multilateral agreements or accession to existing agreements.

…

538 ECSR, Statement of Interpretation on Article 16 of the European Social Charter, 2011/Ob/16 (9 December 2011).

539 ECSR, General Observation regarding Article 17 of the Revised European Social Charter (Article 16 of the European Social Charter 1961), Conclusions XV-2, volume 1 (31 December 2001).

540 ECSR, General Observation regarding Article 17.

541 ECSR, Statement of Interpretation on Article 16 of the Revised European Social Charter (Article 16 of the European Social Charter 1961), Conclusions III (31 July 1973).

542 ECSR, Statement of Interpretation on Article 16.

543 CESCR, Concluding Observations: Ukraine, E/C.12/UKR/CO/5 (4 January 2008), [22].

Article 21

States Parties that recognize and/or permit the system of adoption shall ensure that the best interests of the child shall be the paramount consideration and they shall:

(a) Ensure that the adoption of a child is authorized only by competent authorities who determine, in accordance with applicable law and procedures and on the basis of all pertinent and reliable information, that the adoption is permissible in view of the child's status concerning parents, relatives and legal guardians and that, if required, the persons concerned have given their informed consent to the adoption on the basis of such counselling as may be necessary;

(b) Recognize that inter-country adoption may be considered as an alternative means of child's care, if the child cannot be placed in a foster or an adoptive family or cannot in any suitable manner be cared for in the child's country of origin;

(c) Ensure that the child concerned by inter-country adoption enjoys safeguards and standards equivalent to those existing in the case of national adoption;

(d) Take all appropriate measures to ensure that, in inter-country adoption, the placement does not result in improper financial gain for those involved in it;

(e) Promote, where appropriate, the objectives of the present article by concluding bilateral or multilateral arrangements or agreements, and endeavour, within this framework, to ensure that the placement of the child in another country is carried out by competent authorities or organs.

In addition, the Hague Convention on Protection of Children and Co-operation in Respect of Inter-Country Adoption 1993 establishes safeguards to ensure that inter-country adoptions take place in the best interests of the child and with respect for his or her fundamental rights (including the child's views); requires counselling and relevant consents to be given; enables cooperation between states to respect those safeguards and prevent the abduction, sale or traffic in children; and secures mutual recognition by states of lawful adoptions.[544] Chapter II (Articles 4 to 5) sets out the requirements and procedures for inter-country adoptions.

Regulation of inter-country adoption has been of particular concern in Africa, given its abuse there. Article 24 of the African Charter on the Rights and Welfare of the Child provides:

States Parties which recognize the system of adoption shall ensure that the best interest of the child shall be the paramount consideration and they shall:

(a) establish competent authorities to determine matters of adoption and ensure that the adoption is carried out in conformity with applicable laws and procedures and on the basis of all relevant and reliable information, that the adoption is permissible in view of the child's status concerning parents, relatives and guardians and that, if necessary, the appropriate persons concerned have given their informed consent to the adoption on the basis of appropriate counselling;

[544] Convention on Protection of Children and Co-operation in Respect of Intercountry Adoption (adopted 29 May 1993, 1870 UNTS 167, entered into force 1 May 1995), Article 1.

(b) recognize that inter-country adoption in those States who have ratified or adhered to the International Convention on the Rights of the Child or this Charter may, as the last resort, be considered as an alternative means of a child's care, if the child cannot be placed in a foster or an adoptive family or cannot in any suitable manner be cared for in the child's country of origin;

(c) ensure that the child affected by inter-country adoption enjoys safeguards and standards equivalent to those existing in the case of national adoption;

(d) take all appropriate measures to ensure that in inter-country adoption, the placement does not result in trafficking or improper financial gain for those who try to adopt a child;

(e) promote, where appropriate, the objectives of this Article by concluding bilateral or multilateral arrangements or agreements, and endeavour, within this framework to ensure that the placement of the child in another country is carried out by competent authorities or organs;

(f) establish a machinery to monitor the well-being of the adopted child.

VIOLENCE AND ABUSE AGAINST CHILDREN

Article 10(3) can be understood to require states to protect children against all forms of violence and abuse. The various kinds of violence against children prohibited by international law were mentioned earlier, in relation to the protection of children within families, but apply equally to violence outside the home. The CESCR has consistently condemned all forms of abuse of and violence against children, including corporal punishment in all institutions.[545]

The CESCR has also identified harmful traditional or customary practices engaging Article 10(3). These include low ages of sexual consent;[546] accusations of witchcraft against children;[547] the persecution of albino children;[548] and female genital mutilation (FGM).[549] The CESCR has also described FGM as cruel, inhuman or degrading treatment.[550] It also condemned the 'odious practice' of 'social cleansing' in Colombia, by which criminal groups kill children (among others) thought to be 'disposable'.[551]

The CESCR has advocated measures to heighten awareness among the community, local authorities, doctors, midwives and mothers,[552] to supplement its

545 CESCR, Concluding Observations: Afghanistan, E/C.12/AFG/CO/2-4 (7 June 2010), [28]; Angola, E/C.12/DZA/CO/4 (7 June 2010), [15]; Belgium, E/C.12/BEL/CO/3 (4 January 2008), [18]; Costa Rica, E/C.12/CRI/CO/4 (4 January 2008), [44].

546 CESCR, Concluding Observations: Mexico, E/C.12/MEX/CO/4 (9 June 2006), [21] (age 12).

547 CESCR, Concluding Observations: Angola, E/C.12/AGO/CO/3 (1 December 2008), [25]; Benin, E/C.12/BEN/CO/2 (9 June 2008), [19].

548 CESCR, Concluding Observations: Democratic Republic of Congo, E/C.12/COD/CO/4 (16 December 2009), [28].

549 CESCR, Concluding Observations: Chad, E/C.12/TCD/CO/3 (16 December 2009), [19]; Nigeria, E/C.12/1/Add.23 (16 June 1998), [39]; Senegal, E/C.12/1/Add.62 (24 September 2001), [24].

550 CESCR, Concluding Observations: Chad, E/C.12/TCD/CO/3 (16 December 2009), [19].

551 CESCR, Concluding Observations: Colombia, E/1996/22, E/C.12/1996/18 (1–19 May 1995, 20 November–8 December 1995), [184].

552 CESCR, Concluding Observations: Benin, E/C.12/BEN/CO/2 (9 June 2008), [40].

recommendations to outlaw such practices.[553] In relation to FGM, states have been encouraged to promote alternative 'rite of passage' ceremonies and to combat traditional beliefs about its usefulness in enhancing the marriage prospects of girls.[554] Regionally, Article 21 of the African Charter on the Rights and Welfare of the Child also prohibits harmful social and cultural practices:

1. States Parties to the present Charter shall take all appropriate measures to eliminate harmful social and cultural practices affecting the welfare, dignity, normal growth and development of the child and in particular:

(a) those customs and practices prejudicial to the health or life of the child; and

(b) those customs and practices discriminatory to the child on the grounds of sex or other status.

2. Child marriage and the betrothal of girls and boys shall be prohibited and effective action, including legislation, shall be taken to specify the minimum age of marriage to be 18 years and make registration of all marriages in an official registry compulsory.

The Inter-American Court of Human Rights has found that the vulnerability of girls requires special measures of protection in applying a state's obligation to protect children generally under Article 19 of the American Convention on Human Rights (which bears some similarity to Article 10(3) of the ICESCR). In the *Cotton Field* case, the Court found that Mexico had failed to protect a number of girls found dead in a cotton field in Ciudad Juárez, in the context of a pattern of gender-related violence against hundreds of female victims in the area. The Court stated as follows in relation to child protection:

408. This Tribunal has established that boys and girls have special rights which give rise to specific obligations for the family, society and the State. Moreover, their status requires special protection that must be understood as an additional right that complements all the other rights that the Convention recognizes to each individual. The prevalence of the best interest of the child must be understood as the need to satisfy all the rights of children and adolescents, which obligates the State and affects the interpretation of all the other rights of the Convention when a case concerns minors. Furthermore, the State must pay special attention to the needs and rights of the alleged victims owing to their condition as girls who, as women, belong to a vulnerable group.

409. In this case, the Court finds that the State had the obligation to adopt all the positive measures necessary to ensure the rights of the disappeared girls. Specifically, the State had the obligation to ensure that they were found as soon as possible, once the next of kin had reported that they were missing; above all because the State was aware of the existence of a specific context in which girls were being disappeared.

410. Despite the existence of legislation for the protection of children, together with specific state policies, the Tribunal underscores that the evidence provided by the State does not show that, in this specific case, these measures translated into effective measures for

[553] CESCR, Concluding Observations: Afghanistan, E/C.12/AFG/CO/2-4 (7 June 2010), [31]; Angola, E/C.12/DZA/CO/4 (7 June 2010), [14].

[554] CESCR, Concluding Observations: Kenya, E/C.12/KEN/CO/1 (1 December 2008), [23].

initiating a prompt search, activating all resources to mobilize the different institutions and to deploy domestic mechanisms to obtain information to locate the girls rapidly and, once their bodies were found, to conduct the investigations, and prosecute and punish those responsible effectively and promptly. In summary, the State did not prove that it has proper reaction mechanisms or public policies that would provide the institutions involved with the necessary means to ensure the rights of the girls.[555]

In responding to violence against children in general, Article 19 of the CROC provides for the protection of children against all violence and identifies a variety of protective measures:

1. States Parties shall take all appropriate legislative, administrative, social and educational measures to protect the child from all forms of physical or mental violence, injury or abuse, neglect or negligent treatment, maltreatment or exploitation, including sexual abuse, while in the care of parent(s), legal guardian(s) or any other person who has the care of the child.

2. Such protective measures should, as appropriate, include effective procedures for the establishment of social programmes to provide necessary support for the child and for those who have the care of the child, as well as for other forms of prevention and for identification, reporting, referral, investigation, treatment and follow-up of instances of child maltreatment described heretofore, and, as appropriate, for judicial involvement.

Article 16(2) of the African Charter on the Rights and Welfare of the Child specifically calls on states to establish special monitoring units to support child victims of violence and their carers, 'as well as other forms of prevention and for identification, reporting referral investigation, treatment, and follow-up of instances of child abuse and neglect'.

The CRC has extensively elaborated on the kinds of child protection measures which states should adopt and pursue, including at the legislative, administrative, budgetary, institutional, enforcement, social programme and educational levels.[556] It has specifically called for the establishment of an independent national institution of children's rights, a focal point for coordination of child protection strategies and services, and for child-friendly judicial processes.[557]

The CRC has further provided guidance on the necessary measures to prevent violence against children, including by changing attitudes that tolerate or condone violence, supporting families, and enabling children to protect themselves and access protection services.[558] The investigation of violence or abuse against children must be child-sensitive and not further harm a child, while the treatment of victims may require medical, mental health, social and legal services and support.[559] Due process must also be respected when dealing with violence or

[555] *Gonzalez et al (Cotton Field) v Mexico*, 16 November 2009, IACHR (Ser. A) No. 205, [408]–[410].

[556] CRC, General Comment No. 13 (2011), The right of the child to freedom from all forms of violence (18 April 2011), [41]–[44].

[557] CRC, General Comment No. 13 (2011), [41]–[44].

[558] CRC, General Comment No. 13 (2011), [46]–[47].

[559] CRC, General Comment No. 13 (2011), [51]–[52].

abuse against children, while child-sensitive procedures are necessary, including the use of juvenile or family specialized courts and criminal procedures where appropriate.[560]

CHILD PROTECTION POLICY, STRATEGY OR PLAN

The obligation to fulfil children's rights under Article 10(3) may be understood to require states to adopt a national policy on child protection and a detailed plan for its realization, with attention to disadvantaged groups, and the allocation of sufficient resources to finance it. National policies or plans should also include: (a) national mechanisms to monitor implementation; (b) numerical targets and time frames for implementation; and (c) means of ensuring compliance with national benchmarks and indicators. Such policies should also involve full respect for the principles of accountability, transparency and participation by interested groups, including by involving children in decision-making.

The elements of child protection policy may be drawn from relevant international practice, including in the work of UNICEF, which has an international mandate for children's rights. UNICEF adopted the 'Protective Environmental Framework' in 2002, which defines broad elements that are critical to effective child protection, and which may guide national approaches:

1. *Governmental commitment to fulfilling protection rights*: includes social welfare policies, adequate budgets, public acknowledgement and ratification of international instruments.

2. *Legislation and enforcement*: includes an adequate legislative framework, its consistent implementation, accountability and a lack of impunity.

3. *Attitudes, traditions, customs, behaviour and practices*: includes social norms and traditions that condemn injurious practices and support those that are protective.

4. *Open discussion, including the engagement of media and civil society*: acknowledges silence as a major impediment to securing government commitment, supporting positive practices and ensuring the involvement of children and families.

5. *Children's life skills, knowledge and participation*: includes children, both girls and boys, as actors in their own protection through use of knowledge of their protection rights and ways of avoiding and responding to risks.

6. *Capacity of those in contact with the child*: includes the knowledge, motivation and support needed by families and by community members, teachers, health and social workers and police, in order to protect children.

7. *Basic and Targeted Services*: includes the basic social services, health and education to which children have the right, without discrimination, and also specific services that help to prevent violence and exploitation, and provide care, support and reintegration assistance in situations of violence, abuse and separation.

[560] CRC, General Comment No. 13 (2011), [54]–[56].

8. *Monitoring and oversight*: includes effective systems of monitoring such as data collection, and oversight of trends and responses.[561]

UNICEF acknowledges that low-resource countries may concentrate on defining a minimum package of child protection services, laws, policies and capacities, while wealthier states should concentrate on strengthening and reforming their systems.[562] UNICEF provides human-rights-based tools for states to assist in identifying children's needs and formulating policies. For example, UNICEF's *Toolkit to Map and Assess Child Protection Systems* assists states to assess their performance on policies and law, birth registration, child labour, harmful cultural practices, discrimination, violence and abuse, family and alternative care, migration and trafficking, sexual exploitation, children and justice, and emergencies and armed conflicts.[563]

PROTECTION OF CHILDREN IN ARMED CONFLICT

The CESCR has been concerned about violence against children in armed conflict, such as the large number of children killed in Colombia by assaults, homicides, landmines or in cross-fire between the army and illegal armed groups, as well as sexual violence against girls by those forces.[564]

The ICESCR does not cease to apply during armed conflicts regulated by international humanitarian law (IHL). In conflicts, the obligation to protect children under Article 10(3) of the ICESCR may be partly defined and supplemented by IHL as the special law (*lex specialis*). Article 38 of the CROC expressly incorporates states' IHL obligations concerning children:

1. States Parties undertake to respect and to ensure respect for rules of international humanitarian law applicable to them in armed conflicts which are relevant to the child.

…

4. In accordance with their obligations under international humanitarian law to protect the civilian population in armed conflicts, States Parties shall take all feasible measures to ensure protection and care of children who are affected by an armed conflict.

IHL contains various special rules addressing children.[565] In international armed conflicts, for instance, the Fourth Geneva Convention requires states to take special measures to protect the maintenance, education and religious and cultural rights of children under 15 years, including orphans and those separated from their families, even by arranging their reception in neutral states (Article 24). States must also protect children in occupied territory, including by facilitating the

[561] UNICEF, 'Child Protection Strategy', E/ICEF/2008/5/Rev.1 (20 May 2008), [10].
[562] UNICEF, 'Child Protection Strategy', [14].
[563] UNICEF, 'Toolkit to Map and Assess Child Protection Systems', May 2010, <http://www.unicef.org/protection/57929_58020.html>.
[564] CESCR, Concluding Observations: Colombia, E/C.12/COL/5 (9 January 2009), [15]–[16].
[565] See also UNGA Res. 3318(XXIX), Declaration on the Protection of Women and Children in Emergency and Armed Conflict (1974).

working of relevant institutions; ensuring their identification and registration, and protection of personal status; precluding their enlistment; providing maintenance and education appropriate to the nationality, language and religion of orphaned or separated children; and preserving any preferential measures concerning foods, medical care and protection (Article 50).

Regionally, the African Charter on the Rights and Welfare of the Child also provides for the protection of children in armed conflict, in Article 22:

1. States Parties to this Charter shall undertake to respect and ensure respect for rules of international humanitarian law applicable in armed conflicts which affect the child.

...

3. States Parties to the present Charter shall, in accordance with their obligations under international humanitarian law, protect the civilian population in armed conflicts and shall take all feasible measures to ensure the protection and care of children who are affected by armed conflicts. Such rules shall also apply to children in situations of internal armed conflicts, tension and strife.

In a case involving the massacre of 251 people in an internal armed conflict in Guatemala, the Inter-American Court of Human Rights found that the state had failed to adequately protect the rights of families under Article 17 of the American Convention on Human Rights, where children had been separated from their parents. The Court stated:

187. In relation to the rights of the family, the Court has established in its jurisprudence that the separation of children from their family constitutes, under certain conditions, a violation of his right to a family, enshrined in Article 17 of the American Convention.

...

191. ...the Court notes that, within the context of an internal armed conflict, the State's obligations toward children are defined in Article 4(3) of the Geneva Conventions' Additional Protocol II. This Article establishes that: 'the children will be provided with the care and help they need, and, particularly: [...] (b) the timely measures to facilitate the reunion of the temporarily separated families will be taken [...]'. According to the International Committee of the Red Cross, this obligation has been defined as follows: 'the parties to the conflict should do everything possible to re-establish family ties, that is, not only allow the members of the dispersed families to search for their next of kin, but also facilitate this search.'[566]

ROLE OF PRIVATE ORGANIZATIONS IN CHILD PROTECTION

During the drafting of Article 10(3), Bulgaria proposed that 'responsibility for the maintenance and education of needy children who have lost both parents shall be assumed by the State'.[567] This stimulated discussion about the merits

[566] *Las Dos Erres Massacre case (Preliminary Objections, Merits, Reparations and Costs)*, 24 November 2009, IACHR (Ser. C) No. 211, [187]–[188] and [190]–[191].

[567] UNGA Third Committee Report, A/3525 (9 February 1957), 36.

of cooperation between states and private organizations in realizing children's rights. Saudi Arabia suggested that state responsibility could be direct or indirect, because the state could assist private organizations that cared for orphans.[568] Syria argued that 'it would be unwise to discourage private initiative, which was very active in some countries, by making the State directly and solely responsible for the protection of needy children'.[569] Bulgaria's proposal was rejected,[570] indicating that Article 10(3) allows for private organizations to care for children.

Article 3(1) of the CROC envisages a role for private actors in requiring that the best interests of the child shall be a primary consideration '[i]n all actions concerning children, whether undertaken by public or private social welfare institutions'. Further, Article 5 of the CROC requires states to respect the rights and duties of anyone legally responsible for a child:

> States Parties shall respect the responsibilities, rights and duties of parents or, where applicable, the members of the extended family or community as provided for by local custom, legal guardians or other persons legally responsible for the child, to provide, in a manner consistent with the evolving capacities of the child, appropriate direction and guidance in the exercise by the child of the rights recognized in the present Convention.

As noted earlier, in the area of child labour, employers bear responsibilities to observe minimum age laws and occupational health and safety laws regarding hazardous work. They should conduct their activities on the basis of legislation, administrative measures, codes of conduct and other appropriate measures promoting respect for the rights of mothers, children and families, on a non-discriminatory basis.

In exercising the obligation to protect against violations of Article 10(3), states must take the necessary measures to prevent third parties from interfering with the enjoyment of children's rights, including by adopting the necessary legislative, administrative, judicial, supervision and enforcement measures. The state will bear its own responsibilities for failures to diligently prevent or repress violations of children's rights by private actors. States must also provide public education and information about such rights, to prevent violations.

ECONOMIC EXPLOITATION—CHILD LABOUR

An estimated 215 million children are involved in child labour globally, and 68 million children are not enrolled in primary education.[571] Working may negatively affect a child's right to education and impair their development. Article 10(3) does not prohibit all child labour, recognizing that some children

[568] UNGA Third Committee, A/C.3/SR.735 (21 January 1957), 274 (Saudi Arabia); see also UNGA Third Committee, A/C.3/SR.736 (21 January 1957), 280 (Pakistan).

[569] UNGA Third Committee, A/C.3/SR.736 (21 January 1957), 280 (Syria).

[570] By thirty-two votes to thirteen, with eighteen abstentions: UNGA Third Committee Report, A/3525 (9 February 1957), 43.

[571] ILO, *Giving Globalization a Human Face: General Survey on the Eight Fundamental ILO Conventions Concerning Rights at Work* (Geneva, 2008), Executive Summary, 5.

wish to work, work can be part of a child's preparation for adulthood, and family, social and cultural expectations may accept child labour.[572] In all such cases, work must be voluntary, not harmful, not impair education and be fully paid.

Rather, Article 10(3) prohibits work by children that is 'harmful to their morals or health or dangerous to life or likely to hamper their normal development'. It further requires states to 'set age limits below which the paid employment of child labour should be prohibited'. Where work is not harmful or under-age, it still must be undertaken voluntarily; Article 10(3) works in conjunction with Article 6 of the ICESCR to require that work by children must be freely chosen and entered into. Each of these issues is considered below.

In its General Comment on Article 6 of the ICESCR, the CESCR has highlighted the nexus between the right to work in Article 6, the protection of children under Article 10 and children's right to health under Article 12:

15. The protection of children is covered by article 10 of the Covenant. The Committee recalls its general comment No. 14 (2000) and in particular paragraphs 22 and 23 on children's right to health, and emphasizes the need to protect children from all forms of work that are likely to interfere with their development or physical or mental health. The Committee reaffirms the need to protect children from economic exploitation, to enable them to pursue their full development and acquire technical and vocational education as indicated in article 6, paragraph 2. The Committee also recalls its general comment No. 13 (1999), in particular the definition of technical and vocational education (paras. 15 and 16) as a component of general education. Several international human rights instruments adopted after the ICESCR, such as the Convention on the Rights of the Child, expressly recognize the need to protect children and young people against any form of economic exploitation or forced labour.[573]

Insofar as child labour is permitted, there is also a link to Article 7 of the ICESCR, which provides for safe and healthy conditions of work for all workers. Under that provision also, child labourers are entitled to equal pay for the same work as adults; under-paying children will further amount to 'exploitation' within the meaning of Article 10(3).

As noted by the CESCR, Article 10(3) is related to other international standards. Article 32 of the CROC similarly protects children against 'economic exploitation' or harmful work and requires states to establish a minimum age or ages for work:

1. States Parties recognize the right of the child to be protected from economic exploitation and from performing any work that is likely to be hazardous or to interfere with the child's education, or to be harmful to the child's health or physical, mental, spiritual, moral or social development.

[572] van Bueren, 'Minimum Core Obligations', 153.

[573] CESCR, General Comment No. 18, Article 6 of the International Covenant on Economic, Social and Cultural Rights, E/C.12/GC/18 (6 February 2006).

2. States Parties shall take legislative, administrative, social and educational measures to ensure the implementation of the present article. To this end, and having regard to the relevant provisions of other international instruments, States Parties shall in particular:

(a) Provide for a minimum age or minimum ages for admission to employment;

(b) Provide for appropriate regulation of the hours and conditions of employment;

(c) Provide for appropriate penalties or other sanctions to ensure the effective enforcement of the present article.

Particular forms of social and economic exploitation, such as sexual exploitation and trafficking, are also addressed in the CROC and discussed below. Article 36 of the CROC is a residual obligation on states to protect the child 'against all other forms of exploitation prejudicial to any aspects of the child's welfare'.

In the specialized area of indigenous rights, too, Article 17(2) of the UN Declaration on the Rights of Indigenous Peoples 2007 requires states to take specific measures to protect indigenous children from economic exploitation or hazardous or harmful labour:

States shall in consultation and cooperation with indigenous peoples take specific measures to protect indigenous children from economic exploitation and from performing any work that is likely to be hazardous or to interfere with the child's education, or to be harmful to the child's health or physical, mental, spiritual, moral or social development, taking into account their special vulnerability and the importance of education for their empowerment.

'Work harmful to their morals or health or dangerous to life or likely to hamper their normal development should be punishable by law'

Article 10(3) requires states to punish those who employ children in hazardous work. Article 10(3) does not enumerate the kinds of work which are prohibited, but instead deploys a general formula describing various harms to be avoided. There was not much discussion of concrete examples of such work during the drafting, with ILO standards in the area (as early as 1919 and as late as 1965) backgrounding the discussion, as discussed below.

There was some drafting debate about the term 'morals', included at the suggestion of the Netherlands.[574] While some states thought that 'morals' varied greatly around the world and that the term should thus be avoided,[575] others felt that the term, although 'general', was 'perfectly clear, quite independently of any religious interpretation'.[576] It was suggested that it encompassed a child's 'spiritual well-being'[577] and was to be understood according to a state's particular economic, social and cultural conditions.[578] It was also linked to criminal law

[574] UNGA Third Committee, A/C.3/SR.730 (14 January 1957), 248 (Netherlands); UNGA Third Committee Report, A/3525 (9 February 1957), 33, 36.

[575] UNGA Third Committee, A/C.3/SR.730 (14 January 1957), 249 (Saudi Arabia).

[576] UNGA Third Committee, A/C.3/SR.735 (21 January 1957), 272 (Belgium).

[577] UNGA Third Committee Report, A/3525 (9 February 1957), 40.

[578] UNGA Third Committee, A/C.3/SR.731 (15 January 1957), 255 (Poland).

offences 'against public morals and decency'.[579] Few concrete examples were, however, mentioned.

In contemporary terms, the most obvious areas of work harmful to a child's 'morals' may include sexual exploitation (including prostitution and pornography), narcotics and child soldiering. Certain dangerous industries might also bring related moral hazards for children, such as where the 'freewheeling lifestyle which is so common in remote and unregulated mines exposes them to alcohol abuse, gambling, prostitution and crime'.[580]

In relation to work which is dangerous to the health, life or development of children, ILO standards since 1919 have incrementally identified particularly risky industries. ILO Convention No. 5 concerning Minimum Age (Industry) 1919 first identified industries such as: mines, quarries and extraction; manufacturing, demolition, shipbuilding and electricity; public infrastructure and utilities; and transport of goods or passengers.[581] Subsequent ILO conventions address areas such as agriculture, work at sea, fishing, underground work and non-industrial employment.[582]

One key contemporary standard is ILO Convention No. 138 concerning Minimum Age for Admission to Employment 1973, which requires states to establish a general minimum age of 18 years for 'any type of employment or work which by its nature or the circumstances in which it is carried out is likely to jeopardize the health, safety or morals of young persons' (Article 3(1)). The Convention does not, however, prescribe what work is hazardous, and leaves the matter to be determined 'by national laws or regulations or by the competent authority, after consultation with the organizations of employers and workers concerned, where such exist' (Article 3(2)).

The most recent contemporary standard, ILO Convention No. 182 on the Worst Forms of Child Labour 1999,[583] goes further by specifically identifying 'the worst

[579] UNGA Third Committee, A/C.3/SR.730 (14 January 1957), 251 (Uruguay).

[580] ILO, *Children in Hazardous Work* (Geneva, 2011), xvl.

[581] ILO Convention No. 5 concerning Fixing the Minimum Age for Admission of Children to Industrial Employment (adopted 28 November 1919, entered into force 13 June 1921), Article 1(1).

[582] ILO Convention No. 5; ILO Convention No. 7 fixing the Minimum Age for Admission of Children to Employment at Sea (adopted 8 July 1920, entered into force 27 September 1921); ILO Convention No. 10 concerning the Age for Admission of Children to Employment in Agriculture (adopted 16 November 1921, entered into force 31 August 1923); ILO Convention No. 15 fixing the Minimum Age for the Admission of Young Persons to Employment as Trimmers or Stokers (adopted 11 November 1921, entered into force 20 November 1922); ILO Convention No. 33 concerning the Age for Admission of Children to Non-Industrial Employment (adopted 30 April 1932, entered into force 6 June 1935); ILO Convention No. 58 fixing the Minimum Age for the Admission of Children to Employment at Sea (Revised 1936) (adopted 24 October 1936, entered into force 11 April 1939); ILO Convention No. 59 fixing the Minimum Age for Admission of Children to Industrial Employment (Revised 1937) (adopted 22 June 1937, entered into force 21 February 1941); ILO Convention No. 50 concerning the Age for Admission of Children to Non-Industrial Employment (Revised 1937) (adopted 22 June 1937, entered into force 29 December 1950); ILO Convention No. 112 concerning the Minimum Age for Admission to Employment as Fishermen (adopted 19 June 1959, entered into force 7 November 1961); and ILO Convention No. 123 concerning the Minimum Age for Admission to Employment Underground in Mines (adopted 22 June 1965, entered into force 10 November 1967).

[583] ILO Convention No. 182 concerning the Prohibition and Immediate Action for the Elimination of the Worst Forms of Child Labour (adopted 17 June 1999, entered into force 19 November 2000).

forms of child labour'. Under Article 1, states 'shall take immediate and effective measures to secure the prohibition and elimination of the worst forms of child labour as a matter of urgency'. Article 3 defines the 'worst forms of child labour' as:

(a) all forms of slavery or practices similar to slavery, such as the sale and trafficking of children, debt bondage and serfdom and forced or compulsory labour, including forced or compulsory recruitment of children for use in armed conflict;

(b) the use, procuring or offering of a child for prostitution, for the production of pornography or for pornographic performances;

(c) the use, procuring or offering of a child for illicit activities, in particular for the production and trafficking of drugs as defined in the relevant international treaties;

(d) work which, by its nature or the circumstances in which it is carried out, is likely to harm the health, safety or morals of children.

States must identify these forms of child labour in national laws (Article 3), design programmes to 'eliminate as a priority' the worst forms of child labour (Article 6), and take effective measures of implementation and enforcement (including criminal penalties) (Article 7). The ILO regards Convention Nos. 138 and 182 as 'fundamental', quasi-constitutional standards which all ILO member states must respect, regardless of whether they are parties.[584] Convention No. 182 has wide support, with 174 ratifications.

In interpreting the meaning of hazardous work under Article 3(d) of Convention No. 182, ILO Recommendation 190, although non-binding, lists the following kinds of work:

(a) work which exposes children to physical, psychological or sexual abuse;

(b) work underground, under water, at dangerous heights or in confined spaces;

(c) work with dangerous machinery, equipment and tools, or which involves the manual handling or transport of heavy loads;

(d) work in an unhealthy environment which may, for example, expose children to hazardous substances, agents or processes, or to temperatures, noise levels, or vibrations damaging to their health;

(e) work under particularly difficult conditions such as work for long hours or during the night or work where the child is unreasonably confined to the premises of the employer.[585]

The Recommendation suggests further measures states may wish to take to eliminate these worst forms of child labour, including: national monitoring mechanisms (paragraph 8); inter-agency cooperation (paragraph 9); effective enforcement in the event of breaches, including special supervision of employers or revocation of permits (paragraph 14); international cooperation (paragraphs 11 and 16); and education, training, enforcement in relation to extraterritorial breaches by

[584] ILO, Declaration on Fundamental Principles and Rights at Work (18 June 1998), [2].
[585] ILO Recommendation No. 190 on Worst Forms of Child Labour 1999, [3].

nationals, publicity, complaints procedures, whistle-blower protection and sensitizing of parents (paragraph 15).

Mention must also be made of ILO standards on occupational health and safety generally, which are considered in the chapter of this book on Article 7 of the ICESCR (concerning conditions of work). Such standards are generally not specific to children, but apply to all workers. It should be emphasized, however, that what is not hazardous for an adult may be hazardous for a child,[586] given children's developmental and health vulnerabilities. Thus, exposure to certain toxins, such as mercury in mines, pesticides or herbicides in agriculture, cyanide in fishing, or polybrominated diphenyl ethers at rubbish dumps, may inhibit neurological development.[587]

Hazardous child labour is the largest category of the worst forms of child labour, with an estimated 115 million children aged 5 to 17 working in dangerous conditions—around half of all child labourers worldwide.[588] Around 22,000 children are killed at work annually.[589] Injury rates are typically higher for migrants and minorities than other children.[590]

Around 59 per cent of children in hazardous work are engaged in agriculture (including fishing, forestry, livestock herding, aquaculture, and subsistence and commercial farming).[591] Hazards in agriculture commonly include risks from chemicals and organisms, tools, motorized equipment, animals and plants, carrying heavy loads and dangerous environments (including heights and surfaces, water bodies, ventilation and noise, sun and insects).[592]

The service sector represents 30 per cent of children in hazardous work.[593] Common hazards in domestic service include, for instance, fatigue from long working hours, physical or psychological abuse, sexual exploitation, isolation, cooking risks (such as from fires, stoves or knives), household chemicals and lifting heavy loads (such as laundry, water or other children).[594] Services provided on the street by children bring hazards of dirty and polluted environments, heat and cold, traffic, crime, violence, abuse and exploitation.[595]

Industry represents 11 per cent of children in hazardous work.[596] Hazards include chemicals, fumes, dust, tools, repetitive movements, awkward postures and abuse. In mining and quarrying, dangers include cave-ins, rock-falls, poisoning (such as from mercury, lead or cobalt), asphyxiation, prostitution and drugs.[597] In construction, there are particular dangers on building sites and from construction processes. Other risky industries include shoe-making, leather tanning, garment sweatshops, battery recycling and metal or wood working.

[586] van Bueren, 'Minimum Core Obligations', 154.

[587] ILO, *Children in Hazardous Work* (Geneva, 2011), 23, 27, 35 and 40.

[588] ILO, 'Hazardous Child Labour', <http://www.ilo.org/ipec/facts/WorstFormsofChildLabour/Hazardouschildlabour/lang--en/index.htm>.

[589] ILO, 'Hazardous Child Labour'.

[590] ILO, *Children in Hazardous Work* (Geneva, 2011), 10.

[591] ILO, *Children in Hazardous Work*, 9.

[592] ILO, *Children in Hazardous Work*, 21–2.

[593] ILO, *Children in Hazardous Work*, 9.

[594] ILO, *Children in Hazardous Work*, 22.

[595] ILO, *Children in Hazardous Work*, 38–9.

[596] ILO, *Children in Hazardous Work*, 9.

[597] ILO, *Children in Hazardous Work*, 33.

In monitoring states under the ICESCR, the CESCR has often addressed hazardous child labour,[598] including in domestic service,[599] agriculture,[600] mining,[601] stone-crushing[602] and street begging.[603] It has also expressed concern about child labour generally in many contexts, including children who tend the herds of nomadic herders (*enfants bouviers*) and Koranic students sent out to beg (*muhajirin*);[604] agricultural work by children under 12 years and children between 8 and 15 years working in cotton gins;[605] and those in the sugar cane sector[606] or on tobacco farms.[607]

Child labour is, however, often driven by economic necessity. The CESCR has accordingly urged states to adopt policies which address the root causes of it, such as by: increasing financial assistance to poor families[608] or compensating families that stop receiving income from child labour;[609] raising awareness of the dangers of child labour and the importance of education;[610] and increasing educational opportunities for former child workers.[611]

Regional law also prohibits hazardous child labour. For example, Article 15(1) of the African Charter on the Rights and Welfare of the Child provides that '[e]very child shall be protected from all forms of economic exploitation and from performing any work that is likely to be hazardous or to interfere with the child's physical, mental, spiritual, moral, or social development' and states must take certain measures of protection under Article 15(2).

'Age limits below which the paid employment of child labour should be prohibited'

The final sentence of Article 10(3), which requires states to set age limits below which the paid employment of labour should be prohibited and punishable by

[598] CESCR, Concluding Observations: Afghanistan, E/C.12/AFG/CO/2-4 (7 June 2010), [29]; Angola, E/C.12/DZA/CO/4 (7 June 2010), [17]; Benin, E/C.12/BEN/CO/2 (9 June 2008), [20]; Bolivia, E/C.12/1/Add.60, 21 May 2001, [19]; Bolivia, E/C.12/BOL/CO/2 (8 August 2008), [14(d)]; Brazil, E/C.12/BRA/CO/2 (12 June 2009), [23]; Cambodia, E/C.12/KHM/CO/1 (12 June 2009), [25]; Chad, E/C.12/TCD/CO/3 (16 December 2009), [21].

[599] CESCR, Concluding Observations: Benin, E/C.12/1/Add.78 (5 June 2002), [18]; Benin, E/C.12/BEN/CO/2 (9 June 2008), [20]; Bolivia, E/C.12/1/Add.60 (21 May 2001), [19]; Bolivia, E/C.12/BOL/CO/2 (8 August 2008), [14(d)]; Chad, E/C.12/TCD/CO/3 (16 December 2009), [21].

[600] CESCR, Concluding Observations: Egypt, E/C.12/1/Add.44 (23 May 2000), [21].

[601] CESCR, Concluding Observations: Ukraine, E/C.12/UKR/CO/5 (4 January 2008), [21]; Zambia, E/C.12/1/Add.106 (23 June 2005), [25].

[602] CESCR, Concluding Observations: Zambia, E/C.12/1/Add.106 (23 June 2005), [25].

[603] CESCR, Concluding Observations: Chad, E/C.12/TCD/CO/3 (16 December 2009), [21]; Ukraine, E/C.12/UKR/CO/5 (4 January 2008), [21].

[604] CESCR, Concluding Observations: Chad, E/C.12/TCD/CO/3 (16 December 2009), [21].

[605] CESCR, Concluding Observations: Egypt, E/C.12/1/Add.44 (23 May 2000), [21].

[606] CESCR, Concluding Observations: El Salvador, E/C.12/SLV/CO/2 (27 June 2007), [23].

[607] CESCR, Concluding Observations: Kazakhstan, E/C.12/KAZ/CO/1 (7 June 2010), [27].

[608] CESCR, Concluding Observations: El Salvador, E/C.12/SLV/CO/2 (27 June 2007), [42].

[609] CESCR, Concluding Observations: Bolivia, E/C.12/BOL/CO/2 (8 August 2008), [20(d)].

[610] CESCR, Concluding Observations: Angola, E/C.12/DZA/CO/4 (7 June 2010), [17].

[611] CESCR, Concluding Observations: Afghanistan, E/C.12/AFG/CO/2-4 (7 June 2010), [29]; Brazil, E/C.12/BRA/CO/2 (12 June 2009), [23].

law, caused some debate during the drafting. The United Kingdom preferred a draft text which would only have prohibited harmful child labour but not punished the perpetrators, on the basis that 'the employment of children, with the appropriate safeguards, was justifiable in exceptional cases'.[612] El Salvador likewise thought that not every instance of unlawful child labour would call for criminal action, since often labour inspection 'would suffice to prevent or put an end to the abuse'.[613] However, a strongly worded Romanian amendment was narrowly adopted[614] as the final sentence of Article 10(3).

It was, however, left to states themselves to determine the minimum age for work. The plural reference to 'age limits' in Article 10(3) indicates that a state may set different age limits in different sectors. This is the approach reflected in the various ILO conventions on minimum age in different sectors adopted since 1919.[615] Article 24 of the ICCPR does not specify a minimum age for employment and the HRC asks states simply to indicate the legal age of work, which cannot be 'unreasonably low':

> 4. ... States should also indicate the age at which a child is legally entitled to work and the age at which he is treated as an adult under labour law... However, the Committee notes that the age for the above purposes should not be set unreasonably low and that in any case a State party cannot absolve itself from its obligations under the Covenant regarding persons under the age of 18, notwithstanding that they have reached the age of majority under domestic law.[616]

The most widely accepted contemporary standards are found in ILO Convention No. 138 on Minimum Age 1973, ratified by 166 states. Article 1 requires states to 'pursue a national policy designed to ensure the effective abolition of child labour and to raise progressively the minimum age for admission to employment or work to a level consistent with the fullest physical and mental development of young persons'.

Convention No. 138 then establishes legal minimum ages at which children can engage in different types of work, and this segmented approach is followed in certain regional standards.[617] The basic minimum age is pegged to the age for finishing compulsory schooling, which is generally 15 years (or 14 years in developing countries 'initially') (Article 2(3) to (4)). 'Light' work may be performed by children between 13 and 15 years (or 12 to 14 years in developing countries),

[612] UNGA Third Committee, A/C.3/SR.738 (23 January 1957), 290 (United Kingdom); see also UNGA Third Committee, A/C.3/SR.730 (14 January 1957), 248 (United Kingdom).

[613] UNGA Third Committee, A/C.3/SR.731 (15 January 1957), 254 (El Salvador).

[614] By twenty-five votes to twenty-two, with seventeen abstentions: UNGA Third Committee Report, A/3525 (9 February 1957), 44.

[615] See discussion above.

[616] HRC, General Comment No. 17 (1989).

[617] See, eg, European Social Charter 1961, Article 7(1)–(3), under which states undertake: '(1) to provide that the minimum age of admission to employment shall be 15 years, subject to exceptions for children employed in prescribed light work without harm to their health, morals or education; (2) to provide that a higher minimum age of admission to employment shall be fixed with respect to prescribed occupations regarded as dangerous or unhealthy; (3) to provide that persons who are still subject to compulsory education shall not be employed in such work as would deprive them of the full benefit of their education'.

as long as it does not threaten their health and safety, or hinder their education or vocational orientation and training (Article 7(1) and (4)).

'Hazardous' work (that is, work 'which by its nature or the circumstances in which it is carried out is likely to jeopardise the health, safety or morals of young persons') should not be performed by anyone under 18 years (Article 3(1)). As already noted, what is hazardous work is determined by national authorities in consultation with employers' and workers' organizations (Article 3(2)).

The minimum age for hazardous work may, however, be reduced to 16 years by a state in consultation with employers' and workers' organizations, 'on condition that the health, safety and morals of the young persons concerned are fully protected and that the young persons have received adequate specific instruction or vocational training in the relevant branch of activity' (Article 3(3)). The exception is oddly framed, for if young people are 'fully protected' against hazards, then by definition the work is not hazardous (that is, work 'likely to jeopardise the health, safety or morals of young persons').

The Convention also contains various flexible exceptions for certain work categories or economic sectors (as under Articles 4 to 5). States can thus elect to exclude, for instance, non-commercial agricultural work (such as family and small-scale local farming)—which constitutes the overwhelming majority of child labour globally.[618] Likewise, Article 8 permits individual permits to be granted 'for such purposes as participation in artistic performances'.

In implementing their obligations under Convention No. 138, states must take '[a]ll necessary measures, including the provision of appropriate penalties…to ensure the effective enforcement' of the Convention (Article 9(1)). National law must also define those responsible for ensuring compliance (Article 9(2)) and require employers to keep registers or other documents containing the names and ages or dates of birth of employees less than 18 years (Article 9(3)).

It has been suggested that it is difficult to 'read into' Article 10(3) of the ICESCR the minimum ages in Convention No. 138, because of the small number of states parties.[619] However, Convention No. 138 now has 166 ratifications, representing more than three-quarters of the international community. It can thus be seen as a minimum benchmark, not least because it contains flexible rules according to sector and concessions for developing countries, consistent with the principle of progressive realization under the ICESCR.

In monitoring states, the CESCR has sometimes called on states to ratify and follow the minimum age standards in ILO Convention No. 138, signifying its acceptance of the Convention as a minimum benchmark in the application of Article 10(3).[620] Setting minimum ages also has minimal resource implications and

[618] Colin Fenwick, 'The International Labour Organization: An Integrated Approach to Economic and Social Rights' in Malcolm Langford (ed), *Social Rights Jurisprudence: Emerging Trends in International and Comparative Law* (Cambridge University Press, Cambridge, 2009), 591, 601.

[619] van Bueren, 'Minimum Core Obligations', 155.

[620] CESCR, Concluding Observations: Peru, E/C.12/1/Add.14 (20 May 1997), [34]; Portugal, E/C.12/1/Add.53 (1 December 2000), [22].

can thus be regarded as an obligation of immediate effect under Article 10(3) of the ICESCR,[621] although enforcement and compliance requires some resources, albeit shared by employers' through their record-keeping obligations.

Occasionally, the CESCR has identified particular ages for certain work in national law as being too low. It was concerned that children between 13 and 15 years could perform industrial work in Estonia; agricultural and domestic work could be undertaken from 12 years in Panama; and many children below 16 years were engaged in agriculture and industry in Mexico and that the minimum age should be 15 years.[622] The CESCR has also criticized a discrepancy between the minimum ages for work (16 years) and social security (18 years) in Saint Vincent and the Grenadines, which leaves working children socially unprotected.[623]

The issue is not so much whether Convention No. 138 can be regarded as a minimum standard informing Article 10(3) of the ICESCR, but whether under Convention No. 138 some minimum ages should now be regarded as too low and the available exceptions too generous. ILO Recommendation No. 146 on Minimum Age 1973, for example, encourages states to set the minimum age at the same level for all economic sectors and to progressively raise it to 16 years. This may now be a more appropriate benchmark for the purposes of the human rights-based standards in Article 10(3) of the ICESCR.

Prohibition on forced or compulsory child labour

Even where work is safe and involves a child above the minimum age, it must be undertaken voluntarily by the child. The requirement in Article 10(3) to protect children from 'economic exploitation' implicitly includes a prohibition on forced or compulsory child labour. This is reinforced by Article 6 of the ICCPR, which requires work always to be freely chosen and entered into, and this necessarily includes where it involves children. As noted above, ILO Convention No. 182 also prohibits 'all forms of slavery or practices similar to slavery, such as the sale and trafficking of children, debt bondage and serfdom and forced or compulsory labour', as among the 'worst forms of child labour' (Article 3(a)).

The general considerations concerning the voluntariness of or consent to work were addressed in the earlier chapter on Article 6 and are also relevant to children. The consent of children does, however, raise additional considerations, as the ILO observes:

> 206. …Concerning the criteria for 'offering oneself voluntarily', the Committee of Experts pointed out that with regard to child labour, the question arises whether, and if so, under what circumstances a minor can be considered to have offered himself or herself

[621] van Bueren, 'Minimum Core Obligations', 155.

[622] CESCR, Concluding Observations: Estonia, E/C.12/1/Add.85 (19 December 2002), [21]; Panama, E/C.12/1/Add.64 (24 September 2001), [17]; Mexico, E/C.12/MEX/CO/4 (9 June 2006), [22] and [41].

[623] CESCR, Concluding Observations: Saint Vincent and the Grenadines, E/C.12/1/Add.21 (2 December 1997), [20].

'voluntarily' for work or service and whether the consent of the parents is needed in this regard and whether it is sufficient, and what the sanctions for refusal are…[624]

Relevantly, mention may be made of Article 12(1) of the CROC, by which a child's views are to be given due weight:

States Parties shall assure to the child who is capable of forming his or her own views the right to express those views freely in all matters affecting the child, the views of the child being given due weight in accordance with the age and maturity of the child.

At the same time, the CROC recognizes the 'responsibilities, rights and duties of parents' in decision-making about a child, in Article 5:

States Parties shall respect the responsibilities, rights and duties of parents or, where applicable, the members of the extended family or community as provided for by local custom, legal guardians or other persons legally responsible for the child, to provide, in a manner consistent with the evolving capacities of the child, appropriate direction and guidance in the exercise by the child of the rights recognized in the present Convention.

In some cultures, the family responsibilities of children may include assisting in family agriculture or businesses. Even so, the best interests of the child must be an overriding consideration, not the interests of the parents or family group. Moreover, parents' 'right' to consent to their child working cannot displace the child's right to education (under Article 13 of the ICESCR), or freedom not to work (under Article 6) where the child is capable of making her or his own decision. Moreover, if a child is not yet capable of forming his or her own views in relation to work, it must be queried whether the child is sufficiently mature to undertake any work which parents may wish him or her to perform.

Unlike the law on forced labour by adults, the prohibition on forced child labour is not subject to any exceptions for lawful compulsory labour. This is because Article 11(1) of ILO Convention No. 29 provides that only males over 18 years old 'may be called upon for forced or compulsory labour'. The prohibition is thus absolute.

In monitoring states, the CESCR has occasionally commented on forced child labour under Articles 6 or 10 of the ICESCR. Under Article 6, it was concerned about forced or bonded labour of children under 16 years (thus implicitly referencing the ILO standards) in the Republic of the Congo,[625] and the trafficking of children (as young as 2 years old) for future work on plantations or as house workers in Togo.[626] It was concerned that the abrogation of constitutional protections in the Republic of the Congo removed protections against forced or bonded labour for children under the age of 16 years.[627] It highlighted the vulnerable and

[624] ILO, Report of the Commission of Inquiry appointed under Article 26 of the Constitution of the International Labour Organization to examine the observance by Myanmar of the Forced Labour Convention, 1930 (No. 29) (2 July 1998), [206] ('ILO Commission of Inquiry on Myanmar').

[625] CESCR, Concluding Observations: Republic of the Congo, E/2001/22 (2000), 43 [210].

[626] CESCR, Concluding Observations: Togo, E/2002/22 (2001), 57 [317].

[627] CESCR, Concluding Observations: Republic of the Congo, E/C.12/1/Add.45 (23 May 2000), [19].

difficult circumstances of Sri Lankan children left without their mothers as a result of the slave-like treatment of Sri Lankan women working abroad as domestic helpers.[628] In respect of China, the CESCR condemned a school curriculum activity which forced children to perform civic labour:

23. ... The Committee is also of the view that the 'Diligent Work and Economical Study' (qingong jianxue) programme for schoolchildren constitutes exploitative child labour, in contradiction of the provisions of articles 6 and 7 of the Covenant, and Convention No. 182 concerning the Prohibition and Immediate Action for the Elimination of the Worst Forms of Child Labour of the International Labour Organization (ILO) to which China is a party.[629]

Under Article 10(3), the CESCR was concerned by forced labour by minors in prisons.[630] It has also recommended stricter enforcement of fines and criminal sanctions for those who employ children,[631] increasing labour inspections[632] and creating systems for registering cases of mistreatment.[633]

As might be expected, the CRC has also focused on forced child labour. It has commonly commented on forced child labour in agriculture or the informal sector, such as the large number of child labourers in India, including in bonded labour and in household enterprises, domestic service and agriculture.[634]

The CRC has drawn attention to especially vulnerable groups, such as: refugee, asylum-seeking and unaccompanied children in Georgia; Pygmies and the Kirdi minorities in Cameroon; girls, internally displaced and refugee children, street children, orphans, rural children, *Dalit* bonded labourers (*haliya*), and children from vulnerable castes in Nepal; and *talibés* (students) exploited by their teachers in Mauritania.[635]

Child soldiers

As noted earlier, the forced or compulsory recruitment of children for use in armed conflict is prohibited as one of the worst forms of child labour under ILO Convention No. 182 (Article 3(a)). That instrument does not, however, set a minimum age for lawful child recruitment. The earlier ILO Convention No.

[628] CESCR, Concluding Observations: Sri Lanka, E/1999/22 (1998), 22 [77].

[629] CESCR, Concluding Observations: China, E/C.12/1/Add.107 (13 May 2005), [23].

[630] CESCR, Concluding Observations: Syrian Arab Republic, E/C.12/1/Add.63 (24 September 2001), [18].

[631] CESCR, Concluding Observations: Afghanistan, E/C.12/AFG/CO/2-4 (7 June 2010), [29]; Benin, E/C.12/1/Add.78 (5 June 2002), [38]; Bolivia, E/C.12/BOL/CO/2 (8 August 2008), [20(d)]; Brazil, E/C.12/BRA/CO/2 (12 June 2009), [23]; Cambodia, E/C.12/KHM/CO/1 (12 June 2009), [25].

[632] CESCR, Concluding Observations: Afghanistan, E/C.12/AFG/CO/2-4 (7 June 2010), [29]; Angola, E/C.12/DZA/CO/4 (7 June 2010), [17]; Bolivia, E/C.12/BOL/CO/2 (8 August 2008), [20(d)]; Cambodia, E/C.12/KHM/CO/1 (12 June 2009), [25].

[633] CESCR, Concluding Observations: Netherlands Antilles, E/C.12/NLD/CO/3/Add.1 (31 January 2008), [40].

[634] CRC, Concluding Observations: India, CRC/C/94 (2000), 10 [97].

[635] CRC, Concluding Observations: Georgia, CRC/C/97 (2000), 18 [131]; Cameroon, CRC/C/111 (2001), 71 [383] and [384]; Nepal, CRC/C/150 (2005), 66 [373]–[376]; Mauritania, CRC/C/111 (2001), 8 [76].

29 on Forced Labour 1930 provides that only males over 18 years old 'may be called upon for forced or compulsory labour', including any exception for lawful military conscription (Article 11(1)). The ILO thus concludes that the provision does not permit the military conscription of children under 18 years.[636] In its inquiry on Myanmar, for example, the ILO found that the state had unlawfully forced children as young as 10 to work in support of the military or on public infrastructure.[637]

Article 77(2) of Additional Protocol I 1977 to the Geneva Conventions 1949 prohibits the recruitment of children under 15 years, which is also a war crime within the jurisdiction of the International Criminal Court.[638] Article 38 of the CROC also establishes 15 years as the minimum age for recruitment into military forces, and requires states to take all feasible measures to ensure that children under 15 years do not take a direct part in hostilities:

> 2. States Parties shall take all feasible measures to ensure that persons who have not attained the age of fifteen years do not take a direct part in hostilities.
>
> 3. States Parties shall refrain from recruiting any person who has not attained the age of fifteen years into their armed forces. In recruiting among those persons who have attained the age of fifteen years but who have not attained the age of eighteen years, States Parties shall endeavour to give priority to those who are oldest.

A higher standard is provided in the CROC Optional Protocol on the Involvement of Children in Armed Conflict,[639] which establishes 18 as the minimum age for compulsory recruitment; urges states to raise the minimum age for voluntary recruitment (above the 15 years provided in the CROC); and requires states to take all feasible measures to ensure that members of their armed forces under 18 years do not take a direct part in hostilities. States must also prohibit non-state armed groups from recruiting or using children under the age of 18 years.

Protection against child soldiering is strongest in the African Charter on the Rights and Welfare of the Child, Article 22(2) of which requires states to 'take all necessary measures to ensure that no child shall take a direct part in hostilities and refrain in particular, from recruiting any child'.

In monitoring states, the CESCR has not identified a minimum age at which children may participate in armed conflicts. The abduction or enslavement of children in armed conflicts has been highlighted by the CESCR under Article 6, whether for military or commercial purposes (for example, forced recruitment as soldiers, or the selling of children as servants, agricultural labourers and

[636] ILO Commission of Inquiry on Myanmar, [511] and [206] respectively.

[637] ILO Commission of Inquiry on Myanmar, [511].

[638] Rome Statute of the International Criminal Court (adopted 17 July 1998, 2187 UNTS 3, entered into force 1 July 2002), Article 8(2)(b)(xxxvi) ('use' or 'recruitment').

[639] Optional Protocol to the Convention on the Rights of the Child on the Involvement of Children in Armed Conflict (adopted 25 May 2000, 2173 UNTS 222, entered into force 12 February 2002); see also Free Children from War Conference, The Paris Commitments to Protect Children from Unlawful Recruitment or Use by Armed Forces or Armed Groups and The Paris Principles and Guidelines on Children Associated with Armed Forces or Armed Groups, Paris, February 2007.

concubines in Sudan), including child combatants as young as 9 and the rape of enslaved girls in Liberia.[640]

The CESCR has also commented on child soldiers under Article 10(3), including the recruitment of children by armed groups and forces.[641] It has urged parties to conflicts to cease further recruitment[642] and to immediately release children.[643] The CESCR has also recommended regular follow-up visits to military camps and training centres[644] to monitor compliance with the prohibition on child soldiers, and urged the prosecution and sentencing of those responsible.[645] It has also supported the demobilization, reintegration and rehabilitation of children in military service,[646] to address the psychological and emotional impacts.

'SOCIAL EXPLOITATION'

Sexual exploitation and trafficking

Sexual exploitation and trafficking are forms of both social and economic exploitation. In monitoring states in relation to Article 10(3), the CESCR has often been concerned by the sexual exploitation of children,[647] whether through child prostitution,[648] sex tourism,[649] paedophilia,[650] pornography[651] and including by inducements to leave school (sometimes encouraged by parents).[652] Similar concerns have been expressed under related international instruments by the CRC,[653]

[640] CRC, Concluding Observations: Sudan, CRC/C/121 (2002), 53 [280] and [281]; Liberia, CRC/C/140 (2004), 67 [360] and [361]; Myanmar, CRC/C/140 (2004), 81 [442] and [443].

[641] CESCR, Concluding Observations: Afghanistan, E/C.12/AFG/CO/2-4 (7 June 2010), [30]; Chad, E/C.12/TCD/CO/3 (16 December 2009), [22]; Colombia, E/C.12/COL/CO/5 (7 June 2010), [16]; Democratic Republic of Congo, E/C.12/COD/CO/4 (16 December 2009), [27].

[642] CESCR, Concluding Observations: Afghanistan, E/C.12/AFG/CO/2-4 (7 June 2010), [30]; Colombia, E/C.12/COL/CO/5 (7 June 2010), [16].

[643] CESCR, Concluding Observations: Democratic Republic of Congo, E/C.12/COD/CO/4 (16 December 2009), [27].

[644] CESCR, Concluding Observations: Chad, E/C.12/TCD/CO/3 (16 December 2009), [22].

[645] CESCR, Concluding Observations: Colombia, E/C.12/COL/CO/5 (7 June 2010), [16].

[646] CESCR, Concluding Observations: Afghanistan, E/C.12/AFG/CO/2-4 (7 June 2010), [30]; Chad, E/C.12/TCD/CO/3 (16 December 2009), [22]; Colombia, E/C.12/COL/CO/5 (7 June 2010), [16].

[647] CESCR, Concluding Observations: Belgium, E/C.12/1/Add.54 (1 December 2000), [13]; Brazil, E/C.12/BRA/CO/2 (12 June 2009), [22]; Cambodia, E/C.12/KHM/CO/1 (12 June 2009), [25]; Colombia, E/C.12/COL/CO/5 (7 June 2010), [17]; Czech Republic, E/C.12/1/Add.76 (5 June 2002), [18]; Denmark, E/C.12/1/Add.102 (14 December 2004), [19].

[648] CESCR, Concluding Observations: Belgium, E/C.12/1/Add.54 (1 December 2000), [13]; Afghanistan, E/C.12/AFG/CO/2-4 (7 June 2010), [29]; Chile, E/C.12/1/Add.105 (1 December 2004), [23].

[649] CESCR, Concluding Observations: Sri Lanka, E/C.12/1/Add.24 (16 June 1998), [12].

[650] CESCR, Concluding Observations: Belgium, E/C.12/1/Add.54 (1 December 2000), [13].

[651] CESCR, Concluding Observations: Denmark, E/C.12/1/Add.102 (14 December 2004), [19]; Finland, E/C.12/1/Add.8 (5 December 1996), [16]; Germany, E/C.12/1/Add.29 (4 December 1998), [21].

[652] CESCR, Concluding Observations: Jamaica, E/C.12/1/Add.75 (6 December 2001), [13].

[653] CRC, Concluding Observations: Georgia, CRC/C/97 (2000), 18 [131]; Nepal, CRC/C/150 (2005), 66 [376]; Libyan Arab Jamahiriya, CRC/C/132 (2003), 74 [388].

HRC[654] and CERD (including indigenous children subject to servitude and slavery, child prostitution, trafficking and sale).[655]

With regard to the trafficking of children,[656] the CESCR has expressed concern at the lack of effective control over inter-country adoptions[657] and the risk of illegal adoptions from orphanages,[658] which heighten the danger of commercial or sexual exploitation of children. It has also been concerned about the kidnapping of girls lured by fraudulent marriage or job proposals, or sold into marriage or commercial sex work.[659]

Widely accepted international standards relevant in interpreting 'social exploitation' under Article 10(3) to include sexual exploitation and trafficking stem from the CROC. Article 34 of the CROC requires states to protect children from 'all forms of sexual exploitation and sexual abuse', including inducing or coercing a child to engage in unlawful sexual activity, and using children in prostitution or pornography:

States Parties undertake to protect the child from all forms of sexual exploitation and sexual abuse. For these purposes, States Parties shall in particular take all appropriate national, bilateral and multilateral measures to prevent:

(a) The inducement or coercion of a child to engage in any unlawful sexual activity;

(b) The exploitative use of children in prostitution or other unlawful sexual practices;

(c) The exploitative use of children in pornographic performances and materials.

States must also prevent the abduction, sale or trafficking of children for 'any purpose' (Article 35), which would include forced labour. The CROC Optional Protocol on the Sale of Children, Child Prostitution and Child Pornography[660] further requires states to prohibit 'the sale of children, child prostitution and child pornography' (Article 1) and to criminalize such acts (Article 3). The prohibited acts are defined in Article 2:

For the purposes of the present Protocol:

(a) Sale of children means any act or transaction whereby a child is transferred by any person or group of persons to another for remuneration or any other consideration;

[654] HRC, Concluding Observations: Brazil, A/51/40 vol. I (1996), 44 [336]; Japan, A/54/40 vol. I (1999), 36 [171]; Mali, A/58/40 vol. I (2003), 47 [81(18)]; Philippines, A/59/40 vol. I (2003), 15 [63(13)]; Sri Lanka, A/59/40 vol. I (2003), 30 [66(14)]; Serbia and Montenegro, A/59/40 vol. I (2004), 68 [75(16)]; Lithuania, A/59/40 vol. I (2004), 52 [71(14)]; Thailand, A/60/40 vol. I (2005), 83 [95(20)] and [95(23)].

[655] CERD, Concluding Observations: Venezuela (Bolivarian Republic of), A/60/18 (2005), 71 [381].

[656] CESCR, Concluding Observations: Benin, E/C.12/1/Add.78 (5 June 2002), [18]; Benin, E/C.12/BEN/CO/2 (9 June 2008), [39]; Cambodia, E/C.12/KHM/CO/1 (12 June 2009), [26]; China (including Hong Kong and Macao), E/C.12/1/Add.107 (13 May 2005), [29]; Denmark, E/C.12/1/Add.102 (14 December 2004), [19].

[657] CESCR, Concluding Observations: Azerbaijan, E/C.12/1/Add.20 (22 December 1997), [22].

[658] CESCR, Concluding Observations: Azerbaijan, E/C.12/1/Add.104 (14 December 2004), [25].

[659] CESCR, Concluding Observations: Afghanistan, E/C.12/AFG/CO/2-4 (7 June 2010), [32].

[660] Optional Protocol on the Sale of Children, Child Prostitution and Child Pornography (adopted on 25 May 2000, 2171 UNTS 227, entered into force on 18 January 2002).

(b) Child prostitution means the use of a child in sexual activities for remuneration or any other form of consideration;

(c) Child pornography means any representation, by whatever means, of a child engaged in real or simulated explicit sexual activities or any representation of the sexual parts of a child for primarily sexual purposes.

In criminalizing the sale of children, which is not limited to sale for sexual purposes, states must criminalize '[o]ffering, delivering, or accepting, by whatever means, a child for the purpose of:... [e]engagement... in forced labour' (Article 3(1)(a)(i)(c)). The Protocol does not, however, cover forced labour where it is not connected with the sale of a child, and is thus confined to more traditional slavery-like practices involving ownership.

As regards trafficking in children, the Protocol to Prevent, Suppress and Punish Trafficking in Persons, Especially Women and Children 2000 defines, in Article 3(c), the trafficking in children (persons under 18 years) more protectively than trafficking in general: 'The recruitment, transportation, transfer, harbouring or receipt of a child for the purpose of exploitation shall be considered "trafficking in persons" even if this does not involve any of the means set forth in subparagraph (a) of this article'.[661] The CESCR has called on states to ratify the Protocol.[662]

In responding to concerns about sexual exploitation or trafficking under Article 10(3), the CESCR has most commonly advocated strengthening law enforcement policies,[663] support for victims[664] (including more social workers to help child victims)[665] and child-sensitive judicial procedures when prosecuting these crimes.[666] It has also called on states to adopt national action plans to combat the problem,[667] and to better monitor immigration laws.[668] In the field of extradition, it encouraged Sweden to abolish the dual criminality requirement for the sexual exploitation of minors and women committed by Swedish nationals abroad.[669]

[661] Protocol to Prevent, Suppress and Punish Trafficking in Persons, Especially Women and Children, Supplementing the United Nations Convention Against Transnational Organized Crime (adopted 15 November 2000, A/55/383, entered into force 25 December 2003). Article 3(a) defines 'trafficking in persons' as: 'the recruitment, transportation, transfer, harbouring or receipt of persons, by means of the threat or use of force or other forms of coercion, of abduction, of fraud, of deception, of the abuse of power or of a position of vulnerability or of the giving or receiving of payments or benefits to achieve the consent of a person having control over another person, for the purpose of exploitation. Exploitation shall include, at a minimum, the exploitation of the prostitution of others or other forms of sexual exploitation, forced labour or services, slavery or practices similar to slavery, servitude or the removal of organs'.

[662] CESCR, Concluding Observations: Chile, E/C.12/1/Add.105 (1 December 2004), [49].

[663] CESCR, Concluding Observations: Colombia, E/C.12/COL/CO/5 (7 June 2010), [17].

[664] CESCR, Concluding Observations: Brazil, E/C.12/BRA/CO/2 (12 June 2009), [21]; Chile, E/C.12/1/Add.105 (1 December 2004), [47].

[665] CESCR, Concluding Observations: Greece, E/C.12/1/Add.97 (7 June 2004), [38].

[666] CESCR, Concluding Observations: Brazil, E/C.12/BRA/CO/2 (12 June 2009), [21].

[667] CESCR, Concluding Observations: Honduras, E/C.12/1/Add.57 (21 May 2001), [40]; Hungary, E/C.12/HUN/CO/3 (16 January 2008), [20].

[668] CESCR, Concluding Observations: Republic of Korea, E/C.12/KOR/CO/3 (17 December 2009), [25].

[669] CESCR, Concluding Observations: Sweden, E/C.12/1/Add.70 (30 November 2001), [39].

Notably, Article 39 of the CROC requires states to take 'all appropriate measures to promote physical and psychological recovery and social reintegration of a child victim':

States Parties shall take all appropriate measures to promote physical and psychological recovery and social reintegration of a child victim of: any form of neglect, exploitation, or abuse; torture or any other form of cruel, inhuman or degrading treatment or punishment; or armed conflicts. Such recovery and reintegration shall take place in an environment which fosters the health, self-respect and dignity of the child.

The CESCR has also encouraged the ratification of relevant regional standards, such as the Council of Europe Convention on Action against Trafficking in Human Beings (No. 197).[670] A further relevant regional treaty is the African Charter on the Rights and Welfare of the Child, which prohibits sexual exploitation (Article 27) and the sale, trafficking and abduction of children, as well as the use of children 'in all forms of begging' (Article 29).

Narcotics and exploitation

The protection of children from drug-related exploitation may come within the ambit of Article 10(3) of the ICESCR. Reference may be made to Article 33 of the CROC, which requires states to protect children from the use, production or trafficking of illicit drugs:

States Parties shall take all appropriate measures, including legislative, administrative, social and educational measures, to protect children from the illicit use of narcotic drugs and psychotropic substances as defined in the relevant international treaties, and to prevent the use of children in the illicit production and trafficking of such substances.

Similarly, Article 3(c) of ILO Convention No. 182 lists as a 'worst form' of child labour the 'use, procuring or offering of a child for illicit activities, in particular for the production and trafficking of drugs as defined in the relevant international treaties'. A similar protection is found in Article 28 of the African Charter on the Rights and Welfare of the Child.

'Relevant' international drugs control treaties include the Single Convention on Narcotic Drugs 1961 and Protocol 1972, Convention on Psychotropic Substances 1971 and UN Convention against Illicit Traffic in Narcotic Drugs and Psychotropic Substances 1988.[671] The UN Convention 1988 provides that 'the victimization or use of minors' makes drug offences 'particularly serious' (Article 3(5)).

[670] CESCR, Concluding Observations: Slovenia, E/C.12/SVN/CO/1 (25 January 2006), [33].

[671] Single Convention on Narcotic Drugs (adopted 30 March 1961, 520 UNTS 151, entered into force 13 December 1964) and Protocol amending the Single Convention on Narcotic Drugs (adopted 25 March 1972, 976 UNTS 3, entered into force 8 August 1975); Convention on Psychotropic Substances (adopted 21 February 1971, 1019 UNTS 175, entered into force 16 August 1976); UN Convention against Illicit Traffic in Narcotic Drugs and Psychotropic Substances (adopted 20 December 1988, 1582 UNTS 95, entered into force 11 November 1990).

Because of the peculiarities of the international legal approach to drug control, the protection of children from drugs under Article 10(3) may produce strange results. States must prevent children from being involved in the 'illicit' production and trafficking of drugs covered by international treaties, but not 'licit' production and trafficking. Thus, a child may not work in a 'bootleg' distillery, illegal tobacco farm or marijuana plantation, but can be employed in a lawful beverage or cigarette company, or on a medicinal cannabis crop. The work situation of or risks to the child may be similar, although legal operations may have better labour protections; but that is true of any illegal employment situation, and would not appear to justify special treatment of children working with drugs.

A more serious complication concerns disagreement between states over international drug policy. Those in favour of a 'zero tolerance' approach to drugs will have different views on what are appropriate measures to protect children compared to states that support 'harm reduction'. The latter, for instance, may decriminalize less harmful drugs, or adopt a medicalized, non-criminal, non-punitive approach even to serious drugs (such as 'safe injecting rooms' for drug users, to minimize risks of overdoses or transmissible diseases). The latter approaches raise issues of inconsistency with the international drug treaties, even though empirically they may, depending on the evidence in a given context, better protect child drug users.

International Cooperation and Assistance under Article 10

A state's capacity to fulfil rights relating to families, mothers and children under Article 10 as a whole will depend to some extent on resource and expertise considerations. As for other ICESCR rights, states are required to take steps individually and through international assistance and cooperation (ICESCR, Article 2(1)) to achieve the rights in Article 10, including by treaty action, soft law making, consultation, research and technical assistance (ICESCR, Article 23).[672]

Where states require assistance, they should cooperate with other states as well as relevant international organizations, particularly the ILO (in relation to maternity protection, child labour and social insurance or social security benefits for families), UNICEF (in relation to children), and the Special Representative of the Secretary-General on Violence against Children. In relation to cooperation on children's rights under the CROC, the CRC has urged as follows:

> The Committee calls upon the following partners to support, both financially and technically, child protection programmes, including training, which take full account of the requirements stipulated in article 19 and the Convention more broadly: States parties providing development cooperation; donor institutions (including the World Bank, private sources and foundations); United Nations agencies and organizations; and other international and regional bodies and organizations. This financial and technical support should be provided systematically through strong and equitable partnerships, at the national and international levels. Child rights-based protection programmes should be one of the main

[672] CESCR, General Comment No. 18 (2006), [29].

components in assisting sustainable development in countries receiving international assistance. The Committee also encourages such bodies to continue to work with the Committee, the Special Representative of the Secretary-General on Violence against Children and other international and regional human rights mechanisms to advance this goal.[673]

The CESCR has sometimes called on states to cooperate with particular international actors in specific contexts, such as UNICEF and the ILO in relation to child labour.[674]

Summary of State Obligations under Article 10

As the CESCR has noted in relation to other ICESCR rights, a state enjoys a margin of discretion in assessing which measures are most suitable to meet its specific circumstances.[675] However, the ICESCR clearly imposes a duty on each state party to take whatever steps are necessary to ensure that measures of protection and assistance are provided to families, mothers and children as soon as possible.

Like all human rights, Article 10 imposes three types or levels of obligations on states parties: the obligations to *respect, protect* and *fulfil*. The obligation to *respect* requires states parties to refrain from interfering directly or indirectly with the enjoyment of the rights of families, mothers and children. Specifically, this will include: not denying legal recognition to the family, its ability to live together (including in the immigration, detention, custody and access fields) or the birth registration or nationality of a child; not interfering in the freedom to marry; refraining from dismissing pregnant women or those on maternity leave; not failing to set minimum ages for lawful work by children; and not using child labour or otherwise exploiting children for other purposes (including sexual abuse).

The obligation to *protect* requires states parties to take measures that prevent third parties from interfering with the enjoyment of such rights. States must accordingly legislate to regulate maternity protection and child labour in private enterprises; and to forbid the unlawful recruitment of, or participation in hostilities by, child soldiers. Further, private institutions which are involved in the care of children without families (such as orphanages or alternative care institutions) must be effectively regulated and supervised to ensure that they do not abuse or exploit children and that they respect children's rights. Most importantly, states must also protect children from violence or abuse by parents in the family. Legislation prohibiting discrimination against children or groups of children must be adopted. The state must also take measures to prevent and remedy harmful traditional practices.

The obligation to *fulfil* includes the obligations to provide, facilitate and promote the rights in Article 10. It implies that states parties should adopt

673 CRC, General Comment No. 13 (2011), [74].

674 CESCR, Concluding Observations: Peru, E/C.12/1/Add.14 (20 May 1997), [34]; Paraguay, E/C.12/1/Add.1 (28 May 1996), [27].

675 See, eg, CESCR, General Comment No. 18 (2006), [37].

appropriate legislative, administrative, budgetary, judicial and other measures to ensure their full realization. States are obliged to fulfil (provide) the rights in Article 10 where families, mothers or children are unable, for reasons beyond their control, to realize those rights themselves by the means at their disposal. This includes an obligation to adopt national legislation and policies, strategies or plans for the protection of families and children, with adequate funding to realize such policies over time. Key elements will include: institutions and/or funding for family, maternity and child benefits; childcare and early childhood education services; foster care and alternative care arrangements; and child protection policies.

Remedies

Any person who is a victim of a violation of rights under Article 10 should have access to effective judicial or other appropriate remedies at the national level. This may also involve special mechanisms such as a 'children's commissioner' or ombudsperson, as well as labour and social security mechanisms (including special tribunals) in the case of maternity protection and children at work. All victims of such violations are entitled to adequate reparation, which may take the form of restitution, compensation, satisfaction or guarantees of non-repetition. Certain violations under Article 10 must also be criminally punishable, including unlawful child labour and the sexual exploitation of children.

The incorporation of other relevant international instruments into domestic law may strengthen the effectiveness of measures taken to guarantee the rights in Article 10. The Convention on the Rights of the Child and its Protocols, and ILO conventions on maternity protection and social security for families and children, are particularly relevant. Courts would then be empowered to adjudicate violations of Article 10 by reference to such standards.[676]

Relevant Regional Standards

Regional standards related to the protections for families, mothers and children in Article 10 have been discussed throughout this chapter where relevant. For convenience of reference, the relevant regional standards are extracted in full here.

AFRICA

The African Charter on Human and Peoples' Rights requires the state to protect the family in Article 18:

1. The family shall be the natural unit and basis of society. It shall be protected by the State which shall take care of its physical health and moral.

[676] CESCR, General Comment No. 18 (2006), [49].

2. The State shall have the duty to assist the family which is the custodian of morals and traditional values recognized by the community.

3. The State shall ensure the elimination of every discrimination against women and also ensure the protection of the rights of the woman and the child as stipulated in international declarations and conventions.

4. The aged and the disabled shall also have the right to special measures of protection in keeping with their physical or moral needs.

The African Charter also recognizes individual duties towards the family in Articles 27(1) and 29(1):

Article 27

1. Every individual shall have duties towards his family and society, the State and other legally recognized communities and the international community.

…

Article 29

The individual shall also have the duty:

1. to preserve the harmonious development of the family and to work for the cohesion and respect of the family; to respect his parents at all times, to maintain them in case of need…

Children's rights are more extensively elaborated in the African Charter on the Rights and Welfare of the Child, which provides a general protection for the family in Article 18:

1. The family shall be the natural unit and basis of society. It shall enjoy the protection and support of the State for its establishment and development.

2. States Parties to the present Charter shall take appropriate steps to ensure equality of rights and responsibilities of spouses with regard to children during marriage and in the even of its dissolution. In case of the dissolution, provision shall be made for the necessary protection of the child.

3. No child shall be deprived of maintenance by reference to the parents' marital status.

Alongside state protection and support for the family, the African Children's Charter recognizes the right of children to parental care and protection in Article 19, and outlines parental responsibilities in Article 20 and children's responsibilities in Article 31:

Article 19: Parent Care and Protection

1. Every child shall be entitled to the enjoyment of parental care and protection and shall, whenever possible, have the right to reside with his or her parents. No child shall be separated from his parents against his will, except when a judicial authority determines in accordance with the appropriate law, that such separation is in the best interest of the child.

2. Every child who is separated from one or both parents shall have the right to maintain personal relations and direct contact with both parents on a regular basis.

3. Where separation results from the action of a State Party, the State Party shall provide the child, or if appropriate, another member of the family with essential information concerning the whereabouts of the absent member or members of the family. States Parties shall also ensure that the submission of such a request shall not entail any adverse consequences for the person or persons in whose respect it is made.

4. Where a child is apprehended by a State Party, his parents or guardians shall, as soon as possible, be notified of such apprehension by that State Party.

Article 20: Parental Responsibilities

1. Parents or other persons responsible for the child shall have the primary responsibility of the upbringing and development the child and shall have the duty:

(a) to ensure that the best interests of the child are their basic concern at all times;

(b) to secure, within their abilities and financial capacities, conditions of living necessary to the child's development; and

(c) to ensure that domestic discipline is administered with humanity and in a manner consistent with the inherent dignity of the child.

2. States Parties to the present Charter shall in accordance with their means and national conditions the all appropriate measures;

(a) to assist parents and other persons responsible for the child and in case of need provide material assistance and support programmes particularly with regard to nutrition, health, education, clothing and housing;

(b) to assist parents and others responsible for the child in the performance of child-rearing and ensure the development of institutions responsible for providing care of children; and

(c) to ensure that the children of working parents are provided with care services and facilities.

. . .

Article 31: Responsibility of the Child

Every child shall have responsibilities towards his family and society, the State and other legally recognized communities and the international community. The child, subject to his age and ability, and such limitations as may be contained in the present Charter, shall have the duty;

(a) to work for the cohesion of the family, to respect his parents, superiors and elders at all times and to assist them in case of need;

(b) to serve his national community by placing his physical and intellectual abilities at its service;

(c) to preserve and strengthen social and national solidarity;

(d) to preserve and strengthen African cultural values in his relations with other members of the society, in the spirit of tolerance, dialogue and consultation and to contribute to the moral well-being of society;

(e) to preserve and strengthen the independence and the integrity of his country;

(f) to contribute to the best of his abilities. at all times and at all levels, to the promotion and achievement of African Unity.

Adoption is addressed by Article 24 of the African Children's Charter and the separation of children from parents in Article 25:

Article 24: Adoption

States Parties which recognize the system of adoption shall ensure that the best interest of the child shall be the paramount consideration and they shall:

(a) establish competent authorities to determine matters of adoption and ensure that the adoption is carried out in conformity with applicable laws and procedures and on the basis of all relevant and reliable information, that the adoption is permissible in view of the child's status concerning parents, relatives and guardians and that, if necessary, the appropriate persons concerned have given their informed consent to the adoption on the basis of appropriate counselling;

(b) recognize that inter-country adoption in those States who have ratified or adhered to the International Convention on the Rights of the Child or this Charter may, as the last resort, be considered as an alternative means of a child's care, if the child cannot be placed in a foster or an adoptive family or cannot in any suitable manner be cared for in the child's country of origin;

(c) ensure that the child affected by inter-country adoption enjoys safeguards and standards equivalent to those existing in the case of national adoption;

(d) take all appropriate measures to ensure that in inter-country adoption, the placement does not result in trafficking or improper financial gain for those who try to adopt a child;

(e) promote, where appropriate, the objectives of this Article by concluding bilateral or multilateral arrangements or agreements, and endeavour, within this framework to ensure that the placement of the child in another country is carried out by competent authorities or organs;

(f) establish a machinery to monitor the well-being of the adopted child.

Article 25: Separation from Parents

1. Any child who is permanently or temporarily deprived of his family environment for any reason shall be entitled to special protection and assistance;

2. States Parties to the present Charter:

(a) shall ensure that a child who is parentless, or who is temporarily or permanently deprived of his or her family environment, or who in his or her best interest cannot be brought up or allowed to remain in that environment shall be provided with alternative family care, which could include, among others. foster placement, or placement in suitable institutions for the care of children;

(b) shall take all necessary measures to trace and re-unite children with parents or relatives where separation is caused by internal and external displacement arising from armed conflicts or natural disasters.

3. When considering alternative family care of the child and the best interests of the child, due regard shall be paid to the desirability of continuity in a child's up-bringing and to the child's ethnic, religious or linguistic background.

The remainder of the African Children's Charter addresses the general obligations of states (Article 1), definition of the child (Article 2), non-discrimination (Article 3), best interests of the child (Article 4), rights to survival and development (Article 5), and various civil and political rights (Articles 6 to 10).[677] It also sets out various socio-economic rights, including education (Article 11), leisure, recreation and culture (Article 12), and health (Article 14).

Children are also protected against economic exploitation such as child labour (Article 15) and other forms of exploitation (including sexual exploitation (Article 27), drug abuse (Article 28), and sale, trafficking and abduction (Article 29)). Numerous provisions require the protection of children from violence, such as child abuse and torture (Article 16), harmful social and cultural practices (Article 21), armed conflicts (Article 22), and apartheid and discrimination (Article 26). There are special protections for handicapped (Article 13) and refugee (Article 23) children, children of imprisoned mothers (Article 30) and those affected by juvenile justice (Article 17).

EUROPE

The European Convention on Human Rights requires respect for family life in Article 8:

1. Everyone has the right to respect for his private and family life, his home and his correspondence.

2. There shall be no interference by a public authority with the exercise of this right except such as is in accordance with the law and is necessary in a democratic society in the interests of national security, public safety or the economic well-being of the country, for the prevention of disorder or crime, for the protection of health or morals, or for the protection of the rights and freedoms of others.

The European Social Charter 1961 recognizes the right to protection of children and young persons (Article 7) and employed women (Article 8):

Article 7—The right of children and young persons to protection

With a view to ensuring the effective exercise of the right of children and young persons to protection, the Contracting Parties undertake:

1. to provide that the minimum age of admission to employment shall be 15 years, subject to exceptions for children employed in prescribed light work without harm to their health, morals or education;

2. to provide that a higher minimum age of admission to employment shall be fixed with respect to prescribed occupations regarded as dangerous or unhealthy;

3. to provide that persons who are still subject to compulsory education shall not be employed in such work as would deprive them of the full benefit of their education;

[677] Article 6 (name and nationality), Article 7 (freedom of expression), Article 8 (freedom of association), Article 9 (freedom of thought, conscience and religion) and Article 10 (protection of privacy).

4. to provide that the working hours of persons under 16 years of age shall be limited in accordance with the needs of their development, and particularly with their need for vocational training;

5. to recognise the right of young workers and apprentices to a fair wage or other appropriate allowances;

6. to provide that the time spent by young persons in vocational training during the normal working hours with the consent of the employer shall be treated as forming part of the working day;

7. to provide that employed persons of under 18 years of age shall be entitled to not less than three weeks' annual holiday with pay;

8. to provide that persons under 18 years of age shall not be employed in night work with the exception of certain occupations provided for by national laws or regulations;

9. to provide that persons under 18 years of age employed in occupations prescribed by national laws or regulations shall be subject to regular medical control;

10. to ensure special protection against physical and moral dangers to which children and young persons are exposed, and particularly against those resulting directly or indirectly from their work.

Article 8—The right of employed women to protection

With a view to ensuring the effective exercise of the right of employed women to protection, the Contracting Parties undertake:

1. to provide either by paid leave, by adequate social security benefits or by benefits from public funds for women to take leave before and after childbirth up to a total of at least 12 weeks;

2. to consider it as unlawful for an employer to give a woman notice of dismissal during her absence on maternity leave or to give her notice of dismissal at such a time that the notice would expire during such absence;

3. to provide that mothers who are nursing their infants shall be entitled to sufficient time off for this purpose;

4. (a) to regulate the employment of women workers on night work in industrial employment;

(b) to prohibit the employment of women workers in underground mining, and, as appropriate, on all other work which is unsuitable for them by reason of its dangerous, unhealthy, or arduous nature.

The European Social Charter also recognizes the right of the family to social, legal and economic protection (Article 16), and the rights of mothers and children to social and economic protection (Article 17):

Article 16—The right of the family to social, legal and economic protection

With a view to ensuring the necessary conditions for the full development of the family, which is a fundamental unit of society, the Contracting Parties undertake to promote the economic, legal and social protection of family life by such means as social and family benefits, fiscal arrangements, provision of family housing, benefits for the newly married, and other appropriate means.

Article 17—The right of mothers and children to social and economic protection

With a view to ensuring the effective exercise of the right of mothers and children to social and economic protection, the Contracting Parties will take all appropriate and necessary measures to that end, including the establishment or maintenance of appropriate institutions or services.

The Revised European Social Charter 1996 adds protection and assistance for migrant workers and their families (Article 19).

THE AMERICAS

The American Convention on Human Rights recognizes family rights (Article 17) and the rights of the child (Article 19), with related rights of children to a name (Article 18) and nationality (Article 20):

Article 17. Rights of the Family

1. The family is the natural and fundamental group unit of society and is entitled to protection by society and the state.

2. The right of men and women of marriageable age to marry and to raise a family shall be recognized, if they meet the conditions required by domestic laws, insofar as such conditions do not affect the principle of non-discrimination established in this Convention.

3. No marriage shall be entered into without the free and full consent of the intending spouses.

4. The States Parties shall take appropriate steps to ensure the equality of rights and the adequate balancing of responsibilities of the spouses as to marriage, during marriage, and in the event of its dissolution. In case of dissolution, provision shall be made for the necessary protection of any children solely on the basis of their own best interests.

5. The law shall recognize equal rights for children born out of wedlock and those born in wedlock.

Article 18. Right to a Name

Every person has the right to a given name and to the surnames of his parents or that of one of them. The law shall regulate the manner in which this right shall be ensured for all, by the use of assumed names if necessary.

Article 19. Rights of the Child

Every minor child has the right to the measures of protection required by his condition as a minor on the part of his family, society, and the state.

Article 20. Right to Nationality

1. Every person has the right to a nationality.

2. Every person has the right to the nationality of the state in whose territory he was born if he does not have the right to any other nationality.

3. No one shall be arbitrarily deprived of his nationality or of the right to change it.

The Protocol of San Salvador 1988 gives further protection to families, including for their formation (Article 15) and the rights of children (Article 16):

Article 15—Right to the Formation and the Protection of Families

1. The family is the natural and fundamental element of society and ought to be protected by the State, which should see to the improvement of its spiritual and material conditions.

2. Everyone has the right to form a family, which shall be exercised in accordance with the provisions of the pertinent domestic legislation.

3. The States Parties hereby undertake to accord adequate protection to the family unit and in particular:

   (a) To provide special care and assistance to mothers during a reasonable period before and after childbirth;

   (b) To guarantee adequate nutrition for children at the nursing stage and during school attendance years;

   (c) To adopt special measures for the protection of adolescents in order to ensure the full development of their physical, intellectual and moral capacities;

   (d) To undertake special programs of family training so as to help create a stable and positive environment in which children will receive and develop the values of understanding, solidarity, respect and responsibility.

Article 16—Rights of Children

Every child, whatever his parentage, has the right to the protection that his status as a minor requires from his family, society and the State. Every child has the right to grow under the protection and responsibility of his parents; save in exceptional, judicially-recognized circumstances, a child of young age ought not to be separated from his mother. Every child has the right to free and compulsory education, at least in the elementary phase, and to continue his training at higher levels of the educational system.

13

Article 11: The Right to an Adequate Standard of Living

Article 11

1. The States Parties to the present Covenant recognize the right of everyone to an adequate standard of living for himself and his family, including adequate food, clothing and housing, and to the continuous improvement of living conditions. The States Parties will take appropriate steps to ensure the realization of this right, recognizing to this effect the essential importance of international co-operation based on free consent.

2. The States Parties to the present Covenant, recognizing the fundamental right of everyone to be free from hunger, shall take, individually and through international co-operation, the measures, including specific programmes, which are needed:

(a) To improve methods of production, conservation and distribution of food by making full use of technical and scientific knowledge, by disseminating knowledge of the principles of nutrition and by developing or reforming agrarian systems in such a way as to achieve the most efficient development and utilization of natural resources;

(b) Taking into account the problems of both food-importing and food-exporting countries, to ensure an equitable distribution of world food supplies in relation to need.

Introduction

The scope of Article 11 is immense. It could, in fact, have been even broader, given that initial drafts of the Article drew directly from Article 25(1) of the Universal Declaration of Human Rights, which included the rights to health and social security in its coverage:

Article 25(1)

Everyone has the right to a standard of living adequate for the health and well-being of himself and of his family, including food, clothing, housing and medical care and necessary social services, and the right to security in the event of unemployment, sickness, disability, widowhood, old age or other lack of livelihood in circumstances beyond his control.[1]

However, early in the drafting process it was made clear that the rights to social security and to health warranted their own separate treatment and so they were duly cleaved off into what were to become, respectively, Articles 9 and 12 of the Covenant. Nonetheless, as we show in this chapter, the conditions concerning 'adequate standard of living' that remain in Article 11—especially, when supplemented with stipulations as to how to tackle world hunger—remain both expansive and challenging.

Article 11 is separated into two distinct parts. First, it stipulates that states must recognize and take steps to ensure the realization of the right to an adequate standard of living for individuals and families, and to the continuous improvement of living conditions. It is further specified that such a standard of living requires—but is not restricted to—adequate food, clothing and housing.[2] Of the contenders for what else such a standard requires, the most significant that is not elsewhere provided for in the Covenant is adequate water, which is widely accepted as being implicit in Article 11 and about which there now exists an impressive and growing body of commentary.

Secondly, the Article highlights the combatting of hunger as a matter of particular concern. In subparagraphs 2(a) and (b), it invokes a vast array of means by which food production, conservation and distribution is to be improved and hunger tackled, including the use of technical and scientific methods, nutritional education, agrarian reform, global trade practices and the economics and politics of the equitable distribution of food.

[1] UNGA Res. 217 A(III), Universal Declaration of Human Rights (10 December 1948), Article 25.

[2] The original draft separated out the right to an adequate standard of living and the specific rights to food, clothing and housing into two Articles, but under a series of amendments submitted by a host of states, the two were merged: see UNGA Third Committee, A/3525 (9 February 1957), [120]–[144]

Flowing throughout the Article, there is also a discernible parallel set of obligations on other states and on the international community as a whole to cooperate, coordinate and seek consent to help states realize the right.

As befits such a grave matter as the very subsistence of life,[3] the capacity of Article 11 is wide and deep. But while this scope is both necessary and desirable, it undoubtedly presents a challenge to encapsulate in an instrument designed to bind parties by way of legal obligation.

The tensions between the existential concern of sustaining life and the prosaic matter of how to express it in the form of a legal right capable of implementation and enforcement, are evident in the transcripts of both the UN Commission on Human Rights and the General Assembly's Third Committee's deliberations on the draft of the Article. In fact, during the Commission's first consideration of the Covenant in 1951, a number of states expressed concerns over whether it was at all feasible to draw boundaries around the right, given that the notion of an adequate standard of living would appear to encompass most, if not all, the rights to be included in the Covenant.[4] And while there was some limited debate on this fundamental question, including whether the right ought instead to be expressed as a general provision within the Covenant (or even in the *Preamble*), 'unfortunately', as Mathew Craven notes, 'no such rationalisation process ever took place'.[5] This has resulted, as Craven continues, in 'the somewhat anomalous position of it [Article 11] being a right that appears to have little independent substance'.[6]

The Third Committee's deliberations on the Article in late January 1957,[7] though more specific in focus, were no less revealing of the textual tensions involved in translating ambitions into outcomes. For example, delegates debated whether: (a) the 'family' should be added alongside the individual (no matter that 'everyone' would seem to be sufficient for that task); (b) the second 'adequate' was necessary, to underline (it was argued) the adequacy of food, clothing and housing, to securing an adequate standard of living; and (c) the stipulations that there be a 'continuous improvement of living conditions' and that states parties be obliged to 'take appropriate steps to ensure realization' added anything to the 'take steps' and 'progressive realisation' of all Covenant rights as pronounced in Article 2(1). In fact, as is evident, all of these additional words and phrases made it into the final version of Article 11, which thereby add to its somewhat complicated and overloaded presentation.

[3] A point underlined by several delegates during the drafting of the Article; thus, for example, Mr Ahmed (Pakistan) referred to the rights in Article 11 as lying 'at the root of all civilized existence', and Mr Tsuruoka (Japan) reasoned that 'article 11 had a place distinct from other articles, for it was concerned with matters of life and death': UNGA Third Committee, A/C.3/SR.742 (25 January 1957), [31] and [39], respectively.

[4] See, in particular, UN Commission on Human Rights, E/CN.4/SR.222 (Mr Yu (China)), [17], and E/CN.4/SR.223 (Mr Valenzuela (Chile)), [5], (Mr Cassin (France)), [6], (Mr Metha (India)), [7].

[5] Matthew Craven, *The International Covenant on Economic, Social, and Cultural Rights: A Perspective on Its Development* (Clarendon Press, Oxford, 1995) ('*The ICESCR*'), 292.

[6] Craven, *The ICESCR*, 293.

[7] UNGA Third Committee, A/C.3/SR.740-743 (24–28 January 1957).

There was also considerable debate during these sessions over the express mention of the need for international cooperation, again, involving arguments that such was already a requirement under Article 2(1). Certainly, it was stressed by a number of delegates that international assistance would be needed if those many states in which the majority of the poor did not enjoy an adequate standard of living were to make any meaningful progress towards fulfilling this right.

24. Mr MONTERO (Chile) said that in view of the fundamental nature of the right recognized in article 11, a reference to international co-operation was essential. As the Japanese representative had pointed out at an earlier meeting (740th meeting), some countries—and in particular the under-developed countries—were, with the best will in the world, physically unable to feed, clothe and shelter their people adequately without international assistance. He therefore appealed to the more advanced countries to accept the provision, in the spirit of international solidarity. The article under consideration was the most suitable place in the draft Covenant for the explicit recognition of the fact that the full realization of human rights could not be the work of any one State but must be achieved by co-operation between all States in accordance with the Purposes, Principles and practice of the United Nations.[8]

So it was on the basis of this and similar arguments that the necessity of international cooperation as expressed in Article 2(1) was here restated in Article 11(1). Perhaps the oddest feature of this specific provision, however, was the addition of the phrase 'based on free consent'. This addition appears to have been first proposed by the Syrian delegate (Mr Mufti), who justified doing so by saying that 'it should be made clear that international co-operation should be given voluntarily and freely in accordance with international law and practice'.[9] Despite a number of delegates responding that surely such free consent is implied in the very notion of international cooperation,[10] the addition was made and retained. What is odd about this, and what might be safely said to be unintended (the *travaux préparatoires* are unclear on this point), is that by expressly stating the need for 'consent', the phrase may as much provide an 'out' for developed states who do not wish to assist (or, not as much as they are being pressed to), as it does for developing states to demand sufficient say in the way in which international assistance is to be rendered.

While we may conclude that Article 11(1) is a little overstuffed and perhaps unwieldy, the difficulties presented by the demands of Article 11(2) are of a different order altogether. For it is here, with regard to how to combat world hunger, that the above-mentioned tensions between noble aspiration and implementation in practice are most significantly played out.[11]

[8] UNGA Third Committee, A/C.3/SR.742 (25 January 1957), [24].

[9] UNGA Third Committee, A/C.3/SR.742 (25 January 1957), [31] (per Mr Mufti (Syria)).

[10] UNGA Third Committee, A/C.3/SR.742 (25 January 1957), [39] (per Mr Tsuruoka (Japan)).

[11] The somewhat haphazard and unusually hasty drafting process that spawned Article 11(2) yielded, 'not surprisingly', in the words of Philip Alston (a former Chair of the Committee on Economic, Social and Cultural Rights), 'a relatively confused, and by no means all-embracing mixture of means and ends': Philip Alston, 'International Law and the Human Right to Food' in Philip Alston and Katarina Tomaševski (eds), *The Right to Food* (Martinus Nijhoff Publishers, Dordrecht, 1984), 34.

When the original drafts of the two subsections (a) and (b) of Article 11(2) were first debated by the Third Committee, these concerns were very evident:

52. Mr POPESCU (Romania) emphasised the seriousness of the problem of poverty and hunger in the world. At a time where some groups of countries were enjoying abundance, and when scientific and technical progress had opened immense horizons, it was intolerable that the number of people suffering from poverty and hunger was continually increasing. That situation was contrary to the clearly understood interests of all countries and must be ended.

53. United Nations statistics indicated that about two-thirds of mankind were undernourished and that a greater number of human beings died of hunger in 1963 than ever before. Professor Jan Tinbergen had stated in a recent work that the amount consumed by the majority of the people of Asia, Africa, and a large part of Latin America was only approximately 10 per cent of that consumed by the people of the developed countries; and that the Report on the World Social Situation 1963 (E/CN.5/375 and Add.1-2) pointed out that malnutrition was especially acute in the Far East. That was, of course, a consequence of the colonialist system to which many of those territories had until recently been subjected and which continued to exist in several countries. Despite the improvement recently noted in the quantity of food, its equality [sic] left much to be desired and protein deficiencies caused a great many illnesses, especially among children.

54. That disquieting situation had aroused world public opinion and led to the adoption of a series of measures. The present level of technical development made victory possible in the battle against hunger, if governments acted jointly with international organizations. Nevertheless, no action to that end could be fully successful so long as a considerable proportion of material resources and scientific work continued to be devoted to armaments. An effort must be made to divert to economic and social development the resources at present used for military purposes and, above all, to solve the fundamental problem of hunger.

55. Some important measures had already been taken by various international organizations, especially by FAO, which had launched a world campaign against hunger, to include the World Food Programme within its framework. That organization had also taken steps to send food surpluses to countries in which the population is chronically malnourished. Such measures, Mr Jose de Castro, Independent Chairman of the Council for FAO for 1951–1952, had said, hunger could not be combatted effectively by paternalistic measures designed solely to mitigate the gravity of the problem and to avert a revolt of the starving. For an effective remedy to that evil it was essential to accelerate economic development in general and agricultural production in particular. It was therefore essential to carry out effective agrarian reform, to apply modern techniques to the extraction of natural wealth to train technical and administrative personnel in sufficient quantities and, in addition, to inculcate sound nutritional principles in the people.

56. Mr B. R. Sen, the Director-General of FAO, had recently (1232nd meeting) drawn the Committee's attention to the fact that, while the adoption of the Universal Declaration of Human Rights had done much to ensure the observance of civil and political rights, it had not achieved the same success for economic and social rights. The reason might be that the Universal Declaration did not include the right to freedom from hunger among the fundamental human rights. His delegation therefore considered it essential to include in the draft Covenant on Economic, Social and Cultural Rights, provisions setting forth the main methods

on which the Freedom From Hunger Campaign could be based, in order to give the necessary legal force to the measures already undertaken in that field.[12]

Aside from the notable correspondence these global concerns have with those that still trouble us more than fifty years later,[13] the most striking feature of this extract is the highlighting of the omission of a right to be free from hunger in the UDHR, and the perceived need for that to be rectified in this Covenant. It is especially significant, what is more, that the preferred manner by which that end is to be achieved is by focusing on the means of combatting hunger, rather than—as is more usual in human rights instruments generally, including this Covenant—on the clear statement of right, together with, if anything, an indication of certain conditions under which its implementation may be limited.

Indeed, it was this rather unusual foray into the means of delivery (that is, beyond the general conditions in that respect stipulated in Article 2(1)) that prompted some resistant responses from others in the Third Committee to Mr Popescu's support for the proposition advanced by Mr Sen in paragraph 56 of the above extract. Thus, for example, the Netherlands delegate, Mr Beaufort, while empathizing with the manifest need to address the desperate plight of the world's hungry and also acknowledging that Mr Sen's suggestions were indeed the origin of the two proposed subsections to Article 11(2), nevertheless considered them to be misguided and misplaced. In Mr Beaufort's view, the proposals were 'too detailed' and 'too sweeping' (in respect, in particular, to 2(b)), fitting 'more appropriately in a declaration than in a legally binding instrument'. Expanding upon a similar concern raised earlier by Mr Ataullah from Pakistan,[14] he also questioned whether the substance of such proposals strayed improperly beyond the competence of the Third Committee (and of the Covenant) into the fields administered by the FAO, the WHO and the World Food Programme. Fundamentally, Mr Beaufort was concerned that '[t]here should be a clear distinction between the enunciation of a right and a summing up of the various means of realizing it, and he doubted whether the latter should be included in the draft Covenant'.[15]

Despite other delegates raising similar concerns during debate—notably those from Australia and Austria[16]—the additional subparagraphs were adopted overwhelmingly, by eight-eight votes in favour, none against and

[12] UNGA Third Committee, A/C.3/SR.1266 (18 November 1963), [52]–[56].

[13] That is, except in respect of the numbers of undernourished people worldwide. According to the Food and Agricultural Organization, the number of people chronically undernourished measured across 2010–12 is 868 million (approximately 12.5 per cent of the world's population), and the prevalence of food inadequacy stands at 19.1 per cent of across the globe (that is, some 1.3 billion people): see Food and Agricultural Organization, 'Food Security Indicators', <http://www.fao.org/fileadmin/templates/ess/foodsecurity/Food_Security_Indicators.xlsx>.

[14] UNGA Third Committee, A/C.3/SR.1264 (15 November 1963), [4]; whose particular concern was that in this respect the Third Committee may be engaging in matters that are properly the subject of the UNGA Second ('Economic and Financial') Committee.

[15] UNGA Third Committee, A/C.3/SR.1266 (18 November 1963), [57]–[63].

[16] UNGA Third Committee, A/C.3/SR.1267 (18 November 1963), [8] (per Mr Gilchrist (Australia)), and UNGA Third Committee, A/C.3/SR.1268 (18 November 1963), [8] (per Mr Herndl (Austria)).

only one abstention (Pakistan).[17] Aside, therefore, from Mr Ataullah of Pakistan—who remained unconvinced of the need or appropriateness of the additional text, believing rather, that '[i]mplementation should be left to Governments'[18]—the other sceptics were sufficiently won over to support the motion. As Mr Beaufort of the Netherlands put it, while he retained misgivings as to the 'technical' feasibility of the additional text, 'he wholeheartedly supported the basic purpose of the proposal' and so was content to vote in its favour.[19]

As a result, however, what we have in Article 11 is a right (to an adequate standard of living), accompanied by a call to arms in respect of hunger, together with some indications as to how that war might be waged. The full breadth and depth of these provisions have, as we relate throughout this chapter, provided the Committee on Economic, Social and Cultural Rights, as well as other relevant UN bodies, with particular challenges in terms of offering clear guidance to states as to how the right is to be realized and what are the best ways in practice to tackle hunger.[20] The acuity of these challenges will certainly increase as the Committee engages with individual complaints of breaches of the Article's terms.

In light of the structure of Article 11 and the explanation behind its formulation, the remainder of this chapter is separated into two parts—the first dealing with food and water, and the second with clothing and shelter.

Rights to Food and Water

THE RIGHT TO FOOD

The inclusion of an express reference to the right to food in the Covenant was instigated by China at the Commission stage in 1951. And despite the questions raised against its specific inclusion noted above, it gained sufficiently broad support such that by the time the Article was being considered by the Third Committee in the latter stages of its drafting in 1963, many delegates considered

[17] UNGA Third Committee, A/C.3/SR.1269 (19 November 1963), [2].

[18] UNGA Third Committee, A/C.3/SR.1269 (19 November 1963), [9].

[19] UNGA Third Committee, A/C.3/SR.1269 (19 November 1963), [5].

[20] As Mr Quiambao (Philippines) remarked: 'It was hard to predict what practical effect a provision of that kind would have…'; UNGA Third Committee, A/C.3/SR.1267 (18 November 1963), [6]. Certainly, even from the perspective of obtaining an adequate standard of living as one of the consequences of the alleviation of extreme poverty, the scale and complexity of the issues involved is immense. In their articulation of this perspective, the UN Guiding Principles on Extreme Poverty and Human Rights make the point abundantly clear by stressing the fact that an adequate standard of living is 'an overarching right that encompasses elements essential for human survival, health and physical and intellectual development': Human Rights Council, Final draft of the guiding principles on extreme poverty and human rights, submitted by the Special Rapporteur on extreme poverty and human rights, Magdalena Sepúlveda Carmona, A/HRC/21/39 (18 July 2012), [73]–[74].

it to be the most important right in the whole Covenant.[21] The Australian delegate spoke for many when he proclaimed that 'no human right was worth anything to a starving man'.[22]

The seminal importance of the right continues to be underscored as evidenced in the Committee's General Comment No. 12 on Article 11 (per paragraphs 1 and 4 below). The following extracts from General Comment No. 12 also reflect the difficulties in determining the precise nature of the legal obligations imposed by the Article. Thus, in paragraph 2, the Committee refers to the identification of 'obstacles' to realization, and the 'principal issues' important 'in relation' to the right to adequate food, and impetus for the General Comment being to obtain 'a better definition of the rights relating to food in Article 11'. Expressly declaring what must be done, what must be achieved and how to measure the outcomes are—at least in the context of a General Comment—bridges too far for the Committee.

Introduction and basic premises

1. The human right to adequate food is recognized in several instruments under international law. The International Covenant on Economic, Social and Cultural Rights deals more comprehensively than any other instrument with this right. Pursuant to article 11.1 of the Covenant, States parties recognize 'the right of everyone to an adequate standard of living for himself and his family, including adequate food, clothing and housing, and to the continuous improvement of living conditions', while pursuant to article 11.2 they recognize that more immediate and urgent steps may be needed to ensure 'the fundamental right to freedom from hunger and malnutrition'. The human right to adequate food is of crucial importance for the enjoyment of all rights. It applies to everyone; thus the reference in article 11.1 to 'himself and his family' does not imply any limitation upon the applicability of this right to individuals or to female-headed households.

2. The Committee has accumulated significant information pertaining to the right to adequate food through examination of State parties' reports over the years since 1979. The Committee has noted that while reporting guidelines are available relating to the right to adequate food, only a few States parties have provided information sufficient and precise enough to enable the Committee to determine the prevailing situation in the countries concerned with respect to this right and to identify the obstacles to its realization. This general comment aims to identify some of the principal issues which the Committee considers to be important in relation to the right to adequate food. Its preparation was triggered by the request of Member States during the 1996 World Food Summit for a better definition of the rights relating to food in article 11 of the Covenant, and by a special request to the Committee to give particular attention to the Summit Plan of Action in monitoring the implementation of the specific measures provided for in article 11 of the Covenant.

…

[21] See, eg, Mr Yapou (Israel), who referred to the right as being of 'paramount importance': UNGA Third Committee, A/C.3/SR.1264 (15 November 1963), [7]; and Mr Zalamea (Colombia), who saw the right to be free from hunger as critical, hunger being the 'basic cause of unhappiness and strife in the world': UNGA Third Committee, A/C.3/SR.1267 (18 November 1963), [10].

[22] UNGA Third Committee, A/C.3/SR.1267 (18 November 1963), [8].

4. The Committee affirms that the right to adequate food is indivisibly linked to the inherent dignity of the human person and is indispensable for the fulfilment of other human rights enshrined in the International Bill of Human Rights. It is also inseparable from social justice, requiring the adoption of appropriate economic, environmental and social policies, at both the national and international levels, oriented to the eradication of poverty and the fulfilment of all human rights for all.

...

5. Despite the fact that the international community has frequently reaffirmed the importance of full respect for the right to adequate food, a disturbing gap still exists between the standards set in article 11 of the Covenant and the situation prevailing in many parts of the world. More than 840 million people throughout the world, most of them in developing countries, are chronically hungry; millions of people are suffering from famine as the result of natural disasters, the increasing incidence of civil strife and wars in some regions and the use of food as a political weapon. The Committee observes that while the problems of hunger and malnutrition are often particularly acute in developing countries, malnutrition, under-nutrition and other problems which relate to the right to adequate food and the right to freedom from hunger also exist in some of the most economically developed countries. Fundamentally, the roots of the problem of hunger and malnutrition are not lack of food but lack of access to available food, inter alia because of poverty, by large segments of the world's population.[23]

There are two important points to be drawn from paragraph 5 in this extract. First, the sobering fact that, far from a decrease in the number of chronically malnourished, the intervening fifteen years or so have witnessed a slight increase (to 868 million in 2012, according to the FAO),[24] at a time that almost exactly corresponds with the life of the *Millennium Development Goals* (2000–2015), the very first of which is to 'eradicate poverty and hunger' by, inter alia, 'halving the proportion of people who suffer from hunger'. The second point highlights a recurring theme in the quest to combat hunger and realize the right to food, namely that it is access to food, not its lack, that is so often the cause of hunger. The problem, in other words, lies with the delivery, not the production.

The OHCHR makes clear this point when addressing 'common misconceptions' about the right to food in its 2010 Fact Sheet (second bullet point extracted below), while also stressing (in the first bullet point) the equal importance of access to the opportunity and means by which to obtain food.

B. Common misconceptions about the right to food

- The right to food is NOT the same as a right to be fed. Many assume that the right to food means that Governments have to hand out free food to anyone who needs it. They conclude that this would not be feasible or might cause dependency. This is a misunderstanding. The right to food is not a right to be fed, but primarily the right to feed oneself in dignity. Individuals are expected to meet their own needs, through their own efforts and using their own resources. To be able to do this, a person must

[23] CESCR, General Comment No. 12, The right to adequate food (Article 11), E/C.12/1999/5 (12 May 1999) ('General Comment No.12'), [1]–[2], [4]–[5].

[24] See n. 13 above.

live in conditions that allow him or her either to produce food or to buy it. To produce his or her own food, a person needs land, seeds, water and other resources, and to buy it, one needs money and access to the market. The right to food requires States to provide an enabling environment in which people can use their full potential to produce or procure adequate food for themselves and their families. However, when people are not able to feed themselves with their own means, for instance because of an armed conflict, natural disaster or because they are in detention, the State must provide food directly.

- The denial of the right to food is NOT a result of a lack of food in the world. One might think that people are denied their right to food because there is not enough food to go round. However, according to FAO, the world produces enough food to feed its entire population. The root cause of hunger and malnutrition is not a lack of food but a lack of access to available food. For example, poverty, social exclusion and discrimination often undermine people's access to food, not only in developing countries but also in some of the most economically developed countries where there is an abundance of food. In the longer term, however, States also have to make efforts to enable a sustainable production of food to ensure the availability of food for future generations, considering factors such as population growth, impact of possible climate change and the availability of natural resources.[25]

The notion of food 'adequacy' is, of course, central to the right, and has been interpreted by the Economic, Social and Cultural Rights Committee to incorporate the essential elements of the availability and accessibility of food:

Adequacy and sustainability of food availability and access

7. The concept of adequacy is particularly significant in relation to the right to food since it serves to underline a number of factors which must be taken into account in determining whether particular foods or diets that are accessible can be considered the most appropriate under given circumstances for the purposes of article 11 of the Covenant. The notion of sustainability is intrinsically linked to the notion of adequate food or food security, implying food being accessible for both present and future generations. The precise meaning of 'adequacy' is to a large extent determined by prevailing social, economic, cultural, climatic, ecological and other conditions, while 'sustainability' incorporates the notion of long-term availability and accessibility.

8. The Committee considers that the core content of the right to adequate food implies:

The *availability* of food in a quantity and quality sufficient to satisfy the dietary needs of individuals, free from adverse substances, and acceptable within a given culture;

The *accessibility* of such food in ways that are sustainable and that do not interfere with the enjoyment of other human rights.

[... the General Comment expands on these two elements as follows:]

[25] Office of the UN High Commissioner for Human Rights (OHCHR), 'The Right to Adequate Food', Fact Sheet 34, 2010, 3–4 (footnotes omitted), <http://www.ohchr.org/Documents/Publications/FactSheet34en.pdf>.

12. Availability refers to the possibilities either for feeding oneself directly from productive land or other natural resources, or for well functioning distribution, processing and market systems that can move food from the site of production to where it is needed in accordance with demand.

13. Accessibility encompasses both economic and physical accessibility:

Economic accessibility implies that personal or household financial costs associated with the acquisition of food for an adequate diet should be at a level such that the attainment and satisfaction of other basic needs are not threatened or compromised. Economic accessibility applies to any acquisition pattern or entitlement through which people procure their food and is a measure of the extent to which it is satisfactory for the enjoyment of the right to adequate food. Socially vulnerable groups such as landless persons and other particularly impoverished segments of the population may need attention through special programmes.

Physical accessibility implies that adequate food must be accessible to everyone, including physically vulnerable individuals, such as infants and young children, elderly people, the physically disabled, the terminally ill and persons with persistent medical problems, including the mentally ill. Victims of natural disasters, people living in disaster-prone areas and other specially disadvantaged groups may need special attention and sometimes priority consideration with respect to accessibility of food. A particular vulnerability is that of many indigenous population groups whose access to their ancestral lands may be threatened.[26]

Here it is evident that by determining what constitutes the right to adequate food, the Committee is also pointing to the nature of the responsibilities to realize the right. These, it makes clear, are borne by the state, by way both of the general obligation to realize under Article 2(1) (together with Article 11(1)) and the specific instructions in Article 11(2)). In the remainder of this General Comment, the Committee expands on a number of salient features of states' (and, briefly, international organizations') obligations.[27] It details what 'implementation at the national level' requires (paragraphs 21 to 28)—including noting that while the 'appropriate ways and means of implement[ation]… will inevitably vary significantly from one state to another' (paragraph 21), the obligation to ensure the right to adequate food 'especially for vulnerable population groups and individuals', remains, 'even where a state faces severe resource constraints' (paragraph 28). It points to the importance of adopting national strategies and policies for food security (paragraph 21), and a 'framework law' for their implementation that comprises suitable benchmarks (paragraph 29), and monitoring mechanisms (paragraph 31), as well as 'effective judicial or other appropriate remedies' in the event of non-fulfilment (paragraph 32).

The Committee also points to circumstances in which states would be seen as violating their Covenant obligations in respect of the right to food. Two in particular

[26] CESCR, General Comment No. 12, [7]–[8] and [12]–[13] (emphasis added).
[27] CESCR, General Comment No. 12, [35]–[41].

stand out, not least because both are likely to cause jurisprudential challenges for the Committee if and when they are claimed by victims under cover of the Optional Protocol complaints system. The first of these is that failure 'to ensure the satisfaction of, at the very least, the minimum essential level required to be free from hunger' is a violation, but only, the Committee adds, where the state is 'unwilling' to comply[28] (paragraph 17). Where it is unable, then the Committee offers a let-out provided that the state 'demonstrates that every effort has been made to use all the resources at its disposal [including soliciting international support] in an effort to satisfy, as a matter of priority, those minimum obligations' (paragraph 17).[29]

Responsibilities of the private sector

The second points to what might be referred to as 'ancillary duty-bearers'. The General Comment expressly recognizes the state's obligations not only to ensure that its 'direct' actions are compliant, but also those of non-state entities over which it has regulatory authority (paragraph 19):

> 20. While only States are parties to the Covenant and are thus ultimately accountable for compliance with it, all members of society individuals, families, local communities, non-governmental organizations, civil society organizations, as well as the private business sector have responsibilities in the realization of the right to adequate food. The State should provide an environment that facilitates implementation of these responsibilities. The private business sector—national and transnational—should pursue its activities within the framework of a code of conduct conducive to respect of the right to adequate food, agreed upon jointly with the Government and civil society.[30]

The lines between compliance and violation within each of these two provisions are, and will continue to be, difficult to determine. Perhaps on a case-by-case basis, it will be possible to say with some degree of clarity and certainty when a state has been truly unable to realize the right to adequate food, but in practice that will likely be much more dependent on political, economic and even cultural analyses, than legal. Furthermore, while it may seem reasonable to suggest that the private sector (and especially the private business sector) *should* have responsibilities to respect the right to adequate food, this appears to fall short by failing to follow through with details of how and why. For by not stating what precisely are these private sector responsibilities, including their extent and enforceability, it would seem that mere lip-service is being paid to corporate accountability. Oddly, the very mechanism by which such aspiration can be (and is) translated into legal obligation is not here invoked—that is, the direction under Article 2(1) of the Covenant that a state is under a duty to ensure by

[28] CESCR, General Comment No. 12, [17].

[29] At first this may seem to contradict the provision in para. 28 of the General Comment, as we describe it in the text above, but it seems that the essential difference is that whereas the latter talks merely of 'severe resource constraints', paragraph 17 is triggered only where, in effect, those constraints become such that the state is demonstrably unable (even while willing) to provide protection for the right to adequate food.

[30] CESCR, General Comment No. 12, [20].

all appropriate means—including legislative regulation of private actors within its jurisdiction—the protection, promotion and fulfilment of all rights in the Covenant.[31]

The matter of the role and responsibilities of the corporate sector in the area of the right to an adequate standard of living has been of particular interest to both incumbents of the position of UN Special Rapporteur on the right to food which was established in 2000. Jean Zeigler, who held the position from 2000 to 2008, first pointed to the need for corporations to recognize their obligations regarding the right to food in his 2003 and 2004 Reports to the Commission on Human Rights.[32]

> B. Mechanisms to monitor and demand accountability of transnationals
>
> Under the traditional application of human rights law, it is usually only possible to hold a Government to account for violations of human rights; it is still not well understood how a corporation could be held to account for human rights violations. However, new developments are occurring within human rights law. It is now increasingly understood that there are two key ways of holding corporations to respect human rights—one indirect, the other direct. Corporations can be held to account indirectly, by Governments which have a duty to protect their citizens against any negative impacts on the right to food of third parties. This means that Governments are required to monitor and regulate corporations. Corporations can also be held to account for human rights directly, through the development of direct human rights obligations, intergovernmental instruments and voluntary codes of conduct...[33]

Here again, the reference to corporations being held *directly* is qualified, in the sense that neither is it made clear whether their being 'held to account' is by legal or other means, and if the former, what those means are at the level of international law. In fact, the timing and context is important here, because it was at this very time that a set of so-called human rights 'norms' for transnational corporations and other business enterprises was being advanced by the UN Commission on Human Rights' Sub-Commission on the Promotion and Protection of Human Rights. These norms included an express reference to corporations providing 'workers with remuneration that ensures an adequate standard of living for them and their families...[and that]...[s]uch remuneration shall take due account

[31] Although in an earlier paragraph in General Comment No. 12, the Committee does state: 'The obligation to protect requires measures by the State to ensure that *enterprises* or individuals do not deprive individuals of their access to adequate food' (emphasis added) (CESCR, General Comment No. 12, [15]), without explicitly referring to either Article 2(1) or Article 11(1) (insofar as it repeats the demands of Article 2(1)).

[32] UN Commission on Human Rights: Report submitted by the Special Rapporteur on the right to food, Jean Ziegler, E/CN.4/2003/54 (10 January 2003), [32]; UN Commission on Human Rights: Report submitted by the Special Rapporteur on the right to food, Jean Ziegler, E/CN.4/2004/10 (9 February 2004), [41]–[52], respectively. See also UNGA, Interim report of Mr Jean Ziegler, Special Rapporteur of the Commission on Human Rights on the right to food, A60/350 (12 September 2005), [33].

[33] UN Commission on Human Rights: Report on the right to food, E/CN.4/2004/10 (9 February 2004), [41].

of their needs for adequate living conditions with a view towards progressive improvement.'[34] And while Mr Ziegler (among others), 'urge[d] the Commission to adopt these norms',[35] the norms attracted considerable controversy and were in effect dropped by the Commission.[36] They were replaced with a six-year process whereby a newly appointed Special Representative of the Secretary-General (SRSG) on Human Rights and Transnational Corporations and other Business Enterprises engaged with businesses, civil society and governments, leading to the formulation of a set of Guiding Principles on Business and Human Rights. While these Guiding Principles were adopted by the UN Human Rights Council in 2011, they neither expressly identify specific human rights for which corporations may be responsible for protecting, nor make any claim that corporations might be held directly accountable under international human rights laws for any breaches.[37]

Notwithstanding these broader developments in business and human rights, the specific question of the impact of the private sector on realization of the right has grown in importance and prominence. The second Special Rapporteur on the right to food, Olivier de Schutter, who has held the position since 2008, has invested considerable energy and effort into exposing the significance of this matter and seeking to understand what can and should be done to ensure the right is better protected.

II. The changing context

6. Food systems are currently undergoing deep transformations. The renewed interest in agriculture, from both the public and the private sector, led to foreign direct investment in agriculture rising from an average of US$ 600 million annually in the 1990s, to an average of US$ 3 billion in 2005–2007. The increase in direct investment is part of a larger transformation of the global supply chain in the agrifood sector. Commodity buyers (wholesalers) are larger and more concentrated than previously, and they seek to respond to the requirements of their food industry clients by increased vertical coordination, tightening their control over suppliers. The processing industry is rapidly consolidating, after an initial period during the 1980s and early 1990s during which the parastatal large-scale processors were dismantled. This sector is increasingly globalized and dominated by large transnational corporations. Global retailers and fast-food chains are expanding to reach China, India, Russia, Viet Nam, and increasingly southern and eastern Africa, and diversifying from processed foods to semi-processed foods and, increasingly, fresh produce.

7. In this process of expansion and consolidation, the procurement system too has been modernized: in addition to public standards, private standards have gained increased

[34] UN Commission on Human Rights, Sub-Commission on the Promotion and Protection of Human Rights, Norms on the Responsibilities of Transnational Corporations and Other Business Enterprises with Regard to Human Rights, E/CN.4/Sub.2/2003/12/Rev.2 (26 August 2003), [8].

[35] UN Commission on Human Rights: Report on the right to food, E/CN.4/2004/10 (9 February 2004), Summary.

[36] See David Kinley, Justine Nolan and Natalie Zerial, 'The Politics of Corporate Social Responsibility: Reflections on the United Nations Human Rights Norms for Corporations' (2007) 25(1) *Company and Securities Law Journal*, 30–42.

[37] See further, text at, and content of, n. 39 below.

importance, often imposed through codes of conduct adopted by retailers. Vertical integration has increased, with wholesalers and retailers seeking to secure stability of supply by the use of explicit contracts (long-term arrangements with producers) or techniques such as preferred supplier lists. Procurement is increasingly centralized, as the procurement shed (the area from which companies source) expands from the national to the regional and thence to global networks.

8. As a result of these developments, concentration in the food production and distribution chains has been significantly increasing over the past years. The resulting market structure gives buyers considerable bargaining strength over their suppliers, with potentially severe implications for the welfare both of producers and consumers. Current measures adopted to encourage companies to act responsibly are unable to tackle this structural dimension. Concentration in buying markets is particularly worrying, and even more so than concentration in selling markets, because dominance in buying markets can be achieved with a relatively small market share; for instance, the United Kingdom Groceries Market Investigation concluded in 2000 that retail grocers with as little as 8 per cent of the total retail market have substantial buyer power over sellers.

9. Due to the deeply unequal bargaining positions of food producers and consumers on the one hand, and buyers and retailers on the other hand, the latter can continue to pay relatively low prices for crops even when the prices increase on regional or international markets, and they can continue to charge high prices to consumers even though prices fall on these markets. Thus, one main reason why prices in developing countries have remained high despite the bursting of the bubble in the commodities markets in July 2008—in a number of countries, prices were higher in July 2009 than they were a year earlier—is because of the dominant position of certain traders in these countries. These imbalances of power in the food systems must be corrected. The Special Rapporteur is convinced that the relationships between the actors concerned cannot any longer be based solely on their relative bargaining strength. Instead, they must be collaborative, and based on other modes of communication than price signals.

…

C. The role of employers in respecting the right to food

21. Employers have a responsibility to respect the right to food, even where laws are insufficiently protective of agricultural workers or where the existing labour legislation is inadequately monitored. At present, the globalization of the food economy increases the competitive pressure exercised on suppliers, pushing them to lower wages and downgrade other working conditions, and weakening the ability of unions to resist this downward trend. This can and must be reversed. Its responsibility to respect the right to food implies that a company must not contribute, directly or indirectly, to human rights abuses through its relationship with suppliers. Agribusiness corporations operating at a global level should use their influence on suppliers to ensure that wages and working conditions improve, rather than degrade, as a result of their suppliers joining global value chains. Agribusiness companies could make unilateral undertakings to monitor compliance with certain social standards in the supply chain. They may conclude international framework agreements with global unions. These tools are not a substitute for the enforcement of protective regulatory standards by the State, but they can improve situations that, otherwise, would be even worse.[38]

[38] HRC, Report of the Special Rapporteur on the right to food, Olivier De Schutter, Agribusiness and the right to food, A/HRC/13/33 (22 December 2009), [6]–[9], [21].

Mr de Schutter's repeated references in paragraph 21 above to the actions that corporations *ought* to take in order to respect the right to food is underscored and indeed extended elsewhere in the same report where he talks of the need for major corporate food buyers that are driving the 'supermarketization' of food supply chains worldwide to assist smallholders to comply with the standards they set rather than simply allowing them to be driven out of business (paragraph 37). This entails: (i) the development of appropriate product standards and certification codes such as 'fair trade' within the agricultural sector that promote sustainable smallholder enterprise (paragraphs 38 to 42 and 46 to 48); and (ii) support for 'contract farming', whereby small farmers are 'provided with credit, inputs, and technical assistance by a buyer who typically commits to buy predefined volumes at certain prices, thus ensuring that the producer will have a market and that the investments will pay back' (paragraphs 43 to 45). De Schutter considers his arguments and proposals to be representations of how the principles expounded in the SRSG's 2008 'Protect, Respect and Remedy Framework' for business and human rights can be applied to both states and corporations in the specific circumstance of the right to food.[39]

Food insecurity

Indeed, further on that last point, while the Special Rapporteur has been keen to stress the important role and responsibilities of agribusinesses in the production, accessibility and distribution of food, he has also been careful not, thereby, to overlook the elemental role and responsibilities of states under the Covenant for the protection, respect and fulfilment of the rights it contains. Thus, while it is acknowledged that the heightened focus on the private sector was in part precipitated by the severe and prolonged spike in the cost of staple food commodity prices in 2008, the threats posed by the crisis for the food security not only of those already facing hunger, but also those many more who have barely enough to eat, was a matter that had, ultimately, to be addressed by states, including through their regulation of relevant business entities.

In his earlier, 2008 Report extracted below, Mr de Schutter first places the problem of food insecurity in its wider context and then seeks to define how a human rights approach to the issue (and one especially concerned with the right to food) might achieve greater state accountability for food production, distribution and accessibility, thereby achieving better levels of respect and protection of the right. In this way, de Schutter addresses directly the key questions raised in Article 11(2) of adequate food production and its equitable distribution.

4. It is equally clear that efforts aimed at limiting the increase in prices on international markets are not sufficient. Even before the current crisis, an estimated 852 million people were food-insecure. The current crisis shows that the mismatch between supply of and

[39] Human Rights Council, Protect, Respect and Remedy: A Framework for Business and Human Rights: Report of the Special Representative of the Secretary-General on the issue of human rights and transnational corporations and other business enterprises, John Ruggie, A/HRC/8/5 (7 April 2008), [2]–[3]. The Framework was the precursor to the SRSG's Guiding Principles mentioned above, text at n. 37.

solvent demand for agricultural products may in the future further worsen this situation by making food even less affordable for people whose entitlements are insufficient to allow them to procure sufficient food. The world population, now at 6.7 billion, increases by some 75 million each year; in 2025, there will be 8 billion living on the planet, and 9.2 billion in 2050. It has been estimated that the production of food will have to increase by 50 per cent by 2030, and double by 2050, if an increase growth in demand is to be met. But if a response to the current crisis is sought exclusively in a rise in the overall production of agricultural commodities in order to address the imbalance between the supply and the demand for food as a source of tension on the global commodities markets, it will largely miss its target. This is not only because tackling food insecurity and increasing agricultural investment do not explicitly tackle malnutrition, which affects 2 billion people in the world who suffer from micronutrient deficiency. It is also, and even more importantly, overconsumption and wastage by some, and insufficient purchasing power for the many others, [that is] the main problem, not food shortage. Producing more food will not alleviate the hunger of those who lack the purchasing power required to gain access to the food which is available. Moreover, speaking in aggregate terms obfuscates distributional questions. We need to produce food in order to raise not just the supply of food, but also the purchasing power of those who produce it.

5. In addressing the global food crisis, we should therefore constantly remind ourselves of who the food insecure are, in order to target our efforts at increasing their purchasing power. Most of the food insecure live in rural areas. Agricultural workers are among the most vulnerable, owing due to the often informal character of their employment, depriving them of legal protection from their employers. They amount to 450 million, and represent 40 per cent of the world's agricultural work force. Another important category of food-insecure people are the small-hold farming households. Unless carefully tailored to increase the purchasing power of this category, measures to boost production may lead to investments in large-scale agricultural exploitations, working with technologies and providing markets not accessible to small-holders. There are approximately 500 million small-holder households, totalling 1.5 billion people, living on two hectares of land or less. Many are facing an unprecedented increase in the price of inputs, as a result of the increase of the price of oil and, for livestock farmers, of crops, at the very same moment that, as net food buyers, they are spending larger amounts of their budgets on food. International market price increases will benefit some, particularly in India and China, but not many others, particularly in sub-Saharan Africa. Higher food prices do not always trickle down to the farm-gate, where many poor farmers must sell. To increase their yield, they need access to credit to pay for fertilizer, seeds, and tools. They need access to technology to boost productivity. They will be helped, not by being provided food, but by being supported to produce food, and to sell it at a remunerative price and thus, from their position as net food buyers, become net food sellers. For them, the alternative is clear: to live from farming their small plots, or to join the rapidly expanding slums of the larger cities.

…

8. Adopting a human rights framework can help achieve this objective, because it may guide the redefinition of the policy priorities triggered by the current crisis. The question 'for whose benefit?' is at least as important as the question 'how to produce more?' But there is a risk, in the current situation, that the latter question will be treated as the most pressing and that we focus on solutions that promote the supply of more food, without

paying sufficient attention to the question of who produces, at what price and for whom. This would be a mistake with far-reaching consequences. One of the opportunities created by the current crisis is that investment in agriculture, which has been neglected for many years both in the definition of priorities of official development assistance and in national budgets, will be given in the future the priority it deserves. But how the investments will be channelled, towards whom, and for which purpose, deserves close scrutiny. If, guided by a sense of urgency and a mistaken diagnosis about the challenges facing us, investment is planned exclusively with a view to increasing the supply of food, it could result in the wrong choices. Instead, investment should be guided by the need to promote sustainable forms of agricultural production, benefiting small-holders who are most in need of support, and where the impact on poverty alleviation will be greatest.[40]

Having identified agricultural workers and small land holders as groups that are especially vulnerable to food insecurity, de Schutter proceeds to articulate a number of key features of any state programme aimed at promoting food security and better realizing the right to food—namely, the establishment of relevant legal entitlements to adequate food, the security of land tenure, and the particular needs and rights of women in respect of food.

B. Improving accountability

17. Mapping threats to food security alone does not suffice, however. The human rights approach also leads to an understanding of the requirement of food security in terms of legal entitlements and accountability mechanisms. Ensuring that everyone has access to adequate food is not enough. It is also important that they have so as a matter of right, and that corresponding obligations be imposed on public and private actors who may have an impact on the enjoyment of that right. By ensuring that the hungry and the malnourished have legal claims against those whose actions or inactions have an impact on their situation, this framework creates security, backed by institutional mechanisms. It helps to create the conditions ensuring that people can feed themselves. Ensuring that they can do so as a matter of right rather than as a matter of policy choice is especially important if we take into consideration the capacity to influence decision-makers of the respective groups concerned with food insecurity. It is well known that, in developing countries, small-scale farmers form a large but geographically dispersed group, with little or no access to resources for political lobbying, and face prohibitive transaction costs in the organization of collective action. Urban groups, in contrast, find it easier to mobilize through public protests; so do farmers in industrial economies. With such disparity in access to political influence, a rights-based approach constitutes a necessary insurance against the risk of public policies being biased in favour of the most influential and well-organized interest groups, when they should instead address the needs of those at greatest risk, whether in urban or rural populations.

18. As part of their national strategies, States should adopt a framework legislation ensuring that the right to food is justiciable before national courts or that other forms of redress are available, so that in situations such as the current one, when the prices of food undergo a sudden increase, the other branches of government will not be allowed to remain passive, and so that, in the adoption of measures aimed at realizing the right to

[40] HRC, Report on the right to food, Olivier de Schutter, Building resilience: a human rights framework for world food and nutrition security A/HRC/9/23 (8 September 2008), [4]–[5] and [8].

food, any discrimination in access to food or means for its procurement will be effectively prohibited. By defining in a framework law the obligations corresponding to the right to adequate food with a greater degree of precision, courts or other monitoring mechanisms, such as human rights institutions, will be encouraged to contribute to ensure compliance with the right to adequate food. Such accountability mechanisms may therefore contribute to ensure that, where macro-economic or social policies are misguided or are not well targeted (for instance, because they underestimate the needs of certain segments of the population or of certain regions), this will be identified at an early stage and corrected.

…

C. Securing rights related to the use of land

21. To the extent that the emphasis is on increasing the production of food, the responses to the current global food crisis could, however, lead to new threats to security of land tenure. One danger in the current situation is that, as a result of the renewed interest in agriculture and the race towards the production of agrofuels, competition will increase for land in what has been described as 'an uneven playing field—in many cases between large-scale investors and local land users who often hold no statutory rights over the land they use'. The development of transnational investment in agricultural land, by which countries seek to ensure their food security by buying land abroad, and the development of monocultures for exports increase such pressure even further. In this context, developing countries should be encouraged to ensure security of tenure for all land users. While landowners may gain from the increase in the price of land, it constitutes a threat for landless labourers or for those whose title to the land they cultivate is insecure, and it may make it impossible for small holders to acquire more land in order to increase production. Securing land rights would encourage investors seeking to produce crops for export to opt for contract farming with small-holders, thus contributing to a better livelihood for the producers concerned.

…

D. Women's rights

23. Elsewhere, the previous Special Rapporteur on the right to food explored why the full respect for women's rights is crucial to the enjoyment of the right to adequate food, particularly in its nutritional aspects. As noted by the World Bank, 'in many societies, women bear the primary responsibility for feeding the family, yet without having control of family resources. In many countries, women and girls are also frequently less favoured in the intra-household distribution of food.' The Comprehensive Framework for Action is explicit on this issue. There is a high degree of consensus, therefore, on the need to strengthen women's rights, particularly in rural areas as required under article 14 of the Convention on the Elimination of All Forms of Discrimination against Women, and on the contribution this could make to food and nutrition security. However, many obstacles remain in the implementation at the national level, owing to discriminatory laws or customs. States should be encouraged to move further in this direction by making women's rights an explicit component of their national strategies to respond to the food crisis.[41]

[41] HRC, Report on the right to food, A/HRC/9/23 (8 September 2008), [17]–[18], [21] and [23]. The wide-ranging implications of land tenure, and the attendant obligations on states, are also recognized in the UN's Guiding Principles on Extreme Poverty, formulated by the Special Rapporteur on extreme

Responsibilities of governments

According to the broadly couched terms in Article 11(2), the requirements of states to improve methods of production, conservation and distribution of food, as well as to develop and reform agrarian systems to be more efficient, are to achieved by states both 'individually and through international co-operation'. For states individually, the Committee on Economic, Social and Cultural Rights has outlined its expectations, including, as noted earlier, that states adopt appropriate strategies, policies, monitoring and accountability mechanisms. As noted in the following extracts, a number of Special Rapporteur reports have expanded on these expectations by way of further details and examples of good state practice.

26. The primary obligation to realize the right to food rests with national Governments. The key focus of the guidelines should therefore be national obligations to respect, protect and fulfil the right to food of its own citizens. The first step should be to set up a national strategy for the implementation of the right to food. This would imply a comprehensive review of existing government policies and legislation with respect to the protection of the right to food, before producing an overall policy and framework legislation to ensure comprehensive protection. Examples of good practice and illustrations of the different State obligations to respect, protect and fulfil the right to food could be included in the guidelines to guide the development of a national strategy. A gender-based perspective should also be incorporated into any national strategy. Special attention should be paid to ensuring that national strategies include policies and resources to cope with natural and other disasters, to guard against famine.[42]

At its most basic, the matter of state practice in upholding the right to food can be regarded in two ways—one censorious, the other commendatory. In his 2006 Report to the General Assembly, Mr Zeigler reflects upon both these perspectives, first by explaining his role in dealing with bad state practices, and then offering examples of what he considers to be good (or at least improved) state practice.

9. As the Special Rapporteur's mandate requires him to receive and respond to information on the right to food submitted by governmental and non-governmental organizations (NGOs), the Special Rapporteur has sent out 28 communications to Governments over the last year asking for further information regarding specific allegations of violations of the right to food. The Special Rapporteur views this process as an important means of cooperation with Member States, as it opens a constructive dialogue about specific cases that can be remedied. This year, the majority of the communications were sent jointly with other relevant thematic or country-based special procedures, and were addressed to the Governments of Australia, Brazil, Chile, Colombia, the Democratic Republic of the Congo, the Democratic People's Republic of Korea, Ecuador, India, Indonesia, Israel, the Lao People's Democratic Republic, Mexico, Myanmar, the Philippines, the Republic of Moldova, the Sudan and the United States of America. Communications were also sent to

poverty and human rights, Magdalena Sepúlveda Carmona: Human Rights Council, Final draft of the guiding principles on extreme poverty and human rights, A/HRC/21/39 (18 July 2012), [79]–[80].

[42] UN Commission on Human Rights: Report on the right to food, E/CN.4/2003/54 (10 January 2003), [26].

the European Union. Approximately half related to allegations of violations of the obligation to respect the right to food on the part of State agents, for example, forced evictions from land that inhibited peoples' access to food. The remaining communications related to allegations that relevant authorities failed to protect or fulfil the right to food. The Special Rapporteur appreciated receiving constructive replies, in particular from Australia, Colombia, the Lao People's Democratic Republic, Indonesia and the Philippines, which have either resolved the concerns or initiated a debate about actions that could be taken.

...

II. Positive developments with respect to the right to food

A. Guatemala

13. Following his visit to Guatemala in February 2005, the Special Rapporteur welcomes the commitment of the Government to fight malnutrition and food insecurity and to promulgate a new National Law on Food Security. This Law, which was passed by Congress in May 2005, recognizes the right to food. Its definition of the right to food is grounded in general comment No. 12 of the Committee on Economic, Social and Cultural Rights. It identifies violations of the right to food and establishes a national system for the protection and progressive realization of the right to food. The Law also recommends the strengthening of the Office of the Ombudsman to monitor the protection and progressive realization of the right to food. The Special Rapporteur welcomes the work of the Office of the High Commissioner for Human Rights in Guatemala, FAO and the Grupo Interagencial de Seguridad Alimentaria y Nutricional (Inter-Agency Group on Food and Nutritional Security) on including the right to food in current strategies and programmes.

B. India

14. The Special Rapporteur also welcomes developments in India which he learned about during his visit in August 2005. He was impressed by the full awareness of state and central Governments of their obligations to respect, protect and fulfil human rights, including the right to food. India implements the largest public food distribution system in the world. It has also made a great deal of progress in ensuring access to justice for securing respect for the right to food through decisions of the Supreme Court. In the last 15 years, in its decisions the Court has upheld the right to water of Dalits facing discrimination by the upper castes, the right to a livelihood of traditional fisherpeople struggling against the shrimp industry and the right to a livelihood of members of Scheduled Tribes threatened by the acquisition of land by a private company. More recently, to fulfil the right to food and prevent deaths from starvation, the Court directed all State Governments to fully implement the existing food-based schemes of the central Government [...]. The Special Rapporteur welcomed the opportunity to attend the national Judicial Colloquium on the Right to Food held in Delhi at the initiative of the Right to Food Campaign which brought together 70 senior judges from across India to discuss the right to food.

C. Brazil

15. The Special Rapporteur would also like to bring to the attention of the Assembly developments in Brazil, where the Government's Zero Hunger programme is serving as an important example for worldwide efforts to fight hunger. He welcomes the re-establishment of the National Food and Nutrition Security Council with a specific mandate to combat hunger and malnutrition in Brazil. A new draft law providing for a National Food and Nutrition System, approved in August 2006 by the Federal Commission on Constitution,

Justice and Citizenship, recognizes the right to food and the obligations of the Government to respect, protect, promote, monitor, finance and fulfil the right to food. It also calls for the creation of mechanisms to ensure accountability for meeting these obligations. The Special Rapporteur has been impressed by the participation of the Ministério Público and Brazilian civil society in this process. He believes that the initiative of NGOs to establish the post of a national Special Rapporteur on the right to food within Brazil has had a profound effect on the growing recognition of the right to food as a human right in the country, and serves as an important example for civil society in other countries. He welcomes the holding of the International Conference on Agrarian Reform and Rural Development organized by the Government and FAO in Porto Alegre in March 2006. In the Final Declaration of this conference 95 States recognize that one important way to ensure the fulfilment of the right to food is to establish appropriate land reform to secure access to land for marginalized and vulnerable groups, and to adopt adequate legal frameworks and policies to promote traditional and family agriculture.[43]

The Committee also, unsurprisingly, spends time in its Concluding Observations on states parties' periodic reports relaying its concerns or criticisms of the failures of states (both wealthy and poor) adequately to protect the right to food. Malnutrition (especially among children), absent or ineffective food assistance programmes, including discrimination regarding access to food aid, and the expropriation of farm lands are common problems in many developing countries as the following extracts of Concluding Observations in respect of Angola and Colombia demonstrate. Notably, however, food security problems are not absent in developed states such as Canada, as shown in the extracts below from the Concluding Observations regarding that country.

Angola:

29. The Committee is concerned about the high incidence of acute malnutrition and chronic malnutrition in all the provinces of the State party, particularly affecting children. The Committee notes with concern the reports of widespread hunger in Lunda provinces due to the expropriation of farmlands for the purpose of commercial diamond mining.

The Committee recommends that the State party effectively implement and allocate sufficient resources to relevant programmes and funds to ensure physical and economic access for everyone, especially those from the most disadvantaged social groups, to the minimum essential food, which is sufficient, nutritionally adequate and safe, to ensure freedom from hunger, in line with the Committee's general comment No. 12 (1999) on the right to adequate food as well as its Statement on the world food crisis (E/C.12/2008/1). The Committee also urges the State party to ensure that expropriations of farmer lands do not have a negative impact on the right to food of those who have been expropriated.[44]

Colombia:

21. The Committee is concerned about the high malnutrition rate which affects a considerable number of children and women, in particular among internally displaced groups, as well as persons living in rural areas.

[43] UNGA, Interim report of Special Rapporteur on the right to food, A/61/306 (1 September 2006), [9] and [13]–[15].

[44] CESCR, Concluding observations: Angola, E/C.12/AGO/CO/3 (1 December 2008), [29].

The Committee firmly recommends that the State party adopt an effective national food policy to combat hunger and malnutrition, in particular among children, women, internally displaced persons and persons living in rural areas.

22. The Committee is concerned that the policy encouraging agro-exporting goods, such as agro-fuels, may deprive peasants from cultivating their lands. The Committee is also concerned about the unequal distribution of lands owned by a minority of the population, as well as about the absence of a genuine agrarian reform, as recommended in the previous concluding observations of the Committee (art. 11).

The Committee recommends that the State party develop agricultural policies which prioritize the production of food; implement programmes that protect national food production with incentives for small producers; and ensure the restitution of lands taken from indigenous and Afro-Colombian peoples, as well as peasant communities.[45]

Canada:

[105] Of concern is the evidence of hunger in Canada and the reliance on food banks operated by charitable organizations.

…

[107] The Committee has learned from non-governmental organizations of widespread discrimination in housing against people with children, people on social assistance, people with low incomes, and people who are indebted. Although prohibited by law in many of Canada's provinces, these forms of discrimination are apparently common. A more concerted effort to eliminate such practices would therefore seem to be in order.

…

[112] The Committee is concerned to learn that, in a few cases, courts have ruled that the right to security of the person in the Charter does not protect Canadians from social and economic deprivation, or from infringement of their rights to adequate food, clothing and housing.

[113] The Committee is concerned that provincial human rights legislation has not always been applied in a manner which would provide improved remedies against violations of social and economic rights, in particular concerning the rights of families with children, and the right to an adequate standard of living, including food and housing.

…

E. Suggestions and recommendations

[115] The Committee recommends concerted Government action to eliminate the need for food banks.[46]

Alongside the work of the Committee and of the Special Rapporteurs on the right to food, the UN Food and Agriculture Organization (FAO) has established itself as a leader in the field. In particular, the FAO's 'Voluntary Guidelines to

[45] CESCR, Concluding observations: Colombia, E/C.12/COL/CO/5 (7 June 2010), [21]–[22].

[46] CESCR, Concluding observations: Canada, E/1994/23 (10–28 May 1993, 22 November–10 December 1993), [105], [107], [112]–[113] and [115].

support Member States' efforts to achieve the progressive realization of the right to adequate food' (2004)[47] have come to be seen as a practicable amplification of the 'ways and means' of state implementation that the Committee broadly indicates in paragraphs 21 to 28 of its General Comment No. 12 (as referred to above). The Guidelines are designed to help states build and maintain an enabling environment for the realization of the right to food and the promotion of food security within their individual jurisdictions. In particular, the Guidelines stress the importance of good governance (Guideline 1) and effective policy formulation and administrative practices (Guideline 3) in the delivery of these objectives. In so doing, the Guidelines underscore both the importance of recognizing that it is the *accessibility* of food, more often than its adequacy, that creates a barrier to feeding the hungry, and that in terms of human rights, civil and political rights are vital to the realization of economic, social and cultural rights.

Guideline 1: Democracy, good governance, human rights and the rule of law

…

1.2 States should promote democracy, the rule of law, sustainable development and good governance, and promote and protect human rights and fundamental freedoms in order to empower individuals and civil society to make demands on their governments, devise policies that address their specific needs and ensure the accountability and transparency of governments and state decision-making processes in implementing such policies. States should, in particular, promote freedom of opinion and expression, freedom of information, freedom of the press and freedom of assembly and association, which enhances the progressive realization of the right to adequate food in the context of national food security.

Food should not be used as a tool for political and economic pressure.

…

Guideline 3: Strategies

3.1 States, as appropriate and in consultation with relevant stakeholders and pursuant to their national laws, should consider adopting a national human-rights based strategy for the progressive realization of the right to adequate food in the context of national food security as part of an overarching national development strategy, including poverty reduction strategies, where they exist.

3.2 The elaboration of these strategies should begin with a careful assessment of existing national legislation, policy and administrative measures, current programmes, systematic identification of existing constraints and availability of existing resources. States should formulate the measures necessary to remedy any weakness, and propose an agenda for change and the means for its implementation and evaluation.

[47] As endorsed by Human Rights Council Res. 13/4, The right to food, A/HRC/RES/13/4 (14 April 2010), [41].

3.3 These strategies could include objectives, targets, benchmarks and time frames; and actions to formulate policies, identify and mobilize resources, define institutional mechanisms, allocate responsibilities, coordinate the activities of different actors, and provide for monitoring mechanisms. As appropriate, such strategies could address all aspects of the food system, including the production, processing, distribution, marketing and consumption of safe food. They could also address access to resources and to markets as well as parallel measures in other fields. These strategies should, in particular, address the needs of vulnerable and disadvantaged groups, as well as special situations such as natural disasters and emergencies.

3.4 Where necessary, States should consider adopting and, as appropriate, reviewing a national poverty reduction strategy that specifically addresses access to adequate food.

3.5 States, individually or in cooperation with relevant international organizations, should consider integrating into their poverty reduction strategy a human rights perspective based on the principle of non-discrimination. In raising the standard of living of those below the poverty line, due regard should be given to the need to ensure equality in practice to those who are traditionally disadvantaged and between women and men.

…

3.7 States are encouraged, inter alia and in a sustainable manner, to increase productivity and to revitalize the agriculture sector including livestock, forestry and fisheries through special policies and strategies targeted at small-scale and traditional fishers and farmers in rural areas, and the creation of enabling conditions for private sector participation, with emphasis on human capacity development and the removal of constraints to agricultural production, marketing and distribution.

3.8 In developing these strategies, States are encouraged to consult with civil society organizations and other key stakeholders at national and regional levels including small-scale and traditional farmers, the private sector, women and youth associations, with the aim of promoting their active participation in all aspects of agricultural and food production strategies.

3.9 These strategies should be transparent, inclusive and comprehensive, cut across national policies, programmes and projects, take into account the special needs of girls and women, combine short-term and long-term objectives, and be prepared and implemented in a participatory and accountable manner.

3.10 States should support, including through regional cooperation, the implementation of national strategies for development, in particular for the reduction of poverty and hunger as well as for the progressive realization of the right to adequate food.[48]

The practicability of the work of the FAO has long been a feature of interaction with states. Examples of FAO monitoring of, as well as cooperation and assistance with, states are apparent in many state reports to the Committee, as well as in the Committee's concluding observations, including in respect of Cambodia,[49]

[48] Council of the Food and Agriculture Organisation of the United Nations (127th Session), Voluntary guidelines to support the progressive realization of the right to adequate food in the context of national food security, November 2004.

[49] CESCR, Concluding Observations: Cambodia, E/C.12/KHM/CO/1 (22 May 2009), [15].

Czechoslovakia,[50] the Dominican Republic,[51] Jordan,[52] Republic of Congo,[53] Mongolia,[54] Solomon Islands[55] and Togo.[56] The FAO's Special Programme for Food Security (SPFS), which was established in 1994, and its more recent strategic-oriented Capacity Development Framework,[57] have been central to the organization's endeavours to aid the most food-insecure states to improve food production, distribution and access.[58] Both initiatives are designed to bolster target countries' agricultural infrastructure, technical knowledge and management structure, at both micro and macro levels, and as such, can be seen as integral to those countries' efforts to fulfil the demands of Article 11(2). Thus, for example, in respect of Congo:

> 217. The Committee supports the request by the Government addressed to the United Nations Food and Agriculture Organization (FAO) for a Special Programme for Food Security (SPFS) to facilitate access to food through small-scale low-cost agricultural projects. The Committee notes that a new project formulation mission is planned for the near future to support the national team in the initial preparations for such a programme. The Republic of the Congo can also take advantage of the FAO South-South Cooperation Initiative, which involves the exchange of knowledge, expertise and experience between developing countries.[59]

Examples of recognition by states themselves of their cooperation with the FAO are to be found in the state reports of Cameroon and Argentina:

Cameroon:

> Objectives and specific measures…
>
> 151. As a poverty reduction measure for the rural areas, FAO launched in Cameroon in 1999 the 'Téléfood' initiative, aimed at financing small development projects with funds

[50] CESCR, Concluding Observations: Czechoslovakia, E/C.12/1987/5 (29 October 1986), [166].

[51] CESCR, Concluding Observations: Dominican Republic, E/C.12/1990/8 (26 November–14 December 1990), [236].

[52] CESCR, Concluding Observations: Jordan, E/C.12/1987/5 (26 November–14 December 1990), [81].

[53] CESCR, Concluding Observations: Republic of Congo, E/C.12/1/Add.45 (23 May 2000), [20].

[54] CESCR, Concluding Observations: Mongolia, E/C.12/1/Add.47 (1 September 2000), [14].

[55] CESCR, Concluding Observations: Solomon Islands, E/C.12/1/Add.33 (14 May 1999), [28].

[56] CESCR, Concluding Observations: Togo, E/C.12/1/Add.61 (21 May 2001), [22].

[57] Launched in 2010; see Food and Agriculture Organization of the United Nations, 'Corporate Strategy on Capacity Development' (25 October 2010), <http://www.fao.org/fileadmin/user_upload/capacity_building/Summary_Strategy_PR_E_01.doc>.

[58] As of January 2009, sixteen National Programmes for Food Security—established and run in cooperation with the FAO as part of the SPFS—were operational and almost fifty more were in various stages of planning and formulation. See Food and Agriculture Organization of the United Nations, 'National and Regional Programmes for Food Security' (January 2009), <ftp://ftp.fao.org/docrep/fao/011/i0765e/i0765e04.pdf>. The Capacity Development Framework has focused on increasing long-term sustainability in Africa, emphasizing national ownership and leadership of projects to increase capacity: Food and Agriculture Organization of the United Nations, 'Corporate Strategy on Capacity Development', 1–2. Between 2004 and 2010, the Food and Agriculture Organization implemented over 3,000 field projects in sub-Saharan Africa with budgets of more than US$1 million each: Food and Agriculture Organization of the United Nations, Evaluation of FAO's Activities on Capacity Development in Africa: Final Report (March 2010), 7, <http://www.fao.org/fileadmin/user_upload/capacity_building/PC104-5EvaluationCapacityDevelopmentAfricaK8635E.pdf>.

[59] CESCR, Concluding Observations: Republic of Congo, E/2001/22 (25 April–12 May 2000), [217].

collected during a broadcast organized in connection with the World Food Day on 16 October of every year. In the period 2000–2005, the total cost of projects thus funded amounted to approximately CFAF 77,530,000.

Improvement of the protection of the health of the child…

506. For the implementation of initiatives in this area, the Government has received support from various international and nationals partners (UNAIDS, WHO, UNICEF, Global Fund to Fight AIDS, Tuberculosis and Malaria, European Union, UNFPA, FAO, WFP, African Synergy, AWARE, USAID, CARE, MSP, HKI, GTZ, Rotary International, Plan Cameroon, CIDA, FOREDEN, ADAMS, AAPEC, AUPAES, Chantal Biya Foundation and Cameroon Red Cross). NGOs, associations and traditional chiefs also contributed to mobilizing the population for participation in informal educational discussions.

(a) Enhancing the scope of the education offered…

603. In 2006, activities were carried out on the basis of a partnership among MINPROFF, UNICEF, FAO/WFP, UNFPA150, MINEDUB and MINAS in order to eliminate disparities between boys and girls. Such activities vary among the formal, non-formal and specialized education system.[60]

Argentina:

497. The availability of food in Argentina, as measured by the food balance sheets of the Food and Agriculture Organization of the United Nations (FAO), has historically presented values very close to or in excess of 3,000 kcal. a day per inhabitant. In the most recent period (1997–2001), availability has been 3,174 calories per inhabitant, or 30 per cent more than the average requirement of the population. Apparent consumption of protein is also high (over 100 grams a day per person), while calcium is one of the few nutrients whose availability falls short of the recommended average.[61]

Enforcing the right to food

In terms of meeting the legal obligations imposed by Article 11, the formulation and implementation of policies on food adequacy and access by states is often only half the battle. Enshrining the right in domestic law or otherwise in a format that permits legal enforcement is considered to be an essential complement to any policy initiative. The right to food is incorporated in many national legal systems, sometimes in 'ordinary' law, and sometimes in the constitution. It is also potentially enforceable through instruments of the African and Inter-American human rights systems.

According to the current Special Rapporteur on the right to food, some twenty-four states have incorporated the right explicitly into their constitutions,[62] and many more have constitutional provisions from which one can infer a right

[60] CESCR, State Report: Cameroon, E/C.12/CMR/2-3 (19 July 2010), [151], [506] and [603].

[61] CESCR, State Report: Argentina, E/C.12/ARG/3 (26 January 2011), [497].

[62] UN Special Rapporteur on the right to food, Olivier de Schutter, Countries tackling hunger with a right to food approach: significant progress in implementing the right to food at national scale in Africa, Latin America and South Asia, Briefing Note No. 1, May 2010, 5.

to food.[63] Thus, for example, express provisions are to be found in the constitutions of South Africa (Article 27(1)), Ecuador (Article 13), Brazil (Article 6, as amended in 2010), and Nepal (Interim Constitution 2063 (2007), Article 18) and, implicitly, in the constitutions of India (under Article 21 on the right to life), and Ghana (Article 36(1) on the state's duty to provide welfare and an adequate standard of livelihood), or under constitutionally enshrined Directive Principles of State Policy, as with India (Article 47) and Sri Lanka (Article 27(c)).

Many of these countries—as a well as a number of others who have neither explicit nor implicit constitutional provisions on food—have also enacted framework laws that direct policy and practice across government with a view to securing the right to food. Together, all of these countries can be considered to have adopted what might broadly be called human rights approaches to tackling hunger. Examples include: Brazil's National Food and Nutrition Security Framework Law (2009); Nicaragua's Food Sovereignty, Food Security and Nutrition Law (2009); and Malawi's draft Food Security Bill (2013). Also, in India, a long-debated National Food Security Act 2013 was finally enacted by Parliament in September 2013, following its break-through approval by Executive Order in July 2013. The statute institutes a right to food in the form of access to heavily subsidized food grains for some two-thirds of India's population, as part of a broad-based programme of social protection.[64]

State-based enforcement

Ideally, what should follow these constitutional guarantees, statutory provisions and framework laws for the protection of the right to food are effective mechanisms for their implementation and enforcement. And, indeed, there is now a growing body of domestic jurisprudence on the matter of enforcement. A common theme running through this body of case law—and one that echoes the concerns aired above that often the obstacles to combatting hunger are more to do with access than adequacy—has been complaints raised as to the ineffectiveness or inefficiency of government processes by which food is provided or distributed to those in most need. Thus, in the landmark case of *People's Union for Civil Liberties v Union of India* (2001),[65] the Supreme Court of India held that there existed an implied right to food in the Indian Constitution, and that the state had violated that right by failing adequately to address the dire need for food of millions suffering from a recent severe drought. The state had stockpiled enormous quantities of staple grains, but the public system of distribution of essential foodstuffs had broken down such that it was unable to deliver to those most in

[63] The FAO calculates that thirty-three states have constitutions whose recognition of broader rights—such as adequate standard of living—are considered to 'include' the right to food: Lidija Knuth and Margret Vidar, Food and Agriculture Organisation of the United Nations, *Constitutional and Legal Protection of the Right to Food around the World* (FAO, Rome, 2011), 21.

[64] Available at <http://egazette.nic.in/WriteReadData/2013/E_29_2013_429.pdf>.

[65] *People's Union for Civil Liberties v Union of India*, 28 November 2001, Petition (Civil) No. 196/2001.

need. As a consequence, and over a series of Supreme Court orders spread across many years, the state was compelled to provide immediate, free relief to those in drought-affected communities, to raise the levels of food entitlements generally, and to increase the subsidization of essential foods. What is remarkable about these orders—which thereby obtained the status of legal entitlements enforceable against the state—is the specificity of executive actions demanded by the Court. Significantly, they also contributed to the pressure that led eventually to the enactment of the above-mentioned National Food Security Act in 2013. The following is the text of one of its most significant initial orders issued by the Supreme Court in the case:

After hearing learned counsel for the parties, we issue, as an interim measure, the following directions:

1. TARGETED PUBLIC DISTRIBUTION SYSTEM (TPDS)

(i) It is the case of the Union of India that there has been full compliance with regard to the allotment of foodgrain in relation to the TPDS. However, if any of the States gives a specific instance of non-compliance, the Union of India will do the needful within the framework of the Scheme.

(ii) The States are directed to complete the identification of BPL families, issuing of cards and commencement of distribution of 25 kgs. grain per family per month latest by 1st January, 2002.

(iii) The Delhi Govt. will ensure that TPDS application forms are freely available and are given and received free of charge and there is an effective mechanism in place to ensure speedy and effective redressal of grievances.

2. ANTYODAYA ANNA YOJANA

(i) It is the case of the Union of India that there has been full compliance with regard to the allotment of foodgrain in relation to Antyodaya Anna Yojana. However, if any of the States gives a specific instance of non-compliance, the Union of India will do the needful within the framework of the Scheme.

(ii) We direct the States and the Union Territories to complete identification of beneficiaries, issuing of cards and distribution of grain under this Scheme latest by 1st January, 2002.

(iii) It appears that some Antyodaya beneficiaries may be unable to lift grain because of penury. In such cases, the Centre, the States and the Union Territories are requested to consider giving the quota free after satisfying itself in this behalf.

3. MID DAY MEAL SCHEME (MDMS)

(i) It is the case of the Union of India that there has been full compliance with regard to the Mid Day Meal Scheme (MDMS). However, if any of the States gives a specific instance of non-compliance, the Union of India will do the needful within the framework of the Scheme.

(ii) We direct the State Governments/ Union Territories to implement the Mid-Day Meal Scheme by providing every child in every Government and Government assisted Primary Schools with a prepared mid day meal with a minimum content of 300 calories and 8–12 grams of protein each day of school for a minimum of 200 days. Those Governments providing dry rations instead of cooked meals must within three months start providing cooked meals in all Govt. and Govt. aided Primary Schools in all half the Districts of the State (in order of poverty) and must within a further period of three months extend the provision of cooked meals to the remaining parts of the State.

(iii) We direct the Union of India and the FCI to ensure provision of fair average quality grain for the Scheme on time. The States/Union Territories and the FCI are directed to do joint inspection of food grains. If the food grain is found, on joint inspection, not to be of fair average quality, it will be replaced by the FCI prior to lifting.

4. NATIONAL OLD AGE PENSION SCHEME (NOAPS)

(i) It is the case of the Union of India that there has been full compliance with regard to the National Old Age Pension Scheme. However, if any of the States gives a specific instance of non-compliance, the Union of India will do the needful within the framework of the Scheme.

(ii) The States are directed to identify the beneficiaries and to start making payments latest by 1st January, 2002.

(iii) We direct the State Govts. / Union Territories to make payments promptly by the 7th of each month.

5. ANNAPURNA SCHEME

The States/Union Territories are directed to identify the beneficiaries and distribute the grain latest by 1st January, 2002.

6. INTEGRATED CHILD DEVELOPMENT SCHEME (ICDS)

(i) We direct the State Govts. / Union Territories to implement the Integrated Child Development Scheme (ICDS) in full and to ensure that every ICDS disbursing centre in the country shall provide as under:

(a) Each child up to 6 years of age to get 300 calories and 8–10 gms of protein;

(b) Each adolescent girl to get 500 calories and 20–25 grams of protein;

(c) Each pregnant woman and each nursing mother to get 500 calories & 20–25 grams of protein;

(d) Each malnourished child to get 600 calories and 16–20 grams of protein;

(e) Have a disbursement centre in every settlement.

(ii) It is the case of the Union of India that there has been full compliance of its obligations, if any, under the Scheme. However, if any of the States gives a specific instance of non-compliance, the Union of India will do the needful within the framework of the Scheme.

7. NATIONAL MATERNITY BENEFIT SCHEME (NMBS)

(i) We direct the State Govts. / Union Territories to implement the National Maternity Benefit Scheme (NMBS) by paying all BPL pregnant women Rs. 500/- through the Sarpanch 8–12 weeks prior to delivery for each of the first two births.

(ii) It is the case of the Union of India that there has been full compliance of its obligations under the Scheme. However, if any of the States gives a specific instance of non-compliance, the Union of India will do the needful within the framework of the Scheme.

8. NATIONAL FAMILY BENEFIT SCHEME (NFBS)

(i) We direct the State Govts. / Union Territories to implement the National Family Benefit Scheme and pay a BPL family Rs. 10,000/- within four weeks through a local Sarpanch, whenever the primary bread winner of the family dies.

9. We direct that a copy of this order be translated in regional languages and in English by the respective States/ Union Territories and prominently displayed in all Gram Panchayats, Govt. School Buildings and Fair Price Shops.

10. In order to ensure transparency in selection of beneficiaries and their access to these Schemes, the Gram Panchayats will also display a list of all beneficiaries under the various Schemes. Copies of the Schemes and the list of beneficiaries shall be made available by the Gram Panchayats to members of public for inspection.

11. We direct Doordarshan and AIR to adequately publicise various Schemes and this order. We direct the Chief Secretaries of each of the States and Union Territories to ensure compliance of this order. They will report compliance by filing affidavits in this Court within 8 weeks from today with copies to the Attorney General and counsel for the petitioner.

We grant liberty to the Union of India to file affidavit pursuant to the order of this Court dated 21st November, 2001. List the matter for further orders on 11th February, 2002. In the meanwhile, liberty is granted to the parties to apply for further directions, if any.[66]

The Supreme Court's implication of the right to food was made in respect of the express right to life provided under Article 21 of the Indian Constitution ('no person shall be deprived of his life or personal liberty except according to procedure established by law'), and supported by two Constitutional Directive Principles under Article 39(a) ('the State shall…direct its policy towards securing that the citizen, men and women equally, have the right to an adequate means of livelihood…') and Article 47 ('the State shall regard the raising of the level of nutrition and the standard of living of its people and the improvement of public health as among its primary duties…').

The reasoning behind the adoption of this stance was succinctly expressed by the National Human Rights Commission of India during one of the many hearings that comprised the case: *(NHRC) in the Proceedings of a hearing held on 17 January 2003*:

Article 21 of the Constitution of India guarantees a fundamental right to life and personal liberty. The expression 'Life' in this Article has been judicially interpreted to mean a life with human dignity and not mere survival or animal existence. In the light of this, the

[66] *People's Union for Civil Liberties v Union of India.*

State is obliged to provide for all those minimum requirements which must be satisfied in order to enable a person to live with human dignity, such as education, health care, just and humane conditions of work, protection against exploitation, etc. In the view of the Commission, the Right to Food is inherent to a life with dignity, and Article 21 should be read with Articles 39(a) and 47 to understand the nature of the obligation of the State in order to ensure the effective realization of this right. Article 39(a) of the Constitution enunciated as one of the Directive Principles, fundamental in the governance of the country, requires the State to direct its policy towards securing that the citizens, men and women equally, have the right to an adequate means of livelihood. Article 47 spells out the duty of the State to raise the level of nutrition and the standard of living of its people as a primary responsibility. The citizen's right to be free from hunger enshrined in Article 21 is to be ensured by the fulfillment of the obligation of the State set out in Articles 39(a) and 47. The reading of Article 21 together with Articles 39(a) and 47 places the issue of food security in the correct perspective, thus making the Right to Food a guaranteed Fundamental Right which is enforceable by virtue of the constitutional remedy provided under Article 32 of the Constitution.[67]

In subsequent cases, the right to food has been further iterated and constitutionally embedded within the right to life. Thus, in *Laxmi Mandal v Deen Dayal Harinagar Hospital et al* (2010),[68] the Delhi High Court underscored the importance of the implied rights to food and to health within the Constitution's expressly declared right to life—what the Court termed, 'two inalienable survival rights that form part of the right to life' (paragraph 2). Again, this case concerned the failure of the state to provide access to adequate food for the poorest and most vulnerable, as well as denying them access to basic health care facilities, such that their very right to life is threatened. After overviewing the objectives and deficiencies of the four schemes covering child and maternal welfare that formed the subject matter of the litigation, the Court highlighted the significance of the growing jurisprudence surrounding what constitutes the right to life.

19. ...the Supreme Court has time and again emphasised the importance of the effective implementation of the above schemes meant for the poor. [It] underscore[s] the interrelatedness of the 'right to food' which is what the main PUCL Case was about, and the right to reproductive health of the mother and the right to health of the infant child. There could not be a better illustration of the indivisibility of basic human rights as enshrined in the Constitution of India. Particularly in the context of a welfare State, where the central focus of these centrally sponsored schemes is the economically and socially disadvantaged sections of society, the above orders of the Supreme Court have to be understood as preserving, protecting and enforcing the different facets of the right to life under Article 21 of the Constitution. As already noted, these... petitions focus on two inalienable survival rights that form part of the right to life. One is the right to health, which would include the right to access government (public) health facilities and receive a minimum standard of treatment and care. In particular this would include the enforcement of the reproductive

[67] As reprinted in Colin Gonsalvez, P. Ramesh Kumar and Anup Kumar Srivastava, (eds), *Right to Food* (2nd edn, New Delhi, Human Rights Law Network, 2005), 404–21.

[68] *Laxmi Mandal v Deen Dayal Harinagar Hospital et al* [2010] INDLHC 2983; decided jointly with *Jaitun v Maternity Home MCD, Jangpura et al.*

rights of the mother and the right to nutrition and medical care of the newly born child and continuously thereafter till [sic] the age of about six years. The other facet is the right to food which is seen as integral to the right to life and right to health.[69]

In countries with Constitutions that expressly protect the right to food such as Nepal, the path for litigants to argue and the courts to order that the state provide adequate food at all times is more obvious and direct. But even here, the courts may underline the fundamental importance of the right not only with reference to the intersection of the rights to food and to life, but also by direct appeal to relevant international human rights instruments. Thus, in the case of *Prakash Mani Sharma et al on behalf of Forum for Protection of Public Interest (Pro Public) v Prime Minister and Office of Council of Minister et al* (2008),[70] the Supreme Court of Nepal held that the state had breached not only its obligations under the Interim Constitution 2007 in respect of the right to food and to life,[71] but also Nepal's obligations under the ICESCR, the CRC and the CEDAW. As the following extracts show, after confirming the constitutional basis upon which the right to food exists, and the nature of the obligations thereby imposed on the state—that it must facilitate access to adequate food, rather than necessarily provide it free of charge—the Court concludes by emphasizing the government's additional responsibilities under the relevant international human rights instruments to which it is signatory.[72]

Article 18(3) of the Constitution has provided every person with the right to food regime. The realization of the right to food is not limited only to the availability of food, it is equally important to have access to it. [296]

...

There is no room for dispute that every citizen has the right to food along with the right to live a dignified life. The right to food, however, does not mean that the state is liable to feed morning and evening meals... which is impossible. The right to food is not the right to be fed. In a country like ours which has a mixed and liberal economy imagined by... the Constitution, the states cannot feed both meals free of cost... The state plays the role of just a facilitator and regulator to have access to food. Everyone should be capable to stand on his own as per his needs and aspirations. For this the person, either through the enjoyment of freedom of occupation or producing food himself... made available because of the right economic policy formulated the state... [through, for example]... the duty of the state to provide for seed, fertilizer, irrigation, market, pricing etc for the right under Article 18(3) thereby making the food available and ensuring food security. [297–8]

[69] *Laxmi Mandal*, [19].

[70] *Prakash Mani Sharma et al on behalf of Forum for Protection of Public Interest (Pro Public) v Prime Minister and Office of Council of Minister et al*, 28 November 2008, Writ Petition No. 0065-w0-149 of 2065 BS (2008): while judgment was delivered in 2008, the judgment and reasons were not published until 2011.

[71] Interim Constitution of Nepal 2007, Article 12(1) provides that: 'Every person shall have the right to live with dignity...' and Article 18(3) provides: 'Every citizen shall have the right to food sovereignty as provided for in the law.'

[72] Supreme Court of Nepal, *Some Decisions of the Supreme Court, Nepal,* Volume 12 (2012), 296, 297–8 and 304–5.

The Government should be held responsible not to create any sorts of food crisis in any parts of the country may it be of natural disaster or any other reasons. Nepal is a member signatory of ICESCR and the declarations and conventions like the UDHR (Article 25), CEDAW, the CRC etc, and our own Constitution provides the right to live a dignified life and a right to food regime to every individual as fundamental rights [sic]. [304–5]

Enforcement under regional regimes

Neither the American Convention on Human Rights (1969) nor the African Charter on Human and Peoples' Rights (1986) contains a provision for the right to food in their original formats. The supervisory organs of both, however, have expressly recognized the right in subsequent related instruments, and, what is more, the case law relating to each treaty has been developed so as to read the right to food into other rights (notably the right to life) contained in the relevant instrument.

In the following case of the *Yakye Axa indigenous community of the Enxet-Lengua people v Paraguay* (2005), the Inter-American Court of Human Rights, like the Indian Supreme Court, articulates how the right to food must necessarily be implicated in the right to life, as here provided under the American Convention on Human Rights (ACHR). In so doing, it invokes the reasoning of the UN Committee on Economic, Social and Cultural Rights' General Comments on health (General Comment No. 14), food (General Comment No. 12) and water (General Comment No. 15). In the extracts of the judgment below, the Court also refers to the Additional Protocol to the American Convention on Human Rights in the Area of Economic, Social and Cultural Rights (Protocol of San Salvador) 1988, Article 12 of which expressly recognizes the right to food in much the same way as Article 11 of the ICESCR.[73]

The case was based on claims made by the indigenous Yakye Axa Community that the 'extremely precarious and poor material and economic living conditions' in which its people existed were due in large measure to their access to ancestral lands being denied by the actions of the state. In particular, the state's processing of a land claim lodged by the Community in 1993 had been continually delayed and was not yet settled (paragraph 158(c) of the judgment). Consequently, it was argued (in paragraph 2 of the judgment) that a number of provisions under the ACHR had been infringed, including Articles 4 (Right to Life), 8 (Right to Fair Trial), 21 (Right to Property) and 25 (Judicial Protection) of the American Convention, in combination with the obligations set forth in Articles 1(1)

[73] In notably more direct and economical terms than those employed by its ICESCR cousin, Article 12 of the Additional Protocol to the American Convention on Human Rights in the Area of Economic, Social and Cultural Rights (adopted 17 November 1988, OAS Treaty Series No. 69 (1988), entered into force 16 November 1999) ('San Salvador Protocol'), reads: '1. Everyone has the right to adequate nutrition which guarantees the possibility of enjoying the highest level of physical, emotional and intellectual development. 2. In order to promote the exercise of this right and eradicate malnutrition, the States Parties undertake to improve methods of production, supply and distribution of food, and to this end, agree to promote greater international cooperation in support of the relevant national policies.'

(Obligation to Respect Rights) and 2 (Domestic Legal Effects). In respect of the right to life, it was alleged that:

…the right to life is a basic right, whose protection depends on realization of the other rights. In view of this, the States are under the obligation to ensure the establishment of conditions required for full enjoyment and exercise of that right. This entails positive protection measures by the State. Not taking such measures may create or foster conditions that lead to the death of individuals…[74]

And further, that:

…the right to life has also been abridged, to the detriment of the Community and of its members, by not allowing them to fully exercise the right to access to conditions that would enable each of them to live a decent life. The precarious material conditions and the poverty in which they live today explicitly reflect the lack of full and effective enjoyment of such basic rights as the right to health, the right to food and the right to education. This shortcoming does not allow the Community and its members to enjoy decent living conditions…[75]

In reaching its conclusion that Paraguay had indeed violated Article 4 of the Convention on the right to life (paragraph 241(3)), the court used the following lines of reasoning that highlighted the range of rights—including the right to food—upon which the right to life necessarily depends.

160. Article 4(1) of the Convention establishes that:

[e]very person has the right to have his life respected. This right shall be protected by law and, in general, from the moment of conception. No one shall be arbitrarily deprived of his life.

161. This Court has asserted that the right to life is crucial in the American Convention, for which reason realization of the other rights depends on protection of this one. When the right to life is not respected, all the other rights disappear, because the person entitled to them ceases to exist. Due to the basic nature of this right, approaches that restrict the right to life are not admissible. Essentially, this right includes not only the right of every human being not to be arbitrarily deprived of his life, but also the right that conditions that impede or obstruct access to a decent existence should not be generated.

162. One of the obligations that the State must inescapably undertake as guarantor, to protect and ensure the right to life, is that of generating minimum living conditions that are compatible with the dignity of the human person and of not creating conditions that hinder or impede it. In this regard, the State has the duty to take positive, concrete measures geared toward fulfillment of the right to a decent life, especially in the case of persons who are vulnerable and at risk, whose care becomes a high priority.

163. In the instant case, the Court must establish whether the State generated conditions that worsened the difficulties of access to a decent life for the members of the Yakye Axa Community and whether, in that context, it took appropriate positive measures to fulfill

[74] *Case of the Indigenous Community Yakye Axa v Paraguay*, 17 June 2005, IACHR (Ser. C) No. 125, [158(a)].

[75] *Yakye Axa v Paraguay*, [158(e)].

that obligation, taking into account the especially vulnerable situation in which they were placed, given their different manner of life (different worldview systems than those of Western culture, including their close relationship with the land) and their life aspirations, both individual and collective, in light of the existing international corpus juris regarding the special protection required by the members of the indigenous communities, in view of the provisions set forth in Article 4 of the Convention, in combination with the general duty to respect rights, embodied in Article 1(1) and with the duty of progressive development set forth in Article 26 of that same Convention, and with Articles 10 (Right to Health); 11 (Right to a Healthy Environment); 12 (Right to Food); 13 (Right to Education) and 14 (Right to the Benefits of Culture) of the Additional Protocol to the American Convention, regarding economic, social, and cultural rights, and the pertinent provisions ILO Convention No. 169.

164. In the chapter on proven facts... the Court found that the members of the Yakye Axa Community live in extremely destitute conditions as a consequence of lack of land and access to natural resources, caused by the facts that are the subject matter of this proceeding, as well as the precariousness of the temporary settlement where they have had to remain, waiting for a solution to their land claim. This Court notes that, according to the statements of Esteban López, Tomás Galeano and Inocencia Gómez during the public hearing held in the instant case... the members of the Yakye Axa Community could have been able to obtain part of the means necessary for their subsistence if they had been in possession of their traditional lands. Displacement of the members of the Community from those lands has caused special and grave difficulties to obtain food, primarily because the area where their temporary settlement is located does not have appropriate conditions for cultivation or to practice their traditional subsistence activities, such as hunting, fishing, and gathering. Furthermore, in this settlement the members of the Yakye Axa Community do not have access to appropriate housing with the basic minimum services, such as clean water and toilets. [Paraguay ratified the Additional Protocol to the American Convention on Human Rights regarding Economic, Social and Cultural Rights on June 3, 1997. The Protocol entered into force internationally on November 16, 1999].

165. These conditions have a negative impact on the nutrition required by the members of the Community who are at this settlement... Furthermore, as has been proven in the instant case... there are special deficiencies in the education received by the children and lack of access to health care for the members of the Community for physical and economic reasons.

166. In this regard, the United Nations Committee on Economic, Social, and Cultural Rights, in General Comment 14 on the right to enjoy the highest attainable standard of health, pointed out that:

[i]ndigenous peoples have the right to specific measures to improve their access to health services and care. These health services should be culturally appropriate, taking into account traditional preventive care, healing practices and medicines [...].

[I]n indigenous communities, the health of the individual is often linked to the health of the society as a whole and has a collective dimension. In this regard, the Committee considers that [...] denying them their sources of nutrition and breaking their symbiotic relationship with their lands, has a deleterious effect on their health.

167. Special detriment to the right to health, and closely tied to this, detriment to the right to food and access to clean water, have a major impact on the right to a decent existence and

basic conditions to exercise other human rights, such as the right to education or the right to cultural identity. In the case of indigenous peoples, access to their ancestral lands and to the use and enjoyment of the natural resources found on them is closely linked to obtaining food and access to clean water. In this regard, said Committee on Economic, Social and Cultural Rights has highlighted the special vulnerability of many groups of indigenous peoples whose access to ancestral lands has been threatened and, therefore, their possibility of access to means of obtaining food and clean water [in General Comment 12 (para.13), and General Comment 15 (para.16), respectively].

168. In the previous chapter [of the judgment], this Court established that the State did not guarantee the right of the members of the Yakye Axa Community to communal property. The Court deems that this fact has had a negative effect on the right of the members of the Community to a decent life, because it has deprived them of the possibility of access to their traditional means of subsistence, as well as to use and enjoyment of the natural resources necessary to obtain clean water and to practice traditional medicine to prevent and cure illnesses. Furthermore, the State has not taken the necessary positive measures to ensure that the members of the Yakye Axa Community, during the period in which they have been without territory, have living conditions that are compatible with their dignity, despite the fact that on June 23, 1999 the President of Paraguay issued Decree No. 3.789 that declared a state of emergency in the Community…[76]

In terms of remedial action, the Court ordered that Paraguay had to identify and grant to the Yakye Axa Community suitable traditional land within three years of the judgment,[77] and that in the meantime, or for as long as the community remained landless, 'the State must provide them with the basic services and goods required for their subsistence'.[78]

In light of the growing awareness and promotion of the right to food since at least the early 1980s, it is somewhat curious that no express provision for the right was made in the African Charter on Human and Peoples' Rights, as promulgated in 1986. That said, however, the existence of the right to food has been both inferred in the Charter itself, and has been expressly provided in supplementary human rights instruments to the Charter. In respect of the latter, the African Charter on the Rights and Welfare of the Child (1990) recognizes the right within the context of states' obligations to provide health care and health care services under Article 14(2)(c) and (d):

Article 14 Health and Health Services

…

2. States Parties to the present Charter shall undertake to pursue the full implementation of this right and in particular shall take measures:

…

(c) to ensure the provision of adequate nutrition and safe drinking water;

[76] *Yakye Axa v Paraguay*.

[77] *Yakye Axa v Paraguay*, [241(6)] and [211]–[217].

[78] *Yakye Axa v Paraguay*, [241(7)] and [221].

(d) to combat disease and malnutrition within the framework of primary health care through the application of appropriate technology...[79]

Furthermore, Article 15 of the Protocol to the African Charter on Human and Peoples' Rights on the Rights of Women in Africa (2003) protects the right to food security by requiring states to:

(a) provide women with access to clean drinking water, sources of domestic fuel, land, and the means of producing nutritious food;

(b) establish adequate systems of supply and storage to ensure food security.[80]

The implication of the right to food in the Charter itself was established by the African Commission on Human and Peoples' Rights in the ground breaking case of *The Social and Economic Action Rights Centre (SERAC) v Nigeria*.[81] The case involved multiple claims by the indigenous Ogoni communities from the Niger Delta of human rights violations regarding the rights to life, health and non-discrimination, property, a 'satisfactory environment', and the free disposition of wealth and resources, perpetrated directly by state authorities, or as 'condoned or facilitated' by the state through the actions of its joint venture partners (including a local subsidiary of Royal Dutch Shell Plc) in respect of oil exploration and production in the Delta. In particular, it was alleged that by failing to 'monitor...operations of the oil companies [regarding] safety measures that are standard procedure within the industry',[82] and 'by placing the legal and military powers of the State at the disposal of the oil companies',[83] the Nigerian Government caused or permitted the razing of a number of Ogoni villages, leaving thousands of people homeless and without the means to sustain their livelihoods.[84] Regarding the right to food specifically, the Commission noted the allegations that:

...the Nigerian government has destroyed and threatened Ogoni food sources through a variety of means. The government has participated in irresponsible oil development that has poisoned much of the soil and water upon which Ogoni farming and fishing depended. In their raids on villages, Nigerian security forces have destroyed crops and killed farm animals. The security forces have created a state of terror and insecurity that has made it impossible for many Ogoni villagers to return to their fields and animals. The destruction of farmlands, rivers, crops and animals has created malnutrition and starvation among certain Ogoni Communities.[85]

[79] African Charter on the Rights and Welfare of the Child (adopted 11 July 1990, OAU Doc. CAB/LEG/24.9/49 (1990), entered into force 29 November 1999), Article 14.

[80] Protocol to the African Charter on Human and Peoples' Rights on the Rights of Women in Africa (adopted 11 July 2003).

[81] *Social and Economic Rights Action Center and the Center for Economic and Social Rights v Nigeria* (Communication No. 155/96), (2001) AHRLR 60, 27 October 2001, (African Commission on Human and Peoples' Rights).

[82] *SERAC and CESR v Nigeria*, [4].

[83] *SERAC and CESR v Nigeria*, [2].

[84] *SERAC and CESR v Nigeria*, [7]–[8].

[85] *SERAC and CESR v Nigeria*, [9].

The Commission concluded that Nigeria had indeed violated all the rights mentioned above, including the implied right to food. In respect of the latter, it did so by way of the following reasoning:

64. The Communication argues that the right to food is implicit in the African Charter, in such provisions as the right to life (Art. 4), the right to health (Art. 16) and the right to economic, social and cultural development (Art. 22). By its violation of these rights, the Nigerian Government trampled upon not only the explicitly protected rights but also upon the right to food implicitly guaranteed.

65. The right to food is inseparably linked to the dignity of human beings and is therefore essential for the enjoyment and fulfilment of such other rights as health, education, work and political participation. The African Charter and international law require and bind Nigeria to protect and improve existing food sources and to ensure access to adequate food for all citizens. Without touching on the duty to improve food production and to guarantee access, the minimum core of the right to food requires that the Nigerian Government should not destroy or contaminate food sources. It should not allow private parties to destroy or contaminate food sources, and prevent peoples' efforts to feed themselves.

66. The government's treatment of the Ogonis has violated all three minimum duties of the right to food. The government has destroyed food sources through its security forces and State Oil Company; has allowed private oil companies to destroy food sources; and, through terror, has created significant obstacles to Ogoni communities trying to feed themselves. The Nigerian government has again fallen short of what is expected of it as under the provisions of the African Charter and international human rights standards, and hence, is in violation of the right to food of the Ogonis.[86]

THE RIGHT TO WATER

The conceptualization of the right to water is a relatively new endeavour, with its genesis in the modern era of international human rights being no earlier than the establishment of the Covenant itself—the right to water having never been considered, the *travaux préparatoires* reveal, during the Covenant's formative deliberations.[87] Despite having omitted expressly to include the right to water in the text of Article 11, or anywhere else in the Covenant, considerable effort has since been invested in making clear its necessary implication, not only in Article 11 of the Covenant, but in other international provisions as well. The opening paragraphs of the Committee on Economic, Social and Cultural Rights' 2002 General Comment No. 15, as extracted below, make clear the patent need and importance of such a right, the nature of the right and its various locations in international law texts, including (and especially) alongside the right to food, as an essential component to the right to an adequate standard of living.

1. Water is a limited natural resource and a public good fundamental for life and health. The human right to water is indispensable for leading a life in human dignity. It is a

[86] *SERAC and CESR v Nigeria*, [64]–[66].

[87] For discussion of this apparent silence, see Matthew Craven, 'Some Thoughts on the Emergent Right to Water' in Eibe Riedel and Peter Rothen (eds), *The Human Right to Water* (Berliner Wissenschafts Verlag, Berlin, 2006), Chapter 2.

prerequisite for the realization of other human rights. The Committee has been confronted continually with the widespread denial of the right to water in developing as well as developed countries. Over one billion persons lack access to a basic water supply, while several billion do not have access to adequate sanitation, which is the primary cause of water contamination and diseases linked to water. The continuing contamination, depletion and unequal distribution of water is exacerbating existing poverty. States parties have to adopt effective measures to realize, without discrimination, the right to water, as set out in this general comment.

The legal bases of the right to water

2. The human right to water entitles everyone to sufficient, safe, acceptable, physically accessible and affordable water for personal and domestic uses. An adequate amount of safe water is necessary to prevent death from dehydration, to reduce the risk of water-related disease and to provide for consumption, cooking, personal and domestic hygienic requirements.

3. Article 11, paragraph 1, of the Covenant specifies a number of rights emanating from, and indispensable for, the realization of the right to an adequate standard of living 'including adequate food, clothing and housing'. The use of the word 'including' indicates that this catalogue of rights was not intended to be exhaustive. The right to water clearly falls within the category of guarantees essential for securing an adequate standard of living, particularly since it is one of the most fundamental conditions for survival. Moreover, the Committee has previously recognized that water is a human right contained in article 11, paragraph 1, (see General Comment No. 6 (1995)). The right to water is also inextricably related to the right to the highest attainable standard of health (art. 12, para. 1) and the rights to adequate housing and adequate food (art. 11, para. 1). The right should also be seen in conjunction with other rights enshrined in the International Bill of Human Rights, foremost amongst them the right to life and human dignity.

4. The right to water has been recognized in a wide range of international documents, including treaties, declarations and other standards. For instance, Article 14, paragraph 2, of the Convention on the Elimination of All Forms of Discrimination Against Women stipulates that States parties shall ensure to women the right to 'enjoy adequate living conditions, particularly in relation to [. . .] water supply'. Article 24, paragraph 2, of the Convention on the Rights of the Child requires States parties to combat disease and malnutrition 'through the provision of adequate nutritious foods and clean drinking-water'.[88]

Having implicated the right to water within a number of existing (express) rights in the Covenant and elsewhere, the Committee sought to follow that up with a statement as to the supposed 'normative content' of the right. Thus, in paragraph 10 of General Comment No. 15, the Committee declares that:

The right to water contains both freedoms and entitlements. The freedoms include the right to maintain access to existing water supplies necessary for the right to water, and the right to be free from interference, such as the right to be free from arbitrary disconnections or contamination of water supplies. By contrast, the entitlements include the right to a system

[88] CESCR, General Comment No. 15, The right to water (Articles 11 and 12), E/C.12/2002/11 (20 January 2003) ('General Comment No. 15'), [1]–[4].

of water supply and management that provides equality of opportunity for people to enjoy the right to water.[89]

By invoking the Covenant's umbrella prohibition against discrimination in Article 2(2), the Committee, in paragraphs 13 to 16 of the General Comment, stresses the importance of states ensuring equal access to water for all within their respective jurisdictions, especially women and children, disabled people, refugees, indigenous, nomadic and rural communities, and the poor generally, who, the Committee notes, too often lose out when investment in water services 'disproportionately favour expensive water supply services and facilities that are accessible only to a small, privileged fraction of the population' (paragraph 14).[90]

In any event, the stipulated freedoms and entitlements contained in the right to water must have corresponding duties. As such, and in the absence of any statement as to these duties in the body of the Covenant itself, General Comment No. 15 devotes a considerable amount of its text to describing the precise nature of states' obligations, how they should meet them, and what remedies they ought to provide whenever breaches do occur.

In Part III of the General Comment, the Committee outlines states parties' obligations.[91] First, in terms of their general legal obligations, states must pursue the progressive realization of the right, by way of measures that are expeditious, effective, non-retrogressive and to the maximum of their available resources. Secondly, in terms of their obligations to *respect* the right to water, states must 'refrain from interfering directly or indirectly with the enjoyment of the right to water', by, for example, denying or limiting access to adequate water, diminishing or polluting water or limiting access to, or destroying, water services.[92] What is more, under international humanitarian law, these obligations extend to situations of armed conflict and other emergency circumstances. Thirdly, states must *protect* the right to water by preventing third parties, such as 'individuals, groups, corporations and other entities as well as agents acting under their authority', from interfering in any way with the enjoyment of the right.[93] Significantly, given the prevalence and partiality of

[89] CESCR, General Comment No. 15, [15].

[90] CESCR, General Comment No. 15, [14]. The Special Rapporteur on the right to safe drinking water and sanitation has subsequently expanded on the nature of these types of discrimination, how levels can be measured, and what actions might be taken to combat the discrimination, in UNGA, Report of Catarina de Albuquerque, Special Rapporteur on the human right to safe drinking water and sanitation A/7/270 (8 August 2012), Part IV, [51]–[74]. See also and further, the Special Rapporteur's companion Report to the Human Rights Council (A/HRC/21/24, 2 July 2012), which 'emphasizes that States cannot fully realize the human rights to water and sanitation without addressing stigma as a root cause of discrimination and other human rights violations', Summary, 1.

[91] CESCR, General Comment No. 15, E/C.12/2002/11 (20 January 2003), [17]–[38]. Part IV of the General Comment No. 15 covers 'violations', [39]–[44]. As these violations, naturally, correspond closely with the failing to meet the obligations outlined in Part III, we do not here discuss them further.

[92] CESCR, General Comment No. 15, E/C.12/2002/11 (20 January 2003), [21].

[93] CESCR, General Comment No. 15, [23].

privatization in the water sector, the Committee expands on this form of obligation as follows:

Where water services (such as piped water networks, water tankers, access to rivers and wells) are operated or controlled by third parties, States parties must prevent them from compromising equal, affordable, and physical access to sufficient, safe and acceptable water. To prevent such abuses an effective regulatory system must be established, in conformity with the Covenant and this General Comment, which includes independent monitoring, genuine public participation and imposition of penalties for non-compliance.[94]

Fourthly, regarding their obligations to *fulfil*, the Committee notes that states must institute measures that 'assist individuals and communities to enjoy the right', including 'education concerning the hygienic use of water', the promotion of methods to minimize water wastage, underwriting the affordability of water and ensuring everyone's access to adequate sanitation, all within the domestic political and legal regime that accords 'sufficient recognition' of the right. In reflection of the requirements of Article 11(1) of the Covenant, such recognition should be 'preferably by way of legislative implementation; adopting a national water strategy and plan of action to realize this right; ensuring that water is affordable for everyone; and facilitating improved and sustainable access to water, particularly in rural and deprived urban areas'.[95] The Committee expands on these aspects of national level implementation in Part V of the General Comment,[96] adding that states must establish targets for supplying and improving adequate access to water, monitor performances in reaching those targets, and provide access to appropriate remedies for those who suffer from failed or inadequate delivery, or from other breaches of the right to water. An important feature of this aspect of state obligations concerns the directions provided by the Committee as to the indicators and benchmarks they ought to institute and abide by:

Indicators and benchmarks

53. To assist the monitoring process, right to water indicators should be identified in the national water strategies or plans of action. The indicators should be designed to monitor, at the national and international levels, the State party's obligations under articles 11, paragraph 1, and 12. Indicators should address the different components of adequate water (such as sufficiency, safety and acceptability, affordability and physical accessibility), be disaggregated by the prohibited grounds of discrimination, and cover all persons residing in the State party's territorial jurisdiction or under their control. States parties may obtain guidance on appropriate indicators from the ongoing work of WHO, the Food and Agriculture Organization of the United Nations (FAO), the United Nations Centre for Human Settlements (Habitat), the International Labour Organization (ILO), the United Nations Children's Fund (UNICEF), the United Nations Environment Programme (UNEP), the United Nations Development Programme (UNDP) and the United Nations Commission on Human Rights.

[94] CESCR, General Comment No. 15, [24]. [95] CESCR, General Comment No. 15, [26].
[96] CESCR, General Comment No. 15, [45]–[59].

54. Having identified appropriate right to water indicators, States parties are invited to set appropriate national benchmarks in relation to each indicator. During the periodic reporting procedure, the Committee will engage in a process of 'scoping' with the State party. Scoping involves the joint consideration by the State party and the Committee of the indicators and national benchmarks which will then provide the targets to be achieved during the next reporting period. In the following five years, the State party will use these national benchmarks to help monitor its implementation of the right to water. Thereafter, in the subsequent reporting process, the State party and the Committee will consider whether or not the benchmarks have been achieved, and the reasons for any difficulties that may have been encountered (see General Comment No. 14 (2000), para. 58). Further, when setting benchmarks and preparing their reports, States parties should utilize the extensive information and advisory services of specialized agencies with regard to data collection and disaggregation.[97]

Fifthly, the General Comment stresses the importance that 'states parties recognize the essential role of international cooperation and assistance' to the full realization of the right.[98] And, finally, the Committee articulates in paragraph 37 of the General Comment what it considers to be the core obligations of states in specific respect of the right to water:

Core obligations

37. In General Comment No. 3 (1990), the Committee confirms that States parties have a core obligation to ensure the satisfaction of, at the very least, minimum essential levels of each of the rights enunciated in the Covenant. In the Committee's view, at least a number of core obligations in relation to the right to water can be identified, which are of immediate effect:

(a) To ensure access to the minimum essential amount of water, that is sufficient and safe for personal and domestic uses to prevent disease;

(b) To ensure the right of access to water and water facilities and services on a non-discriminatory basis, especially for disadvantaged or marginalized groups;

(c) To ensure physical access to water facilities or services that provide sufficient, safe and regular water; that have a sufficient number of water outlets to avoid prohibitive waiting times; and that are at a reasonable distance from the household;

(d) To ensure personal security is not threatened when having to physically access to water;

(e) To ensure equitable distribution of all available water facilities and services;

(f) To adopt and implement a national water strategy and plan of action addressing the whole population; the strategy and plan of action should be devised, and periodically reviewed, on the basis of a participatory and transparent process; it should include methods, such as right to water indicators and benchmarks, by which progress can be closely monitored; the process by which the strategy and plan of action are devised, as well as their content, shall give particular attention to all disadvantaged or marginalized groups;

(g) To monitor the extent of the realization, or the non-realization, of the right to water;

[97] CESCR, General Comment No. 15, [53]–[54].

[98] We deal further with the international obligations of the right to an adequate standard of living generally in the last section of the current chapter.

(h) To adopt relatively low-cost targeted water programmes to protect vulnerable and marginalized groups;

(i) To take measures to prevent, treat and control diseases linked to water, in particular ensuring access to adequate sanitation.

The extent to which the General Comment fills in where the text of the Covenant is silent in respect of the right to water has been a matter of some academic and legal debate.[99] The fact is, however, that the right is now sufficiently established in various legal formats[100] such that it is widely accepted as an enforceable right in both international and domestic jurisdictions. Certainly, it is instructive to note in this respect both how often the Committee has raised the right to water in its Concluding Observations on states' periodic reports, and what have been the states' responses. For as Takele Soboka Bulto observes, 'it is clear that the CESCR has taken the silence on the part of *ICESCR* states parties in the face of CESCR's criticisms of their domestic implementation (or violation) of the human right to water as indicative of tacit assent by states to the fact that the *ICESCR* contains the human right to water and consequent state obligations'.[101]

References to the obligations of states to ensure access to adequate water and sanitation are now a common feature of the Committee's Concluding Observations in respect of the periodic reports of many states. The Committee makes frequent criticism of the absence or inadequacy of water services for significant portions of society in certain countries, especially for those people living in slums or shanty towns, as illustrated by the following, fairly typical, extracts from Concluding Observations on the reports of Afghanistan, Angola and Brazil.

Afghanistan:

35. The Committee notes with concern that a high percentage of the population in Afghanistan lack basic services such as drinking water, waste removal, sanitary facilities and electricity, and that due to the lack of sewage systems, water sources are contaminated and unsafe, thus causing serious health problems (art. 11). The Committee urges the State

[99] See, eg, the debate between Stephen Tully and Malcolm Langford across the following four articles: Stephen Tully, 'A Human Right to Access Water? A Critique of General Comment No 15' (2005) 23 (1) *Netherlands Quarterly of Human Rights* 35; Malcolm Langford, 'Ambition That Overleaps Itself—A Response to Stephen Tully's Critique of the General Comment on the Right to Water' (2006) 24(3) *Netherlands Quarterly of Human Rights* 433; Stephen Tully, 'Flighty Purposes and Deeds: A Rejoinder to Malcolm Langford' (2006) 24(3) *Netherlands Quarterly of Human Rights* 461; Malcolm Langford, 'Expectation of Plenty: Response to Stephen Tully' (2006) 24(3) *Netherlands Quarterly of Human Rights* 473.

[100] Including a UN General Assembly resolution adopted in 2010 which expressly 'recognized the right to safe and clean drinking water and sanitation as a human right that is essential for the full enjoyment of life and all human rights'; UNGA Res.64/292 The human right to water and sanitation (3 August 2010).

[101] Takele Soboka Bulto, 'The Emergence of the Human Right to Water in International Human Rights Law: Invention or Discovery?' (2011) 12 *Melbourne Journal of International Law* 290, 306. Bulto notes Eibe Riedel's research, which showed that even in the ten years immediately prior to the adoption of General Comment No. 15 (ie 1993–2002), some 29 per cent of all Concluding Observations (33 out of a total 114), addressed the right to water.

party to provide rural and urban communities with appropriate systems for ensuring access to drinking water and to adequate sanitation infrastructure, in line with the Committee's general comment No. 15 (2002) on the right to water, in particular for low-income, disadvantaged and marginalized individuals and groups, if necessary by seeking international cooperation and assistance.[102]

Angola:

30. The Committee is concerned about the large proportion of the population living in slum conditions and about the lack of effective measures to provide social housing for low-income, vulnerable and marginalized individuals who are living in informal settlements and are frequently deprived of affordable access to adequate water and sanitation.

The Committee recommends that the State party adopt a comprehensive housing plan and policies, and allocate sufficient budgetary resources to ensure its implementation, especially for low-income groups and marginalized individuals and groups. The Committee also recommends that the State party take immediate measures to ensure safe access to adequate water and sanitation in informal settlements in Luanda and other big cities in line with the Committee's general comment No. 15 (2002) on the right to water.[103]

Brazil:

25. The Committee notes with concern that more than 6 million people in the State party live in precarious urban settlements, that there is a large number of homeless people and that significant migration inflows into urban areas have exacerbated the housing shortage. The Committee is further concerned about the absence of adequate measures to provide social housing for low-income families and disadvantaged and marginalized individuals and groups, while acknowledging the State party's efforts in this regard. (art. 11, para. 1)

The Committee recommends that the State party adopt additional measures to deal with the problem of homelessness, ensure adequate access to housing for low-income families, disadvantaged and marginalized individuals and groups and improve the water and sanitation facilities of existing housing units.[104]

More particularly, the committee has also urged states to enshrine the right to water in domestic law so that it becomes a legal entitlement and not merely a desirable policy goal;[105] it has criticized inadequate control by states of the prices charged by private corporations for water services such that significant numbers of people are unable to afford them;[106] and it has taken states to task over their discriminatory behaviour regarding access to water whether within their own territories or in respect of water sources that cross international boundaries.[107]

[102] CESCR, Concluding Observations: Afghanistan, E/C.12/AFG/CO/2-4 (7 June 2010), [35].

[103] CESCR, Concluding Observations: Angola, E/C.12/AGO/CO/3 (1 December 2008), [30].

[104] CESCR, Concluding Observations: Brazil, E/C.12/BRA/CO/2 (12 June 2009).

[105] See CESCR, Concluding Observations: Canada, E/C.12/CAN/CO/4, E/C.12/CAN/CO/5 (22 May 2006), [30].

[106] See CESCR, Concluding Observations: Kenya, E/C.12/KEN/CO/1 (1 December 2008), [30].

[107] See, in respect of water restrictions imposed upon Palestinians and Bedouins: CESCR, Concluding Observations: Israel, E/C.12/1/Add.27 (4 December 1998), [21]–[28]; Israel, E/C.12/1/Add.90 (26 June 2003), [19]–[27] and [40]–[43].

From a policy, and indeed philosophical, point of view, it is not hard to see why so great an effort has been made to retrofit the right to water into the structure and content of the ICESCR. 'Water is', as the United Nations' Fact Sheet 35 on the Right to Water declares in its opening lines, 'the essence of life. Safe drinking water and sanitation are indispensable to sustain life and health, and fundamental to the dignity of all.' The World Health Organization (WHO) adds that:

> …without water, human beings cannot live for more than a few days. It plays a vital role in nearly every function of the body, protecting the immune system—the body's natural defences—and helping remove waste matter. But to do this effectively, water must be accessible and safe. Lack of safe water is a cause of serious illnesses such as diarrhoeal diseases, which kill over 2 million people every year (the vast majority children, mostly in developing countries). Contaminated water, whether drunk or used to cook food, harms people's health. Water is also essential for hygiene, growing food, keeping animals, rest, exercise and relaxation and for a variety of social and cultural reasons.[108]

Access to safe, sufficient and clean water is also considered by the MDGs to be vital for the prospects for development of most of the world's population, more than one-third (ie 2.6 billion) of which, it is estimated by UNICEF, live without sufficient access to clean water or minimally adequate sanitation services.[109]

In striving to achieve MDG 7: 'to ensure environmental sustainability', one of the goal's proclaimed, constitutive targets (Target 7(c)), together with the indicators by which its achievement has been measured, is as follows:

> Target 7.C: Halve, by 2015, the proportion of the population without sustainable access to safe drinking water and basic sanitation
>
> - The world has met the target of halving the proportion of people without access to improved sources of water, five years ahead of schedule.
> - Between 1990 and 2010, more than two billion people gained access to improved drinking water sources.
> - The proportion of people using an improved water source rose from 76 per cent in 1990 to 89 per cent in 2010.
> - Over 40 per cent of all people without improved drinking water live in sub-Saharan Africa.
> - Eleven per cent of the global population—783 million people—remains without access to an improved source of drinking water and, at the current pace, 605 million people will still lack coverage in 2015.
> - Access to improved sanitation facilities increased from 36 per cent in 1990 to 56 per cent in 2010 in the developing regions as a whole. The greatest progress was achieved in Eastern and Southern Asia.

[108] WHO, 'The Right to Water' (2003), <http://www.who.int/water_sanitation_health/en/righttowater.pdf>, 6.

[109] Human Rights Council, Human rights and access to safe drinking water and sanitation, A/HRC/15/L.14 (24 September 2010), Preamble.

- Despite progress, 2.5 billion in developing countries still lack access to improved sanitation facilities.[110]

While, however, not disputing the value of such a goal generally, and the above target specifically, the means by which it is envisaged they are to be met have not been without criticism from a human rights perspective. For example, the Office of the High Commissioner for Human Rights UN Fact Sheet No. 25 on The Right to Water argues, in respect of Target 7(c):

While the content of the MDGs partly resembles some aspects of human rights, a systematic human rights-based approach to understanding and achieving the MDGs remains an unmet challenge. Human rights have not yet played a significant role in supporting and influencing MDG-related activities. In addition, human rights standards require States to ensure that all persons have access without discrimination to safe drinking water and sanitation.

Even if the MDG targets were to be achieved in full, it is important to note that there would still be more than 800 million people without safe drinking water and 1.8 billion people without basic sanitation in 2015.

The United Nations Millennium Project's Task Force on Water and Sanitation has affirmed that access to safe drinking water is a human right and highlighted its importance for achieving the majority of MDGs.[111]

Also, the Special Rapporteur on water and sanitation has criticized the MDG's 'blindspot' regarding discrimination:

[31]. …the Millennium Development Goals are silent on discrimination, inequalities and unjustifiable disparities. At least in theory, many of the targets can be achieved without benefiting a single person with a disability, a single person belonging to an ethnic minority, or a single person living in poverty because their focus on average attainments creates a blind spot in the achievement of equality.

[32]. In her country missions, the Special Rapporteur has noted that specific groups are excluded from access to water and sanitation, often reflecting patterns of discrimination, marginalization and limited political will to ensure substantive equality. These groups can be identified along ethnicity and socioeconomic divides. In some countries, indigenous peoples living on reserves do not have access to water or sanitation services. Dalits often suffer discrimination in accessing water and sanitation, while Roma are most disadvantaged in many European countries. Moreover, the Special Rapporteur's attention has repeatedly been drawn to vast gender inequalities and multiple discrimination, or the compounded impact of various grounds of discrimination on the same individual or group. For instance, women and girls are overwhelmingly tasked with collecting water and are physically and sexually threatened when they fetch water. Persons with disabilities are also disproportionately represented among those who lack access to safe drinking water and sanitation.[112]

[110] UN, The Millennium Development Goals, Target 7(c), <http://www.un.org/millenniumgoals/environ.shtml>. See also UN, The Millennium Development Goals Report 2013, 46–8, <http://www.un.org/millenniumgoals/pdf/report-2013/mdg-report-2013-english.pdf>.

[111] OHCHR, The Right to Water, Fact Sheet 25, August 2010, 29–30, <http://www.ohchr.org/Documents/Publications/FactSheet35en.pdf>.

[112] UNGA, Report of the Special Rapporteur on the human right to safe drinking water and sanitation, A/67/270 (8 August 2012), [31]–[32]

Measuring 'adequacy'

Determining what is 'adequate' in order to satisfy the requirements of the right to water is critical, albeit challenging. The WHO has developed the chart[113] shown in Figure 13.1, below, to provide some guidance as to what adequacy means in practical terms.

Service level	Distance/time	Likely volumes of water collected	Needs met	Intervention priority and actions
No access	More than 1 kilometre/more than 30 minutes round trip	Very low (often below 5 litres per capita per day)	Consumption cannot be assured Hygiene practice compromised Basic consumption may be compromised	**Very high** Provision of basic level service
Basic access	Within 1 kilometre/within 30 minutes round trip	Average unlikely to exceed approximately 20 litres per capita per day	Consumption should be assured Hygiene may be compromised Laundry may occur off-plot – i.e. away from home	**High** Hygiene education Provision of intermediate level of service
Intermediate access	Water provided on-plot through at least one tap (yard level)	Average of approximately 50 litres per capita per day	Consumption assured Hygiene should not be compromised Laundry likely to occur on-plot – i.e. within the confines of the household	**Low** Hygiene promotion still yields health gains Encourage optimal access
Optimal access	Supply of water through multiple taps within the house	Average of 100-200 litres per capita per day	Consumption assured Hygiene should not be compromised Laundry will occur on-plot	**Very low** Hygiene promotion still yields health gains

Source: Howard G, Bartram J. *Domestic water quantity, service level and health.* Geneva, World Health Organization, 2003.

Table 13.1 Service level and quantity of water collected

In addition to the WHO, the quest to understand the nature and extent of the obligations of the right to water, and how best to achieve their fulfilment, has also been promoted by the UN Human Rights Council as well as its predecessor, the Commission on Human Rights. In 2000, the Sub-Commission of the latter established a Special Rapporteur on the right to drinking water supply and sanitation—a position that was held by Mr El Hadji Guissé until 2005. In his final report of July that year, Mr Guissé produced a set of Draft Guidelines for the Realization of the Right to Drinking Water and Sanitation,[114] which 'highlight

[113] WHO, 'The Right to Water' (2003), <http://www.who.int/water_sanitation_health/en/righttowater.pdf>, 29.

[114] UN Commission on Human Rights, Sub-Commission on the Promotion and Protection of Human Rights, Realization of the right to drinking water and sanitation: Report of the Special Rapporteur, El Hadji Guissé, E/CN.4/Sub.2/2005/25 (11 July 2005).

the main and most urgent components of the right to water and sanitation',[115] and that were 'intended to assist government policymakers, international agencies and members of civil society working in the water and sanitation sector to implement the right…'.[116] Article 1 of the Draft Guidelines laid down a definition of the right to water, which although not intended to be 'an exhaustive legal definition of the right',[117] is nevertheless one that has been widely adopted as a working version of such:

1. The right to water and sanitation

    1.1 Everyone has the right to a sufficient quantity of clean water for personal and domestic uses.

    1.2 Everyone has the right to have access to adequate and safe sanitation that is conducive to the protection of public health and the environment.

    1.3 Everyone has the right to a water and sanitation service that is:

    (a) Physically accessible within, or in the immediate vicinity of the household, educational institution, workplace or health institution;

    (b) Of sufficient and culturally acceptable quality;

    (c) In a location where physical security can be guaranteed;

    (d) Supplied at a price that everyone can afford without compromising their ability to acquire other basic goods and services.[118]

Following this proclamation of what the right entails, the Draft Guidelines proceed to outline:

- State actions to implement the right to water and sanitation (Article 2)
- Preventing discrimination and addressing the needs of vulnerable or marginalized groups (Article 3)
- Availability and equitable distribution of water (Article 4)
- Improving access to drinking water supply (Article 5)
- Affordability (Article 6)
- Water quality (Article 7)
- Participatory rights (Article 8)
- Remedies and monitoring (Article 9)
- International obligation and duty of solidarity (Article 10)

Drawing on the broad base established by Mr Guissé, and expanding upon the Draft Guidelines, the UN Human Rights Council, in 2008, appointed an Independent

[115] UN Commission on Human Rights, E/CN.4/Sub.2/2005/25 (11 July 2005), [3], Introduction.
[116] UN Commission on Human Rights, E/CN.4/Sub.2/2005/25 (11 July 2005), [2], Introduction.
[117] UN Commission on Human Rights, E/CN.4/Sub.2/2005/25 (11 July 2005), [3].
[118] UN Commission on Human Rights, E/CN.4/Sub.2/2005/25 (11 July 2005), [1].

Expert (IE) on the Right to Safe Drinking Water and Sanitation (which position was, in 2011, transformed into the Special Rapporteur on the right to safe drinking water and sanitation). In her first report as the IE, Catarina de Albuquerque highlighted the issue of sanitation as a primary concern, noting that not only did its lack or inadequacy threaten the lives, livelihood and health of some 40 per cent of people worldwide, but also undermined the educational capacities of children and the economic fundamentals of many national economies (through increased health and welfare costs and lost productivity of workers).[119] As such, the IE mapped out how and why sanitation is vital to a number of human rights broadly (and the right to water specifically), as well as flagging her intentions in addressing the challenges it poses.

30. The independent expert considers it crucial to explore and identify the human rights obligations regarding sanitation. Human rights law offers a framework by which duty bearers may better understand their obligations and rights holders may be able to better claim their rights. In fact, sanitation can be related to human rights in at least three different ways. First, the enjoyment of a large number of human rights—civil, cultural, economic, political and social—hinges on access to sanitation. Secondly, lack of access to sanitation is frequently a consequence of larger societal discrimination, inequality and exclusion, fundamentally inconsistent with human rights protection. Thirdly, and more fundamentally, lack of access to sanitation constitutes, in itself, a serious human rights concern, as it relates to the inherent dignity of the human being. Sanitation is undoubtedly a matter of human rights and it is the link between the two that the independent expert wishes to further explore, in accordance with her mandate, in the course of 2009.

31. Although lack of access to sanitation is at the origin of the non-realization of basic human rights, the area of sanitation has not been adequately analysed from a human rights perspective. Cultural barriers and the taboo nature of the topic are a serious challenge to examining sanitation. As was stated by the Chairman of the United Nations Secretary-General's Advisory Board on Water and Sanitation (UNSGAB), 'it is time to break through the taboo, to call a spade a spade or a toilet a toilet and start doing something about this unacceptable killer'. The international community cannot shy away from this subject simply because it is uncomfortable, unmentionable, unpopular, or just because it is a very private matter that can be challenging to consider publicly. Sanitation and the human rights obligations concerning this subject must in fact be addressed in a direct and open manner. The independent expert hopes to contribute to this endeavour.[120]

[119] Human Rights Council, Report of the independent expert on the issue of human rights obligations related to access to safe drinking water and sanitation, Catarina de Albuquerque, A/HRC/10/6 (25 February 2009), [22]–[25]. In her Second Report in July 2009, the IE expanded the breadth of rights she saw as impacted by sanitation, and deepened her reasons for believing so: see Human Rights Council, Report of the independent expert on the issue of human rights obligations related to access to safe drinking water and sanitation, Catarina de Albuquerque, A/HRC/12/24 (1 July 2009), [13]–[54]. Further, the IE ventures the argument of the right to sanitation as a distinct right, on the principle basis that its denial threatens to strip an individual of their dignity, and as such strikes at the core of what human rights stand for [55]–[59].

[120] Human Rights Council, Report of the IE on the issue of human rights obligations related to access to safe drinking water and sanitation, Catarina de Albuquerque, A/HRC/10/6 (25 February 2009), [30]–[31].

Having elaborated an argument for why adequate sanitation is a necessary element of the right to water, Ms de Albuquerque then constructs a set of criteria for how to define adequate sanitation in human rights terms, and thereby provide the basis upon which to realize it. It is significant—and, it must be said, both bold and beneficial—that in so doing she articulates what is to be reasonably expected of states to meet the obligation to provide adequate sanitation, and, equally, what is not expected.

A. Defining sanitation in human rights terms

62. Understanding the human rights obligations related to sanitation requires a working definition of sanitation in human rights terms. This definition is drawn from elements related to sanitation as addressed under international human rights law. The independent expert considers that this definition may evolve as the understanding of the human rights obligations related to sanitation continues to develop.

63. The independent expert is of the view that sanitation can be defined as a system for the collection, transport, treatment and disposal or reuse of human excreta and associated hygiene. States must ensure without discrimination that everyone has physical and economic access to sanitation, in all spheres of life, which is safe, hygienic, secure, socially and culturally acceptable, provides privacy and ensures dignity.

64. States are obliged to respect, protect and fulfil human rights as they relate to sanitation.

More concretely, States must, inter alia:

- Refrain from measures which threaten or deny individuals or communities existing access to sanitation. States must also ensure that the management of human excreta does not negatively impact on human rights.
- Ensure that non-State actors act in accordance with human rights obligations related to sanitation, including through the adoption of legislative and other measures to prevent the negative impact of non-State actors on the enjoyment of sanitation. When sanitation services are operated by a private provider, the State must establish an effective regulatory framework.
- Take steps, applying the maximum of available resources, to the progressive realization of economic, social and cultural rights as they relate to sanitation. States must move as expeditiously and effectively as possible towards ensuring access to safe, affordable and acceptable sanitation for all, which provides privacy and dignity. This requires deliberate, concrete and targeted steps towards full realization, in particular with a view to creating an enabling environment for people to realize their rights related to sanitation. Hygiene promotion and education is a critical part of this obligation.
- Carefully consider and justify any retrogressive measures related to the human rights obligations regarding sanitation.
- Take the necessary measures directed towards the full realization of economic, social and cultural rights as they relate to sanitation, inter alia, by according sufficient recognition of human rights obligations related to sanitation in the national political and legal systems, and by immediately developing and adopting a national sanitation strategy and plan of action.

- Provide effective judicial or other appropriate remedies at both the national and international levels in cases of violations of human rights obligations related to sanitation. Victims of violations should be entitled to adequate reparation, including restitution, compensation, satisfaction and/or guarantees of non-repetition.[121]

Paragraphs 65 and 66 of the Report then stress that 'states must realize their human rights obligations related to sanitation in a non-discriminatory manner', in accordance with the terms established generally in respect of the right to water (in paragraphs 13 to 16 of General Comment No. 15), as discussed above, and that all 'concerned individuals and communities' are fully informed and participate in decisions over sanitation and hygiene matters that directly concern them.

67. It is important to state clearly what is not required when considering sanitation in human rights terms:

- States are not obliged to provide everyone with access to a sewerage system. Human rights law does not aim to dictate specific technology options, but instead calls for context-specific solutions.
- States are not obliged to provide individual facilities in every home. This will also depend on the context—sometimes a safe and otherwise adequate facility in the close proximity would suffice as an intermediate step towards full realization of related rights.
- States are not obliged to construct toilets, rather they must create an enabling environment. In fact, it is often argued that demand-led sanitation projects enjoy considerable success. Only in certain conditions, such as extreme poverty or natural disasters, when people, for reasons beyond their control, are genuinely unable to access sanitation through their own means, is the State obliged to actually provide sanitation services.
- States are not obliged to provide sanitation free of charge—those who are in a position to pay must contribute financially or in kind, for example by offering labour for the construction of sanitation systems. Only when people are genuinely unable to pay for sanitation is the State obliged to provide sanitation services free of charge.
- States may decide to privatize sanitation services, but in that case must ensure—through adequate regulation, including effective and accessible complaints procedures—that private actors do not adopt approaches which result in human rights violations.
- States are not required to ensure the full implementation of their human rights obligations related to sanitation immediately. Rather, they must show that they are taking steps to the maximum of their available resources to ensure at least minimum essential levels of sanitation for all people, and they must ensure that they are not discriminating against certain groups in providing access.[122]

[121] Human Rights Council, Report of the IE on the issue of human rights obligations related to access to safe drinking water and sanitation, Catarina de Albuquerque, A/HRC/10/6 (25 February 2009), [62]–[64].

[122] Human Rights Council, Report of the IE on the issue of human rights obligations related to access to safe drinking water and sanitation (25 February 2009), [67].

The questions of the nature, extent and form of states' obligations lie at the heart of all of international human rights law, and so it is with the right to water. It is no surprise, therefore, that so much attention is focused on delineating the practical implications of these questions in an effort thereby to devise measures against which states' performances in meeting the obligations can be gauged. The position of IE/SR on the right to water has been a key figure providing states, individuals and the Economic Social and Cultural Rights Committee itself with guidance in this regard. Extrapolating from her initial remarks on and guidance as to states' obligations as discussed above, the IE later devised a more detailed 'framework for assessing good practices from a human rights perspective, using five normative criteria (availability, quality/safety, acceptability, accessibility and affordability) and five cross-cutting criteria (nondiscrimination, participation, accountability, impact and sustainability).'[123] This was followed in 2011 by a compilation of examples of good practices from across a range of stakeholders (state bodies, international agencies, private service providers and civil society), which act, in effect, as illustrative examples of how the framework works in practice when assessing the merits of legislation, policy planning, service delivery and advocacy, as well as capacity-building, monitoring and litigation.[124]

While, on the one hand, the framework criteria are 'aimed at delineating more clearly the concrete requirements that enable the classification of a certain practice as good',[125] the IE nonetheless stresses that they have been made 'deliberately broad, flexible and adaptable', for, in her view, 'human rights law does not prescribe a particular choice of policy or technology, but instead calls for context-specific solutions'.[126]

There are, further, two key systemic features of the realization of the right to water, which by the combined force of economics and political philosophy, have come to dominate discussions of the means by which the right is implemented. One concerns the respective roles and responsibilities of states and non-state actors (especially corporations) in the provision of adequate water and related services, especially in circumstances where the utility has been fully, or partially, privatized. The other relates to the critical matter of how water and sanitation systems are financed: by whom (public and/or private sponsors), under what conditions and with what levels of accountability? While it true to say that traditionally human rights law professes not to prescribe a particular economic or political philosophy, it is nevertheless neither agnostic, nor neutral, as to the outcomes that result from any particular philosophy that is adopted. Thus, there can

[123] Human Rights Council, Report of the IE on the issue of human rights obligations related to access to safe drinking water and sanitation (1 July 2010).

[124] Human Rights Council, Report of the Special Rapporteur on the human right to safe drinking water and sanitation, Catarina de Albuquerque, A/HRC/18/33/Add.1 (29 June 2011).

[125] Human Rights Council, Report of the IE on the issue of human rights obligations related to access to safe drinking water and sanitation (1 July 2010), [11].

[126] Human Rights Council, Report of the IE on the issue of human rights obligations related to access to safe drinking water and sanitation (1 July 2010), [13].

be no denying that economic, social and political tensions exist between 'human rights and private sector involvement in the water and sanitation sectors'.[127] The human rights implications of financing of water services and their privatization have both been matters upon which the IE/SR has pronounced.[128] In fact, the two matters often intersect. The financing of the building and delivery of water and sanitation utilities, for example, may be obtained—wholly or, more usually, in part—by way of the privatization of the service. This has become an increasingly popular method for states across the globe to underwrite the costs of all kinds of public services, including water, as well as, it is claimed, improving the efficiency and effectiveness of the service. Be that as it may, under international human rights law, states remain responsible for the relevant human rights implications of such undertakings. In the case of the right to water, this amounts to an obligation to implement 'specific measures to regulate service provision and to maintain affordable access for all'.[129]

Indeed, as with the right to food, the involvement of the private sector in the provision of adequate access to, and supply of, water and sanitation services has become a matter of great significance for human rights accountability. In her report on non-state provision of water services, Ms de Albuquerque echoes many of the concerns expressed above by the Special Rapporteur on the right to food. That is, while certainly there is an important and growing awareness at the international level of the broader social responsibilities of corporations, including in respect of human rights, through such initiatives as the United Nations' Global Compact,[130] and the Guiding Principles on Business and Human Rights,[131] and the OECD's Guidelines for Multinational Enterprises,[132] it is the states themselves that bear directly the obligations imposed on them under the international human rights treaties.

B. State obligations

18. The State cannot exempt itself from its human rights obligations by involving non-State actors in service provision. Irrespective of responsibilities of the latter, the State remains the primary duty-bearer for the realization of human rights.

…

[127] Sharmila Murthy, 'The Human Right(s) to Water and Sanitation: History, Meaning and the Controversy Over Privatization' 31(1) (2013) *Berkeley Journal of International Law* 89, 91.

[128] Human Rights Council, Report of the independent expert on the issue of human rights obligations related to access to safe drinking water and sanitation, Catarina de Albuquerque, A/HRC/15/31 (9 June 2010); and UNGA, Report of the Special Rapporteur on the human right to safe drinking water and sanitation, A/66/255 (3 August 2011).

[129] UNGA, Report of the Special Rapporteur on the human right to safe drinking water and sanitation, [65].

[130] See <http://www.unglobalcompact.org>.

[131] Human Rights Council, Guiding Principles on Business and Human Rights: Implementing the United Nations 'Protect, Respect and Remedy' Framework, A/HRC/17/31 (21 March 2011), Annex.

[132] OECD Guidelines for Multinational Enterprises (2011)—see <http://www.oecd.org/daf/inv/mne/48004323.pdf>.

21. When non-State actors are involved in service provision, there is a shift to a stronger focus on the obligation of the State to protect. At the same time, the obligation to fulfil retains its significance with the aim of creating an enabling environment. States have a duty to regulate and monitor providers that they involve in service delivery. Moreover, they may need to adopt supplementary measures depending on the circumstances, for instance to ensure the affordability of services. A comprehensive approach is needed: non-State service providers can be involved, but the State has the obligation to develop an overall (short, medium and long-term) strategy on how to fully realize the rights to water and sanitation. When the State does not directly provide services, its role nevertheless remains obligatory and critical.[133]

Certainly, therefore, states are required to regulate the operations of private sector water providers within their own separate jurisdictions, but they must also encourage, contribute to and obtain guidance from various international initiatives covering business and human rights generally, and the right to water specifically. In respect of the latter, for example, ILO Convention No. 161 (1985) on Occupational Health Services 'underlines the responsibility of employers for the health and safety of their workers, which includes access to safe drinking water and sanitation'.[134] And AquaFed, the International Federation of Private Water Operators, expressly recognizes and supports the human rights to water and sanitation as one of the major challenges faced by its members in their operations in and with states worldwide.[135] More broadly, The CEO Water Mandate, developed under the aegis of the UN Global Compact, addresses not just private sector providers of water services, but also, crucially, water users in both industry and agriculture. Established in 2007, the Mandate is a 'public-private initiative designed to assist companies in the development, implementation, and disclosure of water sustainability policies and practices'.[136]

Implementation and enforcement of the right to water

The right to water is expressly recognized in a number of state constitutions, notably those of Argentina (Article 41 (implicitly)), Belgium (Article 23 (implicitly)), Bolivia (Article 16), the Democratic Republic of Congo (Article 48), Ecuador (Article 12), Kenya (Article 43(1)(d)), the Maldives (Article 23(a)), Nicaragua (Article 105), the Niger (Article 20), South Africa (Art 27(b)(1)) and Uruguay (Article 47). Further, a right to water and, in some cases, sanitation, has been

[133] Human Rights Council, Report of the IE on the issue of human rights obligations related to access to safe drinking water and sanitation (9 June 2010), [18] and [21].

[134] This is the implication made by the OHCHR, The Right to Water, Fact Sheet 35, August 2010, 31, <http://www.ohchr.org/Documents/Publications/FactSheet35en.pdf>.

[135] See <http://www.aquafed.org/page-5-59.html>.

[136] The CEO Water Mandate, <http://ceowatermandate.org/about/>. Although the Mandate does not explicitly refer to human rights in its text, human rights matters have nonetheless been raised in its governance meetings: see Human Rights Council, Report of the IE on the issue of human rights obligations related to access to safe drinking water and sanitation (9 June 2010), n. 21.

recognized (expressly or implicitly) in legislation in other countries, including Algeria, Brazil, France, Hungary, Peru, Uganda and Ukraine. Regulations and policies in many other states, while falling short of enshrining the right to water, nonetheless prioritize access to water and/or sanitation for all, or at least for those in greatest need.[137]

At the domestic level, one of the most significant bodies of jurisprudence on the right to water has been developed by the Indian courts, despite the fact that the right is not expressly recognized in the Indian Constitution. In reasoning parallel to that relating to the right to food discussed above, the Indian courts have interpreted Article 21 of the Constitution, protecting the right to life, as necessarily encompassing both the right to water and to proper sanitation.

The right to life, as courts, including the Supreme Court, have repeatedly stated, entails a life worth living. Adequate food, water and (as we discuss below) housing are all essential considered components of that minimum standard. In *Attakoya Thangal v Union of India*,[138] the High Court of the state of Kerala pronounced that the right to 'sweet' (ie clean) water was one of 'the attributes of the right to life, for these are the basic elements which sustain life itself'.[139] Interpreted as implying a right to water in Article 21 of the Constitution, subsequent judgments of states' High Courts and the Supreme Court have reiterated and expanded the manner and form of the implication, in respect, for example, to the obligation on public authorities to protect against the pollution of water (the Supreme Court in *M C Mehta v Union of India*),[140] and the overuse of groundwater by private sector industry (*Perumatty Grama Panchayat v State of Kerala*),[141] and the state's duty to maintain basic levels of water sanitation in fulfillment of the Constitutional right to life, per *Suo Muto v State of Rajasthan* (noting relevant prior cases):

3. Relying on the decision in *Municipal Council, Ratlam's case* (AIR 1980 SC 1622) (supra), the Supreme Court in *Dr. B.L. Wadehra v. Union of India*, AIR 1996 SC 2969, directed the Municipal Corporation Delhi and the New Delhi Municipal Council to perform its statutory duties of scavenging and cleaning the city. The Supreme Court did not accept the grounds of inadequacy of funds or insufficiency of machinery for non-performance of their statutory obligations.

4. Due to failure of the civic authorities and other bodies to discharge their duties under Article 21 of the Constitution and statutory provisions the quality of life in the city has gone down tremendously. Civic bodies and other authorities have been taking refuge under the purile excuse that they do not have funds to perform their duties. The

[137] See Human Rights Council, Report of the IE on the issue of human rights obligations related to access to safe drinking water and sanitation (25 February 2009), [18]; Human Rights Council, Report of the Special Rapporteur on the human right to safe drinking water and sanitation (29 June 2011), [13]–[23]. For a continually updated compendium of constitutional or legislative guarantees to the right to water in state jurisdictions, see the Information Portal for the Rights to Water and Sanitation: <http://www.righttowater.info/progress-so-far/national-legislation-on-the-right-to-water/>.

[138] (1990) I KLT 580.

[139] *Attakoya Thangal*, 583.

[140] *M C Mehta v Union of India* (2004) 12 SCC 118.

[141] *Perumatty Grama Panchayat v State of Kerala* (2004) 1 KLT 731 (Kerala High Court).

plea of lack of finances is a poor alibi for not performing their statutory duties. The law must be enforced and the fragile plea of lack of finances must be rejected. Inaction of the authorities cannot be tolerated, as that will make mockery of Article 21 of the Constitution and the statutory provisions under which they are obliged to carry out their duties, including duty to provide and maintain civic amenities which make life worth living.[142]

The same insistence on their being immutable minimum standards of water supply and sanitation are also apparent in case law of other countries. Thus, for example, the Belgian Court of Arbitration invoked the right to the protection of a healthy environment under Article 23 of the Constitution to establish that there existed a right of everyone to a minimum supply of drinking water.[143] And courts in both Argentina and South Africa have held that constitutional guarantees of access to adequate water prevent private sector water providers from cutting off supply to customers in the event of the latter's inability to pay for the service.[144]

As with the right to food, provision for the right to water under the regional human rights regimes is indistinct. Neither the American Convention on Human Rights (1969) nor the African Charter on Human and Peoples' Rights (1986) contains an express guarantee of the right to water, although both have developed bodies of jurisprudence that uphold the right by way of its implication in associated rights. Similarly, the Revised European Social Charter (1996) is understood to capture the right to water by way of it being read into the requirement under Article 11 that states ensure the right to the protection of health.[145] This Article stipulates that states must afford such protection by removing 'as far as possible the causes of ill-health', which requirement necessarily entails provision of access to adequate water and sanitation.[146] While the European Convention on Human Rights (1950) covers only civil and political rights, it has been used in

[142] *Suo Muto v State of Rajasthan* [2005] AIR Raj 82 (Rajasthan High Court), [3]–[4].

[143] *Commune de Wemmel, Moniteur Belge*, Arrêt no. 36/98 (24/4/98).

[144] For Argentina, see: *Villavechia de Pérez Lasala, Teresa c/ Obras Sanitarias de Mendoza S.E., s'acción de inconstitucionalidad*, 5 February 1990, Case 45525 (Supreme Court of Mendoza), in which the court upheld a reading of the right to a healthy environment under Article 41 of the Constitution as entailing a non-derogable right to access to adequate water; and *Quevedo, Miguel Angel y otros c/ Aguas Cordobesas S.A., s'acción Amparo Cordoba City*, 8 April 2002 (Civil and Commercial First Instance Court), in which the court held that a private company could not deny water to poor residents in Cordoba merely because they could not pay. For South Africa, see *Residents of Bon Vista Mansions v Southern Metropolitan Local Council* (2002) 6 BCLR 625 (W), in which the Witwatersrand Division of the High Court upheld this extent of the guarantee of the right to water under Article 27(1)(a) of the Constitution.

[145] Revised European Social Charter (adopted 3 May 1996, CETS 163, entered into force 1 July 1999).

[146] The Council of Europe's Committee of Ministers that oversees the implementation of the Charter and hears 'collective complaints' lodged under it has also inferred access to adequate water and sanitation in Article 31 of the Charter, which requires states to 'promote housing of an adequate standard'; see *European Roma Rights Centre (ERRC) v Portugal* (Collective Complaint No. 61/2010), Merits, 30 June 2011 (European Committee of Social Rights). See also the Council of Europe's European Charter on Water Resources (adopted 17 October 2001), which focuses on the need to use water resources responsibly and sustainably, and Article 5 of which confirms the right of everyone to sufficient water for their basic needs.

ways that indirectly uphold the right to water. In *Zander v Sweden*,[147] for example, the European Court of Human Rights found that Sweden had breached elements of the right to a fair trial under Article 6(1) of the Convention by denying claimants access to a legal remedy for the threatened pollution to a water source they used for drinking purposes.[148]

The path traced by the right to water under the African Union's human rights regime is coterminous with that of the right to food. As discussed earlier in this chapter, while neither right is explicitly provided for in the African Charter, both have been inferred in it, and both have also been expressly proclaimed in the Charter's supplementary instruments regarding children's rights and the rights of women. In the seminal case of *SERAC v Nigeria* (2002),[149] the African Commission on Human and Peoples' Rights found that among the many rights that the Nigerian Government had breached by way of its military operations in and around the operations of the Shell Oil company in the Niger Delta was the right to water as embedded in the Charter's rights to health and a clean environment. The Commission did so by upholding the following assertions of the complainants, and with reference to both the terms of the ICESCR (to which Nigeria is a party) and the African Charter:

50. The Complainants allege that the Nigerian government violated the right to health and the right to clean environment as recognized under Articles 16 and 24 of the African Charter by failing to fulfill the minimum duties required by these rights. This, the Complainants allege, the government has done by—

- Directly participating in the contamination of air, water and soil and thereby harming the health of the Ogoni population,
- Failing to protect the Ogoni population from the harm caused by the NNPC Shell Consortium but instead using its security forces to facilitate the damage,
- Failing to provide or permit studies of potential or actual environmental and health risks caused by the oil operations.

Article 16 of the African Charter reads:

'(1) Every individual shall have the right to enjoy the best attainable state of physical and mental health.

(2) States Parties to the present Charter shall take the necessary measures to protect the health of their people and to ensure that they receive medical attention when they are sick.'

Article 24 of the African Charter reads:

'All peoples shall have the right to a general satisfactory environment favourable to their development.'

[147] *Zander v Sweden* (App. 14282/88), 25 November 1993, (1994) 18 EHRR 175.
[148] *Zander v Sweden*, [25]–[29].
[149] *Social and Economic Rights Action Center and the Center for Economic and Social Rights v Nigeria* (Communication No. 155/96), (2001) AHRLR 60, 27 October 2001.

51. These rights recognise the importance of a clean and safe environment that is closely linked to economic and social rights in so far as the environment affects the quality of life and safety of the individual. As has been rightly observed by Alexander Kiss, 'an environment degraded by pollution and defaced by the destruction of all beauty and variety is as contrary to satisfactory living conditions and the development as the breakdown of the fundamental ecologic equilibria is harmful to physical and moral health.'

52. The right to a general satisfactory environment, as guaranteed under Article 24 of the African Charter or the right to a healthy environment, as it is widely known, therefore imposes clear obligations upon a government. It requires the State to take reasonable and other measures to prevent pollution and ecological degradation, to promote conservation, and to secure an ecologically sustainable development and use of natural resources. Article 12 of the International Covenant on Economic, Social and Cultural Rights (ICESCR), to which Nigeria is a party, requires governments to take necessary steps for the improvement of all aspects of environmental and industrial hygiene. The right to enjoy the best attainable state of physical and mental health enunciated in Article 16(1) of the African Charter and the right to a general satisfactory environment favourable to development (Article 16(3)) already noted obligate governments to desist from directly threatening the health and environment of their citizens. The State is under an obligation to respect the just noted rights and this entails largely non-interventionist conduct from the State for example, not from carrying out, sponsoring or tolerating any practice, policy or legal measures violating the integrity of the individual.[150]

In the specific respect of the right to water, the SERAC case was in fact following on from the African Commission's earlier determination in *Free Legal Assistance Group et al v Zaire*,[151] in which it held that the failure to provide safe drinking water constituted a violation of the right to health under Article 16 of the Charter. The implication of the right to water within the terms of the right to health has been further underscored in the 2005 case of *Centre of Housing Evictions and Human Rights (COHRE) v Sudan*,[152] in which the African Commission held that 'the destruction of homes, livestock and farms as well as the poisoning of water sources, such as wells' by state-backed militia during the conflict in Darfur[153] amounted to a violation of Sudan's obligations under Article 16 of the African Charter.

Most recently, the African Commission has expanded the foothold that the right to water and sanitation occupies within the African Charter by expressly referring to it in a pair of 'Guideline' documents. First, in a set of 'implementation' principles and guidelines (akin to the purpose of the CESCR's General Comments), the Commission reflects upon the importance and embeddedness of the right throughout the Charter, and takes considerable care to specify what is

[150] *SERAC and CESR v Nigeria*, [50]–[52].

[151] *Free Legal Assistance Group et al v Zaire*, African Commission Communications 25/89, 47/90, 56/91, 100/93, (1997) 4 IHRR 89, (2000) AHRLR 74 (4 April 1996).

[152] *Sudan Human Rights Organisation and Centre of Housing Evictions and Human Rights (COHRE) v Sudan*, African Commission Communications 296/05, (May 2009), (2009) AHRLR 154.

[153] *Sudan Human Rights Organisation and COHRE v Sudan*, [212].

required of states regarding their broad policy approach to the matter and their handling of particular practical problems of implementation:

I—The right to water and sanitation (Articles 4, 5, 15, 16, 22 and 24)

71. While the African Charter does not directly protect the right to water and sanitation, it is implied in the protections of the right to life, the right to dignity, the right to work, the right to health, the right to economic, social and cultural development and the right to a satisfactory environment.

72. The human right to water entitles everyone to sufficient, safe, acceptable, physically accessible and affordable water for personal and domestic uses. An adequate amount of safe water is necessary to prevent death from dehydration, to reduce the risk of water-related disease and to provide for consumption, cooking, personal and domestic hygienic requirements.

73. The right to water contains both freedoms and entitlements. The freedoms include the right to maintain access to existing water supplies, and the right to be free from interference, such as the right to be free from arbitrary disconnections or contamination of water supplies. The entitlements include the right to a system of water supply and management that provides equality of opportunity for people to enjoy the right to water. Water should be treated as a social and cultural good, and not primarily as an economic good.

74. Everyone has the right to have access to adequate and safe sanitation that is conducive to the protection of public health and the environment. Sanitation comprises at least, a clean toilet or latrine, along with collection, disposal and treatment of human excreta, wastewater, solid waste and storm water removal and hygiene education.

75. The right to water and sanitation imposes the following obligations, among others, on States parties to:

(i) Adopt a national strategy or plan of action to realize the right to water and sanitation

(ii) Adopt comprehensive and integrated strategies and programmes to ensure that there is sufficient and safe water for present and future generations. Such strategies may include: (a) reducing depletion of water resources through unsustainable extraction, diversion and damming; (b) reducing and eliminating contamination of watersheds and water-related eco-systems; (c) monitoring water reserves; (d) ensuring that proposed developments do not interfere with access to adequate water; (e) assessing the impacts of actions that may impinge upon water availability and natural ecosystem watersheds; (g) reducing water wastage in its distribution; (h) response mechanisms for emergency situations; and (i) establishing competent institutions and appropriate institutional arrangements to carry out the strategies and programmes.

(iii) Formulate and implement national water and sanitation strategies and plans of action that should respect, inter alia, the principles of non-discrimination and ensure the right of everyone to participate in decision-making affecting their right to water and sanitation. Communities have the right to determine what type of water and sanitation services they require and how those services should be managed and, where possible, to choose and operate their own services with assistance from the State.

(iv) Improve access to, and promote sustainable use of, water resources and their allocation among users.

(v) Ensure that water, and adequate water and sanitation facilities and services, are within safe physical reach for all sections of the population. Sufficient, safe and acceptable water must be physically accessible within, or in the immediate vicinity, of each household, educational institution, workplace or health institution in a location where physical security can be guaranteed. Sufficient water means water supply for each person that is sufficient and continuous for personal and domestic uses, which normally include drinking, personal sanitation, washing of clothes, food preparation, personal and household hygiene. Safe water is water that, in particular, is free from hazardous substances (micro-organisms, chemical substances and radiological hazards) that could endanger human health, and whose colour, odour and taste are acceptable to users.

(vi) Ensure that all water and sanitation facilities and services are of sufficient quality, culturally appropriate and meet the needs of all groups, including women, children and the elderly. Physical security should not be threatened during access to water and sanitation facilities and services. Water as well as water and sanitation facilities and services, must be affordable for all. These must be accessible to all, including members of vulnerable and disadvantaged groups. These services must be accessible to all.

(vii) Ensure that all levels of government have the necessary resources and skills to discharge their responsibilities. No one should be denied access to water and sanitation because of their housing or land status. Informal human settlements should be upgraded through the provision of water and sanitation services and through assistance with the construction of their own water and sanitation facilities.

(viii) Ensure appropriate water and sanitation pricing policies, including through flexible payment schemes and cross-subsidies from high-income users to low-income users. Subsidize water and sanitation services for low-income households and poor areas that lack the means to secure access to such services. Subsidies should normally be used for connection to distribution networks or for the construction and maintenance of small-scale water supply and sanitation facilities, such as wells, boreholes and latrines.

(ix) Take steps to ensure that local government authorities, and other governance entities not part of central government manage water and sanitation services in their own areas, and under their authority so as to facilitate universal access to water and sanitation in sufficient quantity, quality and continuity, and at an affordable and equitable price. States should promote pro-active citizen involvement in defining water and sanitation policies at the local level in a democratic and inclusive manner. In this regard states parties should increase financing for local water and sanitation infrastructure to address the needs of poor persons and peoples lacking access to water and sanitation; and contribute to developing local government capacity to improve effective water supply and sanitation services.

(x) Ensure that the private ownership of water and sanitation services, or any privatization of water and sanitation services, does not take place in the absence of a clear and efficient regulatory framework that ensures sustainable access to safe, sufficient, physically accessible and affordable water and sanitation. States are obligated to regulate and monitor private water and sanitation providers to ensure that they do not violate the right to access to water and sanitation.

(xi) Ensure that procedures for the disconnection of water and sanitation services are reasonable and only occur after timely and full disclosure of information and include legal recourse and remedies as well as legal assistance.

(xii) Procedures for the disconnection of water must take into account the individual's ability to pay and therefore disconnections for non- payment should not result in a person being denied access to a minimum amount of safe drinking water where that person proves that he or she is unable to pay for these basic services. The quantity of safe drinking water a person can access may be reduced, but full disconnection may only be permissible if there is access to an alternative source which can provide a minimum amount of safe drinking water needed to prevent disease.

(xiii) Progressively extend safe sanitation services, particularly to rural and deprived urban areas, taking into account the needs of women and children.

(xiv) Ensure that disadvantaged and marginalized farmers, including women farmers, have equitable access to water and water management systems, including sustainable rain harvesting and irrigation technology.

(xv) Ensure that there is adequate access to water for subsistence farming and for securing the livelihoods of peoples, including indigenous communities and populations.

(xvi) Take steps on a non-discriminatory basis to prevent threats to health from unsafe and toxic water conditions.

(xvii) Ensure that natural water resources are protected from contamination by harmful substances and pathogenic microbes. This includes strict controls of the use and pollution of water resources for industrial purposes, and especially of extractive industries in rural areas.

(xviii) Monitor and combat situations where aquatic eco-systems serve as a habitat for vectors of diseases wherever they pose a risk to human living environments.

(xix) Ensure access to the minimum essential amount of water that is sufficient and safe for personal and domestic uses to prevent disease.

(xx) Ensure that imprisoned and detained persons have access to sufficient, safe and acceptable water and sanitation. In addition to sufficient water prisoners and detainees should be allowed to bath every day and should be provided with soap, sheets, and detergents for clothes.[154]

The second set of guidelines complement the first, being focused on what is expected of states parties in meeting their reporting obligations under the Charter, including in respect of their regulation and control of private sector water services:

Right to Water and Sanitation

(i) Indicate what legislative and other measures have been taken to ensure access to the minimum essential amount of water, which is sufficient and safe for personal and domestic use, including for preventing disease, together with access to adequate sanitation.

[154] African Commission on Human and Peoples' Rights (48th Session), The Principles and Guidelines on the Implementation of the Economic, Social and Cultural Rights in the African Charter on Human and Peoples' Rights (The Nairobi Guidelines), Nairobi, adopted 26 May 2010.

(ii) Indicate what legislative and other measures have been taken to ensure safe physical access to water facilities or services that provide sufficient, safe and regular water; that have an adequate number of water outlets to avoid prohibitive waiting times; and that are at a reasonable distance from the household, educational institution, workplace or health institution.

(iii) Indicate what legislative and other measures have been taken to ensure that the obligations set out in paras 92 (iv) to (xv) have been complied with, particularly with reference to the obligations to ensure:

(a) That the private ownership of water and sanitation services, or their privatisation, complies with a clear and efficient regulatory framework that ensures sustainable access to safe, sufficient, physically accessible and affordable water and sanitation.

(b) That procedures for the disconnection of water and sanitation services are reasonable and only occur after timely and full disclosure of information and include legal recourse and remedies as well as legal assistance.

(c) That natural water resources are protected from contamination by harmful substances and pathogens. This includes strict controls of the use and pollution of water resources for industrial purposes, and especially of extractive industries in rural areas.[155]

In the absence of an express right to water under the American Convention on Human Rights, the adjudicatory organs of the Convention have sought to instantiate it within the terms of the rights to life (Article 4) and to humane treatment (Article 5).[156] In the *Yakye Axa* case, as discussed and extracted above, the implication of the right to water was constructed alongside that of the right to food in respect of its adequate access for this particular Paraguayan indigenous community.[157] Further, in its Advisory Opinion on the *Legal Status of the Rights of the Child*,[158] the Inter-American Court of Human Rights determined that, for children, Article 4 comprises the 'obligation to provide measures required for life to develop under decent conditions',[159] including, necessarily, the basic means of food and water by which life is sustained. In another case involving children—the *Panchito López Case*[160]—the Court extended this notion by holding that the right to a 'dignified' life for children (and, by implication, adults too) required that even

[155] African Commission on Human and Peoples' Rights (50th Ordinary Session), State Party Reporting Guidelines for Economic, Social and Cultural Rights in the African Charter on Human And Peoples' Rights (Tunis Reporting Guidelines), Banjul, 24 October–7 November 2011.

[156] American Convention on Human Rights (adopted 22 November 1969, 1144 UNTS 143, entered into force 18 July 1978).

[157] *Case of the Indigenous Community Yakye Axa v Paraguay*, 17 June 2005, IACHR (Ser. C) No. 125, [167]–[168].

[158] *Juridical Condition and Human Rights of the Child*, Advisory Opinion, 28 August 2002, OC-17/02.

[159] *Juridical Condition and Human Rights of the Child*, Advisory Opinion, 28 August 2002, OC-17/02, [80].

[160] *Case of Children's Rehabilitation v Paraguay* ('*Panchito López* case'), 2 September 2004, IACHR (Ser. C) No. 63.

in a juvenile detention centre, conditions that are 'grossly inadequate', including deprivation of detainees' access to adequate water and sanitation, amounted to breaches both of the right to life and the right to humane treatment under the Convention.[161]

As under the European Convention on Human Rights, the right to water has also been upheld in the Inter-American system indirectly, by way of application of a state's obligation to provide a remedy for human rights breaches under Article 25(2) of the Convention. In the case of Mapuche Paynemil and Kaxipayiñ Communities, the Inter-American Commission on Human Rights found Argentina to be in breach of Article 25(2) by not complying with national court orders (and an agreement reached under the auspices of the Commission itself) to supply safe and permanent drinking water to the Paynemil Mapuche community whose water sources had been contaminated with heavy metals, including lead and mercury.[162]

Clothing and Housing

CLOTHING

While the rights to food and water concern the essential means of human sustenance, those of housing and clothing are concerned with basic protections against nature's elements. Their apparently equal place within the context of securing an adequate standard of living under Article 11 is somewhat belied by the practice towards the right to clothing. During the Covenant's formative debates, clothing was considered an imperative, with, for example, Mr Cheng Paonan, the Chinese delegate, maintaining that the right is critical for people living in least developed states, especially ones whose economies were predominantly agrarian.[163] However, since then, the right to clothing has largely failed to maintain an independent status, being either overlooked or effectively subsumed within the right to shelter generally and the right to housing specifically. The need for people to be adequately clothed has not diminished, rather the instance of its lack is no longer considered widespread or critical, at least in relation to the other depravations that are typically endured by the poor and destitute. Notably, while there now exist separate UN agencies for the rights to food, water and housing, there is none for the right to clothing.

[161] *Panchito López* case, [170]. The Inter-American Commission on Human Rights has also underscored the obligation of states to respect the right to water in another detention case: *Victor Rosario Congo v Ecuador* (Case 11.427), Report on the Merit No. 63/99, 13 April 1999. This case involved the death of an adult detainee in Ecuador who, while on remand, was assaulted and then left alone in a cell for 'approximately forty days... without food or water' [73]. As a result, the Commission found that Ecuador had breached the right to life under Article 4 of the Convention [84].

[162] *Mapuche Paynemil and Kaxipayiñ Communities*, Case No. 12.010 (5 February 2013) (Inter-American Commission on Human Rights).

[163] UN Commission on Human Rights, E/CN.4/SR.294 (1952), (Cheng Paonan (China)), 5.

In terms of the Committee itself, the situation has been summed up by Mathew Craven in his remark that 'the impression given is that clothing is not a matter in which the State may exercise a great deal of control, nor one that the Committee feels is of great importance'.[164] This is reflected in our survey of the Committee's Concluding Observations on states' reports, in which the few references made to clothing were mostly in the relatively early days of the Committee, and predominantly directed at information gathering—asking states to provide data on and evidence of their implementation of the right. It was as if the Committee was itself trying to work out what the content and meaning of the right might be in practice.[165]

In the last twenty years or so, the right was referred to hardly at all by the Committee other than simply being listed alongside the other two rights (to food and housing) specified in Article 11. The instances in which the Committee has referred to the right in terms of it being more or less a freestanding right have been few and far between. These include, for example, a brief reference in the Committee's 1998 Concluding Observations regarding Sri Lanka to the plight of some 800,000 displaced persons due to the conflict with the Tamil Tigers, which had resulted in many of them 'living in temporary shelters for the past 15 years…lack[ing] basic sanitation, education, food, clothing and health care'.[166] In General Comment No. 5 on Persons with Disabilities, the Committee notes (without further elaboration) that 'the right to adequate clothing…assumes a special significance in the context of persons with disabilities who have particular clothing needs, so as to enable them to function fully and effectively in society'.[167] And, finally, in General Comment No. 19 on the right to social security,[168] the Committee notes in respect of family and support benefits that these would be expected to 'ordinarily cover food, clothing, housing, water and sanitation, or other rights as appropriate'.[169]

Other international human rights instruments also make tangential references to the right to clothing, including: the Convention on the Rights of the Child (1989), Article 27(3) of which instructs states to assist parents and guardians in providing children with 'nutrition, clothing and housing' when the need arises;[170]

[164] Craven, *The ICESCR*, 394.

[165] Nonetheless, some have criticized the neglect of the right as 'baffling given its obvious importance for human well-being': see Stephen James, 'A Forgotten Right? The Right to Clothing in International Law' (2008), unpublished conference paper from the Australian and New Zealand Society of International Law (ANZSIL) Conference: 'Security, Scarcity, Struggle: The Dilemmas of International Law', Canberra, 26–8 June 2008, 1, available at <http://anzsil.anu.edu.au/Conferences/2008/Stephen%20James.pdf>.

[166] CESCR, Concluding Observations: Sri Lanka, E/C.12/1/Add.24 (16 June 1998), [7].

[167] CESCR, General Comment No. 5, Persons with disabilities, E/1995/22 (25 November 1994), Annex IV [33].

[168] CESCR, General Comment No. 19, The right to social security (Article 19), E/C.12/GC/19 (4 February 2008) ('General Comment No. 19').

[169] CESCR, General Comment No. 19, [18].

[170] Convention on the Rights of the Child (adopted 20 November 1989, 1577 UNTS 3, entered into force 2 September 1990), Article 27(3).

the Convention on Rights of Persons with Disabilities (2006), where Article 28 (echoing ICESCR, Article 11) proclaims that 'States Parties recognize the right of persons with disabilities to an adequate standard of living for themselves and their families, including adequate food, clothing and housing';[171] and under the United Nations' Standard Minimum Rules for the Treatment of Prisoners,[172] states are required to ensure that detainees' clothing is clean and hygienic and 'adequate to keep him [or her] in good health… [and] that such clothing shall in no manner be degrading or humiliating' (paragraph 17).[173] Neither the American Convention on Human Rights[174] nor the African Charter on Human and Peoples' Rights makes explicit reference to the right to clothing,[175] although, in respect of the former, the Inter-American Court of Human Rights has implied the right in the 'special measures' provision regarding the rights of the child contained in Article 19 of the Convention.

Finally, the formulations in which the right is found in domestic legal systems is much less determinate than with other rights. Where there exists a constitutional guarantee, then, typically, the right is implied in other, expressly protected rights, such as the right to life (in India (Article 21) and Ireland (Article 40)), the right to work (in Colombia (Article 25)) or a combination of a number of 'democratic' rights, as in Switzerland.[176] Additional protection is also sometimes afforded by the (non-binding) principles of state policy that exist in certain constitutions such as in Bangladesh (Article 15) and Pakistan (Article 38), as well as India (implied in Article 39).

RIGHT TO HOUSING

In contrast to the diminished importance of the right to clothing, the right to housing has risen markedly in prominence. The principal reason for this lies in the nature of the right itself. Housing—a place of shelter and to live in—is fundamental to many aspects of our existence, also being keenly associated with a number of other human rights,[177] including, especially, its 'companion' rights to food and water within Article 11. Housing, as Jessie Hohmann observes, connotes

[171] UN Convention on Rights of Persons with Disabilities (adopted 13 December 2006, 2515 UNTS 3, entered into force 3 May 2008), Article 28.

[172] UN, Standard Minimum Rules for the Treatment of Prisoners, amended E/5988 (13 May 1977).

[173] UN, Standard Minimum Rules for the Treatment of Prisoners, [18], [26] and [17] respectively.

[174] American Convention on Human Rights (adopted 22 November 1969, 1144 UNTS 143, entered into force 18 July 1978).

[175] African Charter on Human and Peoples' Rights (adopted 27 June 1981, 1520 UNTS 217, entered into force 21 October 1986).

[176] See reasoning in *V. v Einwohnergemeinde X und Regierungsrat des Kantons Bern* (BGE/ATF 121 1367) (Swiss Federal Court), [2(b)].

[177] This includes civil and political, as well as economic, social and cultural, rights. Mathew Craven lists the following rights as ones the Committee has 'stressed' as being important to the fulfilment of the right to housing: 'freedom of expression, freedom of association, freedom to take part in public decision-making, freedom to choose one's residence, and freedom from arbitrary and unlawful interference with one's privacy, family, home or correspondence' (Craven, *The ICESCR*, 330).

the essential elements of space, privacy and identity in the social existence of individual human beings. That is, a house, or even just shelter, is somewhere and that space, if adequate, should provide at least a base level of privacy, and through one's association with it, also constitute a primary component in the construction of an individual's social identity.[178] Unsurprisingly, therefore, the right to housing is reiterated in other international human rights instruments, including (as noted in the extract immediately following) the CERD, the CEDAW and the Convention on the Rights of the Child, as well as, since 2000, the International Convention on the Protection of the Rights of All Migrant Workers and Members of Their Families (Article 43(1)(d)) and the Convention on the Rights of Persons with Disabilities (Articles 9 and 28).[179]

The right has indeed attracted considerable attention from the Committee, academics, commentators and specialist housing NGOs, and has done so for three decades or more.[180] It has been the subject of two General Comments, and a Special Rapporteur on adequate housing as a component of the right to an adequate standard of living was established in 2000 by the then UN Commission on Human Rights. The original mandate of the Special Rapporteur, which has been extended repeatedly, is suitably broad in scope:

Commission on Human Rights Resolution 2000/9 (17 April 2000); extracts from para. 7

…

(c) To appoint, for a period of three years, a special rapporteur whose mandate will focus on adequate housing as a component of the right to an adequate standard of living, as reflected in article 25, paragraph 1, of the Universal Declaration of Human Rights, article 11, paragraph 1, of the International Covenant on Economic, Social and Cultural Rights, and article 27, paragraph 3, of the Convention on the Rights of the Child, and on the right to non-discrimination as reflected in article 14, paragraph 2(h) of the Convention on the Elimination of All Forms of Discrimination against Women, and article 5(e) of the International Convention on the Elimination of All Forms of Racial Discrimination;

(d) To request the Special Rapporteur, in the fulfilment of her/his mandate:

(i) To report on the status, throughout the world, of the realization of the rights that are relevant to the mandate, in accordance with the provisions of the relevant instrument, and on developments relating to these rights, including on laws, policies and good practices most beneficial to their enjoyment and difficulties and obstacles encountered

[178] Jessie Hohmann, *The Right to Housing: Laws, Concepts, Possibilities* (Hart, Oxford, 2013), Chapters 6, 7 and 8, which deal with the conceptual perspectives of housing as privacy, identity and space, respectively. As Hohmann puts it, in respect of 'identity', 'the way identity is recognized, socially and legally, is often mediated through relationships with the house and home, both as a physical thing and as an ideological construct' (167).

[179] For a full list of all international human rights instruments that protect the right to housing, including the regional regimes, see UN Office of the High Commissioner for Human Rights and UN Habitat, 'The Right to Adequate Housing', Fact Sheet No. 21/Rev.1, 11–13.

[180] Even by the early 1990s Matthew Craven could state confidently that 'the Committee has dedicated more attention to the right to housing than any other right': Craven, *The ICESCR*, 329.

domestically and internationally, taking into account information received from Governments, organizations and bodies of the United Nations system, other relevant international organizations and non-governmental organizations;

(ii) To promote, as appropriate, cooperation among and assistance to Governments in their efforts to secure these rights;

(iii) To apply a gender perspective in her/his work;

(iv) To develop a regular dialogue and discuss possible areas of collaboration with Governments, relevant United Nations bodies, specialized agencies, international organizations in the field of housing rights, inter alia, the United Nations Centre for Human Settlements (Habitat), non-governmental organizations and international financial institutions, and to make recommendations on the realization of the rights relevant to the mandate;

(v) To identify possible types and sources of financing for relevant advisory services and technical cooperation;

(vi) To facilitate, where appropriate, the inclusion of issues relating to the mandate in relevant United Nations missions, field presences and national offices;

(vii) To submit to the Commission an annual report covering the activities relating to the mandate…

The two General Comments—one, a basal description of the right to housing,[181] the other, an examination of the specific matter of forced evictions[182]—have been vital in defining the scope and content of the right.

General Comment No. 4 in 1991 sets the tone of the right's significance by stating that the right to housing is 'of central importance for the enjoyment of all economic, social and cultural rights' (paragraph 1), and even by 1991, the Committee was able to say (in paragraph 2) that it has already 'accumulate[d] a large amount of information pertaining to this right' drawn from numerous reports of UN bodies and other international organizations as well as from its own assessments of states' periodic reports. No matter this amount of data, and the frequent reaffirmations of importance and necessity of full respect for the right, the Committee laments that 'there remains a disturbingly large gap between the standards set in Article 11(1) of the Covenant and the situation prevailing in many parts of the world' (paragraph 4). In noting that approximately 100 million people worldwide are homeless and that over 1 billion are inadequately housed, the Committee points out that by no means all of these are in developing nations, as 'significant problems of homelessness and inadequate housing also exist in some of the most economically developed societies' (paragraph 4).

What is perhaps even more disturbing is that today, more than twenty years later and despite apparently enormous efforts to address the problem, the situation

[181] CESCR, General Comment No. 4, The right to adequate housing (Article 11(1)), E/1992/23 (25 November–13 December 1992) ('General Comment No. 4'), Annex III.

[182] CESCR, General Comment No. 7, The right to adequate housing (Article 11.1 of the Covenant): forced evictions, E/1998/22 (14 May 1997) ('General Comment No. 7'), Annex IV.

is estimated to have become worse, not better. Although these figures are very hard to calculate with any degree of accuracy, the corresponding figures for today are that homelessness remains at around 100 million, but that the number of inadequately housed has now ballooned to some 1.6 billion.[183]

In this sobering light, the Committee's efforts in General Comment No. 4 to articulate the unconditional nature of the right and the 'seven factors' that constitute housing adequacy are especially poigniant.

6. The right to adequate housing applies to everyone. While the reference to 'himself and his family' reflects assumptions as to gender roles and economic activity patterns commonly accepted in 1966 when the Covenant was adopted, the phrase cannot be read today as implying any limitations upon the applicability of the right to individuals or to female-headed households or other such groups. Thus, the concept of 'family' must be understood in a wide sense. Further, individuals, as well as families, are entitled to adequate housing regardless of age, economic status, group or other affiliation or status and other such factors. In particular, enjoyment of this right must, in accordance with article 2 (2) of the Covenant, not be subject to any form of discrimination.

7. In the Committee's view, the right to housing should not be interpreted in a narrow or restrictive sense which equates it with, for example, the shelter provided by merely having a roof over one's head or views shelter exclusively as a commodity. Rather it should be seen as the right to live somewhere in security, peace and dignity. This is appropriate for at least two reasons. In the first place, the right to housing is integrally linked to other human rights and to the fundamental principles upon which the Covenant is premised. This 'the inherent dignity of the human person' from which the rights in the Covenant are said to derive requires that the term 'housing' be interpreted so as to take account of a variety of other considerations, most importantly that the right to housing should be ensured to all persons irrespective of income or access to economic resources. Secondly, the reference in article 11(1) must be read as referring not just to housing but to adequate housing. As both the Commission on Human Settlements and the Global Strategy for Shelter to the Year 2000 have stated: 'Adequate shelter means... adequate privacy, adequate space, adequate security, adequate lighting and ventilation, adequate basic infrastructure and adequate location with regard to work and basic facilities—all at a reasonable cost'.

8. Thus the concept of adequacy is particularly significant in relation to the right to housing since it serves to underline a number of factors which must be taken into account in determining whether particular forms of shelter can be considered to constitute 'adequate housing' for the purposes of the Covenant. While adequacy is determined in part by social, economic, cultural, climatic, ecological and other factors, the Committee believes that it is nevertheless possible to identify certain aspects of the right that must be taken into account for this purpose in any particular context. They include the following:

(a) Legal security of tenure. Tenure takes a variety of forms, including rental (public and private) accommodation, cooperative housing, lease, owner-occupation, emergency housing and informal settlements, including occupation of land or property. Notwithstanding the type of tenure, all persons should possess a degree of security of tenure which guarantees legal protection against forced eviction, harassment and other

[183] Habitat for Humanity International, FY Annual Report 2012, <http://www.habitat.org/sites/default/files/annual-report-2012.pdf>.

threats. States parties should consequently take immediate measures aimed at conferring legal security of tenure upon those persons and households currently lacking such protection, in genuine consultation with affected persons and groups;

(b) Availability of services, materials, facilities and infrastructure. An adequate house must contain certain facilities essential for health, security, comfort and nutrition. All beneficiaries of the right to adequate housing should have sustainable access to natural and common resources, safe drinking water, energy for cooking, heating and lighting, sanitation and washing facilities, means of food storage, refuse disposal, site drainage and emergency services;

(c) Affordability. Personal or household financial costs associated with housing should be at such a level that the attainment and satisfaction of other basic needs are not threatened or compromised. Steps should be taken by States parties to ensure that the percentage of housing-related costs is, in general, commensurate with income levels. States parties should establish housing subsidies for those unable to obtain affordable housing, as well as forms and levels of housing finance which adequately reflect housing needs. In accordance with the principle of affordability, tenants should be protected by appropriate means against unreasonable rent levels or rent increases. In societies where natural materials constitute the chief sources of building materials for housing, steps should be taken by States parties to ensure the availability of such materials;

(d) Habitability. Adequate housing must be habitable, in terms of providing the inhabitants with adequate space and protecting them from cold, damp, heat, rain, wind or other threats to health, structural hazards, and disease vectors. The physical safety of occupants must be guaranteed as well. The Committee encourages States parties to comprehensively apply the Health Principles of Housing prepared by WHO which view housing as the environmental factor most frequently associated with conditions for disease in epidemiological analyses; i.e. inadequate and deficient housing and living conditions are invariably associated with higher mortality and morbidity rates;

(e) Accessibility. Adequate housing must be accessible to those entitled to it. Disadvantaged groups must be accorded full and sustainable access to adequate housing resources. Thus, such disadvantaged groups as the elderly, children, the physically disabled, the terminally ill, HIV-positive individuals, persons with persistent medical problems, the mentally ill, victims of natural disasters, people living in disaster-prone areas and other groups should be ensured some degree of priority consideration in the housing sphere. Both housing law and policy should take fully into account the special housing needs of these groups. Within many States parties increasing access to land by landless or impoverished segments of the society should constitute a central policy goal. Discernible governmental obligations need to be developed aiming to substantiate the right of all to a secure place to live in peace and dignity, including access to land as an entitlement;

(f) Location. Adequate housing must be in a location which allows access to employment options, health-care services, schools, child-care centres and other social facilities. This is true both in large cities and in rural areas where the temporal and financial costs of getting to and from the place of work can place excessive demands upon the budgets of poor households. Similarly, housing should not be built on polluted sites nor in immediate proximity to pollution sources that threaten the right to health of the inhabitants;

(g) Cultural adequacy. The way housing is constructed, the building materials used and the policies supporting these must appropriately enable the expression of cultural identity and diversity of housing. Activities geared towards development or modernization in the housing sphere should ensure that the cultural dimensions of housing are not sacrificed, and that, inter alia, modern technological facilities, as appropriate are also ensured.[184]

These seven factors set, and remain, the benchmark for realization of the right to housing. Although they largely speak for themselves, they reflect a number of critical aspects of the right. First, in stressing the legal security of tenure, the Committee underscores the importance of securing one's place of abode—whether by legal ownership, rental, leasehold or cooperative arrangement—and the need for redress if eviction is threatened or executed. The significance of this factor, together with its all too frequent violation, was key to the Committee's subsequent work on, and publication of, General Comment No. 7 on forced evictions (see below). Secondly, it is clear that the Committee does not interpret the right to mean that the state is to take the central role in the *provision* of housing. Rather, it is envisaged that state is to construct and implement the policy framework within which the housing provided by the private sector (as supplemented by the state's, mainly, welfare or 'safety net' housing programmes) is made 'affordable' and 'accessible'. Thirdly, the fulfilment of the right to housing requires more than just shelter. As a number of the seven enumerated factors indicate, adequate housing must comprise the provision of essential facilities (such as power, water and sanitation), must be habitable (offering protection against the elements), must be located within reasonable reach of work opportunities and essential social services (for example, regarding health and education), and must be culturally appropriate (in terms of construction and location).

Regarding states' obligations to implement and enforce the right, General Comment No. 4 stresses that 'there are certain steps that must be taken immediately', including, and especially, 'abstention by the Government from certain practices and a commitment to facilitating "self-help" by affected groups' (paragraph 10). Further, as the following extracts from the General Comment relate, states must develop strategies and policies that prioritize the housing needs of the most vulnerable in society, and they must adequately fund, monitor and enforce the implementation of their policies.

11. States parties must give due priority to those social groups living in unfavourable conditions by giving them particular consideration. Policies and legislation should correspondingly not be designed to benefit already advantaged social groups at the expense of others. The Committee is aware that external factors can affect the right to a continuous improvement of living conditions, and that in many States parties overall living conditions declined during the 1980s. However, as noted by the Committee in its General Comment 2 (1990) (E/1990/23, annex III), despite externally caused problems, the obligations under the Covenant continue to apply and are perhaps even more pertinent during times of economic

[184] CESCR, General Comment No. 4, Annex III, [6]–[8].

contraction. It would thus appear to the Committee that a general decline in living and housing conditions, directly attributable to policy and legislative decisions by States parties, and in the absence of accompanying compensatory measures, would be inconsistent with the obligations under the Covenant.

12. While the most appropriate means of achieving the full realization of the right to adequate housing will inevitably vary significantly from one State party to another, the Covenant clearly requires that each State party take whatever steps are necessary for that purpose. This will almost invariably require the adoption of a national housing strategy which, as stated in paragraph 32 of the Global Strategy for Shelter, 'defines the objectives for the development of shelter conditions, identifies the resources available to meet these goals and the most cost-effective way of using them and sets out the responsibilities and time-frame for the implementation of the necessary measures'. Both for reasons of relevance and effectiveness, as well as in order to ensure respect for other human rights, such a strategy should reflect extensive genuine consultation with, and participation by, all of those affected, including the homeless, the inadequately housed and their representatives. Furthermore, steps should be taken to ensure coordination between ministries and regional and local authorities in order to reconcile related policies (economics, agriculture, environment, energy, etc.) with the obligations under article 11 of the Covenant.

13. Effective monitoring of the situation with respect to housing is another obligation of immediate effect. For a State party to satisfy its obligations under article 11(1) it must demonstrate, inter alia, that it has taken whatever steps are necessary, either alone or on the basis of international cooperation, to ascertain the full extent of homelessness and inadequate housing within its jurisdiction. In this regard, the revised general guidelines regarding the form and contents of reports adopted by the Committee (E/C.12/1991/1) emphasize the need to 'provide detailed information about those groups within... society that are vulnerable and disadvantaged with regard to housing'. They include, in particular, homeless persons and families, those inadequately housed and without ready access to basic amenities, those living in 'illegal' settlements, those subject to forced evictions and low-income groups.

14. Measures designed to satisfy a State party's obligations in respect of the right to adequate housing may reflect whatever mix of public and private sector measures considered appropriate. While in some States public financing of housing might most usefully be spent on direct construction of new housing, in most cases, experience has shown the inability of Governments to fully satisfy housing deficits with publicly built housing. The promotion by States parties of 'enabling strategies', combined with a full commitment to obligations under the right to adequate housing, should thus be encouraged. In essence, the obligation is to demonstrate that, in aggregate, the measures being taken are sufficient to realize the right for every individual in the shortest possible time in accordance with the maximum of available resources.

15. Many of the measures that will be required will involve resource allocations and policy initiatives of a general kind. Nevertheless, the role of formal legislative and administrative measures should not be underestimated in this context. The Global Strategy for Shelter (paras. 66–67) has drawn attention to the types of measures that might be taken in this regard and to their importance.

16. In some States, the right to adequate housing is constitutionally entrenched. In such cases the Committee is particularly interested in learning of the legal and practical

significance of such an approach. Details of specific cases and of other ways in which entrenchment has proved helpful should thus be provided.

17. The Committee views many component elements of the right to adequate housing as being at least consistent with the provision of domestic legal remedies. Depending on the legal system, such areas might include, but are not limited to: (a) legal appeals aimed at preventing planned evictions or demolitions through the issuance of court-ordered injunctions; (b) legal procedures seeking compensation following an illegal eviction; (c) complaints against illegal actions carried out or supported by landlords (whether public or private) in relation to rent levels, dwelling maintenance, and racial or other forms of discrimination; (d) allegations of any form of discrimination in the allocation and availability of access to housing; and (e) complaints against landlords concerning unhealthy or inadequate housing conditions. In some legal systems it would also be appropriate to explore the possibility of facilitating class action suits in situations involving significantly increased levels of homelessness.[185]

[NB. the reference in paragraph 15 above to the 'Global Strategy for Shelter' is to a report of the UN Commission on Human Settlements in 1988, which urged states (in paragraphs 66 and 67) to enact appropriate legislation and regulations 'which enables them to produce shelter efficiently and effectively'. The Commission produced a number of subsequent reports, the last of which was in 1997.]

Forced evictions

Reflecting both the importance placed on security of tenure by General Comment No. 4 (as the first of the seven factors, and also in paragraph 18 which states that forced eviction 'can only be justified in the most exceptional circumstances, and in accordance with the relevant principles of international law'), and the continuing and often alarming instances of mass, forced evictions, the Committee published General Comment No. 7 in 1997. Indeed, the Committee observes (in paragraph 4) that:

4. The practice of forced evictions is widespread and affects persons in both developed and developing countries. Owing to the interrelationship and interdependency which exist among all human rights, forced evictions frequently violate other human rights. Thus, while manifestly breaching the rights enshrined in the Covenant, the practice of forced evictions may also result in violations of civil and political rights, such as the right to life, the right to security of the person, the right to non-interference with privacy, family and home and the right to the peaceful enjoyment of possessions.[186]

The Committee notes that 'women, children, youths, older persons, indigenous people, ethnic and other minorities, and other vulnerable individuals and groups all suffer disproportionately from the practice of forced eviction',[187] and that two

[185] CESCR, General Comment No. 4, Annex III, [11]–[17].
[186] CESCR, General Comment No. 7, Annex IV, [4].
[187] CESCR, General Comment No. 7, Annex IV, [10].

especially common causes or reasons for forced evictions are armed conflict (paragraph 6) and (somewhat ironically) economic development (paragraph 7): [188]

6. Many instances of forced eviction are associated with violence, such as evictions resulting from international armed conflicts, internal strife and communal or ethnic violence.[189]

7. Other instances of forced eviction occur in the name of development. Evictions may be carried out in connection with conflict over land rights, development and infrastructure projects, such as the construction of dams or other large-scale energy projects, with land acquisition measures associated with urban renewal, housing renovation, city beautification programmes, the clearing of land for agricultural purposes, unbridled speculation in land, or the holding of major sporting events like the Olympic Games.

In paragraph 1 of General Comment No. 7, the Committee explains its overall purpose: namely, that 'having considered a significant number of reports of forced evictions in recent years, including instances in which it has determined that the obligations of States parties were being violated, the Committee is now in a position to seek to provide further clarification as to the implications of such practices in terms of the obligations contained in the Covenant'. Such clarification the Committee provides by way of first a reiteration of various pronouncements by international organizations on the matter and the particular difficulties encountered in trying to define the term, and then, by the interesting means of explaining the circumstances and conditions under which forced evictions might be considered permissible.

The Committee presents the base prohibition of forced evictions as follows:

9. . . . it is clear that legislation against forced evictions is an essential basis upon which to build a system of effective protection. Such legislation should include measures which (a) provide the greatest possible security of tenure to occupiers of houses and land, (b) conform to the Covenant and (c) are designed to control strictly the circumstances under which evictions may be carried out. The legislation must also apply to all agents acting under the authority of the State or who are accountable to it. Moreover, in view of the increasing trend in some States towards the Government greatly reducing its responsibilities in the housing sector, States parties must ensure that legislative and other measures are adequate to prevent and, if appropriate, punish forced evictions carried out, without appropriate safeguards, by private persons or bodies . . .[190]

In its resolve to make clear to states the seriousness of the matter and the necessity of its regulatory control, the Committee reviews the pronouncements of others on the issue and some of the conceptual and practical problems one encounters in addressing it:

2. The international community has long recognized that the issue of forced evictions is a serious one. In 1976, the United Nations Conference on Human Settlements noted that

[188] CESCR, General Comment No. 7, Annex IV, [6]–[7].

[189] In this regard, the Committee adds, in paragraph 12, that forced evictions and house demolition 'as a punitive measure' are inconsistent with the Covenant, as well as those parts of the Geneva Conventions of 1949 (and 1977 Protocols) that prohibit the displacement of the civilian population and the destruction of private property during times of armed conflict.

[190] CESCR, General Comment No. 7, Annex IV, [9].

special attention should be paid to 'undertaking major clearance operations should take place only when conservation and rehabilitation are not feasible and relocation measures are made'. In 1988, in the Global Strategy for Shelter to the Year 2000, adopted by the General Assembly in its resolution 43/181, the 'fundamental obligation [of Governments] to protect and improve houses and neighbourhoods, rather than damage or destroy them' was recognized. Agenda 21 stated that 'people should be protected by law against unfair eviction from their homes or land'. In the Habitat Agenda Governments committed themselves to 'protecting all people from, and providing legal protection and redress for, forced evictions that are contrary to the law, taking human rights into consideration; [and] when evictions are unavoidable, ensuring, as appropriate, that alternative suitable solutions are provided'. The Commission on Human Rights has also indicated that 'forced evictions are a gross violation of human rights'. However, although these statements are important, they leave open one of the most critical issues, namely that of determining the circumstances under which forced evictions are permissible and of spelling out the types of protection required to ensure respect for the relevant provisions of the Covenant.

3. The use of the term 'forced evictions' is, in some respects, problematic. This expression seeks to convey a sense of arbitrariness and of illegality. To many observers, however, the reference to 'forced evictions' is a tautology, while others have criticized the expression 'illegal evictions' on the ground that it assumes that the relevant law provides adequate protection of the right to housing and conforms with the Covenant, which is by no means always the case. Similarly, it has been suggested that the term 'unfair evictions' is even more subjective by virtue of its failure to refer to any legal framework at all. The international community, especially in the context of the Commission on Human Rights, has opted to refer to 'forced evictions', primarily since all suggested alternatives also suffer from many such defects. The term 'forced evictions' as used throughout this general comment is defined as the permanent or temporary removal against their will of individuals, families and/or communities from the homes and/or land which they occupy, without the provision of, and access to, appropriate forms of legal or other protection. The prohibition on forced evictions does not, however, apply to evictions carried out by force in accordance with the law and in conformity with the provisions of the International Covenants on Human Rights.[191]

As then, to situations where forced evictions may be justifiable, the Committee points to such examples as 'in the case of persistent non-payment of rent or of damage to rented property without any reasonable cause'.[192] The Committee expands on the necessary conditions that must accompany any such action as follows:

5. …Even in situations where it may be necessary to impose limitations on such a right, full compliance with article 4 of the Covenant is required so that any limitations imposed must be 'determined by law only insofar as this may be compatible with the nature of these [i.e. economic, social and cultural] rights and solely for the purpose of promoting the general welfare in a democratic society'.

…

[191] CESCR, General Comment No. 7, Annex IV, [2]–[3].
[192] CESCR, General Comment No. 7, Annex IV, [11].

8. ...The State itself must refrain from forced evictions and ensure that the law is enforced against its agents or third parties who carry out forced evictions (as defined in paragraph 3 above). Moreover, this approach is reinforced by article 17.1 of the International Covenant on Civil and Political Rights which complements the right not to be forcefully evicted without adequate protection. That provision recognizes, inter alia, the right to be protected against 'arbitrary or unlawful interference' with one's home. It is to be noted that the State's obligation to ensure respect for that right is not qualified by considerations relating to its available resources.

...

10. ...The non-discrimination provisions of articles 2.2 and 3 of the Covenant impose an additional obligation upon Governments to ensure that, where evictions do occur, appropriate measures are taken to ensure that no form of discrimination is involved.

...

13. States parties shall ensure, prior to carrying out any evictions, and particularly those involving large groups, that all feasible alternatives are explored in consultation with the affected persons, with a view to avoiding, or at least minimizing, the need to use force. Legal remedies or procedures should be provided to those who are affected by eviction orders. States parties shall also see to it that all the individuals concerned have a right to adequate compensation for any property, both personal and real, which is affected. In this respect, it is pertinent to recall article 2.3 of the International Covenant on Civil and Political Rights, which requires States parties to ensure 'an effective remedy' for persons whose rights have been violated and the obligation upon the 'competent authorities (to) enforce such remedies when granted'.

14. In cases where eviction is considered to be justified, it should be carried out in strict compliance with the relevant provisions of international human rights law and in accordance with general principles of reasonableness and proportionality. In this regard it is especially pertinent to recall General Comment 16 of the Human Rights Committee, relating to article 17 of the International Covenant on Civil and Political Rights, which states that interference with a person's home can only take place 'in cases envisaged by the law'. The Committee observed that the law 'should be in accordance with the provisions, aims and objectives of the Covenant and should be, in any event, reasonable in the particular circumstances'. The Committee also indicated that 'relevant legislation must specify in detail the precise circumstances in which such interferences may be permitted'.

15. Appropriate procedural protection and due process are essential aspects of all human rights but are especially pertinent in relation to a matter such as forced evictions which directly invokes a large number of the rights recognized in both the International Covenants on Human Rights. The Committee considers that the procedural protections which should be applied in relation to forced evictions include: (a) an opportunity for genuine consultation with those affected; (b) adequate and reasonable notice for all affected persons prior to the scheduled date of eviction; (c) information on the proposed evictions, and, where applicable, on the alternative purpose for which the land or housing is to be used, to be made available in reasonable time to all those affected; (d) especially where groups of people are involved, government officials or their representatives to be present during an eviction; (e) all persons carrying out the eviction to be properly identified; (f) evictions not to take place in particularly bad weather or at night unless

the affected persons consent otherwise; (g) provision of legal remedies; and (h) provision, where possible, of legal aid to persons who are in need of it to seek redress from the courts.

16. Evictions should not result in individuals being rendered homeless or vulnerable to the violation of other human rights. Where those affected are unable to provide for themselves, the State party must take all appropriate measures, to the maximum of its available resources, to ensure that adequate alternative housing, resettlement or access to productive land, as the case may be, is available.[193]

So, in sum, while the Committee is adamant that states should prohibit forced evictions as far as is possible, where they do occur the Committee stresses the necessity of the fundamental legal safeguards of: non-arbitrariness, non-discrimination, due process and procedural fairness, including consultation and participation in decision-making, access to remedies, compensation and the provision of adequate rehousing. Such safeguards and conditions have been endorsed and elaborated in the Basic Principles and Guidelines on Development-Based Evictions and Displacement developed by the Special Rapporteur on adequate housing.[194]

The Committee also reserved special attention in the General Comment (paragraphs 17 and 18) for the mass (and often forced) evictions that were, and to a lesser extent still are, occasioned by large-scale development projects backed by international aid agencies like the World Bank. Such projects, typically concern dam building and other major power and utility projects. These were especially controversial during their heyday in the 1970s to the 1990s when not uncommonly tens of thousands of people were removed from their lands and homes.[195] Indigenous and remote communities, already among the most marginalized in many states, were often the most severely affected. 'In this regard', the Committee notes, 'its General Comment No. 2 (1990)...states, *inter alia*, that "international agencies should scrupulously avoid involvement in projects which, for example...promote or reinforce discrimination against individuals or groups contrary to the provisions of the Covenant, or involve large-scale evictions or displacement of persons without the provision of all appropriate protection and compensation. Every effort should be made, at each phase of a development project, to ensure that the rights contained in the Covenant are duly taken into account"'.[196]

[193] CESCR, General Comment No. 7, Annex IV, [5], [8], [10], [13] and [16].

[194] Human Rights Council, Report of the Special Rapporteur on adequate housing as a component of the right to an adequate standard of living, Miloon Kothari, A/HRC/4/18 (11 June 2007), Annex 1, see especially [22], [32], [37], [38], [52], and [55].

[195] As noted by the Special Rapporteur on adequate housing, some 20 per cent of the World Bank's entire portfolio of operations in the early 2000s involved projects 'affecting 2.6 million people through physical or economic displacement': Commission on Human Rights, Report of the Special Rapporteur on adequate housing as a component of the right to an adequate standard of living, Miloon Kothari, E/CN.4/2004/48 (8 March 2004), [30]. Further, see the civil-society-sponsored *Manibeli Declaration* (1994) calling for a moratorium on World Bank funding of large dams, due to—among many reasons—the hundreds of thousands of forcibly displaced persons caused by dam-building; <http://www.internationalrivers.org/es/resources/manibeli-declaration-4334>.

[196] CESCR, General Comment No. 7, Annex IV, [17].

Implementation of the right to housing

From early in its history, the position of the Special Rapporteur on adequate housing has focused on practical means by which the right can be realized. Resolution 2001/28 of the Commission on Human Rights requested that the Special Rapporteur 'give particular emphasis to practical solutions with regard to the implementation of the rights relevant to the mandate, on the basis of pertinent information, notably on best practices, including on domestic legal enforcement of these rights, from Governments, relevant United Nations agencies and non-governmental organizations'.[197] And in order to draw upon such 'best practices', the Commission further called upon states 'to give full effect to housing rights, including through domestic development policies at the appropriate level of government and with international assistance and cooperation, giving particular attention to the individuals, most often women and children, and communities living in extreme poverty, and to security of tenure'.[198]

In fact, there is significant coverage of the right in domestic legal regimes. More than fifty states make provisions for the right or associated governmental obligations in their constitutions,[199] while others provide protection for housing rights through ordinary legislation and policy means.

But no matter these apparently extensive legal protections, significant practical problems remain in terms of their implementation. Both incumbents of the Special Rapporteur post (Miloon Kothari (2000 to 2008) and Raquel Rolnik from 2008) have highlighted a number of recurring challenges that seriously hamper realization of the right to adequate housing.[200] We here concentrate on three of these issues—namely, affordability, discrimination and the consequences of conflict.

Affordability—the privatization and financialization of housing

A major cause of homelessness or inadequate housing in many countries continues to be the prohibitive affordability of housing, both within countries and across

[197] Commission on Human Rights, Report of the Special Rapporteur on adequate housing as a component of the right to an adequate standard of living, Miloon Kothari, E/CN.4/RES/2001/28 (20 April 2001), [5(a)].

[198] Commission on Human Rights, Report of the Special Rapporteur on adequate housing as a component of the right to an adequate standard of living, Miloon Kathari, E/CN.4/RES/2001/28 (20 April 2001), [10(a)].

[199] The OHCHR's Fact Sheet No. 25 on 'Forced Evictions and Human Rights' quotes the following states in this category: 'Afghanistan, Argentina, Bahrain, Bangladesh, Belgium, Bolivia, Brazil, Burkina Faso, Cambodia, Colombia, Costa Rica, Democratic People's Republic of Korea, Dominican Republic, Ecuador, El Salvador, Equatorial Guinea, Fiji, Finland, Greece, Guatemala, Guyana, Haiti, Honduras, Iran (Islamic Republic of), Italy, Kenya, Lithuania, Mali, Mexico, Nepal, Netherlands, Nicaragua, Nigeria, Pakistan, Panama, Paraguay, Peru, Philippines, Poland, Portugal, Qatar, Russian Federation, Sao Tome and Principe, Seychelles, Slovenia, South Africa (draft Constitution), Spain, Sri Lanka, Suriname, Sweden, Turkey, Ukraine, Venezuela and Viet Nam', 26, fn 8.

[200] For a compilation of all reports of the Special Rapporteur, see <http://www.ohchr.org/EN/Issues/Housing/Pages/AnnualReports.aspx>.

countries. In his 2005 Report to the Commission on Human Rights, the Special Rapporteur noted further that:

> ... even where developing countries have successfully attracted a large increase in private capital flows, the rapid growth of cities typically outpaces the provision of adequate housing, resulting in an increased number of the poor living in squatter settlements with no security or civic services. This situation is further aggravated when urban authorities or private operators clear such settlements for commercial use or high-income housing. Moreover, increasing trends towards privatization of housing services and markets typically result in land speculation and the commodification of housing, land and water. The application of user fees for goods such as water, sanitation and electricity, and the repeal of land ceiling and rent control legislation further exacerbate the problem, resulting in increased marginalization of the poor.[201]

The 'financialization' of housing continues to be a matter of concern as reflected in the Special Rapporteur's 2012 Report to the Human Rights Council, in which she notes how the growth of microcredit, especially in developing countries, has made housing finance so much more accessible to the poor. But this newfound 'bankability of the poor' has come at a price. The cost of borrowing through microcredit programmes (though considerably less than through loan sharks) is typically much higher than the interest rates that are normally available in Western countries, and is certainly beyond the means of the very poorest who are most in need of assistance. Even with access to credit, there are still major questions regarding housing affordability, for while:

> ... housing microfinance borrowers increase their housing expenditure substantially ... even after the improvements their dwellings tend to remain segregated from health and education services and employment opportunities and, without secure tenure, they may eventually find themselves evicted (without compensation or relocation) from their improved homes.[202]

A key factor in the increases of both the need and availability of housing finance for the poor has been the massive and worldwide growth in the urbanization of populations, as noted by the Special Rapporteur:

> The majority of the urban poor live in unplanned and unserviced urban settlements and self-produce their habitat incrementally, mobilizing their own material and financial resources. In 2005, over one third (37 per cent) of the urban population in developing countries lived in slums and UN-Habitat estimates that by 2020 the world slum population will reach almost 1 billion.[203]

Above all, there has been a global change in the nature of the state's role in respect of housing, whereby housing is now seen less as a social good and more

[201] Commission on Human Rights Report of the Special Rapporteur on adequate housing as a component of the right to an adequate standard of living, Miloon Kothari, E/CN.4/2005/48 (3 March 2005), [25].

[202] UN General Assembly, Report of the Special Rapporteur on adequate housing as a component of the right to an adequate standard of living, Raquel Rolnik, A/67/286 (10 August 2012), [57].

[203] UN General Assembly, Report of the Special Rapporteur on adequate housing as a component of the right to an adequate standard of living, Raquel Rolnik, A/67/286 (10 August 2012), [49], quoting UN-Habitat, 'State of the World's Cities 2010/2011: Cities for All: Bridging the Urban Divide', Nairobi, 2010, xii.

as a financial commodity. And, as such, the affordability of housing becomes not merely a casualty of financial shocks, but also, as reflected in the 2007/08 global financial crisis, a central cause of the crisis in the first place.

10. Housing finance is now perceived not only as a tool for promoting access to adequate housing but also as critical to the development of the financial sector, and has become a central pillar of the financial market, expanding the terrain for global capital The deregulation, liberalization and internationalization of finance that started in the 1980s had major implications for housing and urban development. Funds for mortgage lending now derive from national and international capital markets and not solely from existing savings and retail finance. These developments have been characterized as the 'financialization' of housing.

11. This process has been accompanied by the conceptual transformation of adequate housing from a social good into a commodity and a strategy for household wealth accumulation and welfare security. Housing has become a financial asset ('real estate'), and housing markets are increasingly regulated so as to promote the financial aspects rather than the social aspects of housing. The real estate sector is perceived as a potential driving force for continued and sustainable economic growth.

12. Yet, market-based housing finance has contributed to a widespread bubble in real estate prices and a decrease in affordability and has done little to promote access to affordable adequate housing for the poorest. Between 1997 and 2004 average housing prices grew by 149 per cent in Spain, 139 per cent in the United Kingdom, 187 per cent in Ireland, 112 per cent in Australia, 65 per cent in the United States and 227 per cent in South Africa. As real estate prices and rents increased and came to be financed through global instead of local financial surpluses, more households faced difficulties in accessing adequate housing in the market. Many observers have pointed to the negative impacts of housing asset dispersion on social stratification and inequality, and the uneven spatial impact of these processes within cities, regions and globally.

13. The affordability crisis was compounded by the erosion, neglect and liberalization of non-market mechanisms for allocating housing resources. Even countries with a long tradition of broad-based social rental housing have redefined their systems to promote ownership, 'free market' principles and competition policies. Thus, there has been a significant reduction in the construction of adequate housing for the poor and most vulnerable groups along with decreasing national budgets and available public funds. In the United States, the budget of the Department of Housing and Urban Development was cut from $83 billion in 1978 to $18 billion in 1983 and between 1996 and 2001, no funding was allocated to public housing construction. The constant reduction in public housing has resulted in long waiting lists, keeping a large number of people in inadequate housing conditions (A/HRC/13/20/Add.4, para. 21; see also A/HRC/10/7). Even in the former Soviet countries, which did not experience a shortage of housing in the short term (following mass privatization), low-income households were soon faced with a huge affordability problem.[204]

[204] UN General Assembly, Report of the Special Rapporteur on adequate housing as a component of the right to an adequate standard of living, Raquel Rolnik, A/67/286 (10 August 2012), [10]–[13].

Discrimination and housing

Discrimination in respect of housing and habitat is a recurrent problem in many countries. Its consequences are suffered disproportionately by minority and/or marginalized groups, including indigenous peoples, ethnic minorities, refugees and non-nationals, and women. In some cases, the discrimination may be direct in that there exist policies or practices that actively promote housing preferences for certain groups while denying access to housing to others. But, equally, discrimination can be indirect, as is often the case with women whose position may be as 'invisible' as it is precarious (or desperate) in terms of housing. The Special Rapporteur has stressed this point repeatedly, as for example in 2005:

46. The factors which increase women's vulnerability to homelessness are multifaceted, and their exact nature varies with differences found in local cultural, economic and legal structures. Structural aspects related to securing the right to adequate housing render invisible the full extent of homelessness, including the threat of homelessness. Addressing women and vulnerability to homelessness must first start with access to the skills, resources and place in the community that allow for the securing of adequate housing. In many places the lack of educational and employment opportunities for women often necessitates economic reliance on family, informal support networks, or a partner or spouse. Such dependence deprives women of the ability to make real choices concerning a range of issues in their lives intimately linked to their well-being, including where and with whom they live. This type of dependency also leaves many women vulnerable to exploitation. Fear of homelessness motivates many women to make life choices they would not otherwise make.

47. Legal provisions and their interpretation increase women's vulnerability to homelessness in many places. A lack of security of tenure as well as the failure to recognize women's property rights inside, outside and upon dissolution of marriage or domestic partnership is a major contributing factor. In situations where women are economically dependent on their partner, and where there are no legal provisions which adequately recognize women's individual interests or joint interests in family assets, including the family home, women can be left vulnerable to homelessness. Even where laws are in place to recognize the interests of women, where one partner is seeking to dissolve a marriage or domestic partnership, women often lack the means to retain adequate legal counsel or access the courts to protect their personal interests. In jurisdictions offering some form of legal aid, this too is often restricted to criminal matters and fails to address family law, systematically disadvantaging women.[205]

And again, building on these points, in 2011 when the Special Rapporteur stressed the importance of social and cultural attitudinal changes to go hand-in-hand with legislative and policy pronouncements:

53. Legislation and gender-sensitive housing law, policy and programming are only the first step. Even where good laws and policies are in place, an important challenge remains in translating them fully into practice. Unfortunately, in terms of implementation, progress

[205] Commission on Human Rights, Report of the Special Rapporteur on adequate housing as a component of the right to an adequate standard of living, Miloon Kothari, E/CN.4/2005/48 (3 March 2005), [46]–[47].

has remained slow. Indeed, during the consultation process for this report, it became clear that even in places where good laws exist, discriminatory social and customary norms continue to hinder the enjoyment of women's right to adequate housing.

54. The existing gaps are complex and difficult to overcome as they are deeply rooted in culture, discriminatory social attitudes and practices, as well as weak or gender-blind systems which delay progress in the realization of the right, and fail to effectively make visible the existing barriers. Those challenges require more than ordinary efforts to enforce laws and put policies into practice; additional actions directed to provoke those changes in cultural patterns are required, and this can be obtained particularly through the combination of awareness-raising and public education, as well as through legal enforcement and legal aid, and provision of appropriate resources through the adoption of specific budgetary measures.[206]

In terms of matters of discrimination on wider grounds, the conditions advocated by the Special Rapporteur in 2002 that states ought to abide by remain apposite:

46. …[The] Special Rapporteur respectfully recommends that Governments and other concerned parties:

(a) Enact or strengthen legislative measures that prohibit racial discrimination in all areas of the public and private sectors, including housing, planning and land policies and provision of building materials, services and housing finance;

(b) Ensure that policies, programmes, and budgetary and financial allocations are carried out in good faith to promote equal access to civic services essential to the realization of the right to adequate housing—including potable water, electricity and sanitation—repeal policies and programmes that promote discriminatory access;

(c) Guarantee access to judicial remedies for violations of the right, such as forced evictions, deliberate denial of civic services, including reparations for damages suffered, in accordance with article 6 of the International Convention on the Elimination of All Forms of Racial Discrimination;

(d) Develop national institutions with adequate resources and mandates to monitor legislative, judicial and administrative services, including to receive complaints, and the capacity and authority to undertake follow-up action;

(e) Undertake affirmative action to diminish, eliminate and compensate for conditions that cause or help to perpetuate discrimination in the realization and retention of the right to adequate housing;

(f) Eliminate barriers to the enjoyment of the right to adequate housing that are disproportionately faced by ethnic and racial minorities and indigenous peoples living in life-threatening and health-threatening housing conditions; special attention needs to be given to particularly vulnerable groups, i.e. persons affected by HIV/AIDS, so that they do not suffer from discrimination in housing;

[206] Human Rights Council, Report of the Special Rapporteur on adequate housing as a component of the right to an adequate standard of living, and on the right to non-discrimination in this context, Raquel Rolnik, A/HRC/19/53 (26 December 2011), [53]–[54].

(g) Remove legal, administrative and social obstacles to women's full and equal right to own land and other property and their right to adequate housing, including through exercise of the right to inheritance, with particular attention to women who face double discrimination, including women with disabilities, HIV/AIDS, minority or other vulnerable status, as well as women who have faced forced evictions;

(h) Ensure in particular that no child will be subjected to discrimination with regard to his or her right to adequate housing on the grounds of his or her parents' race, colour, national or ethnic origin, sex, property or other status, and that special protection and assistance be provided to children living in the streets and those temporarily or permanently deprived of a family environment;

(i) Institutionalize inter-ministerial coordination so as to ensure that the formulation and implementation of economic globalization policies, such as those in the areas of trade, investment, finance, structural adjustment and debt, do not cause the State to contravene covenanted human rights obligations and aggravate living conditions for those people and communities facing discrimination and segregation with regard to housing, land and access to related civic services;

(j) Address the multiple discrimination facing minority, indigenous and distinctly low-income communities the habitability of whose housing is made hazardous by the environmental degradation of the areas where they live, often adjacent to an environmentally degraded workplace;

(k) Institutionalize ethical housing, land-use and planning practices, including the preparation of city and regional master plans, such that segregated residential patterns and discrimination in facilities do not form based on group identity of race, colour, descent, national and ethnic origin—as well as religion. Moreover, it is essential that in the formulation and implementation of these plans, residents enjoy the right to participation, including through participatory budgetary processes, on a basis of non-discrimination and equality;

(l) Provide domestic remedies for violations of the right to adequate housing, including facilities, training for legal practitioners, regulations and procedures, policy guidance, efficient administration of justice, equal court access and public education towards improved prosecution, litigation and other forms of dispute resolution with judicial effect;

(m) Strengthen the efforts to monitor the living conditions of marginalized racial and ethnic groups, particularly with regard to fundamental economic, social and cultural indicators, including housing, and efficiently collect and disaggregate data according to different criteria such as gender, age, ethnicity, etc.; and

(o) Protect and promote economic, social and cultural rights, keeping in mind the interests of the whole population such that no group suffers from discrimination, especially in the particularly odious practice of population transfer and the implantation of alien settlers.[207]

[207] Commission on Human Rights: Report of the Special Rapporteur on adequate housing as a component of the right to an adequate standard of living, Miloon Kothari, E/CN.4/2002/59 (1 March 2002), [46].

Conflict and the consequences for housing

Situations of conflict seriously impact on housing both directly (through destruction or eviction) and indirectly (by way of targeted depravation of housing and related essential services such as power, water and sanitation). The Special Rapporteur provides examples of these effects in the following extracts from a 2005 report:

C. Homelessness as a result of conflict situations

35. The Special Rapporteur has witnessed the effects of conflicts first hand during some of his country missions. In Afghanistan, over two decades of conflicts have resulted in severe destruction and have left houses, public buildings, sanitation and other systems across the country in ruins. As a result, homelessness has become a reality for many. At the same time, urban areas have seen a dramatic growth in population due to the return of refugees, the presence of internally displaced persons who cannot return to their areas of origin, as well as an influx from rural areas of Afghans hoping for better employment possibilities and improved economic and social conditions in general (see E/CN.4/2004/48/Add.2, paragraphs 39–43).

36. Demolition of homes and destruction of property, including land and crops, is not always merely an indirect result of conflict. Housing and land have increasingly become strategic targets. The Special Rapporteur has repeatedly expressed his concern about the demolition of

Palestinian houses and other buildings and the confiscation of Palestinian land becoming a common and widespread measure used by Israel in the occupied Palestinian territories (see E/CN.4/2003/5/Add.1). These acts have left thousands of residents homeless and have harmed the livelihood of thousands more. During 2004, Israel is reported to have demolished 181 homes in the Occupied Territories as a means of punishment and 1,357 homes on the claim of military necessity. These demolitions left an estimated 11,500 Palestinians homeless. Since 1987, Israel is reported to have demolished 4,100 homes, rendering an estimated 28,000 Palestinians homeless.

37. Systematic destruction of private homes, agricultural crops and land and water sources, together with pillage and looting, have also been one of the main features of the human rights violations taking place in Darfur, Sudan, resulting in displacement and homelessness (see E/CN.4/2005/3, paragraphs 70–73). Until security and protection are fully ensured people will not be able to return to their villages. Addressing security considerations must be matched with efforts to ensure the realization of the right to adequate housing, through compensation and reconstruction schemes.

38. In a press briefing on 10 May 2004 regarding the prevailing humanitarian crisis in Colombia, the United Nations Under-Secretary-General for Humanitarian Affairs and Emergency Relief Coordinator stated that among Colombia's nearly 300,000 internally displaced, many were forced into urban slums and shantytowns, living in a 'sea of sewerage and garbage'. Others find themselves entirely homeless and destitute. The crisis of internal displacement is also a crisis of security. The internally displaced constitute a new recruitment base for the guerrilla, paramilitary forces and the drug mafias.[208]

[208] Commission on Human Rights, Report of the Special Rapporteur on adequate housing as a component of the right to an adequate standard of living, Miloon Kothari, E/CN.4/2005/48 (3 March 2005), [35]–[38].

The complexity of these circumstances, together with the urgent need to address their impact on housing, is often somewhat similar to the situations following natural or man-made disasters.[209] In recognizing these factors, the Special Rapporteur has sought to identify the particular needs of the homeless or displaced, and the expected responses of states in these circumstances.

7. The impacts of both conflicts and disasters for the individuals, families and communities affected can be devastating. These include the loss of life and livelihoods; destruction of homes, property and infrastructure; disruption or termination of essential services; and the prolonged and sometimes even permanent forced displacement from land, home and community. Although wealth and power do not offer any immunity from these impacts, it is in most cases the poor and socially disadvantaged who are worst affected; and it is also they who are least able to withstand economic shocks and so generally take the longest to recover.

8. The poor often stand to lose most in disaster contexts because they often have to settle on fragile and exposed land that is highly susceptible to the effects of disasters. When a disaster strikes, their pre-existing vulnerabilities are exacerbated, with women, children and marginalized groups bearing the brunt of the impact. After the disaster, the poor often also find their attempts to return to their homes officially denied on the grounds that return would be unsafe, and/or not permissible as they did not have official proof of a right to live there in the first place. This can have dramatic consequences for the livelihoods of individuals, families and entire communities. In the case of conflicts, the displacement and dispossession of specific groups are often deliberate strategies of one group or side in the conflict against another. This can result in the total destruction and/or secondary occupation of their lands and homes, and obstruction of their attempts to return and reclaim what was theirs.

9. In addition to facing serious humanitarian problems and challenges, victims of disasters and conflicts are often exposed to grave human rights violations, invariably including the right to adequate housing. Humanitarian crises are human rights crises. Notwithstanding, given the concentration of international and national attention, resources and effort they often receive, such crises can also present important human rights opportunities. The World Bank has noted that '... while conflicts unleash horror and suffering, they also destabilize old ways of doing things and create new openings for poor people to get ahead. However, there is a narrow window of opportunity in the aftermath of conflict before old barriers begin to surface' (World Bank, 'Life After Conflict: Surprising Opportunities for Poor People to Escape Poverty,' press release No. 2010/222/SDN (11 January 2010)).[210]

In this respect, the Special Rapporteur adds (later in the same report), that 'the long-term success of post-disaster and post-conflict responses to a great extent

[209] The Special Rapporteur has also conducted a review of the specific housing challenges posed by climate-change events, including the habitat impacts of flooding, landslides, deforestation, drought, spoiled harvests, and access to clean and adequate water: see Human Rights Council, Report of the Special Rapporteur on adequate housing as a component of the right to an adequate standard of living, Raquel Rolnik, A/64/255 (6 August 2009).

[210] Human Rights Council, Report of the Special Rapporteur on adequate housing as a component of the right to an adequate standard of living, and on the right to non-discrimination in this context, Raquel Rolnik, A/HRC/16/42 (20 December 2010).

depends on a properly informed understanding of the local context' (paragraph 36). This requires not just 'high levels of consultation with and direct involvement of the people directly affected in the process of relief and reconstruction' (paragraph 36), but also the appropriate and effective marshalling, coordination and expenditure of 'resources from within countries, bilateral and multilateral international donors, relief agencies and NGOs etc' (paragraph 56). Only thereby will the critical issues of 'security of tenure, location, cultural adequacy and availability of services, facilities and infrastructure' (paragraph 57) be addressed in a manner that will secure both short-term relief and long-term sustainability in terms of housing needs.[211]

States' reports and the Committee's Concluding Observations

These observations of the Special Rapporteurs have been echoed and added to by the Committee's Concluding Observations on states' periodic reports under the Covenant. The malign consequences of conflict for peoples' housing has been highlighted in Committee reports on Afghanistan, Iraq, the Democratic Republic of Congo and Sri Lanka, as well as the perverse effects that conflict, or its threat, can have on state budget allocations, as noted in the Committee's criticism of Angola's defence budget being forty times larger than that of the housing sector, despite the country's urgent need to 'address the acute housing shortage'.[212] Furthermore, the Committee remains critical of the seemingly relentless tendency of states to effect or permit forced evictions without adequate safeguards, such as, for example, in its Concluding Observations regarding Afghanistan,[213] Bolivia,[214] Cambodia,[215] China,[216] Israel,[217] Nigeria and Zimbabwe.[218]

Overall, the right to housing is by far the most common matter of concern raised by the Committee in the context of Article 11's right to an adequate standard of living, being mentioned in respect of very nearly every state. Indeed, in our review of all the Committee's Concluding Observations over the past twenty-five years, housing was mentioned in the context of states' obligations

[211] The matter of 'tenure insecurity' has also been the subject of scrutiny and analysis by the Special Rapporteur, which she considers to be at a crisis point globally, with 'many millions of people [living] under the daily threat of eviction, or in an ambiguous situation where their tenure status can be challenged by authorities or private actors at any time': Human Rights Council, Report of the Special Rapporteur on adequate housing as a component of the right to an adequate standard of living, and on the right to non-discrimination in this context, Raquel Rolnik, A/HRC/22/46 (24 December 2012), [1].

[212] CESCR, Concluding Observations: Algeria, E/C.12/DZA/CO/4 (7 June 2010), [18].

[213] CESCR, Concluding Observations: Afghanistan, E/C.12/AFG/CO/2-4 (7 June 2010), [39].

[214] CESCR, Concluding Observations: Bolivia, E/C.12/BOL/CO/2 (8 August 2008), [14(h)] and [27(h)].

[215] CESCR, Concluding Observations: Cambodia, E/C.12/KHM/CO/1 (12 June 2009), [30]–[31].

[216] CESCR, Concluding Observations: China, E/C.12/1/Add.107 (13 May 2005), [31] and [61].

[217] CESCR, Concluding Observations: Israel, E/C.12/ISR/CO/3 (16 December 2011), [26]–[27].

[218] CESCR, Concluding Observations: Nigeria, E/C.12/1/Add.23 (16 June 1998), [27]; see also Zimbabwe, E/C.12/1/Add.12 (20 May 1997), [13] and [21].

under Article 11 more than three times that of food. And while this is, of course, a crude measure of relative importance, there is no doubting the significance that the Committee invests in the protection of the right to housing. A common and recurring theme in the Committee's deliberations is the matter of the affordability and adequacy of housing for the poor and marginalized in nearly all countries, to greater or lesser extents. Criticisms as well as some commendations are repeatedly made of the adequacy of states' housing policies and programmes in terms of the quantity and quality of housing stock, its relative availability for rural and urban communities as well as its affordability—either directly through provision of low-cost public housing and indirectly, through rent controls and access to low-interest-rate loans.

The state's role is certainly critical in providing or otherwise making available adequate and inexpensive housing, but it is equally clear that there is no political or economic path that will guarantee these ends, as illustrated by the contrasting examples of the Ukraine and Belgium. The experience of the Ukraine over the past twenty-five to thirty years shows how difficult it is to make housing affordable and at the same time adequate. During its time as a republic within the USSR, the Ukraine claimed that as 'State housing was provided free of charge, and that rents did not exceed a third of the real maintenance costs incurred by the State, [t]here were [therefore] no homeless in the Ukraine'.[219] This statement notwithstanding, questions were still asked by the Committee 'concerning housing and difficulties encountered with respect to the continuous improvement of living conditions' (paragraph 104). Following independence in 1990, and the rapid replacement of the communist planned economy with a democratic capitalist state, problems of housing scarcity and affordability arose, especially for the poor and marginalized. These developments are evident in the Committee's Concluding Observations regarding the Ukraine in 1995,[220] 2001 and 2008.[221] In the latter report, the Committee had this to say:

23. The Committee notes with concern that 28 per cent of the population reportedly live below the official poverty line.

24. The Committee is concerned that, in spite of the efforts undertaken by the State party to resettle and integrate formerly deported persons such as Crimean Tatars in the Autonomous Republic of Crimea, most Crimean Tatars have been excluded from the land privatization process, that only a limited number of Crimean Tatars have obtained plots of land, mainly outside areas that were traditionally settled by them, while others face criminal sanctions for squatting on land, and that many Crimean Tatars live in settlements lacking basic infrastructures.

[219] Economic and Social Council Official Records, Ukranian Soviet Socialist Republic, E/C.12/1987/5 (29 October 1986), [105].

[220] CESCR, Concluding Observations: Ukraine, E/C.12/1995/15 (28 December 1995), [27].

[221] CESCR, Concluding Observations: Ukraine, E/C.12/1/Add.65 (24 September 2001), [9]; E/C.12/UKR/CO/5 (4 January 2008).

25. The Committee notes with concern that many Roma live in informal settlements and camps which lack basic infrastructures and services such as safe water, electricity, gas, heating, sewage, garbage disposal and roads, without legal security of tenure and under constant threat of eviction.

26. The Committee is deeply concerned about reports on substandard living conditions and overcrowding in prisons, pre-trial detention centres and centres for refugees and asylum-seekers, including in medical wards for inmates and detainees suffering from tuberculosis.

...

45. The Committee urges the State party to allocate sufficient funds for the implementation of the State Programme to Combat Child Homelessness and Neglect (2006–2010), increase the capacity of and open new centres for homeless children and day centres for street children, ensure access to adequate food, health care and social protection for street children and children deprived of parental care, adopt urgent measures to provide these children and young persons leaving school orphanages with education, accommodation and adequate employment opportunities, and intensify its efforts to improve the living conditions in orphanages and seek alternative solutions for children placed in orphanages, such as foster families or family-type children's homes, and by ensuring an effective procedure of adoption by families.

46. The Committee recommends that the State party allocate sufficient funds for the implementation of its poverty eradication strategy, ensure the full integration of economic, social and cultural rights in the strategy, and specifically address the needs of unemployed persons, women, families with children, pensioners, the rural population, ethnic minorities and other disadvantaged and marginalized individuals and groups. In this regard, the State party is referred to the Committee's Statement on 'Poverty and the International Covenant on Economic, Social and Cultural Rights' (E/C.12/2001/10). The State party is requested to include in its next periodic report updated statistical data, on an annual basis, on the percentage of the population living in poverty, disaggregated by gender, age, number of children per household, number of single-parent households, rural/urban population, and ethnic group.

47. The Committee recommends that the State party allocate sufficient funds for the implementation of the Programme for the Resettlement and Integration of Formerly Deported Persons and ensure that formerly deported persons have equal access to suitable plots of land and adequate housing and to effective remedies for claiming such land and housing. It also recommends that the State party proceed with the adoption of the draft law on compensation of formerly deported persons. The State party should consider repealing the recent law threatening illegal land occupants with several years' imprisonment. It should also ensure that Crimean Tatars living in settlements enjoy legal security of tenure and access to basic infrastructures, including safe water, electricity, gas, heating, sewage and garbage disposal, and roads.

48. The Committee urges the State party to ensure, by legalizing and intensifying its efforts to improve the infrastructures of Roma settlements or through social housing programmes, that all Roma have access to adequate and affordable housing, legal security of tenure, safe water, electricity, gas, heating, sewage and garbage disposal, and roads. The State party should ensure that adequate alternative housing is provided whenever forced

evictions take place, in line with the Committee's general comment No. 7 (1997), and include in its next report disaggregated statistical data, on an annual basis, on the number of forced evictions.[222]

The experience of Belgium shows that, despite long-standing democratic governance, relative wealth and more recently, constitutional protection of housing rights, shortages can still be a chronic problem. Thus, in 1994 the Committee commented:

> Moreover the Committee, while noting with satisfaction that the right to housing has been inscribed in the recently revised Constitution of Belgium, expresses concern at the adequacy of the measures taken to actually enforce that constitutional provision.[223]

Fourteen years later, the situation did not, in the Committee's view, appear to have substantially improved:

> The Committee remains concerned, in spite of the various initiatives undertaken by the State party to increase the supply of social housing units, about the continuing shortage of social housing units for low-income households and other disadvantaged and marginalized individuals and groups, and about the continuing increase of rents in the private rental sector.[224]

The matter of discrimination in terms of housing rights has also been a constant in many Committee observations of states' practices. Thus, in respect of Bolivia, the Committee relayed its concern over 'the large housing shortage, the incidence of forced evictions with respect to peasants and indigenous populations in favour of mining and lumber concessions, and the absence of effective measures to provide social housing for low-income, vulnerable and marginalized groups'.[225] In respect of China, the Committee lamented the fact that despite the country's rapid economic development, inadequate living standards, including housing, still afflicted the rural poor and inland provinces in particular, and that impact on housing of massive infrastructure projects was especially detrimental. Thus, for example, in its 2005 report on China, the Committee declared that it was:

> ... concerned about the reports of forced evictions and insufficient measures to provide compensation or alternative housing to those who have been removed from their homes in the context of urban development projects as well as of rural development projects such as the Three Gorges Project. The Committee is concerned about the number of forced evictions and demolitions that have occurred in anticipation of the 2008 Olympic Games to be hosted by the State party. The Committee further expresses concern about the lack of effective consultations and legal redress for persons affected by forced evictions and demolitions, including those of historic structures, buildings and homes in Lhasa, Tibet. The Committee also regrets that insufficient information was provided on the extent and causes of homelessness in the State party.[226]

[222] CESCR, Concluding Observations: Ukraine, E/C.12/UKR/CO/5 (4 January 2008), [23]–[26], [45]–[47].

[223] CESCR, Concluding Observations: Belgium, E/C.12/1994/7 (31 May 1994), [11].

[224] CESCR, Concluding Observations: Belgium, E/C.12/BEL/CO/3 (4 January 2008), [20].

[225] CESCR, Concluding Observations: Bolivia, E/C.12/1/Add.60 (21 May 2001), 54 [276].

[226] CESCR, Concluding Observations: Peoples Republic of China, E/C.12/1/Add.107 (13 May 2005), [31].

Housing discrimination and lack of adequate consultation on grounds both of poverty and race were also concerns for the Committee with regard to France.

21. The Committee is deeply concerned that persons belonging to racial, ethnic and national minorities, especially migrant workers and persons of immigrant origin, are disproportionately concentrated in poor residential areas characterized by large, low-quality and poorly maintained housing complexes, limited employment opportunities, inadequate access to health care facilities and public transport, under-resourced schools and high exposure to crime and violence.

…

41. The Committee urges the State party to take all appropriate measures, in close consultation with the population concerned, to reduce the phenomenon of residential segregation based on racial, ethnic and national origin, as well as its negative consequences on the living conditions of the affected individuals and groups. In particular, the Committee recommends that the State party take all appropriate measures, in order to:

(a) Improve housing and living conditions in residential areas that are currently racially segregated by facilitating the renovation of existing housing complexes and improving their infrastructures, access to services and employment opportunities;

(b) Support the development of new public housing complexes outside poor, racially segregated areas; and

(c) Ensure the effective implementation of existing legislation to combat discrimination in housing, including discriminatory practices carried out by private actors.

The parlous housing circumstances of the Roma in Europe and the failure of states adequately to address them is also a regular object of the Committee's comments, in respect not just of France (paragraph 24 of the above report), but also Italy[227] and Hungary—in relation to which it has stated:

22. The Committee is deeply concerned that one-fifth of the Roma in the State party [Hungary] live in slum settlements, often without access to running water, adequate sewerage or located close to municipal dumpsites, and that Roma are frequently denied access to social housing, e.g. on the ground that they previously occupied accommodation without legal title or as a result of the distribution of social housing by local governments through public auction at high prices. It is particularly concerned about the increasing number of forced evictions of Roma, often without provision of adequate alternative housing, and about the Constitutional Court's ruling that the need to implement eviction orders takes precedence over the right of children not to be separated from their families and placed in the State care system.

…

[227] CESCR, Concluding Observations: Italy, E/C.12/1/Add.43 (23 May 2000), [10] and [23]; Italy, E/C.12/1/Add.103 (14 December 2004), [24]–[26] and [45]–[48].

45. The Committee urges the State party to adopt and implement remedial measures relating to infrastructure in Roma settlements, extend the application of the Roma Housing and Social Integration Programme to all communities concerned, effectively enforce anti-discrimination legislation in the housing sector, refrain from distributing social housing through public auction at high prices; and increase the availability of social housing, in particular for the Roma. It also urges the State party to ensure that the rights of affected individuals, including children, are safeguarded and that alternative housing is provided whenever forced evictions take place, in line with the Committee's general comment No. 7 (1997) on the right to adequate housing, and to include disaggregated data on the extent of homelessness, the number of forced evictions and arrangements for alternative housing in its next periodic report.[228]

Implementation and compliance indicators

In addition to some general guidance on states' reporting obligations in General Comment No. 7,[229] the specific recommendations provided by the Committee to each state in its Concluding Observations and other communications with individual states, a set of 'practical and operational tools to promote, monitor and implement the human right to adequate housing' has also been developed by the Special Rapporteur on the adequate housing. Prompted by one of the targets in the Millennium Development Goals (Goal 7 on environmental sustainability) which declares that by 2020 states will collectively have 'achieved a significant improvement in the lives of at least 100 million slum dwellers,' the Special Rapporteur formulates three separate instruments.[230] First, a set of Basic Principles and Guidelines on Development-Based Evictions and Displacement, which consolidates and expands the conditions regarding forced evictions discussed earlier in this chapter. Secondly, a Questionnaire on Women and Adequate Housing, which targets the removal of provisions and practices that discriminate against women regarding, in particular, legal security of tenure of land, access to public goods and services, participation in decision-making processes, and access to remedies. And thirdly, a List of Indicative Indicators on the Right to Adequate Housing[231] as follows:

[228] CESCR, Concluding Observations: Hungary, E/C.12/HUN/CO/3 (16 January 2008), [22] and [45].

[229] CESCR, General Comment No. 7, Annex IV, paragraph 19 of which stipulates: 'In accordance with the guidelines for reporting adopted by the Committee, State parties are requested to provide various types of information pertaining directly to the practice of forced evictions. This includes information relating to (a) the "number of persons evicted within the last five years and the number of persons currently lacking legal protection against arbitrary eviction or any other kind of eviction", (b) "legislation concerning the rights of tenants to security of tenure, to protection from eviction" and (c) "legislation prohibiting any form of eviction"'.

[230] All three are contained in Annexes to the Report to the Human Rights Council of the Special Rapporteur on adequate housing as a component of the right to an adequate standard of living, Miloon Kothari, A/HRC/4/18 (7 February 2007), 13–34.

[231] Human Rights Council, Report of the Special Rapporteur on adequate housing as a component of the right to an adequate standard of living, Miloon Kothari, A/HRC/4/18 (7 February 2007), Annex II, 27–8.

Table 13.2 List of illustrative indicators on the right to adequate housing (Article 11(1) ICESCR;* MDG indicators)

Type of Indicator	Habitability	Accessibility to services	Housing affordability	Security of tenure
Structural	• International human rights instruments, relevant to the right to adequate housing, ratified by the State • Date of entry into force and coverage of the right to adequate housing in Supreme Law/Constitution/Bill of Rights • Date of entry into force and coverage of domestic laws relevant to the implementation of the right to adequate housing • Number of registered/operational civil society organizations involved in the promotion and protection of the right to adequate housing			
	• Time frame and coverage of national housing policy statement/strategy for the progressive implementation of measures for the right to adequate housing at different levels of Government, as applicable • Time frame and coverage of national policy on rehabilitation and resettlement			• Date of entry into force and coverage of legislation on security of tenure, equal inheritance and protection against forced eviction
Process	• Number of complaints on the right to adequate housing received, investigated and adjudicated by the national human rights institution/human rights ombudsperson/specialized institution and other administrative mechanisms (created to protect the interests of specific populations groups) in the reporting period • Public expenditure on reconstruction and rehabilitation of displaced persons as a proportion of public development budget • Net ODA for housing received/provided as proportion of public expenditure on housing/gross national income*			
	• Proportions of habitations (cities, towns and villages) covered under provisions of building codes and by-laws	• Proportion of household budget spent on access to utilities, including water supply, sanitation, electricity and garbage disposal	• Proportion of households that receive public housing assistance, including those living in subsidized rented housing and households subsidized for ownership	• Average time taken to settle disputes related to housing and land rights in courts and tribunals

Process (*cont'd*)	• Share of public development budget spent on social/community housing • Increase in habitable area effected through reclamation, including of hazardous sites and change in land use pattern • Addition to habitable area earmarked for social/ community housing during the reporting period	• Proportion of vulnerable households dependent on private sources for water supply • Share of public development budget spent on provision and maintenance of sanitation, water supply, electricity and physical connectivity of habitations	• Proportion of households in self-owned, publicly provided housing and squatter settlements • Average rent of bottom three income deciles as a proportion of the top three	• Number of legal appeals aimed at preventing planned evictions/ demolitions through the issuance of court-ordered injunctions over the reporting period • Number of legal procedures seeking compensation following evictions over the reporting period • Proportion of displaced or evicted persons rehabilitated/ resettled annually over the reporting period
Outcome	• Proportion of population (persons per room or rooms per household) with sufficient living space/ average number of persons per room among targeted households • Proportion of households living in permanent structures in compliance with building codes and by-laws • Proportion of habitations/ households living near hazardous sites	• Proportion of urban population living in slums • Proportion of (rural and urban) population with sustainable access to an improved water source* • Proportion of (rural and urban) population with access to improved sanitation*	• Proportion of households spending more than 'x' % of their monthly income/ expenditure on housing • Annual average of homeless persons per 100,000 population • Proportion of homeless population using public and community-based shelters 'x' being defined normatively for the country context	• Reported cases of 'forced evictions' per 100,000 population (e.g. as reported to United Nations special procedures) over the reporting period • Proportion of households with legally enforceable, contractual, statutory or other protection providing security of tenure/ proportion of households with access to secure tenure* • Proportion of women among individuals with titles to land/ house

Housing rights litigation

In addition to Article 11 in the ICESCR, the right to housing is also referred to in the Convention on the Elimination of all Forms of Racial Discrimination (1965) (Article 5(d)(v)) and the Convention to Eliminate all Forms of Discrimination Against Women (1979) (Article 16(h)). In addition, while the Convention Against Torture (1984) does not mention housing, the Convention's Committee has pronounced on individual complaints that have substantially concerned gross violations of the right to housing that contribute to violations of the torture convention. A number of these cases have been recognized by the Special Rapporteur on adequate housing to be of especial significance—one involving the treatment of Roma in the former Yugoslavia, and another concerning Israel's settlement policy in the Occupied Palestinian Territories.

80. An individual case recently dealt with by the Committee against Torture (CAT) concerns the expulsion and destruction of houses of a Roma settlement in Montenegro (Hajrizi Dzemajl et al. v. Serbia and Montenegro) [Communication No. 161/2000: Yugoslavia, CAT/C/29/D/161/2000, 2 December 2002]. The complainants were 65 persons, all of Romani origin and then nationals of the Federal Republic of Yugoslavia, claiming that articles 1, paragraph 1 and 2, and paragraphs 1, 12, 13, 14 and 16, paragraph 1, of the Convention against Torture and Other Cruel, Inhuman or Degrading Treatment or Punishment had been violated. The destruction of the Roma settlement was a result of the acts of a large mob of several hundred non-Roma, who 'with stones and other objects, first broke windows of cars and houses belonging to Roma and then set them on fire. The crowd also destroyed and set fire to the haystacks, farming and other machines, animal feed sheds, stables, as well as other objects belonging to the Roma', including with explosive devices. Allegedly, police officers were present at the scene, but did not intervene and failed to act in accordance with legal obligations. The Committee concluded that the incident constituted a breach by the State of article 16 of the Convention, i.e. the incidents were labelled as cruel, inhuman or degrading treatment.

81. It should be noted that an individual opinion was issued by two of the members of the Committee, stating that 'the illegal incidents for which the Yugoslav State is responsible constitute "torture" within the meaning of article 1, paragraph 1, of the Convention, not merely "cruel, inhuman or degrading treatment" as covered by article 16. The failure of the State authorities to react to violent evictions, forced displacement and the destruction of homes and property by individuals amounts to unlawful acquiescence which, in our judgement violates article 1, paragraph 1, particularly when read in conjunction with article 2, paragraph 1, of the Convention'. When arguing this point, the two members underline that the suffering inflicted on the victims was 'severe enough to qualify as "torture"', including since the inhabitants 'were forced to abandon their homes in haste given the risk of severe personal and material harm', and since no compensation had been given to the victims. The two reserving members conclude that 'the above amounts to a presumption of "severe suffering", certainly "mental" but also inescapably "physical" in nature even if the victims were not subjected to direct physical aggression' and should therefore have been defined as torture.

82. The Special Rapporteur welcomes the link continuously being made by CAT between forced evictions and breaches of the Convention, including, for example, in the Committee's concluding observations on Israel where it states that 'policies on house demolitions [...] may, in certain instances, amount to cruel, inhuman or degrading treatment or punishment'.

[Conclusions and recommendations of the Committee against Torture: Israel, CAT/C/XXVII/Concl.5, 23 November 2001][232]

At the regional level, none of the principal human rights instruments (namely, the European Convention on Human Rights (1950), the American Convention on Human Rights (1969) and the African Charter on Human and Peoples' Rights (1981)) expressly provide protection for the right to housing. Rather, protection for the right has been derived from other rights that are expressly provided for in these instruments, including, in particular, the rights to privacy, property,[233] health and protection of the family. In addition, several supplementary instruments in the European and African jurisdictions do explicitly refer to the right to housing—that is, the European Convention on the Legal Status of Migrant Workers (1977) (Article 13), the revised European Social Charter (1996) (Part I(31)) and the African Charter on the Rights and Welfare of the Child (1990) (Article 20(2)(a)).

In the case of *Social and Economic Rights Action Centre (SERAC) v Nigeria* (2002),[234] the African Commission on Human and Peoples' Rights made clear the integrated and derivative nature of the right to housing under the African Charter, while also drawing on the relevance of Article 11 of the ICESCR. The case—as described and extracted above in respect of the rights to food and water—concerned the human rights violations of the Ogoni people by the government of Nigeria.

60. Although the right to housing or shelter is not explicitly provided for under the African Charter, the corollary of the combination of the provisions protecting the right to enjoy the best attainable state of mental and physical health, cited under Article 16 [...], the right to property [Article 14], and the protection accorded to the family [Article 18] forbids the wanton destruction of shelter because when housing is destroyed, property, health, and family life are adversely affected. It is thus noted that the combined effect of Articles 14, 16 and 18(1) reads into the Charter a right to shelter or housing which the Nigerian Government has apparently violated.

61. At a very minimum, the right to shelter obliges the Nigerian government not to destroy the housing of its citizens and not to obstruct efforts by individuals or communities to rebuild lost homes. The State's obligation to respect housing rights requires it, and thereby all of its organs and agents, to abstain from carrying out, sponsoring or tolerating any practice, policy or legal measure violating the integrity of the individual or infringing upon his or her freedom to use those material or other resources available to them in a way they find most appropriate to satisfy individual, family, household or community housing needs. Its obligations to protect obliges it to prevent the violation of any individual's right to housing by any other individual or non-state actors like landlords, property developers, and land owners, and where such infringements occur, it should act to preclude further deprivations as well as guaranteeing access to legal remedies. The right to shelter even goes further than

[232] Commission on Human Rights, Report of the Special Rapporteur on adequate housing as a component of the right to an adequate standard of living, Miloon Kothari, E/CN.4/2004/48 (8 March 2004), [80]–[82].

[233] The right to property is enshrined in the American Convention on Human Rights (adopted 22 November 1969, 1144 UNTS 143, entered into force 18 July 1978), Article 21; the African Charter on Human and Peoples' Rights (adopted 27 June 1981, 1520 UNTS 217, entered into force 21 October 1986), Article 14; and the Charter of Fundamental Rights of the European Union (adopted 7 December 2000, OJ C 364/01, entered into force 1 December 2009), Article 17.

[234] *SERAC and CESR v Nigeria* (2001) AHRLR 60, 27 October 2001.

a roof over one's head. It extends to embody the individual's right to be let alone and to live in peace- whether under a roof or not.

62. The protection of the rights guaranteed in Articles 14, 16 and 18(1) leads to the same conclusion. As regards the earlier right, and in the case of the Ogoni People, the Government of Nigeria has failed to fulfil these two minimum obligations. The government has destroyed Ogoni houses and villages and then, through its security forces, obstructed, harassed, beaten and, in some cases, shot and killed innocent citizens who have attempted to return to rebuild their ruined homes. These actions constitute massive violations of the right to shelter, in violation of Articles 14, 16, and 18(1) of the African Charter.

63. The particular violation by the Nigerian Government of the right to adequate housing as implicitly protected in the Charter also encompasses the right to protection against forced evictions. The African Commission draws inspiration from the definition of the term 'forced evictions' by the Committee on Economic Social and Cultural Rights which defines this term as 'the permanent removal against their will of individuals, families and/or communities from the homes and/or which they occupy, without the provision of, and access to, appropriate forms of legal or other protection'. Wherever and whenever they occur, forced evictions are extremely traumatic. They cause physical, psychological and emotional distress; they entail losses of means of economic sustenance and increase impoverishment. They can also cause physical injury and in some cases sporadic deaths…Evictions break up families and increase existing levels of homelessness. In this regard, General Comment No. 4 (1991) of the Committee on Economic, Social and Cultural Rights on the right to adequate housing states that 'all persons should possess a degree of security of tenure which guarantees legal protection against forced eviction, harassment and other threats' (E/1992/23, annex III. Paragraph 8(a)). The conduct of the Nigerian government clearly demonstrates a violation of this right enjoyed by the Ogonis as a collective right.[235]

The African Commission has also pronounced on the matter of States' compliance with the Charter when involved in forced evictions, once again drawing directly on the Committee on Economic Social and Cultural Rights' General Comment Nos. 4 and 7 to support its findings. For example, out of the wide-ranging claims of systematic human rights violations in the case of Sudan Human Rights Organisation and Another v Sudan (2009),[236] the Commission held that Sudan had, by commission and omission, violated the rights to property under Article 14 of the Charter of the indigenous black African tribes in the Darfur region (Western Sudan) by failing to:

refrain […] from the eviction, or demolition of victims' houses and other property. It did not take steps to protect the victims from the constant attacks and bombings, and the rampaging attacks by the Janjaweed militia. It doesn't matter whether they had legal titles to the land, the fact that the victims cannot derive their livelihood from what they possessed for generations means they have been deprived of the use of their property under conditions which are not permitted by article 14.[237]

In the case of *Centre for Minority Rights Development et al v Kenya* (2009),[238] the African Commission held that despite the constitutional safeguard of the right to

[235] *SERAC and CESR v Nigeria*, [60]–[63].

[236] *Sudan Human Rights Organisation and COHRE v Sudan*, (2009) AHRLR 154.

[237] *Sudan Human Rights Organisation and COHRE v Sudan*, [205].

[238] *Centre for Minority Rights Development (Kenya) and Minority Rights Group International on behalf of Endorois Welfare Council v Kenya* (Communication No. 276/2003), (2009) AHRLR 75, 4 February 2010.

property and housing, the Kenyan Government had violated the Charter-protected right to property (Article 14) by forcibly removing the indigenous Endorois from their ancestral lands in the West of the country to make way for game reserves. And despite the fact that the Endorois had established, and, for centuries, practised a sustainable way of life which was inextricably linked to their ancestral land, the state had not provided adequate compensation or suitable alternative land to them.

The right to housing jurisprudence established under the African Charter has both contributed to and, especially, drawn from the development of domestic case law. Thus, for example, the Constitutional Court of South Africa in the watershed case of *Republic of South Africa v Grootboom* (2000)[239] ruled that the protection of the right to housing under the Constitution was violated by the government in respect of its actions regarding the forcible eviction of occupants (including Irene Grootboom) of temporary shelters erected on a local sports field, the destruction of their shacks and possessions, and the inadequacy of plans for, and implementation of, programmes for alternative means of shelter. Section 26 of the Constitution of South Africa provides that everyone has the right of access to adequate housing and that the state has an obligation to take reasonable legislative and other measures to ensure the progressive realization of the right within its available resources. In addition, section 28(1)(c) provides a specific right of shelter to children.

In reaching its determination that the government had failed in its obligations under section 26 (in the particular instance of this case, it effectively subsumed section 28(1)(c)'s right of children to shelter under the broader section 26),[240] the Constitutional Court stressed the interconnectedness of civil and political rights with economic and social rights under the Constitution and the undoubted justiciability of the latter:

> [24] The right of access to adequate housing cannot be seen in isolation. There is a close relationship between it and the other socio-economic rights. Socio-economic rights must all be read together in the setting of the Constitution as a whole. The state is obliged to take positive action to meet the needs of those living in extreme conditions of poverty, homelessness or intolerable housing. Their interconnectedness needs to be taken into account in interpreting the socio-economic rights, and, in particular, in determining whether the state has met its obligations in terms of them.[241]

Under the South African Constitution, the Court is directed to consider relevant international law in its interpretation and application of rights guaranteed by the Constitution. Despite South Africa having only signed, but not ratified, the Covenant, the Court nonetheless confirmed that it considered the notion of 'progressive realization' under the Constitution to be substantially the same as (and in fact

239 *Republic of South Africa v Grootboom et al* (Case CCT 11/00), 2000 (11) BCLR 1169 (CC), 4 October 2000. The Court's judgment was provided by Yacoob J.

240 In respect of section 26, see [69], [88] and [93]; and for reasoning regarding section 28, see [70]–[79].

241 *South Africa v Grootboom*, [24].

was drawn from) that contained in Article 2(1) of the Covenant. Nevertheless, while the Court was both cogniscent of, and keen to use, relevant reports and commentary on ICESCR, Article 11, it was not prepared to endorse the Economic, Social and Cultural Rights Committee's notion of a minimum core obligation in respect of the right to housing, due principally, it declared, to the sheer difficulty of doing so with any degree of precision (paragraphs 31 to 33). Furthermore, it sought to distinguish the slightly different wording used in respect of housing in the two instruments.

[35] The right delineated in section 26(1) [of the Constitution] is a right of 'access to adequate housing' as distinct from the right to adequate housing encapsulated in the Covenant. This difference is significant. It recognises that housing entails more than bricks and mortar. It requires available land, appropriate services such as the provision of water and the removal of sewage and the financing of all of these, including the building of the house itself. For a person to have access to adequate housing all of these conditions need to be met: there must be land, there must be services, there must be a dwelling. Access to land for the purpose of housing is therefore included in the right of access to adequate housing in section 26. A right of access to adequate housing also suggests that it is not only the state who is responsible for the provision of houses, but that other agents within our society, including individuals themselves, must be enabled by legislative and other measures to provide housing. The state must create the conditions for access to adequate housing for people at all economic levels of our society. State policy dealing with housing must therefore take account of different economic levels in our society.

[36] In this regard, there is a difference between the position of those who can afford to pay for housing, even if it is only basic though adequate housing, and those who cannot. For those who can afford to pay for adequate housing, the state's primary obligation lies in unlocking the system, providing access to housing stock and a legislative framework to facilitate self-built houses through planning laws and access to finance. Issues of development and social welfare are raised in respect of those who cannot afford to provide themselves with housing. State policy needs to address both these groups. The poor are particularly vulnerable and their needs require special attention. It is in this context that the relationship between sections 26 and 27 and the other socio-economic rights is most apparent. If under section 27 the state has in place programmes to provide adequate social assistance to those who are otherwise unable to support themselves and their dependents, that would be relevant to the state's obligations in respect of other socio-economic rights.

[37] The state's obligation to provide access to adequate housing depends on context, and may differ from province to province, from city to city, from rural to urban areas and from person to person. Some may need access to land and no more; some may need access to land and building materials; some may need access to finance; some may need access to services such as water, sewage, electricity and roads. What might be appropriate in a rural area where people live together in communities engaging in subsistence farming may not be appropriate in an urban area where people are looking for employment and a place to live.

[38] Subsection (2) speaks to the positive obligation imposed upon the state. It requires the state to devise a comprehensive and workable plan to meet its obligations in terms of the subsection. However subsection (2) also makes it clear that the obligation imposed upon the state is not an absolute or unqualified one. The extent of the state's obligation is defined by three key elements that are considered separately: (a) the obligation to 'take reasonable

legislative and other measures'; (b) 'to achieve the progressive realisation' of the right; and (c) 'within available resources.'[242]

Aside from these invaluable jurisprudential pointers provided by this case, perhaps the most telling feature of Yacoob J.'s reasoning on behalf of the Court was his careful placing of constitutional interpretation in the context of the economic and administrative realities of a still-developing state like South Africa.

[94] I am conscious that it is an extremely difficult task for the state to meet these obligations in the conditions that prevail in our country. This is recognised by the Constitution which expressly provides that the state is not obliged to go beyond available resources or to realise these rights immediately. I stress however, that despite all these qualifications, these are rights, and the Constitution obliges the state to give effect to them. This is an obligation that courts can, and in appropriate circumstances, must enforce.

[95] Neither section 26 nor section 28 entitles the respondents to claim shelter or housing immediately upon demand... However, section 26 does oblige the state to devise and implement a coherent, co-ordinated programme designed to meet its section 26 obligations. The programme that has been adopted and was in force in the Cape Metro [the relevant administrative authority] at the time that this application was brought, fell short of the obligations imposed upon the state by section 26(2) in that it failed to provide for any form of relief to those desperately in need of access to housing.[243]

The limits of the rights to both property and housing have also been subject to analysis in the case of *Leite v Government of Seychelles*,[244] in which the Seychelles Constitutional Court in effect used the 'public interest' in the right to housing under Article 34 of the Constitution as a justification to compulsorily acquire land owned by Mr Leite. The Court dismissed the petitioner's claims that under Article 26 of the Constitution his right to property was protected against such acquisition. It argued that provided Mr Leite was fully compensated (and he did not dispute that he had been), then the state had the power under Article 26(3)(b) to acquire land when in the public interest to do so. In this case, this was substantially satisfied by the plans to build thirty-six housing units on the land intended in part to advance the state's fulfilment of its duty under Article 34 to assist those in need of housing.[245]

Come what may, however, appropriate consultation with, and provision of information to, those affected by actions that compel people to leave their abode is a strict minimum legal requirement. Thus, for example, in *Sesana et al v Attorney-General*,[246] the High Court of Botswana found against the Government for failing to consult with the applicants before summarily terminating the provision of essential services (power, water and sanitation) to their dwellings, on the grounds, in part, that to do so violated their constitutionally protected right to life.[247]

The case law of the American Convention on Human Rights regarding housing has been marked by concerns over the displacement and discriminatory treatment

[242] *South Africa v Grootboom*, [35]–[38]. [243] *South Africa v Grootboom*, [94]–[95].
[244] *Leite v Government of Seychelles and Another* (2003) AHRLR 222 (SyCC 2002), 11 June 2002.
[245] *Leite v Government of Seychelles and Another*, [21]–[22].
[246] *Sesana et al v Attorney-General* (2006) AHRLR 183 (BwHC 2006), 13 December 2006.
[247] *Sesana et al v Attorney-General*, [28]–[29].

of indigenous peoples as a consequence of dispossession, conflict or land acquisitions for commercial uses, such as logging, large-scale farming, hydro-electricity generation and mineral exploration. These cases have usually centered on alleged violations of rights to property (Article 21), life (Article 4) or fair trial (Articles 8 and 25), and have drawn out both the often dire consequences of forced evictions and what governments can do to try to remedy the damage caused.

In two separate cases against Paraguay brought by the Yakye Axa Indigenous Community (in 2005) and the Sawhoyamaxa Indigenous Community (in 2006),[248] the Inter-American Court on Human Rights condemned the government for permitting ancestral lands to be acquired by corporations without due process in terms of adequate reparation and access to remedies, which actions resulted in both communities living in circumstances of squalor without adequate food, clean water, medical care or proper sanitation, and with no access to even basic education services. It held in both cases that Paraguay had violated its obligations to protect the indigenous communities' rights to property (Article 21) and fair trial (Articles 8 and 25), and additionally, in respect of the Sawhoyamaxa, their rights to life and children's rights. The Court ordered the Paraguayan Government to compensate the two communities accordingly, to provide the adequate housing and related services, including and especially medical and sanitation 'necessary for survival', and to 'enact into its domestic laws and within a reasonable time the legislative, administrative or other measures necessary to establish a mechanism to claim restitution of the ancestral lands of the members of indigenous communities, that be efficient in enforcing [sic] their rights over traditional lands'.[249]

In other land, property and housing-related cases, agreements have been reached between the parties before the dispute reached the Court. Thus, in *Community of San Vicente Los Cimientos v Guatemala* (2003), after nearly 700 indigenous families had fled their homes, lands and livestock due to repeated military conflicts across the 1980s and 1990s, a 'friendly settlement' was concluded between the Community and the Government of Guatemala before the Inter-American Commission on Human Rights in which the Government agreed, among other things, 'to provide humanitarian assistance, minimal housing, and basic services through the appropriate official agencies'.[250] In *Mercedes Julia Huenteao Beroiza et al v Chile* (2004), members of the Mapuche Pehuenche people disputed the terms and conditions under which they were to be expelled from their traditional lands in advance of the building of a hydroelectric plant. Their contentions

[248] *Case of the Indigenous Community Yakye Axa v Paraguay*, 17 June 2005, IACHR (Ser. C) No. 125; *Sawhoyamaxa Indigenous Community v Paraguay*, 29 March 2006, IACHR (Ser. C), No. 146, respectively.

[249] *Sawhoyamaxa v Paraguay*, [248(12)]. A similar order was made by the Court in *Yakye Axa v Paraguay*, [242(6)–(14)].

[250] Section 9 of the Agreement, as appended to *Community of San Vicente los Cimientos v Guatemala* (Petition No. 11.197), Friendly Settlement Report No. 68/93, Inter-American Court of Human Rights, 10 October 2003, [36].

included particular concerns regarding housing and led to the following being included in a Memorandum of Understanding registered with the Inter-American Commission between the Government and the Mapuche Pehuenche:

The Government, through the Ministry of Housing and Urban Development, and in accordance with the legal framework in force, shall implement a Housing Program whereunder it shall grant housing subsidies for the construction of homes for the Pehuenche property owners here present, who are relocated as a consequence of the agreed land swaps, as well as for their families…[251]

Another relevant right covered by the Convention is that to free movement and residence (Article 22). Although this right might at first appear similar to the right to housing under Article 11 of the ICESCR, it is in fact peculiarly associated with the freedom of movement under the American Convention. Article 22(1) reads: 'Every person lawfully in the territory of a State Party has the right to move about in it and reside in it, subject to the provisions of the law.' That said, this provision has at times been utilized in a manner that comes close to the constructive protection of the right to adequate housing. In *Ituango Massacres v Colombia* (2006),[252] the government was held responsible for acquiescing to, or assisting, paramilitary groups in their theft of livestock and the destruction of homes in the El Aro and La Granja areas of Colombia and thereby violating its obligations under Article 22, as well as Article 11 (right to privacy and protection against arbitrary interference with one's private life, family and home). In formulating its reasoning, the Court cited with approval the policy requirements of General Comment No. 4 of the Committee on Economic, Social and Cultural Rights, in stating that since many of the inhabitants of the affected areas had lost their homes, 'the state must implement a housing program to provide appropriate housing to the surviving victims'.[253]

The Inter-American Court has also considered a number of cases concerning the conditions endured by prisoners and other detainees in several South American states. Once again, while undoubtedly pertaining to the right to be adequately housed in a general sense, the Court's deliberations have focused on the related rights to life (Article 4) and human treatment (Article 5), as well as the right to fair trial (Articles 8 and 25). In the case of *Juvenile Re-education Institute v Paraguay* (2004),[254] the Court held that Paraguay had violated, inter alia, Articles 4 and 5 of the Convention, as well as Article 19 (which protects the rights of children and minors), for failing to ensure that all the inmates at the institute (the vast majority of whom were not convicted but on remand awaiting trial) had decent living conditions, by exposing inmates to cruel,

[251] Memorandum of Understanding in Friendly Settlement, *Mercedes Julia Huenteao Beroiza et al v Chile* (Petition 4617/02), Friendly Settlement Report No. 30/04, Inter-American Court of Human Rights, 11 March 2004, [34(7)].

[252] *Ituango Massacres v Colombia*, 1 July 2006, IACHR (Ser. C), No. 148.

[253] *Ituango Massacres v Colombia*, [407].

[254] *Juvenile Re-education Institute v Paraguay*, 2 September 2004, IACHR (Ser. C), No. 112.

inhuman and degrading treatment, and by omitting to take the special measures of protection that were required of it where children are concerned.[255] Similarly, in *López Álvarez v Honduras* (2006),[256] the Inter-American Court determined that by detaining Mr López Álvarez in overcrowded prisons, failing to provide him with adequate food, water and hygienic conditions, failing to separate him from convicted inmates, and persisting in detaining him for three months after an appellate court's confirmation of his acquittal, Honduras had violated its obligations under Article 5, as well as Article 7 (right to personal liberty) and Articles 8 and 25 (rights to fair trial and judicial protection respectively).[257]

The European Convention on Human Rights (1950) obliges states to protect everyone's 'right to respect for his private and family life, his home and his correspondence' under Article 8. The reference to respect for one's home, however, has only limited overlap with the notion of the right to adequate housing under the ICESCR. The European Court of Human Rights has indicated that the provision does protect the physical security of the home and one's belongings—so, for example, the destruction of the homes of Greek Cypriots by the Turkish military constituted a violation of Article 8[258]—but it has also indicated that the provision does not encompass the right to a home.[259]

The extent to which Article 8 protects against eviction has also been tested. In *Connors v United Kingdom* (2004), the European Court of Human Rights held that a local authority's forced eviction of gypsies from a caravan site where they had set up home was contrary to Article 8.[260] The Court's concern in this case was with the manner in which the eviction had been executed (by force using sheriffs and the police), and not with the fact that despite permission to establish residence having been granted, the local authority claimed that the conditions of that permission had been broken. In another case involving the accommodation of travellers in the United Kingdom, however, the Court made clear that there exist justifiable limits that a state can place on people establishing residences, noting, specifically, that refusing planning permission to a gypsy to establish a home in a particular area did not amount to a breach of Article 8 provided that the procedure for so determining was fair and reasonable.[261]

The most direct protection of housing rights under the Council of Europe's human rights regime is provided in the Revised European Social Charter. The original European Social Charter of 1961 contained no express provision

[255] *Juvenile Re-education Institute v Paraguay*, 91–8.

[256] *López Álvarez v Honduras*, 1 February 2006, IACHR (Ser. C), No. 141.

[257] *López Álvarez v Honduras*, [225].

[258] *Cyprus v Turkey* (App. 25781/94), 10 May 2001, (2002) 35 EHRR 731.

[259] In *Chapman v United Kingdom* (App. 27238/95), 18 January 2001, in which the Court effectively removed the whole question from its purview by stating that 'whether the State provides funds to enable everyone to have a home is a matter for political not judicial decision' (at [99]).

[260] *Connors v United Kingdom* (App. 66746/01), 27 May 2004, (2005) 40 EHRR 189.

[261] *Buckley v United Kingdom* (App. 20348/92), 25 September 1996, (1997) 23 EHRR 101.

for housing,[262] but under its revision in 1996, a new Article 31 was added, which reads:

Article 31—The right to housing

With a view to ensuring the effective exercise of the right to housing, the Parties undertake to take measures designed:

1. to promote access to housing of an adequate standard;
2. to prevent and reduce homelessness with a view to its gradual elimination;
3. to make the price of housing accessible to those without adequate resources.

The nature and extent of this obligation was investigated in the case of *FEANTSA v France* (2008), which concerned a collective complaint brought by the European Federation of National Organisations Working with the Homeless (FEANTSA) against France regarding the adequacy of the government's housing policies and practices in terms of access to and allocation of housing, habitability standards, and eviction protocols and re-housing programmes. In a wide-ranging and unanimous decision, the Charter's overseeing authority—the European Committee on Social Rights—held that violations had occurred in respect of the following grounds:[263]

(i) …of insufficient progress as regards the eradication of substandard housing and lack of proper amenities of a large number of households;

(ii) …of unsatisfactory implementation of the legislation on the prevention of evictions and the lack of measures to provide rehousing solutions for evicted families;

(iii) …that measures currently in place to reduce the number of homeless are insufficient, both in quantitative and qualitative terms;

(iv) …of insufficient supply of social housing accessible to low-income groups;

(v) …of the malfunctioning of the social housing allocation system, and the related remedies;

(vi) …of the deficient implementation of legislation on stopping places for Travellers.[264]

In response, it should be noted, the French Government indicated that it had already

…taken measures to bring the situation into conformity with the revised Charter and undertakes to follow these up by taking into account the said report, namely by implementing the Act on the enforceable right to housing of 5 March 2007…:

– which establishes an effective appeal in cases of the refusal of social housing to persons in a priority situation;

– which has led to an order issued by the *juge des référés* of the Paris administrative court dated 20 May 2008, in which, for the first time, a mother living with her two

[262] Although Article 16 of the 1961 Charter provided that in 'ensuring the necessary conditions for the full development of the family… Contracting Parties undertake to promote the economic, legal and social protection of family life by such means as… [inter alia] provision of family housing…' This Article remains unchanged in the Revised Charter.

[263] *European Federation of National Organisations Working with the Homeless (FEANTSA) v France* (Complaint No. 39/2006), Merits, 5 December 2007 (European Committee of Social Rights).

[264] In respect of housing laws and practices that overtly discriminate against travellers, or Roma, specifically, the European Committee on Social Rights has also condemned Greece, Italy and Bulgaria, in similar fashions—see, respectively: *European Roma Rights Centre v Greece* (Complaint No. 15/2003), Merits,

children in an emergency accommodation and social reintegration centre has obtained the suspension of a decision of a mediation commission which had considered that her request for social housing did not have 'priority' nor was it 'urgent';

– and which foresees an important programming of budgetary resources to protect against exclusion the most vulnerable persons in a priority situation, such as the homeless or evicted persons of good faith.[265]

In terms then of both the stance of the European Committee on Social Rights and the response of the French Government, this case reflects an apparently much deeper willingness to address the precise policy and practice dimensions of a state's housing programme than is possible either under the ECHR or was possible under the old European Social Charter.

Some of the most influential judgments in domestic law involving housing have been made by the Supreme Court of India concerning the meaning and extent of right to life as protected under Article 21 of the Indian Constitution. The Supreme Court has developed a line of jurisprudence that emphasizes the critical importance of the various elements that make up a life worth living, and not just being alive. Thus, in *Olga Tellis v Bombay Municipal Corporation*,[266] for example, the Court held that:

The sweep of the right to life conferred by Article 21 is wide and far reaching. It does not mean merely that life cannot be extinguished or taken away as, for example, by the imposition and execution of the death sentence, except according to procedure established by law. That is but one aspect of the right to life. An equally important facet of that right is the right to livelihood because, no person can live without the means of living, that is, the means of livelihood. If the right to livelihood is not treated as a part of the constitutional right to life, the easiest way of depriving a person of his right to life would be to deprive him of his means of livelihood to the point of abrogation. Such deprivation would not only denude the life of its effective content and meaningfulness but it would make life impossible to live. And yet, such deprivation would not have to be in accordance with the procedure established by law, if the right to livelihood is not regarded as a part of the right to life. That, which alone makes it possible to live, leave aside what makes like liveable, must be deemed to be an integral component of the right to life.[267]

In reaching this conclusion that the right to livelihood is an essential element to the right to life, the Court relied on the Indian Constitution's so-called 'Directive Principles of State Policy', which though not themselves enforceable, are nonetheless considered constitutive of the right to life which is binding on the state. Specifically, Article 39 states:

39. Certain principles of policy to be followed by the State.

– The State shall, in particular, direct its policy towards securing—

(a) that the citizens, men and women equally, have the right to an adequate means of livelihood;

8 December 2004; *European Roma Rights Centre v Italy* (Complaint No. 27/2004), Merits, 7 December 2005; *European Roma Rights Centre v Bulgaria* (Complaint No. 31/2005), Merits, 18 October 2006.

[265] Report from the European Committee of Social Rights to the Committee of Ministers in relation to *FEANTSA v France*.

[266] (1985) 3 SCC 545.

[267] *Olga Tellis v Bombay Municipal Corp*, [79].

(b) that the ownership and control of the material resources of the community are so distributed as best to subserve the common good;

(c) that the operation of the economic system does not result in the concentration of wealth and means of production to the common detriment;

(d) that there is equal pay for equal work for both men and women;

(e) that the health and strength of workers, men and women, and the tender age of children are not abused and that citizens are not forced by economic necessity to enter avocations unsuited to their age or strength;

(f) that children are given opportunities and facilities to develop in a healthy manner and in conditions of freedom and dignity and that childhood and youth are protected against exploitation and against moral and material abandonment.

The Supreme Court continued, in its judgment in *Olga Tellis*:

The principles contained in Articles 39(a) and 41 [a Directive Principle regarding just and humane working conditions] must be regarded as equally fundamental in the understanding and interpretation of the meaning and content of fundamental rights. If there is an obligation upon the State to secure to the citizens an adequate means of livelihood and the right to work, it would be sheer pendantry to exclude the right to livelihood from the content of the right to life. The State may not, by affirmative action, be compellable to provide adequate means of livelihood or work to the citizens. But, any person who is deprived of his right to livelihood except according to just and fair procedure established by law, can challenge the deprivation as offending the right to life conferred by Article 21.[268]

In terms specifically, of the right to housing, or indeed even a right to reside in a public place, the Court has been circumspect. Thus, in *Olga Tellis*, it condemned only the summary nature of the eviction of the pavement dwellers and the lack of any adequate provision for their subsequent rehousing and general welfare. It stopped short, however, of stipulating that the state is under a positive obligation to provide housing to the homeless or otherwise needy:

No one has the right to make use of a public property for a private purpose without the requisite authorisation and, therefore, it is erroneous to contend that the pavement dwellers have the right to encroach upon pavements by constructing dwellings thereon. Public streets, of which pavements form a part, are primarily dedicated for the purpose of passage and, even the pedestrians have but the limited right of using pavements for the purpose of passing and trepassing. So long as a person does not transgress the limited purpose for which pavements are made, his use thereof is legitimate and lawful. But, if a person puts any public property to a use for which it is not intended and is not authorised so to use it, he becomes a trespasser.[269]

As such, the Court concluded, the local authority was entitled to remove the pavement dwellers. So, while this oft-cited case is important in its recognition of the wide compass of the right to life, the role that the right to adequate housing plays in that endeavour is limited.

[268] *Olga Tellis v Bombay Municipal Corp*, [55].
[269] *Olga Tellis v Bombay Municipal Corp*, [59].

In the subsequent case of *Shantistar Builders v Narayan Khimalal Totame* (1990), the Indian Supreme Court demonstrated a greater willingness to embrace a right to 'reasonable accommodation' as one of the essential elements of the right to life (under Article 21 of the Constitution), and thereby be more prepared to instruct governmental authorities over how they ought to realize that right. In this case, the court required the state authority to attend to the needs of the 'weaker sections'[270] of society as indeed its policy formally obliged it to do.

9. Basic needs of man have traditionally been accepted to be three—food, clothing and shelter. The right to life is guaranteed in any civilized society. That would take within its sweep the right to food, the right to clothing, the right to decent environment and a reasonable accommodation to live in. The difference between the need of an animal and a human being for shelter has to be kept in view. For the animal it is the bare protection of the body; for a human being it has to be a suitable accommodation which would allow him to grow in every aspect—physical, mental and intellectual. The Constitution aims at ensuring fuller development of every child. That would be possible only if the child is in a proper home. It is not necessary that every citizen must be ensured of living in a well-built comfortable house but a reasonable home particularly for people in India can even be mud-built thatched house or a mud-built fire-proof accommodation.

10. With the increase of population and the shift of the rural masses to urban areas over the decades the ratio of poor people without houses in the urban areas has rapidly increased. This is a feature which has become more perceptible after independence. Apart from the fact that people in search of work move to urban agglomerations, availability of amenities and living conveniences also attract people to move from rural areas to cities. Industrialisation is equally responsible for concentration of population around industries. These are feature which are mainly responsible for increase in the homeless urban population. Millions of people today live on the pavements of different cities of India and a greater number live animal like existence in jhuggis.

11. The Planning Commission took note of this situation and was struck by the fact that there was no corresponding rise in accommodation with the growth of population and the shift of the rural people to the cities. The growing realisation of this disparity led to the passing of the Act and acquisition of vacant sites for purposes of housing. Considerable attention has been given in recent years to increasing accommodation though whatever has been done is not at all adequate. The quick growth of urban population overshadows all attempts of increasing accommodation. Sections 20 and 21 of the Act vest power in the State Governments to exempt vacant sites from vesting under the Act for purposes of being taken over if housing schemes are undertaken by owners of vacant urban lands. Section 21 specifically emphasises upon [sic] weaker sections of the people.[271]

All that said, however, India, like many developing countries, continues to struggle to accommodate the slum-dwelling, urban poor in particular, who flock to cities in search of work and opportunity. Thus, despite the official policy (and

[270] A term expressly used in Article 46 of the Constitution which comprises a Directive Principle of State Policy to 'promote with special care the educational and economic interests of the weaker sections of the people'.

[271] *Shanti Star Builders v Narayan K Totame* (1990) 1 SCC 520, [9]–[11].

sometimes because of it), coercion and its consequences are too often resorted to, or permitted, by government authorities. Indeed, the Special Rapporteur on adequate housing noted 'with grave concern' in a 2005 Report:[272]

> ...that Governments continue the practice of mass evictions in cities as a means of creating 'world-class cities', lured by the prospect of international investment. Economic globalization has created competition amongst cities that is to the detriment of the poor. The example of Mumbai, India, is very recent. Between December 2004 and January 2005, 80,000 homes were demolished rendering 300,000 people homeless. For the vast majority of those evicted there was no advance notice, the evictions were violently carried out, and the belongings, including identity cards, of many were damaged or burnt. Those evicted have not been offered alternative accommodation, clearly exacerbating the situation of homelessness in Mumbai. The Chief Minister explained these brutal demolitions as the only way to create a 'world-class' city in the future.

International Cooperation

Although the ICESCR lacks any general stipulation as to jurisdiction of a sort equivalent to that contained in Article 2(1) of the ICCPR,[273] it does make clear its intention that states should cooperate in the fulfilment of the rights contained within it. Thus, Article 2(1) of the ICECSR, as discussed in the chapter on that provision, provides that states shall take steps towards the progressive realization of the Covenant's rights by various means, including 'international assistance and co-operation'. Similar words are used in respect of a number of individual rights, including the right to an adequate standard of living, under Article 11 which in subparagraph (1) refers to the 'essential importance of international co-operation based on free consent' in the realization of the right, and in subparagraph (2) stresses the need for 'international co-operation' in the design and implementation of programmes to combat hunger globally.

While the subject of the potential for arguing that the ICESCR generally, and Article 11 specifically, impose upon states extra-territorial responsibilities has gathered pace in recent years, the fact remains that in terms of legal obligation the Covenant, the Committee and the relevant Special Rapporteurs talk mainly in hope rather than expectation. Certainly, this is a field ripe for debate and development, but it is one which, at present, is dominated more by questions

[272] Commission on Human Rights, Special Rapporteur on adequate housing as a component of the right to an adequate standard of living, Miloon Kathari, Report to the Commission on Human Rights, Miloon Kothari, E/CN.4/2005/48 (3 March 2005), [27].

[273] Which provides: 'Each State Party to the present Covenant undertakes to respect and to ensure to all individuals within its territory *and subject to its jurisdiction* the rights recognized in the present Covenant...' (emphasis added). The Human Rights Committee, in General Comment No. 31 (2004), has interpreted these terms to mean that states are required 'to respect and to ensure the Covenant rights to all persons who may be within their territory *and* to all persons subject to their jurisdiction': HRC, The Nature of the General Legal Obligation Imposed on States Parties to the Covenant, CCPR/C/21/Rev.1/Add. 13 (26 May 2004), [10] (emphasis added). 'This means', the Committee continues, 'that a State party must respect and ensure the rights laid down in the Covenant to anyone within the power or effective control of that State Party, even if not situated within the territory of the State Party' [10].

than answers. As Langford, Coomans and Isa perceptively note, '[e]ven if duties do exist, what sort of obligations flow from the duty in a world of mass poverty and deprivation with limited global resources? Can they be identified with any precision? Who is the duty-bearer when different States have the capacity to assist?'[274]

That said, considerable effort is being invested in delineating just what expectations might legitimately be made of states in terms of their international assistance and cooperation, and why such actions are so important in respect of Article 11. Regarding the right to food, for example, the Economic, Social and Cultural Rights Committee proclaimed in its Statement on the World Food Crisis in 2008[275] that the crisis 'represents a failure to meet the obligations to ensure an equitable distribution of world food supplies in relation to need. The food crisis also reflects failure of national and international policies to ensure physical and economic access to food for all'.[276] It was necessary, therefore, in the opinion of the Committee, that all states take action both to address the immediate causes of the food crisis, individually through national measures, as well as internationally through international cooperation and assistance,[277] *and* 'to pay attention to the longer-term structural causes of the crisis and to focus attention on the gravity of the underlying causes of food insecurity, malnutrition and undernutrition, that have persisted for so long'.[278]

Reflecting the programmatic nature of the obligations imposed on states by Article 11(2) in respect of addressing world hunger, the Committee pursued both of its above appeals to immediate and long-term needs by providing (in paragraphs 11 and 13 respectively) specific suggestions as to what it expects states to do:

11. The Committee therefore urges States to take urgent action, including by:

- Taking immediate action, individually and through international assistance, to ensure freedom from hunger through, inter alia, the provision and distribution of emergency humanitarian aid without discrimination. Humanitarian aid should be provided in cash resources wherever possible.
- Where food aid is provided, care should be taken to ensure that food is purchased locally wherever possible and that it does not become a disincentive for local production. Donor countries should prioritize assistance to States most affected by the food crisis;
- Limiting the rapid rise in food prices by, inter alia, encouraging production of local staple food products for local consumption instead of diverting prime arable land suitable for food crops for the production of agrofuels, as well as the use of food crops

[274] Malcolm Langford, Fons Coomans and Felipe Gómez Isa, 'Extra-Territorial Duties in International Law' in Malcolm Langford, Wouter Vandenhole, Martin Scheinin and Willem van Genugten (eds), *Global Justice, State Duties: The Extra-Territorial Scope of Economic, Social and Cultural Rights in International Law* (Cambridge University Press, New York, 2013), 52.

[275] CESCR, Statement: The World Food Crisis, E/C.12/2008/1 (20 May 2008).

[276] CESCR, Statement: The World Food Crisis, E/C.12/2008/1 (20 May 2008), [9].

[277] CESCR, Statement: The World Food Crisis, E/C.12/2008/1 (20 May 2008), [10].

[278] CESCR, Statement: The World Food Crisis, E/C.12/2008/1 (20 May 2008), [12].

for the production of fuel, and introducing measures to combat speculation in food commodities;

- Establishing an international mechanism of coordination to oversee and coordinate responses to the food crisis and to ensure the equitable distribution of food supplies according to need, and that the policy measures adopted will respect, protect and fulfill the realization of the right to adequate food and freedom from hunger.

…

13. The Committee urges States parties to address the structural causes at the national and international levels, including by:

- Revising the global trade regime under the WTO to ensure that global agricultural trade rules promote, rather than undermine, the right to adequate food and freedom from hunger, especially in developing and net food-importing countries;
- Implementing strategies to combat global climate change that do not negatively affect the right to adequate food and freedom from hunger, but rather promote sustainable agriculture, as required by article 2 of the United Nations Framework Convention on Climate Change;
- Investing in small-scale agriculture, small-scale irrigation and other appropriate technologies to promote the right to adequate food and freedom from hunger for all, including implementing the recommendations of the International Assessment of Agricultural Science and Technology for Development (IAASTD) of 2008.
- Introducing and applying human rights principles, especially those relating to the right to adequate food and freedom from hunger, by undertaking ex ante impact assessments of financial, trade and development policies at both the national and international levels, to ensure that their bilateral and multilateral financial, trade and development commitments do not conflict with their international human rights obligations, particularly under the Covenant.
- Applying and reinforcing the FAO's 'Voluntary Guidelines to Support the Progressive Realization of the Right to Adequate Food in the Context of National Food Security',[279] in the light of the present food crisis.[280]

In its General Comment No. 12 (1999), the Committee separates the various forms of international assistance and cooperation into what states parties ought to do bilaterally and multilaterally, either through their joint and several responsibilities under Articles 55 and 56 of the UN Charter, or their commitments to other relevant international organizations, such as the World Food Programme

[279] Part III of which provides explanations of the importance and role of international cooperation generally, as well as more specific guidance on cooperation in respect of international trade, external debt management, aid coordination, partnerships with civil society and the private sector, and the provision of technical expertise: see Council of the Food and Agriculture Organisation of the United Nations (127th Session), Voluntary Guidelines to Support the Progressive Realization of the Right to Adequate Food in the Context of National Food Security, November 2004, 33–7.

[280] CESCR, Statement: The World Food Crisis, E/C.12/2008/1 (20 May 2008), [11], [13].

and the Food and Agriculture Organization, as well as the World Bank and the IMF:

International obligations

States parties

36 ... States parties should take steps to respect the enjoyment of the right to food in other countries, to protect that right, to facilitate access to food and to provide the necessary aid when required.

37. States parties should refrain at all times from food embargoes or similar measures which endanger conditions for food production and access to food in other countries. Food should never be used as an instrument of political and economic pressure...

States and international organizations

38. States have a joint and individual responsibility, in accordance with the Charter of the United Nations, to cooperate in providing disaster relief and humanitarian assistance in times of emergency, including assistance to refugees and internally displaced persons...

39. Food aid should, as far as possible, be provided in ways which do not adversely affect local producers and local markets, and should be organized in ways that facilitate the return to food self-reliance of the beneficiaries...

The United Nations and other international organizations

41. The international financial institutions, notably the International Monetary Fund (IMF) and the World Bank, should pay greater attention to the protection of the right to food in their lending policies and credit agreements and in international measures to deal with the debt crisis...[281]

The Special Rapporteur on the right to food has been forthright in urging states to take seriously their obligations to cooperate by taking actions that positively promote the provision of and access to food, and refraining from actions that negatively impact on the same goals. In so doing, the Special Rapporteur adopted a broad perspective as to what these actions entail, encompassing, that is, not only states' responsibilities regarding the actions of their own agencies, but also their regulation of the operations of relevant non-state entities that affect food security in other countries.

29. It is certainly clear that in an increasingly globalized world, the actions of one Government can often have repercussions (positive and negative) on the right to food of people in another country (e.g. in the case of agricultural trade). Governments should therefore have a responsibility to ensure that national policies do not have negative effects on the right to food of people in other countries. In the context of extranational obligations, to respect the right to food means that States must not take actions that negatively impact on the right to food of people in another country, (e.g. refrain from food embargoes, or from using food as an instrument of political and economic pressure, or ensuring that their trade relations do not violate the right to food of people in other countries). The obligation to protect implies that States have a duty to regulate their companies and corporations that operate in other countries to prevent violations. The obligation to facilitate access to food requires the State to build a social and

[281] CESCR, General Comment No. 12, E/C.12/1999/5 (12 May 1999), [36]–[41].

international order in which the right to food can be fully realized. States should also take account of their 'extra-national obligations' in their deliberations in multilateral organizations, including the IMF, World Bank and the World Trade Organization (WTO).

30. Therefore, Governments should also have the obligation to refrain from taking action that negatively affects the right to food in other countries. The Committee on Economic, Social and Cultural Rights has stated, for example, that international obligations under the right to food mean that States 'should refrain at all times from food embargoes or similar measures which endanger conditions for food production and access to food in other countries. Food should never be used as an instrument of political and economic pressure.' In the 1993 Vienna Declaration and Programme of Action, States reaffirmed that 'food should not be used as a tool for political pressure'. The long-standing unilateral embargo against Cuba could be seen as a violation of this obligation. Although Cuba has been allowed to import some food from the United States since the disaster of Hurricane Michelle in November 2001, the embargo is nonetheless creating severe problems for the import of adequate foodstuffs to feed Cuba's population. This is the opinion of the General Assembly which, on 12 November 2002, for the eleventh year in a row, condemned the unilateral sanctions of the United States against Cuba and reiterating that these constitute a violation of the Charter of the United Nations and international law. The Special Rapporteur has been invited to make an official visit to Cuba to verify the impact of the embargo on the right to food.[282]

Furthermore, and in respect specifically of international cooperation in development aid, the Special Rapporteur has promoted a human-rights-based approach that would, he argues, not only enhance the level of engagement between donor and target states, but also assure more effective developmental results.[283]

27. The current reform process of international aid is based on the principles of ownership, alignment, harmonization, managing for results, and mutual evaluation, which are made explicit in the Paris Declaration on Aid Effectiveness. An explicit endorsement of a human rights framework for the implementation of these principles could make them more concrete and operational. At a general level, human rights-based approaches to development cooperation recognize people 'as key actors in their own development, rather than passive recipients of commodities and services': they emphasize participation as both a means and a goal; they seek to empower, and thus should combine top-down and bottom-up approaches; both outcomes and processes should be monitored and evaluated, following the adoption of measurable goals and targets in programming; all stakeholders should be involved in analysis; and the programmes should focus on marginalized, disadvantaged, and excluded groups, and aim at reducing disparity. The human right to adequate food in particular should be guiding countries' choices of development strategies, and provide an objective benchmark to evaluate the effectiveness of development efforts, thus improving the accountability of both donors and partners.

[282] Commission on Human Rights: Report of the Special Rapporteur on the right to food, Mr Jean Ziegler, E/CN.4/2003/54 (10 January 2003), [29]–[30].

[283] Human Rights Council, Report of the Special Rapporteur on the right to food, Mr Olivier De Schutter, The role of development cooperation and food aid in realizing the right to adequate food: moving from charity to obligation, A/HRC/10/5 (11 February 2009), [27].

A further example of such exhortation to cooperate is to be found in the recently established Food Assistance Convention (2012),[284] which aims to improve food security between and within countries, by pursuing the following goals:

Article 1

Objectives

The objectives of this Convention are to save lives, reduce hunger, improve food security, and improve the nutritional status of the most vulnerable populations by:

(a) addressing the food and nutritional needs of the most vulnerable populations through commitments made by the Parties to provide food assistance that improves access to, and consumption of, adequate, safe and nutritious food;

(b) ensuring that food assistance provided to the most vulnerable populations is appropriate, timely, effective, efficient, and based on needs and shared principles; and

(c) facilitating information-sharing, cooperation, and coordination, and providing a forum for discussion in order to improve the effective, efficient, and coherent use of the Parties' resources to respond to needs.

Overall, however, it remains the case that while the core content of what the right to food entails is increasingly well defined, the precise jurisdictional boundaries of states' obligations, especially in respect of their extra-territorial responsibility for the actions of corporations within their jurisdiction, remain unclear.[285]

Similar sentiments are echoed in respect of the right to water under Article 11, in respect of which, the Committee's General Comment No. 15 stresses states' responsibilities regarding the extra-territorial actions of private actors (including corporations) over which they have jurisdiction, and in their capacities as members of relevant international organizations, the need for states to promote the right to water in the policy formulation and practices of those bodies. In addition, however, and in recognition of the fundamental imports for the right to water of the trans-boundary management of rivers, lakes and other water sources and repositories, the General Comment also stresses states' duties to assist other states to realize the right to water and, especially, to refrain from actions that inhibit such realization:

International obligations

30. Article 2, paragraph 1, and articles 11, paragraph 1, and 23 of the Covenant require that States parties recognize the essential role of international cooperation and assistance and take joint and separate action to achieve the full realization of the right to water.

31. To comply with their international obligations in relation to the right to water, States parties have to respect the enjoyment of the right in other countries. International cooperation requires States parties to refrain from actions that interfere, directly or indirectly, with

[284] Which came into force in January 2013. As of June 2013, the Convention had been signed by fourteen parties and ratified by eight (namely: Austria, Canada, Denmark, the European Union, Finland, Japan, Switzerland and the United States).

[285] See Smita Narula, 'The Right To Food: Holding Global Actors Accountable Under International' 44 (2006) *Columbia Journal of Transnational Law* 691.

the enjoyment of the right to water in other countries. Any activities undertaken within the State party's jurisdiction should not deprive another country of the ability to realize the right to water for persons in its jurisdiction.

32. States parties should refrain at all times from imposing embargoes or similar measures, that prevent the supply of water, as well as goods and services essential for securing the right to water.* Water should never be used as an instrument of political and economic pressure. In this regard, the Committee recalls its position, stated in its General Comment No. 8 (1997), on the relationship between economic sanctions and respect for economic, social and cultural rights.

* In General Comment No. 8 (1997), the Committee noted the disruptive effect of sanctions upon sanitation supplies and clean drinking water, and that sanctions regimes should provide for repairs to infrastructure essential to provide clean water.

33. Steps should be taken by States parties to prevent their own citizens and companies from violating the right to water of individuals and communities in other countries. Where States parties can take steps to influence other third parties to respect the right, through legal or political means, such steps should be taken in accordance with the Charter of the United Nations and applicable international law.

34. Depending on the availability of resources, States should facilitate realization of the right to water in other countries, for example through provision of water resources, financial and technical assistance, and provide the necessary aid when required. In disaster relief and emergency assistance, including assistance to refugees and displaced persons, priority should be given to Covenant rights, including the provision of adequate water. International assistance should be provided in a manner that is consistent with the Covenant and other human rights standards, and sustainable and culturally appropriate. The economically developed States parties have a special responsibility and interest to assist the poorer developing States in this regard.[286]

35. States parties should ensure that the right to water is given due attention in international agreements and, to that end, should consider the development of further legal instruments. With regard to the conclusion and implementation of other international and regional agreements, States parties should take steps to ensure that these instruments do not adversely impact upon the right to water. Agreements concerning trade liberalization should not curtail or inhibit a country's capacity to ensure the full realization of the right to water.

36. States parties should ensure that their actions as members of international organizations take due account of the right to water. Accordingly, States parties that are members of international financial institutions, notably the International Monetary Fund, the World Bank, and regional development banks, should take steps to ensure that the right to water is taken into account in their lending policies, credit agreements and other international measures.[287]

[286] To this end, the Committee emphasizes that 'it is particularly incumbent on States parties, and other actors in a position to assist, to provide international assistance and cooperation, especially economic and technical which enables developing countries to fulfil their core obligations indicated in paragraph 37 above [that is, a state's "minimum core obligations"]', [38]. Paragraph 37 of General Comment No. 15 is extracted above, text at n. 98.

[287] CESCR, General Comment No. 15, E/C.12/2002/11 (20 January 2003), [30]–[36].

The General Comment adds further a specific exhortation directed at a wide range of such international organizations to cooperate, aid and assist states in the implementation of the right to water:

60. United Nations agencies and other international organizations concerned with water, such as WHO, FAO, UNICEF, UNEP, UN-Habitat, ILO, UNDP, the International Fund for Agricultural Development (IFAD), as well as international organizations concerned with trade such as the World Trade Organization (WTO), should cooperate effectively with States parties, building on their respective expertise, in relation to the implementation of the right to water at the national level. The international financial institutions, notably the International Monetary Fund and the World Bank, should take into account the right to water in their lending policies, credit agreements, structural adjustment programmes and other development projects (see General Comment No. 2 (1990)), so that the enjoyment of the right to water is promoted. When examining the reports of States parties and their ability to meet the obligations to realize the right to water, the Committee will consider the effects of the assistance provided by all other actors. The incorporation of human rights law and principles in the programmes and policies by international organizations will greatly facilitate implementation of the right to water. The role of the International Federation of the Red Cross and Red Crescent Societies, International Committee of the Red Cross, the Office of the United Nations High Commissioner for Refugees (UNHCR), WHO and UNICEF, as well as non-governmental organizations and other associations, is of particular importance in relation to disaster relief and humanitarian assistance in times of emergencies. Priority in the provision of aid, distribution and management of water and water facilities should be given to the most vulnerable or marginalized groups of the population.[288]

As regards the right to adequate housing, the emphasis has been on the assistance that can and ought to be rendered to states by intergovernmental organizations, and the scope for international cooperation between such organizations and states concerning the promotion of the right generally, and preventing forced evictions in particular. Thus, General Comment No. 4 (1991) provides in paragraph 19:

Finally, article 11 (1) concludes with the obligation of States parties to recognize 'the essential importance of international cooperation based on free consent'. Traditionally, less than 5 per cent of all international assistance has been directed towards housing or human settlements, and often the manner by which such funding is provided does little to address the housing needs of disadvantaged groups. States parties, both recipients and providers, should ensure that a substantial proportion of financing is devoted to creating conditions leading to a higher number of persons being adequately housed. International financial institutions promoting measures of structural adjustment should ensure that such measures do not compromise the enjoyment of the right to adequate housing. States parties should, when contemplating international financial cooperation, seek to indicate areas relevant to the right to adequate housing where external financing would have the most effect. Such requests should take full account of the needs and views of the affected groups.[289]

[288] CESCR, General Comment No. 15, [60].

[289] CESCR, General Comment No. 4, E/1992/23 (25 November–13 December 1992), Annex III, [19].

And in the Basic Principles and Guidelines on Development-Based Evictions and Displacement developed by the Special Rapporteur on adequate housing in 2007, Part VIII states:

VIII. Role of the international community, including international organizations

71. The international community bears an obligation to promote, protect and fulfil the human right to housing, land and property. International financial, trade, development and other related institutions and agencies, including member or donor States that have voting rights within such bodies, should take fully into account the prohibition on forced evictions under international human rights law and related standards.

72. International organizations should establish or accede to complaint mechanisms for cases of forced evictions that result from their own practices and policies. Legal remedies should be provided to victims in accordance with those stipulated in these guidelines.

73. Transnational corporations and other business enterprises must respect the human right to adequate housing, including the prohibition on forced evictions, within their respective spheres of activity and influence.[290]

While the promotion of international cooperation and assistance in respect of all the rights covered by the Covenant is certainly a desirable goal, it falls short imposing a clear obligation on states. Thus, the Optional Protocol to the Covenant (OP) offers little by way of defining the nature of the responsibilities imposed on states by the requirement that they ought to provide international assistance and cooperation as per the Covenant's Articles 2(1) and 11(1). As a matter of fact, the relevant provision in the OP (Article 14) focuses more on the responsibilities of the Committee than the duties of the states in this regard, save a rather cryptic reiteration of states' obligation in sub-paragraph 4 of Article 14.

Article 14 International assistance and cooperation

1. The Committee shall transmit, as it may consider appropriate, and with the consent of the State Party concerned, to United Nations specialized agencies, funds and programmes and other competent bodies, its views or recommendations concerning communications and inquiries that indicate a need for technical advice or assistance, along with the State Party's observations and suggestions, if any, on these views or recommendations.

2. The Committee may also bring to the attention of such bodies, with the consent of the State Party concerned, any matter arising out of communications considered under the present Protocol which may assist them in deciding, each within its field of competence, on the advisability of international measures likely to contribute to assisting States Parties in achieving progress in implementation of the rights recognized in the Covenant.

3. A trust fund shall be established in accordance with the relevant procedures of the General Assembly, to be administered in accordance with the financial regulations and rules of the United Nations, with a view to providing expert and technical assistance to

[290] Annex 1 to Report to the Human Rights Council of the Special Rapporteur on adequate housing as a component of the right to an adequate standard of living, Miloon Kothari, A/HRC/4/18 (7 February 2007) [71]–[73].

States Parties, with the consent of the State Party concerned, for the enhanced implementation of the rights contained in the Covenant, thus contributing to building national capacities in the area of economic, social and cultural rights in the context of the present Protocol.

4. The provisions of the present article are without prejudice to the obligations of each State Party to fulfil its obligations under the Covenant.

Certainly, the jurisdictional limitation in the communications provision in Article 2 of the OP to the Covenant, does not appear to envisage any avenue for individuals (or groups) from one state to submit a communication against another state claiming that by the latter's actions their human rights have been infringed upon.[291] It is, therefore, somewhat optimistic in this regard to argue that because Article 2(1) of the Covenant makes no mention of jurisdiction (but rather does refer to international assistance and cooperation), then thereby there is 'no justification to include a jurisdictional limitation in the text of the Optional Protocol'.[292]

The 2011 Maastricht Principles on Extraterritorial Obligations of States in the area of Economic, Social and Cultural Rights also have little to add in respect of international cooperation and assistance, as their focus is on delineating the extent of the extraterritorial obligations of individual states in the field. But, they do reiterate the various formulations of states' cooperative duties stipulated in relevant human rights instruments (including the ICESCR) and agreements establishing relevant international organizations (see principles 15 to 18 and 32), and they make particular mention of the expectations made of states that require assistance (they have an 'obligation to seek international assistance': principle 34) and states that receive such requests, or are otherwise able to assist (they 'must provide international assistance': principle 33).[293]

The end result is that despite all of these initiatives, efforts and exhortations for more effective international cooperation, the responsibilities of states remain more moral than mandatory. As Margot Salomon puts it, '[i]nsofar as this fact reflects the shortcomings of international law, it must first point to nothing more abstruse than a lack of political will,' which lack, it must be said, invariably marks the difference between the protection of human rights and their denial.[294] And so it is with the right to an adequate standard of living under the Covenant.

[291] Article 2 of the OP states: 'Communications may be submitted by or on behalf of individuals or groups of individuals, under the jurisdiction of a State Party, claiming to be victims of a violation of any of the economic, social and cultural rights set forth in the Covenant by that State Party. Where a communication is submitted on behalf of individuals or groups of individuals, this shall be with their consent unless the author can justify acting on their behalf without such consent.'

[292] As advanced by Christian Courtis and Magdalena Sepúlveda, 'Are Extra-Territorial Obligations Reviewable under the Optional Protocol to the ICESCR' (2009) 27(1) *Nordic Journal of Human Rights* 54, 57.

[293] The Principles are a product of the deliberations of non-state experts and while authoritative in terms of their provenance, are nonetheless merely persuasive in respect of the interpretation of the ICECSR rather than binding, having not been formally endorsed by states.

[294] Margot E. Salomon, 'Deprivation, Causation and the Law of International Cooperation' in Langford et al, *Global Justice, State Duties*, 296.

14

Article 12: The Right to Health

Article 12

1. The States Parties to the present Covenant recognize the right of everyone to the enjoyment of the highest attainable standard of physical and mental health.

2. The steps to be taken by the States Parties to the present Covenant to achieve the full realization of this right shall include those necessary for:

(a) The provision for the reduction of the stillbirth-rate and of infant mortality and for the healthy development of the child;

(b) The improvement of all aspects of environmental and industrial hygiene;

(c) The prevention, treatment and control of epidemic, endemic, occupational and other diseases;

(d) The creation of conditions which would assure to all medical service and medical attention in the event of sickness.

Introduction

The history of the specific provision of a right to health in the Covenant is tied up with its broad-based origins in the Universal Declaration on Human Rights (UDHR), in which the rights to health and an adequate standard of living are conjoined in Article 25.[1] As noted at the beginning of the previous chapter, the two rights were separated soon after the UN Commission on Human Rights began the task of transposing the UDHR into binding international instruments. In that process it was manifestly apparent that the two rights, although evidently conceptually intimate, were of such size and complexity on their own that they warranted separate treatment. The enduring nature of the inter-connections between the right to health and a host of other rights in both the ICESCR and the ICCPR is expressly recognized by the Committee, which declared in General Comment No. 14 on the Right to Health (paragraph 3) that:

3. The right to health is closely related to and dependent upon the realization of other human rights, as contained in the International Bill of Rights, including the rights to food, housing, work, education, human dignity, life, non-discrimination, equality, the prohibition against torture, privacy, access to information, and the freedoms of association, assembly and movement. These and other rights and freedoms address integral components of the right to health.[2]

By the time the texts of individual provisions in the Covenants were being considered by the Commission (as well as the UN General Assembly's Third Committee) in the early-to-mid-1950s, there also existed a newly created international body dedicated to promoting health across the globe which was to have a direct and profound effect on the drafting of the right to life in the Covenant. The World Health Organization (WHO), which had been established in 1946, was provided with a mandate to effect 'the attainment by all peoples of the highest

[1] The operative terms of Article 25 provide that 'everyone has a right to a standard of living adequate for the health and well-being of himself and his family, including food, clothing, housing and medical care'. For the full text of Article 25, see Chapter 13 above.

[2] CESCR, General Comment No. 14 on the right to health, E/C.12/2000/4 (11 August 2000) ('General Comment No. 14'). And further, in General Comment No. 15, E/C.12/2002/11 (12 January 2003), on the right to water, the Committee declared that the rights to health and to an adequate standard of living are 'inextricably linked' to the right to water: at [3].

possible level of health'.[3] This was a much more expansive definition of health than was envisaged in the UDHR, stretching significantly beyond obtaining a standard of living merely 'adequate' for health. Essentially, the WHO was, and is, concerned not just with the prevention and eradication of infectious diseases,[4] but also with the proactive responsibility of promoting health and well-being more generally. In its conception of the right to health within the context of the Covenant, the UN Commission on Human Rights was essentially persuaded by this ambitious perspective of the WHO. But in so doing, there was set in train an ongoing perception that the right to health in the Covenant was striving towards two goals that were not necessarily, or always, compatible.

These are, on the one hand, providing a right to individuals to obtain a certain standard of health and health care (as readily inferred from Article 12(1)), and on the other, imposing an obligation on states to ensure a certain standard of health and health care within the community at large (as stated in Article 12(2)). These dual goals, in turn, reflect the core perspectives of the medical profession and public health regulators respectively. As Audrey Chapman puts it, 'medicine focuses primarily on the health status of the individual, generally in the context of physical (and to a lesser extent mental) illness and disability, [whereas] in contrast, public health is concerned with protecting the health of populations and ensuring conditions in which people can be healthy'. Chapman concludes that over the years '[t]his lack of conceptual clarity has complicated both implementation and monitoring of the right to health',[5] albeit that initiatives such as the scholarly journal *Health and Human Rights*, which began publication in 1994, have provided some means by which to expand awareness and knowledge and reconcile differences in perception and practice.[6]

Defining 'Health' and the 'Right to Health'

In fact, during the UN General Assembly Third Committee's consideration of the draft Article on the right to health, deliberations were split roughly equally between concerns over the extent of an individual's right to health, and deliberations as to how best to articulate the obligations of the state to realize the right. There was considerable debate over the content of the right itself in the Article's

[3] Constitution of the World Health Organization ('WHO Constitution') (adopted 22 July 1946, 14 UNTS 185, entered into force 7 April 1948), Article 1.

[4] As stipulated in the Preamble to the WHO Constitution, which provides that '[h]ealth is a state of complete physical, mental and social well-being and not merely the absence of disease or infirmity'.

[5] Audrey Chapman, 'Core Obligations Related to the Right to Health' in Audrey Chapman and Sage Russell (eds), *Core Obligations: Building a Framework for Economic, Social and Cultural Rights* (Intersentia, Antwerp, 2002), 187.

[6] The journal 'provides an inclusive forum for action-oriented dialogue among human rights practitioners. The journal endeavours to increase access to human rights knowledge in the health field by linking an expanded community of readers and contributors'; and it does so not least by being an open access publication. See Health and Human Rights, 'About HHR' (no date), <http://www.hhrjournal.org/about-hhr/>.

first subparagraph. The Commission on Human Rights' submission originally referred to health as 'a state of complete physical, mental and social well-being,' and that everyone's concomitant right was 'to the enjoyment of the highest attainable standard of health'.[7] It also specifically noted that health was more than 'merely the absence of disease or infirmity'. The Third Committee debated a number of amendments to this provision in terms both of form and substance.

The inclusion in the Commission's submission of a definition of health was considered by some as helpful in clarifying the subject matter to which the right applied. However, for a majority of the Committee the definition was considered to be superfluous and in any case unsatisfactory and incomplete, and as such an amendment moved successfully by Afghanistan and the Philippines (A/C.3/L.589) to remove the reference to what health is (and what it is 'merely' not) was adopted. This left the first subparagraph in its current state comprising a sparse statement of the right to health. However, on the nature of the right itself, there was also discussion. Specifically, it was debated whether the right's guarantee of the 'highest attainable standard' was to be merely in relation to 'physical and mental health' or whether it was also to encompass 'social well-being' (as per the Commission's original version), and 'moral well-being' (as per a further amendment of Afghanistan and the Philippines). In the end, though, neither of these additional 'states of health' was endorsed. Social well-being (and a later sub-amendment of 'social health') were rejected for being amorphous and unclear, and moral well-being was widely considered to be inappropriate for an article concerning health,[8] and so was dropped by the amendment's sponsors before any vote was taken.

In respect of sub-paragraph 2 to the Article, the Committee debated various amendments to the four enumerated 'steps' to be taken by states to realize the right to health, as a consequence of which a number of additions and textual changes were made. These included the insertion of the need to reduce stillbirth rates (in paragraph (a)), and the removal of the requirement for improvement of levels of 'nutrition, housing, sanitation, recreation, economic and working conditions' (in paragraph (b)), as each of these matters was specifically dealt with by other provisions in the Covenant (that is, Articles 6 and 7 on the right to, and conditions of, work, and Article 11 on the right to an adequate standard of living). And while the insertion in paragraph (b) of 'industrial hygiene' might be considered also to be covered by Article 7's guarantee of 'safe and healthy working conditions', it was nonetheless thought by the Committee to be broader in scope and closely aligned to the notion of 'environmental hygiene' as already situated in paragraph (b). Similarly, the inclusion of a specific reference to 'occupational diseases' in paragraph (c) was also considered by some to be already adequately covered by Article 7 on working conditions (and Article 9 on the provision of social security), as well as the phrase 'and other diseases' in paragraph (c) itself.

[7] See UN General Assembly, Draft International Covenant on Human Rights: Report of the Third Committee, A/3525 (9 February 1957), [145].

[8] See, eg, the arguments to that end of the representatives of the Netherlands (Mr Beaufort) and the United Kingdom (Mr Hoare) in UN General Assembly Third Committee, A/C.3/SR.746 (30 January 1957).

However, in moving the amendment, Poland successfully argued that while some countries might indeed have reduced the instance of occupational diseases 'to a minimum', it was the case that 'many other countries... were not so fortunate and [had] workers [that] still required special protection', and so specific mention of such diseases should be made.[9]

Reconciling Public Interests and Private Rights

The matter that—somewhat surprisingly—attracted greatest debate was the suggested amendment advanced by Italy and Uruguay (A/C.3/L.590 and Rev.1) that an additional sub-paragraph 3 be inserted into the Article providing safeguards against forced medical treatment.[10] It was argued that neither Article 4 of the Covenant (which deals with permissible limitations in application of the Covenant's provisions) nor Article 7 of the ICCPR (which prohibits not only torture, cruel and unusual punishment, but also non-consensual medical and scientific 'experimentation') provided sufficient protection in this regard and that therefore the amendment was justified. The principle at issue in this debate concerned where the line is to be drawn between the interests of the individual (to refuse treatment) versus those of the wider community (to impose treatment, such as in compulsory vaccination programmes). Although there was some sympathy and support for the proposal, the significant objections raised against its format ultimately proved fatal to its prospects. The amendment's purported imposition of a duty on 'everyone... to care for his health and to undergo appropriate medical treatment' was considered to be out of place in an instrument that otherwise dealt with the imposition of duties on states (not individuals),[11] and was, further, in apparent contradiction to the individual's right to refuse treatment in the second sentence of the amendment.[12] Mr Juvigny, the French representative, expressed this point in the following terms:

> If the duty of a person to care for his health was to be realised by the adoption of legislative measures, the contradiction between the two parts of the amendment, to which the Chilean representative had drawn attention, was even more striking, because on the one hand the

[9] UN General Assembly Third Committee, A/C.3/SR.747 (30 January 1957), [14] (per Mrs Kowalikowa (Poland)).

[10] The text of the amendment, as revised (A/C.3/L.590/Rev.1) read: '3. Everyone is under a duty to care for his health and to undergo appropriate medical treatment. Nothing in this article may be interpreted as authorizing the compulsory imposition of particular medical treatment, except as provided by law for reasons of public health. The law may not go beyond the limits imposed by respect for the human person'.

[11] UN General Assembly Third Committee, A/C.3/SR.747 (30 January 1957)—as per the arguments of Mr Petrzelka (Czechoslovakia), [8], Mr Hamilton (Australia), [11] and Mr Diaz Casanueva (Chile), [30], and A/C.3/SR.746 (30 January 1957), Mr Juvigny (France), [32]. In addition, Mr Morozov (USSR) pointed out quite correctly that '[t]he fact that a person was accorded a right did not, of course, mean that he was obliged to claim it'; UN General Assembly Third Committee, A/C.3/SR.746 (30 January 1957), [25].

[12] See UN General Assembly Third Committee, A/C.3/SR.746 (30 January 1957), Morozov (USSR), [25].

State was urged to legislate in order to oblige a person to care for his health, and on the other the contrary principle was proclaimed, even though with some reservations.[13]

While the amendment was, in the end, comprehensively rejected,[14] the tension it respresents between public policy and individual rights remains a live issue in the field of health today. Thus, for example, compulsory vaccinations against infectious diseases, or mandatory testing, or even restrictions of peoples' movement may be seen as justifiable and permissible under Article 12(2)(c) and (d), but yet be objected to by individuals invoking their right under Article 12(1), on the ground of their different interpretation of the medical benefits of such treatment. What is more, a raft of other civil and political rights might be claimed against such compulsory treatment, such as religious conviction or cultural belief,[15] freedom of movement[16] and the right to a fair trial.[17]

In response, the Committee has recognized the need for guidance on how best to strike a balance between the competing interests of public policy and private rights, both in its Concluding Observations on states' reports (as indicated in footnotes 16 and 17 to the preceding sentence) and in General Comment No. 14 (2000):

Limitations

28. Issues of public health are sometimes used by States as grounds for limiting the exercise of other fundamental rights. The Committee wishes to emphasize that the Covenant's limitation clause, Article 4, is primarily intended to protect the rights of individuals rather than to permit the imposition of limitations by States. Consequently a State party which, for example, restricts the movement of, or incarcerates, persons with transmissible diseases such as HIV/AIDS, refuses to allow doctors to treat persons believed to be opposed to a government, or fails to provide immunization against the community's major infectious diseases, on grounds such as national security or the preservation of public order, has the burden of justifying such serious measures in relation to each of the elements identified in Article 4. Such restrictions must be in accordance with the law, including international human rights standards, compatible with the nature of the rights protected by the Covenant, in the interest of legitimate aims pursued, and strictly necessary for the promotion of the general welfare in a democratic society.

29. In line with Article 5.1, such limitations must be proportional, i.e. the least restrictive alternative must be adopted where several types of limitations are available. Even where such limitations on grounds of protecting public health are basically permitted, they should be of limited duration and subject to review.

[13] UN General Assembly Third Committee, A/C.3/SR.746 (30 January 1957), Morozov (USSR), [33]. The representative of France added that in specific regard to the question of forced sterilization as an example of compulsory medical treatment—to which the Uruguayan representative specifically referred in moving the amendment—that was a matter that in his opinion fell within the ambit of Article 7 of the ICCPR: at [34].

[14] By thirty-five votes against, four for, and twenty-two abstentions: UN General Assembly, Draft International Covenant on Human Rights: Report of the Third Committee, A/3525 (9 February 1957), [156].

[15] Uruguay, State Report on the Implementation of the ICESCR, E/1990/5/Add.7 (13 September 1991), [201(g)].

[16] CESCR, Summary Record of the 19th Meeting, E/C.12/1987/SR.19 (24 March 1987), [52] (Germany).

[17] CESCR, Summary Record of the 12th Meeting, E/C.12/1988/SR.12 (22 February 1988), [8] (Belarus).

Further, in the same General Comment, the Committee recognizes both a general obligation on states to ensure the 'acceptability' of health facilities, goods and services which 'must be respectful of medical ethics and culturally appropriate' (paragraph 12(c)), and a particular duty in respect of indigenous peoples to 'the right to specific measures to improve their access to health services and care [that] should be culturally appropriate, taking into account traditional preventive care, healing practices and medicines' (paragraph 27). The related matter of informed consent has also received attention in this context with the Special Rapporteur on the right of everyone to the enjoyment of the highest attainable standard of physical and mental health (hereinafter, 'the Special Rapporteur on the right to health') stating that:

Informed consent is not mere acceptance of a medical intervention, but a voluntary and sufficiently informed decision, protecting the right of the patient to be involved in medical decision-making, and assigning associated duties and obligations to health-care providers. Its ethical and legal normative justifications stem from its promotion of patient autonomy, self-determination, bodily integrity and well-being.[18]

The extent of an individual's right to health is also limited by the very nature of right itself. That is, while the right-holder's claim encompasses sufficiency in a host of wider socio-economic determinants of health (including food, sanitation and housing), as well as access to adequate health care facilities and services, such as to ensure the 'highest attainable standards of... health', it is not a claim to assurance of the existential circumstance of being healthy. While, on reflection, this is perhaps an obvious point, it nevertheless needs continually to be made to avoid confusion and manage legitimate expectations. As the Committee notes in paragraph 8 of General Comment No. 14:

8. The right to health is not to be understood as a right to be healthy. The right to health contains both freedoms and entitlements. The freedoms include the right to control one's health and body, including sexual and reproductive freedom, and the right to be free from interference, such as the right to be free from torture, non-consensual medical treatment and experimentation. By contrast, the entitlements include the right to a system of health protection which provides equality of opportunity for people to enjoy the highest attainable level of health.

Such a breadth of causal factors, while necessary to recognize, nevertheless poses significant conceptual and practical challenges. The following extract from a report of the Women and Gender Equity Knowledge Network, established as a sub-branch of the WHO Commission on Social Determinants of Health, which focuses on gender, illustrates this point well in the form of the questions it asks and seeks to answer.

However gender intersects with economic inequality, racial or ethnic hierarchy, caste domination, differences based on sexual orientation, and a number of other social markers. Only focusing on economic inequalities across households can seriously distort our

[18] UN General Assembly, Report of the Special Rapporteur on the right of everyone to the enjoyment of the highest attainable standard of physical and mental health, A/64/272 (10 August 2009), [9].

understanding of how inequality works and who actually bears much of its burdens. Health gradients can be significantly different for men and women; medical poverty may not trap women and men to the same extent or in the same way. The standard work on gradients and gaps tells us easily enough that the poor are worse off in terms of both health access and health outcomes than those who are economically better off. But it does not tell us whether the burden of this inequity is borne equally by different caste or racial groups among the poor. Nor does it tell us how the burden of health inequity is shared among different members of poor households. Are women and men, widows and income-earning youths equally trapped by medical poverty? Are they treated alike in the event of catastrophic illness or injury? When health costs go up significantly, as they have in many countries in recent years, do households tighten the belt equally for women and men? And are these patterns similar across different income quintiles? This poses a challenge for policy to ensure not only equity across but also and simultaneously within households. The right to health is affirmed in the Universal Declaration of Human Rights and is part of the WHO's core principles. This report is grounded in the affirmation of equal and universal rights to health for all people, irrespective of economic class, gender, race, ethnicity, caste, sexual orientation, disability, age or location.[19]

The Socio-Economic Context

It is clear, therefore, that the conditions under which the right to health can be realized are complex and dependent on a wide range of highly variable socio-economic factors. This is especially evident when considering what is meant by states' obligations to ensure 'the highest attainable standard of physical and mental health'. In General Comment No. 14, the Committee notes general conditions necessary to 'promote' leading a healthy life (paragraph 4), and then, further, the unavoidably unique circumstances (both social and individual) that comprise any one person's capacity to attain and maintain health (paragraph 9).

4. In drafting article 12 of the Covenant, the Third Committee of the United Nations General Assembly did not adopt the definition of health contained in the preamble to the Constitution of WHO, which conceptualizes health as 'a state of complete physical, mental and social well-being and not merely the absence of disease or infirmity'. However, the reference in article 12.1 of the Covenant to 'the highest attainable standard of physical and mental health' is not confined to the right to health care. On the contrary, the drafting history and the express wording of article 12.2 acknowledge that the right to health embraces a wide range of socio-economic factors that promote conditions in which people can lead a healthy life, and extends to the underlying determinants of health, such as food and nutrition, housing, access to safe and potable water and adequate sanitation, safe and healthy working conditions, and a healthy environment.[20]

[19] Women and Gender Equity Knowledge Network, 'Unequal, Unfair, Ineffective and Inefficient—Gender Inequity in Health: Why it exists and how we can change it' (Final Report to the WHO Commission on Social Determinants of Health) (September 2007), xii–xiii.

[20] Later, in the same General Comment, the Committee highlights s the importance of these 'underlying determinants of health' by formally recognising them as features of what it calls an 'all inclusive'

...

9. The notion of 'the highest attainable standard of health' in article 12.1 takes into account both the individual's biological and socio-economic preconditions and a State's available resources. There are number of aspects which cannot be addressed solely within the relationship between States and individuals; in particular, good health cannot be ensured by a State, nor can States provide protection against every possible cause of human ill health. Thus, genetic factors, individual susceptibility to ill health and the adoption of unhealthy or risky lifestyles may play an important role with respect to an individual's health. Consequently, the right to health must be understood as a right to the enjoyment of variety of facilities, goods, services and conditions necessary for the realization of the highest attainable standard of health.

The Special Rapporteur on the right to health is equally insistent on stressing the importance of the wider socio-economic determinants of health, and especially the fact that a state's obligations under the right to health encompass much more than merely the provision of health care services.

45. The health of populations, communities and individuals requires more than medical care. Equally important are the social, cultural, economic, political and other conditions that make people need medical care in the first place. A WHO commission is currently studying the social determinants of health, such as gender, poverty and social exclusion.[21] Other determinants of health include access to water, sanitation, nutrition, housing and education.

46. In some quarters, the right to the highest attainable standard of health is narrowly understood to mean a right to medical care. However, this view is inconsistent with international human rights law, which encompasses both medicine and public health. The International Covenant on Economic, Social and Cultural Rights, for example, and the Convention on the Rights of the Child clearly affirm that the right to health is more than access to medical care. Specifically, article 24 of the Convention on the Rights of the Child states that the right to health includes access to nutritious food, clean drinking water, environmental sanitation and so on, as well as medical care. Equating the

definition of the right to health: at [11]. See also Committee on the Elimination of All Forms of Discrimination Against Women, General Recommendation No. 24, A/54/38/Rev.1 at chapter 1 (1999), [7], on Women and Health, which stipulates that 'the full realization of women's right to health can be achieved only when States parties fulfil their obligation to respect, protect and promote women's fundamental human right to nutritional well-being throughout their lifespan by means of a food supply that is safe, nutritious and adapted to local conditions'; Committee on the Rights of the Child, General Comment No. 4, CRC/GC/2003/4 (1 July 2003) ('General Comment No.4'), [12] on Adolescent Health, which calls upon states to develop and implement 'programmes to promote the health and development of adolescents by...[inter alia] the provision of material assistance and support with regard to nutrition, clothing and housing'. Each of these Committees is drawing on the specific formulation of the right to health in their own Convention (both of which are very similar to that in Article 12 of the ICESCR), namely, Article 12 of the Convention on the Elimination of All Forms of Discrimination Against Women (CEDAW) (adopted 18 December 1979, 1249 UNTS 13, entered into force 3 September 1981), and Article 24 of the Convention on the Rights of the Child (CRC) (adopted 20 November 1989, 1577 UNTS 3, entered into force 2 September 1990).

[21] The details of (and an extract from) the final report of the Women and Gender Equity Knowledge Network, a sub-branch of the WHO Commission on Social Determinants of Health, are provided above in n. 19 and accompanying text.

right to health with a right to medical care is a misinterpretation of international human rights law.

47. The right to the highest attainable standard of health is an inclusive right extending not only to timely and appropriate medical care but also to the underlying determinants of health, such as access to safe water and adequate sanitation, an adequate supply of safe food, nutrition and housing, healthy occupational and environmental conditions, access to health-related education and information, including on sexual and reproductive health, and freedom from discrimination. In short, the right to health includes both medical care and the underlying determinants of health.

48. In his reports, the Special Rapporteur has consistently looked at medical care and the underlying determinants of health, including the impact of poverty and discrimination on health. However, he has noticed a definite tendency in some Governments, international organizations and elsewhere to devote a disproportionate amount of attention and resources to medical care at the expense of the underlying determinants of health. This is deeply regrettable because both are fundamental elements of the right to the highest attainable standard of health.[22]

The Committee shares and extends this line of reasoning by recognizing both the Realpolitik of how far many people are from living an adequately healthy life (paragraph 5), as well as the ever-changing nature of the challenges facing the realization of the right to health (paragraph 10).

5. The Committee is aware that, for millions of people throughout the world, the full enjoyment of the right to health still remains a distant goal. Moreover, in many cases, especially for those living in poverty, this goal is becoming increasingly remote. The Committee recognizes the formidable structural and other obstacles resulting from international and other factors beyond the control of States that impede the full realization of article 12 in many States parties.

…

10. Since the adoption of the two International Covenants in 1966 the world health situation has changed dramatically and the notion of health has undergone substantial changes and has also widened in scope. More determinants of health are being taken into consideration, such as resource distribution and gender differences. A wider definition of health also takes into account such socially-related concerns as violence and armed conflict. Moreover, formerly unknown diseases, such as Human Immunodeficiency Virus and Acquired Immunodeficiency Syndrome (HIV/AIDS), and others that have become more widespread, such as cancer, as well as the rapid growth of the world population, have created new obstacles for the realization of the right to health which need to be taken into account when interpreting article 12.

[22] UN General Assembly, Report of the Special Rapporteur on health, A/62/214 (8 August 2007), [45]–[48]. In paragraph 50 of the same report, the Special Rapporteur adds: 'Safe water and adequate sanitation are two integral and closely related underlying determinants which are essential for the realization of the right to the highest attainable standard of health. Inadequate access to water and sanitation can threaten life, devastate health, destroy opportunities, undermine human dignity and cause deprivation.'

In an effort to provide further guidance as to how, where and on what to target health initiatives, the Committee has specified in General Comment No. 14 a set of 'special topics of broad application' that relate to Article 12. Again, the range of these categories underscores the broad scope of the right to health.

Article 12. Special topics of broad application

Non-discrimination and equal treatment

18. By virtue of article 2.2 and article 3, the Covenant proscribes any discrimination in access to health care and underlying determinants of health, as well as to means and entitlements for their procurement, on the grounds of race, colour, sex, language, religion, political or other opinion, national or social origin, property, birth, physical or mental disability, health status (including HIV/AIDS), sexual orientation and civil, political, social or other status, which has the intention or effect of nullifying or impairing the equal enjoyment or exercise of the right to health. The Committee stresses that many measures, such as most strategies and programmes designed to eliminate health-related discrimination, can be pursued with minimum resource implications through the adoption, modification or abrogation of legislation or the dissemination of information. The Committee recalls General Comment No. 3, paragraph 12, which states that even in times of severe resource constraints, the vulnerable members of society must be protected by the adoption of relatively low-cost targeted programmes.

19. With respect to the right to health, equality of access to health care and health services has to be emphasized. States have a special obligation to provide those who do not have sufficient means with the necessary health insurance and health-care facilities, and to prevent any discrimination on internationally prohibited grounds in the provision of health care and health services, especially with respect to the core obligations of the right to health. Inappropriate health resource allocation can lead to discrimination that may not be overt. For example, investments should not disproportionately favour expensive curative health services which are often accessible only to a small, privileged fraction of the population, rather than primary and preventive health care benefiting a far larger part of the population.

Gender perspective

20. The Committee recommends that States integrate a gender perspective in their health-related policies, planning, programmes and research in order to promote better health for both women and men. A gender-based approach recognizes that biological and socio-cultural factors play a significant role in influencing the health of men and women. The disaggregation of health and socio-economic data according to sex is essential for identifying and remedying inequalities in health.

Women and the right to health

21. To eliminate discrimination against women, there is a need to develop and implement a comprehensive national strategy for promoting women's right to health throughout their life span. Such a strategy should include interventions aimed at the prevention and treatment of diseases affecting women, as well as policies to provide access to a full range of high quality and affordable health care, including sexual and reproductive services. A major goal should be reducing women's health risks, particularly lowering rates of maternal mortality and protecting women from domestic violence. The realization of women's right to health requires the removal of all barriers interfering with access to health services, education and

information, including in the area of sexual and reproductive health. It is also important to undertake preventive, promotive and remedial action to shield women from the impact of harmful traditional cultural practices and norms that deny them their full reproductive rights.

Children and adolescents

22. Article 12.2(a) outlines the need to take measures to reduce infant mortality and promote the healthy development of infants and children. Subsequent international human rights instruments recognize that children and adolescents have the right to the enjoyment of the highest standard of health and access to facilities for the treatment of illness. The Convention on the Rights of the Child directs States to ensure access to essential health services for the child and his or her family, including pre- and post-natal care for mothers. The Convention links these goals with ensuring access to child-friendly information about preventive and health-promoting behaviour and support to families and communities in implementing these practices. Implementation of the principle of non-discrimination requires that girls, as well as boys, have equal access to adequate nutrition, safe environments, and physical as well as mental health services. There is a need to adopt effective and appropriate measures to abolish harmful traditional practices affecting the health of children, particularly girls, including early marriage, female genital mutilation, preferential feeding and care of male children. Children with disabilities should be given the opportunity to enjoy a fulfilling and decent life and to participate within their community.

23. States parties should provide a safe and supportive environment for adolescents, that ensures the opportunity to participate in decisions affecting their health, to build life-skills, to acquire appropriate information, to receive counselling and to negotiate the health-behaviour choices they make. The realization of the right to health of adolescents is dependent on the development of youth-friendly health care, which respects confidentiality and privacy and includes appropriate sexual and reproductive health services.

24. In all policies and programmes aimed at guaranteeing the right to health of children and adolescents their best interests shall be a primary consideration.

Older persons

25. With regard to the realization of the right to health of older persons, the Committee, in accordance with paragraphs 34 and 35 of General Comment No. 6 (1995), reaffirms the importance of an integrated approach, combining elements of preventive, curative and rehabilitative health treatment. Such measures should be based on periodical check-ups for both sexes; physical as well as psychological rehabilitative measures aimed at maintaining the functionality and autonomy of older persons; and attention and care for chronically and terminally ill persons, sparing them avoidable pain and enabling them to die with dignity.

Persons with disabilities

26. The Committee reaffirms paragraph 34 of its General Comment No. 5, which addresses the issue of persons with disabilities in the context of the right to physical and mental health. Moreover, the Committee stresses the need to ensure that not only the public health sector but also private providers of health services and facilities comply with the principle of non-discrimination in relation to persons with disabilities.

Indigenous peoples

27. In the light of emerging international law and practice and the recent measures taken by States in relation to indigenous peoples, the Committee deems it useful to identify elements that would help to define indigenous peoples' right to health in order better to enable States with indigenous peoples to implement the provisions contained in article 12 of the Covenant. The Committee considers that indigenous peoples have the right to specific measures to improve their access to health services and care. These health services should be culturally appropriate, taking into account traditional preventive care, healing practices and medicines. States should provide resources for indigenous peoples to design, deliver and control such services so that they may enjoy the highest attainable standard of physical and mental health. The vital medicinal plants, animals and minerals necessary to the full enjoyment of health of indigenous peoples should also be protected. The Committee notes that, in indigenous communities, the health of the individual is often linked to the health of the society as a whole and has a collective dimension. In this respect, the Committee considers that development-related activities that lead to the displacement of indigenous peoples against their will from their traditional territories and environment, denying them their sources of nutrition and breaking their symbiotic relationship with their lands, has a deleterious effect on their health.

Evidently, the economic wealth—of individuals as well as states—is a strong determinant of the potential, if not always the practice, of promoting health. The health consequences of disparities between the rich and the poor were the central concern of the 134 state delegates who met at a conference in Alma-Ata (in the former USSR) in September 1978. The eponymous Declaration they signed at the conclusion of the conference has become something of a talisman of what health care should be striving to achieve, and how the right to health might assist in reaching the goal.

Declaration of Alma-Ata, International Conference on Primary Health Care, Alma-Ata, USSR, 1978 (extracts):

…

II

The existing gross inequality in the health status of the people particularly between developed and developing countries as well as within countries is politically, socially and economically unacceptable and is, therefore, of common concern to all countries.

…

IV

The people have the right and duty to participate individually and collectively in the planning and implementation of their health care.

V

Governments have a responsibility for the health of their people which can be fulfilled only by the provision of adequate health and social measures. A main social target of governments, international organizations and the whole world community in the coming decades should be the attainment by all peoples of the world by the year 2000 of a level of health that will permit them to lead a socially and economically productive life. Primary health care is the key to attaining this target as part of development in the spirit of social justice.

VI

Primary health care is essential health care based on practical, scientifically sound and socially acceptable methods and technology made universally accessible to individuals and families in the community through their full participation and at a cost that the community and country can afford to maintain at every stage of their development in the spirit of self-reliance and self-determination. It forms an integral part both of the country's health system, of which it is the central function and main focus, and of the overall social and economic development of the community. It is the first level of contact of individuals, the family and community with the national health system bringing health care as close as possible to where people live and work, and constitutes the first element of a continuing health care process.

The emphasis on the necessity of political action and on policy planning and implementation is the clear message conveyed in the Declaration. And while it may indeed have been foolhardy or ambitious (or both) to have set a deadline for the attainment of something as difficult and intangible as health for all peoples,[23] these imperatives remain today.

The Political and Legal Imperatives

In General Comment No. 14, the Committee has expanded on what it considers to be the nature of the expectations made of states and the obligations placed upon them. In so doing, as the following extracts indicate, it adopts the classic conceptions of human rights duties under international law generally—that is, to 'respect, protect and fulfil', and to cooperate internationally in the spirit of Article 56 of the UN Charter—as well as the more particular duty to ensure the progressive realization of the rights under the ICESCR.

General legal obligations

30. While the Covenant provides for progressive realization and acknowledges the constraints due to the limits of available resources, it also imposes on States parties various obligations which are of immediate effect. States parties have immediate obligations in relation to the right to health, such as the guarantee that the right will be exercised without discrimination of any kind (art. 2.2) and the obligation to take steps (art. 2.1) towards the full realization of article 12. Such steps must be deliberate, concrete and targeted towards the full realization of the right to health.

31. The progressive realization of the right to health over a period of time should not be interpreted as depriving States parties' obligations of all meaningful content. Rather,

[23] This is what Jonathan Wolff remarked upon, ruefully, as an illustration of 'the dangers of setting targets, even if they are twenty-two years away': Jonathan Wolff, *The Human Right to Health* (W. W. Norton, New York, 2012), 8.

progressive realization means that States parties have a specific and continuing obligation to move as expeditiously and effectively as possible towards the full realization of article 12.

32. As with all other rights in the Covenant, there is a strong presumption that retrogressive measures taken in relation to the right to health are not permissible. If any deliberately retrogressive measures are taken, the State party has the burden of proving that they have been introduced after the most careful consideration of all alternatives and that they are duly justified by reference to the totality of the rights provided for in the Covenant in the context of the full use of the State party's maximum available resources.

33. The right to health, like all human rights, imposes three types or levels of obligations on States parties: the obligations to respect, protect and fulfil. In turn, the obligation to fulfil contains obligations to facilitate, provide and promote. The obligation to respect requires States to refrain from interfering directly or indirectly with the enjoyment of the right to health. The obligation to protect requires States to take measures that prevent third parties from interfering with article 12 guarantees. Finally, the obligation to fulfil requires States to adopt appropriate legislative, administrative, budgetary, judicial, promotional and other measures towards the full realization of the right to health.

…

International obligations

38. In its General Comment No. 3, the Committee drew attention to the obligation of all States parties to take steps, individually and through international assistance and cooperation, especially economic and technical, towards the full realization of the rights recognized in the Covenant, such as the right to health. In the spirit of article 56 of the Charter of the United Nations, the specific provisions of the Covenant (articles 12, 2.1, 22 and 23) and the Alma-Ata Declaration on primary health care, States parties should recognize the essential role of international cooperation and comply with their commitment to take joint and separate action to achieve the full realization of the right to health. In this regard, States parties are referred to the Alma-Ata Declaration which proclaims that the existing gross inequality in the health status of the people, particularly between developed and developing countries, as well as within countries, is politically, socially and economically unacceptable and is, therefore, of common concern to all countries.

39. To comply with their international obligations in relation to article 12, States parties have to respect the enjoyment of the right to health in other countries, and to prevent third parties from violating the right in other countries, if they are able to influence these third parties by way of legal or political means, in accordance with the Charter of the United Nations and applicable international law. Depending on the availability of resources, States should facilitate access to essential health facilities, goods and services in other countries, wherever possible and provide the necessary aid when required. States parties should ensure that the right to health is given due attention in international agreements and, to that end, should consider the development of further legal instruments. In relation to the conclusion of other international agreements, States parties should take steps to ensure that these instruments do not adversely impact upon the right to health. Similarly, States parties have an obligation to ensure that their actions as members of international organizations take due account of the right to health. Accordingly, States parties which are members of international financial institutions, notably the International Monetary Fund, the World

Bank, and regional development banks, should pay greater attention to the protection of the right to health in influencing the lending policies, credit agreements and international measures of these institutions.

40. States parties have a joint and individual responsibility, in accordance with the Charter of the United Nations and relevant resolutions of the United Nations General Assembly and of the World Health Assembly, to cooperate in providing disaster relief and humanitarian assistance in times of emergency, including assistance to refugees and internally displaced persons. Each State should contribute to this task to the maximum of its capacities. Priority in the provision of international medical aid, distribution and management of resources, such as safe and potable water, food and medical supplies, and financial aid should be given to the most vulnerable or marginalized groups of the population. Moreover, given that some diseases are easily transmissible beyond the frontiers of a State, the international community has a collective responsibility to address this problem. The economically developed States parties have a special responsibility and interest to assist the poorer developing States in this regard.

41. States parties should refrain at all times from imposing embargoes or similar measures restricting the supply of another State with adequate medicines and medical equipment. Restrictions on such goods should never be used as an instrument of political and economic pressure. In this regard, the Committee recalls its position, stated in General Comment No. 8, on the relationship between economic sanctions and respect for economic, social and cultural rights.[24]

42. While only States are parties to the Covenant and thus ultimately accountable for compliance with it, all members of society—individuals, including health professionals, families, local communities, intergovernmental and non-governmental organizations, civil society organizations, as well as the private business sector—have responsibilities regarding the realization of the right to health. State parties should therefore provide an environment which facilitates the discharge of these responsibilities.

Of particular note in paragraphs 39 to 42 of the above extract are the references to the obligations of states in relation to relevant non-state actors in the field of health, including as members of the International Monetary Fund (IMF), the World Bank and the regional development banks, and in their regulation (including extra-territorial) of 'third parties' (paragraph 39), and 'the private business sector' (paragraph 42). In regard to the latter, there can be no dispute that states are obligated to ensure that alongside public agencies, private actors within their respective territorial jurisdictions are regulated such as to oblige them to protect and promote the right to health. Less clear is the extent to which states possess similar jurisdictional obligations beyond their territorial boundaries, both in respect of their own (public) agencies and relevant private entities as regards upholding the right to health.

The 'responsibility' or 'accountability' for promoting the right to health extra-territorially may be inferred as much from what Article 12 does not say, as what

[24] In CESCR, General Comment No. 8, E/C.12/1997/8 (12 December 1997), the Committee warned that the imposition of economic sanctions against a state—an increasingly common occurrence—should always take account of the ICESCR.

it does say. The Article makes no mention of jurisdictional or territorial limitations to the duties it imposes on states; rather, it couches such duties in broad terms that permit an interpretation of obligations that stretches beyond territorial boundaries. It talks of the recognition, provision, improvement, prevention and creation of various factors that together denote a system of health care that realizes the right to health. That said, the International Court of Justice (ICJ) made it clear in its Advisory Opinion in the Palestinian Wall case (2004)[25] that a state (Israel) which exercises 'effective control' over a territory not internationally recognized as within its national boundaries (the Occupied Palestinian Territory) is obliged to render to all those within that territory the protections guaranteed under international human rights law.[26] And as, in this case, Israel had ratified both the ICCPR and the ICESCR, the Court concluded that Israel was (and is) obliged to provide protection in respect of all of the rights therein—including the right to health under Article 12 of the ICESCR—according to the specific demands of either Covenant.[27]

Further, when these requirements are read in the context of the umbrella requirement of Article 2(1), that states must 'take steps, individually and through international assistance and co-operation' towards realization of the right, then the contention strengthens that some level of extra-territorial obligation has been imposed upon them.[28] Still, this is short of an express duty actively to assist and cooperate internationally—'taking steps' towards such an end is clearly less definitive—no matter how desirable that end might be. What precisely this amounts to in terms of states' duties remains somewhat unclear, although there appears to be some consensus that states are at least bound by a 'do no harm' principle. That is, in the words of the Maastricht Principles on Extraterritorial Obligations of States in the Area of Economic, Social and Cultural Rights 2012, that 'all States have the obligation to refrain from conduct which nullifies or impairs the enjoyment and exercise of economic, social and cultural rights of persons outside their territories'.[29]

[25] *Legal Consequences of the Construction of a Wall in the Occupied Palestinian Territory (Advisory Opinion)* [2004] ICJ Rep 136.

[26] *Palestinian Wall* case, 180. In establishing this to be the case in the present matter, the Court relied expressly and directly on the deliberation of the Committee on Economic, Social and Cultural Rights on this point in its Concluding Observations regarding the reports submitted by Israel under the Covenant. In particular, the Court highlighted the Committee's disputation of Israel's claim that its obligations did *not* extend to the Occupied Territories on account of the fact that as they were in a state of armed conflict, humanitarian law, and not international human rights law, prevailed there: at 180.

[27] *Palestinian Wall* case, 189, 191–2.

[28] In the *Palestinian Wall* case, the ICJ made clear that, at the very least, such cooperation demands that states do not interfere with the capacities of other states to fulfil their obligations under the international human rights treaties, including the ICESCR, stating that Israel 'is under an obligation not to raise any obstacle to the exercise of such rights in those fields where competence has been transferred to Palestinian authorities': 180.

[29] Maastricht Principles on Extraterritorial Obligations of States in the Area of Economic, Social and Cultural Rights (5 March 2012), Principle 20 ('Direct Interference'). Principle 21 ('Indirect Interference') further asserts that states must refrain from conduct that causes third parties (other states or international organizations) to interfere with another state's fulfilment of its obligations under the ICESCR. A similar negatively couched 'legal responsibility' of states is identified by Judith Bueno de

Notably, the Maastricht Principles also refer to the extra-territorial obligations of states regarding the actions of 'non-state actors' over which they exercise—or might reasonably be expected to exercise—jurisdiction. Thus, mirroring the obligation quoted immediately above, they refer, in Principle 24, to states' duty to 'take necessary measures to ensure that non-State actors... such as private individuals and organisations and transnational corporations and other business enterprises, do not nullify or impair the enjoyment of economic, social and cultural rights'.[30] Further, the Maastricht Principles also refer to states' responsibilities regarding 'the acts and omissions of non-state actors acting on the instructions or under the direction or control of the state' (Principle 12(a)) and in regard to instituting measures not just to prevent human rights abuses by non-state actors, but also 'to hold them to account for any such abuses, and to ensure an effective remedy for those affected' (Principle 27).

Translation of Context and Obligations into Action

Beyond recognizing the broad socio-economic context in which the right to health exists and the spelling out of its attendant legal obligations, the Committee has also formulated a set of broad policy objectives for the guidance of states in their realization of the right. The Committee laid out four 'interrelated and essential elements' of the right to health, in paragraph 12 of General Comment No. 14, while acknowledging that their 'precise application... will depend on the conditions prevailing in a particular State'. We here extract all four, although we will elaborate upon only three ('Availability', 'Accessibility', and 'Quality'), as the fourth ('Acceptability') has, in practice, a narrow application that offers little more than is provided by the other three categories, especially accessibility (in terms of cultural appropriateness and gender and life-cycle sensitivity) and quality (in terms of respect for medical ethics).[31]

Mesquita, Paul Hunt and Rajat Khosla, 'The Human Right Responsibility of International Assistance and Cooperation in Health' in Mark Gibney and Sigrun Skogly (eds), *Universal Human Rights and Extraterritorial Obligations* (University of Pennsylvania Press, Pennsylvania, 2010), at 105.

[30] Principle 24 also refers to Principle 25, which outlines the various purported duties of states regarding their conduct, and their regulation of others' conduct, extraterritorially in the realm of economic, social and cultural rights.

[31] The redundancy of 'acceptability' as a separate category is further borne out by the manner in which the right to health is framed in four other human rights instruments. The words 'acceptable' or 'acceptability' are not used in any of the relevant articles of the CEDAW, the CRC, the Convention on the Elimination of All Forms of Racial Discrimination (ICERD) (adopted 7 March 1966, 660 UNTS 195, entered into force 4 January 1969) or the Convention on the Rights of Persons with Disabilities (CRPD) (adopted 30 March 2007, 2515 UNTS 3, entered into force 3 May 2008). And while the word 'appropriate' is used in each, the context of its employment makes clear that the concerns are with accessibility and/or quality of the health care provided rather than anything peculiarly 'acceptable'. Thus, the focus is entirely on accessibility through non-discrimination in the case of the ICERD (Articles 2 and 5(e)(iv)); mainly so in respect of the CEDAW (Article 12, including a specific reference to save the specific reference to pregnancy and post-natal health care); a mixture of accessibility and quality of care in the CRPD (Article 25, stressing non-discrimination as well as the 'range, quality and standard of free or affordable health care'); and a strong focus on quality in the case of the CRC

General Comment No. 14, paragraph 12 states:

(a) *Availability*. Functioning public health and health-care facilities, goods and services, as well as programmes, have to be available in sufficient quantity within the State party. The precise nature of the facilities, goods and services will vary depending on numerous factors, including the State party's developmental level. They will include, however, the underlying determinants of health, such as safe and potable drinking water and adequate sanitation facilities, hospitals, clinics and other health-related buildings, trained medical and professional personnel receiving domestically competitive salaries, and essential drugs, as defined by the WHO Action Programme on Essential Drugs.

(b) *Accessibility*. Health facilities, goods and services have to be accessible to everyone without discrimination, within the jurisdiction of the State party. Accessibility has four overlapping dimensions:

(i) *Non-discrimination*: health facilities, goods and services must be accessible to all, especially the most vulnerable or marginalized sections of the population, in law and in fact, without discrimination on any of the prohibited grounds.

(ii) *Physical accessibility*: health facilities, goods and services must be within safe physical reach for all sections of the population, especially vulnerable or marginalized groups, such as ethnic minorities and indigenous populations, women, children, adolescents, older persons, persons with disabilities and persons with HIV/AIDS. Accessibility also implies that medical services and underlying determinants of health, such as safe and potable water and adequate sanitation facilities, are within safe physical reach, including in rural areas. Accessibility further includes adequate access to buildings for persons with disabilities.

(iii) *Economic accessibility (affordability)*: health facilities, goods and services must be affordable for all. Payment for health-care services, as well as services related to the underlying determinants of health, has to be based on the principle of equity, ensuring that these services, whether privately or publicly provided, are affordable for all, including socially disadvantaged groups. Equity demands that poorer households should not be disproportionately burdened with health expenses as compared to richer households.

(iv) *Information accessibility*: accessibility includes the right to seek, receive and impart information and ideas concerning health issues. However, accessibility of information should not impair the right to have personal health data treated with confidentiality.

(c) *Acceptability*. All health facilities, goods and services must be respectful of medical ethics and culturally appropriate, i.e. respectful of the culture of individuals, minorities, peoples and communities, sensitive to gender and life-cycle requirements, as well as being designed to respect confidentiality and improve the health status of those concerned.

(Article 24, covering preventive, adequate and informative health care, and in respect of the only (implicit) reference to culture, to take steps towards 'abolishing traditional practices prejudicial to the health of children'). Note further, in respect of indigenous cultural appropriateness, our brief discussion earlier in this chapter under 'The socio-economic context'.

(d) *Quality*. As well as being culturally acceptable, health facilities, goods and services must also be scientifically and medically appropriate and of good quality. This requires, *inter alia*, skilled medical personnel, scientifically approved and unexpired drugs and hospital equipment, safe and potable water, and adequate sanitation.

Using this categorization of essential elements of the right to health (save 'acceptability' as explained), we now expand upon what is, can and must be done to implement the right satisfactorily.

Availability

The foundational feature of any health care system that respects the right to health must clearly be that the appropriate resources, facilities and services are made available in the first place. The matter of availability boils down to addressing the dual questions of whether the state has suitable and sufficient resources, and whether it has the capacity and willingness to utilize them appropriately and effectively.

SUFFICIENCY

Economic, institutional, administrative and skills-based resources are all relevant here, and it is to the maximum of their availability that Article 2(1) of the Covenant is referring when it imposes the obligation on states to achieve 'progressively the full realisation' of all rights in the Covenant. As we established in Chapter 3 on Article 2(1), this is a multilayered and complex matter to understand, let alone to implement and enforce. So, as we see in paragraphs 30, 31 and 32 of General Comment No. 14 (as extracted above), while the Committee recognizes states' 'constraints due to the limits of available resources', there are nonetheless 'various obligations... of immediate effect', such as positively taking steps towards full realization, and doing so in a non-discriminatory manner. And where—invariably (even if regrettably)—retrogressive measures are resorted to, states' parties are burdened with the obligation to justify such measures and to demonstrate that in any event, the maximum available resources are being deployed.

In its Concluding Observations on states' reports, the Committee repeatedly refers to the need for states to improve the availability of and support for health facilities through increases in resource allocations to the sector. More specifically, for example, the Committee has pressed states to increase financial resources allocated to public health programmes;[32] urged states 'to address the scarcity of water problems, in particular the sustainable management of the available water resources' given the grave impact of water scarcity on people's

[32] CESCR, Concluding Observations: Bolivia, E/C.12/1/Add.60 (21 May 2001), [42]; Ecuador, E/C.12/1/Add.100 (7 June 2004), [29]; Georgia, E/C.12/1/Add.83 (19 December 2002), [24]; Uruguay, E/C.12/1/Add.18 (22 December 1997), [10].

health;[33] welcomed the diversion of resources to 'social welfare measures, particularly in the fields of health and education';[34] and queried whether states are striking the most appropriate balance between the providing of funding for public health care systems and regulating the cost of private health schemes.[35] The Committee has also raised concerns about the availability and adequacy of health care resources across a range of issues, including (and particularly) matters that clearly fall within the realm of the states' core obligations as outlined in paragraphs 43 and 44 of General Comment No. 14 (as extracted and discussed below), including: health care facilities for women, especially focusing on sexual and reproductive health;[36] for children;[37] for rural[38] and indigenous[39] communities; and in respect of appropriate provision for mental health care.[40]

To a very significant extent, availability is recognized as being directly related to – indeed causative of - the level of a state's development. The strength of this linkage is such that, as the Special Rapporteur on the right to health puts it, 'securing a certain level of health-related development is a prerequisite for the overall economic development of a country'. Thus, he continues:

For instance, in Africa, it is estimated that the HIV/AIDS pandemic has reduced the economic growth rate by between two to four per cent continent-wide. Similarly, it has been estimated that the long-term negative effects of malaria result in a decrease in gross national product of up to 1.3 per cent in certain affected regions. The importance of particular aspects of health as they relate to poverty, and in turn, development, has also been well documented. For example, securing the sexual and reproductive health of populations has an integral role in eliminating poverty and promoting economic growth, alongside its direct effects on individuals' health. Ensuring access to reproductive services, including family planning, is a vital step in disrupting the 'repetitive cycle' of poverty, inequality and slow economic growth that is perpetuated by limited reproductive choices. It has also been observed that development policies designed to improve economic conditions and living standards of communities can often have unintended effects on health; in particular, they can create additional health risks for vulnerable groups, which is known to compromise the welfare objectives of development policies.

...

[33] CESCR, Concluding Observations: Yemen, E/C.12/1/Add.92 (12 December 2003), [18]–[19], [37] and [38].

[34] CESCR, Concluding Observations: Guatemala, E/C.12/1/Add.3 (28 May 1996), [25].

[35] CESCR, Concluding Observations: Finland, E/C.12/1/Add.52 (1 December 2000), [31].

[36] CESCR, Concluding Observations: Cambodia, E/C.12/KHM/CO/1 (12 June 2009), [19] and [32]; Nepal, E/C.12/1/Add.66 (24 September 2001), [32]–[35] and [55]; Nepal, E/C.12/NPL/CO/2 (16 January 2008), [25]–[26] and [45]–[46].

[37] CESCR, Concluding Observations: Bolivia, E/C.12/1/Add.60 (21 May 2001), [22] and [42]; Bolivia, E/C.12/BOL/CO/2 (8 August 2008), [22] and [35]; Madagascar, E/C.12/MDG/CO/2 (16 December 2009), [29]–[30].

[38] CESCR, Concluding Observations: China, E/C.12/1/Add.107 (13 May 2005), [32], [60]; Uzbekistan, E/C.12/UZB/CO/1 (24 January 2006), [60]; Paraguay, E/C.12/1/Add.1 (28 May 1996), [16] and [28].

[39] CESCR, Concluding Observations: Costa Rica, E/C.12/CRI/CO/4 (4 January 2008), [26]–[27]; Australia, E/C.12/2000/21 (31 August 2000), [380]; Australia, E/C.12/AUS/CO/4 (12 June 2009), [28].

[40] CESCR, Concluding Observations: China, E/C.12/1/Add.58 (21 May 2001), [20] and [45]; China, E/C.12/1/Add.107 (13 May 2005), [35] and [64]; Latvia, E/C.12/LVA/CO/1 (7 January 2008), [29] and [54].

6. As this role of development policies in creating or exacerbating 'diseases of poverty', alongside health problems associated with industrialization, has become increasingly acknowledged, more holistic approaches to development have been sought out, and the potential for the right to health to inform and guide development practice has increased. Indeed, the ability of people to enjoy an adequate level of health is today broadly recognized as a key development goal in itself.[41]

While the intertwining of the development and the right to health in this way has been one of the vital components in the thinking behind the human-rights-based approach to development,[42] it is unclear whether and how this has impacted on the availability of health-related resources. What has become clear, however, is that economic development alone—no matter how advanced—is not sufficient to address the human rights issues related to health.

It was this concern, and in particular with the states' and others' obligations in respect of their establishment, maintenance and advancement of public health systems, that was the driving force behind the 1986 Ottawa Charter for Health Promotion. In its focus on industrialized nations, the Charter emphasizes the 'positive' aspects of health—that is, living healthy lifestyles (and not simply disease- and injury-free ones), and what 'social and personal resources, as well as physical capacities' need to be invested in achieving that goal. The Charter adopts an expanded perspective on the prerequisites of a healthy life, including a 'stable eco-system, sustainable resources, and social justice, and equity', as well as the more standard necessities of food, shelter, education, income and freedom from violence. It also adopts a holistic view of how we—that is everyone (states, non-state organizations, communities and individuals)—are to 'create supportive environments' that promote health:

Our societies are complex and interrelated. Health cannot be separated from other goals. The inextricable links between people and their environment constitutes the basis for a socioecological approach to health. The overall guiding principle for the world, nations, regions and communities alike, is the need to encourage reciprocal maintenance—to take care of each other, our communities and our natural environment. The conservation of natural resources throughout the world should be emphasized as a global responsibility.

Changing patterns of life, work and leisure have a significant impact on health. Work and leisure should be a source of health for people. The way society organizes work should help create a healthy society. Health promotion generates living and working conditions that are safe, stimulating, satisfying and enjoyable.

Systematic assessment of the health impact of a rapidly changing environment—particularly in areas of technology, work, energy production and urbanization—is essential and must be followed by action to ensure positive benefit to the health of the public. The

[41] Human Rights Council, Report of the Special Rapporteur on the right of everyone to the enjoyment of the highest attainable standard of physical and mental health, A/HRC/17/25 (12 April 2011), [4] and [6].

[42] As expressed in the Report of the Special Rapporteur, per n. 41 above, [7]–[13]; Benjamin Mason Fox Meier and Ashley M. Fox, 'Development as Health: Employing the Collective Right to Development to Achieve the Goals of the Individual Right to Health' (2008) 30(2) *Human Rights Quarterly* 259.

protection of the natural and built environments and the conservation of natural resources must be addressed in any health promotion strategy.[43]

It is true that the Charter's philosophical view of health promotion is not easily directly translated into the legal obligations such as are provided under Article 12 of the Covenant, but as Paul Hunt (a former Special Rapporteur on the right to health) and Gunilla Backman have argued, it played its part in the 'evolutionary process' of the understanding of 'the connections between public health and human rights' in the relatively early days of the quest.[44]

WILLINGNESS

Although obviously essential, the adequacy of resources addresses only half of the availability question. The capacity and willingness of a state to direct them effectively and efficiently towards the promotion and protection of the right to health is another matter altogether. Such willingness hangs largely on the commitment and competence of a state's political, administrative and legal apparatus. For even with constrained resources, the expectation is that states must nonetheless take steps to realize the right, at least to the extent that the core obligations (as mentioned above) demand. For those states whose resources are more abundant, therefore, the expectations are correspondingly higher. The capacity or 'willingness' to deliver, in other words, is an irreducible commitment, whereas it is acknowledged that resource capacity is limited to (widely) varying degrees. Thus, as the Committee proclaims in its 2007 Statement on the obligation to take steps to the maximum available resources:

4. The 'availability of resources', although an important qualifier to the obligation to take steps, does not alter the immediacy of the obligation, nor can resource constraints alone justify inaction. Where the available resources are demonstrably inadequate, the obligation remains for a State party to ensure the widest possible enjoyment of economic, social and cultural rights under the prevailing circumstances. The Committee has already emphasized that, even in times of severe resource constraints, States parties must protect the most disadvantaged and marginalized members or groups of society by adopting relatively low-cost targeted programmes.[45]

Further, the Committee has made clear that as a matter of principle, 'a state that is unwilling to use the maximum of its available resources for the realization of the right to health is in violation of its obligations under article 12'.[46]

Classically, the articulation of states' obligations as to intention in the human rights context is achieved by way of the familiar framework that they have duties

[43] Ottawa Charter for Health Promotion (Ottawa, 21 November 1986), Part 2 ('What Health Action Means').

[44] Paul Hunt and Gunilla Backman, 'Health Systems and the Right to the Highest Standard of Health' in Andrew Clapham, Mary Robinson, Claire Mahon and Scott Jerbi (eds), *Realizing the Right to Health* (Rüffer & Rub, Zurich, 2009), 42.

[45] CESCR, An Evaluation of the Obligation to Take Steps to the 'Maximum of Available Resources' under an Optional Protocol to the Covenant, E/C.12/2007/1 (10 May 2007), [4].

[46] CESCR, General Comment No. 14, [47].

to 'respect, protect, fulfil' the relevant right. Thus, the Committee stipulates in General Comment No. 14 how this framework applies in respect of the right to health under what it calls 'specific legal obligations':

34. In particular, States are under the obligation to respect the right to health by, inter alia, refraining from denying or limiting equal access for all persons, including prisoners or detainees, minorities, asylum seekers and illegal immigrants, to preventive, curative and palliative health services; abstaining from enforcing discriminatory practices as a State policy; and abstaining from imposing discriminatory practices relating to women's health status and needs. Furthermore, obligations to respect include a State's obligation to refrain from prohibiting or impeding traditional preventive care, healing practices and medicines, from marketing unsafe drugs and from applying coercive medical treatments, unless on an exceptional basis for the treatment of mental illness or the prevention and control of communicable diseases. Such exceptional cases should be subject to specific and restrictive conditions, respecting best practices and applicable international standards, including the Principles for the Protection of Persons with Mental Illness and the Improvement of Mental Health Care. In addition, States should refrain from limiting access to contraceptives and other means of maintaining sexual and reproductive health, from censoring, withholding or intentionally misrepresenting health-related information, including sexual education and information, as well as from preventing people's participation in health-related matters. States should also refrain from unlawfully polluting air, water and soil, e.g. through industrial waste from State-owned facilities, from using or testing nuclear, biological or chemical weapons if such testing results in the release of substances harmful to human health, and from limiting access to health services as a punitive measure, e.g. during armed conflicts in violation of international humanitarian law.

35. Obligations to protect include, inter alia, the duties of States to adopt legislation or to take other measures ensuring equal access to health care and health-related services provided by third parties; to ensure that privatization of the health sector does not constitute a threat to the availability, accessibility, acceptability and quality of health facilities, goods and services; to control the marketing of medical equipment and medicines by third parties; and to ensure that medical practitioners and other health professionals meet appropriate standards of education, skill and ethical codes of conduct. States are also obliged to ensure that harmful social or traditional practices do not interfere with access to pre- and postnatal care and family-planning; to prevent third parties from coercing women to undergo traditional practices, e.g. female genital mutilation;[47] and to take measures to protect all vulnerable or marginalized groups of society, in particular women, children,

[47] See WHO Fact Sheet No. 241 on Female Genital Mutilation (2012), <http://www.who.int/mediacentre/factsheets/fs241/en/>, which declares that, in the WHO's opinion, whatever the cultural demands or pressures regarding the practice, it yields no health benefits, only harm. It states: 'FGM has no health benefits, and it harms girls and women in many ways. It involves removing and damaging healthy and normal female genital tissue, and interferes with the natural functions of girls' and women's bodies. Immediate complications can include severe pain, shock, haemorrhage (bleeding), tetanus or sepsis (bacterial infection), urine retention, open sores in the genital region and injury to nearby genital tissue. Long-term consequences can include: recurrent bladder and urinary tract infections; cysts; infertility; an increased risk of childbirth complications and newborn deaths; the need for later surgeries. For example, the FGM procedure that seals or narrows a vaginal opening needs to be cut open later to allow for sexual intercourse and childbirth. Sometimes it is stitched again several times, including after childbirth, hence the woman goes through repeated opening and closing procedures, further increasing and repeated both immediate and long-term risks.'

adolescents and older persons, in the light of gender-based expressions of violence. States should also ensure that third parties do not limit people's access to health-related information and services.

36. The obligation to fulfil requires States parties, inter alia, to give sufficient recognition to the right to health in the national political and legal systems, preferably by way of legislative implementation, and to adopt a national health policy with a detailed plan for realizing the right to health. States must ensure provision of health care, including immunization programmes against the major infectious diseases, and ensure equal access for all to the underlying determinants of health, such as nutritiously safe food and potable drinking water, basic sanitation and adequate housing and living conditions. Public health infrastructures should provide for sexual and reproductive health services, including safe motherhood, particularly in rural areas. States have to ensure the appropriate training of doctors and other medical personnel, the provision of a sufficient number of hospitals, clinics and other health-related facilities, and the promotion and support of the establishment of institutions providing counselling and mental health services, with due regard to equitable distribution throughout the country. Further obligations include the provision of a public, private or mixed health insurance system which is affordable for all, the promotion of medical research and health education, as well as information campaigns, in particular with respect to HIV/AIDS, sexual and reproductive health, traditional practices, domestic violence, the abuse of alcohol and the use of cigarettes, drugs and other harmful substances. States are also required to adopt measures against environmental and occupational health hazards and against any other threat as demonstrated by epidemiological data. For this purpose they should formulate and implement national policies aimed at reducing and eliminating pollution of air, water and soil, including pollution by heavy metals such as lead from gasoline. Furthermore, States parties are required to formulate, implement and periodically review a coherent national policy to minimize the risk of occupational accidents and diseases, as well as to provide a coherent national policy on occupational safety and health services.[48]

These specifications of what a state should provide are admirably detailed and helpful in providing guidance to states, individuals and the Committee itself as to the type and levels of actions states must take and services they must provide. At the same time, the range of these specifications is vast—stretching from areas of health care that require particular attention (for women, sexual and reproductive health, and mental health), through the promotion of healthy living as well as the regulation of health-impacting activities (such as environmental pollution and the use of weaponry) and other social and economic 'underlying determinants of health' as discussed earlier, to appropriate education and training of health care providers and professionals, the provision of suitable health information and guidance to the general public. Perhaps the most abiding message of these obligations is, however, the insistence on what might best be called good governance. States

[48] Under this heading of 'General Obligations', the Committee includes a further paragraph in General Comment No. 14 (paragraph 37) on the matter of the obligation to fulfil. In so doing, it purports to parse this obligation still further, into obligations to fulfil (facilitate), to fulfil (provide) and to fulfil (promote). In point of fact, however, this somewhat indulgent and confusing exercise adds nothing to the obligations articulated in [34]–[36], and it is for this reason that we have chosen not to include this paragraph in the extracted material above.

must recognize the right to health in their political and legal systems, are required to institute national health care policies of universal application, establish appropriate institutions to manage and dispense health care, adequately fund and otherwise ensure affordability of health care, and regulate third-party health providers, especially following privatization or the establishment of public-private partnerships in the sector. The latter point regarding the widening scope of health care providers and other contributors to the health care system is now very much a central feature of what comprises the scope and interests of the health sector in many countries. Thus, for example, a WHO report in 2007 entitled 'Everybody's Business', which sought to 'clarify and strengthen the WHO's role in health systems in a changing world',[49] was as keen to recognize the growing importance of the non-public sector, as it was to continue to encourage more investment in health from public funds. The report stated that 'while more resources are needed, government ministers are also looking for ways of doing more with existing resources. They are seeking innovative ways of harnessing and focusing the energies of communities, non-governmental organizations (NGOs) and the private sector.'[50]

Funding responsibilities

At the root of the old and new initiatives for making health care facilities more readily available, the matter of funding is always to be found. Thus, later in the same report, the WHO spends time canvassing, comparing and contrasting the various options not only for increasing funding, but also using existing resources more efficiently and effectively.

There is growing interest in the array of domestic financing mechanisms that can be drawn upon to move towards universal coverage, including tax-based funding, social health insurance, community or micro-insurance, micro-credit and conditional cash transfers. All of these mechanisms make major demands on managerial capacity. On the other hand, where providers depend largely on out-of-pocket payments for their income, there is over-provision of services for people who can afford to pay, and lack of care for those who cannot.

Much of the increase in investment by external partners has focused on particular diseases or health conditions. The global health landscape has been transformed in the last ten years with the emergence of multiple, billion-dollar global health partnerships such as the Global Fund and the GAVI Alliance. These have helped generate growing political support for increasing access to care and treatment for many critical health conditions, and have also thrown a spotlight on longstanding systems issues such as logistics, procurement and staffing. Moreover the growing demands for provision of lifelong treatments highlights the need for policies that protect people from catastrophic spending.

'Scaling-up' is not just about increasing spending

It is increasingly recognized that scaling-up is not just about increasing investment. Close scrutiny of what is involved points to a set of health systems challenges, most of which are equally pertinent in higher as well as low-income settings.

[49] WHO, 'Everybody's Business: Strengthening Health Systems to Improve Health Outcomes' (2007), v.

[50] WHO, 'Everybody's Business', v.

Countries both rich and poor are looking for ways of doing more with existing resources. In many health systems, existing health workers could be more productive if they had access to critical material and information resources, clearly defined roles and responsibilities, better supervision and an ability to delegate tasks more appropriately. Changes in overall intervention-mix and skill mix could create efficiencies.

In many instances, extending coverage or quality cannot be achieved simply by replicating existing models for service delivery or focusing only on the public sector. In addition, decision makers seek innovative ways to engage with communities, NGOs and the private sector. Promising experiences, such as working with informal providers to expand TB care, the social marketing of bed-nets or contracting with NGOs, need to be shared. It is important to take note of what did and did not work in the past. Careful analysis is needed about which local initiatives are genuinely amenable for replication and expansion. Multiple barriers cannot all be addressed or overcome at once. Judgements have to be made between pushing to quickly get specific outcomes and building systems and institutions. Managing the tension between saving lives and livelihoods and starting the process of re-building the state is a particular challenge in fragile states.[51]

The Special Rapporteur on the right to health has also specifically addressed the question of finance in a 2012 Report in which he identified three particular issues as crucial to understanding and improving the funding of the sector and thereby 'ensuring universal access to good quality health facilities, goods and services'.[52] These three issues were: the raising of funds, the pooling of funds and their allocation. In so doing, the Special Rapporteur assessed both the challenges and opportunities of balancing private and public funding sources, as well as the questions of access to, and delivery of, international funding assistance. After first underlining the fundamental importance of 'adequate, equitable and sustainable financing for health' (paragraph 1), and the states' obligation to ensure as much, the Report proceeds in paragraphs 2 to 14 as follows:

2. The contemporary landscape of health financing is characterized by persistent deficits and recurring challenges in financing health systems throughout the world.

Public spending on health is too low in many States because of low budget prioritization for health and, in some cases, the unavailability of adequate public funds in absolute terms. Deficits in governance are also central to many States' failure to finance health adequately. Widespread corruption, tax loopholes and weak tax administration, characterized by high rates of tax evasion, often diminish States' capacity to raise revenues and allocate adequate public funds towards health. Many States are overly dependent on out-of-pocket payments from users and international funding to finance their health systems. International funding for health, however, is unpredictable and unsustainable, as the recent financial crisis has demonstrated, and out-of-pocket payments for health goods and services disproportionately impact on the poor, who must pay considerably larger proportions of their income on health care than wealthy patients. As a result, poor households often experience financial catastrophe and impoverishment due to out-of-pocket payments, resulting in a chilling effect that discourages many from seeking health care in the first place.

[51] WHO, 'Everybody's Business', 8.

[52] UN General Assembly, Interim Report of the Special Rapporteur on the right of everyone to the enjoyment of the highest attainable standard of physical and mental health, A/67/302 (13 August 2012), Summary.

3. The right to health approach to health financing recognizes that an appropriate balance must be achieved between public and private financing for health, as well as between public and private administration of health facilities, goods and services. However, the global trend towards privatization in health systems poses significant risks to the equitable availability and accessibility of health facilities, goods and services, especially for the poor and other vulnerable or marginalized groups. In many cases, privatization has led to increased out-of-pocket payments for health goods and services, disproportionate investment in secondary and tertiary care sectors at the expense of primary health care, and increased disparity in the availability of health facilities, goods and services among rural, remote and urban areas.

4. The right to heath approach to health financing is especially critical in the light of these global trends and challenges in financing for health. It provides a framework to ensure the prioritization of health in State budgets, strengthened by the active and informed participation of affected individuals and communities in the formulation, implementation, monitoring and evaluation of health budgets. The approach requires the equitable allocation of health funds and resources and recognizes the essential role international assistance plays in ensuring that adequate funds and technical resources are available for health globally, particularly for low income States. The approach emphasizes the importance of prioritizing funding for primary health care in striking a balance among financing the primary, secondary and tertiary care sectors. Finally, the right to health approach recognizes the resource divide among rural, remote and urban areas and requires States to equitably allocate health funds and resources to rural and remote areas to ensure the availability and accessibility of good quality health facilities, goods and services in those areas based on the principle of non-discrimination.

II. Conceptual framework

5. Health financing is a central component of the right to health and instrumental to full realization of the right to health as articulated in article 12 of the International Covenant on Economic, Social and Cultural Rights, elaborated by General Comment No. 14 of the Committee on Economic, Social and Cultural Rights. Numerous other international and regional instruments, such as the Declaration of Alma-Ata adopted at the International Conference on Primary Health Care in 1978 and the Abuja Declaration on HIV/AIDS, Tuberculosis and Other Related Infectious Diseases, adopted by the African Union in 2001, have also recognized the centrality of health financing to the stability and effectiveness of health systems and meeting international development goals. States therefore have an obligation to ensure adequate, equitable and sustainable funding for health. The primary concerns of health financing are: how States ensure that adequate funds are available for health and the sources from which they raise those funds; how the funds are pooled; and how funds and resources are allocated within health systems to ensure universal access to good quality health facilities, goods and services. The right to health approach provides a conceptual framework through which each of these key concerns may be addressed.

A. Ensuring adequate funds and prioritizing health financing

6. States have an obligation under the right to health to ensure that adequate funds are available for health and to prioritize financing for health in their budgets. That obligation is a necessary prerequisite to the realization of nearly every aspect of the right to health and required under States' obligation to make use of maximum available resources to ensure full realization of the right (General Comment No. 14, para. 33). As elaborated in General

Comment No. 14, the right to health includes numerous entitlements, such as the availability of good quality health facilities and access to essential medicines, which require positive outlays by the State. Adequate public funding is necessary in order to realize these positive entitlements. Insufficient expenditure or misallocation of public resources may result in the lack of enjoyment of the right to health by individuals or groups, particularly the vulnerable or marginalized, and amount to a violation of the State's obligation to fulfil the right to health (General Comment No. 14, para. 52).

7. In order to make use of maximum available resources, States must therefore take all necessary steps to raise adequate revenue and mobilize resources for health and ensure that health financing is correspondingly prioritized in national and subnational budgets. Budget prioritization requires States to set aside a significant portion of general government expenditures towards spending on health and prioritize health alongside other core funding commitments, such as spending on education, social security and defence. States have a positive obligation in this regard to facilitate the active and informed participation of affected individuals and communities in the formulation, implementation, monitoring and evaluation of health budgets. States should also ensure transparency in the formulation, implementation, monitoring and evaluation of budgets for health. In order to ensure accountability for the implementation of national and subnational health budgets and related laws and policies, States should also develop and implement mechanisms that allow or provide for independent auditing and oversight of those instruments.

8. The obligation to prioritize funding or health in State budgets is closely linked to the principle of progressive realization, which establishes a specific and continuing obligation for States to move as expeditiously and effectively as possible towards the full realization of the right to health of all persons, without discrimination and taking into account constraints due to the limits of available resources (General Comment No. 14, paras. 30 and 31, and General Comment No. 3, para. 9). In order to facilitate progressive realization of the right to health for all persons, States should make use of the maximum available funds and resources to realize the right to health, which requires successfully raising funds and ensuring that they are allocated to health through budget prioritization. States unwilling to utilize the maximum of their available resources towards realization of the right to health are in violation of their obligations under the right (General Comment No. 14, para. 47).

9. The obligation to ensure that adequate funds are available for health and to prioritize financing for health should be informed by the core obligations of the right to health (General Comment No. 14, paras. 43–45). Core obligations are non-derogable and represent the minimum essential levels which States are required to meet in order to be in compliance with the right to health. Core obligations include positive and negative entitlements and address distributional and equity concerns. Positive entitlements, such as the obligation to ensure access to basic shelter, housing and sanitation, and an adequate supply of safe and potable water, often require States to utilize significant funds and resources towards their realization. Core obligations that establish negative entitlements and address distributional concerns, such as the obligation to ensure equitable allocation of, and non-discriminatory access to, good quality health facilities, goods and services assume the existence of such facilities, goods and services, and thus also require significant financial outlays from States. States should therefore ensure that adequate funds are available for health and prioritize financing for health in order to meet at least these core obligations of the right to health. In this sense, core obligations establish a funding baseline below which States would be considered in violation of their obligations under the right to health.

B. Pooling and allocation of health funds and resources

10. The obligation to ensure the equitable allocation of health facilities, goods and services for all persons without discrimination is a core obligation under the right to health. The right to access good quality health facilities, goods and services on a non-discriminatory basis, particularly for vulnerable or marginalized groups, including, among others, ethnic, racial, religious and sexual minority groups, women, children and the poor, constitutes an additional core obligation for States. In order to meet these core obligations under the right to health, States must ensure the equitable allocation of health funds and resources towards achieving universal access to good quality health facilities, goods and services, in accordance with the principle of non-discrimination and with special attention to the needs of vulnerable or marginalized populations. Inequitable allocation of health funds and resources may lead to indirect discrimination within health systems, particularly with respect to vulnerable or marginalized groups who often lack the social and political means to challenge the inequitable allocation of public resources (General Comment No. 14, para. 19).

11. Equitable allocation of funds and resources for health may be achieved through the pooling of health funds collected through prepayment schemes. Pooling allows for the cross-subsidization of financial risks associated with health care among different groups across large populations and the transfer of health funds from the rich to the poor and the healthy to the sick. Cross-subsidization of financial risks thus protects vulnerable or marginalized groups, such as the poor, from catastrophic health expenditures and ensures access to good quality health facilities, goods and services that may otherwise be financially inaccessible. Pooling of funds for health in order to facilitate the cross-subsidization of health and financial risks is thus an essential method by which States may ensure the equitable allocation of health funds and resources as required under the right to health.

12. General Comment No. 14 of the Committee on Economic, Social and Cultural Rights recognizes that investments in health should not disproportionately favour expensive curative care services, which are often accessible only to a small fraction of the population, over primary and preventive health care, which benefit a far larger part of the population. Primary health-care services are generally less costly than secondary and tertiary care, which by definition require health-care workers with specialized training, sophisticated diagnostic equipment and significant physical health infrastructure. Investment in primary health care is thus more cost efficient in the long run because it prevents illness and promotes general health, which reduces the need for more costly secondary and tertiary care. [...] The resulting savings may be reinvested in the health system, possibly in the form of additional health-care subsidies for the poor. The right to health thus requires an efficient allocation of health funds and resources between primary, secondary and tertiary care sectors, with an emphasis on primary health care.

13. States should allocate health funds and resources towards ensuring good quality health facilities, goods and services are available and easily accessible for rural and remote populations. The significant disparity in health outcomes among rural and remote populations and their urban counterparts in many States is well documented.[...] This is due to a number of factors, including inadequate investment in health infrastructure and the lack of qualified health workers in rural and remote areas. This problem is compounded by the fact that rural and remote populations often comprise vulnerable or marginalized groups, such as the poor, ethnic and racial minorities, and indigenous populations, who tend to be poorer

than those in urban areas.[. . .] In accordance with the right to health approach, States must therefore ensure health funds and resources are equitably allocated among rural, remote and urban areas.

C. International assistance

14. The right to health approach recognizes the essential role that international assistance plays in ensuring that adequate funds and resources are available for health globally, particularly in developing States. In the spirit of Article 56 of the Charter of the United Nations, articles 2 (1), 12, 22 and 23 of the International Covenant on Economic, Social and Cultural Rights, and the Declaration of Alma-Ata, States should recognize the essential role of international cooperation and comply with their commitments to take joint and separate action to achieve full realization of the right to health globally. In this regard, the Declaration of Alma-Ata proclaims that gross inequalities in health among various groups, particularly between developed and developing countries, but within countries as well, is politically, socially and economically unacceptable and must be of common concern to all States. The right to health approach requires States to cooperate internationally in order to ensure the availability of sustainable international funding for health. This includes a responsibility to pool funds internationally from compulsory contributions by States, based upon their ability to pay, and allocate funds to States, based upon their need, in order to achieve cross-subsidization of resources for health globally.

Accessibility

The adequacy of health funding also has a direct impact on accessibility of the right to health, although the emphasis here is on the capacity of the users of the health system to be able to afford to access the services available. Their capacity to do so depends not just on affording any point-of-service fees and the costs of medicine, but also on the costs they may incur in reaching the service in the first place (for example, travel, food and accommodation costs), and even on the costs related to their securing access to the fundamental social determinants to a basically healthy life, such as adequate food and water, sanitation, housing and clothing, as well as physical safety and security. Such costs, even when relatively small, can nevertheless present very real barriers to access for many, especially the poorest who often have the greatest health needs.

Aside from this effective discrimination against the poor, access can also critically be denied through direct and indirect discrimination against particular sectors of society(whether poor or not), as is too often the case with women and children, certain ethnic or indigenous minorities, certain castes or socially marginalized groups (based on sexuality or on health status (for example, persons with disabilities or suffering from HIV/AIDs)) and immigrants.

The significance of the denial of access, even where health services are available, to the quest to realize the right to health is reflected in the Committee's stipulation of what it considers to be the 'core obligations' of states regarding the right to health in General Comment No. 14, which, as the extracts below demonstrate, focus on the matters of accessibility, provision and distribution.

Core Obligations

43. In General Comment No. 3, the Committee confirms that States parties have a core obligation to ensure the satisfaction of, at the very least, minimum essential levels of each of the rights enunciated in the Covenant, including essential primary health care. Read in conjunction with more contemporary instruments, such as the Programme of Action of the International Conference on Population and Development, the Alma-Ata Declaration provides compelling guidance on the core obligations arising from article 12. Accordingly, in the Committee's view, these core obligations include at least the following obligations:

(a) To ensure the right of access to health facilities, goods and services on a non-discriminatory basis, especially for vulnerable or marginalized groups;

(b) To ensure access to the minimum essential food which is nutritionally adequate and safe, to ensure freedom from hunger to everyone;

(c) To ensure access to basic shelter, housing and sanitation, and an adequate supply of safe and potable water;

(d) To provide essential drugs, as from time to time defined under the WHO Action Programme on Essential Drugs;

(e) To ensure equitable distribution of all health facilities, goods and services;

(f) To adopt and implement a national public health strategy and plan of action, on the basis of epidemiological evidence, addressing the health concerns of the whole population; the strategy and plan of action shall be devised, and periodically reviewed, on the basis of a participatory and transparent process; they shall include methods, such as right to health indicators and benchmarks, by which progress can be closely monitored; the process by which the strategy and plan of action are devised, as well as their content, shall give particular attention to all vulnerable or marginalized groups.

44. The Committee also confirms that the following are obligations of comparable priority:

(a) To ensure reproductive, maternal (pre-natal as well as post-natal) and child health care;

(b) To provide immunization against the major infectious diseases occurring in the community;

(c) To take measures to prevent, treat and control epidemic and endemic diseases;

(d) To provide education and access to information concerning the main health problems in the community, including methods of preventing and controlling them;

(e) To provide appropriate training for health personnel, including education on health and human rights.[53]

[53] It has been suggested that 'these core obligations reflect the actual practice of very many states at their domestic law level, and may be regarded as part of customary international law or even as general principles of law in the sense of Article 38(1)(c) of the Statute of the International Court of Justice': Eibe Riedel, 'The Human Right to Health: Conceptual Foundations' in Clapham et al, *Realizing the Right to Health*, 32. As far as we are aware, however, such arguments have not been raised, let alone accepted before any international tribunal or domestic superior court.

And once again the Committee underscores the imperative that those states which are able (namely the richer states) ought to render assistance by way both of bilateral and multilateral means, to other (mainly poorer) states to enable them to fulfil these core obligations:

45. For the avoidance of any doubt, the Committee wishes to emphasize that it is particularly incumbent on States parties and other actors in a position to assist, to provide 'international assistance and cooperation, especially economic and technical' which enable developing countries to fulfil their core and other obligations indicated in paragraphs 43 and 44 above.

The insistence on 'equity', 'non-discrimination' and accessibility to 'everyone' in these core obligations reiterates the focus on combatting discrimination expressed by the Committee earlier in General Comment No. 14 (paragraphs 18 to 27) in which it referred to 'Special topics of broad application', as extracted and discussed above under 'The socio-economic context'. The Special Rapporteur has also picked a number of these topics for further attention, including persons with mental disabilities, the health concerns of the elderly, and a broad swathe of issues covering sexual orientation, sex workers and sexual, reproductive and maternal health.

REGARDING MENTAL DISABILITIES

Thus, for example, relatively early in his tenure as the Special Rapporteur on the right to health, Paul Hunt issued a report (in 2005) on persons with mental disabilities who constitute, he noted, 'a group that is among the most neglected, marginalized and vulnerable' in almost every society.[54] Recognizing the size, gravity and complexity of the task of securing the highest attainable standard of mental health, he sets out the freedoms and entitlements that are owed to people with mental disabilities, as well as the specific expectations regarding accessibility to adequate and appropriate health care services.[55]

6. One in every four persons will suffer from a mental disorder at some stage in his or her life. Moreover, the incidence of such disorders is increasing. Today, about 450 million people around the world suffer from mental or neurological disorders, or from psychosocial problems. Very few of them are receiving treatment, care and support—and if they are, it is often seriously inappropriate. Mental and behavioural disorders are estimated to account for 12 per cent of the global burden of disease, yet the mental health budget of most countries is less than 1 per cent of their total health expenditure. Mental health care and support services are often not covered by health insurance. More than 40 per cent of countries have no mental health policy and over 30 per cent have no mental health programme. Over 90 per cent of countries have no mental health policy that includes children and adolescents. In short, mental health is among the most grossly neglected elements of the right to health.

[54] Commission on Human Rights, Report of the Special Rapporteur on the right of everyone to the enjoyment of the highest attainable standard of physical and mental health, E/CN.4/2005/51 (11 February 2005), Summary.

[55] Report of the Special Rapporteur, per n. 54 above, [6]–[13]. The same report also expands on three mental disability issues that demand particular attention, namely, intellectual disability, the right to community integration, and consent to treatment: [76]–[90].

7. Persons with intellectual disability are among the most neglected—the most 'invisible' in our communities. Consistent with this neglect, there are no estimates for the burden of intellectual disability, but what evidence there is suggests it is substantial. Intellectual disability can place severe personal, economic and social burdens on both individuals and their families.

8. Where mental health care and support services are available, users are vulnerable to violations of their human rights within these settings. This is particularly true in segregated service systems and residential institutions, such as psychiatric hospitals, institutions for people with intellectual disabilities, nursing homes, social care facilities, orphanages, and prisons.

9. The Special Rapporteur has received numerous accounts of the long-term, inappropriate institutionalization of persons with mental disabilities in psychiatric hospitals and other institutions where they have been subjected to human rights abuses, including: rape and sexual abuse by other users or staff; forced sterilizations; being chained to soiled beds for long periods of time, and, in some cases, being held inside cages; violence and torture; the administration of treatment without informed consent; unmodified use (i.e. without anaesthesia or muscle relaxants) of electro-convulsive therapy (ECT); grossly inadequate sanitation; and a lack of food. In one European country last year, 18 patients at a psychiatric hospital died, from causes including malnutrition and hypothermia.

10. While abuse is particularly rife in large psychiatric hospitals and other residential institutions, there is also increasing information about human rights violations sustained by persons with mental disabilities in community-based facilities. As countries move to community-based care and support, violations in this context will inevitably become more numerous unless appropriate safeguards are introduced.

11. Also alarming is the high rate of persons with mental disabilities, as well as the high rate of suicides, in prisons. In many cases, persons with severe mental disabilities who have not committed a crime, or who have committed only a minor offence, are misdirected towards prison rather than appropriate mental health care or support services. Prison conditions—such as overcrowding, lack of privacy, enforced isolation and violence—tend to exacerbate mental disabilities. However, there is often little access to even rudimentary mental health care and support services. Recent jurisprudence testifies to the vulnerabilities of persons with mental disabilities in detention to the violation of a range of their human rights.

12. Other groups also face particular vulnerabilities. For example, women with mental disabilities are especially vulnerable to forced sterilization and sexual violence, a violation of their sexual and reproductive health rights. Ethnic and racial minorities often face discrimination in access to, and treatment in, mental health care and support services. Indigenous populations are frequently ignored, with no specialist development of psychiatric and support services despite acute needs that are manifest in increasing suicide rates and overrepresentation in high-security mental health facilities.

13. Mental disabilities are common in all countries and may have a dramatic impact on the lives of individuals and their families. In addition to sometimes distressing limitations, stigmatization of various conditions often leads to discrimination against those affected—and this in turn may lead to their marginalization. It is this interaction between personal and societal limitations that gives rise to disability, and often denies those

affected equal opportunities to enjoy a wide range of human rights and fundamental freedoms, including the rights to education, work, recognition as a person before the law, privacy, social security, adequate housing, adequate nutrition, and liberty. Where such disability-based stigma compounds discrimination on other grounds, such as gender, race and ethnicity, those affected are particularly vulnerable to violations of their human rights.

The fact that the enormity of the problem of inadequate health care for mentally disabled people is so often unknown is due, to a significant degree, to the denial or neglect of their freedoms and entitlements under the right to health. As such, the Special Rapporteur continues in the same report:

Entitlements

42. The right to health includes an entitlement to a system of health protection, including health care and the underlying determinants of health, which provides equality of opportunity for people to enjoy the highest attainable standard of health. Crucially, care and support services—as well as medical attention—play a vital role in ensuring the health and dignity of persons with mental disabilities.

43. States should take steps to ensure a full package of community-based mental health care and support services conducive to health, dignity, and inclusion, including medication, psychotherapy, ambulatory services, hospital care for acute admissions, residential facilities, rehabilitation for persons with psychiatric disabilities, programmes to maximize the independence and skills of persons with intellectual disabilities, supported housing and employment, income support, inclusive and appropriate education for children with intellectual disabilities, and respite care for families looking after a person with a mental disability 24 hours a day. In this way, unnecessary institutionalization can be avoided.

44. Scaling up interventions to ensure equality of opportunity for the enjoyment of the right to health will require training adequate numbers of professionals, including psychiatrists, clinical psychologists, psychiatric nurses, psychiatric social workers, occupational therapists, speech therapists, behavioural therapists, as well as carers, in order to work towards the care and full integration of individuals with mental disabilities in the community. General practitioners, and other primary care providers, should be provided with essential mental health-care and disability sensitization training to enable them to provide front-line mental and physical health care to persons with mental disabilities.

45. As well as an entitlement to health care, the right to health includes an entitlement to the underlying determinants of health, including adequate sanitation, safe water and adequate food and shelter. Persons with mental disabilities are disproportionately affected by poverty, which is usually characterized by deprivations of these entitlements. Also, the conditions in psychiatric hospitals, as well as other institutions used by persons with mental disabilities, are often grossly inadequate from this point of view.[56]

In respect of the specific matter of the accessibility of health care services for people with mental disabilities, the Special Rapporteur's Report enumerates a set

[56] Report of the Special Rapporteur, as per n. 54 above, [42]–[45].

of essential provisions that States must effect, including and especially combatting discrimination, if the right to health is to be realized for this sector of society:

46(b) *Accessibility* has four dimensions. First, health-care facilities, goods and services, including support services, must be accessible physically and geographically, in other words, in safe physical and geographical reach of persons with disabilities. This has especially important implications for community-based care. Second, health facilities, goods and services, including psychotropic drugs, must be economically accessible (i.e. affordable) to users. Mental health care and support services are often neither subsidized by the State, nor covered by health insurance, meaning that they can be unaffordable to most of those who need it. Third, mental and physical health-care services should also be accessible without discrimination on any of the prohibited grounds. States may need to take affirmative action to ensure equality of access for all individuals and groups, such as ethnic and racial minorities in need of care and support. States should ensure that persons with disabilities get the same level of medical care within the same system as other members of society, and do not face discrimination on the basis of presumptions of their quality of life and potential. A fourth dimension concerns the accessibility of information. This entitlement is often denied to persons with mental disabilities because they are wrongly judged to lack the capacity to make or participate in any decisions about their own treatment and care. Information on health (and other) matters, including diagnosis and treatment, must be accessible to persons with mental disabilities, and the parents of children with mental disabilities…

Non-discrimination and equality

51. International human rights law proscribes discrimination in access to health care and the underlying determinants of health, and to the means for their procurement, on grounds including physical and mental disability, and health status.

52. Various forms of stigma and discrimination continue to undermine the realization of the right to health for persons with mental disabilities. For example, they often face discrimination in access to general health-care services, or stigmatizing attitudes within these services, which may dissuade them from seeking care in the first place. Stigma and discrimination within the community, schools and workplaces can also act as a barrier to persons seeking social support, diagnosis and treatment.

53. While the majority of families provide deeply caring and supportive environments for family members with mental disabilities, in some cases stigma may lead to inappropriate institutionalization of persons with mental disabilities against their will, including sometimes in institutions which have inadequate facilities for treatment and care, and where their dignity and other human rights are at risk.

54. Decisions to isolate or segregate persons with mental disabilities, including through unnecessary institutionalization, are inherently discriminatory and contrary to the right of community integration enshrined in international standards. Segregation and isolation in itself can also entrench stigma surrounding mental disability…

55. A lack of accurate information about mental disability, as well as inadequate support services, often fuels these decisions. The dissemination of information about mental disability, and the human rights of persons with disabilities, is an important strategy for combating stigma and discrimination. States have an obligation 'to provide education and

access to information concerning the main health problems in the community'. The provision of human rights and disability awareness training for health workers, as well as staff in related sectors, is also essential for ensuring equal access to care, and the respect of the human rights and dignity of persons with mental disabilities within care.

56. Under international human rights law, States not only have an obligation to prohibit discrimination, they also have a positive obligation to ensure equality of opportunity for the enjoyment of the right to health by persons with mental disabilities. For example, as well as being entitled to the same health-care services as other members of society, the right to health gives rise to an entitlement of persons with mental disabilities to have access to, and to benefit from, those medical and social services which promote their independence and autonomy, prevent further disabilities and support their social integration.

57. This may demand special measures for particular groups. For example, States should ensure that adolescents with mental disabilities or psychosocial problems have access to necessary services that are sensitive to their needs. The Committee on the Rights of the Child has stressed the particular importance of paying particular attention to, among others, the special needs relating to the sexuality of adolescents with disabilities.

58. Inappropriate resource allocation can lead to inadvertent discrimination. Crucially, the small budgetary allocations that most countries accord to mental health is a significant barrier to persons with mental disabilities enjoying their right to health on the basis of equality of opportunity.[57]

REGARDING SEXUAL, REPRODUCTIVE AND MATERNAL HEALTH

The accessibility of health care services and facilities in the area of sexual, reproductive and maternal health is another matter of enormous size and importance. No fewer than three of the Millennium Development Goals directly concern this field—promoting maternal health (MDG 5) and the health of children (MDG 4), and combatting HIV/AIDs and other diseases (MDG 6)[58]—and while progress is being made towards each of these,[59] the global situation still remains grave:

Preventable and treatable injuries and diseases are overwhelming in sub-Saharan Africa, the Indian subcontinent, and other impoverished areas of the world. In a single year, nearly 7 million children die before age five, close to 300,000 women die in pregnancy or childbirth, and approximately 4 million people died of AIDS, malaria, or tuberculosis. By 2020, 70% of deaths in the developing world will be from non-communicable diseases. Life expectancy in sub-Saharan Africa is 56 years, almost a quarter-century less than in high-income countries. Billions of people still lack access to fundamental human needs. In 2010, 870 million people were suffering from chronic hunger, 780 million people lacked

[57] Report of the Special Rapporteur, as per n. 54 above, [42]–[45].

[58] To which list one might add, as noted by the Special Rapporteur in his 2004 Report on sexual and reproductive health, the goals to tackle extreme poverty (MDG 1) and promote gender equality (MDG 3), which bear on the underlying determinants of health: Commission on Human Rights, Report of the Special Rapporteur on the right of everyone to the enjoyment of the highest attainable standard of physical and mental health, E/CN.4/2004/49 (16 February 2004), [8].

[59] See UN, Millennium Development Goals Report (New York, 2013), 4, which notes 'remarkable gains' in respect of combatting diseases; 'big gains' in respect of children's health, and declining maternal mortality ratios. Overall, however, it adds that 'progress in many areas is far from sufficient'.

access to clean water, and 2.5 billion people did not have access to proper sanitation facilities. A woman in sub-Saharan Africa is nearly 100 times more likely to die in pregnancy or childbirth during the course of her lifetime than a woman in a developed country, while a child born in Africa is 18 times more likely to die before she reaches age five than a child born in a high-income country.[60]

At an International Conference on Population and Development held in Cairo in 1994, certain landmark statements on, and definitions of, sexual and reproductive health were adopted which stressed the importance of couples and individuals to have access to adequate family planning advice, assistance and medical support without discrimination or coercion. The corresponding sections of the resultant Cairo Declaration were considered to be so significant and still relevant by the Special Rapporteur that he quoted them in full in his 2004 report on the subject:

7.2. Reproductive health is a state of complete physical, mental and social well-being and not merely the absence of disease or infirmity, in all matters relating to the reproductive system and to its functions and processes. Reproductive health therefore implies that people are able to have a satisfying and safe sex life and that they have the capability to reproduce and the freedom to decide if, when and how often to do so. Implicit in the last condition are the right of men and women to be informed and to have access to safe, effective, affordable and acceptable methods of family planning of their choice, as well as other methods of their choice for regulation of fertility which are not against the law, and the right of access to appropriate health-care services that will enable women to go safely through pregnancy and childbirth, and provide couples with the best chance of having a healthy infant. In line with the above definition of reproductive health, reproductive health care is defined as the constellation of methods, techniques and services that contribute to reproductive health and well-being by preventing and solving reproductive health problems. It also includes sexual health, the purpose of which is the enhancement of life and personal relations, and not merely counselling and care related to reproduction and sexually transmitted diseases.

7.3. Bearing in mind the above definition, reproductive rights embrace certain human rights that are already recognized in national laws, international human rights documents and other consensus documents. These rights rest on the recognition of the basic right of all couples and individuals to decide freely and responsibly the number, spacing and timing of their children and to have the information and means to do so, and the right to attain the highest standard of sexual and reproductive health. It also includes their right to make decisions concerning reproduction free of discrimination, coercion and violence, as expressed in human rights documents. In the exercise of this right, they should take into account the needs of their living and future children and their responsibilities towards the community. The promotion of the responsible exercise of these rights for all people should be the fundamental basis for government- and community-supported policies and programmes in the area of reproductive health, including family planning.[61]

[60] As noted by the Joint Action and Learning Initiative on National and Global Responsibilities for Health, 'About JALI and a Framework Convention on Global Health' (no date), <http://www.jalihealth.org/about/index.html>.

[61] Commission on Human Rights, Report of the Special Rapporteur on the right of everyone to the enjoyment of the highest attainable standard of physical and mental health, E/CN.4/2004/49 (16 February 2004), [18], quoting relevant paragraphs of Organisation of Islamic Cooperation, Cairo Declaration on Human Rights in Islam (5 August 1990). See also the same Special Rapporteur Report at [19], in which it cites, and adds to, similar sentiments as expressed in the Beijing Platform for Action (15 September 1995), as adopted at Fourth World Conference on Women in Beijing.

While this was, and remains, a statement of what ought to be, the situation in the field is, as the Special Rapporteur notes later in the same report, often very different and challenging:

14. Many of the numerous obstacles to sexual and reproductive health are interrelated and entrenched. They operate at different levels: clinical care, the level of health systems, and the underlying determinants of health. In addition to biological factors, social and economic conditions play a significant role in determining women's sexual and reproductive health. The low social status of girls and women frequently contribute to their sexual and reproductive ill health. Many women experience violence during pregnancy, which may give rise to miscarriage, premature labour and low birth weight. Some traditional views about sexuality are obstacles to the provision of sexual and reproductive health services, including reliable information, and these views have an especially damaging impact upon adolescents. Poverty is associated with inequitable access to both health services and the underlying determinants of health. Too often, improvements in public health services disproportionately benefit those who are better off.

His concern in this 2004 Report was therefore to underline the relevant entitlements under the right to health:

28. The right to health includes an entitlement to a system of health protection, including health care and the underlying determinants of health, which provides equality of opportunity for people to enjoy the highest attainable level of health. For example, women should have equal access, in law and fact, to information on sexual and reproductive health issues.

29. Thus, States have an obligation to ensure reproductive health and maternal and child health services, including appropriate services for women in connection with pregnancy, granting free services where necessary. More particularly, States should improve a wide range of sexual and reproductive health services, including access to family planning, pre- and post-natal care, emergency obstetric services and access to information. The Special Rapporteur urges all duty-holders also to ensure access to such vital health services as voluntary testing, counselling and treatment for sexually transmitted infections, including HIV/AIDS, and breast and reproductive system cancers, as well as infertility treatment.[62]

The states' obligations in this regard also encompass a prohibition against the criminalization of certain sexual or reproductive behaviour or services rendered, as such action invariably negatively impacts on the capacity of affected persons to access adequate and appropriate healthcare. In a 2011 report on the subject, the Special Rapporteur notes that '[c]riminal laws penalizing and restricting induced abortion are the paradigmatic examples of impermissible barriers to the realization of women's right to health and must be eliminated, [because] [t]hese laws infringe women's dignity and autonomy by severely restricting decision-making by women in respect of their sexual and reproductive health'.[63]

[62] Commission on Human Rights, Report of the Special Rapporteur on the right of everyone to the enjoyment of the highest attainable standard of physical and mental health, E/CN.4/2004/49 (16 February 2004), [28]–[29].

[63] UN General Assembly, Report of the Special Rapporteur on the right of everyone to the enjoyment of the highest attainable standard of physical and mental health, A/66/254 (3 August 2011), [21]. The report goes on to examine in detail the right to health implications of criminalization of abortion or related actions: at [21]–[43].

In respect of the related issue of access to maternal health care, the Special Rapporteur added in another report,[64] commentary on the implications of the right to health for the responsibility of states to reduce rates of maternal mortality. That is, both as to expectations made of states regarding the health care system itself:

13. The right to the highest attainable standard of health entitles women to services in connection with pregnancy and the post-natal period, and to other services and information on sexual and reproductive health. These entitlements encompass the key technical interventions for the prevention of maternal mortality, including access to a skilled birth attendant, emergency obstetric care, education and information on sexual and reproductive health, safe abortion services where not against the law, and other sexual and reproductive health-care services.

And also, of the wider determinants of adequate health:

18. The right to health is not just a right to health care, but an entitlement to other social, economic, cultural and political determinants of health. These include participation in health-related decision-making processes, information on sexual and reproductive health, literacy, nutrition, non-discrimination and gender equality. The majority of these determinants have a direct influence on access to the health services that are essential for preventing maternal mortality. Some, such as nutrition, can be a direct cause of maternal mortality.

Two further areas of discrimination that inhibit access to health care services and facilities addressed by the Special Rapporteur have been those of: older persons; and the criminalization of same-sex conduct, sexual orientation and gender identity.

ACCESS ISSUES FOR OLDER PERSONS

After observing that 'the world population is ageing at a steady and significant pace' and that as regards the realization of the right to health (among many other matters), this constitutes 'a harbinger of a quiet demographic revolution',[65] the Special Rapporteur sounds a note of warning over the current and growing crisis of older persons' access to adequate health care worldwide.

7. …It owes much to the significant gains achieved in many areas which have substantially increased longevity but will have far-reaching and unpredictable consequences for all countries, developed and developing alike. A rapidly ageing population presents significant challenges for the global community, in a world that is already affected by various social, economic, cultural and political challenges. The immediate consequences of longer life expectancy include increases in the prevalence of chronic and non-communicable diseases and disabilities, which, if unaddressed, could place significant burdens on health systems, strain pension and social security systems, increase demand for primary health care and put pressure on the availability and affordability of long-term care.

[64] UN General Assembly, Report of the Special Rapporteur on the right of everyone to the enjoyment of the highest attainable standard of physical and mental health on maternal health, A/61/338 (13 September 2006).

[65] UN General Assembly, Report of the Special Rapporteur on the right of everyone to the enjoyment of the highest attainable standard of physical and mental health on older persons, A/HRC/18/37 (4 July 2011), [5] and [7], respectively.

8. Developing countries will be predominantly affected by the resulting epidemiological transition, when non-communicable diseases amongst older persons increase. The broader population will however continue to struggle with communicable diseases, particularly infectious diseases and other illnesses related to poverty. Developing age-friendly services and settings, and promotion of health care and preventive medicine among older persons will strengthen the efforts of developing countries to deal with the complications of chronic and terminal non-communicable illnesses. In order to address the challenge adequately, it is essential for States to prepare themselves to meet the needs of older persons, train health professionals in old-age care, and formulate sustainable policies for long-term care.[66]

Reiterating the specific reference to the protection of the health rights of older persons in paragraph 25 of General Comment No. 14 (as extracted above), and the Committee's General Comment No. 6 (1995) which examines in detail the economic, social and cultural rights of the elderly more generally, the Special Rapporteur nevertheless stresses 'their vulnerability to discrimination and exclusion'. In terms of securing their access to adequate health facilities, goods and services, therefore, he continues (in paragraph 25 of the report) to say that this:

...includes physical, financial and information components. Older persons may be unable to access health care because of the location of services or their limited physical mobility. Poverty may also exacerbate older persons' inability to access healthcare, particularly where social security does not exist. Finally, information accessibility refers to the right to seek, receive and impart information regarding health issues. With regard to older persons, it means that health-related information should be tailored to suit their needs and communicated to them in an appropriate, comprehensible manner allowing them to make fully informed decisions about their health condition and treatment.

ACCESS ISSUES FOR SEX WORKERS, SEXUAL ORIENTATION AND GENDER IDENTITY

The criminalization of certain activities related to sexual conduct, orientation and identity has significant negative consequences on access to adequate health services for affected persons. Often resulting from—and further entrenching—social stigmatization of these groups, such laws marginalize these members of society's access to health care and tend to justify their ill-treatment or neglect.

In a 2010 Report that addressed these issues together, Anand Grover, the second holder of the post of Special Rapporteur on the right to health, noted the similar detrimental effects of criminalization and stigmatization of both same-sex relationships and sex workers.[67] In respect of the former:

22. Criminalization may not be the sole reason behind stigma, but it certainly perpetuates it, through the reinforcement of existing prejudices and stereotypes. Same-sex conduct was

[66] UN General Assembly, Report of the Special Rapporteur, per previous footnote, [7]–[8].

[67] UN General Assembly, Report of the Special Rapporteur on the right of everyone to the enjoyment of the highest attainable standard of physical and mental health, A/HRC/14/20 (27 April 2010), [22], [24] and [27].

long considered a psychiatric disorder; until recently, the world's major professional psychological classification system retained homosexuality as a psychological disorder, which speaks to how deeply this stigma was embedded.

23. Stigmatization prevents legislative and policymaking institutions from adequately addressing health-related matters in communities that are especially vulnerable to the infringement of the enjoyment of the right to health. Where same-sex conduct is illegal, sexual orientation may be treated as a problem that needs to be corrected, ignored or used to legitimize violence directed towards these individuals. Attempts to 'cure' those who engage in same-sex conduct are not only inappropriate, but have the potential to cause significant psychological distress and increase stigmatization of these vulnerable groups.

And in respect of sex workers:

27. Sex workers remain subject to stigma and marginalization, and are at significant risk of experiencing violence in the course of their work, often as a result of criminalization. As with other criminalized practices, the sex-work sector invariably restructures itself so that those involved may evade punishment. In doing so, access to health services is impeded and occupational risk increases. Basic rights afforded to other workers are also denied to sex workers because of criminalization, as illegal work does not afford the protections that legal work requires, such as occupational health and safety standards.

ACCESS TO ESSENTIAL MEDICINES

Over the past twenty years or so, the question of access to essential medicines has grown to become a matter of intense interest and debate within the field of health and beyond. One WHO report estimates that there are some 2 billion people worldwide who lack access to essential medicines.[68] The matter is in fact as complex as it is significant, involving a matrix of competing interests that range from those who would benefit from the medicine and the pressure on public authorities to ensure that access to such medicines is secured (or at least not denied), to the commercial and intellectual property interests of the pharmaceutical corporations who research and develop the drugs in the first place and the concomitant interests of government regulators to ensure the safety and effectiveness of the drugs produced. Deep in the heart of this matrix lies the right to health.

One might consider the 'right' of adequate access to essential medicines to be 'a derivative right from the rights to health and life',[69] and thereby constitute a matter of acute need and a topic of especial importance. In fact, the derivation is as much drawn from a more diffuse source within the ICESCR—namely, Article 15 on the right to benefit from scientific progress and its applications and products.[70] In particular, sub-paragraphs 1(b) and (c) of Article 15 mark out two of the most important sides in the right to health debate over access to essential medicines.

[68] WHO, 'WHO Medicines Strategy: Countries at the Core, 2004–07' (2004), 3.

[69] This position is advanced in Stephen Marks, 'Access to Essential Medicines as a Component of the Right to Health' in Clapham et al, *Realizing the Right to Health*, 94.

[70] See Chapter 17 in this volume.

That is, where Article 15(1)(b) reads: '...the right of everyone...(b) to enjoy the benefits of scientific progress and its applications', it is clearly referring to the states' public interest needs to protect and promote community health at large. While, on the other hand, Article 15(1)(c)'s proclamation on '...the right of everyone...(c) to benefit from the protection of the moral and material interests resulting from any scientific...production of which he is the author', is concerned to protect the interests of innovators and manufacturers of drugs—that is, essentially, pharmaceutical companies. Stephen Marks characterizes this 'apparent contradiction' as the '"right" of pharmaceutical companies to earn a profit from the drugs they develop by setting prices that render medicines inaccessible to the destitute sick' versus the '"right" of those destitute sick to benefit from the development of the new drugs'.[71] 'The way out of this dilemma', Marks suggests:

> ...is to distinguish intellectual property rights from human rights and consider them a temporary monopoly established for the valid social purpose of encouraging scientific invention and artistic creation. In other words, an IPR [intellectual property right] is a legally protected interest of a lower order than a human right, which implies a superior moral and legal claim.[72]

The Committee on Economic, Social and Cultural Rights has framed the problem as a balancing exercise, but with, in the end, a clear bias towards human rights. In its General Comment No. 17 (2005) on the right of everyone to benefit from the protection of the moral and material interests resulting from any scientific, literary or artistic production of which he or she is the author (Article 15, paragraph 1 (c), of the Covenant), the Committee counsels that the moral and material interests enshrined in Article 15 'cannot be isolated from the other rights recognized in the Covenant'. States are 'obliged to strike an adequate balance between their obligations under Article 15, paragraph 1(c), on one hand, and under the other provisions of the Covenant, on the other hand, with a view to promoting and protecting the full range of rights guaranteed in the Covenant'.[73] In the present context, these 'other provisions' include not only the right to 'enjoy the benefits' under Article 15(1)(b), but also the right to health under Article 12. Placing this specific matter in the broader context of intellectual property rights versus human rights debate, the Committee continues:

> 35. ...In striking this balance, the private interests of authors should not be unduly favoured and the public interest in enjoying broad access to their productions should be given due consideration. States parties should therefore ensure that their legal or other regimes for the protection of the moral and material interests resulting from one's scientific, literary or artistic productions constitute no impediment to their ability to comply with their core obligations in relation to the rights to food, health and education, as well as to take part in cultural life and to enjoy the benefits of scientific progress and its applications, or any other right enshrined in the Covenant. Ultimately, intellectual property is a social product and has a social function. States parties thus have a duty to prevent unreasonably

[71] Marks, 'Access to Essential Medicines', 87. [72] Marks, 'Access to Essential Medicines', 87.
[73] CESCR, General Comment No. 17, E/C.12/GC/17 (12 January 2006) ('General Comment No. 17'), [35].

high costs for access to essential medicines, plant seeds or other means of food production, or for schoolbooks and learning materials, from undermining the rights of large segments of the population to health, food and education.[74]

In a similar vein, the UN Millennium Development Goals Gap Taskforce Reports have also consistently approached the matter from a public health perspective, prioritizing access to medicines in the poorest and most deprived nations and communities, while being careful not to deny valid corporate interest. So, for example, in its 2011 Report, the Taskforce stresses the importance of generic medicines (ie those produced outside the normal restrictions of the patent-holder) in offering 'the potential to achieve equivalent health outcomes at lower cost, provided their quality is assured',[75] and while acknowledging the significant steps some pharmaceutical companies have taken towards differential pricing of their products and innovate research ventures focusing on developing medicines to combat diseases common in poor states, it also urges companies greatly to expand their 'disclosure of information in key areas such as marketing and promotional activities, lobbying policies and practices, and intellectual property and competition policies, all of which could have an impact on access to and rational use of medicines'.[76]

Unsurprisingly, the WHO also takes a public-health-oriented approach to this balancing act in its definition of essential medicines or drugs, which it declares 'are those that satisfy the health care needs of the majority of the population; they should therefore be available at all times in adequate amounts and in the appropriate dosage forms, and at a price that individuals and the community can afford'.[77] Similarly, in a resolution adopted in 2001, the UN Commission on Human Rights sought to stress the imperative that states take concerted and effective action to combat pandemic diseases with all the means at their disposal, including where privately sourced. The resolution, in part, provides that the Commission:

1. Recognizes that access to medication in the context of pandemics such as HIV/AIDS, tuberculosis and malaria is one fundamental element for achieving progressively the full realization of the right of everyone to the enjoyment of the highest attainable standard of physical and mental health;

…

3. Also calls upon States to develop and implement national strategies, in accordance with applicable international law, including international agreements acceded to, in order progressively to realize access for all to prevention-related goods, services and information as well as access to comprehensive treatment, care and support for all individuals infected and affected by pandemics such as HIV/AIDS, tuberculosis and malaria;

[74] CESCR, General Comment No. 17, [35]. Also, earlier in the same General Comment, the Committee underlines its unambiguous view of the superiority of human rights claims when it proclaims that 'in contrast to human rights, intellectual property rights are generally of a temporary nature, and can be revoked, licensed or assigned to someone else': at [2].

[75] Millennium Development Goal Gap Task Force ('MDG Gap Task Force'), 'The Global Partnership for Development: Time to Deliver' (2011), 54.

[76] MDG Gap Task Force, 'The Global Partnership for Development', 58.

[77] WHO Expert Committee, Ninth Report: The Use of Essential Drugs (WHO Technical Report Series No. 895, Geneva, 2000), <http://apps.who.int/medicinedocs/en/d/Js2281e/#Js2281e>.

…

5. Affirms the importance of public health interests in both pharmaceutical and health policies;

6. Calls upon States to pursue policies, in accordance with applicable international law, including international agreements acceded to, which would promote:

(a) The availability, in sufficient quantities, of pharmaceutical products and medical technologies used to treat pandemics such as HIV/AIDS, tuberculosis and malaria or the most common opportunistic infections that accompany them;

(b) The accessibility and affordability for all without discrimination, including the most vulnerable or socially disadvantaged groups of the population, of pharmaceutical products or medical technologies used to treat pandemics such as HIV/AIDS, tuberculosis, malaria or the most common opportunistic infections that accompany them;

(c) The assurance that pharmaceutical products or medical technologies used to treat pandemics such as HIV/AIDS, tuberculosis, malaria or the most common opportunistic infections that accompany them, irrespective of their sources and countries of origin, are scientifically and medically appropriate and of good quality;

7. Calls upon States, at the national level, on a non-discriminatory basis, in accordance with applicable international law, including international agreements acceded to:

(a) To refrain from taking measures which would deny or limit equal access for all persons to preventive, curative or palliative pharmaceutical products or medical technologies used to treat pandemics such as HIV/AIDS, tuberculosis, malaria or the most common opportunistic infections that accompany them;

(b) To adopt and implement legislation or other measures, in accordance with applicable international law, including international agreements acceded to, to safeguard access to such preventive, curative or palliative pharmaceutical products or medical technologies from any limitations by third parties;

(c) To adopt all appropriate positive measures, to the maximum of the resources allocated for this purpose, to promote effective access to such preventive, curative or palliative pharmaceutical products or medical technologies.[78]

While the key task of how states are to determine how such availability and adequacy is to be obtained and maintained appears to be less of a concern in these proclamations than the (undeniably vital) task of stating that such facilities ought to be made available, come what may, there is increasing attention being paid to the practicalities of achieving the right balance. This has been especially so at the level of international cooperation and assistance, spurred on by the potential and sometimes actual conflicts between the WTO's intellectual property rights regime—known as TRIPS (Trade-Related aspects of Intellectual Property

[78] Commission on Human Rights Resolution 2004/26, Access to Medication in the Context of Pandemics such as HIV/AIDS, Tuberculosis and Malaria, E/CN.4/RES/2004/26 (23 April 2004). Significantly, the only member state of the Commission that did *not* vote for the Resolution was the United States, which abstained.

rights)—and the various human rights regimes that demand states secure the highest attainable standards of health.

The 1994 TRIPS Agreement has a number of built-in mechanisms to permit states, in effect, to bypass patent rights, including by means of the system of so-called 'compulsory licensing'. The potential capacity of that provision, however, was not fully realized and exploited until a watershed event in March 2001 when thirty-nine pharmaceutical companies initiated legal action in the High Court in Pretoria against the Government of South Africa, claiming that the then recent amendments to the country's Medicines Act[79] permitting the government to override or evade existing patent rights in respect of certain essential medicines (and in particular anti-retroviral HIV/AIDS drugs) transgressed the state's obligations under TRIPS, as incorporated in South African law. Reflecting a serious error of judgment on the part of the corporations, they were forced to drop the case barely two months later in April 2001 after a worldwide outcry had ensued at the perceived rapacity of the companies (whose combined global profits exceed the total GDP of South Africa) in the face of a government trying to tackle an HIV/AIDS epidemic of potentially terrifying proportions.[80]

In point of fact, in the Preamble to TRIPS, member states declare their recognition of 'the special needs of the least-developed country Members in respect of maximum flexibility in the domestic implementation of laws and regulations in order to enable them to create a sound and viable technological base'. Article 31 of TRIPS (entitled 'Other Uses without Authorization of the Right Holder') translates this 'flexibility' in the specific circumstance of seeking to evade or override the patent restrictions, including pharmaceutical patents over essential medicines, as follows:

Article 35

Where the law of a Member allows for other use of the subject matter of a patent without the authorization of the right holder, including use by the government or third parties authorized by the government, the following provisions shall be respected:

…

(b) such use may only be permitted if, prior to such use, the proposed user has made efforts to obtain authorization from the right holder on reasonable commercial terms and conditions and that such efforts have not been successful within a reasonable period of time. This requirement may be waived by a Member in the case of a national emergency or other circumstances of extreme urgency or in cases of public non-commercial use. In situations of national emergency or other circumstances of extreme urgency, the right holder shall, nevertheless, be notified as soon as reasonably practicable. In the case of public non-commercial use, where the government or contractor, without making a patent search,

[79] Medicines and Related Substances Control Amendment Act No. 90 (1997), which granted the government powers to enable domestic manufacture of generic drugs or their importation from producers in other countries.

[80] See Sarah Joseph, 'Pharmaceutical Corporations and Access to Drugs: The "Fourth Wave" of Corporate Human Rights Scrutiny' (2003) 25 *Human Rights Quarterly* 425, 443–4.

knows or has demonstrable grounds to know that a valid patent is or will be used by or for the government, the right holder shall be informed promptly.

It was the emergency and urgency conditions of this subsection that the South African Government would have likely been able successfully to invoke, had the case brought against it by the thirty-nine pharmaceutical companies proceeded to trial.

Perhaps the most significant consequence of this high profile case was the impetus it provided for what was to become the Declaration on the TRIPS Agreement and Public Health, concluded at the WTO's Doha Ministerial Meeting on 14 November 2001. The imbroglio in South Africa brought pressure to bear on the trade ministers not so much to change TRIPS, but rather to reiterate and clarify the meaning and extent of the Article 31 provisions as they then stood (and still stand). Thus, paragraph 4 of the 2001 'Doha Declaration' reads:

We agree that the TRIPS Agreement does not and should not prevent members from taking measures to protect public health. Accordingly, while reiterating our commitment to the TRIPS Agreement, we affirm that the Agreement can and should be interpreted and implemented in a manner supportive of WTO members' right to protect public health and, in particular, to promote access to medicines for all.

In this connection, we reaffirm the right of WTO members to use, to the full, the provisions in the TRIPS Agreement, which provide flexibility for this purpose.

To leave no doubt as to the implications of this reaffirmation, the Declaration elaborates (in paragraph 5) upon what such 'flexibility' entails—namely, that:

(a) In applying the customary rules of interpretation of public international law, each provision of the TRIPS Agreement shall be read in the light of the object and purpose of the Agreement as expressed, in particular, in its objectives and principles.

(b) Each member has the right to grant compulsory licences and the freedom to determine the grounds upon which such licences are granted.

(c) Each member has the right to determine what constitutes a national emergency or other circumstances of extreme urgency, it being understood that public health crises, including those relating to HIV/AIDS, tuberculosis, malaria and other epidemics, can represent a national emergency or other circumstances of extreme urgency…[81]

[81] In fact, there exist within various articles of the TRIPS a range of so-called 'flexibilities' potentially available to WTO member states that relate to access to patented or patentable essential medicines. See UN General Assembly, Report of the Special Rapporteur on the right of everyone to the enjoyment of the highest attainable standard of physical and mental health on the impact of TRIPS on the right to health, A/HRC/11/12 (31 March 2009), [25]–[55], which explains in detail how these can and do operate under seven categories of 'flexibility'. These are: (1) the use of transition periods during which member states are granted extended deadlines before they need to comply with the patent protections afforded by TRIPS; (2) relative freedom to determine what is patentable subject matter; (3) compulsory licensing; (4) power to determine when intellectual property rights have been 'exhausted' and to permit 'parallel importation' of otherwise patented medicines; (5) limited discretion to determine exceptions to the rights of patent holders; (6) the power to determine the basis upon which patent claims can be opposed or existing patents revoked; and (7) so-called 'pro-competitive' measures, which allow states to use competition laws to restrict the monopolistic features of patent law.

Some evidence of the relative success of this promotion of a view that prefers the need to combat extreme public health threats to the need to protect (at least in full) the commercial interests of patent holders is now apparent. A 2009 report of the Special Rapporteur on the impact of TRIPS on the right to health, for example, had this to say about the use of HIV medicines:

20. The example of HIV medicines is particularly illustrative. In 2001, when the HIV crisis was at its peak and the need for antiretrovirals (ARVs) was the most acute, it was the availability of cheaper generic ARVs from developing countries that led to a reduction in prices from over US$10,000 per patient per year to less than US$350 per patient per year for a first-line combination therapy. Today generic competition has helped reduce prices of first generation ARVs by more than 99 per cent. The availability of generic medicines from developing countries like Brazil, India, South Africa and Thailand has exerted a downward pressure on prices and increased the range of affordable options for national treatment programmes. Generic manufacturers have also been able to produce fixed-dose combinations of ARVs, which are easier to administer and use in developing countries and LDCs, including some combinations that are not available from patentees. The importance of generic medicines continues to be underscored today by their prominence in international medicine supply programmes.[82]

That said, there is also evident reluctance, even antagonism, on the part of some pharmaceutical corporations to cooperate in initiatives that seek to strike a balance between commercial and public health or human rights interests. In his final report as Special Rapporteur, Paul Hunt, noted, for example, 'the regrettable refusal of some pharmaceutical companies to engage' in a collaborative project that he had engineered (together with Mary Robinson, the former UN High Commissioner for Human Rights) in 2008. This was despite the fact that the project sought to address an acknowledged problem facing companies, as well as governments and rights activists, namely:

How can pharmaceutical companies sensibly be asked to respect their human rights responsibilities in relation to access to medicines without much more specific guidance, as well as the identification of good practices? How can they be monitored, and held to account, if their human rights responsibilities in relation to access to medicines are unclear?[83]

Further, as Hunt's successor as Special Rapporteur, Anand Grover, points out in a subsequent report, the growing use of bilateral trade agreements tend, under pressure from the corporate interests pressing their case on Western governments, to ignore or dilute the TRIPS flexibilities that benefit developing nations, or the imposition of added patent protection to the TRIPS conditions (known as 'TRIPS-plus').[84]

[82] UN General Assembly, Report of the Special Rapporteur on the right of everyone to the enjoyment of the highest attainable standard of physical and mental health, A/HRC/11/12 (31 March 2009), [20].

[83] UN General Assembly, Report of the Special Rapporteur on the right of everyone to the enjoyment of the highest attainable standard of physical and mental health, A/63/263 (11 August 2008), [33]. It should be noted that two companies, Novartis and NovoNordisk, were willing to engage in the project: see [32]. In the same report, and flowing from the collaborate project mentioned, Hunt proposes a set of Human Rights Guidelines for Pharmaceutical Companies in relation to Access to Medicines which seek to provide guidance on how to address these very questions: see Annex, 15–25.

[84] For Grover's detailed description of these tactics and their consequences, see UN General Assembly, Report of the Special Rapporteur on the right of everyone to the enjoyment of the highest attainable standard of physical and mental health, A/HRC/11/12 (31 March 2009), [67]–[93].

Quality

Alongside availability and accessibility (and appropriateness), the quality of health care services and facilities is integral to realizing the highest attainable standard of physical and mental health. The standards of preventive, remedial and rehabilitative action and attention that any health care system can and does deliver in practice will obviously vary enormously on account of a wide range of factors. We might intuitively suppose this much, but it is in fact borne out by the evidence of the Committee's Concluding Observations on states' periodic reports over the past twenty years or so. A sample of these illustrates the breadth and depth of differences between states in the concerns as to quality raised by the Committee.

RECURRING THEMES

An examination of the last twenty years of the Committee's Concluding Observations regarding states parties' periodic reports reveals a number of recurring themes regarding the issue of the quality of health under the right to health. Among the most common of these are:

- lack of adequate sexual and reproductive health care and education,[85] sometimes in the face of repressive legal regimes that severely restrict, or even criminalize, abortions, and inadequate provision of family planning advice and services;[86]
- poor standards of maternal and infant health care,[87] especially in countries where high morbidity rates (often associated with illegal or clandestine abortions services)[88] point to significant problems in quality and coverage;

[85] CESCR, Concluding Observations: Argentina, E/C.12/1/Add.38 (8 December 1999), [24] and [38]; Benin, E/C.12/1/Add.78 (5 June 2002), [23] and [42]; Bolivia, E/C.12/1/Add.60 (21 May 2001), [23] and [43]; Bolivia, E/C.12/BOL/CO/2 (8 August 2008), [27](f); Brazil, E/C.12/BRA/CO/2 (12 June 2009), [23]; Cambodia, E/C.12/KHM/CO/1 (12 June 2009), [30]; Chile, E/C.12/1/Add.105 (1 December 2004), [54]; Colombia, E/C.12/1/Add.74 (6 December 2001), [24]; Macedonia, E/C.12/MKD/CO/1 (15 January 2008), [25]–[26] and [45]–[46]; Georgia, E/C.12/1/Add.42 (17 May 2000), [18] and [30]; Panama, E/C.12/1/Add.64 (24 September 2001), [20]; Philippines, E/C.12/PHL/CO/4 (1 December 2008), [31]; Poland, E/C.12/1/Add.82 (19 December 2002), [28]–[29]; Kazakhstan, E/C.12/KAZ/CO/1 (7 June 2010), [33]; Kenya, E/C.12/KEN/CO/1 (1 December 2008), [33].

[86] CESCR, Concluding Observations: Benin, E/C.12/1/Add.78 (5 June 2002), [23] and [42]; Bolivia, E/C.12/1/Add.60 (21 May 2001), [22]; Brazil, E/C.12/1/Add.87 (26 June 2003), [29]; Philippines, E/C.12/PHL/CO/4 (1 December 2008), [31]; People's Republic of China, E/C.12/1/Add.107 (13 May 2005), [36] and [65]; Poland, E/C.12/1/Add.26 (16 June 1998), [12]; Poland, E/C.12/1/Add.82 (19 December 2002), [29]; Poland, E/C.12/POL/CO/5 (2 December 2009), [28]; Mexico, E/C.12/MEX/CO/4 (9 June 2006), [25] and [44].

[87] CESCR, Concluding Observations: Bolivia, E/C.12/BOL/CO/2 (8 August 2008), [22]; Cambodia, E/C.12/KHM/CO/1 (12 June 2009), [29] and [32]; Colombia, E/C.12/COL/CO/5 (7 June 2010), [25]; Democratic People's Republic of Korea, E/C.12/1/Add.95 (12 December 2003), [22]–[23] and [43]–[44]; Nicaragua, E/C.12/NIC/CO/4 (28 November 2008), [27]; Panama, E/C.12/1/Add.64 (24 September 2001), [20]; Philippines, E/C.12/1995/7 (7 June 1995), [31]; Poland, E/C.12/POL/CO/5 (2 December 2009), [24]; Kenya, E/C.12/KEN/CO/1 (1 December 2008), [32]; Madagascar, E/C.12/MDG/CO/2 (16 December 2009), [29]; Mexico, E/C.12/MEX/CO/4 (9 June 2006), [23]; Ukraine, E/C.12/1/Add.65 (24 September 2001), [18].

[88] See especially CESCR Concluding Observations: Brazil, E/C.12/1/Add.87 (26 June 2003), [29]; Philippines, E/C.12/PHL/CO/4 (1 December 2008), [31]; PRC, E/C.12/1/Add.107 (13 May 2005), [36] and [65]; Mexico, E/C.12/MEX/CO/4 (9 June 2006), [25] and [44].

– the absence, or very poor quality, of health care services for the mentally ill, including endemic discrimination and abuse in psychiatric institutions;[89]

– chronic lack or absence of health care services in rural areas in many countries,[90] as well as deep discrimination in service provision where it does exist against such groups as indigenous peoples,[91] Roma,[92] migrants,[93] lower castes and ethnic minorities,[94] prisoners,[95] and disabled people,[96] as well as women and children;[97]

– severe deficiencies in essential social and welfare determinants of health, especially regarding access to adequate food, water and sanitation.[98]

[89] CESCR, Concluding Observations: Argentina, E/C.12/1/Add.38 (8 December 1999), [23]; Cyprus, E/C.12/1/Add.28 (4 December 1998), [15]; Georgia, E/C.12/1/Add.83 (19 December 2002), [25]; Kazakhstan, E/C.12/KAZ/CO/1 (7 June 2010), [32]; Paraguay, E/C.12/PRY/CO/3 (4 January 2008), [22]; Poland, E/C.12/POL/CO/5 (2 December 2009), [24]; People's Republic of China, E/C.12/1/Add.107 (13 May 2005), [35]; Uzbekistan, E/C.12/UZB/CO/1 (24 January 2006), [35], [66].

[90] CESCR, Concluding Observations: Angola, E/C.12/DZA/CO/4 (7 June 2010), [20]; Finland, E/C.12/1/Add.52 (1 December 2000), [20]; Guinea, E/C.12/1/Add.5 (28 May 1996), [26]; Moldova, E/C.12/1/Add.91 (12 December 2006), [46]; Madagascar, E/C.12/MDG/CO/2 (16 December 2009), [29]; Nepal, E/C.12/1/Add.66 (24 September 2001), [31]–[32] and [55]; Nepal, E/C.12/NPL/CO/2 (16 January 2008), [46]; China (including Hong Kong and Macao), E/C.12/1/Add.107 (13 May 2005), [60]; Russian Federation, E/C.12/1/Add.94 (12 December 2003), [31] and [59]; Ukraine, E/C.12/UKR/CO/5 (4 January 2008), [27] and [50]; Yemen, E/C.12/1/Add.92 (12 December 2003), [15].

[91] CESCR, Concluding Observations: Colombia, E/C.12/COL/CO/5 (7 June 2010), [25]; Russian Federation, E/C.12/1/Add.94 (12 December 2003), [31]; Brazil, E/C.12/BRA/CO/2 (12 June 2009), [28].

[92] CESCR, Concluding Observations: Greece, E/C.12/1/Add.97 (7 June 2004), [24] and [46]; Hungary, E/C.12/HUN/CO/3 (16 January 2008), [25]; Macedonia, E/C.12/MKD/CO/1 (15 January 2008), [26] and [46]; Serbia and Montenegro, E/C.12/1/Add.108 (23 June 2005), [12]–[13].

[93] CESCR, Concluding Observations: Belgium, E/C.12/BEL/CO/3 (4 January 2008), [21] and [35]; France, E/C.12/FRA/CO/3 (9 June 2008), [26]; UK, E/C.12/1/Add.79 (5 June 2002), [21].

[94] CESCR, Concluding Observations: Nepal, E/C.12/NPL/CO/2 (16 January 2008), [24]; India, E/C.12/IND/CO/5 (8 August 2008), [27].

[95] CESCR, Concluding Observations: Cambodia, E/C.12/KHM/CO/1 (12 June 2009), [33]; Moldova, E/C.12/1/Add.91 (12 December 2003), [25]; Russian Federation, E/C.12/1/Add.13 (20 May 1997), [26]; Russian Federation, E/C.12/1/Add.94 (12 December 2003), [33]; Trinidad and Tobago, E/C.12/1/Add.80 (5 June 2002), [26]; Ukraine, E/C.12/1/Add.80 (5 June 2002), [29]; Uzbekistan, E/C.12/UZB/CO/1 (24 January 2006), [34]; Yemen, E/C.12/1/Add.92 (12 December 2003), [18].

[96] CESCR, Concluding Observations: Finland, E/C.12/1/Add.52 (1 December 2000), [31]; Guatemala, E/C.12/1/Add.3 (28 May 1996), [21]; UK (Hong Kong), E/C.12/1/Add.10 (6 December 1996), [30]; China (Hong Kong), E/C.12/1/Add.58 (21 May 2001), [20].

[97] CESCR, Concluding Observations: Paraguay, E/C.12/PRY/CO/3 (4 January 2008), [22]; Ukraine, E/C.12/1/Add.65 (24 September 2001), [18]; Guinea, E/C.12/1/Add.5 (28 May 1996), [21]; Madagascar, E/C.12/MDG/CO/2 (16 December 2009), [29]; Yemen, E/C.12/1/Add.92 (12 December 2003), [34].

[98] CESCR, Concluding Observations: Chad, E/C.12/TCD/CO/3 (16 December 2009), [31]; Costa Rica, E/C.12/CRI/CO/4 (4 January 2008), [26]; Dominican Republic, E/C.12/1/Add.6 (6 December 1996), [24]; Guatemala, E/C.12/1/Add.3 (28 May 1996), [21]; Guinea, E/C.12/1/Add.5 (28 May 1996), [21]; India, E/C.12/IND/CO/5 (8 August 2008), [34]; Iraq, E/C.12/1/Add.17 (12 December 1997), [22]; Libyan Arab Jamahiriya, E/C.12/LYB/CO/2 (25 January 2006), [18]; Mali, E/C.12/1994/17 (21 December 1994), [13]; Nepal, E/C.12/1/Add.66 (24 September 2001), [27]; China (including Hong Kong and Macao), E/C.12/1/Add.107 (13 May 2005), [34]; Solomon Islands, E/C.12/1/Add.33 (14 May 1999), [22]; Solomon Islands, E/C.12/1/Add.84 (19 December 2002), [13]; Sri Lanka, E/C.12/1/Add.24 (16 June 1990), [7]; Yemen, E/C.12/1/Add.92 (12 December 2003), [19].

In addition, and perhaps most significantly of all, are the Committee's recurrent complaints as to the very poor standards of health care across all aspects of the health systems in many countries, there being, in these cases, too few or poorly equipped health centres, clinics and hospitals, in terms of basic facilities,[99] access to and availability of drugs,[100] and the training of health personnel,[101] as well as chronic public underfunding,[102] and/or the prohibitive costs of private sector health care;[103] highly differential coverage, nearly always preferring urban to rural communities in respect of provision of services;[104] and the absence of, or major deficiencies in, health care planning, leading, for example, to the failure of immunization and vaccination programmes and the consequent increases in levels of infectious and preventable diseases.[105]

As the footnotes to each of the above-itemized problems attest, the concerns are widespread and deep across nearly all member states. There are, as the Committee notes, cases of gross neglect where large swathes of a country's population are without any health care at all, or that which exists is utterly inadequate—for example, in North Korea (noting 'the high rate of children under 5 that are chronically malnourished (45 per cent according to government statistics), as well as the high incidence of poverty-related diseases');[106] India (noting 'that, despite the economic growth achieved by the State party, health-care expenditures remain exceptionally low at around 1 per cent of GDP, and that a significant proportion

[99] CESCR, Concluding Observations: Angola, E/C.12/DZA/CO/4 (7 June 2010), [20]; Argentina, E/C.12/1/Add.38 (8 December 1999), [23]; Chad, E/C.12/TCD/CO/3 (16 December 2009), [29]; Ecuador, E/C.12/1/Add.100 (7 June 2004), [29]; El Salvador, E/C.12/SLV/CO/2 (27 June 2007), [24]; Georgia, E/C.12/1/Add.83 (19 December 2002), [24]; Russian Federation, E/C.12/1/Add.94 (12 December 2003), [31]; Senegal, E/C.12/1/Add.62 (24 September 2001), [56]; Togo, E/C.12/1/Add.61 (21 May 2001), [16]; Trinidad and Tobago, E/C.12/1/Add.80 (5 June 2002), [31]; Yemen, E/C.12/1/Add.92 (12 December 2003), [15].

[100] CESCR, Concluding Observations: Russian Federation, E/C.12/1/Add.13 (20 May 1997), [28]; Russian Federation, E/C.12/1/Add.94 (12 December 2003), [31]; Republic of Korea, E/C.12/KOR/CO/3 (17 December 2009), [30]; Trinidad and Tobago, E/C.12/1/Add.80 (5 June 2002), [31]; China (including Hong Kong and Macao), E/C.12/1/Add.107 (13 May 2005), [87].

[101] CESCR, Concluding Observations: Benin, E/C.12/1/Add.78 (5 June 2002), [24]; Nepal, E/C.12/1/Add.66 (24 September 2001), [26]; Nigeria, E/C.12/1/Add.23 (16 June 1998), [28]; Uruguay, E/C.12/1/Add.18 (22 December 1997), [10].

[102] CESCR, Concluding Observations: Democratic People's Republic of Korea, E/C.12/1/Add.95 (12 December 2003), as reflected in comments at [22], [43]; Ecuador, E/C.12/1/Add.100 (7 June 2004), [29]; Georgia, E/C.12/1/Add.83 (19 December 2002), [24]; India, E/C.12/IND/CO/5 (8 August 2008), [33]; Nepal, E/C.12/1/Add.66 (24 September 2001), [33]–[34]; Nigeria, E/C.12/1/Add.23 (16 June 1998), [28]; Philippines, E/C.12/1995/7 (7 June 1995), [21]; Russian Federation, E/C.12/1/Add.13 (20 May 1997), [28]; Uruguay, E/C.12/1/Add.18 (22 December 1997), [10].

[103] CESCR, Concluding Observations: El Salvador, E/C.12/SLV/CO/2 (27 June 2007), [24]; Republic of Korea, E/C.12/1/Add.59 (21 May 2001), [26]; Republic of Korea, E/C.12/KOR/CO/3 (17 December 2009), [30]; Switzerland, E/C.12/1/Add.30 (7 December 1998), [24]; Uzbekistan, E/C.12/UZB/CO/1 (24 January 2006), [29].

[104] See n. 88 above, and accompanying text.

[105] CESCR, Concluding Observations: Colombia, E/C.12/1/Add.74 (6 December 2001), [25]; Democratic Republic of the Congo, E/C.12/COD/CO/4 (16 December 2009), [34]; Kenya, E/C.12/KEN/CO/1 (1 December 2008), [32]; Kyrgyzstan, E/C.12/1/Add.49 (1 September 2000), [22]; Suriname, E/C.12/1995/6 (7 June 1995), [19]–[20].

[106] CESCR, Concluding Observations: Democratic People's Republic of Korea, E/C.12/1/Add.95 (12 December 2003), [22]–[23].

of the population continues to have limited or no access to basic health services, resulting in alarmingly high rates of maternal and infant mortality, as well as high incidences of tuberculosis and other communicable diseases');[107] Nepal (where 'the Committee notes with regret that 29 per cent of the population has no access to safe water, 90 per cent has no access to health services and 84 per cent has no access to sanitation');[108] and Nigeria (noting that 'gross under-funding and inadequate management of health services during the last decade had led to the rapid deterioration of health infrastructures in hospitals').[109] More usually, however, health care systems are in place in some form or other, but are fundamentally hampered by lack of adequate resources of all kinds and the chronic under-capacity of services and facilities to meet demand. Thus, the Committee's remarks in respect of Georgia in 2002 are representative of a great many states:

Georgia[110]

24. The Committee expresses deep concern about the insufficiency of material and technical resources, medication, hygienic and sanitary conditions and food in hospitals, as well as about the low wages of the medical staff, resulting in the common practice of charging informal fees for basic health-care services that are formally provided free of charge. A particular negative effect of such informal fees is that it puts basic health care even further beyond the reach of the poorest and most disadvantaged groups of society.

So too is much (although of course not all) of the Committee's even fuller examination of the extent of the health care problems that face Moldova in its efforts to realize the right to health under the Covenant, as also are the Committee's responses to the circumstance:

Republic of Moldova[111]

24. The Committee is concerned about the deterioration of the public health system and notes with regret that conditions in hospitals, especially psychiatric hospitals, are inadequate.

25. The Committee is alarmed about the rising incidence of tuberculosis in the State party and notes with particular concern the acuteness of this problem in prisons where the infection rate is more than 40 times higher than the national average, according to the 2003 Baseline Study on the Human Rights Status in the Republic of Moldova.

26. The Committee is concerned about the rising incidence of HIV/AIDS and sexually transmitted diseases in the State party. In this regard, it is also concerned that sex education classes held in urban areas are almost non-existent in rural areas.

27. The Committee is concerned about the continuing high level of infant and maternal mortality. It is also concerned that the number of abortions remains high (15.6 per 1,000

[107] CESCR, Concluding Observations: India, E/C.12/IND/CO/5 (8 August 2008), [33]. See also in the same source [38] and [73].

[108] CESCR, Concluding Observations: Nepal, E/C.12/1/Add.66 (24 September 2001), [27].

[109] CESCR, Concluding Observations: Nigeria, E/C.12/1/Add.23 (16 June 1998), [28].

[110] CESCR, Concluding Observations: Georgia E/C.12/1/Add.83 (19 December 2002), [24].

[111] CESCR, Concluding Observations: Republic of Moldova, E/C.12/1/Add 91 (12 December 2003), [24]–[28] and [46]–[50].

women of fertile age in 2002), notwithstanding the ongoing programmes in the area of reproductive health.

28. The Committee is concerned that drug abuse is a serious problem in the State party, with the number of drug addicts having more than doubled in the last five years despite the establishment of an interdepartmental commission to fight drug addiction in 2000 and the launch of a programme to fight drug addiction and the drugs business in the period 2003–2004.

…

46. The Committee recommends that the State party take effective measures to ensure the quality, affordability and accessibility of health services, especially in rural areas. In this respect, the Committee draws the attention of the State party to its general comment No. 14 (2000) on the right to the highest attainable standard of health and requests detailed information, on a disaggregated and comparative basis, on progress made in the second periodic report.

47. The Committee recommends that the State party intensify its efforts under the National Programme on Tuberculosis Prophylaxis and Control to combat the spread of tuberculosis, including by ensuring the availability of medicines and adequate sanitary conditions in prisons.

48. The Committee recommends that the State party intensify its efforts to combat the spread of HIV/AIDS and other sexually transmitted diseases, including through public information campaigns and by ensuring that sex education is also introduced to schools in rural areas.

49. The Committee urges the State party to reinforce its efforts to reduce infant and maternal mortality by increasing health coverage for women and children. The Committee calls upon the State party to strengthen efforts to promote awareness of sexual and reproductive health, safe contraceptive methods and the health risk of using abortion as a method of birth control, and to report on the results of such measures in its next periodic report.

50. The Committee calls on the State party to ensure the effective implementation of programmes to prevent and combat drug abuse, especially among young people. It requests the State party to provide disaggregated and comparative data on this problem in its next periodic report.

IMPORTANCE OF RESOURCES

A major cause of such inadequacies in many states is the severe lack of resources, especially funding. The gravity, as well as complexity, of this situation—which impacts the rich as well as poor states—is captured in the following extract from the Special Rapporteur's 2012 report on health financing:

2. The contemporary landscape of health financing is characterized by persistent deficits and recurring challenges in financing health systems throughout the world. Public spending on health is too low in many States because of low budget prioritization for health and, in some cases, the unavailability of adequate public funds in absolute terms. Deficits in governance are also central to many States' failure to finance health adequately. Widespread corruption, tax loopholes and weak tax administration, characterized by high rates of tax evasion, often diminish States' capacity to raise revenues and allocate adequate public funds towards health. Many States are overly dependent on out-of-pocket payments from users and international funding to finance their health systems. International funding for health, however, is unpredictable and unsustainable, as the recent financial crisis has

demonstrated, and out-of-pocket payments for health goods and services disproportionately impact on the poor, who must pay considerably larger proportions of their income on health care than wealthy patients. As a result, poor households often experience financial catastrophe and impoverishment due to out-of-pocket payments, resulting in a chilling effect that discourages many from seeking health care in the first place.

Although, clearly, adequate funding is vital to the achievement and maintenance of an effective and efficient system of health care, as a matter of fact, and as our above survey of Committee Concluding Observations makes clear, just about everything affects the 'quality' of health care.[112] This poses a challenge to those—the Committee included—who seek to provide some practical direction to states as to how they ought to meet the demands of ensuring the right to health of sufficient quality. The key to meeting this challenge lies largely in one's capacity to identify and then focus on addressing certain priority matters, as evidenced by what problems are facing states on the ground. Drawing on the terms provided in the text of Article 12 itself, and reflecting many of the 'lessons learnt' from its depository of states' periodic reports, the Committee has used part of General Comment No. 14 (as extracted below) to compile what it intends to be a focused and usable guide as to states' obligations to improve the quality of their health care services and facilities.

OBLIGATIONS REGARDING 'QUALITY'

Article 12(2) provides baseline standards of the health care obligations borne by states which are, in the words of the Committee, 'illustrative' and 'non-exhaustive' (General Comment No. 14, paragraph 7), and provide 'guidance in the action to be taken by states' (paragraph 13). To this end, the Committee (in General Comment No. 14) briefly expands on each of the four subcategories of health issues and attendant obligations identified in Article 12(2), emphasizing in respect of each, the importance of preventive measures, education and the dissemination of information, as much as the provision of adequate curative facilities and services:

Article 12.2(a)
The right to maternal, child and reproductive health

14. The provision for the reduction of the stillbirth rate and of infant mortality and for the healthy development of the child' (art. 12.2(a)) may be understood as requiring measures

[112] Indeed, the range of other factors identified by the Committee in its Concluding Observations of states' reports that we have *not* already mentioned prove this very point. These include, eg, the various detrimental health impacts of: trade sanctions (Iraq, E/C.12/1/Add.17 (12 December 1997), [8]–[10]), trade liberalization (Colombia, E/C.12/1/Add.74 (29 November 2001), [9]; Costa Rica, E/C.12/CRI/CO/4 (19 November 2007), [27]; Ecuador, E/1991/23 (1990), [136]; India, E/C.12/IND/CO/5 (8 August 2008), [46]; Morocco, E/C.12/1/Add.55 (1 December 2000), [38]), major industrial accidents (India, E/C.12/IND/CO/5 (8 August 2008), [59]), military conflict (Afghanistan, E/C.12/AFG/CO/2-4 (21 May 2010), [12]) and civil war (Sri Lanka, E/C.12/1/Add.24 (16 June 1998), [5]–[7] and [21], also emphasizing the extremely high rate of youth suicide alcohol dependence, adolescent crime, child abuse, sexual disorders and domestic violence against women (at [14]); Sri Lanka, E/C.12/LKA/CO/2-4 (9 December 2010), [28], [29], [35] and [36]).

to improve child and maternal health, sexual and reproductive health services, including access to family planning, pre- and post-natal care, emergency obstetric services and access to information, as well as to resources necessary to act on that information.

Article 12.2(b)

The right to healthy natural and workplace environments

15. 'The improvement of all aspects of environmental and industrial hygiene' (art. 12.2(b)) comprises, inter alia, preventive measures in respect of occupational accidents and diseases; the requirement to ensure an adequate supply of safe and potable water and basic sanitation; the prevention and reduction of the population's exposure to harmful substances such as radiation and harmful chemicals or other detrimental environmental conditions that directly or indirectly impact upon human health. Furthermore, industrial hygiene refers to the minimization, so far as is reasonably practicable, of the causes of health hazards inherent in the working environment. Article 12.2(b) also embraces adequate housing and safe and hygienic working conditions, an adequate supply of food and proper nutrition, and discourages the abuse of alcohol, and the use of tobacco, drugs and other harmful substances.

Article 12.2(c)

The right to prevention, treatment and control of diseases

16. 'The prevention, treatment and control of epidemic, endemic, occupational and other diseases' (art. 12.2(c)) requires the establishment of prevention and education programmes for behaviour-related health concerns such as sexually transmitted diseases, in particular HIV/AIDS, and those adversely affecting sexual and reproductive health, and the promotion of social determinants of good health, such as environmental safety, education, economic development and gender equity. The right to treatment includes the creation of a system of urgent medical care in cases of accidents, epidemics and similar health hazards, and the provision of disaster relief and humanitarian assistance in emergency situations. The control of diseases refers to States' individual and joint efforts to, inter alia, make available relevant technologies, using and improving epidemiological surveillance and data collection on a disaggregated basis, the implementation or enhancement of immunization programmes and other strategies of infectious disease control.

Article 12.2(d)

The right to health facilities, goods and services

17. 'The creation of conditions which would assure to all medical service and medical attention in the event of sickness' (art. 12.2(d)), both physical and mental, includes the provision of equal and timely access to basic preventive, curative, rehabilitative health services and health education; regular screening programmes; appropriate treatment of prevalent diseases, illnesses, injuries and disabilities, preferably at community level; the provision of essential drugs; and appropriate mental health treatment and care. A further important aspect is the improvement and furtherance of participation of the population in the provision of preventive and curative health services, such as the organization of the health sector, the insurance system and, in particular, participation in political decisions relating to the right to health taken at both the community and national levels.

THE ILO AND OCCUPATIONAL HEALTH

Of these four issues, three ((a), (c) and (d)) are especially prominent in our assessment of Concluding Observations above. The fourth ((b) workplace health) has a relatively long history in international human rights laws to the extent that they encompass international labour rights.[113] The International Labour Organization (ILO) has a nearly ninety-year record of international standard-setting in the field, including in occupational health and safety. Among the most important of its relevant Conventions in this respect are: ILO Convention No. 155 concerning Occupational Safety and Health (1981),[114] ILO Convention No. 161 concerning Occupational Health Services (1985),[115] ILO Convention No. 169 concerning Indigenous and Tribal Peoples Convention (1989)[116] (in which Article 20 urges states to prevent discrimination in terms of provision of 'medical and social assistance, occupational safety and health', and Article 25 prescribes that governments provide culturally sensitive health care assistance that is participatory and community based), and ILO Convention No. 182 concerning the Worst Forms of Child Labour (1999),[117] Article 3(d) of which includes 'work which, by its nature or the circumstances in which it is carried out, is likely to harm the health, safety or morals of children' as one of the criteria that constitutes a prohibited (worst) form of child labour.[118]

The Revised European Social Charter (1996)[119] also expressly protects occupational health and safety, the original 1961 terms of which, under Article 3, remained unchanged after the Charter's revision in the mid 1990s.

Article 3—The right to safe and healthy working conditions

With a view to ensuring the effective exercise of the right to safe and healthy working conditions, the Parties undertake, in consultation with employers' and workers' organisations:

1. to formulate, implement and periodically review a coherent national policy on occupational safety, occupational health and the working environment. The primary aim of this policy shall be to improve occupational safety and health and to prevent accidents and injury to health arising out of, linked with or occurring in the course of work, particularly by minimising the causes of hazards inherent in the working environment;

[113] On which point, see Chapter 9 above on the right to just and favourable conditions of work.

[114] ILO Convention No. 155 concerning Occupational Safety and Health (adopted 22 June 1981, entered into force 11 August 1983).

[115] ILO Convention No. 161 concerning Occupational Health Services (adopted 25 June 1985, entered into force 17 February 1988).

[116] ILO Convention No. 169 concerning Indigenous and Tribal Peoples Convention (adopted 27 June 1989, entered into force 5 September 1991).

[117] ILO Convention No. 182 concerning the Worst Forms of Child Labour (adopted 17 June 1999, 19 November 2000).

[118] While the first three of these Conventions have relatively low levels of state ratifications (ILO No. 155 has sixty ratifications, ILO No. 161 has thirty-one, and ILO No. 169 has twenty-two), the last mentioned—ILO No. 182—which is deemed by the ILO to be one of the eight so-called 'Fundamental Conventions', has been ratified by 177 of the 185 member states of the ILO.

[119] Revised European Social Charter, (adopted 3 May 1996, CETS 163, entered into force 1 July 1999).

2. to issue safety and health regulations;

3. to provide for the enforcement of such regulations by measures of supervision;

4. to promote the progressive development of occupational health services for all workers with essentially preventive and advisory functions.

The Charter has been ratified or acceded to by thirty-three of the forty-seven member states of the Council of Europe.[120]

MATERNAL HEALTH

In respect of the particular issue of enhancing the quality of maternal health services, the Special Rapporteur, while acknowledging the inter-reliance of the right to health and the Millennium Development Goal 5 to improve maternal health, presents a detailed argument as to how the former makes a 'constructive contribution' to the latter.

27. The Millennium Project Task Force on Child Health and Maternal Health, charged with developing recommendations for Goal 5, is unequivocal in its recognition of the role of human rights, including the right to health, in policymaking to reduce maternal mortality. Other actors have also advocated a rights-based approach to health policymaking, and some have taken steps to integrate human rights into their maternal mortality policies and programmes.

28. There are several reasons why the right to health has a constructive contribution to make in the context of maternal health policymaking:

(a) On account of its grounding in law, widespread acceptance by the international community and detailed framework of relevant norms and obligations, the right to health can help legitimize policies and programmes that prevent maternal mortality;

(b) The right-to-health principles of equality and non-discrimination have three important roles to play in policies to reduce maternal mortality. First, they underpin programmes that promote more equitable distribution of health care, including provision in rural or poor areas, or areas with high indigenous or minority populations. Second, they underpin prioritization of interventions—such as emergency obstetric care—that can guarantee women's enjoyment of the right to health on the basis of non-discrimination and equality. Third, policies which promote non-discrimination and equality—as well as dignity, cultural sensitivity, privacy and confidentiality—in the clinical setting, can improve patient-provider relationships and encourage women to seek health care;

(c) The right to health includes an entitlement to participate in health policymaking at the local, national and international levels. Participation by relevant stakeholders, including women, will help develop more effective and sustainable programmes, reduce exclusion and enhance accountability;

[120] Twelve countries have signed, but have not followed through with ratification of the Charter. These include: Denmark, Germany, Greece, Poland, Spain and the United Kingdom. Liechtenstein and Switzerland have neither signed nor ratified the Charter.

(d) Monitoring and accountability are integral features of the right to health and can help reduce maternal mortality. The right to health demands accountability of various stakeholders, including health-care providers, local health authorities, national Governments, international organizations and civil society. Accessible and effective accountability mechanisms—including courts, tribunals, health ombudsmen, impact assessments and policy review processes—can all help enhance access to health care; and

(e) A right-to-health approach to reducing maternal mortality requires appropriate indicators to monitor progress made, and to highlight where policy adjustments may be needed. The scope of this report does not permit a detailed analysis of which indicators are needed. The Special Rapporteur wishes to refer the General Assembly to his report to the Commission on Human Rights (E/CN.4/2006/48, paras. 22–61 and annex [extracted, in part, at n. 140 below]), which sets out a methodology for a rights-based approach to health indicators, including in relation to the reproductive health strategy endorsed by the World Health Assembly in May 2004.

29. In short, a policy that is animated by the right to health is likely to be equitable, inclusive, non-discriminatory, participatory and evidence-based. In the context of maternal mortality policies, these features help to empower women and ensure that policies are likely to be sustainable, robust and effective.[121]

INTERNATIONAL ASSISTANCE AND COOPERATION

For those many states which have difficulties in marshalling sufficient resources to build and maintain even a basic system of health care, international assistance and cooperation is often a vital source of funding, training, advice and expertise upon which they draw. What is more, from the perspective of the Covenant—that is, as expressly provided in Article 2(1) and implicitly in Article 12—it is believed that the member states have a responsibility to render such assistance and cooperation. Thus, as the Special Rapporteur notes in paragraph 14 of his 2012 report on health financing: 'the right to health approach requires States to cooperate internationally in order to ensure the availability of sustainable international funding for health', and this 'includes a responsibility to pool funds internationally from compulsory contributions by States, based upon their ability to pay, and allocate funds to States, based upon their need, in order to achieve cross-subsidization of resources for health globally'.[122]

Later in the same report, the Special Rapporteur stresses the obligatory nature of this responsibility, while, at the same time, identifying various problems associated with its delivery and offering suggestions as to how these might be overcome, including by way of 'pooling of international funds', as discussed earlier.

22. Under the right to health, States have an obligation to cooperate internationally towards ensuring the availability of sustainable international funding for health. International

[121] UN General Assembly, Report of the Special Rapporteur on the right of everyone to the enjoyment of the highest attainable standard of physical and mental health, A/61/338 (13 September 2006), [27]–[29].

[122] UN General Assembly, Report of the Special Rapporteur on the right of everyone to the enjoyment of the highest attainable standard of physical and mental health, A/67/302 (13 August 2012), [14].

assistance is among the main sources of funding for health in many developing States. Many of these States lack sufficient health funds and resources to meet domestic health needs and thus depend heavily upon international assistance. Moreover, given the level and rate of development in some low-income States, they will be unable to raise adequate funds domestically to meet domestic health needs in the near future. Realization of the right to health in the developing world is thus also dependent upon the availability of sustainable international funding for health, which should ultimately be realized through an obligatory, treaty-based regime founded upon the principle of global solidarity.

23. Existing international funding practices present a number of problems. Donor States, multilateral donor institutions, international financial institutions and other funders continue to engage in practices that undermine full realization of the right to health. In many instances, funders fail to focus their activities on the health needs of recipient States and direct assistance towards health systems development, inadequately incorporate the inputs of affected communities in their activities, and attach conditionalities to the receipt of funding for health.

24. International funders should ensure that their activities respect the right to health. The activities of funders should therefore be directed towards meeting domestic health needs and promoting the development of self-sustaining interventions and health systems. Towards that end, donors should incorporate the participation of civil society and affected communities in their activities in order to ensure health interventions are responsive and sustainable and in accordance with the right to health. Donors should also abstain from attaching pernicious conditionalities to the receipt of international assistance.

25. International donors tend to focus on short-term interventions addressing specific health issues without adequate focus on strengthening health systems. In some States, this has resulted in an overdependence on international funding and the underdevelopment of domestic health systems, many of which are incapable of meeting even basic health needs in the absence of international assistance. Moreover, States that have become over-dependent on international funding for health may be less likely to prioritize health in their budgets, which is critical to the long-term sustainability of domestic health systems.

26. Many low-income States lack adequate funds and resources for health in absolute terms. Other States may at times face severe resource shortfalls that require international funding to resolve. However, in many cases, even low-income States may mobilize funds beyond those currently allocated for health through budget prioritization. Moreover, some States possess sufficient resources but have simply failed to mobilize and allocate adequate funds for health equitably. While the right to health approach requires States to cooperate internationally towards ensuring the availability of sustainable international funding for health, recipient States should also take all possible steps to ensure domestic resource self-sufficiency in order to avoid overdependence on international funding.

27. International assistance is often conditioned on recipient States adopting policies in line with the social, political or economic interests and ideologies of donors. Conditional aid may require recipient States to implement specific health strategies preferred by donors in order to obtain funds. Donor-driven strategies, however, may not be aligned with the health needs of recipient States and may instead distort domestic health priorities. For example, donor funds earmarked for abstinence-only programmes in AIDS-affected countries promote the benefits of abstaining from sexual activity until marriage, but are required to withhold valuable information about the health benefits of condoms and contraception

on the premise that such information contradicts the message of abstinence. Studies have found abstinence-only programmes to be ineffective in preventing HIV and that withholding information about contraceptives places young people at increased risk of pregnancy and sexually transmitted infections.

28. Another bilateral assistance fund directed towards combating HIV/AIDS, does not grant funds to organizations that do not have a policy explicitly opposing sex work. However, sex workers are among the most high-risk groups for HIV and have played a critical role in combating HIV transmission. They must therefore be fully integrated into all HIV prevention efforts in order to ensure that interventions are responsive, sustainable and in line with the right to health. Donor States should therefore not be driven by social, political or economic ideologies when designing and implementing health interventions. In accordance with the right to health, donors should instead ensure that they implement the most effective health strategies available given the needs of the recipient State as articulated by local stakeholders.

29. In many instances, as a result of macroeconomic conditions attached to loans from international financial institutions, international assistance for health does not result in increased public spending on health, but is instead used by States to build up reserves. Studies indicate that each additional $1 of aid for health adds only approximately $0.37 to health budgets in recipient States, and less than $0.01 in States under the advice of the International Monetary Fund. For example, in order to meet health-related Millennium Development Goals, one State would have needed to increase its total revenue by 20 per cent and allocate 15 per cent of the increased amount towards health. However, conditions attached to macroeconomic loans required the Ministry of Health to freeze health budgets moving forward. Restrictions on State health spending of this nature infringe upon the right to health because they disproportionately impact the poor, who rely more heavily on the availability of public health facilities, goods, and services than other groups.

Pooling international funds for health

30. International funding for health is inconsistent and insecure. Donor interventions are often fragmented and poorly coordinated. The insecurity of international funding has been highlighted by the recent global financial crisis, which led, in part, to the cancellation of Round 11 of the Global Fund to Fight AIDS, Tuberculosis and Malaria. Inconsistent international funding for health places States that rely heavily on international assistance at risk of severe funding shortfalls during global economic downturns. Fragmentation of donor interventions is illustrated by the situation in one State, where 50 donors operate, 19 of which directly provide assistance to the Government through budget support and 31 of which provide aid through isolated individual mechanisms or agreements. Poorly coordinated donor interventions lead to redundant spending, inefficient allocation of health funds and resources, and the failure of initiatives to address domestic health needs effectively.

31. In order to cooperate towards ensuring the availability of sustainable international funding for health as required by the right to health, States should pool funds for health internationally. International cooperation in the form of a single global pool or multiple coordinated pools would facilitate the cross-subsidization of health systems in developing States and allow for the coordination of donor activities in recipient States. International cooperation in the form of global pooling of funds for health is critically needed at this time in order to meet the global disease burden and promote the development of sustainable domestic health systems.

32. The Global Fund and the International Drug Purchase Facility (UNITAID) represent two successful examples of global pooling that have had significant positive impacts in the fight against HIV/AIDS, tuberculosis and malaria globally. Both the Global Fund and UNITAID have collected and pooled significant resources from donor States and through innovative financing mechanisms and allocated funds and resources based on need. Under programmes funded by the Global Fund, 3.3 million people living with HIV received antiretroviral treatments in 2011 alone and 9.3 million smear-positive cases of tuberculosis were detected and treated between 2010 and 2012. UNITAID has provided child-friendly treatment to 400,000 children living with HIV and delivered 46 million artemisinin-based combination therapies to first-line purchasers of malaria medications. Moreover, in contrast to bilateral aid and assistance from international financial institutions, the Global Fund and UNITAID have removed conditionalities and increased levels of transparency and stakeholder participation in funding processes and programmatic activities in accordance with the right to health approach to health financing.

33. In order to shift the global paradigm of international assistance for health from a donor-based charity regime towards an obligatory system based on the principle of solidarity, global pooling mechanisms should be founded upon international or regional treaties under which States incur legal obligations to contribute to the pool according to their ability to pay and through which funds are allocated based upon need. Such a shift is necessary in order to ensure the availability of sustainable international funding as required by the right to health. In order to promote ownership and accountability within the regime, each State would contribute to the fund regardless of its income level and all funding and programmatic processes must be transparent and include the active and informed participation of civil society and affected communities. In order to realize the right to health globally, States should therefore take all necessary steps towards the development of treaty-based global pooling mechanisms, comprising compulsory progressive contributions allocated based upon need and driven by transparent, participatory processes.[123]

OBLIGATIONS OF INTERNATIONAL ORGANIZATIONS

A key mechanism for international cooperation in the field of health care quality is what states can do through relevant international organizations, and what those organizations can do themselves. In respect of the latter, General Comment No. 14 has this to say about the obligations of the wide range of international actors other than states parties whose functions and operations bear on the right to health:

63. The role of the United Nations agencies and programmes, and in particular the key function assigned to WHO in realizing the right to health at the international, regional and country levels, is of particular importance, as is the function of UNICEF in relation to the right to health of children. When formulating and implementing their right to health national strategies, States parties should avail themselves of technical assistance and cooperation of WHO. Further, when preparing their reports, States parties should utilize the extensive information and advisory services of WHO with regard to data collection, disaggregation, and the development of right to health indicators and benchmarks.

[123] UN General Assembly, Report of the Special Rapporteur on the right of everyone to the enjoyment of the highest attainable standard of physical and mental health A/67/302 (13 August 2012), [22]–[33].

64. Moreover, coordinated efforts for the realization of the right to health should be maintained to enhance the interaction among all the actors concerned, including the various components of civil society. In conformity with articles 22 and 23 of the Covenant, WHO, The International Labour Organization, the United Nations Development Programme, UNICEF, the United Nations Population Fund, the World Bank, regional development banks, the International Monetary Fund, the World Trade Organization and other relevant bodies within the United Nations system, should cooperate effectively with States parties, building on their respective expertise, in relation to the implementation of the right to health at the national level, with due respect to their individual mandates. In particular, the international financial institutions, notably the World Bank and the International Monetary Fund, should pay greater attention to the protection of the right to health in their lending policies, credit agreements and structural adjustment programmes. When examining the reports of States parties and their ability to meet the obligations under article 12, the Committee will consider the effects of the assistance provided by all other actors. The adoption of a human rights-based approach by United Nations specialized agencies, programmes and bodies will greatly facilitate implementation of the right to health. In the course of its examination of States parties' reports, the Committee will also consider the role of health professional associations and other non-governmental organizations in relation to the States' obligations under article 12.

65. The role of WHO, the Office of the United Nations High Commissioner for Refugees, the International Committee of the Red Cross/Red Crescent and UNICEF, as well as non governmental organizations and national medical associations, is of particular importance in relation to disaster relief and humanitarian assistance in times of emergencies, including assistance to refugees and internally displaced persons. Priority in the provision of international medical aid, distribution and management of resources, such as safe and potable water, food and medical supplies, and financial aid should be given to the most vulnerable or marginalized groups of the population.

Realizing the Right to Health: Implementation, Monitoring and Enforcement

In the final section in this chapter, we assess how and how well the right to health is realized, primarily at the level of state actions and activities, but also through certain international processes. We do so by way of three steps: first by analyzing the requirements and practice of states' implementation of national health care plans; secondly, by assessing means and methods of monitoring and evaluation of standards of health and health care; and thirdly, by reviewing the levels of accountability and enforcement of the right to health through international and domestic laws and institutions. These steps are reflected in a section of the Special Rapporteur's 2008 report on health systems and the right to the highest attainable standard of health,[124] entitled 'Leadership, governance, stewardship'

[124] Human Rights Council, Report of the Special Rapporteur on the right of everyone to the enjoyment of the highest attainable standard of physical and mental health, A/HRC/7/11 (31 January 2008).

(paragraphs 87 to 106), which outlines the planning, monitoring and accountability (enforcement) components of a viable health system:

87. This is 'arguably the most complex but critical building block of any health system'. It encompasses many elements, including planning and accountability.

(a) Planning

88. In the Special Rapporteur's experience, this is one of the weakest features of the development and strengthening of health systems. With a few honourable exceptions, the record of health planning is poor, while the history of health planning is surprisingly short. Many States do not have comprehensive, up-to-date health plans. Where they exist, plans 'often fail to be implemented and remain grand designs on paper. Elsewhere plans may be implemented but fail to respond to the real needs of the population.'

89. However, from the perspective of the right to the highest attainable standard of health, effective planning is absolutely critical. Progressive realization and resource availability—two inescapable components of the international right to health—cannot be addressed without planning.

90. Recognizing the critical role of effective planning, the Committee on Economic, Social and Cultural Rights designated the preparation of a health 'strategy and plan of action' a core obligation arising from the right to the highest attainable standard of health. The Committee also encouraged high-income States to provide international assistance 'to enable developing countries to fulfil their core…obligations', including the preparation of a health plan. According to the Declaration of Alma-Ata: 'All governments should formulate national policies, strategies and plans of action to launch and sustain primary health care as part of a comprehensive national health system and in coordination with other sectors.'

91. Health planning is complex and many of its elements are important from the perspective of the right to the highest attainable standard of health, including the following.

92. The entire planning process must be as participatory and transparent as possible.

93. It is very important that the health needs of disadvantaged individuals, communities and populations are given due attention. Also, effective measures must be taken to ensure their active and informed participation throughout the planning process. Both the process and plan must be sensitive to cultural difference.

94. Prior to the drafting of the plan, there must be a health situational analysis informed by suitably disaggregated data. The analysis should identify, for example, the characteristics of the population (e.g. birth, death and fertility rates), their health needs (e.g. incidence and prevalence by disease), and the public and private health-related services presently available (e.g. the capacity of different facilities).

95. The right to the highest attainable standard of health encompasses an obligation on the State to generate health research and development that addresses, for example, the health needs of disadvantaged individuals, communities and populations. Health research and development includes classical medical research into drugs, vaccines and diagnostics, as well as operational or implementation research into the social, economic, cultural, political

and policy issues that determine access to medical care and the effectiveness of public health interventions. Implementation research, which has an important role to play with a view to dismantling societal obstacles to health interventions and technologies, should be taken into account when drafting the national health plan.

96. The plan must include certain features such as clear objectives and how they are to be achieved, time frames, indicators and benchmarks to measure achievement, effective coordination mechanisms, reporting procedures, a detailed budget that is attached to the plan, financing arrangements (national and international), evaluation arrangements, and one or more accountability devices. In order to complete the plan, there will have to be a process for prioritizing competing health needs.

97. Before their finalization, key elements of the draft plan must be subject to an impact assessment to ensure that they are likely to be consistent with the State's national and international legal obligations, including those relating to the right to the highest attainable standard of health. For example, if the draft plan proposes the introduction of user fees for health services, it is vital that an impact assessment is undertaken to anticipate the likely impact of user fees on access to health services for those living in poverty. If the assessment confirms that user fees are likely to hinder access, the draft plan must be revised before adoption; otherwise, it is likely to be inconsistent with the State's obligations arising from the right to the highest attainable standard of health.

98. Of course, planning is only the means to an end: an effective, integrated health system that is accessible to all. The main task is implementation. Evaluation, monitoring and accountability can help to ensure that all those responsible for implementation discharge their duties as planned, and that any unintended consequences are swiftly identified and addressed.

(b) Monitoring and accountability

99. As already discussed, monitoring and accountability have a crucial role to play in relation to human rights and health systems. Accountability provides individuals and communities with an opportunity to understand how those with responsibilities have discharged their duties. Equally, it provides those with responsibilities the opportunity to explain what they have done and why. Where mistakes have been made, accountability requires redress. But accountability is not a matter of blame and punishment. It is a process that helps to identify what works, so it can be repeated, and what does not, so it can be revised. It is a way of checking that reasonable balances are fairly struck.

100. In the context of health systems, there are many different types of accountability mechanisms, including health commissioners, democratically elected local health councils, public hearings, patients' committees, impact assessments, judicial proceedings, and so on. An institution as complex and important as a health system requires a range of effective, transparent, accessible, independent accountability mechanisms. The media and civil society organizations have a crucial role to play.

101. Accountability in respect of health systems is often extremely weak. Sometimes the same body provides health services, regulates and holds to account. In some cases, accountability is little more than a device to check that health funds were spent as they should have been. Of course, that is important. But human rights accountability is much broader. It is also concerned with ensuring that health systems are improving, and the right

to the highest attainable standard of health is being progressively realized, for all, including disadvantaged individuals, communities and populations.

102. In some States, the private health sector, while playing a very important role, is largely unregulated. Crucially, the requirement of human rights accountability extends to both the public and private health sectors. Additionally, it is not confined to national bodies; it also extends to international actors working on health-related issues.

103. Accountability mechanisms are urgently needed for all those—public, private, national and international—working on health-related issues. The design of appropriate, independent accountability mechanisms demands creativity and imagination. Often associated with accountability, lawyers must be willing to understand the distinctive characteristics and challenges of health systems, and learn from the rich experience of medicine and public health.

104. The issue of accountability gives rise to two related points.

105. First, the right to the highest attainable standard of health should be recognized in national law. This is very important because such recognition gives rise to legal accountability for those with responsibilities for health systems. As is well known, the right is recognized in the Constitution of WHO, as well as the Declaration of Alma-Ata. It is also recognized in numerous binding international human rights treaties, including the Convention on the Rights of the Child, which has been ratified by every State in the world, except for two (the United States of America and Somalia). The right to the highest attainable standard of health is also protected by numerous national constitutions. It should be recognized in the national law of all States.

106. Second, although important, legal recognition of the right to the highest attainable standard of health is usually confined to a very general formulation that does not set out in any detail what is required of those with responsibilities for health. For this reason, a State must not only recognize the right to health in national law but also ensure that there are more detailed provisions clarifying what society expects by way of health-related services and facilities. For example, there will have to be provisions relating to water quality and quantity, blood safety, essential medicines, the quality of medical care, and numerous other issues encompassed by the right to the highest attainable standard of health. Such clarification may be provided by laws, regulations, protocols, guidelines, codes of conduct and so on. WHO has published important standards on a range of health issues. Obviously, clarification is important for providers, so they know what is expected of them. It is also important for those for whom the service or facility is intended, so they know what they can legitimately expect. Once the standards are reasonably clear, it is easier (and fairer) to hold accountable those with responsibilities for their achievement.

IMPLEMENTATION THROUGH NATIONAL HEALTH CARE PLANNING

It will be recalled that one of the 'core obligations' identified by the Committee in General Comment No. 14 (in paragraph 43, as extracted above) was the requirement that states 'adopt and implement a national public health strategy and plan of action', using 'epidemiological evidence', that is comprehensive in its coverage, participatory and transparent, and is periodically reviewed against 'right to health indicators and benchmarks'. This echoes the Alma-Ata Declaration proclamation that states' obligations in this respect comprise:

VIII

All governments should formulate national policies, strategies and plans of action to launch and sustain primary health care as part of a comprehensive national health system and in coordination with other sectors. To this end, it will be necessary to exercise political will, to mobilize the country's resources and to use available external resources rationally.

IX

All countries should cooperate in a spirit of partnership and service to ensure primary health care for all people since the attainment of health by people in any one country directly concerns and benefits every other country. In this context the joint WHO/UNICEF report on primary health care constitutes a solid basis for the further development and operation of primary health care throughout the world.

Indeed, a significant contribution to the capacity and uptake of states in formulating such national plans has been made by the work of the WHO, which has been at the forefront of establishing model health policies and programmes of action. Thus, in just six years between 2008 and 2013, the WHO published more than 100 guidelines, policy statements and recommendations relating to states' and communities' health policies or clinical interventions. These publications have ranged across just about every major (and many less obviously so) issue of public health concern, from controlling epidemics, administering immunization programmes, maternal and child health and welfare, and preparing for influenza pandemics, through guidelines on the treatment of tuberculosis, malaria, hepatitis, measles and rubella, as well as providing vitamin and vital minerals supplements to children and pregnant women, to infection control, safe abortions, blood transfusions, the treatment of mental disorders and recommendations on air quality, hand hygiene, physical activity, malnutrition, pain management and diagnosing HIV in children.[125]

In respect of national health plans in the poorest countries battling high levels of poverty, in particular, the WHO also devised a set of Human Rights, Health and Poverty Reduction Strategies in 2005, which outline approaches that states should take in formulating 'pro-poor health strategies that are based on human rights principles' and thereby 'recognize and address the reality of the most marginalized or vulnerable groups' (page 13). In the preparation of any national plan, the report urges states first to develop a participatory framework within which to formulate a health strategy that embraces 'every individual, no matter how poor or marginalized'. For 'without the participation of the poor, national policy planners run the risk of basing their strategies and policies on incorrect assumptions

[125] For a record of WHO publications, see WHO, 'Documents Listed Alphabetically' (2013), <http://www.who.int/publications/guidelines/atoz/en/index.html>. Further, the WHO Annual World Health Reports cover particular themes for each year: see the collection of prior reports at WHO, 'World Health Report Archive' (2013), <http://www.who.int/whr/previous/en/>.

and misunderstandings while overlooking opportunities that may exist to make a real difference and bring about genuine change' (page 22).

Notably, these features are reflected in the United Nations' Guiding Principles on Extreme Poverty,[126] regarding how states should combat the extensive and particular impacts of the instance of poverty on the right to health:

J. Right to the highest attainable standard of physical and mental health

81. In a clear example of the vicious circle of poverty, persons experiencing ill health are more likely to become poor, while persons living in poverty are more vulnerable to accidents, diseases and disability. Limited access to physical and mental health care, including medicines, insufficient nutrition and unsafe living environments deeply affect the health of persons living in poverty and impair their ability to engage in income-generating or productive livelihood activities. Women and girls carry a disproportionate care responsibility when health-care facilities are lacking or inaccessible and thus often must forego education or formal employment to provide care.

82. States should:

(a) Take multidimensional measures to tackle the relationship between ill health and poverty, recognizing the many and varied determinants of health and the agency and autonomy of persons living in poverty;

(b) Enhance the accessibility and quality of preventive and curative health care for persons living in poverty, including sexual and reproductive health care and mental health care;

(c) Ensure that persons living in poverty have access to safe and affordable medicines and that inability to pay does not prevent access to essential health care and medicine;

(d) Establish health-care facilities within the safe physical reach of communities living in poverty, including in rural areas and slums, and ensure that such facilities have all resources necessary for their proper functioning;

(e) Take special measures to target the main health conditions affecting persons living in poverty, including neglected diseases. This should include free immunization, educational programmes and training for health practitioners to identify and treat such illnesses;

(f) Implement specific and well-resourced policies to tackle gender-based violence, including accessible preventive and treatment services that protect the dignity and privacy of persons living in poverty;

(g) Provide tailor-made services for groups whose access to health services may raise particular challenges, such as language, geographical barriers, cultural barriers, age, discrimination or existing health status. Women living in poverty should have access to high-quality sexual and reproductive health services and information.

[126] As submitted in Human Rights Council, Final Draft of the Guiding Principles on Extreme Poverty and Human Rights, submitted by the Special Rapporteur on extreme poverty and human rights, A/HRC/21/39 (18 July 2012).

BASIC PRINCIPLES OF HEALTH CARE PLANNING

The WHO report on Human Rights, Health and Poverty Reduction Strategies mentioned earlier properly recognizes that in developing and executing a national health plan, 'the exact detail of the health component of each [plan]. . . will vary depending upon each country's context and specific health threats' (page 26). But that said, it continues:

Any policy-maker or planner working within the MOH [Ministry of Health] will be familiar with the main elements of a health policy and may well have experience in tailoring the policy specifically to meet the needs of the poor. Bringing a human rights approach to the task, however, gives the policy or strategy an additional dimension that extends to tackling the underlying causes, some of which may not normally fall within the remit of a health policy or be under the mandate of the MOH. It also lays out a clear scope of obligations on the part of the government that can provide a helpful framework for policy-makers on the one hand, and demonstrate a solid public commitment to human rights principles on the other.

Human rights instruments state that a government has three clear overriding duties or obligations when endeavouring to realize the human rights of its population. Using the right to health as an example and as the entry point for our analysis, the government concerned has the obligation:

- to respect: by refraining from any activity or policy that directly or indirectly may jeopardize an individual's capacity to enjoy the right to health;
- to protect: by taking measures to ensure risks to health are minimized and that no other party is able to interfere with anyone's right to health;
- to fulfil: by providing, facilitating and promoting all the necessary resources and systems required to meet the health needs of all individuals (page 25).

'Drawing on [the] deepening experience [of health workers], and informed by health good practices', the Special Rapporteur on the right to health has expanded at length on what he considers to be the key principles that underpin 'the general approach of the right to the highest attainable standard of health towards the strengthening of health systems'.[127] A large part of his 2008 report on health systems (paragraphs 36 to 66) is dedicated to outlining seventeen such principles, ranging from the need for transparency, participation and non-discrimination, through the importance of preventive policies, agency coordination and international cooperation, to states' core obligations and legal duties. These principles are then followed in the report by what might be viewed as guidance as to best practice policies and standards—referred to as 'the "building blocks" of a health system' in the Special Rapporteur's report:

67. Informed by health good practices, the preceding section outlines the general approach of the right to the highest attainable standard of health towards the strengthening of health

[127] Human Rights Council, Report of the Special Rapporteur on the right of everyone to the enjoyment of the highest attainable standard of physical and mental health, A/HRC/7/11 (31 January 2008), [37].

systems. This general approach has to be consistently and systematically applied across the numerous elements that together constitute a functioning health system.

68. What are these functional elements of a health system? The health literature on this issue is very extensive. For its part, WHO [in Everybody's Business: Strengthening Health Systems to Improve Health Outcomes, WHO, 2007, p. 3] identifies 'six essential building blocks' which together make up a health system:

(a) Health services. 'Good health services are those which deliver effective, safe, quality personal and non-personal health interventions to those who need them, when and where needed, with minimum waste of resources.' Non-personal health interventions include, for example, safe water and adequate sanitation;

(b) Health workforce. 'A well-performing health workforce is one which works in ways that are responsive, fair and efficient to achieve the best health outcomes possible, given available resources and circumstances, i.e. there are sufficient numbers and mix of staff, fairly distributed; they are competent, responsive and productive';[128]

(c) Health information system. 'A well-functioning health information system is one that ensures the production, analysis, dissemination and use of reliable and timely information on health determinants, health systems performance and health status';

(d) Medical products, vaccines and technologies. 'A well-functioning health system ensures equitable access to essential medical products, vaccines and technologies of assured quality, safety, efficacy and cost-effectiveness, and their scientifically sound and cost-effective use';

(e) Health financing. 'A good health financing system raises adequate funds for health, in ways that ensure people can use needed services, and are protected from financial catastrophe or impoverishment associated with having to pay for them';

(f) Leadership, governance, stewardship. This 'involves ensuring strategic policy frameworks exist and are combined with effective oversight coalition-building, the provision of appropriate regulations and incentives, attention to system-design, and accountability'.

69. Although some of these formulations may be subject to debate, for the purposes of this report these 'building blocks' are a useful way of looking at a health system. Of course, each 'building block' has generated a huge literature over many years.

70. For present purposes, three short points demand emphasis. First, these are not only 'building blocks' for a health system, they are also 'building blocks' for the right to the highest attainable standard of health. Like a health system, the right to health requires health services, health workers, health information, medical products, financing and stewardship.

71. Second, in practice, the 'building blocks' might not have all the features required by the right to the highest attainable standard of health. For example, a country might have a health information system, one of the WHO 'building blocks'. But the information system might not include appropriately disaggregated data, which is one of the requirements of the

[128] On this specific issue, the report devotes a further page-and-a-half of description and of direction-giving to states: see Human Rights Council, Report of the Special Rapporteur, A/HRC/7/11 (31 January 2008), [75]–[86].

right to health. In short, an essential 'building block' might be in place, but without all the features required by international human rights law.

72. Third, the crucial challenge is to apply—or integrate—the right to the highest attainable standard of health, as well as other human rights, across the six 'building blocks'. The general approach outlined in the preceding section has to be consistently and systematically applied to health services, health workers, health information, medical products, financing and stewardship—all the elements that together constitute a functioning health system.

73. The systematic application of the right to health to the six 'building blocks' is likely to have a variety of results. In some cases, the right to health will reinforce existing features of the 'building blocks' that routinely receive the attention they deserve. In other cases, the application of the right will identify existing features of the 'building blocks' that tend to be overlooked in practice and that require much more attention, such as the disaggregation of data on appropriate grounds. It is also possible that the application of the right may identify features that, although important, are not usually regarded as forming any part of the six 'building blocks'.

Together, these general and particularized reports comprise the essential elements of national health care plans, in which respect the WHO also offers direct and practical assistance to states through individual country reviews of health strategies and collaborations between governments and the WHO.[129] Such bespoke analyses and/or assistance have been conducted in respect of nearly every country. Typically, the WHO provides only country profiles and some indication of particular risk factors (like alcohol, tobacco or road traffic casualties) of the richer states whose health systems are comparatively well catered for. Whereas in respect of least-developed and middle-income states it will additionally establish a cooperation strategy which involves greater levels of scrutiny of, and assistance for, the state's health care system. Thus, for example, in respect of Malaysia (a middle-income economy), the WHO Country Co-operation Strategy (CCS) 2009–13 assesses the country's health care planning and delivery as follows (pages 13–14):

Malaysia is an upper-middle income country with a stable political system and democratically elected government. The Outline Perspective Plan and the Ninth Malaysia Development Plan articulate the national priorities which include (among others), promoting growth with equity, strengthening human resource development, improving the standard and sustainability of quality of life and pursuing environmentally sustainable development. The health status in Malaysia is relatively good, being on target to achieve the Millennium Development Goals (MDGs). An extensive and comprehensive primary health care (PHC) system provides good access to care. Total health expenditure (THE) is only 4.3% of GDP, with about 45% from the public sector, but 40% of THE is out of pocket from private households. The national health priorities include enhancing the health care delivery system to increase access to quality care, and reducing the disease burden, both communicable and non-communicable diseases. The key health challenges are posed by the changing disease pattern with high prevalence of non-communicable diseases and their risk factors, a rapidly growing private sector and high proportion of health expenditure being out of pocket, and a large population of migrant workers who are at high risk of communicable diseases.

[129] For an archive of the WHO profiles on each country, including the ones extracted below, see WHO, 'Countries' (2013), <http://www.who.int/countries/en/>.

Malaysia's rapid economic growth has reduced its need for development assistance, and the health sector receives a miniscule proportion of such financial assistance. During the past decade, WHO support has changed focus from the provision of fellowships and scholarships for capacity building, to selective technical and policy advice and advocacy. The increasing complexities of health issues in the country necessitate inputs requiring more sophisticated technical expertise.

WHO has focused on policy advice on critical issues and selected technical issues during the previous CCS period. Major policy advice has been on issues such as HIV/AIDS, International Health Regulations (IHR), trade and health sector issues related to liberalization. Technical issues addressed include adoption of international standards and norms such as the Framework Convention on Tobacco Control (FCTC),[130] strengthening of technical and managerial capacity (such as for food safety), and monitoring health situation (such as HIV/AIDS Burden of disease). Additionally support has been provided to key health institutions to play a leading role at regional and international levels, with several Malaysian institutions now taking the lead in policy and capacity development in the region and in ASEAN.

The Strategic Approach for the period 2009-2013 continues and deepens the direction developed during the previous CCS (2006–2008). A Strategic Agenda has been agreed and it has two arms. The first arm covers issues on which WHO will provide support to Malaysia. The second arm identifies issues on which WHO will support Malaysia's participation and contributions in regional and international collaboration, with such collaboration providing opportunities for Malaysia to share its experiences and lessons with other countries while also learning from others. While it is envisaged that Malaysia would make significant contributions in this second arm, strong support would be needed from all the three levels of WHO to make this arm a success. Malaysia would derive benefit from mutual learning and from WHO technical support for such initiatives. The issues identified in each arm are based on the priority needs, as well as the capacity and interest of Malaysia and WHO. In summary, the issues are listed below.

First arm: WHO support for Malaysian priority areas:

1. Development and strengthening of the health system and health policy related to:
   - Health reform and health care financing
   - Inter-sectoral action in addressing health inequities
   - Strategic planning and coordination for human resource development
   - Capacity building for evidence based policy and practice
   - Health information and knowledge management
2. Communicable disease control focusing on:
   - HIV/AIDS and Sexually Transmitted Infections (STI)
   - Surveillance and response to outbreaks of emerging diseases and International Health Regulations (IHR) including Asia-Pacific Strategy on Emerging Diseases (APSED and APSED 2010)

[130] Framework Convention on Tobacco Control (adopted 21 May 2003, 2302 UNTS 166, entered into force 27 February 2005). As of September 2013, the FCTC has 178 states parties to it.

- Vector-borne diseases: Prevention and Control of Dengue, Malaria Elimination and Lymphatic Filariasis Elimination

3. Prevention and Control of Non-communicable disease (NCD), and their risk factors and promotion of healthy lifestyles

Second Arm: Malaysia's participation in-and contribution to-regional and international collaboration with WHO support towards mutual learning:

- Health system governance
- Quality Improvement
- Primary Health Care (PHC)
- Maternal, newborn and child health, adolescent health and reproductive health
- Nutrition
- Food safety and Quality
- Pharmaceuticals
- Environmental health
- Harm Reduction Programmes for Injecting Drugs Users

In each of the areas specified, important programmatic areas have been identified which will be the focus of policy or technical inputs (First Arm) and the utilization of Malaysia's lessons and achievements with WHO's support at the regional and global levels (Second Arm).

In respect of Zambia, a much poorer state, the WHO Country Co-operation Strategy 2008–13 first assesses the state of the country's health care policy and planning, and then summarizes the challenges faced by the health sector to improve its level of service:

2.4.1 National Health Policy and Planning

The National Health Strategy Plan 2006–2010 constitutes a summary chapter of Vision 2030 and the Fifth National Development Plan. The targets to be achieved under the Vision 2030 include attaining health MDGs, increased access to health facilities and availability of health workers. The NHSP 2006–2010 identifies twelve (12) priority interventions for attaining the health improvement through effective coordination, implementation and monitoring of health services. The objectives of Health Systems Governance were:

- To provide a comprehensive policy and legal framework for effective coordination, implementation and monitoring of health services;
- To ensure efficient and effective organization and management of health service delivery at all levels;
- To ensure that the different situations and requirements of men and women are catered for so as to promote gender sensitivity and equity in delivery and access to health services; and,
- To strengthen SWAp management and coordinating mechanisms in order to improve health sector performance.

Zambia has a mature Sector-wide Approach (SWAp) mechanism. The MoH coordinates all planning activities, using a range of medium and short-term plans for the sector. The sector uses the Medium-Term Expenditure Framework (MTEF) budget to allocate resources for implementation. Support is needed to allocate resources across facilities in their districts. Costs of inputs are provided and districts are advised to use annual inflation rates, but recent fuel price increases have had an impact on the spending power of districts. All known resources that come under MoH management are included in the MoH resource envelope and the MTEF. (p. 10)

…

2.5 Summary of challenges in the health sector

The health sector in Zambia was faced with several challenges such as the high burden of preventable diseases, particularly in the areas of HIV, malaria, TB, diarrhoeal and respiratory diseases. The situation for TB is improving but case detection remains low, especially in children. Knowledge on HIV status and use of counselling and testing services is inadequate. Indoor residual spraying for malaria prevention has proved an effective intervention but is applied in a limited number of districts. There is also increasing burden of non- communicable diseases, particularly diabetes, obesity and hypertension. The current maternal and child mortality levels remain high and Zambia is unlikely to attain the related MDGs at current rate of reduction. The deaths are mostly occurring at the perinatal stage. Maternal deaths are mostly caused by clinical factors. Information on adolescent sexuality needs to be scaled up. Access to the different components of IMCI [Integrated Management of Child Illness] services is not adequately available. Prevalence of malnutrition among children and pregnant women remains high. EPI [Expanded Program on Immunization] coverage is up but there are significant variations between districts. Cold chain storage capacity at the national, provincial and district levels is less than desired and will be further challenged in the light of the possible introduction of new vaccines.

The persistent inadequate availability of skilled health professionals has resulted in low access to health services in all communities and facilities. The profile shows an aging professional cohort, particularly among medical staff. The training institutions are insufficient to meet the projected needs, with most of them operating below capacity. They are also poorly distributed, particularly among rural and urban areas. Physical access to functional health centres is poor in rural areas. Where they exist in urban areas, their capacity is limited leading to congestion in facilities. There is still lack of specialist care in key areas responsible for high disease burden e.g. cardiovascular and renal conditions, and a number of diagnostic procedures still require sending patients abroad at a high cost. There are difficulties in the referral systems with geographical barriers (terrain, transport, etc.,) to access.

Health financing is below acceptable levels for programme implementation. Out of pocket expenditure is high. Donor support is a significant component of the budget; however, it is mainly earmarked for a few programme areas. The existing health information systems need to be strengthened at all levels. (p. 13)

PLANNING FOR PRIMARY HEALTH CARE

The content and boundaries of 'primary health care' (as highlighted in earlier extracts from the Alma-Ata Declaration, and as reflected in the above two country analyses) is a key element in a state's national health plan or strategy, which ideally, the Alma-Ata Declaration goes on to suggest:

1. reflects and evolves from the economic conditions and sociocultural and political characteristics of the country and its communities and is based on the application of the relevant results of social, biomedical and health services research and public health experience;

2. addresses the main health problems in the community, providing promotive, preventive, curative and rehabilitative services accordingly;

3. includes at least: education concerning prevailing health problems and the methods of preventing and controlling them; promotion of food supply and proper nutrition; an adequate supply of safe water and basic sanitation; maternal and child health care, including family planning; immunization against the major infectious diseases; prevention and control of locally endemic diseases; appropriate treatment of common diseases and injuries; and provision of essential drugs;

4. involves, in addition to the health sector, all related sectors and aspects of national and community development, in particular agriculture, animal husbandry, food, industry, education, housing, public works, communications and other sectors; and demands the coordinated efforts of all those sectors;

5. requires and promotes maximum community and individual self-reliance and participation in the planning, organization, operation and control of primary health care, making fullest use of local, national and other available resources; and to this end develops through appropriate education the ability of communities to participate;

6. should be sustained by integrated, functional and mutually supportive referral systems, leading to the progressive improvement of comprehensive health care for all, and giving priority to those most in need;

7. relies, at local and referral levels, on health workers, including physicians, nurses, midwives, auxiliaries and community workers as applicable, as well as traditional practitioners as needed, suitably trained socially and technically to work as a health team and to respond to the expressed health needs of the community.

The matter of how national health plans ought to be structured and implemented is also of critical importance to their success. It is for this reason that the Committee, in General Comment No. 14, stresses the importance of an overarching legislative framework through which relevant institutions, policies and practices dealing with health ought to be mediated.

Framework legislation

53. The most appropriate feasible measures to implement the right to health will vary significantly from one State to another. Every State has a margin of discretion in assessing which measures are most suitable to meet its specific circumstances. The Covenant, however, clearly imposes a duty on each State to take whatever steps are necessary to ensure that everyone has access to health facilities, goods and services so that they can enjoy, as soon as possible, the highest attainable standard of physical and mental health. This requires the adoption of a national strategy to ensure to all the enjoyment of the right to health, based on human rights principles which define the objectives of that strategy, and the formulation of policies and corresponding right to health indicators and benchmarks.

The national health strategy should also identify the resources available to attain defined objectives, as well as the most cost-effective way of using those resources.

54. The formulation and implementation of national health strategies and plans of action should respect, inter alia, the principles of non-discrimination and people's participation. In particular, the right of individuals and groups to participate in decision-making processes, which may affect their development, must be an integral component of any policy, programme or strategy developed to discharge governmental obligations under article 12. Promoting health must involve effective community action in setting priorities, making decisions, planning, implementing and evaluating strategies to achieve better health. Effective provision of health services can only be assured if people's participation is secured by States.

55. The national health strategy and plan of action should also be based on the principles of accountability, transparency and independence of the judiciary, since good governance is essential to the effective implementation of all human rights, including the realization of the right to health. In order to create a favourable climate for the realization of the right, States parties should take appropriate steps to ensure that the private business sector and civil society are aware of, and consider the importance of, the right to health in pursuing their activities.

56. States should consider adopting a framework law to operationalize their right to health national strategy. The framework law should establish national mechanisms for monitoring the implementation of national health strategies and plans of action. It should include provisions on the targets to be achieved and the time-frame for their achievement; the means by which right to health benchmarks could be achieved; the intended collaboration with civil society, including health experts, the private sector and international organizations; institutional responsibility for the implementation of the right to health national strategy and plan of action; and possible recourse procedures. In monitoring progress towards the realization of the right to health, States parties should identify the factors and difficulties affecting implementation of their obligations.

MONITORING, EVALUATION AND THE USE OF INDICATORS

National health care planning requires data to be established in the first place, and monitoring and evaluation thereafter, to ensure that its goals are being achieved, or if not, providing the information as to why not. As the Special Rapporteur on the right to health puts it:[131]

7. The United Nations Development Programme (UNDP) Human Development Report 2000: Human Rights and Human Development, devotes a chapter to, and makes a compelling case for, the careful use of human rights indicators: 'Statistical indicators are a powerful tool in the struggle for human rights. They make it possible for people and organizations—from grass-roots activists and civil society to governments and the United Nations—to identify important actors and hold them accountable for their actions.' Indicators, it continues, can be used as tools for:

- Making better policies and monitoring progress;
- Identifying unintended impacts of laws, policies and practices;

[131] UN General Assembly, Report of the Special Rapporteur on the right of everyone to the enjoyment of the highest attainable standard of physical and mental health, A/58/427 (10 October 2003), [7].

- Identifying which actors are having an impact on the realization of rights;
- Revealing whether the obligations of these actors are being met;
- Giving early warning of potential violations, prompting preventive action;
- Enhancing social consensus on difficult trade-offs to be made in the face of resource constraints;
- Exposing issues that had been neglected or silenced.

Crucially, human rights indicators can help States, and others, recognize when national and international policy adjustments are required.

In fact, the inclusion of performance indicators and benchmarks are now established features of many national, regional and global health plans. The three health-related MDGs (together with their respective targets) to reduce child mortality (MDG3), to improve maternal health (MDG 5) and to combat HIV/AIDS, malaria and other diseases (MDG 6), are a set of meta-indicators. As are the WHO's Global Health Indicators, upon which it bases its annualized World Health Statistics reports that measure individual country and global aggregate levels in respect of nearly 100 key health issues organized around ten themes, namely:

1. life expectancy and mortality;
2. cause-specific mortality and morbidity;
3. selected infectious diseases;
4. health service coverage;
5. risk factors;
6. health workforce, infrastructure and essential medicines;
7. health expenditure;
8. health inequities;
9. demographic and socio-economic statistics; and
10. health information systems and data availability.[132]

Building on the content of Article 12(2)—which comprises, in effect, a set of four high level indicators[133]—the Economic, Social and Cultural Rights Committee also stresses the importance of formulating, using and reviewing health indicators in General Comment No. 14:

Right to health indicators and benchmarks

57. National health strategies should identify appropriate right to health indicators and benchmarks. The indicators should be designed to monitor, at the national and international

[132] See, eg, WHO, 'World Health Statistics Report 2012: Part III—Global Health Indicators' (2012), <http://www.who.int/healthinfo/EN_WHS2012_Part3.pdf>.

[133] Namely, to improve the health of newborns, infants and children; to improve environmental and industrial hygiene; to prevent, treat and control disease; and to institute universal health care.

levels, the State party's obligations under article 12. States may obtain guidance on appropriate right to health indicators, which should address different aspects of the right to health, from the ongoing work of WHO and the United Nations Children's Fund (UNICEF) in this field. Right to health indicators require disaggregation on the prohibited grounds of discrimination.

58. Having identified appropriate right to health indicators, States parties are invited to set appropriate national benchmarks in relation to each indicator. During the periodic reporting procedure the Committee will engage in a process of scoping with the State party. Scoping involves the joint consideration by the State party and the Committee of the indicators and national benchmarks which will then provide the targets to be achieved during the next reporting period. In the following five years, the State party will use these national benchmarks to help monitor its implementation of article 12. Thereafter, in the subsequent reporting process, the State party and the Committee will consider whether or not the benchmarks have been achieved, and the reasons for any difficulties that may have been encountered.

As a matter of fact, the Committee has been assiduous in its frequent requests of states—rich and poor alike—for more statistical data on their health systems as it tries to build up national and global pictures of the state of peoples' health and the health care services being provided to them. Although some states certainly find it harder than others to collect and deliver such data in their periodic reports, a great many do so effectively. Interestingly, and importantly, as states respond with data, the Committee uses it not only to understand more clearly the health issues in the relevant country, but also to delve deeper into particular health problems and ask the state for still more information and explanation, as illustrated by the following extract from the Committee's Concluding Observations on Australia's fourth periodic report under the Covenant:[134]

28. In spite of the State party's commitment to 'close the gap' in key health indicators between indigenous and non-indigenous people, the Committee notes with concern the continuing high levels of ill health among indigenous people, in particular women and children.(arts. 2, para. 2; and 12)

The Committee calls on the State party to take immediate steps to improve the health situation of indigenous people, in particular women and children, including by implementing a human rights framework that ensures access to the social determinants of health such as housing, safe drinking water, electricity and effective sanitation systems. Further, the Committee invites the State party to identify disaggregated health indicators and appropriate national benchmarks in relation to the right to health, in line with the Committee's general comment No. 14, and to include information on the process of identifying such indicators and benchmarks in its next periodic report.

The Committee has been equally keen in urging states to adopt appropriate health indicators and benchmarks from which this data can be drawn and against which states (and the Committee) can measure their performance in providing for health needs.

[134] CESCR, Concluding Observations: Australia, E/C.12/AUS/CO/4 (12 June 2009), [28].

Obviously, these indicators vary from country to country, as circumstances dictate, but for many, the use of indicators is part of their administrative requirements of review and assessment in their delivery of all government services, including health. For example, the United Kingdom's Care Quality Commission undertakes thousands of on-site inspections and interviews each year as it continually assesses the standards of service delivered throughout the country across a range of health-related areas, including all National Health Service trusts (and all the facilities they operate and services they provide (including hospitals, surgeries and clinics)), dental care services and mental health care, and social care services.[135]

The setting of benchmarks and the assessing of performance can also be greatly enhanced when significant contributions are made to the process by non-governmental bodies and individuals. The following pair of extracts from a global survey of civil society-based accountability initiatives in the field of health illustrates such inputs in Brazil and India (even aside the superfluity of acronyms in the latter).[136]

Brazil

The Brazilian Health Councils System acknowledges the contribution citizens can make to accountability through the presence of health councils at the municipal, state and national levels. Mandated by law, representatives of civil society (50 per cent), health workers (25 per cent) and government officials and contracted out service providers (25 per cent), come together at the monthly meetings of the health councils to make binding decisions, approve budgets and health plans, and play a role in ensuring accountability. In December 2000, municipal health councils were operational in 5,451 municipalities, with approximately 88,000 council members.

The health councils are linked institutionally to the executive agencies—the National Health Council, State Health Councils, and Municipal Health Councils. The health councils' actions are guided by the recommendations from the health conferences, which take place at the three levels of government, with the broad participation of several social sectors. These conferences are convened every four years by the executive branch to evaluate the health situation and propose guidelines for the formulation of health policy. The monthly health councils also make it possible for the public to voice its demands, as they are open to the public. Whilst only elected council members are entitled to vote, all those present at the monthly meetings have a right to express an opinion. As the meetings are open to the public, the health councils permit greater adaptation of the programs offered by the system. Many public health units and public hospitals have also been setting up councils or other advisory bodies with significant representation of users.

[135] The results of these surveys and assessments are published in annual reports. For the most recent report and links to previous reports, see Care Quality Commission, 'Annual Report 2012/13' (2013), <http://www.cqc.org.uk/public/reports-surveys-and-reviews/reports/annual-report-2012/13>.

[136] Helen Potts, 'Accountability and the Right to the Highest Attainable Standard of Health' (University of Essex Human Rights Centre, 2008), 22 and 16, respectively, <http://www.womenslinkworldwide.org/pdf_programs/en_prog_rr_col_pubs_accountability.pdf>.

India

The Jan Swasthya Abhiyan (JSA or People's Health Movement-India) has had an ongoing process of critical engagement with the National Rural Health Mission framework (NRHM) in the form of the People's Rural Health Watch (PRHW), which is an independent initiative by JSA to audit the state of rural public health services periodically, particularly in the light of the official NRHM initiative. This auditing is independent of the official framework and has been conceptualised and implemented entirely by JSA. This programme has been implemented in seven northern states and involves JSA member organisations independently collecting information about the activities conducted under the NHRM, both at the state and national levels. Two rounds of these periodic surveys have been completed so far.

Interviews are conducted with health care providers in community health centres (CHCs) and primary health care centres (PHCs); patients in the CHC or PHC; village-based health workers; and people in the village community. The information collected from the CHCs and PHCs covers the following broad areas: the availability of health centres in the selected area; the availability of staff and personnel in these health centres; the availability of infrastructure, services and medicines in these centres; women and children's health services and their management; problems faced by the doctors and other personnel in performing their duties; and the changes being introduced by the NRHM. The questionnaire for the village health workers covers the broad areas of socio-economic background, selection process, quality of training, actual activities and tasks, and interaction with other health personnel. The questionnaires for patients and village community members deal with accessibility, availability and quality of health services in their respective areas. The survey information is then included in reports which are made publicly available and which serve a dual purpose. First, the reports assist with ensuring public awareness regarding implementation of the NRHM. Secondly, the reports assist with maintaining pressure on the government to be accountable for the promises of the NRHM.

General Comment No.14's broad guidelines as to indicators have been variously elaborated upon and supplemented, including by way of considerable investment in the formulation of a 'human rights-based approach' to right to health indicators. This last-mentioned effort has certainly added to the content and scope of right to health indicators, but has, it must be said, added little in terms of providing a new or alternative perspective on the matter. This much has been recognized by, for example, the Special Rapporteur on the right to health (as per the following extract from a 2006 Report), albeit by way of introduction to an assessment of the discrete features of a so-called 'human rights based approach' to right to health indicators.[137]

27. A human rights-based approach to health indicators is not a radical departure from existing indicator methodologies. Rather, it uses many commonly used health indicators,

[137] Human Rights Commission, Report of the Special Rapporteur on the right of everyone to the enjoyment of the highest attainable standard of physical and mental health, E/CN.4/2006/48 (3 March 2006). The assessment referred to is contained in [48]–[50] of this report, which itself draws on the Special Rapporteur's earlier analysis of right to health indicators *simpliciter*—that is, without the added 'human rights-based approach' perspective—in his earlier report, UN General Assembly, Report of the Special Rapporteur on the right of everyone to the enjoyment of the highest attainable standard of physical and mental health, A/58/427 (10 October 2003), [5]–[63]. In this, it is indeed difficult to distinguish between what the Special Rapporteur labels a 'human rights-based approach to health indicators', and the Committee's 'right to health indicators', which, as CESCR, General Comment No. 14, [57] makes clear, also require disaggregation ('on the prohibited grounds of discrimination').

adapts them so far as necessary (e.g. by requiring disaggregation), and adds some new indicators to monitor issues (e.g. participation and accountability) that otherwise tend to be neglected. In short, a human rights-based approach to health indicators reinforces, enhances and supplements commonly used indicators.

In relation to right to health in the specific circumstances of using a human-rights-based approach to poverty reduction, the UN Office of the High Commissioner for Human Rights (OHCHR) has drawn up a number of targets and indicators that complement the broader guidance provided in the General Comment:[138]

C. Key targets and indicators

Target 1: All people to have access to adequate and affordable primary health care

Indicators:

- Life expectancy at birth
- Proportion of public expenditure on primary health care
- Proportion of poor people not covered by any kind of pre-payment mechanisms, by non-discretionary interventions (e.g., exemption schemes, cash subsidies, vouchers) in relation to health user fees, or by privately funded health insurance
- Number of primary health care units per thousand population
- Number of doctors per thousand population
- Proportion of poor people with access to affordable essential drugs

Target 2: To eliminate avoidable child mortality

Indicators:

- Under-five mortality rate
- Infant mortality rate
- Proportion of under-five children immunized against communicable diseases

Target 3: To eliminate avoidable maternal mortality

Indicators:

- Maternal mortality ratio
- Proportion of births attended by skilled health personnel
- Proportion of mothers with access to pre- and post-natal medical care facilities

Target 4: All men and women of reproductive age to have access to safe and effective methods of contraception

Indicator:

The rate of use of safe and effective methods of contraception among poor couples of reproductive age who wish to use contraceptives

[138] OHCHR, Principles and Guidelines for a Human Rights Based Approach to Poverty Reduction Strategies, HR/PUB/06/12 (2006), [178].

Target 5: To eliminate HIV/AIDS

Indicators:

- HIV prevalence among pregnant women
- Condom use rate
- Number of children orphaned by HIV/AIDS

Target 6: To eliminate the incidence of other communicable diseases

Indicators:

- Prevalence and mortality rate associated with communicable diseases
- Proportion of people with access to clean, safe drinking water
- Proportion of people with access to adequate sanitation
- Proportion of people immunized against communicable diseases

Target 7: To eliminate gender inequality in access to health care

Indicators:

- Sex ratio (overall, birth and juvenile)
- Disability-adjusted life years lost for men and women
- Ratio of women and men treated in medical institutions

The OHCHR report notes that as 'ill health is constitutive of poverty if the lack of command over economic resources plays a role in its causation . . . [so] the right to health has a crucial role to play in relation to poverty reduction' (paragraph 173). These indicators, it argues, can be used to monitor and evaluate the means by which states in which poverty is prevalent, or even just present, can go about realizing the right to health.[139]

In fact, the field of health indictors has become somewhat overcrowded in recent years, which, as the Special Rapporteur noted in 2006, leads to a number of difficulties, not the least of which is the 'problem of terminology'. After explaining the nature of this problem, the Special Rapporteur provides a suggested road map out of the morass:[140]

51. The literature reveals a multitude of health indicators. But there is a more fundamental difficulty. There is no commonly agreed and consistent way of categorizing and labeling different types of health indicators. For example, the following categories and labels for indicators can be found: performance, statistical, variable, process, conduct, outcome,

[139] The report goes on to add a set of 'key features of a strategy for realizing the right to health', including improving the supply, accessibility, affordability and effectiveness of health services for the poor, as well as promoting policies that 'bear positively on the underlying determinants of health, entailing particular benefits for the poor': OHCHR, Principles and Guidelines for a Human Rights Based Approach to Poverty Reduction Strategies, HR/PUB/06/12 (2006), [179]–[183].

[140] Human Rights Commission, Report of the Special Rapporteur on the right of everyone to the enjoyment of the highest attainable standard of physical and mental health, E/CN.4/2006/48 (3 March 2006), [51]–[57].

output, result, achievement, structural, screening, qualitative, quantitative, core and rated. The same indicator may appear in several categories. This multiplicity of overlapping labels is very confusing. Crucially, it confines meaningful discussion to a small elite of health experts. The lack of a common approach to the classification of health indicators represents a challenge to those who wish to introduce a simple, consistent and rational system for human rights-based health indicators.

52. If progress is to be made, there must be a degree of terminological clarity and consistency. In 2003, the Special Rapporteur suggested that special attention should be devoted to the following three categories of indicators: structural, process and outcome indicators. While there is no unanimity in the health literature, these categories and labels are widely understood. They are also relatively straightforward...

53. In the following paragraphs, the Special Rapporteur provides definitions of structural, process and outcome indicators. He accepts that it is not always easy to draw a neat line between these categories. No doubt the definitions will need further tightening. Nonetheless, he suggests that what follows will serve as working definitions.

54. Structural indicators address whether or not key structures and mechanisms that are necessary for, or conducive to, the realization of the right to health, are in place. They are often (but not always) framed as a question generating a yes/no answer. For example, they may address: the ratification of international treaties that include the right to health; the adoption of national laws and policies that expressly promote and protect the right to health; or the existence of basic institutional mechanisms that facilitate the realization of the right to health, including regulatory agencies.

55. Process indicators measure programmes, activities and interventions. They measure, as it were, State effort. For example, the following are process indicators: the proportion of births attended by skilled health personnel; the number of facilities per 500,000 population providing basic obstetric care; the percentage of pregnant women counselled and tested for HIV; the percentage of people provided with health information on maternal and newborn care, family planning services and sexually transmitted infections; the number of training programmes and public campaigns on sexual and reproductive health rights organized by a national human rights institution in the last five years. Such process indicators can help to predict health outcomes.

56. Outcome indicators measure the impact of programmes, activities and interventions on health status and related issues. Outcome indicators include maternal mortality, child mortality, HIV prevalence rates, and the percentage of women who know about contraceptive methods.

57. While structural indicators will often be framed as a question generating a yes/no answer, process and outcome indicators will often be used in conjunction with benchmarks or targets to measure change over time. However, there is no conceptual reason why all three types of indicators cannot either generate a yes/no answer or be used with benchmarks to measure change over time.

This is indeed the structural format adopted in the OHCHR's important recent work on human rights indicators, in which the set of 'illustrative indicators' on the right to health that it lays out are categorized as structural, process or outcomes-based, in their application to the five key themes identified for health (sexual and reproductive health; child mortality and health care; natural and occupational environment; prevention, treatment and control of diseases; and accessibility to health facilities and essential medicines).[141]

This latter OHCHR report provides an extensive review of the object, theory and practice of the use of indicators. It also, importantly, advocates care and restraint in choice of indicators, reflecting the concern of many that 'indicator fatigue' may be working against the essential task of winning the support of agencies and organizations to use indicators to collect the data in the first place.[142]

For instance, sometimes a single indicator may be adequate to cover more than one attribute of a right; in other cases several may be required to cover just one attribute. In such instances, to the extent that substantive conceptual requirements are met, indicators that capture more than one attribute of a right could be selected with a view to limiting their total number... Moreover, not all illustrative indicators developed for a right in this Guide [as above, in respect of the right to health] need to be used. For example, the actual choice of indicators to monitor treaty compliance could be made by a State party in consultation with the treaty body concerned while taking into account the country's context, its implementation priorities and statistical considerations on data availability.[143]

ENFORCEMENT, VIOLATIONS AND REMEDIES

As the above discussions of plans, strategies, monitoring and evaluation attest, a state's accountability for the standard and performance of its health care policies and practices operates at the political level as well as that of legal obligation. This is true also of the right to health insofar as it is realized through a state's health care performance. That said, however, this section of the chapter focuses on the opportunities for, and examples of, enforcement of legal obligations through various courts and tribunal bodies at the national and international levels, and in respect of the right to health in various legal settings: in domestic constitutional law and ordinary legislation, as well as in international human rights law (relating to a number of different treaties) and even international trade law. All of these will, to greater or lesser extents, serve as jurisprudential guides in the coming years to the Committee on Economic, Social and Cultural Rights as it develops its own body of case law regarding the right to health under the Optional Protocol.

In General Comment No. 14, the Committee sets out the legal basis upon which the right to health is founded, what constitutes a violation of the right and how and when those violations are to be addressed and remedies provided.

III. Violations

46. When the normative content of article 12 (Part I) is applied to the obligations of States parties (Part II), a dynamic process is set in motion which facilitates identification of

[141] OHCHR, Human Rights Indicators: A Guide to Measurement and Implementation ('Human Rights Indicators'), HR/PUB/12/5 (2012), 90. Notably, the chosen health themes broadly reflect the 'steps to be taken by states' in Article 12(2) of the ICESCR.

[142] See, eg, Riedel, 'The Human Right to Health: Conceptual Foundations', 35–6.

[143] OHCHR, Human Rights Indicators, 72.

violations of the right to health. The following paragraphs provide illustrations of violations of article 12.

47. In determining which actions or omissions amount to a violation of the right to health, it is important to distinguish the inability from the unwillingness of a State party to comply with its obligations under article 12. This follows from article 12.1, which speaks of the highest attainable standard of health, as well as from article 2.1 of the Covenant, which obliges each State party to take the necessary steps to the maximum of its available resources. A State which is unwilling to use the maximum of its available resources for the realization of the right to health is in violation of its obligations under article 12. If resource constraints render it impossible for a State to comply fully with its Covenant obligations, it has the burden of justifying that every effort has nevertheless been made to use all available resources at its disposal in order to satisfy, as a matter of priority, the obligations outlined above. It should be stressed, however, that a State party cannot, under any circumstances whatsoever, justify its non-compliance with the core obligations set out in paragraph 43 above, which are non-derogable.

48. Violations of the right to health can occur through the direct action of States or other entities insufficiently regulated by States. The adoption of any retrogressive measures incompatible with the core obligations under the right to health, outlined in paragraph 43 above, constitutes a violation of the right to health. Violations through acts of commission include the formal repeal or suspension of legislation necessary for the continued enjoyment of the right to health or the adoption of legislation or policies which are manifestly incompatible with pre-existing domestic or international legal obligations in relation to the right to health.

49. Violations of the right to health can also occur through the omission or failure of States to take necessary measures arising from legal obligations. Violations through acts of omission include the failure to take appropriate steps towards the full realization of everyone's right to the enjoyment of the highest attainable standard of physical and mental health, the failure to have a national policy on occupational safety and health as well as occupational health services, and the failure to enforce relevant laws.

Violations of the obligation to respect

50. Violations of the obligation to respect are those State actions, policies or laws that contravene the standards set out in article 12 of the Covenant and are likely to result in bodily harm, unnecessary morbidity and preventable mortality. Examples include the denial of access to health facilities, goods and services to particular individuals or groups as a result of de jure or de facto discrimination; the deliberate withholding or misrepresentation of information vital to health protection or treatment; the suspension of legislation or the adoption of laws or policies that interfere with the enjoyment of any of the components of the right to health; and the failure of the State to take into account its legal obligations regarding the right to health when entering into bilateral or multilateral agreements with other States, international organizations and other entities, such as multinational corporations.

Violations of the obligation to protect

51. Violations of the obligation to protect follow from the failure of a State to take all necessary measures to safeguard persons within their jurisdiction from infringements of the right to health by third parties. This category includes such omissions as the failure to regulate the activities of individuals, groups or corporations so as to prevent them from violating the right to health of others; the failure to protect consumers and workers from practices detrimental to health, e.g. by employers and manufacturers of medicines or food;

the failure to discourage production, marketing and consumption of tobacco, narcotics and other harmful substances; the failure to protect women against violence or to prosecute perpetrators; the failure to discourage the continued observance of harmful traditional medical or cultural practices; and the failure to enact or enforce laws to prevent the pollution of water, air and soil by extractive and manufacturing industries.

Violations of the obligation to fulfil

52. Violations of the obligation to fulfil occur through the failure of States parties to take all necessary steps to ensure the realization of the right to health. Examples include the failure to adopt or implement a national health policy designed to ensure the right to health for everyone; insufficient expenditure or misallocation of public resources which results in the non-enjoyment of the right to health by individuals or groups, particularly the vulnerable or marginalized; the failure to monitor the realization of the right to health at the national level, for example by identifying right to health indicators and benchmarks; the failure to take measures to reduce the inequitable distribution of health facilities, goods and services; the failure to adopt a gender-sensitive approach to health; and the failure to reduce infant and maternal mortality rates.

…

Remedies and accountability

59. Any person or group victim of a violation of the right to health should have access to effective judicial or other appropriate remedies at both national and international levels. All victims of such violations should be entitled to adequate reparation, which may take the form of restitution, compensation, satisfaction or guarantees of non-repetition. National ombudsmen, human rights commissions, consumer forums, patients' rights associations or similar institutions should address violations of the right to health.

60. The incorporation in the domestic legal order of international instruments recognizing the right to health can significantly enhance the scope and effectiveness of remedial measures and should be encouraged in all cases. Incorporation enables courts to adjudicate violations of the right to health, or at least its core obligations, by direct reference to the Covenant.

61. Judges and members of the legal profession should be encouraged by States parties to pay greater attention to violations of the right to health in the exercise of their functions.

62. States parties should respect, protect, facilitate and promote the work of human rights advocates and other members of civil society with a view to assisting vulnerable or marginalized groups in the realization of their right to health.

We turn now to assess how these responsibilities as to violations of the right to health are mediated through domestic and international courts and tribunals.

Domestic enforcement

It has been calculated that more than two-thirds of the world's constitutions[144] make some reference to the right to health, either explicitly (for example, South

[144] The MDG Gap Task Force estimates that 'health is a fundamental human right recognized in at least 135 national constitutions': MDG Gap Task Force, 'Delivering on the Global Partnership for Achieving the Millennium Development Goals' (2008), 42.

Africa),[145] implicitly (for example Germany)[146] or, alternatively, nominate the protection or promotion of health or health care as important policy goals (for example India).[147] Certainly, as the Special Rapporteur put it in 2008, 'the right to the highest attainable standard of health is... protected by numerous national constitutions'.[148] The right to health or to access to health care is, further, enshrined in the ordinary legislation of even more states, either as an amplification of its constitutional expression, or as a free-standing provision, as for example in Indonesia's National Social Security System Law No. 40 of 2004, which provides health insurance for the entire population, including free health care for the poor, the United Kingdom's National Health Service (Primary Care) Act 1977,[149] which maintains the country's system of universal health care and regulates its delivery, or, alternatively, the Danish Patients' Rights Act 1998, which protects patients' rights to dignity, autonomy and integrity.[150]

With this extensive and varied legislative grounding, it appears that the justiciability of the right to health, far from being a problem, has grown and flourished. Health-related litigation is now commonly pursued in domestic courts on the grounds of negligence or medical malpractice, failure to provide adequate health care and (what amounts to the same thing) failure to make basic health care affordable for the most vulnerable, and refusal to provide emergency medical assistance. The legal forms in which such litigation is pursued range across constitutional rights guarantees (including writs of *amparo* and *tutelas*—see following paragraph), ordinary legislation covering non-discrimination, access to information, privacy and fairness under administrative law, criminal law (for example, criminal negligence, assault or manslaughter), common law tort law, class actions and contract law.

That said, there are vast differences between states as to how enforcement through litigation in the courts is promoted. Thus, whereas in Colombia huge numbers of individual cases have been initiated through the system of simplified and expedited individual writs, known as *tutelas*, seeking remedies for claimed

[145] Article 27 of the Constitution of South Africa provides a guarantee to access to health care and emergency medical treatment. For the text and analysis of the application of this provision, see text below accompanying n. 162.

[146] Article 2 of the Basic Law of the Federal Republic of Germany provides that: '[e]veryone has the right to life and to physical integrity', which has been interpreted necessarily to imply a guarantee of a basic level of health care.

[147] Part IV of the Constitution of India contains a number of 'Directive Principles of State Policy', including to protect the health of individual adults (Article 39(e)), to protect the health of children (Article 39(f)) and to improve public health (Article 47).

[148] Human Rights Council, Report of the Special Rapporteur on the right of everyone to the enjoyment of the highest attainable standard of physical and mental health, A/HRC/7/11 (31 January 2008), [105].

[149] This Act repeals and replaces the National Health Service Act 1946 by which the United Kingdom's original NHS was established.

[150] Similar patients' rights legislation exists in a number of other European states, including Belgium, Lithuania and Romania. The voluntary, NGO-devised European Charter of Patients' Rights (November 2002) aims to promote the assurance under Article 35 of the Charter of Fundamental Rights of the European Union (adopted 18 December 2000, 2000/C 364/01, entered into force 1 December 2009), that states implement 'a high level of human health protection'.

breaches of the constitutional and other legislative protections of rights of access to adequate health care. The use of the similarly styled, but much more restrictive, writ of *amparo*, available in other Latin-American jurisdictions, has yielded fewer health cases in respect, for example, of Brazil (and far fewer in respect of Argentina), despite the constitutional protections of the right to life and to health also existing in these two countries. Still fewer cases, especially in respect of their constitutional protections of the right to life and to health, are filed in the Indian and South African courts (as discussed below). Yet, the volume of cases is no necessary guide as to the impact of litigation on the enforcement of health laws or improvement of health standards, especially for those most in need.

Thus, for example, on the one hand, tutela litigation in Colombia has confirmed the extent of the state's obligation to provide access to health care for children (under Article 44 of the Constitution), to encompass free vaccination programmes for children in the poorest areas; that a private health care company had to supply a hearing aid to a child free of charge even if the device was excluded from the compulsory health plan; and, further, that health providers (both public and private) may be compelled to cover the costs of specialized overseas medical treatment of children provided that the circumstances are sufficiently grave, the treatment is not available in Colombia, there is a strong likelihood of its success, and that the individuals are unable to cover the costs themselves.[151] Invoking the Colombian constitutional obligations to preserve the dignity of the individual (under Articles 1, 2 and 21) and the delivery of health services that are 'efficient, universal and co-operative' (under Article 49), tutela litigation has also been successfully employed to compel public and private health care institutions to make available free retroviral medication to adult HIV/AIDS patients who cannot afford them, again, even though the relevant medicines are not included on the free compulsory health plan.[152]

On the other hand, in many other respects the astronomical numbers of tutela cases filed have yielded no more than was due under existing laws or jurisprudence, and, in any case, seemed to have largely favoured the better off rather than the poorest. This was one of the conclusions reached by Alicia Ely Yamin, Oscar Parra-Vera and Camila Gianella in their detailed study of the judicial protection of the right to health in Colombia:

...with respect to the majority of the nearly 800,000 cases filed between 1999 and 2009, judges were enforcing either clear, pre-existing legal obligations—laid out in policies

[151] These cases and the use of *tutelas* in health litigation generally is discussed in Magdalena Sepúlveda, 'Colombia: The Constitutional Court's Role in Addressing Social Justice' in Malcolm Langford (ed), *Social Rights Jurisprudence: Emerging Trends in International and Comparative Law* (Cambridge University Press, Cambridge, 2008), 152–3. Sepúlveda notes, tellingly, that as compared to the more restrictive approach of the South African Constitutional Court in *Soobramoney* (which we discuss below), the reasoning of the Colombian Constitutional Court makes it clear that 'when life is in danger, the right to health is justiciable, notwithstanding the budgetary issues that the enforcement of the right may raise'; at 153, n. 71.

[152] Sepúlveda, 'Colombia', 157.

designed and enacted by the political branches of government—or obligations that have been read into the POS [the national social insurance scheme] over years of jurisprudence.

…

As the tutelas are awarded on a first-come, first-served basis and not all treatments are, or could be, universalized, the Court can be justifiably criticized for awarding health benefits based on the morally irrelevant criterion of who possesses greater access to justice. This inequity has been exacerbated greatly by the fact that those who have historically benefited from the tutelas are the better-off, who have a more comprehensive defined benefit package.[153]

There has also been a 'rights revolution' in health litigation in Brazil since the mid 2000s, with the courts showing great willingness to uphold claims based on enshrined constitutional rights or on ordinary legislation, although in terms of the sheer volume of cases, nothing like the same magnitude as in Colombia. Here, too, the cases are being filed predominantly by richer individuals and tend to focus on access to medicines, medical equipment and surgical procedures (including overseas), as well as dietary needs and hygiene products. Octavio Motta Ferraz concludes her study of health litigation in Brazil and its 'winners' and 'losers' by stating that, in respect of the former, 'we can say with some confidence…that they are neither those most deprived of health services, nor the most disadvantaged in terms of other social determinants of health'. She adds that, 'the total absence or paucity of judicialization in the regions, states and municipalities of Brazil where human development is lowest shows that those at the bottom of the socio-economic ladder are not going to court, whether individually or through public attorneys and NGOs, to claim their right to health'.[154]

Argentinian courts, in contrast, entertain a relatively small number of health litigation cases, and while, by this different way, some of the same distributive imbalances are nevertheless evident, there is also more reason to see the wider enforcement impacts of litigation. So, for example, in the joint cases of *Menores Comunidad Paynemil / accion de amparo Expte*. 311-CA-1997,[155] an Appeals Court held that the constitutionally protected right to health of both the adults (the primary case) and children (the amparo) of the indigenous Paynemil

[153] Alicia Ely Yamin, Oscar Parra-Vera and Camila Gianella, 'Colombia: The Judicial Protection of the Right to Health: An Elusive Promise?' in Alicia Ely Yamin and Sri Gloppen (eds), *Litigating Health Rights: Can Courts Bring More Justice to Health?* (Harvard University Press, Massachusetts, 2011), 113, 114.

[154] Octavio L Motta Ferraz, 'Brazil: Health Inequalities and Courts: The Social Impact of the Judicialization of Health' in Yamin and Gloppen, *Litigating Health Rights*, 99. Florian Hoffman and Fernando Bentes would appear to agree in light of their analysis of socio-economic rights in Brazil when they conclude that 'social rights litigation will continue to play an at once transformative and destabilizing role, true to the syncretism that characterizes so much of Brazil'; Florian Hoffman and Fernando Bentes, 'Accountability for Social and Economic Rights in Brazil' in Varun Gauri and Daniel Brinks (eds), *Courting Social Rights: Judicial Enforcement of Social and Economic Rights in the Developing World* (Cambridge University Press, Cambridge, 2008), 145.

[155] This, in fact. is a pair of cases heard and decided jointly, *Children of the Paynemil Community /Amparo*, 19 May 1997, File 311-CA-1997 (Second Chamber of Appeals for Civil Matters of the Province of Neuquen, Argentina).

community had been violated by the state's neglect in remedying a situation of high-level pollution of the community's drinking water source caused by a private oil corporation working nearby. The court concluded that 'even though the Government has performed some activities as to the pollution situation, in fact there has been a failure in adopting timely measures in accordance with the gravity of the problem'.[156]

In the case of *Viceconti v Ministry of Health and Social Welfare*,[157] Ms Viceconti, Argentina's national Ombudsman, successfully sought a court order compelling the government to institute protective measures in areas exposed to hemorrhagic fever, including immediate production and distribution of the Candid 1 vaccine to the more than 3.5 million affected people. The Federal Court of Appeals based its decision on the constitutional protection of the right to health. Notably, in granting the order under cover of the state's constitutional obligations, the Federal Court of Appeals relied expressly on the fact that the ICESCR, and within it the guarantee of the right to health under Article 12, had primacy in domestic law by virtue of its constitutional incorporation.[158]

The capacity of health litigation to impact large numbers of people, especially the poor or otherwise vulnerable, is likewise evidenced in cases before the Indian and South African courts.[159] In *Minister of Health v Treatment Action Campaign (TAC)*,[160] the Constitutional Court of South Africa held the government's restricted access to nevirapine, an anti-retroviral drug designed to prevent mother-child HIV transmission, constituted a breach of section 27(1)(a) of the Constitution, which provides that 'everyone has the right to have access to (a) health care services, including reproductive health care…'. Although the Court understood the research-based reasons advanced by the government as to why the medication was not made universally available, it nevertheless concluded that the need was so desperate and so great that such comprehensive coverage was required as quickly as possible:

> [68] …The fact that the research and training sites will provide crucial data on which a comprehensive programme for mother-to-child transmission can be developed and, if financially feasible, implemented is clearly of importance to government and to the country. So too is ongoing research into safety, efficacy and resistance. This does not mean, however, that until the best programme has been formulated and the necessary funds and infrastructure provided for the implementation of that programme, nevirapine must be withheld from

156 *Children of the Paynemil Community/Amparo.*

157 *Viceconti v Ministry of Health and Social Welfare*, 2 June 1998, Case no. 31.777/96 (Federal Court of Appeals, Argentina).

158 *Viceconti v Ministry of Health and Social Welfare.*

159 According to the fascinating comparative empirical research conducted by Daniel Brinks and Varun Gauri on social (including health) litigation in a number of developing countries, including India and South Africa, the litigation in these two states is substantially 'pro-poor', and significantly better on this score than Brazil, for example: see Daniel Brinks and Varun Gauri, 'The Law's Majestic Equality? The Distributive Impact of Litigating Social and Economic Rights', World Bank Policy Research Working Paper No. 5999 (2012).

160 *Minister of Health et al v Treatment Action Campaign et al* (No. 2), 5 July 2002, 2002 (5) SA 721 (Constitutional Court of South Africa).

mothers and children who do not have access to the research and training sites. Nor can it reasonably be withheld until medical research has been completed. A programme for the realisation of socio-economic rights must 'be balanced and flexible and make appropriate provision for attention to…crises and to short, medium and long term needs. A programme that excludes a significant segment of society cannot be said to be reasonable.'

[69] The applicants do not suggest that nevirapine should be administered indiscriminately to mothers and babies throughout the public sector. They accept that the drug should be administered only to mothers who are shown to be HIV-positive and that it should not be administered unless it is medically indicated and, where necessary, counselling is available to the mother to enable her to take an informed decision as to whether or not to accept the treatment recommended. Those conditions form part of the order made by the High Court.[161]

A critical feature in the Court's reasoning was the fact that the financial impost on the government to provide full coverage was minimal, as the drug was provided free to the state by the manufacturer for a period of five years.[162] In this respect, the TAC case was materially distinct from *Soobramoney v Minister of Health KwaZulu Natal*,[163] in which the same Court was prepared to countenance the restrictions the provincial government authorities had placed on access to medical treatment (renal dialysis, in that case) on account of the fact that the treatment was expensive and resources were limited, and the policy employed was fair and reasonable in the circumstances. The facts of the case are vital, and were laid out by Chaskalson P. at the beginning of the judgment:

[1] The appellant, a 41 year old unemployed man, is a diabetic who suffers from ischaemic heart disease and cerebro-vascular disease which caused him to have a stroke during 1996. In 1996 his kidneys also failed. Sadly his condition is irreversible and he is now in the final stages of chronic renal failure. His life could be prolonged by means of regular renal dialysis. He has sought such treatment from the renal unit of the Addington state hospital in Durban. The hospital can, however, only provide dialysis treatment to a limited number of patients. The renal unit has 20 dialysis machines available to it, and some of these machines are in poor condition. Each treatment takes four hours and a further two hours have to be allowed for the cleaning of a machine, before it can be used again for other treatment. Because of the limited facilities that are available for kidney dialysis the hospital has been unable to provide the appellant with the treatment he has requested.

[2] The reasons given by the hospital for this are set out in the respondent's answering affidavit deposed to by Doctor Saraladevi Naicker, a specialist physician and nephrologist in the field of renal medicine who has worked at Addington Hospital for 18 years and who is currently the President of the South African Renal Society. In her affidavit Dr Naicker says that Addington Hospital does not have enough resources to provide dialysis treatment for all patients suffering from chronic renal failure. Additional dialysis machines and more

[161] *Minister of Health v Treatment Action Campaign*, [68]–[69]. The quoted passage at the end of [68] comes from a decision of the same court, *Government of the Republic of South Africa et al v Grootboom et al*, 4 October 2000, 2001 (1) SA 46 (CC), [43].

[162] *Minister of Health v Treatment Action Campaign*, [48].

[163] *Soobramoney v Minister of Health KwaZulu Natal*, 27 November 1997, 1998 (1) SA 765 (CC) (Constitutional Court of South Africa).

trained nursing staff are required to enable it to do this, but the hospital budget does not make provision for such expenditure. The hospital would like to have its budget increased but it has been told by the provincial health department that funds are not available for this purpose.

[3] Because of the shortage of resources the hospital follows a set policy in regard to the use of the dialysis resources. Only patients who suffer from acute renal failure, which can be treated and remedied by renal dialysis are given automatic access to renal dialysis at the hospital. Those patients who, like the appellant, suffer from chronic renal failure which is irreversible are not admitted automatically to the renal programme.

The appellant had claimed that as section 27(3) of the Constitution provides that 'no one may be refused emergency medical treatment', his right would be violated if he was so denied. Further, and as an inevitable consequence, his right to life under section 11 would also be transgressed. The Court, however, took the view that:

[11] What is apparent from these provisions is that the obligations imposed on the state by sections 26 and 27 in regard to access to housing, health care, food, water and social security are dependent upon the resources available for such purposes, and that the corresponding rights themselves are limited by reason of the lack of resources. Given this lack of resources and the significant demands on them that have already been referred to, an unqualified obligation to meet these needs would not presently be capable of being fulfilled. This is the context within which section 27(3) must be construed.

[12] The appellant urges us to hold that patients who suffer from terminal illnesses and require treatment such as renal dialysis to prolong their lives are entitled in terms of section 27(3) to be provided with such treatment by the state, and that the state is required to provide funding and resources necessary for the discharge of this obligation.

[13] The words 'emergency medical treatment' may possibly be open to a broad construction which would include ongoing treatment of chronic illnesses for the purpose of prolonging life. But this is not their ordinary meaning, and if this had been the purpose which section 27(3) was intended to serve, one would have expected that to have been expressed in positive and specific terms.

Chaskalson P. then concludes:

[21] The applicant suffers from chronic renal failure. To be kept alive by dialysis he would require such treatment two to three times a week. This is not an emergency which calls for immediate remedial treatment. It is an ongoing state of affairs resulting from a deterioration of the applicant's renal function which is incurable. In my view section 27(3) does not apply to these facts.[164]

In yet another seminal South African health rights case, *B et al v Minister of Correctional Services*,[165] this time before the High Court, the Court held that while the state was obliged to provide HIV-positive prisoners with anti-retroviral medication, this was not an absolute right (not least because no such absolute right existed

[164] The other two judges on the Court concurred with Chaskalson P.'s reasoning.

[165] *B et al v Minister of Correctional Services*, 17 April 1997, 1997 (4) SA 441 (C) (High Court, Cape of Good Hope Provincial Division).

for the rest of society), and was limited by what the state could reasonably afford. Thus, it maintained that:

> [49] ... If the prison authorities should, therefore, make out a case that as a result of budgetary constraints, they cannot afford a particular form of medical treatment or that the provision of such medical treatment would place an unwarranted burden on the State, the Court may very well decide that the less effective medical treatment which is affordable to the State must in the circumstances be accepted as 'sufficient' or 'adequate medical treatment'.

Such 'resources realism' is less evident in Indian judicial thinking regarding health litigation. This is due, in part, to the 'gravity of the health care crisis' in India and to the general failure of effective enforcement mechanisms regarding those cases in which health rights have been upheld. This is according to the conclusions reached by Sharanjeet Parmar and Namita Wahi in their study of health litigation in India.[166] However, they also conclude that 'health rights litigation does *not* appear to be deepening health inequities between competing health interests'.[167] Certainly, there are a number of cases that illustrate apparent progress in reversing legislative injustices and correcting policy failures.

For example, in a series of cases in the 1980s and early 1990s, the Supreme Court of India employed an expansive interpretation of the constitutional right to life (Article 21) to include living with dignity and some base level of health and health care,[168] before finally, in 1996, stating definitively, in *Paschim Banga Khet Mazdoor Samity v State of West Bengal*,[169] that the right to life enshrined in the Indian Constitution (Article 21) elevates the preservation of human life to a level of paramount importance, and imposes, thereby, an obligation on the state to safeguard the right to life of every person. The following extract sets out the salient facts of the case and the reasoning of the court.

> [9]. The Constitution envisages the establishment of a welfare State at the federal level as well as at the State level. In a welfare State the primary duty of the Government is to secure the welfare of the people. Providing adequate medical facilities of the people is an essential part of the obligations undertaken by the Government in a welfare State. The Government discharges this obligation by running hospitals and health centres which provide medical care to the person seeking to avail those facilities. Article 21 imposes an obligation on the State to safeguard the right to life of every person. Preservation of

[166] Sharanjeet Parmar and Namita Wahi, 'India: Citizens and the Right to Health: Between Promise and Progress?' in Yamin and Gloppen, *Litigating Health Rights*, 155–89.

[167] Parmar and Wahi, 'India: Citizens and the Right to Health', 183.

[168] These cases (all from the Supreme Court of India), and the health issues they raised, included *Municipal Council, Ratlam v Shri Vardhichand et al*, 29 July 1980, (1981) SCR (1) 97 (health impacts of grossly inadequate sanitation facilities); *Francis Coralie Mullin v Union Territory of Delhi*, 13 January 1981, (1981) 2 SCR 516 (prisoners' health care); *Paramanand Katara v Union of India*, 28 August 1989, (1989) 4 SCR 286 (provision of emergency health care); *Subhash Kumar v State of Bihar et al*, 9 January 1991, (1991) SCR (1) 5 (health impacts of river water pollution); and *CESC Ltd v Subash Chandra Bose*, 15 November 1991, (1992) AIR SC 573 (defining health as a complete state of physical, mental and social well-being and not merely the absence of disease or infirmity).

[169] *Paschim Banga Khet Mazdoor Samity v State of West Bengal*, 6 May 1996, (1996) 4 SCC 37 (Supreme Court of India).

human life is thus of paramount importance. The Government hospitals run by the State and the Medical Officers employed therein are duty bound to extend medical assistance for preserving human life. Failure on the part of a Government hospital to provide timely medical treatment to a person in need of such treatment results in violation of his right to life guaranteed under Article 21. In the present case there was breach of the said right of Hakim Seikh guaranteed under Article 21 when he was denied treatment at the various Government hospitals which were approached even though his condition was very serious at that time and he was in need of immediate medical attention. Since the said denial of the right of Hakim Seikh guaranteed under Article 21 was by officers of the State in hospitals run by the State, the State cannot avoid its responsibility for such denial of the constitutional right of Hakim Seikh.

…

[16] It is no doubt true that financial resources are needed for providing these facilities. But at the same time it cannot be ignored that it is the constitutional obligation of the State to provide adequate medical services to the people. Whatever is necessary for this purpose has to be done. In the context of the constitutional obligation to provide free legal aid to a poor accused this Court has held that the State cannot avoid its constitutional obligation in that regard on account of financial constraints. (See *Khatri (II) v. State of Bihar*, (1981) 1 SCC 627 at p. 631: (AIR 1981 SC 928 at p.931)). The said observations would apply with equal, if not greater, force in the matter of discharge of constitutional obligation of the State to provide medical aid to preserve human life. In the matter of allocation of funds for medical services the said constitutional obligation of the State has to be kept in view. It is necessary that a time bound plan for providing these services should be chalked out keeping in view the recommendations of the Committee as well as the requirements for ensuring availability of proper medical services in this regard as indicated by us and steps should be taken to implement the same…

17. The Union of India is a party to these proceedings. Since it is the joint obligation of the Centre as well as the States to provide medical services it is expected that the Union of India would render the necessary assistance in the improvement of the medical services in the country on those lines.

By so deciding, the Supreme Court would seem to be giving preference to legal principle over economic realities; or rather, it may be seen as seeking to influence allocations in the latter by pressing home the importance of the former. And, indeed, the Supreme Court has since made it clear, in *Kapila Hingorani v the State of Bihar*,[170] that budgetary constraints are not a legitimate reason to qualify the right to health as embedded in the constitutional right to life, when to limit the right leads directly to its egregious violation. Thus, in this case, the deaths from starvation of public sector employees, whose salary payments were significantly in arrears, were attributed directly to the state. Appeals to financial stringency, it is clear, simply don't cut it when people are dying.

Evidently, litigating health rights in domestic courts has become both widespread and moderately successful in terms of securing respect for the right to

[170] *Kapila Hingorani v the State of Bihar*, 13 January 2005, (2003) 6 SCC 1 (Supreme Court of India).

health for a widening range of individuals and groups, including the poorest and most marginalized. But litigation, as Thérèse Murphy points out, also has its limits:

Complexity is also inevitable given the challenge of inequality and inequity. For some, the rising number of health rights cases simply sharpens the fear that a justiciable right to health, rather than addressing the social injustice that is 'killing people on a grand scale', will instead compound it. If those who are able to access the courts turn to law in increasing numbers in order to secure 'their' drugs, 'their' treatment, and, more broadly, 'their' right to health, this—the critics point out—will simply distort health budgets and presumably a range of other budgets as well.[171]

While the skyrocketing health care costs in nearly all Western states is caused by a host of factors, one of them is certainly the significant increases in tortious action in, for example, the United States (even absent a constitutional guarantee of the right to life), and the knock-on effect this has on health insurance premiums for service providers and individual consumers alike.[172] The recent trajectory of the health care system of a middle-income economy like Costa Rica (also without constitutional protection of health rights) is sobering reading, having built up an enviably equitable national universal health care system from the 1970s, it has been under greater pressure in recent times for reasons that some believe are closely related to the exponential rise in, and success of, low cost, open access health litigation over the last fifteen years or so, leading to claims of the 'harming [of] the health system by forcing the reallocation of funds away from general health priorities to high cost treatments of uncommon illnesses'.[173] While, in his study of these claims, Bruce Wilson sees 'no concrete evidence' of this occurring,[174] he acknowledges the possibility and its continuing threat.[175]

International enforcement

In addition to the ICESCR, the right to health or to the highest attainable standard of health is recognized in four of the United Nations' core international human rights treaties: the ICERD (Article 5(e)(iv)); the CEDAW (Article 12 (as well as Article 10(f)); the CRC (Article 24); and the CRPD (Article 25).[176]

Further, the interdependency of the right to health's relationship with other rights, such as the rights to life, food and water, as well as adequate sanitation and housing, is evident not only in the jurisprudence of some domestic legal

[171] Thérèse Murphy, *Health and Human Rights* (Hart, Oxford, 2013), 50.

[172] See, eg, Mary M. Pozarycki, 'Rising Health Care Costs' (2006) 15(2) *Annals of Health Law* 331, 333–4.

[173] Bruce M. Wilson, 'Costa Rica: Health Rights Litigation: Causes and Consequences' in Yamin and Gloppen, *Litigating Health Rights*, 133.

[174] Wilson, 'Costa Rica: Health Rights Litigation', 150.

[175] Noting, eg, the courts' 'continued deafness to...budgetary concerns': Wilson, 'Costa Rica: Health Rights Litigation', 146.

[176] Furthermore, and in addition to the ICESCR, the CRC, in Article 24, expressly recognizes the responsibility of states to take account of 'the needs of developing countries' in their realization of the right to health.

systems' rights regimes, but under international human rights regimes as well. Certainly, if one takes a broad perspective on the scope of the right to health, then the matrix of related rights and instruments, encompassing such social and environmental determinants as, for example, tobacco control and climate change, as well as all the obligations associated with providing medical care and treatment, is very extensive.[177]

Thus, for example, the African Commission on Human and Peoples' Rights held in one of its earliest decisions, that the African Charter's guarantee of the right to health under Article 16 encompasses a state's duties to 'provide basic services such as safe drinking water and electricity', as well access to adequate medicines.[178] The African Commission has also held that the environmental degradation that leads directly to human health problems is a violation of Article 16. In *Social and Economic Action Rights Centre (SERAC) v Nigeria* (2002), the Commission maintained that environmental pollution caused by extensive oil and gas exploration activities conducted over many decades in the Niger Delta by a government consortium with Shell Petroleum Development Corporation had resulted in the 'contamination of water, soil and air [which] has had serious short and long-term health impacts, including skin infections, gastrointestinal and respiratory ailments, and increased risk of cancers, and neurological and reproductive problems'.[179]

Poor environmental management and protection has also been held by the European Court of Human Rights in *López Ostra v Spain* to be a sufficient basis to breach a state's obligation under the European Convention on Human Rights to respect people's private and family lives. The 'unbearable' living conditions endured by a local community in Spain living next to a privately owned tannery waste treatment plant were apparently causing serious health problems and an unjustified interference with family life under Article 8 of the Convention.[180] While the casual link between the plant and the health problems suffered by the locals was not unequivocally established, and it was acknowledged that private and family life can be seriously disrupted without necessarily endangering people's health (paragraph 51), the Court nevertheless determined that 'the State did not succeed in striking a fair balance between the interest of the town's economic

[177] Notably, in this respect, Article 11 of the 1996 Revised European Social Charter holds states responsible not just for 'ensuring the effective exercise of the right to health', but to do so 'in co-operation with public or private organisations', and additionally 'to remove as far as possible the causes of ill-health', and to promote health education and 'encourage…individual responsibility in matters of health'.

[178] Which duties in this case, the state was failing to fulfil: *Free Legal Assistance Group et al v Zaire*, 4 April 1996, Communication Nos. 25/89, 47/90, 56/91, 100/93, (2000) AHRLR 74 (African Commission on Human and Peoples' Rights), [47].

[179] *Social and Economic Action Rights Centre (SERAC) v Nigeria*, 27 May 2002, Communication No. 155/96, (2001) AHRLR 6 (African Commission on Human and Peoples' Rights), [2]. While noting that 'the intervention of multinational corporations may be a potentially positive force for development if the State and the people concerned are ever mindful of the common good and the sacred rights of individuals and communities', (at [60]), the Commission nonetheless held Nigeria to have been in violation of Article 16 (among a number of Articles) of the Charter.

[180] *López Ostra v Spain* (App. 16798/90), (1995) 20 EHHR 277, [8].

well-being—that of having a waste-treatment plant—and the applicant's effective enjoyment of her right to respect for her home and her private and family life' (paragraph 58).

In addition to private and family life, there are also other civil and political rights that overlap and intersect with the right to health. For example, the European Court of Human Rights has read a number of health rights into the protection of the right to life under Article 2 of the European Convention on Human Rights. A number of these have been usefully summarized by the Court in *Nitecki v Poland* (2002):[181]

The Court recalls that the first sentence of Article 2 enjoins the State not only to refrain from the intentional and unlawful taking of life, but also to take appropriate steps to safeguard the lives of those within its jurisdiction. It cannot be excluded that the acts and omissions of the authorities in the field of health care policy may in certain circumstances engage their responsibility under Article 2 (see *Powell v. the United Kingdom* [decision], no. 45305/99, 4.5.2000).

The Court has held in cases involving allegations of medical malpractice that the State's positive obligations under Article 2 to protect life include the requirement for hospitals to have regulations for the protection of their patients' lives and also the obligation to establish an effective judicial system for establishing the cause of a death which occurs in hospital and any liability on the part of the medical practitioners concerned (see, among other authorities, *Erikson v. Italy*, [decision], no. 37900/97, 26.10.1999; *Calvelli and Ciglio v. Italy* [GC], no. 32967/96, § 49, ECtHR 2002).

Furthermore, with respect to the scope of the State's positive obligations in the provision of health care, the Court has stated that an issue may arise under Article 2 where it is shown that the authorities of a Contracting State put an individual's life at risk through the denial of health care which they have undertaken to make available to the population generally (see *Cyprus v. Turkey* [GC], no. 25781/94, § 219, ECtHR 2001-IV).

Another set of examples relating to the protection against torture, cruel, inhuman or degrading treatment or punishment under Article 7 of the ICCPR, and against torture in Article 1 of the Convention Against Torture (CAT), bear on the right to health, albeit *in extremis*. This is reflected in the case law of individual complaints established by both the UN Human Rights Committee and the Committee against Torture, which frequently make reference to the physical and mental health and welfare of those subjected to such treatment.[182]

[181] *Nitecki v Poland* (App. 65653/01), 21 March 2002 (First Section Decision as to Admissibility), <http://echr.ketse.com/doc/65653.01-en-20020321/view/>.

[182] See chapter 9 on torture of Sarah Joseph and Melissa Castan, *The International Covenant on Civil and Political Rights: Cases, Materials and Commentary* (3rd edn, Oxford University Press, Oxford, 2013), 215–328, which covers not only the jurisprudence concerning the International Covenant on Civil and Political Rights (adopted 16 December 1966, 999 UNTS 171, entered into force 23 March 1976) and the UN Convention against Torture and Other Cruel, Inhuman or Degrading Treatment or Punishment (adopted 10 December 1984, 1456 UNTS 85, entered into force 26 June 1987), but also relevant considerations of the prohibition of torture under Article 7(2)(e) of the Rome Statute of the International Criminal Court (adopted 17 July 1998, 2187 UNTS 90, entered into force 1 July 2002).

The related rights regarding conditions of detention, as well as deportation, extradition or refoulement, also give rise to health concerns. Thus, for example, in *Brown v Jamaica* (1999), the Human Rights Committee found that the respondent state had violated death row inmate Mr Brown's rights under Articles 7 (protection against inhuman treatment) and 10 (to be treated with humanity when in detention) of the ICCPR:

3.9 In March of 1997, while on death row at St. Catherine's District Prison, the author's belongings were destroyed by the wardens in the contexts of a search exercise carried out following an escape bid made by other prisoners. The author's asthma pump and other medication were destroyed, and despite numerous complaints to the prison authorities these have not been replaced. Moreover, the author states that he has suffered repeated asthma attacks since his arrival at St. Catherine's prison and he complains that the warders have been slow in responding to his requests for assistance, have refused to take him to hospital and on some occasions have denied medication. In particular, it is alleged that the author has not received an inhaler and a pump, despite a prescription by the prison doctor.[183]

In the case of *Lantsova v The Russian Federation* (2002), the Human Rights Committee found that the inhuman conditions under which Mr Lantsova had been held pending his trial, and which had led to his death in custody, constituted a violation of his right to life under Article 6 of the ICCPR. In respect of the right to adequate medical care implied in the right to life, the Committee stated that:

9.2 Concerning the death of Mr. Lantsova, the Committee notes the author's allegations, on the strength of testimony by several fellow detainees, that after the deterioration of the health of the author's son, he received medical care only during the last few minutes of his life, that the prison authorities had refused such care during the preceding days and that this situation caused his death. It also takes note of the information provided by the State party, namely that several inquiries were carried out into the causes of the death, i.e. acute pneumonia leading to cardiac insufficiency, and that Mr. Lantsova had not requested medical assistance. The Committee affirms that it is incumbent on States to ensure the right of life of detainees, and not incumbent on the latter to request protection. The stated intention of the State party to improve conditions has no impact in the assessment of this case. The Committee notes that the State party has not refuted the causal link between the conditions of the detention of Mr. Lantsova and the fatal deterioration of his state of health. Further, even if the Committee starts from the assertion of the State party that neither Mr. Lantsova himself nor his co-detainees had requested medical help in time, the essential fact remains that the State party by arresting and detaining individuals takes the responsibility to care for their life. It is up to the State party by organizing its detention facilities to know about the state of health of the detainees as far as may be reasonably expected. Lack of financial means cannot reduce this responsibility. The Committee considers that a properly functioning medical service within the detention centre could and should have known about the dangerous change in the state of health of Mr. Lantsova. It considers that the State party failed to take appropriate measures to protect Mr. Lantsova's life during the period he spent in the

[183] HRC, *Brown v Jamaica*, Communication No. 775/1997, CCPR/C/65/D/775/1997 (11 May 1999), [3.9].

detention centre. Consequently, the Human Rights Committee concludes that, in this case, there has been a violation of paragraph 1 of article 6 of the Covenant.[184]

Similarly, the African Commission on Human and Peoples' Rights in the *Mauritanian* case (2000) held that:

122. The State's responsibility in the event of detention is even more evident to the extent that detention centres are its exclusive preserve, hence the physical integrity and welfare of detainees is the responsibility of the competent public authorities. Some prisoners died as a result of the lack of medical attention. The general state of health of the prisoners deteriorated due to the lack of sufficient fool; they had neither blankets nor adequate hygiene. The Mauritanian state is directly responsible for this state of affairs and the government has not denied these facts. Consequently, the Commission considers that there was a violation of Article 16 [of the African Charter of Human and Peoples' Rights which protects an individual's right to health].[185]

Casting the jurisdictional net still wider, the European Court of Human Rights has held that the obligations regarding health care implicit within the European Convention on Human Rights' Article 3 protection against torture or inhuman or degrading treatment apply when a state is considering deportation of a non-national who is seriously ill with HIV/AIDS, even if (indeed, especially if) he has just been released from prison following the conclusion of his sentence for a drug-trafficking offence and during which time he had been receiving appropriate medical care. In *D v United Kingdom* (1997),[186] and after considering the 'health and sanitation problems which beset the population of St Kitts' (paragraph 52) (of which the applicant was a native), the Court concluded that 'the removal of the applicant to St Kitts would give rise to a violation of Article 3' (paragraph 59), because the resulting 'abrupt withdrawal' of high level medical care (paragraph 52) would 'expose him to the very real risk of dying under most distressing circumstances and would thus amount to inhuman treatment' (paragraph 53). Significantly, this was despite the substance of the counterclaims of the UK Government—namely, that while it 'did not dispute the fact that the removal of the applicant to St Kitts and the consequential loss of the current medical treatment would hasten his death. [It maintained that]...the threat to his life expectancy stemmed not from factors for which the Government could be held responsible but from his own fatal illness in conjunction with the lack of adequate medical treatment in the receiving country' (paragraph 57).

A decade later, a apparently very similar state party argument was to receive a more sympathetic reception from the European Court of Human Rights, when in *N v United Kingdom* (2008) it upheld the UK Government's decision to deport an

[184] HRC, *Yekaterina Pavlovna Lantsova v Russian Federation*, Communication No. 763/1997, CCPR/C/74/D/763/1997 (15 April 2002), [9.2]; the author of the communication was the mother of the deceased.

[185] *Malawi African Association et al v Mauritania*, 11 May 2000, Communication Nos. 4/9, 61/91, 96/93, 98/93, 164/97, 196/97, 210/98 (African Commission on Human and Peoples' Rights), [122]. For the full text of Article 16 of the African Charter on Human and Peoples' Rights (adopted 27 June 1981, 1520 UNTS 217, entered into force 21 October 1986), see n. 191 below.

[186] *D v United Kingdom* (App. 30240/96), 2 May 1997, (1997) 24 EHRR 423.

illegal immigrant to her native Uganda after she had arrived nine years earlier in a condition of serious ill-health (HIV-positive and suffering disseminated tuberculosis) and been treated for these ailments as well as later complications including cancer, and making a complete recovery. Her asylum claim had been dismissed during that period. After reviewing a line of similar cases, including *D v United Kingdom*, involving member states seeking to deport non-nationals to countries in which their health care would be inferior to that which they were receiving in the member state, the court reached the following conclusion:

46. The Court observes at the outset that, although the applicant applied for, and was refused, asylum in the United Kingdom, she does not complain before the Court that her removal to Uganda would put her at risk of deliberate, politically motivated, ill-treatment. Her claim under Article 3 is based solely on her serious medical condition and the lack of sufficient treatment available for it in her home country.

47. In 1998 the applicant was diagnosed as having two AIDS-defining illnesses and a high level of immunosuppression. As a result of the medical treatment she has received in the United Kingdom her condition is now stable. She is fit to travel and will remain fit as long as she continues to receive the basic treatment she needs. The evidence before the national courts indicated, however, that if the applicant were to be deprived of her present medication her condition would rapidly deteriorate and she would suffer ill heath, discomfort, pain and death within a few years…

48. According to information collated by WHO… antiretroviral medication is available in Uganda, although through lack of resources it is received by only half of those in need. The applicant claims that she would be unable to afford the treatment and that it would not be available to her in the rural area from which she comes. It appears that she has family members in Uganda, although she claims that they would not be willing or able to care for her if she were seriously ill.

49. The United Kingdom authorities have provided the applicant with medical and social assistance at public expense during the nine-year period it has taken for her asylum application and claims under Articles 3 and 8 of the Convention to be determined by the domestic courts and this Court. However, this does not in itself entail a duty on the part of the respondent State to continue to provide for her.

50. The Court accepts that the quality of the applicant's life, and her life expectancy, would be affected if she were returned to Uganda. The applicant is not, however, at the present time critically ill. The rapidity of the deterioration which she would suffer and the extent to which she would be able to obtain access to medical treatment, support and care, including help from relatives, must involve a certain degree of speculation, particularly in view of the constantly evolving situation as regards the treatment of HIV and AIDS worldwide.

51. In the Court's view, the applicant's case cannot be distinguished from those cited in paragraphs 36–41 above. It does not disclose very exceptional circumstances, such as in *D. v. the United Kingdom* (cited above), and the implementation of the decision to remove the applicant to Uganda would not give rise to a violation of Article 3 of the Convention.[187]

[187] *N v United Kingdom* (App. 26565/05), 27 May 2008, (2008) 47 EHRR 39. The Court also dismissed the applicant's claim under Article 8 as unnecessary to consider, given its determination in respect of Article 3. Note that in a joint dissenting judgment, three members of the Grand Chamber

Reflecting on the reasoning in this case as well as a number of other similarly decided cases under the ECHR, Manisuli Ssenyonjo observes that 'while the reason is not always explicitly stated, it appears to be based on the allegation that finding a breach of Article 3 in cases involving claims of health care in other states would open up the floodgates to medical immigration and make Europe vulnerable to becoming the "sick-bay" of the world'.[188]

The obligations to respect the right to health are especially onerous in circumstances where the state agencies have custody, or effective control, over individuals' lives, such as with prisoners and other detainees, as illustrated above, but also regarding children in care or patients in psychiatric or mental health institutions. Thus, in *Purohit and Moore v The Gambia* (2003), the African Commission on Human and Peoples' Rights held that the inadequate and inhuman treatment of psychiatric patients under outdated legislation (the Lunatics Detention Act 1917 (LDA), a colonial statute still in force) amounted to a breach of the state's obligations to protect individual and family health under Articles 16 and 18, respectively, of the African Charter on Human and Peoples' Rights:[189]

83. In the instant case, it is clear that the scheme of the LDA is lacking in terms of therapeutic objectives as well as provision of matching resources and programmes of treatment of persons with mental disabilities, a situation that the Respondent State does not deny but which never-the-less falls short of satisfying the requirements laid down in Articles 16 and 18(4) of the African Charter.

84. The African Commission would however like to state that it is aware that millions of people in Africa are not enjoying the right to health maximally because African countries are generally faced with the problem of poverty which renders them incapable to provide the necessary amenities, infrastructure and resources that facilitate the full enjoyment of this right. Therefore, having due regard to this depressing but real state of affairs, the African Commission would like to read into Article 16 the obligation on part of States party to the African Charter to take concrete and targeted steps, while taking full advantage of its available resources, to ensure that the right to health is fully realised in all its aspects without discrimination of any kind.

held that 'the distinguishing of the present case from that of *D v the United Kingdom* is…misconceived' (at [25] of the Joint Dissenting Opinion of Judges Tulkens, Bonello and Spielmann), leading to their conclusion that there was a breach of Article 3.

188 Manisuli Ssenyonjo, *Economic, Social and Cultural Rights in International Law* (Hart, Oxford, 2009), 338.

189 These read:

Article 16: 1. Every individual shall have the right to enjoy the best attainable state of physical and mental health. 2. States Parties to the present Charter shall take the necessary measures to protect the health of their people and to ensure that they receive medical attention when they are sick;

and

Article 18: 1. The family shall be the natural unit and basis of society. It shall be protected by the State which shall take care of its physical health and moral. 2. The State shall have the duty to assist the family which is the custodian of morals and traditional values recognized by the community. 3. The State shall ensure the elimination of every discrimination against women and also ensure the protection of the rights of the woman and the child as stipulated in international declarations and conventions. 4. The aged and the disabled shall also have the right to special measures of protection in keeping with their physical or moral needs.

85. The African Commission commends the Respondent State's disclosure that there is no significant shortage of drug supplies at Campama and that in the event that there are drug shortages, all efforts are made to alleviate the problem. Furthermore, that it has taken steps to improve the nature of care given to mental health patients held at Campama. The Respondent State also informed the African Commission that it is fully aware of the outdated aspects of the LDA and has therefore long taken administrative steps to complement and/or reform the archaic parts of the LDA. This is however not enough because the rights and freedoms of human beings are at stake. Persons with mental illnesses should never be denied their right to proper health care, which is crucial for their survival and their assimilation into and acceptance by the wider society.

Inadequate and unhealthy conditions of detention have also been raised in the context of the American Convention on Human Rights. However, in the absence of an express right to health in that Convention,[190] complaints submitted to the Inter-American Commission and Court regarding standards of health or health care have relied upon the Convention's protection of the right to life under Article 4 ('no one shall be arbitrarily deprived of his life'), and the right to humane treatment under Article 5, the first two clauses of which provide that:

1. Every person has the right to have his physical, mental, and moral integrity respected.

2. No one shall be subjected to torture or to cruel, inhuman, or degrading punishment or treatment. All persons deprived of their liberty shall be treated with respect for the inherent dignity of the human person.

Thus, in the *Panchito López* case, the atrocious conditions of a Paraguayan detention centre for minors, which had serious consequences for their physical and mental health, were held by the Inter-American Court to be so inhumane and degrading, that they were contrary not only to Article 5 of the Convention, but also the right to life under Article 4. The Court made clear the link between the two rights in this case by stressing the state's failure in 'exposing all the inmates at the Center to cruel, inhuman and degrading treatment and to unfit living conditions that were prejudicial to their right to life, their growth and development and their life plans'.[191] It held, further, that these inhuman conditions were, in large part,

[190] Although the right is expressly provided in the Additional Protocol to the American Convention on Human Rights in the Area of Economic, Social and Cultural Rights ('Protocol of San Salvador') (adopted 17 November 1988, OAS Treaty Series No. 69, entered into force 16 November 1999), Article 10 of which guarantees that everyone has the right to health, comprising 'the enjoyment of the highest level of physical, mental and social well-being'. On the application of this provision by the Court, see discussion of the case of *Albán Cornejo v Ecuador*, below at n. 194 and accompanying text.

[191] *Case of Children's Rehabilitation v Paraguay*, 2 September 2004, Series C No. 63 (Inter-American Court of Human Rights) ('*Panchito López* case'), [176]. In addition, the Court held Paraguay to be in breach of its specific obligation to protect children under Article 19 of the Convention. In this respect, and especially in light of the Court's reasoning quoted in the text above regarding the health requirements of Articles 4 and 5, the Court echoes the views of the CRC in its General Comment on Adolescent Health and Development, the essential aim of which it states is 'to identify the main human rights that need to be promoted and protected in order to ensure that adolescents do enjoy the highest attainable standard of health, develop in a well-balanced manner, and are adequately prepared to enter adulthood and assume a constructive role in their communities and in society at large': CRC, General Comment No. 4, [4].

due to the state not providing 'the proper health care that any person deprived of his or her liberty must have', let alone 'the regular medical supervision that would ensure the children's normal growth and development so essential to their future'.[192]

States' responsibilities for the provision of adequate health care for patients have also been upheld under the same Articles of the Inter-American Convention. Significantly, this responsibility is one borne by the state irrespective of whether the hospital or clinic is publically or privately operated. In both of the following cases, the impugned health care provider was a private entity, and yet in both the Inter-American Court held the state to be liable for the breaches. In *Ximenes-Lopes v Brazil*, Damião Ximenes-Lopes, a young mentally ill person who had been hospitalized in a private psychiatric clinic that operated within the public health system of Brazil, was found dead three days after admission. In holding that the clinic's unhygienic conditions and the neglectful and incompetent treatment that Mr Ximenes-Lopes received during his time there had contributed directly to his death, the Court presented the following argument:[193]

> [89] As to the persons who are under medical treatment, and since health is a public interest the protection of which is a duty of the States, these must prevent third parties from unduly interfering with the enjoyment of the rights to life and personal integrity, which are particularly vulnerable when a person is undergoing health treatment. The Court considers that the States must regulate and supervise all activities related to the health care given to the individuals under the jurisdiction thereof, as a special duty to protect life and personal integrity, regardless of the public or private nature of the entity giving such health care.
>
> [90] The failure to regulate and supervise such activities gives rise to international liability, as the States are liable for the acts performed by both public and private entities which give medical assistance, since under the American Convention international liability comprises the acts performed by private entities acting in a State capacity, as well as the acts committed by third parties when the State fails to fulfill its duty to regulate and supervise them. Therefore, the duty of the States to regulate these acts is not limited to public hospitals, but includes any and all health care institutions.
>
> [91] Under the State coverage, '[h]ealth is a right due to everyone and the State's duty, which is guaranteed through social and economic policies which have the purpose of reducing health risks and guaranteeing the universal and egalitarian access to health programs and services aimed at ensuring health promotion, protection, and recovery,' as provided for by Article 196 of its Constitution. Furthermore, in accordance with Article 197 thereof, it is 'the responsibility of the Power of the State, according to law, to provide for the regulation, supervision and control of such health programs and services [... and their] implementation must be carried out either directly or through third parties, and by private natural or artificial persons.'

[192] *Panchito López* case [173].

[193] *Ximenes-Lopes v Brazil,* 4 July 2006, Series C No. 149 (Inter-American Court of Human Rights), [89]–[91]

The death of a patient in a private hospital was also at the heart of the case of *Albán Cornejo et al v Ecuador*.[194] Laura Susana Albán Cornejo died a few days after being admitted to a private hospital located in Quito. On admission, she had exhibited symptoms of bacterial meningitis and it was alleged that her death was caused directly by the medication she was incorrectly prescribed by physicians in the hospital to treat the condition. In formulating its opinion, the Inter-American Court underscored the fact that it:

> …has repeatedly stated that the right to life [as protected by Article 4 of the Convention] is a fundamental human right, the enjoyment and exercise of which is a prerequisite for the exercise of all other rights. Personal integrity is essential for the enjoyment of human life. In turn, the rights to life and humane treatment are directly and immediately linked to human health care.[195]

After adding that the implied right to health care in the Convention itself is further supported by its express provision in Article 10 of the 1988 Additional Protocol to the American Convention on Human Rights in the Area of Economic, Social and Cultural Rights,[196] the Court held that the state was indeed to be held liable for the medical malpractice that led to Albán Cornejo's death (paragraphs 50 and 109), not least because it had failed adequately to supervize the provision of health care services by a private operator, but also that at the relevant time there existed no appropriate legislation providing for such oversight, and specifically, no legislation regarding medical malpractice:

> States must adopt the necessary measures, among which is the enactment of criminal laws and the creation of a judicial system to prevent and punish the violation of fundamental rights, such as the right to life and humane treatment. As far as substantive criminal law is concerned, such purpose is realized through the enactment of adequate criminal descriptions in accordance with criminal legal provisions, which meet the requirements of punitive law in a democratic society and which are adequate for the protection of goods and legal interests, from a criminal perspective. As far as procedural criminal law is concerned, it is necessary to have the effective resources to ensure access to justice and the full satisfaction of legitimate claims in a timely manner.[197]

The Inter-American Court has also held states responsible for the degrading, unhygienic and, in some cases, fatal conditions suffered by specific groups within society that government authorities have either caused or failed to prevent or correct. This was the situation, for example, with indigenous peoples in two notable cases before the Court, both involving Paraguay.[198] In *Yakye Axa indigenous*

[194] *Albán Cornejo et al v Ecuador*, 22 November 2007, Series C No. 171 (Inter-American Court of Human Rights).

[195] *Cornejo v Ecuador*, [117].

[196] For the text of which, see above, n. 192.

[197] *Cornejo v Ecuador*, [135].

[198] The two cases, both heard by the Inter-American Court of Human Rights, are *Case of the Indigenous Community Yakye Axa v Paraguay*, 17 June 2005, Series C No. 125; *Sawhoyamaxa Indigenous Community v Paraguay*, 29 March 2006, Series C No. 146. In these cases the Court built upon the similar arguments and reasoning it advanced ten years earlier in the comparable case of *Yanomami Indians v Brazil*, 5 March 1985, Case No. 7615 (Inter-American Commission on Human Rights).

community v Paraguay and *Sawhoyamaxa Indigenous Community v Paraguay*, which concerned the appalling conditions under which the communities were forced to live after they were removed from their traditional lands, the Court held the state responsible for failing to address both the manner in which the communities were dispossessed of their lands, and the gross violations of their rights to health, food, housing, sanitation and education that followed. Further discussion of the facts and findings of both of these cases are to be found throughout the previous chapter on the right to an adequate standard of living under Article 11.

A state's responsibility to ensure that free, informed and prior consent is provided by patients to non-emergency, invasive medical procedures has also been upheld by international human rights tribunals. Thus, for example, in *AS v Hungary*,[199] the UN Committee on the Elimination of Discrimination against Women found that the failure of hospital personnel to make it clear to a female patient who had consented to a caesarean section to remove a foetus which had died at the onset of labour, that she was also consenting to sterilization, was attributable to the state. The patient, a Roma, with limited education, was presented with the additional, barely legible, consent request while on the operating table and already in a state of some distress. The Committee found that the relevant legislation, policies and protocols were inadequate in failing to prevent such an occurrence, and that in consequence the state was found to have violated both the right to access to health care services under Article 12 of the Convention and 'access to specific educational information to help to ensure the health and well-being of families, including information and advice on family planning' as provided by Article 10(f).[200]

The right to health has also found some limited protection in cases involving international trade law. Article XX of the General Agreement on Tariffs and Trade 1947 (GATT), which falls within the ambit of the WTO, stipulates a number of permissible exceptions to the otherwise stringent demands that states reduce and remove their restrictions on trade between each other. Included in this list of exceptions is where it is deemed 'necessary to protect human, animal or plant life or health' (GATT, Article XX(b)).[201] There has been a series of cases that have passed through the WTO's dispute settlement process involving states claiming that their trade-restrictive actions have been justified on the grounds of protecting human health under this provision and/or the related provision in the same Article 'relating to the conservation of exhaustible natural resources if such measures are

[199] Committee on the Elimination of All Forms of Discrimination Against Women, *AS v Hungary*, Communication No. 4/2004, CEDAW/C/36/D/4/2004 (29 August 2008).

[200] The Committee also relied on the provisions of its General Recommendation No. 24 (1999), which refer specifically to an individual woman's right to be fully informed and to have access to quality health care services, which respect her dignity and are sensitive to her needs and perspectives and specify that 'States parties should not permit forms of coercion, such as non-consensual sterilization', [11.3].

[201] There is an identical provision in the GATT's sister treaty, the General Agreement on Trade in Services (adopted 15 April 1994, 1869 UNTS 183, contained in Marrakesh Agreement Establishing the World Trade Organization, adopted 15 April 1994, 1867 UNTS 154, Annex 1B, entered into force 1 January 1995), Article XIV(b).

made effective in conjunction with restrictions on domestic production or consumption' (Article XX(g)). These include:[202]

- *Thailand—Cigarettes*—a case brought by the United States against Thailand's ban on the importation of cigarettes which the Thai Government argued was justified under its public health policy to reduce the consumption of tobacco which was harmful to health, and therefore permissible under GATT, Article XX(b). Although the WTO dispute panel did not deny the importance of the objective, it found against Thailand on the basis that it sought only to ban imported cigarettes and not the sale of local produced cigarettes and that, further, other less trade-restrictive avenues were open to the government in order to achieve the goals of its public health policy.[203]
- *US—Gasoline*—a case brought by Venezuela and Brazil challenging a US law regulating the composition and levels of emissions of gasoline that was introduced with the aim of controlling and reducing air pollution in the United States. The challenge was unsuccessful and the US regulation was upheld.[204]
- *EC—Asbestos*—a case brought by Canada against the (then) European Communities (EC) regarding the EC's ban on asbestos-containing building products. The WTO Appellate Body upheld the EC regulation on the grounds that it was justified in order to protect human health, both in respect of construction workers and the community at large.[205]
- *Brazil—Retreaded Tyres*—a case brought by the European Communities against Brazil's prohibition on the importation of retreaded tyres. Brazil argued, successfully, that the ban was necessary because the storage and warehousing of imported retreaded tyres provided a ready breeding ground for mosquitos,

[202] For further discussion of these, and other, cases concerning the use of concerns to protect public health as a means to justify trade restrictions under international trade laws, see Jeffery Atik, 'Trade and Health' in Daniel Bethlehem, Donald McRae, Rodney Neufeld and Isabelle Van Damme (eds), *The Oxford Handbook of International Trade Law* (Oxford University Press, Oxford, 2008), 598–618.

[203] GATT Panel Report, *Thailand—Restriction on importation of and internal taxes on cigarettes*, DS10/R, ruling adopted 7 November 1990, BISD 37S/200. Regarding the current WTO, Dispute Settlement, Dispute DS434 *Australia—Certain Measures Concerning Trademarks and Other Plain Packaging Requirements Applicable to Tobacco Products and Packaging*, as raised by the Ukraine, and joined by Honduras, the Dominican Republic and Cuba in 2012, it seems likely that Australia will be able successfully to defend the plain packaging legislation by claiming, inter alia, that its object is to discourage smoking and thereby protect human health, as per GATT, Article XX(b): see Tania Voon and Andrew Mitchell, 'Implications of WTO Law for Plain Packaging of Tobacco Products' in Andrew Mitchell, Tania Voon and Jonathan Liberman (eds), *Public Health and Plain Packaging of Cigarettes: Legal Issues* (Edward Elgar, Cheltenham, 2012), nn. 101–16 and corresponding text.

[204] WTO, Dispute Settlement, Appellate Body Report, *United States—Standards for Reformulated and Conventional Gasoline* (WT/DS2/AB/R) and the panel report on 'United States—Standards for Reformulated and Conventional Gasoline' (WT/DS2/R) as modified by the Appellate Body report, ruling adopted 20 May 1996.

[205] WTO, Dispute Settlement, Dispute DS135 *European Communities— Measures affecting asbestos and asbestos-containing products*, ruling adopted on 5 April 2001.

which increased the instance of mosquito-borne diseases. The import ban was, however, otherwise found to transgress non-discriminatory provisions elsewhere in the GATT.[206]

Although this is, as yet, a fairly meagre extent of coverage of what might be broadly called the right to health, the ground may have been laid for some future, more robust protection under the apparatus of the WTO. Thus, as Sarah Joseph has argued, with self-conscious optimism, 'a broad interpretation of Article XX(b) might permit measures which promote all human rights that protect physical and mental security, such as the right to be free from torture and certain prohibitions on labour rights abuses'.[207] TRIPS is not, of course, the only means by which to secure access to new or novel medicines (or even older and tried and tested ones) for those who cannot afford them, but it is certainly an important way, and one yet to be fully developed.[208]

Framework Convention on Global Health

A final word in this chapter is dedicated to the future of global health care; specifically, that is, in respect of the proposal for a Framework Convention on Global Health (FCGH). The brainchild of academics and activists in the field, lead by Larry Gostin of Georgetown Law School, and being promoted by the Joint Action and Learning Initiative on National and Global Responsibilities for Health (JALI), the Framework Convention seeks to redress the perceived inadequacy of current global governance on health and international law's weak responses to the 'persistence of…an unconscionable level of avoidable deaths' worldwide[209] and the enduring inequities in health care and the social environments that allow them to happen. The FCGH seeks to establish a framework setting out health norms and priorities, the social determinants required for good health, and the means for better enforcement and compliance. The intention is to set these standards at the global level, with a view to them being tailored to suit individual country circumstances. This 'vital task of constructing the norms and processes of an FCGH', as Larry Gostin and Eric Friedman put it,[210] still requires an enormous amount of work:

> Ultimately, though, a broad coalition of leading states, civil society organizations, and academic institutions will have to develop the ideas. Without a bottom-up, inclusive process, a treaty of this breathtaking scope and historic impact could never succeed politically. What is most important in formulating a treaty that successfully responds to the imperatives of

[206] WTO, Dispute Settlement, Dispute DS332 *Brazil—Measures Affecting Imports of Retreaded Tyres*, ruling adopted 17 December 2007.

[207] Sarah Joseph, *Blame it on the WTO? A Human Rights Critique* (Oxford University Press, Oxford, 2011), 110.

[208] On which prospects and possibilities, see John Tobin, *The Right to Health in International Law* (Oxford University Press, Oxford, 2012), 366–7.

[209] Lawrence O. Gostin and Eric A. Friedman, 'Towards a Framework Convention on Global Health: A Transformative Agenda for Global Health Justice' (2013) 13 *Yale Journal of Health Policy, Law and Ethics* 1, 4.

[210] Gostin and Friedman, 'Towards a Framework Convention on Global Health', 74.

human rights and global justice is that it captures the views and aspirations of the people whose health is most imperiled under current governance arrangements.[211]

What, perhaps, this initiative demonstrates above all is that while Article 12 of the Covenant is certainly insufficient on its own to address the health needs and ambitions invested in the right to health, it is a vital part of the enterprise, and one, what is more, that the FCGH aims to support and expand upon.

211 Gostin and Friedman, 'Towards a Framework Convention on Global Health', 74.

15

Article 13: The Right to Education

Article 13

1. The States Parties to the present Covenant recognize the right of everyone to education. They agree that education shall be directed to the full development of the human personality and the sense of its dignity, and shall strengthen the respect for human rights and fundamental freedoms. They further agree that education shall enable all persons to participate effectively in a free society, promote understanding, tolerance and friendship among all nations and all racial, ethnic or religious groups, and further the activities of the United Nations for the maintenance of peace.

2. The States Parties to the present Covenant recognize that, with a view to achieving the full realization of this right:

(a) Primary education shall be compulsory and available free to all;

(b) Secondary education in its different forms, including technical and vocational secondary education, shall be made generally available and accessible to all by every appropriate means, and in particular by the progressive introduction of free education;

(c) Higher education shall be made equally accessible to all, on the basis of capacity, by every appropriate means, and in particular by the progressive introduction of free education;

(d) Fundamental education shall be encouraged or intensified as far as possible for those persons who have not received or completed the whole period of their primary education;

(e) The development of a system of schools at all levels shall be actively pursued, an adequate fellowship system shall be established, and the material conditions of teaching staff shall be continuously improved.

3. The States Parties to the present Covenant undertake to have respect for the liberty of parents and, when applicable, legal guardians to choose for their children schools, other than those established by the public authorities, which conform to such minimum educational standards as may be laid down or approved by the State and to ensure the religious and moral education of their children in conformity with their own convictions.

4. No part of this article shall be construed so as to interfere with the liberty of individuals and bodies to establish and direct educational institutions, subject always to the observance of the principles set forth in paragraph I of this article and to the requirement that the education given in such institutions shall conform to such minimum standards as may be laid down by the State.

Article 13 is the longest in the Covenant and it makes detailed provision concerning a wide range of issues related to education. The Article lays down specific requirements for different levels of education: primary, secondary, higher and fundamental education (Article 13(2)). It also establishes general principles applicable to all levels of education, stipulating the ends to which education should be directed (Article 13(1)), guaranteeing the liberty of parents to choose schools which educate their children in accordance with their religious and moral convictions (Article 13(3)), and protecting the freedom of all individuals and bodies to establish private schools (Article 13(4)).

Background and Context

The right to education is often considered a particularly important right, and it is one which receives wide support. The importance of the right to education lies both in the importance of education in and of itself, and in its ability to contribute to the enjoyment of other human rights. As the Committee has explained in General Comment No. 13 on the right to education:

> Education is both a human right in itself and an indispensable means of realizing other human rights. As an empowerment right, education is the primary vehicle by which economically and socially marginalized adults and children can lift themselves out of poverty and obtain the means to participate fully in their communities. Education has a vital role in empowering women, safeguarding children from exploitative and hazardous labour and sexual exploitation, promoting human rights and democracy, protecting the environment, and controlling population growth. Increasingly, education is recognized as one of the best financial investments States can make. But the importance of education is not just practical: a well-educated, enlightened and active mind, able to wander freely and widely, is one of the joys and rewards of human existence.[1]

The fact that education affects the enjoyment of other human rights has led to it being termed a 'multiplier right'. In the words of the former Special Rapporteur on the right to education, Katerina Tomaševski:

> Education operates as a multiplier, enhancing the enjoyment of all individual rights and freedoms where the right to education is effectively guaranteed, while depriving people of the enjoyment of many rights and freedoms where the right to education is denied or violated.[2]

The importance of education was recognized in the UN Charter—which requires the United Nations to promote 'international, cultural and educational cooperation'[3]—and in the subsequent establishment of the UN Educational, Scientific and Cultural Organization (UNESCO). The Preamble to the UNESCO Constitution notes that 'the wide diffusion of culture, and the education of humanity for justice and liberty and peace are indispensable to the dignity of man and constitute a sacred duty which all the nations must fulfil in a spirit of mutual assistance and concern'. It also indicates that the states parties to the Constitution believe 'in full and equal

[1] CESCR, General Comment No. 13, The right to education (Article 13 of the Covenant), E/C.12/1999/10 (8 December 1990) ('General Comment No. 13'), [1].

[2] Katerina Tomaševski, *Removing Obstacles in the Way of the Right to Education (Right to Education Primers No. 1)* (Novum Grafiska, Gothenburg, 2001), 9.

[3] Charter of the United Nations (adopted 26 June 1945, 1 UNTS XVI, entered into force 24 October 1945), Article 55(b).

opportunities for education for all'. Further, Article 1(2) of the Constitution indicates that UNESCO will:

(b) Give fresh impulse to popular education and to the spread of culture:

By collaborating with Members, at their request, in the development of educational activities;

By instituting collaboration among the nations to advance the ideal of equality of educational opportunity without regard to race, sex or any distinctions, economic or social;

By suggesting educational methods best suited to prepare the children of the world for the responsibilities of freedom;

The right to education, as such, was first recognized in the Universal Declaration of Human Rights ('UDHR'), Article 26:

(1) Everyone has the right to education. Education shall be free, at least in the elementary and fundamental stages. Elementary education shall be compulsory. Technical and professional education shall be made generally available and higher education shall be equally accessible to all on the basis of merit.

(2) Education shall be directed to the full development of the human personality and to the strengthening of respect for human rights and fundamental freedoms. It shall promote understanding, tolerance and friendship among all nations, racial or religious groups, and shall further the activities of the United Nations for the maintenance of peace.

(3) Parents have a prior right to choose the kind of education that shall be given to their children.[4]

Article 13 of the ICESCR offers a binding and more detailed elaboration of the general right to education recognized in the UDHR.

The right to education has also been recognized in the Convention on the Rights of the Child ('CROC'). Article 28 of the CROC provides:

1. States Parties recognize the right of the child to education, and with a view to achieving this right progressively and on the basis of equal opportunity, they shall, in particular:

(a) Make primary education compulsory and available free to all;

(b) Encourage the development of different forms of secondary education, including general and vocational education, make them available and accessible to every child, and take appropriate measures such as the introduction of free education and offering financial assistance in case of need;

(c) Make higher education accessible to all on the basis of capacity by every appropriate means;

(d) Make educational and vocational information and guidance available and accessible to all children;

[4] UNGA Res. 217 A(III), Universal Declaration of Human Rights (10 December 1948), Article 26.

(e) Take measures to encourage regular attendance at schools and the reduction of drop-out rates.

2. States Parties shall take all appropriate measures to ensure that school discipline is administered in a manner consistent with the child's human dignity and in conformity with the present Convention.

3. States Parties shall promote and encourage international cooperation in matters relating to education, in particular with a view to contributing to the elimination of ignorance and illiteracy throughout the world and facilitating access to scientific and technical knowledge and modern teaching methods. In this regard, particular account shall be taken of the needs of developing countries.[5]

Article 29 of the CROC then sets out the ends to which education should be directed, reflecting Article 13(1) of the ICESCR and Article 26(2) of the UDHR.

As might be expected, UNESCO has done considerable work in relation to education and is responsible for a number of binding international conventions, most notably the UNESCO Convention against Discrimination in Education. In seeking to address discrimination in education, the Convention makes wide-ranging provision regarding the implementation of education within states. Thus, Article 4 of the Convention is in terms quite similar to that of Article 13 of the ICESCR:

The States Parties to this Convention undertake furthermore to formulate, develop and apply a national policy which, by methods appropriate to the circumstances and to national usage, will tend to promote equality of opportunity and of treatment in the matter of education and in particular:

(a) To make primary education free and compulsory; make secondary education in its different forms generally available and accessible to all; make higher education equally accessible to all on the basis of individual capacity; assure compliance by all with the obligation to attend school prescribed by law;

(b) To ensure that the standards of education are equivalent in all public education institutions of the same level, and that the conditions relating to the quality of education provided are also equivalent;

(c) To encourage and intensify by appropriate methods the education of persons who have not received any primary education or who have not completed the entire primary education course and the continuation of their education on the basis of individual capacity;

(d) To provide training for the teaching profession without discrimination.[6]

Other relevant documents adopted by UNESCO include binding instruments, such as the Convention on Technical and Vocational Education,[7] and a range of

[5] Convention on the Rights of the Child (adopted 20 November 1989, 1577 UNTS 3, entered into force 2 September 1990), Article 28.

[6] UNESCO Convention against Discrimination in Education (adopted 14 December 1960, 429 UNTS 93, entered into force 22 May 1962), Article 4.

[7] UNESCO Convention on Technical and Vocational Education (adopted 10 November 1989, 1649 UNTS 143, entered into force 29 August 1991).

non-binding recommendations, including the Recommendation Concerning the Status of Teachers,[8] the Recommendation on the Development of Adult Education[9] and the Recommendation Concerning the Status of Higher-Education Teaching Personnel.[10]

At the international level, the right to education has also been affirmed in a range of non-binding documents and declarations, most notably the 1990 World Declaration on Education for All,[11] which was reaffirmed ten years later in the 2000 Dakar Framework for Action.[12]

The right to education is also well protected within regional human rights systems. Article 2 of Protocol 1 to the European Convention for the Protection of Human Rights and Fundamental Freedoms ('ECHR') provides:

> No person shall be denied the right to education. In the exercise of any functions which it assumes in relation to education and teaching, the State shall respect the right of parents to ensure such education and teaching in conformity with their own religious and philosophical convictions.[13]

Although the right is formulated in negative terms ('shall not be denied'), the European Court of Human Rights held in the *Belgian Linguistics* case[14] that Article 2 of Protocol 1 provides positive rights of access to educational institutions existing at a particular time and rights to an effective education:

> In spite of its negative formulation, this provision uses the term 'right' and speaks of a 'right to education'. Likewise, the Preamble to the Protocol specifies that the objective of the Protocol lies in the collective enforcement of 'rights and freedoms'. There is therefore no doubt that Article 2 does enshrine a right…

> The negative formulation indicates…that the Contracting Parties do not recognise such a right to education as would require them to establish, at their own expense, or to subsidise, education of any particular type or at any particular level. However, it cannot be concluded from this that the State has no positive obligation to ensure respect for such a right as is protected by Article 2 . . .

[8] UNESCO Special Intergovernmental Conference, Recommendation Concerning the Status of Teachers, Paris, 5 October 1966.

[9] UNESCO General Conference (19th Session), Recommendation on the Development of Adult Education, Nairobi, 26 November 1976.

[10] UNESCO General Conference (29th Session), Recommendation Concerning the Status of Higher-Education Teaching Personnel, Paris, 11 November 1997.

[11] World Conference on Education for All: Meeting Basic Learning Needs, World Declaration on Education for All and Framework for Action to Meet Basic Learning Needs ('World Declaration on Education for All'), Jomtien, Thailand, 5–9 March 1990.

[12] World Education Forum, The Dakar Framework for Action: Education for All: Meeting Our Collective Commitments, Dakar, Senegal, 26–8 April 2000.

[13] European Convention for the Protection of Human Rights and Fundamental Freedoms (ECHR) (adopted 4 November 1950, 213 UNTS 2, entered into force 3 September 1953), Protocol 1 (adopted 20 March 1954, 213 UNTS 262, entered into force 18 May 1954), Article 2.

[14] *Case Relating to Certain Aspects of the Laws on the Use of Languages in Education in Belgium (No. 2)* (Apps. 1474/62, 1677/62, 1691/62, 1769/63, 1994/63 and 2126/64) ('*Belgian Linguistics* case'), 23 July 1968, (1968) 1 EHRR 252.

The first sentence of Article 2... consequently guarantees, in the first place, a right of access to educational institutions existing at a given time, but such access constitutes only a part of the right to education. For the 'right to education' to be effective, it is further necessary that, inter alia, the individual who is the beneficiary should have the possibility of drawing profit from the education received...[15]

The right to education is also protected under Article 17 of the Revised European Social Charter[16] and Article 14 of the Charter of Fundamental Rights of the European Union.[17]

Within the Inter-American human rights system, the right to education is protected in Article 13 of the Additional Protocol to the American Convention on Human Rights in the Area of Economic, Social and Cultural Rights (the 'San Salvador Protocol'), in terms similar to those used in Article 13 of the ICESCR:

1. Everyone has the right to education.

2. The States Parties to this Protocol agree that education should be directed towards the full development of the human personality and human dignity and should strengthen respect for human rights, ideological pluralism, fundamental freedoms, justice and peace. They further agree that education ought to enable everyone to participate effectively in a democratic and pluralistic society and achieve a decent existence and should foster understanding, tolerance and friendship among all nations and all racial, ethnic or religious groups and promote activities for the maintenance of peace.

3. The States Parties to this Protocol recognize that in order to achieve the full exercise of the right to education:

(a) Primary education should be compulsory and accessible to all without cost;

(b) Secondary education in its different forms, including technical and vocational secondary education, should be made generally available and accessible to all by every appropriate means, and in particular, by the progressive introduction of free education;

(c) Higher education should be made equally accessible to all, on the basis of individual capacity, by every appropriate means, and in particular, by the progressive introduction of free education;

(d) Basic education should be encouraged or intensified as far as possible for those persons who have not received or completed the whole cycle of primary instruction;

(e) Programs of special education should be established for the handicapped, so as to provide special instruction and training to persons with physical disabilities or mental deficiencies.

4. In conformity with the domestic legislation of the States Parties, parents should have the right to select the type of education to be given to their children, provided that it conforms to the principles set forth above.

[15] *Belgian Linguistics* case, 280–81.

[16] Revised European Social Charter (adopted 3 May 1996, CETS 163, entered into force 1 July 1999), Article 17.

[17] Charter of Fundamental Rights of the European Union (adopted 7 December 2000, OJ C 364/01, entered into force 1 December 2009), Article 14.

5. Nothing in this Protocol shall be interpreted as a restriction of the freedom of individuals and entities to establish and direct educational institutions in accordance with the domestic legislation of the States Parties.[18]

Unlike many of the other provisions in the San Salvador Protocol, Article 13 is justiciable, such that violations of this right are subject to the system of individual petitions applicable to the American Convention on Human Rights.[19] The right to education is also protected in the American Declaration on the Rights and Duties of Man, Article XII of which states:

Every person has the right to an education, which should be based on the principles of liberty, morality and human solidarity.

Likewise every person has the right to an education that will prepare him to attain a decent life, to raise his standard of living, and to be a useful member of society.

The right to an education includes the right to equality of opportunity in every case, in accordance with natural talents, merit and the desire to utilize the resources that the state or the community is in a position to provide.

Every person has the right to receive, free, at least a primary education.[20]

In the African Charter on Human and Peoples' Rights, Article 17(1) provides simply that '[e]very individual shall have the right to education'.[21] The African Charter on the Rights and Welfare of the Child, Article 11, offers a more detailed elaboration of the right:

1. Every child shall have the right to an education.
2. The education of the child shall be directed to:

   (a) the promotion and development of the child's personality, talents and mental and physical abilities to their fullest potential;

   (b) fostering respect for human rights and fundamental freedoms with particular reference to those set out in the provisions of various African instruments on human and peoples' rights and international human rights declarations and conventions;

   (c) the preservation and strengthening of positive African morals, traditional values and cultures;

   (d) the preparation of the child for responsible life in a free society, in the spirit of understanding tolerance, dialogue, mutual respect and friendship among all peoples ethnic, tribal and religious groups;

   (e) the preservation of national independence and territorial integrity;

[18] Additional Protocol to the American Convention on Human Rights in the Area of Economic, Social and Cultural Rights ('San Salvador Protocol') (adopted 17 November 1988, OAS Treaty Series No. 69 (1988), entered into force 16 November 1999), Articles 13.

[19] San Salvador Protocol, Article 19(6).

[20] Ninth International Conference of American States, American Declaration on the Rights and Duties of Man, Bogota, Colombia, 2 May 1948, Article 12.

[21] African Charter on Human and Peoples' Rights (adopted 27 June 1981, 1520 UNTS 217, entered into force 21 October 1986).

(f) the promotion and achievements of African Unity and Solidarity;

(g) the development of respect for the environment and natural resources;

(h) the promotion of the child's understanding of primary health care.

3. States Parties to the present Charter shall take all appropriate measures with a view to achieving the full realization of this right and shall in particular:

(a) provide free and compulsory basic education;

(b) encourage the development of secondary education in its different forms and to progressively make it free and accessible to all;

(c) make the higher education accessible to all on the basis of capacity and ability by every appropriate means;

(d) take measures to encourage regular attendance at schools and the reduction of drop-out rates;

(e) take special measures in respect of female, gifted and disadvantaged children, to ensure equal access to education for all sections of the community.

4. States Parties to the present Charter shall respect the rights and duties of parents, and where applicable, of legal guardians to choose for their children's schools, other than those established by public authorities, which conform to such minimum standards may be approved by the State, to ensure the religious and moral education of the child in a manner with the evolving capacities of the child.

5. States Parties to the present Charter shall take all appropriate measures to ensure that a child who is subjected to schools or parental discipline shall be treated with humanity and with respect for the inherent dignity of the child and in conformity with the present Charter.

6. States Parties to the present Charter shall have all appropriate measures to ensure that children who become pregnant before completing their education shall have an opportunity to continue with their education on the basis of their individual ability.

7. No part of this Article shall be construed as to interfere with the liberty of individuals and bodies to establish and direct educational institutions subject to the observance of the principles set out in paragraph I of this Article and the requirement that the education given in such institutions shall conform to such minimum standards as may be laid down by the States.[22]

A range of other international instruments protect the right to education in specific contexts, or protect particular aspects of human rights in education. These are discussed in more detail below.

Article 13(1)

Article 13(1) indicates the ends to which education should be directed. According to the *travaux préparatoires*, '[i]t was considered necessary to lay down the

[22] African Charter on the Rights and Welfare of the Child (adopted 11 July 1990, OAU Doc. CAB/LEG/24.9/49 (1990), entered into force 29 November 1999), Article 11.

objectives of education at the beginning of…[article 13], although the view was expressed that paragraph 1, mainly declaratory in character, was out of place in a legal instrument'.[23]

Similar provisions are found in Article 26(2) of the UDHR, Article 13(2) of the San Salvador Protocol to the American Convention on Human Rights, and Article 11(2) of the African Charter on the Rights and Welfare of the Child, as set out above, and in Article 29 of the Convention on the Rights of the Child, which provides as follows:

1. States Parties agree that the education of the child shall be directed to:

(a) The development of the child's personality, talents and mental and physical abilities to their fullest potential;

(b) The development of respect for human rights and fundamental freedoms, and for the principles enshrined in the Charter of the United Nations;

(c) The development of respect for the child's parents, his or her own cultural identity, language and values, for the national values of the country in which the child is living, the country from which he or she may originate, and for civilizations different from his or her own;

(d) The preparation of the child for responsible life in a free society, in the spirit of understanding, peace, tolerance, equality of sexes, and friendship among all peoples, ethnic, national and religious groups and persons of indigenous origin;

(e) The development of respect for the natural environment.

Similar statements concerning the ends to which education should be directed are found in the World Declaration on Education for All,[24] the Vienna Declaration and Programme of Action,[25] and the Plan of Action for the United Nations Decade for Human Rights Education.[26] According to the Committee in General Comment No. 13:

While all these texts closely correspond to article 13(1) of the Covenant, they also include elements which are not expressly provided for in article 13(1), such as specific references to gender equality and respect for the environment. These new elements are implicit in, and reflect a contemporary interpretation of article 13(1). The Committee obtains support for this point of view from the widespread endorsement that the previously mentioned texts have received from all regions of the world.[27]

More generally, the Committee has indicated in General Comment No. 13:

States parties agree that all education, whether public or private, formal or non-formal, shall be directed towards the aims and objectives identified in article 13(1). The Committee

[23] UNGA, Draft International Covenants on Human Rights: Report of the Third Committee (Rapporteur Mr Carlow Manuel Cox (Peru)), A/3764 (5 December 1957), 8.

[24] World Declaration on Education for All, Article 1.

[25] UNGA, World Conference on Human Rights, Vienna Declaration and Programme of Action, A/CONF.157/23 (25 June 1993), Part I [33] and Part II [80].

[26] UNGA, Plan of Action for the United Nations Decade for Human Rights Education, A/51/506/Add.1 (12 December 1996), [2].

[27] CESCR, General Comment No. 13, [5].

notes that these educational objectives reflect the fundamental purposes and principles of the United Nations as enshrined in Articles 1 and 2 of the Charter. For the most part, they are also found in article 26(2) of the Universal Declaration of Human Rights, although article 13(1) adds to the Declaration in three respects: education shall be directed to the human personality's 'sense of dignity', it shall 'enable all persons to participate effectively in a free society', and it shall promote understanding among all 'ethnic' groups, as well as nations and racial and religious groups. Of those educational objectives which are common to article 26(2) of the Universal Declaration of Human Rights and article 13(1) of the Covenant, perhaps the most fundamental is that 'education shall be directed to the full development of the human personality'.[28]

Similarly, the Committee on the Rights of the Child has indicated in its General Comment No. 1 on Article 29(1):

1. Article 29, paragraph 1, of the Convention on the Rights of the Child is of far-reaching importance. The aims of education that it sets out, which have been agreed to by all States parties, promote, support and protect the core value of the Convention: the human dignity innate in every child and his or her equal and inalienable rights…

2. Article 29(1) not only adds to the right to education recognized in article 28 a qualitative dimension which reflects the rights and inherent dignity of the child; it also insists upon the need for education to be child-centred, child-friendly and empowering, and it highlights the need for educational processes to be based upon the very principles it enunciates. The education to which every child has a right is one designed to provide the child with life skills, to strengthen the child's capacity to enjoy the full range of human rights and to promote a culture which is infused by appropriate human rights values…

3. The child's right to education is not only a matter of access (art. 28) but also of content. An education with its contents firmly rooted in the values of article 29(1) is for every child an indispensable tool for her or his efforts to achieve in the course of her or his life a balanced, human rights-friendly response to the challenges that accompany a period of fundamental change driven by globalization, new technologies and related phenomena…

4. Article 29(1) states that the States parties agree that education should be directed to a wide range of values. This agreement overcomes the boundaries of religion, nation and culture built across many parts of the world. At first sight, some of the diverse values expressed in article 29(1) might be thought to be in conflict with one another in certain situations. Thus, efforts to promote understanding, tolerance and friendship among all peoples, to which paragraph (1)(d) refers, might not always be automatically compatible with policies designed, in accordance with paragraph (1)(c), to develop respect for the child's own cultural identity, language and values, for the national values of the country in which the child is living, the country from which he or she may originate, and for civilizations different from his or her own. But in fact, part of the importance of this provision lies precisely in its recognition of the need for a balanced approach to education and one which succeeds in reconciling diverse values through dialogue and respect for difference. Moreover, children are capable of playing a unique role in bridging many of the differences that have historically separated groups of people from one another.[29]

[28] CESCR, General Comment No. 13, [4].

[29] Committee on the Rights of the Child (CRC), General Comment No. 1, CRC/GC/2001/1 (17 April 2001), [1]–[4].

The issues raised by Article 13(1) are considered by the CESCR in its monitoring of state reports: the Committee inquires into the school curriculum with a view to assessing the extent to which the curriculum is directed towards the ends set out in Article 13(1). Thus, in relation to Georgia in 2000:

The Committee notes with concern that in the new secondary school curriculum there appears to be an imbalance between the amount of time devoted to military training (three units) and to 'fundamentals of justice' (one unit).[30]

And in relation to Japan:

The Committee urges the State party to ensure that school textbooks and other teaching materials present issues in a fair and balanced manner which reflects the aims and objectives of education, as set out in Article 13(1) of the Covenant, the Committee's General Comment No. 13 and General Comment No. 1 of the Committee on the Rights of the Child.[31]

The Committee has repeatedly expressed concern about discriminatory educational practices which do not appear to 'promote understanding, tolerance and friendship among all nations and all racial, ethnic or religious groups'. So, for example, in relation to the United Kingdom:

The Committee expresses its concern that the educational structure in Northern Ireland is heavily segregated with most Protestants attending Protestant schools and most Catholics attending Catholic schools and only approximately two per cent of the school population attending integrated schools.[32]

And in its Concluding Observations on Israel in 2003:

The Committee...encourages the State party to develop the system of mixed schools for Jewish and Arab pupils, in order to promote understanding, tolerance and friendship among the citizens of the country.[33]

The Committee has also interpreted Article 13(1) as requiring a human rights education. Thus, the Guidelines on Treaty-Specific Documents to be Submitted by States Parties under Articles 16 and 17 of the International Covenant on Economic, Social and Cultural Rights ('Guidelines on Treaty-Specific Documents') ask states to:

Indicate to what extent the form and substance of education in the State party are directed towards the aims and objectives identified in Article 13, paragraph 1, and whether school curricula include education on economic, social and cultural rights.[34]

[30] CESCR, Concluding Observations: Georgia, E/C.12/1/Add.42 (17 May 2000), [19].

[31] CESCR, Concluding Observations: Japan, E/C.12/1/Add.67 (24 September 2001), [59].

[32] CESCR, Concluding Observations: United Kingdom of Great Britain and Northern Ireland, E/C.12/1/Add.19 (12 December 1997), [18]; see also Bosnia and Herzegovina, E/C.12/BIH/CO/1 (24 January 2006), [28] and [50]; Serbia and Montenegro, E/C.12/1/Add.108 (23 June 2005), [64].

[33] CESCR, Concluding Observations: Israel, E/C.12/1/Add.90 (26 June 2003), [45].

[34] CESCR, Guidelines on Treaty-Specific Documents to be submitted by States Parties under Articles 16 and 17 of the International Covenant on Economic, Social and Cultural Rights ('Guidelines on Treaty-Specific Documents'), E/C.12/2008/2 (24 March 2009), [58].

In its Concluding Observations, the Committee frequently stresses the need for states to provide human rights education. So, for example, in its Concluding Observations on Nepal in 2008, the Committee:

> ... urges that human rights be introduced at all levels of education, both as a subject and as a methodology of instruction, reflecting values of participation and social inclusion. The Committee stresses the value of education as a tool for national reconciliation, the eradication of harmful feudal practices, the promotion of respect for the dignity of all persons and groups, as well as the building of skills to enhance future employment prospects.[35]

Article 13(2)

Article 13(2) sets out in detail the requirements for achieving the right to education in respect of different levels of education: primary, secondary, technical and vocational education, higher education and fundamental education. The Article provides that states 'recognize' these requirements. The *travaux* indicate that this change from the previous wording ('it is understood that') was intended to strengthen the Article, by making clear that the measures set out in Article 13(2) were to be progressively realized by states, in accordance with Article 2 of the Covenant.[36]

OVERALL APPROACH—'4A' SCHEME

Although the Article sets out different obligations relating to each level of education, it is clear that there are certain key aspects of the right to education which are equally applicable to all levels. According to General Comment No. 13, 'education in all its forms and at all levels shall exhibit the following interrelated and essential features', namely: availability, accessibility, acceptability and adaptability.[37] This '4A' scheme for conceptualizing the right to education was developed in the work of the Special Rapporteur on the right to education, Katerina Tomaševski,[38] and by the Committee.

According to General Comment No. 13, *availability* of education means that:

> ... functioning educational institutions and programmes have to be available in sufficient quantity within the jurisdiction of the State party. What they require to function depends upon numerous factors, including the developmental context within which they operate; for example, all institutions and programmes are likely to require buildings or

[35] CESCR, Concluding Observations: Nepal, E/C.12/NPL/CO/2 (16 January 2008), [47]; see also China, E/C.12/1/Add.107 (13 May 2005), [102]; Colombia, E/C.12/1995/18 (8 December 1995), [199]; Solomon Islands, E/C.12/1/Add.84 (19 December 2002), [31]; Israel, E/C.12/1/Add.90 (26 June 2003), [44].

[36] UNGA, Draft International Covenants on Human Rights: Report of the Third Committee (Rapporteur Mr Carlow Manuel Cox (Peru)), A/3764 (5 December 1957), 8.

[37] CESCR, General Comment No. 13, [6].

[38] Commission on Human Rights, Preliminary Report of the Special Rapporteur on the right to education, E/CN.4/1999/49 (13 January 1999), [42]–[74].

other protection from the elements, sanitation facilities for both sexes, safe drinking water, trained teachers receiving domestically competitive salaries, teaching materials, and so on; while some will also require facilities such as a library, computer facilities and information technology...[39]

The focus is therefore on the availability of educational infrastructure, as discussed in more detail below.

Accessibility of education involves three key elements: non-discrimination, physical accessibility and economic accessibility. According to General Comment No. 13:

Accessibility—educational institutions and programmes have to be accessible to everyone, without discrimination, within the jurisdiction of the State party. Accessibility has three overlapping dimensions:

(i) Non-discrimination—education must be accessible to all, especially the most vulnerable groups, in law and fact, without discrimination on any of the prohibited grounds (see paras. 31–37 on non-discrimination);

(ii) Physical accessibility—education has to be within safe physical reach, either by attendance at some reasonably convenient geographic location (e.g. a neighbourhood school) or via modern technology (e.g. access to a 'distance learning' programme);

(iii) Economic accessibility—education has to be affordable to all. This dimension of accessibility is subject to the differential wording of article 13(2) in relation to primary, secondary and higher education: whereas primary education shall be available 'free to all', States parties are required to progressively introduce free secondary and higher education...[40]

In many ways, physical and economic barriers to accessibility also involve discrimination in terms of access to education, as the Special Rapporteur on the right to education noted in his report on the promotion of equality of opportunity in education.[41] Issues of accessibility are therefore considered in more detail in the context of the discussion of non-discrimination below.

Acceptability of education means, according to General Comment No. 13, that:

...the form and substance of education, including curricula and teaching methods, have to be acceptable (e.g. relevant, culturally appropriate and of good quality) to students and, in appropriate cases, parents; this is subject to the educational objectives required by article 13(1) and such minimum educational standards as may be approved by the State (see art. 13(3) and (4)).[42]

This embraces a number of issues which are discussed in more detail below, such as: the quality of education; the need for education to be culturally appropriate for all, including minorities and indigenous groups—and, in particular, the need for education in, or of, the languages of these groups; the need for schools to

[39] CESCR, General Comment No. 13, [6(a)]. [40] CESCR, General Comment No. 13, [6(b)].

[41] Human Rights Council, Report of the Special Rapporteur on the right to education on the promotion of equality of opportunity in education, A/HRC/17/29 (18 April 2011), [53]–[62].

[42] CESCR, General Comment No. 13, [6(c)].

respect the religious convictions of students and parents; and the avoidance of corporal punishment. These last two aspects of acceptability clearly overlap to a considerable extent with the rights of parents under Article 13(3). The question of acceptability also raises a number of issues from the rights of the child perspective, as General Comment No. 1 of the Committee on the Rights of the Child indicates:

> The curriculum must be of direct relevance to the child's social, cultural, environmental and economic context and to his or her present and future needs and take full account of the child's evolving capacities; teaching methods should be tailored to the different needs of different children. Education must also be aimed at ensuring that essential life skills are learned by every child and that no child leaves school without being equipped to face the challenges that he or she can expect to be confronted with in life.[43]

In its Concluding Observations, the CESCR has considered a range of other issues relating to acceptability of education, including, for example, concerns about conditions in school and pressures placed on students due to the competitive nature of education. So, for example, in relation to Japan, the Committee 'is concerned about the frequently excessively competitive and stressful nature of all levels of education, which results in school absence, illness, and even in suicide by students'.[44]

Quality of education is another important aspect of acceptability of education, and the Committee frequently expresses concern regarding educational standards. For example, in relation to the Republic of Korea:

> The Committee notes with concern that the low quality of education in public schools is compelling families to supplement the education of their children with private instruction.[45]

A further issue related to the acceptability of education concerns the treatment of pregnant students. The need to adopt appropriate mechanisms to ensure that pregnant girls can continue their education has been noted by the CESCR[46] and by the Committee on the Rights of the Child.[47] The issue is explicitly addressed in Article 11(6) of the African Charter on the Rights and Welfare of the Child, which provides that:

> States Parties to the present Charter shall have all appropriate measures to ensure that children who become pregnant before completing their education shall have an opportunity to continue with their education on the basis of their individual ability.

[43] CESCR, General Comment No. 13, [9].

[44] CESCR, Concluding Observations: Japan, E/C.12/1/Add.67 (24 September 2001), [31]; see also Republic of Korea, E/C.12/KOR/CO/3 (17 December 2009), [34].

[45] CESCR, Concluding Observations: Republic of Korea, E/C.12/1/Add.59 (21 May 2001), [27]. See also, eg, CESCR, Concluding Observations: Ukraine, E/C.12/1/Add.65 (24 September 2001), [17]; Russian Federation, E/C.12/1/Add.13 (20 May 1997), [29].

[46] See, eg, CESCR, Concluding Observations: Kenya, E/C.12/KEN/CO/1 (1 December 2008), [34].

[47] CRC, Concluding Observations: Guyana, CRC/C/15/Add.224 (30 January 2004), [48(b)]; see also Indonesia, CRC/C/15/Add.223 (30 January 2004), [63(c)].

The need to ensure that schools do not penalize pregnant girls by treating pregnancy as a disciplinary offence has been highlighted in the work of the Special Rapporteur on the right to education.[48] In this context, a decision of the Supreme Court of Colombia, which found that penalization of pregnant girls by suspension and removal from mainstream schooling, is worth noting. In the case of *Martinez Martinez y Suarez Robayo v Collegio Cuidad de Cali*,[49] the Court found that:

...although a suspension from school attendance does not imply a definitive loss of the right to education, it does imply the provision of instruction to the pregnant schoolgirl in conditions which are stigmatizing and discriminatory in comparison with other pupils in her ability to benefit from [the right to education]...The conversion of pregnancy—through school regulations—into a ground for punishment violates fundamental rights...to education.[50]

Adaptability of education essentially refers to the need for education to be flexible. According to General Comment No. 13:

[E]ducation has to be flexible so it can adapt to the needs of changing societies and communities and respond to the needs of students within their diverse social and cultural settings.[51]

One particular issue of concern in this context is the need for education to accommodate the needs of working children. This is specifically identified in the work of the Special Rapporteur,[52] and is reflected in the Concluding Observations of the Committee. So, for example, in relation to El Salvador:

22. Although child labour is often necessary for the survival of the family, it is one of the factors hampering the implementation of Articles 13 and 14 of the Covenant, and the Committee is disturbed by the apparent lack of action by the authorities to remedy the situation...

34. It is the Committee's opinion that measures should be taken by the authorities to enable working children to receive an adequate education.[53]

This issue is also addressed in the work of the International Labour Organization (ILO). In particular, ILO Convention 182 concerning the Prohibition and Immediate Action for the Elimination of the Worst Forms of Child Labour (1999),

[48] Commission on Human Rights, Progress Report of the Special Rapporteur on the right to education, E/CN.4/2000/6 (1 February 2000), [56]–[60].

[49] *Martinez Martinez y Suarez Robayo v Collegio Cuidad de Cali*, 11 November 1998, Case No. T-177814 (Supreme Court of Colombia).

[50] See Commission on Human Rights, Progress Report of the Special Rapporteur on the right to education, E/CN.4/2000/6 (1 February 2000), [60]. See also the decision of the Botswana Court of Appeals in *R v Tatu Shabani*, Criminal Sessions Case No. 322 of 2003 (PC) (unreported), referred to in Human Rights Council, Report of the Special Rapporteur on the right to education on justiciability of the right to education, A/HRC/23/35 (10 May 2013), [58].

[51] CESCR, General Comment No. 13, [6(d)].

[52] Commission on Human Rights, Progress Report of the Special Rapporteur on the right to education, E/CN.4/2000/6 (1 February 2000), [61]–[65].

[53] CESCR, Concluding Observations: El Salvador, E/C.12/1/Add.4 (28 May 1996), [22] and [34]; see also Egypt, E/C.12/1/Add.44 (23 May 2000), [21]; Benin, E/C.12/1/Add.78 (5 June 2002), [19]; Uruguay, E/C.12/1994/3 (30 May 1994), [8]; Jamaica, E/C.12/1/Add.75 (6 December 2001), [13].

emphasizes the obligations of states to ensure access to free basic education for all children.[54]

Other issues related to the adaptability of education concern the need to take appropriate measures to deliver education to children in areas suffering from conflict or natural disasters. So, for example, in its Concluding Observations on Afghanistan, the Committee indicated that it was 'deeply concerned about the increase in the number of child victims of attacks against schools by insurgents' and recommended that the 'State party should improve security for children in school as well as on their way to and from school'.[55] And in relation to the Democratic People's Republic of Korea, the Committee 'calls upon the State party to continue its effort in assisting those children who have suffered from the consequences of natural disasters to return to school'.[56] The Special Rapporteur on the right to education has also prepared a special report concerning the right to education in emergency situations, namely, situations arising out of armed conflict or natural disaster.[57] This report confirms that 'states have an obligation to respect, protect and fulfil the right to education, whether or not an emergency situation prevails'.[58]

In addition to analyzing the right to education in terms of this '4A' scheme of availability, accessibility, acceptability and adaptability, the Committee has provided further guidance on the obligations of states in relation to the right to education using the typology of obligations to respect, protect and fulfil. According to General Comment No. 13:

> In relation to article 13(2), States have obligations to respect, protect and fulfil each of the 'essential features' (availability, accessibility, acceptability, adaptability) of the right to education. By way of illustration, a State must respect the availability of education by not closing private schools; protect the accessibility of education by ensuring that third parties, including parents and employers, do not stop girls from going to school; fulfil (facilitate) the acceptability of education by taking positive measures to ensure that education is culturally appropriate for minorities and indigenous peoples, and of good quality for all; fulfil (provide) the adaptability of education by designing and providing resources for curricula which reflect the contemporary needs of students in a changing world; and fulfil (provide) the availability of education by actively developing a system of schools, including building classrooms, delivering programmes, providing teaching materials, training teachers and paying them domestically competitive salaries.[59]

[54] International Labour Conference (87th Session), Convention concerning the Prohibition and Immediate Action for the Elimination of the Worst Forms of Child Labour, No. 182, Geneva, 17 June 1999, Article 7.

[55] CESCR, Concluding Observations: Afghanistan, E/C.12/AFG/CO/24 (7 June 2010), [43]; see also Sri Lanka, E/C.12/1/Add.24 (16 June 1998), [7].

[56] CESCR, Concluding Observations: Democratic People's Republic of Korea, E/C.12/1/Add.95 (12 December 2003), [40].

[57] Human Rights Council, Report of the Special Rapporteur on the right to education in emergency situations, A/HRC/8/10 (20 May 2008).

[58] Human Rights Council, Report of the Special Rapporteur on the right to education in emergency situations, A/HRC/8/10, [37].

[59] CESCR, General Comment No. 13, [50].

The Committee has also clarified what it considers to be the 'minimum core obligation' of states in relation to the right to education as follows:

In the context of article 13, this core includes an obligation: to ensure the right of access to public educational institutions and programmes on a non-discriminatory basis; to ensure that education conforms to the objectives set out in article 13(1); to provide primary education for all in accordance with article 13(2)(a); to adopt and implement a national educational strategy which includes provision for secondary, higher and fundamental education; and to ensure free choice of education without interference from the State or third parties, subject to conformity with 'minimum educational standards' (art. 13(3) and (4)).[60]

LEVELS OF EDUCATION

While the general obligations set out above are applicable to all levels of education, Article 13(2) provides specific guidance on measures to be taken in relation to different levels of education.

Primary education—Article 13(2)(a)

Under Article 13(2)(a), primary education shall be compulsory and available free to all.

According to General Comment No. 13:

The Committee obtains guidance on the proper interpretation of the term 'primary education' from the World Declaration on Education for All which states: 'The main delivery system for the basic education of children outside the family is primary schooling. Primary education must be universal, ensure that the basic learning needs of all children are satisfied, and take into account the culture, needs and opportunities of the community' (art. 5). '[B]asic learning needs' are defined in article 1 of the World Declaration. While primary education is not synonymous with basic education, there is a close correspondence between the two. In this regard, the Committee endorses the position taken by UNICEF: 'Primary education is the most important component of basic education.'[61]

The Committee thus equates primary education with the education necessary to obtain 'basic learning needs' as defined in the World Declaration on Education for All:

These needs comprise both essential learning tools (such as literacy, oral expression, numeracy, and problem-solving) and the basic learning content (such as knowledge, skills, values, and attitudes) required by human beings to be able to survive, to develop their full capacities, to live and work in dignity, to participate fully in development, to improve the quality of their lives, to make informed decisions, and to continue learning.[62]

The meaning of 'free' is considered in the Committee's General Comment No. 11 on Article 14 of the Covenant:

Free of charge. The nature of this requirement is unequivocal. The right is expressly formulated so as to ensure the availability of primary education without charge to the child,

[60] CESCR, General Comment No. 13, [57]. [61] CESCR, General Comment No. 13, [9].
[62] World Declaration on Education for All, Article 1(1).

parents or guardians. Fees imposed by the Government, the local authorities or the school, and other direct costs, constitute disincentives to the enjoyment of the right and may jeopardize its realization. They are also often highly regressive in effect. Their elimination is a matter which must be addressed by the required plan of action. Indirect costs, such as compulsory levies on parents (sometimes portrayed as being voluntary, when in fact they are not), or the obligation to wear a relatively expensive school uniform, can also fall into the same category. Other indirect costs may be permissible, subject to the Committee's examination on a case-by-case basis.[63]

In other words, both direct and indirect costs relating to education may need to be met by the state in order for states to comply with their obligations under Article 13(2)(a).

The term 'compulsory' is also considered in General Comment No. 11:

Compulsory. The element of compulsion serves to highlight the fact that neither parents, nor guardians, nor the State are entitled to treat as optional the decision as to whether the child should have access to primary education. Similarly, the prohibition of gender discrimination in access to education, required also by articles 2 and 3 of the Covenant, is further underlined by this requirement. It should be emphasized, however, that the education offered must be adequate in quality, relevant to the child and must promote the realization of the child's other rights.[64]

According to the Committee, the obligation to provide free and compulsory primary education is part of the minimum core obligation of states under Article 13.[65] This obligation is also reinforced by Article 14 of the Covenant which requires states to adopt plans of action for the progressive implementation of free and compulsory primary education.

Further guidance on the approach which the Committee takes to Article 13(2)(a) is provided by the Guidelines on Treaty-Specific Documents. Paragraph 59 asks states to indicate in particular:

(a) The level or grade until which education is compulsory and free for all;

(b) Any direct costs such as school fees, as well as the measures taken to eliminate them; and

(c) Any indirect costs (e.g. expenses for school books, uniforms, transport, special fees such as exam fees, contributions to district education boards, etc.) and the measures taken to alleviate the impact of such costs on children from poorer households.

Secondary education—Article 13(2)(b)

Article 13(2)(b) provides that secondary education 'shall be made generally available and accessible to all by every appropriate means, and in particular by the progressive introduction of free education'. According to General Comment No. 13:

The phrase 'generally available' signifies, firstly, that secondary education is not dependent on a student's apparent capacity or ability and, secondly, that secondary education

[63] CESCR, General Comment No. 11, Plans of Action for Primary Education (Article 14), E/1992/23 (10 May 1999), [7].

[64] CESCR, General Comment No. 11, [6].

[65] CESCR, General Comment No. 13, [57].

will be distributed throughout the State in such a way that it is available on the same basis to all.[66]

The reference to 'progressive introduction of free education' means, according to General Comment No. 13, that although states should prioritize the provision of free primary education, they must also take steps to achieve free secondary and higher education.[67]

Technical and vocational education—Article 13(2)(b)

Article 1(a) of the UNESCO Convention on Technical and Vocational Education indicates that technical and vocational education consists of:

[A]ll forms and levels of the educational process involving, in addition to general knowledge, the study of technologies and related sciences and the acquisition of practical skills, know-how, attitudes and understanding relating to occupations in the various sectors of economic and social life.[68]

This definition is adopted by the Committee in General Comment No. 13, in which the Committee notes that technical and vocational education ('TVE') 'forms part of both the right to education and the right to work'.[69] This link between TVE and employment is also emphasized in the report on technical and vocational education and training of the Special Rapporteur on the right to education,[70] and is reflected in the approach to TVE in ILO instruments such as the Human Resources Development Convention 1975[71] and the Social Policy (Basic Aims and Standards) Convention 1962.[72]

The inclusion of TVE in the right to education essentially reflects the need for education to be flexible and to meet the diverse needs of students. As the Special Rapporteur noted in his special report on TVE:

International experience demonstrates that adapting to an increasingly diversified student population calls for providing various learning pathways, including in technical and vocational subjects. New approaches to education and training are crucial to meet the demand for new skills in an increasingly knowledge- and skills-based society.[73]

Under Article 13(2)(b), technical and vocational education, which forms part of secondary education, must be 'generally available'. The Committee provides further guidance on TVE in General Comment No. 13 as follows:

[T]he right to TVE includes the following aspects:

(a) It enables students to acquire knowledge and skills which contribute to their personal development, self-reliance and employability and enhances the productivity

[66] CESCR, General Comment No. 13, [13]. [67] CESCR, General Comment No. 13, [14].

[68] UNESCO Convention on Technical and Vocational Education, Article (1)(a).

[69] CESCR, General Comment No. 13, [15].

[70] UNGA, Report of the Special Rapporteur on the right to education, A/67/310 (15 August 2012).

[71] International Labour Conference (60th Session), Human Resources Development Convention 1975, No. 142, Geneva, 23 June 1975.

[72] International Labour Conference (46th Session), Social Policy (Basic Aims and Standards) Convention 1962, No. 117, Geneva, 22 June 1962.

[73] UNGA, Report of the Special Rapporteur on the right to education, A/67/310 (15 August 2012), [10].

of their families and communities, including the State party's economic and social development;

(b) It takes account of the educational, cultural and social background of the population concerned; the skills, knowledge and levels of qualification needed in the various sectors of the economy; and occupational health, safety and welfare;

(c) Provides retraining for adults whose current knowledge and skills have become obsolete owing to technological, economic, employment, social or other changes;

(d) It consists of programmes which give students, especially those from developing countries, the opportunity to receive TVE in other States, with a view to the appropriate transfer and adaptation of technology;

(e) It consists, in the context of the Covenant's non-discrimination and equality provisions, of programmes which promote the TVE of women, girls, out-of-school youth, unemployed youth, the children of migrant workers, refugees, persons with disabilities and other disadvantaged groups.[74]

Other international instruments and programmes also address the issue of TVE. Most notable in this context is the UNESCO Convention on Technical and Vocational Education, and the UNESCO Revised Recommendation concerning Technical and Vocational Education.[75] UNESCO has also adopted a five-year strategy for the TVE sector, and in 2012 organized the Third International Congress on Technical and Vocational Education and Training, 'Transforming TVET: Building Skills for Work and Life'. The outcome document of that congress[76] 'provides new guidance to States on transforming technical and vocational education and training'.[77]

Higher education—Article 13(2)(c)

Under Article 13(2)(c), 'higher education shall be made equally accessible to all, on the basis of capacity, by every appropriate means, and in particular by the progressive introduction of free education'.

Unlike secondary education, higher education need not be 'generally available', but only 'accessible to all, on the basis of capacity'. According to General Comment No. 13, '[t]he "capacity" of individuals should be assessed by reference to all their relevant expertise and experience'.[78] This means that it is possible to adopt conditions, including particularly academic prerequisites, to restrict access to higher education. There is a body of case law to this effect under the

[74] CESCR, General Comment No. 13, [16].

[75] UNESCO General Conference (18th Session), Revised Recommendation concerning Technical and Vocational Education, Paris, 19 November 1974.

[76] UNESCO Third International Congress on Technical and Vocational Education and Training, Shanghai Consensus: Recommendations of the Third International Congress on Technical and Vocational Education and Training, Shanghai, 14–16 May 2012.

[77] UNGA, Report of the Special Rapporteur on the right to education, A/67/310 (15 August 2012), [16].

[78] CESCR, General Comment No. 13, [19].

ECHR.[79] Most recently, in the case of *Tarantino et al v Italy*,[80] the European Court of Human Rights upheld regulations restricting access to certain faculties, such as medicine and dentistry, by establishing quotas for admission and requiring applicants to pass an entrance examination. The Court found that such regulations were legitimate and did not constitute a violation of the right to education under Article 2 of Protocol 1 of the ECHR. The Court confirmed its general approach to such cases as follows:

43. The Court reiterates that the guarantees of Article 2 of Protocol No. 1 apply to existing institutions of higher education within the member States of the Council of Europe and that access to any institution of higher education existing at a given time is an inherent part of the right set out in the first sentence of Article 2 of Protocol No. 1. . .

44. In spite of its importance, this right is not, however, absolute, but may be subject to limitations; these are permitted by implication since the right of access 'by its very nature calls for regulation by the State'. . . Admittedly, the regulation of educational institutions may vary in time and in place, inter alia, according to the needs and resources of the community and the distinctive features of different levels of education. Consequently, the Contracting States enjoy a certain margin of appreciation in this sphere, although the final decision as to the observance of the Convention's requirements rests with the Court. . .

45. In order to ensure that the restrictions that are imposed do not curtail the right in question to such an extent as to impair its very essence and deprive it of its effectiveness, the Court must satisfy itself that they are foreseeable for those concerned and pursue a legitimate aim. . . Furthermore, a limitation will only be compatible with Article 2 of Protocol No. 1 if there is a reasonable relationship of proportionality between the means employed and the aim sought to be achieved. . .

46. The Court notes that Article 2 of Protocol No. 1 in any event permits limiting access to universities to those who duly applied for entrance and passed the examination. . .[81]

The Court found that the measures in question in this case were foreseeable and pursued the legitimate aim of 'achieving high levels of professionalism, by ensuring a minimum and adequate educational level in universities running in appropriate conditions, which is in the general interest'.[82] The Court considered that the measures imposed 'were not disproportionate and that in applying those measures the State did not exceed its margin of appreciation'.[83]

Fundamental education—Article 13(2)(d)

Article 13(2)(d) requires states to 'encourage' or 'intensify' fundamental education 'for those persons who have not received or completed the whole period of their primary education'.

[79] See, eg, *Patel v United Kingdom* (App. 8844/80), 9 December 1980, (1982) 4 EHRR 256; *X v United Kingdom* (App. 8874/80), 9 December 1980 (1982) 4 EHRR 252.

[80] *Tarantino et al v Italy* (Apps. 25851/09, 29284/09 and 64090/09), ECtHR 2 April 2013.

[81] *Tarantino v Italy*, [43]–[46].

[82] *Tarantino v Italy*, [48].

[83] *Tarantino v Italy*, [58].

According to General Comment No. 13:

22. In general terms, fundamental education corresponds to basic education as set out in the World Declaration on Education For All. By virtue of article 13(2)(d), individuals 'who have not received or completed the whole period of their primary education' have a right to fundamental education, or basic education as defined in the World Declaration on Education for All.

23. Since everyone has the right to the satisfaction of their 'basic learning needs' as understood by the World Declaration, the right to fundamental education is not confined to those 'who have not received or completed the whole period of their primary education'. The right to fundamental education extends to all those who have not yet satisfied their 'basic learning needs'.

24. It should be emphasized that enjoyment of the right to fundamental education is not limited by age or gender; it extends to children, youth and adults, including older persons. Fundamental education, therefore, is an integral component of adult education and life-long learning. Because fundamental education is a right of all age groups, curricula and delivery systems must be devised which are suitable for students of all ages.[84]

As Ssenyonjo has noted, the language of the Article—'fundamental education shall be encouraged or intensified as far as possible'—does not suggest a heavy obligation on the part of the state when compared with its obligations in relation to other levels of education.[85]

Other levels of education

Although not specifically mentioned in Article 13, the Committee has also inferred obligations for states to provide preschool[86] and continuing education,[87] as part of the right to education.

Article 13(2)(e)

Article 13(2)(e) provides for general state obligations to ensure the achievement of the right to education as set out in the other provisions of Article 13(2). It requires states to 'actively pursue' the development of 'a system of schools at all levels', to establish 'an adequate fellowship system', and to improve the material conditions of teaching staff.

According to General Comment No. 13:

25. The requirement that the 'development of a system of schools at all levels shall be actively pursued' means that a State party is obliged to have an overall developmental strategy for its

[84] CESCR, General Comment No. 13, [22]–[24].

[85] Manisuli Ssenyonjo, *Economic, Social and Cultural Rights in International Law* (Hart, Oxford, 2009), 380.

[86] See, eg, CESCR, Concluding Observations: United Kingdom of Great Britain and Northern Ireland, E/C.12/1994/20 (9 December 1994), [276]; Republic of Moldova, E/C.12/1/Add.91 (12 December 2003), [29]; Australia, E/C.12/AUS/CO/4 (12 June 2009), [31]; Norway, E/C.12/1/Add.109 (23 June 2005), [33].

[87] CESCR, Concluding Observations: Luxembourg, E/C.12/1/Add.22 (12 December 1997), [24].

school system. The strategy must encompass schooling at all levels, but the Covenant requires States parties to prioritize primary education (see para. 51). '[A]ctively pursued' suggests that the overall strategy should attract a degree of governmental priority and, in any event, must be implemented with vigour.

26. The requirement that 'an adequate fellowship system shall be established' should be read with the Covenant's non-discrimination and equality provisions; the fellowship system should enhance equality of educational access for individuals from disadvantaged groups.[88]

PARTICULAR ISSUES

The Committee's general approach

When considering state reports in relation to the right to education, the Committee's general approach is often to start with indicators which may suggest problems with fulfillment of the right to education in the state, in particular, rates of enrolment, literacy and drop-outs from education. So, for example, in relation to Mali:

With regard to the right to education recognized in Article 13 of the Covenant, the Committee is concerned about the high rate of illiteracy (adult illiteracy averaged 68%; males 59%, female 76.1%) in Mali…The rate of school enrolment in Mali is among the lowest in the world. Enrolment in primary schools included only 15% of children in the relevant age group (males 17%, females 14%); secondary enrolment is equivalent to only 7% of children in the appropriate age group (males 10%, females 5%). Many students receive higher education abroad, mainly in France and Senegal. Repeat and drop-out rates are very high; only 7% of pupils complete the primary education cycle each year.[89]

Similarly, in relation to Tunisia, the Committee has noted:

Despite the marked progress in the area of education, the Committee notes that illiteracy still affects one-third of the population, 42% of women and 23% of men, and that serious disparities continue to exist between the literacy rates of boys and girls at all age levels and between urban and rural areas. It also notes the serious problem of school drop-out, and especially that half of those enrolled in primary schools do not continue with secondary education. In this regard, the Committee is concerned about students who drop out at the end of the first cycle of basic education.[90]

The Committee has demonstrated a particular concern with the need to ensure *literacy*. The Guidelines on Treaty-Specific Documents require states to '[i]ndicate the measures taken to promote literacy, as well as adult and continuing education, in a life-long perspective'.[91] And in its Concluding Observations, the Committee has repeatedly expressed concern about high rates of illiteracy,[92] and requested

[88] CESCR, General Comment No. 13, [25]–[26].

[89] CESCR, Concluding Observations: Mali, E/C.12/1994/17 (21 December 1994), [15]; see also, eg, Senegal, E/C.12/1/Add.64 (24 September 2001), [34].

[90] CESCR, Concluding Observations: Tunisia, E/C.12/1/Add.36 (14 May 1990), [17].

[91] CESCR, Guidelines on Treaty-Specific Documents, [62].

[92] See, eg, CESCR, Concluding Observations: Brazil, E/C.12/1/Add.87 (20 June 2003), [39]; Bolivia, E/C.12/1/Add.60 (21 May 2001), [25].

states to 'adopt effective measures to combat illiteracy',[93] including establishing literacy programmes for adults.[94]

The Committee also looks at the amount of money allocated for education under states' budgets as an indicator of whether the state is complying with its obligations in relation to the right to education. So, for example, in relation to Angola:

> The Committee regrets that the budget allocated to the education decreased between 2004 and 2006, despite the rapidly rising number of children in the school age...The Committee recommends that the State party...increase public expenditure on education in general.[95]

And in relation to Korea:

> The Committee is disturbed by a range of features of the Korean education system. Only primary education is provided free of charge. However, given the strength of the Korean economy it appears appropriate that free education should also extend to the secondary and higher sectors.[96]

In this context, the Committee has also expressed concern about the effect of structural adjustment agreements entered into with organizations such as the IMF.[97]

Educational infrastructure

As noted above, the requirement that education be 'available' obliges states to provide adequate educational infrastructure: 'functioning educational institutions and programmes have to be available in sufficient quantity within the jurisdiction of the State party'.[98]

This requirement will clearly not be met where states fail to provide schools or other educational establishments, or close existing establishments. Thus, in a case before the African Commission on Human and Peoples' Rights, *Free Legal Assistance Group et al v Zaire*,[99] the Commission found that the closure of secondary schools and universities for a period of two years, allegedly due to mismanagement of public finances by the government, amounted to a violation of the right to education under Article 17 of the African Charter.[100] Similarly, in the

[93] CESCR, Concluding Observations: Brazil, E/C.12/1/Add.87 (20 June 2003), [63].

[94] See, eg, CESCR, Concluding Observations: Saint Vincent and the Grenadines, E/C.12/1/Add.21 (2 December 1997), [27]; Senegal, E/C.12/1/Add.62 (24 September 2001), [57]; India, E/C.12/IND/CO/5 (8 August 2008), [82]; Bolivia, E/C.12/1/Add.60 (21 May 2001), [44].

[95] CESCR, Concluding Observations: Angola, E/C.12/AGO/CO/3 (1 December 2008), [39].

[96] CESCR, Concluding Observations: Republic of Korea, E/C.12/1995/3 (7 June 1995), [13]. See also, eg, CESCR, Concluding Observations: Dominican Republic, E/C.12/1/Add.6 (6 December 1996), [17]; Ukraine, E/C.12/1/Add.65 (24 September 2001), [17]–[32]; Jamaica, E/C.12/1/Add.75 (6 December 2001), [19]; Latvia, E/C.12/LVA/CO/1 (7 January 2008), [30].

[97] See, eg, CESCR, Concluding Observations: Senegal, E/C.12/1993/18 (5 January 1994), [7].

[98] CESCR, General Comment No. 13, [6(a)].

[99] *Free Legal Assistance Group et al v Zaire*, African Commission on Human and Peoples' Rights, Communication Nos. 25/89, 47/90, 56/91, 100/93, (1997) 4 IHRR 89, (2000) AHRLR 74, 4 April 1996.

[100] *Free Legal Assistance Group v Zaire*, [48].

case of *Democratic Republic of the Congo v Burundi, Rwanda and Uganda*,[101] the Commission found that the activities of armed forces of Burundi, Rwanda and Uganda in Congolese provinces caused violations of the right to education, as a result of 'the general disruption of life and state of war that took place while the forces of the respondent states were occupying and in control of the eastern provinces of the complainant state'.[102] At the national level, the Constitutional Court of South Africa has required arrangements to be made to secure the right to basic education for students where their school was to be evicted from the land on which it was located.[103]

More generally, failure by states to provide adequate educational infrastructure, or progressively to improve existing infrastructure, will raise issues under Article 13(2). In particular, the Committee in its Concluding Observations has focused on facilities available for education, and the availability, education and remuneration of teachers. On the issue of facilities, for example, the Committee has noted, in relation to the Republic of the Congo, that:

> 23. The Committee is profoundly dissatisfied with the education system in the Congo. Although the Congo used to have quite a developed education system, that has seriously deteriorated as result of economic mismanagement, the shortage of resources and political unrest. According to the delegation, there are fewer children enrolling in school, a shortage of teachers and teaching materials, and the school buildings are in a deplorable state.
>
> ...
>
> 29. The Committee urges the State party to pay due attention to the rehabilitation of the educational infrastructure by allocating the necessary funds for teachers' salaries, teaching materials and school building repairs.[104]

In relation to Nigeria, the Committee expressed concern that:

> Schoolchildren often have to carry their desks and chairs from their homes to the school...Recent poor educational quality is due partly to little teacher attention being devoted to school work because of poor salaries, leading to incessant strikes and school closures.[105]

The Committee has also highlighted as problematic 'obsolete teaching materials and equipment in schools and colleges',[106] 'low levels of remuneration for teachers',[107] 'inadequacy of pedagogical tools'[108] and 'excessive numbers of students per class and per teacher'.[109]

[101] *Democratic Republic of the Congo v Burundi, Rwanda and Uganda*, African Commission on Human and Peoples' Rights, Communication No. 227/99, (2004) AHRLR 19, 29 May 2003.

[102] *Democratic Republic of the Congo v Burundi, Rwanda and Uganda*, [88].

[103] *Governing Body of the Juma Musjid Primary School et al v Ahmed Asruf Essay N.O. et al*, 11 April 2011, 2011 (8) BCLR 761.

[104] CESCR, Concluding Observations: Republic of the Congo, E/C.12/1/Add.45 (23 May 2000), [23] and [29].

[105] CESCR, Concluding Observations: Nigeria, E/C.12/1/Add.23 (16 June 1998), [31].

[106] CESCR, Concluding Observations: Ukraine, E/C.12/1/Add.65 (24 September 2001), [17].

[107] CESCR, Concluding Observations: Ukraine, E/C.12/1/Add.65 (24 September 2001), [17].

[108] CESCR, Concluding Observations: Tunisia, E/C.12/1/Add.36 (14 May 1999), [28].

[109] CESCR, Concluding Observations: Tunisia, E/C.12/1/Add.36 (14 May 1999), [28].

Similar issues relating to educational infrastructure have been raised by regional human rights bodies monitoring the right to education. To cite just one example, the European Committee of Social Rights, which monitors state compliance with the European Social Charter, noted, in finding conditions in the Republic of Moldova not to be compliant with Article 17(2) of the Revised European Social Charter:

States need to ensure a high quality of teaching…The Committee notes…that closures of educational institutions, inadequate transportation and poor conditions prevent children from receiving an education. In most cases, kindergartens are being closed due to insufficient funding, and those that continue to operate do not provide year-round programmes. Moreover, the facilities are also deteriorating with heating shortages and poor sanitation…[110]

Non-discrimination

The need to guarantee equality of access to education is a key element of the right to education. According to General Comment No. 13:

The prohibition against discrimination enshrined in article 2(2) of the Covenant is subject to neither progressive realization nor the availability of resources; it applies fully and immediately to all aspects of education and encompasses all internationally prohibited grounds of discrimination.[111]

The importance of equal access to education for all is also reflected in other international instruments, most notably the UNESCO Convention against Discrimination in Education, which specifically seeks to address this issue. Similarly, in relation to the CROC, the Committee on the Rights of the Child has specifically indicated that non-discrimination is an essential aspect of the right to education:

Discrimination on the basis of any of the grounds listed in article 2 of the Convention, whether it is overt or hidden, offends the human dignity of the child and is capable of undermining or even destroying the capacity of the child to benefit from educational opportunities. While denying a child's access to educational opportunities is primarily a matter which relates to article 28 of the Convention, there are many ways in which failure to comply with the principles contained in article 29(1) can have a similar effect. To take an extreme example, gender discrimination can be reinforced by practices such as a curriculum which is inconsistent with the principles of gender equality, by arrangements which limit the benefits girls can obtain from the educational opportunities offered, and by unsafe or unfriendly environments which discourage girls' participation. Discrimination against children with disabilities is also pervasive in many formal educational systems and in a great many informal educational settings, including in the home. Children with HIV/AIDS are also heavily discriminated against in both settings. All such discriminatory practices are in direct contradiction with the requirements in article 29(1)(a) that education be directed to the development of the child's personality, talents and mental and physical abilities to their fullest potential.[112]

[110] European Committee of Social Rights, Conclusions 2005—Moldova, Volume 2 (9 March 2005), 472.

[111] CESCR, General Comment No. 13, [31].

[112] CRC, General Comment No. 1, CRC/GC/2001/1 (17 April 2001), [10].

The issue of equality of opportunity in education has also been the subject of a special report by the Special Rapporteur on the right to education,[113] and issues of equality of opportunity in education have been considered extensively in national jurisprudence.[114]

The Guidelines on Treaty-Specific Documents indicate that the Committee is concerned with discriminatory practices which affect a range of different groups.[115] The Committee's Concluding Observations on Kenya are indicative of the general approach adopted by the Committee:

> The Committee notes with concern that children from poor families, pregnant girls, children living in remote rural areas and in informal settlements, nomadic children, children with disabilities, refugee children and internally displaced children have limited to access to education…The Committee recommends that the State party (a) increase the funds allocated to bursaries and textbook subsidies for children from poor families, as well as to school transportation and mid-day meals in remote rural and deprived urban areas; (b) facilitate the readmission of girls who dropped out of school due to pregnancy by supporting them in finding adequate arrangements for the care of their babies; (c) ensure adequate access for nomadic children to mobile schools, including in the north eastern Province; and (d) cater for the special needs to children with disabilities and integrate refugee children and internally displaced children in the regular school system.[116]

It is therefore clear that the Committee is concerned with all forms of discrimination in relation to education. So, for example, the Committee has expressed concern about discrimination on the basis of sexual orientation[117] and discrimination against children in homes or institutions.[118] However, there are other categories of discrimination with which the Committee and other international bodies have expressed particular concern in their work, namely, discrimination on the basis of: geographical location; economic circumstances; disability; sex; citizenship or residence status; membership of a minority group; religion; and detention.

[113] Human Rights Council, Report of the Special Rapporteur on the right to education on the promotion of equality of opportunity in education, A/HRC/17/29 (18 April 2011).

[114] Eg, in the historic case of *Brown v Board of Education*, 34 US 483 (1954), the US Supreme Court found that segregation in education, such that black and white children attended separate educational facilities, was 'inherently unequal'. See also *Campaign for Fiscal Equity v The State of New York*, 719 NYS 2d 475 (2001); the decision of the Indian Supreme Court in *Km. Chitra Gosh and Another v Union of India et al* (1969) 2 SCC 228, cited in the report of the Special Rapporteur on the right to education on justiciability of the right to education, A/HRC/23/35 (10 May 2013), [46]; and the South African case of *Motala and Another v University of Natal* (1995) (3) BCLR 374 (D), cited in Human Rights Council, Report of the Special Rapporteur on the right to education on the promotion of equality of opportunity in education, A/HRC/17/29 (18 April 2011), [68], which upheld the acceptability of affirmative action in education to protect previously disadvantaged persons.

[115] CESCR, Guidelines on Treaty-Specific Documents, [63]–[65].

[116] CESCR, Concluding Observations: Kenya, E/C.12/KEN/CO/1 (1 December 2008), [34]; see also, eg, former Yugoslav Republic of Macedonia, E/C.12/MKD/CO/1 (15 January 2008), [27]–[28] and [47]–[48].

[117] CESCR, Concluding Observations: Poland, E/C.12/POL/CO/5 (2 December 2009), [32].

[118] CESCR, Concluding Observations: Ukraine, E/C.12/1995/15 (28 December 1995), [21]; see also Democratic People's Republic of Korea, E/C.12/1/Add.95 (12 December 2003), [41].

Geographical location

The Committee is concerned to ensure that those living in rural and regional areas have equal access to education. In its Concluding Observations on Guatemala, for example, the Committee expressed concern 'that only 30% of children living in rural communities complete primary education' and urged the state to hire 'additional teachers to fully cover rural areas'.[119] This aspect of non-discrimination overlaps with the requirement that education be 'physically accessible', that is, according to General Comment No. 13: 'education has to be within safe physical reach, either by attendance at some reasonably convenient geographic location (e.g. a neighbourhood school) or via modern technology (e.g. access to a 'distance learning' programme)'.[120] The issue of physical barriers to education, including '[i]nadequate public transportation', which is 'particularly acute in rural areas',[121] is also addressed in the report of the Special Rapporteur on the right to education on the promotion of equality of opportunity in education.[122]

Conversely, the Committee is concerned about overcrowding and other measures which may affect the quality of education in urban centres. Thus, in relation to Angola, while the Committee is 'concerned at the lack of schools and training of teachers, especially in remote areas and slums settlements',[123] it is also concerned that 'in the most populated wilayas the student-to-teacher ratio is very high—sometimes up to forty students per class'.[124] Overall:

> The Committee recommends that the State party take urgent measures to address regional disparities in access to education and enrolment rates through the creation of new establishments and the expansion of the school transport system.[125]

In general terms, then, the Committee in concerned about disparities between urban and rural areas.[126] In particular, according to General Comment No. 13:

> Sharp disparities in spending policies that result in differing qualities of education for persons residing in different geographic locations may constitute discrimination under the Covenant.[127]

Economic circumstances

According to General Comment No. 13, 'education has to be affordable to all'.[128] This reflects the wording of Article 13, under which primary education shall be

[119] CESCR, Concluding Observations: Guatemala, E/C.12/1/Add.93 (12 December 2003), [27] and [45].
[120] CESCR, General Comment No. 13, [6(b)(ii)].
[121] Human Rights Council, Report of the Special Rapporteur on the right to education on the promotion of equality of opportunity in education, A/HRC/17/29 (18 April 2011), [53].
[122] Human Rights Council, Report of the Special Rapporteur on the right to education on the promotion of equality of opportunity in education, A/HRC/17/29 (18 April 2011), [53]–[55].
[123] CESCR, Concluding Observations: Angola, E/C.12/AGO/CO/3 (1 December 2008), [39].
[124] CESCR, Concluding Observations: Angola, E/C.12/DZA/CO/4 (7 June 2010), [21].
[125] CESCR, Concluding Observations: Angola, E/C.12/DZA/CO/4 (7 June 2010), [21].
[126] CESCR, Concluding Observations: Paraguay, E/C.12/1/Add.1 (28 May 1996), [17].
[127] CESCR, General Comment No. 13, [35].
[128] CESCR, General Comment No. 13, [6(b)(iii)].

available 'free to all', while states are required progressively to introduce free secondary and higher education. As noted above, this requires the removal of both direct and indirect costs associated with education.

The importance of providing free education is also emphasized in regional instruments. Article 13 of the San Salvador Protocol to the American Convention on Human Rights and Article 11 of the African Charter on the Rights and Welfare of the Child address this issue in similar terms to those in the ICESCR. In the European context, the Revised European Social Charter, Article 17(2), requires the provision of 'free primary and secondary education'. The Charter of Fundamental Rights of the European Union, Article 14(2), indicates that the right to education 'includes the possibility to receive free compulsory education'.

This engages the issue of economic accessibility, discussed above, as well as issues of non-discrimination. According to the Special Rapporteur:

56. Surveys in various countries point to financial constraints—direct and indirect costs of schooling—as a central reason for children being out of school or dropping out. Tuition fees appear as the most obvious financial obstacle, and the accumulation of indirect costs, such as those related to transportation, school materials, uniform and other indirect contributions, undermine access to education opportunities. Besides, disparities in the provisions for public education contribute to unequal opportunities for many students receiving education in poorly resourced schools, as compared to well-resourced ones.

57. Even if primary or basic education were to be accessible free of cost, such access cannot be universalized effectively unless financial support in the form of grants and bursaries is provided to the children who are excluded, in particular those who are victims of extreme poverty. Furthermore, targeting elimination of child labour in order to safeguard mandatory education is particularly relevant.[129]

The Committee has, in its work, expressed concern regarding the imposition of fees and indirect costs of education, and particularly the impact of such costs on access to education for poorer sectors of the population. So, for example, in relation to Mauritius, the Committee:

…notes that the Mauritian school system is extremely competitive, which leads to widespread, Government-encouraged and costly private tuition and thus renders access to secondary and tertiary education more difficult for the poorer segments of the population. The Committee is also concerned about the re-introduction of fees at the tertiary level of education, which constitutes a deliberately retrogressive step.[130]

Similarly, in relation to Korea:

The Committee is concerned about the high associated costs of education required to be paid by parents. It is also concerned about information regarding the deepening inequality in education and the fact that the chances of entering a high-level university for students are often determined by their parents' ability afford after-school tutoring or private education. The Committee recommends that the State party accelerate its efforts to ensure that education

[129] Human Rights Council, Report of the Special Rapporteur on the right to education on the promotion of equality of opportunity in education, A/HRC/17/29 (18 April 2011), [56]–[57].

[130] CESCR, Concluding Observations: Mauritius, E/C.12/1994/8 (31 May 1994), [16].

is equally accessible to all and without discrimination, on the basis of ability, not financial capacity. It also recommends that the State party...strengthen the public education system and provide financial support to low-income families to cover the associated costs of education.[131]

The Committee frequently expresses concern about tuition fees for higher education, particularly where these are introduced or increased. In relation to Canada, for example:

The Committee views also with concern the fact that tuition fees for university education in Canada have dramatically increased in the past few years, making it very difficult for those in need to attend university in the absence of a loan or grant. A further subject of concern is the significant increase in the average student debt on graduation.[132]

And in relation to Bulgaria, the Committee 'is concerned that the fees introduced in higher education may represent a serious obstacle for disadvantaged groups of society seeking such an education'.[133]

The Committee has also expressed concern about the need to ensure equality as between public and private schools, in the context of increasing privatization of education, as discussed further below in the context of Article 13(4).

Disability

The Committee's General Comment No. 5 on Persons with Disabilities[134] provides:

35. School programmes in many countries today recognize that persons with disabilities can best be educated within the general education system. Thus the Standard Rules [Standard Rules on the Equalization of Opportunities for Persons with Disabilities, annexed to General Assembly resolution 48/96 of 20 December 1993] provide that 'States should recognize the principle of equal primary, secondary and tertiary educational opportunities for children, youth and adults with disabilities, in integrated settings'. In order to implement such an approach, States should ensure that teachers are trained to educate children with disabilities within regular schools and that the necessary equipment and support are available to bring person with disabilities up to the same level of education as their non-disabled peers. In the case of deaf children, for example, sign language should be recognized as a separate language to which the children should have access and whose importance should be acknowledged in their overall social environment.

This approach is endorsed by General Comment No. 13.[135]

131 CESCR, Concluding Observations: Republic of Korea, E/C.12/KOR/CO/3 (17 December 2009), [33]; see also Colombia, E/C.12/COL/CO/5 (7 June 2010), [29].

132 CESCR, Concluding Observations: Canada, E/C.12/1/Add.31 (10 December 1998), [39]; note also Canada, E/C.12/CAN/CO/4-E/C.12/CAN/CO/5 (22 May 2006), [31]: 'the Committee while noting that scholarships, bursaries, loans and other types of supports are provided to disadvantaged and marginalized individuals and groups, expresses concern about the discriminatory impact of tuition fee increases on low-income persons in many provinces and territories since 1998'.

133 CESCR, Concluding Observations: Bulgaria, E/C.12/1/Add.37 (8 December 1999), [21]; see also Germany, E/C.12/1/Add.29 (4 December 1998), [22]; Germany, E/C.12/1/Add.68 (24 September 2001), [29] and [47].

134 CESCR, General Comment No. 5, Persons with disabilities, E/1994/22 (9 December 1994) ('General Comment No. 5').

135 CESCR, General Comment No. 13, [36].

Within a regional context, the specific rights of persons with disabilities in relation to the right to education are recognized in Article 13(3)(e) of the San Salvador Protocol to the American Convention on Human Rights, which provides that '[p]rograms of special education should be established for the handicapped, so as to provide special instruction and training to persons with physical disabilities or mental deficiencies'. At the universal level, these rights are also recognized, and elaborated in more detail, in Article 24 of the Convention on the Rights of Persons with Disabilities:

1. States Parties recognize the right of persons with disabilities to education. With a view to realizing this right without discrimination and on the basis of equal opportunity, States Parties shall ensure an inclusive education system at all levels and life long learning directed to:

(a) The full development of human potential and sense of dignity and self-worth, and the strengthening of respect for human rights, fundamental freedoms and human diversity;

(b) The development by persons with disabilities of their personality, talents and creativity, as well as their mental and physical abilities, to their fullest potential;

(c) Enabling persons with disabilities to participate effectively in a free society.

2. In realizing this right, States Parties shall ensure that:

(a) Persons with disabilities are not excluded from the general education system on the basis of disability, and that children with disabilities are not excluded from free and compulsory primary education, or from secondary education, on the basis of disability;

(b) Persons with disabilities can access an inclusive, quality and free primary education and secondary education on an equal basis with others in the communities in which they live;

(c) Reasonable accommodation of the individual's requirements is provided;

(d) Persons with disabilities receive the support required, within the general education system, to facilitate their effective education;

(e) Effective individualized support measures are provided in environments that maximize academic and social development, consistent with the goal of full inclusion.

3. States Parties shall enable persons with disabilities to learn life and social development skills to facilitate their full and equal participation in education and as members of the community. To this end, States Parties shall take appropriate measures, including:

(a) Facilitating the learning of Braille, alternative script, augmentative and alternative modes, means and formats of communication and orientation and mobility skills, and facilitating peer support and mentoring;

(b) Facilitating the learning of sign language and the promotion of the linguistic identity of the deaf community;

(c) Ensuring that the education of persons, and in particular children, who are blind, deaf or deafblind, is delivered in the most appropriate languages and modes and means of communication for the individual, and in environments which maximize academic and social development.

4. In order to help ensure the realization of this right, States Parties shall take appropriate measures to employ teachers, including teachers with disabilities, who are qualified in sign language and/or Braille, and to train professionals and staff who work at all levels of education. Such training shall incorporate disability awareness and the use of appropriate augmentative and alternative modes, means and formats of communication, educational techniques and materials to support persons with disabilities.

5. States Parties shall ensure that persons with disabilities are able to access general tertiary education, vocational training, adult education and lifelong learning without discrimination and on an equal basis with others. To this end, States Parties shall ensure that reasonable accommodation is provided to persons with disabilities.[136]

The rights of disabled persons in relation to education are also recognized in various non-binding instruments, including the Declaration on the Rights of Disabled Persons[137] and the Standard Rules on the Equalization of Opportunities for Persons with Disabilities.[138]

A key theme which emerges from the international instruments and jurisprudence on the right to education of those with disabilities is the need to integrate persons with disabilities into mainstream education wherever possible. This is confirmed in the report of the Special Rapporteur on the right to education of persons with disabilities, which stresses that persons with disabilities have the right to 'inclusive education'.[139] According to the Special Rapporteur, the concept of inclusive education involves both integrating those with disabilities into mainstream education, and making appropriate and relevant education available to such groups within this education system.[140] The need to integrate persons with disabilities is also emphasized in the work of the Committee. The Committee's Concluding Observations on Mauritius provide a good example of the Committee's approach:

The Committee recommends that the State party strengthen its efforts to eliminate situations that may be discriminatory against children with disabilities and take steps to ensure that all children with disabilities can, as appropriate, study in mainstream schools. In order to implement this approach, the State party should ensure that teachers are trained to educate children with disabilities within regular schools, in line with the Committee's General Comment No. 5 (1994) on persons with disabilities.[141]

[136] Convention on the Rights of Persons with Disabilities (adopted 13 December 2006, 2515 UNTS 3, entered into force 3 May 2008).

[137] UNGA Res. 3447 (XXX), Declaration on the Rights of Disabled Persons, A/RES/3447(XXX) (9 December 1975), Article 6.

[138] UNGA Res. 48/96, Annexure: Standard Rules on the Equalization of Opportunities for Persons with Disabilities, A/RES/48/9 (20 December 1993).

[139] Human Rights Council, Report of the Special Rapporteur on the right to education on the equalization of opportunities for persons with disabilities, A/HRC/4/29 (19 February 2007).

[140] Human Rights Council, Report of the Special Rapporteur on the right to education on the equalization of opportunities for persons with disabilities, A/HRC/4/29, [10].

[141] CESCR, Concluding Observations: Mauritius, E/C.12/MUS/CO/4 (8 June 2010), [30]; see also, eg, Madagascar, E/C.12/MDG/CO/2 (16 December 2009), [31]; Australia, E/C.12/1993/9 (3 June 1993), [9].

The specific rights of persons with disabilities in relation to education have been the subject of two cases brought before the European Committee of Social Rights ('the Social Committee'). These cases confirm the need to ensure that persons with disabilities are educated in mainstream schools where possible, and offer further insight into the application of the right to education to persons with disabilities.

In the first case, *Autism–Europe v France*,[142] the Social Committee considered measures taken by the French Government to accommodate individuals with autism within the education system. Autism-Europe argued that children with autism were rarely integrated into mainstream education, and special education institutions and services were inadequate and received insufficient financial support. They also argued that early intervention to assist children with autism in France was 'virtually non-existent'.[143] The Social Committee noted that Article 15 of the Revised Social Charter, which addresses the rights of persons with disabilities, specifically mentioned the need for education for such persons. Under that Article, states undertake:

> ...to take the necessary measures to provide persons with disabilities with guidance, education and vocational training in the framework of general schemes wherever possible or, where this is not possible, through specialized bodies, public or private.

The Social Committee made the following general observations on the rights of persons with disabilities to education under the Charter:

> 48. ...The underlying vision of Article 15 is one of equal citizenship for persons with disabilities and, fittingly, the primary rights are those of 'independence, social integration and participation in the life of the community'. Securing a right to education for children and others with disabilities plays an obviously important role in advancing these citizenship rights. This explains why education is now specifically mentioned in the revised Article 15 and why such an emphasis is placed on achieving that education 'in the framework of general schemes, wherever possible'. It should be noted that Article 15 applies to all persons with disabilities regardless of the nature and origin of their disability and irrespective of their age. It thus clearly covers both children and adults with autism.
>
> 49. Article 17 [which contains the right to education for children and young persons] is predicated on the need to ensure that children and young persons grow up in an environment which encourages the 'full development of their personality and of their physical and mental capacities'. This approach is just as important for children with disabilities as it is for others and arguably more in circumstances where the effects of ineffective or untimely intervention are ever likely to be undone. The Committee views Article 17, which deals more generally, *inter alia*, with the right to education for all, as also embodying the modern approach of mainstreaming. Article 17§1, in particular, requires the establishment and maintenance of sufficient and adequate institutions and services for the purpose of education. Since Article 17§1 deals only with children and young persons it is important to read it in conjunction with Article 15§1 as far as adults are concerned.[144]

[142] *Autism–Europe v France*, Complaint No. 13/2002, 4 November 2003 (European Committee of Social Rights).

[143] *Autism–Europe v France*, [32].

[144] *Autism–Europe v France*, [48]–[49].

Noting that 'the implementation of the Charter requires the State parties to take not merely legal action but also practical action to give full effect to the rights recognized in the Charter',[145] the Social Committee found:

53. …When the achievement of one of the rights in question is exceptionally complex and particularly expensive to resolve, a State Party must take measures that allows it to achieve the objectives of the Charter within a reasonable time, with measurable progress and to an extent consistent with the maximum use of available resources. States Parties must be particularly mindful of the impact that their choices will have for groups with heightened vulnerabilities as well as for others persons affected including, especially, their families on whom falls the heaviest burden in the event of institutional shortcomings.

54. In the light of the afore-mentioned, the Committee notes that in the case of autistic children and adults, notwithstanding a national debate going back more than twenty years about the number of persons concerned and the relevant strategies required, and even after the enactment of the Disabled Persons Policy Act of 30 June 1975, France has failed to achieve sufficient progress in advancing the provision of education for persons with autism. It specifically notes that most of the French official documents, in particular those submitted during the procedure, still use a more restrictive definition of autism than that adopted by the World Health Organisation and that there are still insufficient official statistics with which to rationally measure progress through time. The Committee considers that the fact that the establishments specialising in the education and care of disabled children (particularly those with autism) are not in general financed from the same budget as normal schools, does not in itself amount to discrimination, since it is primarily for States themselves to decide on the modalities of funding.

Nevertheless, it considers, as the authorities themselves acknowledge, and whether a broad or narrow definition of autism is adopted, that the proportion of children with autism being educated in either general or specialist schools is much lower than in the case of other children, whether or not disabled. It is also established, and not contested by the authorities, that there is a chronic shortage of care and support facilities for autistic adults.

…

For these reasons, the Committee concludes by 11 votes to 2 that the situation constitutes a violation of Articles 15§1 and 17§1 whether alone or read in combination with Article E of the revised European Social Charter [which contains a prohibition on discrimination].

In the case of *Mental Disability Advocacy Center (MDAC) v Bulgaria*,[146] the Social Committee drew on the findings in the *Autism–Europe* case in finding the situation in Bulgaria not to be in conformity with Article 17(2) of the Revised Charter because children with moderate, severe or profound intellectual disabilities living in homes for mentally disabled children ('HMDCs') had limited access to education. Only 2.8 per cent of these children were being taught in mainstream primary schools, while only 3.4 per cent were in special schools.[147] In addition, ordinary

[145] *Autism–Europe v France*, [53].

[146] *Mental Disability Advocacy Center (MDAC) v Bulgaria*, Complaint No. 41/2007, 3 June 2008 (European Committee of Social Rights).

[147] *MDAC v Bulgaria*, [33].

schools were not equipped to deal with the needs of these children, and those who attended special schools within the homes were not eligible for diplomas attesting completion of primary school education, and were therefore prevented from entering secondary education. The decision draws on, and affirms, the approach taken in the *Autism-Europe* case. In particular, it reiterates the importance of educating persons with disabilities in mainstream schools where possible; the fact that the rights of persons with disabilities must be ensured not only in law but also in practice; and that where it is 'exceptionally complex and expensive' to secure the rights concerned, measures taken by the state must meet the three criteria of reasonable time frame, measurable progress and financing in accordance with maximum use of available resources:

35. Firstly, as regards taking special account of children with disabilities, the Committee points out that, while it is acceptable for a distinction to be made between children with and without disabilities in the application of Article 17§2, the integration of children with disabilities into mainstream schools in which arrangements are made to cater for their special needs should be the norm and teaching in specialised schools must be the exception…

36. In addition, for any special education that is set up to be in conformity with Article 17§2, the children concerned must be given sufficient instruction and training and complete their schooling in equivalent proportions to those of children in mainstream schools…

37. The Committee considers that all education provided by states must fulfil the criteria of availability, accessibility, acceptability and adaptability… In the present case, the criteria of accessibility and adaptability are at stake, i.e. educational institutions and curricula have to be accessible to everyone, without discrimination and teaching has to be designed to respond to children with special needs.

38. As regards the respect for the right to education of intellectually disabled children residing in HMDCs, the Committee takes note of the efforts made by the Government, particularly through the adoption of legislation and the setting up of action plans. It considers this to be a necessary first step but one that is insufficient to bring a situation into conformity with the Revised Charter. It reiterates that 'the aim and purpose of the Charter, being a human rights protection instrument, is to protect rights not merely theoretically, but also in fact'…

39. The Committee points out that when it is exceptionally complex and expensive to secure one of the rights protected by the Revised Charter, the measures taken by the state to achieve the Revised Charter's aims must fulfil the following three criteria: '(i) a reasonable timeframe, (ii) a measurable progress and (iii) a financing consistent with the maximum use of available resources'… It also recalls that 'States Parties must be particularly mindful of the impact that their choices will have for groups with heightened vulnerabilities' and that they must also take 'practical action to give full effect to the rights recognised in the Charter'…

43. … The Committee notes that only 2.8% of the children with intellectual disabilities residing in HMDCs are integrated in mainstream primary schools, which is extremely low whereas integration should be the norm. Mainstream educational institutions and

curricula are not accessible in practice to these children. There also appears to be insufficient evidence to show real attempts to integrate these children into mainstream education. The Committee considers therefore that the criterion of accessibility is not fulfilled.

44. For the very few children integrated into mainstream primary schools, the way in which they are dealt with should be suited to their special needs. The Committee finds on this point in particular that teachers have not been trained sufficiently to teach intellectually disabled children and teaching materials are inadequate in mainstream schools. These schools are therefore not suited to meet the needs of children with intellectual disabilities and hence to provide their education. The Committee concludes that neither therefore is the criterion of adaptability met.

45. The Committee notes that only 3.4% of children with intellectual disabilities residing in HMDCs attend the special classes set up for them. Despite the fact that special classes should not be the norm but only an exception to mainstream education, the figure is very low and demonstrates that special education is not accessible to children with intellectual disabilities residing in HMDCs.

46. As to the educational activities that intellectually disabled children follow within the HMDCs, the Committee takes note that the HMDCs are not themselves to be regarded as educational institutions, that, consequently, the children are ineligible for a diploma attesting completion of primary school education and that they are therefore prevented from entering secondary education... The Committee concludes that the activities pursued by intellectually disabled children living in HMDCs who attend neither a mainstream school nor a special class cannot be considered to be a form of education.

47. As to the Government's argument that the right of children with intellectual disabilities residing in HMDCs to education is being implemented progressively, the Committee is aware of Bulgaria's financial constraints. It notes however that any progress that has been made has been very slow and mainly concerns the adoption of legislation and policies (or action plans), with little or no implementation. It would have been possible to take some specific steps at no excessive additional cost (for example HMDC directors and the municipal officials to whom HMDCs and primary schools are accountable could have been informed about and given training on the new legislation and action plans)... Progress is therefore patently insufficient at the current rate and there is no prospect that the situation will be in conformity with article 17§2 within a reasonable time. Consequently, the Committee considers that the measures taken do not fulfil the three criteria referred to above, i.e. a reasonable timeframe, measurable progress and financing consistent with the maximum use of available resources...

48. Consequently, the Committee holds that the situation in Bulgaria constitutes a violation of Article 17§2 of the Revised Charter because children with moderate, severe or profound intellectual disabilities residing in HMDCs do not have the effective right to an education.[148]

[148] *MDAC v Bulgaria*, [35]–[48].

Sex

According to the Special Rapporteur on the right to education, 'women constitute the majority of those who remain deprived of education'.[149]

The obligations of states in relation to the right to education for women are set out in detail in the Convention on the Elimination of All Forms of Discrimination Against Women ('CEDAW'), Article 10:

> States Parties shall take all appropriate measures to eliminate discrimination against women in order to ensure to them equal rights with men in the field of education and in particular to ensure, on a basis of equality of men and women:
>
> (a) The same conditions for career and vocational guidance, for access to studies and for the achievement of diplomas in educational establishments of all categories in rural as well as in urban areas; this equality shall be ensured in pre-school, general, technical, professional and higher technical education, as well as in all types of vocational training;
>
> (b) Access to the same curricula, the same examinations, teaching staff with qualifications of the same standard and school premises and equipment of the same quality;
>
> (c) The elimination of any stereotyped concept of the roles of men and women at all levels and in all forms of education by encouraging coeducation and other types of education which will help to achieve this aim and, in particular, by the revision of textbooks and school programmes and the adaptation of teaching methods;
>
> (d) The same opportunities to benefit from scholarships and other study grants;
>
> (e) The same opportunities for access to programmes of continuing education, including adult and functional literacy programmes, particularly those aimed at reducing, at the earliest possible time, any gap in education existing between men and women;
>
> (f) The reduction of female student drop-out rates and the organization of programmes for girls and women who have left school prematurely;
>
> (g) The same opportunities to participate actively in sports and physical education;
>
> (h) Access to specific educational information to help to ensure the health and well-being of families, including information and advice on family planning.[150]

The Committee's General Comment No. 13 indicates that the Committee interprets the non-discrimination obligations in relation to Article 13 in light of the CEDAW.[151] This is reflected in the Guidelines on Treaty-Specific Documents, which ask states to:

> Indicate the measures taken to ensure the same admission criteria for boys and girls at all levels of education, and to raise awareness among parents, teachers and decision-makers on the value of educating girls.[152]

[149] Human Rights Council, Report of the Special Rapporteur on the right to education on the promotion of equality of opportunity in education, A/HRC/17/29 (18 April 2011), [47].

[150] Convention on the Elimination of All Forms of Discrimination Against Women (CEDAW) (adopted 18 December 1979, 1249 UNTS 13, entered into force 3 September 1981), Article 10.

[151] CESCR, General Comment No. 13, [31].

[152] CESCR, Guidelines on Treaty-Specific Documents, [64].

The importance of ensuring equal access to education for boys and girls is stressed in a range of other international instruments, including the Millennium Development Goals, the second of which is:

To ensure that, by... [2015], children everywhere, boys and girls alike, will be able to complete a full course of primary schooling and that girls and boys will have equal access to all levels of education.[153]

The issue of girls' right to education has also been the subject of a specific report by the Special Rapporteur on the right to education.[154] In that report, the Special Rapporteur notes a number of factors which contribute to gender inequality in education, and recommends that states take measures to address these. In particular, he notes that:

57. Even though gender inequality in education has special local and regional features, some characteristics are common to many countries, such as poverty (which itself accounts for many forms of exclusion), dangerous school environments and many patriarchal effects such as curricular stereotyping, parental unwillingness to invest or take an interest in girls' education, child labour, discriminatory social and cultural practices, restrictions on girls' freedom of movement and expression and, of course, wars and emergencies.

...

66. The discrimination girls encountered in the school environment is also due to a lack of educational models that have a cultural focus and are respectful of diversity; to the long distances girls must travel to get to school; to the lack of safe transport; to the sparse recruitment of women teachers; to the limited attention paid to girls with special educational needs; to the absence of thorough, continual gender awareness-raising and training for male and female teachers; to the scant interest taken in attracting back and retaining pregnant teenagers and adolescent mothers; to the lack of sex education; and to the costs of registration, uniforms, food, textbooks and teaching materials that families must defray, which affect girls more unfavourably.[155]

The need to ensure equal access to education, regardless of gender, is frequently emphasized in the Committee's Concluding Observations. For example, in relation to Afghanistan:

The Committee, while noticing the efforts made by the State party to improve and promote access to education and reduce gender disparities, notes with concern and in particular that the right to education is not guaranteed in the State party without discrimination, and is also concerned at the poor situation of education in Afghanistan. In particular, the Committee is deeply concerned about the... throwing of acid to prevent girls and female teachers from going to school... The Committee recommends that the State party... take adequate steps

[153] UN Millennium Declaration, General Assembly Resolution 55/2, A/RES/55/2 (18 September 2000), 19.

[154] Commission on Human Rights, Report of the Special Rapporteur on the right to education on girls' right to education, E/CN.4/2006/45 (8 February 2006).

[155] Commission on Human Rights, Report of the Special Rapporteur on the right to education on girls' right to education, E/CN.4/2006/45 (8 February 2006), [57] and [66]. See also Human Rights Council, Report of the Special Rapporteur on the right to education on the promotion of equality of opportunity in education, A/HRC/17/29 (18 April 2011), especially at [47].

to encourage the school enrollment of girls, including by providing facilities in schools (for example, separate toilets for girls) and by training and recruiting female teachers, in particular in rural areas.[156]

And in relation to Cameroon:

The Committee is concerned about the high level of illiteracy still existing in Cameroon. It also notes with deep concern the cultural preference given to the education of male children. This is reflected in the higher illiteracy rate of women, which is 49.9% compared with 30% for men.[157]

The Committee is particularly aware of parental attitudes and other cultural factors which limit women's access to education. In relation to Kyrgyzstan:

[T]he Committee is concerned about the phenomenon of children dropping out of school to provide for their families. The situation of girls is particularly alarming, as their access to education is being curtailed by a revival of the tradition of early marriage, and a decrease in the prestige of having a formal education.[158]

Similarly, in relation to the Former Yugoslav Republic of Macedonia:

The Committee urges the State party to…promote universal school attendance through intensified awareness-raising campaigns for parents on the importance of education and their obligation to send their children, including girls, to school.[159]

Similar observations have been made by the Committee on the Elimination of Discrimination Against Women in its monitoring of state reports under that Convention. The CEDAW Committee has also noted the particular problem of girls dropping out of school due to pregnancy, discussed above in relation to the acceptability of education. The Committee's comments on Zambia exemplify its general approach in this area:

246. Despite the State party's effort in the area of education, the Committee is concerned at the low rate of female literacy, the low enrollment of girls in school in rural and urban areas and the high drop-out rate of girls due to pregnancy. These negative factors are reinforced by stereotyping in textbooks. It notes that education is a key to the advancement of women and that the low level of education of women and girls remains one of the most serious impediments to their full enjoyment of human rights.

247. The Committee urges the State party to strengthen its efforts to improve the literacy level of girls and women in rural and urban areas, to ensure equal access of girls and young women to all levels of education and to prevent girls dropping out of school. It encourages the State party to introduce further special measures in the areas of education, including incentives for parents to send girls to school and to encourage the recruitment of more qualified women teachers.[160]

[156] CESCR, Concluding Observations: Afghanistan, E/C.12/AFG/CO/2–4 (7 June 2010), [43].

[157] CESCR, Concluding Observations: Cameroon, E/C.12/1/Add.40 (8 December 1999), [29].

[158] CESCR, Concluding Observations: Kyrgyzstan, E/C.12/1/Add.49 (1 September 2000), [23].

[159] CESCR, Concluding Observations: Former Yugoslav Republic of Macedonia, E/C.12/MKD/CO/1 (15 January 2008), [47].

[160] UNGA, Report of the Committee on the Elimination of Discrimination against Women, A/57/38 Part II (2002) 107, [246]–[247].

Citizenship or residence status

The particular situation of non-nationals, including immigrants, asylum seekers and those with no residence papers, has been the subject of considerable attention by the Committee, and within jurisprudence on the right to education more broadly. General Comment No. 13 'confirms that the principle of non-discrimination extends to all persons of school age residing in the territory of a State party, including non-nationals, and irrespective of their legal status'.[161]

The rights of non-nationals to education are recognized in a range of international legal instruments. Under Article 3(e) of the UNESCO Convention against Discrimination in Education, states undertake to 'give foreign nationals resident within their territory the same access to education as that given to their own nationals'. Similarly, the International Convention on the Protection of the Rights of All Migrant Workers and Members of their Families, Article 30,[162] provides that:

> Each child of a migrant worker shall have the basic right of access to education on the basis of equality of treatment with nationals of the State concerned. Access to public pre-school educational institutions or schools shall not be refused or limited by reason of the irregular situation with respect to stay or employment of either parent or by reason of the irregularity of the child's stay in the State of employment.

Other international instruments which protect the right to education, such as the Convention on the Rights of the Child, provide that nationality is a prohibited basis for discrimination in enjoyment of the right.[163] Further, the Convention on the Elimination of All Forms of Racial Discrimination, Article 5(e)(v) provides:

> States Parties undertake to prohibit and to eliminate racial discrimination in all its forms and to guarantee the right of everyone, without distinction as to race, colour, or national or ethnic origin, to equality before the law, notably in the enjoyment of the following rights:... The right to education and training.[164]

And the Committee on the Elimination of Racial Discrimination, in its General Recommendation XXX: Discrimination against Non-Citizens,[165] recommends that states:

> 29. Remove obstacles that prevent the enjoyment of economic, social and cultural rights by non-citizens, notably in the areas of education...

[161] CESCR, General Comment No. 13, [34].

[162] International Convention on the Protection of the Rights of All Migrant Workers and Members of their Families (adopted 18 December 1990, 2220 UNTS 3, entered into force 1 July 2003), Article 30; see also Article 43.

[163] Convention on the Rights of the Child, Article 2.

[164] Convention on the Elimination of All Forms of Racial Discrimination (adopted 21 December 1965, 660 UNTS 195, entered into force 4 January 1969), Article 5(e)(v).

[165] UN Committee on the Elimination of Racial Discrimination (CERD) (65th Session), General Recommendation XXX: Discrimination against Non-Citizens, 2004, [29]–[31].

30. Ensure that public educational institutions are open to non-citizens and children of undocumented immigrants residing in the territory of a state party;

31. Avoid segregated schooling and different standards of treatment being applied to non-citizens on grounds of race, color, descent and national or ethnic origin in elementary and secondary school and with respect to access to higher education.

Concern for the position of non-nationals[166] and immigrants[167] is evident in the Concluding Observations of the Committee. In particular, the Committee has shown interest in the position of refugees and asylum seekers. So, for example, in relation to Senegal, the Committee 'is concerned that…children of asylum seekers who have not yet been granted refugee status cannot enroll in school unless they are able to pay tuition fees'.[168]

Similarly, in relation to Canada:

The Committee is concerned that loan programmes for post-secondary education are available only to Canadian citizens and permanent residents and that recognized refugees who do not have permanent residence status, as well as asylum seekers, are ineligible for these loan programmes.[169]

These comments demonstrate that the Committee is not only concerned with situations where non-nationals are unable to enroll in educational institutions, but also with situations where non-nationals are required to meet costs associated with education where nationals are not. The permissibility of charging fees to non-nationals for education which is provided free of charge to nationals was considered by the European Court of Human Rights in the case of *Ponomaryov v Bulgaria*.[170] The applicants in that case were two Russian boys who, following the divorce of their parents, had moved with their mother to Bulgaria where she married a Bulgarian national. The mother obtained a permanent residence permit and the sons were entitled to live in Bulgaria, where they attended primary and secondary schools. In 2005, while they were attending secondary school, the boys were asked to pay school fees, even though secondary education was free for Bulgarian nationals. The Court acknowledged that Bulgaria did not necessarily need to provide free secondary education; however, once the state voluntarily decided to provide such education free of charge, it could not do so on a discriminatory basis.[171] The Court then turned to consider whether charging secondary school fees to non-nationals was justified (in light of resource or other considerations) or,

[166] See, eg, CESCR, Concluding Observations: Azerbaijan, E/C.12/1/Add.104 (14 December 2004), [33] and [59]; Kuwait, E/C.12/1/Add.98 (7 June 2004), [26], [46].

[167] See, eg, CESCR, Concluding Observations: United Kingdom of Great Britain and Northern Ireland (Hong Kong), E/C.12/1/Add.10 (6 December 1996), [31] and [44]; Liechtenstein, E/C.12/LIE/CO/1 (9 June 2006), [20].

[168] CESCR, Concluding Observations: Senegal, E/C.12/1/Add.62 (24 September 2001), [33].

[169] CESCR, Concluding Observations: Canada, E/C.12/1/Add.31 (10 December 1998), [39]; see also Norway, E/C.12/1/Add.109 (23 June 2005), [22] and [43]; Serbia and Montenegro, E/C.12/1/Add.108 (23 June 2005), [37] and [64].

[170] *Ponomaryov v Bulgaria* (App. 5335/05) ECtHR 21 June 2011.

[171] *Ponomaryov v Bulgaria*, [53].

alternatively, constituted impermissible discrimination with respect to the enjoyment of the right to education, contrary to Article 14 of the ECHR:

54. …[A] State may have legitimate reasons for curtailing the use of resource-hungry public services—such as welfare programmes, public benefits and health care—by short-term and illegal immigrants, who, as a rule, do not contribute to their funding. It may also, in certain circumstances, justifiably differentiate between different categories of aliens residing in its territory. For instance, the preferential treatment of nationals of Member States of the European Union—some of whom were exempted from school fees when Bulgaria acceded to the Union…may be said to be based on an objective and reasonable justification, because the Union forms a special legal order, which has, moreover, established its own citizenship…

55. Although similar arguments apply to a certain extent in the field of education—which is one of the most important public services in a modern State—they cannot be transposed there without qualification. It is true that education is an activity that is complex to organise and expensive to run, whereas the resources that the authorities can devote to it are necessarily finite. It is also true that in deciding how to regulate access to education, and in particular whether or not to charge fees for it and to whom, a State must strike a balance between, on the one hand, the educational needs of those under its jurisdiction and, on the other, its limited capacity to accommodate them. However, the Court cannot overlook the fact that, unlike some other public services…education is a right that enjoys direct protection under the Convention…

56. In the Court's view, the State's margin of appreciation in this domain increases with the level of education, in inverse proportion to the importance of that education for those concerned and for society at large. Thus, at the university level, which to this day remains optional for many people, higher fees for aliens—and indeed fees in general—seem to be commonplace and can, in the present circumstances, be considered fully justified. The opposite goes for primary schooling, which provides basic literacy and numeracy—as well as integration into and first experiences of society—and is compulsory in most countries…

57. Secondary education, which is in issue in the present case, falls between those two extremes. The distinction is confirmed…by the differentiation between those three levels of education in the International Covenant on Economic, Social and Cultural Rights…However, the Court is mindful of the fact that with more and more countries now moving towards what has been described as a 'knowledge-based' society, secondary education plays an ever-increasing role in successful personal development and in the social and professional integration of the individuals concerned. Indeed, in a modern society, having no more than basic knowledge and skills constitutes a barrier to successful personal and professional development. It prevents the persons concerned from adjusting to their environment and entails far-reaching consequences for their social and economic well-being.

58. These considerations militate in favour of stricter scrutiny by the Court of the proportionality of the measure affecting the applicants.

59. In assessing that proportionality the Court does not need, in the very specific circumstances of this case, to determine whether the Bulgarian State is entitled to deprive all unlawfully residing aliens of educational benefits—such as free education—which it has agreed to provide to its nationals and certain limited categories of aliens. It is not the Court's

role to consider in the abstract whether national law conforms to the Convention…It must confine its attention, as far as possible, to the particular circumstances of the case before it…

60. On that point, the Court observes at the outset that the applicants were not in the position of individuals arriving in the country unlawfully and then laying claim to the use of its public services, including free schooling…Even when the applicants found themselves, somewhat inadvertently, in the situation of aliens lacking permanent residence permits…the authorities had no substantive objection to their remaining in Bulgaria and apparently never had any serious intention of deporting them…Indeed, at the material time the applicants had taken steps to regularise their situation…Thus, any considerations relating to the need to stem or reverse the flow of illegal immigration clearly did not apply to the applicants' case…

61. Nor can it be said that the applicants tried to abuse the Bulgarian educational system…It was not their choice to settle in Bulgaria and pursue their education there; they came to live in the country at a very young age, because their mother had married a Bulgarian national…The applicants could not realistically choose to go to another country and carry on their secondary studies there…Moreover, there is no indication that the applicants, who were fully integrated in Bulgarian society and spoke fluent Bulgarian…had any special educational needs which would have required additional financing for their schools.

62. However, the authorities did not take any of these matters into account…

63. The Court, for its part, finds that in the specific circumstances of the present case the requirement for the applicants to pay fees for their secondary education on account of their nationality and immigration status was not justified. There has therefore been a violation of Article 14 of the Convention taken in conjunction with Article 2 of Protocol No. 1.[172]

Discrimination against migrants on the basis that they lack residence papers or other relevant documents would also seem to be impermissible under international law. Thus, in the case of *Timishev v Russia*,[173] the European Court of Human Rights found that the refusal to admit Chechen migrant children to school in the neighbouring republic to which they had moved, on the basis that their father did not have the required residence papers, constituted a violation of the right to education. Similarly, in the case of *The Yean and Bosico Children v Dominican Republic*,[174] the Inter-American Court for Human Rights found a breach of the American Convention on Human Rights when the applicants, girls born in the Dominican Republic to Haitian immigrant mothers, were refused birth certificates by the Dominican Civil Registry. The birth certificates would have established that they were citizens of the Dominican Republic and thus entitled them to enrol in school. The Court found that the state's refusal to grant the birth certificates

172 *Ponomaryov v Bulgaria*, [54]–[63].

173 *Timishev v Russia* (Apps. 55762/00 and 55974/00), 13 December 2005, (2007) 44 EHRR 37.

174 *The Yean and Bosico Children v Dominican Republic*, 8 September 2005, IACHR Series C No. 130.

denied the girls the right to a nationality, and so deprived them of basic rights of citizenship, including the right to education, as protected under Article XII of the Declaration on the Rights and Duties of Man and Article 13 of the San Salvador Protocol to the American Convention on Human Rights. The Court noted that:

> [T]he vulnerability to which the children were exposed as a result of the lack of nationality and juridical personality was also reflected, in the case of the child Violeta Bosico, by the fact that she was prevented from attending day school at the Palavé School during the 1998–1999 school year…It is worth noting that, according to the child's right to special protection embodied in Article 19 of the American Convention, interpreted in light of the Convention on the Rights of the Child and the Additional Protocol to the American Convention on Human Rights in the Area of Economic, Social and Cultural Rights, in relation to the obligation to ensure progressive development contained in Article 26 of the American Convention, the State must provide free primary education to all children in an appropriate environment and in the conditions necessary to ensure their full intellectual development.[175]

The Special Rapporteur on the right to education has specifically considered the right to education for migrants, refugees and asylum-seekers, and has prepared a special report on the right to education for these groups.[176] In his report, the Special Rapporteur expresses concern not only regarding policies which discriminate against non-nationals in terms of access to education, as considered above, but also circumstances which affect the quality and acceptability of education provided to non-nationals, such as: failure to provide special instruction in the language of the host country; failure to offer mother tongue education; failure to tailor curricula to the special needs of these groups;[177] and lack of qualified staff in, for example, schools in refugee camps.[178]

Membership of a minority group

Discrimination against minority and indigenous groups is of particular concern in relation to the right to education. The protection of minorities' rights in relation to education has a long history in international law, dating back to the inter-war minority treaties and the jurisprudence of the Permanent Court of International Justice.[179] In contemporary international law, the rights of minority and indigenous groups in relation to education are protected in a number of binding and non-binding international instruments.

[175] *The Yean and Bosico Children v Dominican Republic*, 185.

[176] Human Rights Council, Report of the Special Rapporteur on the right to education of migrants, refugees and asylum-seekers, A/HRC/14/25/Corr.1 (12 May 2010).

[177] Human Rights Council, Report of the Special Rapporteur on the right to education, A/HRC/14/25/Corr.1, [43]–[48]. Language issues in relation to education are discussed in more detail in the context of discrimination against minorities, below.

[178] Human Rights Council, Report of the Special Rapporteur on the right to education, A/HRC/14/25/Corr.1, [50].

[179] *Minority Schools in Albania*, Advisory Opinion, [1935] PCIJ (ser. A/B) No. 64; *Treatment of Polish Nationals and Other Persons of Polish Origin or Speech in the Danzig Territory*, Advisory Opinion, [1933] PCIJ (ser. A/B) No. 44; *Rights of Minorities in Upper Silesia (Minority Schools)*, Judgment, [1928] PCIJ (ser. A) No. 15.

As noted above, Article 5(e)(v) of the Convention on the Elimination of All Forms of Racial Discrimination prohibits discrimination in relation to enjoyment of the right to education on the basis of 'national or ethnic origin'. Similarly, Article 1 of the UNESCO Convention against Discrimination in Education indicates that 'race' and 'national or social origin' are prohibited grounds of discrimination under that Convention. Further, Article 5(c) of the UNESCO Convention specifically provides for the right of minorities to carry on their own educational activities:

It is essential to recognize the right of members of national minorities to carry on their own educational activities, including the maintenance of schools and, depending on the educational policy of each State, the use or the teaching of their own language, provided however:

(i) That this right is not exercised in a manner which prevents the members of these minorities from understanding the culture and language of the community as a whole and from participating in its activities, or which prejudices national sovereignty;

(ii) That the standard of education is not lower than the general standard laid down or approved by the competent authorities; and

(iii) That attendance at such schools is optional.

The International Labour Organization (ILO) Indigenous and Tribal Peoples Convention 1989[180] provides, in relation to 'indigenous and tribal peoples':

Article 26

Measures shall be taken to ensure that members of the peoples concerned have the opportunity to acquire education at all levels on at least an equal footing with the rest of the national community.

Article 27

1. Education programmes and services for the peoples concerned shall be developed and implemented in co-operation with them to address their special needs, and shall incorporate their histories, their knowledge and technologies, their value systems and their further social, economic and cultural aspirations.

2. The competent authority shall ensure the training of members of these peoples and their involvement in the formulation and implementation of education programmes, with a view to the progressive transfer of responsibility for the conduct of these programmes to these peoples as appropriate.

3. In addition, governments shall recognise the right of these peoples to establish their own educational institutions and facilities, provided that such institutions meet minimum standards established by the competent authority in consultation with these peoples. Appropriate resources shall be provided for this purpose.

Article 28

1. Children belonging to the peoples concerned shall, wherever practicable, be taught to read and write in their own indigenous language or in the language most commonly used

[180] ILO Convention Concerning Indigenous and Tribal Peoples in Independent Countries (adopted 27 June 1989, 72 ILO Official Bull. 59, entered into force 5 September 1991) ('ILO Convention No 169' or 'Indigenous and Tribal Peoples Convention').

by the group to which they belong. When this is not practicable, the competent authorities shall undertake consultations with these peoples with a view to the adoption of measures to achieve this objective.

2. Adequate measures shall be taken to ensure that these peoples have the opportunity to attain fluency in the national language or in one of the official languages of the country.

3. Measures shall be taken to preserve and promote the development and practice of the indigenous languages of the peoples concerned.

Article 29

The imparting of general knowledge and skills that will help children belonging to the peoples concerned to participate fully and on an equal footing in their own community and in the national community shall be an aim of education for these peoples.

Similar obligations concerning indigenous peoples' rights to education are contained in the UN Declaration on the Rights of Indigenous Peoples:[181]

Article 14

1. Indigenous peoples have the right to establish and control their educational systems and institutions providing education in their own languages, in a manner appropriate to their cultural methods of teaching and learning.

2. Indigenous individuals, particularly children, have the right to all levels and forms of education of the State without discrimination.

3. States shall, in conjunction with indigenous peoples, take effective measures, in order for indigenous individuals, particularly children, including those living outside their communities, to have access, when possible, to an education in their own culture and provided in their own language.

And in relation to minority groups generally, the UN Declaration on the Rights of Persons Belonging to National or Ethnic, Religious and Linguistic Minorities,[182] Article 4, provides:

1. States shall take measures where required to ensure that persons belonging to minorities may exercise fully and effectively all their human rights and fundamental freedoms without any discrimination and in full equality before the law.

…

3. States should take appropriate measures so that, wherever possible, persons belonging to minorities may have adequate opportunities to learn their mother tongue or to have instruction in their mother tongue.

4. States should, where appropriate, take measures in the field of education, in order to encourage knowledge of the history, traditions, language and culture of the minorities

[181] UNGA Res. 61/295, UN Declaration on the Rights of Indigenous Peoples, A/RES/61/295 (13 September 2007).

[182] UNGA Res. 47/135, UN Declaration on the Rights of Persons Belonging to National or Ethnic, Religious and Linguistic Minorities, A/RES/47/135 (18 December 1992).

existing within their territory. Persons belonging to minorities should have adequate opportunities to gain knowledge of the society as a whole.

At the regional level, the European Framework Convention for the Protection of National Minorities[183] provides:

Article 12

1. The Parties shall, where appropriate, take measures in the fields of education and research to foster knowledge of the culture, history, language and religion of their national minorities and of the majority.

2. In this context the Parties shall *inter alia* provide adequate opportunities for teacher training and access to textbooks, and facilitate contacts among students and teachers of different communities.

3. The Parties undertake to promote equal opportunities for access to education at all levels for persons belonging to national minorities.

Article 13

1. Within the framework of their education systems, the Parties shall recognise that persons belonging to a national minority have the right to set up and to manage their own private educational and training establishments.

2. The exercise of this right shall not entail any financial obligation for the Parties.

Article 14

1. The Parties undertake to recognise that every person belonging to a national minority has the right to learn his or her minority language.

2. In areas inhabited by persons belonging to national minorities traditionally or in substantial numbers, if there is sufficient demand, the Parties shall endeavour to ensure, as far as possible and within the framework of their education systems, that persons belonging to those minorities have adequate opportunities for being taught the minority language or for receiving instruction in this language.

3. Paragraph 2 of this article shall be implemented without prejudice to the learning of the official language or the teaching in this language.

This international legal framework highlights a number of issues related to the right to education for minorities and indigenous groups which are reflected in the work of the CESCR. In particular, it indicates that the rights of minorities in relation to education include both the right to establish their own private educational and training establishments, and the right to access, and profit from, mainstream education on the basis of equality. As regards the first of these, within the ICESCR framework, the right to establish private educational institutions is guaranteed to all under Article 13(4), and is considered in more detail below.

As regards the right to access, and profit from, mainstream education, there are clearly a range of ways in which minorities may be discriminated against in

[183] European Framework Convention for the Protection of National Minorities (FCNM) (adopted 1 February 1995, ETS 157, entered into force 1 February 1998).

relation to their enjoyment of the right to education. Some are mentioned specifically in the Guidelines on Treaty-Specific Documents, which ask states to:

Indicate…the steps taken to prevent lower educational standards for [minority and indigenous] children, their segregation in special classes, and their exclusion from mainstream education.[184]

Most obviously, minorities may be the victims of direct discrimination. So, for example, in its Concluding Observations in relation to Japan, the Committee expressed concern:

…about the fact that minority schools, such as Korean schools, are not officially recognized, even when they adhere to the national education curriculum, and that they therefore neither receive central government subsidies nor are able to provide qualification for university entrance examinations.[185]

Similarly, the Opinion of the Committee on the Elimination of Racial Discrimination in *Murat Er v Denmark* concerned an allegation of direct racial discrimination on the part of a technical training college.[186] The petitioner in the case was of Turkish origin and was studying carpentry at Copenhagen Technical School. Part of the course of study involved traineeships in private companies. The applicant complained that the school accepted instructions from employers not to send trainees of non-Danish origin. He argued before the Committee that this amounted to discrimination in relation to education and training. The Committee found that the petitioner's chances of obtaining an internship were indeed more limited than other students as a result of his ethnicity, and that this constituted racial discrimination and a violation of his rights under Article 5(e)(v) of the CERD.

Short of direct discrimination, however, a range of other factors may lead to minority groups being unable to profit from their education on the basis of equality. These include economic, cultural and linguistic barriers, and the particularly vulnerable situation in which many minority groups find themselves, as suggested in the following Concluding Observations of the Committee with respect to France:

28. The Committee notes with concern that significant disparities in terms of school performance and drop-out rates continue to exist between French pupils and pupils belonging to racial, ethnic or national minorities, in spite of the efforts made by the State party to address the social and economic inequalities existing in the field of education.

…

49. The Committee recommends that the State party adopt all appropriate measures to reduce the significant disparities in terms of school performance between French pupils and pupils belonging to racial, ethnic or national minorities in the field of education, inter

[184] CESCR, Guidelines on Treaty-Specific Documents, [63].

[185] CESCR, Concluding Observations: Japan, E/C.12/1/Add.67 (24 September 2001), [32]; see also, eg, Finland, E/C.12/1/Add.8 (5 December 1996), [17] and [24]; UN Interim Administration Mission in Kosovo, E/C.12/UNK/CO/1 (1 December 2008), [31].

[186] *Murat Er v Denmark,* CERD Communication No. 40/2007, 8 August 2007, CERD/C/71/D/40/2007.

alia by intensifying the provision of French-language courses for those students who lack adequate French-language proficiency and avoiding the overrepresentation of minority students in classes for children with learning difficulties. The Committee further recommends that the State party undertake further studies on the correlation between school failure and social environment, with a view to elaborating effective strategies aimed at reducing the disproportionate drop-out rates affecting minority pupils.[187]

The work of the Committee, however, reveals that there are two issues, in particular, in relation to enjoyment of the right to education by minorities, with which the Committee is especially concerned: the languages in which education is conducted, and the specific situation of the Roma, as a particularly marginalized and disadvantaged minority group.

Language issues

There are two ways in which the language used in education impacts upon minority groups. In the first place, if education is not available in the language spoken by minority groups, but only the dominant language of the state, then this may affect access by minority groups to education. According to the Special Rapporteur on the right to education:

> The lack of education in mother-tongue or native language is often a source of exclusion. This is particularly relevant for minorities and migrants…[A]vailable experience shows that a child learns better in his or her mother tongue in the formative stages and initial period of education.[188]

As a result, the Committee has demonstrated a particular concern to ensure that children from minority groups receive adequate instruction in the dominant language, so as to profit from their education. So, for example, in relation to Liechtenstein:

> The Committee encourages the State party to continue reducing linguistic barriers through intensive German-language training for immigrant children, to offer appropriate catch-up classes…[189]

Similarly, in relation to the Netherlands Antilles:

> 52. The Committee expresses its concern at the increase in the school dropout rate, the causes of which include the difficulties which have emerged in education due to the existence of several tongues spoken as first languages on the islands and the use of Dutch as the language of education.
>
> …
>
> 57. The Committee encourages the government, in addressing the school dropout problem, to expedite the implementation of its programme for education in the students' mother tongues along with the progressive introduction of Dutch.[190]

[187] CESCR, Concluding Observations: France, E/C.12/FRA/CO/3 (9 June 2008), [28] and [49].

[188] Human Rights Council, Report of the Special Rapporteur on the right to education on the promotion of equality of opportunity in education, A/HRC/17/29 (18 April 2011), [63].

[189] CESCR, Concluding Observations: Liechtenstein, E/C.12/LIE/CO/1 (9 June 2006), [36]; see also France, E/C.12/FRA/CO/3 (9 June 2008), [49].

[190] CESCR, Concluding Observations: Netherlands Antilles, E/C.12/1/Add.25 (16 June 1998), [52] and [57].

Arguably, however, the more significant aspect of language use in education, from the perspective of minority groups, concerns the possibility for minority groups to receive instruction in, or of, their mother tongue. This issue, which relates to the acceptability of education, is a significant one. The rights of minorities to education in, or of, their mother tongue are protected by several provisions within international law, as noted above.[191] There are also clear statements in the Committee's Concluding Observations to the effect that minority groups are entitled to education in their own language. So, for example, in relation to Kosovo:

> The Committee recommends that UNMIK [United Nations Interim Administration Mission in Kosovo] identify funds and advise the relevant Kosovo authorities on the urgent need to... ensure that children from non-Serbian minority communities, in particular Roma, Ashkali and Egyptian children, have adequate opportunities at all levels of education to receive instruction in or of their mother tongue and on their history and culture, that sufficient teaching staff and textbooks are available for that purpose, and that the cultures and traditions of minority communities are adequately reflected in the revised curriculum.[192]

And in relation to Greece:

> 28. The Committee is concerned that a high percentage of Roma and Turkish-speaking children are not enrolled in school, or drop out at a very early stage of their schooling. While it is possible to receive bilingual instruction in Turkish and Greek at the two Muslim minority secondary schools in Thrace, the Committee notes with concern that no such possibility exists at the primary level or outside Thrace, and that members of other linguistic groups have no possibility to learn their mother tongue at school.
>
> ...
>
> 50. The Committee urges the State party to take effective measures to increase school attendance by Roma and Turkish-speaking children, including at the secondary level, to ensure, to the extent possible, that children belonging to minority linguistic groups have an opportunity to learn their mother tongue, including regional dialects, at school, and to ensure an adequate staffing with teachers specialized in multicultural education.[193]

A key case on this issue is the decision of the European Court of Human Rights in *Belgian Linguistics*.[194] The case arose out of the division of the Belgian state into different linguistic regions, in order to defuse tensions between the

[191] See, eg, Article 5(c) of the UNESCO Convention against Discrimination in Education; Article 28 of the ILO Indigenous and Tribal Peoples Convention; Article 14(1) and (3) of the UN Declaration on the Rights of Indigenous Peoples; Article 4(3) of the UN Declaration on the Rights of Persons Belonging to National or Ethnic, Religious and Linguistic Minorities; and Article 14 of the European Framework Convention for the Protection of National Minorities.

[192] CESCR, Concluding Observations: United Nations Interim Administration Mission in Kosovo (UNMIK), E/C.12/UNK/CO/1 (1 December 2008), [31].

[193] CESCR, Concluding Observations: Greece, E/C.12/1/Add.97 (7 June 2004), [28] and [50]; see also, eg, Serbia and Montenegro, E/C.12/1/Add.108 (23 June 2005), [64]; Estonia, E/C.12/1/Add.85 (19 December 2002), [32].

[194] *Case Relating to Certain Aspects of the Laws on the Use of Languages in Education in Belgium (No. 2)* ('*Belgian Linguistics* case') (Apps. 1474/62, 1677/62, 1691/62, 1769/63, 1994/63 and 2126/64), 23 July 1968, (1968) 1 EHRR 252.

different linguistic groups (French speakers and Flemish speakers). The case resulted from six separate applications by French-speaking Belgians living in the Flemish-speaking region, who complained about Belgian language laws which effectively prevented their children from obtaining education in French. They claimed that this constituted discrimination contrary to Article 14 of the ECHR, with respect to the right to education under Article 2 of Protocol 1.

The Court found that the right to education does not include the right to access education in a particular language, but merely the right to access educational institutions existing at a given time:

> 3. ... the first sentence of Article 2 (P1-2) does not specify the language in which education must be conducted in order that the right to education should be respected... However the right to education would be meaningless if it did not imply in favour of its beneficiaries, the right to be educated in the national language or in one of the national languages, as the case may be.
>
> ...
>
> 11. In the present case the Court notes that Article 14, even when read in conjunction with Article 2 of the Protocol... does not have the effect of guaranteeing to a child or to his parent the right to obtain instruction in a language of his choice. The object of these two Articles... read in conjunction, is more limited: it is to ensure that the right to education shall be secured by each Contracting Party to everyone within its jurisdiction without discrimination on the ground, for instance, of language... [T]o interpret the two provisions as conferring on everyone within the jurisdiction of a State a right to obtain education in the language of his own choice would lead to absurd results, for it would be open to anyone to claim any language of instruction in any of the territories of the Contracting Parties.[195]

The Court went on to find that the language laws were not discriminatory, as there were 'objective and reasonable justifications' for the distinction in treatment between French and Flemish speakers, namely the need to maintain the Belgian system of territorial monolingualism.

Subsequent case law of the European Court of Human Rights has repeated and confirmed the position as set out in *Belgian Linguistics*.[196] However, some more recent judgments have suggested that, at least in particular cases, there is a right to education in the language of one's choice. Thus, in the case of *Cyprus v Turkey*, the Court found that the abolition of Greek-language secondary schools in Turkish-controlled northern Cyprus 'must be considered in effect to be a denial of the substance of the right [to education]',[197] for although Greek-language primary schools were still available, and Greek-Cypriot children could attend secondary schools in English or Turkish, 'the authorities must no doubt be aware that it is the wish of Greek-Cypriot parents that the schooling of their children

[195] *Belgian Linguistics* case, [3] and [11].

[196] See, eg, *Skender v Former Yugoslav Republic of Macedonia* (App. 62059/00) ECtHR 22 November 2001.

[197] *Cyprus v Turkey* (App. 25781/94), 10 May 2001, (2002) 35 EHRR 30, [278].

be completed through the medium of the Greek language'.[198] The general view is that the Court's finding in this case was exceptional, based on:

> ... the prior existence of such [Greek-language secondary] schools and their abolition by the Turkish authorities; an international agreement to allow the Greek Cypriot authorities to provide such education in the north, fulfilment of which the Turkish authorities prevented; and the denial of the right to return to Northern Cyprus of Greek Cypriot children who went to the southern part of the island for their education.[199]

However, the European Court of Human Rights has again suggested that there may, in certain cases, be a right to education in a particular language, in the recent case of *Catan et al v Moldova and Russia*.[200] The case is important not only for the Court's comments on the right to education in a particular language, but also for its discussion on the rights of minorities in relation to education generally, and indeed on the right to education as a whole. The case concerned the disputed territory of Transdniestria, officially part of the territory of Moldova, but under the effective control of the Russian-supported administration, the Moldovan Republic of Transdniestria ('MRT'). In 1994, the MRT introduced a law banning the use of the Latin script in schools and requiring use of the Cyrillic script for the Moldovan language, although such a version of the language was an artificial creation not used anywhere else. Following the introduction of this law, a number of schools sought to teach children of Moldovan ethnicity using the Latin script. These schools were subject to a variety of oppressive measures by the MRT authorities:

> In the summer of 2004, the schools were closed and premises besieged and subsequently stormed by 'MRT' police. Teachers were arrested and detained and Latin script materials were seized and destroyed. Some parents lost their jobs because of their decision to send their children to Moldovan language schools.[201]

The applicants in the case were affected parents and teachers, who claimed, inter alia, that the failure of the MRT authorities to provide education in the official Moldovan language affected the substance of the right to education.[202] The Court found that:

> 137. ... although the text of Article 2 of Protocol No. 1 does not specify the language in which education must be conducted, the right to education would be meaningless if it did not imply in favour of its beneficiaries, the right to be educated in the national language or in one of the national languages, as the case may be (*Case 'relating to certain aspects of the laws on the use of languages in education in Belgium'*, cited above, § 3).
>
> ...

[198] *Cyprus v Turkey*, [278].

[199] Geoff Gilbert, 'The Burgeoning Minority Rights Jurisprudence of the European Court of Human Rights' (2002) 24 *Human Rights Quarterly* 736, 762. For further discussion of this somewhat confusing judgment, see Fernand de Varennes, 'Linguistic Identity and Language Rights' in Marc Weller (ed), *Universal Minority Rights: A Commentary on the Jurisprudence of International Courts and Treaty Bodies* (Oxford University Press, Oxford, 2007), 312.

[200] *Catan et al v Moldova and Russia* (Apps. 43370/04, 8252/05 and 18454/06), 19 October 2012, (2013) 57 EHRR 4.

[201] *Catan v Moldova and Russia*, [126].

[202] *Catan v Moldova and Russia*, [140]–[141].

142. While it is difficult for the Court to establish in detail the facts relating to the applicants' experiences following the reopening of the schools, it nonetheless notes the following. First, Article 6 of the '"MRT" Law on Languages' was in force and the use of the Latin alphabet constituted an offence in the 'MRT'... Secondly, it is clear that the schools had to move to new buildings, with the Alexandru cel Bun School divided between three sites and pupils at the Ştefan cel Mare School having to travel 40 kilometres each day. Thirdly, according to figures provided by the Moldovan Government, the number of pupils enrolled in the two schools still in 'MRT' controlled territory approximately halved between 2007 and 2011 and there has also been a significant reduction in children studying in Moldovan/Romanian throughout Transdniestria. Although it appears that Transdniestria has an ageing population and that Moldovans in particular are emigrating... the Court considers that the 50% attendance drop at Evrica and Alexandru cel Bun Schools is too high to be explained by demographic factors alone. For the Court, these uncontested facts serve to corroborate the general thrust of the allegations contained in the 81 affidavits submitted by the applicant parents and pupils, describing the constant harassment they suffered.

143. The schools were at all times registered with the Moldovan Ministry of Education, using a curriculum set by that Ministry and providing teaching in the first official language of Moldova. The Court therefore considers that the forced closure of the schools, based on the '"MRT" Law on languages'... and the subsequent measures of harassment constituted interferences with the applicant pupils' rights of access to educational institutions existing at a given time and to be educated in their national language... In addition, the Court considers that these measures amounted to an interference with the applicant parents' rights to ensure their children's education and teaching in accordance with their philosophical convictions... The applicant parents in this case wanted their children to be educated in the official language of their country, which was also their own mother tongue. Instead, they were placed in the invidious position of having to choose, on the one hand, between sending their children to schools where they would face the disadvantage of pursuing their entire secondary education in a combination of language and alphabet which they consider artificial and which is unrecognised anywhere else in the world, using teaching materials produced in Soviet times or, alternatively, subjecting their children to long journeys and/or substandard facilities, harassment and intimidation.

144. There is no evidence before the Court to suggest that the measures taken by the 'MRT' authorities in respect of these schools pursued a legitimate aim. Indeed, it appears that the 'MRT''s language policy, as applied to these schools, was intended to enforce the Russification of the language and culture of the Moldovan community living in Transdniestria, in accordance with the 'MRT''s overall political objectives of uniting with Russia and separating from Moldova. Given the fundamental importance of primary and secondary education for each child's personal development and future success, it was impermissible to interrupt these children's schooling and force them and their parents to make such difficult choices with the sole purpose of entrenching the separatist ideology.[203]

The Court thus found that there had been a violation of the right to education, under Article 2 of Protocol 1. Although it is clear that the Court was influenced by the fact that the Moldovan language was the official language of Moldova, suggesting that the result may have been different in relation to claims for education in other

[203] *Catan v Moldova and Russia*, [143]–[145].

languages, the case nonetheless shows a greater preparedness, on the part of the Court, to find a violation of the right to education on the basis of language policy.

In this context, it is worth noting that the right to education in one's own language is in fact guaranteed in several national legal systems. So, for example, the Constitution of the Republic of South Africa, section 29(2), provides that '[e]veryone has the right to receive education in the official language or languages of their choice in public educational institutions where that education is reasonably practicable'. This provision was considered by the South African Constitutional Court in the case of *Head of Department: Mpumalanga Department of Education and Another v Hoerskool Ermelo and Another*.[204] The Court in that case required the governing body of a school to reconsider its language policy, under which the school provided instruction only in Afrikaans, and to consider providing instruction in English also. The regional and national jurisprudence therefore suggests a trend towards greater recognition of the right to education in one's own language. Given the CESCR's comments on this issue in its Concluding Observations, it seems likely that it would adopt a similar approach.

Roma

The particular situation of the Roma community is worthy of special mention as it offers an excellent case study of the general approach taken by the Committee and other international bodies to the right to education for minority groups. The Roma represent a particularly marginalized and vulnerable minority, subject to multiple and overlapping forms of discrimination and disadvantage. The way in which the right to education for this group is dealt with by the relevant bodies therefore highlights a range of issues relevant to the position of minority groups generally. In addition, the international legal materials on the right to education for the Roma offer useful discussion about the issue of when differential treatment allegedly for the benefit of minority groups, such as segregation with respect to schooling, will amount to unlawful discrimination.

There is a considerable body of Concluding Observations, together with a series of cases before the European Court of Human Rights, considering the rights of the Roma in relation to education. So, for example, the Committee's Concluding Observations on the Ukraine indicate that:

> 31. The Committee is concerned about reports on the high drop-out rate among Roma children in primary and secondary education, the frequent refusal to enrol Roma children in mainstream schools, and their segregation in special classes or placement in special schools for children with mental disabilities…
>
> 54. The Committee recommends that the State party adopt special measures, including subsidies for textbooks and other educational tools, in order to increase school attendance

[204] *Head of Department: Mpumalanga Department of Education v Hoërskool Ermelo*, 14 October 2009, 2010 (2) SA 415. The case of *Gauteng Provincial Legislature In re: Gauteng School Education Bill of 1995* (CCT39/95), 4 April 1996, 1996 (3) SA 165, discussed further below in the context of Article 13(4), also concerned the rights of different linguistic groups to education in their own language.

by Roma children at the pre-school, primary and secondary levels, combat discrimination against Roma pupils, promote their admission to mainstream schools and classes, raise awareness among Roma families on the importance of education, including for girls, and provide additional catch-up and Ukrainian and Russian language classes for Roma pupils.[205]

Similarly, in relation to Finland:

19. The Committee notes with concern the high drop-out rate of Roma children, and in particular of Roma girls, despite the efforts undertaken by the State party to improve access to education of Roma children. The Committee is deeply concerned that according to reports received, Roma children tend to be channeled towards special education more than other children due to the perception of teachers that such children are difficult or need special attention.

...

28. The Committee recommends that the State party intensify its efforts to improve access to inclusive education for Roma children, inter alia by: (a) taking immediate steps to eliminate negative prejudices and stereotypes regarding Roma and their contribution to society; (b) facilitating the recruitment of Roma teachers so as to ensure, to the widest extent possible, adequate opportunities for Roma children to receive instruction in their native language; (c) increasing the availability of school books in the Romani language; and (d) organizing special training for teachers to increase their knowledge about the culture and traditions of Roma and to raise their sensitivity to the needs of Roma children.[206]

As suggested in these Concluding Observations, a particular manifestation of discrimination against, and marginalization of, Roma is the practice of tending to segregate them; in particular, the fact that Roma children are disproportionately represented in special schools for mentally handicapped children. The disproportionate representation of Roma children in these schools appears to be widespread through Europe and has been the subject of a number of cases before the European Court of Human Rights. At issue in each of these cases was the question of whether there were 'objective and reasonable justifications' for this differential treatment of Roma children, such that the differential treatment would not violate the prohibition on discrimination in Article 14 of the ECHR.

The case of *D.H. v Czech Republic*[207] concerned eighteen Roma children who were placed in special schools. The applicants claimed that Roma children were vastly over-represented in special schools, and that this effectively amounted to segregation as 'their channelling to special schools was...often quasi-automatic'.[208] As a result, these children were 'relegated to educational

[205] CESCR, Concluding Observations: Ukraine, E/C.12/UKR/CO/5 (4 January 2008), [31] and [54].

[206] CESCR, Concluding Observations: Finland, E/C.12/FIN/CO/5 (16 January 2008), [19] and [28]; see also, eg, Slovakia, E/C.12/1/Add.81 (19 December 2002), [18] and [33]; Slovenia, E/C.12/SKV/CO/1 (25 January 2006), [24]; and Bosnia and Herzegovina, E/C.12/BIH/CO/1 (24 January 2006), [29] and [51]. See also, eg, CERD, Concluding Observations: Poland, A/58/18 (2003) 35, [163]; United Kingdom of Great Britain and Northern Ireland, A/58/18 (2003) 88, [542]; Slovakia, A/59/18 (2004) 70, [385].

[207] *D.H. v Czech Republic* (App. 57325/00), 13 November 2007, (2008) 47 EHRR 3.

[208] *D.H. v Czech Republic*, [63].

facilities designed for other purposes, offering little opportunity for skills training or educational preparation and therefore very limited opportunity for further study or employment'.[209] In considering whether this situation amounted to discrimination in relation to the right to education, the Court first noted the particularly vulnerable situation of the Roma and found that this gives rise to obligations of special protection on the part of the state:

> The Court notes that as a result of their turbulent history and constant uprooting the Roma have become a specific type of disadvantaged and vulnerable minority...As the Court has noted in previous cases, they therefore require special protection...[T]his protection also extends to the sphere of education. The present case therefore warrants particular attention, especially as when the applications were lodged with the Court the applicants were minor children for whom the right to education was of paramount importance.[210]

The Court went on to note that:

> Even if the exact percentage of Roma children in special schools at the material time remains difficult to establish, their number was disproportionately high. Moreover, Roma pupils formed a majority of the pupils in special schools. Despite being couched in neutral terms, the relevant statutory provisions therefore had considerably more impact in practice on Roma children than on non-Roma children and resulted in statistically disproportionate number of placements of the former in special schools.[211]

On this basis, the Court found a discriminatory effect. The question was then whether there was an 'objective and reasonable justification' for the difference in treatment between Roma and non-Roma students. The government argued that the applicants were placed in special schools as a result of low intellectual capacity, determined on the basis of tests.[212] However, the Court noted that 'the tests used to assess the children's learning abilities or difficulties have given rise to controversy and continue to be the subject to scientific debate and research'.[213] In particular, there were suggestions that the tests were culturally biased. As a result:

> The Court considers that, at the very least, there is a danger that the tests were biased and that the results were not analysed in the light of the particularities and special characteristics of the Roma children who sat them. In these circumstances, the tests in question cannot serve as justification for the impugned difference in treatment.[214]

The Court then went on to consider whether the measures in question fell within the state's 'margin of appreciation':

> 206. ...whenever discretion capable of interfering with the enjoyment of a Convention right is conferred on national authorities, the procedural safeguards available to the individual will be especially material in determining whether the respondent State has, when fixing the regulatory framework, remained within its margin of appreciation...

[209] *D.H. v Czech Republic*, [63].
[210] *D.H. v Czech Republic*, [182].
[211] *D.H. v Czech Republic*, [193].
[212] *D.H. v Czech Republic*, [197].
[213] *D.H. v Czech Republic*, [199].
[214] *D.H. v Czech Republic*, [201].

207. The facts of the instant case indicate that the schooling arrangements for Roma children were not attended by safeguards...that would ensure that, in the exercise of its margin of appreciation in the education sphere, the State took into account their special needs as members of a disadvantaged class...Furthermore, as a result of the arrangements the applicants were placed in schools for children with mental disabilities where a more basic curriculum was followed than in ordinary schools and where they were isolated from pupils from the wider population. As a result, they received an education which compounded their difficulties and compromised their subsequent personal development instead of tackling their real problems or helping them to integrate into the ordinary schools and develop the skills that would facilitate life among the majority population. Indeed, the Government have implicitly admitted that job opportunities are more limited for pupils from special schools.

208. In these circumstances and while recognising the efforts made by the Czech authorities to ensure that Roma children receive schooling, the Court is not satisfied that the difference in treatment between Roma children and non-Roma children was objectively and reasonably justified and that there existed a reasonable relationship of proportionality between the means used and the aim pursued. In that connection, it notes with interest that the new legislation has abolished special schools and provides for children with special educational needs, including socially disadvantaged children, to be educated in ordinary schools.

209. Lastly, since it has been established that the relevant legislation as applied in practice at the material time had a disproportionately prejudicial effect on the Roma community, the Court considers that the applicants as members of that community necessarily suffered the same discriminatory treatment. Accordingly, it does not need to examine their individual cases.

210. Consequently, there has been a violation in the instant case of Article 14 of the Convention taken in conjunction with Article 2 of Protocol No. 1 as regards each of the applicants.

In the later case of *Orsus v Croatia*,[215] Roma children were segregated into separate classes, allegedly on account of their limited knowledge of the Croatian language. Although Croatia argued that the segregation was necessary to assist these students, the Court found that such segregation could only be justified 'if it served the purpose of bringing their command of the Croatian language up to an adequate level and then securing their immediate transfer to a mixed class'.[216] Since there was evidence that this was not the case, the Court found a violation of Article 14 taken together with Article 2 of Protocol 1 of the ECHR.

A good summary of the Court's approach is set out in the recent case of *Horváth and Kiss v Hungary*.[217] The facts of this case largely reflect those of *D.H. v Czech Republic*: two students of Roma origin complained that their placement in special schools for those with intellectual disabilities was inappropriate and amounted to discrimination. The Court noted that:

102. ...as a result of their turbulent history and constant uprooting, the Roma have become a specific type of disadvantaged and vulnerable minority. They therefore require special

[215] *Orsus v Croatia* (App. 15766/03), 16 March 2010, (2011) 52 EHRR 7.
[216] *Orsus v Croatia*, [172].
[217] *Horváth and Kiss v Hungary* (App. 11146/11), 29 January 2013, (2013) 57 EHRR 31.

protection. Their vulnerable position means that special consideration should be given to their needs and their different lifestyle both in the relevant regulatory framework and in reaching decisions in particular cases…

…

104. In the context of the right to education of members of groups which suffered past discrimination in education with continuing effects, structural deficiencies call for the implementation of positive measures in order, *inter alia*, to assist the applicants with any difficulties they encountered in following the school curriculum. These obligations are particularly stringent where there is an actual history of direct discrimination. Therefore, some additional steps are needed in order to address these problems, such as active and structured involvement on the part of the relevant social services…

…

127. The facts of the instant case indicate that the schooling arrangements for Roma applicants with allegedly mild mental disability or learning disability were not attended by adequate safeguards that would ensure that, in the exercise of its margin of appreciation in the education sphere, the State took into account their special needs as members of a disadvantaged class…Furthermore, as a result of the arrangements, the applicants were placed in schools for children with mental disabilities where a more basic curriculum was followed than in ordinary schools and where they were isolated from pupils from the wider population. As a consequence, they received an education which did not offer the necessary guarantees stemming from the positive obligations of the State to undo a history of racial segregation in special schools. The education provided might have compounded their difficulties and compromised their subsequent personal development instead of helping them to integrate into the ordinary schools and develop the skills that would facilitate life among the majority population…

128. Since it has been established that the relevant legislation, as applied in practice at the material time, had a disproportionately prejudicial effect on the Roma community, and that the State, in a situation of *prima facie* discrimination, failed to prove that it has provided the guarantees needed to avoid the misdiagnosis and misplacement of the Roma applicants, the Court considers that the applicants necessarily suffered from the discriminatory treatment. In this connection—and with regard to the vulnerability of persons with mental disabilities as such, as well as their past history of discrimination and prejudice—the Court also recalls its considerations pronounced in the case of *Alajos Kiss v. Hungary* (no. 38832/06, 20 May 2010):

'[I]f a restriction on fundamental rights applies to a particularly vulnerable group in society, who have suffered considerable discrimination in the past, such as the mentally disabled, then the State's margin of appreciation is substantially narrower and it must have very weighty reasons for the restrictions in question… [T]he treatment as a single class of those with intellectual or mental disabilities is a questionable classification, and the curtailment of their rights must be subject to strict scrutiny.' (paragraphs 42 and 44).

129. Consequently, there has been a violation in the instant case of Article 14 of the Convention taken in conjunction with Article 2 of Protocol No. 1 in respect of each of the applicants.

The Court has also found that segregation of Roma children more generally—that is, simply into separate schools, not necessarily special schools—may amount to a violation of the right to education, read in light of the prohibition on discrimination in Article 14 of the Convention. Thus, in the recent case of *Lavida et al v Greece*, the Court found a violation where Roma children were restricted to attending a primary school attended solely by other Roma.[218] The Court found that the state's refusal to take measures to combat segregation amounted to discrimination and a violation of the right to education. The Court reached similar findings in the case of *Sampani et al v Greece*,[219] and in cases where the authorities initially failed to enrol a group of Roma children for a full academic year, and subsequently placed them in special classes in a school annex.[220]

Religion

Religion is a prohibited ground of discrimination under Article 2(2) of the Covenant, so such discrimination is impermissible in relation to the right to education. Discrimination on the basis of religion may also amount to a violation of rights to freedom of religion under, for example, Article 18 of the ICCPR. This general obligation, on the part of states, to protect against discrimination on the basis of religion in relation to education, is reinforced by the specific obligation in Article 13(3), which provides for the right of parents and guardians 'to ensure the religious and moral education of their children in conformity with their own convictions'. This specific provision, which has generated considerable discussion and jurisprudence, is discussed in more detail below.

Direct discrimination, for example, limiting access to educational institutions to persons of a particular religion, is clearly prohibited. Thus, in the case of *Tengur v The Minister of Education and Another*,[221] the Supreme Court of Mauritius, interpreting the Mauritian Constitution in light of international law and, in particular, Article 13 of the ICESCR, found that reserving for Catholics 50 per cent of places in state-funded Roman Catholic secondary schools constituted unlawful discrimination against non-Catholics.[222]

But what of measures which indirectly affect the ability of those of a particular religion to access, or profit from, educational opportunities, such as regulations prohibiting the wearing of religious dress? The main issue which has arisen in this context concerns regulations which effectively prohibit the wearing of Islamic headscarves in schools and other educational institutions. Regulations such as those in France, which prohibit the wearing of overtly religious symbols in schools, clearly affect the ability of Muslim women and girls to attend such institutions. This has been noted in the Concluding Observations of bodies including the Human Rights Committee, Committee on the Elimination of Racial Discrimination and Committee

[218] *Lavida et al v Greece* (App. 7973/10) ECtHR 30 May 2013.
[219] *Sampani et al v Greece* (App. 59608/09) ECtHR 11 December 2012.
[220] *Sampanis et al v Greece* (App. 32526/05) ECtHR 5 June 2008.
[221] *Tengur v The Minister of Education and Another*, Record No. 77387, 2002 SCJ 48 (Supreme Court of Mauritius).
[222] On appeal, the decision was affirmed by the Privy Council: *Bishop of Roman Catholic Diocese of Port Louis v S. Tengur*, 3 February 2004, Privy Council Appeal No. 21 of 2003.

on the Rights of the Child,[223] all of which have expressed concern at the impact of such measures on enjoyment of the right to education by these groups.

This issue has been considered in the key case before the European Court of Human Rights of *Şahin v Turkey*.[224] In that case, Leyla Şahin, a medical student at Istanbul University and a practising Muslim, was refused access to lectures and exams because she wore a headscarf, in contravention of university regulations. She complained to the European Court of Human Rights that this violated both her right to freedom of religion, under Article 9 of the ECHR, and her right to education, under Article 2 of Protocol 1. In relation to her claim under Article 9, the Court found that, although there was an interference with her right to manifest her religion, the measures in question pursued the legitimate aim of protecting the rights and freedoms of others and maintaining public order, as the purpose of the regulations was to maintain the secular character of the university and thus the equality of all students. The measures therefore fell within the state's margin of appreciation. The Court then considered the complaint in relation to Article 2 of Protocol 1 and noted:

157. . . . [T]he Court is able to accept that the regulations on the basis of which the applicant was refused access to various lectures and examinations for wearing the Islamic headscarf constituted a restriction on her right to education, notwithstanding the fact that she had had access to the university and been able to read the subject of her choice in accordance with the results she had achieved in the university entrance examination. However, an analysis of the case by reference to the right to education cannot in this instance be divorced from the conclusion reached by the Court with respect to Article 9 . . . as the considerations taken into account under that provision are clearly applicable to the complaint under Article 2 of Protocol No. 1, which complaint consists of criticism of the regulation concerned that takes much the same form as that made with respect to Article 9.

158. In that connection, the Court has already found that the restriction was foreseeable to those concerned and pursued the legitimate aims of protecting the rights and freedoms of others and maintaining public order. . . The obvious purpose of the restriction was to preserve the secular character of educational institutions.

159. As regards the principle of proportionality, the Court found in paragraphs 118 to 121 above that there was a reasonable relationship of proportionality between the means used and the aim pursued. In so finding, it relied in particular on the following factors which are clearly relevant here. Firstly, the measures in question manifestly did not hinder the students in performing the duties imposed by the habitual forms of religious observance. Secondly, the decision-making process for applying the internal regulations satisfied, so far as was possible, the requirement to weigh up the various interests at stake. The university authorities judiciously sought a means whereby they could avoid having to turn away students wearing the headscarf and at the same time honour their obligation to protect the rights of others and the interests of the education system. Lastly, the process also appears to have been accompanied by safeguards—the rule requiring conformity with statute and judicial review—that were apt to protect the students' interests . . .

[223] See, eg, Human Rights Committee, Concluding Observations: France, CCPR/C/FRA/CO/4 (31 July 2008), [23]; CERD Committee, Concluding Observations: France, CERD/C/FRA/CO/16 (18 April 2005), [18]; CRC Committee, Concluding Observations: France, CRC/C/155/Add.240 (30 June 2004), [25]–[26].

[224] *Şahin v Turkey* (App. 44774/98), 10 November 2005, (2007) 44 EHRR 5.

160. It would, furthermore, be unrealistic to imagine that the applicant, a medical student, was unaware of Istanbul University's internal regulations restricting the places where religious dress could be worn or had not been sufficiently informed about the reasons for their introduction. She could reasonably have foreseen that she ran the risk of being refused access to lectures and examinations if, as subsequently happened, she continued to wear the Islamic headscarf after 23 February 1998.

161. Consequently, the restriction in question did not impair the very essence of the applicant's right to education…

162. In conclusion, there has been no violation of the first sentence of Article 2 of Protocol No. 1.

The Court therefore tied its finding in relation to the right to education to its finding in relation to the right to manifest one's religion. This, along with other aspects of the majority's decision, was heavily criticized in the dissenting judgment of Judge Tulkens:

16. The Grand Chamber adopted 'by analogy' its reasoning on the existence of interference under Article 9 of the Convention…I am not entirely satisfied that the reasoning with regard to religious freedom 'is clearly applicable' to the right to education…

17. …I will not pursue here the debate concerning the right to freedom of religion, but will confine myself to highlighting the additional elements that concerned the proportionality of the limitations that were imposed on the applicant's right to education.

I would begin by noting that before refusing the applicant access to lectures and examinations, the authorities should have used other means either to encourage her (through mediation, for example) to remove her headscarf and pursue her studies, or to ensure that public order was maintained on the university premises if it was genuinely at risk. The fact of the matter is that no attempt was made to try measures that would have had a less drastic effect on the applicant's right to education in the instant case. My second point is that it is common ground that by making the applicant's pursuit of her studies conditional on removing the headscarf and by refusing her access to the university if she failed to comply with this requirement, the authorities forced the applicant to leave the country and complete her studies at Vienna University. She was thus left with no alternative…Lastly, the Grand Chamber does not weigh up the competing interests, namely, on the one hand, the damage sustained by the applicant—who was deprived of any possibility of completing her studies in Turkey because of her religious convictions and also maintained that it was unlikely that she would be able to return to her country to practise her profession owing to the difficulties that existed there in obtaining recognition for foreign diplomas—and, on the other, the benefit to be gained by Turkish society from prohibiting the applicant from wearing the headscarf on the university premises.

In these circumstances, it can reasonably be argued that the applicant's exclusion from lectures and examinations and, consequently, from the university itself, rendered her right to education ineffective and, therefore, impaired the very essence of that right.

This dissenting position has received considerable support in the literature.[225] However, more recent jurisprudence of the Court, such as the case of *Lautsi v*

[225] See, eg, Jill Marshall, 'Conditions for Freedom: European Human Rights Law and the Islamic Headscarf Debate' (2008) 30 *Human Rights Quarterly* 631; Niraj Nathwani, 'Islamic Headscarves and Human Rights: A Critical Analysis of the Relevant Case Law of the European Court of Human

Italy,[226] discussed further below, suggests that the Court may continue to grant a large margin of appreciation to states in this area. It is to be hoped that the entry into force of the Optional Protocol represents an opportunity for the CESCR to develop a different approach, reflecting the Concluding Observations of the relevant international treaty bodies.

Detention

As the Special Rapporteur on the right to education has noted, persons in detention constitute 'a group subject to discrimination generally and to discrimination in the provision of education specifically'.[227] In spite of this, however, the right to education of persons in detention has received little attention, with the notable exception of a special report of the Special Rapporteur on this issue.[228] According to the Special Rapporteur, although instruments such as the Basic Principles for the Treatment of Prisoners, adopted by the General Assembly in 1990,[229] and the Standard Minimum Rules for the Treatment of Prisoners, adopted by the Economic and Social Council in 1957,[230] seek to ensure the right to education of persons in detention:

> Despite variations between penal systems, it is clear that, for all, the provision of education for persons in detention is inherently complex and, where it does take place, it does so in an environment inherently hostile to its liberating potential. Frequently, inadequate attention and resources, both human and financial, dedicated to adequate education, combined with the damaging impact of detention, exacerbate often low levels of self-esteem and motivation of learners and create major challenges for prison administrators, staff and learners alike.[231]

The Special Rapporteur therefore makes a number of recommendations to improve the protection of the right to education of persons in detention. In particular:

> The Special Rapporteur recommends that authorities in charge of public education:
>
> (a) Make available to all detainees, whether sentenced or in remand, education programmes that would cover at least the curriculum of compulsory education at the primary and, if possible, at the secondary level also;

Rights' (2007) 25 *Netherlands Quarterly of Human Rights* 221; Ben Saul, 'Wearing Thin: Restrictions on Headscarves and Other Religious Symbols' in J. McAdam (ed), *Forced Migration, Human Rights and Security* (Hart, Oxford, 2008), 181–212; Ssenyonjo, *Economic, Social and Cultural Rights in International Law*, 395–8.

[226] *Lautsi et al v Italy* (App. 30814/06), 18 March 2011, (2012) 54 EHRR 3.

[227] Human Rights Council, Report of the Special Rapporteur on the right to education of persons in detention, A/HRC/11/8 (2 April 2009), 2.

[228] Human Rights Council, Report of the Special Rapporteur on the right to education of persons in detention, A/HRC/11/8 (2 April 2009). An application under the ECHR, which would have raised the issue directly, was rejected for non-exhaustion of domestic remedies: *X v Austria* (App. 4511/70), 24 May 1971, (1972) 38 CD 84.

[229] UNGA Res. 45/111, Basic Principles for the Treatment of Prisoners, A/RES/45/111 (14 December 1990), Article 6.

[230] UN Economic and Social Council, Standard Minimum Rules for the Treatment of Prisoners, Res. 663 c (XXIV) (31 July 1957), Rules 77(1) and (2).

[231] Human Rights Council, Report of the Special Rapporteur on the right to education of persons in detention, A/HRC/11/8 (2 April 2009), [6].

(b) Together with the institutions of detention, arrange comprehensive education programmes aimed at the development of the full potential of each detainee. These should aim also to minimize the negative impact of incarceration, improve prospects of reintegration, rehabilitation, self-esteem and morale.[232]

Corporal punishment

The right to education would seem to encompass a prohibition on the use of corporal punishment in educational institutions. This is specifically provided in some of the relevant instruments. Thus, Article 28(2) of the Convention on the Rights of the Child provides:

States Parties shall take all appropriate measures to ensure that school discipline is administered in a manner consistent with the child's human dignity and in conformity with the present Convention.

And the Committee on the Rights of the Child has indicated in its General Comment No. 1:

Education must also be provided in a way that respects the strict limits on discipline reflected in article 28(2) and promotes non-violence in school. The Committee has repeatedly made clear in its concluding observations that the use of corporal punishment does not respect the inherent dignity of the child nor the strict limits on school discipline. Compliance with the values recognized in article 29(1) clearly requires that schools be child-friendly in the fullest sense of the term and that they be consistent in all respects with the dignity of the child. The participation of children in school life, the creation of school communities and student councils, peer education and peer counselling, and the involvement of children in school disciplinary proceedings should be promoted as part of the process of learning and experiencing the realization of rights.[233]

At the regional level, Article 11(5) of the African Charter on the Rights and Welfare of the Child provides:

States Parties to the present Charter shall take all appropriate measures to ensure that a child who is subjected to schools or parental discipline shall be treated with humanity and with respect for the inherent dignity of the child and in conformity with the present Charter.

Although Article 13 of the ICESCR does not specifically mention the issue of corporal punishment, General Comment No. 13 indicates that:

In the Committee's view, corporal punishment is inconsistent with the fundamental guiding principle of international human rights law enshrined in the Preambles to the Universal Declaration of Human Rights and both Covenants: the dignity of the individual. Other aspects of school discipline may also be inconsistent with human dignity, such as public humiliation. Nor should any form of discipline breach other rights under the Covenant, such as the right to food. A State party is required to take measures to ensure that discipline

[232] Human Rights Council, Report of the Special Rapporteur on the right to education of persons in detention, A/HRC/11/8 (2 April 2009), [91].

[233] CRC, General Comment No. 1, [8].

which is inconsistent with the Covenant does not occur in any public or private educational institution within its jurisdiction. The Committee welcomes initiatives taken by some States parties which actively encourage schools to introduce 'positive', non-violent approaches to school discipline.[234]

The Committee has reflected this approach in its Concluding Observations. So, for example, in relation to Trinidad and Tobago:

While the Committee welcomes the abolition of corporal punishment in schools, it is concerned at the continued resort to corporal punishment at home...[235]

The issue of corporal punishment in schools also raises issues of the freedom of parents to ensure their children's education in accordance with their convictions, under Article 13(3). The case law of the European Court of Human Rights on the issue of corporal punishment is discussed in this context, below.

Academic freedom

The Committee has indicated in General Comment No. 13 that academic freedom is an important aspect of the right to education:

38. In the light of its examination of numerous States parties' reports, the Committee has formed the view that the right to education can only be enjoyed if accompanied by the academic freedom of staff and students. Accordingly, even though the issue is not explicitly mentioned in article 13, it is appropriate and necessary for the Committee to make some observations about academic freedom. The following remarks give particular attention to institutions of higher education because, in the Committee's experience, staff and students in higher education are especially vulnerable to political and other pressures which undermine academic freedom. The Committee wishes to emphasize, however, that staff and students throughout the education sector are entitled to academic freedom and many of the following observations have general application.

39. Members of the academic community, individually or collectively, are free to pursue, develop and transmit knowledge and ideas, through research, teaching, study, discussion, documentation, production, creation or writing. Academic freedom includes the liberty of individuals to express freely opinions about the institution or system in which they work, to fulfil their functions without discrimination or fear of repression by the State or any other actor, to participate in professional or representative academic bodies, and to enjoy all the internationally recognized human rights applicable to other individuals in the same jurisdiction. The enjoyment of academic freedom carries with it obligations, such as the duty to respect the academic freedom of others, to ensure the fair discussion of contrary views, and to treat all without discrimination on any of the prohibited grounds.

40. The enjoyment of academic freedom requires the autonomy of institutions of higher education. Autonomy is that degree of self-governance necessary for effective decision-making by institutions of higher education in relation to their academic work, standards, management and related activities. Self-governance, however, must be consistent with systems of public accountability, especially in respect of funding provided by the

[234] CESCR, General Comment No. 13, [41].

[235] CESCR, Concluding Observations: Trinidad and Tobago, E/C.12/1/Add.80 (5 June 2002), [29].

State. Given the substantial public investments made in higher education, an appropriate balance has to be struck between institutional autonomy and accountability. While there is no single model, institutional arrangements should be fair, just and equitable, and as transparent and participatory as possible.

This approach is reflected in the Concluding Observations of the Committee. So, for example, in relation to the Republic of Korea, the Committee:

…is concerned about the absence of self-regulation and diversity in university education in arts and culture, following the request of the Ministry of Culture, Sports and Tourism to the Korean National University of Arts to solely concentrate on 'practical education'. The Committee, while noting the information provided by the State party and the need for general audits, recommends that universities be guaranteed the freedom to exercise fully their academic authority and control their curriculum and teaching methods.[236]

The issue of academic freedom also engages other rights, most notably freedom of expression, but also rights to participate in cultural life and the benefits of scientific progress, which are discussed in the chapter on Article 15, below.

Article 13(3)

Article 13(3) protects the rights of parents in relation to their children's schooling. These rights are also protected under a range of international and regional instruments. For example, the UNESCO Convention against Discrimination in Education, Article 5(1)(b) provides:

It is essential to respect the liberty of parents and, where applicable, of legal guardians, firstly to choose for their children institutions other than those maintained by the public authorities but conforming to such minimum educational standards as may be laid down or approved by the competent authorities and, secondly, to ensure in a manner consistent with the procedures followed in the State for the application of its legislation, the religious and moral education of the children in conformity with their own convictions; and no person or group of persons should be compelled to receive religious instruction inconsistent with his or their convictions…

Similarly, Article 2 of Protocol 1 of the ECHR provides:

In the exercise of any functions which it assumes in relation to education and to teaching, the State shall respect the right of parents to ensure such education and teaching in conformity with their own religious and philosophical convictions.

Article 14(3) of the Charter of Fundamental Rights of the European Union, Article 13(4) of the San Salvador Protocol to the American Convention on Human Rights and Article 11(4) of the African Charter on the Rights and Welfare of the Child all contain similar provisions.

[236] CESCR, Concluding Observations: Republic of Korea, E/C.12/KOR/CO/3 (17 December 2009), [35].

As articulated in Article 13(3), there are two aspects to this right, as General Comment No. 13 notes:

28. Article 13(3) has two elements, one of which is that States parties undertake to respect the liberty of parents and guardians to ensure the religious and moral education of their children in conformity with their own convictions…

29. The second element of article 13(3) is the liberty of parents and guardians to choose other than public schools for their children, provided the schools conform to 'such minimum educational standards as may be laid down or approved by the State'. This has to be read with the complementary provision, article 13(4), which affirms 'the liberty of individuals and bodies to establish and direct educational institutions'.

The second of these, the liberty of parents to choose private schools for their children, is relatively uncontroversial. As indicated in the General Comment, this right intersects with, and is complemented by, the right to establish private schools under Article 13(4), discussed further below.

The liberty of parents to ensure their children's education in conformity with their convictions has given rise to more detailed consideration in the literature and the jurisprudence. This aspect of the right to education engages elements of freedom of religion, and indeed its terms are mirrored in Article 18(4) of the ICCPR, which provides:

The States Parties to the present Covenant undertake to have respect for the liberty of parents and, when applicable, legal guardians to ensure the religious and moral education of their children in conformity with their own convictions.

Further, the jurisprudence of the European Court of Human Rights has indicated that Article 2 of Protocol 1 is the *lex specialis* in relation to Article 9 (freedom of religion) in the context of education. In the case of *Lautsi v Italy*,[237] which concerned the compulsory display of crucifixes in state schools in Italy:

59. The Court reiterates that in the area of education and teaching Article 2 of Protocol No. 1 is in principle the *lex specialis* in relation to Article 9 of the Convention. That is so at least where, as in the present case, the dispute concerns the obligation laid on Contracting States by the second sentence of Article 2 to respect, when exercising the functions they assume in that area, the right of parents to ensure such education and teaching in conformity with their own religious and philosophical convictions…

The complaint in question should therefore be examined mainly from the standpoint of the second sentence of Article 2 of Protocol No. 1…

60. Nevertheless, that provision should be read in the light not only of the first sentence of the same Article, but also, in particular, of Article 9 of the Convention…which guarantees freedom of thought, conscience and religion, including the freedom not to belong to a religion, and which imposes on Contracting States a 'duty of neutrality and impartiality'.

[237] *Lautsi et al v Italy* (App. 30814/06), 18 March 2011, (2012) 54 EHRR 3.

In that connection, it should be pointed out that States have responsibility for ensuring, neutrally and impartially, the exercise of various religions, faiths and beliefs. Their role is to help maintain public order, religious harmony and tolerance in a democratic society…

DEFINITIONS

'Respect'

Article 13(3) requires states to 'respect' the liberty of parents to ensure their children's education in accordance with their convictions. On the issue of what constitutes 'respect', the jurisprudence of the European Court of Human Rights is instructive. In the case of *Campbell and Cosans v United Kingdom*,[238] the Court noted that 'respect':

…means more than 'acknowledge' or 'taken into account'; in addition to a primarily negative undertaking, it implies some positive obligation on the part of the State…This being so, the duty to respect parental convictions in this sphere cannot be overridden by the alleged necessity of striking a balance between the conflicting views involved.[239]

In terms of the scope of this obligation to respect the liberty of parents, the European Court of Human Rights has indicated that it applies to all functions which the state exercises in relation to education, including not just matters of curriculum, but also matters of discipline and administration. Thus, in the case of *Kjeldsen, Busk Madsen and Pedersen v Denmark*,[240] the Court found that Article 2 of Protocol 1 'applies to each of the State's functions in relation to education and to teaching' and 'enjoins the State to respect parent's convictions, be they religious or philosophical, throughout the entire State education programme'.[241]

'Liberty'

Significantly, Article 13(3) refers to the 'liberty', not 'right', of parents in relation to their children's education. According to the *travaux préparatoires*, the drafters 'preferred the word "liberty" to the word "right", since, in their view, the latter word might imply an obligation for the States Parties to grant material assistance to private schools'.[242]

'Convictions'

The term 'convictions' is not defined in the Covenant or other international instruments addressing this issue. However, the issue of what constitutes 'convictions'

[238] *Campbell and Cosans v United Kingdom* (App. 7511/76), 25 February 1982, (1982) 4 EHRR 293.
[239] *Campbell and Cosans v UK*, [37(a)].
[240] *Kjeldsen, Busk Madsen and Pedersen v Denmark*, 7 December 1976, (1976) 1 EHRR 711.
[241] *Kjeldsen, Busk Madsen and Pedersen v Denmark*, [51]. See also *Campbell and Cosans v UK*, [33]–[35].
[242] UNGA, Draft International Covenants on Human Rights: Report of the Third Committee (Rapporteur Mr Carlow Manuel Cox (Peru)), A/3764 (5 December 1957), 9.

has been dealt with by the European Court of Human Rights in the context of cases under Article 2 of Protocol 1 of the ECHR. The case of *Campbell and Cosans v United Kingdom*[243] was brought by two mothers who objected to the use of corporal punishment in schools. They argued that the use of corporal punishment in state-funded schools in Scotland amounted to a failure to respect their rights to ensure the education of their children in conformity with their philosophical convictions. The question therefore arose whether a belief that corporal punishment should not be used amounted to a philosophical 'conviction'. The Court found:

36. …In its ordinary meaning the word 'convictions', taken on its own, is not synonymous with the words 'opinions' and 'ideas', such as are utilised in Article 10…of the Convention, which guarantees freedom of expression; it is more akin to the term 'beliefs' (in the French text: 'convictions') appearing in Article 9…which guarantees freedom of thought, conscience and religion—and denotes views that attain a certain level of cogency, seriousness, cohesion and importance.

As regards the adjective 'philosophical', it is not capable of exhaustive definition and little assistance as to its precise significance is to be gleaned from the *travaux préparatoires*. The Commission pointed out that the word 'philosophy' bears numerous meanings: it is used to allude to a fully-fledged system of thought or, rather loosely, to views on more or less trivial matters. The Court agrees with the Commission that neither of these two extremes can be adopted for the purposes of interpreting Article 2 (P1-2): the former would too narrowly restrict the scope of a right that is guaranteed to all parents and the latter might result in the inclusion of matters of insufficient weight or substance.

Having regard to the Convention as a whole…the expression 'philosophical convictions' in the present context denotes, in the Court's opinion, such convictions as are worthy of respect in a 'democratic society'…and are not incompatible with human dignity; in addition, they must not conflict with the fundamental right of the child to education, the whole of Article 2 (P1-2) being dominated by its first sentence…

The applicants' views relate to a weighty and substantial aspect of human life and behaviour, namely the integrity of the person, the propriety or otherwise of the infliction of corporal punishment and the exclusion of the distress which the risk of such punishment entails. They are views which satisfy each of the various criteria listed above; it is this that distinguishes them from opinions that might be held on other methods of discipline or on discipline in general.

Article 13(3) does not refer to 'philosophical convictions', but rather to 'religious and moral education' in accordance with parents' 'convictions'. Nonetheless, the case law of the European Court of Human Rights on the issue of what constitutes a 'conviction' should be relevant to the interpretation of Article 13(3).

In relation to the meaning of 'religious convictions', the jurisprudence of the European Court of Human Rights is again useful. In the case of *Valsamis v Greece*,[244] the Court equated 'religious convictions' with the beliefs associated

[243] *Campbell and Cosans v UK*.
[244] *Valsamis v Greece* (App. 21787/93), 18 December 1996, (1997) 24 EHRR 294.

with a 'known religion'.[245] On the question of what constitutes a religion, the Human Rights Committee's General Comment No. 22 on the right to freedom of thought, conscience and religion[246] is also instructive:

Article 18 protects theistic, non-theistic and atheistic beliefs, as well as the right not to profess any religion or belief. The terms 'belief' and 'religion' are to be broadly construed. Article 18 is not limited in its application to traditional religions or to religions and beliefs with institutional characteristics or practices analogous to those of traditional religions. The Committee therefore views with concern any tendency to discriminate against any religion or belief for any reason, including the fact that they are newly established, or represent religious minorities that may be the subject of hostility on the part of a predominant religious community.[247]

PARTICULAR ISSUES

Curriculum

One of the main issues which arises in relation to the liberty of parents to ensure the religious and moral education of children in accordance with their convictions concerns the curriculum used in schools for the teaching of religion and related subjects. General Comment No. 13 provides as follows:

Article 13(3) has two elements, one of which is that States parties undertake to respect the liberty of parents and guardians to ensure the religious and moral education of their children in conformity with their own convictions. The Committee is of the view that this element of article 13(3) permits public school instruction in subjects such as the general history of religions and ethics if it is given in an unbiased and objective way, respectful of the freedoms of opinion, conscience and expression. It notes that public education that includes instruction in a particular religion or belief is inconsistent with article 13(3) unless provision is made for non-discriminatory exemptions or alternatives that would accommodate the wishes of parents and guardians.[248]

Similarly, according to the Human Rights Committee's General Comment No. 22:

The Committee is of the view that article 18.4 permits public school instruction in subjects such as the general history of religions and ethics if it is given in a neutral and objective way. The liberty of parents or legal guardians to ensure that their children receive a religious and moral education in conformity with their own convictions, set forth in article 18.4, is related to the guarantees of the freedom to teach a religion or belief stated in article 18.1. The Committee notes that public education that includes instruction in a particular religion or belief is inconsistent with article 18.4 unless provision is made for non-discriminatory exemptions or alternatives that would accommodate the wishes of parents and guardians.[249]

[245] *Valsamis v Greece*, [26].

[246] Human Rights Committee, General Comment No. 22, The right to freedom of thought, conscience and religion (Article 18), CCPR/C/21/Rev.1/Add.4 (30 July 1993).

[247] Human Rights Committee, General Comment No. 22, [2].

[248] CESCR, General Comment No. 13, [28].

[249] Human Rights Committee, General Comment No. 22, [6].

This issue has not been raised directly before the CESCR. However, guidance as to the approach the Committee may take can be gained from the jurisprudence of the European Court of Human Rights. The leading case on this issue is that of *Kjeldsen, Busk Madsen and Pedersen v Denmark*,[250] which concerned legislation introducing compulsory sex education in schools in Denmark. The case was brought by parents who argued that this infringed their right to ensure education and teaching in conformity with their religious and philosophical convictions. In considering the scope of the second sentence of Article 2 of Protocol 1, the Court found that the essence of this provision was to ensure pluralism in education and to protect against indoctrination:

50. …The second sentence of Article 2 (P1-2) aims in short at safeguarding the possibility of pluralism in education which possibility is essential for the preservation of the 'democratic society' as conceived by the Convention. In view of the power of the modern State, it is above all through State teaching that this aim must be realised.

…

53. [T]he setting and planning of the curriculum fall in principle within the competence of the Contracting States. This mainly involves questions of expediency on which it is not for the Court to rule and whose solution may legitimately vary according to the country and the era. In particular, the second sentence of Article 2 of the Protocol (P1-2) does not prevent States from imparting through teaching or education information or knowledge of a directly or indirectly religious or philosophical kind. It does not even permit parents to object to the integration of such teaching or education in the school curriculum, for otherwise all institutionalised teaching would run the risk of proving impracticable. In fact, it seems very difficult for many subjects taught at school not to have, to a greater or lesser extent, some philosophical complexion or implications. The same is true of religious affinities if one remembers the existence of religions forming a very broad dogmatic and moral entity which has or may have answers to every question of a philosophical, cosmological or moral nature.

The second sentence of Article 2 (P1-2) implies on the other hand that the State, in fulfilling the functions assumed by it in regard to education and teaching, must take care that information or knowledge included in the curriculum is conveyed in an objective, critical and pluralistic manner. The State is forbidden to pursue an aim of indoctrination that might be considered as not respecting parents' religious and philosophical convictions. That is the limit that must not be exceeded.

Applying this approach to the facts of the case, the Court found that there was no violation of the right to education:

54. …[T]he Danish State, by providing children in good time with explanations it considers useful, is attempting to warn them against phenomena it views as disturbing, for example, the excessive frequency of births out of wedlock, induced abortions and venereal diseases. The public authorities wish to enable pupils, when the time comes, 'to take care of themselves and show consideration for others in that respect', 'not…[to] land themselves or others in difficulties solely on account of lack of knowledge'…

These considerations are indeed of a moral order, but they are very general in character and do not entail overstepping the bounds of what a democratic State may regard as the public

[250] *Kjeldsen, Busk Madsen and Pedersen v Denmark*, 7 December 1976, (1976) 1 EHRR 711.

interest. Examination of the legislation in dispute establishes in fact that it in no way amounts to an attempt at indoctrination aimed at advocating a specific kind of sexual behaviour. It does not make a point of exalting sex or inciting pupils to indulge precociously in practices that are dangerous for their stability, health or future or that many parents consider reprehensible. Further, it does not affect the right of parents to enlighten and advise their children, to exercise with regard to their children natural parental functions as educators, or to guide their children on a path in line with the parents' own religious or philosophical convictions.

Certainly, abuses can occur as to the manner in which the provisions in force are applied by a given school or teacher and the competent authorities have a duty to take the utmost care to see to it that parents' religious and philosophical convictions are not disregarded at this level by carelessness, lack of judgment or misplaced proselytism. However, it follows from the Commission's decisions on the admissibility of the applications that the Court is not at present seised of a problem of this kind…

The Court consequently reaches the conclusion that the disputed legislation in itself in no way offends the applicants' religious and philosophical convictions to the extent forbidden by the second sentence of Article 2 of the Protocol (P1-2), interpreted in the light of its first sentence and of the whole of the Convention.

Besides, the Danish State preserves an important expedient for parents who, in the name of their creed or opinions, wish to dissociate their children from integrated sex education; it allows parents either to entrust their children to private schools, which are bound by less strict obligations and moreover heavily subsidised by the State (paragraphs 15, 18 and 34 above), or to educate them or have them educated at home, subject to suffering the undeniable sacrifices and inconveniences caused by recourse to one of those alternative solutions.

The opposite conclusion was reached in the case of *Folgerø v Norway*,[251] which concerned the compulsory teaching of a subject on Christianity, religion and philosophy ('KRL') in Norwegian schools. The curriculum was weighted in favour of study of Christianity, and a number of parents, members of the Norwegian Humanist Association, objected that this violated their rights under Article 2 of Protocol 1. Although there was the possibility of obtaining a partial exemption from the subject, for lessons involving instruction in Christianity, the parents argued that they should be able to obtain full exemption from the subject for their children. The Court found that there was 'a clear preponderance of Christianity in the composition of the subject'.[252] The Court then continued:

96. The question then arises whether the imbalance highlighted above could be said to have been brought to a level acceptable under Article 2 of Protocol No. 1 by the possibility for pupils to request partial exemption from the KRL subject under section 2–4(4) of the Education Act 1998. Under this provision '[a] pupil shall, on the submission of a written parental note, be granted exemption from those parts of the teaching in the particular school concerned that they, from the point of view of their own religion or philosophy of life, consider as amounting to the practice of another religion or adherence to another philosophy of life'.

…

[251] *Folgerø et al v Norway* (App. 15472/02) ECtHR 29 June 2007.
[252] *Folgerø v Norway*, [91].

97. In this connection the Court notes that the operation of the partial-exemption arrangement presupposed, firstly, that the parents concerned be adequately informed of the details of the lesson plans to be able to identify and notify to the school in advance those parts of the teaching that would be incompatible with their own convictions and beliefs. This could be a challenging task…

98. Secondly…it was a condition for obtaining partial exemption that the parents give reasonable grounds for their request…[I]nherent in the condition to give reasonable grounds was a risk that the parents might feel compelled to disclose to the school authorities intimate aspects of their own religious and philosophical convictions. The risk of such compulsion was all the more present in view of the difficulties highlighted above for parents in identifying the parts of the teaching that they considered as amounting to the practice of another religion or adherence to another philosophy of life. In addition, the question whether a request for exemption was reasonable was apparently a potential breeding ground for conflict, a situation that parents might prefer simply to avoid by not expressing a wish for exemption.

99. Thirdly, the Court observes that even in the event that a parental note requesting partial exemption was deemed reasonable, this did not necessarily mean that the pupil concerned would be exempted from the part of the curriculum in question…

100. In the light of the above, the Court finds that the system of partial exemption was capable of subjecting the parents concerned to a heavy burden with a risk of undue exposure of their private life and that the potential for conflict was likely to deter them from making such requests…

102. Against this background, notwithstanding the many laudable legislative purposes stated in connection with the introduction of the KRL subject in the ordinary primary and lower secondary schools, it does not appear that the respondent State took sufficient care that information and knowledge included in the curriculum be conveyed in an objective, critical and pluralistic manner for the purposes of Article 2 of Protocol No. 1.

Accordingly, the Court finds that the refusal to grant the applicant parents full exemption from the KRL subject for their children gave rise to a violation of Article 2 of Protocol No. 1.

The Court reached similar conclusions in the case of *Zengin v Turkey*,[253] which concerned compulsory classes in religious culture and ethics which were based on the teaching of Sunni Islam, and for which the applicants, as followers of the Alevi Islamic faith, were unable to obtain exemption.

Other

Again, in the absence of direct consideration by the Committee, the jurisprudence of the European Court is useful for exploring the relevant issues. The display of religious symbols in schools was considered in the case of *Lautsi v Italy*,[254] which concerned the display of crucifixes in classrooms in state schools. In that case, the Court acknowledged that:

[I]t is true that by prescribing the presence of crucifixes in State-school classrooms—a sign which, whether or not it is accorded in addition a secular symbolic value, undoubtedly

[253] *Hasan and Eylem Zengin v Turkey* (App. 1448/04), 9 October 2007, (2008) 46 EHRR 44.
[254] *Lautsi et al v Italy* (App. 30814/06), 18 March 2011, (2012) 54 EHRR 3.

refers to Christianity—the regulations confer on the country's majority religion preponderant visibility in the school environment.[255]

However, the Court went on to note that:

71. ... That is not in itself sufficient, however, to denote a process of indoctrination on the respondent State's part and establish a breach of the requirements of Article 2 of Protocol No. 1.

...

72. [A] crucifix on a wall is an essentially passive symbol... It cannot be deemed to have an influence on pupils comparable to that of didactic speech or participation in religious activities...

...

74. Moreover, the effects of the greater visibility which the presence of the crucifix gives to Christianity in schools needs to be further placed in perspective by consideration of the following points. Firstly, the presence of crucifixes is not associated with compulsory teaching about Christianity... Secondly, according to the indications provided by the Government Italy opens up the school environment in parallel to other religions. The Government indicated in this connection that it was not forbidden for pupils to wear Islamic headscarves or other symbols or apparel having a religious connotation; alternative arrangements were possible to help schooling fit in with non-majority religious practices; the beginning and end of Ramadan were 'often celebrated' in schools; and optional religious education could be organised in schools for 'all recognised religious creeds'... Moreover, there was nothing to suggest that the authorities were intolerant of pupils who believed in other religions, were non-believers or who held non-religious philosophical convictions.

In addition, the applicants did not assert that the presence of the crucifix in classrooms had encouraged the development of teaching practices with a proselytising tendency, or claim that the second and third applicants had ever experienced a tendentious reference to that presence by a teacher in the exercise of his or her functions.

75. Lastly, the Court notes that the first applicant retained in full her right as a parent to enlighten and advise her children, to exercise in their regard her natural functions as educator and to guide them on a path in line with her own philosophical convictions...

76. It follows from the foregoing that, in deciding to keep crucifixes in the classrooms of the State school attended by the first applicant's children, the authorities acted within the limits of the margin of appreciation left to the respondent State in the context of its obligation to respect, in the exercise of the functions it assumes in relation to education and teaching, the right of parents to ensure such education and teaching in conformity with their own religious and philosophical convictions.

The Court therefore granted a significant margin of appreciation to the state, suggesting that findings of a violation of the right to education on the basis of religious matters not relating to school curriculum may be limited. This certainly reflects the position in the case of *Valsamis v Greece*.[256] In that case, the Court

[255] *Lautsi et al v Italy*, [71].

[256] *Valsamis v Greece* (App. 21787/93), 18 December 1996, (1997) 24 EHRR 294.

found no violation of Article 2 of Protocol 1 where the daughter of Jehovah's Witnesses was punished by her school for not attending a school parade for Greek National Day, although attending such a parade would be contrary to the religious beliefs of Jehovah's Witnesses. The Court found that there was nothing in the requirement to attend the parade that 'could offend the applicants' pacifist convictions to an extent prohibited by the second sentence of Article 2 of Protocol 1'.[257]

Article 13(4)

Article 13(4) protects the right of individuals and bodies to establish private schools. It was not included in the original draft of the Covenant submitted by the Commission on Human Rights, but was added later as:

> The view was expressed that, while paragraph 3 acknowledged the existence of private schools, the article should explicitly recognize, in a new paragraph, the liberty of individuals and bodies to establish and direct educational institutions.[258]

Article 13(4) therefore needs to be read in conjunction with Article 13(3), which protects the right of parents to choose private schools for their children, discussed above.[259]

The right to establish private schools has a long history in international law. It can be traced to the inter-war minorities treaties and in this context was affirmed by the Permanent Court of International Justice.[260] It is thus closely associated with the rights of minorities in relation to education, as discussed above (although, as expressed in the ICESCR, the right applies equally to all). The right to establish private schools is recognized in many international instruments, including the UNESCO Convention against Discrimination in Education, Article 5(c) (with respect to minorities); Article 14(3) of the Charter of Fundamental Rights of the European Union; Article 13(5) of the San Salvador Protocol to the American Convention on Human Rights; and Article 17(7) of the African Charter on the Rights and Welfare of the Child. Although it is not explicitly recognized in Article 2 of Protocol 1 of the ECHR, the European Commission of Human Rights has interpreted the Article as including a right to establish private schools: see *Ingrid Jordebo Foundation of Christians Schools and Ingrid Jordebo v Sweden*.[261]

[257] *Valsamis v Greece*, [31].

[258] UNGA, Draft International Covenants on Human Rights: Report of the Third Committee (Rapporteur Mr Carlos Manuel Cox (Peru)), A/3764 (5 December 1957), 10.

[259] CESCR, General Comment No. 13, [29].

[260] See, eg, *Minority Schools in Albania*, Advisory Opinion, [1935] PCIJ (ser. A/B) No. 64.

[261] *Ingrid Jordebo Foundation of Christians Schools and Ingrid Jordebo v Sweden*, 51 DR 125 (1987).

Article 13(4) has been interpreted by the Committee as follows, according to General Comment No. 13:

29. The second element of article 13(3) is the liberty of parents and guardians to choose other than public schools for their children, provided the schools conform to 'such minimum educational standards as may be laid down or approved by the State'. This has to be read with the complementary provision, article 13(4), which affirms 'the liberty of individuals and bodies to establish and direct educational institutions', provided the institutions conform to the educational objectives set out in article 13(1) and certain minimum standards. These minimum standards may relate to issues such as admission, curricula and the recognition of certificates. In their turn, these standards must be consistent with the educational objectives set out in article 13(1).

30. Under article 13(4), everyone, including non-nationals, has the liberty to establish and direct educational institutions. The liberty also extends to 'bodies', i.e. legal persons or entities. It includes the right to establish and direct all types of educational institutions, including nurseries, universities and institutions for adult education. Given the principles of non-discrimination, equal opportunity and effective participation in society for all, the State has an obligation to ensure that the liberty set out in article 13(4) does not lead to extreme disparities of educational opportunity for some groups in society.

It is clear from the *travaux préparatoires* that Article 13 does not 'imply an obligation for the States Parties to grant material assistance to private schools'.[262] However, if the state chooses to fund private schools, it must do so on a non-discriminatory basis, in line with its other obligations under Article 13 and Article 2(2) of the Covenant and under other provisions of international law. Thus, in a case which concerned Canada's provision of public funding to Roman Catholic schools but not schools of other faiths, such as Jewish schools, the Human Rights Committee found that:

[T]he Covenant does not oblige States parties to fund schools which are established on a religious basis. However, if a State party chooses to provide public funding to religious schools, it should make this funding available without discrimination.[263]

This issue was also considered by the Supreme Court of Mauritius in the case of *Tengur v The Minister of Education and Another*.[264] The case concerned the fact

[262] UNGA, Draft International Covenants on Human Rights: Report of the Third Committee (Rapporteur Mr Carlos Manuel Cox (Peru)), A/3764 (5 December 1957), 9. It is also clear that there is no obligation on the state to establish schools of a particular type. This latter issue arose in a case before the South African Constitutional Court, *Gauteng Provincial Legislature In re: Gauteng School Education Bill of 1995* (CCT39/95), 4 April 1996, 1996 (3) SA 165, which concerned the equivalent provision of the interim South African Constitution, section 32(c), which provided that 'every person shall have the right to establish, where practicable, educational institutions based on a common culture, language or religion'. The petitioners argued that this meant that every person could demand from the state the right to have established schools based on a common culture, language or religion. However, the Court rejected this interpretation of section 32(c), taking into account the position under international law (see, in particular, the judgment of Justice Sachs), which, it found, simply permitted members of minority groups to establish their own schools.

[263] Human Rights Committee, *Arieh Hollis Waldman v Canada*, Communication No. 694/1996, CCPR/C/67/D/694/1996 (5 November 1999), [10.6].

[264] Record No. 77387, Supreme Court of Mauritius, 2002 SCJ 48.

that 50 per cent of places in Roman Catholic secondary schools were reserved for Catholics, although the schools were funded by the state. The Supreme Court of Mauritius interpreted the relevant provisions of the Mauritian Constitution in light of Article 13 of the ICESCR, and found that the measures in question constituted unlawful discrimination against non-Catholics. On appeal, the decision was affirmed by the Privy Council.[265]

Similarly, the CESCR has suggested that, in the case of minority schools, states may need to take positive measures to support such schools (presumably in order to realize the objective of non-discrimination). So, for example, in relation to Japan:

> The Committee...recommends that the State party officially recognize minority schools, in particular Korean schools, when they comply with the national education curriculum, and consequently make available to them subsidies and other financial assistance, and also recognize their school leaving certificates as university entrance examination qualifications.[266]

Further, where states choose to fund private schools, it is important that this does not lead to discrimination, in terms of quality of education, between public and private schools. In this context, the Committee has expressed concern about the general phenomenon of privatization of education and the effect of this on equality of access to educational opportunities. Thus, in relation to Italy, the Committee has noted:

> With regard to the public funding of private schools, the Committee reminds the State party that any such funding must be without discrimination on any of the prohibited grounds.[267]

Similarly, in relation to Australia:

> The Committee is concerned about the effects of funding accorded to non-government schools on the quality of education in government schools.[268]

Conclusion

The broad scope of Article 13, and the detailed nature of its provisions, reflects the importance accorded to the right to education within international law and policy. Unlike many other economic, social and cultural rights, the right to education has generated significant jurisprudence, largely as a result of the fact that it is justiciable within the framework of the ECHR system, as well as within various national legal systems. In interpreting Article 13, guidance is therefore to be obtained not only from General Comment No. 13 and Concluding Observations

[265] *Bishop of Roman Catholic Diocese of Port Louis v S. Tengur*, 3 February 2004, Privy Council Appeal No. 21 of 2003.
[266] CESCR, Concluding Observations: Japan, E/C.12/1/Add.67 (24 September 2001), [60].
[267] CESCR, Concluding Observations: Italy, E/C.12/1/Add.43 (23 May 2000), [35].
[268] CESCR, Concluding Observations: Australia, E/C.12/1993/9 (3 June 1993), [10].

of the Committee, but also from the jurisprudence, and in particular, decisions of the European Court of Human Rights.

This body of material suggests that Article 13 is likely to be a fertile ground for individual complaints under the Optional Protocol. This is particularly so with respect to Articles 13(3) and (4), which are not subject to progressive realization and impose clear obligations on states to guarantee individuals' rights in relation to education. This is to be welcomed for, in the words of the Special Rapporteur:

> The enjoyment of the right to education is often least accessible to those who need it most—disadvantaged and marginalized groups and, above all, children from poor families. It therefore requires enforcement in case of its breaches or violations…As such, the Special Rapporteur would like to underline the important role that adjudication plays in the effective realization of the right to education, and in ensuring that it is given effect to. He considers it vital to improve access to justice for all those whose right to education is not fully protected and respected.[269]

[269] Human Rights Council, Report of the Special Rapporteur on the right to education on justiciability of the right to education, A/HRC/23/35 (10 May 2013), [2]–[3].

16

Article 14: Implementation of the Right to Free, Compulsory Primary Education

Article 14

Each State Party to the present Covenant which, at the time of becoming a Party, has not been able to secure in its metropolitan territory or other territories under its jurisdiction compulsory primary education, free of charge, undertakes, within two years, to work out and adopt a detailed plan of action for the progressive implementation, within a reasonable number of years, to be fixed in the plan, of the principle of compulsory education free of charge for all.

Article 14 is an unusual provision, in that it does not set out the content of a right, but rather provides for the implementation of the right to free, compulsory primary education contained in Article 13(2)(a). Article 14 requires states which have not been able to secure free, compulsory primary education to all within their jurisdiction to adopt a detailed plan of action to ensure the progressive implementation of this right.

Background

It is clear from the *travaux préparatoires* that the drafters of the Covenant were aware that Article 14 was 'unique and exceptional in comparison with the other provisions of the draft Covenant, since it defined a method of giving effect to the right to education proclaimed in the preceding Article'.[1] However, it was felt that

[1] UNGA Third Committee, A/C.3/SR.789, 23 October 1957, 138 (France).

the inclusion of Article 14 in the Covenant was warranted 'in view of the basic importance of the right to education'.[2]

A number of objections were raised to the inclusion of the Article.[3] The objections were summarized by the representative of the United Nations Educational, Scientific and Cultural Organization (UNESCO) as follows:

The criticisms of substance were of three kinds: legal objections, practical objections and objections from the point of view of international action... From the legal point of view, it had been maintained that... [Article 14] conflicted with the principle of progressive implementation, which was implicit in the draft Covenant and explicit in [Article 13]... On practical grounds, it had been objected that if States were obliged to adopt a plan, they might find that it was too rigid... From the point of view of international action, it had been objected that UNESCO was... dealing with the question... [There was also a] contention that technical assistance was preferable to educational planning...[4]

The response to these objections underlines the drafters' view of the critical importance of the right to education. According to the French representative:

15. ... However exceptional it might be, it [Article 14] was nevertheless justified by certain practical reasons which the opponents of the Article had themselves advanced. If the percentage of illiteracy in the world was as high as it was said to be, it was not a bad idea to show, by adopting a provision which would be somewhat more binding on the States parties to the Covenant, that there was a firm resolve to persevere systematically in the anti-illiteracy campaign.

16. However, that was not the only or even the strongest argument which could be advanced in favour of including... [Article 14]. The Commission on Human Rights had considered that the draft Covenant on Economic, Social and Cultural Rights was, to a large extent, a program of future action which should contain a general definition of those rights but should leave it to the competent specialized agencies to give effect to each specific right. Some articles, such as that concerning social security, were very brief and contained no implementing provisions, since it had been thought that the ILO, through the facilities it had had for many years, was capable of making great efforts in that field, and was in fact already doing so. The authors of the draft, on the other hand, had considered that UNESCO, being a very young organization at the time, without such efficient methods of implementation and supervision, needed guidance in applying the articles concerning education...

18. The existing wording of... [Article 14] did not weaken the notion of progressive implementation: it completed and clarified that notion by defining the stages which must be completed in order to attain a specific goal. There was no great difficulty in determining those stages in advance in the field of education, since population statistics made it possible to predict, for example, without great risk of error, how many places would be required in schools within six years. In any case, a plan ought not to be rigid; some margin for error should be left...

[2] UNGA Third Committee, A/C.3/SR.790, 24 October 1957, 143 (UNESCO).

[3] See, eg, UNGA Third Committee, A/C.3/SR.789, 23 October 1957, 137 (United Kingdom); 138 (Australia).

[4] UNGA Third Committee, A/C.3/SR.790, 24 October 1957, 143–4 (UNESCO).

19. In conclusion...the plan provided for in [Article 14] did not constitute a rigid obligation. It was only a general plan which would reflect the willingness of each State to do only what was possible, but, in fact, to do it.[5]

Ultimately, of course, the proponents of Article 14 prevailed, and the Article was adopted by an overwhelming majority: sixty votes to three, with eight abstentions. Overall:

The majority of the representatives agreed that the fundamental character of the right to primary education justified the inclusion of a special implementation clause, even though similar provisions were not made with regard to other rights.[6]

The *travaux* thus contain numerous statements emphasizing the importance of primary education and of literacy.[7] So, for example, the representative of UNESCO noted that:

It had been maintained that it was unnecessary to include a special implementing article as no such article had been included for the other rights. The right to primary education was, however, a special case. It was a fundamental right, without which the others could hardly be exercised and it should be given priority over all other. Speaking on United Nations Day...to adopt such a principle would be a fitting way to celebrate the day.[8]

Bulgaria proposed amendments which would have extended the scope of Article 14 to adult education, by rendering states which had not achieved 'conditions of general literacy' subject to the obligation to prepare detailed plans of action for ensuring progressive implementation of the principle of free, compulsory education for all. However, this amendment was ultimately rejected, as it was 'considered likely to exceed the resources of many States'.[9] As it stands, Article 14 thus emphasizes the importance of primary education, and requires states to prioritize the provision of such education free of charge.

Context

The essence of Article 14 is that it requires states to prepare a plan for achieving free, compulsory primary education for all. This is often referred to as the goal of 'universal primary education'. This emphasis on achieving universal primary

[5] UNGA Third Committee, A/C.3/SR.789, 23 October 1957, 138–9 (France). See also UNGA Third Committee, A/C.3/SR.790, 24 October 1957, 143–4 (UNESCO).

[6] UNGA, Draft International Covenants on Human Rights: Report of the Third Committee (Rapporteur Mr Carlow Manuel Cox (Peru)), A/3764 (5 December 1957), 18.

[7] UNGA Third Committee, A/C.3/SR.789, 23 October 1957, 139 (Saudi Arabia); UNGA Third Committee, A/C.3/SR.790, 24 October 1957, 146 (Indonesia); 147–8 (Japan).

[8] UNGA Third Committee, A/C.3/SR.790, 24 October 1957, 144.

[9] UNGA, Draft International Covenants on Human Rights: Report of the Third Committee (Rapporteur Mr Carlow Manuel Cox (Peru)), A/3764 (5 December 1957), 18.

education is reflected in a range of international agreements and political commitments. For example, the second Millennium Development Goal is:

To ensure that, by... [2015], children everywhere, boys and girls alike, will be able to complete a full course of primary schooling and that girls and boys will have equal access to all levels of education.[10]

A number of other programmes and initiatives, such as the Secretary-General's Global Education First Initiative, seek to support this goal.

The World Declaration on Education for All: Meeting Basic Learning Needs,[11] provides that: 'Every person—child, youth and adult—shall be able to benefit from educational opportunities designed to meet their basic learning needs'.[12] According to Article III, paragraph 1:

Basic education should be provided to all children, youth and adults. To this end, basic education services of quality should be expanded and consistent measures must be taken to reduce disparities.

Critically, Article V notes:

The main delivery system for the basic education of children outside the family is primary schooling. Primary education must be universal, ensure that the basic learning needs of all children are satisfied, and take into account the culture, needs, and opportunities of the community.

Similarly, the 2000 Dakar Framework for Action[13] sets out specific goals for achieving education for all. According to the Commentary to the Framework, the second of those goals is to ensure that 'by 2015 all children, particularly girls, children in difficult circumstances and those belonging to ethnic minorities, have access to and complete free and compulsory primary education of good quality'. States therefore commit themselves to achieving universal primary education by 2015.[14]

The Dakar Framework for Action also provides a more recent iteration of the Article 14 obligation to draw up plans of action to achieve universal primary education. Paragraph 9 of the Framework provides as follows:

Drawing on the evidence accumulated during the national and regional EFA [Education for All] assessments, and building on existing national sector strategies, all States will be requested to develop or strengthen existing national plans of action by 2002 at the latest...The plans will address problems associated with the chronic under-financing of basic education by establishing budget priorities that reflect a commitment to achieving

[10] UNGA Res. 55/2, United Nations Millennium Declaration, A/RES/55/2 (18 September 2000), [19].

[11] World Conference on Education for All: Meeting Basic Learning Needs, World Declaration on Education for All and Framework for Action to Meet Basic Learning Needs ('World Declaration on Education for All'), Jomtien, Thailand, 5–9 March 1990.

[12] World Declaration on Education for All, Article I, [1].

[13] World Education Forum, The Dakar Framework for Action: Education for All: Meeting Our Collective Commitments, Dakar, Senegal, 26–8 April 2000 ('The Dakar Framework for Action').

[14] The Dakar Framework for Action: Expanded Commentary, 15–16 [32]–[33].

EFA goals and targets at the earliest possible date, and no later than 2015. They will also set out clear strategies for overcoming the special problems facing those currently excluded from educational opportunities…

This obligation reinforces that assumed by states under Article 14. Thus, in its Concluding Observations, the CESCR often ties states' obligations under Article 14 to the obligations which they have assumed under the Dakar Framework. So, for example, in relation to Venezuela:

The Committee recommends that the State party implement, with the assistance of the United Nations Educational, Scientific and Cultural Organization, a comprehensive National Education for All Plan as required by the Dakar Framework for Action, and to reflect in the Plan Articles 13 and 14 of the Covenant and the Committee's General Comments 11 and 13.[15]

Similarly, in relation to Nepal:

The State party is urged to adopt a comprehensive National Education for All (EFA) Plan, as anticipated by paragraph 16 of the Dakar Framework for Action. When formulating and implementing its EFA Plan, the State party is urged to take into account the Committee's General Comments Nos. 11 and 13 and General Comment No. 1 of the Committee on the Rights of the Child, and to establish an effective monitoring system for the Plan. The State party is also encouraged to continue the technical advice and assistance from UNESCO in relation to both the formulation and implementation of its EFA Plan.[16]

The broader international legal and policy framework is also relevant to interpreting the scope of Article 14. As noted above in relation to Article 13, the term 'primary education' is not defined in the Covenant. However, in light of these later instruments and frameworks, primary education must be understood as encompassing 'basic education', as provided in the World Declaration on Education for All.[17]

Interpretation and Application by the CESCR

GENERAL

The obligation contained in Article 14 is clearly an obligation of conduct, perhaps the clearest example of an obligation of conduct contained in the Covenant. Article 14 requires states to adopt a detailed plan of action for the progressive implementation of free, compulsory primary education. The Committee has given guidance on what this involves in its General Comment No. 11:

8. Adoption of a detailed plan. The State party is required to adopt a plan of action within two years. This must be interpreted as meaning within two years of the Covenant's entry into force

[15] CESCR, Concluding Observations: Venezuela, E/C.12/1/Add.56 (21 May 2001), [30].

[16] CESCR, Concluding Observations: Nepal, E/C.12/1/Add.66 (24 September 2001), [58]. See also CESCR, Concluding Observations: Yemen, E/C.12/1/Add.92 (12 December 2003), [43]; Nigeria, E/C.12/1/Add.23 (16 June 1998), [41]; Senegal, E/C.12/1/Add.62 (24 September 2001), [59]; Syrian Arab Republic, E/C.12/1/Add.63 (24 September 2001), [44].

[17] World Declaration on Education for All, Article 1(1).

of the State concerned, or within two years of a subsequent change in circumstances which has led to the non-observance of the relevant obligation. This obligation is a continuing one and States parties to which the provision is relevant by virtue of the prevailing situation are not absolved from the obligation as a result of their past failure to act within the two year limit. The plan must cover all of the actions which are necessary in order to secure each of the requisite component parts of the right and must be sufficiently detailed so as to ensure the comprehensive realization of the right. Participation of all sections of civil society in the drawing up of the plan is vital and some means of periodically reviewing progress and ensuring accountability are essential. Without those elements, the significance of the article would be undermined.

…

10. Progressive implementation. The plan of action must be aimed at securing the progressive implementation of the right to compulsory primary education, free of charge, under article 14. Unlike the provision in article 2.1, however, article 14 specifies that the target date must be 'within a reasonable number of years' and moreover, that the timeframe must 'be fixed in the plan'. In other words, the plan must specifically set out a series of targeted implementation dates for each stage of the progressive implementation of the plan. This underscores both the importance and the relative inflexibility of the obligation in question. Moreover, it needs to be stressed in this regard that the State party's other obligations, such as non-discrimination, are required to be implemented fully and immediately.[18]

A particular issue arises as to whether states which have provided for free, compulsory primary education in their legislation, but have not been able to implement it in practice, are required to undertake the measures set out in Article 14. It is clear from the *travaux* that the drafters intended Article 14, and the obligations contained therein, to apply in this situation. According to the representative of UNESCO:

To the question whether the obligation to work out a plan would apply to States which had not yet been able to put the principle of compulsory primary education fully into effect, although they had passed legislation on the subject, UNESCO had replied that the Article should be interpreted as applying to all States which had not yet succeeded in making primary education free and compulsory, whether or not they had passed legislation on the subject.[19]

This interpretation is also evident in the Committee's Concluding Observations, and translates into a broader concern, on the part of the Committee, with situations where 'the principle of free primary education guaranteed by law is not always applied'.[20] So, for example, in relation to India, the Committee 'urges the State party to continue to make determined efforts to achieve universal primary education'[21] as:

The Committee is concerned that, despite the efforts made by the State party to achieve universal primary education, including the adoption of the Constitution (86th Amendment) Act in 2002 which makes the right to primary education a fundamental right, and the 'Sarva Shikasha Abhiyan' (Education for All) program, aimed at achieving 100% primary enrolment, the wide disparity in enrolment and dropout rates in primary school continue to

[18] CESCR, General Comment No. 11, Plans of action for primary education (Article 14), E/C.12/1999/4 (10 May 1999) ('General Comment No. 11'), [8] and [10].

[19] UNGA Third Committee, A/C.3/SR.790, 24 October 1957, 143 (UNESCO).

[20] CESCR, Concluding Observations: Guinea, E/C.12/1/Add.5 (28 May 1996), [23].

[21] CESCR, Concluding Observations: India, E/C.12/IND/CO/5 (8 August 2008), [40].

persist, negatively affecting, in particular, girls, Muslim children and children belonging to scheduled castes and scheduled tribes.[22]

It is clear that the key obligation under Article 14 is to 'adopt a detailed plan', and the Committee frequently reminds states in which free, compulsory primary education is not secured of their obligations in this respect. So, for example, in relation to Zimbabwe:

The Committee reminds the State party that, as a signatory to the Covenant, it is committed to ensure compulsory, free primary education to all children in Zimbabwe…[T]he Committee invites Zimbabwe to submit to it within a year a plan of action and a progress report as to the implementation of this obligation.[23]

In terms of the content of the plan, the General Comment provides that the plan 'must cover all of the actions which are necessary in order to secure each of the requisite component parts of the right'.[24] Further guidance as to the sorts of matters which should be covered can be obtained from the Committee's Concluding Observations. Thus, in relation to Nepal, the Committee has stressed the importance of 'concrete benchmarks through which progress can be measured'.[25]

The Committee's Concluding Observations on Brazil in relation to Article 13(2)(a) are also instructive in terms of the sorts of steps which the Committee considers states should take in planning for universal primary education:

The Committee is concerned that 43% of children between 7 and 14 years of age do not complete the eighth grade of basic education at the proper age, despite the State party's efforts to ensure the provision of compulsory elementary education free of charge and its programs to encourage parents and caregivers to enrol young children in primary school…The Committee recommends that the State party:

(a) conduct a study to establish the full range of factors which contribute to children failing to complete primary school at the proper age;

(b) draw up policies and implement strategies to address the factors identified;

(c) include, in its next periodic report, information on the measures taken under subparagraphs (a) and (b) above and any progress achieved.[26]

'COMPULSORY'

On the meaning of the requirement that primary education be 'compulsory', General Comment No. 11 provides as follows:

6. Compulsory. The element of compulsion serves to highlight the fact that neither parents, nor guardians, nor the State are entitled to treat as optional the decision as to whether the child

[22] CESCR, Concluding Observations: India, E/C.12/IND/CO/5 (8 August 2008), [40].
[23] CESCR, Concluding Observations: Zimbabwe, E/C.12/1/Add.12 (20 May 1997), [22].
[24] CESCR, General Comment No. 11, [8].
[25] CESCR, Concluding Observations: Nepal, E/C.12/NPL/CO/2 (16 January 2008), [47]. See also CESCR, Concluding Observations: Colombia, E/C.12/1/Add.74 (6 December 2001), [48]; Gambia, E/C.12/1994/9 (31 May 1994), [17]; Zambia, E/C.12/1/Add.106 (23 June 2005), [54].
[26] CESCR, Concluding Observations: Brazil, E/C.12/BRA/CO/2 (12 June 2009), [31].

should have access to primary education. Similarly, the prohibition of gender discrimination in access to education, required also by articles 2 and 3 of the Covenant, is further underlined by this requirement. It should be emphasized, however, that the education offered must be adequate in quality, relevant to the child and must promote the realization of the child's other rights.

The Committee's Concluding Observations indicate that the Committee is concerned where this requirement of Article 14 is not satisfied, even if primary education is free of charge. Thus, in relation to Nepal, the Committee has noted 'with concern that the State party has yet to adopt a policy of compulsory education'[27] and:

The Committee calls upon the State party to introduce not only free but also compulsory education, in conformity with Articles 13 and 14 of the Covenant, and to specify in its third periodic report by when it plans to achieve this.[28]

It is clear that the Committee envisages the 'element of compulsion' in relation to 'compulsory' education as being provided for by legislation. Thus, in relation to Saint Vincent and the Grenadines:

Concerning the right to education, the Committee notes with concern that, as mentioned by the State party in its report to CEDAW, there is no legal requirement that children attend school.[29]

Legislation providing for compulsory education should also stipulate ages for admission to, and completion of, primary education, as the Committee noted in its Concluding Observations in relation to Kuwait:

25. The Committee is concerned that ages for admission and completion of free compulsory primary to intermediate education have not been clearly set.

…

45. The Committee recommends that the State party set ages for admission to, and completion of, free compulsory primary to intermediate education. In this regard, the Committee refers the State party to its General Comment No. 11 (1999)…[30]

'FREE'

General Comment No. 11 gives the following guidance on the meaning of 'free of charge':

7. Free of charge. The nature of this requirement is unequivocal. The right is expressly formulated so as to ensure the availability of primary education without charge to the child, parents or guardians. Fees imposed by the Government, the local authorities or the school, and other direct costs, constitute disincentives to the enjoyment of the right and may jeopardize its realization. They are also often highly regressive in effect. Their elimination is a matter which must be addressed by the required plan of action. Indirect costs, such as compulsory levies on parents (sometimes portrayed as being voluntary, when in fact they are

[27] CESCR, Concluding Observations: Nepal, E/C.12/NPL/CO/2 (16 January 2008), [27].

[28] CESCR, Concluding Observations: Nepal, E/C.12/NPL/CO/2 (16 January 2008), [47]. See also, eg, CESCR, Concluding Observations: Solomon Islands, E/C.12/1/Add.84 (19 December 2002), [14].

[29] CESCR, Concluding Observations: Saint Vincent and the Grenadines, E/C.12/1/Add.21 (2 December 1997), [27].

[30] CESCR, Concluding Observations: Kuwait, E/C.12/1/Add.98 (7 June 2004), [26] and [45].

not), or the obligation to wear a relatively expensive school uniform, can also fall into the same category. Other indirect costs may be permissible, subject to the Committee's examination on a case-by-case basis. This provision of compulsory primary education in no way conflicts with the right recognized in article 13.3 of the Covenant for parents and guardians 'to choose for their children schools other than those established by the public authorities'.

It is clear from this statement from the Committee that providing education 'free of charge' requires the elimination of both direct and indirect costs associated with education. In relation to direct costs, the Committee's Concluding Observations on Cameroon are indicative of the Committee's general approach:

27. The Committee notes with deep concern that there is no legislation in Cameroon which provides for free primary education. The Committee regrets the requirement of a parental contribution in the form of compulsory fees levied by primary schools which, in view of high levels of poverty, greatly restrict access to primary education, particularly for girls.

...

43. The Committee recommends that the Government take effective measures to end all forms of compulsory parental contribution for primary education. In this regard, the Committee urges the State party to allocate increased resources to education, in particular for infrastructure and human resources, especially in rural areas...[31]

The Committee has also expressed concern about situations where schools levy 'unofficial fees'. Thus, in relation to Cambodia:

The Committee notes with concern that low salaries are considered to be one of the reasons for the continuation of the collection of unofficial fees in many schools.[32]

In relation to indirect costs, the Committee has noted, for example, in relation to Georgia:

26. ...The Committee is concerned that, although primary education should be provided free of charge, as stipulated by law and in Article 14 of the Covenant, parents are faced with payments for various purposes....

45. The Committee recommends that the State party undertake measures to ensure that access to free primary education is not impeded in reality by additional material costs and by informal fees.[33]

The Committee has expressed concern about a range of indirect costs including 'the cost of textbooks, stationery and teaching materials [which] is unaffordable for many parents and makes primary education inaccessible to many'.[34] So, for example, in relation to Colombia:

The Committee is concerned that access to free and compulsory education is not fully ensured, as families continue to pay for the provision of educational services such as

[31] CESCR, Concluding Observations: Cameroon, E/C.12/1/Add.40 (8 December 1999), [27] and [43]. See also, eg, CESCR, Concluding Observations: Democratic Republic of the Congo, E/C.12/COD/CO/4 (16 December 2009), [35].

[32] CESCR, Concluding Observations: Cambodia, E/C.12/KHM/CO/1 (12 June 2009), [35].

[33] CESCR, Concluding Observations: Georgia, E/C.12/1/Add.83 (19 December 2002), [26] and [45].

[34] CESCR, Concluding Observations: Solomon Islands, E/C.12/1/Add.84 (19 December 2002), [14].

school exams, reports, carnet, certifications and the use of equipment based on their incomes...The Committee recommends that the State party take immediate measures to ensure access of all children without discrimination, to free and compulsory primary education.[35]

NON-DISCRIMINATION

As noted above in relation to Article 13, states are required to implement the right to education without discrimination, such that education is available equally to all. As a result, it would seem that the plan to be adopted by states under Article 14 must be one which seeks to ensure free, compulsory primary education for all on the basis of equality and without discrimination. This approach is confirmed by other international legal and policy frameworks seeking to secure universal primary education, which emphasize the need to provide education for all. Thus, the Millennium Development Goals stress the need to ensure primary education for 'boys and girls alike',[36] while the Commentary to the Dakar Framework for Action seeks to ensure that 'by 2015 all children, *particularly girls, children in difficult circumstances and those belonging to ethnic minorities*, have access to and complete free and compulsory primary education'.[37]

The need to ensure free, compulsory primary education to all without discrimination is also stressed in some Concluding Observations of the Committee. For example, in relation to Kuwait, the Committee has expressed concern that the state 'does not provide free compulsory education to non-Kuwaiti children as a right enshrined in the Covenant'.[38] Similarly, in relation to India:

40. The Committee is concerned that, despite the efforts made by the State party to achieve universal primary education...the wide disparity in enrolment and dropout rates in primary schools continue to persist...

...

80. The Committee urges the State party to continue to make determined efforts to achieve universal primary education, compulsory and free of charge, by, inter alia, taking further initiatives to eliminate child marriages, child labour, especially of school-aged children, and targeting disadvantaged and marginalized groups in particular.[39]

And in relation to China:

The Committee is concerned about the continued irregularities in the State party's provision of universal access to free compulsory primary education, in particular with regard

[35] CESCR, Concluding Observations: Colombia, E/C.12/COL/CO/5 (7 June 2010), [29]. See also CESCR, Concluding Observations: El Salvador, E/C.12/SLV/CO/2 (27 June 2007), [26]; Nepal, E/C.12/NPL/CO/2 (16 January 2008), [27]; Nigeria, E/C.12/1/Add.23 (16 June 1998), [31].

[36] UNGA Res. 55/2, United Nations Millennium Declaration, A/RES/55/2 (18 September 2000), [19].

[37] The Dakar Framework for Action: Expanded Commentary, Goal 2 (emphasis added). See further [32] and [33].

[38] CESCR, Concluding Observations: Kuwait, E/C.12/1/Add.98 (7 June 2004), [26].

[39] CESCR, Concluding Observations: India, E/C.12/IND/CO/5 (8 August 2008), [40] and [80].

to rural communities, minority regions, disadvantaged families and internal migrant populations.[40]

THE QUESTION OF RESOURCES

A state is not able to escape its obligation under Article 14 on the basis that it lacks sufficient resources. According to General Comment No. 11:

9. Obligations. A State party cannot escape the unequivocal obligation to adopt a plan of action on the grounds that the necessary resources are not available. If the obligation could be avoided in this way, there would be no justification for the unique requirement contained in article 14 which applies, almost by definition, to situations characterized by inadequate financial resources.[41]

In its Concluding Observations, the Committee emphasizes the unequivocal nature of this obligation. So, for example, in relation to the Solomon Islands:

While noting that the lack of financial resources due to the prevailing economic crisis in Solomon Islands leaves little scope to the State party for providing adequate educational services, the Committee nevertheless is concerned about the absence of compulsory primary education in Solomon Islands, with merely 60% of school age children having access to primary education. The Committee would consequently like to draw the attention of the Government to its obligations under Articles 13, paragraph 2(a) and 14 of the Covenant, which stipulate that primary education shall be compulsory and free of charge, and to its General Comment No. 11…[42]

Similarly, in relation to Zimbabwe, in the context of 'concern about cutbacks in educational expenditure, which result in non-compliance with Article 13, paragraph 2(a) of the Covenant, requiring free, compulsory and universal primary education':[43]

Even though the Committee is aware of the current difficulties in Zimbabwe and the State party's efforts in this field, the Committee invites Zimbabwe to submit to it within a year a plan of action and a progress report as to the implementation of this obligation.[44]

INTERNATIONAL ASSISTANCE

States are expected to seek, and to receive, international assistance to enable them to comply with their obligations under Article 14 and to achieve the goal of universal primary education. General Comment No. 11 provides:

9. …the reference to 'international assistance and cooperation' in article 2.1 and to 'international action' in article 23 of the Covenant are of particular relevance in this situation.

[40] CESCR, Concluding Observations: China, E/C.12/1/Add.107 (13 May 2005), [37]. See also CESCR, Concluding Observations: Morocco, E/C.12/1/Add.55 (1 December 2000), [55]; Paraguay, E/C.12/1/Add.1 (28 May 1996), [17].

[41] CESCR, General Comment No. 11, [9].

[42] CESCR, Concluding Observations: Solomon Islands, E/C.12/1/Add.33 (14 May 1999), [23].

[43] CESCR, Concluding Observations: Zimbabwe, E/C.12/1/Add.12 (20 May 1997), [14].

[44] CESCR, Concluding Observations: Zimbabwe, E/C.12/1/Add.12 (20 May 1997), [22].

Where a State party is clearly lacking in the financial resources and/or expertise required to 'work out and adopt' a detailed plan, the international community has a clear obligation to assist.

...

11. The Committee calls upon every State party to which article 14 is relevant to ensure that its terms are fully complied with and that the resulting plan of action is submitted to the Committee as an integral part of the reports required under the Covenant. Further, in appropriate cases, the Committee encourages States parties to seek the assistance of relevant international agencies, including the International Labour Organization (ILO), the United Nations Development Programme (UNDP), the United Nations Educational, Scientific and Cultural Organization (UNESCO), the United Nations Children's Fund (UNICEF), the International Monetary Fund (IMF) and the World Bank, in relation both to the preparation of plans of action under article 14 and their subsequent implementation. The Committee also calls upon the relevant international agencies to assist States parties to the greatest extent possible to meet their obligations on an urgent basis.

The importance of international assistance is also emphasized in the World Declaration on Education for All and the Dakar Framework for Action. The World Declaration on Education for All, Article X provides:

1. Meeting basic learning needs constitutes a common and universal human responsibility. It requires international solidarity and equitable and fair economic relations in order to redress existing economic disparities...

2. Substantial and long-term increases in resources for basic education will be needed. The world community, including intergovernmental agencies and institutions, has an urgent responsibility to alleviate the constraints that prevent some countries from achieving the goal of education for all. It will mean the adoption of measures that augment the national budgets of the poorest countries or serve to relieve heavy debt burdens....

And the Dakar Framework for Action provides that, for countries with 'significant challenges...special technical support will be provided by the international community'.[45] It goes on to stipulate that:

[P]artner members of the international community undertake to work in a consistent, co-ordinated and coherent manner. Each partner will contribute according to its comparative advantage in support of the National EFA Plans to ensure that resource gaps are filled.[46]

As a result, the Committee urges states to seek and utilize international assistance where necessary. So, for example, in relation to the Solomon Islands, the Committee:

[U]rges the State party to take steps to ensure that all children are able to fully exercise their right to free and compulsory primary education, in accordance with Article 14 of the Covenant, and to seek assistance from United Nations Educational, Scientific and Cultural Organization in this regard.[47]

[45] The Dakar Framework for Action, [16]. [46] The Dakar Framework for Action, [17].
[47] CESCR, Concluding Observations: Solomon Island, E/C.12/1/Add.84 (19 December 2002), [28].

Conclusion

Article 14 emphasizes the importance of the right to free, compulsory primary education by requiring states to draw up concrete plans for the realization of this right. This reflects the priority given to the achievement of free, compulsory primary education for all in other international instruments and political commitments. In spite of these commitments, however, the goal of universal primary education has not been achieved. In 2011, 57 million children of primary school age were not in school, and, based on current figures and trends, it appears that the Millennium Development Goal of universal primary education by 2015 will not be met.[48] As a result, Article 14 has not become redundant, as its drafters might have hoped or expected, but continues to play an important role in pushing states to take concrete measures towards the achievement of free, compulsory primary education for all.

[48] The Millennium Development Goals Report 2013, 14, <http://www.un.org/millenniumgoals/pdf/report-2013/mdg-report-2013-english.pdf>.

17

Article 15: Cultural Rights

Article 15

1. The States Parties to the present Covenant recognize the right of everyone:

(a) To take part in cultural life;

(b) To enjoy the benefits of scientific progress and its applications;

(c) To benefit from the protection of the moral and material interests resulting from any scientific, literary or artistic production of which he is the author.

2. The steps to be taken by the States Parties to the present Covenant to achieve the full realization of this right shall include those necessary for the conservation, the development and the diffusion of science and culture.

3. The States Parties to the present Covenant undertake to respect the freedom indispensable for scientific research and creative activity.

4. The States Parties to the present Covenant recognize the benefits to be derived from the encouragement and development of international contacts and co-operation in the scientific and cultural fields.

Article 15 is the only Article of the Covenant which deals with 'cultural rights'. It contains three separate rights: the right to take part in cultural life (Article 15(1)(a)); the right to enjoy the benefits of scientific progress and its applications (Article 15(1)(b)); and the right to benefit from the protection of the moral and material interests resulting from any scientific, literary or artistic production of which an individual is the author (Article 15(1)(c)).

Background and Context

Article 15 reflects, in binding form, the right embodied in Article 27 of the Universal Declaration of Human Rights (UDHR):

> (1) Everyone has the right freely to participate in the cultural life of the community, to enjoy the arts and to share in scientific advancement and its benefits.
>
> (2) Everyone has the right to the protection of the moral and material interests resulting from any scientific, literary or artistic production of which he is the author.[1]

[1] UNGA Res. 217 A (III), Universal Declaration of Human Rights, A/810 (10 December 1948) (UDHR), Article 27.

The importance of culture was recognized in the United Nations Charter—which requires the United Nations to promote 'international cultural and educational cooperation'[2]—and in the subsequent establishment of the United Nations Educational, Scientific and Cultural Organization (UNESCO). Article 1 of the UNESCO Constitution describes the purposes and functions of that organization as follows:

> 1. The purpose of the Organization is to contribute to peace and security by promoting collaboration among the nations through education, science and culture...
>
> 2. To realize this purpose the Organization will:
>
> (a) Collaborate in the work of advancing the mutual knowledge and understanding of peoples, through all means of mass communication, and to that end recommend such international agreements as may be necessary to promote the free flow of ideas by word and image;
>
> (b) Give fresh impulse to popular education and to the spread of culture...
>
> (c) Maintain, increase and diffuse knowledge:
>
> By assuring the conservation and protection of the world's inheritance of books, works of art and monuments of history and science, and recommending to the nations concerned the necessary international conventions;
>
> By encouraging cooperation among the nations in all branches of intellectual activity, including the international exchange of persons active in the fields of education, science and culture and the exchange of publications, objects of artistic and scientific interest and other materials of information;
>
> By initiating methods of international cooperation calculated to give the people of all countries access to the printed and published materials produced by any of them.

Article 15 can be seen as furthering these ideas and principles through the provision of an individual human right to participate in culture and science. And indeed an initial draft of Article 15, which was considered by the Commission on Human Rights when formulating the draft Covenant to be considered by state representatives, was prepared by UNESCO.[3]

Article 15(1)(a)

'The States Parties to the present Covenant recognize the right of everyone to take part in cultural life.'

Most discussion of Article 15, both by United Nations treaty bodies and within academic literature, focuses on the right to participate in cultural life. At the international level, this right is protected not only under the ICESCR, but also by

[2] Charter of the United Nations (adopted 26 June 1945, 1 UNTS XVI, entered into force 24 October 1945), Article 55(b).

[3] See UNGA Third Committee, A/C.3/SR.797 (31 October 1957), [13].

Article 27(1) of the UDHR, set out above. The right is also secured to particular groups by: Article 5(e)(vi) of the International Convention on the Elimination of All Forms of Racial Discrimination;[4] Article 13(c) of the Convention on the Elimination of All Forms of Discrimination against Women;[5] Article 31 of the Convention on the Rights of the Child;[6] Articles 43(1)(g) and 45(1)(d) of the International Convention on the Protection of the Rights of All Migrant Workers and Members of Their Families;[7] and Article 30 of the Convention on the Rights of Persons with Disabilities.[8]

The right to participate in cultural life is also recognized in a range of non-binding or 'soft law' instruments, most notably the Recommendation on Participation by the People at Large in Cultural Life and their Contribution to It, adopted by the General Conference of UNESCO in 1976,[9] and the Universal Declaration on Cultural Diversity, adopted by the General Conference of UNESCO in 2001.[10] In addition, the UN General Assembly has adopted a series of resolutions on Human Rights and Cultural Diversity,[11] which support the right to participate in cultural life.

At the regional level, the right is protected by Article 17(2) of the African Charter on Human and Peoples' Rights,[12] Article 14(1)(a) of the Additional Protocol to the American Convention on Human Rights in the Area of Economic, Social and Cultural Rights ('San Salvador Protocol'),[13] and Article 42(1) of the Arab Charter on Human Rights.[14] Although there is no explicit protection for cultural rights within the European human rights system, the European Court of Human Rights has protected rights to culture and cultural identity by means of the right to private and family life in Article 8 of the European Convention

[4] International Convention on the Elimination of All Forms of Racial Discrimination (adopted 21 December 1965, 660 UNTS 195, entered into force 4 January 1969).

[5] Convention on the Elimination of All Forms of Discrimination Against Women (adopted 18 December 1979, 1249 UNTS 13, entered into force 3 September 1981).

[6] Convention on the Rights of the Child (adopted 20 November 1989, 1577 UNTS 3, entered into force 2 September 1990).

[7] International Convention on the Protection of the Rights of All Migrants and Members of Their Families (adopted 18 December 1990, 2220 UNTS 39481, entered into force 1 July 2003).

[8] Convention on the Rights of Persons with Disabilities (adopted 13 December 2006, 2515 UNTS 3, entered into force 3 May 2008).

[9] UNESCO, Recommendation on Participation by the People at Large in Cultural Life and their Contribution to it (26 November 1976). See especially Article 4.

[10] UNESCO, Universal Declaration on Cultural Diversity (2 November 2001). See especially Article 5.

[11] From UNGA Res. 55/91, Human Rights and Cultural Diversity, A/RES/55/91 (4 December 2000) to UNGA Res. 66/154, Human Rights and Cultural Diversity, A/RES/66/154 (19 December 2011).

[12] African Charter on Human and Peoples' Rights (adopted 27 June 1981, 1520 UNTS 217, entered into force 21 October 1986). See also Article 17(3).

[13] Additional Protocol to the American Convention on Human Rights in the Area of Economic, Social and Cultural Rights (adopted 17 November 1988, 28 ILM 156 (1989), entered into force 16 November 1999) ('San Salvador Protocol').

[14] League of Arab States, Arab Charter on Human Rights (adopted 22 May 2004, 18 HRLJ 151 (1997), entered into force 15 March 2008).

for the Protection of Human Rights and Fundamental Freedoms.[15] Thus, in *Chapman v United Kingdom*,[16] in which the applicant, who was a gypsy, complained about state measures affecting the stationing of her caravan, the Grand Chamber stated:

> The Court considers that the applicant's occupation of her caravan is an integral part of her ethnic identity as a Gypsy, reinforcing the long tradition of that minority of following a travelling lifestyle... Measures affecting the applicant's stationing of her caravan therefore have an impact going beyond the right to respect for her home. They also affect her ability to maintain her identity as a Gypsy and to lead her private and family life in accordance with that tradition.[17]

The European Court of Human Rights has also protected aspects of the right to take part in cultural life through use of Article 10 (right to freedom of expression).[18]

To the extent that the right protects the interests of minority groups in practising their own culture, it is also guaranteed by minority rights provisions, most notably Article 27 of the International Covenant on Civil and Political Rights (ICCPR):

> In those States in which ethnic, religious or linguistic minorities exist, persons belonging to such minorities shall not be denied the right, in community with the other members of their group, to enjoy their own culture, to profess and practise their own religion, or to use their own language.[19]

Other relevant minority rights instruments include: the International Labour Organization Indigenous and Tribal Peoples Convention 1989;[20] the UN Declaration on the Rights of Persons Belonging to National or Ethnic, Religious or Linguistic Minorities;[21] the UN Declaration on the Rights of Indigenous Peoples;[22] and, within the European context, the European Framework Convention for the Protection of National Minorities.[23]

[15] European Convention for the Protection of Human Rights and Fundamental Freedoms (adopted 4 November 1950, 213 UNTS 2, entered into force 3 September 1953) (ECHR).

[16] (App. 27238/95), 18 January 2001, (2001) 33 EHRR 18.

[17] *Chapman v United Kingdom*, [73].

[18] See, eg, *Khurshid Mustafa and Tarzibachi v Sweden* (App. 23883/06), 16 December 2008, (2011) 52 EHRR 24.

[19] International Covenant on Civil and Political Rights (adopted 16 December 1966, 999 UNTS 171, entered into force 23 March 1976) (ICCPR), Article 27.

[20] ILO Convention No. 169 concerning Indigenous and Tribal Peoples in Independent Countries (adopted 27 June 1989, entered into force 5 September 1991) ('Indigenous and Tribal Peoples Convention'). See, eg, Article 5.

[21] UNGA Res. 47/135, Declaration on the Rights of Persons Belonging to National or Ethnic, Religious and Linguistic Minorities, A/RES/47/135 (18 December 1992), Articles 1, 2(1) and 2(2).

[22] UNGA Res. 61/295, Declaration on the Rights of Indigenous Peoples, A/RES/61/295 (13 September 2007), Articles 5 and 8.

[23] Council of Europe, Framework Convention for the Protection of National Minorities (adopted 1 February 1995, ETS 157, entered into force 1 February 1998), Article 5. See also Article 4(2).

DEFINITIONS

'Cultural life'

The key issue which arises in relation to the interpretation of Article 15 concerns what is meant by the word 'culture' in Article 15(2) and its corollary in Article 15(1)(a), 'cultural life'. In particular, the *travaux préparatoires* indicate that there was, from the outset, uncertainty as to whether the 'cultural life' referred to in Article 15 included only cultural *products*, such that the essence of Article 15 is a right of access to art, theatre and other cultural expressions; or whether it included culture in the anthropological sense, as a way of life, such that the right includes the rights of nations and minority groups to maintain their particular cultural traditions. The issue is summarized well in the reported comments of the Japanese representative during discussions in the Third Committee:

> The meaning of the words 'the right... to take part in cultural life' was not, however, clear... The words 'take part' were suitable in the case of political or economic activities but not in the case of cultural life, which was an integral part of human life. If the intention had been to refer to the external aspects of culture, it might be preferable to replace the words 'in cultural life' by the words 'in cultural activities', or to add the words 'of the community', which were to be found in article 27, paragraph 1, of the Universal Declaration of Human Rights.[24]

It seems clear that the drafters of Article 15 generally understood culture in terms of its external manifestations. Thus, the representative of the UN Secretariat explained to the Third Committee that the term 'cultural life' was used as an abbreviation of 'manifestations of national and international cultural life', the terminology which had been used in UNESCO's preliminary draft.[25] And the majority of discussion during negotiation of the text focused on cultural products and expressions and the need to ensure access to these by all sectors of the population. However, it was also clear that some representatives thought that the text should cover culture as a way of life. Thus, the Iranian representative noted that:

> In her view, the word 'culture' as used in the article referred not to the humanities or the arts, but to the moral, intellectual and aesthetic experiences inherited by various groups from the past and enhanced by them.[26]

However, she went on to say that '[i]f that view was correct, the original text was inadequate'.[27]

The text was not, ultimately, amended to accommodate such concerns. In spite of this, the CESCR has interpreted Article 15 as including the right of groups to maintain their particular cultural practices and traditions. At the seventh session of the Committee, there was a day of general discussion on Article 15, during which several speakers indicated that culture should be interpreted in this way.[28]

[24] UNGA Third Committee, A/C.3/SR.796 (31 October 1957), 173–4.

[25] See UNGA Third Committee, A/C.3/SR.797 (31 October 1957), 178 ([13]).

[26] UNGA Third Committee, A/C.3/SR.799 (4 November 1957), 189–90.

[27] UNGA Third Committee, A/C.3/SR.799 (4 November 1957), 190 ([25]).

[28] See Chapter VII, 'General Discussion on the Right to Take Part in Cultural Life as Recognized in Article 15 of the International Covenant on Economic, Social and Cultural Rights' in CESCR, Report on the Seventh Session, E/1993/22 (1993), [202]–[223]. See, especially, [204] and [209].

The Committee endorsed this approach, concluding that 'culture meant a way of life', in other words 'a world view representing the totality of a person's encounter with the external forces affecting his life and that of his community'.[29]

This approach to the concept of 'culture' is confirmed in General Comment No. 21 on the right of everyone to take part in cultural life:

11. In the Committee's view, culture is a broad, inclusive concept encompassing all manifestations of human existence. The expression 'cultural life' is an explicit reference to culture as a living process, historical, dynamic and evolving, with a past, a present and a future.

12. The concept of culture must be seen not as a series of isolated manifestations or hermetic compartments, but as an interactive process whereby individuals and communities, while preserving their specificities and purposes, give expression to the culture of humanity. This concept takes account of the individuality and otherness of culture as the creation and product of society.

13. The Committee considers that culture, for the purpose of implementing Article 15(1)(a), encompasses, inter alia, ways of life, language, oral and written literature, music and song, non-verbal communication, religion or belief systems, rites and ceremonies, sport and games, methods of production or technology, natural and man-made environments, food, clothing and shelter and the arts, customs and traditions through which individuals, groups of individuals and communities express their humanity and the meaning they give to their existence, and build their world view representing their encounter with the external forces affecting their lives. Culture shapes and mirrors the values of well-being and the economic, social and political life of individuals, groups of individuals and communities.[30]

This approach reflects that taken by UNESCO, as articulated, for example, in the Preamble to the UNESCO Recommendation on Participation by the People at Large in Cultural Life and Their Contribution to It, which notes that 'culture is not limited to access to works of art and the humanities, but is at one and the same time the acquisition of knowledge, the demand for a way of life and the need to communicate'.

To the extent that the right to participate in cultural life concerns rights of access to external manifestations of a particular culture, a further question arises as to whether it is only 'high' culture to which access is to be guaranteed, or whether the term includes participation in popular culture also. It is clear from the *travaux* that '[w]hat was envisaged by the drafters of the right to take part in cultural life was the democratization of culture—that is, access for all to a preordained canon of "great" works that had previously been the sole preserve of a fortunate elite'.[31]

[29] CESCR, Report on the Seventh Session, E/1993/22 (1993), [213].

[30] CESCR, General Comment No. 21, Right of everyone to take part in cultural life (art. 15, para. 1(a), of the International Covenant on Economic, Social and Cultural Rights), E/C.12/GC/21 (21 December 2009) ('General Comment No. 21').

[31] Roger O'Keefe, 'The "Right to Take Part in Cultural Life" under Article 15 of the ICESCR' (1998) 47(4) *International and Comparative Law Quarterly* 904, 912.

In practice, however, the Committee has for some time been equally concerned with participation in popular culture. Thus, General Comment No. 21 notes that the cultural goods and services, to which Article 15 seeks to secure access, include 'cinemas and sports stadiums' and 'folklore'.[32] And the Guidelines on Treaty-Specific Documents to be Submitted by States Parties under Articles 16 and 17 of the International Covenant on Economic, Social and Cultural Rights ('Guidelines on Treaty-Specific Documents')[33] ask states to provide information on measures to promote participation in, for example, cinema and sports events.[34] When reviewing state reports, the Committee has therefore inquired into support for, and access to, many different forms of popular culture, including media,[35] television,[36] sport[37] and 'leisure'[38] activities. In General Comment No. 5 on persons with disabilities,[39] the Committee includes tourism[40] and going to restaurants[41] as elements of cultural life. The Special Rapporteur in the field of cultural rights has also linked cultural rights to the right to rest and 'leisure' in Article 24 of the UDHR.[42]

'Everyone'

Within the academic literature, there has been considerable debate as to whether cultural rights are individual or collective rights.[43] As the Special Rapporteur in the field of cultural rights has noted:

> One debate that constantly arises in international human rights law, in particular when it concerns cultural rights, relates to the collective dimensions of rights—referring to the collective exercise of individual rights on the one hand, and the existence of collective rights per se—understood as group rights—on the other hand.[44]

Traditionally, the rights protected in the ICCPR and ICESCR were understood as individual rights, and in the context of cultural rights this approach is reflected

[32] CESCR, General Comment No. 21, [16(a)].

[33] CESCR, Guidelines on Treaty-Specific Documents to be Submitted by States Parties under Articles 16 and 17 of the ICESCR ('Guidelines on Treaty-Specific Documents'), E/C.12/2008/2 (24 March 2009).

[34] CESCR, Guidelines on Treaty-Specific Documents, [67(a)].

[35] See, eg, CESCR, Report on the Sixth Session, E/1992/23 (25 November–13 December 1991), [310] (Colombia); CESCR, Report on the Fifth Session, E/1991/23 (26 November–14 December 1990), [79] (Jordan).

[36] See, eg, CESCR, Report on the Fifth Session, E/1991/23 (26 November–14 December 1990), [80] (Jordan).

[37] See, eg, CESCR, Report on the Sixth Session, E/1992/23 (25 November–13 December 1991), [248] (Sweden).

[38] See, eg, CESCR, Report on the Seventh Session, E/1993/22 (23 November–11 December 1992), [73] (Belarus).

[39] CESCR, General Comment No. 5, Persons with disabilities, E/1994/22 (9 December 1994) ('General Comment No. 5').

[40] CESCR, General Comment No. 5, [36].

[41] CESCR, General Comment No. 5, [38].

[42] Human Rights Council, Report of the Independent Expert in the Field of Cultural Rights, A/HRC/14/36 (22 March 2010), [18].

[43] O'Keefe, 'The "Right to Take Part in Cultural Life" under Article 15 of the ICESCR', 917.

[44] Human Rights Council, Report of the Independent Expert in the Field of Cultural Rights, A/HRC/14/36 (22 March 2010), [10].

in the fact that Article 27 of the ICCPR is considered to be an individual right.[45] However, if cultural rights include rights to enjoy a particular cultural tradition and way of life, then it is clear that aspects of these rights are collective in nature, as they can only be enjoyed in community with other members of the cultural group. And, indeed, complaints to the Human Rights Committee concerning violations of Article 27 are often brought by, or on behalf of, communities.[46]

In General Comment No. 21, the Committee clarifies that the right to participate in cultural life has both individual and collective elements:

> [T]he Committee recognizes that the term 'everyone' in the first line of Article 15 may denote the individual or the collective; in other words, cultural rights may be exercised by a person (a) as an individual, (b) in association with others, or (c) within a community or group, as such.[47]

And in relation to indigenous peoples, the General Comment specifically notes that:

> States parties should take measures to guarantee that the exercise of the right to take part in cultural life takes due account of the values of cultural life, which may be strongly communal, or which can only be expressed and enjoyed as a community by indigenous peoples. The strong communal dimension of indigenous peoples' cultural life is indispensable to their existence, well-being and full development.[48]

The fact that cultural rights have both individual and collective dimensions is also noted in the only case, at the international or national level, to have considered the right to take part in cultural life, namely the decision of the African Commission on Human and Peoples' Rights in *Centre For Minority Rights Development (Kenya) and Minority Rights Group International On Behalf of Endorois Welfare Council v Kenya* ('*Endorois* case').[49] In relation to the cultural rights in Article 17 of the African Charter, the Commission:

> [N]otes that Article 17 of the Charter is of a dual dimension in both its individual and collective nature, protecting, on the one hand, individuals' participation in the cultural life of their community and, on the other hand, obliging the state to promote and protect traditional values recognized by a community.[50]

If rights to participate in cultural life are both individual and collective, this raises the possibility of conflict between individual and collective rights to culture. This issue has arisen in several Article 27 cases before the Human Rights Committee (HRC). In the case of *Lovelace v Canada*,[51] the author of the communication was born and registered as a 'Maliseet Indian', which gave her certain rights under

[45] See HRC, General Comment No. 23, the rights of minorities, CCPR/C/21/Rev.1/Add.5 (8 April 1994) ('General Comment No. 23'), [3.1].

[46] See, eg, *Chief Ominayak and the Lubicon Lake Band v Canada*, HRC Communication No. 167/84 (26 March 1990).

[47] CESCR, General Comment No. 21, [9].

[48] CESCR, General Comment No. 21, [36].

[49] African Commission on Human and Peoples' Rights Communication No. 276/2003, (2009) AHRLR 75, 4 February 2010.

[50] *Endorois* case, [241].

[51] HRC Communication No. 24/77 (30 July 1981).

the relevant legislation, including the right to live on an Indian reserve. Following her marriage to a non-Indian, she lost these rights, and was thus not entitled to return to the reserve, even when her marriage ended. The author claimed that this constituted a violation of her rights under Article 27 to enjoy her own culture. However, the measures she complained of were designed, in part, to preserve the identity of the Indian tribe, and thus to ensure their collective right to enjoy their culture. The HRC indicated that measures affecting the right of an individual to enjoy their own culture 'must have both a reasonable and objective justification and be consistent with the other provisions of the Covenant'.[52] Applying this test to the facts of the case, the Committee found:

> Whatever may be the merits of the Indian Act in other respects, it does not seem to the Committee that to deny Sandra Lovelace the right to reside on the reserve is reasonable, or necessary to preserve the identity of the tribe. The Committee therefore concludes that to prevent her recognition as belonging to the band is an unjustifiable denial of her rights under Article 27 of the Covenant, read in the context of the other provisions referred to.[53]

Similarly, in the case of *Kitok v Sweden*,[54] the HRC was required to consider whether legislation which restricted rights to engage in reindeer husbandry, a traditional activity of the indigenous Sami people, to Sami who have reindeer husbandry as their 'permanent occupation' and have not 'gone over to any other main economic activity'[55] interfered with the Article 27 rights of the author, who had left full-time reindeer farming for financial reasons. According to the HRC:

> In resolving this problem, in which there is an apparent conflict between the legislation, which seems to protect the rights of the minority as a whole, and its application to a single member of that minority, the Committee has been guided by the *ratio decidendi* in the *Lovelace* case, namely, that a restriction upon the right of an individual member of a minority must be shown to have a reasonable and objective justification and to be necessary for the continued viability and welfare of the minority as a whole. After a careful review of all the elements involved in this case, the Committee is of the view that there is no violation of article 27 by the State party. In this context, the Committee notes that Mr. Kitok is permitted, albeit not as of right, to graze and farm his reindeer, to hunt and to fish.[56]

Conflict between the cultural rights of minority groups as a whole and those of their members also arose in the case of *Mahuika v New Zealand*.[57] The case was brought by a number of Maori individuals who claimed that their traditional rights to fish were affected by legislation based on an agreement between the New

[52] *Lovelace v Canada*, [16].
[53] *Lovelace v Canada*, [17].
[54] HRC Communication No. 197/85 (27 July 1988).
[55] See *Kitok v Sweden*, [9.6].
[56] *Kitok v Sweden*, [9.8].
[57] HRC Communication No. 547/93 (27 October 1993).

Zealand Government and Maori representatives. Although the majority of Maori tribes supported the agreement, those bringing this case did not. According to the Committee:

In such circumstances, where the right of individuals to enjoy their own culture is in conflict with the exercise of parallel rights by other members of the minority group, or of the minority as a whole, the Committee may consider whether the limitation in issue is in the interests of all members of the minority and whether there is reasonable and objective justification for its application to the individuals who claim to be adversely affected.[58]

On the facts, the HRC found that there had been no violation of Article 27.

If such an issue arose before the CESCR, it seems likely that the Committee would follow the HRC on this point. In particular, the test formulated in *Mahuika v New Zealand*, set out above, seems to offer an appropriate way of reconciling the conflicting cultural claims of individuals and members of the group as whole.

'To take part'

The Committee has clarified, in General Comment No. 21, that the right 'to take part' in cultural life has three main components: participation in, access to and contribution to cultural life:

(a) *Participation* covers in particular the right of everyone—alone, or in association with others or as a community—to act freely, to choose his or her own identity, to identify or not with one or several communities or to change that choice, to take part in the political life of society, to engage in one's own cultural practices and to express oneself in the language of one's choice. Everyone also has the right to seek and develop cultural knowledge and expressions and to share them with others, as well as to act creatively and take part in creative activity;

(b) *Access* covers in particular the right of everyone—alone, in association with others or as a community—to know and understand his or her own culture and that of others through education and information, and to receive quality education and training with due regard for cultural identity. Everyone has also the right to learn about forms of expression and dissemination through any technical medium of information or communication, to follow a way of life associated with the use of cultural goods and resources such as land, water, biodiversity, language or specific institutions, and to benefit from the cultural heritage and the creation of other individuals and communities;

(c) *Contribution to cultural life* refers to the right of everyone to be involved in creating the spiritual, material, intellectual and emotional expressions of the community. This is supported by the right to take part in the development of the community to which a person belongs, and in the definition, elaboration and implementation of policies and decisions that have an impact on the exercise of a person's cultural rights.[59]

[58] *Mahuika v New Zealand*, [9.6].

[59] CESCR, General Comment No. 21, [15].

NATURE OF STATE OBLIGATIONS

Article 15 not only requires states to refrain from interfering with the rights of individuals and groups to participate in cultural life; it also imposes positive obligations on states to take steps to ensure such participation. According to General Comment No. 21:

The right to take part in cultural life can be characterized as a freedom. In order for this right to be ensured, it requires from the State Party both abstention (i.e. non-interference with the exercise of cultural practices and with access to cultural goods and services) and positive action (ensuring preconditions for participation, facilitation and promotion of cultural life, and access to and preservation of cultural goods).[60]

More specifically, the Committee has analyzed state obligations under Article 15 in terms of the obligations to respect, protect and fulfil the right:

The right of everyone to take part in cultural life, like the other rights enshrined in the Covenant, imposes three types or levels of obligations on States Parties: (a) the obligation to respect; (b) the obligation to protect; and (c) the obligation to fulfil. The obligation to respect requires States Parties to refrain from interfering, directly or indirectly, with the enjoyment of the right to take part in cultural life. The obligation to protect requires States Parties to take steps to prevent third parties from interfering in the right to take part in cultural life. Lastly, the obligation to fulfil requires States Parties to take appropriate legislative, administrative, judicial, budgetary, promotional and other measures aimed at the full realization of the right enshrined in Article 15, paragraph 1(a) of the Covenant.[61]

The Committee has also outlined the 'necessary conditions for the full realization of the right of everyone to take part in cultural life on the basis of equality and non-discrimination',[62] indicating that the right to take part in cultural life requires availability, accessibility, acceptability, adaptability and appropriateness of cultural programmes:

(a) *Availability* is the presence of cultural goods and services that are open for everyone to enjoy and benefit from, including libraries, museums, theatres, cinemas and sports stadiums; literature, including folklore, and the arts in all forms; the shared open spaces essential to cultural interaction, such as parks, squares, avenues and streets; nature's gifts, such as seas, lakes, rivers, mountains, forests and nature reserves, including the flora and fauna found there, which give nations their character and biodiversity; intangible cultural goods, such as languages, customs, traditions, beliefs, knowledge and history, as well as values, which make up identity and contribute to the cultural diversity of individuals and communities. Of all the cultural goods, one of special value is the productive intercultural kinship that arises where diverse groups, minorities and communities can freely share the same territory;

(b) *Accessibility* consists of effective and concrete opportunities for individuals and communities to enjoy culture fully, within physical and financial reach for all in both urban

[60] CESCR, General Comment No. 21, [6].

[61] CESCR, General Comment No. 21, [48]. See further [49]–[55], which set out the relevant obligations in more detail.

[62] CESCR, General Comment No. 21, [16].

and rural areas, without discrimination. It is essential, in this regard, that access for older persons and persons with disabilities, as well as for those who live in poverty, is provided and facilitated. Accessibility also includes the right of everyone to seek, receive and share information on all manifestations of culture in the language of the person's choice, and the access of communities to means of expressions and dissemination.

(c) *Acceptability* entails that the laws, policies, strategies, programmes and measures adopted by the State party for the enjoyment of cultural rights should be formulated and implemented in such a way as to be acceptable to the individuals and communities involved. In this regard, consultations should be held with the individuals and communities concerned in order to ensure that the measures to protect cultural diversity are acceptable to them;

(d) *Adaptability* refers to the flexibility and relevance of strategies, policies, programmes and measures adopted by the State party in any area of cultural life, which must be respectful of the cultural diversity of individuals and communities;

(e) *Appropriateness* refers to the realization of a specific human right in a way that is pertinent and suitable to a given cultural modality or context, that is, respectful of the culture and cultural rights of individuals and communities, including minorities and indigenous peoples. The Committee has in many instances referred to the notion of cultural appropriateness (or cultural acceptability or adequacy) in past general comments, in relation in particular to the rights to food, health, water, housing and education. The way in which rights are implemented may also have an impact on cultural life and cultural diversity. The Committee wishes to stress in this regard the need to take into account, as far as possible, cultural values attached to, inter alia, food and food consumption, the use of water, the way health and education services are provided and the way housing is designed and constructed.[63]

The Committee has also clarified what it considers to be the 'minimum core obligation' in relation to the right as follows:

[T]he Committee considers that article 15, paragraph 1(a), of the Covenant entails at least the obligation to create and promote an environment within which a person individually, or in association with others, or within a community or group, can participate in the culture of their choice, which includes the following core obligations applicable with immediate effect:

(a) To take legislative and any other necessary steps to guarantee non-discrimination and gender equality in the enjoyment of the right of everyone to take part in cultural life;

(b) To respect the right of everyone to identify or not identify themselves with one or more communities, and the right to change their choice;

(c) To respect and protect the right of everyone to engage in their own cultural practices, while respecting human rights which entails, in particular, respecting freedom of thought, belief and religion; freedom of opinion and expression; a person's right to use the language of his or her choice; freedom of association and peaceful assembly; and freedom to choose and set up educational establishments;

[63] CESCR, General Comment No. 21, [16].

(d) To eliminate any barriers or obstacles that inhibit or restrict a person's access to the person's own culture or to other cultures, without discrimination and without consideration for frontiers of any kind;

(e) To allow and encourage the participation of persons belonging to minority groups, indigenous peoples or to other communities in the design and implementation of laws and policies that affect them. In particular, States parties should obtain their free and informed prior consent when the preservation of their cultural resources, especially those associated with their way of life and cultural expression, are at risk.[64]

PARTICULAR ISSUES

As noted above, the Committee, in its work, considers culture both in the narrow sense of cultural products and in the broader sense of culture as a way of life. In relation to the former, particular issues identified by the Committee include the need for infrastructure to support cultural activities, the importance of protecting cultural heritage, and the need to ensure creative freedom. In relation to the latter, the Committee has focused on the rights of minority and indigenous groups to maintain and develop their traditional cultures and practices (including, in particular, their own language and their access to ancestral lands and resources), as well as the need to protect national cultures as a whole.[65] Underpinning the Committee's approach to culture in both senses is the overarching requirement of non-discrimination in the enjoyment of the right to participate in cultural life.

Cultural infrastructure

A key obligation on states with respect to the right to take part in cultural life involves the provision of, and support to, cultural infrastructure, such as museums, art galleries, publishing houses, and so on. The work of the Committee indicates that states are expected to support cultural infrastructure through the allocation of funds, together with the implementation of appropriate policies and legislation.

Thus, General Comment No. 21 notes that the realization of the right to take part in cultural life requires 'the presence of cultural goods and services that are open for everyone to enjoy and benefit from, including libraries, museums, theatres, cinemas and sports stadiums'.[66] And the Guidelines on Treaty-Specific Documents require states to provide 'information on the institutional infrastructure to promote popular participation in, and access to, cultural life'.[67]

[64] CESCR, General Comment No. 21, [55].

[65] This general mapping of the issues considered by the Committee draws on the excellent analysis of the Committee's work in relation to Article 15 in O'Keefe, 'The "Right to Take Part in Cultural Life" under Article 15 of the ICESCR'.

[66] CESCR, General Comment No. 21, [16].

[67] CESCR, Guidelines on Treaty-Specific Documents, [67].

More specifically, the General Comment indicates that states are expected to ensure the availability of cultural infrastructure by taking concrete measures, including the provision of financial support:

States Parties are under an obligation to facilitate the right of everyone to take part in cultural life by taking a wide range of positive measures, including financial measures, that would contribute to the realization of this right, such as:

(a) Adopting... measures aimed at establishing and supporting public institutions and the cultural infrastructure necessary for the implementation of such policies...

(d) Granting assistance, financial or other, to artists, public and private organizations... cultural associations, trade unions and other individuals and institutions engaged in... creative activities.[68]

The Committee's discussion of state reports and Concluding Observations are instructive in this regard. So, for example, in relation to Colombia in 1991:

Members of the Committee asked the representatives of the State Party to give details of legislative and other measures which the Government had taken to ensure that everyone could exercise the right to take part in the cultural life of his choice and to express his own culture. They asked what information was available on: (a) funds to promote cultural development and the participation of everyone in cultural life, including public aid to private initiative; (b) the institutional infrastructure established to apply measures to promote the participation of everyone in culture—cultural centres, museums, libraries, theatres, cinemas and handicraft centres...[69]

And in relation to Brazil, in 2009:

The Committee recommends that the State Party take measures to encourage the broader participation of its citizens in cultural life, inter alia, by: (a) Ensuring the wider availability of cultural resources and assets, particularly in smaller cities and regions, and ensuring, in this regard, special provision through subsidies and other forms of assistance for those who lack the means to participate in the cultural activities of their choice...[70]

On the issue of funding, the Committee has shown itself prepared to ask very specific questions about the percentage of the national budget allocated to cultural activities and whether this is sufficient.[71]

The Committee has also indicated that the resources necessary to ensure the right to take part in cultural life include the human resources of artists, authors and other creators. The infrastructure states are expected to provide therefore includes educational facilities to train those interested in pursuing careers in the cultural sphere, and the Guidelines on Treaty-Specific Documents require states

[68] CESCR, General Comment No. 21, [52].

[69] CESCR, Report on the Sixth Session, E/1992/23 (25 November–13 December 1991), [310] (Colombia). See also, eg, [284] (Spain).

[70] CESCR, Concluding Observations: Brazil, E/C.12/BRA/CO/2 (12 June 2009), [33]. See also, eg, Mauritius, E/C.12/MUS/CO/4 (8 June 2010), [31].

[71] See, eg, CESCR, Report on the Sixth Session, E/1992/23 (25 November–13 December 1991), [247]–[248] (Sweden) and [284] (Spain).

to 'provide information on school and professional education in the field of culture and the arts'.[72]

In addition, the Committee seems to interpret state obligations in this area in light of Article 15(4), under which states 'recognize the benefits to be derived from the encouragement and development of international contacts and cooperation in the…cultural fields'. Thus, the Committee has inquired into the extent to which cultural activities have been undertaken with the support of, or in cooperation with, international organizations, such as UNESCO,[73] and has also asked whether state cultural policies are aimed at disseminating cultural works beyond state borders.[74]

Cultural heritage

The Committee has made clear that Article 15(1)(a) imposes obligations on states to preserve and promote cultural heritage. In this respect, the right reinforces state obligations recognized in a number of international instruments which seek to protect cultural heritage. These include the Convention Concerning the Protection of the World Cultural and Natural Heritage,[75] the Convention on the Protection of the Underwater Cultural Heritage,[76] and the Convention on the Safeguarding of the Intangible Cultural Heritage,[77] together with non-binding instruments such as the UNESCO Declaration on the Intentional Destruction of Cultural Heritage.[78]

According to General Comment No. 21:

> States Parties are obliged to:
>
> (a) Respect and protect cultural heritage in all its forms, in times of war and peace, and natural disasters;
>
> Cultural heritage must be preserved, developed, enriched and transmitted to future generations… Such obligations include the care, preservation and restoration of historical sites, monuments, works of art and literary works, among others.
>
> (b) Respect and protect cultural heritage of all groups and communities, in particular the most disadvantaged and marginalized individuals and groups, in economic development and environmental policies and programmes…[79]

[72] CESCR, Guidelines on Treaty-Specific Documents, [69]. The importance of this aspect of the right to participate in cultural life was established in the early work of the Committee: see, eg, CESCR, Report on the Sixth Session, E/1992/23 (25 November–13 December 1991), [249] (Sweden); CESCR, Report on the Third Session, E/1989/22 (6–24 February 1989), [307] (Trinidad and Tobago).

[73] See, eg, CESCR, Report on the Fifth Session, E/1991/23 (26 November–14 December 1990), [154] (Ecuador).

[74] See, eg, CESCR, Report on the Sixth Session, E/1992/23 (25 November–13 December 1991), [284] (Spain).

[75] Convention Concerning the Protection of the World Cultural and Natural Heritage (adopted 16 November 1972, 1037 UNTS 151, entered into force 17 December 1975).

[76] Convention on the Protection of the Underwater Cultural Heritage (adopted 2 November 2001, 2562 UNTS 3, entered into force 2 January 2009).

[77] Convention on the Safeguarding of the Intangible Cultural Heritage (adopted 17 October 2003, 2368 UNTS 1, entered into force 20 April 2006).

[78] UNESCO, Declaration on the Intentional Destruction of Cultural Heritage (17 October 2003).

[79] CESCR, General Comment No. 21, [50].

The General Comment further notes that the obligation to fulfil the right to participate in cultural life requires states to adopt '[p]rogrammes aimed at preserving and restoring cultural heritage'.[80]

The Guidelines on Treaty-Specific Documents also indicate that states have obligations to enhance access to cultural heritage and to ensure knowledge of cultural heritage is transmitted as widely as possible. Thus, the Guidelines ask states to provide information on measures taken 'to enhance access to the cultural heritage of mankind, including through new information technologies such as the Internet'.[81]

The approach taken by the Committee to the issue of cultural heritage is well illustrated by its Concluding Observations on Afghanistan in 2010:

> The Committee…notes with concern that, over the past several decades, many areas and elements of the cultural heritage of the State Party were illegally excavated, vandalized, looted, deliberately destroyed or simply allowed to deteriorate without protection…The Committee also recommends that the State Party enhance its current practice with regard to the registration and protection of historical monuments and archaeological sites and pursue its efforts to facilitate the return of the objects illegally exported from Afghanistan. The Committee also recommends that the State Party establish mechanisms to coordinate the activities of Government agencies and ministries in regard to illicit excavation and export of cultural property.[82]

Similarly, in relation to Iraq, the Committee has expressed 'alarm' at the 'destruction of the cultural heritage of religious communities and minorities'.[83]

One particular issue which has been noted by the Committee concerns the need for states to protect their *linguistic* heritage. Thus, in relation to Benin in 2002, the Committee considered it 'worrying that the State Party is not making enough effort to preserve the diversity of language in the country, and not taking steps to ensure that some of them do not disappear altogether'.[84] Similarly, in relation to France:

> The Committee reiterates the recommendation…that the State Party increase its efforts to preserve and promote regional and minority languages and cultural heritage, inter alia by ensuring that sufficient financial and human resources be allocated to the teaching of regional and minority languages and cultures in public schools and to TV and radio broadcasting in these languages.[85]

The issue of cultural heritage has also been the subject of a specific report by the Special Rapporteur in the field of cultural rights.[86] Noting that states have

80 CESCR, General Comment No. 21, [54].

81 CESCR, Guidelines on Treaty-Specific Documents, [67(b)].

82 CESCR, Concluding Observations: Afghanistan, E/C.12/AFG/CO/2-4 (7 June 2010), [44].

83 CESCR, Concluding Observations: Iraq, E/C.12/1994/6 (30 May 1994), [12]. See also Angola, E/C.12/AGO/CO/3 (1 December 2008), [40].

84 CESCR, Concluding Observations: Benin, E/C.12/1/Add.78 (5 June 2002), [27]; see also [47]. See also Benin, E/C.12/BEN/CO/2 (9 June 2008), [28].

85 CESCR, Concluding Observations: France, E/C.12/FRA/CO/3 (9 June 2008), [51].

86 Human Rights Council, Report of the Independent Expert in the Field of Cultural Rights, A/HRC/17/38 (21 March 2011).

an obligation to ensure access to cultural heritage, the Special Rapporteur has indicated:

[T]he following must be ensured: (a) physical access to cultural heritage, which may be complemented by access through information technologies; (b) economic access, which means that access should be affordable to all; (c) information access, which refers to the right to seek, receive and impart information on cultural heritage, without borders; and (d) access to decision making and monitoring procedures...[87]

Creative freedom

The right to creative freedom is implicit in the right to take part in cultural life under Article 15(1)(a). The obligations of states in this regard are reinforced by Article 15(2), which provides that states shall take steps necessary for the conservation, the development, and the diffusion' of culture, and, more explicitly, by Article 15(3), under which states 'undertake to reinforce the freedom indispensable for...creative activity'.

This element of the right clearly overlaps, to a large extent, with the right to freedom of expression, as protected in a range of international instruments, including Article 19(2) of the ICCPR. As with the right to freedom of expression, there are two aspects to this element of the right to take part in cultural life: the right to create and the right to have access to the cultural creations of others.

According to General Comment No. 21:

The obligation to respect [the right to take part in cultural life] includes the adoption of specific measures aimed at achieving respect for the right of everyone, individually or in association with others or within a community or group:...

(b) To enjoy freedom of opinion, freedom of expression in the language or languages of their choice, and the right to seek, receive and impart information and ideas of all kinds and forms including art forms, regardless of frontiers of any kind;

This implies the right of all persons to have access to, and to participate in, varied information exchanges, and to have access to cultural goods and services, understood as vectors of identity, values and meaning.

(c) To enjoy the freedom to create, individually, in association with others, or within a community or group, which implies that States Parties must abolish censorship of cultural activities in the arts and other forms of expression, if any;

This obligation is closely related to the duty of States Parties, under Article 15, paragraph 3, 'to respect the freedom indispensable for scientific research and creative activity'.[88]

[87] HRC, Report of the Independent Expert in the Field of Cultural Rights, A/HRC/17/38 (21 March 2011), [60]. See also the detailed discussion of the 'right to have access to and enjoy cultural heritage' in the Special Rapporteur's report on Morocco: Human Rights Council, Report of the Independent Expert in the Field of Cultural Rights, Addendum: Mission to Morocco (5–16 September 2011), A/HRC/20/26/Add.2 (2 May 2012), [42]–[50].

[88] CESCR, General Comment No. 21, [49].

A large range of practices can affect creative freedom. As the Special Rapporteur noted in her report on the right to freedom of artistic expression and creativity:[89]

Restrictions can be imposed at various stages of the artistic creation, from the development of the idea through to production, performance, publication and distribution. Restrictions on artistic freedoms can result from oppressive laws and regulations, but can also be the outcome of a fear of physical or economic coercion.[90]

The work of the Committee indicates that it is, first and foremost, concerned with censorship, which has a clear and direct impact on creative freedom, together with measures directed specifically at artists and others engaged in creative activity. So, for example, in relation to Korea:

The Committee is concerned that the National Security Law is being used to curtail the activities of intellectuals and artists. Under this law, not only are their works being censored, confiscated or destroyed, but the intellectuals and artists themselves are being subjected to criminal prosecution.[91]

Similarly, in relation to Kenya:

The Committee...regrets the frequent interventions by the government in cultural life through, for example, the banning of plays and the prohibition of certain books and periodicals.[92]

The Committee has also expressed concern regarding a range of lesser measures, which may nonetheless affect creative freedom and freedom of expression. For example, in relation to Australia:

The Committee expresses concern over provisions of the Federal Customs Regulations which prohibit the importation of certain materials...The practical application of these provisions could run counter to freedom of artistic creation and performance.[93]

And in relation to Iraq:

[T]he Committee is concerned that clarification remains to be given by the State Party as to the compatibility of the steps taken by the Government in its exercise of control over the choice and broadcasting of minority language radio programmes with the implementation of the provisions of the Covenant, including its Article 15, paragraph 2.[94]

[89] Human Rights Council, Report of the Special Rapporteur in the Field of Cultural Rights, The right to freedom of artistic expression and creativity ('Report of the Special Rapporteur on the right to freedom of artistic expression and creativity'), A/HRC/23/34 (14 March 2013).

[90] HRC, Report of the Special Rapporteur on the right to freedom of artistic expression and creativity, [53].

[91] CESCR, Concluding Observations: Republic of Korea, E/C.12/1/Add.59 (21 May 2001), [32].

[92] CESCR, Concluding Observations: Kenya, E/C.12/1993/6 (3 June 1993), [19]. See also Libyan Arab Jamahiriya, E/C.12/1/Add.15 (20 May 1997), [18]; Tunisia, E/C.12/1/Add.36 (14 May 1999), [19]; Egypt, E/C.12/1/Add.44 (23 May 2000), [25] and [41].

[93] CESCR, Concluding Observations: Australia, E/C.12/1993/9 (3 June 1993), [12].

[94] CESCR, Concluding Observations: Iraq, E/C.12/1994/6 (30 May 1994), [13]. See also Iran, E/C.12/1993/7 (9 June 1993), [7] re. fatwahs.

In recent years, the Committee has also shown particular concern regarding restrictions on access to the Internet.[95]

The Special Rapporteur's report on this issue is also instructive in terms of the sorts of practices which may amount to a restriction on creative freedom. She identifies, in particular, unclear regulations; prior censorship; classification and rating (when used as 'tools of oppression'[96]); regulation over the use of public space for cultural purposes; restrictions on mobility, such as travel restrictions for artists; and economic and financial issues as possible causes of restrictions on the enjoyment of this right.[97]

Minority and indigenous groups

The Committee has expressed particular concern regarding the rights of minority groups and indigenous peoples to maintain and develop their own culture and way of life. This is probably the single most commonly raised issue in the Committee's Concluding Observations on Article 15.

The position in international law is summarized well in the report of the Special Rapporteur in the field of cultural rights on her mission to Brazil:

> Ensuring the cultural rights of persons belonging to specific cultural communities who differ from dominant majorities (Afro-descendant communities, indigenous peoples and other groups) implies providing them with the possibilities for bringing their own individual and collective cultural viewpoints to the shaping of cultural and social developments, while preserving in parallel those elements of their culture that they desire to maintain. It also implies promoting and protecting the rights of minorities and indigenous peoples recognized at the international level, which protect minorities and indigenous peoples' culture understood as a way of life, including their language, religion and system of beliefs, traditions, customs and other artistic and cultural manifestations.[98]

More specifically, General Comment No. 21 provides:

> 32. In the Committee's view, Article 15, paragraph 1(a) of the Covenant also includes the right of minorities and of persons belonging to minorities to take part in the cultural life of society, and also to conserve, promote and develop their own culture. This right entails the obligation of States Parties to recognize, respect and protect minority cultures as an essential component of the identity of the States themselves. Consequently, minorities have the right to their cultural diversity, traditions, customs, religion, forms of education, languages, communication media (press, radio, television, Internet) and other manifestations of their cultural identity and membership.
>
> 33. Minorities, as well as persons belonging to minorities, have the right not only to their own identity but also to development in all areas of cultural life. Any programme

[95] CESCR, Concluding Observations: China, E/C.12/1/Add.107 (13 May 2005), [39]; Libyan Arab Jamahiriya, E/C.12/LYB/CO/2 (25 January 2006), [21].

[96] Report of the Special Rapporteur on the right to freedom of artistic expression and creativity, [64].

[97] See Report of the Special Rapporteur on the right to freedom of artistic expression and creativity, [53]–[84].

[98] Human Rights Council, Report of the Independent Expert in the Field of Cultural Rights, Addendum: Mission to Brazil, A/HRC/1738/Add.1 (21 March 2011), [66].

intended to promote the constructive integration of minorities and persons belonging to minorities into the society of a State Party should thus be based on inclusion, participation and non-discrimination, with a view to preserving the distinctive character of minority cultures.[99]

In relation to indigenous peoples, in particular, the General Comment provides as follows:

Indigenous peoples have the right to act collectively to ensure respect for their right to maintain, control, protect and develop their cultural heritage, traditional knowledge and traditional cultural expressions, as well as the manifestations of their sciences, technologies and cultures, including human and genetic resources, seeds, medicines, knowledge of the properties of fauna and flora, oral traditions, literature, designs, sports and traditional games, and visual and performing arts. States parties should respect the principle of free, prior and informed consent of indigenous peoples in all matters covered by their specific rights.[100]

In its Concluding Observations, the Committee frequently expresses concern about the position of minority and indigenous groups, both generally, and in particular with respect to the maintenance of their cultural heritage. For example, in relation to France:

29. The Committee remains concerned about the lack of official recognition of minorities within the territory of the State Party. With specific regard to cultural rights, the Committee further notes with concern that some of these rights are not respected…

50. The Committee…recommends that the State Party consider reviewing its position with regard to the recognition of minorities under the Constitution, and recognize officially the need to protect the cultural diversity of all minority groups under the jurisdiction of the State Party, in accordance with the provisions of Article 15.[101]

And in relation to Hungary:

The Committee recommends that the State Party take appropriate measures, including education and awareness-raising campaigns, to integrate the values of minority cultures into the national culture, while at the same time preserving the cultural identity of its minorities.[102]

The Committee has even suggested that states are required to take measures to protect minority groups outside their own jurisdiction. For example, the Committee has inquired whether Sweden 'had taken any steps to ease the marginalization that the Gypsy population often suffered in other European countries'.[103]

[99] CESCR, General Comment No. 21. [100] CESCR, General Comment No. 21, [37].

[101] CESCR, Concluding Observations: France, E/C.12/FRA/CO/3 (9 June 2008), [29] and [50].

[102] CESCR, Concluding Observations: Hungary, E/C.12/HUN/CO/3 (16 January 2008), [53]. See also Syrian Arab Republic, E/C.12/1/Add.63 (24 September 2001), [45]; Belgium, E/C.12/BEL/CO/3 (4 January 2008), [37]; Ukraine, E/C.12/UKR/CO/5 (4 January 2008), [59]; Kenya, E/C.12/KEN/CO/1 (1 December 2008), [35].

[103] CESCR, Report on the Sixth Session, E/1992/23 (25 November–13 December 1991), [248] (Sweden).

This may reflect the emphasis on 'international contacts and co-operation' in Article 15(4).

In addition, the Committee has emphasized the importance of allowing persons from minority and indigenous groups to participate in decision-making processes. According to the General Comment, the minimum core obligations associated with the right to take part in cultural life include an obligation for states:

> To allow and encourage the participation of persons belonging to minority groups, indigenous peoples or to other communities in the design and implementation of laws and policies that affect them. In particular, States Parties should obtain their free and informed prior consent when the preservation of their cultural resources, especially those associated with their way of life and cultural expression, are at risk.[104]

In addition to this general concern for the position of minority groups and their ability to maintain and practise their traditional ways of life, the Committee's work has identified two particular issues regarding the cultural rights of minorities: the right of minority groups to use and maintain their own language (including, in particular, in the context of education); and the rights of indigenous peoples to ancestral lands and natural resources which form part of their culture.

Language

The rights of minority groups to use their own language are provided for in a number of international legal instruments, both binding and non-binding. These include Article 27 of the ICCPR; the UN Declaration on the Rights of Persons Belonging to National or Ethnic, Religious and Linguistic Minorities;[105] the UN Declaration on the Rights of Indigenous Peoples;[106] the International Labour Organization Indigenous and Tribal Peoples Convention;[107] the European Framework Convention for the Protection of National Minorities;[108] and the 1990 Copenhagen Document produced by the Organization for Security and Cooperation in Europe,[109] and the subsequent 1998 Oslo Recommendations on the Linguistic Rights of National Minorities.[110] Reflecting this body of law, the Committee has, when considering Article 15(1)(a), paid special attention to the possibilities for minority and indigenous groups to use and maintain their own language.

The Committee's comments in this context have focused on the general need to preserve minority languages, including, in particular, indigenous and endangered

[104] CESCR, General Comment No. 21, [55(e)].

[105] Declaration of the Rights of Persons Belonging to National or Ethnic, Religious and Linguistic Minorities, Article 2(1).

[106] Declaration on the Rights of Indigenous Peoples, Article 13.

[107] ILO Indigenous and Tribal Peoples Convention, Article 28.

[108] European Framework Convention for the Protection of National Minorities, Article 10.

[109] Conference on Security and Co-operation in Europe, Document of the Copenhagen Meeting of the Conference on the Human Dimension (29 June 1990) 29 ILM 1305, Article 32.

[110] Organization for Security and Co-operation in Europe, Oslo Recommendations Regarding the Linguistic Rights of National Minorities (February 1998).

languages,[111] together with a range of more specific issues. Thus, the Committee has expressed concern about the ability of minority groups to use their mother tongue in communications with public authorities,[112] and in the media;[113] and the possibility for minorities to give their children names in their mother tongue, and to have those names registered.[114] In some circumstances, the Committee has suggested that minority languages should be recognized as official languages by states.[115]

The most common observation by the Committee, however, concerns the importance of allowing for the use of minority and indigenous languages in education. This is significant both because language barriers can prevent minority groups from accessing or benefiting from education, and because failure to teach minority languages can lead to their decline and eventual disappearance. This dual importance of education in minority languages is made clear in the Committee's comments on Cambodia:

> The Committee notes that primary education continues to be a problem for the various ethnic minorities in the north and east of the country, where there are 20 minority languages spoken by these groups as their mother tongue while the formal education curriculum has only used Khmer as the medium of instruction. The Committee also notes with concern that indigenous communities may lose their culture and language as a result of a lack of education and information in their own languages.[116]

The issue of minority language use in education is raised in many of the Committee's Concluding Observations,[117] and is discussed further in the chapter on the right to education, above.

The Committee's 2009 Concluding Observations on Australia are indicative of the general approach the Committee takes to issues regarding the use of minority and indigenous languages. The Committee's comments cover both the general need to preserve endangered languages, and the specific steps through which this can be accomplished, including in the context of education:

> The Committee notes with concern that according to the National Indigenous Languages Survey, only about 145 of the original estimated 250 indigenous languages exist today in the State Party, and most of them are critically endangered...The Committee recommends that the State Party: (a) strengthen its efforts to guarantee the indigenous peoples' rights under Article 1 and 15 to enjoy their identity and culture, including through the

[111] See, eg, CESCR, Concluding Observations: Canada, E/C.12/CAN/CO/4 (22 May 2006), [33]; Australia, E/C.12/AUS/CO/4 (12 June 1999), [33].

[112] See, eg, CESCR, Concluding Observations: Bolivia, E/C.12/1/Add.60 (21 May 2001), [24] and [45]; Honduras, E/C.12/1/Add.57 (21 May 2001), [29] and [52].

[113] See, eg, CESCR, Concluding Observations: Iraq, E/C.12/1994/6 (30 May 1994), [13]; Libyan Arab Jamahiriya, E/C.12/LYB/CO/2 (25 January 2006), [23].

[114] See, eg, CESCR, Concluding Observations: Libyan Arab Jamahiriya, E/C.12/LYB/CO/2 (25 January 2006), [24] and [42]; Morocco, E/C.12/MAR/CO/3 (4 September 2006), [32] and [59].

[115] See, eg, CESCR, Concluding Observations: Angola, E/C.12/DZA/CO/4 (7 June 2010), [22].

[116] CESCR, Concluding Observations: Cambodia, E/C.12/KHM/CO/1 (12 June 2009), [34].

[117] See, eg, CESCR, Concluding Observations: Japan, E/C.12/1/Add.67 (24 September 2001), [32] and [60]; Ecuador, E/C.12/1/Add.100 (7 June 2004), [58].

preservation of their traditional languages; (b) consider improving the Maintenance of Indigenous Languages and Records Program; (c) preserve and promote bilingual education in schools.[118]

Rights of indigenous peoples to ancestral lands and natural resources

Noting that the cultures of indigenous peoples are often tied to their ancestral lands, the Committee has interpreted the right to take part in cultural life as encompassing, in appropriate cases, the right of indigenous peoples to their ancestral lands and natural resources:

According to General Comment No. 21:

> The strong communal dimension of indigenous peoples' cultural life is indispensable to their existence, well-being and full development, and includes the right to the lands, territories and resources which they have traditionally owned, occupied or otherwise used or acquired. Indigenous peoples' cultural values and rights associated with their ancestral lands and their relationship with nature should be regarded with respect and protected, in order to prevent the degradation of their particular way of life, including their means of subsistence, the loss of their natural resources and, ultimately, their cultural identity. States Parties must therefore take measures to recognize and protect the rights of indigenous peoples to own, develop, control and use their communal lands, territories and resources, and, where they have been otherwise inhabited or used without their free and informed consent, take steps to return these lands and territories.[119]

This approach is reflected in the Committee's Concluding Observations. For example, in relation to the Democratic Republic of the Congo:

> The Committee is deeply concerned that the systematic and abusive exploitation of forest resources in the State Party has negatively affected the lands and the way of life of numerous indigenous peoples, especially the pygmies living in the Province of Equateur, impeding the enjoyment of their rights as well as their material and spiritual relationship with nature and, ultimately their own cultural identity. The Committee recommends that the State party adopt legislation and measures to recognize the status of pygmies and other indigenous peoples living in the State Party, in order to protect their ancestral lands as well as their own cultural identity.[120]

Similarly, in relation to Chad:

> The Committee is concerned about the system of exploitation of natural resources in the State party, which adversely affects the land and the way of life of indigenous peoples, depriving them of rights related to their ancestral land and cultural identity. The Committee recommends that the State party adopt specific measures to protect the cultural identity and ancestral land of the indigenous population.[121]

[118] CESCR, Concluding Observations: Australia, E/C.12/AUS/CO/4 (12 June 2009), [33].

[119] CESCR, General Comment No. 21, [36].

[120] CESCR, Concluding Observations: Democratic Republic of the Congo, E/C.12/COD/CO/4 (16 December 2009), [36].

[121] CESCR, Concluding Observations: Chad, E/C.12/TCD/CO/3 (16 December 2009), [35]. See also Sweden, E/C.12/SWE/CO/5 (1 December 2008), [15]; Australia, E/C.12/AUS/CO/4 (12 June 2009), [32]; Madagascar, E/C.12/MDG/CO/2 (16 December 2009), [33].

The connection between indigenous culture and rights to land and natural resources is also acknowledged in the work of other international and regional bodies. The Human Rights Committee's General Comment No. 23 on the rights of minorities, for example, notes that:

> With regard to the exercise of the cultural rights protected under article 27, the Committee observes that culture manifests itself in many forms, including a particular way of life associated with the use of land resources, especially in the case of indigenous peoples. That right may include such traditional activities as fishing or hunting and the right to live in reserves protected by law.[122]

Further, in a number of cases before the Human Rights Committee, indigenous peoples have claimed that interference with their ancestral lands, and with their ability to dispose of natural resources through traditional activities such as reindeer herding and fishing, constitute violations of Article 27 of the ICCPR, which provides that 'persons belonging to…minorities shall not be denied the right, in community with the other members of their group, to enjoy their own culture'. So, for example, in *Chief Ominayak and the Lubicon Lake Band v Canada*, the HRC found that expropriations of traditional lands of the Lubicon Lake Band for the purposes of private oil and gas exploration 'threaten the way of life and culture of the Lubicon Lake Band, and constitute a violation of article 27 so long as they continue'.[123]

Similarly, in the case of *Länsman v Finland*,[124] the HRC considered whether quarrying on lands traditionally used by indigenous Sami people for reindeer husbandry would constitute a violation of Article 27. The HRC noted that 'reindeer husbandry is an essential element of [Sami] culture'[125] and further that 'mountain Riutusvaara [where quarrying was to be carried out] continues to have a spiritual significance relevant to their culture'.[126] On the facts, the Committee found that the impact of the quarrying was not so substantial as to deny the authors the right to enjoy their own culture. However, the Committee noted that:

> [I]f mining activities…were to be approved on a large scale and significantly expanded by those companies to which exploitation permits have been issued, then this may constitute a violation of the authors' rights under article 27, in particular of their right to enjoy their own culture.[127]

In subsequent cases, the HRC considered the impact on traditional reindeer husbandry of logging,[128] and state measures denying access to traditional grazing lands in favour of private property interests.[129] Again, on the facts of each case,

122 HRC, General Comment No. 23, [7].

123 *Chief Ominayak and the Lubicon Lake Band v Canada*, HRC Communication No. 167/84 (26 March 1990), [33].

124 HRC Communication No. 511/92 (8 November 1994).

125 *Länsman v Finland*, [9.2].

126 *Länsman v Finland*, [9.3].

127 *Länsman v Finland*, [9.8].

128 *Länsman v Finland*, HRC Communication No. 671/95 (30 October 1996); *Äärelä and Näkkäläjärvi v Finland*, HRC Communication No. 779/97 (24 October 2001); *Länsman v Finland*, HRC Communication No. 1023/01 (17 March 2005).

129 *Jonassen v Norway*, HRC Communication No. 942/00 (25 October 2002).

the Committee found no violation of Article 27. However, it is clear that the Committee accepted that the complaints fell within the scope of Article 27, and that claims to enjoy one's own culture could include claims relating to the land and natural resources necessary to engage in traditional cultural activities. Similarly, in *Mahuika v New Zealand*, the HRC considered whether legislation which restricted the fishing rights of Maori tribes amounted to a violation of Article 27. Although the Committee found no violation on the facts, it acknowledged that 'the use and control of fisheries is an essential element of [Maori] culture',[130] such that restriction of access to fish stocks could, in an appropriate case, be contrary to Article 27.

Within the African human rights system, the significance of ancestral lands to the culture of indigenous peoples was the subject of the decision of the African Commission on Human and Peoples' Rights in the *Endorois* case. As noted above, this case is significant as it is the only case—at either the international or national level—to have expressly considered the right to take part in cultural life (in this case, under Article 17(2) and (3) of the African Charter). The case was brought on behalf of the Endorois, a community of indigenous people who were forcibly removed from their ancestral lands around the Lake Bogoria area in Kenya when the Kenyan Government gazetted those areas in order to create a game reserve for tourists. The complainants argued that this violated numerous rights under the African Charter, including the rights to cultural life under Article 17(2) and (3). The basis for this claim was that the cultural practices and pastoralist way of life of the Endorois were inextricably connected with access to their ancestral lands:

> The Complainants state that the area surrounding Lake Bogoria is fertile land, providing green pasture and medicinal salt licks, which help raise healthy cattle. The Complainants state that Lake Bogoria is central to the Endorois religious and traditional practices. They state that the community's historical prayer sites, places for circumcision rituals, and other cultural ceremonies are around Lake Bogoria. These sites were used on a weekly or monthly basis for smaller local ceremonies, and on an annual basis for cultural festivities involving Endorois from the whole region. The Complainants claim that the Endorois believe that the spirits of all Endorois, no matter where they are buried, live on in the Lake, with annual festivals taking place at the Lake. The Complainants further claim that the Endorois believe that the Monchongoi forest is considered the birthplace of the Endorois and the settlement of the first Endorois community.[131]

Further:

> The Complainants claim that land for the Endorois is held in very high esteem, since tribal land, in addition to securing subsistence and livelihood, is seen as sacred, being inextricably linked to the cultural integrity of the community and its traditional way of life. Land, they claim, belongs to the community and not the individual and is essential to the preservation and survival as a traditional people. The Complainants claim that the Endorois health, livelihood, religion and culture are all intimately connected with their traditional

[130] *Mahuika v New Zealand*, HRC Communication No. 547/93 (27 October 1993), [9.3].
[131] *Endorois* case, [6].

land, as grazing lands, sacred religious sites and plants used for traditional medicine are all situated around the shores of Lake Bogoria.[132]

On the issue of the connection of the Endorois with their ancestral lands, the Commission found as follows:

After studying all the submissions of the Complainants and the Respondent State, the African Commission is of the view that Endorois culture, religion, and traditional way of life are intimately intertwined with their ancestral lands—Lake Bogoria and the surrounding area. It agrees that Lake Bogoria and the Monchongoi Forest are central to the Endorois' way of life and without access to their ancestral land, the Endorois are unable to fully exercise their cultural and religious rights, and feel disconnected from their land and ancestors.[133]

Having established this connection, the Commission turned to consider the substance of the complaint regarding the right to take part in cultural life:

239. The Complainants allege that the Endorois' cultural rights have been violated on two counts: first, the community has faced systematic restrictions on access to cultural sites and, second, that the cultural rights of the community have been violated by the serious damage caused by the Kenyan Authorities to their pastoralist way of life.

…

241. The African Commission is of the view that protecting human rights goes beyond the duty not to destroy or deliberately weaken minority groups, but requires respect for, and protection of, their religious and cultural heritage essential to their group identity, including buildings and sites such as libraries, churches, mosques, temples and synagogues.

…

244. The African Commission notes that a common theme that usually runs through the debate about culture and its violation is the association with one's ancestral land. It notes that its own Working Group on Indigenous Populations/Communities has observed that dispossession of land and its resources is 'a major human rights problem for indigenous peoples.' It further notes that a Report from the Working Group has also emphasized that dispossession 'threatens the economic, social and *cultural survival* of indigenous pastoralist and hunter-gatherer communities.'

…

249. In its analysis of Article 17 of the African Charter, the African Commission is aware that unlike Articles 8 and 14, Article 17 has no claw-back clause. The absence of a claw-back clause is an indication that the drafters of the Charter envisaged few, if any, circumstances in which it would be appropriate to limit a people's right to culture. It further notes that even if the Respondent State were to put some limitation on the exercise of such a right, the restriction must be proportionate to a legitimate aim that does not interfere adversely on the exercise of a community's cultural rights. Thus, even if the creation of the Game Reserve constitutes a legitimate aim, the Respondent State's failure to secure access, as of right, for the celebration of the cultural festival and rituals cannot be deemed proportionate to that aim. The Commission is of the view that the cultural activities of the Endorois community

[132] *Endorois* case, [16]. [133] *Endorois* case, [156].

pose no harm to the ecosystem of the Game Reserve and the restriction of cultural rights could not be justified, especially as no suitable alternative was given to the community.

250. It is the opinion of the African Commission that the Respondent State has overlooked that the universal appeal of great culture lies in its particulars and that imposing burdensome laws or rules on culture undermines its enduring aspects. The Respondent State has not taken into consideration the fact that by restricting access to Lake Bogoria, it has denied the community access to an integrated system of beliefs, values, norms, mores, traditions and artifacts closely linked to access to the Lake.

251. By forcing the community to live on semi-arid lands without access to medicinal salt licks and other vital resources for the health of their livestock, the Respondent State have created a major threat to the Endorois pastoralist way of life. It is of the view that the very essence of the Endorois' right to culture has been denied, rendering the right, to all intents and purposes, illusory. Accordingly, the Respondent State is found to have violated Article 17(2) and (3) of the Charter.

In this way, the right to take part in cultural life was used to protect indigenous peoples' access to ancestral lands and natural resources.

The close relationship between indigenous peoples' cultural identity and access to their ancestral lands and natural resources has also been recognized within the Inter-American human rights system. Within that system, however, the right to culture, recognized in the San Salvador Protocol, is not justiciable before the Inter-American Commission on Human Rights or Inter-American Court of Human Rights.[134] As a result, the relevant cases have considered the issue in different terms, using the concept of indigenous peoples' cultural connection to the land to found property rights in relation to ancestral lands, thus bringing indigenous land claims within the right to property under Article 21 of the American Convention on Human Rights. The reasoning of the Inter-American Court of Human Rights is clearly set out in the *Case of the Yakye Axa Indigenous Community v Paraguay*:[135]

130. ILO Convention No. 169 contains numerous provisions pertaining to the right of indigenous communities to communal property, which is addressed in this case, and said provisions can shed light on the content and scope of Article 21 of the American Convention. The State ratified and included said Convention 169 in its domestic legislation by means of Law No. 234/93.

131. Applying said criteria, this Court has underlined that the close relationship of indigenous peoples with the land must be acknowledged and understood as the fundamental basis for their culture, spiritual life, wholeness, economic survival, and preservation and transmission to future generations.

135. The culture of the members of the indigenous communities directly relates to a specific way of being, seeing, and acting in the world, developed on the basis of their close relationship with their traditional territories and the resources therein, not only because they are their main means of subsistence, but also because they are part of their worldview, their religiosity, and therefore, of their cultural identity.

[134] See San Salvador Protocol, Article 19(6).

[135] 17 June 2005, IACHR Series C No. 125.

136. The above relates to the provision set forth in Article 13 of ILO Convention No. 169, that the States must respect 'the special importance for the cultures and spiritual values of the peoples concerned of their relationship with the lands or territories, or both as applicable, which they occupy or otherwise use, and in particular the collective aspects of this relationship'.

137. Therefore, the close ties of indigenous peoples with their traditional territories and the natural resources therein associated with their culture, as well as the components derived from them, must be safeguarded by Article 21 of the American Convention. In this regard, the Court has previously asserted that the term 'property' used in said Article 21 includes 'those material things which can be possessed, as well as any right which may be part of a person's patrimony; that concept includes all movables and immovables, corporeal and incorporeal elements and any other intangible object capable of having value'.[136]

Protection for national cultures

It is not only minority cultures which the Committee seeks to protect in relation to the right to take part in cultural life, but also national cultures as a whole. So, for example, in relation to Rwanda, the Committee 'wanted to know what steps were being taken to develop and protect national culture'.[137] And with regard to Jordan, the Committee:

[W]ished to know if any television material was locally produced or whether it was all imported; what role satellite and cable television played; and what was done to protect local culture from being overwhelmed by television transmissions.[138]

The Committee has also, for example, inquired into the effect of tourism on national culture and the enjoyment of cultural rights.[139]

This interest in protecting national cultures from foreign influences can be seen to reflect concerns within international law more generally regarding the protection of cultural diversity in the context of increasing globalization, with the associated risk of cultural homogenization. These concerns would seem to lie behind the development of the Universal Declaration on Cultural Diversity, which explicitly links cultural rights and the protection of cultural diversity.[140] Some of the principles in this Declaration are restated, in binding form, in the Convention on the Protection and Promotion of the Diversity of Cultural Expressions.[141] This Convention aims to protect cultural diversity, particularly in the context of

[136] *Yakye Axa v Paraguay*. See also *Case of the Moiwana Community v Suriname*, 15 June 2005, IACHR Series C No. 124, [130]–[134]; *Case of the Sawhoya Maxa Indigenous Community v Paraguay,* 29 March 2006, IACHR Series C No. 146, [118]; *Case of the Saramaka People v Suriname*, 28 November 2007, IACHR Series C No. 172 and 185.

[137] CESCR, Report on the Third Session, E/1989/22 (6–24 February 1989), [188] (Rwanda).

[138] CESCR, Report on the Fifth Session, E/1991/23 (26 November–14 December 1990), [80] (Jordan). See also, eg, CESCR, Report on the Sixth Session, E/1992/23 (25 November–13 December 1991), [248] (Sweden).

[139] CESCR, Report on the Third Session, E/1989/22 (6–24 February 1989), [307] (Trinidad and Tobago).

[140] See especially UNESCO Universal Declaration on Cultural Diversity, Articles 4, 5 and 6.

[141] Convention on the Protection and Promotion of the Diversity of Cultural Expressions (adopted 20 October 2005, 2440 UNTS 311, entered into force 18 March 2007).

globalization of trade, and gives states the right to adopt measures to protect cultural diversity on their territories, including 'all appropriate measures' where cultural expressions are 'in need of urgent safeguarding'.[142]

The connection between globalization and threats to rights under the Covenant, including cultural rights, is made explicit in the Committee's Concluding Observations on Mexico in 1994:

> The Committee recommends in particular that the State party should take energetic steps to mitigate any negative impact that the North American Free Trade Agreement (NAFTA) might have on the enjoyment of the rights set out in the Covenant.[143]

Against this background, repeated references in General Comment No. 21 to the fact that the right to take part in cultural life requires states to protect cultural diversity can be read to include state obligations to protect national cultures. For example:

> States Parties are under an obligation to facilitate the right of everyone to take part in cultural life by taking a wide range of positive measures…that will contribute to the realization of this right, such as:
>
> (a) Adopting policies for the protection and promotion of cultural diversity, and facilitating access to a rich and diversified range of cultural expressions.[144]

The concern to protect culture in the face of the perceived threat of cultural homogenization arising from globalization, and in particular increased trade in cultural services, is also reflected in paragraph 50(b) of General Comment No. 21, which indicates that:

> Particular attention should be paid to the adverse consequences of globalization, undue privatization of goods and services, and deregulation on the right to participate in cultural life.

The Special Rapporteur in the field of cultural rights has also addressed this issue, noting that:

> There is a growing perception that globalization leads to cultural homogenization. This raises the question of how best to assess the accuracy of such a perception and what measures, if any, are required to ensure the enjoyment of cultural rights in this context.[145]

In particular, difficult questions arise as to how to balance the need to protect national cultures against the importance of freedom of expression and the free circulation of ideas. In this context, it should also be noted that, under Article 15(4), states recognize the benefits of 'encouragement and development of international contacts and co-operation in the scientific and cultural fields'. Ultimately, however, the Committee appears aware of the need to strike a delicate

[142] Convention on the Protection and Promotion of the Diversity of Cultural Expressions, Article 8.
[143] CESCR, Concluding Observations: Mexico, E/C.12/1993/16 (5 January 1994), [11].
[144] CESCR, General Comment No. 21, [52].
[145] Human Rights Council, Report of the Independent Expert in the Field of Cultural Rights, A/HRC/14/36 (22 March 2010), [44].

balance in this area, and 'has adroitly balanced the right to enjoy a distinctive national culture with the competing demands for the freedom to receive outside cultural input and for cultural development'.[146]

Non-discrimination

The requirement to guarantee the rights contained in the ICESCR without discrimination is, as noted above in Chapter 4 on Article 2(2), an immediate obligation, not subject to progressive realization. The requirement to ensure equal access to culture for all is therefore central to the right to take part in cultural life, and much of the Committee's work on Article 15(1)(a) has focused on this issue. Since violations of this aspect of the right are relatively easy to identify, discrimination in access to cultural life also seems likely to feature prominently in any Article 15 complaints under the Optional Protocol.

According to General Comment No. 21, accessibility of culture requires 'effective and concrete opportunities for individuals and communities to enjoy culture fully, within physical and financial reach for all in both urban and rural areas, without discrimination'.[147] Further:

21. Article 2, paragraph 2, and Article 3 of the Covenant prohibit any discrimination in the exercise of the right of everyone to take part in cultural life on the grounds of race, colour, sex, language, religion, political or other opinion, national or social origin, property, birth or other status.

22. In particular, no one shall be discriminated against because he or she chooses to belong, or not to belong, to a given cultural community or group, or to practise or not to practise a particular cultural activity. Likewise, no one shall be excluded from access to cultural practices, goods and services.

23. The Committee emphasizes that the elimination of all forms of discrimination in order to guarantee the exercise of the right of everyone to take part in cultural life can, in many cases, be achieved with limited resources by the adoption, amendment or repeal of legislation, or through publicity and information... [E]ven in times of severe resource constraints, the most disadvantaged and marginalized individuals and groups can and indeed must be protected by the adoption of relatively low-cost targeted programmes.

The General Comment then goes on to consider in detail 'persons and communities requiring special protection',[148] namely women, children, older persons, persons with disabilities, minorities, migrants, indigenous peoples and persons living in poverty.

Concerns to ensure equality of access for all are also reflected in the Guidelines on Treaty-Specific Documents, which ask states to:

Provide information on the institutional infrastructure to promote popular participation in, and access to, cultural life, especially at the community level, including in rural and

[146] O'Keefe, 'The "Right to Take Part in Cultural Life" under Article 15 of the ICESCR', 922.
[147] CESCR, General Comment No. 21, [16(b)].
[148] CESCR, General Comment No. 21, [25]–[39].

deprived urban areas. In this regard, indicate the measures taken to promote broad participation in, and access to, cultural goods, institutions and activities, including measures taken:

(a) To ensure that access to concerts, theatre, cinema, sport events and other cultural activities is affordable for all segments of the population;

. . .

(c) To encourage participation in cultural life by children, including children from poorer families, and migrant or refugee children; and

(d) To eliminate physical, social and communication barriers preventing older persons and persons with disabilities from fully participating in cultural life.[149]

Particular issues concerning the cultural rights of minority and indigenous groups have been discussed above. The Committee has also offered guidance on measures to ensure equality of access for other groups which may suffer discrimination in this area.

Women

In relation to women's enjoyment of the right to participate in cultural life, the Committee has indicated that this requires 'the elimination of institutional and legal obstacles as well as those based on negative practices, including those attributed to customs and traditions, that prevent women from participating fully in cultural life'.[150] The Special Rapporteur has also prepared a specific report on the cultural rights of women.[151] According to the Special Rapporteur:

Women's perspectives and contributions must move from the margins of cultural life to the centre of the processes that create, interpret and shape culture. In order to ensure that the dominant culture of their societies is based on gender equality, the tendency to marginalize women's concerns and silence their voices must be overcome, obstructions impeding their equal participation in public life eliminated and their underrepresentation in the institutions and processes defining the culture of their communities surmounted. Women must be recognized as, and supported to be, equal spokespersons vested with the authority to determine which of the community's traditions are to be respected, protected and transmitted to future generations.[152]

Children

According to General Comment No. 21:

26. Children play a fundamental role as the bearers and transmitters of cultural values from generation to generation. States parties should take all the steps necessary to stimulate

[149] CESCR, Guidelines on Treaty-Specific Documents, [67].

[150] CESCR, General Comment No. 21, [25]. See also CESCR, General Comment No. 16, The equal right of men and women to the enjoyment of all economic, social and cultural rights (art. 3 of the International Covenant on Economic, Social and Cultural Rights), E/C.12/2005/4 (11 August 2005), [31].

[151] UNGA, Report of the Special Rapporteur in the Field of Cultural Rights, A/67/287 (10 August 2012).

[152] UNGA, Report of the Special Rapporteur in the Field of Cultural Rights, A/67/287 (10 August 2012), [25].

and develop children's full potential in the area of cultural life, with due regard for the rights and responsibilities of their parents or guardians. In particular, when taking into consideration their obligations under the Covenant and other human rights instruments on the right to education, including with regard to the aims of education, States should recall that the fundamental aim of educational development is the transmission and enrichment of common cultural and moral values in which the individual and society find their identity and worth. Thus, education must be culturally appropriate, include human rights education, enable children to develop their personality and cultural identity and to learn and understand cultural values and practices of the communities to which they belong, as well as those of other communities and societies.

27. The Committee wishes to recall in this regard that educational programmes of States parties should respect the cultural specificities of national or ethnic, linguistic and religious minorities as well as indigenous peoples, and incorporate in those programmes their history, knowledge and technologies, as well as their social, economic and cultural values and aspirations. Such programmes should be included in school curricula for all, not only for minorities and indigenous peoples. States parties should adopt measures and spare no effort to ensure that educational programmes for minorities and indigenous groups are conducted on or in their own language, taking into consideration the wishes expressed by communities and in the international human rights standards in this area. Educational programmes should also transmit the necessary knowledge to enable everyone to participate fully and on an equal footing in their own and in national communities.

Older persons

According to General Comment No. 21:

28. The Committee is of the view that States parties to the Covenant are obligated to pay particular attention to the promotion and protection of the cultural rights of older persons. The Committee emphasizes the important role that older persons continue to play in most societies by reason of their creative, artistic and intellectual abilities, and as the transmitters of information, knowledge, traditions and cultural values. Consequently, the Committee attaches particular importance to the message contained in recommendations 44 and 48 of the Vienna International Plan of Action on Aging, calling for the development of programmes featuring older persons as teachers and transmitters of knowledge, culture and spiritual values, and encouraging Governments and international organizations to support programmes aimed at providing older persons with easier physical access to cultural institutions (such as museums, theatres, concert halls and cinemas).

29. The Committee therefore urges States parties to take account of the recommendations contained in the United Nations Principles for Older Persons, and in particular of principle 7, that older persons should remain integrated in society, participate actively in the formulation and implementation of policies that directly affect their well-being and share their knowledge and skills with younger generations; and principle 16, that older persons should have access to the educational, cultural, spiritual and recreational resources of society.[153]

[153] See also CESCR, General Comment No. 6, The economic, social and cultural rights of older persons, E/1996/33 (12 August 1995) ('General Comment No. 6'), especially [39]–[41].

Persons with disabilities

According to the Committee's General Comment No. 5 on persons with disabilities:

36. The Standard Rules [on the Equalization of Opportunities for Persons with Disabilities] provide that 'States should ensure that persons with disabilities have the opportunity to utilize their creative, artistic and intellectual potential, not only for their own benefit, but also for the enrichment of their community, be they in urban or rural areas... States should promote the accessibility to and availability of places for cultural performances and services... [Rule 10, paras 1–2] The same applies to places for recreation, sports and tourism.

37. The right to full participation in cultural and recreational life for persons with disabilities further requires that communication barriers be eliminated to the greatest extent possible. Useful measures in this regard might include 'the use of talking books, papers written in simple language and with clear format and colours for persons with mental disability, [and] adapted television and theatre for deaf persons'. [See A/47/415, para 79]

38. In order to facilitate the equal participation in cultural life of persons with disabilities, Governments should inform and educate the general public about disability. In particular, measures must be taken to dispel prejudices or superstitious beliefs against persons with disabilities, for example those that view epilepsy as a form of spirit possession or a child with disabilities as a form of punishment visited upon the family. Similarly, the general public should be educated to accept that persons with disabilities have as much right as any other person to make use of restaurants, hotels, recreation centres and cultural venues.[154]

Migrants

According to General Comment No. 21:

34. States parties should pay particular attention to the protection of the cultural identities of migrants, as well as their language, religion and folklore, and of their right to hold cultural, artistic and intercultural events. States parties should not prevent migrants from maintaining their cultural links with their countries of origin.

35. As education is intrinsically related to culture, the Committee recommends that States parties adopt appropriate measures to enable the children of migrants to attend, on a basis of equal treatment, State-run educational institutions and programmes.

Persons living in poverty

According to General Comment No. 21:

38. The Committee considers that every person or group of persons is endowed with a cultural richness inherent in their humanity and therefore can make, and continues to make, a significant contribution to the development of culture. Nevertheless, it must be borne in mind that, in practice, poverty seriously restricts the ability of a person or a group of persons to exercise the right to take part in, gain access and contribute to, on equal terms, all spheres of cultural life, and more importantly, seriously affects their hopes for the future and their ability to enjoy effectively their own culture. The common underlying theme in

[154] CESCR, General Comment No. 5. See further CESCR, General Comment No. 21, [30]–[31].

the experience of persons living in poverty is a sense of powerlessness that is often a consequence of their situation. Awareness of their human rights, and particularly the right of every person to take part in cultural life, can significantly empower persons or groups of persons living in poverty.

39. Culture as a social product must be brought within the reach of all, on the basis of equality, non-discrimination and participation. Therefore, in implementing the legal obligations enshrined in article 15, paragraph 1(a), of the Covenant, States parties must adopt, without delay, concrete measures to ensure adequate protection and the full exercise of the right of persons living in poverty and their communities to enjoy and take part in cultural life.

General—barriers to access

In addition to considering issues of discrimination against certain groups in relation to the right to participate in cultural life, the Committee has also considered more generally the issue of barriers to access to culture, which affect the ability of individuals to participate in cultural life. In particular, the Committee has focused on financial, physical, geographical and linguistic barriers to access.

In relation to financial barriers to access, the Committee has emphasized that states must ensure that the cost of cultural activities does not prevent individuals from participating in cultural life, and has encouraged states to offer subsidies to overcome difficulties in this regard. So, for example, in relation to Guinea, the Committee has expressed concern that '[a]ccess to culture remains difficult, as demonstrated, for example, by the high price of publications'.[155] And in relation to Brazil:

The Committee notes with concern that the enjoyment of the right to cultural life under Article 15 of the Covenant is largely limited to the educated and/or affluent segments of society in the State Party… The Committee recommends… special provision through subsidies and other forms of assistance for those who lack the means to participate in the cultural activities of their choice.[156]

On the question of physical barriers to access, the Committee has focused, in particular, on issues of access for the elderly and persons with disabilities.[157] In this context, it is clear that the Committee will be concerned with issues such as wheelchair access to cultural venues, and 'adapted television and theatre for deaf persons'.[158]

As regards geographical barriers to access, the Committee has expressed concern regarding disparities in terms of the provision of cultural activities between rural and urban areas. So, for example, in relation to Brazil:

The Committee notes with concern… that cultural resources and assets are concentrated in large cities, with relatively little provision being made for smaller regions and towns… The

[155] CESCR, Concluding Observations: Guinea, E/C.12/1/Add.5 (28 May 1996), [24].

[156] CESCR, Concluding Observations: Brazil, E/C.12/BRA/Co/2 (12 June 2009), [33]. See also Kazakhstan, E/C.12/KAZ/CO/1 (7 June 2010), [37].

[157] See CESCR, General Comment No. 21, [28] and [31]; CESCR, General Comment No. 5, [36]–[37]; and CESCR, General Comment No. 6, [40].

[158] CESCR, General Comment No. 5, [37].

Committee recommends that the State Party take measures to encourage the broader participation of its citizens in cultural life, inter alia, by: (a) ensuring the wider availability of cultural resources and assets, particularly in smaller cities and regions.[159]

Finally, the Committee has expressed particular concern regarding language barriers which impede access to culture. So, for example, in its 1995 monitoring of Mauritius, the Committee raised questions regarding a short-story writing competition which formed part of a series of measures organized to promote cultural activity, but which did not allow short stories to be submitted in Creole.[160] Similarly, the Committee has expressed concern regarding prohibitions on the use of the Amazigh language in the media in Libya,[161] and has inquired into the percentage of cultural programmes available in the Guarani language in Paraguay.[162]

RELATIONSHIP TO OTHER RIGHTS

It is clear from General Comment No. 21 that an important aspect of the right to take part in cultural life involves the need to take cultural factors into account in the realization of other rights. In other words, the right to take part in cultural life informs and influences the content of other human rights. Thus, according to the General Comment, 'appropriateness' is a key element of realization of the right to take part in cultural life:

Appropriateness refers to the realization of a specific human right in a way that is pertinent and suitable to a given cultural modality or context, that is, respectful of the culture and cultural rights of individuals and communities, including minorities and indigenous peoples. The Committee has in many instances referred to the notion of cultural appropriateness (or cultural acceptability or adequacy) in past general comments, in relation in particular to the rights to food, health, water, housing and education. The way in which rights are implemented may also have an impact on cultural life and cultural diversity. The Committee wishes to stress in this regard the need to take into account, as far as possible, cultural values attached to, inter alia, food and food consumption, the use of water, the way health and education services are provided and the way housing is designed and constructed.[163]

At the same time, however, the right to take part in cultural life cannot be used to limit the scope of other rights under international human rights law. According to General Comment No. 21:

18. The Committee wishes to recall that, while account must be taken of national and regional particularities and various historical, cultural and religious backgrounds, it is

[159] CESCR, Concluding Observations: Brazil, E/C.12/BRA/CO/2 (12 June 2009), [33]. See also, eg, CESCR, Report on the Sixth Session, E/1992/23 (25 November–13 December 1991), [189] and [247].

[160] CESCR, Summary Record of the 40th Meeting: Mauritius, E/C.12/1995/SR.40 (30 November 1995), [41].

[161] CESCR, Concluding Observations: Libya, E/C.12/LYB/CO/2 (25 January 2006), [23].

[162] CESCR, Summary Record of the 4th Meeting: Paraguay, E/C.12/1996/SR.4 (6 May 1996), [31]–[37] and [43].

[163] CESCR, General Comment No. 21, [16(e)].

the duty of States, regardless of their political, economic or cultural systems, to promote and protect all human rights and fundamental freedoms. Thus, no one may invoke cultural diversity to infringe upon human rights guaranteed by international law, nor to limit their scope.

19. Applying limitations to the right of everyone to take part in cultural life may be necessary in certain circumstances, in particular in the case of negative practices, including those attributed to customs and traditions, that infringe upon other human rights. Such limitations must pursue a legitimate aim, be compatible with the nature of this right and be strictly necessary for the promotion of general welfare in a democratic society, in accordance with article 4 of the Covenant. Any limitations must therefore be proportionate, meaning that the least restrictive measures must be taken when several types of limitations may be imposed.[164]

The Committee thus demonstrates awareness of concerns that the right to take part in cultural life can be interpreted as allowing for extreme cultural relativism, which would undermine the protection of universal human rights. The Committee therefore seeks to balance the need to take cultural concerns into account when interpreting human rights with the need to ensure universal, minimum standards in the enjoyment of all rights.

This issue of the universalism/cultural relativism of human rights is addressed in more detail in the work of the Special Rapporteur in the field of cultural rights:

32. The principle of universality of human rights, one of the core principles of international human rights law, on the one hand, and cultural rights and cultural diversity on the other, are sometimes considered as opposed. This view stems partly from a misplaced tendency to equate cultural diversity with cultural relativism, which has the effect of raising fears and misunderstandings regarding the recognition and implementation of cultural rights.

33. According to the Vienna Declaration and Programme of Action (1993), while the significance of national and regional particularities and various historical, cultural and religious backgrounds must be borne in mind, it is the duty of the States, regardless of their political, economic and cultural systems, to promote and protect all human rights and fundamental freedoms (part. I, sect. 5). In particular, this entails, as enshrined in the Universal Declaration on Cultural Diversity (art. 4), and reiterated in resolution 10/23 of the Human Rights Council (para. 4), that no one may invoke cultural diversity to infringe upon human rights guaranteed by international law, nor to limit their scope…

34. Therefore, not all cultural practices can be considered as protected in international human rights law. For example, in accordance with article 5 of the Convention on the Elimination of All Forms of Discrimination against Women, States 'shall take all appropriate measures to modify the social and cultural patterns of conduct of men and women, with a view to achieving the elimination of prejudices and customary and all other practices which are based on the idea of the inferiority or the superiority of either of the sexes or on stereotyped roles for men and women'…

[164] CESCR, General Comment No. 21, [18]–[19].

35. Cultural rights may be subjected to limitations in certain circumstances. However, as in the case of any limitations in international human rights law, this should be a last resort only and be in accordance with certain conditions…

36. …[I]dentifying exactly which cultural practices should be considered as contrary to human rights is not always a simple task. At the national level, such an identification process requires, inter alia, a legal framework indicating principles on the basis of which cultural rights may be limited and an independent judiciary able to adopt an informed decision on the basis of such a legal framework, as well as international human rights law, taking into consideration the practice of international human rights supervisory bodies. The law alone does not suffice, however. Policy measures allowing for an informed, open and participatory debate to take place within a given society and/or community and encouraging a modification of cultural patterns or practices which are detrimental to the enjoyment of human rights are also necessary. What is particularly needed at the community level is the reinforcement of positive elements of culture while raising awareness of the oppressive nature of certain practices pursued in the name of culture through a process of 'cultural negotiation' involving families, intellectuals and community leaders. Such a process can create the space for new interpretations to arise and for developing good cultural practices, in particular those that are able to foster the implementation of universal human rights in various cultural contexts.[165]

Article 15(1)(b)

'The States Parties to the present Covenant recognize the right of everyone to enjoy the benefits of scientific progress and its applications.'

The 'right to science' is generally considered as somewhat separate from the cultural rights contained in other parts of Article 15. However, the formulation of this right can be seen to be driven by the same general considerations which led to the founding of UNESCO, discussed above, to advance access to science and culture for all.[166] As the Special Rapporteur in the field of cultural rights has noted, the right to science and the right to participate in the cultural life of the community are 'inherently interlinked, since both relate to the pursuit of knowledge and understanding and to human creativity in a constantly changing world'.[167]

[165] Human Rights Council, Report of the Independent Expert in the Field of Cultural Rights, A/HRC/14/36 (March 2010).

[166] Although the immediate origins of the right to take part in science are often traced to the post-war period and concern the way in which scientific discoveries could be misused to cause human suffering. One of the earliest references to this issue in international instruments can be seen in a resolution of the Inter-American Conference on the Problems of War and Peace held in Mexico City in 1945, which declared the 'duty of the State to protect the citizen against the use of scientific discoveries in a manner to create fear and unrest'. See further Richard Pierre Claude, 'Scientists' Rights and the Human Right to the Benefits of Science' in Audrey Chapman and Sage Russell (eds), *Core Obligations: Building a Framework for Economic, Social and Cultural Rights* (Intersentia, Antwerp, 2002), 250–1.

[167] Human Rights Council, Report of the Special Rapporteur in the Field of Cultural Rights on the right to enjoy the benefits of scientific progress and its applications, A/HRC/24/26 (14 May 2012), [3]. See further [16]–[20].

The right to science is protected in other international instruments, most notably Article 27(1) of the UDHR:

Everyone has the right freely to participate in the cultural life of the community, to enjoy the arts and to share in scientific advancement and its benefits.

The right is also recognized in regional human rights instruments. The Charter of the Organization of American States provides that states 'shall extend among themselves the benefits of science and technology by encouraging exchange and utilization of scientific and technological knowledge'.[168] Article 14 of the San Salvador Protocol to the American Convention on Human Rights provides that 'the States Parties to this Protocol recognize the right of everyone to enjoy the benefits of scientific and technological progress'. The American Declaration on the Rights and Duties of Man provides for the right of every person 'to participate in the benefits that result from intellectual progress, especially scientific discoveries'.[169] And Article 42 of the Arab Charter on Human Rights recognizes the right in substantially the same terms as those contained in the ICESCR, recognizing, for example, the right 'to take part in cultural life and to enjoy the benefits of scientific progress and its application'.[170] Although other regional human rights systems do not offer general protection in terms of the right to science, they do contain some provisions that protect aspects of this right. For example, Article 13 of the Charter of Fundamental Rights of the European Union indicates that scientific research should be 'free of constraint'.[171]

Aspects of the right to science are also recognized in non-binding instruments, most notably the UN Declaration on the Use of Scientific and Technological Progress in the Interests of Peace and For The Benefit of Mankind.[172] The protection provided by the right is also complimented by more specific instruments adopted within the context of UNESCO, including the Universal Declaration on the Human Genome and Human Rights,[173] the Universal Declaration on Bioethics and Human Rights[174] and the UNESCO Recommendation on the Status of Scientific Researchers.[175]

In general terms, there has been very little consideration of the right to science in the work of the CESCR, and the right has also been largely neglected in the

[168] Charter of the Organization of American States (adopted 30 April 1048, 119 UNTS 3, entered into force 13 December 1951), as amended, Article 38.

[169] Organization of American States, American Declaration on the Rights and Duties of Man (2 May 1948), Article XIII.

[170] League of Arab States, Arab Charter on Human Rights (adopted 22 May 2004, 18 HRLJ 151 (1997), entered into force 15 March 2008), Article 42(1).

[171] Charter of Fundamental Rights of the European Union (adopted 7 December 2000, OJ C 364/01, entered into force 1 December 2009), Article 13.

[172] UNGA Res. 3384(XXX), Declaration on the Use of Scientific and Technological Progress in the Interests of Peace and For The Benefit of Mankind, A/RES/3384(XXX) (10 November 1975) ('UN Declaration on the Use of Scientific and Technological Progress in the Interests of Peace and For The Benefit of Mankind').

[173] UNESCO, Universal Declaration on the Human Genome and Human Rights, 11 November 1997.

[174] UNESCO, Universal Declaration on Bioethics and Human Rights, 19 October 2005.

[175] UNESCO, Recommendation on the Status of Scientific Researchers, 20 November 1974.

academic literature.[176] However, between June 2007 and July 2009, UNESCO initiated three expert meetings on the issue, which led to the formulation of the Venice Statement on the Right to Enjoy the Benefits of Scientific Progress and its Applications ('the Venice Statement').[177] This Statement, together with the 2012 Report of the Special Rapporteur in the field of cultural rights on the right to enjoy the benefits of scientific progress and its applications,[178] have assisted in clarifying the content of the right.

DEFINITIONS

According to the Special Rapporteur in the field of cultural rights:

Science must be understood as knowledge that is testable and refutable, in all fields of inquiry, including social sciences, and encompassing all research. The terms 'benefits' of science and 'scientific progress' convey the idea of a positive impact on the well-being of people and the realization of their human rights. The 'benefits' of science encompass not only scientific results and outcomes but also the scientific process, its methodologies and tools.[179]

This broad approach is supported by the Venice Statement, which provides that the 'right is applicable to all fields of science and its applications'.[180]

NATURE OF STATE OBLIGATIONS

The Venice Statement provides an overview of the normative content of the right as follows:

13. The normative content should be directed towards the following:

(a) Creation of an enabling and participatory environment for the conservation, development and diffusion of science and technology, which implies *inter alia* academic and scientific freedom, including freedoms of opinion and expression, to seek, receive and impart information, association and movement; equal access and participation of all public and private actors; and capacity-building and education.

(b) Enjoyment of the applications of the benefits of scientific progress, which implies *inter alia* non-discriminatory access to the benefits of scientific progress and its applications, including technology transfer and capacity-building.

[176] See Amrei Müller, 'Remarks on the Venner Statement on the Right to Enjoy the Benefits of Scientific Progress and its Applications (Article 15(1)(b) ICESCR)' (2010) 10 *Human Rights Law Review* 765–6.

[177] Available at: <http://shr.aaas.org/article15/Reference_Materials/VeniceStatement_July2009.pdf> (accessed 29 August 2013).

[178] Human Rights Council, Report of the Special Rapporteur in the Field of Cultural Rights on the right to enjoy the benefits of scientific progress and its applications ('Report of the Special Rapporteur on the right to science'), A/HRC/20/26 (14 May 2012).

[179] Human Rights Council, Report of the Special Rapporteur on the right to science, [24].

[180] Venice Statement, [12(a)].

(c) Protection from abuse and adverse effects of science and its applications. Areas of contemporary controversy include, for example, stem cell research, nanotechnologies, nuclear energy, GMOs, climate change, generic seeds that can be reused, cloning, ethics of science and technology, new technologies in the working environment. The possibility of adverse effects of science in these and other regards requires that impact assessments should be seen as an integral part of the development of science.

The Venice Statement thus indicates that there are three aspects to this right: freedom of scientific research and communication; enjoyment of the benefits of scientific progress; and protection from adverse effects of science. It is also apparent that there are two distinct sets of rights-holders in relation to this right: scientists; and the general population who may benefit or otherwise from scientific discoveries.

This framework of issues is reflected in the work of the Committee, which in addition emphasizes the importance of non-discrimination in relation to the enjoyment of all aspects of the right. The Guidelines on Treaty-Specific Documents thus require states to indicate:

(a) The measures taken to ensure affordable access to the benefits of scientific progress and its application for everyone, including disadvantaged and marginalized individuals and groups; and

(b) The measures taken to prevent the use of scientific and technical progress for purposes which are contrary to the enjoyment of human dignity and human rights.[181]

As regards the specific obligations which Article 15(1)(b) imposes on states, the Venice Statement provides as follows:

14. The duty to *respect* should include:

(a) to respect the freedoms indispensable for scientific research and creative activity, such as freedom of thought, to hold opinions without interference, and to seek, receive, and impart information and ideas of all kinds;

(b) to respect the right of scientists to form and join professional societies and associations, as well as academic autonomy;

(c) to respect the freedom of the scientific community and its individual members to collaborate with others both within and across the country's borders, including the freed exchange of information, research ideas and results;

(d) to take appropriate measures to prevent the use of science and technology in a manner that could limit or interfere with the enjoyment of the human rights and fundamental freedoms.

15. The duty to *protect* should include:

(a) to take measures, including legislative measures, to prevent and preclude the utilization by third parties of science and technologies to the detriment of human

[181] Guidelines on Treaty-Specific Documents, [70].

rights and fundamental freedoms and the dignity of the human person by third parties;

(b) to take measures to ensure the protection of the human rights of people subject to research activities by entities, whether public or private, in particular the right to information and free and informed consent.

16. The duty to *fulfill* should include:

(a) to adopt a legal and policy framework and to establish institutions to promote the development and diffusion of science and technology in a manner consistent with fundamental human rights. The relevant policies should be periodically reviewed on the basis of a participatory and transparent process, with particular attention to the status and needs of disadvantaged and marginalized groups;

(b) to promote access to the benefits of science and its applications on a nondiscriminatory basis including measures necessary to address the needs of disadvantaged and marginalized groups;

(c) to monitor the potential harmful effects of science and technology, to effectively react to the findings and inform the public in a transparent way;

(d) to take measures to encourage and strengthen international cooperation and assistance in science and technology to the benefit of all people and to comply in this regard with the States' obligations under international law;

(e) to provide opportunities for public engagement in decision-making about science and technology and their development;

(f) to institute effective science curricula at all levels of the educational system, particularly in the State-sponsored schools, leading to development of the skills necessary to engage in scientific research.[182]

PARTICULAR ISSUES

The following discussion will consider each of the three aspects of the right identified in the Venice Statement (freedom of scientific research and communication; enjoyment of the benefits of scientific progress; and protection from adverse effects of science), as well as the general requirements of non-discrimination and international cooperation.

Freedom of scientific research and communication

It is clear that academic freedom and freedom of expression are important aspects of the right to science. This reflects Article 15(3), under which states 'undertake to respect the freedom indispensable for scientific research and creative activity'. The freedoms to be protected include both those of scientists and those of the general public seeking to access scientific research and information.

[182] Venice Statement, [14]–[16].

As regards the rights of scientists, the Committee has emphasized, in particular, the importance of academic freedom. Thus, in relation to Kenya, the Committee expressed:

[I]ts deep concern about the fact that, according to information available to it, academic freedom in Kenya is still seriously curtailed through intimidation and a variety of measures such as the need for academics to obtain official research and travel clearance.[183]

Similarly, in relation to Nigeria, the Committee has indicated concern that:

The military authorities have found intellectuals, journalists, university professors and university students to be easy targets for repression or persecution on the pretext that they constitute the most vociferous and dangerous political opposition. One of the major university campuses has been put under military guardianship. Universities have suffered repeated and long periods of closure.[184]

In addition to requiring respect for academic freedom, the Committee has also examined the way in which states treat scientists and researchers more generally. So, for example, the Committee has expressed concern about the phenomenon of a 'brain drain' from particular states.[185] In a similar vein, the Committee, in relation to Germany in 1998:

...notes with alarm that only 12% of public servants in the science and technology sector of the former German Democratic Republic, including teachers, scientists and professionals, have been re-employed and the rest remain without employment or adequate compensation or a satisfactory pension plan. It is feared that the majority of the affected people may have been dismissed from their positions for political rather than for professional or economic reasons.[186]

The Committee thus considers not only aspects of academic freedom, but also more general concerns regarding the practical and economic conditions faced by scientists, which may affect their work and thus scientific progress.

The right of the general public to access scientific research and information is the corollary of scientists' right to academic freedom. It overlaps substantially with concerns about freedom of information identified in relation to Article 15(1)(a), above, particularly relating to access to the Internet. Thus, in relation to China:

39. The Committee notes with deep concern the restrictions placed on access to information with regard to academic research, foreign and domestic publications and the Internet.

...

68. The Committee urges the State Party to remove restrictions on freedom of information and expression in the State Party, to enable all persons under its jurisdiction to take part in

[183] CESCR, Concluding Observations: Kenya, E/C.12/1993/6 (3 June 1993), [19].

[184] CESCR, Concluding Observations: Nigeria, E/C.12/1/Add. 23 (16 June 1998), [33].

[185] See, eg, CESCR, Concluding Observations: Nigeria, E/C.12/1/Add. 23 (16 June 1998), [33]; CESCR, Report on the Seventh Session, E/1993/22 (23 November–11 December 1992), [147] (Hungary).

[186] CESCR, Concluding Observations: Germany, E/C.12/1/Add.29 (4 December 1998), [16].

cultural life, enjoy the benefits of scientific progress and its applications, and benefit from the protection of the moral and material interests resulting from any scientific, literary or artistic production of which he or she is the author.[187]

Enjoyment of the benefits of scientific progress

It is clear from the wording of Article 15(1)(b) that the drafters were concerned to protect the rights of both scientists and the general public who would be benefiting from their discoveries.

The right of everyone to share in the benefits of scientific progress and its applications clearly raises a wide range of issues, including, for example, access to advances in medical technology (discussed further below in relation to non-discrimination). Another particular issue which the Committee early identified as relevant in this context is the use of scientific discoveries to protect the environment. Thus, in relation to Belarus, the Committee:

> [W]ished to know whether legislative and other measures had been taken to protect the environment and also thereby to guarantee the rights enunciated in Article 15.[188]

Similarly, in relation to Colombia, the Committee inquired into 'measures intended to contribute to the maintenance of a healthy and clean environment and the institutional infrastructure established for that purpose'.[189]

Another important aspect of ensuring 'everyone' enjoys the benefits of scientific progress is public participation in decision-making about science and its uses. Thus, the Venice Statement indicates that the duty to fulfil the right to science imposes obligations on states to 'provide opportunities for public engagement in decision-making about science and technology and their development'.[190] And the Special Rapporteur repeatedly emphasizes the importance of participation in her work:

> 22. Indeed, one key aspect of the right to science relates to the opportunities given to individuals and peoples to make informed decisions after considering both the possible improvements offered by scientific advances and their potential side effects or dangerous usages. One important aspect of the discussion is determining what is to be regarded as 'benefits' or 'scientific progress'. This consideration must be guided by instruments such as Limburg principle 11, stressing that popular participation at all stages is 'indispensable to achieving progress in realizing economic, social and cultural rights'…
>
> 43. Reasons of the importance of the participation of individuals, communities and peoples in science-related decision-making include, in particular (a) the obligation to protect all

[187] CESCR, Concluding Observations: China, E/C.12/1/Add.107 (13 May 2005), [39] and [68].

[188] CESCR, Report on the Seventh Session, E/1993/22 (23 November–11 December 1992), [73] (Belarus).

[189] CESCR, Report on the Sixth Session, E/1992/23 (25 November–13 December 1991), [311] (Colombia). See also CESCR, Report on the Sixth Session, E/1992/23 (25 November–13 December 1991), [152] (Democratic People's Republic of Korea).

[190] Venice Statement, [16(e)].

persons, including marginalized populations, such as indigenous peoples, against the negative consequences of scientific testing or applications on, in particular, their food security, health or environment; and (b) the need to ensure that scientific research is conducted on key issues, including for the most vulnerable. Major decisions regarding funding and research priorities, science policies, emerging areas of research, and new technological applications should entail a participatory process.[191]

Protection from adverse effects of science

It is clear from the Guidelines on Treaty-Specific Documents, which specifically require states to provide information on the 'measures taken to prevent the use of scientific and technical progress for purposes which are contrary to the enjoyment of human dignity and human rights',[192] that the right to enjoy the 'benefits' of science includes the right to be protected from the adverse effects of scientific discoveries. This interpretation of Article 15(1)(b) is also supported by the Venice Statement, as set out above.

This aspect of the right to science is supported by more detailed provisions in the UN Declaration on the Use of Scientific and Technological Progress in the Interests of Peace and for the Benefit of Mankind,[193] which provides that:

2. All States shall take appropriate measures to prevent the use of scientific and technological developments, particularly by the State organs, to limit or interfere with the enjoyment of the human rights and fundamental freedoms of the individual as enshrined in the Universal Declaration of Human Rights, the International Covenants on Human Rights and other relevant international instruments.

…

4. All States shall refrain from any acts involving the use of scientific and technological achievements for the purposes of violating the sovereignty and territorial integrity of other States, interfering in their internal affairs, waging aggressive wars, suppressing national liberation movements or pursuing a policy of racial discrimination. Such acts are not only a flagrant violation of the Charter of the United Nations and principles of international law, but constitute an inadmissible distortion of the purposes that should guide scientific and technological developments for the benefit of mankind.

…

6. All States shall take measures to extend the benefits of science and technology to all strata of the population and to protect them, both socially and materially, from possible harmful effects of the misuse of scientific and technological developments, including their misuse to infringe upon the rights of the individual or of the group, particularly with regard to respect for privacy and the protection of the human personality and its physical and intellectual integrity.

[191] Human Rights Council, Report of the Special Rapporteur on the right to science, [22] and [43].
[192] Guidelines on Treaty-Specific Documents, [70(b)].
[193] UN Declaration on the Use of Scientific and Technological Progress in the Interests of Peace and for the Benefit of Mankind, [2], [4], [6] and [8].

…

8. All States shall take effective measures, including legislative measures, to prevent and preclude the utilization of scientific and technological achievements to the detriment of human rights and fundamental freedoms and the dignity of the human person.

The issue of protection from the adverse effects of science is also considered in some detail in the work of the Special Rapporteur.[194]

The Concluding Observations of the Committee in relation to the Democratic People's Republic of Korea in 1991 are indicative of the approach which the Committee takes to this issue:

Members of the Committee requested an indication of what measures had been taken to prevent the use of scientific and technical progress for purposes contrary to the enjoyment of all human rights, including the rights to life, health, liberty of person, privacy and other similar rights…[195]

Non-discrimination

As noted previously, non-discrimination in respect of all economic, social and cultural rights is an immediate obligation for states, and the issue of non-discrimination is stressed repeatedly in relation to the right to science. Thus, the Venice Statement indicates that states should:

[P]romote access to the benefits of science and its applications on a nondiscriminatory basis including measures necessary to address the needs of disadvantaged and marginalized groups.[196]

And the UN Declaration on the Use of Scientific and Technological Progress in the Interests of Peace and For The Benefit of Mankind provides:

All States shall take the necessary measures, including legislative measures, to ensure that the utilization of scientific and technological achievements promotes the fullest realization of human rights and fundamental freedoms without any discrimination whatsoever on grounds of race, sex, language or religious beliefs.[197]

The importance of equality in relation to the right to science has also been considered in the work of the Special Rapporteur:

30. States should ensure that the benefits of science are physically available and economically affordable on a non-discrimination basis.

31. The non-discrimination obligation demands eliminating both de jure and de facto barriers. In particular, positive steps must be taken for marginalized populations, such as people living in poverty and persons with disabilities, as well as the elderly, women and

[194] Human Rights Council, Report of the Special Rapporteur on the right to science, [49]–[55].
[195] CESCR, Report on the Sixth Session, E/1992/23 (25 November–13 December 1991), [153] (Democratic People's Republic of Korea).
[196] Venice Statement, [16(b)].
[197] UN Declaration on the Use of Scientific and Technological Progress in the Interests of Peace and For The Benefit of Mankind, Article 7.

children, to ensure non-discriminatory access to scientific information, processes and products. Specific measures encompass eliciting the priority needs of such populations through a consultative process and facilitating targeted research by both public and private sector institutions.[198]

The work of the CESCR in considering state reports indicates that the Committee is particularly concerned to ensure the right of the most disadvantaged to access science and its benefits. Thus, the Committee has inquired into:

[W]hat measures had been taken to guarantee the exercise of the right of everyone, particularly in the most disadvantaged sectors of the country, to enjoy the benefits of scientific progress and its application.[199]

The need to ensure equality as between men and women in relation to access to science and its benefits has also been a focus in the work of international bodies. In particular, the Committee on the Elimination of Discrimination Against Women has repeatedly expressed concern about the access of women and girls to science education and careers. So, for example, in relation to Bhutan:

The Committee encourages the State party... to take all necessary measures to increase the number of women in secondary and tertiary education in the country, including in technology- and science-related courses, in order to ensure that girls and women are accorded an equal opportunity to study, develop and benefit from science and technology.[200]

Similarly, in relation to Sri Lanka, the Committee has expressed concern about 'the underrepresentation of women in engineering and technology-related courses in tertiary education'.[201]

The principle of non-discrimination also raises a range of specific issues in relation to the right to science. Of particular significance in recent times has been the problem of unequal access to the Internet and information technology, that is, the so-called 'digital divide'. According to the Special Rapporteur, '[s]ignificant gaps in computer use and access to the Internet for reasons of income, education, gender and geographic location persist'.[202] As a result:

36. Access to the Internet and information communication technologies is an increasingly important area of action. The Committee on Economic Social and Cultural Rights stressed that Governments must respect and protect freedom of information and expression, including on the Internet to ensure the implementation of article 15 of the Covenant. With the Internet emerging as a critical platform for scientific and cultural flows and exchanges, freedom of access to it and maintaining its open architecture are important for upholding the right of people to science and culture.[203]

198 Human Rights Council, Report of the Special Rapporteur on the right to science, [30]–[31].

199 CESCR, Report on the Fifth Session, E/1991/23 (26 November–14 December 1990), [79] (Jordan).

200 CEDAW, Concluding Observations: Bhutan, A/59/38 (2004), [114]. See also, eg, CEDAW, Concluding Observations: Germany, A/59/38 (2004), [396]; and CEDAW, Concluding Observations: Canada, A/59/38 (2004), [343].

201 CEDAW, Concluding Observations: Sri Lanka, A/57/38 (2002), [280] and [281].

202 Human Rights Council, Report of the Special Rapporteur on the right to science, [37].

203 Human Rights Council, Report of the Special Rapporteur on the right to science, [36].

Other specific issues concerning equality in enjoyment of the right to science are identified in the Venice Statement:

3. The acceleration of the production of knowledge in the context of globalization has increased the effects on human rights in both positive and negative ways, with consequences for inequalities among and within States and across generations. We have identified many examples of these conflicting trends, including the following:

(i) In the area of food production, although scientific advances have significantly increased crop yields, they may also reduce crop genetic diversity, widen the gap between poor farmers and large-scale producers, and thus affect the right to food.

(ii) Scientific advances in medicine have helped to cure more diseases and enhance the quality of life. However, these advances are driven primarily by market considerations that often do not correspond to the health needs of the world's population as a whole, thus affecting the right to health.

(iii) Advances in information and communication technologies have expanded opportunities for education, freedom of expression and trade. But they have also widened the 'digital gap,' and facilitated infringements of privacy, incitement to hatred and censorship, and thus affect the full spectrum of human rights as well as cultural diversity.

4. Significant disparities are increasing among States concerning the availability of resources, capabilities, and infrastructure necessary to engage in research and development. The acceleration of scientific progress is widening the divide between the most and least scientifically and technologically advanced societies. The resulting lack of access reduces the ability to enjoy human rights, including the ability to hold governments accountable, particularly for the direction of scientific progress and its impact on human rights.

International cooperation

Consistent with Article 15(4), under which states 'recognize the benefits to be derived from the encouragement and development of international contacts and cooperation in the scientific and cultural fields', the Committee has emphasized the importance of international cooperation in the field of science. So, for example, in its monitoring of state reports, the Committee has asked about opportunities for scientists to learn about 'scientific achievements realized in other countries'.[204]

The importance of such international cooperation was stressed by the drafters of the Covenant, with Article 15(4) being added to the text pursuant to amendments suggested in the Third Committee.[205] The original amendment called for 'mutual contacts between scientific and cultural experts'. This was subsequently altered to refer to contacts 'in the scientific and cultural fields' to make clear 'that cultural and scientific relations between nations would not be in the hands only of

[204] CESCR, Report on the Sixth Session, E/1992/23 (25 November–13 December 1991), [153] (Democratic People's Republic of Korea).

[205] UNGA, Draft International Covenants on Human Rights: Report of the Third Committee (Rapporteur Mr Carlos Manuel Cox (Peru)), A/3764 (5 December 1957), [73].

experts chosen by the Governments and would therefore be as extensive and free as possible'.[206]

The Venice Statement confirms that states should:

[T]ake measures to encourage and strengthen international cooperation and assistance in science and technology to the benefit of all people and to comply in this regard with the States' obligations under international law.[207]

States' obligations in this regard would include those under the Declaration on the Use of Scientific and Technological Progress in the Interests of Peace and For The Benefit of Mankind:

1. All States shall promote international co-operation to ensure that the results of scientific and technological developments are used in the interests of strengthening international peace and security, freedom and independence, and also for the purpose of the economic and social development of peoples and the realization of human rights and freedoms in accordance with the Charter of the United Nations.

...

5. All States shall co-operate in the establishment, strengthening and development of the scientific and technological capacity of developing countries with a view to accelerating the realization of the social and economic rights of the peoples of those countries.

In stressing the importance of international cooperation, the Committee emphasizes, in particular, the need to share the benefits of science among nations, through measures such as transfers of technology from developed to developing nations. As the Special Rapporteur has indicated:

66. The need to promote everyone's access to science and its applications raises the issue of the sharing of benefits and the transfer of scientific knowledge and technologies.

...

68. The implied obligation for developing countries is the prioritization of the development, importation and dissemination of simple and inexpensive technologies that can improve the life of marginalized populations, rather than innovations that disproportionately favour educated and economically affluent individuals and regions. The corresponding obligation for industrialized States is to comply with their international legal obligations through the provision of direct aid, financial and material, as well as the development of international collaborative models of research and development for the benefit of developing countries and their populations.[208]

RELATIONSHIP TO OTHER RIGHTS

As noted above, the right to science overlaps with, and is reinforced by, rights of freedom of expression, and the state obligations contained in Article 15(3). It may also be relevant to the interpretation and application of other rights contained in

206 UNGA Third Committee, A/C.3/SR.798 (1 November 1957) (Sweden), [21].
207 Venice Statement, Article 16(d).
208 Human Rights Council, Report of the Special Rapporteur on the right to science, [66] and [68].

the ICESCR, notably the right to freedom from hunger under Article 11, which specifically provides that states shall take measures:

> To improve methods of production, conservation and distribution of food by making full use of technical and scientific knowledge, by disseminating knowledge of the principles of nutrition and by developing or reforming agrarian systems in such a way as to achieve the most efficient development and utilization of natural resources.[209]

At the same time, however, the right may conflict with intellectual property rights, including those recognized in Article 15(1)(c), which may restrict public access to scientific discoveries and their benefits. As the Venice Statement notes:

> The right to enjoy the benefits of scientific progress and its applications may create tensions with the intellectual property regime, which is a temporary monopoly with a valuable social function that should be managed in accordance with a common responsibility to prevent the unacceptable prioritization of profit for some over benefit for all.[210]

This issue has been addressed in some detail in the work of the Special Rapporteur,[211] who has noted:

> 56. Concern has been widely expressed about the conflict between the right to science and intellectual property rights, in particular since the adoption of the WTO Agreement on Trade-Related Aspects of Intellectual Property Rights (TRIPS). Bilateral and/or regional trade and investment agreements containing 'TRIPS plus' provisions or restricting TRIPS flexibilities can also pose problems. The potential of intellectual property regimes to obstruct new technological solutions to critical human problems such as food, water, health, chemical safety, energy and climate change requires attention.
>
> 57. The rights of authors protected by human rights instruments are not to be equated with 'intellectual property rights'; both intellectual property rights and authors' rights may, if necessary, be limited to uphold other rights. The intellectual property regime is a temporary monopoly that 'should be managed in accordance with a common responsibility to prevent the unacceptable prioritization of profit for some over benefit for all'.[212]

Issues of concern which have been raised in this context include the effect of intellectual property regimes on access to medicines, and the assertion of intellectual property rights over the traditional knowledge of indigenous peoples, known as 'bioprospecting'.[213]

Article 15(1)(c)

'The States Parties to the present Covenant recognize the right of everyone to benefit from the protection of the moral and material interests resulting from any scientific, literary or artistic production of which he is the author.'

[209] ICESCR, Article 11(2)(a).

[210] Venice Statement, [10].

[211] Human Rights Council, Report of the Special Rapporteur on the right to science, [56]–[65].

[212] Human Rights Council, Report of the Special Rapporteur on the right to science, [56]–[57].

[213] See Human Rights Council, Report of the Special Rapporteur on the right to science, [64].

The authors' rights enshrined in Article 15(1)(c) are also recognized, in identical terms, in Article 27(2) of the UDHR and Article 14(1)(c) of the San Salvador Protocol. They are also protected by Article 13 of the American Declaration on the Rights and Duties of Man, which provides that:

Every person has the right to take part in the cultural life of the community, to enjoy the arts, and to participate in the benefits that result from intellectual progress, especially scientific discoveries.

He likewise has the right to the protection of his moral and material interests as regards his inventions or any literary, scientific or artistic works of which he is the author.

However, authors' rights are not included in the protection for cultural rights in other regional human rights instruments. And international protection for the rights contained in Article 15(1)(c) is generally found in instruments dealing with intellectual property rather than human rights. Of particular note in this context are treaties prepared under the auspices of the World Intellectual Property Organization, such as the Berne Convention for the Protection of Literary and Artistic Works.[214]

The inclusion of intellectual property-type rights in the Covenant was controversial, and an analysis of the history indicates considerable difference of opinion among the drafters as to whether these rights should in fact constitute human rights. The draft Covenant submitted to the Third Committee by the Commission on Human Rights did not include the present Article 15(1)(c). The Uruguayan and Costa Rican representatives co-sponsored an amendment introducing the intellectual property provision, on the basis that the UDHR recognized such a right, and that the right was complementary to the other rights recognized in what is now Article 15.[215] This received widespread support, in particular from the French delegation and from UNESCO. However, others, in particular the socialist bloc, objected to its inclusion on the basis that the general rights of the public protected under the other provisions of what is now Article 15 should not have property rights included with them. Ultimately, the provision was included. The final vote was thirty-nine to nine, with twenty-four delegations abstaining from the vote.

The status of this human right in international law is therefore somewhat controversial. However, General Comment No. 17 on the right of everyone to benefit from the protection of the moral and material interests resulting from any scientific, literary or artistic production of which he or she is the author confirms:

1. The right of everyone to benefit from the protection of the moral and material interests resulting from any scientific, literary or artistic production of which he or she is the author is a human right, which derives from the inherent dignity and worth of all

[214] Berne Convention for the Protection of Literary and Artistic Works (adopted September 9, 1886, revised July 24, 1971, 1161 UNTS 30, as revised in 1979).

[215] See UNGA, Draft International Covenants on Human Rights: Report of the Third Committee (Rapporteur Mr Carlos Manuel Cox (Peru)), A/3764 (5 December 1957), [76].

persons. This fact distinguishes article 15, paragraph 1(c), and other human rights from most legal entitlements recognized in intellectual property systems. Human rights are fundamental, inalienable and universal entitlements belonging to individuals and, under certain circumstances, groups of individuals and communities. Human rights are fundamental as they are inherent to the human person as such, whereas intellectual property rights are first and foremost means by which States seek to provide incentives for inventiveness and creativity, encourage the dissemination of creative and innovative productions, as well as the development of cultural identities, and preserve the integrity of scientific, literary and artistic productions for the benefit of society as a whole.

2. In contrast to human rights, intellectual property rights are generally of a temporary nature, and can be revoked, licensed or assigned to someone else. While under most intellectual property systems, intellectual property rights, often with the exception of moral rights, may be allocated, limited in time and scope, traded, amended and even forfeited, human rights are timeless expressions of fundamental entitlements of the human person. Whereas the human right to benefit from the protection of the moral and material interests resulting from one's scientific, literary and artistic productions safeguards the personal link between authors and their creations and between peoples, communities, or other groups and their collective cultural heritage, as well as their basic material interests which are necessary to enable authors to enjoy an adequate standard of living, intellectual property regimes primarily protect business and corporate interests and investments. Moreover, the scope of protection of the moral and material interests of the author provided for by article 15, paragraph 1(c), does not necessarily coincide with what is referred to as intellectual property rights under national legislation or international agreements.

3. It is therefore important not to equate intellectual property rights with the human right recognized in article 15, paragraph 1(c)...[216]

DEFINITIONS

'Author'

According to General Comment No. 17:

The Committee considers that only the 'author', namely the creator, whether man or woman, individual or group of individuals, of scientific, literary or artistic productions, such as, inter alia, writers and artists, can be the beneficiary of the protection of article 15, paragraph 1(c).[217]

In other words, only natural persons who have created works can benefit from this protection. The General Comment also indicates that the right can be enjoyed by groups of individuals or communities.[218]

[216] CESCR, General Comment No. 17, The right of everyone to benefit from the protection of the moral and material interests resulting from any scientific, literary or artistic production of which he or she is the author (article 15, paragraph 1(c) of the Covenant), E/C.12/GC/17 (12 January 2006) ('General Comment No. 17'), [1]–[3].

[217] CESCR, General Comment No. 17, [7]. [218] CESCR, General Comment No. 17, [8].

'Any scientific, literary or artistic production'

According to General Comment No. 17, the term 'any scientific, literary or artistic production':

[R]efers to creations of the human mind, that is to 'scientific productions', such as scientific publications and innovations, including knowledge, innovations and practices of indigenous and local communities, and 'literary and artistic productions', such as, inter alia, poems, novels, paintings, sculptures, musical compositions, theatrical and cinematographic works, performances and oral traditions.[219]

'Benefit from the protection'

The Committee gives considerable flexibility to states in determining what sort of measures to take to protect the rights of authors under Article 15(1)(c):

The Committee considers that article 15, paragraph 1(c), recognizes the right of authors to benefit from some kind of protection of the moral and material interests resulting from their scientific, literary or artistic productions, without specifying the modalities of such protection. In order not to render this provision devoid of any meaning, the protection afforded needs to be effective in securing for authors the moral and material interests resulting from their productions. However, the protection under article 15, paragraph 1(c), need not necessarily reflect the level and means of protection found in present copyright, patent and other intellectual property regimes, as long as the protection available is suited to secure for authors the moral and material interests resulting from their productions...[220]

'Moral interests'

According to General Comment No. 17, the moral interests protected by Article 15(1)(c) are twofold:

[T]he right of authors to be recognized as the creators of their scientific, literary and artistic productions and to object to any distortion, mutilation or other modification of, or other derogatory action in relation to, such productions, which would be prejudicial to their honour and reputation.[221]

'Material interests'

According to General Comment No. 17:

15. The protection of 'material interests' of authors in article 15, paragraph 1(c), reflects the close linkage of this provision with the right to own property, as recognized in article 17 of the Universal Declaration of Human Rights and in regional human rights instruments, as well as with the right of any worker to adequate remuneration (art. 7(a)). Unlike other human rights, the material interests of authors are not directly linked to the personality of the creator, but contribute to the enjoyment of the right to an adequate standard of living (art. 11, para. 1).

[219] CESCR, General Comment No. 17, [9]. [220] CESCR, General Comment No. 17, [10].
[221] CESCR, General Comment No. 17, [13].

16. The term of protection of material interests under article 15, paragraph 1(c), need not extend over the entire lifespan of an author. Rather, the purpose of enabling authors to enjoy an adequate standard of living can also be achieved through one-time payments or by vesting an author, for a limited period of time, with the exclusive right to exploit his scientific, literary or artistic production.

NATURE OF STATE OBLIGATIONS

The Committee, in General Comment No. 17, has given the following overview of the elements of the right protected under Article 15(1)(c):

The right to the protection of the moral and material interests of authors contains the following essential and interrelated elements, the precise application of which will depend on the economic, social and cultural conditions prevailing in a particular State party:

(a) *Availability*. Adequate legislation and regulations, as well as effective administrative, judicial or other appropriate remedies, for the protection of the moral and material interests of authors must be available within the jurisdiction of the States parties;

(b) *Accessibility*. Administrative, judicial or other appropriate remedies for the protection of the moral and material interests resulting from scientific, literary or artistic productions must be accessible to all authors. Accessibility has four [sic] overlapping dimensions:

(i) Physical accessibility: national courts and agencies responsible for the protection of the moral and material interests resulting from the scientific, literary or artistic productions of authors must be at the disposal of all segments of society, including authors with disabilities;

(ii) Economic accessibility (affordability): access to such remedies must be affordable for all, including disadvantaged and marginalized groups. For example, where a State party decides to meet the requirements of article 15, paragraph 1(c), through traditional forms of intellectual property protection, related administrative and legal costs must be based on the principle of equity, ensuring that these remedies are affordable for all;

(iii) Accessibility of information: accessibility includes the right to seek, receive and impart information on the structure and functioning of the legal or policy regime to protect the moral and material interests of authors resulting from their scientific, literary and artistic productions, including information on relevant legislation and procedures. Such information should be understandable to everyone and should be published also in the languages of linguistic minorities and indigenous peoples;

(c) *Quality of protection*. Procedures for the protection of the moral and material interests of authors should be administered competently and expeditiously by judges and other relevant authorities.

More specifically, General Comment No. 17 outlines the nature of states' obligations under Article 15(1)(c) as follows:

30. States parties are under an obligation to *respect* the human right to benefit from the protection of the moral and material interests of authors by, inter alia, abstaining from

infringing the right of authors to be recognized as the creators of their scientific, literary or artistic productions and to object to any distortion, mutilation or other modification of, or other derogatory action in relation to, their productions that would be prejudicial to their honour or reputation. States parties must abstain from unjustifiably interfering with the material interests of authors, which are necessary to enable those authors to enjoy an adequate standard of living.

31. Obligations to *protect* include the duty of States parties to ensure the effective protection of the moral and material interests of authors against infringement by third parties. In particular, States parties must prevent third parties from infringing the right of authors to claim authorship of their scientific, literary or artistic productions, and from distorting, mutilating or otherwise modifying, or taking any derogatory action in relation to such productions in a manner that would be prejudicial to the author's honour or reputation. Similarly, States parties are obliged to prevent third parties from infringing the material interests of authors resulting from their productions. To that effect, States parties must prevent the unauthorized use of scientific, literary and artistic productions that are easily accessible or reproducible through modern communication and reproduction technologies, e.g. by establishing systems of collective administration of authors' rights or by adopting legislation requiring users to inform authors of any use made of their productions and to remunerate them adequately. States parties must ensure that third parties adequately compensate authors for any unreasonable prejudice suffered as a consequence of the unauthorized use of their productions.

...

34. The obligation to *fulfil* (provide) requires States parties to provide administrative, judicial or other appropriate remedies in order to enable authors to claim the moral and material interests resulting from their scientific, literary or artistic productions and to seek and obtain effective redress in cases of violation of these interests. States parties are also required to *fulfil* (facilitate) the right in article 15, paragraph 1(c), e.g. by taking financial and other positive measures which facilitate the formation of professional and other associations representing the moral and material interests of authors, including disadvantaged and marginalized authors, in line with article 8, paragraph 1(a), of the Covenant. The obligation to *fulfil* (promote) requires States parties to ensure the right of authors of scientific, literary and artistic productions to take part in the conduct of public affairs and in any significant decision-making processes that have an impact on their rights and legitimate interests, and to consult these individuals or groups or their elected representatives prior to the adoption of any significant decisions affecting their rights under article 15, paragraph 1(c).

The Committee has also clarified what it considers to be the 'minimum core obligation' in relation to the right as follows:

(a) To take legislative and other necessary steps to ensure the effective protection of the moral and material interests of authors;

(b) To protect the rights of authors to be recognized as the creators of their scientific, literary and artistic productions and to object to any distortion, mutilation or other modification of, or other derogatory action in relation to, their productions that would be prejudicial to their honour or reputation;

(c) To respect and protect the basic material interests of authors resulting from their scientific, literary or artistic productions, which are necessary to enable those authors to enjoy an adequate standard of living;

(d) To ensure equal access, particularly for authors belonging to disadvantaged and marginalized groups, to administrative, judicial or other appropriate remedies enabling authors to seek and obtain redress in case their moral and material interests have been infringed;

(e) To strike an adequate balance between the effective protection of the moral and material interests of authors and States parties' obligations in relation to the rights to food, health and education, as well as the rights to take part in cultural life and to enjoy the benefits of scientific progress and its applications, or any other right recognized in the Covenant.[222]

PARTICULAR ISSUES

The above extracts from the General Comment suggest that the Committee focuses, in particular, on at least two issues. The first is the need for legislative measures and judicial or administrative remedies to ensure the protection of authors' rights.[223]

The second is the need to implement the right on a non-discriminatory basis. In practice, this has led to concern on the part of the Committee with physical and economic accessibility of authors' protection, together with the need for information regarding such protection to be in the languages of linguistic minorities.[224] The Committee has also focused on the need to protect the particular intellectual property interests of indigenous peoples. Thus, General Comment No. 17 provides:

With regard to the right to benefit from the protection of the moral and material interests resulting from any scientific, literary or artistic production of indigenous peoples, States parties should adopt measures to ensure the effective protection of the interests of indigenous peoples relating to their productions, which are often expressions of their cultural heritage and traditional knowledge. In adopting measures to protect scientific, literary and artistic productions of indigenous peoples, States parties should take into account their preferences. Such protection might include the adoption of measures to recognize, register and protect the individual or collective authorship of indigenous peoples under national intellectual property rights regimes and should prevent the unauthorized use of scientific, literary and artistic productions of indigenous peoples by third parties. In implementing these protection measures, States parties should respect the principle of free, prior and informed consent of the indigenous authors concerned and the oral or other customary forms of transmission of scientific, literary or artistic production; where appropriate, they should provide for the collective administration by indigenous peoples of the benefits derived from their productions.[225]

So, for example, in relation to Bolivia:

The Committee recommends that the State party should develop a special intellectual property regime that protects the collective rights of the indigenous peoples, including

[222] CESCR, General Comment No. 17, [39].
[223] See further CESCR, General Comment No. 17, [47] and [48].
[224] See CESCR, General Comment No. 17, [18(b)].
[225] CESCR, General Comment No. 17, [32].

their scientific products and traditional knowledge and traditional medicine. To this end the Committee recommends that a registry of intellectual property rights of indigenous peoples should be opened and that the State party should ensure that the profit derived therefrom benefit them directly.[226]

Similarly, in relation to Mexico:

27. The Committee notes with concern that the collective authorship of indigenous peoples of their traditional knowledge and cultural heritage is not protected by the Federal Copyright Act or in other legislation of the State party…

46. The Committee recommends that the State party consider the adoption of legislation to recognize, register and protect the collective authorship of indigenous peoples of their traditional knowledge and cultural heritage and to prevent the unauthorized use of scientific, literary and artistic productions of indigenous peoples by third parties.[227]

RELATIONSHIP TO OTHER RIGHTS

As the Committee has indicated, the rights protected by Article 15(1)(c) are closely related to other rights protected under the Covenant and in international law, notably rights to work and rights to an adequate standard of living, as protection for the material interests of authors is designed to protect these rights.[228]

At the same time, however, as noted previously, protection of these rights may conflict with protection of other rights guaranteed in international law. In this respect, the Committee has indicated that:

35. The right of authors to benefit from the protection of the moral and material interests resulting from their scientific, literary and artistic productions cannot be isolated from the other rights recognized in the Covenant. States parties are therefore obliged to strike an adequate balance between their obligations under article 15, paragraph 1(c), on one hand, and under the other provisions of the Covenant, on the other hand, with a view to promoting and protecting the full range of rights guaranteed in the Covenant. In striking this balance, the private interests of authors should not be unduly favoured and the public interest in enjoying broad access to their productions should be given due consideration. States parties should therefore ensure that their legal or other regimes for the protection of the moral and material interests resulting from one's scientific, literary or artistic productions constitute no impediment to their ability to comply with their core obligations in relation to the rights to food, health and education, as well as to take part in cultural life and to enjoy the benefits of scientific progress and its applications, or any other right enshrined in the Covenant. Ultimately, intellectual property is a social product and has a social function. States parties thus have a duty to prevent unreasonably high costs for access to essential medicines, plant seeds or other means of food production, or for schoolbooks and learning materials, from undermining the rights of large segments of the population to health, food and education. Moreover, States parties should prevent the use of scientific and technical

[226] CESCR, Concluding Observations: Bolivia, E/C.12/BOL/CO/2 (8 August 2008), [37].
[227] CESCR, Concluding Observations: Mexico, E/C.12/MEX/CO/4 (9 June 2006), [27] and [46].
[228] See CESCR, General Comment No. 17, [15].

progress for purposes contrary to human rights and dignity, including the rights to life, health and privacy, e.g. by excluding inventions from patentability whenever their commercialization would jeopardize the full realization of these rights. States parties should, in particular, consider to what extent the patenting of the human body and its parts would affect their obligations under the Covenant or under other relevant international human rights instruments.[229]

Conclusion

Article 15 protects a range of human interests relating to cultural, scientific and creative endeavours. To date, the Committee has focused overwhelmingly on the right to participate in cultural life under Article 15(1)(a), devoting relatively little attention to the rights under Article 15(1)(b) and (c). However, in light of the increasing importance of access to technology and other scientific developments, reflected in the preparation of the Venice Statement, and the associated intellectual property issues, it will be interesting to see if the Committee's practice in this respect shifts over time.

It will also be interesting to see whether, and how, Article 15 is invoked in communications under the Optional Protocol. In this context, it is clear that some elements of Article 15 lend themselves to justiciability better than others. As O'Keefe has noted, with respect to the right to take part in cultural life:

In modern—indeed, post-modern—societies characterized by radical cultural pluralism, governmental decisions as to the allocation of limited resources to cultural ends implicate an almost bewildering array of competing interests, and necessarily involve trade-off and compromise. They are, in short, the stuff of political judgment, not legal adjudication.[230]

On the other hand, complaints about state measures which affect the rights of minority and indigenous groups to enjoy their own culture have already been the subject of cases before the Human Rights Committee.[231] And the requirement of non-discrimination imposes a concrete and immediate obligation on states, thus making it an ideal subject for adjudication. In this respect, complaints under the Optional Protocol may provide a mechanism for developing the Committee's approach to, and understanding of, the rights protected under Article 15.

[229] CESCR, General Comment No. 17, [35].

[230] Roger O'Keefe, 'Cultural Life, Right to Participate in, International Protection', *Max Planck Encyclopedia of Public International Law*, online entry, <http://www.mpepil.com>.

[231] See, eg, *Kitok v Sweden*, HRC Communication No. 197/85 (27 July 1988); *Länsman v Finland*, HRC Communication No. 511/92 (8 November 1994); and *Mahuika v New Zealand*, HRC Communication No. 547/93 (27 October 1993), discussed above.

Bibliography

Alston, Philip, 'International Law and the Human Right to Food' in Philip Alston and Katarina Tomaševski (eds), *The Right to Food* (Martinus Nijhoff, Dordrecht, 1984)

Anderson, Benedict, *Imagined Communities: Reflections on the Origin and Spread of Nationalism* (Verso, London, 2006)

Apps, Patricia and Rees, Ray, 'Gender, Time Use, and Public Policy over the Life Cycle' (2005) 21 *Oxford Review of Economic Policy* 439

Apps, Patricia, Mendolia, Silvia and Walker, Ian, 'The Impact of Pre-school on Adolescents' Outcomes', Institute for the Study of Labour, IZA Discussion Paper No. 6971 (October 2012)

Aquafed, 'Human Right to Safe Drinking Water and Sanitation' (23 October 2012), <http://www.aquafed.org/page-5-59.html>

Ashiagbor, Diamond, 'The Right to Work' in Grainne de Burca and Bruno de Witte (eds), *Social Rights in Europe* (Oxford University Press, Oxford, 2005)

Australian Human Rights and Equal Opportunity Commission, *Bringing Them Home: Report of the National Inquiry into the Separation of Aboriginal and Torres Strait Islander Children from Their Families* (April 1997)

Australian Human Rights Commission, *Immigration Detention at Villawood 2011* (Australian Human Rights Commission, Sydney, 2011)

Baderin, Mashood, *International Human Rights and Islam* (Oxford University Press, Oxford, 2005)

Balakrishnan, Radhika, Elson, Diane, Heintz, James and Lusiani, Nicholas, 'Maximum Available Resources and Human Rights: Analytical Report' (Centre for Women's Global Leadership, Rutgers, The State University of New Jersey, New Brunswick, 2011)

Baldwin, Clive and Morel, Cynthia, 'Group Rights' in Malcolm Evans and Rachel Murray (eds), *The African Charter on Human and People's Rights: The System in Practice, 1986–2006* (Cambridge University Press, Cambridge, 2010)

Bamber, Greg and Sheldon, Peter, 'Collective Bargaining: An International Analysis' in Roger Blanpain (ed), *Comparative Labour Law and Industrial Relations in Industrialized Market Economies* (Kluwer, The Hague, 2007)

Bartels, Lorand, 'Trade and Human Rights' in Daniel Bethlehem, Donald McRae, Rodney Neufeld and Isabelle Van Damme (eds), *The Oxford Handbook of International Trade Law* (Oxford University Press, Oxford, 2009)

Bayefsky, Anne, 'The Principle of Equality or Non-Discrimination in International Law' (1990) 11 *Human Rights Law Journal* 1

Beveridge, William, 'Social Insurance and Allied Services', Report to the UK Parliament (November 1942)

Bleiberg, Benjamin, 'Unveiling the Real Issue: Evaluating the European Court of Human Rights' Decision to Enforce the Turkish Headscarf Ban in *Leyla Sahin v Turkey*' (2005) 91 *Cornell Law Review* 129

Brand, Danie and Heyns, Christof (eds), *Socio-Economic Rights in South Africa* (Pretoria University Press, Pretoria, 2005)

Brunner, Lisl, 'The Rise of Peoples' Rights in the Americas: The Saramaka People Decision of the Inter-American Court of Human Rights' (2008) 7 *Chinese Journal of International Law* 699

Bulto, Takele Soboka, 'The Emergence of the Human Right to Water in International Human Rights Law: Invention or Discovery?' (2011) 12 *Melbourne Journal of International Law* 290

Cassese, Antonio, *Self-Determination of Peoples: A Legal Reappraisal* (Oxford University Press, Oxford, 1996)

Claude, Richard Pierre, 'Scientists' Rights and the Human Right to the Benefits of Science' in Audrey Chapman and Sage Russell (eds), *Core Obligations: Building a Framework for Economic, Social and Cultural Rights* (Intersentia, Antwerp, 2002)

Courtis, Christian and Sepúlveda, Magdalena, 'Are Extra-Territorial Obligations Reviewable under the Optional Protocol to the ICESCR?' (2009) 27(1) *Nordic Journal of Human Rights* 54

Craven, Matthew, 'Some Thoughts on the Emergent Right to Water' in Eibe Riedel and Peter Rothen (eds), *The Human Right to Water* (Berliner Wissenschafts, Berlin, 2006)

Craven, Matthew, *The International Covenant on Economic, Social and Cultural Rights: A Perspective on Its Development* (Clarendon Press, Oxford, 1995)

Crawford, James, 'The Right of Self-Determination in International Law: Its Development and Future' in Philip Alston (ed), *People's Rights* (Oxford University Press, Oxford, 2001)

Crawford, James, *Brownlie's Principles of Public International Law* (8th edn, Oxford University Press, Oxford, 2012)

Dankwa, Emmanuel Victor, 'Working Paper on Article 2(3) of the International Covenant on Economic, Social and Cultural Rights' (1987) 9(2) *Human Rights Quarterly* 230

de Varennes, Fernand, 'Linguistic Identity and Language Rights' in Marc Weller (ed), *Universal Minority Rights: A Commentary on the Jurisprudence of International Courts and Treaty Bodies* (Oxford University Press, Oxford, 2007)

Desta, Melaku Geboye, 'Commodities, International Regulation of Production and Trade', *Max Planck Encyclopedia of Public International Law Online*, online entry, <http://www.mpepil.com>

Socorro Dikono, Maria, 'A Rights-Based Approach towards Budget Analysis', Paper commissioned by the International Human Rights Internship Program (1999), <http://www.equalinrights.org/uploads/tx_wizzresources/Diokno_1999_RBA_to_budget_Analysis.pdf>

Dolzer, Rudolf and Schreuer, Christoph, *Principles of International Investment Law* (Oxford University Press, Oxford, 2008)

Doumbia-Henry, Cleopatra and Gravel, Eric, 'Free Trade Agreements and Labour Rights: Recent Developments' (2006) 145 *International Labour Review* 185

Dowell-Jones, Mary, *Contextualising the International Covenant on Economic, Social and Cultural Rights: Assessing the Economic Deficit* (Martinus Nijhoff, Leiden, 2004)

Drzewicki, Krzysztof, 'The Right to Work and Rights in Work' in Asbjørn Eide, Catarina Krause and Allan Rosas (eds), *Economic, Social and Cultural Rights* (2nd edn, Kluwer, The Hague, 2001)

Eriksson, Maja Kirilova, 'Family Rights and the United Nations Covenant on Economic, Social and Cultural Rights: Article 10(1)' in Audrey Chapman and Sage Russell (eds), *Core Obligations: Building a Framework for Economic, Social and Cultural Rights* (Intersentia, Antwerp, 2001)

Fenwick, Colin, 'The International Labour Organisation: An Integrated Approach to Economic and Social Rights' in Malcolm Langford (ed), *Social Rights Jurisprudence: Emerging Trends in International and Comparative Law* (Cambridge University Press, Cambridge, 2008)

Foscarinis, Maria, Paul, Brad, Porter, Bruce and Scherer, Andrew, 'The Human Right to Housing: Making the Case in U.S. Advocacy' (2004) 38 *Clearinghouse Review* 97

Foster, Caroline, 'Articulating Self-Determination in the Draft Declaration on the Rights of Indigenous Peoples' (2001) 12 *European Journal of International Law* 141

Free the Slaves, *The Congo Report: Slavery in Minerals* (June 2011)

Gearty, Conor and Mantouvalou, Virginia, *Debating Social Rights* (Hart, Oxford, 2011)

Gernigon, Bernard, Odero, Alberto and Guido, Horacio, *ILO Principles Concerning the Right to Strike* (International Labour Organization, Geneva, 2000)

Gilbert, Geoff, 'The Burgeoning Minority Rights Jurisprudence of the European Court of Human Rights' (2002) 24 *Human Rights Quarterly* 736

Gonsalvez, Colin, Kumar, P. Ramesh and Srivastava, Anup Kumar (eds), *Right to Food* (2nd edn, Human Rights Law Network, New Delhi, 2005)

Gopalakrishnan, Ramapriya, 'Enforcing Labour Rights through Human Rights Norms: The Approach of the Supreme Court of India' in Colin Fenwick and

Tonia Novitz (eds), *Human Rights at Work: Perspectives on Law and Regulation* (Hart, Oxford, 2010)

Gray, Christine, *International Law and the Use of Force* (3rd edn, Oxford University Press, Oxford, 2008)

Habitat for Humanity International, Annual Report 2012, <http://www.habitat.org/sites/default/files/annual-report-2012.pdf>

Hammer, Nikolaus, 'International Framework Agreements: Global Industrial Relations between Rights and Bargaining' (2005) 11 *Transfer* 511

Human Rights Watch, *The Curse of Gold: Democratic Republic of Congo* (Human Rights Watch, New York, 2005)

Harris, David, O'Boyle, Michael, Bates, Edward and Buckley, Carla, *Law of the European Convention on Human Rights* (2nd edn, Oxford University Press, Oxford, 2009)

Harvey, Philip, 'Benchmarking the Right to Work' in Shareen Hertel and Lanse Minkler (eds), *Economic Rights: Conceptual, Measurement and Policy Issues* (Cambridge University Press, Cambridge, 2007)

Hathaway, James, *The Rights of Refugees under International Law* (Cambridge University Press, Cambridge, 2011)

Hayter, Susan and Stoevska, Valentina, *Social Dialogue Indicators: International Statistical Inquiry 2008–09—Technical Brief* (ILO, Geneva, 2011)

Henkin, Louis (ed), *The International Bill of Rights: The Covenant on Civil and Political Rights* (Columbia University Press, New York, 1981)

Henrard, Kristin, 'Minorities, International Protection', *Max Planck Encyclopedia of Public International Law Online*, online entry, <http://www.mpepil.com>

Heredero, Gómez, *Social Security as a Human Right: The Protection Afforded by the European Convention on Human Rights* (Council of Europe, Strasbourg, 2007)

Hohmann, Jessie, *The Right to Housing: Laws, Concepts, Possibilities* (Hart, Oxford, 2013)

Human Rights and Equal Opportunity Commission, *A Last Resort? Report of the National Inquiry into Children in Immigration Detention* (13 May 2004)

Human Rights and Equal Opportunity Commission (Australia), 'Social Justice Report 2007' (2008), Chapter 3: 'The Northern Territory "Emergency Response" Intervention—A Human Rights Analysis'

Hunt, Jo, 'Fair and Just Working Conditions' in Tamara Hervey and Jeff Kremer (eds), *Economic and Social Rights under the EU Charter of Fundamental Rights: A Legal Perspective* (Hart, Oxford, 2003)

Industrial Arbitration Court (Singapore), 'Collective Agreements Sample Clauses' (20 August 2013), <http://www.iac.gov.sg/Pages/SampleClauses.aspx#Part11>

Jennings, Robert and Watts, Arthur, *Oppenheim's International Law* (9th edn, Pearson Education, London, 1996), vol. II: Peace

Joseph, Sarah and Castan, Melissa, *The International Covenant on Civil and Political Rights: Cases, Materials and Commentary* (2nd edn, Oxford University Press, Oxford, 2005)

Joseph, Sarah and Castan, Melissa, *The International Covenant on Civil and Political Rights: Cases, Materials and Commentary* (3rd edn, Oxford University Press, Oxford, 2013)

Joseph, Sarah, 'UN Covenants and Labour Rights' in Fenwick, Colin and Novitz, Tonia (eds), *Human Rights at Work: Perspectives on Law and Regulation* (Hart, Oxford, 2010)

Kapuy, Klaus, Pieters, Danny and Zaglmayer, Bernhard, *Social Security Cases in Europe: The European Court of Human Rights* (Intersentia, Antwerp, 2007)

Kinley, David, Nolan, Justine and Zerial, Natalie, 'The Politics of Corporate Social Responsibility: Reflections on the United Nations Human Rights Norms for Corporations' (2007) 25(1) *Company and Securities Law Journal* 30

Klerk, Yvonne, 'Working Paper on Article 2(2) and Article 3 of the International Covenant on Economic, Social and Cultural Rights' (1987) 9 *Human Rights Quarterly* 250

Koch, Ida Elisabeth, *Human Rights as Indivisible Rights: The Protection of Socio-Economic Rights under the European Convention on Human Rights* (Martinus Nijhoff, Leiden, 2009)

Lamarche, Lucie, 'The Right to Social Security in the International Covenant on Economic, Social and Cultural Rights' in Audrey Chapman and Sage Russell (eds), *Core Obligations: Building a Framework for Economic, Social and Cultural Rights* (Intersentia, Antwerp, 2002)

Langford, Malcolm, 'Expectation of Plenty: Response to Stephen Tully' (2006) 24(3) *Netherlands Quarterly of Human Rights* 473

Langford, Malcolm, 'Ambition That Overleaps Itself—A Response to Stephen Tully's Critique of the General Comment on the Right to Water' (2006) 24(3) *Netherlands Quarterly of Human Rights* 433

Langford, Malcolm, 'The Right to Social Security and Implications for Law, Policy and Practice' in Eibe Riedel (ed), *Social Security as a Human Right: Drafting a General Comment on Article 9 ICESCR—Some Challenges* (SpringerVerlag, Berlin, 2007)

Langford, Malcolm, Coomans, Fons and Gómez Isa, Felipe, 'Extra-Territorial Duties in International Law' in Malcolm Langford, Wouter Vandenhole, Martin Scheinin and Willem van Genugten (eds), *Global Justice, State Duties: The Extra-Territorial Scope of Economic, Social and Cultural Rights in International Law* (Cambridge University Press, New York, 2013)

Lee, Helen, 'Why Finnish babies sleep in cardboard boxes', *BBC News* (4 June 2013)

Marceau, Gabrielle, 'Trade and Labour' in Daniel Bethlehem, Donald McRae, Rodney Neufeld and Isabelle Van Damme (eds), *The Oxford Handbook of International Trade Law* (Oxford University Press, Oxford, 2009)

Marshall, Jill, 'Conditions for Freedom: European Human Rights Law and the Islamic Headscarf Debate' (2008) 30 *Human Rights Quarterly* 635

Martin, Lisa, 'UN concerned about NT intervention', *Sydney Morning Herald* (29 August 2012), <http://news.smh.com.au/breaking-news-national/un-concerned-about-nt-intervention-20120829-250kk.html>

Miller, Jane, 'Family Obligations in Europe', *Findings*, Social Policy Research 107, Joseph Rowntree Foundation, New York, November 1996

Müller, Amrei, 'Remarks on the Venner Statement on the Right to Enjoy the Benefits of Scientific Progress and Its Applications (Article 15(1)(b) ICESCR)' (2010) 10 *Human Rights Law Review* 765

Mundlak, Guy, 'The Right to Work—The Value of Work' in Daphne Barak-Erez and Aeyal Gross (eds), *Exploring Social Rights: Between Theory and Practice* (Hart, Oxford, 2011)

Murray, Rachel and Evans, Malcolm (eds), *Documents of the African Commission on Human and Peoples' Rights: Volume 2* (Hart, Oregon, 2009)

Murthy, Sharmila, 'The Human Right(s) to Water and Sanitation: History, Meaning and the Controversy Over Privatization' (2013) 31(1) *Berkeley Journal of International Law* 89

Narula, Smita, 'The Right To Food: Holding Global Actors Accountable Under International' (2006) 44 *Columbia Journal of Transnational Law* 691

Nathwani, Niraj, 'Islamic Headscarves and Human Rights: A Critical Analysis of the Relevant Case Law of the European Court of Human Rights' (2007) 25 *Netherland Quarterly of Human Rights* 221

Novitz, Tonia, 'Protection of Workers under Regional Human Rights Systems: An Assessment of Evolving and Divergent Practices' in Colin Fenwick and Tonia Novitz (eds), *Human Rights at Work: Perspectives on Law and Regulation* (Hart, Oxford, 2010)

Nowak, Manfred, *UN Covenant on Civil and Political Rights: CCPR Commentary* (2nd edn, Clarendon, Oxford, 2005)

Nussberger, Angelika, 'Work, Right to, International Protection', *Max Planck Encyclopedia of Public International Law*, online entry, <http://www.mpepil.com>

O'Keefe, Roger, 'Cultural Life, Right to Participate in, International Protection', *Max Planck Encyclopaedia of Public International Law*, online entry, <http://www.mpepil.com>

O'Keefe, Roger, 'The "Right to Take Part in Cultural Life" under Article 15 of the ICESCR' (1998) 47(4) *International and Comparative Law Quarterly* 904

Obenland, Wolfgang, 'Taxes and Human Rights', Info Steuergerechtigkeit #08e, Policy Brief, Global Policy Forum and Tax Justice Network Germany, February 2013

Olaniyan, Kolawole, 'Civil and Political Rights in the African Charter: Articles 8–14' in Malcolm Evans and Rachel Murray (eds), *The African Charter on Human and People's Rights: The System in Practice 1986–2006* (2nd edn, Cambridge University Press, Cambridge, 2010)

Centre for Economic and Social Rights, 'OPERA Framework', <http://www.cescr.org/section.php?id=179>

Ostner, Ilona, Reif, Michael and Turba, Hannu, 'Family Policies in Germany', Third Report for the Project 'Welfare Policies and Employment in the Context of Family Change' (8–9 October 2003)

Pellet, Alain and Miron, Alina, 'Sanctions', *Max Planck Encyclopedia of Public International Law Online*, online entry, <http://www.mpepil.com>

Pellet, Alain, 'The Opinions of the Badinter Arbitration Committee: A Second Breath for the Self-Determination of Peoples' (1992) 3 *European Journal of International Law* 178

Pictet, Jean (ed), *Commentary: IV Geneva Convention Relative to the Protection of Civilian Persons in Time of War* (ICRC, Geneva, 1958)

Queen's University Belfast, *Budget Analysis and the Advancement of Economic and Social Rights in Northern Ireland*, <http://www.qub.ac.uk/schools/SchoolofLaw/Research/HumanRightsCentre/ResearchProjects/BudgetAnalysis/>

Ragazzi, Maurizio, 'Financial Institutions, International', *Max Planck Encyclopedia of Public International Law Online*, online entry, <http://www.mpepil.com>

Rajagopal, Balakrishnan, *International Law from Below: Development, Social Movements and Third World Resistance* (Cambridge University Press, Cambridge, 2004)

Rishmawi, Mervat, 'The Arab Charter on Human Rights and the League of Arab States: Update' (2010) 10 *Human Rights Law Review* 169

Ryan, Bernard, 'The Charter and Collective Labour Law' in Tamara Hervey and Jeff Kremer (eds), *Economic and Social Rights under the EU Charter of Fundamental Rights: A Legal Perspective* (Hart, Oxford, 2003)

Rynhart, Gary, 'International Employers' Organizations' in Roger Blanpain (ed), *Comparative Labour Law and Industrial Relations in Industrialized Market Economies* (Kluwer, Netherlands, 2007)

Salomon, Margot E., 'Deprivation, Causation and the Law of International Cooperation' in Malcolm Langford, Wouter Vandenhole, Martin Scheinin and Willem van Genugten (eds), *Global Justice, State Duties: The Extra-Territorial Scope of Economic, Social and Cultural Rights in International Law* (Cambridge University Press, New York, 2013)

Saul, Ben, 'The International Crime of Genocide in Australian Law' (2000) 22 *Sydney Law Review* 527

Saul, Ben, 'Wearing Thin: Restrictions on Headscarves and Other Religious Symbols' in Jane McAdam (ed), *Forced Migration and Human Rights* (Hart, Oxford, 2008)

Scheinin, Martin, 'The Right to Social Security' in Asbjorn Eide, Catarina Krause and Allan Rosas (eds), *Economic, Social and Cultural Rights: A Textbook* (2nd edn, Kluwer, The Hague, 2001)

Schreuer, Christoph, 'Investments: International Protection', *Max Planck Encyclopedia of Public International Law Online*, online entry, <http://www.mpepil.com>

Schrijver, Nico, *Sovereignty over Natural Resources: Balancing Rights and Duties* (Cambridge University Press, Cambridge, 2008)

Sen, Amartya, 'Human Rights and the Limits of the Law' (2006) 27(6) *Cardozo Law Review* 2913

Siegel, Richard, 'The Right to Work: Core Minimum Obligations' in Audrey Chapman and Sage Russell (eds), *Core Obligations: Building a Framework for Economic, Social and Cultural Rights* (Intersentia, Antwerp, 2002)

Simma, Bruno, Khan, Daniel-Erasmus, Nolte, Georg and Paulus, Andreas (eds), *The Charter of the United Nations: A Commentary* (3rd edn, Oxford University Press, Oxford, 2012)

Social and Economic Rights Fulfilment Index, <http://serfindex.org/data>

Ssenyonjo, Manisuli, 'Economic, Social and Cultural Rights' in Mashood Baderin and Manisuli Ssenyonjo (eds), *International Human Rights Law: Six Decades after the UDHR and Beyond* (Ashgate, Surrey, 2010)

Ssenyonjo, Manisuli, *Economic, Social and Cultural Rights in International Law* (Hart, Oxford, 2009)

Tabucanon, Gil, 'The Banaban Resettlement: Implications for Pacific Environmental Migration' (2012) 35 *Pacific Studies* 1

The Rights to Water and Sanitation, 'The rights to water and sanitation in national law', <http://www.righttowater.info/progress-so-far/national-legislation-on-the-right-to-water/>

Thürer, Daniel and Burri, Thomas, 'Self-Determination', *Max Planck Encyclopedia of Public International Law Online*, online entry, <http://www.mpepil.com>

Tomaševski, Katerina, *Removing Obstacles in the Way of the Right to Education (Right to Education Primers No. 1)* (Novum Grafiska, Gothenburg, 2001)

Tooze, Jennifer, 'Social Security and Social Assistance' in Tamara Hervey and Jeff Kenner (eds), *Economic and Social Rights under the EU Charter of Fundamental Rights* (Hart, Oxford, 2003)

Tully, Stephen, 'A Human Right to Access Water? A Critique of General Comment No 15' (2005) 23(1) *Netherlands Quarterly of Human Rights* 35

Tully, Stephen, 'Flighty Purposes and Deeds: A Rejoinder to Malcolm Langford' (2006) 24(3) *Netherlands Quarterly of Human Rights* 461

Umozurike, Oji, *Self-Determination in International Law* (Archon Books, Connecticut, 1972)

US Department of State, *2011 Human Rights Report: Democratic Republic of the Congo* (24 May 2012), <http://www.state.gov/j/drl/rls/hrrpt/2011/af/186183.htm>

van Bueren, Geraldine, 'The Minimum Core Obligations of States under Article 10(3) of the International Covenant on Civil and Political Rights' in Audrey Chapman and Sage Russell (eds), *Core Obligations: Building a Framework for Economic, Social and Cultural Rights* (Intersentia, Antwerp, 2002)

van Dijk, Pieter, van Hoof, Fried, van Rijn, Arjen and Zwaak, Leo (eds), *Theory and Practice of the European Convention on Human Rights* (4th edn, Intersentia, Antwerp, 2006)

Viljoen, Frans, *International Human Rights in Africa* (Oxford University Press, Oxford, 2007)

Villalpando, Santiago M., 'Forced/Slave Labour', *Max Planck Encyclopedia of Public International Law* online entry, <http://www.mpepil.com>

Weller, Marc, *Escaping the Self-Determination Trap* (Martinus Nijhoff, Leiden, 2008)

Index